D0852022

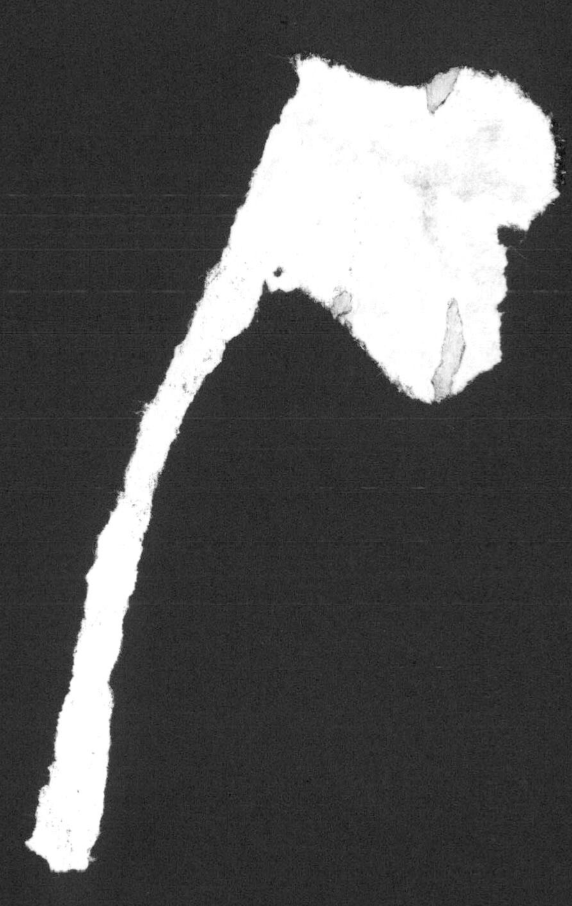

The Encyclopedic Atlas of

WINE

A comprehensive guide to the
world's greatest wines and wineries

Chief Consultant

Catherine Fallis MS

GLOBAL BOOK PUBLISHING

Publisher	Gordon Cheers
Associate Publisher	Margaret Olds
Art Director	Stan Lamond
Managing Editor	Susan Page
Editors	Denise Imwold Fiona Doig
Cover Design	Stan Lamond
Picture Research	Gordon Cheers
Photo library	Alan Edwards
International Rights	Dee Rogers
Production	Bernard Roberts

Photographers
Glenn A. Baker, Gilbert Bel-Bachir, Rob Blakers, John Borthwick, Ken Brass, Adam Bruzzone, Claver Carroll, Craig Cranko, Frank Dalgity, Steven Elphick, Jean-Paul Gollin, Richard Humphrys, David Keith Jones, Brian Jordan, Ionas Kaltenbach, Mike Langford, Gary Lewis, Andre Martin, David McGonigal, Craig Potton, Janet Price, Christo Reid, Don Skirrow, Ken Stepnell, Oliver Strewe, Jon Wyand, James Young

First published in 2004 by
Global Book Publishing Pty Ltd
1/181 High Street
Willoughby, 2068
NSW, Australia
phone: 61 2 9967 3100 fax: 61 2 9967 5891
email: rightsmanager@globalpub.com.au

ISBN 1 74048 050 3

For all sales, please contact:
Global Book Publishing Pty Ltd
phone: 61 2 9967 3100 fax: 61 2 9967 5891
email: rightsmanager@globalpub.com.au

Printed in Hong Kong by Sing Cheong Printing Co. Ltd

Photographers: The publisher would be pleased to hear from photographers interested in supplying photographs that could be included our books. Email editor@globalpub.com.au

Captions for images in the preliminary pages

Page 1: Fermentation vessel containing 1986 cabernet at Concha y Toro, a Maipo Valley producer in Chile.

Pages 2/3: Tying vines Portuguese fashion, near Felgueiras, Minho, Portugal.

Pages 4/5: Corks designed to hold sulfur pellets. The pellets burn in barrels to sterilize them, but the amount used has to be carefully controlled.

Pages 6/7 (right): Grape picking on steep slopes near Kobern, Mosel, Germany.

Page 10: Vineyards plunge down to the Mosel River at Urzig, Germany

Contributors

Catherine Fallis MS, author and educator, is also known as the grape goddess®. She is founder and president of Planet Grape® LLC, guest host on NBC-11 TV's "In Wine Country," and is a Culinary Institute of America-Greystone Adjunct Instructor. Catherine created the grape goddess guides to good living® to give all Earthlings a chance to learn about life's simpler and more decadent palate pleasures without the intimidation factor. Enjoy grape goddess guides as a series of 1-minute daily email lessons complete with images and audio. Free sample lessons at: www.planetgrape.com http://www.planetgrape.com or http://workplacelanguage.com/social-skills/winebasics.htm

Dr. Patrick Farrell MW, a medical doctor by training, is one of a handful of Masters of Wine living in the US He has followed California's wine-producing regions carefully since moving to the Golden State in 1988. He is a past program and professional session chairman of the Society of Wine Educators and actively teaches about wine. Patrick has judged wine competitions internationally and keeps a busy schedule visiting the world's wine regions. He is currently combining his wine and medical training in writing a book on wine and health.

Rebecca Chapa is a San Francisco-based wine consultant whose clients include some major hotels. She is a contributing editor for *Wine & Spirits* and writes freelance for *Santé*, www.SpiritsUSA.com, and has a bi-monthly column in *SOMA* magazine. She was co-program chair of the Society of Wine Educators Conference in San Jose, California, in August 2000. She has completed the Higher Certificate towards the Master of Wine degree given by the Wine and Spirits Education Trust in England and is one of a handful of Americans to have completed the Diploma course of study.

Peter Forrestal was the founding editor of *The Wine Magazine* and is now its associate editor. As a freelance wine and food writer, he has written *A Taste of the Margaret River,* co-authored *The Western Table*, and edited *Discover Australia: Wineries*. He is a former president of the Wine Press Club of Western Australia, a member of the Circle of Wine Writers, and the Australian Society of Wine Educators. He has been wine correspondent for the *West Australian*, the *Western Review*, and the *Perth Weekly*.

Maureen Ashley MW started tasting wine as a hobby in the 1970s and entered the wine trade in 1979. She became a Master of Wine in 1984, also attaining the Tim Derouet Award for the excellence of her results. She became a freelance writer in 1986. One of the foremost Italian wine experts, she now lives in Rome. Maureen has written three books in the Touring in Wine Country series as well as *Italian Wines*, in the Sainsbury's Regional Wine Guides series. She writes widely for international audiences, leads wine tours in Italy, and gives talks and tutored tastings.

Tony Aspler, based in Toronto, is the editor of *Winetidings* magazine, wine columnist for the *Toronto Star*, and creator of the Air Ontario Wine Awards. He is a member of the Advisory Board for Masters of Wine (North America). Tony contributed to Jancis Robinson's *Oxford Companion To Wine*, and the *Larousse Encyclopedia of Wine*. He is himself the author of several books on wine, including *Guide to New World Wines*, *Vintage Canada*, *Travels With My Corkscrew*, *The Wine Lover's Companion*, and *The Wine Lover Dines*. He also writes murder mysteries about a wine writer/detective. His website is at www.tonyaspler.com.

James Aufenast writes for *Harpers Wine & Spirit Weekly*, the UK's major wine trade magazine, on emerging wine areas including the south of France, Israel, and Canada. He specializes in Eastern Europe, and has visited Romania and Bulgaria to investigate the wine industries in those countries. He also writes for *The Times* Weekend section on food and drink, and reviews restaurants for the *Who Drinks Where Crushguide,* a London restaurant guide. James has written a cocktail book for Quarto Publishing. He lives in London.

Helena Baker, a native of Prague, holds a Diploma from the Wine and Spirit Education Trust in London, is one of the founders of the Prague Wine Society and the Slow Food Convivium of Prague. Helena is also a freelance wine writer, columnist, wine taster at international wine competitions, consultant, and lecturer. She has translated the *Encyclopedia of Czech and Moravian Wines*, by professor Vilém Kraus, and published her own *Pocket Guide 2000 to the Wines and Winemakers of the Czech Republic,* which she is currently translating into English. She lives in a country house just outside Prague.

Jeffrey Benson spent the last 30 years traveling to virtually every wine growing country in the world as buying director for a large wine importing company. Specializing in wines from outside Europe, he was responsible for developing new export markets for such countries as India, Canada, and Zimbabwe. He has co-authored three books on his favorite wines, *Sauternes*, *Saint Emilion/Pomerol,* and *The Sweet Wines of Bordeaux*. He is now a wine consultant to various hotel groups around the world and travels extensively lecturing and contributing articles to various international wine publications.

Stephen Brook worked as an editor in the US and Britain before becoming a freelance writer specializing in travel and wine. His *Liquid Gold: Dessert Wines of the World* won the Andre Simon Award in 1987. Other awards include the Bunch Award for wine writer of the year in 1996. He is the author of *Sauvignon Blanc and Sémillon* and the *Wine Companion to Southern France*, *Sauternes and the Other Sweet Wines of Bordeaux*, and *The Wines of California*. He lives in London, where he is a regular contributing editor for *Decanter* and writes on wine for *Condé Nast Traveller*.

Jim Budd started writing about wine in 1988, having previously taught English in London. He contributes to a number of specialty drinks magazines, including *Wine & Spirit International*, *Decanter*, and *Harpers Wine & Spirit Weekly*, and contributes to a number of internet sites, including decanter.com and madaboutwine.com. He wrote *Appreciating Fine Wines*, and contributed to *Oz Clarke's Pocket Wine Book*, the Oz Clarke CD ROM, and *Oz Clarke's Encyclopedia of Wine*. In 1997 he won Le Prix du Champagne Lanson Noble Cuvée for investigating bogus Champagne investment schemes. Jim now has a website (www.investdrinks.org) about drinks investments.

Steve Charters MW qualified as a lawyer in the UK, but was seduced by the allure of wine, and worked in retail and wine education in both London and Sydney. He is one of only 240 members of the Institute of Masters of Wine in the world, and one of only 12 in Australia, having passed its rigorous theory and tasting examination in 1997. Steve now lectures in Wine Studies at Edith Cowan University, in Perth, Australia. His courses cover the understanding and appreciation of wine, its varying worldwide styles, and marketing and selling wine.

Michael Fridjhon is chairman of the South African Wine Industry Trust and an international wine judge. He is the convenor of the South African Airways selection panel, a regular columnist for *Business Day*, and a contributor to the *Financial Mail*, *Wine*, *Wine & Spirit International*, *Harpers Wine & Spirit Weekly*, and *Decanter*. He wrote *The Penguin Book of South African Wine*, is co-author of *Conspiracy of Giants—An Analysis of the South African Liquor Industry*, and a contributor to the *John Platter South Africa Wine Guide*, *The Complete Book of South African Wine*, *Hugh Johnson's Wine Companion*, and the new *Oxford Companion to Wine*.

Ken Gargett, based on the Gold Coast in Queensland, Australia, is a lawyer as well as a contributor to *The Wine Magazine*, *Discover Australia: Wineries,* and other publications. Ken also has a weekly column in the Queensland *Courier Mail*. He is a wine educator for the Wine Society in Queensland and conducts training and consults within the industry, as well as judging. He was the 1993 winner of the Vin de Champagne Award and has conducted numerous Australian wine promotions and seminars.

Harold Heckle pursued his love of romance languages and literature at the universities of Bristol and King's College (England). After working with the British Council in Perú and a subsidiary of the Bank of England, he became a theater producer, then went on to research, write, and broadcast for BBC Radio. One feature, *The Grape Debate*, led to wine journalism. He has chaired The Wine Club since its inception. Today, Harold writes for *Wine & Spirit International* and *Decanter*, and is columnist for the Spanish newspaper, *El Mundo*. He lives in England and grows his own organic vegetables.

Brian Jordan became interested in wine in the early 1980s when he purchased a hotel restaurant in Britain's west country, and subsequently was twice winner and twice runner-up for the best wine list in the UK. He began writing about wine in the 1990s, subsequently expanding into international judging, consultancy, photography, lecturing, broadcasting, and organizing wine competitions. As a freelance wine writer, his articles have appeared in every significant wine-oriented magazine in the UK as well as several in other countries.

James Lawther MW, based in Bordeaux, France, cut his teeth in the wine trade retailing wine at Steven Spurrier's Caves de la Madeleine in Paris, and as a lecturer at the Académie du Vin. He was the first Englishman to pass the Master of Wine examination while resident in France (1993). He is now an independent wine consultant, writer, and contributing editor to *Decanter*. He is the author of the *Bordeaux Wine Companion* and has contributed to the recent edition of *The Wine Atlas of France*. James also leads tours in the French wine regions.

Alex Liddell has lived in France, Portugal and Italy and travels the wine countries of the world for six months of the year. He is the author of *Port Wine Quintas of the Douro*, and *Madeira*. One of Alex' most recent publications is

Wines of Hungary. He is a member of the Circle of Wine Writers and contributes to Australia's *The Wine Magazine*.

Wink Lorch has worked in the world of wine for over 20 years, in the last 15 or so as a writer and educator. She was one of the two contributing editors for Williams-Sonoma's *The Wine Guide*, published by Time-Life in 1999. She currently writes for trade and consumer magazines in the UK. Wink is a founding member of the Association of Wine Educators in the UK and regularly leads tutored tastings and wine courses. She divides her time between her chalet in the French Alps (close to Savoie, Jura, and Swiss vineyards) and a *pied-à-terre* in England.

Nico Manessis, born on the island of Corfu, has been active in the international wine business for over 20 years in Europe and the US. His first book, *The Greek Wine Guide*, published in 1994, has been instrumental in bringing quality Greek wine to international attention. More recently, he has written *The Illustrated Greek Wine Book*. He also regularly contributes to newspapers and *Decanter*, and lectures frequently on the new wines of his native country, appearing often at the Université de Vin in France. He is a member of l'Académie Internationale du Vin and lives in Geneva, Switzerland.

Giles MacDonogh is a historian and the author of several books on Germany, including lives of Frederick the Great and the Kaiser and histories of Prussia and Berlin. He is also a wine writer, contributing a regular column to the *Financial Times* and *Punch*, as well as writing occasional articles for *Decanter*, *Wine*, and other specialized magazines. He is the author of three books on wine, two of them on Austria: *The Wine and Food of Austria* and *New Wines from the Old World*. One of his most recent books, *Portuguese Table Wines*, explores Portugal's transformation to a producer of note.

Kate McIntyre learned firsthand about vineyards and wineries growing up from the age of nine on her family's estate on Victoria's Mornington Peninsula. She began her career in the wine industry at Philip Murphy Wine and Spirits in 1996. In 1998 she was the inaugural winner of the Negociants Working with Wine Fellowship. She is now studying for the Master of Wine exam and is a regular contributor to *The Wine Magazine*. In 1999 she was wine writer for *Women's Weekly* and is an occasional contributor to *Divine* magazine. She was also a contributor to *Discover Australia: Wineries*.

Alex Mitchell credits her involvement in the 1998 Negociants Working With Wine program as being the turning point in her career in wine. It exposed her to an unprecedented range of imported wines and winning its prestigious Wine Writing Prize has led to her writing regularly for *The Wine Magazine*. After many years of nursing and four years in wine retail, she now has her own business. She has taught wine studies at Swinburne University and has contributed to two books. She plans to complete a Bachelor of Oenology and intends to become a winemaker.

Sally Marden is a professionally trained journalist who cut her writing teeth on regional UK newspapers. She turned to drink in 1990 when she joined leading trade publication *Off Licence News*. She has traveled extensively to wine regions throughout Europe, the US, Chile and Australia, and, as well as writing for a range of wine publications in the UK, has co-presented a food and drink television series for Channel 4 in the UK. In 1998 she moved to the Barossa, where she now writes and consults for a specialist wine marketing company, as well as contributing regularly to various publications, including *The Wine Magazine* and *Le Vigneron*.

Jasper Morris MW joined the UK wine trade in 1979 and founded his company, Morris & Verdin Ltd, two years later. The plan was to import wines from all over France but he rapidly developed a heavy bias towards Burgundy. He has also developed a strong second string in Californian wines. Since becoming a Master of Wine in 1985, he has been much in demand as a writer and lecturer. He regularly contributes to *Decanter* magazine and was responsible for the Burgundy entries in the *Oxford Companion to Wine*.

Jeremy Oliver is an independent Australian wine writer, broadcaster, author, and speaker. Since 1984, when he became the world's youngest published wine author, he has written nine books and has contributed wine columns to dozens of magazines and newspapers. In addition to his self-published annual guide to Australian wine, *The OnWine Australian Wine Annual*, and his bi-monthly newsletter, *Jeremy Oliver's OnWine Report*, he currently contributes to *The Wine Magazine*, *Personal Investment*, and *The Australian Way*. He is also a speaker and master of ceremonies at wine presentations and has a comprehensive and independent wine website at www.onwine.com.au.

Anthony Peregrine comes from Lancashire in Northern England, and studied political sciences before working as a teacher in Mexico City. On his return to England, he wrote for several newspapers before moving to France in 1988. He now lives near Montpellier in the Languedoc region where he freelances for the British press, covering wine, food, and travel. His work appears in the *Daily Telegraph*, the *Daily Mail*, *Decanter*, *Wine & Spirit International*, and on BBC Radio 4.

John Radford has been writing about wine professionally since 1977, after an earlier career in the wine trade. He has a special interest in the wines of Spain and Portugal and contributed chapters on Iberia to the *Larousse Encyclopedia of Wine* and *Hugh Johnson's Wine Companion*. His book, *The New Spain*, won the Glenfiddich, Lanson, and Versailles Cookbook Fair prizes in 1999. He co-wrote the *Mitchell Beazley Pocket Guide to Fortified and Sweet Wines* and writes for *Decanter*, *Wine*, and other specialty magazines in the UK. He lives in the south coast of England.

Margaret Rand has been writing about wine for 20 years. She has edited *Wine*, and *Wine & Spirit International*, is wine editor of *Oz Clarke's Wine Guide*, and was founding editor of *Whisky Magazine*. She contributes to a wide range of publications, including *The Sunday Times* (UK), the *Daily Telegraph*, and *Wine*. She wrote the audio guide for Vinopolis, London's major wine exhibit.Recent publications include an introductory guide to wine, which she co-authored with Robert Joseph; and the best selling *Grapes and Wines*, co-authored with Oz Clarke.

Michele Round was an art teacher before pursuing her fascination for food and wine as a consultant, writer, and commentator. She is a regular contributor to *The Wine Magazine*, writes a weekly food column for a Tasmanian newspaper, and has written about wine for a variety of national publications. Through her work in gastronomy as a cook, writer and teacher, she became passionate about the synergy between food and wine. Born and raised in Tasmania, Michele became well known as a champion of the developing island wine industry through a weekly ABC Radio wine segment.

Joanna Simon is an award-winning wine writer for *The Sunday Times* (UK), for which she writes a weekly column, and a contributor to many other publications worldwide. She is a former editor of two leading UK wine magazines, *Wine* and *Wine & Spirit International*, and is author of *Wine with Food* and *Discovering Wine*. She is also a broadcaster, presenting *The Bottle Uncorked* in 1999, BBC Radio 4's first series devoted to wine. When not writing, tasting, talking about wine, or visiting the world's vineyards, she escapes from London to a beautiful and remote part of France.

Marguerite Thomas is the author of *Wineries of the Eastern States*. She is travel editor of *The Wine News* and she writes "Tastings," a food and wine column for the *Los Angeles Times* Syndicate International. She is a regular contributor on food and wine to various US publications, including *Saveur*, *Country Home*, and *Time Out New York*. She was raised in France and California, and now resides in New York, where she has been nominated to receive the prestigious James Beard Award for wine journalism.

Joelle Thomson is a freelance wine writer in Auckland, New Zealand. She started writing about wine for the weekly arts newspaper, *Capital Times*, in the mid-1990s and worked full-time in food and design magazines in New Zealand prior to her freelance career. She published her first book, *Joelle Thomson's Under $15 Wine Guide*, in 1999 and has since written *Weekends for Wine Lovers*. She is currently wine writer for the *Christchurch Press*, *Grocer's Review*, *SHE*, and *NZ Home & Entertaining*, and a regular contributor to *The Wine Magazine*.

Roger Voss, one of Britain's leading wine and food writers, is European editor for the New York-based *Wine Enthusiast* magazine and writes for UK magazines such as *Decanter* and *Harpers Wine & Spirit Weekly*. He has been an editor of the Consumers' Associations' *Which? Wine Guide* for four years and has also written *Wine and Food of France* and *The Wines of the Loire*, as well as guides to port and sherry, and chardonnay and cabernet. Upcoming publications include a fifth edition of his guide to the wines of the Loire, Alsace, and the Rhône. He lives in the Bordeaux region of France.

Dr. Paul White, originally from Oregon, captained the Oxford University Blind Wine Tasting Team while completing a doctorate at Oxford University. He developed his analytical skills further as a judge at London's International Wine Challenge. Based in Wellington, he is currently a columnist for the *New Zealand Herald*, and contributes to the *Oregonian* and other media throughout Australasia, the US and Europe. He also publishes an online wine tasting guide at www.winesense.co.nz. His senior judging credits include London's International Wine Challenge, the Sydney International Top 100, and Sydney Royal Easter Show.

Simon Woods is a former electronics design engineer who picked up the wine bug while traveling in Australia in 1988 and has hardly put a glass down since. He spent the early 1990s coordinating London's International Wine Challenge, the world's biggest wine competition, and is now co-editor of *Which? Wine Guide*, as well as being a regular columnist for *Wine*. He has judged at wine competitions in France, England and Australia and has also appeared on radio and television both at home and abroad. He lives in the Pennines in the North of England.

Contents

Tiny underground wine cellars dot the landscape in northwest Spain.

The World of Wine

The History of Wine

More than any other drink across the world, wine fascinates, entices and seduces. Tea and coffee have their rituals, beer and water quench the thirst, whisky and brandy intoxicate, but none of these attract so many connoisseurs, stimulate such fellowship, or even give so much pleasure as wine. More books are written about wine than about any other drink, and more wine is tasted in the formalized rituals of sniff and slurp than any other beverage on the planet.

RIGHT: Recioto and retsina; modern wine styles that most resemble wines drunk in ancient times.

It is too easy, while we enjoy a glass of chilled chardonnay, to ignore where it came from, how it was made, or the cultural background that spawned it. However, wine is rooted in history, and it has a dynamic relationship to both those cultures who have drunk it for millennia and those who have enjoyed it for less than 100 years.

Wine was probably first made in the region of the Caucasus Mountains between Europe and Asia, roughly in present-day Georgia or Kurdistan. The current best evidence for its origin suggests that it was being made there perhaps 8,000 years ago. Some archeologists think beer was made before wine because barley, which is essential for making beer, was a key initial crop in the diet of our ancestors. Mead, made from honey, and palm wine were also important early beverages. Nevertheless, wine has a venerable history.

It is likely that the first winemaker would have been a woman, for women would probably have been responsible for gathering fruit and nuts in Neolithic society. The usual hypothesis is that a few bunches of wild grapes were stored in a clay pot and forgotten for a few days. They began to ferment, probably by carbonic maceration. As juice ran out, yeast fermentation may have begun. After a few days, the owner of the pot remembered the grapes and, perhaps feeling thirsty, she drank the juice that had accumulated at the bottom. Although it may not have been very pleasant, it made her feel strangely euphoric. Thus the first wine, and maybe the first alcoholic drink, probably was born.

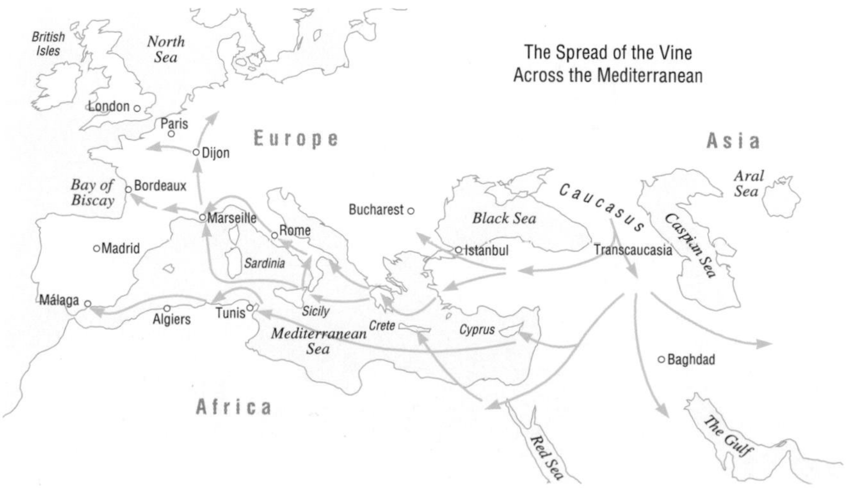

At first, wine would have been made on a haphazard basis, probably from the wild vines of the region. Initially, its limited availability, depending on grapes occurring naturally, would have confined its use to special occasions. Later, when wine was made from cultivated grapes, its use would have become much more widespread.

WINE AS A COMMODITY

As Neolithic society became more developed with the more efficient cultivation of crops, so it began to create surplus product and afford certain individuals the opportunity to trade that surplus. The climate around cities like Ur and Babylon, among the earliest centers of civilization in the Middle East, was too hot for production of the balanced grapes needed to produce good wine, but places such as these had the wealth to purchase it, and in this way, wine became a commodity.

The first wine trader might have lived in one of the cities of Sumer, in what is now southern Iraq. Located on major rivers like the Tigris and Euphrates, these cities irrigated their crops, and became arteries of trade. Wine producers there would load up reed boats with their large pots of the magic liquid and float it downstream to the great centers of the south.

Wine spread rapidly throughout the Mediterranean world. It was produced by the Egyptians, though only for their rich, and then later by the Greeks, who produced it for all classes. The austere early Romans were suspicious of it, but wine had become popular well before the time of Caesar, and was again a huge source of wealth for those who produced it (using slave labor) on a large scale.

The wine drunk in the ancient world would not have resembled most of the wines we drink today. The taste then was for sweeter wine. It may well have had a lower alcohol level, and would regularly have been mixed with other substances such as honey, spices, and sometimes even seawater!

The Roman Empire, and its efficient transport network, encouraged not only the trade of wine but also the spreading of the vine. Even before Roman arrival, Greek traders had brought the vine to the southern areas of France, but then the *pax Romana* spread it throughout all of France and Spain—and possibly encouraged the use of wild vines in Germany. By the end of the third century AD, wine was being made in many of the places we now see as its traditional home: Bordeaux, Burgundy, the Mosel Valley and Jeréz. Eventually, these areas started to send wine back to Rome itself.

Critical to this spread was a revolution in the method of transporting wine. The early storage of all liquids, including wine, was in long thin clay jars, known as *amphorae*. However, a new form of container appeared from France in the second century AD. Barrels, invented by the Celts, were the technological advance necessary to distribute cheap, mass-produced wine to the burgeoning masses of the Roman Empire.

THE INFLUENCE OF THE CHURCH

As Europe entered the Middle Ages, the trade in wine that declined during the Dark Ages slowly resumed. Rich and heady Mediterranean wines such as malmsey, which was a sweet wine from Greece, became particularly popular in northern Europe. Meanwhile the Church became important in both the production and distribution of wine. In the monasteries, monks observed and studied the natural world, and these observations and studies led to an understanding of, and later highly developed skills in, viticulture.

ABOVE: *Thirsty pilgrims can choose between wine or water at a monastery on the way to Santiago de Compostela in Galacia, Spain.*

The Abbey of Citeaux, founded by the Cistercian order in 1098, sits just outside the Côte d'Or, the heartland of the Burgundy wine region. Originally seeking simple, austere lives, the monks later became wealthy as the laity bequeathed property (including vineyards) to the abbey. By the end of the twelfth century the Church owned much of the land in the village of Vougeot. At the same time, the abbey became a staging post for travelers. Consequently visitors sampled the wines and the monks' reputation spread, stimulating demand for their produce. Their influence lasted until the French Revolution of 1789.

A new era in wine followed Columbus' voyage to the Americas in 1492. By the end of 1521, there were vineyards in Mexico; by 1548 they could be found in Chile; by 1769 they were in California. The Dutch made wine in the Cape of Good Hope in 1659, and vine cuttings were taken on from there by the first European settlers traveling to the new southern lands of Australia and New Zealand.

BELOW: *Traditional Portuguese* barcos rabelos *(flat-bottomed port boats), used to transport young port down the river Douro.*

THE SCIENTIFIC REVOLUTION

The seventeenth and eighteenth centuries saw the scientific and industrial revolutions. In this period, empirical work allowed the development of the greatest sparkling wine in the world in Champagne, and yet more growth in the wine trade. At the same time, the rise of the middle classes provided a burgeoning market for what until then had been predominantly consumed by those who had produced it. The influence of this nascent consumer revolution can be seen by the early nineteenth century, when the two most expensive wines in the world were tokay and constantia; these came not from France or Italy, but from Hungary and South Africa. Sixty years later, the spread of railways led to the next development. When wines produced in Italy or the south of France could be delivered in Berlin or London or Paris within 24 hours, producers were no longer restricted to seeking a market only in the nearest town.

One other very important legacy of the nineteenth century was the work of Louis Pasteur. Enology as a science is based on biochemistry, and was one of the later branches of science to develop. Louis Pasteur contributed substantially to our ability to control the processes involved in winemaking—and thus our ability to make good wine. He was a scientist of wide interests, and one who enjoyed wine as well.

Pasteur didn't discover yeasts, but he showed that microscopic organisms were responsible for fermentations. When he was commissioned by the French government to investigate wine spoilage, he discovered the various bacteria that cause it and offered means of preventing their activity. It was due to this man more than any other that winemaking became a science, and that the drink we now enjoy can be produced so reliably and cheaply.

What had been a golden age came to an end in the 1860s when the pest phylloxera arrived from North America. It first ravaged vineyards in France, and then moved through the rest of Europe, until the solution of grafting was discovered. At the same time, the growing trade in wine provoked widespread fraud, as producers of cheap wine tried to pass their product off as *grand vin*. Then came war, and Prohibition in the US—and general depression to wine producers around the world.

The response to the fraud problem in Europe was to develop a system to protect the producers of quality wine by guaranteeing its origin. This process, which developed into the French Appellation system, also gave rise to the European idea of labeling "quality" wine, which has a specific demarcated origin, and "table" wine, which does not. The European system is the basis for quality control in other parts of the world, for example, the American Viticultural Areas (AVAs) in the US.

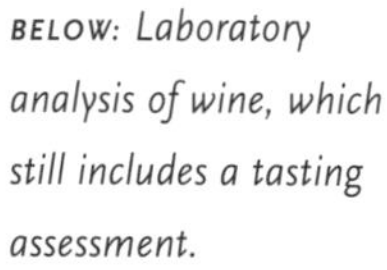

BELOW: *Laboratory analysis of wine, which still includes a tasting assessment.*

WINE TODAY

The last century has consolidated the impact of developments in the scientific, technological and transport worlds. Discoveries of the scientific basis for malolactic fermentation and for keeping oxygen away from wine have altered what we drink—as has the fact that Jacob's Creek Chardonnay can be shipped from Australia to the UK for less than 10p per bottle (US15¢). Perhaps the main change since the Second World War, however, has been in the way wine is consumed. Mediterranean countries have traditionally consumed a lot of wine, but in England wine was considered a drink for the aristocrats, in Australia for alcoholics and in the US it had been banned under Prohibition. However, the impact of war (during which many young men were introduced to wine), along with growing disposable income and the rapid development of technology (making cheap but fruity wine commonplace), all spread wine drinking. In the last decade, this has extended to include Japan, China and Southeast Asia. It is now normal for shoppers in a UK supermarket to pick up a bottle to drink with their evening meal—something their parents would never have done. The spread of wine consumption has spawned an industry of education in the subject. Writers like Hugh Johnson are owed a large debt by the wine industry for making this product so well understood.

WHY DO WE DRINK WINE?

Technically, alcohol is a depressant, acting on the nervous system in a similar way to some tranquilizers, and in moderate amounts creating a feeling of contentment, cheerfulness and camaraderie. But alcohol is also present—in stronger form—in spirits. So why do we not drink spirits exclusively? Because there are other reasons for drinking wine—magic, for example. In earlier times people did not understand the process of fermentation, and believed that when they drank wine, gods had taken over their bodies. The relationship between wine and ritual continues in the communion service of the Christian Church today.

Another reason was that wine was safer to drink than water. Until the development of pure water supplies 160 years ago, water carried all kinds of bacteria, causing dysentery, cholera and typhoid. The alcohol content of wine, however, sustains very few bacteria and none of them are harmful. So wine became the safe drink of choice in the Mediterranean countries, just as beer was in northern Europe.

As wine became the daily drink, a natural relationship grew between wine and different styles of food. In Spain, for instance, inland regions make full-bodied red wines to go with their heavy food, which is often based on lamb. Their white wines—rioja is a good example—are traditionally also full-bodied to match the fleshy river fish of the central areas. Coastal regions produce lighter wines. The crisp, fresh, albariño-based wines of Galicia in the northwest of Spain and the sparkling cava of Catalonia are classic examples which marry better with the seafood or shellfish of those areas.

***ABOVE:** Wine drinking the Spanish way!*

We cannot avoid mentioning the relationship of wine to status. Throughout history there has been a tension between wine as an elite beverage and wine for consumption by the masses. In ancient Egypt, wine tended to be the preserve of the rich. In Greece, it was everyone's everyday drink. From the eighteenth century on in the United Kingdom—later in other northern European and English-speaking countries—wine was associated with the moneyed classes, while even the peasants drank it daily in southern countries. For the former it became associated with pretension and snobbery, giving rise to ideas of connoisseurship and "tasting"—concepts that would have been completely alien to most of the world's wine drinkers.

WORLD WINE PRODUCTION AND CONSUMPTION [1]

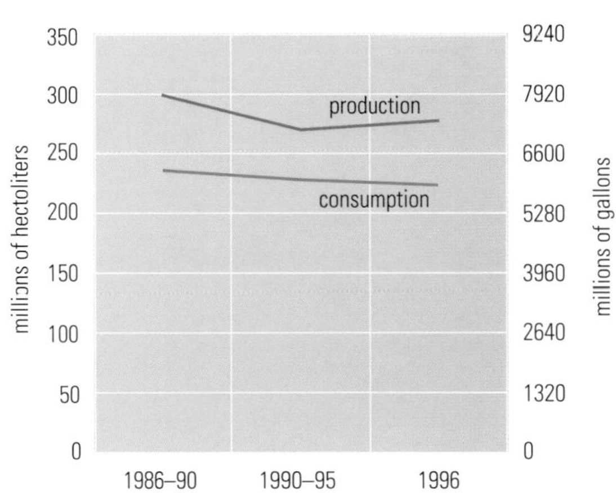

WINE CONSUMPTION TRENDS PER CAPITA IN THREE COUNTRIES [2]

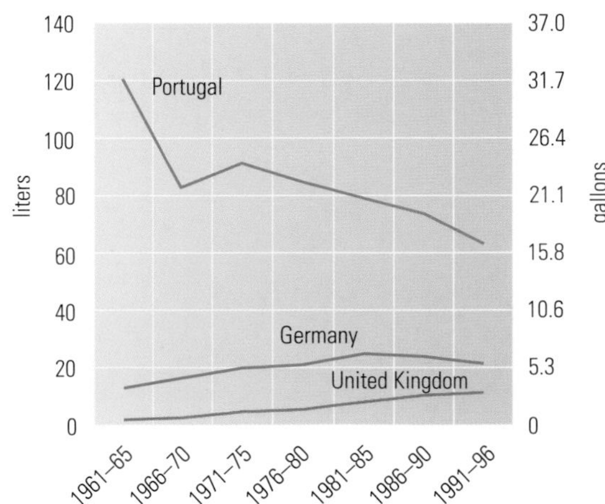

1 Figures from the Wine Institute, California, based on information from the Organisation for Wine and the Vine, Paris.
2 Based on Berger, Anderson and Stringer, "Trends in the World Wine Market," 1961-96, CIES, Adelaide, 1998.

ABOVE: The Martinborough Wine and Music Festival, New Zealand, takes on a European influence!

National tastes vary, and there are even different cultural tastes within the same country. The volume of wine consumed also varies between countries; but these consumption patterns are subject to change. Since the mid-1980s, it has been clear that there is a process of "convergence," with respect to alcohol consumption, between different cultures. For example, it has been found that beer drinkers have the occasional bottle of wine, confirmed wine-lovers take a beer now and then, both sometimes try spirits and spirit drinkers themselves may indulge in both wine and beer.

Consumption trends in three different countries reveal that, in a typical southern European wine-producing country such as Portugal, consumption has halved over about 35 years. In Germany, on the other hand, a country which makes and imports wine, there has been a steady growth in the amount drunk. From the small base in the United Kingdom, there has been rapid growth, particularly in the last ten years. Worldwide, in the long term, if markets in China and the United States grow, then overall consumption may increase. In the countries of Southeast Asia recently there has been a dramatic increase in the consumption of red wine.

Tastes in wine vary considerably. As a rule, Germans like their white wine light and slightly sweet. Italians enjoy their whites dry and rather neutral, to match but not dominate their food. Traditionally, the Portuguese and some eastern Europeans prefer their whites heavy and oxidized. Australians like very fruity wines, while the French opt for some restraint. All of this is good news for wine-lovers, for it means there are many types of wine to explore and, for each style you dislike, there will be many others you will appreciate.

Winemakers catering to the international market are producing wines for different national tastes. An Australian producer of a large-consumption branded chardonnay can adjust the residual sugar levels in the drink for each market so that it is comparatively sweet for the Japanese market, has some noticeable softness for the domestic or Scandinavian market, rather less for the United States and is fairly dry for the UK market.

RIGHT: A visitor gets a feel for traditional pressing at a Californian wine festival.

Grapes and Viticulture

In producing wine, there's a perceived tension between what occurs "naturally" and what results from human intervention. Broadly, the debate is between the role of nature (environment and grape variety), and what the viticulturist and winemaker can do. In practice, this is a false dichotomy. For a commercial wine that is made on a large scale and sells for less than US$10, the essential element is the ability of the winemaker to maximize the character of the variety. For expensive, high-quality wines the varietal character should shine through, but the winemaker may also need enough restraint to reveal the environmental influences. In examining how wine is made, it becomes apparent that the relative importance of these factors will vary from wine to wine.

THE ENVIRONMENT FOR GROWING GRAPES

Vines need a temperate climate and generally flourish best between 30 and 50 degrees of latitude in the northern hemisphere and between 30 and 40 degrees in the southern hemisphere (because of its greater maritime influence). Altitude reduces the average temperature by 2°F (0.6°C) for each 330 feet (100 m), so vines tend to be planted at lower levels except in the warmest climates. Vines must also have access either to a reasonable rainfall, ideally concentrated in winter, or irrigation.

Before examining the various natural conditions that affect vines, it is useful to examine the concept of *terroir*. This French term, related to *terre*, the word for soil, is more correctly translated as "region." The term encompasses the entire natural environment of the vine—the climate, soil, site and topography of the vineyard where it grows. It is a useful concept for some wines, but it also provokes much meaningless debate. Diehard *terroiristes*, usually perceived to be extreme Europhiles, claim that wine must reflect the specific site on which the grapes are grown. Their opponents, crudely caricatured as technocrats, retort that all you need to grow wine grapes is a decent warm climate and a regular supply of water (from irrigation, if necessary).

Whatever the merits of either argument, the reality is that most winemakers don't limit their production to grapes from single regions. At the end of the 1990s, even in France—the bastion of *terroir*-based wines—50 percent of all wine sold was *vin de table*, which is not marketable under a region of origin. However, in California and the southern hemisphere, many wine producers continue to claim that the specific topographies and soils which characterize their own particular vineyards make their wines distinctive.

ABOVE: Beautiful Rippon Vineyard, Otago. In New Zealand, two companies produce three-quarters of all wine.

WORLD DISTRIBUTION OF VINEYARDS AND INFLUENCE OF CLIMATE

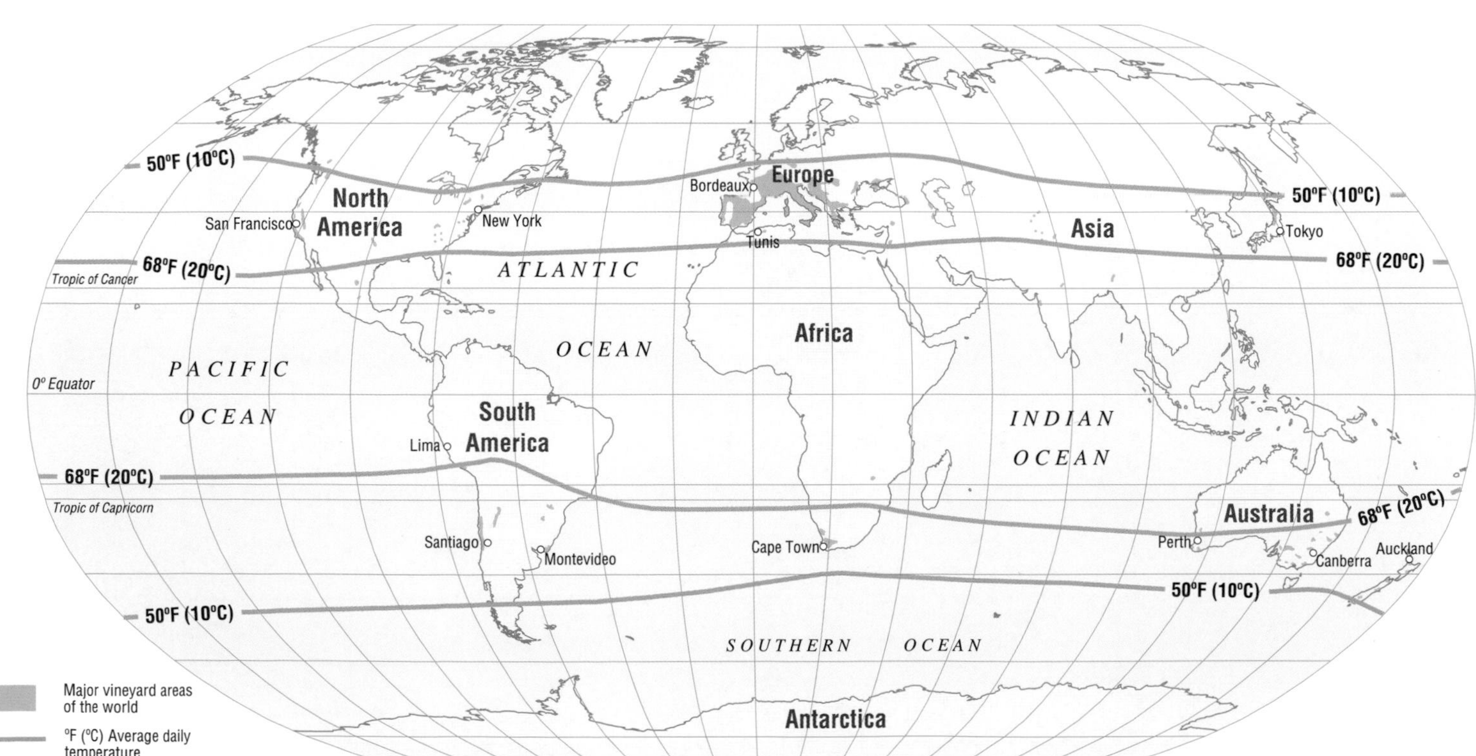

ABOVE: *"God's Stairway," the Scala Dei winery, Priorato, Spain, in a protected, mountainous basin.*

The average bottle of wine is sold for under US$10 per bottle. At that price, it is enough to know that it comes from Languedoc or southeast Australia. There is no doubt that at the top 1 percent of all wine sold, the specific site does influence the wine, modifying structure slightly and adding nuances of flavor. It is also true that some of the greatest wines are sold with only the broadest connection to a specific *terroir*—vintage port, champagne and Penfolds' Grange among them.

Climate

Climate is the most immediately obvious of all the environmental factors which affects vines; it includes temperature, sunshine, rainfall, frost and the impact of wind.

Vines are dormant below about 50°F (10°C), and ripening occurs only above about 63°F (17°C). Vine function diminishes above 75°F (24°C), and the vine may shut down entirely at temperatures higher than about 90°F (32°C). Sunshine is related to heat, but is not the same. Photosynthesis requires sunlight, not heat, so hot cloudy climates are not ideal for producing wine grapes. Sunny days well into fall are crucial, as harvest may take place late in September, or even into October (March or April in the southern hemisphere).

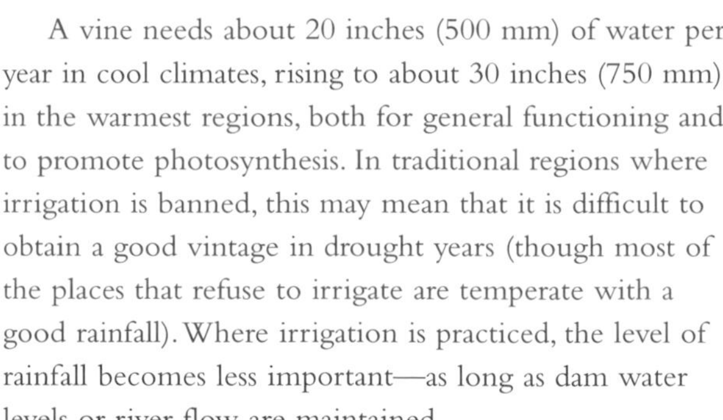

A vine needs about 20 inches (500 mm) of water per year in cool climates, rising to about 30 inches (750 mm) in the warmest regions, both for general functioning and to promote photosynthesis. In traditional regions where irrigation is banned, this may mean that it is difficult to obtain a good vintage in drought years (though most of the places that refuse to irrigate are temperate with a good rainfall). Where irrigation is practiced, the level of rainfall becomes less important—as long as dam water levels or river flow are maintained.

Frost affects the quantity of wine more than the quality. Winter frosts are rarely a problem, but a frost late in spring can literally nip a crop in the bud by burning off the spring shoots. In 1991, the yields in Touraine in the Loire Valley were about 10 percent of normal because a severe frost that struck on April 21–22 destroyed most shoots.

The impact of frosts can be mitigated by good site selection, or by artificial means. The most basic of these is using hot braziers in the vineyards to raise the temperature, while one of the more technologically advanced ways is aspersion—spraying the shoots with water, which freezes and, paradoxically, insulates them against the worst of the cold.

Wind may cool the vines, or burn them when the wind is warm, and at its worst can rip leaves off. While it is not a general problem, it may be recurrent in specific regions such as the Rhône Valley, where the Mistral can

CLOCKWISE FROM RIGHT: *Riverside vineyards in Germany; vines in maritime Bordeaux; flat vineyards in the hot south of California; bush vines in Mediterranean southern France.*

whip down towards the Mediterranean, stressing the vines and impeding ripening. Winds can also be beneficial in a warm climate, as in the Hunter region in Australia, where the valley funnels in sea breezes to moderate the heat of the sun.

Comparing climates between different wine regions is fraught with difficulty, and has to take account of temperature and temperature variability, sunlight and sun angle, rainfall, wind and various other factors. One can roughly categorize wine regions in four ways—maritime, continental, Mediterranean and hot inland. The charts on the right give examples of each, using four wine regions—Bordeaux, the Rheingau, Provence and the Riverland in Australia. The information covers just four of the many variables involved: the number of sunshine hours during summer, the mean July temperature (January for the Riverland), the mean winter temperature and the annual rainfall.

CLIMATIC VARIABLES IN FOUR MAJOR WINE-GROWING REGIONS [3]

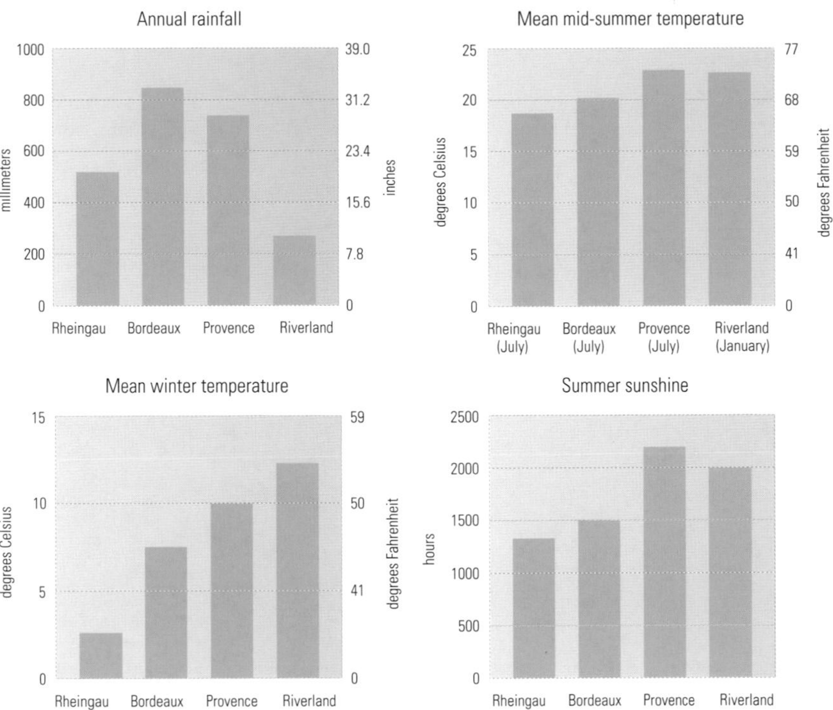

From this, it becomes apparent that Bordeaux and the Rheingau have broadly similar summer temperatures (the former is a bit hotter, and has marginally more sunshine), but the continental climate is markedly colder in winter. The Mediterranean and hot inland climates are both warmer in summer, and noticeably warmer in winter. The maritime climate, with its proximity to the ocean, is the wettest, but the Mediterranean is also quite wet (though it is in fact rather drier in summer, which is why it has the highest number of sunshine hours). The inland region has the least rainfall, and irrigation is essential here.

It is impossible to use climatic modeling to predict exactly what varieties will be used, and which wines will be made, but the wines of each of these nominated regions shows something about their climate:

Rheingau produces delicate, light but intensely flavorful white wines, based on riesling.

Bordeaux has a range of full whites, fine cabernet and merlot-based reds and dessert wines.

Provence boasts robust but flavorful reds, and some tasty rosés.

Riverland produces some good wines, but it concentrates on the production of bulk wine.

An important distinction must be made between the climate of a wine region and its weather. The climate is the average of all the weather factors over a long period. It allows one to predict what is likely to happen to a vineyard planted there and, therefore, is a key indicator of site selection. The weather is what happens in a particular year, and it will inevitably deviate from the climatic norms. Thus, 1987 in Bordeaux was wetter than normal, especially in autumn, so that cabernet sauvignon grapes did not ripen properly. On the other hand, 1990 in the same region was warmer and sunnier than usual, resulting in an early and large crop of high-quality grapes. That is how the impact of weather leads to vintage variation, though it is more of an issue in marginal climates. In warmer regions, there is likely to be less variation from one year to the next.

Soil

The most important benefit offered by soil is also the most overlooked, and that is anchorage. The ability to root the vine into the ground is essential. Beyond that, however, the key element is drainage. Vines don't like to be waterlogged and respond badly in those conditions. Additionally, if drainage is poor and there is heavy rain near harvest, the grapes are likely to soak up extra water and dilute their other components, thus reducing the quality of the resulting wine. Drainage can be modified.

Vines can tolerate quite a wide range of soil pH levels, from about 5.5 (acidic) to around 8.5 (alkaline), but it may be better to adjust the soil at either end of the spectrum, and particular rootstocks may be required to cope with extreme situations. Nutrient content is also critical. Vines need a supply of various elements, most notably nitrogen, but also phosphorus, potassium and various metals.

However, excessive fertilizer—particularly too much nitrogen—promotes vigorous vine canopy growth that may shade the bunches of grapes and inhibit ripening. Likewise, too much potassium in the soil will reduce the acid level in juice—and consequently in the wine—making it less balanced and stable, and reducing its aging potential. This has been a major problem in the vineyards of Burgundy in the last few decades after intemperate

3 Based on J. Gladstones, "Viticulture and Environment," Winetitles, Adelaide, 1992.

The Rheingau—a classic example of the importance of site

Although it is quite a large region, the Rheingau in Germany is a good example of how site can modify the overall climate and situation of a wine region. In this case, it turns an area in what is a very marginal latitude into one of the country's prime wine regions. The site modifies the position in a number of ways:

- *The river Rhine, which generally flows south–north through Germany, turns east–west at this point. This gives some riverside slopes a southerly aspect, maximizing sun exposure at the warmest part of the day.*
- *The Taunus Mountains to the north protect the vineyards from the cold winds that blow down from the Arctic.*
- *The river provides airflow, reducing air pockets, thus limiting the development of frosts.*
- *The river provides some reflected light onto the slopes, which is crucial to aid the final ripening in a cool northern fall.*
- *The river encourages mists in some years, which are necessary for the development of "noble rot" to make great botrytized sweet wines.*

use of fertilizer in the region in the years following the Second World War.

Modern viticulturists monitor soil structure and composition, and moderate water supply and nutrient addition (which often come through the same pipe) accordingly. There is a view among some commentators, however—though it is hard to adduce concrete evidence for it—that the best wine comes from the vineyards which are manipulated the least.

The ideal soil, therefore, has good drainage, with access to retained water at some depth if irrigation is not an option. It should have a balanced texture—neither too much clay, which will waterlog, nor too much sand, which drains well but does not retain nutrients. It has reasonable access to essential elements, but is not so fertile that it promotes luxuriant canopy growth. As well, it should not be overly limey or acidic. In many ways (except for the lime content), chalky soil is close to perfect, but the only substantial wine region where it predominates is Champagne.

One common myth needs to be nailed. There is no evidence that the soil in the vineyard conveys flavor to the wine. Mosel wines may be described as "slatey," or chablis as "flinty," but that is not because slate or flint in the soil imparts flavor. It is possible, though unproven, that chemical component of the soil may influence nuances of taste, but it is not true that soil conveys its flavor to the wine.

Site and topography

The site of a vineyard mediates between the predominant soil and the overall climate of the region. By dint of a particular aspect, the climate may have, say, a more south-facing aspect than is general, or the soil may be modified by erosion. The winding Mosel Valley offers many sites; the best are those with a southerly aspect on a hillside. The flatter parts of the region make less fine, less intense wine.

Other factors can also be decisive. Isolated hills encourage airflow, thus reducing the chance of frosts in late spring. Rivers also reduce the likelihood of frosts as they tend to raise the prevailing temperature slightly through airflow. Altitude can also be decisive; a rise of 330 feet (100 m) reduces the average temperature by 2°F (0.6°C). Site can be modified by human intervention. Trees are often planted to act as wind-breaks. Eroded soil can be taken from the foot of a slope back up to the top.

BELOW: *Soil profile showing different "horizons" in Costers del Segre, Spain.*

BELOW CENTER: *The world-famous "Terra Rossa" (red soil) of Coonawarra, Australia, provides excellent drainage.*

BELOW RIGHT: *Vineyards planted in sand in the Clarendon Hills, South Australia.*

VINE AND VARIETY

The grape

The grape variety is of vital importance in shaping wine styles. At its most basic, it determines the color of the wine: you cannot get red wine from white grapes (although you can get white wine from red grapes). After that, choice of grape influences the levels of acidity, alcohol and (in red wines) tannin, as well as the body and style of the wine. The variety also determines how the winemaker will approach the wine. Few winemakers would age riesling in oak or put it through malolactic fermentation. Conversely, no winemaker is going to prevent the malolactic fermentation in cabernet sauvignon, and most will give it some oak treatment.

The typical wine grape is quite small. Even with white wines, some flavor comes from the skin, and a low juice-to-skin ratio enhances those characters. In black grapes (also known as red grapes), the skin gives the wine its tannin and color. Thicker skins and/or smaller grapes mean deeper color and more tannic wine.

The variety, of course, also gives the wine its core flavors. Each variety may have a range of typical aromas and tastes—its "flavor spectrum." No wine will display all of these flavors, but a reasonably good wine should show at least one or two flavors to give good varietal character, and a complex wine will display more.

The flavor spectrum for shiraz, for instance, includes herbs, mint, spice, pepper, raspberry, cherry, mulberry, blackberry, plum, cassis, black olives, aniseed, liquorice,

The typical composition of a grape[4]

Water	75.00%
Sugars	22.00%
Acids	
-Tartaric	0.6%
-Malic	0.5%
Total	1.10%
Nitrogenous matter	0.80%
Phenolics	0.05%
Minerals	0.50%
Other matter	0.55%

Note that this is for a grape of average ripeness, and will vary according to variety and location.

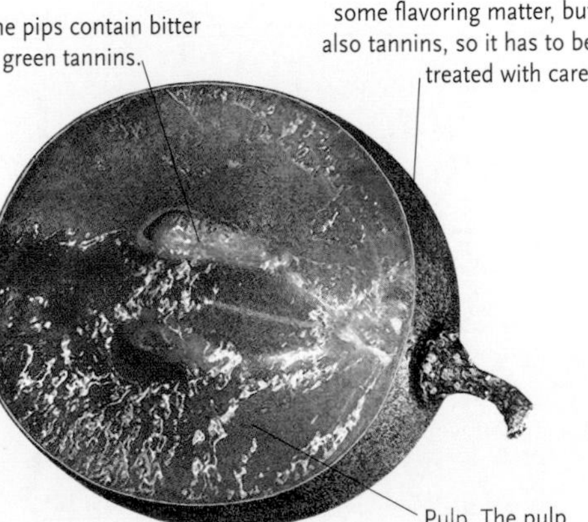

CABERNET SAUVIGNON

ABOVE: *Precipitous terraced slopes of the Mosel Valley, Germany.*

4 Based on P. Iland and P. Gago, "Australian Wine—From the Vine to the Glass," Patrick Iland Promotions, Adelaide, 1997.

LEFT TO RIGHT: Grenache. Malbec. Petit verdot. Pinot noir.

LEFT TO RIGHT: Hand picked syrah, awaiting crushing. Tannat. Tempranillo. Zinfandel.

ABOVE (LEFT TO RIGHT): Cabernet franc—almost ripe. Cabernet sauvignon.

prune, stewed plum, chocolate, jammy and raisin.[5] The primary fruit in shiraz develops, roughly, in that order, moving generally from fruit grown in a cool climate (or which may be underripe) to fruit from warm areas (which may be too ripe).

Though there may be some overlap between varieties, the flavor spectrum differs from variety to variety. Thus, shiraz may show a white pepper character, but cabernet sauvignon should not. Both types of wine, however, may display plummy or curranty flavors.

The condition of the fruit is also important. In cool regions, underripe fruit will give harsh green characters and, if it is damp, disease may well dull or spoil the wine. In hot climates, the overripe grapes may give hot alcohol and jammy flavors lacking balance and complexity.

While the variety shapes the style of wine, the climate modifies how each variety develops. Riesling grows well in a very cool climate because it can become flavor-ripe while it is barely physiologically ripe. Thus, intense rieslings are made in northern Germany with a potential alcohol content of a comparatively low 9 percent and showing a comparatively low level of sugar content at ripeness. But the same variety also flourishes in the Clare Valley—a warm, if not hot, region of South Australia—where it makes fuller but still intense styles of wines.

5 Based on Coombes and Dry, "Viticulture in Australia," Vol. 2, Winetitles, Adelaide, 1992.

Red grape varieties

Barbera Widely planted in Italy and California but only makes characterful wines in Piedmont.

Cabernet franc Overlooked sibling of the next red variety, but contributes a lot to Bordeaux wines, and makes interesting, underrated wines in the Loire Valley.

Cabernet sauvignon The most ubiquitous red variety in the world. Bordeaux is its heartland, but upstarts in California, Tuscany and Australia are staking a claim.

Gamay Makes fruity (and occasionally ageworthy) wines in Beaujolais, whose wines are misunderstood.

Grenache The most planted red variety in the world, but concentrated in France and Spain. Only makes great wine in Châteauneuf-du-Pape, but is attracting some interest in Australia.

Lambrusco This can be better than you might expect, but you really have to search out the best examples. Otherwise, it's a frothy, sweet, insubstantial wine for cola drinkers.

Malbec A minor player in southwest France (including Bordeaux), but malbec is the major player in Argentina.

Merlot This is the "other" great red variety of Bordeaux, but it is responsible for its priciest wines. Now relocating to California, but yet to be granted residency elsewhere in the world.

Mourvèdre Little-known grape from southern France and Spain that gives tannic backbone to blends. Attracting attention in Australia and California.

Nebbiolo High acid, high tannin variety which makes complex long-lived wines in Piedmont, but hasn't repeated the feat elsewhere in the world.

Petit verdot A minor but high-quality component in the Bordeaux mix; it is also being investigated in emerging wine regions.

Pinotage South Africa's very own variety, a crossing of the productive cinsault and exacting pinot noir. This grape can make some good wines, but often results in jammy or tart nonentities.

Pinot meunier Least well known but most widely planted grape in Champagne. Traditionally treated as second rate, but Krug at least is proud of pinot meunier's role in its wine.

Pinot noir The classic red grape of Burgundy, but one of the fussiest varieties to manage. It has captivated obsessives across the world, but only New Zealand and parts of the USA seem to be making headway with it.

Sangiovese Widely planted in Italy, and capable of making great savory wines in Tuscany. Attracting cautious interest elsewhere.

Syrah/shiraz Makes stunning wines in the northern Rhône and Australia. An increasingly popular variety, sometimes to blend, in other parts of the world.

Tannat Hard tannic variety in southwest France that, with age, turns in some complex, interesting wines.

Tempranillo The great grape of Rioja, it is also producing good wines in other parts of Spain and northern Portugal.

Touriga naçional Portugal's great indigenous variety. A key component of port, but also used for increasingly good table wines.

Zinfandel California's very own variety (though it also appears as the primitivo in southern Italy). Makes juicy, brambly, powerfully alcoholic wines.

White grape varieties

Chardonnay The most desired grape variety in the world, originating in Burgundy but now widespread. Makes full-bodied, potentially complex wines.

Chenin blanc Makes great wine in the Loire Valley and much ordinary (but occasionally good) wine in South Africa.

Colombard A good workhorse variety in the south of France; it is also widely planted for making neutral wines in South Africa, California and Australia.

Furmint Described as "fiery," this is the great variety of Hungarian tokay and has potential for table wine.

Garganega Neutral variety, but can make wines of great texture and character in Soave.

Gewürztraminer A most distinctive variety, with lychee and rose-petal characters. At its best in Alsace. Planted widely but not densely elsewhere.

Malvasia Heavy but interesting variety, little known but widely planted in southern Europe.

Marsanne Mainstay of white wines in the northern Rhône Valley, and surprisingly concentrated in central Victoria, Australia.

Melon de bourgogne The variety of muscadet. Neutral and light.

Müller-thurgau Widely planted, early ripening, but mediocre "flowery" variety. Planted mainly in Germany but with an outpost in New Zealand.

Muscadelle Generally a minor supporting variety, but the grape behind the great fortified tokays of Australia.

Muscat A wide family of grapes, but at its best (*muscat blanc à petits grains*) responsible for dry aromatic

BELOW (LEFT TO RIGHT): Chardonnay. Furmint in Tokaji—yet to ripen fully. Dark tinted gewürztraminer. Hand-picking malvasia. Muscadelle.

BOTTOM (LEFT TO RIGHT): Pink muscat grapes. Pinot gris. Riesling. Sémillon waiting to be processed. Viognier.

A year in the life of a vine

RIGHT: *The pruned vine is dormant in winter, allowing it to preserve its strength for the next season.*

BELOW: *The "set": the flower heads form into nascent grapes. Poor weather can lead to the failure of bunches to form, or irregularly developing bunches.*

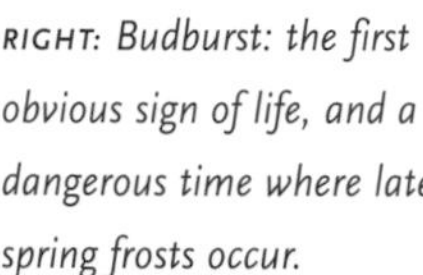

RIGHT: *Budburst: the first obvious sign of life, and a dangerous time where late spring frosts occur.*

BELOW: *Grapes ripening on the vine following* veraison*—the point at which their color changes. Now the sugar levels in the bunches increase, and acidity becomes proportionately less important.*

ABOVE: *Spring growth: the vine is focusing its energies on the development of shoots and foliage.*

RIGHT: *The apparently insignificant vine flowers.*

RIGHT: *A vineyard in late fall, following harvest, and just prior to leaf-fall.*

wines in Alsace, good sparkling wine in Asti and great fortified wines in southern France and Australia.

Palomino Boring, but it does make exciting sherry.

Pinot blanc Restrained variety, at its best in Alsace and Italy. Now the subject of interesting experiments in the United States.

Pinot gris Makes full-bodied, slightly aromatic wines. Best in Alsace, but also used in Italy, central Europe, Oregon, and attracting attention elsewhere.

Riesling The world's greatest white variety, making stunning, focused wines (from dry to very sweet) in Germany, Alsace, Austria and Australia. Misunderstood and mistreated elsewhere.

Sauvignon blanc A classic in the central Loire and New Zealand. Other regions are still trying.

Sémillon Makes great wines in Bordeaux (in particular botrytized dessert wines) and the Hunter Valley in Australia. Ignored elsewhere.

Trebbiano The world's most widely planted and boring white grape variety. Ideal for cognac.

Viognier Makes full-bodied and aromatic white centered on the northern Rhône, but now attracting attention elsewhere in the world, especially in California.

Chardonnay around the world

A good example of how one type of grape can make different styles of wine when grown in different surroundings is given by the most versatile of varieties, chardonnay, which is grown in a diversity of environments.

Adelaide Hills Good natural acidity combined with ripe fruit make a typical, comparatively ripe Australian wine with good aging potential.

Carneros The mists of the San Francisco Bay moderate what would otherwise be a hot climate, making for well-structured wines that still show some generosity of fruit.

Chablis The steely table wines of this cool region have a firm acidity that allows them to develop into some of the longest living whites available.

Champagne In this cool region of France, the grape makes acidic and delicate base wine for the greatest sparkling wines of the world.

Hunter Valley One of the warmest regions of Australia produces big chardonnays with a typical "peaches and cream" character.

Languedoc In southern France, the chardonnay grape produces melon and butter characters that reflect burgundy without its great structural balance and intensity.

Marlborough In this dry region of New Zealand, chardonnay produces wines that may echo some of the Australian fruit styles, but with an extra vein of acidity.

Meursault In the Côte d'Or, the heartland of Burgundy, the grape produces buttery, nutty wines with a streak of acidity.

Napa Valley Just 20 miles (32 km) north of Carneros, in California, chardonnay becomes full, ripe and generous, but without the tautness of the wines from farther south.

ABOVE: Planting a grafted vine in a stony Spanish vineyard.

The vine

The grapevine *Vitis vinifera*, originally native to east Asia, is now the most commonly cultivated species across the world. Within the *vinifera* species are thousands of varieties, possibly as many as 10,000, although few of them are used to make wine. Only 200 varieties are recorded as being significant in France.

The varieties commonly used for winemaking have developed over the centuries. Sometimes they have appeared naturally, sometimes encouraged by grape growers. The pinot family, for instance, is prone to mutation. Pinot meunier and pinot gris came from pinot noir; pinot blanc from pinot gris.

For the last century or so, it has been possible to create specific new varieties by taking the pollen from one and fertilizing the flower of another variety, and planting out the resulting seeds. The two most famous of these crossings are probably müller-thurgau, now the most widely planted grape in Germany, and pinotage in South Africa. Both will occasionally make good wine, but they are generally used as workhorse varieties. The problem with new varieties is that the viticulturists who produce them are searching for higher yields or early ripening rather than enhanced flavor, structure or quality in the resulting wine.

It is now also possible to produce hybrids—vines that have as their parents both a *Vitis vinifera* vine and another species, invariably one from North America. This is done to create vines with resistance to specific pests, diseases or weather conditions. Traditionally, hybrids are perceived to make poor wine and are prohibited for the production of "quality" wine in Europe. In practice, some of these grapes—seyval blanc in the United Kingdom is an example—can make fair, if not great, wine.

Most viticultural attention these days is focused not on new varieties, but on the genetic manipulation of existing varieties. It should be possible to exclude from chardonnay the genes that make it prone to rots and other fungal diseases, thus reducing the costs of growing the grapes and guaranteeing more regular quality. Inevitably, this raises the spectre of labeling problems, with consumers seeking information about genetically manipulated wine. Less acknowledged is the likelihood that, as with most other viticultural developments,

ABOVE: *Vines planted along the contours, to reduce erosion, high above a Basque village.*

modifications will be developed to aid the grape grower—primarily by encouraging larger yields—rather than the consumer, who would rather see the development of more intense, complex and harmonious wines.

The most important part of the vine's cycle is the process of ripening, which is what creates the final wine—and it is particularly important in the period following *véraison* (the key stage at which the grape skins begin to turn black, or to become translucent if they are white grapes). After *véraison*, when the vine normally has sufficient reserves of sugar, the surplus is sent into the grapes. This is eventually converted to alcohol, making grape juice into wine.

Ripening, however, is crucial for more than just sugar accumulation. The acidity is very high in developing grapes, but the relative acid levels drop with the ripening process, allowing a balanced wine to develop. In cool grape-growing regions, poor weather during summer can limit ripening. If this happens, the resulting wines will be unbalanced or will have to be treated to reduce the acidity. Conversely, in hot regions, the acidity may drop too much and have to be replaced.

Ripening also allows the various flavor components of the grape to develop. At the same time, the phenolic compounds that give red wines their color and tannin also increase, with the tannins developing from green and coarse to ripe and smooth. Red wine made from insufficiently ripened grapes will be found to have a harsh, bitter, tannic structure.

IN THE VINEYARD

Site selection

Before a vine is even planted, the choice of site for the vineyard is crucial. In addition to the factors detailed previously (under site and topography), such as avoiding frosts and guaranteeing good drainage—there are economic factors to consider. Can a vineyard be harvested mechanically? Is there ready access to a market; or, if a cellar door is planned, will there be substantial passing trade? What does the land cost? In Champagne, for example, you will pay much more per acre than you would in Languedoc.

These factors have little importance in the classic regions of Europe. Here, vineyards have been planted for centuries—even millennia—and inherited land is the rule. But elsewhere in the world, including the distant reaches of the south of France or Spain and parts of eastern Europe, site selection for enterprising new grape growers is very relevant.

Many tests can be done before planting—for instance, testing to assess drainage, pH and nutrient content. When the tests are completed the land can be prepared—this might be deep ploughing to break up the soil, digging in lime or having the land treated for nematodes or other pests.

Rootstocks

In Europe and California, and often in other parts of the world, grapevines will invariably be grafted on to other rootstocks before planting. The technique of grafting has been known to horticulturists for centuries, and essentially is the insertion of the shoot of one species into the branch of another. This can be done to allow, for instance, two or three varieties of apple to grow out of one tree trunk. In viticulture, it allows shoots from *Vinifera* vines to be grafted onto the roots of another vine species, often in order to gain resistance to pests, disease or other conditions.

The main reason for grafting in viticulture is to avoid phylloxera, but rootstocks can also benefit vines planted in soils with a high lime content by minimizing the effect of lime in inhibiting the uptake of some essential elements. Other rootstocks can help the vine to cope with summer aridity or high salinity.

Planting

The orientation within which vines will be planted is done with two—sometimes contradictory—aims. The first is to optimize the angle to sun; to be at 90° to the midday sun is generally considered to be ideal. However, it is also better to plant along a slope rather than down it, as rows of vines down a slope will facilitate erosion.

In Europe, vines are traditionally close-spaced, sometimes as many as 20,000 per acre (10,000 per ha). The theory is that this increases the pressure on the vines, which has the effect of limiting yields, and thus guaranteeing quality. In practice, much less dense planting is used in many regions, especially where machines are used for harvesting and other forms of vineyard management. It is also the case that, while dense planting is preferable in the poor vineyard soils of Europe, wider spacing will, in fact, induce the vine to give its best in high-potential soils.

Pruning and training

Pruning allows the viticulturist to determine how productive the vine is to be for the next season, offering the opportunity for a greater or lesser yield. It is also the precursor to training the vine, creating the "architecture" of the canopy to allow for various forms of management.

Training determines how the vine is to be shaped. It may be along a wire, with just one cane or cordon or a number of them, or it may be in bush form, which is excellent for conserving the vine's resources in arid regions, but not a good shape for a vineyard that is mechanized. Canopy management techniques are designed to open grapes up to sunlight, or to encourage airflow to inhibit diseases that stem from humidity.

Irrigation

As with the subject of *terroir*, irrigation is now very much a non-issue, despite the traditional resistance to it that has existed in Europe. Opponents of irrigation would argue the dangers of increasing yield excessively

LEFT: *Newly planted vines, protected from damage in plastic tubes, with posts ready for trellis wires. It will take another two years before these vines bear usable fruit.*

by using extra water, but supporters are aware that it needs to be controlled carefully according to the style of wine being made. It is also worth remembering that the regions in which irrigation is banned tend to be those with a temperate climate and regular, year-round rainfall. Much high-quality Australian and Chilean wine would not exist substantially without irrigation. Interestingly, Spain has now relaxed its ban on irrigation, and the practice has started to appear in other parts of the European Union.

The oldest method of irrigation, known since ancient times, was flood irrigation, which was later developed into irrigation by furrow, channelling water along rows by the vines. This system needs flattish land to work effectively, and vineyards are more often planted on slopes. Spray irrigation was developed over the last 40 years (often with mobile sprinklers), and then drip irrigation, with a pipe along each row of vines dropping water into the soil, was introduced.

The advantages of the drip system are precision, simplicity and the ability to apply other products such as liquid fertilizer along with the water. The system is very responsive, and can be used to a greater or lesser extent according to need.

Many grape growers—especially those committed to quality—would argue that they only resort to irrigation in the driest seasons, except in the first three years of the vine's life, when it is essential to establish the young plant. However, it remains a useful tool in the ever-expanding viticultural armory.

RIGHT: Netting protects the vines at the Amisfield Lake Hayes vineyard, Central Otago, New Zealand.

BELOW: Cleaning buckets to prevent the spread of disease, Maximin Grünhäuser Estate, Saar, Germany.

Soil management

Historically, the land between vine rows has been kept free of vegetation. This was useful in dry climates where grass and weeds would otherwise compete with the vines for limited water supplies. However, it has been found that a mid-row crop inhibits soil erosion and makes it easier to get mechanical access without churning up the soil. Careful choice of the crop (grass, clover or rye) allows cutting or digging-in the greenery to create a nutritious mulch. This is more natural than inorganic fertilizers, which are still widely used. Soil compacts with time, so it may be necessary to plough or even deep-rip it to facilitate airflow and drainage. Unfortunately, loosening the soil can also promote erosion.

Diseases and disorders

Much of the viticulturist's time is spent ensuring the good health of the vine. Four types of disease, as well as some disorders, can affect grape vines. The largest group, fungal disease, is caused by microscopic filament-shaped organisms. They include rots, oidium and peronospera.

Rots (especially grey rot) attack the whole vine and spread rapidly. Rot starts from dead material (often dead flowers from late spring) and needs humidity to develop. It reduces yields and can impair the color and flavor of wine. It spreads particularly fast when berries are split, which may result from bird activity or rapid berry growth after high autumn rainfall. It is controlled by sprays and pre-empted by good canopy management.

Oidium is a powdery mildew that splits berries and inhibits bunch growth. Uniquely for fungal diseases, it does not need humidity, just warmth and shade. It is now easily inhibited by dusting with sulfur if caught early.

Peronospera is a downy mildew that requires warm, humid conditions. A cottony growth appears on the underside of leaves and inhibits plant growth. It is easily controlled with copper-based sprays.

Bacterial diseases are few in number. The most virulent is Pierce's disease, which kills vines and is incurable, and is a particular problem in the United States. Leaves develop dead spots, which enlarge, causing leaf fall. It is spread by small insects called leafhoppers and occurs especially in vineyards near streams (the bacteria grow in water).

Viral diseases, including fanleaf virus and leafroll virus, are of recent origin (dating from about 1890) when rootstocks began to be used. They tend to be spread by cuttings from infected plants, although insects like nematodes may pass them on. They do not necessarily kill, but may weaken vines and reduce yields. The only effective treatment is to heat-treat vine stock to create virus-free material. Fanleaf virus, which may be spread by nematodes, causes malformed growth in the form of fan-like deformed leaves that cause poor set and small bunches. Cabernet sauvignon vines are particularly sensitive to this disease. It is a major problem in the Napa Valley and Burgundy. So far, the only cure that has been discovered is to uproot the whole vineyard, fumigate and replant it with virus-free stock. With the onset of leafroll virus, often spread by mealy bugs, leaves roll downwards and discolor. It is now widespread, especially in humid regions. Although it rarely kills vines, it reduces yields and delays ripening.

Vine disorders, including chlorosis, *coulure* and *millerandage*, also occur. These are not diseases, but environmental problems that can afflict vines.

Chlorosis is common in chalky soils which inhibit iron uptake from the soil, thus limiting the development of chlorophyll, causing the yellowing of leaves and poor photosynthesis.

Coulure and *millerandage* refer to poor berry formation resulting from inadequate fertilization of flowers or poor fruit set. It results from poor carbohydrate supply due to inadequate photosynthesis at the time of flowering, usually because of poor weather.

Vine pests

Vines are vulnerable to many animal and insect pests. Birds pick holes in fruit; rabbits and deer nibble shoots; and insects defoliate or attack berries and roots. Critically, pests can also act as vectors, or carriers, of a disease. Different pests are active in different countries and regions, but the one with a worldwide impact on the wine industry is phylloxera.

This small louse, native to North America, lives on the roots of American vine species. Here, vines have become tolerant to the insect and, as it feeds off the roots, they callous over with no lasting damage. However, in other parts of the world vines have no natural protection against this pest and it has caused great destruction.

Phylloxera spread to France in the early 1860s, probably from an imported vine from North America, starting in a vineyard in Marseilles. In searching for food, the American parasite had discovered *Vinifera* vines and started feeding from their roots. Its life-cycle—a single female can lay up to 20 million eggs in a season—was enough to ensure a rapid progress throughout the entire country (it had reached all parts within 30 years) and then on through Europe.

The French puzzled for years about how to deal with it. They discovered that phylloxera would not tolerate sandy soil, but in practical terms this knowledge was of little use. It could be dealt with by flooding a vineyard for 100 days, but again, that was rarely possible or practical. Certain chemicals injected into the soil would kill it—carbon disulfide was found to be the best—but they were expensive, dangerous and had only temporary impact. The solution was to graft scions of *Vitis vinifera* varieties onto rootstocks from native American vines. That way, growers were able to keep their syrah or chardonnay grapes but could now protect them from devastation.

In the interim, however, hundreds of thousands of acres of vine had been lost, never to be replanted, and the viticultural map of Europe changed. Old, often high-quality varieties, like carmenere in Bordeaux, disappeared because they could be replanted with more productive vines.

BELOW: Grapes growing at Chateau Tahbilk in Australia, where one vineyard dates back to the mid-nineteenth century.

Winemaking

HARVEST AND CRUSHING

The first stage in the process of making wine is to harvest the grapes. This can be done either by machine or by hand. Neither of these methods is technically "better" than the other; it just depends on where you are and what kind of wine you choose to make.

Mechanical harvesting is usually fine on flat or undulating vineyard sites. It is quick (one person can do in four hours what may take six to ten days to complete if done by hand), and therefore cheaper. It allows you to harvest at night, which is useful in warm climates to minimize oxidation. It generally preserves the fruit quality almost as well as hand-picked fruit. Hand-picking does, however, allow more selectivity and ensures that you pick whole bunches without any juice starting to run, which is all but inevitable with the vigorous harvesters.

The decision whether or not to pick by machine generally boils down to factors other than that of quality. Traditionally, grapes have been hand-picked in California because of the availability of cheap Mexican labor. In the flat land of the Muscadet region, producing wines that generally sell in the lower price bracket, most picking is done by machine. Usually, vineyards in Australia are picked by machine, but a quality producer may hand-pick for extra selectivity. In the steep parts of the Mosel Valley, it is impossible to get machines on the slopes. In Champagne, where whole, unbroken bunches are essential for the sparkling wine, hand-picking is the order of the day.

The various types of mechanical harvesters all work by straddling the vines, while a number of vibrating beaters strike the vine trunks vigorously to dislodge the grapes. Generally, the bunch stalks remain on the plant. The grapes fall into trays under the beaters, and are then carried up into hoppers at the top of each side of the harvester. Every few rows, the hoppers are emptied into a trailer, which carries the grapes back to the winery.

Most vineyards are close to the wineries that serve them, but transporting the grapes becomes an issue when they are some distance away. Adding sulfur dioxide to inhibit the oxidation process, then blanketing them under an inert gas in a closed container allows them to be shipped over long distances without much damage, although there could still be a quality problem with broken or rotten grapes. Often, large producers will have white grapes pressed and then transported to a winery as juice. In Champagne, where grapes need to be dealt with quickly to guarantee a good base wine, they are often pressed at press-houses in the middle of vineyards. At the winery, the grapes may be sorted (a process called *triage*) to eliminate rotten or unripe bunches. Appellation regulations in Chateauneuf-du-Pâpe make it compulsory to exclude 10 percent of the grapes to enhance quality.

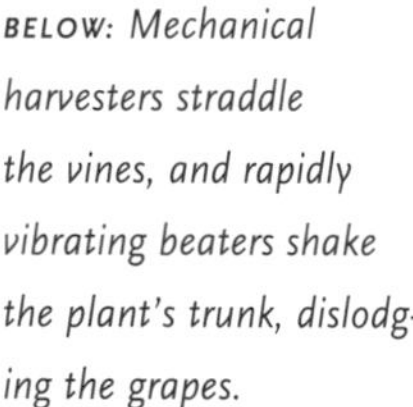

BELOW: Mechanical harvesters straddle the vines, and rapidly vibrating beaters shake the plant's trunk, dislodging the grapes.

The first stage at the winery is to destem and crush the grapes. Crushing does not press juice out of the grapes; it is merely designed to split open the skins to encourage some juice to run out naturally. Destemming is almost always carried out because the bunch stems carry tannins that may be quite green and could leach out into the juice and taint the wine. However, some of the stems are left in with some red wines. With wines that require whole-bunch pressing—as with sparkling wines, or some white wines where the winemaker wants to emphasize delicate fruit—the stems remain, but a fast, gentle pressing precludes any phenolic uptake from them.

WHITE WINE FERMENTATION

White grapes are pumped from the crusher to the press, initially without any pressure. The grapes merely sit (or get turned if it is a rotary press) to encourage juice to flow out naturally. This is the "free-run juice" that provides the freshest, most delicate wine. After it has been allowed to run out, pressure is applied, and a number of pressings will probably be carried out. The pressed juice is fermented separately from the free-run juice to ensure that, if it is too harsh, it does not spoil the more elegant wine made from the free-run juice.

Often the grapes in a particular region will not have the necessary balance to give a wine the right structure. The juice, or must, can be modified to ensure that the resulting wine is well structured. This includes:

Enrichment This increases the sugar content of the must, which increases the final alcohol content of the wine. Generally, it is done by adding sugar to the ferment (chaptalization), but sometimes it is done by adding concentrated grape juice. Chaptalization is common in Europe—especially the cool north—and allowed in New Zealand, but banned in Australia. Enrichment doesn't sweeten the wine, it only increases its alcohol level.

Acidification In warm climates, the acid level of the grapes may drop to too low a level before the grapes have attained flavor ripeness. Therefore, acid can be added to the must, which both maintains its freshness

BELOW: Grapes need to be taken to the winery fast once picked: the Swiss way.

Presses

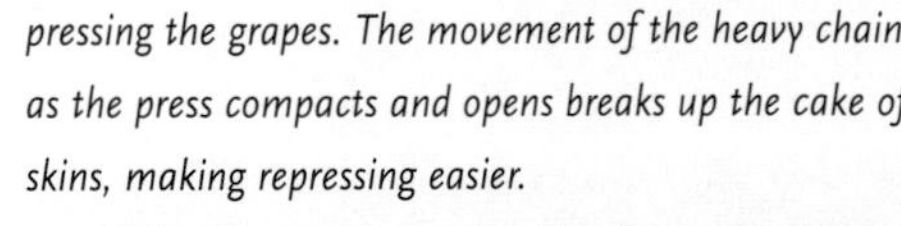

Presses come in different forms. The most traditional type is the basket press, which is still used in Champagne, and by anyone who wants a fast but gentle press. A more recent development is the vaslin press, comprising a cylinder with plates at each end that are pulled together by metal chains, thus compressing the grapes. The movement of the heavy chains as the press compacts and opens breaks up the cake of skins, making repressing easier.

Today the most common style of press is probably the air-bag (bladder) press. A thick rubber membrane lies in a cylinder that is filled with grapes. The membrane is then blown up, compacting the grapes and extracting the juice. The advantage is that it is gentle—avoiding the extraction of bitter phenolics from the pips and stems—but it is also efficient. These days, the process is computerized, and the winemaker can preset the machine for a number of pressings at different pressures.

EXTREME LEFT: A traditional "basket" press in Spain, with the marc (pressed grape skins and residue) spilling out after a pressing.

LEFT: Mats used to contain the grapes in a basket press, drying after use.

White wine fermentation

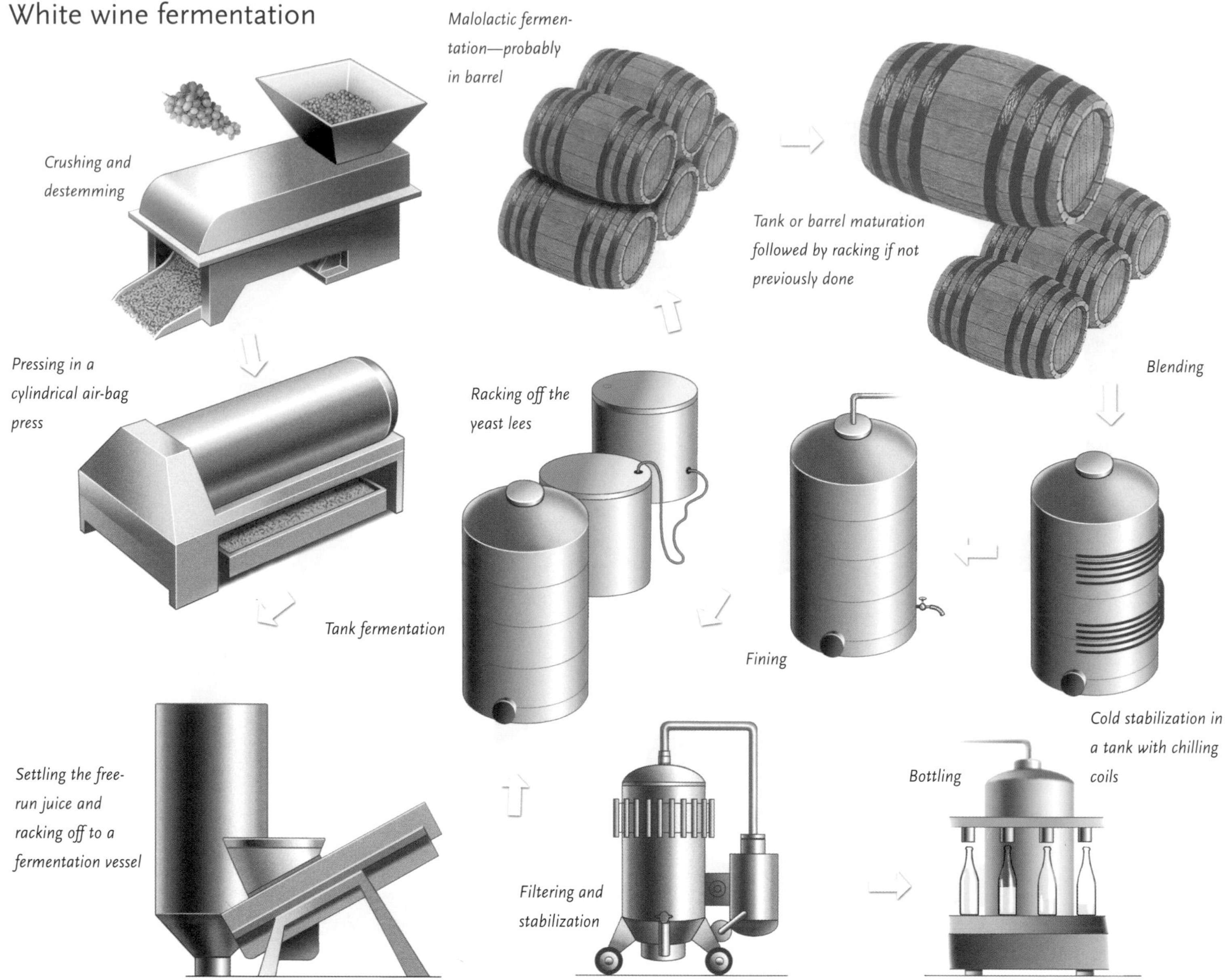

and protects it from bacterial spoilage. Acidification is frequently practiced in warm wine-producing areas such as Australia, but is rare in northern Europe.

Deacidification In cool areas, the process of ripening may not reduce acid levels sufficiently, and the resulting wine would be too searing. In that event acid can be removed from the must.

Must adjustment is not designed to alter the taste of wine, but rather to modify its structure. In small amounts, it improves the wine without being detectable; but it is noticeable in higher amounts and can have a detrimental effect on the wine.

RED WINE FERMENTATION

A key element in the production of red wine is the extraction of the phenolics, a process which happens mainly during maceration of the grape must and skins. Generally, winemakers are looking for the presence of three factors: an appropriate color, the right amount of tannins and the suitable fineness of tannins. Red grape varieties that tend to have thicker skins are more likely to produce deeper color and firmer tannins in the wine, although ripeness and the level of yield also affect this. The major difference between making red and white wine is, therefore, that the former includes skins in the fermentation process, while the latter relies on juice only.

The fermentation temperature for red wines is generally higher than that for whites. This is necessary to help extract the color and tannin from the skins, but the heat sacrifices some of the aromatic elements which are therefore less likely to show in red wines. The temperature varies from the low 70s F (20s C), which enhances the ripe primary fruit aromas of the wine up to 90°F (32°C), which evaporates some of the primary fruit characters, but offers more complexity and help in creating a finer structure in the wine.

Winemakers have several methods to aid the uptake of phenols in the wine, generally relying on the fact that

Red wine fermentation

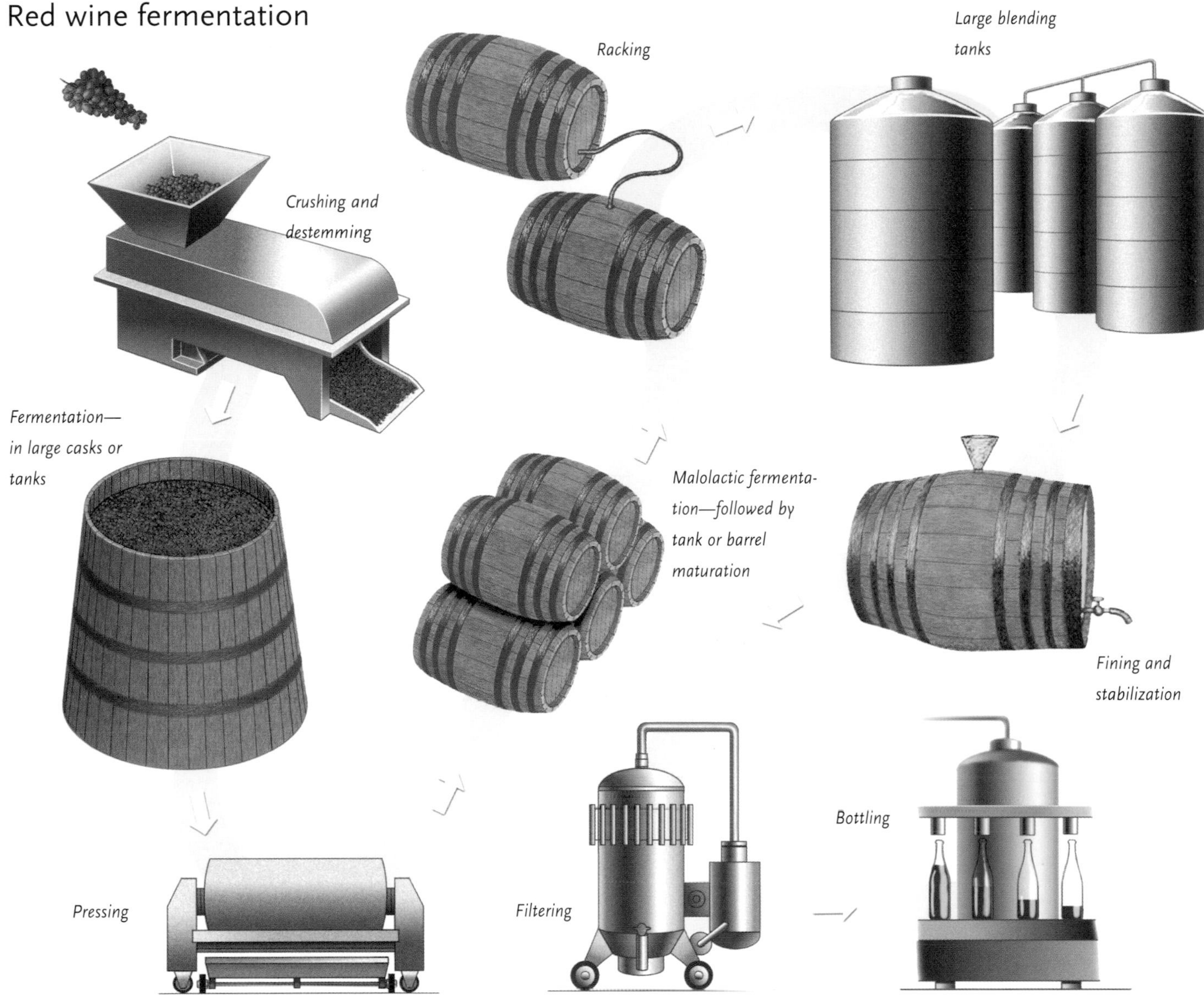

the skins, stalks and other solid matter tend to form a "cap" on the top of the must in the fermentation tank:

Pumping must over Involves taking wine from the bottom of the fermentation tank and spraying it over the cap. This action increases the extraction of phenolics.

Plunging Pushing the cap down into the must to enable more contact.

Header boards A series of boards at right angles to each other that is used to keep the cap constantly submerged below the top of the must.

Rotofermenting This is the modern method, and is essentially a fermentation tank tipped on its side that can rotate occasionally to tumble the cap. Care has to be taken to ensure that this is not overdone, as this would over-extract phenolics.

Other methods can be adopted to increase phenolic content. The wine can be *saignéed*; a small amount of juice is taken off at the start of fermentation, thus increasing the skin-to-juice ratio. Outside Europe, tannin is also often added in powder form to improve the structure.

Following the end of fermentation, or sometimes just before it is completed, the red wine is pumped off the skins, which are then run into a press. Red press wine is generally much harsher than the other wine because the process of pressing extracts more tannins, although the resulting wine may be quite deep-colored and flavorful. As a result, only a portion may be added back to the final blend to avoid making the finished wine too coarse.

At some point after the end of fermentation, a second process—called "malolactic fermentation"—may also be used on the wine. Almost all red wines undergo this, as may some more full-bodied whites. This results from the activity not of yeasts, but of bacteria. New wine contains a number of acids; the most important is tartaric acid, but another is malic acid that is a green, sharp and apple-like. The activity of lactic bacteria converts the malic acid into softer, creamier lactic acid. Red wines do not need green acidity, which is why the process is

ABOVE: *One of the procedures for monitoring fermentation: pinot noir nearing the end of the process in Burgundy, France.*

encouraged for them. With some white wines, malolactic fermentation is discouraged to preserve their fresh, lively character, but with others, it may be encouraged, either completely or partially, because the creamier, buttery components it imparts give extra complexity to the wine. These days the winemaker can easily control the process.

How fermentation works

Fermentation is the conversion of sugar into alcohol and carbon dioxide. It is catalyzed by yeast—minute microflora—which consume sugar as food and give out alcohol as a result. In the process, the yeast cells multiply rapidly, speeding up the process of fermentation so that, by the time it finishes, there may be hundreds of thousands of yeast cells per cubic inch of wine. The fermentation also creates a great deal of heat, which usually needs to be controlled because the yeasts may die if the temperature exceeds 95°F (35°C).

Fermentation ends naturally when either all the yeast nutrients (predominantly sugar) are used up, or when the alcohol level reaches a point where it poisons the yeasts—usually around 15 percent abv (alcohol by volume)—or when a combination of sugar and alcohol exhausts the yeasts. It can also be ended by heating the wine to kill the yeasts, by dosing them with very high levels of sulfur dioxide, or by filtering them out.

Almost invariably, the process begins these days with the winemaker adding specially prepared yeast to the juice. This has the advantage of ensuring a quick start to the ferment, precluding spoilage and giving the winemaker more control over the process. Occasionally, winemakers use natural yeasts, which are sometimes considered to give more flavor complexity to the finished wines.

A key component in managing fermentation is the control of temperature. White wines are usually fermented at lower temperatures than red, to preserve their aromatic and fruity qualities.

In the past, wine was generally aged in huge wooden vats, usually open-topped to let the carbon dioxide escape. Now other inert containers are more common, usually stainless steel, which can be kept clean easily, and can be cooled without difficulty during fermentation.

Sometimes the winemaker will opt for barrel fermentation. This involves the whole or, more commonly, the last part of fermentation in small barrels. This gives some of the character of oak to the wine—the oak flavors will be subtle and more completely integrated because the wine is fermented in and not just aged in oak. Given the difficulty of transferring red must—including skins—into barrels with small bung-holes, the practice is usually reserved for white wines. Some reds—especially pinots—may be pressed before the completion of fermentation and then pumped into barrels, where the yeast cells finish the process.

MATURATION

All wine needs a period to settle down following fermentation, during which it may undergo some treatments. For light, fresh wines, this period of maturation

Oak

When wine-lovers talk about oak today, they are really referring to the impact of new oak barrels on the wine. Oak is an excellent wood for storing liquids: it is flexible and malleable and, crucially, it can be made watertight. For wine, it has the additional advantage of adding oak flavors—creamy, vanillin, cedary and spicy. This sometimes gives wine a desirable complexity. Oak contains tannins, so it also gives additional phenols to the wine, which is something makers of white wine in particular must treat with care.

The oak for barrels generally comes from two countries, France and the USA. The trees used are of different oak species, and there are often different methods of seasoning the wood, so the two types provide varying components to the wine. As a general rule, American oak offers more overt vanillin and coconut components to the wine, whereas French oak tends to be more restrained, with spicy, cedary characters predominating. The size of barrel also has an impact on this, with small barrels like the widely used Bordeaux-style barrique of 60 gallons (225 l) offering a greater surface-to-wine ratio than larger ones, and thus more easily imparting oak qualities to the wine. Winemakers these days tend to match oak type to wine. Rioja and Australian shiraz are often aged in

American oak. Chardonnay and cabernet are more likely to be aged in French oak.

Assembling a barrel involves heating the inside of the staves, often with an open flame, to make them bend easily. This chars the insides of the barrel, and the level of charring can affect the wine. Thus, barrels come with a high, medium or low toast; the high-toasted barrels tend to impart a distinctly smoky style to the wine.

Clearly, the longer that the wine is in the barrel, the higher the uptake of flavor and tannin. This part of the aging process has to be very carefully monitored by the winemaker to avoid the oak characters dominating the fruit aroma and flavor of the wine.

LEFT: *Planks of oak for barrels are left to mature outside the factory for at least four to five years.*

may only be a few weeks, but can last for up to three years for some wines before bottling takes place. There are several ways in which such maturation can occur.

Barrel Barrels may be made of oak (of various types) or chestnut, and rarely of some other woods. Oak allows minute oxygen contact with the wine via the staves. This both helps it to stabilize naturally and develops the flavor components. Traditionally, the oak was rarely new.

Tank Large stainless steel tanks are completely inert; wine can be stored for a fairly long period without losing freshness.

Bottle Wine is rarely stored for long in bottle. It is usually out on the store shelves as soon as possible after bottling.

ABOVE: *Blending port. This process is critical, with the objective that the final wine must be better than the sum of its parts.*

FINISHING

Wine goes through a number of processes before it is bottled. Critical to the final style of the wine is how it is blended. Almost all wines, including the most expensive vintages in the world, are blended in some form or other. What is essential is that any blend should be better balanced and more complex than the sum of its parts. Otherwise, the blend does not really succeed. Unfortunately, blending is sometimes carried out merely to stretch the quantity of the wine, with the result that the quality of the best constituents is reduced, not enhanced.

Most often, wine is blended from a number of vineyards and/or varieties. Different sites produce slight variations in the wine, even when the same variety is used. They may be more or less tannic or acidic and produce different flavor components so that structural balance and complexity can be improved by the blend. Different grape varieties may give complementary aspects. In both Bordeaux and outside Europe, sémillon, which gives weight, texture and aging ability, is regularly blended with sauvignon blanc, which gives acidity, freshness and fruit to the youthful incarnation of the wine. At this stage, some of the press wine may also be added. It may offer fuller flavors, but too much in the blend may provide unacceptably coarse phenolics for either red or white wines, so it needs to be handled with discretion.

Less often, wine may be blended across vintages—tawny port and champagne are classic examples of this. Even for table wine, however, most countries allow other vintages to be blended into a wine; in Australia and South Africa, 15 percent of wine from a previous year can be used in this way.

It is critical to stabilize a wine; otherwise, the wine may become spoiled, develop haze or not show at its best. Several operations may be included in this process.

Fining This process uses substances with one electrical charge (positive or negative) to attract substances that are suspended in the wine and have the opposite charge. Thus, bentonite (a powdered clay) may be added to white wines to attract and remove proteins that exist in the wine that could cause a haze after bottling. With red wine, a number of substances, including egg white, may be added to remove some of the coarser tannins or phenolic bitterness.

Filtration This extracts solids that may exist in the wine, often of minute size, including yeast cells and bacteria. A number of filtration methods may be adopted, including coarse filtration, which only extracts the largest particles, and centrifuging, spinning the wine at very high speed, to push solids out of the wine. Filtration is the subject of great debate. Opponents say it rips the guts out of the wine, and supporters claim it is essential to guarantee a stable, attractive drink. While it may modify some of the fine nuances of top-quality wine, as a general rule, it does nothing but ensure its drinkability.

LEFT: *Stainless steel containers are now used by many producers for the aging and fermentation of wine.*

Additives Like most food, almost all wine has some chemical addition to ensure its freshness, and sometimes to act against bacterial or yeast spoilage. The most common such additive is sulfur dioxide, which has been used at least since ancient Roman times to ward off oxidation and guarantee a lively, enjoyable wine. In most cases, sulfur dioxide is a perfectly safe substance, but chronic asthmatics may experience a reaction to it. Additionally, excessive quantities can dull wine and give it a "burnt match" smell. Generally today, precise measurement and using it in combination with forms of ascorbic acid (vitamin C, which also acts as a preservative) ensures freshness without detrimental effects.

Cold stabilization For complex chemical reasons, wine that is chilled tends to deposit crystals of potassium bitartrate. These are harmless, but consumers tend to find them unsightly and may even be concerned that they are fragments of glass. A number of treatments can be carried out to remove the tartrates. Most involve chilling the wine so the tartrates precipitate out so they can be filtered out of the finished product.

From all the foregoing information, it should be clear that effective analysis is a key tool in the winemaker's armory. Many simple tests are carried out—to obtain rough alcohol level, or to assess the progress of malolactic fermentation—in even the smallest of wineries. More complex tests may have to be done, or at least confirmed, by an external laboratory, although the largest companies today have highly equipped in-house facilities. For many situations, both to satisfy domestic or export authorities, or to deal with subsequent problems that may occur, a winery must have precise measurements of various components of the wine or additives to it.

BELOW: A bottling line, Greece. Bottling usually occurs immediately after the final filtration.

BOTTLING

The final stage in the process is to get the drink into the bottle. This is generally done just after a final filtration and, ideally, is carried out in sterile conditions to ensure no damage to the wine occurs. These days, the whole process is mechanized, and large companies have their own bottling lines in constant use. Small companies may transport their wine to larger ones for bottling, or use a mobile bottling plant.

Bottles come in many shapes and sizes. The standard size is 28 fluid ounces (750 ml)—about 6–7 glasses. A half bottle is 14 fluid ounces (375 ml). Some wines have their own sized bottles—the *clavelin* for *vin jeaune* Jura wine is traditionally 24 fluid ounces (640 ml). A magnum is 56 fluid ounces (1.5 l)—an excellent size for the slow aging of wine. There are also larger—and more unwieldy—sizes.

There is debate about how bottles are closed. Cork—a flexible and effective stopper—has been used for at least 300 years. Its problem is that it can cause cork taint, which at best dulls the wine and at worst makes it less attractive than ditch water.

Because it affects between 2 and 5 percent of wine bottled, potentially one bottle in each case of wine you buy could be tainted. To avert this, many wine companies are exploring other options, such as synthetic corks and even crown seals. While these may be fine for short-term storage, no one is sure about their long-term impact on wine that is designed to age. They may be too effective at keeping out oxygen (a small amount passes by the cork, and helps to catalyze the necessary aging process in the bottle). It is possible that they could also add off flavors to the wine. Perhaps we will have a clearer idea of their effect in 25 years' time.

The chief problem with alternative closures may be rooted in ritual. Drawing a blue piece of plastic from a bottle—or pulling off a crown seal—doesn't have the same impact or drama as extracting a cork. Meanwhile, the cork industry is claiming to be tackling the issue.

AGING

The final part of the process for any wine is its development in bottle. Most wines, whether red or white, are designed to be drunk young and, although a few months in bottle probably benefits their integration, they are best consumed within two years or so. Only a few wines will benefit obviously from aging.

The development of wine in bottle is still little understood. However, it can best be summarized as a slow oxidation. Once the oxygen is used up, other chemical changes take place in what is called a reductive environment. The danger in this is that the oxidizing process will reduce the wine to a dull liquid which will not be drunk (the ultimate fate of all lifeless wine), or

even a vinegar. The first precondition for aging wine, therefore, is a component to slow down its oxidative development. With both white and red wines, but more essentially with whites, acidity performs this function by preserving freshness. In red wine, the phenolics also protect the wine because they tend to react with the oxygen before other flavorful components of the wine do. This means that the white wines which age the longest tend to be those with high acidity—rieslings, Loire chenin blancs and Hunter Valley sémillons. With red wines, it follows that the more tannic varieties—cabernets and merlots, nebbiolo and syrah—age the longest. However, this may also be dependent on the style of wine. Many sweet, alcoholic dessert wines will age well, and madeira is possibly the longest lived of all.

With white wine, the impact of time is to deepen its color through lemon to gold and finally to amber. The reverse is true with red wine: with age, it moves from deep purple, via ruby and mahogany to tawny. In both cases, if the wine is brown the process has gone too far and the wine is oxidized, unless it is a fortified wine, in which case brown may be acceptable.

The second requirement for aging wine is that it has sufficient flavor complexity to make it worth keeping. An inexpensive cabernet sauvignon from almost anywhere in the world may have enough tannin to allow it to age, but it will lose its fruitiness with time, and develop no interesting new flavors to make it enjoyable. Some quite expensive wines are deliberately made to be drunk young and are the more enjoyable for it; they will seem little different, and certainly no better, after some years.

Critically, with red wines, the process of aging causes the phenolics in the wine to polymerize—that is, the tannin and coloring material form large chains of molecules. With time, these polymers become so large that they can no longer remain suspended in the liquid, so they fall out as deposits. So wines that may be astringent, or even unpleasant, when young soften with time and become more attractive. Youthful ports, barolos and many cabernet-based wines can seem horrible at two years of age, but sublime at 15. There is a tendency today to think that "real" red wine has to be chock full of tannins to be taken seriously. However, most red styles are designed to be aged and soft, and will be more exciting for it.

The alcohol and sugar in sweet wines also acts as a preservative, and helps them to age for a particularly long time. Sparkling wines can also age well because the pressure of carbon dioxide helps marginalize oxygen activity, and their particularly high acidity preserves freshness. With time, they acquire toasty, biscuity aromas, and ultimately even mushroomy characters. While they may lose some fizz, they can remain exciting, fascinating wines.

ABOVE: *Different wine bottle shapes have a cultural rather than practical significance.*

The World's Best Reds

Red wine is made in many different places around the world, with varying levels of success. Some regions have been recognized as producers of top quality wines for many years, while other areas have only attained that status much more recently.

For example, in Burgundy the vineyard of Clos de Vougeot was enclosed sometime in the 1300s. It is classified as Grand Cru, the very highest level in Burgundy's appellation system. (In Bordeaux the highest ranking is Premier Cru, in a classification system which was complied in 1885. This ranking is exemplified by the superb Chateau Latour.)

By comparison, California's Napa Valley in the US is a much younger winemaking region. The first commercial winery was built in the area as relatively recent as 1861. The Robert Mondavi Winery, which opened in 1966, is the largest exporter of premium wine in the region.

Australia is also regarded as part of winemaking's New World. That country's most acclaimed red, Penfold's Grange Hermitage from the Barossa Valley in South Australia, was inspired by the best wines of Bordeaux, and is much sought after. This wine was first made in the 1950s.

Reflecting Italy's long and fragmented history, the wines from each region are highly individual, using specific indigenous grape varieties. Nebbiolo, for

LEFT TO RIGHT: Patrizi Barolo; Domaine Jacques Prieur Clos Vougeot: Chateau Latour Grand Vin; Robert Mondavi Cabernet Sauvignon; Alejandro Fernandez Pesquera; Puente Alto Don Melchor; Penfolds Grange Hermitage.

example, is emblematic of Piedmont, with the Barolo and Barbaresco zones recognized as being the producers of the best quality wines. Those from Barolo are considered a little fuller and more powerful than the more refined wines of Barbaresco.

Spain is another European country with a long tradition of winemaking. The wines from Ribera del Duero, in Castilla-León, are some of the most prestigious, exemplified by Pesquero, a wine which is made entirely from tempranillo grapes.

Spain also introduced red wine to Chile. Their wine industry is a rapidly expanding one, with the Maipo Valley region near Santiago probably best known. Concha y Toro is one of the most outstanding winemakers here.

The World's Best Whites

White wines, as with reds, are produced the world over, and greatly vary in quality. Various regions of the Old World, long renowned for particular wines, now find themselves rivals in the far more recently established estates to be found in the New World.

Perhaps most synonymous the world over with celebrations and superlative wine is the Champagne region of France. Located here is the Veuve Clicquot Ponsardin estate, and La Grande Dame is its prestige cuvée. A wine of great fineness and balance, it still displays the famed yellow label devised by Madame Clicquot herself. She took control of the house after the death of her husband in 1805 (*veuve* is French for "widow").

The greatest rieslings originate in the Mosel–Saar–Ruwer region of Germany, and the most expensive and renowned of these are from the famous vineyards of the Bernkastel district, where around a dozen different producers make and sell Bernkasteler Doctor riesling auslese.

Italy's finest moscato originates near Asti, in the Piedmont region. Moscato d' Asti is a light and elegant beverage, excellent with desserts. Among dessert wines, however, France's Chateau d'Yquem, from the Graves district, south of Bordeaux, which specializes in sauternes, is regarded as one of the world's best.

LEFT TO RIGHT: *Veuve Clicquot Ponsardin La Grande Dame; Domaine Jacques Prieur Montrachet; Chateau d'Yquem Sauternes; Lauerburg Berncastler Doctor; Marcarini Moscato d'Asti; Leeuwin Estate Art Series Chardonnay; Cloudy Bay, and Stag's Leap Chardonnay.*

Western Australia's Margaret River region is said to be "for wine lovers who seek class and finesse." Here the Leeuwin Estate, renowned for wines of great complexity, produces the Art Series Chardonnay, regarded as one of Australia's best.

Marlborough is New Zealand's best known wine region, famed for its sauvignon blanc. The highly regarded Cloudy Bay winery produces a sauvignon blanc that has achieved something of a cult-status since its release in 1985, and its chardonnay is also much vaunted.

California's most famous wine region is Napa Valley, one of the greatest districts being the Stag's Leap district. Though renowned for its legendary 1973 Stag's Leap Cabernet Sauvignon which was ranked as best in the world by French judges, the Stag's Leap Wine Cellars Chardonnay is also excellent.

The Silverado Trail, Napa Valley, California.

United States of America

United States of America

ABOVE: *Flying the flag in honor of a bountiful grape harvest.*

Impressed by the abundance of grapevines found in North America, Leif Ericson, the Norse explorer, named the land "Vinland" (Vineland) around the year 1000. The name proved prophetic as the United States is now the fourth-largest wine producer worldwide, and its impact upon the vine has loomed large. Phylloxera, Prohibition, the University of California at Davis and American scientific and economic clout have helped shape the American and the international wine industries.

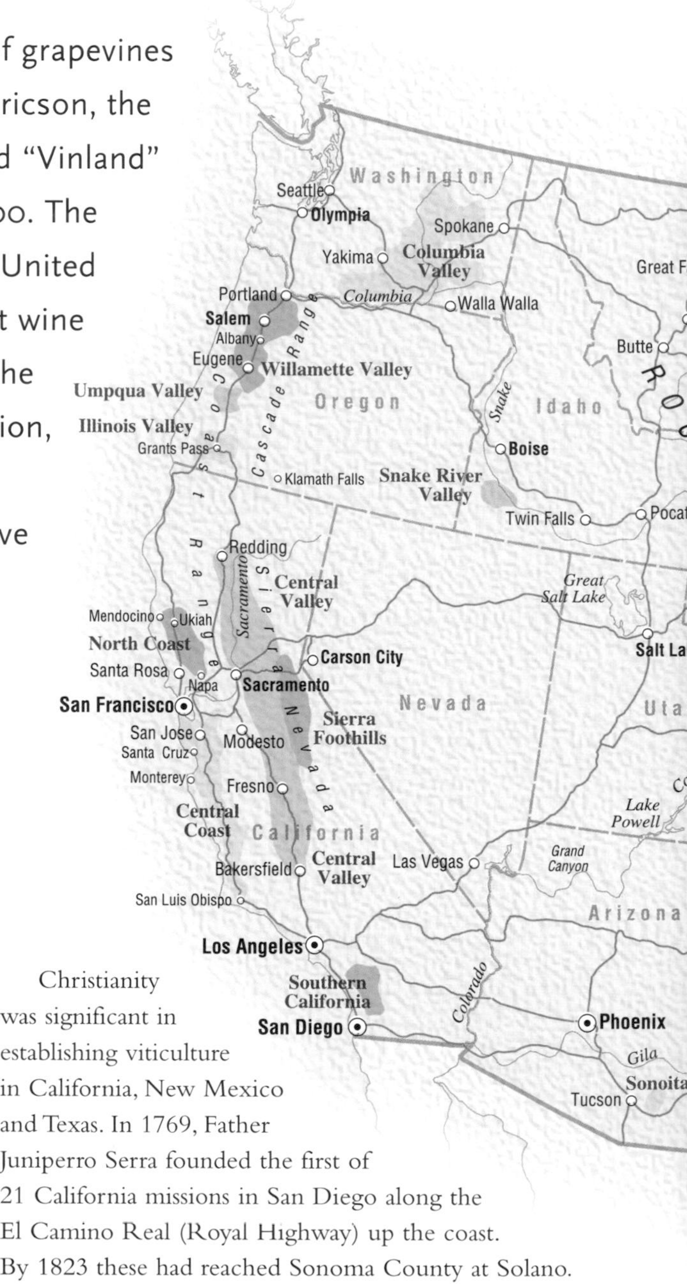

Early European settlers celebrated the abundance of grapevines, though they were dismayed that the native varieties produced wine with an unpleasant "foxy" characteristic. Grape vines traveled back and forth across the Atlantic. In the late 1800s the great regions of Europe were decimated by the root louse phylloxera—a native of North American soils, taken to Europe via cuttings. Although native American vines are resistant to the louse, the pest infested European vineyards. America, though, while being the source of the devastation was also the source of the cure in the form of resistant rootstock for grafting.

California dominates the American wine industry and the ascendancy of the vine in the United States is directly linked to California's history. Early colonists soon turned from native varieties to imported grape varieties and winemaking expertise from Europe for their wine needs. Repeated attempts to establish the European vine on the east coast failed, despite heroic attempts by the likes of Thomas Jefferson. Fungal diseases and phylloxera proved insurmountable until as recently as 40 years ago.

Christianity was significant in establishing viticulture in California, New Mexico and Texas. In 1769, Father Juniperro Serra founded the first of 21 California missions in San Diego along the El Camino Real (Royal Highway) up the coast. By 1823 these had reached Sonoma County at Solano.

In 1833 the missions were secularized by the Mexican government and the Solano vineyard fell into the hands of General Vallejo, who became a prominent grower. A small-scale wine industry evolved, particularly in the Los Angeles region, where vines were irrigated by the Los Angeles River.

Meanwhile, production in Ohio reached its peak in the 1850s. A challenging climate, industrial expansion and the rise of California combined to check production in the east. In 1848 the California goldrush began—the state's population grew thirty-fold and winemaking boomed. The mission grape dominated the state's viticulture, producing better sweet wine and brandy than table wine.

European varieties were imported as early as 1833, when Jean Louis Vignes, a French cooper, brought in non-mission vines. *Vitis vinifera* varieties were planted during the next two decades. Some believe that Sonoma producer Agoston Haraszthy—"father of California viticulture"—was the source of new varieties, but by 1861, when he traveled to Europe in search of cuttings, they were already in California.

ABOVE: Aerial view showing contour of Napa Valley, California.

1 Hudson River Region
2 Western Connecticut Highlands
3 Southeastern New England
4 Central Delaware Valley
5 Lancaster Valley
6 Cumberland Valley
7 Catoctin
8 Shenandoah Valley
9 Northern Neck George Washington Birthplace
10 Monticello
11 North Fork of Roanoke
12 Rocky Knob

NORTH

200 miles (320 kilometers)

ABOVE: *Eberle vineyards, Paso Robles, California.*

RIGHT: *A specially designed cup for sampling wine from tanks or vats.*

During the 1880s, the University of California, with Professor Eugene W. Hilgard, was the guiding light. By 1880, zinfandel, which probably arrived between 1852 and 1855, was the first choice of quality-minded vineyard owners. The first *vinifera* plantings in Washington State took place in 1876.

In the early 1900s, Sonoma was the wine center of the United States. French, Swiss and Italian winemakers greatly improved wine quality and California wine was winning awards in Europe. With Prohibition (1919–1933) came darkness for the industry. Some wineries survived by producing sacramental and medicinal wines; some were saved by selling grapes for home winemaking. There was a shift to grapes with high yields and fruit that survived shipping—petite sirah, carignane and alicante bouchet. Curiously, alcohol consumption increased during Prohibition. Organized crime boomed, monopolizing alcohol distribution.

Prohibition was a serious blow to the wine industry, and recovery was slow as the nation had developed a preference for spirits in the meantime.

In 1948 Zellerbach's Hanzell Winery (north of Sonoma) was planted with pinot noir and chardonnay. The temperature and humidity in the cellar mimicked that of Burgundy. Hanzell produced the first quality chardonnay, laying the groundwork for the later boom. The 1950s saw a revival of the industry. Quality improved as plantings increased, and better winery hygiene, use of stainless-steel equipment, temperature control and commercial yeast came into greater acceptance.

The 1960s heralded the modern era of wine production with Joe Heitz and Robert Mondavi opening wineries in the Napa Valley. Mondavi embarked upon vineyard and winery trials in a successful quest for quality. Chateau Ste Michelle and Columbia Winery first put Washington State on the map. Gallo greatly impacted the industry by introducing chablis blanc and hearty burgundy in 1964. In 1973 Moët & Chandon began production of Chandon Sparkling Wine in Napa Valley and was the first champagne house in the United States. The 1973 vintage produced California wines that shook the wine world by winning the famed Paris tasting. This 1976 competition pitted California chardonnay and cabernet sauvignon against top wines from Burgundy and Bordeaux. The French judges ranked the 1973 Stag's Leap Cabernet Sauvignon the top red and the 1973 Château Montelena Chardonnay the top white, thus creating a fantastic marketing bonanza for the California wine industry.

The unstoppable David Lett and other pinot noir specialists established vineyards and wineries in Oregon during the early 1970s. Further California expansion took place in 1979 with Opus One, a joint venture between Mondavi and Baron Philippe de Rothschild. Producers from other parts of the world have followed with ventures in California, including Torres, Moueix, Perrin, Antinori and Southcorp.

Prices stagnated in the late 1980s as supply exceeded demand. A new strain of phylloxera, biotype-B, appeared in Napa Valley and spread throughout California and into Oregon. As most of California's vines were planted on AXR-1 or *Vitis vinifera* stock, this created much damage. Luckily, the spread of phylloxera and the time to vine death takes years, allowing the existing vineyards to be ripped out and replanted with resistant rootstock. Producers faced enormous debts that forced them into partnerships and restructured corporations. Nevertheless, replanting has afforded them the opportunity to rethink variety, clone, rootstock, spacing, trellising, aspect and irrigation, so quality should improve markedly.

Meanwhile, quality and quantity greatly improved in Oregon, Washington, New York (Finger Lakes and Long Island), and Virginia, and impressive efforts have come from New Mexico and Texas.

Production in the early 1990s gained momentum when economic expansion brought increased demand. After a flurry of reports on the benefits of moderate wine consumption, red wines, such as cabernet sauvignon, pinot noir, zinfandel, and, particularly, merlot, became especially popular with health-conscious consumers. With producers trying to hold onto export market gains and maintain dominance in domestic markets, some of them bought wine or vineyards in the Languedoc region of France, to help with production shortfalls. In spite of increased replanting costs and increased Bordeaux prices and increased demand, record sales and record prices led to record profits.

Currently another threat looms, Pierce's disease, particularly because of a new vector, the glassy-winged sharpshooter. Previous epidemics of Pierce's disease occurred from 1892 to 1906 and in the 1930s, wiping out thriving vineyards in Anaheim, California.

Despite some ideal climates for growing quality wine grapes, the American wine industry has had to grapple with many challenges. To date, the three "Ps," Prohibition, phylloxera, and Pierce's disease, have been the most overpowering. California—the state and its wine industry—continues to be an innovative, dominant, and resilient force. With a new wave of viticulture and a melding of the science and art of winemaking, the future of world-class wine from America appears to be a promising one.

LEFT: The grape harvest, Carneros, California.

BELOW: Vines are sometimes netted to protect the fruit from birds until harvest time.

ABOVE: *Pickers work their way along rows of ripening fruit, harvesting with care.*

WASHINGTON STATE

PAUL WHITE

At the beginning of the millennium Washington State's phenomenal growth saw one new winery opening every 13 days. During the past 20 years a base of 19 wineries has grown to 240, with an increase in vineyard area from 5,000 to 29,000 acres (2,023 to 11,745 ha). Currently ranked second in premium varietal production within the US, Washington State now exports its wine to over 40 countries.

ABOVE: *Ivy grows over a long-disused wine press.*

History

The growing of *Vitis vinifera* here can be documented from 1876 when Italian immigrants brought cinsault to Walla Walla. Washington's modern history begins with associated vintners Pommerelle and Nawico, the precursors of Chateau Ste Michelle and Columbia Winery, which demonstrated the viability of *vinifera* varietals progressively throughout the 1950s and 1960s. Thereafter, Washington's reputation for excellence in wines spread from its delicately perfumed rieslings and elegant chardonnays in the 1970s and 1980s, powerful merlots and cabernet sauvignon in the 1990s, and recently, for world class syrah.

Landscape and climate

Washington's geology has been much influenced over time by volcanic activity and flood erosion on a massive scale. Lava flows provided basalt foundations for both the gentle slopes and sharply etched east–west ridges now covered in vines. As glaciers retreated 16,000 years ago, they left behind a free-draining gravel bed up to 250 feet (76 m) deep, with shallow, stone-studded, sandy topsoil—just perfect for low-vigor grape growing.

Washington State is divided climatically by the volcanoes of the Cascade Mountains. These effectively capture the clouds flowing off the Pacific Ocean, soaking western Washington with some 50 inches (127 cm) of rain annually, and leaving less than 8 inches (20 cm) to fall on eastern Washington's Columbia River basin.

The generously irrigated, ever-sunny Columbia River Valley contains 99.9 percent of Washington's vineyards. The Columbia's growing season is marked by an intense early ripening period followed by a long, gentle "Indian summer" finish. Cool nights and consistent conditions create the deep perfumes, crystal-clear fruit flavors and excellent natural acidity that define Washington's cool-climate wine styles.

Wines and vines

Eastern Washington's wine styles are defined by intense, vibrant fruit, juicy natural acids and lavish oak treatment. They were at one time seen as relatively inexpensive alternatives to California wines, but that is no longer he case. The state's most-planted grapes, merlot and chardonnay, generally show elegant style, varietal purity, fine structure and balance. Both cabernet sauvignon and franc are bottled as straight varietals and/or combined with merlot in "Meritage" blends, among the most bordeaux-like in the country. Although difficult varietals to sell, Washington's sauvignon blanc, chenin blanc and sémillon are among the finest examples in the US.

Newcomers syrah, malbec and viognier show tremendous promise, but nebbiolo and sangiovese have, so far, been less consistent. Experimental plantings of carmenère, marsanne, rousanne and mourvèdre suggest that these have great potential. More serious treatment of grenache, cinsault and lemberger (blaufränkisch) has brought new life to these older, workhorse grapes. Relatively small quantities of other varieties are grown in western Washington's milder, wetter regions.

Yakima Valley

Washington's largest AVA (American Viticultural Area) is the Columbia Valley with 25,000 acres (10,125 ha) of vines planted inside a total area of 10.7 million acres (4,333,500 ha). It was conceived as a blanket appellation for virtually all of the state's vineyards. Within this large area are three smaller, more climatically distinctive AVAs: the semi-arid Yakima Valley, Walla Walla River Valley and Red Mountain. Relatively cooler than the surrounding Columbia AVA, the Yakima Valley produces about 40 percent of the state's wine. The region is bounded by the evocatively named Rattlesnake Hills and Horse Heaven Hills.

HOGUE CELLARS

Established **1982** ***Owners*** **Hogue family** ***Production*** **400,000 cases** ***Vineyard area*** **1,800 acres (729 ha)**

One of the leaders in the region, Hogue is a largish winery with the will and ability to do small-batch winemaking. All of the wines show crystal-clear varietal characters, understated elegance and are inexpensive for their quality. Highlights include riesling from 26-year-old vines; a spicy, fleshy fumé blanc; leesy, creamy, crisp chardonnay; a more intense, nutty, complex Vineyard Selections Chardonnay; a blackberry and vanilla syrah with fine tannins; minty, juicy merlot; and a meaty, mocca, tobacco-tinged Genesis Cabernet Franc that is soft and deeply juicy.

KIONA

Established **1979** ***Owners*** **Holmes and Williams families** ***Production*** **NA** ***Vineyard area*** **30 acres (12 ha)**

Kiona is sited in chalky, high-pH soil on one of Yakima's driest, hottest sites, Red Mountain. Its lemberger vines are the oldest in the state and its cabernet grapes are considered among the best produced. Known for solid, well-made, fruit-forward, excellent-value wines, with strengths especially in late-harvested riesling, chenin blanc and lemberger wines.

Other Washington Producers

CANOE RIDGE

Established **1993** ***Owner*** **Chalone Wine Group** ***Production*** **32,000 cases** ***Vineyard area*** **156 acres (63 ha)**

Originally it was planned to grow only merlot, but Canoe Ridge has since also produced distinctive cabernet and chardonnay. The strong pinot noir experience of former Acacia Winery winemaker John Abbott now shapes deeply perfumed, velvety, elegant merlots. His chardonnays have a classic delicacy and purity, with crisp apple characters and fine-boned textures. Although underrated and underpriced, Canoe Ridge's cabernets show ripe blackcurrant characters, impressive mid-palates and fine structures.

ABOVE: *Itinerant pickers from Mexico, here working at Hogue Cellars, follow the grape harvest up the west coast.*

DELILLE CELLARS/ CHALEUR ESTATE

Established **1992** ***Owners*** **Charles and Greg Lill, Jay Soloff, Christopher Upchurch** ***Production*** **3,574 cases** ***Vineyard area*** **NA**

Sharply focused, site-specific, unfiltered wines have brought DeLille to the fore of Washington's more serious producers. Best wines include a super-concentrated, deeply integrated savory Chaleur (cabernet sauvignon/merlot/cabernet franc), a counterpoint to the plummy merlot-dominant D2. Chaleur Doyenne Syrah shows classic blackberry and white pepper aromas and a typically firm dusty tannic palate. The estate also produces a classy, beautifully balanced sauvignon/sémillon white.

> *WINE, n. Fermented grape-juice known to the Women's Christian Union as "liquor" sometimes as "rum." Wine, madam, is God's next best gift to man.*
>
> AMBROSE BIERCE (1842–1914), *The Devil's Dictionary*

L'ECOLE NO 41

Established **1983** ***Owners*** **Clubb family** ***Production*** **17,000 cases** ***Vineyard area*** **NA**

Marty Clubb makes Washington's best sémillons—ripe and rich-textured Fries Sémillon and barrel-fermented L'Ecole No 41 Sémillon, with green walnut and citrus characters. Another steal is the beeswax, melon and citrusy chenin blanc. Reds show strength through a finely structured Seven Hills Merlot; expansive Apogee merlot/cabernet blend; and meaty, smooth, viscous Walla Walla Cabernet Sauvignon.

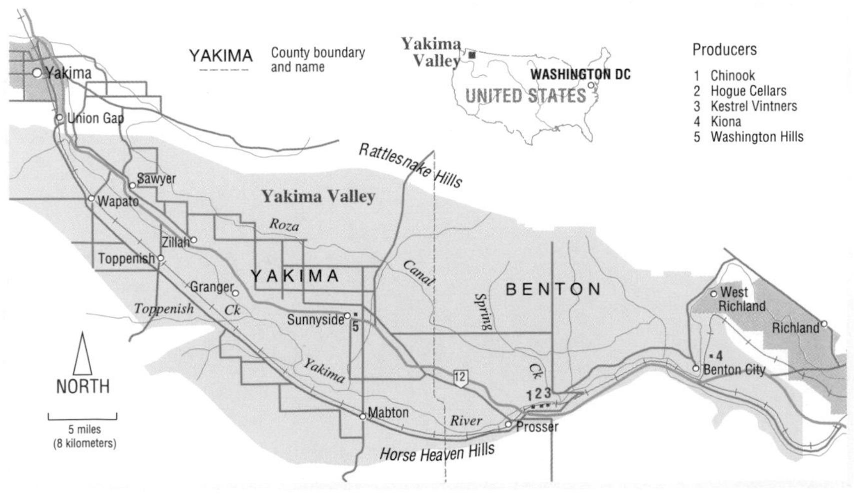

ABOVE: *For premium wines, winemakers prefer that the grapes are picked by hand.*

QUILCEDA CREEK VINTNERS

Established 1979 **Owners** Golitzen family **Production** NA **Vineyard area** NA

Alex Golitzen and his son Paul make Washington's most famous cabernet sauvignons. French oaked, unfined, unfiltered, these complex, densely structured wines are consistently composed of fruit from the state's best sites: Kiona, Mercer, Klipsum and Ciel du Cheval.

WATERBROOK WINERY

Established 1984 **Owners** Rendal family **Production** 27,000 cases **Vineyard area** 14 acres (6 ha)

This is one of Walla Walla's original boutique wineries and maintains top quality at sharp prices. Best value wines include a light, grassy, seamless sauvignon blanc (23 percent sémillon) and a nutty, melt-in-your-mouth chardonnay. The merlot, cabernet sauvignon and Red Mountain "Meritage" show focused varietal characters and nice tannins.

GLEN FIONA

Established 1995 **Owner** Ronald White, Tony Weeks, Berle "Rusty" Figgins **Production** 3,000 cases **Vineyard area** NA

Rusty Figgins studied winemaking at Wagga Wagga in Australia, and now mainly produces variant blends of syrah, spiced by grenache, cinsault or viognier. Vinification style takes its cue from the vintage, following an eclectic Franco-Australian mix of cold maceration, basket pressing, wild and rhône yeast fermentation in neutral old oak, resulting in personality-filled wines, including a peppery, concentrated Columbia Valley Syrah and a fleshy, broadly perfumed Walla Walla Syrah blend (5 percent viognier).

Regional Dozen

QUALITY WINES

- Columbia Winery Otis Cabernet Sauvignon
- Eroica Riesling (Chateau St Michelle & Dr Ernst Loosen)
- Fidelitis Meritage
- Leonetti Merlot
- Quilceda Creek Cabernet Sauvignon
- Zefina Serience White

BEST VALUE WINES

- Avery Johannisberg Riesling
- Columbia Winery Viognier Red Willow
- De Lille Chaleur Estate Meritage White
- L'Ecole No 41 Barrel-Fermented Sémillon
- Hogue Cellars Syrah
- Waterbrook Sauvignon Blanc

LEONETTI CELLAR

Established 1977 **Owners** Gary and Nancy Figgins **Production** 5,500 cases **Vineyard area** NA

Leonetti is Walla Walla's oldest winery and has its oldest merlot vines. The original vineyard, which was planted in 1974, is managed through intensive low-yield viticultural practices. Recent plantings have added petit verdot, cabernet franc, syrah and carmenère. Stylistically, Leonetti's cabernet sauvignon, cabernet sauvignon reserve, merlot and sangiovese are big, powerful and oak-driven, with layers of opulent fruit. These are seriously sought-after wines.

RIGHT: *Tightly bunched white grapes.*

ANDREW WILL

Established 1989 **Owner** Chris Camarda **Production** 350 cases **Vineyard area** NA

This Vashon Island winery makes tiny quantities of vineyard-designated wines from Ciel du Cheval, Boushey, Klipsun and Pepper Bridge. Carmarda's supple, plummy, finely structured merlots, as well as Sorella, a cabernet sauvignon-dominated merlot/franc blend, and sangiovese and chenin blanc are all highly sought after.

WOODWARD CANYON

Established 1981 **Owner** Richard Small **Vineyard area** NA

Richard Small, one of Washington's great boutique winemakers, helped put Washington merlot, cabernet, and chardonnay on the premium map. Drawing low-yield fruit primarily from the lower Columbia and Walla Walla areas and a high-density planted home vineyard, wines are unfiltered, unfined, and not acidified. Woodward Celilo Chardonnay shows complex savory characters and is finely structured, counterpointing a fat, fleshy, peachy Walla Walla Chardonnay. Woodward Canyon reds include a juicy, chocolatey merlot with explosive midpalate; a dark, dense old-vine cabernet; and Charbonneau, which is a complex, silky, seamless merlot/cabernet sauvignon/franc blend.

Other significant producers in this State include Cayuse, Chinook, Kestrel Vintners, Washington Hills, Bookwalter, Corus Brands, Dunham, Hedges, Mathews, McCrea Cellars, Salishan Vineyards, Seven Hills Winery and Stimson Lane Vineyards & Estates.

OREGON

PAUL WHITE

Oregon has long held a reputation for progressivism and non-conformity in North America, so it should come as no surprise that its wine industry grows the world's most difficult grape—pinot noir—in a hostile environment. As well as embracing harsh growing conditions, Oregonians imposed some of the world's toughest labeling laws on themselves in the 1970s, with varietal content and stated region of origin set at 100 percent. Although varietal content was eventually relaxed to 90 percent, with cabernet sauvignon given dispensation down to 75 percent, these parameters remain high by world standards.

History

Although Oregon's first *Vitis vinifera* was planted in 1847, only a handful of early vineyards and wineries survived past Prohibition, and even some of these petered out later. The modern industry began in the 1960s and scored a breakthrough when Eyrie Vineyards' 1975 Pinot Noir achieved second place within a top flight of Cru-class burgundies at the Gault/Millau Wine Olympics in France in 1979. The late 1980s brought steady growth and the mid-1990s saw progress through improved viticulture in evening out previous difficulties with vintage variation. Now ranked fourth in US production with an annual output of nearly one million cases, Oregon has over 170 wineries, with 383 vineyards and 10,000 acres (4,050 ha) planted in *vinifera* varieties.

Landscape and climate

Like Washington, Oregon is climatically divided into dry eastern and wet western halves by the volcanic Cascade Mountains, which block clouds generated by the Pacific Ocean and cast a rain shadow over the great western valley. This maritime influence is somewhat mitigated by Oregon's northern position at the 45th parallel, which contributes lengthened days, indirect sunlight and a broad diurnal temperature range within a long growing season. It is cooler and wetter than both Washington and California, although the growing season is relatively dry, peaking with 90°F (32°C) temperatures in July that gradually taper into warm autumnal days and cool nights.

Vines and wines

Winemaking in Oregon tends to follow traditional Burgundian practices, primarily using barrels of French or Oregon oak. The wineries are small and labor-intensive operations. Virtually all of the wineries produce pinot noirs in a style that echoes perfumes, structures and textures found in Burgundy. These wines often require up to seven years to open up, with many capable of evolving for a decade or more. Chaptalization is allowed, but rarely applied.

Pinot gris, Oregon's most exciting variety, is made in a style based on barrel and tank fermentation. Other Alsatian varieties, pinot blanc, gewürztraminer and riesling, have thrived in the cool climate, and show consistently ripe, well-focused varietal characters in well-executed dry styles. Both riesling and gewürztraminer are often good value in semi-sweet, late-harvest and icewine styles. Recently introduced Burgundian chardonnay clones have brought fuller, better balanced wines. Both white and red wines show subdued European fruit characters with nicely balanced acidity.

Regional Dozen

QUALITY WINES

Archery Summit Single Vineyard Pinot Noirs
Beaux Frères Pinot Noir
Domaine Drouhin Pinot Noir and Cuvée Laurene
Eyrie Pinot Meunier
Ponzi Reserve Pinot Noir
Ken Wright Single Vineyard Pinot Noirs

BEST VALUE WINES

Amity Pinot Blanc
Argyle Reserve Riesling
Bridgeview Dry Gewürztraminer
Firesteed Pinot Noir
Foris Chardonnay
Rex Hill Kings Ridge Pinot Gris

Willamette Valley

Some 60 miles (96 km) wide and 100 miles (160 km) deep, the wet Willamette Valley AVA (40 inches/102 cm precipitation per annum) is home to 150 wineries. Almost all focus primarily on pinot noir, with riesling, chardonnay, pinot gris, pinot blanc, sauvignon blanc and gewürztraminer fleshing out their portfolios. Vineyards are planted in relatively infertile soil on gentle slopes, primarily clustered around the Red Hills of Dundee,

BELOW: Multihued fall foliage dazzling in the sunshine.

with the rest scattered throughout Yamhill County, Washington County and the Eola Hills.

ARCHERY SUMMIT WINERY

Established **1995** ***Owners*** **Andrus family** ***Production*** **10,000 cases** ***Vineyard area*** **100 acres (40 ha)**

Echoing Domaine Drouhin (see below) with a monumental, gravity-fed winery driven by California style and capital, Archery Summit is the brainchild of Gary Andrus of Pine Ridge in the Napa Valley. Its strength lies in a range of single-vineyard pinot noirs, infused with spicy oak and jam-packed with fruit complexity and layers of texture. Expensive, but very smart wines.

RIGHT: Overflowing, fermenting barrel of wine.

ARGYLE WINERY

Established **1986** ***Owners*** **Brian Croser and Cal Knudsen** ***Production*** **33,000 cases** ***Vineyard area*** **120 acres (49 ha)**

Visionary Australian winemaker Brian Croser, of Petaluma, created the Argyle Winery intending to make *méthode champenoise* from chardonnay and pinot noir, but has subsequently attracted as much attention for his equally high-quality still wines, chardonnay and riesling.

BEAUX FRÈRES

Established **1988** ***Owners*** **Mike Etzel, Robert M. Parker and Robert Roy** ***Production*** **3,000 cases** ***Vineyard area*** **30 acres (12 ha)**

High-quality Beaux Frères established its close-planted, multi-clone, low-yield vineyard for optimum grape production. The pinot noir is unfined, unfiltered and dominated by new oak, in an opulent forward-fruit, high-alcohol style. Sulfur levels are deliberately kept low.

BETHEL HEIGHTS

Established **1977** ***Owners*** **Caastel, Web and Dudley families** ***Production*** **10,000 cases** ***Vineyard area*** **50 acres (20 ha)**

Pioneers of the important Eola Hills region, Bethel Heights winery produces multi-clone, low-cropping, estate-grown pinot noir. The best of the bunch includes the old-vine Southeast Block Reserve and Flat Block, both of which are full-flavored and structured to age brilliantly.

DOMAINE DROUHIN

Established **1987** ***Owner*** **Joseph Drouhin** ***Production*** **12,200 cases** ***Vineyard area*** **74 acres (30 ha)**

Domaine Drouhin represents the greatest and most undisputed recognition by France of Oregon's potential. In 1987, Burgundian *négociant* house Joseph Drouhin planted a vineyard in Dundee with double the normal vine density in the United States, then built a monumental, state-of-the-art, gravity-fed winery. Drouhin's pinots, now considered Oregon benchmarks, show an elegantly underplayed, multi-layered complexity that consistently ranks among the best produced anywhere outside Burgundy. Cuvée Laurene, a wine of outstanding quality, is made only in top vintages.

BELOW: Black grapes still increasing in sweetness late in the season.

EYRIE VINEYARDS

Established **1966** ***Owners*** **Lett family** ***Production*** **8,000–10,000 cases** ***Vineyard area*** **50 acres (20 ha)**

Visionary founding father of Oregon pinot noir, David Lett, deserves equal credit for similarly establishing the Alsatian varietals pinot gris, muscat and riesling. Lett follows traditional Burgundian winemaking practices, opting for a lighter, more delicately perfumed style of pinot noir. Tight and austere while young, these wines often begin to blossom only at 5–10 years of age. Eyrie's pinot meunier ranks among the best produced anywhere and his ground-breaking pinot gris is an area benchmark.

PANTHER CREEK CELLARS

Established **1986** ***Owners*** **Kaplan family** ***Production*** **7,300 cases** ***Vineyard area*** **Grapes are bought in**

Panther Creek Cellars produces high-quality, unfiltered, low-production, low-yield (less than 180 cases), single-vineyard, ageworthy pinot noirs with generous fruit and balanced structures. Worth seeking out is Melón, made from the melon de bourgogne grape.

PONZI VINEYARD

Established **1974** ***Owners*** **Ponzi family** ***Production*** **7,200 cases** ***Vineyard area*** **NA**

Ponzi has stuck with chardonnay, pinot gris, pinot noir and riesling planted in 1970. Its velvety, red fruit, smoky bacon, mushroomy pinot noir consistently ranks among Oregon's most complex. Other wines show rich textures and clean ripe fruit.

REX HILL VINEYARDS

Established **1982** ***Owner*** **Paul Hart** ***Production*** **40,000 cases** ***Vineyard area*** **400 acres (162 ha)**

All Rex Hill wines show excellent fruit purity and fine balance. Pinot noirs show distinct *terroir* characters through a single-vineyard range and multi-layered complexity at Reserve level. Whites include a crisp unoaked sauvignon, varietally focused pinot gris and pinot blanc, and a fine-boned chardonnay. Bargain label Kings Ridge wines are very well made, easy drinking and sharply priced.

ST INNOCENT WINERY

Established **1988** ***Owners*** **Mark Vlossak** ***Production*** **7,000 cases** ***Vineyard area*** **NA**

Sharing winemaker Mark Vlossak with Panther Creek, the quality and styles of this winery are based on a different fruit source and made into a wide range of single-vineyard, concentrated, fine-grained pinot noirs, chardonnays and pinot gris.

WILLAMETTE VALLEY VINEYARDS

Established **1988** ***Owners*** **Shareholders** ***Production*** **85,000 cases** ***Vineyard area*** **50 acres (20 ha)**

This winery goes from strength to strength. Fruit is drawn from two vineyards and is intensively managed. From its beginning, WVV has shown steady improvement across a range of wines, with strengths in pinot noir, pinot gris, chardonnay and riesling.

Producers
1 Amity Vineyard
2 Archery Summit Winery
3 Argyle Winery
4 Beaux Frères
5 Bethel Heights
6 Cameron
7 Domaine Drouhin
8 Elk Cove Vineyards
9 Evesham Wood
10 Eyrie Vineyards
11 Rex Hill Vineyards
12 King Estate Winery
13 Panther Creek Cellars
14 Ponzi Vineyard
15 St Innocent Winery
16 Willamette Valley Vineyards
17 Ken Wright Winery

10 miles (16 kilometers)

KEN WRIGHT WINERY

Established **1994** ***Owner*** **Ken Wright Cellars** ***Production*** **7,000 cases** ***Vineyard area*** **28 acres (11.5 ha)**

Ken Wright draws grapes from a wide range of microclimates and soil types, producing single-vineyard pinot noirs that clearly delineate *terroir* differences within the Willamette Valley. The wines are complex and condensed and the melony chardonnay and pinot blanc are excellent.

Other Oregon Producers

The Umpqua Valley AVA mainly produces pinot noir, cabernet sauvignon, chardonnay, riesling and sauvignon blanc. Farther south, in the hotter, drier and more elevated Rogue Valley, riesling, gewürztraminer, pinot gris, cabernet sauvignon, chardonnay, cabernet franc, merlot and sémillon are favored. The state's eastern vineyards, near Columbia Gorge and the Walla Walla AVA, generally sell their grapes to Washington wineries.

BRIDGEVIEW VINEYARDS

Established **1980** ***Owners*** **Kerivan family and Ernie Brodie** ***Production*** **64,000 cases** ***Vineyard area*** **74 acres (30 ha)**

This southern Illinois Valley winery consistently produces some of Oregon's best-value varietals from a closely planted vineyard. The riesling, pinot noir and chardonnay are well-made, ripely flavored and sharply priced. They are among Oregon's best value wines.

ABOVE: *New vine plantings in Oregon to replace vines attacked by the phylloxera biotype-B strain.*

Other significant producers in Oregon include Amity Vineyard, Cameron, Elk Cove Vineyards, Evesham Wood, King Estate Winery and Henry Estate Winery.

ABOVE: *Widely spaced vine rows make it easy to harvest the grapes mechanically.*

IDAHO

CATHERINE FALLIS MS

Idaho is on a similar latitude to Bordeaux. Its wineries fall under the state classification of AO, or Appellation of Origin. Idaho is officially a subzone of tri-state Pacific Northwest with Oregon and Washington. Ste Chapelle Winery along with the Idaho Grape Growers and Wine Producers Commission (17 wineries and 20 growers) is currently determining boundaries in order to complete a multi-AVA application. Snake River Valley and two sub-AVAs of Sunny Slope and Arena Valley, a moon crater 20 minutes northwest of the Oregon border, are proposed.

The Pacific Northwest is the second-largest area in North America for *vinifera* grape production, with more than 45,000 acres (18,210 ha) under vine across the three states. Not unexpectedly, Idaho's contribution is the smallest. Growth is slow, as the industry is in a stranglehold by the local legislature. Several hundred thousand acres of affordable, plantable land with available water lie fallow. But interest from larger, outside businesses is increasing.

Varieties in production in Idaho include cabernet franc, cabernet sauvignon, chardonnay, chenin blanc, lemberger (blaufrankisch), gewürztraminer, merlot, pinot gris, pinot noir, riesling, sauvignon blanc, sémillon and syrah. Experimental plantings of tempranillo, valdespino, viognier and zinfandel are showing great promise.

Regional Dozen

QUALITY WINES

- Carmela Vineyards Cabernet Franc, Riesling and Sémillon
- Koenig Vineyards Zinfandel
- Pend d'Oreille Chardonnay
- Sawtooth Riesling
- South Hills/Hegy's Pinot Noir
- Ste Chapelle Reserve Syrah Reserve Series

BEST VALUE WINES

- Camas Winery Hog Heaven White
- Carmela Vineyards Lemberger
- Pend d'Oreille Bistro Rouge Red Table Wine
- Sawtooth Chenin Blanc
- South Hill/Hegy's Chenin Blanc
- Ste Chapelle Dry Riesling Winemaker's Series

History

In 1862, gold was discovered and vines were planted—French and German immigrants were credited with bringing cuttings from Europe. Their expertise paid off. At the 1898 Chicago World's Fair a Clearwater River Valley wine won a prize and at the 1904 International Exposition a local wine placed second behind Château Cheval Blanc. Prohibition delivered the first blow to the industry in the 1920s. In 1971 the industry began to recover from its second handicap by gaining freedom from the state-monopoly liquor stores. Wines could now be sold in food outlets, and grape growing was re-established. Ste Chapelle produced the first commercial wines in 1976 and several others began production in the 1980s.

There are still fewer than 20 commercial wineries in Idaho. With 57 percent of residents teetotal Mormons, producers must market their wines outside the state in competition with more widely accepted and recognized Oregon and Washington wines.

Landscape and climate

The wine industry is in two segments, with the growers in the southwest clustered around Boise—in Gooding, Twin Falls, Owyhee, Ada and Canyon counties. Canyon County, just south of Nampa, especially the Dry Lake Valley subzone, is slightly warmer than the Snake River vineyards. Ste Chapelle is a big customer in this area. The wineries, conversely, are set up in the central west.

The climate is inhospitable, rainfall is low and severe winters delay bud break. However, sixteen hours a day of intense sunshine is common, offsetting the cold temperatures. The area is classified low Region II on the

Winkler-Amerine scale. To the east, the Rocky Mountains protect the area from arctic storms but winters are long and challenging.

Vines and wines

High-stress climatic conditions (high altitude and abundant sunshine) produce unique wines with both high natural alcohol and high natural acidity. Fully ripe, bone-dry, high-acid, characterful riesling is a specialty, but it is not as popular as the chardonnays, which range from lean and tart to rich, viscous, oaky and buttery. Bordeaux varietals are coming into their own, though many are bolstered with Washington fruit. Ste Chapelle produces Idaho/Washington labeled merlot and cabernet sauvignon. Camas and other wineries produce solely from Washington State fruit. Idaho is one of four places in the world where all the vineyards are planted on their own roots. The nutrient-deficient soil is inhospitable to the vine louse, phylloxera.

Snake River Valley

Snake River Valley is currently the most important and certainly the most well-known of the wine-producing regions in Idaho, but it is worth noting that regions in the southwest are emerging and at present provide huge quantities of fruit for the Snake River Valley wineries.

Most of Idaho's wineries are clustered near the Washington and Oregon borders in the high mountain valleys of the Snake and Clearwater rivers and are concentrated in an area rather appropriately named Sunny Slope. These rivers provide a climate-tempering influence in the region.

The most desirable vineyard sites can be found in south-facing hillsides along the Snake River, where convection currents pull freezing air off the hillsides during winter and cool the vines during summer.

STE CHAPELLE WINERY

Established **1976** ***Owner*** **Canadaigua** ***Production*** **135,000 cases** ***Vineyard area*** **640 acres (259 ha) plus, 600 acres (242 ha) newly planted**

Ste Chapelle Winery in Caldwell, named for La Sainte Chapelle, or Saint's Chapel, built by Louis IX in thirteenth-century Paris, was Idaho's first and is now its largest winery. Ste Chapelle is replanting or directing the redevelopment of more than 1,000 acres (404 ha) of the original vineyard sites first discovered in the nineteenth century. Winemaker Chuck Devlin joined Ste Chapelle Winery just before harvest in 2000. He sees syrah and riesling as the varietals with the most potential for the area, and there are plans afoot to increase production to 300,000 cases a year.

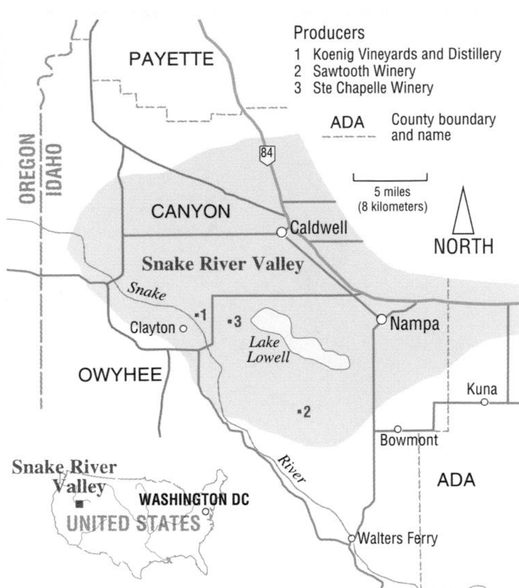

Other Idaho Producers

CAMAS WINERY

Established **1983** ***Owner*** **Stuart L. Scott** ***Production*** **3,700 cases** ***Vineyard area*** **Grapes are bought in**

The Scotts purchase grapes from independent growers and crush them in the field. They gather wild huckleberries, elderberries and plums in the nearby Clearwater, St Joe and Kaniksu National Forests. Their eclectic range of wines includes both *vinifera* varietals and fruit wines, handmade sparkling wines, honey meads and an Ethiopian hopped honey wine.

Camas is one of the oldest wineries in the state, taking its name from the local lily, which at one time was widespread on the Palouse Hills.

PEND D'OREILLE WINERY

Established **1995** ***Owners*** **Stephen and Julie Meyer** ***Production*** **2,000 cases** ***Vineyard area*** **Grapes are bought in**

Stephen and Julie's shared experiences in winemaking include the 1985 harvest in Meursault and seven years at Roudon-Smith Winery in the Santa Cruz Mountains. Chardonnay, pinot noir, merlot, cabernet franc, cabernet sauvignon, a bordeaux red blend and a "bistro" blend are all handcrafted using traditional French methods. The Meyers purchase local fruit for chardonnay and pinot noir, but their most notable wines to date are made with fruit from Columbia Valley, Washington.

Other Idaho producers of significance include Koenig Vineyards; Sawtooth Winery; Carmela Vineyards; and South Hill/Hegy's Winery, which is one of Idaho's smallest wineries. Here, fruit is pressed with an antique Italian press, and all wine is bottled, labeled and corked by hand.

LEFT: A healthy bloom on ripening black grapes.

CALIFORNIA

The Golden State's vinous impact looms large, despite the checkered history of the wine industry over the past 100 years. The University of California (UC) at Davis has influenced several generations of winemakers from around the world. California was at the forefront of modern, hygienic winery practices that revolutionized warm climate wine production. California has been a trendsetter, for good or for bad, in the development of the clean, fruity and overtly oaked style of wine now produced in many parts of the world. Californian wine continues to be the model by which the world's largest economy sets its palate.

RIGHT: The official seal of the state of California.

The journey from the Californian mission vineyards of the eighteenth century to the present day of heady prices and record profits has been difficult. Cycles of boom and bust have been created by markets, disease, politics, war, folly, insight and forward thinking. Prohibition (1919–33) had effects upon the American wine industry which linger to this day. A modern wine industry arose during the 1950s and 1960s and grew in fits and starts, only to be hit with phylloxera biotype-B during the 1990s. Resilient as ever, Californians view this as an expensive lesson and opportunity to improve upon the past's viticultural mistakes. Replanting and record profits have softened the phylloxera blow.

RIGHT: The vivid colors of fall at a Talley family vineyard, in California.

More than 556,000 acres (22,180 ha) of wine grapes are planted in California. The state is the fourth largest wine producer in the world after France, Italy and Spain. Californian wine accounts for 91 percent of production and 72 percent of wine sales in the US. Ninety-eight percent of US wine exports hale from California and these have increased five-fold in value and three-fold in volume since 1990.

In 2002, 65 percent of the California crush was red grapes and 35 percent was white grapes. Chardonnay was by far the leading white variety over colombard and chenin blanc. Cabernet sauvignon was the leading red, and was slightly ahead of zinfandel.

Landscape and climate

Understanding the Californian climate is not easy. Two myths need dispelling—first, that autumn is cooler than summer, second, that bathing beauties in skimpy bathing suits frolick in the ocean. The reality? Autumn is frequently warmer than summer, especially near the Pacific coast. Surface water temperatures are cold, 50–60°F (10–16°C), for most of the year along the California coast. This is due to a combination of factors resulting in warm surface water being pushed away from the shore and out to sea. Only in the south, and then only for a month or two during summer, does one venture into the Pacific Ocean without a wetsuit.

Two mountain ranges that impact upon the state's viticulture—the westernmost is aptly named the Coastal Range and the range farther inland is the Sierra Nevada Range. Between these two is the famed Central Valley, one of the great agricultural regions on earth. The Coastal Range runs parallel to the Pacific Ocean along most of California's coastline. Up to 4,000 feet (1,221 m) in elevation, it can be a major obstacle to the cooling influence of the Pacific Ocean. The famous inversion layer of the Los Angeles basin and the resulting smog are testament to this effect.

The cool to cold coastal water temperatures influence climate in two ways. Air over the water is cooled and water vapor condenses to form a marine layer, which cools the morning to early afternoon and reduces sunshine in affected regions. The cool air also serves onshore breezes that are typically 20–30 miles per hour (32–48 km per hour) when maximal in late afternoon. The cooling effect is profound enough so that homes built along the coast, south of Los Angeles, do not require air conditioning.

As the inland is warmed by the day's sunshine two forces are created to promote this powerful onshore wind. A temperature gradient between the cool coastline and the warm to hot interior is formed. As the hot inland air rises, a pressure gradient combines with the temperature gradient to generate the cooling breeze from the Pacific Ocean.

The Coastal Range, which helps to create the cooling of the Pacific Ocean's surface, also helps to moderate the effect of these breezes on the interior of California. In those areas where the mountains run parallel to the coast, the onshore breeze is blocked and only the coastal plain is cooled, but at several locations the Coastal Range turns perpendicular and permits the cooling effect of the onshore wind to permeate inland. Similarly, gaps in the Coastal Range—the most famous being Golden Gate in San Francisco—also permit the cool afternoon and evening breezes to gain entry to the interior valleys of the state.

West to east orientation is thus more important in terms of temperature along coastal California, than north to south. While southern California is warmer than central and north, coastal regions of the south are cooler than inland regions of the north.

During the early autumn, the Pacific high usually weakens, lessening both the marine layer and the onshore winds. This results in net autumn warming. The regional weather pattern may further change when a strong inland high and a weakening Pacific high create a pattern of offshore winds. Both daily maximum and minimum temperatures increase during these periods.

Petite sirah "peh teet sear ahh"

Though many connect petite sirah with syrah, a red grape that earned its reputation in France's Rhône Valley for the sultry, smoky wines of Côte Rôtie and Hermitage, the two are not related. America's petite sirah had, in the 1980's, also been incorrectly linked with durif, another rhône varietal with similar characteristics. A typical California petite sirah from Mendocino, such as Guenoc or Parducci, is medium-bodied and juicy, while those from Sonoma such as Foppiano or Napa Valley's Louis Martini are medium-to-full bodied and supple. The lavishly oaked Stag's Leap Napa Valley bottling is very rich with sweet flavors and barrel tannins, and is about double the price of the less-oaky versions. At the lighter end of the spectrum, Bogle is very accessible and fruity.

Climate is of supreme importance to Californian viticulture. Areas with significant coastal effects—Carneros, Sonoma, Arroyo Grande and Santa Barbara—may indeed have cooler summer temperatures than such classic regions as Bordeaux and Burgundy. Cool evening temperatures cause grapes to retain good natural acidity levels.

Although summer temperatures may be lower in such coastal regions than classic regions, or even cool regions like Oregon, autumn climate patterns differ markedly. Whereas daily maximal temperatures decrease, sometimes markedly, during the autumn in the classic regions in Europe and in the Pacific Northwest, the reverse tends to take place during the early fall period in coastal California. This allows for continued ripening, usually with cool evening temperatures. Under such conditions, and depending upon how long the "hang time" is prolonged, it is possible to obtain grapes with a ripe flavor profile suggesting a warm climate, while retaining the acidity of a cooler climate.

Thus, climate and aspect play greater roles than soil type in influencing viticulture in California. The coastal mountains and valleys were under the Pacific Ocean 250 million years ago. Great earthquakes caused by the interaction of the Pacific and North American tectonic plates, moved what are now Napa and Sonoma Valleys, and much of the coast, eastward. Marked volcanic activity has further complicated the geological picture. Soils vary markedly and include shale, sandstone, limestone, sandy loams, clay loams, gravel, granite, sand and volcanic. Short distances may yield much variation among soil types.

ABOVE: New plantings at Chalone Vineyards, California, backed by the Pinnacles National Monument.

ABOVE: *Schied Vineyards along Route 25, California.*

RIGHT: *A sign at Clairborne & Churchill Winery, California.*

Vines and wines

Since the 1850s California has experienced a metamorphosis in varieties and styles of wine. Sweet and fortified wines from the mission grape gave way to the ever-versatile zinfandel. The fortunes of riesling, colombard and chenin blanc have risen and fallen. Zinfandel, chardonnay and cabernet sauvignon finished the twentieth century as dominant in the blush, white and red table wine categories. Sweet and fortified wines have gone out of fashion though some very good examples remain.

Generalizations regarding style miss wines on the vanguard, which may be the standard bearers 20 years hence. General styles do exist, especially since many winemakers were trained at either UC Davis or Fresno State. There is increasing cross-pollination with producers in France, Italy, Australia and South America; this has blurred some of the boundaries both geographically and stylistically. As new plantings mature and new opinion makers appear, these styles should evolve too.

Wine critics play a vital role in the development of style. Critics have immense power in setting wine styles—retailers and producers use critic-generated scores to sell wines. Producers then try to emulate the high scoring win; this is a situation not unique to the US.

Varietal wines (those with at least 75 percent of the variety on the label) have long been dominant in California. But changing styles means that a cabernet sauvignon wine is now more likely to contain merlot, sometimes all five red Bordeaux standards. In homage to Côte Rôtie, syrah producers are increasingly blending up to 10–15 percent viognier. Most varietal labeled chardonnay and pinot noir are not blended.

Meritage wines are blends of bordeaux varieties, either red (cabernet sauvignon, cabernet franc, merlot, malbec, petite verdot) or white (sauvignon blanc, sémillon, muscadelle) which must meet legal criteria.

Wine laws

California's wine is subject to both state and federal laws. The Bureau of Alcohol, Tobacco and Firearms (BATF) has a powerful regulatory role in both designation and distribution. American viticultural areas (AVAs) are awarded by BATF, and are based on geography and history. AVAs were established in 1978. There are now 145 in total, 87 of them in California.

Varietal and place of origin fall under state and federal laws, with the more stringent standard being that to which the industry is held. Wine labeled as California must be entirely made from grapes grown within the state.

The content standard for county of origin or varietal designation is 75 percent. A wine containing 75 percent cabernet sauvignon and 25 percent merlot may be labeled as varietal cabernet sauvignon. One with 70 percent cabernet sauvignon and 30 percent merlot may not carry a single varietal designation. Such a wine can be labeled with no varietal description or with the relevant percentages. An AVA origin labeled wine carries an 85 percent or more content requirement. A designated vineyard (for example, Martha's Vineyard) is even more stringent: 95 percent of the grapes originate from the designated vineyard.

Wineries are not obliged to state what varieties, by percentage, went into making any wine, as long as at least 75 percent is from the varietal named on the label. Increasingly, though, wineries do detail the varietal breakdown.

The laws governing the distribution of wine are being hotly contested at state and federal levels, by those who seek to reduce regulation and open up markets and those trying to protect their tax revenue or distribution interests.

With good friends . . .
And good food on the board,
and good wine in the pitcher,
we may well ask: When shall we
live if not now?

M. F. K FISHER,
The Art of Living

The three-tiered system—producer/importer, wholesaler and retailer—was set up to increase competition and counter organized crime. Distribution is controlled at federal, state and local levels—this is all a throwback to the repeal of Prohibition in 1933.

Under the three-tiered system, a producer or importer may only sell to a wholesale distributor (except for cellar door sales by a producer), who may then sell to a retailer, who may then sell to the consumer. Protagonists in all levels of the system actively lobby government to protect their turf. Those who lobby well may gain exceptions to the system. Some states, such as Pennsylvania and Vermont, directly control retailing via a government-enforced monopoly. A confusing system it is!

Viticulture

California is a prime location for viticulture, with its dry, warm climate. Dry weather keeps many diseases and pests at bay; sunshine and lack of rain during the growing season allows long "hang time." Without imminent disease or weather pressures, Californian viticulturalists can wait to pick at the optimal time of ripeness for almost every vintage.

Although history has offered challenges to California's winegrowers, their flexibility and adaptation to their physical environment has yielded success. Since the experiences of the pioneers of California viticulture were diminished due to Prohibition, winegrowers were very open to research and innovation. As a result, the face of California viticulture has been forever changed. Additionally, the trend in the winery towards "wine is grown not made" has placed greater emphasis on vineyard practices.

ABOVE: *A self-explanatory road sign.*

Although Prohibition created a lapse in California's wine production, the greatest challenge to the industry is and has been phylloxera—a grape-root louse which begins as a nuisance reducing yields, but eventually kills the vine. Once thought resistant to phylloxera, AxR1 rootstock began to fail in the mid-1980s falling prey to "biotype-B," a new mutation.

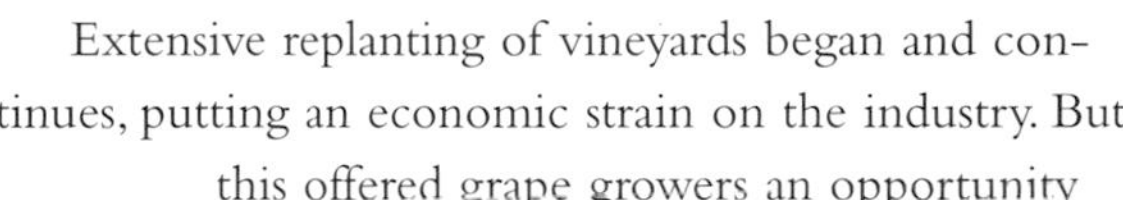

Extensive replanting of vineyards began and continues, putting an economic strain on the industry. But this offered grape growers an opportunity to regroup. Much of the previous vine material had been planted according to guidelines intended for bulk wine or raisin production. With replanting, viticulturalists could determine the best match of site to vine and rootstock materials. Greater diversity of plant material is now available. Clones of varieties such as the Dijon series from Burgundy have recently been introduced and may improve grape quality. More international varieties are being used as growers propagate their own vine and rootstock materials. Sharing of information is a vital and common occurrence.

BELOW: *Companion planting of vines and roses at Wild Horse Vineyard, San Luis Obispo, California.*

RIGHT: *Protected from the elements—newly planted vines at Edna Valley, California.*

As California's vineyards are replanted, training and pruning methods are also getting a facelift. California "sprawl" originated as the popular "anti-training" of vines—they grew wild with much less guidance from the viticulturalist. With technology and mechanization, the need for tractors, rippers and other machinery necessitated more orderly vine training. Many producers moved to a three-wire system to allow for canopy management. These training systems improve air circulation, decrease disease pressure and the need for spraying, and help let more light into the canopy. Quality has improved with less vegetal flavors, less vine vigor and greater ripeness. New forms of trellising and pruning are adopted from other regions. Most vineyards are tractor-friendly and mechanization has increased, but harvesting for premium production is mostly done by hand.

ABOVE: *A barrel sign announcing the entrance to Paragon Vineyards in the Edna Valley, California.*

Traditionally, California has benefitted from a large labor force of migrant farm workers at harvest time, but lately, fewer are available. More vineyards are employing full-time workers or hiring vineyard management companies to provide a core group of trained workers.

California's generally warm and dry climate keeps disease pressure from becoming a major threat. Despite this, in the early days chemicals were used in great quantities at the mere hint of danger. Overuse led to chemicals killing good insects as well as bad, and the creation of the "super-bug" as insects became immune to stronger chemicals. In recent years, environmental, governmental and consumer pressures have forced vine growers to explore more natural means of disease and pest control. Now the focus is on sustainable agriculture, agriculture with an eye toward the environment while allowing chemical intervention when necessary. Some growers have embraced organic or biodynamic agricultural methods. At any rate, California viticulturalists have become more aware of the delicate balance of the ecosystem and, as a result, are more considerate in terms of vineyard practices.

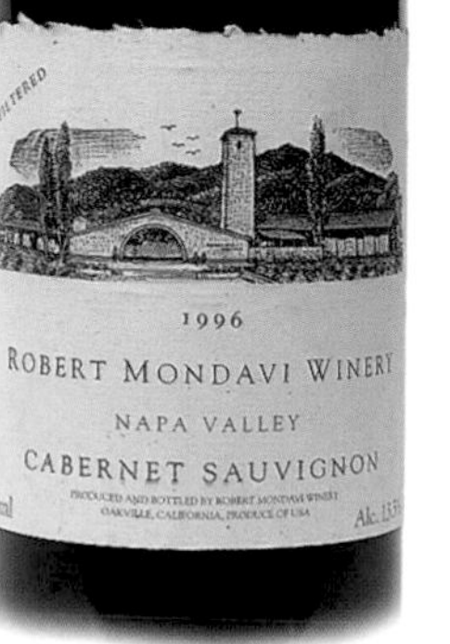

Major vineyard problems still exist. Frost, sunburn, birds, mold and mildew are kept to a minimum via physical or chemical means. But the two major players are still phylloxera and Pierce's disease. Although not forgotten, the dread of phylloxera has been supplanted with a new fear—Pierce's disease. It is spread by a bacterium transported by the blue-green sharpshooter. Once it has taken hold there is no current treatment for it. Most prevalent in riparian areas, the bugs infect nearby vineyards and there is the fear that new vectors, like the glassy-winged sharpshooter, will travel up the highway system to ravage more vineyards.

Irrigation is commonly used in most of California with the exception of a few dry-farmed sites. Weather in the state is distinct from most other wine regions in that there is often little or no rain during the growing season, the majority falling during the winter. Without irrigation, vine growing would be near impossible and controlled drip irrigation allows careful control of watering. Strict legislation controls water rights, however, sufficient water may not always be available.

Although many innovations of agricultural techniques have been offered to California's viticulturalists, in recent years the movement has been towards a balance of tradition and technology. Lacking a thorough and consistent history, California has been looking abroad for expertise. They have gleaned a wealth of information and have brought it home. The upcoming challenges will be met and conquered with this openness to new ideas.

AROMATIC & NON-BARREL FERMENTED WHITE WINES

As in much of the world, the modern technique includes crushing and destemming followed by some period of cold settling. Of note is the fact that vineyards and wineries are usually in close proximity. Skin contact has usually been frowned upon although some producers opt for purposeful contact to improve aromatics.

Most fermentations are inoculated with one of the many strains of commercial yeast and a cool, temperature-controlled fermentation employed to yield a clean, fruity wine. Smaller producers are increasingly successful in spontaneous ferments. Malolactic fermentation may be inoculated or, less commonly, occur spontaneously. Many producers block the secondary fermentation in this style of wine, often with sterile filtration.

Less expensive styles of chardonnay and other varieties may then receive the kiss of oak. Oak chips at the lower end and several months of *barrique* maturation for somewhat more upscale wines. French and American oak are both used.

BARREL FERMENTED WHITES

At the upper end, chardonnay is barrel fermented, usually in new and newish French *barriques*. Cool rooms and cellars are increasingly used for temperature control. Most are still inoculated, though there is a trend toward more spontaneous fermentations. Lees stirring and contact are used to variable degrees. More producers are opting not to filter their wines. It is not uncommon for other varieties such as sauvignon blanc, marsanne, pinot blanc, pinot gris and others to be so treated.

Technical skill varies between producers though the trend is for less overt diacetyl notes and for more judicious use of oak. When well made, California chardonnay is a world class wine.

BLUSH AND ROSÉ WINES

White zinfandel is the benchmark here. Most are treated as aromatic white wines, fewer are back blended with red wine. Fermentations are often stopped to leave the wines off dry. Sterile filtration and early bottling are normal. Increasingly, dry versions are made from varieties such as pinot noir, sangiovese and cabernet sauvignon.

PINOT NOIR AND OTHER RED WINES

After either crush/destem or whole cluster pressing, temperature-controlled warm (80°F [30°C] or more) fermentation is performed in open top, stainless steel vessels. Punching down is performed for extraction and a limited post-fermentation maceration may be employed. Increasing numbers of producers ferment spontaneously.

French oak maturation in new and used barrels for 9–12 months is common. American oak barrels are increasingly used. Oak chips are employed at the lower end. Increasingly, producers bottle their wines unfined and unfiltered, though finishing techniques are variable.

Other varieties (such as zinfandel, syrah and grenache) may be produced in a similar manner, often with an increased frequency of punching down, slightly lower fermentation temperatures and a longer post-fermentation maceration.

CABERNET SAUVIGNON AND OTHER REDS

Bordeaux is used as a model here, though most fermentations are inoculated. Closed top fermenters are employed. Fermentation temperatures are warm yet controlled. Pumping over is used for extraction. Post-fermentation maceration tends to be two to four weeks, or longer.

ABOVE: *Postbox and sign for the Lazy Creek Vineyards, Mendocino.*

Oak barrels, oak staves and oak chips are all employed with barrel maturation regimens at one year, though this varies. Clarification is via a combination of racking, fining and filtration, though increasingly wines are unfiltered.

Other varieties, particularly merlot, cabernet franc, sangiovese, zinfandel and syrah are treated in a similar manner, though often with shorter macerations, more American oak and shorter periods of barrel maturation. Wines at the top end tend to be treated in a manner very similar to top cabernet sauvignon.

SPARKLING WINES

Inexpensive wines are cleanly produced using bulk methods. French champagne houses, transplanted cava producers and American concerns produce sparkling wines using traditional techniques.

SWEET AND FORTIFIED WINES

Modern techniques are employed, with one innovation being cryo extraction, whereby an icewine is induced by placing harvested grapes into freezers and then continuing production as per an icewine.

BELOW: *The Sunstone Vineyard, California, tasting room is reminiscent of those in the countryside around Provence, France.*

Mendocino and Lake County

REBECCA CHAPA

Forty-one wineries have their home in Mendocino, north of Sonoma County and 90 miles (145 km) north of San Francisco. The region is possibly the most geographically diverse in California with mountain ranges, valleys and lakes producing a wide variety of terrains and climates. Most vineyards are located on hillsides, with only 15 percent of producers growing grapes on the valley floor. Of 2,248,000 acres (909,753 ha) of available agricultural land, only 16,156 acres (6,543 ha) are planted as vineyards. There are 300 of these, with 25 percent of acreage certified organic. No single producer in Mendocino farms more than 1,000 acres (405 ha). Varietal selection is diverse, with gewürztraminer, petite sirah, syrah, riesling and zinfandel appearing as often as pinot noir, chardonnay, sauvignon blanc and cabernet sauvignon. The vineyard area of Lake County, to the east of Mendocino, covers about 5,500 acres (2,225 ha).

BELOW: Vines at the Navarro Vineyards, Mendocino.

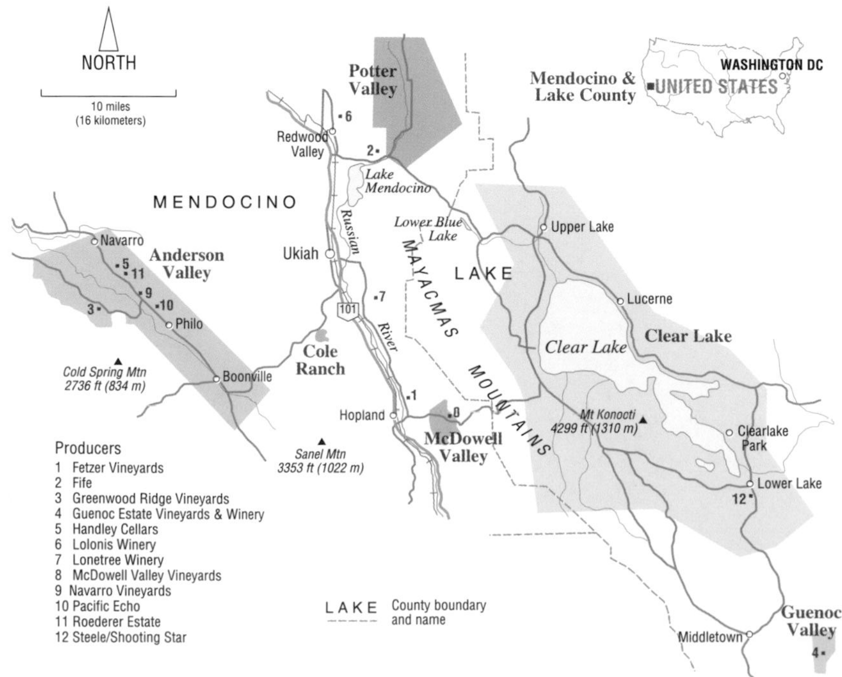

History

First planted under vine in the 1850s following the gold rush, Mendocino's grape growers concentrated on cultivating the hillsides in order to leave room for other crops on the flatlands. Since the region was isolated, wines were generally sold locally, missing out on exposure to major markets gained by more easily accessible wineries in Napa and Sonoma. Prohibition shut down most wineries until the 1960s. At this time, better transport created a surge in Mendocino's wine industry. For the first time wineries began focusing on making their own wine rather than selling grapes to bulk producers. In recent years there has been a renewal of interest and investment in Mendocino wines—a sign of better things to come.

The first vineyards in Lake County were planted in the 1870s but were ripped out to provide room for other crops when Prohibition took hold. Although slow to recover—today Lake County still has only six wineries—investment in vineyard land by some large companies is growing, as is the buying of fruit for labels such as Fetzer and Robert Mondavi.

Climate and landscape

Climate throughout the Mendocino region is diverse, ranging from cool to cold on the coast and at higher altitudes, to warmer temperatures on the valley floors. Cool nights retain acidity in the fruit, while warm days allow for ripeness. Rhône varieties such as viognier and grenache do well in warmer areas like the McDowell Valley, while cooler regions such as the northwest section of the Anderson Valley are planted with cool-climate varieties including pinot noir. Soils are similar to those of Sonoma County with light texture, sand, gravel and powdery consistencies and tend to be well drained. Rainfall is about 37 inches (94 cm) per annum.

To the east of Mendocino, Lake County is well known for cool nights and hot days during the growing season. From the west the county is shielded from fog and moisture by the Mayacamas Mountains. Similarly, Clear Lake moderates the climatic influence on Lake County's vineyards.

FIFE, MENDOCINO

Established **1996** ***Owner*** **Dennis Fife** ***Production*** **10,000 cases** ***Vineyard area*** **13 acres (5 ha)**

Fife uses great fruit and minimum handling to make some fierce reds. The Redhead Zinfandel, named partly after the brick-red soil it grows in, is spicy and fiery without the coarse texture of some zinfandels. MAX is a blend of syrah, petite sirah, charbono and zinfandel.

LEFT: A tasting room for the environmentally aware—all of Fetzer's Vineyards are farmed organically.

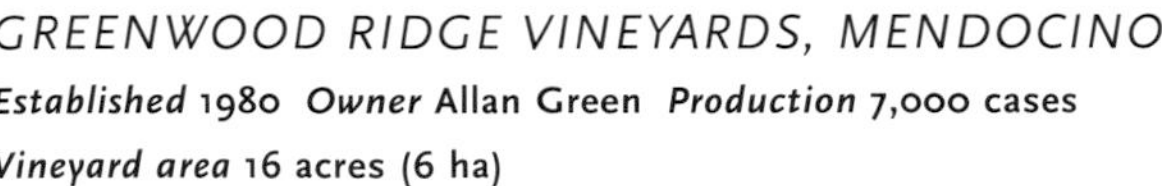

GREENWOOD RIDGE VINEYARDS, MENDOCINO

Established **1980** ***Owner*** **Allan Green** ***Production*** **7,000 cases** ***Vineyard area*** **16 acres (6 ha)**

Allan Green is a great advocate of his region and every year since 1983 has held the large and very entertaining California Wine Tasting Championships at his winery. He makes fantastic wines too and Greenwood Ridge—which sits about 1,400 feet (427 m) above sea level, above the fog and frost—is well known for its pinot noir and zinfandel. It was the first winery to release wines under the Mendocino Ridge appellation in 1998.

GUENOC ESTATE VINEYARDS & WINERY, LAKE COUNTY

Established **1982** ***Owner*** **Orville Magoon** ***Production*** **100,000 cases** ***Vineyard area*** **340 acres (138 ha)**

The Guenoc Estate, includes some of California's oldest vineyards. Lillie Langtry, actress and winemaker, owned the property from 1888 to 1906. Elevations range from about 800 to 1,500 feet (244 to 457 m), and soils are rocky and alluvial. The region's warm days and rather cool nights are great for growing bordeaux varieties and specific emphasis has been placed on carmenère. In 1981, Guenoc Valley was recognized as an AVA, the first in the US owned by a single proprietorship.

LOLONIS WINERY, MENDOCINO

Established **1920** ***Owner*** **Petros Lolonis** ***Production*** **30,000 cases** ***Vineyard area*** **300 acres (121 ha)**

Lolonis has been in the business of growing vines since before Prohibition. The winery itself was started in 1982. Lolonis is strongly opposed to using chemicals for most pest control, preferring to use natural methods such as ladybugs and praying mantis to control leaf hoppers and spiders.

MCDOWELL VALLEY VINEYARDS, MENDOCINO

Established **1970** ***Owners*** **Bill and Vicky Crawford** ***Production*** **18,400 cases** ***Vineyard area*** **250 acres (101 ha)**

McDowell Valley Vineyards farms 90 of its acres (36 ha) organically, and makes wines from traditional rhône varieties like grenache, syrah and viognier. Especially popular is its grenache rosé, a tasty dry alternative to white zinfandel.

NAVARRO VINEYARDS, MENDOCINO

Established **1974** ***Owners*** **Deborah Cahn and Ted Bennett** ***Production*** **32,000–35,000 cases** ***Vineyard area*** **60 acres (24 ha)**

Navarro produces many styles from dry to vendange tardive, and even makes grape juice. Vineyard management includes natural methods of pest control. Pinot noir from Navarro is offered in both traditional and newer styles, and the gewürztraminer is excellent. All wines are consistently of a high quality.

ROEDERER ESTATE, MENDOCINO

Established **1982** ***Owners*** **Champagne Louis Roederer** ***Production*** **70,000 cases** ***Vineyard area*** **350 acres (142 ha)**

As the first investment by the Champenois in Mendocino, Jean-Claude Rouzaud believed firmly that Anderson Valley was the perfect place for his Californian *méthode champenoise* property. Great care is taken to produce optimal grapes and to vinify in the French style. The wines are perhaps California's most elegant, and often indistinguishable from French champagne.

Other significant producers in Mendocino and Lake County include Fetzer Vineyards, Handley Cellars, Lonetree Winery, Pacific Echo and Steele/Shooting Star.

Regional Dozen

QUALITY WINES

Christine Woods Pinot Noir, Anderson Valley
Eaglepoint Ranch Petite Sirah
Elke Pinot Donnelly
Creek Pinot Noir
Navarro Vineyards Late Harvest Gewürztraminer
Roessler Blue Jay Pinot Noir, Anderson Valley
Lolonis Petros

BEST VALUE WINES

Chance Creek Sangiovese, Redwood Valley
Dunnewood Cabernet Sauvignon
Esterlina Riesling Cole Ranch
Handley Pinot Noir
Husch Pinot Noir
Roederer Estate Brut

BELOW: A vineyard in the fall at the Roederer Estate, Mendocino.

ABOVE: *Vineyard at the Benziger Family Winery, Sonoma Valley, which aims to create affordable premium wines.*

Sonoma County

REBECCA CHAPA

Sonoma County is north of San Francisco and west of Napa Valley, adjacent to the Pacific coast. The region has 180 wineries on 48,000 acres (19,440 ha) and produces 133,000 tons (135,660 t) annually. Although on a grand scale geographically, Sonoma has more small wineries than Napa. And although it is quieter than the Napa Valley in the middle of the summer tourist season, Sonoma is the hot spot for grape growing in California. Significant vineyard plantings are concentrating on producing prime grapes for the premium segment of the market.

History

Although Sonoma's wine history began before that of the Napa Valley, it was on a much smaller scale. Here, instead of wealthy investors concentrating only on wine, many of the area's pioneers were Italian farmers who grew grapes with a variety of other crops. In 1823, the last, most northerly Californian mission was built in Sonoma, creating more of a focus on the growing of grapes. Soon after, William Hill planted the first non-mission varieties in Sonoma.

RIGHT: *California's oldest premium winery established in 1857 is the Buena Vista Winery in Sonoma Valley.*

In 1857, Count Agoston Haraszthy, a Hungarian who became known as the "father" of the Californian wine industry, arrived in Sonoma and started the Buena Vista winery. He was influential in bringing vine material back to California from Europe and the 100,000 cuttings (about 350 varieties) he imported from France, Italy and Spain changed viticulture in Sonoma for ever. A surge in plantings followed, resulting in production levels of 132,000 tons (119,724 t) of grapes from a total of 180 wineries, and plantings by around 750 vineyards of 49,000 acres (19,845 ha). These levels dwindled after Prohibition, never to regain their vast numbers. Today, however, the future in Sonoma looks promising with an increase in the number of big-name wineries doing business here, including Gallo, the largest wine company in the world.

Climate and landscape

Slightly cooler than Napa Valley, cool sites in Sonoma County are excellent for growing more delicate grape varieties. The climate varies dramatically according to individual appellation—fog and offshore breezes keeping temperatures low by the ocean, near gaps in the Coastal Range and to the south near Carneros.

BENZIGER FAMILY WINERY

Established **1981** ***Owners*** **the Benziger family** ***Production*** **180,000 cases** ***Vineyard area*** **65 acres (26 ha)**

Originally, Mike Benziger bought wine in bulk to sell under the Glen Ellen label. It became a successful brand on its own and was sold to Heublein. Now the Benzigers can finally concentrate on their original intention, which is to create affordable premium wines. Merlot and chardonnay offer exceptional value.

CHALK HILL WINERY

Established **1972** ***Owners*** **Frederick and Peggy Furth** ***Production*** **75,000 cases** ***Vineyard area*** **300 acres (121 ha)**

Chalk Hill was granted a viticultural appellation in 1984. Chalk Hill Winery produces the only 100 percent estate-bottled wines in this appellation. The site is also known for conducting one of the largest private clonal experiments in the US in which 17 chardonnay clones are being studied. Vineyards sit at 200–600 feet (60–185 m) elevation and plantings run up and over the hillsides rather than on terraces, in order to protect the natural shape of the hills. Chalk Hill is most appreciated for its white wines—sauvignon blanc, chardonnay and pinot gris. It also produces a botrytized sémillon with exquisite peach and apricot flavors.

DEHLINGER WINERY

Established **1975** ***Owner*** **Tom Dehlinger** ***Production*** **7,000 cases** ***Vineyard area*** **50 acres (20 ha)**

Taking advantage of the cool and foggy weather of the Russian River Valley, the vines at Dehlinger produce outstanding chardonnay, pinot noir and syrah. Winemaking techniques aim to extract as much flavor as possible from the grapes and on this prime site, there's much to be had.

FERRARI-CARANO VINEYARDS & WINERY

Established **1981** ***Owners*** **Don and Rhonda Carano** ***Production*** **150,000 cases** ***Vineyard area*** **1,200 acres (486 ha)**

Don and Rhonda Carano from Reno, Nevada, have made their mark on the region by producing a number of great wines. Best known for its chardonnay, the winery also produces a Reserve Fumé Blanc with 100 percent barrel fermentation and extended lees aging. Winemaker George Bursick has worked wonders with sangiovese for Siena, a proprietary wine. Memories of the Reno area inspired a rare sweet dessert wine called El Dorado Gold, almost impossible to find.

FLOWERS WINERY

Established **1990** ***Owners*** **Joan and Walt Flowers** ***Production*** **10,000 cases** ***Vineyard area*** **23 acres (9 ha)**

Flowers is one of the pioneers of the rugged Sonoma Coast near Jenner, where the Russian River flows into the Pacific Ocean, the winery enjoys an altitude just higher than the fog line and benefits from the best of both worlds—natural air conditioning and plenty of sunshine. Look out for Perennial, a blend that changes yearly but usually includes zinfandel, pinot noir and pinot meunier.

HANZELL VINEYARDS

Established **1953** ***Owners*** **Barbara and Alex deBrye** ***Production*** **2,700 cases** ***Vineyard area*** **26 acres (10 ha)**

These vineyards were originally established by J. D. Zellerbach, whose passion for burgundy brought changes to Californian winemaking and continues to be a force in the winemaking at Hanzell. Small French barrels and stainless steel equipment were just a few of his early innovations. Pinot noir and chardonnay are recommended.

IRON HORSE VINEYARDS

Established **1978** ***Owners*** **Sterling family and Forrest Tancer** ***Production*** **36,000–45,000 cases** ***Vineyard area*** **246 acres (100 ha)**

Audrey and Barry Sterling and Forrest Tancer founded this winery in Sonoma's Green Valley in 1979 with the goal of making unique high quality wines. Only estate-grown grapes and those from Forrest's mother's ranch, T-bar-T, in Alexander Valley, are used to ensure high-quality fruit. Iron Horse is particularly noted for its sparkling wine.

JORDAN VINEYARD & WINERY

Established **1972** ***Owner*** **Tom Jordan** ***Production*** **8,000 cases** ***Vineyard area*** **275 acres (111 ha)**

Located in the Alexander Valley, Jordan is a top producer of cabernet sauvignon and chardonnay and strives to

Regional Dozen

- Amphora Zinfandel Dry Creek Valley
- Chalk Hill Cabernet Sauvignon, Chalk Hill
- Dehlinger Pinot Noir Russian River Valley
- De Lorimier Merlot Alexander Valley
- Dry Creek Vineyards DCV-3 Sauvignon Blanc Dry Creek Valley
- Flowers Camp Meeting Ridge Pinot Noir Sonoma Coast
- Hanzell Chardonnay Sonoma Valley
- Iron Horse Vineyards Brut Green Valley
- Korbel Chardonnay Champagne Brut, Russian River Valley
- Landmark Damaris Reserve Chardonnay Sonoma County
- Mazzocco Zinfandel Dry Creek Valley
- Peterson Zinfandel Dry Creek Valley

LEFT: Vineyards in every direction in the Sonoma Valley, California.

BELOW: Gardens leading to the tasting room at Ferrari-Carano Winery.

RIGHT: Statue of St Francis, after whom the St Francis Winery, Sonoma County, was named.

produce wines that go well with food. The region has a long growing season with sufficient warmth for ripeness and fog to retain acidity. The site was originally planted with plums, but is now covered with rows of cabernet sauvignon, cabernet franc, merlot and chardonnay. Jordan's cabernet is very drinkable in its youth, but ages successfully as well. When the 1978 was made, skeptics believed it was too well integrated to age but a tasting of that vintage today proves that older wines don't need tannin and harshness to mature well.

LAUREL GLEN VINEYARD

Established **1981** ***Owner*** **Patrick Campbell** ***Production*** **4,000 cases** ***Vineyard area*** **35 acres (14 ha)**

Laurel Glen produces 100 percent estate-grown wines from 30-year-old vines and sells them under the Laurel Glen and Counterpoint labels. As well, it uses grapes from Chile and Argentina to make a red blend called Terra Rossa and REDS ("a wine for the people"), a bistro-style wine. Syrah and sangiovese are experimental varieties currently being used to add aromatics.

PETER MICHAEL

Established **1983** ***Owner*** **Sir Peter Michael** ***Production*** **7,000–9,000 cases** ***Vineyard area*** **76 acres (31 ha)**

Peter Michael is one of those producers whose wines sell out in seconds. Wines are made with traditional methods on mountain vineyards with limited production, thus the demand exceeds supply without fail. Vines grow on 45° slopes for the most part and elevations of 2,000 feet (610 m) allow for long slow ripening. Rocky volcanic soils further control vine vigor and productivity. Chardonnays include Mon Plaisir and Belle Côte, and if you see Point Rouge, buy it. A bordeaux-style blend, Les Pavots, and L'Après Midi, a sauvignon blanc, are also winners.

RAVENSWOOD WINERY

Established **1976** ***Owners*** **Constellation/Canadaigua** ***Production*** **250,000 cases** ***Vineyard area*** **18 acres (7 ha)**

Most of the fruit is purchased, often from dry-farmed sites with 70 to 100-year-old vines. The Ravenswood logo—"No wimpy wines"—is borne out in its powerful zinfandels, ranging from complex vineyard-designates to a great-value zinfandel from Lodi. Although about three-quarters of the production is zinfandel, Ravenswood also does wonders with bordeaux varieties, especially its Gregory Cabernet Sauvignon, which has a hint of mint, and its stalwart merlot from the famed Sangiacomo Vineyard in Carneros. Every wine this winery puts out tends to be at least good quality if not outstanding.

ST FRANCIS

Established **1979** ***Owners*** **Joseph Martin, Lloyd Canton and Kobrand Corp.** ***Production*** **200,000 cases** ***Vineyard area*** **800 acres (324 ha)**

Named after the patron saint of the last mission on the California trail, St Francis was built in 1979. While it is noted for producing fruity yet firm red wines, St Francis may be better known as the first premium winery to experiment with synthetic corks. It now uses them for its entire production. Old Vine Zinfandel is chocolatey and full in body.

BELOW: Stored wine casks at Ferrari-Carano Winery, Sonoma County.

SIMI WINERY

Established **1876** ***Owners*** **Constellation/Canandaigua** ***Production*** **120,000 cases** ***Vineyard area*** **300 acres (121 ha)**

Simi was founded by two Tuscan brothers, Giuseppe and Pietro

Simi. Cellars were built in 1890, however, in the meantime, the first few vintages were made in San Francisco. Sendal is a tasty white bordeaux blend.

SONOMA-CUTRER VINEYARDS

Established **1973** ***Owners*** **Brown-Forman** ***Production*** **80,000 cases** ***Vineyard area*** **400 acres (162 ha)**

Sonoma-Cutrer has always been at the forefront of innovation, with cooling tunnels, sorting tables, membrane presses and the like, making its wines state-of-the-art. One of California's first wineries to concentrate on only one variety, it was also the first to vineyard-designate chardonnay. The Russian River Ranches bottling is the standby, while the Cutrer Vineyard label has more intensity and needs more time to come around. Wines from Les Pierres Vineyard have a mineral note reminiscent of white burgundy. The last two wines took so long to evolve that a new cellar was built specifically for their barrel aging.

TOPOLOS AT RUSSIAN RIVER VINEYARDS

Established **1978** ***Owner*** **Michael Topolos** ***Production*** **18,000 cases** ***Vineyard area*** **27 acres (11 ha)**

The Russian River Vineyards have existed since 1963. Owned by the Topolos family since 1978, they are now the source for environmentally friendly wines with most of the production organic and with some bio-dynamic plantings. Dry-farmed old vines produce deep purple berries that pack a punch in the Piner Heights Zinfandel. Other wines include sauvignon blanc, pinot noir and charbono.

UNTI VINEYARDS & WINERY

Established **1998** ***Owners*** **Unti family** ***Production*** **3,600 cases** ***Vineyard area*** **26 acres (10 ha)**

Newcomer Unti is making a name for itself with a line of powerful reds including zinfandel and syrah from Dry Creek Valley. The families planted these grapes along with sangiovese for the simple reason that it's what they enjoy drinking. Early reports suggest that consumers agree with them. Oak is restrained in order to keep the wines drinkable upon release.

Other notable producers in Sonoma County include David Bynum Winery, Carmenet Vineyards, Gallo of Sonoma, Hafner Vineyard, Kistler Vineyards, Landmark, Lynmar at Quail Hill Vineyard, Marimar Torres Estate, Seghesio Family Vineyards, Stonestreet and Williams & Selyem Winery.

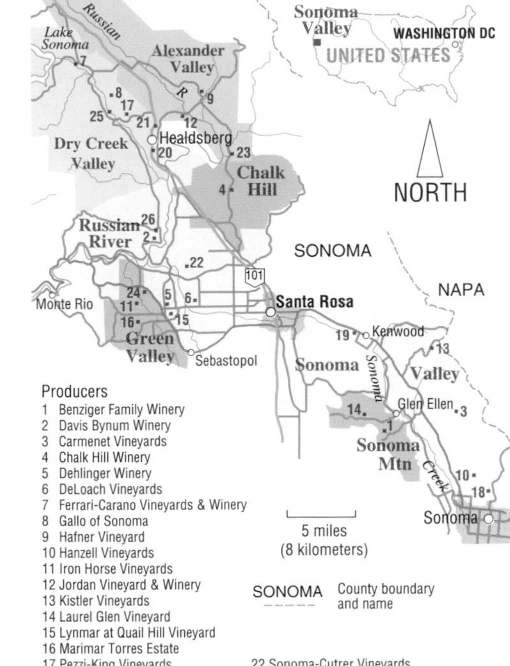

Zinfandel

Zinfandel, affectionately called "zin" by Americans had long been considered a native grape. When proven to be Vitis vinifera, *and so by definition, not native to America, theories on its importation abounded. Eventually, DNA analysis confirmed that zinfandel was identical to Apuglia's primitivo, though Italian records could only trace the primitivo variety back some 150 years. Searches along the Dalmatian coast brought samples of the plavac mali vine back for analysis which demonstrated the variety to be an offspring of zinfandel. Finally, in 2001, further detective work proved that zinfandel was the Croatian variety crljenak. Today top zinfandels come from vines up to 100 years old, from Sonoma, Amador County and Paso Robles.*

BELOW: *Grape harvest at Ravenswood Winery, Sonoma Valley.*

ABOVE: *Lush Napa Valley vineyards surrounding winery buildings.*

Napa Valley

REBECCA CHAPA

Known around the world as the top premium wine-growing region in North America, the Napa Valley's diversity of appellations and wine styles defies definition. Some believe that with time, Napa Valley's diversity will be further made evident by appellations as detailed as those of Burgundy. A favorable climate and the talent of its winemakers contribute to its fame, though the scourge of phylloxera has forced Napa's viticulturalists to review their choice of varieties and to concentrate on more strategic plantings.

RIGHT: *The Napa region welcomes many visitors each year.*

History

The Valley was originally settled by Wappo Indians who called it Napa, meaning "Land of Plenty," a name that was adopted by future settlers. Napa's first homestead and the first property to plant grapevines was established by George Yount, for whom the town of Yountville is named, in 1836. In 1861, the first commercial winery was built by Charles Krug in St Helena and by 1889 there were more than 140 wineries in Napa Valley. Phylloxera hit with devastating effect in the early 1890s and in 1920 Prohibition put many wineries out of business. These were hard setbacks to overcome—by 1960 wineries numbered a mere 25. However, by 1990 the wine industry had picked up and over 200 were operating. Today, the number has swelled to over 250, with 40,016 acres (16,206 ha) of a total of 297,000 acres (120,285 ha) under vine, yielding around 129,000 tons (131,580 t) of fruit.

During Napa's evolution the Napa Valley Vintners Association, formed in 1943, and the Napa Valley Grape Growers Association, formed in 1975, were integral at marketing and improving the wines of the region.

They remain a driving force. An ordinance in 1968, promoting agriculture as the prime use of land, protects 30,000 acres (12,150 ha) of land for grape growing and further regulations are in force to thwart erosion. Currently, the latest battle is in trying to prevent certain producers from using the name "Napa" if their wines do not meet the requirements of the grape source.

Climate and landscape

Napa Valley includes part of the Carneros region at the mouth of San Pablo Bay. It stretches about 30 miles (48 km) to the northwest and is a mere 5 miles (8 km) wide near the city of Napa, narrowing to 1 mile (1.6 km) near Calistoga. To the west, the valley is bounded by the green forests of the Mayacamas Mountains that separate it from Sonoma Valley and to the east, the much drier and rugged Vaca range.

Climate is primarily Mediterranean—warm, dry summers; wet, cool winters. Rain is rare during the growing season and most occurs from October through May. Fog, drawn up the valley as the air heats up inland during the day, is pulled in from the bay, and can be seen in the more southerly areas. Its effect is to keep the vines cool, which retains the natural acidity in the fruit. Nights tend to be cool and the days warm, allowing for slow ripening. Traveling north from Carneros to Calistoga in summer, the temperature can increase 1 degree per mile.

Soils are diverse—there were up to 32 different types at the last count—created from volcanic eruptions and earth movements. Many faults cross the area. Volcanic ash and lava were deposited especially along the Mayacamas. Soils are less deep and rockier on the mountainsides than in the valley, stressing the vines, a condition which some believe produces better-quality wines. Sub-appellations of the valley include Atlas Peak, Howell Mountain, Los Carneros, Mount Veeder, Oakville, Rutherford, St Helena, Spring Mountain District, Stags Leap District and Wild Horse Valley. New appellations are continually being proposed.

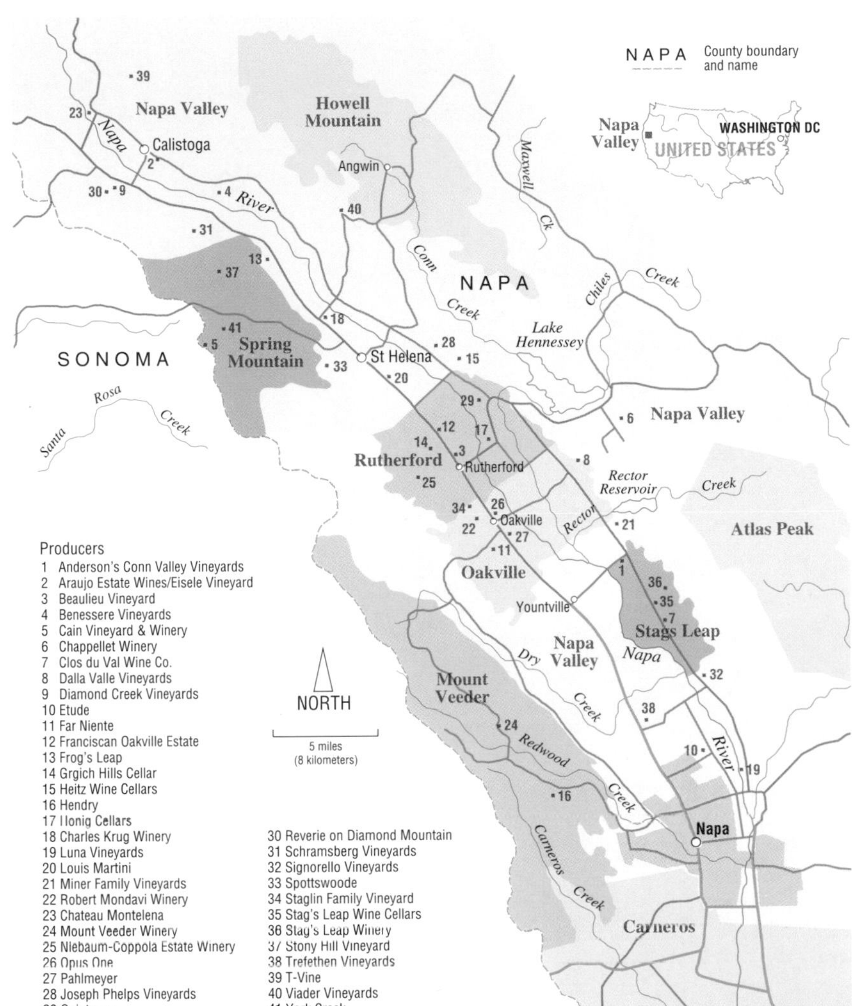

BEAULIEU VINEYARD

Established **1900** ***Owners*** **Diageo** ***Production*** **1.1 million cases** ***Vineyard area*** **1,200 acres (486 ha)**

Georges de Latour from Bordeaux established Beaulieu Vineyard in 1900 and was instrumental in importing grafted vines from France that were phylloxera-resistant. His business survived Prohibition by making high-grade altar wine for the Catholic Church. In 1938, André Tchelistcheff, an innovator who taught others techniques such as malolactic fermentation, cold fermentation and filtration, joined Beaulieu. The founder's vision lives on in the winery's prestigious Georges de Latour Private Reserve Cabernet Sauvignon.

BENESSERE VINEYARDS

Established **1995** ***Owners*** **John and Ellen Benish** ***Production*** **2,500 cases** ***Vineyard area*** **36 acres (15 ha)**

Benessere is at the forefront of the Italian varietal craze. Winemaker Chris Dearden makes a killer sangiovese. He has a little help from some friends, though. His two consultants are both on Italy's DOCG tasting board and help Benessere adapt Italian viticultural practices to California's microclimates. The result is a sangiovese with cherry aromas reminiscent of Italy's best. Though still in its infancy, Benessere Vineyards can be expected to master the variety.

ABOVE: *Experience the delights of Napa Valley by riding the wine train.*

CAIN VINEYARD & WINERY

Established **1980** ***Owners*** **Jim and Nancy Meadlock** ***Production*** **18,000 cases** ***Vineyard area*** **84 acres (34 ha)**

Cain Five—a meritage produced from the Spring Mountain District which is a blend of all five major bordeaux varieties—is Cain Vineyard & Winery's most

respected wine. Thin soils on the steep mountain slopes keep yields from these vineyards lower and elevations of up to 2,100 feet (640 m) help to keep the vines cool, resulting in concentrated and complex fruit. Cain Cuvée, a lighter style, is a great alternative to Cain Five and Cain Musqué is 100 percent sauvignon blanc from the floral musqué clone grown in Monterey.

CHAPPELLET WINERY

Established **1967** ***Owners*** **Don and Molly Chappellet** ***Production*** **30,000 cases** ***Vineyard area*** **110 acres (44 ha)**

Chappellet was the second winery built in Napa Valley after Prohibition. This is a beautiful property on Pritchard Hill overlooking Lake Hennessey to the east of Napa Valley. Vineyards are at elevations from 800 to 1,800 feet (245 to 550 m) and 50 percent are dry-farmed. The Old Vine Cuvée Chenin Blanc, from vines planted in the 1960s, is proof that quality chenin blanc can be produced in Napa Valley. A moelleux-style chenin blanc is also outstanding.

ABOVE: *An old wine press in the grounds of the Napa Wine Company.*

CLOS DU VAL WINE CO.

Established **1972** ***Owner*** **John Goelet** ***Production*** **75,000 cases** ***Vineyard area*** **300 acres (121 ha)**

The Bordelais heritage of Clos du Val's general manager, Bernard Portet, has enabled the company to master bordeaux varieties, especially cabernet sauvignon. The winery produces an elegant cabernet sauvignon from Stag's Leap fruit, well balanced in structure with integrated oak influence. Its Carneros Pinot Noir is firm and rich in structure. The wine has great acidity, and is much better paired with a rack of lamb than salmon. Ariadne is a sémillon/sauvignon blanc blend with refreshing acidity and a rich mouthfeel. These wines are meant to be accessible, with restrained alcohol and wood aging that matches the wine rather than overpowering it.

DALLA VALLE VINEYARDS

Established **1986** ***Owner*** **Naoko Dalla Valle** ***Production*** **3,300 cases** ***Vineyard area*** **25 acres (10 ha)**

The winery specializes in cabernet sauvignon blended with some cabernet franc and merlot, but Dalla also makes Pietre Rosse, a spectacular sangiovese. Its cabernet sauvignon and a small proprietary bottling called Maya are collectors' items at auctions. Both wines are long-lived, lean and tannic in their youth, but will develop exceptional grace with some age.

During one of my treks through Afghanistan, we lost our corkscrew. We were compelled to live on food and water for several days.

CUTHBERT J. TWILLIE
(W. C. Fields, 1880–1946)
in My Little Chickadee (1940)

DIAMOND CREEK VINEYARDS

Established **1968** ***Owners*** **Al and Boots Brounstein** ***Production*** **3,000 cases** ***Vineyard area*** **20 acres (8 ha)**

Originally a pharmacist, Al decided to pursue his passion for wine and waterfalls and has accomplished both in a vineyard oasis with man-made waterfalls. He was one of the first to focus attention on *terroir* in California and his site contains three distinct soil types, after which he has named his wines—Gravelly Meadow, Red Rock Terrace and Volcanic Hill. They are some of the first of California's vineyard-designated wines and the winery is California's first cabernet-only estate.

FAR NIENTE

Established **1885** ***Owners*** **Gil Nickel, Dirk Hampson and Larry Maguire** ***Production*** **35,000–40,000 cases** ***Vineyard area*** **200 acres (81 ha)**

Far Niente was originally founded in 1885, but fell into disrepair after closing during Prohibition. In 1979, Gil Nickel purchased the estate and set about restoring it. Now Far Niente produces cabernet sauvignon and a rich creamy chardonnay with ripe tropical fruit-flavors. The winery focuses on moving wine through gravity

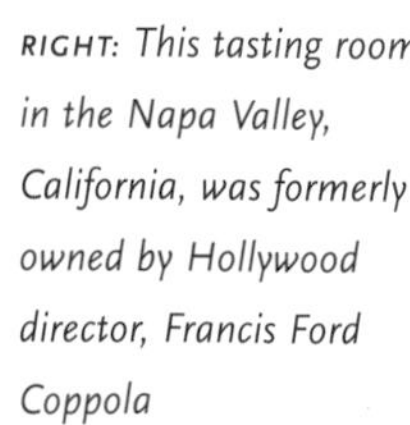

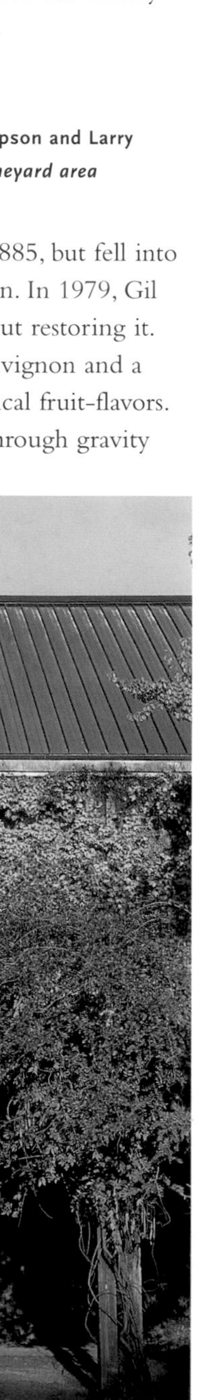

RIGHT: *This tasting room in the Napa Valley, California, was formerly owned by Hollywood director, Francis Ford Coppola*

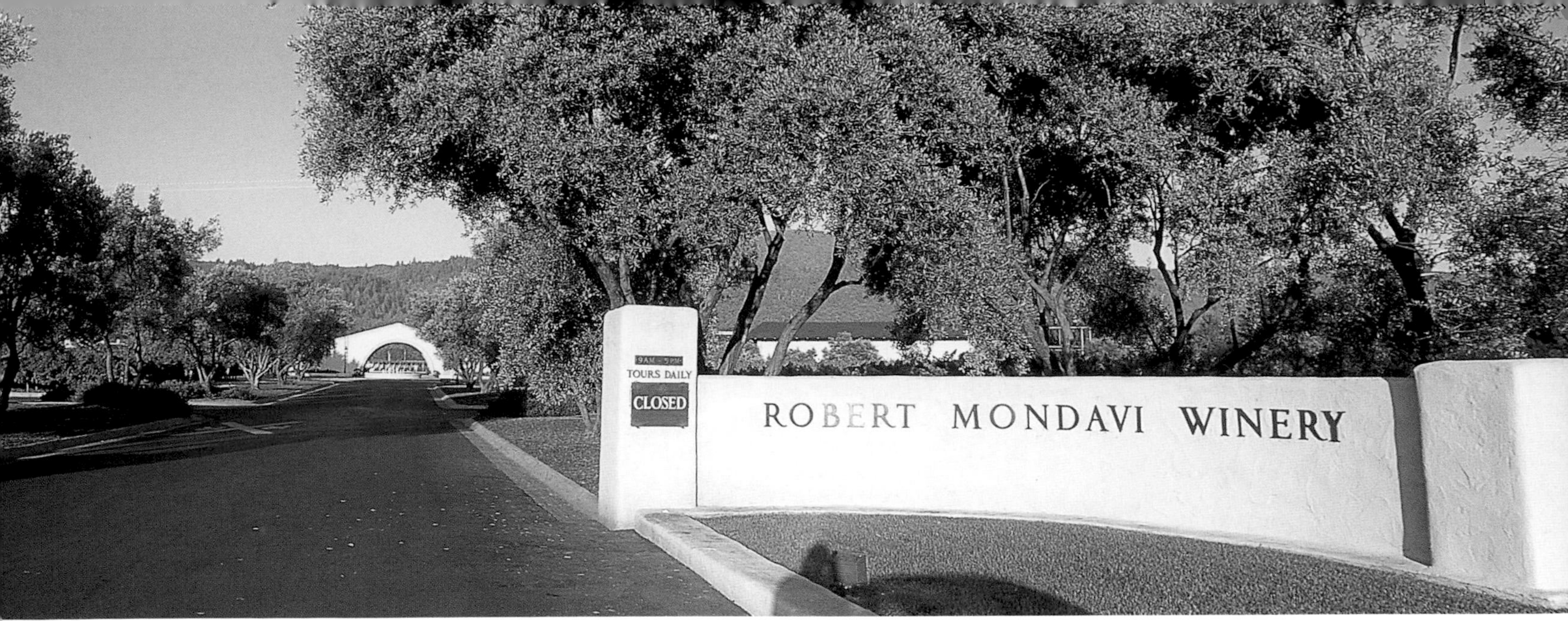

ABOVE: Entrance to the winery of one of California's most influential winemakers.

to ensure more gentle handling. In 1989, Dolce, a botrytized dessert wine made from sémillon and sauvignon blanc, was created, proving that sauternes-style wines can be made in California.

HEITZ WINE CELLARS

Established **1961** ***Owners*** **Heitz family** ***Production*** **40,000 cases** ***Vineyard area*** **335 acres (136 ha)**

This company was originally in the business of finishing wines for others, but, in 1965, made the decision to make its first cabernet sauvignon. In 1968, it produced a stellar vintage from Martha's Vineyard grapes (and was the only winery to receive fruit from there) and the Martha's Vineyard bottling is now a well-known commodity on the auction scene. Heitz has also made wines from Stag's Leap Wine Cellar's Fay Vineyard, and Bella Oaks. Heitz wines typically have a very distinctive mint and eucalyptus character.

HENDRY

Established **1992** ***Owners*** **George Hendry, Susan Ridley and Jeff Miller** ***Production*** **6,000 cases** ***Vineyard area*** **123 acres (50 ha)**

This boutique winery is a favorite among lovers of cabernet sauvignon, zinfandel and pinot noir. Its location, between Mount Veeder and Carneros, results in wines with concentrated mountain fruit, yet with bright refreshing acidity. Due to contrasting *terroir*, Hendry split the vineyard into blocks and the wines are intended to show the different characters of these.

LANG & REED WINE CO.

Established **1996** ***Owners*** **John and Tracey Skupny** ***Production*** **2,000 cases** ***Vineyard area*** **NA**

Tracey and John Skupny have created a demand for cabernet franc in California, even if it is only for their version. All grapes are contracted from optimal fruit sources and the ripe black fruit character of their wines is true to the variety, without any overly green or herbaceous character, demonstrating the delicacy cabernet franc can achieve when yields are limited.

LOUIS MARTINI

Established **1922** ***Owners*** **Gallo** ***Production*** **150,000 cases** ***Vineyard area*** **600 acres (243 ha)**

Louis P. Martini began clonal trials on pinot noir and chardonnay in 1948, resulting in the UC Davis chardonnay clone 108 which is now widespread throughout California. Martini is also believed to have been the first to plant pinot noir. Martini's primary vineyard sites are in Sonoma Valley, Monte Rosso, Russian River Valley, Los Vinedos del Rio, Napa's Chiles Valley, Glen Oaks and in Napa's Pope Valley. Its line of classic varietals and Reserve wines are excellent value, especially the Reserve Cabernet Sauvignon.

MIURA

Established **1997** ***Owner*** **Emmanuel Kemiji** ***Production*** **2,500 cases** ***Vineyard area*** **NA**

Miura, named after the breeder of the most famous fighting bulls in Spain, is a reminder of Master Sommelier Emmanuel Kemiji's European heritage. Once employed by the Ritz Carlton San Francisco, he now uses his expert palate to create distinctive wines from some of California's best vineyards. Currently, he produces merlot from Carneros, pinot noir from Pisoni Ranch and chardonnay fashioned after white burgundy. A bordeaux-style blend is the only departure from the single-vineyard/single-variety theme.

ROBERT MONDAVI WINERY

Established **1966** ***Owners*** **Public shareholders** ***Production*** **350,000 cases** ***Vineyard area*** **1,500 acres (607 ha)**

Robert Mondavi is one of the most influential people in California's winemaking history. In 1943, he joined the Charles Krug winery owned by his family and learned about California winemaking. A trip to Bordeaux in 1962 inspired him to pursue his own goals and in 1966 he opened his own

Regional Dozen

- Benessere Sangiovese
- Chappellet Signature Cabernet Sauvignon
- Chateau Montelena Cabernet Sauvignon
- Detert Family Vineyards Cabernet Franc
- Hendry Block 7 Zinfandel
- Lail Vineyards J. Daniel Cuvée
- Lewis Cellars Cabernet Sauvignon
- Long Vineyards Sangiovese
- Schramsberg Brut Rosé
- Spyglass Cabernet Sauvignon
- Stag's Leap Wine Cellars Artemis Cabernet Sauvignon
- Storybook Mountain Vineyards Zinfandel

ABOVE: The intoxicating sight of fruit on the vine at a vineyard in Napa Valley.

winery. Robert Mondavi has never rested on his laurels and his experiments into almost every aspect of viticulture and vinification have contributed significant technological advances to the region. In 1979, he went into partnership with Baron Philippe de Rothschild of Chateau Mouton-Rothschild to create Opus One. Recently Mondavi expanded to Chile and Italy and now covers all levels of the market, from value wines such as Woodbridge to prestige *cuvées* like Opus. Special projects include a winery that specializes in Italian varieties and a collaboration with NASA to use aerial imagery to pinpoint phylloxera's spread through vineyards. Mondavi was the visionary behind Copia, the American Center for Food, Wine, and the Arts. Robert Mondavi Winery is currently the largest exporter of premium California wine, reaching more than 90 countries.

CHATEAU MONTELENA

Established **1882** ***Owners*** **Barrett family** ***Production*** **35,000 cases** ***Vineyard area*** **120 acres (49 ha)**

Chateau Montelena is renowned for the famous Paris Tasting of 1976, when its second vintage of modern chardonnay, the 1973, won as the top white wine. Although this spurred the growth of chardonnay as a premium California wine, Chateau Montelena is probably just as acclaimed for its red wines, and the cabernet sauvignon has been proven to age extraordinarily well in vertical tastings. As a result, this is one of the first California wineries to offer its cabernet *en primeur* and it has been quite successful.

OPUS ONE

Established **1979** ***Owners*** **Baroness Philippine de Rothschild and Robert Mondavi** ***Production*** **30,000 cases** ***Vineyard area*** **104 acres (42 ha)**

The scale of this winery is awesome, considering it is solely devoted to the production of just one wine—a meritage or cabernet blend. The wine is made with the utmost care, from densely spaced vines, hand-picked and sorted fruit to careful vinification and 18 months aging in French oak. Opus is aged 18 months in bottle before release. Even though luscious upon release, Opus One has the capacity to age. The 1979 and 1980, the first releases, remain vibrant and alive today.

PATZ & HALL WINE CO.

Established **1988** ***Owners*** **Donald and Heather Patz, James Hall and Anne Moses** ***Production*** **10,000 cases** ***Vineyard area*** **NA**

Patz & Hall could be listed under almost any region, as their fruit hails from California's top sources, but they are based in Napa where their first wine, a 1988 Napa Valley Chardonnay made from the Caldwell Vineyard, was born. The Patz & Hall Wine Co. has formed close relationships with their growers in an effort to produce the best pinot noir and chardonnay possible. Their wines have gained a huge following.

JOSEPH PHELPS VINEYARDS

Established **1973** ***Owners*** **Joseph Phelps family** ***Production*** **85,000–100,000 cases** ***Vineyard area*** **395 acres (160 ha)**

In 1974, Phelps produced Insignia, the first proprietary bordeaux-style blend from California. In that same year, Phelps produced California's first syrah, and put rhône-style wines on the map with the Vin du Mistral line. Le Mistral, a rhône blend, is a great example, and the Phelps viognier shows exceptional richness and floral character. Phelps also makes high-quality cabernet sauvignon, sauvignon blanc and many others, including a line of late-harvest dessert wines. Both Insignia and Backus Cabernet Sauvignon are the top-of-the-line reds, suitable for long cellaring.

LEFT: *Winemakers in Napa Valley wax lyrical about their produce.*

QUINTESSA

Established **1990** ***Owner*** **Agustin Huneeus *Production* 1,500 cases *Vineyard area* 280 acres (113 ha)**

Owned by Agustin Huneeus and marketed and distributed by Franciscan Estates, this special property is in the Rutherford appellation and has distinctively different soils, elevations and microclimates. Quintessa wines are elegant in style and improving each year as the vines age.

SCHRAMSBERG VINEYARDS

Established **1862** ***Owner*** **Jamie Davies *Production* 48,000 cases *Vineyard area* 54 acres (22 ha)**

In 1965, when the late Jack Davies and his wife, Jamie, purchased the property they realized that not many wineries were making *méthode champenoise* wines in California. They decided to go for this corner of the market and to concentrate on exceptional fruit quality. By 1967, they released the first California sparkling wine produced with chardonnay that had a vintage date. In 1971, they were first to produce a California *blanc de noirs*. Their J. Schram bottling rivals the best French champagne.

SPOTTSWOODE

Established **1882** ***Owner*** **Mary Weber Novak *Production* 6,000 cases *Vineyard area* 40 acres (16 ha)**

Located to the west of St Helena, Spottswoode was named after the Spotts family who purchased the estate

BELOW: *Futuristic Opus One vineyards and tasting rooms.*

in 1910. The vineyards were replanted by the current owner which was followed by the first vintage of cabernet sauvignon in 1982. The vineyard is organically farmed.

STAGLIN FAMILY VINEYARD

Established **1985** ***Owners*** **Shari and Garen Staglin** ***Production*** **9,000 cases** ***Vineyard area*** **50 acres (20 ha)**

The Staglin family make limited quantities of some exquisite wines. Their cabernet sauvignon has lush fruit flavors but with sufficient power to enable it to age, and the chardonnay is well balanced in oak with focused fruit. The sangiovese, named Stagliano, is a benchmark for the variety but is only available in very small quantities. Minimal handling highlights the essence of this excellent fruit source.

STAG'S LEAP WINE CELLARS

Established **1972** ***Owners*** **Warren and Barbara Winiarski** ***Production*** **65,000 cases** ***Vineyard area*** **180 acres (73 ha)**

Warren Winiarski is famous, not only for the victory of his 1973 Cabernet Sauvignon at the Paris Tasting in 1976, but because he has always been ahead of the pack in producing wines of optimal quality in Napa Valley. While well known for the longevity of Stag's Leap Cask 23 Cabernet, SLV and Fay Vineyard wines are also gaining ground.

T-VINE

Established **1992** ***Owner*** **Greg Brown** ***Production*** **3,500–4,000 cases** ***Vineyard area*** **NA**

You have to love a winery whose winemaker delivers the wine in person. Not only is he the delivery guy, but

BELOW: *Napa Valley–home of California's oldest established and most productive wineries.*

multi-talented Greg Brown is also the sales and marketing team, vineyard manager, accountant and winemaker. He seems to enjoy this situation, though, since all of his resources go into the end product rather than to a large staff. And the wine really is evidence of this. A grenache blended with some petite sirah for color and weight is a joy. Zinfandel is mouthwatering yet ultra-ripe.

YORK CREEK

***Established* 1991 *Owner* Fritz Maytag *Production* 600–700 cases *Vineyard area* 125 acres (51 ha)**

Fritz Maytag started York Creek long after his Maytag blue cheese and Anchor Steam Brewery were popular. The winery specializes in a full-bodied red blend from grapes grown at the top of Spring Mountain, which is an ecologically diverse site that Maytag proudly notes has 24 tree species, commemorating them on his wine labels. One of the only wineries to produce a worthwhile Californian port, the York Creek version is made primarily of zinfandel and petite sirah fortified with brandy from the estate vineyard.

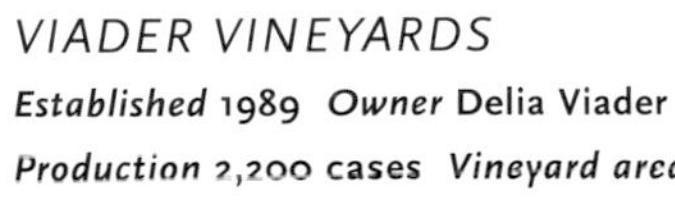

VIADER VINEYARDS

***Established* 1989 *Owner* Delia Viader *Production* 2,200 cases *Vineyard area* 23 acres (9 ha)**

Delia Viader was born in South America and she has created an estate that produces a St-Émilion-style cabernet sauvignon/cabernet franc blend from Howell Mountain fruit. Fruit is grown on steep hillsides at 1,100 feet (335 m) above sea level. Contrary to most plantings in California, the rows run up and over hillsides, rather than across, for maximum sun exposure. Vines are closely spaced with 2,000 plants per acre (809 per ha) planted in primarily volcanic soils. The fruit is organically farmed in order "to maintain the fine balance between struggle and survival, which results in grapes and finally wines of character and distinction." The high proportion of cabernet franc in the blend (about 40 percent) makes Viader unique among other California proprietary reds.

ABOVE: A stark winter scene in a Napa valley vineyard.

Long Vineyards

The odds of a speedboat landing in the vineyards in Napa Valley are about the same as a 1977 Napa Chardonnay tasting fresh. Had I only known that I would observe both on the drive up to Long Vineyards on Pritchard Hill! On a sunny winter day between massive storms causing flooding on the valley floor and ice patches on the road, a small group including J W Apple of the New York Times and his wife Betty, Barney and Bella Rhodes, Joel Fleischman, founding winemaker Zelma Long and her partner Philip Freese, current winemaker Sandi Belcher, and Pat and Bob Long gathered in their living room overlooking Lake Hennessy for a tasting of Chardonnays from 1977 to 2000. Zelma Long, the founding mother of Napa Valley (just as Robert Mondavi is in my view the founding father) said that tasting through this historic flight of wines "was like looking at seven different children all at different points in their lives." Across the board, the Chardonnay's were elegant in style, soft and supple in texture, showing tropical fruit, specifically papaya, mango, and guava attributed to the vineyard just adjacent to the house, with an earthy streak sometimes showing itself as squash or root vegetables, and pleasant, tingly acidity. Differences really reflected oak-usage philosophy. Long Vineyards Chardonnay was the first barrel-fermented Chardonnay in Napa Valley, and, surprisingly, is today one of the most elegant, with truly refreshing understated use of oak. How nice to taste the subtle expression of earth rather than the overdone, points-driven manipulation of man.

Other notable producers in Napa Valley include Anderson's Conn Valley Vineyards, Araujo Estate Wines/Eisele Vineyard, Corison Wines, Detert Family Vineyards, Frog's Leap, Grgich Hills Cellar, Honig Cellars, Lail Family Vineyards, Lewis Cellars, Long Vineyards, Luna Vineyards, Miner Family Vineyards, Pahlmeyer, Reverie on Diamond Mountain, Stony Hill Vineyard, and Storybook Mountain Vineyards.

Carneros

REBECCA CHAPA

Carneros straddles Napa and Sonoma Counties at their southernmost points and huddles closely around the San Pablo Bay, a northern part of the San Francisco Bay. Totalling 36,900 acres (14,944 ha), of which 15,147 acres (6,138 ha) are suitable for viticulture—currently 6,200 acres (2,511 ha) are planted. Of this, 48 percent is planted with chardonnay, 32 percent with pinot noir, 5 percent with cabernet sauvignon and 6 percent with merlot.

RIGHT: *Robert Mondavi was one of the first large companies to invest in Carneros after it was declared an AVA.*

History

Carneros' first winery, the Winter Winery, was built in 1870. Between the late 1870s and 1880s, infestations of phylloxera stopped the industry in its tracks, ravaging almost all the vineyards. The advent of Prohibition also prevented further development of wineries. A resurgence in investment started in the 1960s and it was in full force by the 1980s, when development reached its current pace.

Carneros was defined as an AVA in 1983 and after that occurred, investment in the area took off with purchases of land by large companies such as Freixenet and Robert Mondavi. In 1985, the Carneros Quality Alliance, which is quite possibly California's most effective viticultural appellation marketing association, was born.

Regional Dozen

QUALITY WINES

Beaulieu Vineyards Carneros Pinot Noir
Domaine Carneros la Rève Brut
Domaine Chandon Blanc de Noirs
Gloria Ferrer Royal Cuvée Brut
Joseph Phelps Vineyards Los Carneros Chardonnay
Robert Sinskey Merlot
Haven's Merlot
Liparita Carneros Chardonnay

BEST VALUE WINES

Acacia Pinot Noir
Cline Carneros Syrah
Gloria Ferrer Blanc de Noirs
Saintsbury Garnet Pinot Noir

RIGHT: *Growers note special features and attach these to the end of the vineyard rows.*

Climate and landscape

The boundaries of Carneros were delineated by its distinctive climate, due to the effects of the bay and differences in elevation. Producers in Carneros thus used climatic rather than historical or political differences as a method for defining their borders. As a result, the character of Carneros wines is special and recognizable. The area's rather interesting microclimate is influenced by the San Pablo Bay, which has a moderating effect on temperature in spring and winter, helping to lengthen the growing season. In the summer, fog rolls off the bay to cool the vineyards in the mornings and afternoons. However, proximity to the bay also creates wind in certain parts of Carneros where it stresses the vines. Elsewhere, it helps prevent rot on the vines by drying out dew from the morning fog.

The region consists of low-lying land at sea level near the bay and rolling hills to the north, that reach 1,000 feet (305 m) in the westerly hills. Soils are mostly clay-based and usually shallow. Carneros is Region I and is ideal for cooler climate grape varieties such as pinot noir and chardonnay. Winemakers are also exploring other varieties, notably merlot. Carneros has a much lower annual rainfall than both Napa and Sonoma Counties so irrigation is vital.

ACACIA

Established **1979** ***Owner*** **Chalone Wine Group** ***Production*** **60,000 cases** ***Vineyard area*** **100 acres (40 ha)**

Acacia is known for vineyard-designated pinot noir and for chardonnay. The year 1986 saw the launch of a refreshing brut sparkling wine, and in 1991 Acacia finally began sharing their zinfandel—they had been making it on the side for 10 years—with the public. Although chardonnay is the money-maker, making up 60–65 percent of production, pinot noir is the soul of the winery. The Beckstoffer Vineyard vines, part of the original Martini Ranch, are some of Carneros' oldest pinot noir. As a result, its wines are intensely concentrated and complex.

DOMAINE CARNEROS BY TAITTINGER

Established **1987** ***Owner*** **Champagne Taittinger & Kobrand Corp.** ***Production*** **45,000 cases** ***Vineyard area*** **110 acres (44 ha)**

Lightness and delicacy are the goals for Domaine Carneros wines. Most *cuvées* are primarily pinot noir with some chardonnay and pinot meunier. Production includes a premium *méthode champenoise* and a proprietary *blanc de blancs*, la Rève. The Domaine Carneros still pinot noir rivals other top California favorites.

DOMAINE CHANDON

Established **1973** ***Owner*** **Louis Vuitton Moet-Hennessy** ***Production*** **350,000 cases** ***Vineyard area*** **1,100 acres (445 ha)**

Domaine Chandon is probably the most recognized sparkling wine producer in California. A leader in innovation, and with the resources of Moët et Chandon at its disposal, Domaine Chandon has been able to greatly enhance *méthode champenoise* production throughout California. Its still pinot meunier, with its bright jammy fruit, is helping to create a following for that grape.

GLORIA FERRER

Established **1982** ***Owner*** **Freixenet S.A.** ***Production*** **82,000 cases** ***Vineyard area*** **335 acres (136 ha)**

The Ferrer family from Spain, owners of Freixenet, S.A., are the largest producers of *méthode champenoise* wine in the world. The wines tend to rely heavily on pinot noir in the blend and are exceptional value for this quality of wine, not only in California, but internationally. The Royal Cuvée is a particularly good aperitif.

HAVENS WINE CELLARS

Established **1984** ***Owners*** **Michael and Kathryn Havens, Jon and Russell Scott** ***Production*** **16,000 cases** ***Vineyard area*** **5 acres (2 ha)**

At 5 acres, Havens is small, but its merlot is a wonderful example of how the intense flavors of Carneros merlot can be tamed. In a sea of merlot that often tastes nothing like the grape, here is an example that is very true to the variety.

SAINTSBURY

Established **1981** ***Owners*** **Richard A. Ward and David W. Graves** ***Production*** **48,000 cases** ***Vineyard area*** **55 acres (22 ha)**

Although Saintsbury makes chardonnay, it is best known for its pinot noir which makes up two-thirds of its output. Three styles are made—Garnet, for light, easy drinking; Carneros, rich and firm; and Reserve, the richest. Grapes come from 12 vineyards, and a gentle handling regimen is thought to be the key to its success. A special bottling of Brown Ranch Pinot Noir has been produced since 1996.

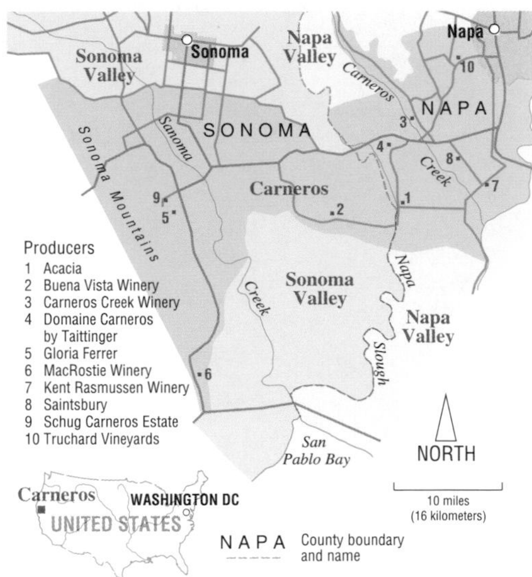

ROBERT SINSKEY VINEYARDS

Established **1986** ***Owners*** **Robert M. Sinskey and Robert M. Sinskey Jr** ***Production*** **25,000 cases** ***Vineyard area*** **150 acres (61 ha)**

Sinskey produces incredibly silky textured pinot noir, as well as merlot which has become a standard for the variety. Most wines come from Carneros plantings, which provides the wines with vivacious acidity. The chardonnay is very clean in flavor, one of the few from California to be made without malolactic fermentation.

TRUCHARD VINEYARDS

Established **1989** ***Owners*** **Tony and Jo Ann Truchard** ***Production*** **11,000 cases** ***Vineyard area*** **250 acres (101 ha)**

Initially, Truchard provided grapes to other well-known wineries, but now produces its own. It is on the right track, especially with pinot noir and spicy syrah. Truchard uses estate fruit for its own wines and sells the remainder.

Other notable producers include Buena Vista Winery, Carneros Creek Winery, MacRostie Winery, Kent Rasmussen Winery, Saintsbury and Schug Carneros Estate.

BELOW: Skilled workers hand picking grapes, which ensures only fruit of high quality is used in the production of premium wines.

Central Valley

CATHERINE FALLIS MS

The Central Valley AVA runs 400 miles (645 km) north to south, or nearly three-quarters the length of the state of California. The spectacular Sierra Nevada range to the east protects this massive AVA from the desert climate of Nevada and the coastal ranges to the west soften the effects from marine influences. The demarcation begins just north of Redding at Shasta Lake, near the Oregon border and runs to Bakersfield in the south (just north of Los Angeles). This AVA is divided into two subzones—north, the smaller cool Sacramento River Valley; south, the hot multi-county San Joaquin Valley.

Fine wine production centers around Sacramento River Valley. With the exception of Yolo county, which borders the southern tip of Mendocino County, the prime growing zones here are from 70 to 100 miles (112 to 160 km) east to northeast of San Francisco Bay. Six of the eight AVAs are here—Clarksburg (which includes the sub-AVA Merritt Island), Dunnigan Hills, Suisin Valley and Solano County-Green Valley, and Lodi. Grapes from Yolo and Sacramento Counties and the northern half of San Joaquin County are sought after by fine-wine producers of the north and central coasts.

Clarksburg AVA fruit is prized by 30 major wineries including Gallo, Beringer, Sebastiani, Glen Ellen, Mondavi Woodbridge, Clos du Bois, Louis Martini and Baron Herzog. Sutter Home and Korbel Champagne Cellars have their own vineyards in the area.

Lodi AVA, which overlaps Sacramento and San Joaquin Counties, stands unsurpassed for premium varietals including chardonnay, sauvignon blanc, cabernet sauvignon, merlot and zinfandel. It produces more than Napa and Sonoma combined. Only recently producers such as Burgess, Clos du Val, M. Cosentino, J. Lohr, Ravenswood and Turley have credited Lodi as the fruit source on their wine labels.

The southern half of the AVA is the San Joaquin Valley. This flat, hot, high-volume area includes the southern tip of San Joaquin County (south of Lodi and Stockton), Stanislaus County with Modesto and the high-elevation two-winery Diablo Grande AVA, Merced County, Madera County and Fresno County with its namesake city of Fresno. The Madera AVA overlaps parts of Madera and Fresno Counties. The southernmost area comprises Kings, Tulare and Kern Counties and extends just south of Bakersfield.

Sixty percent of California's grape tonnage (including raisin and table) is generated in the Central Valley, as is 60 percent of the state's chardonnay. Colombard and chenin blanc dropped from 60 to just 30 percent in the last few years, while plantings of chardonnay, cabernet sauvignon, and merlot have increased 21 percent. With the current glut of wine grapes causing plummeting prices, 50,000 acres (20,250 ha) of vineyards were recently pulled out, and many growers were forced to let their crops rot on the vine.

Colombard is the most widely planted varietal, followed by chenin blanc. Sauvignon blanc, sémillon, muscat, chardonnay, zinfandel, grenache, barbera, carignane, carnelian, cabernet sauvignon, merlot, mourvèdre,

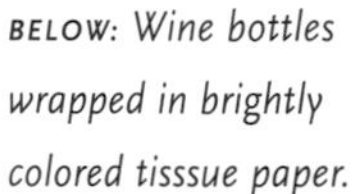

BELOW: *Wine bottles wrapped in brightly colored tisssue paper.*

petite sirah and ruby cabernet are also widely planted. Planting of pinot gris, sangiovese, viognier and syrah is on the rise. Thompson seedless, classified as "raisin-type grapes" by California's Agricultural Statistical Service, covers 267,000 acres (108,050 ha) and is included in production figures by the mass producers in the south.

ABOVE: *The grape-vine leaf in fall.*

History

If not for the dams built over a century ago to trap melting snow from the Sierra Foothills, and the network of irrigation canals feeding most of the valley's vineyards, this flat, arid land would not have thrived. Leon Adams in *The Wines of America* calls it "more fabulously productive than the delta of the Nile." The 1850s saw many wineries being established in Lodi and farther south in the valley. Flame tokay put Lodi on the map and until the late 1970s was dominant in the area. Germans, Italians and Armenians began producing vast quantities of sweet, fortified and sparkling wine for mass consumption.

Unlike much of Napa and Sonoma Valleys, Central Valley growers have long histories in the wine industry, some going back two centuries. Central Valley producers survived Prohibition by shipping fruit to the east. Young Mondavi and Gallo family members bragged of how many cases they could pack in a day. After Prohibition, the rival families turned their attention to agribusiness and mass production of inexpensive, well marketed wines. Thunderbird, Ripple, Boone's Farm, Tott's and Cook's filled the cups of the masses for decades. In the 1960s and 1970s premium North Coast producers looked towards Lodi zinfandel for its extra power and depth. And today they are coming back in droves.

Landscape and climate

The Sacramento River Valley is a warm inland area, classified as Region IV on the heat summation scale, similar to the Mediterranean district Languedoc-Roussillon. Temperatures climb to 100°F (38°C) during the peak of summer. However, the nearby Golden Gate Gap sends its fog and marine breezes as far inland as Lodi. In the summer months cool westerly "carquinez" breezes moderate the climate in Lodi. Clarksburg AVA also has a long, dry growing season, warm summer days, rich alluvial soils and cooling delta breezes on summer evenings. In January and February the multitude of waterways and rivers create fog conditions.

LEFT: *Wine grapes in full delicious bloom.*

The San Joaquin Valley is classified as Region IV on the Winkler-Amerine scale, warming to Region V in the deep southern plains. The valley floor flatlands of fertile sandy loam are marked with a network of irrigation canals and levees harnessing water from inland rivers and Sierra Nevada snow melts.

Vines and wines

The Sacramento River Valley produces premium whites and reds. Regional style markers are balance, softer tannins in the reds, dry, restrained and rich fruit character and moderate oak usage. Clarksburg AVA produces good chenin blanc and the Clarksburg chardonnay is worth watching. Dunnigan Hills AVA is notable for the rhône-style and late-harvest wines of R. H. Phillips. Suisin Valley and Solano County–Green Valley AVAs each have one winery and are beginning to establish their identity—a task which is not easy in the shadow of their famous neighbor, Napa Valley.

Zinfandel and carignane grown in Lodi is some of the finest anywhere in the state, even at the current high tonnage levels. Most of the Lodi reds exhibit softer tannins, have a distinct varietal character and tend to be more judiciously oaked than their rather showy neighbors.

The latest techniques in trellising, irrigation and pest management are in full use in the Sacramento River Valley. The Lodi Woodbridge Winegrape Commission has launched the industry's only district-wide Integrated Pest Management program to reduce pesticide and herbicide usage. Fertile alluvial soil, heat and irrigated vines yield large crops. Eight tons per acre (20 t per ha) is standard; quality conscious producers are at half that or less. Surprisingly even the oldest head-trained, dry-farmed

RIGHT: Gloves are an essential piece of equipment when picking grapes by hand.

vines are still capable of high yields. Industrial farming including flood irrigation, pesticide application by plane and machine harvesting dominate in the San Joaquin Valley.

Upscale winemaking, with an emphasis on experimentation, artistry and premium winemaking techniques, dominates in the north. Conversely, science and control are prevalent in the south, where continuous bulk production techniques yield consistent quality at low prices. California is far better at large scale production than any region in the world.

Regional Dozen

QUALITY WINES

Capay Valley Vineyards Viognier
Clayton Lodi Zinfandel
Jessie's Grove Lodi Reserve Old Vine Zinfandel
Lucas Lodi Old Vine Zinfandel
St Amant Lodi Barbera
St Amant Mohr-Fry Ranch Lodi Old Vine Zinfandel

BEST VALUE WINES

Bogle Clarksburg Chenin Blanc
Ficklin Madera Vintage Port
McManis Family Vineyards Chardonnay
Phillips Vineyards Lodi Old Vine Carignane
R. H. Phillips Dunnigan Hills Night Harvest Sauvignon Blanc
Quady Starboard Madera Port

JESSIE'S GROVE

Established **1998** ***Owner*** **Greg Burns** ***Production*** **2,500 cases** ***Vineyard area*** **320 acres (130 ha)**

A 32-acre (13 ha) live oak grove was the inspiration for the winery's name. The grove and vines planted in 1890 remain to this day. Part of one small patch of organically farmed estate zinfandel goes to Turley each year for their "Spenker Vineyards Lodi Zinfandel." Greg Burns calls his wine from this same patch "Royalty." Burns is crafting world-class zinfandel, and transforming the 1830 barn into a winery and tasting room.

LUCAS WINERY AND VINEYARD

Established **1978** ***Owner*** **David Lucas** ***Production*** **NA** ***Vineyard area*** **20 acres (8.1 ha) old vine, 10 acres (4.1 ha) new plantation**

Lucas' old-vine zinfandel was one of the first to gain notice for the region. He is now building a winery that is designed to nurture and coddle zinfandel. He also produces a most quaffable chardonnay.

RIGHT: The Central Valley's ripened offerings.

PHILLIPS VINEYARDS

Established **1984** ***Owners*** **Phillips family** ***Production*** **2,700 cases** ***Vineyard area*** **170 acres (68.8 ha)**

Phillips Vineyards uses outstanding varietal old-vine carignane, newly planted syrah, along with the usual suspects of cabernet sauvignon, chardonnay and white zinfandel for their wines; also, the not so usual blends such as "Don's special blend/Lodi red," from carignane, syrah and symphony. All are straightforward, honest and ready to drink wines.

QUADY WINERY

Established **1977** ***Owners*** **Quady family** ***Production*** **15,000 cases** ***Vineyard area*** **NA**

Electra, Elysium and Essensia are Quady's muscat line. Elysium is a fortified black muscat—rich, deep and syrupy. Essensia is a paler, more delicate and floral fortified orange muscat. Electra is light, fizzy and frothy, modeled after Moscato d'Asti. Quady Starboard Port is made of tinta cao, tinta alvarelho and tinta rouriz from Amador, as are the vintage and non-vintage bottlings.

ST AMANT WINERY

Established **1980** ***Owners*** **Richard and Barbara St Amant Spencer** ***Production*** **4,500 cases** ***Vineyard area*** **34 acres (13.8 ha)**

This winery produces excellent old-vine zinfandel, smoky, deep and low acid barbera, rich and decadent viognier, ripe and briny roussanne and a port-style wine from five port varietals in open-top fermenters à la Portugal. In fact, St Amant uses these *lagare*-like low, wide vats to help integrate the tannins on all their reds. St Amant also bottles a Mohr-Fry Ranch Zinfandel—this is a winery to watch.

Other significant producers in Central Valley include Capay Valley Vineyards, Clayton Vineyards, Delicato Vineyards, Isom Ranch and Gallo.

Sierra Foothills

REBECCA CHAPA & CATHERINE FALLIS MS

The Sierra Foothills, with about 50 wineries, is small in comparison with other Californian regions. It spans the counties of Yuba, Nevada, El Dorado, Amador, Calaveras, Tuolumne and Mariposa. Rustic country roads wind through pastoral scenes recalling a past era.

Climate ranges from Region III to Region IV and varied exposures and elevations create significant fluctuations over the region. Nights are often cold even in summertime, with cold air coming from the peaks of the Sierra Nevada mountains directly into the vineyards.

Pressure from purchasers of fruit have pushed growers in the region to produce more zinfandel, barbera, sangiovese, syrah and cabernet varieties. The region's wines tend to be less oaky than those from other Californian regions, with rich, dense fruit characters. Old-vine wines have outstanding concentration and Italian and Rhône styles are gaining popularity.

There are four AVAs in the region: North Yuba, El Dorado, Fiddletown and California Shenandoah Valley. In 2001, the 250-acre (101 ha) Fair Play AVA was approved in El Dorado County. Eleven wineries in the region focus on mountain-grown fruit. At 2,000 to 3,000 feet (610 to 915 m), Fair Play has the highest average elevation of any California appellation.

WINE REGIONS

North Yuba

North Yuba was established as an AVA in 1988. Annual rainfall is relatively high, and with well-drained soils, sauvignon blanc and riesling do very well. North Yuba is generally synonymous with the beautiful winery of Renaissance, which has terraced hillsides planted from 1,700 to 2,300 feet (520 to 755 m) with 27 distinct plots. Twelve plots are planted to cabernet sauvignon, which has become winemaker Ben Gideon's specialty. Late harvest sauvignon blanc and recently released viognier and syrah are less rustic and austere.

El Dorado

El Dorado was granted an AVA in 1983. Most of its 16 wineries are east and southeast of Placerville. All are more than 1,400 feet (460 m) above sea level. Prohibition left this AVA a shell with a mere 12 acres (5 ha) under cultivation, until the Boeger family built their estate. Currently about 416 acres (168 ha) are part of El Dorado County. Cool nights help the grapes retain high acidity, yet the grapes have no problems ripening; soils are mainly granitic, deep and well drained. El Dorado is a prime site for Italian varieties.

EDMUNDS ST JOHN VINEYARDS

Established **1985** ***Owners*** **Steve Edmunds and Cornelia St John**
Production **4,000 cases** ***Vineyard area*** **no estate acreage**

Recent investment in El Dorado, in land called "The Higher Ground" will provide fruit to replace supplies from Napa and Sonoma. The winery has a long-held reputation for rhône varietals, most notably a Sonoma Valley Durrell Vineyard syrah. El Dorado production includes a Wylie-Fenaughty syrah: Wylie is near

Regional Dozen

QUALITY WINES

Domaine de la Terre Rouge Sentinel Oak Vineyard Shenandoah Valley Syrah
Edmunds St John Wylie-Fenaughty El Dorado Syrah
Karly Pokerflats Amador Zinfandel
Renwood Winery Granpère Amador Zinfandel
Shenandoah Vineyards Vintners Selection Amador Zinfandel
Sobon Estates Rocky Top Amador Zinfandel

BEST VALUE WINES

Black Sheep Calaveras County Zinfandel
Deaver Vineyards Amador County Barbera
Montevina Amador County Barbera
Montevina Amador County Brioso Zinfandel
Perry Creek Vineyards Zin Man El Dorado Zinfandel
Vino Noceto Amador County Sangiovese

LEFT: An old jug, used by winemakers for topping up wine barrels.

BELOW: The Sierra Nevada mountains were initially settled by seekers of gold, many of whom later turned to grape growing.

RIGHT: A hand picker displays the grape harvest.

Georgetown and Fenaughty near Placerville; a Matagrano Vineyard sangiovese: Matagrano is near Lotus; and a St Johnson Vineyard pinot grigio. Another popular wine is a "Rocks and Gravel" côtes-du-rhône style blend of syrah, grenache and mourvèdre.

California Shenandoah Valley

The Bureau of Alcohol, Tobacco and Firearms has ruled that the "Shenandoah Valley of the West" must be labeled as California Shenandoah Valley in order to prevent confusion with "Shenandoah Valley" on the east coast. The region has 1,300 acres (526 ha) that overlap El Dorado and Amador counties. The AVA was founded in 1983. Snowy winters give way to warm springs, which allow for growth, and cool night air flowing from the Sierra Nevadas preserves the grapes' high acidity. The region's total expanse stretches over 10,000 acres (4047 ha).

SHENANDOAH VINEYARDS/SOBON ESTATE

Established **1977** ***Owners*** **Leon and Shirley Sobon** ***Production*** **38,000 cases** ***Vineyard area*** **167 acres (67.5 ha) plus 146 acres (59 ha) organically farmed**

Sobon Estate is the oldest winery in America with continuous production since 1856 and today it is the prestige label for the house. The Sobon family moved here from Los Altos in 1977. Leon's love of zinfandel led him to Amador County, where the old vines, rocky soil and long growing season combine to produce some of the most complex zins anywhere in the world. The Sobon Estate's Rocky Top, Cougar Hill and Lubenko bottlings are each reflective of a particular old-vine zinfandel site. Shenandoah sangiovese planted on an old lava flow is intensely varietal, with leather and mint rounding out the luscious dark cherry flavors.

BELOW: A barrel with half pressed shiraz grapes.

Amador County

Amador County is home to Shenandoah Valley and Fiddletown AVAs and is a key source of old-vine zinfandel. High annual rainfall enables dry farming. Spring frost is common, but zinfandel fares well because it buds late. Amador County's grape acreage increased during Prohibition by supplying grapes for home winemaking.

MONTEVINA WINERY

Established **1973** ***Owners*** **Trinchero family** ***Production*** **90,000 cases** ***Vineyard area*** **600 acres (243 ha)**

This was the first post-Prohibition winery in Amador. In 1905, 100 acres (40.5 ha) of zinfandel was planted; cabernet sauvignon in the 1960s; and recently plantings included barbera, sangiovese and syrah. The vineyards were CCOF-certified (California Certified Organic Farmers) for ten years until a recent uncontrollable dust mite problem. Montevina is famous for its affordable barbera and zinfandel, and esoteric bottlings such as aglianico, freisa, refosco and aleatico. The premium Terra d'Oro line is well structured and dense.

CHARLES SPINETTA

Established **1984** ***Owner*** **Charles Spinetta** ***Production*** **5,000 cases** ***Vineyard area*** **80 acres (32 ha)**

Charles is a fifth generation winemaker whose forebears worked with the Gallos and Mondavis, who also originated here in Amador. Old-vine zinfandel and barbera are highlights, as is chenin blanc released in three styles.

STORY WINERY

Established **1971** ***Owners*** **Bruce and Jan Tichenor** ***Production*** **2,500 cases** ***Vineyard area*** **42 acres (17 ha)**

Some of these hilltop vineyards date back to the early 1900s and include the oldest mission vines in the state. Vines as thick as trees stretch their thick, gnarly arms up to five feet (1.6 m). Both a dry and a sweet mission are produced from this block, as well as a zinfandel/mission blend called "miss-zin" but straight zinfandel is of most interest, especially that from the Picnic Hill vineyard. Sonora Winery has been purchasing fruit from this vineyard since 1995 for their old-vine zinfandel release. Newer plantings include barbera and sangiovese.

VINO NOCETO

Established **1990** ***Owners*** **Jim and Suzy Gullet** ***Production*** **2,800 cases** ***Vineyard area*** **21 acres (8.5 ha)**

Indigenous nut trees on the property inspired the Italian "noce" in the winery's name. Jim Gullet has quickly established a reputation for ripe, round, strawberry and cherry-laden sangiovese in an elegant, lightly oaked style, in contrast with most of the North Coast sangioveses

ABOVE: *Donner Lake in the Sierra Nevada mountains.*

whose overt oakiness masks varietal character and charm. Vino Noceto's version sells out within weeks each year. A new *riserva* sangiovese is made from selected lots with extended aging. In summer, they make frivolo, a sparkling moscato. The winery here custom crushes several batches of fruit for North Coast producer Folio a Deux each year.

Calaveras County

Just south of Amador, this region is about 500 acres (202 ha) and has seven wineries. Cooler temperatures make Calaveras County a Region II (Winkler-Amerine heat summation scale), which is particularly good for chardonnay and sauvignon blanc—both would thrive on the limestone and volcanic soils.

BLACK SHEEP WINERY

Established **1986** ***Owners*** **Dave and Jan Olson** ***Production*** **3,900 cases** ***Vineyard area*** **no estate acreage**

Black Sheep is consistently producing small lots of very well-priced quality zinfandel here near the town of Murphys. The showy Amador County zin comes from the Clockspring Vineyard in the Shenandoah Valley; it's aged exclusively in American oak; the Calaveras County zinfandel is aged half in American and half in French oak and has a hint of black pepper. A 100 percent French colombard called True Frogs Lily Pad White is a snob-buster—a slightly sweet white quaffer.

Tuolumne County

SONORA WINERY AND PORT WORKS

Established **1986** ***Owners*** **Private Partnership** ***Production*** **4,000 cases** ***Vineyard area*** **3 acres (1.2 ha)**

Originally named "Chateau Garaj," Sonora has established a sound reputation for vintage port produced with the same varietals and techniques as those in the renowned Douro Valley in the north of Portugal. They are also known for old-vine zinfandels. Newer projects include a vinho tinto, a dry red from three port varietals, which has met with much critical acclaim, and a tawny port. Sonora is located halfway between Stockton and the Yosemite National Park.

Other significant producers in the Sierra Foothills include Perry Creek Vineyards and Dobra Zemlja.

San Francisco Bay

CATHERINE FALLIS MS

That the very mention of San Francisco conjures up images of the magnificent Golden Gate Bridge, rugged coastline and some of the best wining and dining in North America, was not lost on those who petitioned for this AVA. Awarded in 1999, the BATF's approval of this AVA has met with controversy from the industry. The area overlaps five counties which border the San Francisco Bay—San Francisco, San Mateo, Santa Clara, Alameda, Contra Costa and parts of Santa Cruz and San Benito. Vineyards are planted on 5,800 of the 1,566,720 acres (634,043 ha) in the region and there are 39 wineries.

Export-minded Wente family of the Livermore Valley led the petition, convinced that buyers would recognize one of the world's favorite tourist attractions on labels, whereas the Livermore Valley appellation would mean little. But is there more substance than just the conviction that the tourist symbols would promote sales?

In fact, the Golden Gate Gap is the only break in North America's western coastal range. This unique opening to the cool Pacific Ocean has far-reaching effects, providing a source of cool air and fog which travels into the sometimes baking Central Valley as the hot air rises. Imagine, if you will, a clockface, with the gap at the Golden Gate Bridge at the 9:00 position. At the 12:00 to 1:00 position, this marine influence heads up into San Pablo Bay and into Carneros and the Napa Valley. At 2:00 the cool air and fog funnels into Lodi. At 3:00, Contra Costa County is the beneficiary, followed by the Livermore Valley at 4:00. So, with as much proximity to the cooling source as Napa and with similar daily temperatures, the case seemed assured for this AVA not to be lumped into the vast Central Coast AVA.

BELOW: San Francisco's Golden Gate Bridge was completed in 1937. The length of the main span of suspended structure is 4,200 feet (1,280 m).

In addition to bringing more recognition to Livermore Valley itself, this new AVA is also home to several other appellation "orphans." Producers in the western Livermore Valley whose acreage falls outside the current delineation previously deferred to the Central Coast AVA. Now they can use the San Francisco Bay appellation. The Wente and Concannon vineyards in Livermore Valley are phasing in this use on their labels. The Livermore Valley Winegrowers Association would like to see "San Francisco Bay–Livermore Valley" as the origin noted.

Other appellation orphans include those from Contra Costa County—a lone producer in Martinez, the Conrad Viano Winery—and all of the wines produced from Oakley fruit including those from Bonny Doon, Cline Cellars, Jade Mountain and Rosenblum Cellars.

Contra Costa County

Lumped into the larger Central Coast AVA until 1999—and now included in the slightly smaller San Francisco Bay AVA—the century old vineyards that remain in this community are shrinking daily. Pre-Prohibition, more than 6,000 acres (2,428 ha) were planted and the area was home to 27 wineries. Today some 1,500 acres (607 ha) are planted to zinfandel, mourvèdre, carignane—"kerrigan" in local dialect—alicante bouchet, chardonnay and palomino, but not a single winery remains.

Contra Costa County is an important source of old-vine zinfandel and rhône varietals. However, vineyard growth has been threatened—strip malls and housing developments have left very little room for agriculture. Still, there are many in the area who share an intense sense of loss about this and, thankfully, a revival may be imminent—500 acres (202 ha) of new vineyards have been planted in the last few years.

One of California's finest pre-Prohibition wine regions, Contra Costa County was first planted by Marsh in 1846. Strentzel from Poland, naturalist Muir and educator Swett followed over the next few decades. In the late 1890s Christian Brothers began making wine. Many Italians settled in the area and with them came fine winemaking traditions. They planted the bulk of what remains today, especially zinfandel and mourvèdre. It's only in the last few decades that the area has been recognized as a source of premium fruit. The Rhône Ranger movement started in Oakley, with old-vine mourvèdre, still a much sought after old-vine fruit source.

Vineyards in Oakley are on flatlands at the confluence of the Sacramento and San Joaquin rivers and have very deep sandy soil. A soft breeze comes through each afternoon and evenings are 10–35°F (2–12°C) cooler than afternoons. Fog sometimes comes up on the water, but it doesn't come out onto the vines. Winter rainfall is usually 10 inches (25 cm) providing ideal conditions.

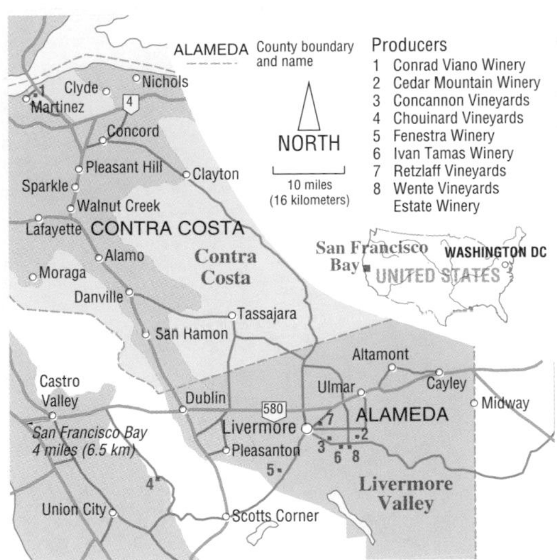

ABOVE: *Victorian architecture features in these houses facing Alamo Square, San Francisco.*

Vines and wines

Mourvèdre is around a century old here and finds particular success. It has to struggle to ripen and produces a small crop. Carignane too, maintains acidity, allowing its particular varietal character to come through.

Old vines of all types are common and give dense, richly fruited wines. Lower end blends are reminiscent of days when wine was made of field blends mixed with water. The premium "zins" and mourvèdre's represent the other extreme, fashioned into super extracted, lavishly oaked and expensive wines. Cline's Small Berry Mourvèdre has a distinctive chocolate mint note, which, with its almost port-like alcohol, makes it a wonderful wine to enjoy after dinner. All but the low end wines have marked longevity.

Most vines are gnarly, dry farmed and have taken 75 to 120 years of head-pruning. Light sandy soil allows for deep root penetration by vines and facilitates drainage. Crops are small, with an average of 1.5 tons per acre (3.75 t per ha). Fruit is hand harvested, with alicante bouchet proving especially challenging.

ROSENBLUM CELLARS

Established **1973** ***Owners*** **Kent and Kathy Rosenblum** ***Production*** **60,000 cases** ***Vineyard area*** **no estate vineyards**

The Rosenblums started making wine at home and now make wine out of a warehouse near Oakland, with fruit from Ukiah to Santa Barbara. Two of their four signature zins come from vineyards in Oakley—Carla's and Continente; Henry's is from Napa Valley and Maggie's is from Sonoma. The wines have deliberately soft tannins and take full advantage of the 25 percent allowable blending, adding zin, cabernet sauvignon, or carignane.

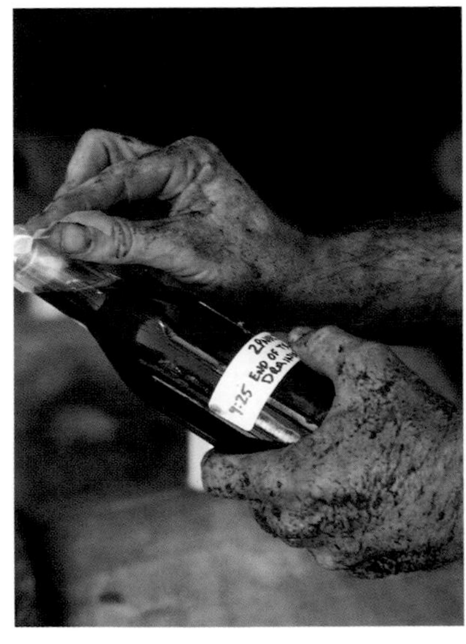

LEFT: *A small, sample bottle of pinot noir.*

Livermore Valley

The Livermore Valley AVA demarcates a 10 x 15 mile (16 x 24 km) transverse valley nestled into the base of San Francisco Bay's coastal ranges. This and the similar west to east openings at Santa Barbara are the only two transverse coastal valleys in the state.

Unlike San Jose, whose fate was loss of vineyards, housing developers here have actually stimulated the growth of vineyards. In a unique wine country model developers must contribute a percentage of land to permanent agriculture and make a donation to a land trust for each home that they want to build.

Current delineation of the AVA covers 96,000 acres (38,850 ha), of which 5,000 acres (2,023 ha) are planted to vines today. Growth will cap at 8,000 acres (3,238 ha) at the first phase of current plan build-out. Varieties planted include the famous d'Yquem-cutting sauvignon blanc and sémillon, Wente clone chardonnay, cabernet sauvignon and the first varietally labeled petite sirah. Secondary varietals include malvasia bianca, pinot gris, merlot and zinfandel. New plantings are primarily syrah and sangiovese. More than 650,000 cases are produced using local fruit, with Concannon, Ivan Tamas and Wente leading in volume. Local grape supply cannot meet demand, so producers often source fruit from Monterey and Lodi and some of the smaller producers form co-operatives with larger wineries for better buying power.

Regional Dozen

QUALITY WINES

Bonny Doon Vineyards Old Telegram Mourvèdre
Cline Cellars Live Oak Vineyard Zinfandel
Cline Cellars Small Berry Mourvèdre
Cline Cellars Bridgehead Vineyard Zinfandel
Jacuzzi Reserve Zinfandel
Jade Mountain Mourvèdre
Rosenblum Carla's Reserve Zinfandel
Turley Duarte Zinfandel

BEST VALUE WINES

Cotes d'Oakley Vin Blanc, Vin Gris and Vin Rouge
Cline Cellars Ancient Vines Zinfandel
Rosenblum Chateau La Paws Cote du Bone Mourvèdre
Viano Vineyards Zinfandel

ABOVE: *San Francisco's cable cars and Alcatraz prison in the background.*

History

California's wine pioneers discovered the rocky, well-drained soil and ideal climate of the Livermore Valley in the 1800s just when Wells Fargo gold trains, horse-runners and bandits were running through the area.

Over 100 years ago the Wente and Concannon families, and others, started making wine here. Today these families are still the leaders of the Livermore Valley.

Wente selected a Montpellier clone originating in Burgundy's Corton-Charlemagne. This clone produced over one-third of all Californian chardonnay even in the 1960s. Wetmore of Cresta Blanca vineyard brought sémillon and sauvignon blanc cuttings back from Chateau d'Yquem in Bordeaux. His wines won gold medals in the Paris Exposition of 1889. This notoriety brought a second gold rush to the state, especially to the Livermore Valley.

By 1900 more than 20 wineries and 20,000 acres (80,940 ha) were in production. The few that survived the first challenge of phylloxera faced a second blow—Prohibition. A few survived selling sacramental wine and shipping fruit to the east coast for winemaking.

Regional Best

- Cedar Mountain Blanches Vineyard Cabernet Sauvignon
- Chouinard Chardonnay
- Concannon Petite Sirah
- Elliston Pinot Gris
- Fenestra Sémillon
- Garre Grenache
- Ivan Tamas Trebbiano
- Retzlaff Cabernet Sauvignon
- Stony Ridge Malvasia Bianca
- Wente Crane Ridge Reserve Merlot

Landscape and climate

The Livermore Valley is a west to east valley that draws in the cool marine layer from the nearby Golden Gate Gap (mirroring the Napa and Sonoma Valleys with the map sideways). Morning fog gives way to warm and sometimes baking hot afternoon sun. The heat stays for about four to five hours, but from these five to ten days each year, the average moves upwards. Unlike the North Coast, however, cool marine breezes bring the temperature down dramatically. The evenings are cool to cold, especially in July. Cooler evening temperatures in summer allow grapes to retain high natural acidity. Most of the Livermore Valley is classified as Region III, though locals quip that "we are region II-and-a-half."

With deep gravelly sedimentary soil the area has been historically compared to the Graves region of Bordeaux in France—primarily gravel with shale ridges in the western canyons. Pockets of heavy clay, red clay and loam, and rock and loam are scattered throughout the valley floor.

Vines and wines

Cabernet sauvignon is the signature red wine, with petite sirah a close second. The bordeaux varietals sémillon and sauvignon blanc represent the leading whites. In the cooler, foggier zones growers plant chardonnay and merlot. Petite sirah has performed well here. New plantings of syrah and pinot gris are showing early promise.

Chardonnay is richer and of higher alcohol than those from Sonoma and less markedly oaked than those of Napa. Pear and melons are better descriptors than the guava and pineapple of Arroyo Seco in Monterey. The Wente clone gives characteristics of apples, peaches and bananas. Cabernet sauvignon is beautifully round with classic dark berry fruit and balanced acidity. Lavishly oaked examples are few and far between, even at the super premium level.

Rhône Rangers

Now a consumer-friendly organization with elaborate tastings, a newsletter, and a website, this term initially referred to a handful of California winemakers who dared to produce wine from such Rhône Valley varieties as marsanne, syrah, rousanne, viognier, grenache and others.

Owing to the climate and the recent successes of Australian shiraz on world markets, rhône varieties are booming in California. At the 2004 Rhône Ranger tasting in San Francisco, 150 producers poured hundreds of different offerings of Rhône-inspired wines. The Hospice du Rhône is an educational and charitable event, held in Paso Robles, that brings international Rhône-inspired producers and consumers together each June.

LEFT: *The luscious beauty of the raw material.*

Gravelly soil provides excellent drainage and heat retention into the cooler evening. Many growers are in transition from the Californian sprawl to a divided canopy. Permanent overhead irrigation systems were invented here and are common. Many vineyards are farmed organically, but few mention this on their labels. Growers are constantly on guard to prevent the return of phylloxera to the area.

Livermore Valley growers were the first in the nation to machine harvest and to field crush and press. Large scale night harvesting is common. Many winemakers draw on fruit sources outside of the AVA, especially from Monterey, Lodi and the Santa Cruz Mountains. There is intense competition for local fruit from all points, most notably from the North Coast.

Vinification styles vary dramatically. Overall, restraint is the word of the day. Experimentation with techniques, tanks, yeast strains, is ongoing and information is accessible to anyone who asks. Styles run the gamut from whites made in a squeaky clean mass production style to reds made in small lots with extended maceration, press fractions and bottled unfiltered. Little mention is made of native yeast fermentations. Oak use varies. The smaller producers on a shoestring budget use American barrels and French innerstaves.

CEDAR MOUNTAIN WINERY

Established 1990 **Owners** Earl and Linda Ault **Production** 4,000 cases **Vineyard area** 17 acres (6.8 ha)

Earl and Linda Ault represent two of the valley's PH.D.s. Linda quips "It doesn't take a rocket scientist to make wine, but it helps." Cedar Mountain Winery's signature wine is a cabernet sauvignon, which ages beautifully and has consistently been awarded gold medals. While cabernet sauvignon may have put Cedar Mountain on the map, they have also garnered national accolades for port wines such as Cabernet Royale, made from fruit from their estate.

CHOUINARD VINEYARDS

(Currently outside the LV AVA)
Established 1985 **Owners** George and Caroline Chouinard **Production** 5,500 cases **Vineyard area** 6.5 acres (2.6 ha)

During his career as an architect, George designed several wineries. The Chouinards were drawn to this area because of its similarities to the climate of the Napa Valley without the price tag. Their isolated 100 acre (40.4 ha) estate perched at the top of the Walpert Ridge is far removed from "civilization." Picnics and hiking are encouraged, as is sampling the deeply flavored, elegant, estate chardonnay and cabernet sauvignon.

WENTE VINEYARDS ESTATE WINERY

Established 1883 **Owners** Wente family **Production** 300,000 cases **Vineyard area** 2000 acres (809 ha)

Certainly the "Robert Mondavi" of Livermore Valley, the Wente family is integrally part of the region. Carolyn Wente petitioned for the AVA status. The Wente family has an undying commitment to their area and to quality, that started well over 100 years ago. Today over 80 percent of California's sauvignon blanc, sémillon and chardonnay originates from the Wente (and former Cresta Blanca) clones. Concentrations are especially high in the North Coast. The family sells 100,000 cases domestically; the remaining 200,000 are sold in 150 countries. Recently the family purchased the famous Cresta Blanca Winery, a state historic landmark and restored it and its original sandstone caves as a sparkling wine facility.

LEFT: *This colored crystal glass is from the period between 1900 and 1930.*

Other notable producers in the San Francisco AVA include Cline Cellars, Conrad Viano Winery, Colcannon Vineyards, Fenestra Winery, Ivan Tamas Winery and Retzlaff Vineyards.

BELOW: *Part of the processing—running off newly pressed shiraz grapes.*

North Central Coast

CATHERINE FALLIS MS

California's North Central Coast begins at San Francisco Bay and ends north of Paso Robles in Monterey. The section covers the Santa Cruz Mountains and the adjacent Santa Clara Valley wine regions, the land between the Pacific Ocean and the Diablo Ranges just south of San Francisco which includes San Mateo, Santa Cruz, Santa Clara and parts of San Benito counties.

RIGHT: *Hand-picked grapes in California.*

Vineyards in the remote Santa Cruz Mountains, just as in the metropolis of San Jose, and Silicon Valley—are few and far between. Wineries, however, abound. Santa Cruz boasts 51 and Santa Clara 21. Winemakers use the abundant vineyards of Monterey County as their primary source of fruit.

SANTA CLARA VALLEY

This is "the valley," the only valley to the locals, who live encapsulated in their unique environment. Santa Clara Valley is the Silicon Valley—no vineyards (except for a few patches to the south near "garlic capital" Gilroy in the San Ysidro AVA)—every square inch of land serves the techmasters.

The Santa Clara Valley AVA covers 332,800 acres about (134,680 ha), including San Ysidro sub-AVA at 2,340 acres (947 ha) and part of Pacheco Pass AVA, a small valley that overlaps Santa Clara and San Benito counties. Vine area is small—an estimated 200 acres (81 ha), most of this in San Ysidro clustered in the southeast near Gilroy and inland and north of the mouth of Monterey Bay. The powerful marine influence, drawn in along the Pajaro River, cools the warm plains. This area is known as the Hecker Pass, after the 152 Highway you will find traces of another era, much like a deserted Highway 29 in Napa Valley, with boarded-up houses and abandoned vineyards.

An exception is the inviting tourist-oriented Zanger Casa de Fruta, which farms more than grapes. Sarah's Vineyard, famous for chardonnay is here, and the grenache for Bonny Doon's Clos de Gilroy is farmed nearby. The largest wineries in the valley are Mirassou and J. Lohr—showplaces housing offices rather than functioning wineries; grape growing and winemaking activities take place in Monterey or in the Livermore Valley.

History

The Santa Clara Wine Growers Association states proudly that Santa Clara Valley is "the oldest continuously producing region in the state," although the landscape has changed dramatically over time. Franciscan friars planted at the Mission Santa Clara de Asis in 1777 and provided vine cuttings to other locals, many of whom were French immigrants. By the 1830s the Santa Clara Valley, with its bustling village of San Jose, was the hub of the California wine industry. To the north, in San Mateo County, Emmet Rixford planted "La Questa Vineyards" at Woodside in the late 1800s. His cabernet sauvignons were a benchmark for the era and are still referred to. Three acres (1.2 ha) of the original vineyards are still farmed by the Mullen family.

A Frenchman, Antoine Delmas, brought over cuttings to replace the mission vines. Unfortunately this spread phylloxera and by the 1890s many of the vineyards were destroyed. The remaining vineyards were grafted over to resistant American rootstock and by the early 1900s there were more than 100 wineries and 8,500 acres (3,440 ha) of vines.

After Prohibition, when many survived by selling

BELOW: *The russet tones of these vine leaves herald the impending fall harvest.*

sacramental wine or grapes to home winemakers, there were still 61 wineries in business. One of the most historic and beautiful is the Paul Masson Mountain Winery in the Santa Cruz Mountain foothills near Saratoga. This winery hosted a "Music in the Vineyards" concert series for several decades. Like fellow winemaking colleagues, they have now relocated to Monterey. Governor Leland Stanford's old cellar is now a bank in the Stanford shopping center and this beautiful rural environment has become a congested metropolis in just two decades.

COOPER-GARROD VINEYARDS

Established 1994 Owners Cooper and Garrod families Production 3,000 cases Vineyard area 21 acres (8.5 ha)

The Garrod family purchased land from the Mount Eden Orchard and Vineyard Company in 1893. Following his great-grandfather's footsteps, Jan Garrod began replanting the estate vineyards in the 1980s. Today these unirrigated hillside vineyards are planted to chardonnay, cabernet sauvignon and cabernet franc, each of which are vinted and bottled separately.

J. LOHR WINERY

Established 1974 Owner Jerry Lohr Production 550,000 cases Vineyard area 1,735 acres (702 ha)

Once a research scientist at NASA, while developing land and building custom homes in Santa Clara, Santa Cruz and Monterey, Jerry Lohr was investigating the best grape-growing regions of California. He planted in Monterey, but established his winery in San Jose. Winemaker Jeff Meier crafts single-vineyard estates, Cypress, and a de-alcoholized line, Ariel. Best sellers include a fairly dry Bay Mist Riesling and a valdiguie, formerly known as gamay. Paso Robles Syrah shows promise.

SANTA CRUZ MOUNTAINS

Hippies and hitchhikers share granola and clove cigarettes with suddenly rich computer fiends. As if in a Berkeley that time forgot, spirituality, hemp and incense reign supreme in this isolated corner of the world, where the softer, gentler atmosphere suits the highly creative and fuels the fires of the iconoclastic. Getting here is an effort. This dizzying mountain terrain is not for the lazy You will suffer badly in anything but a low-slung, sleek, growling sports car; your high-center-of-gravity 4WD will mark you as fair game as you try to maneuver it through these vertiginous and sometimes excruciatingly narrow passes.

The Santa Cruz Mountains play host to America's premier mountain vineyard area. In 1981, AVA status, the first based on geophysical and climatic factors, was granted. Elevation contour lines at 400 feet (122 m) in the west and 400–800 feet (122–244 m) along the eastern face mark the borders and surround the Santa Cruz Mountain range from Half Moon Bay in the north, to Mount Madonna near Watsonville in the south.

LEFT: Late-harvest grapes shrivel and sweeten on the vines.

The 350,000 acre (141,640 ha) AVA covers parts of three counties, San Mateo, Santa Cruz and Santa Clara. Locals estimate that about 750 acres (304 ha) are under vine, mostly in terraces on the steep hillsides above the fog line at daybreak. Sub-AVA Ben Lomond Mountain covers 38,400 acres (15,540 ha) northwest of Santa Cruz, 70 acres (28 ha) of which are planted to vines. Vineyard expansion is unlikely. Pierce's disease continues its devastation through the area and the struggle for urban development is ongoing. Total production is just under 500,000 cases per year.

> *I made a mental note to watch which bottle became empty soonest, sometimes a more telling evaluation system than any other.*
>
> GERALD ASHER, *On Wine*

History

The Santa Cruz Mountains were first recognized as a premium wine-producing region in the late 1800s. Many local wines won awards throughout the century at events such as the San Francisco and Paris exhibitions. Much later, in the famous 1976 Paris challenge of California vs. France, two of the 11 wines chosen to represent California's best were local. "Count" Haraszthy, prominent in California winemaking, planted his "San Mateo County" vineyard here at the southern tip of the San Andreas Lake in 1854, but 40 wineries and as many as 4,000 acres (1,418 ha) of vines barely survived Prohibition. Many original vineyards, which grew alongside grain, corn, potatoes, beans and sugarbeets,

Regional Best

- Bonny Doon Vineyards Clos de Gilroy Grenache
- Cooper-Garrod Cabernet Franc
- Jory Winery Syrah
- Thomas Kruse Brut Méthode Champenoise
- J. Lohr Cypress California Chardonnay
- Solis Winery Estate Sangiovese
- Storr's Mann Vineyard Merlot
- Testarossa Cuvée Niclaire Reserve Pinot Noir

ABOVE: Fall paints the leaves in autumnal beauty.

are now planted with Christmas trees. One of the oldest and largest Santa Cruz wineries, Martinelli, founded in 1868 in Watsonville, today produces only apple cider and apple juice. Luckily, visionary Martin Ray, who had grown up in the Mount Eden foothills, purchased the Paul Masson Champagne Company right after Prohibition and started producing 100 percent varietal table wines. His pinot noir was notable and made international news. Ray brought partners in during the 1960s in an effort to expand. They, in turn, began to take over his vineyards, renaming the estate Mount Eden Vineyards in 1972. Martin Ray is credited with creating the boutique winery model. Today's visionaries include Jeffrey and Eleanor Patterson, owners of Mount Eden Vineyards, Paul Draper of Ridge Vineyards, Kathryn Kennedy and Randall Grahm of Bonny Doon.

Landscape and climate

AVA borders are defined according to elevation contour lines. Many of the vineyards are as high as 2,000 feet (610 m) with spectacular views of San Francisco and San Jose. Steep-sloping vineyards face in all directions with the west always cooler than the low-lying inland eastern side. Constant ocean breezes and maritime fog has facilitated the spread of Pierce's disease, which has all but ravaged these coastal vineyards. Up into the ridges, especially to the east, the climate cools down substantially. Most of the AVA is classified as Region I on the Winkler-Amerine heat summation scale. The soils vary from sandy to heavy clay to barren rocky shale. Shallow soil and the cool climate restrict yields to about 2 tons per acre (5 t per ha).

Vines and wines

One of America's cooler climate vineyard regions, the area's reputation rests on its pinot noir and, more recently, chardonnay. The long-lived intense, brooding and tarry cabernet sauvignons of Kathryn Kennedy, Ridge Vineyards and Mount Eden, however, are stealing the spotlight.

Randall Grahm resists what he calls the ever-monotonous and monochromatic chardonnay and cabernet sauvignon. He first planted pinot noir here at the coastal vineyards of Bonny Doon. Results were not impressive so the young idealist switched to rhône, Italian types and some obscure varietals. His vineyards were one of the first to fall victim to Pierce's disease and he now sources fruit from Monterey (as do most producers), Washington State, Spain, France, Contra Costa and Germany.

The average growing season is 300 days; some years, harvest continues well after Thanksgiving. The challenge is great in this cool, rugged terrain and individual styles vary greatly, but all agree that the fruit, not the winemaker, is responsible for greatness. In the 1960s, the industry learned about the winery; in the 1990s the vineyard was the focus. Most vinification is typical of California approaches, but a few small producers still release rustic reds with untamed mountain tannins.

BONNY DOON VINEYARD

Established **1983** ***Owners*** **Grahm family** ***Production*** **190,000 cases** ***Vineyard area*** **70 acres (28.3 ha) bearing, 70 acres (28.3 ha) newly planted in Monterey**

Iconoclast and self-proclaimed "tortured flower child" Randall Grahm has single-handedly brought more attention to the Santa Cruz Mountains than anyone else. His newsletter reaches far-flung corners of the world; there are doon-heads everywhere! Luckily, his production is vast enough to reach the legions of devoted fans. His determination comes in the face of great challenges: Pierce's disease, which caused total devastation of vineyards at Bonny Doon, and an ill-fated winery plan for Pleasanton in the Livermore Valley. He jokes about his current "winery," a former granola factory in an outlying area of Santa Cruz on the "wrong" side of the tracks. The tasting room up at Bonny Doon remains and is well worth the drive. Look forward to the next chapter about life on Planet Doon, where, Grahm says, living is all about taking chances.

KATHRYN KENNEDY WINERY

Established **1973** ***Owner*** **Kathryn Kennedy** ***Production*** **3,800 cases** ***Vineyard area*** **8 acres (3.2 ha)**

After viticultural courses at UC Davis, Kathryn planted own-rooted cabernet sauvignon on inland rolling foothills near Saratoga, with its moderate marine influence. This small scale encourages intense involvement with all aspects of production—pruning by hand and bottling unfiltered. In 1981, Kathryn's youngest son, Marty Mathis, became winemaker. In addition to long-time cult-status cabernet sauvignon and lateral, a blend of cabernet franc and merlot, recent releases include a richly structured Maridon Vineyard syrah and a crisp, dry chenin blanc/viognier blend.

MOUNT EDEN VINEYARDS

Established **1972** ***Owners*** **Jeffrey and Eleanor Patterson (major shareholders)** ***Production*** **15,000 cases** ***Vineyard area*** **42 acres (17 ha)**

Martin Ray developed this former Paul Masson property into a dramatic ridgetop wine estate in the 1940s and 1950s. Partners came in to facilitate the planned expansion in the early 1960s and proceeded to take over; in 1972 they formed Mount Eden. Patterson, president in 1993, crafts two styles of chardonnay: a French-style estate version that fools burgundy fans with its nutty, erotic notes, and the much fruitier, more forward California style "MacGregor Vineyard" bottling. The estate cabernet is deeply colored, lusciously fruited and velvety. The wines are notable for their longevity, and the Pattersons promote the concept of wine enjoyment at the table through photo and poetry exhibitions.

RIDGE VINEYARDS

Established **1959** ***Owner*** **A. Otsuka** ***Production*** **55,000 cases** ***Vineyard area*** **60 acres (24.3 ha)**

Paul Draper's wines are very popular with the British trade, notably Hugh Johnson, Harry Waugh and Jancis Robinson, particularly his Montebello Cabernet Sauvignon, from estate-grown, old-vine fruit that is very restrained early in its life. Americans, according to Draper, prefer the showier, more opulent, corporal zinfandels. Wine from each plot in this fractured limestone ridge is identified and tasted before blending. Other releases include a series of North and Central Coast zinfandels, an alicante, chardonnay, grenache, mataro, petite sirah and syrah.

Other significant producers in North Central Coast include Mirassou Vineyards and Champagne Cellars, Clos Tita and David Bruce Winery.

Regional Best

- Bonny Doon Vineyards Le Cigare Volante California
- Clos Tita Estate Pinot Noir
- Kathryn Kennedy Lateral
- Kathryn Kennedy Maridon Vineyard Syrah
- Kathryn Kennedy Meritage
- Mount Eden Reserve Cabernet Sauvignon
- Ridge Montebello Cabernet Sauvignon
- Thunder Mountain Cabernet Sauvignon

LEFT: *Grapes ripening in the sunshine.*

ABOVE: *Hand-picking grapes in San Benito County—a labor intensive operation.*

RIGHT: *A bust of author John Steinbeck, Cannery Row, in downtown Monterey.*

Monterey County

CATHERINE FALLIS MS

A world-class jazz festival, the Laguna Seca speedway and international golf tournaments draw visitors to the Monterey Peninsula as does the wild and untamed coastal beauty, but it won't be long before wine steals the spotlight. Only 100 miles (160 km) from San Francisco, and just one hour from the heart of Silicon Valley, this sophisticated yet cozy cluster of oceanfront villages is one of America's favorite vacation spots. Big Sur, Carmel, Pebble Beach, Spanish Bay, Pacific Grove, and Cannery Row in Monterey are the hot spots for tourists and locals alike. Venture inland, though, to an as yet undiscovered destination—Monterey's glorious wine country.

Franciscan friars planted the first vines here at Soledad Mission in the 1800s. In 1915 Francis Will Silvear planted muscat and thompson seedless, then, after Prohibition, chardonnay and pinot noir, with the idea of producing sparkling wine at what is now Chalone Vineyards. The full potential of the region was widely recognized in the 1950s and 1960s, after a 1944 UC Davis study conducted by Professor A. J. Winkler and Maynard A. Amerine. They reported a climatic range here from low Region I near Monterey Bay to low Region III at King City—comparable with Napa, Sonoma, Burgundy and Bordeaux. The report came at a time when demand for table wine was increasing as steadily as the demand for new housing developments, especially in the Livermore and Santa Clara valleys. Wente, Paul Masson, Mirassou, and J. Lohr initially sought land for vineyards here.

California coastal living is far different from what one might imagine. Fleece and fireplaces, hot cocoa and wool are more appropriate than hot little bikinis and ice-cold beer. The Monterey Peninsula coastline is cool, humid and foggy most of the year, especially in the morning. The sun is shining brightly, however, about 10 miles (16 km) inland. This is the pot of gold at the end of the rainbow; warm sun soaks the chill out of your bones. This is Steinbeck country. All you see for miles are rows of grape vines. You may encounter the occasional horseman on this former cattle-grazing land. And you certainly will have the chance to try some of the best Mexican food on the planet—Monterey is a former Mexican territory and many vineyard crews are second- and third-generation workers. English is a second language in the towns and villages. What you won't see quite yet are the bells and whistles of an established wine country. Apart from the sophisticated Carmel Valley, restaurants and accommodations are few and far between, as are tasting rooms and gift shops.

The wine industry here is concentrated in the Monterey and San Benito counties primarily where the vast Salinas Valley draws the marine influence into the warmer inland. A few scattered AVAs have found remote sites at cooler, high elevations where grapes struggle to ripen at all, but when they do, they have unique qualities and a distinct signature of their origin.

Monterey and surrounding areas fall under the larger North Central Coast AVA. Monterey County ends just 30 miles (48 km) north of Paso Robles, the beginning of the South Central Coast.

The six AVAs of San Benito County are San Benito; Paicines; Cienega Valley and its sub-appellation, Lime Kiln Valley; Mount Harlan; and Pacheco Pass, a small valley overlapping with Santa Clara County. Mount Harlan is the county's most relevant AVA, home of Josh Jensens' world-famous Claera Winery, and Pietra Santa, Enz, De Rose, and Flint wineries. The seven AVAs of Monterey County are Monterey (which is geographically located in the Salinas Valley) and its four sub-AVAs of Arroyo Seco, Hames Valley, San Lucas, and the Santa Lucia Highlands, plus Chalone and Carmel Valley.

Monterey County was sixth of the top ten counties in California in 1998 with wine grape coverage at 134,699 acres (54,5112 ha). Demarcated acreage includes Monterey AVA 35,758 acres (14,470 ha), which does not include figures for Arroyo Seco 18,240 acres (7,380 ha), Hames Valley 10,240 acres (4,144 ha); San Lucas 33,920 acres (13,470 ha); and Santa Lucia Highlands 22,000 acres (8,900 ha). Carmel Valley wine grape cultivation is a substantial 19,200 acres (7,770 ha); Chalone 8,540 acres (3,456 ha). San Benito County includes the San Benito AVA at 45,000 acres (18,211 ha) (which includes sub-AVAs Cienega Valley, its sub-AVA Lime Kiln Valley and Paicines); Pacheco Pass at 3,200 acres (1,295 ha) and Mount Harlan at 7,440 acres (3,010 ha).

Monterey County was fourth in the US top ten in 1998 for grape sale revenues, after Sonoma, San Joaquin and Napa at US$168,970,808. Monterey enjoys particular success with burgundian varietals pinot noir and chardonnay from the Santa Lucia Highlands, and bordeaux varietals cabernet sauvignon and sauvignon blanc from the Carmel Valley. Chardonnay is the most widely planted, at 14,555 acres (5,890 ha). Cabernet sauvignon is the second most widely planted, at 3,607 acres (1,460 ha) and merlot is third at 2,990 acres (1,210 ha). Secondary varietals include gewürztraminer, inzolia, muscat blanc/canelli, sémillon, viognier, white riesling, malvasia bianca, orange muscat, valdiguie, petite sirah, nebbiolo and petit verdot.

This vast area is finally becoming recognized as a significant contributor to the California wine industry. Monterey walks proudly if still a bit awkwardly among her more stylish North Coast neighbors.

LEFT: A statue commemorating Father Juniperro Serra, founder of some of California's early missions.

Landscape and climate

The Salinas Valley, or Monterey AVA, bears a striking resemblance to the Napa Valley. The wide mouth of the valley is too cool for grape growing. Like San Francisco, where you need a sweater especially in the summer, it bears the full brunt of strong marine influences. Heading due south along the 101 Freeway into the heart of the 12 mile (19 km) wide valley brings you to Soledad—the center and the outpost in the first round of expansion inland. At the base of the Santa Lucia mountain range to the west, or the Coastal Range, a handful of wineries have nestled into the foothills and have successfully petitioned for AVA status.

These Santa Lucia bench vineyards are planted on terraces facing southeast, giving extended exposure to the sun before afternoon breezes from the Pacific lower the temperature. Farther south, with Greenfield as the base, is Arroyo Seco, which begins with a narrow Santa

RIGHT: The old bell at Soledad Mission was cast in Mexico in the seventeenth century.

Lucia canyon then flattens out over the valley floor. Bordeaux varietals thrive at the warmer terraced canyon mouth; oddly named "Greenfield Potatoes" or 3–4 inch (7–10 cm) cobblestones mark the soil in the plains. Their drainage and heat-retaining qualities give chardonnay and riesling their signature tropical character.

Wente is a major force in this area, producing 20,000 cases of Arroyo Seco Brut Reserve sparkling wine each year. Continuing south to King City, the San Lucas AVA straddles the freeway rather than tucking up into the coastal foothills. Its vineyards are set into alluvial fans and terraces ranging from 500–1,200 feet (152–366 m). The valley floor proper is just too windy here for fine wine production. Shale and sandstone soil, warm days and cool nights give deeply colored and flavored bordeaux varietals, chardonnay and syrah.

Hames Valley marks the southern tip of the valley near Bradley. Once again nestled up into the foothills and thus protected from the Salinas Valley winds, Hames Valley is similar to southern neighbor Paso Robles in its shaly loam soil and warm climate. Cabernet sauvignon here is intense. The world's largest contiguous vineyard, San Bernabe, (8,300 planted acres—3,361 ha) between King City and San Lucas, is owned by Central Valley's Delicato Vineyards which produces one-third of the total output of Monterey. This vineyard is referred to as the "Hope Diamond" in the industry. San Bernabe's *terroir* is unique. Much of the vineyard is on ancient, though now stabilized, Aeolian sand dune remnants (65 percent of San Bernabe soil is of this type). Nowhere else in the county is this soil type found in such an uninterrupted expanse. It is the most diverse single vineyard in the world, an absolutely remarkable matrix of soils and 22 distinct microclimates.

BELOW: Winery sign and "château" buildings in Carmel valley.

Chalone AVA is a one-winery appellation 1,800 feet (550 m) above Soledad in the Gavilan Mountain range near the eerie dormant volcano, the Pinnacles National Monument. Clay, decomposed granite, quartz crystals and limestone in the soil coupled with a long, cool growing season allow particular success with chardonnay, pinot noir and chenin blanc.

Carmel Valley has a long history of cabernet sauvignon going back to Father Juniperro Serra in the 1800s. Well-drained gravelly terraces, very warm days and very cool nights, especially in the Cachagua district (Esselen Indian word for Hidden Springs), produce intensely varietal cabernet sauvignons, merlots and sauvignon blancs. The Tularcitos Ridge to the northeast provides additional physical isolation and protection from the nearby Pacific Ocean.

San Benito County's most important AVA is Mount Harlan, a single winery appellation. Josh Jensen's Calera vineyards are planted in limestone outcrops 2,200 feet (720 m) up into the Gavilan Range across the San Benito County line. At this elevation temperatures are low even in the peak of summer. Drop back down into nearby Hollister to the north and feel the baking heat.

A common factor throughout Monterey and San Benito counties is lack of rainfall. The average rainfall is 10 inches (4 cm), not enough to ripen grapes. Judicious use of irrigation from the massive underground river, the Salinas, provides balance between growth of vines and maturation of the grape.

Vines and wines

The long growing season with short daily bursts of heat gives intense varietal character if crops are restrained and the fruit reaches full maturity on the vine. Well-developed colors, excellent balance of sugar and acid, fruit true to the natural flavor of the varietal and the ability to age are becoming the descriptors for Monterey.

Bordeaux varietals thrive in the warmer Carmel and southern Salinas Valley locations with their hot, dry days and cool nights. Burgundian varietals show restraint in the higher elevations, but give full throttle, showy, ripe, opulent expressions closer to the valley floor, where less day-to-night variation in temperature exists. Rhône and Italian varietals show early promise, especially syrah, which is vibrantly fruity, sometimes smoky and not nearly as heavily oaked as it is in the North Coast. Anyone who has tasted through library collections

of Chalone, Calera, or Durney will attest to their incredible longevity. The potential is strong across the board as Monterey struggles through adolescence and comes into adulthood.

Budbreak is two weeks earlier than other California regions; harvest is two weeks later. Grapes here have up until recently been farmed primarily for tonnage, not for fine wine. Unlimited water from the underground Salinas River fed overhead irrigation systems, allowing for plentiful production. However, the large-volume production caused imbalance in the vines; foliage grew out of control, too, and caused the Monterey "veggies" or the green bell pepper or even asparagus character prevalent in many early cabernet sauvignons and sauvignon blancs. Implementation of better farming techniques, including the use of new clonal material, tighter spacing, better trellising (better air and sun penetration into the grapes), controlled canopies and judicious irrigation has allowed for fully ripe, highly evolved fruit.

Vinification techniques reflect the golden era of California winemaking. Winemakers are taking less and less credit for their successes. Far from the ego-driven wine styles of the North Coast, where a "signature style" is mandated by deep-pocket marketing types, here the attitude is more like "I have only to look to the vineyard to make good wine. With better fruit, we will have better wine."

The Robert Mondavi Winery is credited with the creation of the Central Coast Vineyard Team, or CCVT, which investigates ways to reduce pesticide use. Its Positive Points System measures integrated farm management and its positive environmental effects in Monterey as well as in San Luis Obispo and Santa Barbara County.

BERNARDUS WINERY

***Established* 1990 *Owner* Bernardus Marinus Pon *Production* 50,000 cases *Vineyard area* 52 acres (21 ha)**

Pon owned the oldest "wynkoper" distribution house in his native Holland and visited Bordeaux regularly to buy stock. One of his dreams was to create a red wine of equal quality to the finest from Bordeaux. He chose the Carmel Valley for its strong track record of producing intense, complex and long-lived cabernet sauvignon and merlot. The recently released Marinus shows great promise. His respect for nature is reflected in his vineyard approaches and has also led to the preservation of more than 300 live oaks on this former Native American land in the Cachagua Valley.

CALERA

***Established* 1975 *Owner* Josh Jensen *Production* 30,000 cases *Vineyard area* 47 acres (19 ha); 28 acres (11.3 ha) newly planted**

Early viognier pioneer and burgundy fanatic, Josh Jensen, chose Mount Harlan high up in the Gavilan Mountains for the site of his vineyard. He named this former limestone quarry and kiln, Calera, (Spanish for lime kiln). Jensen's early success with vineyard-designated pinot noir and chardonnay as well as America's first world-class viognier helped focus attention on San Benito County as a fine wine producing region. Calera single-vineyard pinot noirs are some of the longest lived in America, certainly rivalling their peers in the Côte d'Or.

ABOVE: The Big Sur coastline attracts numerous visitors but many remain unaware that it is just a short journey inland into the glorious wine region of Monterey County.

Regional Dozen

QUALITY WINES

Bernardus Marinus Cabernet Sauvignon/Merlot/Cabernet Franc
Calera Jensen Mount Harlan Pinot Noir
Galante Red Rose Hill Carmel Valley Cabernet Sauvignon
Joullian Carmel Valley Cabernet Sauvignon
Morgan Reserve Pinot Noir
Pisoni Pinot Noir

BEST VALUE WINES

Jekel FOS Reserve Chardonnay
J. Lohr Bay Mist Monterey White Riesling
Monterra San Bernabe Ranch Syrah
Morgan Monterey/Sonoma Sauvignon Blanc
Paraiso Chardonay
Ventana Gold Stripe Chardonnay

RIGHT: Well-tended vineyards in the Carmel Valley.

CHALONE

Established **1960** ***Owners*** **Château Lafite-Rothschild 50 percent, 12,000 shareholders 50 percent** ***Production*** **35,000 cases** ***Vineyard area*** **326 acres (132 ha)**

Winemaker Dan Karlsen modestly credits his well-drained limestone based soils, high altitudes and mature vines—not his talents—for the benchmark chenin blanc, chardonnay, pinot blanc and pinot noir. Despite his challenges—his remote vineyards are susceptible to gophers, birds, snakes and wild boar—he does manage to turn out outstanding wines. Chalone Vineyard is the oldest producing vineyard in Monterey County, has its own AVA, and is located 1,800 feet (549 m) above the Salinas Valley floor in the Gavilan Mountains.

GALANTE VINEYARDS

Established **1994** ***Owners*** **Galante family** ***Production*** **5,000 cases** ***Vineyard area*** **70 acres (28 ha)**

Jack Galante is a fifth-generation Californian. His grandfather, J. F. Devendorf, was the founder of Carmel. The family purchased this former cattle ranch in Carmel Valley in 1969 and in 1983, planted the vineyards, but Jack waited ten years before making his first release. He hired winemaker Greg Vita, a graduate of UC Davis, and vineyard manager Eliud Ortiz, a native of Guatemala, to complete the team. Estate wines include Blackjack Pasture, Red Rose Hill and Rancho Galante cabernet sauvignons. The Rancho Galante is drinkable right out of the gate; the others would benefit from a few years in the cellar, especially the more tannic Red Rose bottling. All three are intense, deeply fruited, rich, balanced wines that represent a benchmark for the region and for the state. Galante is also well known for its quality cut garden roses, grown beside the vines and shipped all over the country.

ABOVE: A saint's niche at Carmel Mission.

JOULLIAN

Established **1982** ***Owners*** **Ed Joullian and Dick Sias** ***Production*** **12,000 cases** ***Vineyard area*** **40 acres (16.2 ha)**

For the partnership of the Joullian and Sias families of Oklahoma City, this 655-acre (265-ha) estate in the heart of Carmel Valley is a dream come true. After extensive and expensive contouring and terracing, the families planted 40 acres (16.2 ha) to primarily bordeaux varietals, with a small area going to chardonnay, zinfandel and petite sirah. Winemaker Ridge Watson, who was apprenticed at Château Carbonnieux in the Graves district of Bordeaux, France is turning out truly world-class sauvignon blanc and cabernet sauvignon. He is tinkering with petite sirah because he likes what another "Ridge"—namely, Paul Draper's Ridge Vineyards—does with it.

MORGAN

Established **1982** ***Owners*** **Dan and Donna Lee** ***Production*** **50,000 cases** ***Vineyard area*** **65 acres (26.3 ha)**

Morgan chardonnay and pinot noirs have earned accolades for many years. Winemaker Dean De Korth, a burgundy fanatic—he worked with Olivier LeFlaive, Pierre Morey and Dominique Lafon before settling in Monterey—is best known for his Reserve Pinot Noir and Chardonnay. His newly released syrah and pinot gris are sure to keep the press humming and the consumers lining up at the door. Morgan is Dan's mother's maiden name. The vineyards are in the Santa Lucia Highlands.

PARAISO SPRINGS VINEYARDS

Established **1987** ***Owners*** **Rich and Claudia Smith** ***Production*** **20,000 cases** ***Vineyard area*** **400 acres (162 ha)**

The Smith family is very active in the wine grape-growing community locally, nationally and internationally. Their estate vineyard in the Santa Lucia Highlands is just two miles (3.2 km) from historic Soledad Mission, site of Monterey's first vineyard. Winemaker Zorn makes the benchmark riesling of the county. In fact, the bone-dry, rich, petrolly riesling caught the attention of connoisseurs around the globe. Answering to consumer demand, however, the winery recently reverted to an off-dry style. Paraiso Springs is renowned for its elegant, deeply flavored pinot noir, syrah, chardonnay and pinot blanc. Zorn makes Cobblestone Chardonnay, a joint venture with the Levine family (Arroyo Seco), as well as own-label Tria with winemaker Bill Knuttel of Chalk Hill.

Other significant producers in Monterey County include Cloninger, Hahn Estates/Smith & Hook Winery, Heller Estate/Durney Vineyards, Lockwood, Meador Estate, Pisoni and Robert Talbott Vineyards.

South Central Coast

PATRICK FARRELL MW

LEFT: A Wine Trail guides visitors in the area.

California's central coast runs from Santa Barbara in the south to Santa Cruz in the north. Two counties comprise the South Central Coast: San Luis Obispo (SLO) in the north and Santa Barbara (SB) in the south. Proximity to the cooling effect of coastal waters and breezes is particularly marked in these regions. The transverse orientation of the coastal mountain range allows the channeling of cool marine-influenced air inland, resulting in cool climates in the westerly reaches of the Santa Ynez, Santa Maria, Los Alamos and Edna valleys. Long growing seasons (up to 190 days), sunshine and relative warmth in the fall ensure ripe grapes with good retained natural acidities. Paso Robles, on the Coastal Range's easterly side, is less influenced by the Pacific and has a much warmer climate. The region has expanded rapidly and has attracted outside investment. Recognized for their quality, grapes from the central coast are shipped throughout the state.

San Luis Obispo County has four AVAs: Edna Valley, Arroyo Grande, Paso Robles and York Mountain. Edna Valley and Arroyo Grande are adjacent and have many shared characteristics, including a joint vintners' and grape growers' association. York Mountain is a small, one-winery AVA in western Paso Robles.

EDNA VALLEY AND ARROYO GRANDE

Located next to the charming university town of San Luis Obispo, Edna Valley was granted AVA status in 1982. Arroyo Grande is located just to its south. Together they cover 2,000 acres (810 ha). With missions nearby, viticulture in these regions dates back to 1859, when French immigrant Pierre Dalladet planted vines in San Luis Obispo.

Edna Valley's development as a wine-producing region really began in the late 1960s, with the Niven family being particularly prominent. The Nivens are owners of the 1,000-acre (405-ha) Paragon Vineyard and have formed two important strategic alliances, the first being a partnership with the publicly traded Chalone Wine Group in the formation of Edna Valley Winery in 1980. The most recent partnership occurred more than 10 years ago when Australia's giant Southcorp bought into the Seven Peaks Winery.

Arroyo Grande has also been involved in international partnerships. Maison Deutz was a 1982 Franco-American joint venture involving the Deutz Champagne house. Currently owned by other Frenchmen and renamed Laetitia, this one-time sparkling-wine-only specialist now also produces table wines.

Edna Valley is Region I–II on the Winkler-Amerine heat summation scale. The east-to-west valley opens up to the cooling effects of the Pacific Ocean at Morro Bay 15 miles (24 km) away. Arroyo Grande's climate varies significantly as one moves inland. Westerly Laetitia is only about 2 miles (3.2 km) from the Pacific and is Region I for most vintages. Talley is 8 miles (12.9 km) from the coast and is Region I–II. Saucelito Canyon is another 12 or so miles (about 19 km) inland and is a warm Region III. Soils consist of sandy and clay loams over limestone that was once under the ocean and contains abundant marine deposits.

Regional Best

QUALITY WINES

- Edna Valley Winery Reserve Chardonnay
- Laetitia Estate Pinot Noir Reserve
- Laetitia Cuvée "M" Sparkling Wine
- Saucelito Canyon Zinfandel
- Talley Reserve Pinot Noir, Chardonnay

BEST VALUE WINES

- Seven Peaks Chardonnay, Merlot, Shiraz
- Corbett Canyon Chardonnay, White Zinfandel, Cabernet Sauvignon
- Oupe Roussanne Edna Valley

Vines and wines

Edna Valley and Arroyo Grande represent a continuum of viticulture from the 1970s to the present era. Saucelito

BELOW: Laetitia vineyards where chardonnay, pinot blanc and pinot noir are the main plantings.

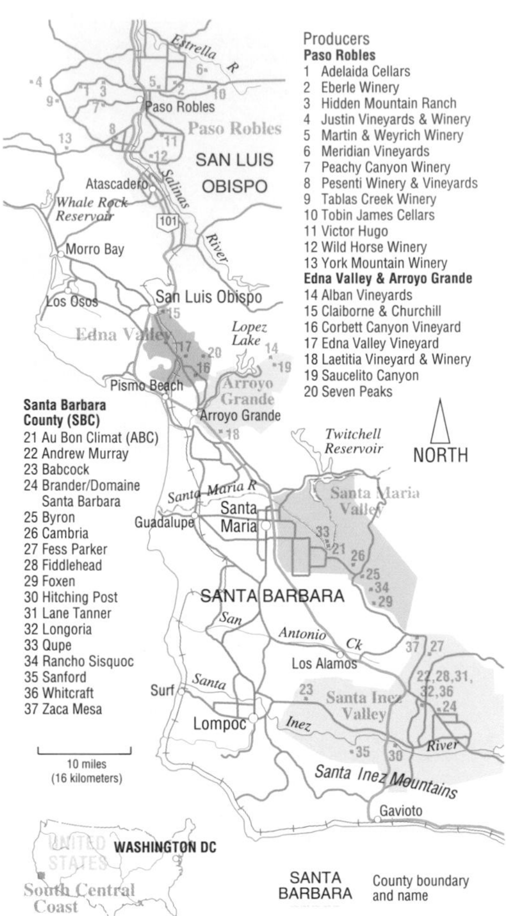

ABOVE RIGHT: Extensive vineyards near Paso Robles.

Canyon is an exception with its 100-year-old zinfandel vines. More recent plantings have included newer clones and altered spacing as in the rest of the state. Modern techniques mirror much of California with some notable exceptions. Maison Deutz brought classic champagne-production techniques to the region. These, along with traditional techniques from Burgundy, continue to be practiced at Laetitia by the French winemaker there. Seven Peaks has an Australian winemaker producing wines in the Roseworthy tradition.

ALBAN VINEYARDS

Established **1986** ***Owner*** **John Alban** ***Production*** **5,000 cases** ***Vineyard area*** **60 acres (24.3 ha)**

Rhône enthusiast John Alban reports having been "hooked" by his first Condrieu tasted during his studies at Fresno State University. A post-graduation stint in France's Rhône Valley further confirmed John's passion. Alban winery was the first all-rhône variety winery in California. Grenache, syrah, viognier and roussanne are produced. Wines are well made and good value.

RIGHT: A traditional wine decanter resting on its stand.

EDNA VALLEY VINEYARD

Established **1979** ***Owners*** **Chalone Wine Group and the Niven family** ***Production*** **100,000 cases** ***Vineyard area*** **1,000 acres (405 ha)**

The wines here are well made, well priced and reliable for chardonnay and pinot noir. A traditional-method sparkling wine available at the winery is also good.

SAUCELITO CANYON

Established **1974** ***Owners*** **Bill and Nancy Greenough** ***Production*** **2,000 cases** ***Vineyard area*** **8 acres (3.2 ha)**

Located in the upper and warmer reaches of Arroyo Grande, Saucelito Canyon boasts 100-year-old zinfandel vines. The zinfandel is rich and ripe, with characteristic brambly fruit that has tobacco and spice notes. It competes well with other examples statewide.

PASO ROBLES

Paso Robles, the largest of the San Luis Obispo County AVAs, consists of 20,000 acres (8,100 ha) planted. In 2004, 3 million cases were produced by 76 wineries. This represents remarkable growth, up from 6,500 acres (2,633 ha) and 25 wineries in 1994. Grapes are processed locally as well as being shipped throughout the state.

Here, the Coastal Range is oriented north to south, with only a small opening to the cooling effects of the Pacific Ocean at the Templeton Gap. Paso Robles is thus a warm region, with a history of producing better red wines, particularly full-throttle zinfandels, than whites.

Unlike Santa Barbara County, where the rich and famous from Hollywood may be found relaxing and riding horses in the latest fashions, Paso Robles is real cowboy country with nary a powdered and perfumed starlet in sight. Producers seem more blue collar as well, although corporate giant Beringer has a major stake in Paso Robles in Meridian. The hilly and somewhat cooler west side is divided from the flatter east side by Highway 46.

Paso Robles' vinous traditions date back to the eighteenth and nineteenth centuries. Just 8 miles (13 km) outside Paso Robles proper is the mission San Miguel, where the first grapes were grown in 1797. Current traditions of dry-farmed zinfandel grown on the west side's rolling hills were begun in the 1880s by Andrew York. French and Italian immigrants followed suit over the next several decades. Despite Prohibition, some vineyards were planted, on their own roots, in the 1920s only to succumb to a phylloxera outbreak during the 1940s. Vineyards were then replanted onto resistant Rupestris St George rootstock. Such vineyards are excellent sources of old-vine zinfandel and include Pesenti, Martinelli and the Dusi Ranch. The west side hills were preferred for vineyards as they provided some frost protection. Zinfandel was a favored variety partly because of its large second crop, which provided additional insurance against the first being hit by frost.

Growth occurred on the flatter, hotter and drier east side in the 1970s. Under the guidance of University of California at Davis' Professor Olmo, vineyards were planted on their own roots, with overhead sprinklers for irrigation and frost protection. Gary Eberle, then winemaker at Estrella River, was one of the first to plant syrah and cabernet sauvignon. The 1980s saw continued growth on both the east and west sides. Justin was established on the west side and drip irrigation and cabernet franc were introduced. In the late 1980s, Martin Brothers and Caparone introduced Italian varieties such as nebbiolo, sangiovese and pinot grigio. In 1989, phylloxera biotype-A (not the genetically changed biotype-B that had already struck Napa and Sonoma) struck Paso Robles.

Planting and replanting occurred through the 1990s. The region did well as the nation turned to red wine. Zinfandel, cabernet and merlot plantings all increased. New rootstocks, new clones, new varieties and higher-density plantings were all the rage. Canopy management had become a common catchword. The 1990s also saw the arrival of the Perrin family from the famed Château Beaucastel in southern France. The family teamed with importer Robert Haas of Vineyard Brands. The new venture, Tablas Creek, includes rhône varieties imported from Beaucastel and has shown early promise.

Paso Robles is the warmest of California's coastal valleys and stands at Region III–IV on the Winkler-Amerine scale, but this is just part of the story. In summertime, daytime maximum temperatures may reach as high as 100°F (38°C) but the minimum temperature on the same day may be as low as 45°F (7°C). Diurnal variation is marked, usually 40–50°F (4–10°C). Cool air makes its way through the Templeton Gap in the late afternoon to early evening. By mid-evening, a sweatshirt or sweater are needed for outdoors. The early morning is very cool and thus it takes a while for the land and vines to heat up.

The west side is hilly and somewhat cooler than the flat east side. Well-drained soils are of low-to-moderate vigor. Sandy or clay loam soils are based on the degradation of granite, serpentine, shale or sandstone. Those based upon shale are most common. Rainfall occurs mostly during the winter. Western vineyards average 30 inches (76 cm), while the east side receives a paltry 9 inches (23 cm) annually.

LEFT: A picnic at Meridian Vineyards, Paso Robles.

Vines and wines

Planted varieties include zinfandel, chardonnay and the classic varieties from Bordeaux, the Rhône Valley and central–northern Italy. Older, phylloxera-resistant plantings are on Rupestris St George rootstock. Own-rooted vines are either scheduled for replanting or are doomed to repeat history. A host of resistant rootstocks is being utilized, including 110R, 140R, 1103P and 3309C. Nematodes can cause problems in this area and this may influence the choice of rootstock.

Overhead sprinklers are used for frost protection, particularly on the east side. New plantings tend to be at higher densities than the old 8 x 10 feet (2.4 x 3.1 m)

Regional Best

QUALITY WINES

Hidden Mountain Ranch (Dusi Ranch Vineyard) Zinfandel
Ridge Zinfandel
Justin Vineyards Justinification
Eberle Syrah, Viognier
Meridian Syrah

BEST VALUE WINES

Pesenti Estate Zinfandel
Martin & Weyrich Moscoto
Peachy Canyon Incredible Red Bin 106

BELOW: New plantings at Paso Robles.

RIGHT: Overhead-trained sauvignon blanc vines in the Santa Ynez Valley, California.

plantings. Since the climate is warm and dry, there is little disease pressure and many growers are opting for an organic approach. Cover crops and decreased spraying are popular measures. Netting is increasingly used to protect vines from bird damage.

Techniques vary little from other parts of California. Oak is commonly used as a seasoning. Better efforts are being made to use oak in a supporting role and to allow the underlying fruit to speak for the wine. Many smaller producers are making their wines with an eye to minimizing such interventions as fining and filtering. Many also try to keep sulfur dioxide at a minimum.

EBERLE WINERY

Established **1983** ***Owner*** **Gary Eberle** ***Production*** **25,000 cases** ***Vineyard area*** **42 acres (17 ha)**

Gary Eberle, once a lineman on Penn State's football team, was involved in the planting at the Estrella River Winery and was one of the first to introduce syrah to the region. His wines are good across the board and very reliable, and his ripe-styled cabernet ages very well. The syrah and viognier are regional standards.

ABOVE: The crest of Martin & Weyrich Winery.

MARTIN & WEYRICH WINERY

Established **1981** ***Owners*** **David and Mary Weyrich** ***Production*** **28,000 cases** ***Vineyard area*** **190 acres (77 ha)**

Among the first to specialize in Italian varieties, Martin & Weyrich produces moscato, pinot grigio, sangiovese and nebbiolo. The moscato is delightfully floral, fizzy, somewhat sweet and well priced. Pinot grigio is cleanly made from Paso Robles and Santa Barbara fruit, which lend natural acidity to this nicely balanced wine. Reds have been rustic.

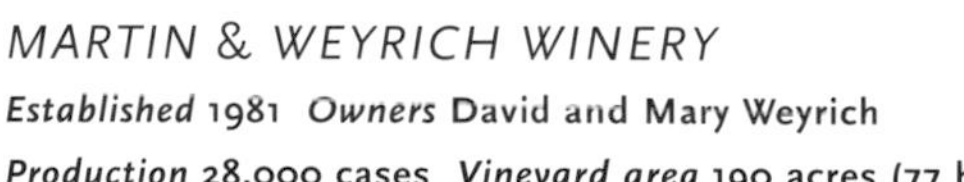

PEACHY CANYON WINERY

Established **1988** ***Owners*** **Doug and Nancy Beckett** ***Production*** **30,000 cases** ***Vineyard area*** **88 acres (36 ha)**

Although good bordeaux varietals and blended wines are made here, the real interest lies in zinfandel. Peachy Canyon has a well-deserved reputation for putting some wonderful zinfandel fruit in the bottle. Expansion is in the works with the purchase of Twin Hills Winery.

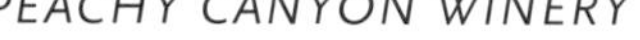

TOBIN JAMES CELLARS

Established **1987** ***Owners*** **Tobin James and the Silver family** ***Production*** **20,000 cases** ***Vineyard area*** **16 acres (6.5 ha)**

Tobin James was formerly the winemaker at Peachy Canyon and continues to produce some of the region's most exciting zinfandels. The wines tend to be bold and firm with piercing fruit. Chardonnay and cabernet are less successful here. Playing off the legend of Jesse James and the shared surname is the James Gang Reserve Zinfandel.

WILD HORSE WINERY

Established **1983** ***Owners*** **Ken and Tricia Volks** ***Production*** **85,000 case** ***Vineyard area*** **50 acres (20 ha)**

Wild Horse is a reliable source of well-made and well-priced merlot and cabernet sauvignon. Syrah and mourvèdre are relatively recent, and successful, additions. Both Rhône-inspired wines are well structured with true varietal character and good intensity of ripe fruit.

YORK MOUNTAIN WINERY

Established **1882** ***Owner*** **Max Goldman** ***Production*** **4,000 cases** ***Vineyard area*** **5 acres (2 ha)**

Established by Andrew York as the Ascension Winery, York Mountain Winery is the region's oldest winery in continuous operation and was the first commercial winery in the region. Owing to the winery's location in far western and cooler Paso Robles, and its long history, York Mountain Winery was awarded its own AVA in 1983.

SANTA BARBARA COUNTY (SBC)

Santa Barbara AVA's are Santa Ynez Valley, Santa Maria Valley; and the new AVA Santa Rita Hills with 500 acres (202 ha) bearing fruit. The Santa Barbara wine industry is growing rapidly, up from 46 wineries in 1998 to 76 in 2004. Located 90 miles (145 km) north of Los Angeles, Santa Barbara's vineyards seem far removed from the hustle and bustle of "La-La Land." Half-an-hour's drive northeast of beautiful Santa Barbara, the region is unusual in that the Coastal Range is perpendicular to the coastline. Cool maritime air and morning fogs yield some of California's cooler vineyards.

This expanding region consists of 21,000 acres (7,290 ha) of vine plantings producing in excess of a million cases of wine each year. Chardonnay and pinot noir are the primary varieties, though fine examples of both rhône and bordeaux varieties may also be found. Some 55 percent of the region's harvest is crushed elsewhere. Local wine volume increased 230 percent between 1992 and 1998.

Although there were vineyards for Santa Barbara's mission at the end of the eighteenth century, the region currently planted did not participate in the statewide wine boom of the mid-to-late nineteenth century. In 1892, nearby Carpenteria claimed the world's largest grapevine, a 50-year-old mission vine with a trunk 9 feet (2.7 m) in circumference, producing up to 10 tons (9 t) annually. Novelty aside, modern history dates back to the early 1960s with plantings in the Santa Maria and Santa Ynez valleys. Wineries followed in the 1970s. Vineyards were initially planted with a host of varieties, cabernet sauvignon being the most commonly planted. The cool climate, coupled with excessive canopies, made for unripe, vegetative cabernet, which damaged the region's reputation.

With the nationwide boom in chardonnay during the 1970s and 1980s, the regional reputation improved markedly, as chardonnay does very well in the cool climate. Pinot noir plantings increased with critical

The wines they are a-changin'

Wine styles continue to evolve in the golden state. Top white burgundy was used as a model by quality-seeking California winemakers from the 1960s onwards. Ripe, warm-climate fruit was subjected to the full set of winemaking techniques employed in Burgundy to flesh out cool-climate chardonnay; the resulting wines were often too rich and alcoholic.

Phylloxera-induced replanting and changes in fashion have shifted top-quality chardonnay growing to much cooler regions such as the Russian River Valley, Carneros and Santa Barbara County. A more gentle hand from the winemaker, together with crisper, cooler climate fruit has led to the development of more balanced yet distinctive wines which compete with the best chardonnay worldwide.

BELOW: *Byron Estate vineyards cling to the slopes, Santa Maria Valley.*

acclaim. Vineyards expanded throughout the remainder of the century. Large concerns from northern California were drawn to the region. Robert Mondavi purchased Byron and greatly expanded plantings. Kendall-Jackson established Cambria while Beringer planted chardonnay and pinot noir for the Meridian brand.

Santa Barbara sits at the demarcation between central and southern California. The natural expectation is that vineyards here would be warmer than those north of San Francisco, but they are not. In fact, westerly vineyards in the Santa Maria and Santa Ynez valleys are among the coolest in California. Broccoli ripens in the very cool, far-western portions of these coastal valleys, but wine grapes don't.

ABOVE: *Outside of Burgundy, pinot noir is making headway only in New Zealand and the US.*

The opening of the Santa Maria Valley is much larger than the Santa Ynez Valley, which accounts for cooler conditions at similar distances from the coast. Thus as one moves farther inland, conditions change from untenable for grape growing to Region I on the heat summation scale to Region II. As coastal influences fall off inland, temperatures rise rapidly, yielding Regions III and IV.

There are mesas and rolling hills with altitudes to 1,500 feet (457.5 m). Higher altitudes and northerly slopes will be cooler, although proximity to the coast is still the most important factor. Growers are increasingly planting on hillsides. Santa Barbara County is dry, only receiving from 8 to 10 inches (20 to 25 cm) of rain a year, mostly from November to March. Soils are variable, tending toward sandy loams. The growing season is long. In 1997, budbreak was a little early, occurring on the first of February. The harvest of early varieties such as chardonnay began in early September, while syrah was harvested several weeks later. In 1999, the length of time from budbreak to harvest was between 170 and 192 days, depending on location and variety.

More so than in northern California, Santa Barbara is prone to some of the warmest temperatures during the fall. Maximum temperatures may be 85–90°F (29–32°C), cooling off to 50°F (10°C) at night. This gives an extended growing season that allows chardonnay, pinot noir and syrah to ripen. Vintage influences which varieties ripen to their optimum.

Regional Best

- Au Bon Climat Bien Nacido Pinot Noir
- Babcock Grand Cuvée
- Brander Cuvée Natalie Sauvignon Blanc
- Bonaccorsi Syrah
- Brewer Clifton Syrah
- Clos Pepe Pinot Noir
- Gainey Vineyards Riesling
- Hitching Post Pinot Noir
- Longoria Cuvée Blues Cabernet Franc
- Melville Pinot Noir

Vines and wines

Chardonnay here combines ripeness with good-to-very-good retained natural acidity. Most are barrel fermented with the better wines having a balance between apple, pear or tropical fruit notes and oak. Many other white varieties are treated like chardonnay with the better efforts enabling the fruit to show through the influence of new oak.

Pinot noir in Santa Barbara has had a spiced-tea note added to very good underlying berry fruit. This seems to have been a function of planting material. New clones do not have the herbal notes and are nicely perfumed. Overall, the style is fairly robust and occasionally somewhat rustic. Better producers, such as Au Bon Climat, Longoria or Lane Tanner, produce some of California's best efforts from this elusive variety.

Merlot, cabernet franc and cabernet sauvignon are certainly less ripe than their Napa counterparts. Herbaceousness has been problematic in the past but planting on warmer sites and better canopy management is yielding riper fruit. Syrah shows promise here, exemplified by Qupe's string of successes. Warmer vintages add smoked-meat aromas to clean-berry fruit. Cooler vintages tend toward peppery notes. The better wines have good acidity and balanced tannins. Some new to the variety, particularly with the 1997 and 1998 vintages, had problems with dominant green tannins. Styles will certainly evolve as newer clones and plantings mature.

Vineyards planted during the 1970s through to the early 1990s were not planted on rootstock. Phylloxera was discovered in 1994 but has spread slowly on the sandy soils. New plantings were at higher densities, involved a variety of rootstocks, new varieties and different clonal selections of such standards as chardonnay and pinot noir.

AU BON CLIMAT (ABC)

Established **1982** ***Owners*** **Morgan and Jim Clendenen** ***Production*** **24,320 cases** ***Vineyard area*** **43 acres (17 ha)**

Jim Clendenen produces some of California's best pinot noir and chardonnay. His pinot noir brims with

berry fruit and shows intense yet delicate flavors, balance and length. His chardonnay demonstrates power and finesse, while retaining good acidity and balance. Additionally, Jim is part of the brains trust that combines the talents of ABC, Qupe, Makor, Il Podere de Olivos, Vita Nova and the Hitching Post. Other ventures include Vita Nova and Ici La Bas. Vita Nova has been successful with Italian varieties and bordeaux blends. Its Acceomicus, a blend of petite verdot and cabernet sauvignon, shows nice cassis fruit.

LEFT: A winery sign invites visitors to sample the wares of this large estate.

BABCOCK

Established **1984** ***Owners*** **the Babcock family** ***Production*** **12,000 cases** ***Vineyard area*** **70 acres (28 ha)**

Brian Babcock's chardonnay and pinot noir, especially the Grande Cuvée, are excellent wines. Brian also produced fine dry rieslings until phylloxera struck. The 11 Oaks Sauvignon Blanc is one of the state's best, and Italian varieties show promise.

FOXEN

Established **1987** ***Owners*** **Bill Wathen and Richard Dore** ***Production*** **12,000 cases** ***Vineyard area*** **15 acres (6 ha)**

Foxen produces bold, well-crafted wines. Chardonnay is uniformly excellent; pinot noir is muscular and ages well. Foxen's bordeaux blends prove that given the right site, these varieties can do well here. The barrel-fermented chenin blanc is one of the best examples in the state.

HITCHING POST

Established **1991** ***Owners*** **Frank Ostini and Gray Hartley** ***Production*** **2,600 cases** ***Vineyard area*** **NA**

Frank Ostini is owner and chef of the two restaurants for which the wines are named. The smokiness from the grill matches game notes in the very well made pinot noir to a tee. The local pinots are a perfect match for barbecued meats, particularly steak and ostrich.

LONGORIA

Established **1982** ***Owners*** **Rick and Diana Longoria** ***Production*** **3,500 cases** ***Vineyard area*** **8 acres (3.2 ha)**

Rick Longoria's pinot noir is one of the region's best, as are his merlot and cabernet franc. The 2001 Pinot Noir Reserve from the Bien Nacido vineyard combines expansive notes of smoky game, berry fruit and oak on the palate with good balance and length of finish.

QUPE

Established **1982** ***Owner*** **Bob Lindquist** ***Production*** **17,000 cases** ***Vineyard area*** **12 acres (4.9 ha)**

Qupe means golden poppy in the local Chumash Indian language. Bob Lindquist, the rock-solid counterpoint to Jim Clendenen's flamboyance, produces very good chardonnay, and is one of California's leading "Rhône Rangers." He also makes fine viognier, syrah, marsanne and red rhône blends. His syrah is the region's benchmark, with berry aromatics and smoked-meat flavors framed in oak.

ZACA MESA

Established **1973** ***Owners*** **the Cushman family** ***Production*** **37,617 cases** ***Vineyard area*** **247 acres (100 ha)**

Winemaker Dan Gehrs, who arrived several years ago, is making good chardonnay, viognier and roussanne. Even better is the syrah, which is known for intensity of berry, smoky flavors reminiscent of the northern Rhône.

Other significant producers in South Central Coast include Claiborne & Churchill, Corbett Canyon Vineyard, Laetitia Vineyard & Winery, Seven Peaks (Edna Valley and Arroyo Grande); Adelaida Cellars, Hidden Mountain Ranch, Justin Vineyards and Winery, Meridian Vineyards, Pesenti Winery and Vineyards, Tablas Creek Winery, Victor Hugo (Paso Robles); Andrew Murray, Brander/Domaine Santa Barbara, Byron, Cambria, Fiddlehead, Lane Tanner, Ranchio Sisquoc and Whitcraft (Santa Barbara County).

LEFT: Chardonnay, pinot noir, and syrah are the main grapes grown on Cambria Winery's sweeping slopes.

Southern California

PATRICK FARRELL MW

Southern California has a rich wine history. Production flourished in Los Angeles and Orange counties through the early part of the 1900s until the advent of Pierce's disease, then aptly named Anaheim disease, wiped out commercial grape growing in Orange County. Escalating real estate prices and suburban sprawl led to the demise of commercial viticulture in Los Angeles County. Other than curiosities such as good cabernet sauvignon grown in Beverly Hills or Malibu, Temecula and Cucamonga are Southern California's AVAs of significance. Ever-growing metropolitan Los Angeles chips away at Cucamonga's old vines—first planted in 1838—offering them an uncertain future. Pierce's disease has ravaged Temecula and places this improving region in great peril. Yet, both regions are important from historical and current viticultural perspectives.

Regional Best

QUALITY WINES

Hart Barbera, Mourvèdre, Syrah, Zinfandel
Thornton Vintage Blanc de Blanc
Mount Palomar Cortese
Orfila Syrah, Viognier

BEST VALUE WINES

Hart Grenache Rosé
Galleano Zinfandel, Grenache Rosé
Mount Polomar Port

Los Angeles has long been the population and commercial center of California. The state's first wine industry, which retained primacy until the latter nineteenth century, developed here. Cucamonga was known for strong, sweet wines; sandy soil discouraged phylloxera and encouraged expansion in the late nineteenth century, increasing four-fold 1870–1890. As the greater Los Angeles area grew during the twentieth century, vineyard area shrank from 20,000 acres (8,093 ha) in 1960 to 1,000 (405 ha) in 1997.

BELOW: Vines displaying fall color, Southern California.

Temecula's experimentation with vineyards began in the 1960s. Industrialist Ely Callaway first planted vines in 1969 and by 1974 had a winery. However, Temecula languished in the shadow of Napa, Sonoma and Santa Barbara counties. Quality has been improving, but the discovery of Pierce's disease, and especially of a new vector, the glassy-winged sharpshooter, has cast a pall over the region.

The San Gabriel and San Bernardino Mountains—in the greater Los Angeles area—create a favorable climate and a smog-causing inversion layer even though they are 50 miles (80 km) from the coast. The cooling effects of the Pacific Ocean yields a temperature gradient from the cool coast to the very warm mountain foothills.

The Cucamonga Valley sits near the eastern edge of this plain and is very warm, though evenings are cooled by Pacific breezes. At the Temecula Valley cooler air from the coast comes some 22 miles (35 km) inland through a gap in the mountains. Temecula is a warm region; its altitude of 1,400–1,600 feet (427–488 m) also contributes to the moderate climate.

Vines and wines

The Cucamonga Valley still contains 1,000 acres (405 ha) of vines, with old, dry-farmed vines maintaining such rhône varieties as mourvèdre, syrah, grenache, and cinsault. Old-vine mission grapes are still found and provide a vital link to the past. Deep sandy soils have protected the vines from phylloxera. The absence of citrus and other hosts for the leafhopper have also kept Pierce's disease away, though not from Temecula.

Viticulture in Temecula has seen quality improvement over the past decade, particularly with new varieties. Although chardonnay has been successful—65 percent of plantings—the shift to rhône and Italian varieties better suited to the warm climate has yielded the best wines to date. Viognier here has been high quality, clean and fruity with variable amounts of oak. Chenin blanc produces a clean, floral, fruity wine with good retained acidity. Cabernet sauvignon and merlot from Temecula—though not as successful as petite sirah or zinfandel—have improved and produce rich, alcoholic, and tannic wines.

Old-vine palomino and several Portuguese varieties provide excellent material for fortified wines from Cucamonga. Sherry- and port-style wines have richness and length of finish. They are some of the state's best.

Sparkling, sweet, and fortified wines are all represented in Cucamonga and Temecula, with table wines having the greatest economic impact.

The real excitement comes from other varieties. Cucamonga produces alcoholic, full-throttle rhône-style wines from old-vine grenache, syrah, cinsault, carignane and mourvèdre. Temecula has also produced good wines from the same rhône varieties, as well as barbera, sangiovese, and cortese.

CUCAMONGA VALLEY

The Cucamonga Valley's 1,000 acres (405 ha) has vines scattered amid freeways, the Ontario airport, industrial developments and new housing. The city of Rancho Cucamonga is its hub. This warm region sits 30–45 miles (48–72 km) east on the I-15 interstate from Temecula. Though in decline as a viticultural region, it remains an important source of old-vine grenache, mourvèdre, syrah, zinfandel and mission for the state. Cucamonga fruit is shipped to winemakers in Temecula, Napa, Sonoma and on the Central Coast.

GALLEANO WINERY

Established **1927** ***Owner*** **Don Galleano** ***Production*** **9,000 cases** ***Vineyard area*** **100 acres (40.1 ha) owned; 500 acres (202 ha) leased**

Galleano is a producer of note—it is a resource for dry-farmed, old-vine rhône varieties and zinfandel. The Galleano winery and housing buildings are historic landmarks under siege from industrial expansion. Wine prices are very reasonable. The grenache rosé has attracted many medals; it is dry, clean and packed with peppery, berry grenache. Zinfandel, grenache, carignane and mourvèdre—barrel and vat—demonstrate purity of varietal fruit and great character.

TEMECULA VALLEY

Temecula in the Luiseno Indian language means "where the sun shines through the mist." Cool air from the Pacific moderates temperatures from late afternoon via the Rainbow and Santa Margarita gaps in the coastal mountain ranges. Well-drained granite soils and low rainfall necessitate irrigation. Phylloxera has not been a problem here, despite many own-rooted vines. Pierce's disease remains the primary challenge to the more than 3,000 acres (1,214 ha) of vines and 28 varieties. More than 200 acres (80 ha) were lost in 1999 to the glassy-winged sharpshooter with about 30 percent of vines affected.

LEFT: A major advantage of mechanical harvesting is that it can be carried out 24 hours a day.

CILURZO VINEYARD & WINERY

Established **1968 (vineyard), 1978 (winery)** ***Owner*** **Vincenzo Cilurzo** ***Production*** **10,000 cases** ***Vineyard area*** **40 acres (16.1 ha)**

The Cilurzo family runs a pleasant tasting room. Wine quality is much improved in recent years while prices remain reasonable. The chardonnay, sauvignon blanc, chenin blanc and old-vine zinfandel all drink well. Red wines, including merlot, reserve merlot and petite sirah Reserve, demonstrate ripe fruit, power and balance. The late-harvest petite sirah is a delight.

HART WINERY

Established **1974 (vineyard), 1980 (winery)** ***Owners*** **Hart family** ***Production*** **4,000 cases** ***Vineyard area*** **11 acres (4.5 ha)**

Hart has a reputation for the best quality production in Temecula. Every wine has balance and delightful fruit that is allowed to take center stage, with judicious use of oak. The grenache rosé is one of California's best blush wines. Viognier demonstrates wonderful apricot aromatics with refreshing acidity and balance. Red rhône varieties are all well made, as is barbera. With rare exceptions, cellar-door prices represent very good value.

SAN PASQUAL VALLEY

Located 15 miles (24 km) from the Pacific Ocean, the San Pasqual Valley AVA is cooler than either Temecula or Cucamonga. This is the newest up-and-coming area.

ORFILA VINEYARDS & WINERY

Established **1994** ***Owner*** **Alejandro Orfila** ***Production*** **10,000 cases** ***Vineyard area*** **40 areas (16 ha)**

Orfila's wines have been turning heads in recent years. Its syrah and viognier have had rave reviews and won handfuls of medals. The merlot and sangiovese are also well done.

Other producers of note in southern California include J. Filippi Winery, Callaway Vineyard & Winery, Maurice Carrie Vineyard & Winery, Mount Palomar Winery, Temecula Crest Winery and Thornton Winery.

ABOVE: *Tending the vines at Brimstone Hill Winery on the Shawangunk Wine Trail, New York.*

RIGHT: *Riesling grapes, among the earliest grown in the Eastern United States.*

EASTERN UNITED STATES

PATRICK FARRELL MW

In the early 1990s the wine industry in the eastern United States was restricted to a few isolated vintners producing regional curiosities with a modest local following. Aggressively flavored and usually sweet, wines were almost always made from native American grapes (principally *Vitis labrusca*) and/or French–American hybrids. Today the European *Vitis vinifera* dominates the east and its wines are attracting critical acclaim, both internationally and in upscale restaurants.

The whites showed the earliest promise, especially riesling, chardonnay and the hybrids seyval and vidal. More recently, however, red wines—cabernet sauvignon, cabernet franc and merlot—have also improved. The rise of the region's best is an inspiring tale that combines equal parts technology, foresight, good farming and good fortune.

History

Wine has been made in the US since Europeans arrived. The colonists found grapes in the new land—there are more grape varieties in the region between the Atlantic coast and the Rocky Mountains than anywhere else on earth. Unfortunately, these grapes produced wine with unappealing aromas and flavors, described as "foxy." The current scientific view is that the culprit is o-amino acetophenone. European cuttings were brought to Virginia in 1619, and for 350 years America struggled to establish a viable commercial wine industry. Freezing winters and hot, humid summers took their toll, but the worst enemy was disease. While native grapes were resistant to Pierce's disease, black rot, phylloxera, mildews and other indigenous fungal problems, the European imports were not.

Once phylloxera was brought under control in the late 1800s, California's wine industry soared. In the cooler, damper eastern states, *vinifera* vines remained an impossible dream and viticulturists turned to hybrids. With improved vineyard practices, the industry began to flourish, particularly around Lake Erie and the Finger Lakes.

Yet before the boom had really begun, it was all over. In 1920 the 18th Amendment to the Constitution of the United States was enacted, prohibiting the manufacture, sale, transportation or importation of alcoholic beverages. Prohibition lasted until 1933, when the 21st Constitutional Amendment, repealing the 18th, was passed. During the 13 dry years, thousands of wineries across

America were forced to shut; a hundred or so in California and New York survived by making sacramental wines for the clergy, medicinal wines for pharmacies, wine-based health "tonics" and fresh grape juice concentrate. Some wineries pressed grapes into "wine bricks" for sale to home winemakers—heads of households were allowed to make 200 gallons (757 l) of wine annually for personal use.

With Prohibition repealed, California began to rebuild its wine industry. In the east, progress was slow—vineyards had been ripped out, winemaking equipment broken, winemaking skills forgotten. Until farm winery Acts were passed (mostly in the 1970s), state winery licenses were prohibitively expensive for all but the largest wineries. State and local laws regulated a host of activities such as days and times wineries could open and they could not sell wine direct to consumers (see below).

Leon Adams, in The Wines of America, writes that the American wine industry was "reborn in ruins." Many eastern wineries replaced native grape varieties with hybrids. Philip Wagner, founder of Boordy Vineyards in Maryland, helped develop and promote hybrids as a more palate-pleasing alternative to the labrusca grapes. But they were still a long way from the flavor profile of wines from Europe or California.

Change in the east came via an émigré from the Ukraine. Dr Konstantin Frank had successfully grown *vinifera* grapes back home—freezing winters could not be the reason European vines died in eastern America, he said. Disease and pests were the problem, and these could be controlled by modern science.

One of the few to listen was Charles Fournier. Formerly chief winemaker at Veuve Clicquot, Fournier came to Gold Seal Vineyards in New York's Finger Lakes in 1934. Gold Seal, founded as the Urbana Wine Company in 1865, had prospered until Prohibition, and Fournier's mission was to recapture its former greatness. Fournier hired Frank in 1953, and together they began grafting grapes onto cold-resistant rootstock found locally and in Canada; they also initiated new trellis-training methods.

In 1957, when temperatures around the Finger Lakes dropped to –25°F (–4°C) about a third of the buds on local native and hybrid vines perished, but the *vinifera* vines that Frank and Fournier had planted were relatively unscathed. Winemaking on the eastern coast suddenly shifted course.

ABOVE: New York City is only about 40 miles (65 km) south of the Hudson River AVA.

It was almost 30 years before various states in the east began to cultivate vines in earnest. Virginia maintained a modest wine industry until Prohibition, but struggled to regain momentum after Repeal (early vintners were Thomas Jefferson and George Washington). Only in the past decade or so has growth surged: in 1976, for example, Virginia had six wineries; by 1999 it had 60.

Ninety percent of all American wine is produced in California. With the remaining 10 percent divided among the other 47 wine-producing states, the output from each is a comparative trickle. For example, Sakonnet, the largest winery in New England, produces 50,000 cases a year—the output for a medium-sized California winery. An average eastern winery turns out 6,000–8,000 cases annually. Yet production continues at an astonishing rate. In 1995, for example, Virginia produced 75,000 cases; by 1998 the figure was 214,340 cases. Other states may soon be producing wine commercially. Vermont, whose climate was considered too extreme for viticulture, has recently seen successful plantings of *vinifera*.

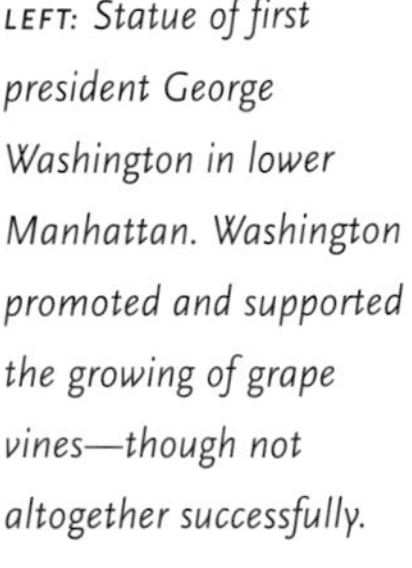

LEFT: Statue of first president George Washington in lower Manhattan. Washington promoted and supported the growing of grape vines—though not altogether successfully.

Factors driving the extraordinary recent boom include the strong economy of the late 1980s and 1990s, technological advances, improvements in winemaking techniques and vineyard practices, the lifting of some restrictive laws, and the increased education and interest of consumers. Support and assistance from state governments, in particular New York and Virginia, and scientific and practical help from Cornell University and Virginia Institute of Technology, have also played critical roles.

Landscape and climate

There are three distinct viticultural areas: Benchlands, Atlantic Uplands, and Mountains. The Benchlands are benches of sand, sediment, and stone formed from debris left by drifting glaciers thousands of years ago. The Benchlands include the coastal sections of Rhode Island, Long Island, New Jersey, Connecticut, Virginia and southeastern Massachusetts. Weather here is usually temperate. Farther inland, the viticultural region around Lake Erie very much resembles the Benchlands.

The Atlantic Uplands is a vast plateau between the coastal zones of the Atlantic Ocean and the eastern mountain ranges. The Uplands has mineral-rich, well-drained soils and a relatively long growing season. Viticultural Uplands include northern New Jersey, the Delaware River Valley, much of Pennsylvania, Maryland, northern and central Virginia, Connecticut, and the Hudson River Valley and Finger Lakes regions of New York.

The Mountains' high altitudes and harsh climate make grape growing difficult, but in certain isolated microclimates in the mountains of Virginia and central Pennsylvania the right combination of soil and sunlight provides a hospitable environment for vines.

I know never to take a wine for granted. Drawing a cork is like attendance at a concert or at a play that one knows well, when there is all the uncertainty of no two performances ever being quite the same. That is why the French say, "There are no good wines, only good bottles."

GERALD ASHER, *On Wine, 1982.*

Vines and wines

The best white grapes in the east include chardonnay, with a wide stylistic range, although wines lack the fruitiness of California wine. Riesling (dry, semidry, or sweet) is well-suited to the cooler regions around Lake Erie and the Finger Lakes. Gewürztraminer, especially from New England and the Finger Lakes areas, can yield fragrant and delicate wines. Seyval blanc can resemble a fragrant blend of chardonnay and pinot blanc. But vidal blanc promises most—especially grapes from the Finger Lakes or the mountains of Virginia—as a late-harvest or icewine with intense honeyed flavors and bracing acidity. Vignoles also makes outstanding late-harvest and icewine.

The best red grapes include merlot, the dominant red in Virginia and on Long Island, where it can produce full-bodied lively single-varietal wines and is important in red blends. Cabernet franc is often quite thin and herbaceous, but is improving. Sometimes good as a single varietal, cabernet sauvignon is at its best in bordeaux-style blends. Pinot noir is starting to show but is very dependent on a good weather, full ripeness and low yields—as well as superior winemaking.

Laws

Laws regulating the marketing, sales and distribution of wine are extremely complex. One lasting effect of Prohibition is that the regulation of liquor laws remains

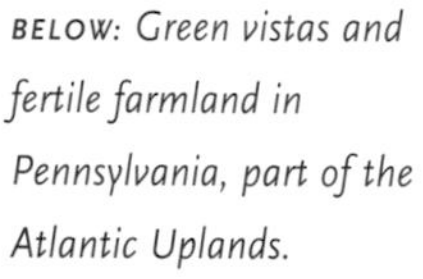

BELOW: *Green vistas and fertile farmland in Pennsylvania, part of the Atlantic Uplands.*

under the jurisdiction of individual states, resulting in a frustrating tangle that varies from state to state, even community to community.

Nationally, wine is under the control of the Bureau of Alcohol, Tobacco and Firearms (BATF) which regulates the way it is taxed, classified, marketed, labeled, sold and consumed. Joining BATF regulations are state and local statutes, with the infamous three-tier marketing system that links manufacturers (producers, vintners, *négociants*), wholesalers/distributors and retailers. Encouraged by these last groups, most states forbid or partially restrict shipment of wine direct to consumers, which is most harmful to wineries in the east. With so many states, and so many different wineries, allowing sales direct from winery to consumer seems like the logical solution, but powerful lobby groups resist rationalization of the laws.

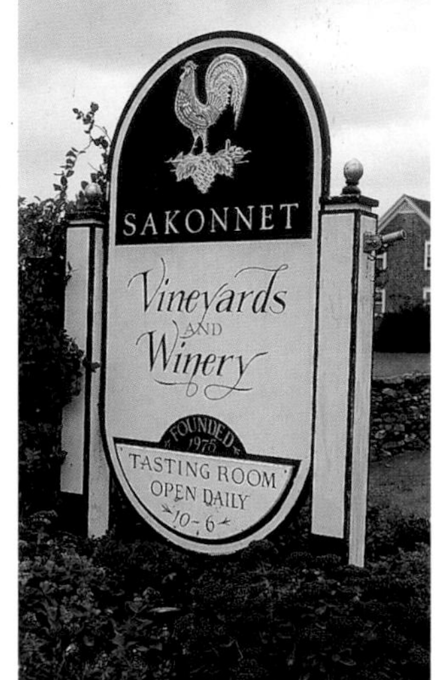

LEFT: A vineyard sign welcomes visitors to the winery of New England's largest producer.

New York State

New York state is arguably the most promising wine-producing state in the east. Along with Virginia, it has led the eastern states in wine production since the repeal of Prohibition. Locals even seem to have acquired a taste for the foxy wines produced in the early days. Although wine production goes back 170 years, two-thirds of the state's 150 wineries have been established since 1985. The industry is a work in progress; certain varietals, for example, riesling from the Finger Lakes, may be better suited to the east than to West Coast climes.

BEDELL CELLARS

Established **1980** ***Owners*** **John and Susan Bedell** ***Production*** **8,500 cases** ***Vineyard area*** **30 acres (12 ha)**

John "Kip" Bedell began full-time winemaking in 1990 and has had a great influence on other Long Island vintners, particularly in overcoming the variability of eastern growing seasons. His merlot, chardonnay, cabernet and a riesling dessert wine ("Eis") are outstanding.

FOX RUN VINEYARDS

Established **1990** ***Owners*** **Scott Osborne and Andy Hale** ***Production*** **14,000 cases** ***Vineyard area*** **50 acres (20 ha)**

One of Finger Lake's most exciting wineries, Fox Run was bought by Scott Osborne in 1994. Canadian-born winemaker Peter Bell was trained in Australia (at Charles Sturt University). Fox Run's aromatic and crisp riesling demonstrates its excellent potential in this region. The *blanc de blancs* is a refreshing sparkler and recent vintages of reserve pinot noir have been showing well.

DR. FRANK'S VINIFERA WINE CELLARS/ CHÂTEAU FRANK

Established **1963** ***Owners*** **Frank family** ***Vineyard area*** **76 acres (31 ha)**

The riesling and gewürztraminer from here are among the region's best. Recent chardonnays have been crisp and flavorful. Sister winery, Château Frank, makes sprightly sparklers.

MILLBROOK VINEYARDS & WINERY

Established **1985** ***Owners*** **John and Kathe Dyson** ***Production*** **15,500 cases** ***Vineyard area*** **52 acres (21 ha)**

This winery was formerly an old dairy farm in the Hudson River region. Among Millbrook's productions are an oaky chardonnay, a fragrant, full-bodied tokay and a cabernet franc infused with sweet berry overtones.

HERMANN J. WIEMER VINEYARD, INC.

Established **1980** ***Owner*** **Hermann J. Wiemer** ***Production*** **12,000 cases** ***Vineyard area*** **65 acres (26 ha)**

A native of Germany's Moselle region, and arguably the most respected vintner in the east, Wiemer is at home with the cool climate and glacial soils of the Finger Lakes. Riesling and gewürztraminer reminiscent of Alsace, as well as trocken beerenauslese-style late-harvest riesling are stunners. Recent chardonnay has also been most impressive.

WOLFFER ESTATE

Established **1992** ***Owner*** **Christian Wolffer** ***Production*** **9,000 cases** ***Vineyard area*** **50 acres (20 ha)**

Formerly Sagpond Vineyards, this is the most important winery on Long Island's South Fork. Winemaker Roman Roth's production is admirably restricted to a few varietals, a flinty and refreshing chardonnay and a merlot with juicy cherry flavors. The sparkling has elegance and structure.

OTHER EASTERN PRODUCERS

BARBOURSVILLE VINEYARDS, VIRGINIA

Established **1976** ***Owners*** **Zonin family** ***Production*** **25,000 cases** ***Vineyard area*** **120 acres (48.6 ha)**

Founded by Zonin, Italian winemakers, Barboursville was the first producer to succeed with *vinifera* varieties in Virginia. Winemaker Luca Paschina produces Italian classics—pinot

Regional Best

- Anthony Road Wine Company Late Harvest Vignoles
- Barboursville Vineyards Pinot Grigio
- Bedell Cellars "Eis"
- Boordy Vineyards Seyval
- Chamard Vineyards Cabernet Franc
- Clover Hill Vineyards and Winery Concord
- Clinton Vineyards Seyval
- Fox Run Vineyards Reserve Pinot Noir
- Hermann J. Wiemer Vineyard Chardonnay
- Horton Vineyards Norton
- Linden Vineyards Sauvignon Blanc
- McGregor Vineyards Sparkling Riesling
- Presque Isle Wine Cellars Cabernet Franc/Petite Sirah
- Sakonnet Vineyards Fumé Blanc (Vidal)
- Sharpe Hill Vineyard Select Late Harvest
- Wolffer Estate/Sagpond Vineyards Merlot
- Wolffer Estate Brut Rosé

a native grape that produces inky purple wine redolent of plums and cherries, is a favorite.

SAKONNET VINEYARDS, NEW ENGLAND

Established **1985** ***Owners*** **Susan and Earl Samson** ***Production*** **50,000 cases** ***Vineyard area*** **45 acres (18 ha)**

The Samsons are dedicated to making and marketing eastern wine. Winemaker John Sotello, formerly with California's prestigious Iron Horse, has helped guide Sakonnet's evolution. Among its best wines are fragrant gewürztraminer, peachy vidal blanc, elegant fumé blanc and rich chardonnay.

Other producers in Eastern United States include Linden Vineyards, Palmer Vineyards, Westport Vineyards and White Hall Vineyards.

ABOVE: *Vineyards at Augusta, Missouri. This is one the Midwest's strongest wine-producing states.*

grigio, sangiovese and barbera, as well as chardonnay, merlot, pinot noir, cabernet franc and cabernet sauvignon. Good vintages of lush dessert wines—philéo (muscat, riesling and malvasia) and malvasia reserve.

CHADDSFORD WINERY, PENNSYLVANIA

Established **1982** ***Owners*** **Eric and Lee Miller** ***Production*** **30,000 cases** ***Vineyard area*** **30 acres (12 ha)**

Like many eastern wineries Chaddsford produces an astonishing range of wines from hybrid and *vinifera* grapes. Good vintages produce fruity pinot grigio and high-end chardonnays, as well as some complex cabernet blends.

BELOW: *Building drystone walls is a skill taken from the Old World to the New by early settlers.*

HORTON VINEYARDS, VIRGINIA

Established **1993** ***Owners*** **Dennis and Sharon Horton** ***Production*** **25,000 cases** ***Vineyard area*** **100 acres (40.5 ha)**

From a few vines planted in 1983, the winery is today one of Virginia's success stories. Dennis Horton concentrates on viognier, marsanne, syrah, mourvèdre, grenache and malbec. Another hot-climate success is touriga nacional. Horton's norton,

Other US Regions

THE SOUTHWEST

The Southwest is the oldest wine-producing region in the US. Spanish missionaries planted grapes in New Mexico in the 1500s, and in Texas in the 1600s. Scores of vineyards and wineries thrived until Prohibition. Replanting did not begin in earnest until the 1970s. Today Texas is the fifth-largest wine-producing state in the US with more than 3,000 acres (1,214 ha) of mostly *vinifera* grapes and 55 commercial wineries. New Mexico has 28 wineries and strong foreign investment (especially from France). Colorado has 48 wineries with most of its 132 vineyards sited on the state's western slopes.

The Southwest, where the sun shines intensely from cloudless skies, has the warmest summer weather of any grape-growing region in the US, yet winters can be bitterly cold. The lack of water in parched areas is a problem for vines. Best growing sites combine high altitude, dry air and relatively cool temperatures during the growing season.

As in most other states, restrictive laws make selling wine a challenge, although this is starting to change. In Arizona, for example, recent changes in state law will make it easier for vintners to sell their wine direct within the state itself.

Chardonnay, cabernet sauvignon and merlot all do well in most of the southwestern viticultural regions. Sauvignon blanc, chenin blanc and riesling are also favored. Zinfandel is gaining a foothold, particularly in western Texas, and syrah, sangiovese and tempranillo all show promise. Good dessert wines, especially fortified port-style wines, are quite successful in areas where the hot summers and cold winters resemble the climate in the Douro Valley in Portugal.

CALLAGHAN, ARIZONA

Established **1991** ***Owner*** **Kent Callaghan** ***Production*** **1500–2,000 cases** ***Vineyard area*** **17 acres (7 ha)**

Callaghan is by far the most visible of the handful of wineries in Arizona. The winery's specialty is well-structured tannic blends of cabernet sauvignon with merlot and cabernet franc. Syrah looks extremely promising and recent plantings of petit verdot, mourvèdre, tempranillo and touriga francesca also seem headed for success.

COLORADO CELLARS, COLORADO

Established **1978** ***Owners*** **Richard and Padte Turley** ***Production*** **10,000 cases** ***Vineyard area*** **20 acres (8 ha)**

The state's oldest winery and perhaps its largest, Colorado Cellars' wines include dry riesling, chardonnay, merlot and port. A perennial bestseller is Road Kill Red, a semi-sweet lemberger.

FALL CREEK VINEYARDS, TEXAS

Established **1975** ***Owners*** **Ed and Susan Auler** ***Production*** **35,000 cases** ***Vineyard area*** **65 acres (26 ha)**

Fall Creek produces chardonnay, chenin blanc, riesling, cabernet sauvignon and merlot. Of particular note is the high-end and very limited Meritus, a blend of merlot, cabernet sauvignon and malbec.

THE MIDWEST

The weather is always a challenge in the Midwestern states, but recent viticultural research, advances in cool-climate production technology and a string of good vintages have all contributed to some outstanding progress.

The Midwest's strongest wine-producing states are Ohio, Michigan and Missouri. In the early 1800s, Ohio was an important producer of native and hybrid wine grapes, especially the catawba. By the 1850s, it was the leading wine-producing state in the US, but 75 years later disease and Prohibition had destroyed most of the region's wine industry. Serious rebuilding did not begin until the 1970s, but Ohio is now booming—it boasts 70 wineries.

Michigan had only a few wineries before Prohibition, but boutique wineries are now thriving, particularly in the southwestern corner of Lake Michigan's shoreline.

In Missouri, the first wines were made in 1823 by French Jesuits. Stone Hill, the state's leading wine estate, was founded in 1847, however, it also succumbed to Prohibition and became a mushroom farm.

The stable temperatures of the Great Lakes' deep waters warm the air blowing across the lakes, reducing the threat of late spring and early fall frosts and prolonging the growing season. In winter, heavy snow packs insulate the dormant vines.

Because of the severe Midwest winters, cool-climate grapes do best. Hybrids dominate, but *vinifera* types are gaining a following. White wines are riesling, chardonnay, gewürztraminer, seyval and vignoles. Pinot noir (for sparkling wine) and cabernet franc lead red *vinifera* plantings.

The Midwest's prospects are bright, as Ohio has introduced initiatives and incentives that have effectively promoted viticulture and winemaking. Neighboring states are beginning to follow suit.

BELOW: *Freshly harvested gewürztraminer grapes.*

FIRELANDS WINE COMPANY, OHIO

Established **1987** ***Owner*** **Paramount Distillery** ***Production*** **NA** ***Vineyard area*** **210 acres (85 ha)**

This company grows most of its grapes on North Bass Island, on Lake Erie. The focus is almost entirely on *vinifera*—riesling, cabernet sauvignon, cabernet franc, chardonnay, gewürztraminer and Italian-style unoaked pinot grigio.

Notable producers in Other US Regions include Two Rivers Winery (Colorado); Chalet Débonné Vineyards, Harpersfield Vineyard (both Ohio); Peninsula Cellars, Chateau Grand Traverse, L. Mawby Vineyards, St Julian Wine Company (all Michigan); The Wallersheim Wine Company (Wisconsin); and Stonehill Winery (Missouri).

BELOW: *Expanses of well-spaced, trained vines–typical of a United States' vineyard.*

Picking riesling icewine grapes on the Niagara Peninsula, Ontario.

Canada

Melville I.
Banks Island
Prince of Wales Island
Admundsen Gulf
Victoria Island
Gulf of Boothia
Baffin Island
Foxe Basin
Netilling Lake
Repulse Bay
Cape Dorset
Southampton Island
Baker Lake
Salluit
Killiniq
Fort McPherson
Mackenzie
Mackenzie Mountains
Great Bear Lake
Koidern
Mt Logan 19,550 ft (5959 m)
Haines Junction
Whitehorse
Fort Simpson
Yellowknife
Great Slave Lake
Dubawnt Lake
Watson Lake
Hay River
Yathkyed Lake
CANADA
HUDSON BAY
Nueltin Lake
ROCKY MOUNTAINS
Peace
Lake Athabasca
Wollaston Lake
Churchill
Cree Lake
Reindeer Lake
Peace River
Athabasca
Churchill
Nelson
Queen Charlotte Islands
Churchill Lake
Fort Severn
Belcher Islands
Lake Minto
Lake Bienville
Réservoir de la Grande 2
James Bay
Eastmain
La Ronge
Severn
Mt Waddington 13,176 ft (4016 m)
Edmonton
Grand Rapids
Cedar Lake
Lake Winnipeg
Waskaganish
Moose Factory
Albany
Fraser
Kamloops
Vancouver Island
Saskatoon
Lake Winnipegosis
Fraser Valley
Lake Okanagan
Kelowna
Calgary
Vancouver
Okanagan Valley
Victoria
Medicine Hat
Regina
Lake Manitoba
Winnipeg
Kenora
Lake Seul
Lake Nipigon
Cochrane
Lake of the Woods
Thunder Bay
Lake Superior
Sudbury
OTTAWA
Lake Huron
Lake Michigan
Toronto
St Catharines
Hamilton
Niagara Falls
Lake Erie North Shore & Pelee Island
Niagara Peninsula
Lake Erie
NORTH
200 miles
(320 kilometers)

Canada

TONY ASPLER

ABOVE: *This delightful café spills out onto the sidewalk in Québec's quaint old quarter.*

Canada's potential as a wine-producing country was recognized back in 1867 when a wine from Ontario received high praise from judges at the French exposition in Paris. Nevertheless, the wine industry spent the next century making inferior wines. Then, in 1991, an Ontario dessert wine—the 1989 Inniskillin Vidal Icewine—won the grand prix d'honneur at the Vinexpo in Bordeaux.

Conscientious producers have worked together to develop an appellation system based on European models. The Vintners' Quality Alliance (VQA) governs the use of geographic or varietal designations, grape types and viticultural and winemaking practices. With the recent official recognition of VQA Canada, international acceptance is growing rapidly. However, the sale of alcoholic beverages in Canada is controlled by provincial mono-polies (although this is not the case in Alberta, where it is privatized) and, consequently, wine prices carry heavy markups. These monopoly markup systems are so inflexible that many Canadian wines are sold only in the province of origin.

Wine is made in four distinct zones across Canada where microclimates provide respite from winter's icy blast. Ontario has the lion's share, with 80 percent of the country's wineries located on the Niagara Peninsula. The remaining three areas are in British Columbia, Québec and Nova Scotia. Because of the marginal climate, both hybrid and *vinifera* grape varieties are used, with emphasis on the latter. In the past the emphasis was on white grape varieties, although several reds—notably cabernet franc, pinot noir and gamay—have now been found to produce well.

LEFT: *Signs mark the wine routes in the various wine regions throughout Canada.*

Landscape and climate

Winter is the most critical climatic factor influencing the production of wine in Canada. Even the most vine-conducive regions are susceptible to the occasional spell of –4°F (–20°C) weather. Where wine is most successfully produced, large bodies of water provide some degree of protection against extreme cold and spring frost.

Canada's Niagara Peninsula is on the same latitude as the Midi in France and Italy's Tuscany, but lacks the benefit of a balmy Mediterranean climate. Fortunately, the certainty of freezing temperatures has benefited the industry by assuring the production of icewine consistently every year. That vines can survive in Ontario at all is due to the mitigating influence of the lakes Ontario and Erie. In British Columbia, winemaking is dominated by tiny wineries, the majority of which sell their entire capacity at the farm gate. Most of the production occurs in the Okanagan Valley, which is located on the same latitude as France's Champagne,

BELOW: *Riesling icewine grapes on the Niagara Peninsula, Ontario.*

History

Experience has shown that wine from indigenous North American grapes comes up short on palatability. If it is true that Lief Ericsson's crew made wine from the grapes they found in 1001, they could be forgiven for a hearty endorsement of the wine's virtues after their harsh crossing of the Atlantic Ocean.

When the first stalwart Europeans arrived and settled in and around Québec and Montréal in the sixteenth century, wine was among one of their many deprivations. As in many areas of European settlement, the Catholic Church was instrumental in early wine production. In Canada, these early wines were based on local grapes and, according to the Jesuit missionaries, they were suitable only for mass. Since then, vineyardists have been searching for more desirable grape types that can survive the harsh climate, and experimentation has identified zones where vinifera vines can thrive.

Winemaking began in earnest in Ontario when Count Justin de Courtney purchased and expanded on some 1811 plantings near Toronto. He had some success in the 1860s producing wines from European varieties. Meanwhile, the regions that produce Ontario's wine today were being established on the Niagara Peninsula and Pelee Island. However, Ontario wine producers faced an uphill battle against the growing temperance movement. The struggle lasted for over 30 years, profoundly affecting the nature of the wines produced, and the results are still seen in the government monopoly on alcohol sales introduced in the early 1940s.

In British Columbia, winery development took a similar path if on a smaller scale. The first vineyard in BC's Okanagan Valley was planted in the nineteenth century by the Oblate fathers to make wine for sacramental purposes. Commercial ventures were established around Lake Okanagan, then other areas followed on Vancouver Island and on some smaller islands between Vancouver Island and the mainland. Much of the early wine industry centered on fruit other than grapes, and it wasn't until an oversupply of apples in the 1930s caused prices to drop that farmers turned to grapes.

In the 1960s light and sweet sparkling wines, such as the 7 percent alcohol sparkler Baby Duck, became the rage in North America. Fortunately, it was a temporary fad and consumers gradually started to demand greater variety, which was fulfilled by an increase in imported European table wines. Many Canadian vineyards have now reached the levels of maturity that support the development of superpremium wines. The concomitant investment in technology has moved the Canadian wine industry into a position where it can compete with confidence at the international level.

ABOVE: *Nineteenth-century cut-glass decanter*

but the altitude and semi-desert environment give Okanagan wines their unique character. Lively flavors and high acidity result from the fluctuation between hot daytime and very cool nighttime temperatures. Lake Okanagan, about 62 miles (100 km) long, provides a moderating influence on the climate.

The climates of Québec and Nova Scotia are less conducive to vine growing, particularly *vinifera* varieties. In Québec, the hybrids seyval, vidal and maréchal foch exhibit the required characteristics. However, even they must be hilled up with earth during the freezing winter and then uncovered for the growing season. In the maritime province Nova Scotia, the industry survives by blending local wines with imported wines, but homegrown specialties are produced. Two hardy Russian varieties, michurinetz and severny from the genus *Amurensis*, are cultivated locally.

Vines and wines

Some very palatable wines are made with vidal, seyval blanc, maréchal foch, and baco noir (early French vines that were cross-pollinated with indigenous varieties). Many single varietal wines are produced in all wine-growing regions in Canada, while blends of classic Bordeaux varieties, particularly reds, are increasing in Ontario and British Columbia. Proprietary blends are

RIGHT: *Niagara Falls, with American Falls on the left and Horseshoe Falls on the right. Over half of Canada's wineries are located on the Niagara Peninsula within a short distance of the Falls.*

made for the lower price ranges, but are not entitled to a VQA designation. Preferred *vinifera* grapes are mostly French and German varietals. Hybrids are grown in all provinces and are the mainstay of the industry in Québec and Nova Scotia. A few specified, high-quality hybrids are permitted by VQA Canada.

Laws

To varying degrees, the governments in Canadian provinces control the sale of alcoholic beverages, however, winery owners have designed a set of standards regarding the production of wine. The Vintners' Quality Alliance (VQA) was established in Ontario in 1989 as a voluntary set of regulations. The VQA Act passed the Ontario provincial legislature in the spring of 1990, to become law in mid-2000. A similar system has been adopted in British Columbia, with some minor variance in criteria. VQA Canada, formerly a group working under the umbrella of the Canadian Wine Institute and representing the interests of Ontario and British Columbia to assist primarily with export market development, became official in June 1999. Both provinces have adopted a national VQA wine standard, and the group is working to bring in Nova Scotia and Québec. In March 2004, VQA Canada authorized the use of controversial screw caps on VQA wines. The mandate of the new body is to work on national VQA regulatory issues, quality standards, legal and trademark protection, and inter-provincial and international trade issues on behalf of the Canadian wine industry. VQA is to Canada what AOC is to France and DOCG is to Italy. Regulations are designed to guarantee superior quality wines, affecting all areas of quality control in winemaking, from what grapes can be used and where they can be cultivated, to the taste of the finished wine and the labeling on the bottle.

Wine is one of the most civilized things in the world and one of the most natural things of the world that has been brought to the greatest perfection, and it offers a greater range for enjoyment and appreciation than, possibly, any other purely sensory thing.

ERNEST HEMINGWAY (1899–1961), *Death in the Afternoon*

ABOVE: *Poplar Grove, Naramata Bench, Okanagan Valley, British Columbia*

ABOVE: *Vineyards at Naramata in the Okanagan Valley support a range of grape types, from syrah to ehrenfelser.*

BRITISH COLUMBIA

Although much of BC's early wine was made from fruit other than grapes, a determined handful of purists persisted in seeking the appropriate varietals and the most suitable locations. Those locations have been largely confined to the Okanagan Valley, with a few vineyards established in the Fraser Valley, and on Vancouver Island.

One of many significant events that changed BC's wine industry in the twentieth century was the Canada–US Free Trade Agreement. The agreement, signed in 1988, caused a major crisis as it became apparent that continued dependence on hybrid varieties would not provide a competitive edge in the liberalized market. Eventually, growers tore up about 65 percent of their acreage and replanted with *vinifera* vines. Many of these new *vinifera* plantings leaned more toward French varietals, such as pinot blanc, chardonnay and pinot gris. Consequently, more of the wineries started to produce drier, French-style wines. Initial plantings of reds in the warmer, southern end of the Okanagan Valley are promising. Pinot noir, cabernet franc, merlot and cabernet sauvignon are all in demand.

ABOVE: *Freshly harvested gewürztraminer grapes.*

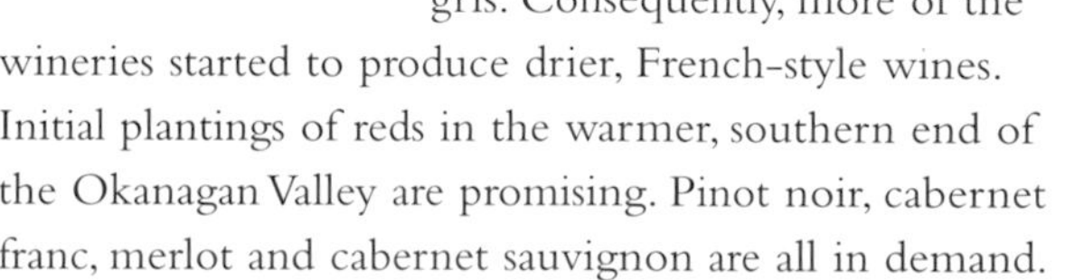

The 1993 International Wine and Spirits Competition in London confirmed the fact that the BC wine industry had come of age when it conferred the Avery Trophy for Best Chardonnay in the World on the 1992 Mission Hill Grand Reserve Chardonnay.

Okanagan Valley

The majority of wineries in British Columbia are found in the Okanagan Valley, parts of which experience near-desert conditions. Etched out by a retreating glacier, this long, steep valley runs north–south, nearly equidistant from the Rocky Mountains to the east and the Pacific coast to the west. The southernmost tip of the valley reaches almost to the United States border. Lake Okanagan stretches for about 62 miles (100 km) and is a mitigating influence on climatic extremes. Predictable summers provide a favorable environment for vines.

In the warmest area, south of Lake Okanagan, the average annual rainfall is low, a meagre 6 inches (15 cm), making irrigation a necessity. At the southernmost point of the valley, Osoyoos Lake is a mitigating influence in winter. Just north of this, part of the west side of the valley is called the "Golden Mile" for its row of contiguous wine properties. Further to the north, the area around Okanagan Falls and Vaseaux Lake also enjoys reliably hot daytime temperatures. Continuing north, Naramata supports a wide range of grape types from hardy ehrenfelser to heat-loving syrah. Kelowna, in central Okanagan, is slightly cooler and from there north, crisp, flavorful German-style whites abound. Pinot noir and chardonnay are also cultivated successfully.

Significant producers in the Okanagan Valley, in addition those below, include Andrés Wines, Calona Wines, Cedar Creek Estate Winery, Gehringer Brothers Estate Winery, Gray Monk Cellars, Inniskillin Okanagan Vineyards, Kettle Valley Winery, Nichol Vineyard & Farm Winery, St Hubertus Estate Winery, Summerhill Estate Winery and Wild Goose Vineyards.

BLUE MOUNTAIN VINEYARD & CELLARS

Established 1991 **Owners** the Mavety family **Production** 12,000 cases **Vineyard area** 60 acres (24 ha)

A Burgundy-like climate, an established vineyard of pinot blanc, pinot gris, chardonnay and pinot noir and a talented father (Ian) and son (Mark) team of winemakers have made Blue Mountain one of the Okanagan Valley's leading producers. When long-term grape growers Ian and Jane Mavety decided to make their own wine, they barrel-fermented their pinot blanc and their pinot gris and launched a stunning pinot noir. They also make some commendable sparkling wines.

BURROWING OWL VINEYARDS

Established 1994 **Owners** the Wyse family and partners **Production** 12,000 cases **Vineyard area** 290 acres (117 ha)

This vineyard has proven to the world that BC can produce great reds, in this case, merlot. The Wyse family's winery uses gravity flow to move the wine through the winemaking process. Talented winemaker Bill Dyer, who has a master's degree in enology from the University of California at Davis and worked for around ten years at Sterling Vineyards in the Napa Valley, is extremely enthusiastic about both the soil and the climate at Burrowing Owl Vineyards.

LEFT: A warning sign to be taken seriously—collision with a bull moose can cause a great deal of damage to vehicles and their occupants.

DOMAINE COMBRET

Established 1993 **Owner** Robert Combret **Production** 10,000 cases **Vineyard area** 30 acres (12 ha)

Originally from Provence, the Combret family has been in Canada since 1992. From their first Canadian vintage, 1993, they won a silver medal at the Challenge International du Vin at Blaye-Bourg in Bordeaux for a riesling made in the Alsatian style. Their chardonnay from the same vintage did well in an annual challenge held in Burgundy. Robert Combret's son Olivier, who trained at Montpellier, fulfils Domaine Combret's winemaking responsibilities.

HAINLE VINEYARDS

Established 1978 **Owners** the Hainle Family **Production** 5,500 cases **Vineyard area** 18.5 acres (7.5 ha)

Hainle Vineyards produced Canada's first icewine in 1977 and went into commercial production the following year. Walter Hainle died in a hiking accident in 1995, and his son Tilman is now at the helm. He trained at Weisberg and worked at Uniake Cellars (which later became Cedar Creek Estate Winery) until 1985, when he joined the family enterprise. In 1991, Tilman introduced champagne method sparklers from pinot blanc, chardonnay, pinot noir and pinot meunier. Hainle Vineyards are certified organic and Tilman uses as little sulphur dioxide as possible in production.

Producers
1 Andrés Wines
2 Blue Mountain Vineyard & Cellars
3 Burrowing Owl Vineyards
4 Calona Wines
5 Cedar Creek Estate Winery
6 Domaine Combret
7 Gehringer Brothers Estate Winery
8 Gray Monk Cellars
9 Hainle Vineyards
10 Inniskillin Okanagan Vineyards
11 Kettle Valley Winery
12 Lang Vineyards
13 Mission Hill Winery
14 Nichol Vineyard & Farm Winery
15 Poplar Grove Farm Winery
16 Quails' Gate Estate Winery
17 St-Hubertus Estate Winery
18 St-Laszlo Vineyards
19 Sumac Ridge Estate Winery
20 Summerhill Estate Winery
21 Tinhorn Creek Vineyards
22 Vincor International
23 Wild Goose Vineyards

NORTH
10 miles (16 kilometers)
Vernon, Coldstream, Okanagan Lake, Oyama, Okanagan Centre, Winfield, Kelowna, Westbank, Peachland, Naramata, Trout, Summerland, Penticon, Skaha Lake, Kaleden, Okanagan Falls, Olalla, Vaseaux Lake, Keremeos, CANADA, Cawston, Oliver, Hayes, Osoyoos Lake, Osoyoos, UNITED STATES, Oroville, Okanagan Valley, OTTAWA

LANG VINEYARDS

Established 1993 **Owners** Gunther and Kristina Lang **Production** 5,000 cases **Vineyard area** 15 acres (6.1 ha)

After coming to Canada from Germany in 1980, the Langs bought an Okanagan vineyard. They replaced existing vines with new grape varieties and made wine as a hobby. In the late 1980s, the Langs and their neighbors, the Klokockas of Hillside Estate Winery, campaigned for legal changes to allow grape growers to develop small wineries on their properties. After legislation was passed, they built a winery where they could showcase rieslings and other *vinifera*-based wines.

MISSION HILL WINERY

Established 1981 **Owner** A. von Mandl **Production** 205,000 cases **Vineyard area** 600 acres (243 ha) owned or controlled

Inspired by Robert Mondavi in the Napa Valley and the tradition of the French château, Anthony von Mandl's

ABOVE: Still at Mission Hill Winery, Okanagan Valley, British Columbia.

focus for Mission Hill is quality and innovation. The decision to hire New Zealand winemaker John Simes in 1992 was immediately rewarded when his first vintage, 1992 Mission Hill Grand Reserve Chardonnay, won the Avery Trophy for Best Chardonnay worldwide.

POPLAR GROVE FARM WINERY

Established **1997** ***Owners*** **Ian and Gitta Sutherland *Production* 1,500 cases *Vineyard area* 7 acres (3 ha)**

Ian Sutherland's grape mix is two-thirds red to one-third white, and his aim is to keep the winery small. The composition of the clay loam soil in his vineyard is much like that of St-Emilion, so Ian planted merlot and cabernet franc. White grapes are chardonnay and pinot gris. He launched his first chardonnay with resounding success.

QUAILS' GATE ESTATE WINERY

Established **1989** ***Owner*** **Dick Stewart *Production* 60,000 cases *Vineyard area* 115 acres (47 ha)**

Few winemakers believed in 1989 that there was a future for red varietals in BC. But the search for the perfect pinot noir inspired Quails' Gate founder Dick Stewart and his son Ben to research new varietal clones and experiment with canopy management and high-density planting. Winemaking benefited from the talents of two Australian winemakers, first Jeff Martin, then Peter Draper, who died suddenly during the 1999 harvest. The crush was completed by Simon Osika, on loan from BRL Hardy's Houghton Winery in Western Australia.

ST LASZLO VINEYARDS

Established **1970s** ***Owners*** **the Ritlop family *Production* 5,000 cases *Vineyard area* 10 acres (4 ha)**

The first crush from this vineyard planted to both hybrid and *vinifera* grapes was in 1978. Joe Ritlop does not use chemicals in the vineyard and avoids sulphides, sorbates and preservatives in the winery. He also prefers to allow the natural yeasts to produce fermentation in his full-bodied wines. He makes some remarkable late-harvested wines, including a tokay aszu.

SUMAC RIDGE ESTATE WINERY

Established **1979** ***Owner*** **Vincor International Inc. *Production* 50,000 cases *Vineyard area* 131 acres (53 ha)**

Sumac Ridge, the first medium-size winery in BC, was sold in early 2000 to Vincor International Inc., Canada's largest wine company. It was established by Harry McWatters, who, in 1991, went into partnership with Bob Wareham to develop Black Sage Vineyards, 115 acres (47 ha) of some of the best vineyard land in Canada and the major source of grapes for Sumac Ridge. Black Sage is planted with premium varietals, mostly red, including cabernet sauvignon, cabernet franc, merlot, pinot noir and malbec. Its white varieties include chardonnay, pinot blanc and sauvignon blanc. Oak is an important element in the Sumac Ridge style.

TINHORN CREEK VINEYARDS

Established **1993** ***Owners*** **Bob and Barbara Shaunessy and Kenn and Sandra Oldfield *Production* 40,000 cases *Vineyard area* 160 acres (65 ha)**

Influenced by the success of the Napa Valley, winery founder Bob Shaunessy started buying up existing vineyards at a time when small growers were bearing the brunt of the pull-out program. The Shaunessys then went into partnership with Kenn and Sandra Oldfield, and now Sandra is winemaker and Kenn is viticulturalist and general manager. In a few short years, the partners have acquired many accolades for their wines. The California influence is evident in their use of American oak and in the concentrated flavor of the wines.

VINCOR INTERNATIONAL (JACKSON-TRIGGS)

Established **1982** ***Owner*** **Vincor International Inc. *Production* 2 million cases *Vineyard area* 750 acres (304 ha) owned or leased**

Vincor's winery in Oliver went into production in 1982, drawing on grapes from the Inkameep vineyard farmed by the Osoyoos Indian Band. In 1996, the company signed a lease agreement with the band to develop some 2,000 acres

(810 ha) on the Osoyoos Lake Bench. In the southernmost tip of the Okanagan Valley, this area benefits from long hours of sunlight, high daytime heat and cool nights. When fully developed, this land has the potential to double the supply of high-quality grapes in British Columbia. These Vincor vineyards will be dedicated to super- and ultra-premium chardonnay, pinot noir, merlot, cabernet sauvignon and sauvignon blanc.

Other BC Regions

VANCOUVER ISLAND

The Cowichan Valley on Vancouver Island and the few wineries on nearby smaller islands enjoy a climate more like that of Ontario's Niagara Peninsula than that of the Okanagan, with mild overnight temperatures. The wines from this area show soft acids and rich fruit flavors. Wineries are a fairly new phenomenon for Vancouver Island, but their initial results indicate that this region has considerable potential.

VENTURI-SCHULZE VINEYARDS

Established **1993** ***Owners*** **Giordano Venturi and Marilyn Schulze** ***Production*** **500 cases** ***Vineyard area*** **20 acres (8 ha)**

Giordano Venturi, an electronics instructor from Italy, and his wife Marilyn Schulze, an Australian-born microbioligist, bought a pretty 100-year old farm at Cowichan Bay and planted 25 different grape varieties. From those, the 11 best performers were chosen—pinot noir, auxerrois, pinot gris, schönberger, madeleine sylvaner, siegerrebe, ortega, kerner, chasselas, gewürztraminer and madeleine angevin—to remain in this organically farmed vineyard. Only very small quantities of handcrafted wines are produced at Venturi-Schulze.

FRASER VALLEY

The Fraser Valley is within half an hour's drive of Vancouver, and is a more temperate and humid area than the Okanagan Valley, producing wines with a softer flavor profile than those from the Okanagan. There are two wineries in this region, one grows vines and the other vinifies Okanagan fruit.

DOMAINE DE CHABERTON

Established **1991** ***Owner*** **Claude Violet** ***Production*** **25,000 cases** ***Vineyard area*** **55 acres (22 ha)**

When Claude Violet came to British Columbia from his native France, he transported 350 years of winemaking heritage to the Fraser Valley. Domaine de Chaberton is the only winery growing grapes in this British Columbia designation just north of the United States border. The wines, from bacchus, madeleine angevine, madeleine sylvaner, ortega, chardonnay and chasselas doré, are sold locally as well as being exported to places such as France and Japan.

Regional Dozen

QUALITY WINES

Blue Mountain Pinot Noir
Cedar Creek Platinum Reserve Chardonnay
Gehringer Riesling Icewine
Mission Hill Chardonnay Reserve
Quails' Gate Pinot Noir Family Reserve
Sumac Ridge Meritage
Vincor Jackson-Triggs Merlot

BEST VALUE WINES

Calona Vineyards Artist Reserve Chardonnay
Gray Monk Unwooded Chardonnay
Hawthorne Mountain Chardonnay
Hester Creek Estate Pinot Blanc
St Hubertus Riesling
Sumac Ridge Gewürztraminer Private Reserve
Tinhorn Creek Gewürztraminer

BELOW: Irrigation at the Vincor plantings, Osoyoos, Okanagan Valley, British Columbia

ONTARIO

The wine industry in Ontario looked extremely promising in 1867, when the judges at the French exposition in Paris recorded that the Canadian wine submitted by Count Justin de Courtney "resembled more the great French table wines than any other foreign wines" that they had tasted. During the time de Courtney was seeking favour in Europe, a small handful of vineyardists had discovered the potential of the Niagara Peninsula. At the turn of the century, there were 35 commercial wineries operating there. The grape variety most commonly used then was the concord, an indigenous labrusca variety, which is virtually indestructible, and which makes better jelly than wine.

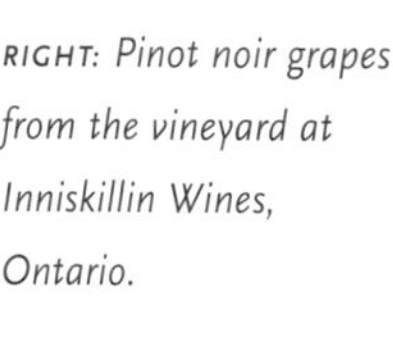

RIGHT: Pinot noir grapes from the vineyard at Inniskillin Wines, Ontario.

Coincident with the growth of wineries, however, came an increasingly strong temperance movement. The movement's influence culminated in the Ontario Temperance Act of 1916 prohibiting the sales of beverage alcohol. During the 1930s alcoholic beverages were legalized, but sales were restricted to government-run shops in a monopoly system. It has been liberalized somewhat over the years, but tight control remains over selection and pricing.

The wine-producing areas of Ontario benefit from the proximity of two of the Great Lakes, Ontario and Erie. In the summer, the lakes absorb and hold enough heat to cushion winter's frigid attack. The exchange of warm and cool air creates a constant flow that benefits most of the areas where vines are grown.

In the late 1970s, the provincial government's wine-industry assistance program included five-year interest-free loans to replant vineyards with *vinifera* and superior hybrid vines. Most growers planted white grapes known to be cold resistant, but some planted a broad range of white varietals and a number of reds.

Now that it has been shown that the vines can thrive, the percentage of red grapes planted has increased significantly. Favored red varieties are cabernet franc, pinot noir, merlot, cabernet sauvignon, gamay noir, baco noir, maréchal foch, and a few plantings of syrah. Favored white varieties are chardonnay, riesling, pinot blanc, pinot gris, gewürztraminer, chenin blanc, sémillon and vidal.

Niagara Peninsula

Lake Ontario's influence diminishes inland, on a level plain where cold air can settle. Spring frosts are a problem here—protective measures such as using fans to move the air are sometimes needed. In summer, temperatures rise quickly and fruit matures well—the heat contributes to ripeness, and translates into intense flavors. Chardonnay, for example, can show tropical nuances not found in the cooler Niagara Bench vineyards farther inland. There the terrain slopes up the Niagara Escarpment—the area has good drainage and the incline causes constant air circulation, almost eliminating spring frost and humidity-related disease. The cooler environment there encourages the acid needed for balance and elegance; the warmer temperatures of the plain give more intensity and richness. A series of benches thought to provide superior fruit are delineated along the Escarpment, including the Vineland Double Bench, St David's Bench and the already well-known Beamsville Bench.

Significant producers located on the Niagara Peninsula, in addition to those below, include Château des Charmes, East Dell Estates, Hernder Estate Wines, Kittling Ridge Estate Wines & Spirits, Konzelmann Winery, Lakeview Cellars Estate Winery, Magnotta Winery, Marynissen Estates, Peninsula Ridge Estates Winery and Strewn Estate Winery.

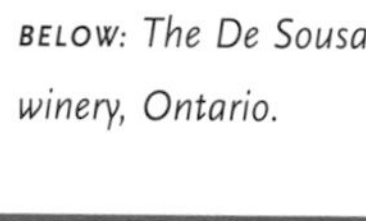

BELOW: The De Sousa winery, Ontario.

CAVE SPRING CELLARS

Established **1986** ***Owners*** **Len Pennachetti and Angelo Pavan** ***Production*** **60,000 cases** ***Vineyard area*** **155 acres (63 ha)**

Cave Spring Cellars' ultra-premium wines exhibit concentrated fruit, reflecting their bench *terroir* and winemaker Angelo Pavan's signature elegance. Cave Spring is one of the few medium-sized wineries in Niagara to use only *vinifera* varieties.

HENRY OF PELHAM

Established **1983** ***Owners*** **the Speck family** ***Production*** **70,000 cases** ***Vineyard area*** **225 acres (91 ha)**

Paul, Matthew and Daniel Speck are direct descendants of Nicholas Smith, who was deeded land by the Crown for his loyalist stance in the war of 1776. The Specks and winemaker Ron Giesbrecht concentrate on chardonnay, riesling, cabernet sauvignon and baco noir. They are recognized as the region's best producer of baco noir.

HILLEBRAND ESTATES

Established **1981** ***Owners*** **Andrés Wines** ***Production*** **340,000 cases** ***Vineyard area*** **30 acres (12 ha)**

Hillebrand, founded in 1979, was sold in the early 1980s to Underberg of Switzerland. The little winery invested in technology and grew considerably. Then in 1994, Andrés Wines bought Hillebrand. Although now a large winery, it focuses on VQA wines and varietals.

INNISKILLIN WINES INC.

Established **1975** ***Owners*** **Vincor International Inc.** ***Production*** **150,000 cases** ***Vineyard area*** **120 acres (49 ha)**

Inniskillin started the quality wine revolution in Canada when Donald Ziraldo and Karl Kaiser applied for a boutique winery license—the industry was then dominated by large companies. Donald and Karl introduced well-made varietal wines and, later, single-vineyard labels. When 1989 Inniskillin's Vidal Icewine won a gold medal at Vinexpo in 1991, Canada was finally recognized as a cool-climate wine-producing country.

MALIVOIRE WINE COMPANY

Established **1998** ***Owners*** **Martin Malivoire and Moira Saganski** ***Production*** **2,000 cases** ***Vineyard area*** **65 acres (26 ha)**

Martin Malivoire erected a large Quonset hut on a slope of the escarpment, where he takes advantage of gravity to limit the need for pumps. The winery focuses on premium wines from gewürztraminer, chardonnay, pinot noir and pinot gris. Under the direction of the talented consultant winemaker, Ann Sperling, the wines reflect elegance and balance. Ann has bottled several wines using both natural and synthetic corks and will compare them over the course of their maturation.

PELLER ESTATES

Established **1991** ***Owner*** **Andrés Wines** ***Production*** **750,000 cases** ***Vineyard area*** **240 acres (97 ha)**

Andrés Wines, founded by Andrew Peller in 1961, became famous for its success with Baby Duck, a low-alcohol sweet sparkler that enjoyed enormous success in

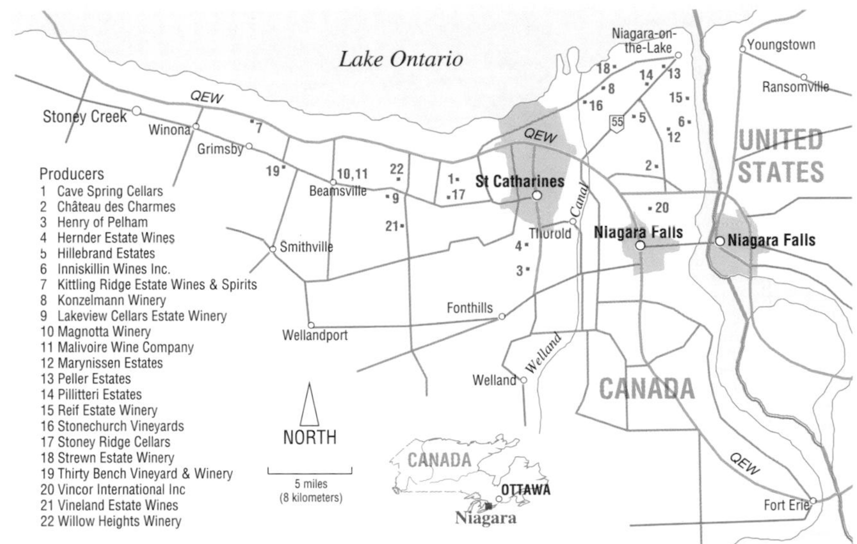

ABOVE: *Wine education at Hillebrand Estates, Ontario.*

Icewine

Half of Canada's wineries are clustered together in the Niagara Peninsula. Known for decades as Canada's Banana Belt, the region is experiencing unprecedented growth. While garnering international attention as a producer of world-class icewine—the extreme climate facilitates production of this supersweet yet piercingly acidic wine—the jury is still out on its dry whites and reds. As with other developing regions, most local producers look to the superripe, highly extracted, and highly alcoholic styles popularized by the American wine press as their role models, rather than focusing on developing signature styles.

In June 2000, the Canadian Wine Institute, the German Deutscher Weinbauverband and the Austrian Vsterreichischer Weinbauverband agreed to set voluntary international standards for making icewine following traditional practices so the wine would stand apart from fraudulent and low-quality versions.

ABOVE: *Reif Estate Winery, Ontario.*

the 1970s. To change their image, Andrés developed a line of VQA wines under the Peller Estates label. In 1994, Andrés expanded their line by buying Hillebrand Estates Winery. Branded labels and competitively priced VQA wines are widely available across the province.

RIGHT: *Pillitteri Estates Winery, Ontario.*

PILLITTERI ESTATES WINERY

Established **1993** ***Owner*** **Gary Pillitteri** ***Production*** **20,000 cases** ***Vineyard area*** **37 acres (15 ha)**

Winery founder Gary Pillitteri came to Canada from Sicily after the Second World War and started growing grapes in the Niagara. Already a reputed amateur winemaker, Gary inaugurated his winery in 1993. A second generation of Pillitteris and their spouses now manage the vineyards, farm market, bakery, greenhouse and tasting room. Winemaker Sue-Ann Staff produces a range of wines including barrel-aged chardonnay, riesling dry, pinot grigio, vidal sussreserve, gewürztraminer icewine and cabernet sauvignon.

Regional Dozen

QUALITY WINES

Cave Spring Riesling Dry
Château des Charmes Cabernet Franc
Henry of Pelham Riesling Icewine
Inniskillin Vidal Pearl Icewine
Stoney Ridge Gewürztraminer Barrel-Fermented Icewine
Willow Creek Vidal Icewine

BEST VALUE WINES

Cave Spring Gamay
Hillebrand Estates Trius Brut
Malivoire Old Vine Foch
Pillitteri Cabernet Franc
Peninsula Ridge Chardonnay
Vineland Estate Dry Riesling

REIF ESTATE WINERY

Established **1983** ***Owner*** **Ewald Reif** ***Production*** **35,000 cases** ***Vineyard area*** **135 acres (55 ha)**

Ewald Reif brought 13 generations of winemaking tradition with him when he emigrated to Canada from Germany. His scenic vineyard benefits from the effects of Lake Ontario. In 1987, Ewald's nephew Klaus took up winemaking duties and immediately gained a reputation for himself with a stunning vidal icewine that was subsequently included in Robert Parker's top ten of the year. He now shares winemaking responsibilities with Roberto de Domenico.

STONECHURCH VINEYARDS

Established **1990** ***Owners*** **the Hunse family** ***Production*** **30,000 cases** ***Vineyard area*** **150 acres (61 ha)**

Grape growers since 1972, the Hunse family operates one of the largest estate wineries in Ontario; 85 percent of production is VQA. Their production of chardonnay, riesling, vidal late harvest, pinot noir, reserve cabernet sauvignon and other wines grew from 500 cases to 30,000 cases between 1990 and 1995.

STONEY RIDGE CELLARS

Established **1985** ***Owners*** **Cuesta Corporation** ***Production*** **70,000 cases** ***Vineyard area*** **134 acres (54 ha)**

When winemaker Jim Warren founded Stoney Ridge Cellars he produced 500 cases from a tin shed. In 1990, he went into partnership with grape grower Murray Puddicombe and they built a winery in Winona. They sold the winery to Ottawa investors in 1998, with Jim continuing as chief winemaker. They produce 52 different wines, mostly varietally-named from well-known French and German varieties, from three lines: Stoney Ridge Cellars, Cuesta Estates for premium wines and Woods End, a lower priced range.

THIRTY BENCH VINEYARD & WINERY

Established **1994** ***Owners*** **Dr Tom Muckle, Yorgos Papageorgiou, Frank Zeritsch and Deborah Paskus** ***Production*** **7,000 cases** ***Vineyard area*** **40 acres (16 ha)**

This tiny winery boasts the driest vineyard on the bench. Riesling is the emphasis here and all styles are made. Increasing quantities of vidal, chardonnay and a range of red *vinifera* wines are also made. The winery's philosophy emphasizes extensive cropping and long barrel aging.

VINELAND ESTATE WINES

Established **1988** ***Owner*** **John Howard** ***Production*** **30,000 cases (potential 70,000)** ***Vineyard area*** **300 acres (122 ha)**

Perched high on the side of the Niagara Escarpment, this winery has an unimpaired view of Lake Ontario. The constant flow of air from the lake protects vineyards near the escarpment by minimizing the effects of extreme heat and cold, and vines thrive on the well-drained slope of clay and loam. Riesling is the most planted grape and Winemaker Brian Schmidt is expanding the repertoire of red and white varieties with notable success.

WILLOW HEIGHTS WINERY

Established **1994** ***Owners*** **Ron and Avis Speranzini** ***Production*** **6,000 cases** ***Vineyard area*** **12 acres (5 ha)**

Ron Speranzini's goal is to emulate the wines of Burgundy and, after practicing for many years as an amateur, he now makes very limited quantities of handcrafted pinot. In 1998, the yield was thinned to 2 tons per acre (35 hl/ha), and the resulting wine showed delicate red berry fruit with a very elegant, balanced structure. Besides pinot noir, Willow Heights' wines include chardonnay, riesling, vidal, gewürztraminer, merlot and cabernet franc.

Other Ontario Regions

LAKE ERIE NORTH SHORE & PELEE ISLAND

In the Lake Erie North Shore and Pelee Island regions, summer temperatures are warmer than those of Niagara. However, Lake Erie is considerably shallower than Lake Ontario and consequently cools more quickly in winter. In colder years, the lake freezes over and ice packs often surround Pelee Island.

COLIO WINES OF CANADA

Established **1978** ***Owners*** **Enzo DeLuca and Joe Berardo** ***Production*** **200,000 cases** ***Vineyard area*** **180 acres (73 ha)**

The Colio vineyards are located within the North Shore Lake Erie VQA appellation, but the winery buys grapes from all three of Ontario's delimited grape-growing areas. Many of Colio's wines are brand-named and sold within the lower price ranges, but they still manage to escape the ordinary by reason of winemaker Carlo Negri's flair. The Colio Estates Vineyard label, a line established in 1999, introduced premium and ultra-premium wines. It includes a line of red and white varietals and a vidal icewine. The winery now has a considerable export market.

PELEE ISLAND WINERY

Established **1980** ***Owner*** **Wolf von Teichman** ***Production*** **200,000 cases** ***Vineyard area*** **500 acres (202 ha)**

While not exactly Mediterranean in climate, Pelee Island does enjoy the longest growing season and some of the hottest daytime temperatures in Canada. Chardonnay and a number of German varietals were among the first varieties planted, but reds now form an important part of the portfolio. Pelee Island has the largest plantings of *vinifera* vines of any Ontario winery, and their VQA bottlings are very competitively priced. Winemaking is under the direction of Walter Schmoranz.

Regional Best

Colio Cabernet Franc
Leblanc Riesling
Pelee Island Gamay/Zweigelt
Pelee Island Pinot Noir

BELOW: Chardonnay grapes, Ontario.

ABOVE: *Notre-Dame de Québec Basilica-Cathedral is the center of the oldest parish in North America.*

Other Canadian Regions

QUÉBEC

Québec has a difficult climate for vine growing, particularly of *Vitis vinifera* varieties. Winter is vine-splittingly cold, with many days of 5°F (-20°C). Summers are short and often humid. The region in which grapes are grown is situated on a vast glacial plain to the south and southeast of Montréal. The western sector of this plain—the Montérégie—is slightly warmer than the neighboring Eastern Townships, where vineyards are clustered around Dunham. Experience has shown that some grape varieties that grow well in the Montérégie are not so successful in the Townships.

RIGHT: *Riesling grapes.*

Vinifera varieties are in the minority here, although some growers do have microclimates where auxerrois, chardonnay and riesling can thrive. The preferred white grape hybrids are seyval blanc, vidal, cayuga, geisenheim, éona and cliche-vandal; de chaunac, maréchal foch, st croix, seyval noir, baco noir and chancellor are favored for reds. One advantage of the cold is that in some of the lesser varieties, the least attractive characteristics are minimized, particularly a musky odor termed "foxy."

Notable producers in Québec, in addition to those listed below, include Vignoble Dietrich-Jooss, Vignoble Morou, and Domaine des Côtes D'Ardoise where riesling and gamay are grown as well as a number of successful hybrids.

DOMAINE DES CÔTES D'ARDOISE

Established **1984** ***Owner*** **Jacques Papillon** ***Production*** **1,600 cases** ***Vineyard area*** **20 acres (8 ha)**

Planted in 1980 in the Dunham area by Christian Barthomeuf, this vineyard was the first in the province. It enjoys a microclimate warm enough to support *vinifera* varieties and has the advantage of a protective horseshoe shape. Riesling and gamay are grown, and a number of successful hybrids. The name Côtes d'Ardoise refers to the slate that is contained in the soil. Current owner Jacques Papillon has hired Vera Klokocka and John Fletcher, former owners of Hillside Estate Winery in British Columbia, to oversee production of one of the broadest ranges produced by a Québec winery.

VIGNOBLE LES ARPENTS DE NEIGE

Established **1992** ***Owner*** **Gilles Séguin** ***Production*** **2,000 cases** ***Vineyard area*** **12 acres (5 ha)**

King Louis XIV's advisors, referring to Québec, may not have thought that a few acres of snow were worth fighting for, but Les Arpents de Neige owner, Gilles Séguin, thinks his few acres of snow are well worth the effort. Working with French winemaker Jean-Paul Martin, Les Arpents de Neiges makes an excellent seyval and some blended wines from hybrids.

VIGNOBLE DE L'ORPAILLEUR

Established **1982** ***Owners*** **Hervé Durand, Frank Furtado and Pierre Rodrigue** ***Production*** **6,500 cases** ***Vineyard area*** **24 acres (10 ha)**

This winery's name came from a statement by Québecois folk singer, Gilles Vigneault, who once said that, "Making wine in Québec is like panning for gold." But founder Hervé Durand must be a successful prospector, because l'Orpailleur has become the leading winery in the province. Originally from the south of France, Durand studied enology in Dijon, then went to Argentina to teach it before coming to Québec to practice it. Marc Grau, who hails from France, has been winemaker since 1991. L'Orpailleur's Seyval is a standard-setter in Québec.

LA VITACÉE

Established **1979** ***Owners*** **Réjean Gagnon and Alain Loiselle** ***Production*** **200 cases** ***Vineyard area*** **10 acres (4 ha)**

This winery in the Montérégie may be tiny, but it is important in terms of experimental planting. To discover which varieties can survive the winter without hilling, owners and winemakers Réjean and Alain Loiselle have trained hybrids to high trellises, then strung a line of 60-watt light bulbs along the top to ward off frost. From their experimentation, they have selected some hybrids such as de chaunac and st croix for increased plantings and plan to quadruple the vineyard size. They work with enologist Luc Rolland in the production of the wine and use Missouri oak to age the reds.

NOVA SCOTIA

Although Nova Scotia's climate is only marginally suitable for growing grapes, the hardy Russian varieties michurinetz and severny do thrive here. Also, trials have shown that certain resistant *vinifera* vines can grow in protected microclimates.

Wineries are located in the Annapolis Valley, bordering the Bay of Fundy, and on the northeast shore overlooking the Northumberland Strait between Nova Scotia and Prince Edward Island. In both cases sheltered waters provide the necessary mitigating forces. A climatic advantage here is the slow ripening of grapes over a cool summer benefits the flavor and structure of the wine.

Only about 300 acres (121 ha) of vines are growing in the province. Plantings of early-ripening *vinifera* vines are increasing. Grapes of choice are seyval blanc, new york muscat, l'acadie blanc and geisenheim clone gm for whites. The most widely planted red varieties are michurinetz and maréchal foch.

A significant Nova Scotian producer, in addition to Sainte Famille Wines (below), is Jost Vineyards, which is planted mostly with hybrids such as baco noir and seyval.

SAINTE FAMILLE WINES

Established **1989** ***Owners*** **Suzanne and Doug Corkum** ***Production*** **4,500 cases** ***Vineyard area*** **30 acres (12 ha)**

This tiny winery is situated within the confines of an old Acadian village founded in 1680. The vineyard's protected site on a south-facing slope by the Avon River allows chardonnay, riesling and cabernet franc as well as a selection of hybrids to thrive. Winemaker Suzanne Corkum leans towards clean, crisp whites and barrel-aged reds. She uses Nevers, Limousin and Allier oak, and has plans to try some barrel fermentation for the whites.

BELOW: *Château Frontenac, Québec City, Québec.*

The colorful tasting room at the Pisano winery, Montevideo, Uruguay.

Mexico and South America

ABOVE: *Preparing new vineyards for planting, Mexico.*

was called la California, an area far better suited to viticulture than the warmer south. One of the priests charged with establishing vineyards around the missions of New Spain was Juan Ugarte and he most probably planted the first mission grapes in northern Mexico and California. In fact, the oldest surviving winery in Mexico, the Bodega Marqués de Aguayo, was founded in 1593. Today it produces only a tiny amount of wine, most of which, as is often the case in Mexico, is reserved for distilling into brandy.

Today, major worldwide producers such as Domecq, González Byass, Hennessy and Martell all have significant investments in Mexico. Sparkling wine interests have also entered the market with not inconsiderable force, including Freixenet and Martini & Rossi. These firms pick early to ensure acidity in their grapes. Cinzano and Seagrams are equally well-established.

Wine regions

Baja California in the northwest and the high-altitude valleys of the Sierra Madre offer the best potential for winemaking. Their slightly cooler nights give enologists at least a chance of capturing something like the varietal aromas so sought after.

Baja California has a climate and topography as well suited to large-scale quality viticulture as Mexico can muster. More than 10,000 acres (4,000 ha) are planted here, mainly near Ensenada in the Guadalupe Valley. Bodegas de Santo Tomás makes commendable chardonnay and some cabernet sauvignon that, although not aromatically perfect, is passable. Bodegas de Santo Tomás and Monte Xanic give Mexican winemaking a diversity that is evident in the varieties used. You can find wines from chardonnay to viognier, from barbera through cabernet sauvignon to pinot noir here. Bodega Santa Tomás alone grows 14 different varieties. L. A. Cetto makes Mexico's most memorable and recommendable range of wines. Their nebbiolo and petit syrah have met with some critical success, although not every harvest has yielded a wine you could express full confidence in, which gives some idea of the difficulties enologists have to work against. Stainless steel has brought significant improvements in Mexico, as wine storage used to be one of the prime causes for the wholesale oxidation of wines kept in tanks at relatively high temperatures. Earlier bottling is another factor that is influencing wines positively.

Laguna, Torreón, has seen recent investment at Bodega Vergel. New vinification equipment struggles admirably to coax aromatic life out of grapes that grow in a warm climate, even those that have been planted at some altitude.

Parras Valley, Saltillo, north of Mexico City, is almost certainly America's earliest viticultural enclave. An altitude of 1,500 feet (458 m) comes to the rescue here. Still, brandy remains king. Of historical note is Bodegas de San Lorenzo, founded in 1626. Viñedos San Marcos is quite a modern establishment, producing reasonable sparkling wine and some modest cabernet sauvignon.

San Juan del Río takes viticulture to 6,000 feet (1,830 m), allowing for somewhat more aromatic potential in the grapes near harvest time. Cavas de San Juan makes some interesting cabernet sauvignon and tentative pinot noir under the Hidalgo label here. Its Carte Blanche sparkling wine is worthy of note.

RIGHT: *Corked bottles of chardonnay stored at Château Camou, Guadalupe Valley, Mexico.*

Sonora is home to extensive plantations of the Thompson seedless variety. This is mostly edible grape and brandy territory.

Zacatecas and Aguascalientes plateaus grow grapes at up to 7,000 feet (2,135 m). Bodegas Altiplano has some reasonable wines. A new region called Querétaro may yet provide further potential for aromatic properties in varietals that have been carefully selected.

PERÚ

As the focal point of Spain's imperial presence in South America, Perú was the first country on the continent of South America to benefit from viticulture. The first vineyards were planted there in the 1540s, however climatic conditions did not favor the production of quality wine. But with the advent of distillation into grape brandy, the prospects for viticulture changed considerably.

The Pisco Valley, 100 miles (160 km) south of the capital, Lima, proved a suitable spot for cultivating moscatel, torontel, albillo and a host of lesser-known grape varieties, all destined to be distilled into a spirit also called Pisco.

Landscape and climate

Perú is divided into three main geographical areas: coastal (bordering the Pacific to the west), central mountain (made up of two huge cordilleras of the Andes with an altiplano or high-altitude plain) and the Amazon Basin (to the east). All viticulture of note takes place in the coastal area, reaching up into the foothills of the Andes. This area is made up of a sandy-alluvial strip of varying width, punctuated by oases arising wherever rivers flow down with life-giving water from the Andes. Winter temperatures remain too high for vines to go into full dormancy, which makes it difficult to restrain vigor, although careful monitoring of anhydrous stress can yield reasonable results. Most Pisco producers can obtain two harvests per year.

Vines and wines

The main force in Peruvian winemaking today is Tacama, based a short distance outside the city of Ica. Stainless steel and temperature control have transformed production, which can total 792,000 gallons (3 million liters). Varietal malbec and blends such as Gran Vino Tinto Reserva Especial form the backbone of Tacama's quality production. Other producers include Viña Ocucaje, also based in Ica; Canepa in Tacna; and Fábrica Nacional de Licores in Surco.

BRAZIL

If big is beautiful, Brazil has it all. Commercially, demographically and geographically, Brazil is a giant. Artistically and musically its contribution cannot be ignored. With 180 million people, all determined to make their mark on life, this is hardly surprising. The eighth-largest economy in the world (twice the size of Russia's) is certainly a place to sell wine.

Although Brazilian interest in wine is still nascent, with the annual consumption currently at less than half a gallon (2 l) per capita, the potential for growth is plain to see. What is also clear to those in charge of the Brazilian economy is that even this small amount multiplied by 180 million would mean a hemorrhage of hard-earned currency if all that wine had to be imported. Fortunately for the exchequer, although perhaps not so for the wine-lover, Brazil is South America's third-largest wine producer after Argentina and Chile.

Landscape and climate

Brazil is not ideal for viticulture—the climate is far too moist and hot, and it is difficult to find varietal character in grapes grown in such conditions—so viticulture is concentrated in the cooler southernmost regions. There are two main clusters: Rio Grande do Sul, which includes the hilly Serra Gaucha region, and Frontera. Even here humidity, rainfall and heat can cause problems, particularly near harvest. While Serra Gaucha

ABOVE: *Reaping the rewards of the season.*

CENTER: *A wineskin popular in earlier times; they are little more than a curiosity these days.*

BELOW: *Vineyard at Pedro Domecq, Baja California, Mexico.*

ABOVE: *The vineyards and winery buildings at Establecimineto Juanico, Canelones, Uruguay.*

developed as a result of immigrant settlement, Frontera was chosen for its viticultural potential on slightly more scientific grounds and so holds most promise. There have also been some attempts at tropical viticulture near Recife, but these have yet to attract serious attention.

Vines and wines

Only the bravest or those with the most to gain pit themselves against the elements to make wine in Brazil. Market leaders such as Remy Martin and Moët & Chandon are all found here. Sparkling wine is made to reasonably high standards and Serra Gaucha may be better suited to this type of production than to still wine. The Aurora co-operative is based in Bento Gonçalves and makes a commendable effort to market still wines.

The *parrera*, or traditional overhead vine-training, is being discarded in favor of more advanced styles in an effort to improve fruit quality. Fruit is certainly the key to the future of the industry here, where there is so often a need to chaptalize.

Regional Best

QUALITY WINES

Chardonnay del Museo Carrau
Preludio Juanico
Sauvignon Blanc Castillo Viejo
Tannat RPF, Pisano
Tannat Viejo Stagnari

BEST VALUE WINES

Cabernet Franc Castillo Viejo
Cabernet Sauvignon Calvinor
Cabernet Sauvignon Stagnari
Merlot Abuelo Don Domingo, Falcone
Merlot De Lucca

URUGUAY

When wine buyers first started to trace wines from interesting places around the world, few would have considered this small cosmopolitan country. Despite this, Uruguayan wines have been a presence at international wine fairs for longer than those of Argentina. Its winemakers have succeeded in penetrating even the most demanding markets with products that are imaginative and well made. With an annual domestic wine consumption of some 8 gallons (30 l) per head, international winelovers are lucky to see any of it. The future holds great promise for this tiny producer nation, which was first settled in 1726 by 25 families from the Canary Isles. With them came the knowledge of how to make wine in difficult conditions.

From wine
what sudden friendship
springs.

JOHN GAY *(1685–1732)*
Fables

Vines and wines

Uruguay has eight wine regions encompassing fifteen smaller subregions. The most important of these regions are Canelones, Montevideo, Colonia and Artigas. There are over 24,700 acres (10,000 ha) of vineyards planted, divided among 370 bodegas. Total annual production is about 24 million gallons (91 million l) per year.

While Uruguay may not have the ideal, dry and sunny conditions found in central Argentina or Chile, careful vineyard techniques allow for more than adequate viticultural conditions. Rainfall, especially toward the Brazilian border, causes some problems. One solution adopted in 1984 was to train vines on the Lyre system, known here as the Lira. This system, invented in 1970 by Dr Alain Garbonneau, optimizes photosynthetic effect and foliage aeration. To date, about 865 acres (350 ha) have been planted and are growing under this system, the most significant area anywhere in the world. Another important fact is that tannat planted by Pascual Harriague in 1838 has adapted very well to its local environment and has gone on to make exceptionally smooth and velvety wine with depth and complexity. Today there is more tannat planted here than anywhere else.

LEFT: Daniel Pisano corks a bottle in the cellars at the family-owned Pisano winery, Uruguay.

CALVINOR, ARTIGAS

Established **1975** ***Owners*** **Cooperative** ***Production*** **177,780 cases** ***Vineyard area*** **346 acres (140 ha)**

An impressive bodega in a warm and humid area near the Brazilian border, this big modern winery takes full advantage of vineyards that must be carefully managed to produce quality fruit at the optimum moment. The results are surprisingly good, especially when you realize that Calvinor mainly aims to reach the value-for-money market. If they set their minds to it, Calvinor could aim even higher with their wines.

IRURTIA, COLONIA

Established **1913** ***Owners*** **the Irurtia family** ***Production*** **500,000 cases** ***Vineyard area*** **865 acres (350 ha)**

This bodega harnesses cabernet franc (probably the country's second-best grape) and tannat to good effect. Try the Posada del Virrey Tannat.

LOS CERROS DE SAN JUAN, COLONIA

Established **1854** ***Owners*** **the Terra family** ***Production*** **111,110 cases** ***Vineyard area*** **198 acres (80 ha)**

This concern is deserving of inclusion in history books and maybe even the list of World Heritage sites. The ancient winery is near the beautiful town of Colonia, by the mouth of the River Plate. Deep below the old stone building lies a large cistern encircled by a complex of Edwardian copper piping. The remarkable thing is that in the early 1900s a German winemaker was trying to cool his fermentations by means of cold water. He collected the winter rainfall off the roof and stored it in the underground cistern at close to freezing point. During fermentation he would draw water out through specially designed pipes, driving the flow with steam pumps, to chill the fermenters. This is surely one of the earliest sophisticated temperature-controlled fermentation systems. Today's winemaker, Estela de Frutos, makes deep and chewy tannat wines from grapes grown in what are among the most interesting and picturesque vineyards in Uruguay.

ESTABLECIMINETO JUANICÓ, CANELONES

Established **1979** ***Owners*** **the Deicas family** ***Production*** **355,555 cases** ***Vineyard area*** **544 acres (220 ha), plus 988 acres (400 ha) managed**

With its impressive vineyards, this winery exudes an air of efficiency and enthusiasm. It made a name for itself by selling to Britain's extremely demanding chain store, Marks & Spencer. Wines such as the exquisite Preludio demonstrate clear vision and attention to detail, down to using the tiniest percentage of petit verdot to complement a tannat, cabernet franc and cabernet sauvignon blend.

Other significant wine producers in Uruguay include Castel Pujol, Pisano (both Montevideo); Stagnari (Canelones); and Castillo Viejo.

BELOW: Vineyard workers grafting cabernet sauvignon onto phylloxera-resistant rootstock; Casa Madero, Pajas Valley.

The foreman oversees the harvest in the vineyards at Viña Los Vascos, Santiago, Chile.

Chile and Argentina

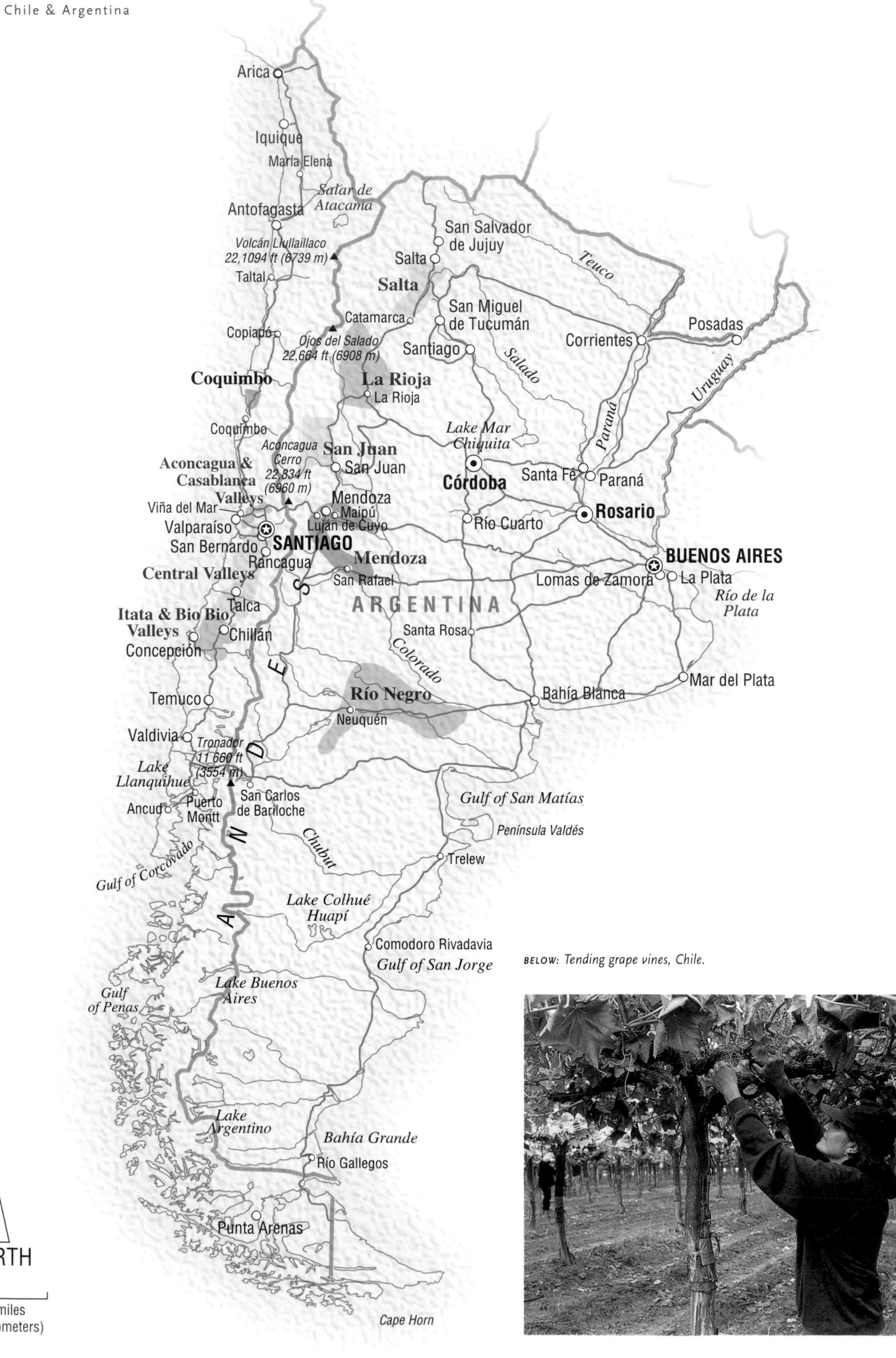

BELOW: *Tending grape vines, Chile.*

Chile and Argentina

HAROLD HECKLE

ABOVE: *Winemaker Raoul de la Mota in the cellars at Bodegas & Cavas de Weinert, Mendoza, Argentina.*

Chile's winemaking heritage goes back to the arrival of the Spanish conquistadors in the sixteenth century. However it is only since the early 1980s that the country has been seen as a "viticultural paradise." Chile's geographic isolation has meant that it is one of only a few wine regions in the world to remain phylloxera-free, and the wines produced here—blockbuster merlots, splendid carmenères and great-value sauvignon blancs—have today emerged as powerful products worldwide.

When Argentine wine began to appear in the international market, few consumers realized the magnitude of the phenomenon involved. In wine terms, this was the last great undiscovered land. Its size and isolation are subjects that merit special attention, but even more intriguing for the wine lover is the potential within such a vast viticultural landscape.

LEFT: *A mold-blown green goblet.*

CHILE

Chile's location on the southwestern extremity of Latin America lends it an air of isolation, reinforced by the Andes mountain range rising to unbelievable heights in the east. A smaller ridge rises to 3,000 feet (900 m) above sea level on the forward edge of the landmass, and between this ridge and the Andes lies a longitudinal depression called a "valley." This valley extends southward from latitude 32° to 42°, where it begins to submerge and form fjord-like inlets.

The protected environment created between the two ranges provides a shelter for flora and fauna. The only problem is that low rainfall levels limit life to a semi-arid existence on newly exposed and poor soil in most of the valley. The violence of the geological forces that created the Andes means that much of the surface is not so much soil as the chaotic remnants of smashed and tortured rock.

Agriculture

It is difficult to be precise about the age of human settlement in the valley. Recent research, mainly from new archeological digs nearby in Argentina, has uncovered much new evidence that will take time to decipher fully. It seems that human beings have existed in the area for longer than was previously thought. What is certain is that different human settlements clustered along the coast and the valley, all the way down to Tierra del Fuego, surviving by fishing and limited agriculture. Several tribes became dominant and grew in size and sophistication. Some of

BELOW: *Loading grapes at harvest time, Proviar Vineyards, Mendoza.*

ABOVE: Vines at the Bodega Errazuriz Panquehue, Aconcagua Valley, in the Coquimbo region.

these tribes were very spirited and not only survived colonization, but in some cases, for example the dark-eyed Araucanos, were never completely subdued by the colonizers. A number of important tribes, such as the Araucanos and the Mapuche, are extant to this day, although fairly well assimilated into the population.

Agriculture moved to a totally different level of complexity after the arrival of the Incas, who seem to have been exceptionally talented agriculturists with a positive genius for irrigation. Whatever agriculture was already in existence was transformed dramatically under the Incas' administration and influence. The Incas harnessed the available water with an intricate array of canals, dams and storage tanks; they even devised a legal framework that ensured its equitable distribution and guaranteed that water was available to all.

Naturally enough, this development transformed agriculture and the underlying ecology of the valley. Silt from the rivers improved the fertility of the land and farming became an established way of life. By the time the Spanish conquistadors arrived in about 1536, comfortable subsistence was no longer an issue and the indigenous population would have stood at 500,000 approximately.

Advanced viticulture

When Napoleon intervened in Spain, placing his brother on the throne, Spain's American colonies felt a shiver of apprehension and a desire to break away. While turmoil gradually built up in Latin America, Chile began its process of secession on September 18, 1810. By February 12, 1818, it was at last free to determine its own destiny.

In the early 1830s, a forward-thinking Frenchman named Claude Gay obtained the backing of the Chilean government to establish a nursery for botanical species from around the world. Called the Quinta Normal, it was to play a decisive role in South American, and even world, viticulture. A wide range of botanical specimens was brought in, including a fairly complete compendium of grape varieties. This collection of plants, isolated from the infections that later ravaged vineyards across the world, proved invaluable in restocking nursery vineyards in Europe. This fine effort was aided by the work begun under the instigation of Silvestre Ochagavía Echazarreta, a wealthy Chilean landowner of Basque ancestry. Determined to make wines similar to those he had sampled while on a grand tour of Europe, Echazarreta imported a good supply of cuttings of the classic varietals, along with a French winemaker.

Looking back, it is difficult to imagine the disaster for European agriculture that was the phylloxera infestation of little more than a century ago. Whole rural populations were plunged into despair, even starvation, and never again would vines grow trouble-free in European soil. In the catastrophe's aftermath, Europe turned to Chile for virus-free vine cuttings.

Landscape and climate

Located at a latitude of between 32°30' and 38° south, Chile's vineyards are a similar distance from the equator as some of their northern hemisphere equivalents. The effect of the Pacific currents and the significant barrier to continental heating by the Andes ensure a cooler environment than seems possible. The Humboldt Current in particular brings the cooling influence of the Antarctic to Chile's coastal regions.

The great altitude of the Andes inevitably traps and precipitates clouds and atmospheric humidity as high-altitude rain and snow. As temperatures fluctuate, melting snow runs down the slopes and makes its way to the sea. The consequences flowing from this are in several ways important to life in the valley. The water creates oases, and the erosion at higher altitudes fills the rivers with silt which they disgorge in the valley, providing a more attractive *milieu* for plant life. Significantly, the rivers breach the second ridge on their way to the sea, opening the ecosystem of the valley to maritime influences, which helps to temper the natural tendency toward desertification. Once daylight temperatures rise in the valley, rising hot air draws in cooling, humid air from the coast, while at night the effect is reversed. In the wettest areas annual rainfall averages are generally below 32 inches (800 mm). The rainy season comes in winter and its effects are felt mostly in the south and to a lesser extent in the west, in the shadow of the coastal ridge.

ABOVE: *Vineyards at Cousiño Macul, in the Maipo Valley near Suntlago.*

Spanish influence

Chile's population grew rapidly throughout the eighteenth and nineteenth centuries principally through European migration. The first lot of immigrants came chiefly from Spain and was composed to a great extent of Basque families. The next lot of immigrants came more from Germany, England and Italy. Fortunes made by exploiting Chile's natural wealth gave rise to a status-conscious, land-owning class that felt it was appropriate to include wine-making estates in its portfolios. Eventually, about ten such powerful families (principally Basque) controlled fruit and wine production in Chile.

Over time, the per capita consumption of wine in Chile increased to the point where it became attractive to the exchequer from a taxation point of view. Slowly, as taxes increased, the incentive to be bold and invest receded from the Chilean wine industry.

The arrival of the vine

The spot chosen by the conquering Spaniards for the new capital city, Santiago de Chile, was strategically placed at the northern edge of the valley, from then on to be known as el Valle Central, the central valley. Each of the smaller valleys criss-crossing the Valle Central retained the name of its river, some reflecting the pre-Columbian cultures that had once flourished there.

To begin with, viticulture was not an imperative in Chile. Although vines were imported into Mexico early on, the first Spaniards to arrive in South America were much more interested in the glint of gold. The political reality they faced was also pretty snarled. Some vines were inevitably imported with other foodstuffs and would have entered South America via Perú. It is generally assumed that vines arrived near Santiago de Chile in the mid-sixteenth century. To complicate matters even further, by the seventeenth century Spain dictated that no wine should be produced in the new lands of las indias, *the Indies, in an effort to protect and even boost domestic wine production in the Iberian Peninsula. It is difficult to imagine how the instigators of this law ever imagined it could be enforced.*

The first varieties grown appear to have been grapes for eating. What is certain is that it was always going to be difficult to enforce the letter of the law in such a vast expanse of land. Research suggests that small vineyards, producing wine for personal consumption, were soon in full swing around the early settlements. Another factor in the early spread of viticulture involves the Church. As an integral part of the holy sacrament, wine simply had to be available for the communion service. Early missions would have ensured a supply of wine by one means or another. In fact, the grape variety that proliferated in the Viceroyalty of New Spain (which later became Mexico) and its northernmost province of La California is to this day known as "mission." This same variety is known as "país" in Chile and "criolla chica" in Argentina.

As more settlers arrived from Europe, mainly migrants from the harsh, southwestern provinces of Spain, grape-growing became quite a well-established adjunct to farming. We can imagine that wine-making was equally prevalent. Evidence of this can be found in a recommendation sent by the Governor of Chile in 1678, exhorting Spain to lift the ban on vineyards so as to encourage the establishment of more homesteads or estancias. By this stage it must have been obvious that grapes were well-suited to the environment. A lack of humidity during the vegetative and fruit cycles led to healthy bunches come harvest time, the dry conditions reducing the risk of fungal infections to an absolute minimum. The absence of downy and powdery mildew would have meant bigger yields and much healthier crops than were possible in Europe.

Carmenère

The vigorous carmenère is the grape variety behind many of Chile's finest red wines. It produces deeply flavored, smooth, carmine-colored wines. For many years carmenère was mislabeled as merlot, but is now coming into its own. Agustin Hunees, President of Veramonte Winery, says "It's a great grape, but it's one dimensional. It has the best mouthfeel of any red; low in acidity but with lots of flavor. We have three choices: eliminate it, promote it as our national grape or use it as a unique component in blends. I think the future lies in our last option."

ABOVE: *Laborers in the vineyard. Women pruning vines near Santiago.*

Toward the end of the 1960s, investment in the industry was very slow and quality was generally patchy. Still, Chile's reputation was already beginning to take shape, and it was possible to find some respectable wine at good prices. Chile eventually descended into a disastrous period of political and economic turmoil that led to little wine being exported and even less money being directed to vineyards and wineries.

Modernization

Nothing remains the same for long in regions as promising as Chile. Fresh blood, a commitment to improving quality and expanding markets, and new investment have all been rewarded. Playing its strongest hand, Chile began by improving and marketing its red wines. It was cabernet sauvignon that appeared first. Beguiling and pure aroma came along with its great color. Initially, cabernet was harvested slightly early, leading to capsicum and tomato bush aromas. These were formerly considered faults in the wine but are now, to some extent thanks to Chilean cabernets, enjoyed by wine lovers all over the world.

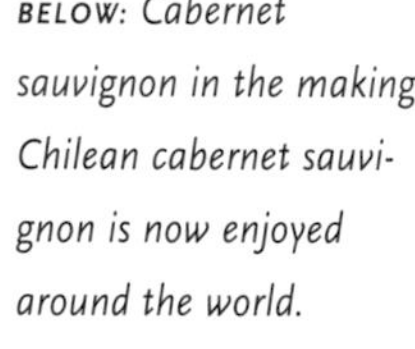

BELOW: *Cabernet sauvignon in the making. Chilean cabernet sauvignon is now enjoyed around the world.*

Next, Chile turned to white wines. By this time new money was being invested in new areas such as Casablanca. Research had shown that cooler areas would help produce aromatically charged white wines. Although Casablanca was farther north and nearer the equator, it was cooled by the maritime influences that had proved so successful in New Zealand. The gamble paid off.

Sauvignon blanc was the variety of choice in many of the new plantations. And the results were more than encouraging. In Britain and the United States, Chilean sauvignon blanc became a hit in the wine-bar and health-club circuits—this was certainly a major breakthrough for the country.

Not content with simply conquering middle markets, Chile joined hands with some of the greatest stars in the firmament of enology to tackle the top end of the market. So a new generation of Chilean super-wines was born. Names like Château Lafite-Rothschild, Château Mouton-Rothschild, Lurton, Robert Mondavi, Marnier Lapostolle and others were all folded into the fabric of Chilean wine. As these wines emerged—towering wines aimed at capturing exclusive markets—the price of Chilean wines generally began to rise.

Great names have been added to the nomenclature of serious winemaking. Caballo Loco, Montes Alpha "M," Almaviva, Domus Aurea, Finis Terrae and Seña all stand as testaments to the unimpeachable quality of Chilean wine.

Argentina might have its malbec, South Africa its pinotage and Uruguay its tannat, but Chile has great-value sauvignon blanc and very accessible merlot and carmenère. All of these wines come together under the umbrella of top wines of increasing sophistication.

Central Valleys & Other Regions

MAIPO VALLEY

This is perhaps the best-known name in Chilean wine, mainly because the valley is nearest to the capital, Santiago. As many of the original bodegas were built within a day's drive of the city, many are dotted around Maipo and its subregions, including Llano de Maipo and Buin. Today, those regions which are offering higher-quality fruit deserve greater recognition.

CONCHA Y TORO

Established **1883** ***Owners*** **Public company** ***Production*** **11,000,000 cases** ***Vineyard area*** **8,154 acres (3,300 ha)**

Another Maipo bodega with a great history, its Puente Alto vineyard provides grapes for the Marqués de Casa Concha Cabernet Sauvignon, for Don Melchor and Casillero del Diablo. These are wines that seldom disappoint. Cabernet sauvignon (and a great barrel-fermented sauvignon blanc) form the basis of these quality wines. A less-expensive line called Trio also offers great value for money. When it comes to high-quality wine, Concha y Toro has linked up with none other than Château Mouton-Rothschild to produce Almaviva. The inside of this winery looks a bit like Opus One, in California. The vineyard forms part of Puente Alto. To ensure that quality control is kept up to its legendary standards, it is Mouton that calls the shots here. As a consequence, some very high prices are paid for Almaviva wines. By all accounts, the price is worth paying. Every vintage has seen discernible improvement in quality.

VIÑA AQUITANIA

Owners **Paul Pontalier (of Château Margaux) and Bruno Prats (of Cos D'Estournel)**

This bodega produces another interesting wine that is well worth keeping an eye on: Paul Bruno, named after the two joint owners of the estate. The grapes are from vines adjacent to those of Domus Aurea on the Quebrada Macul and the first vintage was in 1994. From all accounts, the first vintages have had some teething problems evident in blind tastings, where the wines haven't done terribly well. It seems that both the 1997 and 1998 vintages may have righted the problems, but only time will tell. The 1998 vintage is the first to be widely available on the international market.

COUSIÑO MACUL

Established **1856** ***Owners*** **the Cousiño family** ***Production*** **200,000 cases** ***Vineyard area*** **1,359 acres (550 ha)**

Domus Aurea is produced from a single vineyard on the Quebrada de Macul slope—it is a wine full of promise.

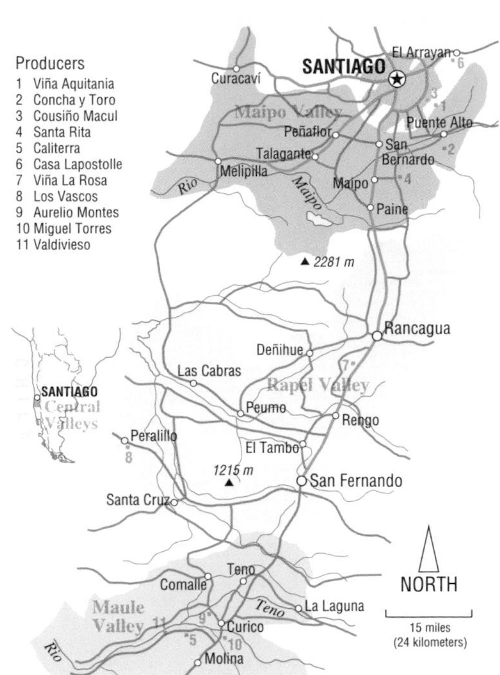

LEFT: Cabernet sauvignon vines growing at Viña Los Vascos near Santiago.

Regional Dozen

QUALITY WINES

Almaviva, Baron Philippe de Rothschild and Viña Concha y Toro
Clos Apalta, Casa Lapostolle
Cordillera, Miguel Torres
Montes Alpha M
Robert Mondavi—Eduardo Chadwick, Seña
Triple C, Santa Rita

BEST VALUE WINES

Concha y Toro Explorer Pinot Noir
Errazuriz Wild Ferment Chardonnay
Miguel Torres Cordillera
Sauvignon Blanc from Casa Lapostolle, Viña Casablanca or Viña Carmen
Valdivieso Caballo Loco
Viña Gracia Merlot

This wine is the result of a venture to make a single-vineyard wine that expresses the unique *terroir* of the Maipo Valley. Cousiño Macul has also joined forces with the Lurton brothers to produce Finis Terrae, an expensive super-premium wine which follows the bordeaux blend and which has engendered many good reviews.

SANTA RITA

Established **1880** ***Owners*** **Cristalerías de Chile S. A. 56.1%, Bayona S. A. 23.5%, others 20.4%**
Production **6 million cases** ***Vineyard area*** **4,940 acres (2,000 ha) not all producing**

The range of wines here, from the value-for-money 120 Selection (that includes a seductive pinot noir from Casablanca) to the recently released Triple C, are worthy ambassadors for Chilean enology. Medalla Real is a line that offers more quality and concentration than 120, as does Santa Rita Reserva. Note that Reserva in this case simply means "good wine" and is not subject to strictly defined standards imposed by a regulatory body. The winery brings fruit in from vineyards spread throughout the valley, notably from Casablanca, Rapel and Maule. Interestingly, the wines are now labeled as coming from specific, denominated areas. For example, according to the labels, Santa Rita Reserva Sauvignon Blanc comes from DO Valle del Maule, and Triple C (Premium Red Wine) from DO Valle del Maipo. The latter is quite an impressive wine.

RIGHT: Sauvignon blanc grapes ready for crushing; this variety has been enormously successful for the Chilean wine trade.

RAPEL VALLEY

Farther south, and slightly cooler than Maipo is Rapel. This vine-growing area is subdivided further, with Cachapoal to the north and Colchagua to the south. The most important wineries have major vineyard holdings here, including Santa Rita, Santa Emiliana and Undurraga. There is no doubt of the depth and concentration that wines from this valley can achieve. Cono Sur succeed in making interesting pinot noir at 13 percent by volume. Smaller, "boutique" wineries, such as Luis Felipe Edwards, are also worth keeping an eye on. Based in Colchagua, they make a good-value cabernet sauvignon called Pupilla. Greater concentration is to be found in Luis Felipe Edwards Cabernet Sauvignon, while topping the list is the Cabernet Sauvignon Reserva. Luis Felipe Edwards' Spectrum is broadened by carmenère and the chardonnay.

CALITERRA

Established **1989** ***Owners*** **Errazuriz Panquehue**
Production **and** ***Vineyard area*** **NA**

A fusion between Chile and California, in 1996 Caliterra became a joint venture between the Chadwick and Mondavi families. Winemaker Miguel Rencoret oversees a sparkling new state-of-the-art winery in the Arboleda del Guique, Colchagua Valley and new plantations have enabled the establishment to supply 50 percent of its needs. The facilities look space-age, especially when illuminated at night. For the time being, sauvignon and chardonnay are complemented with merlot and cabernet. In the future syrah, malbec, sangiovese and carmenère will bolster the existing range. Grapes are obtained from all of Chile's producing areas. This bodega has a capacity of 1,663,200 gallons (6.3 million l), but as yet there are no facilities for oak aging. An eyecatching array of gleaming stainless-steel tanks, ranging in capacity from 2,750 to 22,000 gallons (12,500 to 100,000 l), makes up the rows. All of these tanks can be heated to hasten malolactic fermentation. The Reservas are sent away to barrels in Curicó and San Felipe, Panquehue.

CASA LAPOSTOLLE

Established **1994** ***Owners*** **Marnier-Lapostolle (Grand Marnier), France and Rabat family, Chile** ***Production*** **180,000 cases**
Vineyard area **741 acres (300 ha)**

Some ventures succeed in capturing the imagination of wine lovers the world over. One such is Casa Lapostolle. This winery set off something of a chain reaction that generated headlines all over the world with the launching of its superb Cuvée Alexandre Merlot. So seductive is this wine that some wine experts consider it a good alternative to Pétrus. Reactions are perhaps a little more subdued these days, but Casa Lapostolle continues to

LEFT: Reaping the harvest. Picking cabernet sauvignon, Viña Los Vascos.

put forward great wines at what amounts to very affordable prices. Casa Lapostolle's more recent Clos Apalta takes its Carmenère/Merlot to an unfiltered and highly concentrated level of quality. The first vintage of this very attractive wine was 1997.

VIÑA LA ROSA

Established **1824** ***Owners*** **the Ossa family and Señor Recaredo Ossa** ***Production*** **480,000 cases** ***Vineyard area*** **1,483 acres (600 ha), increasing**

The winery lies 75 miles (120 km) south of the capital Santiago in the Rapel Valley. Palm trees native to Chile surround the vineyards, making Viña la Rosa a memorable landmark. It is from these palm plantings that the bodega gained its inspiration to name a new range of wines, La Palmería.

Chardonnay, cabernet sauvignon and merlot have been developed with an eye to the export markets. La Rosa is still owned by the founding family, who planted vines for the first time in the 1830s. With a capacity of 3,432,000 gallons (13 million l), this bodega is certainly worth knowing about, especially as it has access to good-quality, recent plantings of syrah, merlot, carmenère and cabernet sauvignon varieties.

LOS VASCOS

Established **1982** ***Owners*** **Domaines Barons de Rothschild (Lafite) & Viña Santa Rita** ***Production*** **400,000 cases** ***Vineyard area*** **1235 acres (500 ha), only 741 acres (300 ha) are producing**

Los Vascos is another headline-grabbing establishment, but if you consider the fact that Château Lafite-Rothschild has been a partner since 1988, this is hardly surprising.

MAULE VALLEY

With the arrival of Miguel Torres in this region, history began to change for Chilean winemaking. Torres settled in Curicó, situated directly south of Colchagua, although his vineyards are slightly to the east and closer to the cooling influence of the Andes. Maule contains other regions that are equally interesting, such as Cauquenes, Linares, Lontue, Parral and Talca. More than 61,775 acres (25,000 ha) make up this viticultural region.

AURELIO MONTES, CURICÓ

Established **1988** ***Owners*** **Douglas Murray, Alfredo Vidaurre, Aurelio Montes and Pedro Grand** ***Production*** **280,000 cases** ***Vineyard area*** **544 acres (220 ha)**

The vineyards contain some immaculate rows of recently planted clones. The quality of Aurelio's wines is beyond doubt. His Montes Alpha Cabernet Sauvignon is vivid and concentrated. His super premium Montes Alpha "M" has one drawback, it seems to be made to age for … well, no one has tasted one nearing maturity. The whole range is closed tight. There will be some stunning wines when they open up. While waiting for this happy event, you might like to try his refined sauvignon blanc or malbec.

BELOW: Barrel room at Cousiño Macul, a traditional bodega which still produces promising wines.

***Above:** Vats being sulfured at the winery of Errazuriz Panquehue, Coquimbo.*

MIGUEL TORRES, CURICÓ

***Established** 1979 **Owners** the Torres family **Vineyard area** 740 acres (300 ha)*

Torres is pursuing some interesting projects. For example, his Maquehua Chardonnay is fermented in small *barriques* of new Nevers oak and kept on lees for eight months. What makes this wine particularly attractive is the fact that it is made from a very careful clonal selection. After nearly two decades of careful identification, isolation and propagation, Torres selected three clones to make this wine: clone RC32, from Rio Claro, the coldest mountainside vineyard; clone SFN64, from the San Francisco del Norte estate; and clone Ma18, from the Maquehua estate. In terms of *tinto*, Cordillera is made from ancient cariñena vines from high up, nestled among the foothills of the Andes. The wine's *assemblage* combines the qualities of the old cariñena (60 percent) with syrah (30 percent) and merlot, the intention is to bring out the depth and finesse that ancient vines can lend to a wine, also pre-phylloxera cariñena provides a potent link with the Torres family's Catalonian ancestry.

VALDIVIESO, LONTUE

***Established** 1879 Owners the Mitjans, Gil and Coderch families **Production** 600,000 cases **Vineyard area** 494 acres (200 ha)*

Lontue is just to the south of Curicó, and here Jorge Coderch makes a fine selection of wines. The Barrel Selection malbec provides proof that you don't have to go all the way to Argentina for supple and deep malbec. Valdivieso Single Vineyard Reserve Cabernet Franc or Merlot are very attractive wines. Top of the list is Caballo Loco. Vinified in a bordeaux style, the wine is produced only in good years from Valdivieso's very best grapes. Fermented only in small quantities, it sells out very fast. Usually Caballo Loco sports a number on the label, depending on which release it is. The third release, for example, is labeled Caballo Loco No 3.

***Right:** Grape harvesting boxes wait beneath the vines for the pickers.*

COQUIMBO

This is the most northerly region in Chile. Too hot to make viable quality wine, the grapes grown here are used to make another famous drink, Pisco. Basically, Pisco is an *aguardiente*, literally a "firewater." It is distilled from muscat and pedro ximénez grapes. The process takes place in pot stills to give four categories of Pisco: Gran Pisco (43 percent by volume), Reservado (40 percent), Especial (35 percent) and Selección (30 percent). As an aperitif, Pisco is second to none.

Farther south, and straddling the Aconcagua River, the Aconcagua Valley is the most northerly of Chile's quality wine regions. Inland from the coast lie the Don Maximiano vineyards of Errazuriz at Viña Panquehue.

ERRAZURIZ PANQUEHUE, VIÑA PANQUEHUE

Established **1870** ***Owners*** **the Chadwick family** ***Production*** **405,000 cases** ***Vineyard area*** **927 acres (375 ha)**

The real class of this Coquimbo bodega can be seen in the uniform quality of its array of wines, from delicate and quite special Wild Ferment Chardonnay (made with natural yeasts), to characterful sauvignon blanc and chardonnay. The high spots are in the reds. These now include pinot noir, syrah, a Curicó Merlot that would please anyone, Aconcagua Merlot Reserva to blow the cobwebs away, and some gloriously aromatic cabernet blends, culminating in the Seña that combines cabernet with 10 percent carmenère and a touch of merlot.

CASABLANCA VALLEY

While nearer the coast, this is still technically part of Aconcagua. West of Santiago and south of Valparaiso and Viña del Mar, the location is just south of 33° latitude. Despite its apparently northern location, this region's success centers on a river valley that opens directly onto the Pacific Ocean. As as result, it is exposed to maritime effects almost continuously, which creates fog and mist. This results in 200 days of bright sunshine a year compared with 300 days farther inland.

Planting began in the Casablanca Valley in the early 1980s, concentrating on white grapes. Initially, chardonnay was the grape of choice, but since then considerable plantations of sauvignon blanc have gone in as a result of its relative success in the export markets. Some cabernet sauvignon and merlot complement the white grape varieties grown here.

Some wines are labeled as coming simply from the Valle Central. This is the safest and most honest way of describing wines made from fruit that might include grapes trucked in or bought from specialist growers in suitable vineyards up and down the valley. An example of this is the Vistasur Merlot, made by Vistamar. This however is not the case with the more upmarket wines such as Casa Lapostolle's Chardonnay and the Chardonnay Cuvée Alexandre, which clearly display "Casablanca Valley" on the label. Here, Michel Rolland has used French oak *barriques* to draw out local expression from single-vineyard Casablanca fruit.

VIÑA CASABLANCA

Established **1992** ***Owners*** **Viña Santa Carolina S. A.** ***Production*** **80,000 cases** ***Vineyard area*** **148 acres (60 ha), plus 544 acres (220 ha) under long-term lease**

Viña Casablanca was set up by Santa Carolina to exploit the success the region has had with the white varieties. Winemaker Ignacio Recabarren has guided this bodega to international acclaim, using fruit from the Santa Isabel Estate, but red grapes are brought in from other areas to enhance local bodegas' tinto vinification.

BÍO-BÍO VALLEY

ABOVE: *A view of the barrel room at Santa Carolina.*

This is the southernmost viticultural region of Chile. Once dedicated to the more humble varieties of grapes, such as moscatel de alejandria and país, recent times have witnessed a much keener interest in developing quality plantations in the region. New wineries are continuously springing up in Chile, despite the fact that there is a limit to the soils available for the planting of vines. One can find test plantings of 20 different varieties in the Bio-Bio Valley, mourvèdre and viognier are among them.

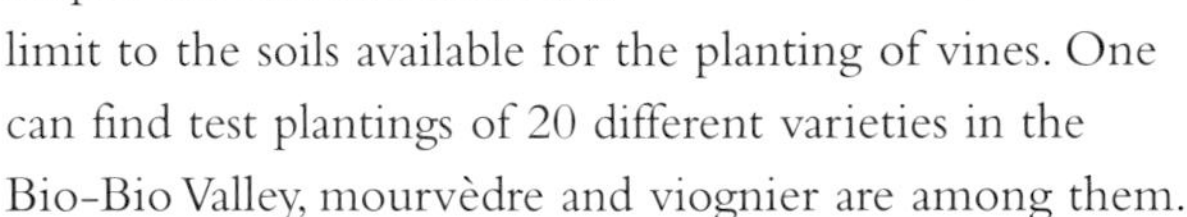

VIÑA GRACIA

Owners **Cópora Wineries** ***Production*** **and** ***Vineyard area*** **NA**

Córpora established Viña Gracia, an exceptionally stylish winery, to vinify fruit from vineyards in Aconcagua, Maipo, Cachapoal, and, notably, Bío-Bío. The winery is run by Jacques Antoine Toublanc, a Frenchman. The bodega has a total capacity of 1.25 million gallons (4 7 million l). Experimentation with yeasts has achieved some interesting results. One is a *barrique*-fermented chardonnay from Tatiwe made using yeast 1080, a culture native to Portugal's Vinho Verde.

LEFT: *Chardonnay, one of the popular white grapes in Chile, being harvested.*

ABOVE: The road from Salta to Cafayate, Salta.

ARGENTINA

Argentina is of great importance to the wine world because of the amount of land dedicated to the vine, the quantity of wine produced, the diversity of *terroir* involved, the specific varietals grown, and, as a result, the styles of wine possible. It ranks with the United States as the world's fourth-largest wine producer, after Italy, France and Spain, so it is rather surprising to find that until very recently it exported almost no wine.

Things are changing fast. No one can be in any doubt that, despite a stumbling start, Argentine wine will soon form an important part in the broad spectrum of international wines available to consumers around the world. How far Argentina will choose to go and how great it will become are questions to exercise the mind and stir the imagination.

The arrival of the vine

Vines were well-established in the Mendoza region by the sixteenth century, probably brought in by Juan Cédron, a Spanish priest. Although these early wines were intended for local consumption, word began to spread that they were better than some made elsewhere.

Things progressed slowly until 1880 when French botanist Aimé Pouget introduced the first French varieties. He chose Mendoza as the site for new plantations and discovered that top-quality vines thrived. One such variety that did particularly well in the western and northwestern areas of Mendoza was *la uva francesa,* the French grape, or malbec. Such was the perceived quality of this adapted variety that much of the red-grape plantations were dedicated to it, especially around Mendoza city and in neighboring Luján de Cuyo. Grown at around 2,623 feet (800 m) above sea level, it produced a lusty red wine, full of color and vibrancy that survived well in barrel, bottle and the leather pouch.

Following the completion of a rail link to Buenos Aires, a great explosion in wine-related activity began in Mendoza with a rapid proliferation of vineyards and bodegas. Quality was not initially sacrificed to profit. However, by the early twentieth century, wine consumption in Argentina had peaked at nearly 26.4 gallons (100 l) per capita, and with little regard for quality the industry went head-on into mass production. Good-quality vineyards, including prize malbec plots, were grubbed up and replaced with whatever yielded the most grapes.

The collapse began in 1980, with the national economy struggling and Argentina's foreign policy taking several turns for the worse. The huge Grupo Greco collapsed, bankrupting Bodega Arizu; other collapses followed. By 1988, the wine industry had sunk into the doldrums. There are still vast, untended, overgrown vineyards and abandoned workers' houses dotted around San Rafael in Mendoza.

What though youth gave love and roses, Age still leaves us friends and wine.

THOMAS MOORE (1779–1852), *National Airs, Spring and Autumn*

From this low point Argentina has risen once again to merit inclusion in international markets, though it is still dogged by political and economic strife.

Landscape and climate

Argentina is sometimes referred to as six continents crammed into one immense country, so diverse and extensive is its geography. The country sweeps from north of the Tropic of Capricorn (21° 46') to Tierra del Fuego at latitude 55° 03' south, and from sea level to a towering 22,816 feet (6,959 m) (Mount Aconcagua). The variety within this nation includes the widest imaginable spread of climatic conditions.

Argentine vineyards have been spared the devastation of phylloxera, although it certainly exists—you can occasionally see the mites clinging onto *vinifera* roots when you pull them up, but they seem to be kept well in check by several factors. Perhaps most crucial is the flood irrigation system used to water the vineyards here. Being aerobic, phylloxera probably detests being flooded. Global warming is a worry, though, as water runoff from the Andes appears to be diminishing with the warmer weather, an effect that is quite noticeable in Argentina. This has led to many growers opting for drip irrigation. In these cases most growers have taken the precaution of grafting vines onto resistant American rootstock.

Wine regions

Within Argentina are five main wine-producing regions spread over 15 geographically very different provinces.

Mendoza is responsible for about 95 percent of all exports because its 1,038 bodegas produce 75 percent of Argentina's wines, and it was the first region to adapt to higher-quality production. In the main, Mendoza vineyard care is natural and attuned to modern health and ecological considerations—brilliant sunshine and dry weather help keep diseases at bay. In some regions conditions are suited to developing wine styles of character.

San Juan, to the north of Mendoza, has yet to provide wine lovers with a winery of note. This situation may change soon, as massive investment has gone into planting international varietals in new, well-irrigated vineyards. When El Niño brought bad weather to Mendoza, San Juan came to the rescue with fruit of reasonable quality.

La Rioja is famous for its torrontés grape, locally called torrontés riojano. Originally this area supplied cheap wines for mass consumption on the domestic market but has now begun to move upmarket. The Co-operativa La Riojana is the largest in America. With a sizeable research budget, it is now a major presence on export markets, providing good-value wines at modest prices. Their Santa Florentina Torrontés has tamed the wildest excesses of the variety (using native yeasts) and offers a charming aperitif wine. Red wines are benefiting from antipodean techniques.

Salta is composed of many valleys, including Valles Calchaquíes, surely one of the most beautiful wine-producing valleys on earth. Bodegas Etchart (also found in Mendoza) has its principal winery here. Outstanding among its fine wines is the older, more mature style Arnaldo B. Etchart. This wine blends malbec with varying quantities of cabernet sauvignon and other French varietals to give quite an active nose and a well-rounded palate—Michel Rolland helped shape these wines. Etchart has made an art of torrontés wines and this variety is at its most subtle here. Varietal cabernet sauvignon has won positive comment and continues to improve.

Río Negro, in the south of Patagonia, contains a wine region of great promise. A deep rift valley protects the region around the General Roca, providing a macroclimate that seems to favour viticulture and soft fruits

BELOW: Sémillon arriving in boxes at the Weinert bodega.

ABOVE: *Redeemable tokens given to grape pickers at Finca Flichman, Mendoza.*

exceptionally well. The main producer here is Humberto Canale. From quality fruit come wines with some delicacy and a great deal of promise. With greater investment in the winery, who knows what may be possible. Another venture worthy of note is the French-owned Fabre-Montmayou, maker of the well-received Infinitus wines.

MENDOZA

Mendoza's wine-producing regions can be divided roughly into three areas: the main cluster in the north, more or less surrounding the sprawling city of Mendoza, one higher up and closer to the Andes to the west, and one to the south, toward the middle of the province.

The cluster around the city straddles the Mendoza and Tunuyán rivers and includes two of Mendoza's three DOs *(Denominación de Origen)*, Luján de Cuyo and Maipú. This area is itself subdivided into three regions.

La Zona Alta, properly known as Región de la Zona Alta del Río Mendoza, but also referred to as Primera Zona, the First Zone. It is blessed with some of the most picturesque vineyards in the world. The snow-capped Andes and the lower Cordón de Plata range act as a spectacular backdrop. The visual effect is made more striking by the fact that the area devoted to viticulture is flat, perfect cycling country. The soil is made up of the moraine and waterborne deposits eroded from the Andes. The surface is a very pale tan, fine, sandy, almost clay-like crust with negligible organic matter. It drains well and is suitable for high-quality wine. More than 300 bodegas cultivate almost 50,000 acres (20,235 ha) of vineyards in this area.

Región del Norte and ***Región del Este*** are lower than the Zona Alta and together encompass 210,000 acres (84,985 ha) dedicated to viticulture. Soils of the Región del Norte tend to be less porous and permeable than the other regions, favoring young fruity wines, both white and red. The Región del Este has a more complex soil structure. Some areas have deep upper layers with good water retention; others have solid rock strata near the surface and poor water retention.

Región del Valle de Uco (the Uco Valley Region), nearest the Andes, to the east, is divided into Tupungato, Tunuyán and San Carlos. At 3,300 feet (1,006 m) above sea level, this is the highest of Mendoza's regions and is currently attracting the most attention. Its soils are stony, alluvial sediments that produce quality wines. There are now more than 3,500 acres (1,417 ha) of vineyards in the region.

Región del Sur in the south is divided into General Alvear and San Rafael, Mendoza's third DO. At an altitude of 2,600 feet (793 m) above sea level and with sandy soils, the region can yield wines of delicate fragrance.

Vines and wines

It goes without saying that in any wine area as large as Mendoza there will be a bewildering array of grape varieties grown. The Zona Alta imparts special characteristics to many of the varieties grown there. Those that reach standards of world-class include bonarda, malbec, chardonnay and tempranillo (or tempranilla). Local

BELOW: *Pickers with boxes filled to the brim, wait for the truck at Proviar Vineyards.*

Susana Balbo

In a country dominated by male winemakers, Susana Balbo stands out for her incredible skill and experience. For 20 years, Susana produced wines for Argentina's top bodegas, and planned and built the most innovative winery in the nation, Bodega Catena. Susana was the first Argentine winemaker to be hired as a consultant to make wine outside of Argentina. Currently she is concentrating on her own label, Bodega Susana Balbo. Her current releases are Malbec, Cabernet Sauvignon and Brioso, which means "tenacity or strength of spirit."

torrontés grapes are somewhat more delicate than some found in other provinces.

The Región del Norte produces lively chenin blanc, ugni blanc and sangiovese. You will also see a great deal of pedro ximénez. The Región del Este specializes in cabernet sauvignon, syrah, sangiovese, chenin blanc, chardonnay and some less-than-typical sauvignon blanc. The cooler Valle de Uco yields chardonnay, merlot and malbec. The Región del Sur can claim some chardonnay, cabernet sauvignon and bonarda.

The powerhouse of Argentine winemaking today, Mendoza is in a state of constant dynamic flux with new entities starting all the time and old ones folding or merging with others. Starting in San Rafael, many *mendocino* bodegas are making quite an impact with the quality of their wines.

Nicolás Catena's holding company now controls about 25 percent of Argentina's top-quality vineyards with international varietals as well as substantial vineyard holdings in San Juan. Catena has reached this dominant position by employing a mix of strategies including careful investment, stealth, corporate buy-outs and even hostile takeovers. His stable now features some of the most remarkable wineries in all of Argentina, which include Bodega Catena, Bodega Escorihuela and Bodega Esmeralda.

BODEGAS Y VIÑEDOS SANTA ANA, GUAYMALLÉN

***Established* 1891 *Owners* Santa Carolina (Chile) and Luis Alfredo Pulenta *Vineyard area* NA**

This large bodega in the grand Argentine style has its own railroad siding and still sends trainloads of wine to Buenos Aires. Bought with Chilean (Santa Carolina) money, it has been modernized to a high standard, with a keen eye to exporting. While its current wines are still in a transitional stage, the future looks promising. A 100 percent syrah is packed full of deep, attractive fruit.

BODEGA BALBI, SAN RAFAEL

***Established* 1930 *Owner* Allied Domecq *Production* bought-in grapes**

Highly efficient and well thought out, this bodega's aim is to make good-value wines for everyday drinking. Balbi is singularly successful with a range of bright, well-made white wines. They also make a rosé that sells well in most markets, a rare thing. Their reds are approachable, clean and well-focused. Allied Domecq has helped transform this bodega.

BODEGAS VALENTÍN BIANCHI, SAN RAFAEL

***Established* 1928 *Owners* the Bianchi family *Vineyard area* 865 acres (350 ha)**

This old bodega is something of a rabbit warren, cramped and labyrinthine, in the middle of town. A long list of wines show the definable house style of vinification here and it isn't to everyone's taste. That said, they manage to extract some good fruit, for example, from wine made from Elsa's Vineyard grapes (look for this on the label). Recent attempts to take the wines further upmarket include building a modern

ABOVE: Vineyards lining the road at Chandon, Mendoza.

Regional Dozen

QUALITY WINES

Catena Alta Cabernet Sauvignon
Cheval des Andes Bordeaux Blend
Bodegas Chandon Baron B Sparkling Wine
Mapema Primera Zona Bordeaux Blend
Terrazas de Los Andes Gran Cabernet Sauvignon
Tikal Jubilo Bordeaux Blend

BEST VALUE WINES

La Agrícola Q Tempranillo
Balbi Malbec
Susana Balbo Malbec
Catena Malbec
Bodega Salentein Merlot
Etchart Torrontés

wine plant on the outskirts of the city, where they are beginning to produce some commendable traditional method sparkling wine. The range they call Famiglia Bianchi reflects their Italianate family roots.

BODEGA CATENA

Established **1999** ***Owner*** **Nicolás Catena**
Vineyard area **NA**

The newest and without a doubt the most innovative winery in Argentina, Susana Balbo (of Bodegas Martins) planned and built this bodega on a budget in record time, the first woman to head such an important and ambitious project in the country. Its cavernous hall boasts the latest vinification equipment imaginable, including computer-controlled robots that crush grapes directly above the gravity-fed tanks and later sink the caps individually for each tank. The design brings to mind a Maya pyramid. Without question, the wines emerging from here are bound to provide another quantum leap in terms of quality. The winery nestles beside Catena's Agrelo vineyards, not too far from the Tupungato plantations.

BODEGA CHANDON, AGRELO, LUJÁN DE CUYO

Established **1959** ***Owners*** **Moët & Chandon** ***Production*** **Millions of cases** ***Vineyard area*** **c.1,235 acres (c.500 ha)**

This was Moët & Chandon's first venture outside France, causing outrage in their home country at the

time (they don't use the traditional method to make sparkling wine). Today Bodega Chandon provides the domestic market with its top-selling charmat-style sparkler. The varietal chardonnay is very clean and is a great success in restaurants.

BELOW: Workers loading trucks with cabernet sauvignon at Finca Flichman, Maipú.

NAVARRO CORREAS, MAIPÚ

Established **c.1798** ***Owners*** **CINBA** ***Vineyard area*** **Small holdings in Luján de Cuyo, Maipú and Tupungato**

This bodega's current vineyards include the land that was once Tiburcio Benegas' famous bodega El Trapiche. The drinks company CINBA has invested heavily to bring this once-struggling company back into the winemaking limelight. Its bottle-fermented 100 percent pinot noir (with a blush) is Argentina's best bubbly. Though successful on the domestic market, the reds and whites have still to overcome their fusty image.

DOLIUM, AGRELO

Established **1998** ***Owner*** **Mario Giadorou** ***Vineyard area*** **NA**

Financed and constructed by retired stainless-steel engineer Mario Giadorou, this impressive bodega was built largely underground, which, while adding to the expense, has obvious benefits. With a design allowing for adaptation to future technological improvements, this state-of-the-art bodega ran into teething problems with its first harvest because of the eccentricities of Giadorou's ex-partner. To repair the damage Giadorou turned to Susana Balbo to sort out the problems, and now the venture's future looks brighter.

BODEGA ESMERALDA

Established **1970s** ***Owner*** **Nicolás Catena** ***Vineyard area*** **NA**

Formerly Catena's flagship enterprise, where Pedro Marchevsky and José Galante, with assessment by Paul Hobbs, crafted Argentina's best wines. In the Catena Alta range, the chardonnay is right up there with other

LEFT: *Vines in flower, early spring.*

world-class wines; the malbec is definitive; and the cabernet sauvignon sets new standards. Below this category are Catena wines, providing extraordinary complexity for the price. Alamos Ridge wines fill the next medium-price bracket with some aplomb, and below these the bodega produces an interesting range of wines called Argento, which should not be missed.

BODEGAS ETCHART, PERDRIEL, LUJÁN DE CUYO

Established **1938 (Salta), 1992 (Mendoza)** ***Owners*** **Pernord Ricard** ***Production*** **666,667 cases** ***Vineyard area*** **138 acres (56 ha)**

This firm has two bodegas, one in Mendoza, the other in northern Salta. The firm's best work is done at the bodega in Salta.

FINCA FLICHMAN, MAIPÚ

Established **1873** ***Owners*** **Sogrape, Portugal** ***Production*** **1,000,000 cases** ***Vineyard area*** **494 acres (200 ha)**

The vineyards here are an interesting patchwork. Some very poor, stony soil has recently been planted with selected clones and provided with drip irrigation. After transformation by its new owners, there will undoubtedly be some interesting wines made in the next few years, with more vineyard area being planted. Another vineyard is, in contrast, covered over with topsoil which was specially carted in early last century. Sogrape will no doubt sharpen the image of the wines.

BODEGAS Y VIÑEDOS GOYENECHEA, SAN RAFAEL

Established **1868** ***Owners*** **the Goyenechea family** ***Vineyard area*** **250 acres (100 ha)**

Traditional Basque-influenced styles of winemaking are maintained here. The Goyenechea family has been here for generations and the old bodega shows its history. Some of the not inconsiderable stretches of vineyards are covered with anti-hail mesh. Investment has recently been directed toward vineyard care, leaving winery modernization for later, so the better wines tend to be the younger ones that go into bottle rapidly. A bright and lingering chardonnay is worth trying and the young reds are full of good fruit.

BODEGA NORTON, LUJÁN DE CUYO

Established **c.1890** ***Owners*** **the Swarowski family** ***Vineyard area*** **74 acres (30 ha) Agrelo, plus 395+ acres (160+ ha) Luján de Cuyo**

Heavy investment in new and replanted vineyards, together with a new vinification plant, promises a bright future for this bodega. Norton Privada is a bordeaux-style wine that ages very well in bottle, and the chardonnay has also come a long way, with improvement showing in recent vintages. Lighter and less exalted wines, such as the vivacious torrontés, provide depth to a line that also includes a very acceptable sparkling wine.

TRAPICHE, MENDOZA (MAIPÚ)

Established **c.1900** ***Owners*** **Luis Alfredo Pulenta and others** ***Vineyard area*** **1,235 acres (500 ha)**

Peñaflor is the largest bodega in Mendoza and Trapiche is an appendage to it. The family behind this landmark winery has seen turbulent times engulf their operations. A buy-out headed by a branch of the family with links in the US seems to have stabilized things a bit. While the family has business interests in other fields, wine was the basis of its fortune. Today family members are producing quite an array of wines, from basic mass-produced tetra bricks called Thermidor (with the local nickname of Terminator) to some fine products under the Trapiche label. The bodega appears to be in two minds about whether to leave Trapiche as its premium line or whether it should upgrade the Peñaflor line to a similar level.

ABOVE: *A harvest worker takes a moment to reflect while waiting for the truck.*

BODEGAS & CAVAS DE WEINERT, CARRODILLA, LUJÁN DE CUYO

Established **1976** ***Owners*** **Bernardo Weinert** ***Vineyard area*** **NA**

When Michel Rolland helped make wines here, wine writers such as Robert Parker gave them a good write-up. Since then the winery has gone through an up-and-down period. Enologist Raul de la Mota has now left, making way for new blood. Some of the wines (made from good quality fruit) are deep and well extracted, but quality has been variable, mainly because the winery has yet to modernize. Old wood is still used to store wine, at times to very good effect, at others less than convincing. Carrascal is a traditional line and some premium malbec is also sold.

The mountainous countryside of Iroulégay. This appellation in the Southwest region of France has potential for rapid growth in the near future.

France

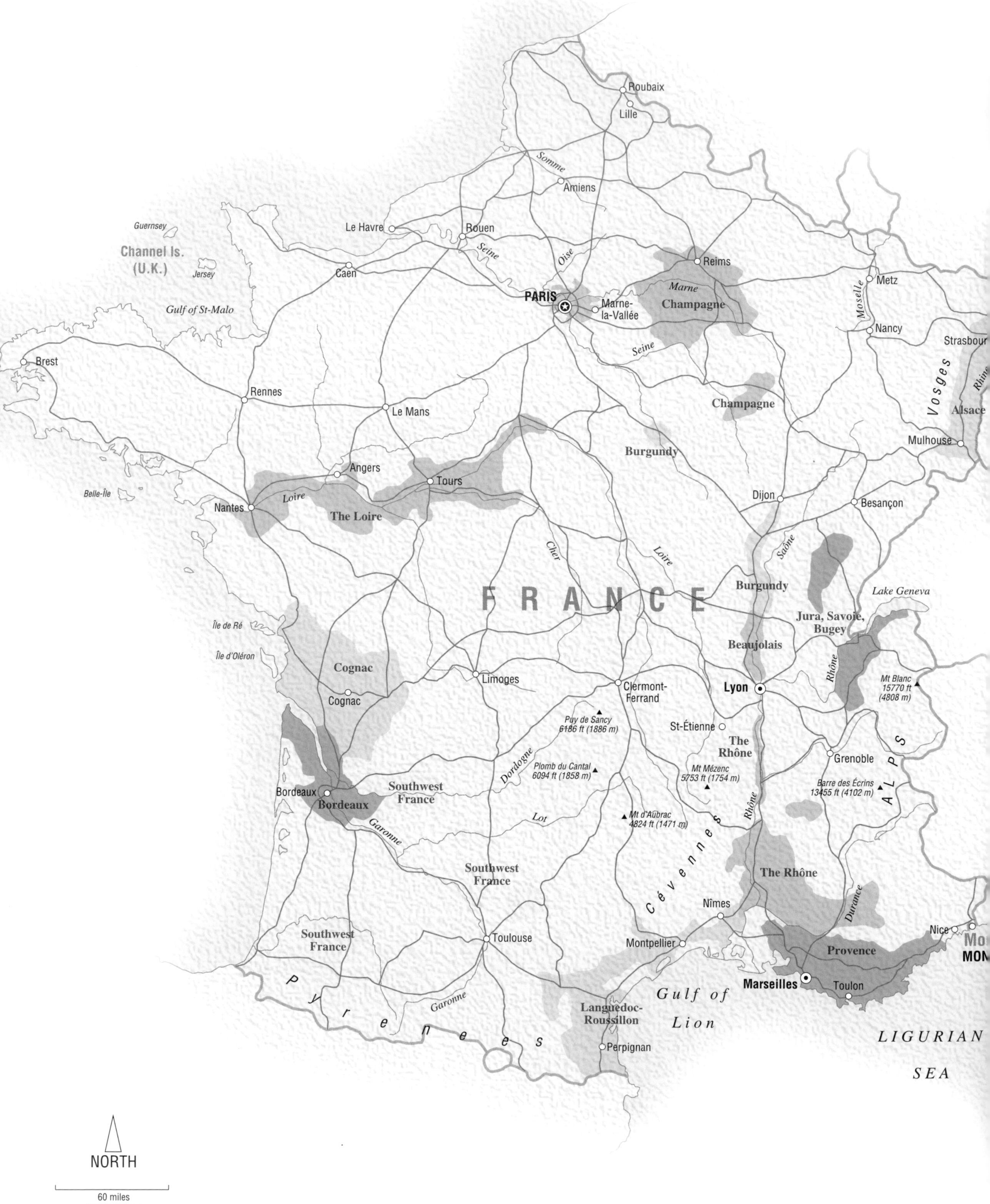

FRANCE
PARIS
Roubaix
Lille
Amiens
Somme
Le Havre
Rouen
Seine
Oise
Reims
Marne
Champagne
Marne-la-Vallée
Seine
Champagne
Metz
Moselle
Nancy
Strasbourg
Vosges
Rhine
Alsace
Mulhouse
Guernsey
Channel Is. (U.K.)
Jersey
Caen
Gulf of St-Malo
Brest
Rennes
Le Mans
Burgundy
Angers
Tours
Belle-Île
Nantes
Loire
The Loire
Dijon
Besançon
Cher
Loire
Saône
Burgundy
Lake Geneva
Jura, Savoie, Bugey
Beaujolais
Île de Ré
Île d'Oléron
Cognac
Cognac
Limoges
Clermont-Ferrand
Lyon
Rhône
Mt Blanc 15770 ft (4808 m)
Puy de Sancy 6186 ft (1886 m)
St-Étienne
The Rhône
Grenoble
ALPS
Plomb du Cantal 6094 ft (1858 m)
Mt Mézenc 5753 ft (1754 m)
Barre des Écrins 13455 ft (4102 m)
Dordogne
Bordeaux
Bordeaux
Southwest France
Garonne
Lot
Mt d'Aubrac 4824 ft (1471 m)
Rhône
Cévennes
The Rhône
Durance
Southwest France
Nîmes
Nice
Southwest France
Toulouse
Montpellier
Provence
Marseilles
Toulon
Pyrenees
Garonne
Languedoc-Roussillon
Gulf of Lion
Perpignan
LIGURIAN SEA
NORTH
60 miles (96 kilometers)

France

France's pre-eminence as a winemaking country proves that there is more to status than size. True, it is the number one wine exporter in the world, it ranks second in per-capita level of consumption and produces more wine than any other country. Italy's output has sometimes been greater and Spain has a larger percentage of its land under vine, but it is France that reigns supreme, because more truly great wines are produced here that have set the standard for the rest of the world to follow.

ABOVE: Appellation rules seek to maintain quality by controlling winemaking procedures.

This doesn't mean that France produces only wines of enviable quality. Although winemaking standards have improved enormously in the last two decades—through measures such as the control of fermentation temperatures which allows the harvesting of riper grapes—some very poor wines are still produced. In part, this most certainly can be attributed to the country's highly variable climate.

LEFT: At work in the Taine-Hermitage vineyards, Rhône Valley.

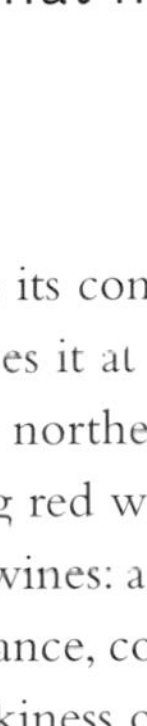

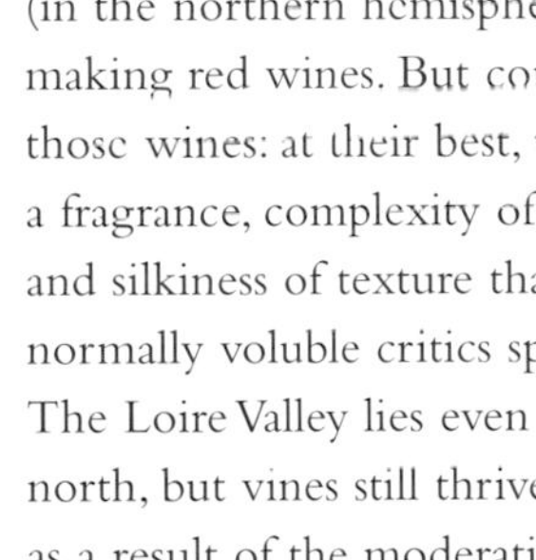

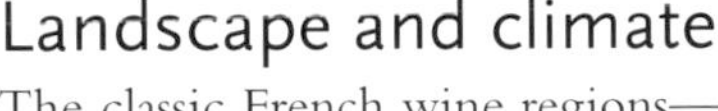

Landscape and climate

The classic French wine regions—including Bordeaux, Burgundy and Champagne—are all close to the geographical limits of successful vine-growing. In poor years, the grapes just do not see enough sun and warmth to get perfectly ripe. In other years, all might be progressing well and then devastating hail tears through the vineyards, as occurred in part of St-Émilion in September 1999, or torrential downpours arrive just before the harvest, as happened in much of the Médoc in the same year.

Yet, to talk of a marginal climate is misleading, for France encompasses an extraordinary range of terrain and weather patterns, which is precisely why its winemaking practices are so complex and its wines so diverse. Bordeaux, for example, on the west coast, has a maritime climate. The prevailing dampness means that disease is a perennial threat, but one such infestation, *Botrytis cinerea* (noble rot), is a boon for the sweet-wine producers of sauternes. Burgundy, inland to the north and east, is cooler than Bordeaux; so much so that its continental climate, with relatively high rainfall, places it at the northern limit (in the northern hemisphere) for making red wines. But consider those wines: at their best, they have a fragrance, complexity of flavor and silkiness of texture that leaves normally voluble critics speechless. The Loire Valley lies even farther north, but vines still thrive there as a result of the moderating influences of moist Atlantic breezes and the expansive river and its tributaries. In France's most northerly wine region, Champagne, the grapes barely ripen each year, but that's rarely a cause for concern—high-acid, relatively low-sugar grapes are perfect raw material for the finest sparkling wines.

BELOW: Many French estates are known as châteaux, whether or not they incorporate the grand style of residence that the term implies.

French producers rarely consider climate in isolation, however. What counts is *terroir*, the complete package of soil and subsoil, aspect and altitude, climate and mesoclimate—and any other natural feature that might affect the vines. The soils and geology of French vineyards are at least as varied as the climates. For instance, Burgundy and Jura have limestone, Beaujolais and the northern Rhône sit on granite, Champagne has chalk, the Médoc has gravel, and some of the vineyards in Châteauneuf-du-Pape are covered with huge, smooth stones for as far as the eye can see.

No single soil type produces the best wine, but if there is one characteristic that France's finer vineyards share, it is that they tend to be located on poor soils where little else will thrive—in particular, on poor soils on slopes that can retain some water without becoming waterlogged. Thus, in regions such as Alsace, Burgundy and Beaujolais, the best vineyards (often called *crus*) tend to be on the hillsides and the more ordinary vineyards on flatter ground. Similarly, the exciting new *domaines* that have made a name for themselves in Languedoc in recent years are not located on the coastal plains but on the inland *coteaux*, or hills.

As any producer in any one of these regions would tell you, however, these are generalizations. There is no such thing as a single-soil region. As a result, most of the important French winegrowing areas have been divided into subregions based on the characteristics of their *terroirs*. Such distinctions form the basis of France's national classification system, known as *appellation d'origine contrôlée*, often abbreviated to AC or AOC.

Appellations and other classifications

The appellation system was created in 1935, after nearly 30 years of piecemeal and pragmatic legislation, to protect the authenticity of wines and the livelihoods of their producers. It does this by defining boundaries and, within each area, stipulating the permitted grape varieties, yields and alcohol content; cultivation, vinification and maturation practices; and labeling procedures.

Fine distinctions may result in a large number of subregions. In Bordeaux, for example, in addition to the generic Bordeaux appellation, there are 56 smaller appellations. Burgundy, which is less than a quarter the size of Bordeaux, has no fewer than 98 appellations, some of them tiny but nevertheless divided between many

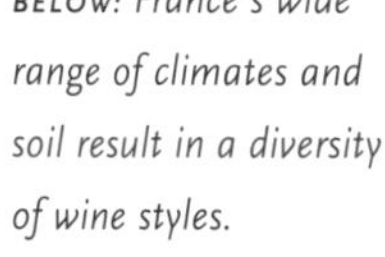

BELOW: *France's wide range of climates and soil result in a diversity of wine styles.*

owners. That makes Bordeaux probably the most complex of all French regions.

As far as the consumer is concerned, *appellation d'origine contrôlée* guarantees the origin and style of a wine—at least in theory. What it does not do, in theory or practice, is guarantee a wine's quality, and in many appellations, such as generic Bordeaux or Anjou Rosé, the standards are clearly inadequate.

In the past—as recently as ten years ago—it could be said that the tighter the specifications of an individual appellation, the better its wines would be. Now, anyone who toes that line does so with less conviction, simply because the appellation authorities, often under the influence of local vested interests, have sometimes shown themselves to be pointlessly, even harmfully, intractable. In Provence, for example, the leading estate, Domaine de Trévallon, was refused appellation status on the grounds that its blend contained "too much" cabernet sauvignon.

Unless the authorities display some common sense flexibility (as they have done recently in some places, such as Madiran), it can be difficult for dynamic, quality conscious winemakers to innovate, improve their wines, or even just label them differently—labeling by grape variety, for example, is almost never permitted for appellation wines (with the exception of AC Alsace, where the practice is traditional and where there is only one principal appellation). This state of affairs has led some producers to opt for the less prestigious but much less restrictive *vin de pays* (VDP) classification. This was created in 1979 as an intermediate category between *vin de table*, the most basic of French wine, and AC. (There is also a small category called *vin délimité de qualité supérieure*, or VDQS, which was intended to be for novice or probationary appellations, but it dwindles with every promotion to AC.) *Vin de pays* was introduced principally to encourage producers of *vins de table* to raise their standards, especially in the vast Languedoc-Roussillon area in the south, and overall it has worked extremely well, now accounting for three in every ten bottles of French wine. These include wines labeled by grape variety, or *vins de cépages* as they are known locally. The French tend to be dismissive of varietal wines, insisting that wine is much more than mere grapes—it is *terroir*—but recently they have had to acknowledge that these wines are commercially successful. So *vins de pays* such as Chardonnay Vin de Pays d'Oc now compete with varietal wines from countries like Australia, Chile and Argentina, and have become one of the recent success stories of French wine.

As complicated and absurd as it may sometimes appear, *appellation d'origine contrôlée* is definitely not all bad. If it were, you can be sure it would not have spawned so many similar appellation systems around the world. Furthermore, it has played a critical role in protecting the identity and reputation of French wines, both at home and overseas.

Joanna Simon

ABOVE: *Vineyards above the town of Taine with the Rhône in the background.*

ABOVE: *Champagne bottles are stored in angled racks so that sediment falls into the bottle neck.*

Champagne

KEN GARGETT & PETER FORRESTAL

Champagne's effervescent charm has conquered the globe. Whenever a celebration of any sort takes place in the modern world, you can be certain that the sound of champagne corks popping will not be far away. Weddings, births, anniversaries—victories of any nature whatsoever—all call for a bottle of the world's best bubbly.

Champagne originates from the province of the same name in northeastern France, which lies just 100 miles (160 km) to the east of Paris. It encompasses the five departments of Marne, Haute-Marne, Seine-et-Marne, Aisne and Aube and centers on the towns of Reims and Épernay, where most of the champagne houses are based. This region has been producing wine for hundreds of years, but it was only in the seventeenth century that the natural process that gives rise to the bubbles began to be understood, and only in the nineteenth century that sparkling wine became Champagne's principal product. Over the past 300 years, the procedure for making champagne has evolved and gradually been refined. Today, only wines made following the local appellation laws and originating in the viticultural region of Champagne are allowed to use that name.

History

Pope Urban II, pontiff from 1088 to 1099, declared that there was never a better wine than that produced in Aÿ—although, given that he was a Champenois, he might just have been a little biased. In the *Bataille des Vins*, written around 1200, Henri d'Andelys rated wines from Épernay, Reims and Hautvillers among the very best in all of Europe.

Around the first half of the sixteenth century, Pope Leo X, Charles V of Spain, François I of France, and Henry VIII of England all owned vineyards in Champagne. A batch of *vin d'Aÿ* sent to Henry VIII's chancellor, Cardinal Wolsey, in 1518, was the first recorded shipment of wine from Champagne to England. Henri IV (1553–1610) became the first French king to introduce wine from Champagne to his court.

The first notable producer of champagne as we know it, was Ruinart, founded in 1729 (though Gosset had been producing still wine since at least 1584 and remains the oldest Champagne house operating today). Others were established soon afterward, including the houses now known as Taittinger (in 1734), Moët et Chandon (in 1743), later followed by Veuve Clicquot (in 1772).

Demand grew mostly in the late nineteenth century, which was a glorious time for Champagne. The dawn of the twentieth century saw a lot of unrest among growers from the Aube district, who had been excluded from Champagne, and simmering discontent finally erupted

Méthode champenoise

England was the first country to develop a taste for sparkling wine. During the period following the Restoration of 1660, young wines from Champagne were usually imported in barrels during winter, by which time the cold climate had arrested fermentation. Once spring arrived, however, the wine, by now transferred to bottles, would warm again and the yeasts would be reactivated. Fermentation would then restart, producing carbonic gas. In France, this usually caused the bottle to open or shatter; in England, however, cork stoppers and much stronger glass were already in widespread use, so the wine could develop further.

The process of secondary fermentation probably began to be understood in France soon afterward. This discovery is traditionally attributed to Dom Pérignon but contrary to legend, he did not invent champagne. However, he did make several significant contributions to its development.

For a long period, the still wines of Champagne remained in greater demand. This situation only changed following several technical innovations in the early nineteenth century, including the process of remuage *(or riddling), which allowed producers to remove the sediment that forms during secondary fermentation without emptying the bottle. The production process is strictly regulated. Once the beginning date for harvesting is announced, usually mid-September, handpicked grapes go to nearby press houses. The juice goes through* débourbage*, or settling out, followed by fermentation. After racking, the* assemblage*, or blending, takes place, then bottling, when the* liqueur de tirage *(a solution of yeast and sugar) is added to initiate secondary fermentation. Bottles are sealed with a crown cap or the traditional agrafe cork and placed in cellars to spend time on lees and build complexity. Dead yeast cells are worked down to the top of the inverted bottle (*remuage*), which is then dipped in freezing brine. The cap is then removed and the frozen plug of sediment flies out (*dégorgement*). A small quantity of wine plus sugar (the* liqueur d'expedition*) is then added, with the amount of sugar determining the eventual sweetness of the champagne. Levels range from dry (Brut), a bit sweeter (extra dry) or very sweet (demi-sec). Until 1850, all champagne was sweet. A few houses release zero-dosage champagnes labeled Sauvage, Extra Brut or Brut Nature. Extra Brut was allowed 0-6 grams/liter residual sugar but new CIVC regulations allow Extra Brut 3-6 grams/liter and Brut Nature 0-3 grams/liter. Bottles are then corked, muzzled with a protective wire cage, labeled, and shipped off to every corner of the globe.*

TOP: *Champagne must be served chilled.*

LEFT: *Riddling shakes dead yeast cells into the neck.*

in 1911 when 5,000 Aube growers marched on Champagne. The dispute ended and eventually the Aube was incorporated into the region of Champagne.

Since World War II, the region has prospered, and recently, the industry has been rationalized and there have been amazing improvements in the yield and quality of the harvest. Yet, at the same time, the distinctive character of champagne remains much as it was in the late nineteenth century, though the current preference is for drier styles.

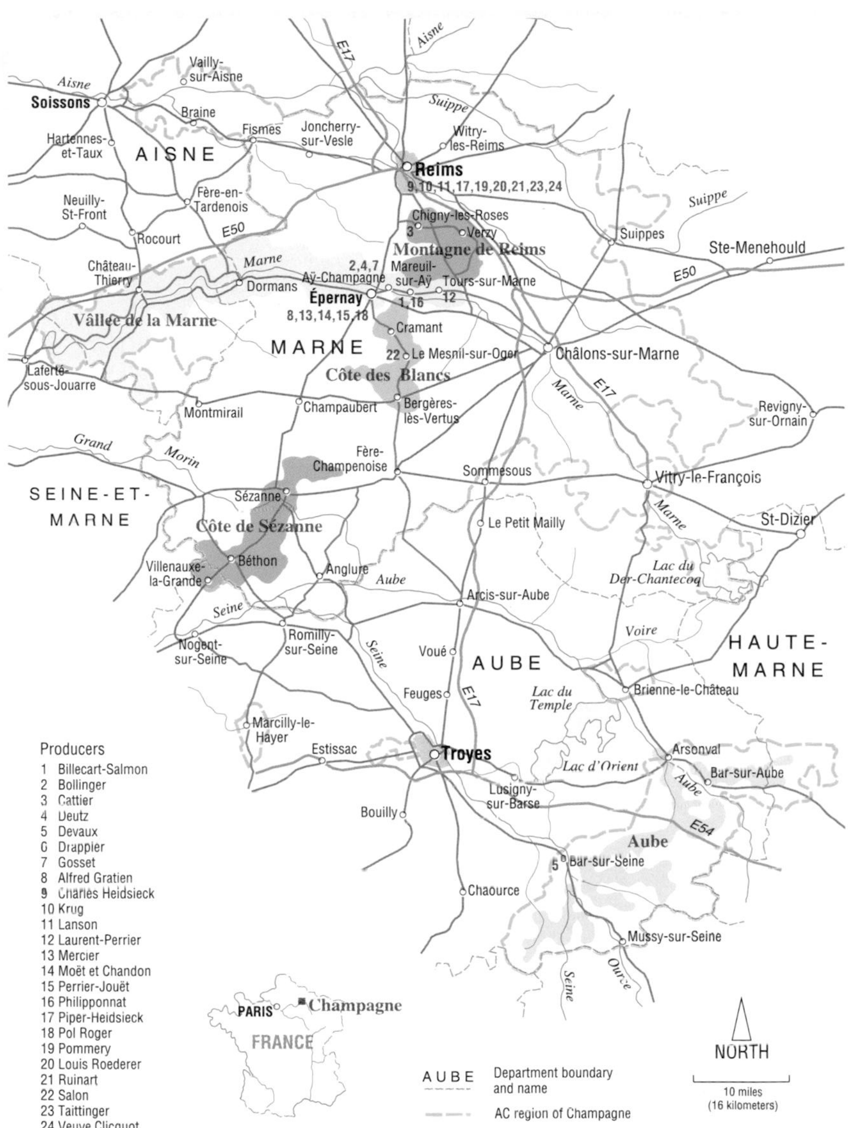

Landscape and Climate

Perhaps more than in any other winegrowing area, Champagne's *terroir*—its unique combination of geology, climate, hydrology and environment—directly determines the style of its wine. Champagne lies near the northern limits of the wine-producing world, where the mean annual temperature of 50°F (10°C) is barely sufficient to ripen grapes. Furthermore, Atlantic mildness and continental harshness interact here, creating a highly variable climate that is compounded by the undulating terrain. Only in certain areas do topography, aspect and other factors such as the presence of forests (which stabilize temperatures and supply moisture) create a *terroir* fit for ripening vines. At the same time, these marginal conditions have turned out to be highly appropriate for the production of champagne: the cool temperatures produce high levels of acidity that are perfect for sparkling wine, and subregional variations result in distinctive styles that lend themselves to blending.

By far the most significant influence on the character of the wine is the geological makeup of the soil. Champagne's chalk subsoils originally formed as the floor of an ancient ocean, which retreated about 70 million years ago. Earthquakes 20 and 10 million years ago pushed some of these marine sediments, known as belemnite chalk, to the surface, creating the area's undulating terrain. Most of the land now has a thin layer of surface soil over a deep layer of belemnite chalk (except in the Aube, where the soils are clay), which may be hundreds of feet thick in places.

Belemnite subsoils are thought to be the source of much of the fineness and lightness that characterize champagne. They provide excellent drainage, adequate moisture retention, and—critically in such a marginal climate—absorb heat from the sun by day and slowly release it at night, thereby warming the vines at the coldest time of day.

Vineyards and classifications

The Champenois' determination to protect their famous wine is legendary, and numerous restrictions have been placed on production processes and the use of the name. Recently, these have been tightened in response to challenges from other regions and to counter the suggestion that not all champagne is what it should be.

In 1927 the boundaries of the viticultural area of Champagne were legally defined. This allowed the appellation to have a size of 84,155 acres (34,057 ha), but in reality only about 76,600 acres (31,000 ha) were available for vineyards—roads, schools and housing occupied much of the rest. By the 1990s, around 71,660 acres (29,000 ha) were under cultivation—almost 2 percent of France's total vineyard area. Very little land suitable for vines now remains in Champagne.

There are five major wine-producing districts: Côte des Blancs, Montagne de Reims, Vallée de la Marne, Côte de Sézanne and the Aube. These cover more than 300 villages, 261 houses and 44 co-operatives. Around 5,000 growers make and sell their own wine; another 14,000 sell only grapes.

The CIVC (Comité Interprofessionnel du Vin de Champagne) was formed in 1942 and regulates vineyard practices, marketing, vinification methods and maturation. The villages are rated (the *Echelle des Crus*) for the

ABOVE: *Fall colors swathe the elegant exterior of a residence in the town of Épernay.*

quality of vineyards and grapes, and this then determines the price. Each year CIVC gives a price for the vintage, and they determine when to pick. Depending on the grade given, the growers get that percentage of the price. A 100 percent rating equals 100 percent of the price for the grapes, and also equals Grand Cru status; 90–99 percent is Premier Cru and 80–89 percent is Deuxième Cru.

In 1919, laws entitling the Champagne region to its own appellation were passed. Legislation in 1927 made Champagne one of the earliest appellations in France; it is still the only one permitted to omit the phrase *appellation d'origine contrôlée* or the initials AC or AOC from its labels.

Under Champagne appellation rules, up to 673 gallons (2,550 l) of juice from a pressing of 8,820 pounds (4,000 kg) can be used. The first 541 gallons (2,050 l) are the *cuvée;* the next 132 gallons (500 l) are the *taille.* Till 1992, a second *taille* of a further 44 gallons (166 l) was permitted. Nonvintage wines must spend fifteen months on lees, vintage champagnes three years—better producers usually extend these periods to three and five years respectively. One hundred percent of a vintage wine must come from the stated vintage.

Vines and wines

Only three kinds of grape variety are actually permitted in Champagne, they are pinot noir, pinot meunier and chardonnay. Pinot noir makes up 38 percent of plantings. It gives champagne structure, weight, power and backbone, plus a richness of flavor. Pinot noir does especially well in the Montagne de Reims and is the most planted variety in the Aube.

Pinot meunier covers 35 percent of the vineyards, and is dominant in the Vallée de la Marne. It is an undervalued grape that few houses admit to using (though most do); it provides fruit flavor in the midpalate and sometimes a slightly earthy character. It is particularly useful in cold years due to its ripening ability, although there is justifiable concern that it matures too quickly.

Chardonnay, which makes up 27 percent of the vineyard (though this percentage increases in the Grands Crus), is the only variety that is used regularly on its own in a champagne, the *blanc de blancs*. At its best, the grape is characterized by elegance, delicacy, finesse and refinement. It also contributes to the acidity of the wine and is essential to the length of the finish. The Côte des Blancs is almost entirely devoted to chardonnay.

Around 80 percent of champagnes are nonvintage blends—which is why the name of the producer rather than the vineyard appears on the label. The Champenois are master blenders, skillfully combining wines from different grapes, vineyards and vintages. This is a clear case of necessity being the mother of invention, as over the years local producers had to use blending to deal with the vagaries of the climate and the limited output of most growers. Wine from a poor vintage can be turned into an outstanding product by blending with wines from superior vintages. In doing so, the blenders add their own signatures to the wines and create house styles.

Because the *terroir* is so variable, grape varieties will have different characteristics when they are grown in different vineyards. This can be useful in creating a blend, for example, chardonnay grown on the Côte des Blancs has a steely backbone, yet on the Montagne de Reims and in some parts of the Vallée de Marne it produces a much fuller wine.

Around 1870, some houses started bottling particularly good years separately, in doing so, they created vintage champagnes for the first time. Today, these are released, on average, four or five times a decade. Other styles of champagne include rosé, *blanc de blancs*, and the unusual *blanc de noirs*, which is made only from black grapes. Most houses also issue prestige *cuvées*, a practice that began when Moët et Chandon released the 1921 Dom Pérignon in 1937. The Champagne region also makes small quantities of still reds, rosés and whites, as well as ratafia and *eaux-de-vie*.

BOLLINGER

Established **1829** ***Owner*** **Société Jacques Bollinger** ***Production*** **100,000 cases** ***Vineyard area*** **356 acres (144 ha)**

It seems this is the favorite tipple of everyone from James Bond to the Ab Fab set, Bollinger Champagnes are among the most impressive available. The style is distinctive: rich, complex and heavily reliant on pinot The prestige R.D. (*récemment dégorgé*) is effectively the vintage wine (Grande Année) given additional time on lees to develop further complexity. The Grande Année is also mixed with still pinot noir to produce a very powerful rosé that can sometimes, however, seem out of balance. The rare Vieilles Vignes Françaises is an exceptionally rich, powerful and complex 100 percent pinot noir made from nongrafted bush vines.

GOSSET

Established **1584** ***Owner*** **Rémy-Cointreau** ***Production*** **50,000 cases** ***Vineyard area*** **30 acres (12 ha)**

Gosset has an even longer history, albeit as a maker of still wines, than Ruinart (generally considered to be the oldest champagne producer) and remained in family hands until as recently as 1994, when it was sold to Rémy-Cointreau. The Grand Reserve shows more power and depth than the slightly sweet Brut Excellence, but the stars here are the vintage wines, which includes the recently introduced Célebris and the muscular Grand Millésime. Occasionally, Gosset produces special releases, such as the gloriously rich Quatrième Centenaire. The packaging is always fabulous.

KRUG

Established **1843** ***Owner*** **LVMH** ***Production*** **50,000 cases** ***Vineyard area*** **49 acres (20 ha)**

Although ownership of this house passed from the family to Rémy-Cointreau and thence to LVMH (in 1999), the company is still managed by brothers Henri and Rémi Krug. The Krugs are traditionalists who ferment in 54-gallon (205-l) oak casks and allow no malolactic fermentation or filtration. Substantial reserves enable them to blend close to 50 wines from numerous vintages to produce their monumental Grande Cuvée. Vintage Krug is one of the world's great wines, exhibiting delicacy and finesse with a tight structure, steely backbone, great richness, depth of flavor, power and complexity. The classy and expensive 100 percent chardonnay Clos du Mesnil, with its creamy texture and underlying strength, is a rarity, as it comes from a single, walled vineyard.

BELOW: *The house of Bollinger is the source of some of the world's most prestigious champagnes.*

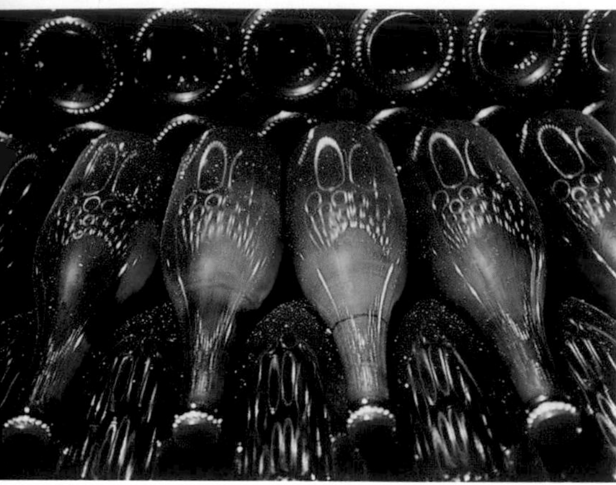

ABOVE: *Sealed with crown caps, bottles of Moët et Chandon undergo secondary fermentation.*

MOËT ET CHANDON

Established **1743** ***Owner*** **LVMH**
Production **2 million cases**
Vineyard area **1,520 (615 ha)**

Moët et Chandon is the largest of the Champagne houses and was the first (in 1962) to be floated on the Paris stockmarket. It claims that a bottle of its champagne is popped somewhere in the world every few of seconds. The nonvintage Brut Impérial may on occasion be inconsistent—hardly surprising given the vast quantities produced—but vintage Moët is admirable, its bold citrus flavors and strong acidity ensuring that it matures superbly. The flagship, Dom Pérignon, is also outstanding, displaying delicate lemon citrus flavors, rich creamy texture, great finesse and balance, and gentle and most refreshing acidity.

PHILIPPONNAT

Established **1910** ***Owner*** **Boizel Chanoine Champagne** ***Production*** **40,000 cases** ***Vineyard area*** **30 acres (12 ha)**

Philipponnat's flagship wine, the Clos des Goisses, is sourced from the Marne Valley vineyard of the same name. Floral, almost tropical when young, it develops powerful, toasty flavors and a creamy, honeyed texture with age. Le Reflet is ripe and approachable and it includes any fruit from the Clos des Goisses which is not used in prestige wine. Both the brut and rosé are soft, easy-drinking wines. The sale of Philipponnat in 1997 has seen the dynamic Bruno Paillard take the helm, a move likely to result in further improvement in the wines.

POL ROGER

Established **1849** ***Owner*** **NA** ***Production*** **110,000 cases**
Vineyard area **210 acres (85 ha)**

This small, charming family establishment makes what were Winston Churchill's favorite champagnes, a connection that is commemorated in the name of the prestige *cuvée*, Sir Winston Churchill. Released in 1984, this displays power and finesse, accompanied by layers of flavor that linger on the palate and in the memory. The rest of the range is equally impressive. The White Foil is a medium-bodied nonvintage with some floral characters and persistent flavors; the vintage is pristine, intense and tightly structured when young, and develops a biscuity toastiness with age. The Blanc de Chardonnay combines lemony freshness, an exquisitely creamy texture and impressive intensity.

LOUIS ROEDERER

Established **1760** ***Owners*** **the Roederer family** ***Production*** **220,000 cases** ***Vineyard area*** **470 acres (190 ha)**

Louis Roederer is undoubtedly one of the great houses of Champagne and its range of wines is superb. The Brut Premier, with its tight structure, power, and biscuity, yeasty flavors, is invariably one of the top nonvintage champagnes. Likewise, the vintage is outstanding, showing finesse, balance and intensity of flavor. For many people, however, the pinnacle, not only of the Roederer portfolio but of champagne, is the superb Cristal. Sold

RIGHT: *This monument at the house of Moët et Chandon commemorates one of the great figures in Champagne's history, Dom Pérignon.*

Beyond celebrations

The explosive pop of the cork, the shimmering bubbles, and market image of champagne all point to the world's celebratory wine par excellence. One of the best kept secrets in the world of wine is how wonderful champagne can be with food. From omelets to caviar to smoked salmon to chicken with a cream sauce, champagne is a joy. If one is to drink wine with sushi, champagne (nonvintage) is the only choice. Blue cheese with champagne is an earthly delight. With the added weight of pinot noir and skin contact, rosé champagne can take on a surprising array of red meats! An evening of joy can arise from piecing together a meal pairing different champagnes with all courses encountered.

in a clear (though not crystal!) bottle wrapped in yellow cellophane to protect the wine from ultraviolet light, it is the embodiment of elegance—subtle, yet powerful; delicate, but intense; restrained, yet opulent. It also displays a soft, creamy texture and gentle, lingering acidity. Cristal is a memorable drinking experience.

RUINART

Established **1729** ***Owner*** **LVMH** ***Production*** **160,000 cases** ***Vineyard area*** **37 acres (15 ha)**

The oldest of Champagne houses boasts impressive early connections, as founder Nicholas Ruinart's uncle was a close friend of Dom Pérignon. Although it is now part of a worldwide enterprise, Ruinart retains its identity as a small, quality house. The flagship wine, Dom Ruinart, a *blanc de blancs*, is outstanding.

TAITTINGER

Established **1734** ***Owners*** **Taittinger family** ***Production*** **NA** ***Vineyard area*** **633 acres (256 ha)**

The prestige wines of Taittinger are the Comtes de Champagne, a 100 percent chardonnay wine, and the

100 percent pinot noir Comtes de Champagne Rosé. The former undergoes malolactic fermentation and, unusually for champagne, includes a portion of wine that has been matured in new oak; this gives it an enticing, creamy texture to match its delicacy and finesse. The rosé is fuller and a lot more powerful. When youthful, the vintage wine has citrus and yeast flavors, and crisp, fresh acidity on the finish.

VEUVE CLICQUOT

Established **1772** ***Owner*** **LVMH** ***Production*** **750,000 cases** ***Vineyard area*** **702 acres (284 ha)**

Madame Clicquot assumed control of this house in 1805 at the tender age of 27, following the death of her husband François (veuve means "widow" in French). During the next half-century, she transformed the company and the industry with her energy and innovations. Today, Veuve Clicquot is best known for its rich pinot-dominated champagnes, including the distinctive Yellow Label Brut nonvintage. The vintage is consistently excellent, it is delicate, yet intense, balanced, yet powerful, crisp and dry, yet soft and refreshing. The prestige *cuvée*, La Grande Dame, is a wine of enormous finesse and balance with firm structure and biscuity, yeasty flavors; it comes within a hair's breath of the great champagnes.

Other recommended producers in Champagne include Perrier-Jouët, Salon, Billecart-Salmon, Charles Heidsieck, Cattier, Deutz, Devaux, Drappier, Alfred Gratien, Lanson, Laurent-Perrier, Mercier, Piper-Heidsieck and Pommery.

Regional Dozen

QUALITY WINES

- Bollinger Vielles Vignes Blanc de Noir Vintage
- Krug Grand Cuvée
- Pol Roger Cuvée Sir Winston Churchill Vintage
- Pommery Cuvée Louise Vintage
- Louis Roederer Cristal Vintage
- Dom Ruinart R de Ruinart Vintage

BEST VALUE WINES

- Deutz Brut Rosé Vintage
- Gosset Brut Reserve nv
- Jacquesson Blanc de Blancs nv
- Bruno Paillard Brut nv
- Philipponnat Royale Reserve Brut nv
- Veuve Clicquot Gold Label Vintage Reserve

TOP: Louis Roederer offers an outstanding range, including the famous prestige cuvée, Cristal.

LEFT: The intricately carved barrel graces the entrance hall in the house of Mercier.

The Loire

ROGER VOSS

The French have a saying: "The Loire is a queen and the kings of France have loved her." It's an accurate—if probably politically incorrect—description of the intimate relationship that France has with its longest and arguably most beautiful river, which flows past some of the most stupendous and most characteristic French landscape. Quiet and peaceful, the Loire is the last natural, undammed great river of Europe. The language spoken in the regions of Anjou and Touraine, through which the river flows, is regarded as the purest, clearest form of French. The great cities of Orléans, Tours, Nantes and Angers are some of the most historic in the country, and they, and their castles, the grand châteaux for which the Loire Valley is most famous, are a reminder of the country's glorious past.

ABOVE: *The vineyards of Sancerre are renowned for their dry white wines.*

The River Loire also provides a mild mesoclimate for wine production. While the country to the north and south is too inhospitable for the vine, the Loire Valley and the valleys of the river's main tributaries are just those few vital degrees warmer in summer and winter, allowing grapes to flourish. There are few hills in the region, so moist, warm air from the Atlantic Ocean can spread far up into the interior, moderating the climate. It is this special and privileged mesoclimate that is also responsible for the milky blue light that has made the Loire region such an inspiration for generations of painters and travelers alike.

The Loire wine region extends from Montbrison in the Côtes du Forez, just across the mountains from Beaujolais, all the way to the Atlantic Ocean. Throughout that region, vineyards line the river and its tributaries—the Allier, Cher, Indre, Vienne, Sèvre Nantaise and Loir. In total, approximately 124,618 acres (50,433 ha) of vines produce what can be described as Loire wines. These cover every style imaginable—dry and sweet white, light red and rich red, dry and sweet sparkling—and include 87 different appellations. But all share certain characteristics: freshness, fruitiness and zing, and all are very much northern, cool-climate wines.

Grape varieties

If Loire wine styles are varied, so are the region's grape varieties. The list of obscure Loire grapes is fascinating and almost endless. The tressallier of Saint-Pourçain; the romorantin of Cour-Cheverny; the pineau d'aunis, pineau menu and groslot of Touraine; the gros plant of the Pays Nantais—all are rare species that make wines with unusual, sometimes exotic flavors. However, the finest wines in the Loire are produced from three grape varieties that never seem to achieve such quality elsewhere in France. Perhaps the fact that the Loire is at the limits of grape-growing brings out the best in chenin blanc, cabernet franc and sauvignon blanc.

The great whites of the Coteaux du Layon, savennières, vouvray and montlouis are all based on chenin blanc. The intense acidity of the wines when young, whether sweet or dry, gives them an extraordinary ability to age. Cabernet franc is able to strut its stuff in the quartet of red-wine appellations of Saumur-Champigny, Bourgueil, St-Nicolas-de-Bourgueil and Chinon. The styles of these wines vary from the lighter produce of Saumur-Champigny to the velvet richness of truly great Chinon.

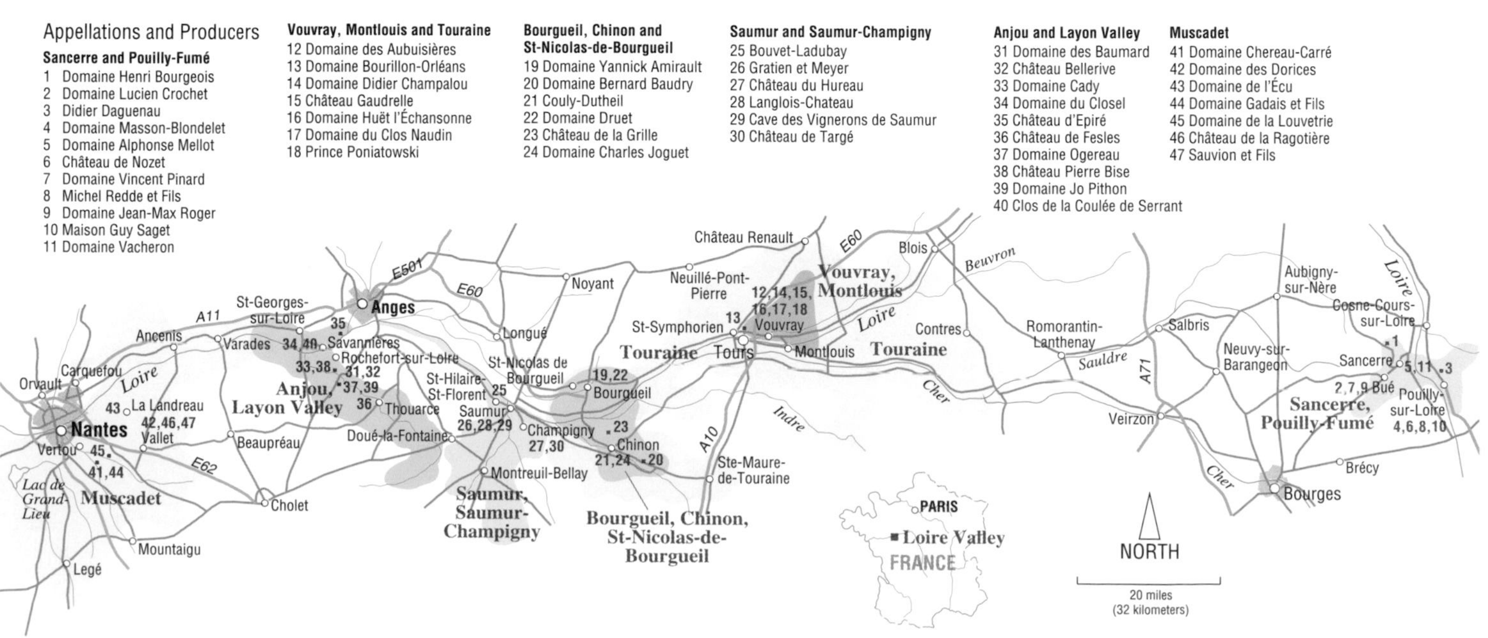

ABOVE: *Magnificent Azay-le-Rideau is one of the Loire Valley's most splendid châteaux.*

Sauvignon blanc's spiritual home is in the vineyards of Sancerre and Pouilly-sur-Loire. Here, the wines never have warm-climate, tropical-fruit flavors; instead they are crisper and more herbaceous. However, an increasing number of good producers are obtaining plenty of concentration, and some have even been experimenting with wood. Pouilly-fumé tends to be softer and richer than sancerre, and also ages better. Three other major grape varieties encountered in the Loire are muscadet or melon de bourgogne, pinot noir and gamay.

Made for aging

Just because Loire wines, when young, are fresh and fruity, doesn't mean that they do not age; on the contrary, most Loire whites develop well. This is particularly true of chenin-blanc-based wines from Savennières, the Coteaux du Layon (including Quarts de Chaume and Bonnezeaux) and Vouvray. Experts often suggest that, after an initial fruity spell, these wines go through a dumb period, meaning a period when they do not show their best at between two and five years of age. After that, the very best examples can be expected to age for upward of 20 years.

Other Loire white wines also have quite surprisingly long lives. The sauvignon blanc-based wines of Pouilly-Fumé, for example, do not begin to show their true character until they are somewhere around three years old. Sancerre whites mature and fade more quickly, as does muscadet, although in the best vintages the top *cuvées* will develop and mature.

Loire reds can also develop well. The better wines from Chinon and Bourgueil age as well as many Bordeaux reds, and the lighter wines of Saumur-Champigny and St-Nicolas-de-Bourgueil will continue to develop for at least ten years, maybe more, depending on the vintage. The reds of Sancerre are less long-lived, although a few producers who have cut yields and wood-aged the wines can produce 10- or 15-year-old examples that still have youthful fruit.

Vintage counts

Vintage affects the Loire Valley wines more than those from other regions of France. The very cool climate coupled with varieties that are not easily ripened make for a challenge. Underripe vintages are common, yet can produce "food friendly" wines. Sauvignon blanc is then lighter in color, more acidic and less fruity. Mineral notes become more pronounced. Cabernet franc is also lighter and crisper, having a more weedy aromatic profile. Riper vintages have deeper color, especially the cabernet franc. Sauvignon becomes rounder while still crisp. Mineral notes give way to lime fruit. Cabernet franc, when riper, is more deeply colored (a relative term in the Loire) and less astringent. Aromas and flavors shift to raspberries and lead pencil. Vintage counts, especially in the Loire, so be careful.

ABOVE: Vineyards cover almost every hillside around the historic walled town of Sancerre.

APPELLATIONS AND PRODUCERS

The Loire's 87 appellations include some famous names and some rarities. Among the latter are the scattered VDQS' areas of Châteaumeillant (red and rosé wines made near La Châtre in the Cher department), Coteaux di Giennois (red, rosé and white wines from just north of Pouilly-sur-Loire), Vin de l'Orléanais (red, rosé and white wines from around the city of Orléans—the closest Loire vineyards to Paris) and Vin du Thouarsais (more red, rosé and white wines, this time made south of the main Anjou vineyards). Travelers to the region may, if they persevere, come across these and other remnants of what were often much larger vineyard areas until phylloxera and economic difficulties put paid to them.

There are two major Loire-wide appellations. Crémant de Loire applies to traditional method sparkling wines with a generally higher level of quality than those of Saumur, and Vin de Pays du Jardin de la France applies to varietally labeled wines (in particular chardonnay). Otherwise, the Loire's appellations can be conveniently grouped under the following headings.

Sancerre, Pouilly-Fumé and the vineyards of the Center

Sauvignon blanc and pinot noir are the stars in these vineyards. The two principal appellations are Sancerre (whites, reds and rosés) and Pouilly-Fumé (whites only). Other lesser appellations are Menetou-Salon (whites, reds and rosés), Quincy (whites only) and Reuilly (whites, reds and rosés). All these wines combine richness, freshness and acidity. The whites have the characteristic gooseberry and grapefruit flavors of sauvignon blanc, those of Pouilly-Fumé being fuller, fatter and more long-lived than those of Sancerre, while those from Reuilly, Quincy and Menetou-Salon are generally soft and round. The reds, from pinot noir, are lightweight burgundy lookalikes, only rarely achieving more than passing attractiveness.

DOMAINE LUCIEN CROCHET

Established **NA** ***Owners*** **the Crochet family** ***Production*** **21,000 cases** ***Vineyard area*** **84 acres (34 ha)**

Sancerres here are full-bodied and concentrated, and the *négociant* wines, made from purchased grapes, are pleasant enough. However, the emphasis is on the *domaine* wines, from vineyards that include parts of some of the best in Bué. The Le Chêne Cuvée comes from the Chêne Marchand vineyard, whereas the Sancerre Prestige is a blend from the best lots.

DIDIER DAGUENEAU

Established **1980s** ***Owner*** **Didier Dagueneau** ***Production*** **4,200 cases** ***Vineyard area*** **28.4 acres (11.5 ha)**

Didier Dagueneau's wines are among the great white wines of France. The range of different *cuvées*, many of which are wood-aged, begins with Cailloux, named for the soil from which it comes, and moves through increasingly complex, long-lasting wines: Le Bois Renard (formerly known as Le Bois Menard), Silex (again named after the soil), Pur Sang and, most remarkable of all, Astéroïde.

DOMAINE ALPHONSE MELLOT

Established **Seventeenth century** ***Owners*** **the Mellot family**
Production **25,000 cases** ***Vineyard area*** **120 acres (50 ha)**

There have been 19 Alphonses at the head of this family company, whose cellars and shop in the center of Sancerre are among the most prominent of any Sancerrois producer. The current Alphonse has changed the whole nature of his wines, reducing yields and pushing up quality to a remarkable extent. The wines, produced from the Domaine la Moussière are top-quality sancerre, the result of considerable research into the right clones and of picking superripe fruit at harvest-time. The nineteenth Alphonse, now in charge of wine-making, has even had a *cuvée* named after him, Sancerre Génération XIX.

CHÂTEAU DE NOZET

Established **NA** ***Owners*** **the de Ladoucette family** ***Production*** **100,000 cases** ***Vineyard area*** **257 acres (104 ha)**

Based in their showpiece nineteenth-century château, the de Ladoucette family are the biggest players in Pouilly and also own the firms of Comte Lafon in Sancerre, Marc Brédif in Vouvray and Albert Pic in Chablis. When Château du Nozet came out with its top *cuvée*, Pouilly-Fumé Baron de L, in 1973, it shone like a beacon among much second-rate Loire wine. If it no longer shines so brightly, that is because standards have risen across the region. The rest of the Nozet range is made from purchased grapes and is generally of a good standard.

MICHEL REDDE ET FILS

Established **Nineteenth century** ***Owners*** **the Redde family**
Production **21,000 cases** ***Vineyard area*** **87 acres (35 ha)**

The Redde family runs a smart, modern operation that turns out a wide range of excellent-quality Pouilly-Fumé. The main part of the vineyard is on the slopes that face south onto the Loire. The top *cuvée*, Cuvée Majorum, made only in the best years, has excellent ripeness and depth, while the light *cuvée*, La Moynerie (named after the estate), is spicier and less complex. The Reddes also make Sancerre and Les Tuilières, as well as the rare, chasselas-based Pouilly-sur-Loire.

DOMAINE GUY SAGET

Established **NA** ***Owner*** **Jean-Louis Saget** ***Production*** **330,000 cases** ***Vineyard area*** **94 acres (38 ha)**

From the production figures above, it is easy to deduce that Guy Saget's main business is a *négociant*. He produces a wide range of wines from most of the major appellations in the Loire; all are competent or better. But his starting point was Pouilly-Fumé, and that is where his winery is located. Three of his Pouilly-Fumé *cuvées*—Chantalouette, Les Roches and Marie de Beauregard—have steadily improved in quality and now compare well with the appellation's top wines. Recently, Saget purchased Domaine de la Perrière which also produces an attractive range of wines.

ABOVE: A crate of 1997 Domaine Alphonse Mellot Sancerre, ready for shipping.

TOP: The nineteenth Alphonse Mellot examines some of the wine in his cellar.

DOMAINE VACHERON

Established **NA** ***Owners*** **the Vacheron family** ***Production*** **22,000 cases** ***Vineyard area*** **89 acres (36 ha)**

From the Vacheron cellars, in the heart of the town of Sancerre, issues a range that includes the best red *cuvée* in the area, a wine that is one of the few to justify the fuss made about Sancerre reds. Aged in *barriques*, it also develops well in bottle—10- and even 15-year-old examples are still in their early maturity. The whites shouldn't be forgotten either and are generally fresh, clean and minerally. The Vacherons have made wine for generations, and Jean-Louis, Denis and Jean-Dominique continually update their production methods, filling the ancient, rambling cellars with stainless steel tanks and modern presses.

LEFT: The town of Pouilly-sur-Loire, center of the world-famous Pouilly-Fumé appellation.

ABOVE: *The Loire's long, winding journey takes it through attractive towns such as Saumur.*

Gravières are among the best wines in the appellation, full of super-mature fruit that provides great richness. Bertrand Couly, in charge of vinification on the estate, also makes the other *cuvées* such as Domaine René Couly, as well as the *négociant* wines that come from Chinon, Bourgueil and St-Nicolas-de-Bourgueil.

DOMAINE CHARLES JOGUET

Established **NA** ***Owner*** **Jacques Genet** ***Production*** **9,000 cases** ***Vineyard area*** **91 acres (37 ha)**

Although Charles Joguet himself has entered semi-retirement, the estate that bears his name continues to produce some of the best wines in Chinon. In ascending order of power and richness, the Joguet *cuvées* are: Chinon Terroir, Cuvée du Clos de la Cure, Cuvée Clos du Chêne Vert, Les Varennes du Grand Clos and Clos de la Dioterie. The distinguishing characteristics of all Joguet wines are the suppleness and ripeness of the tannins.

Saumur and Saumur-Champigny

The westernmost vineyards of Anjou are normally treated separately from the rest of the province. The three principal appellations in this area are Saumur for white wines from chenin blanc and red wines from cabernet franc; Saumur-Champigny for quality red wines, similar to those of St-Nicolas-de-Bourgueil; and Saumur Mousseux for sparkling wines made mainly from chenin blanc. Saumur Mousseux is one of the largest sparkling wine appellations in France, producing on average 12 million bottles a year.

The best use of bad wine is to drive away poor relations.
ANONYMOUS

GRATIEN ET MEYER

Established **1864** ***Owners*** **the Gratien family** ***Production*** **170,000 cases** ***Vineyard area*** **49 acres (20 ha)**

One of the largest producers of sparkling saumur, Gratien et Meyer has recently shown a definite hike in quality. Wines such as Cuvée Flamme, the vintage Cuvée de Minuit and the Crémant de Loire Cuvée Royale are the result of significant financial investment and working with contract growers to improve their viticulture and hence the quality of the fruit. A departure for this company—under the same family ownership as Champagne Alfred Gratien—was the development of a range of still wines from the estate under the name Château Gratien.

LANGLOIS-CHATEAU

Established **1885** ***Owner*** **Bollinger** ***Production*** **70,000 cases** ***Vineyard area*** **161 acres (65 ha)**

Drawing on vineyards in Saumur, Saumur-Champigny, Sancerre and Muscadet, Langlois makes a range of still wines, of which the most exciting are the red saumur and saumur-champigny. Following the traditions of its parent company, the firm also makes sparkling wine, but instead of making the local saumur, it produces crémant de loire to a high standard. The best is Cuvée Quadrille, a blend of chenin blanc, chardonnay, cabernet franc and cabernet sauvignon.

CAVE DES VIGNERONS DE SAUMUR

Established **1957** ***Owner*** **Co-operative of 300 members** ***Production*** **1 million cases** ***Vineyard area*** **3,460 acres (1,400 ha)**

The huge cellar complex of the Saumur co-operative at St-Cyr-en-Bourg is not only big, it is also one of the most modern in France. Using its 6 miles (10 km) of underground cellars, gravity-fed pumps and huge state-of-the-art vinification and press rooms, the co-operative makes a range of wines from all over the Saumur and Saumur-Champigny appellations, as well as Rosé de Loire and some sparkling wines. The most successful are the red and white saumur, and the deliciously fruity rosés.

Anjou and the Layon valley

An enormous variety of wines comes under the Anjou banner. The two principal styles are whites (both dry and sweet) from chenin blanc, and reds from cabernet franc. The jewels are the sweet-white-wine vineyards concentrated around the Layon valley in the following appellations: Bonnezeaux, Quarts de Chaume, Coteaux du Layon (including village appellations such as Coteaux du Layon Chaume, Coteaux du Layon St-Lambert-du-Lattay and Coteaux du Layon St-Aubin-de-Luigné) and Coteaux de l'Aubance. Across the Loire from the Layon vineyards lies the tiny enclave of Savennières, which produces dry white wines from chenin blanc, often seen as the purest expression of that grape variety.

The local reds are grouped under the Anjou Rouge and superior Anjou Villages appellations. Huge quantities of semisweet, generally indifferent anjou rosé have given a bad name to a region that can and does produce great wines.

DOMAINE DES BAUMARD

Established **NA** ***Owners*** **the Baumard family** ***Production*** **15,000 cases** ***Vineyard area*** **99 acres (40 ha)**

This *domaine* is at the top of the tree in the Layon valley. Florent Baumard makes the valley's best and most consistent range at the sixteenth-century family home in Rochefort-sur-Loire. The Quarts de Chaume has the characteristic intensity of this great sweet wine and develops beautifully after ten years in bottle. The two savennières, Clos St-Yves and Clos du Papillon, are lighter than some wines from this appellation and therefore more appealing when young. Clos Ste-Catherine is a deliciously balanced coteaux du layon. The Baumards also make red anjou and a crémant de loire.

CHÂTEAU D'EPIRÉ

Established **NA** ***Owners*** **the Bizard family** ***Production*** **5,000 cases** ***Vineyard area*** **25 acres (10 ha)**

This *domaine* has been owned by the Bizard family for over a century. Based in a fine château in the village of Epiré, it includes 20 acres (8 ha) of chenin blanc for savennières and 5 acres (2 ha) of cabernet franc for an anjou rouge, Clos de la Cerisaie. The wines are designed for long-term aging, and the savennières is at its best after 10 years. The chateau also produces medium-dry and sweet wines in good years.

CHÂTEAU DE FESLES

Established **NA** ***Owner*** **Bernard Germain** ***Production*** **33,000 cases** ***Vineyard area*** **87 acres (35 ha)**

ABOVE: *A rainbow points to the pot of gold amid the Quarts de Chaume vineyards in Anjou.*

The benchmark *domaine* for the ultrasweet bonnezeaux, Château de Fesles has undergone a series of changes in the past decade. From being owned by the Boivin family, it passed briefly through the hands of Parisian pâtissier Gaston Lenôtre (who spent millions renovating both the cellar and the château), before landing in the lap of Bernard Germain, whose family owns 11 estates in Bordeaux as well as others in the Coteaux du Layon. The bonnezeaux of Château de Fesles is the star of the range, which also includes a rosé d'anjou, an anjou rouge and an anjou villages.

DOMAINE OGEREAU

Established **Early twentieth century** ***Owner*** **Vincent Ogereau** ***Production*** **5,800 cases** ***Vineyard area*** **57 acres (23 ha)**

Vincent Ogereau believes in making wines with balance. From his vineyards in the Coteaux du Layon village of St-Lambert-du-Lattay, he is able to conjure wines that

BELOW: *Exceptional sweet white wines come from the vineyards of the Layon Valley in Anjou.*

ABOVE: *The Loire is at the limit of winegrowing in western France and winters can be chilly.*

combine lightness and elegance with sweet, sometimes botrytized flavors. Whole-cluster maceration before fermentation adds concentration to the likes of the Coteaux du Layon St-Lambert and the top-of-the-range Prestige. Half the production is good-quality anjou rouge and anjou villages.

CLOS DE LA COULÉE DE SERRANT

Established **Twelfth century** ***Owners*** **the Joly family** ***Production*** **1,700 cases** ***Vineyard area*** **35 acres (14 ha)**

Nicolas Joly, who manages his family's property, is a passionate, articulate advocate for biodynamic cultivation, and his ongoing attempts to promote this practice regularly arouse controversy and debate in the Anjou area. In addition, Joly has to deal with the responsibility of making wine in one of just three single-vineyard appellations in the whole of France. This wine, Savennières Coulée de Serrant, made from chenin blanc, comes from a precipitous 17-acre (7-ha) slope in the Savennières vineyards. Recent vintages have revealed enormously rich, dry, full-bodied wines, which last, seemingly, forever. Among the other wines originating from the Joly family cellars, the Savennières Roches aux Moines and the minerally Savennières Becherelle stand out.

RIGHT: *Local producers sample each others' wares at an informal picnic in the Pays Nantais.*

Muscadet

The westernmost vineyards, in the Pays Nantais region around Nantes, are devoted almost entirely to white wines. There are four Muscadet appellations, all using the muscadet or melon de bourgogne grape. In order of importance, they are Muscadet de Sèvre et Maine, Muscadet Côtes de Grand Lieu, Muscadet des Coteaux de la Loire and Muscadet. Muscadet de Sèvre et Maine and Muscadet Côtes de Grand Lieu are bottled on lees, straight from the unracked, unfiltered cask or tank in which they were fermented, giving a slight prickle and extra freshness to the taste.

Gros Plant is another important appellation in the Pays Nantais. Here, an ultradry, crisp white is produced from gros plant grapes.

DOMAINE DE LA LOUVETRIE

Established **NA** ***Owner*** **Joseph Landron** ***Production*** **12,500 cases** ***Vineyard area*** **62 acres (25 ha)**

Joseph Landron makes several muscadets, each one from grapes grown in a particular soil type. The lightest and freshest, Cuvée Amphibolite, is bottled without any chaptalization or filtration. Hard, rocky orthogneiss soils are used to produce the fatter Hermine d'Or, which

carries the seal of approval of the society of the same name, and the old-vine Fief du Breuil wines. The Landrons also own Clos du Château de la Carizière, where equally fine muscadet is produced.

CHÂTEAU DE LA RAGOTIÈRE

Established **NA** ***Owners*** **the Couillaud brothers** ***Production*** **40,000 cases** ***Vineyard area*** **161 acres (65 ha)**

The Couillaud brothers—Bernard, François and Michel—own two Muscadet properties, Château de la Ragotière and the much less well-known Château la Morinière. From the first comes classic, rich, fat muscadet, including one *cuvée*, Auguste Couillaud, that is aged in wood. From the second property issues a *vin de pays* made from chardonnay, which, in warm years, seems almost akin to chablis. At the top of the range is a superb bottling of the best selection from Château de la Ragotière, which is aged on, and racked straight off the lees.

SAUVION ET FILS

Established **1965** ***Owners*** **the Sauvion family** ***Production*** **15,000 cases** ***Vineyard area*** **74 acres (30 ha)**

This is one of the best-known names in Muscadet. The vineyards at the family property of Château du Cléray Sauvion near Vallet produce a reserve wine. The other top *cuvée* is Cardinal Richard, which is made from wines selected by a panel of tasters. The Découverte range consists of *négociant* wines, again they are chosen by a tasting panel. The Sauvions also make Allégorie, a barrel-fermented muscadet, which has the distinctive vanilla-and-toast taste that muscadet connoisseurs either love or loathe.

Other good producers in the Loire are Domaine Henri Bourgeois, Domaine Masson-Blondelet, Domaine Vincent Pinard, Domaine Jean-Max Roger, Domaine des Aubuisières, Château de la Grille, Château Gaudrelle, Domaine Bourillon-Orléans, Domaine du Clos Naudin, Domaine Yannick Amirault, Domaine Druet, Bouvet-Ladubay, Château du Hureau, Château de Targé, Château Bellerive, Domaine Cady, Chateaux Pierre Bise, Domaine Jo Pithon, Domaine Chereau-Carré, Domaine des Dorices, Domaine de l'Écu, Domaine Gadais et Fils and Domaine du Closel.

Regional Dozen

Domaine des Baumard Coteaux du Layon Clos de Ste-Catherine
Château Pierre Bise Quarts de Chaume
Domaine Couly-Dutheil Chinon Clos de l'Écho
Domaine Didier Dagueneau Pur Sang, Blanc Fumé de Pouilly
Domaine Druet Bourgueil Grand Mont
Château de Fesles Bonnezeaux Château de Fesles
Domaine Huët-L'Échansonne Vouvray Clos du Bourg Demi-sec
Domaine René-Noël Legrand Saumur-Champigny Les Rogelins
Domaine du Clos Naudin Vouvray Moelleux Réserve
Château de la Ragotière Muscadet de Sèvre et Maine
Coulée de Serrant Savennières Coulée de Serrant
Domaine Vacheron Sancerre Les Romains

LEFT: There are few hills in the Loire Valley, which allows warm moist air from the Atlantic to flow through the region, moderating the climate.

ABOVE: The vineyards of Biard are part of Cognac's most important cru, Grande Champagne.

Cognac

ANTHONY PEREGRINE

Cognac, the spirit with the highest self-esteem of any in the world, was in turmoil as the twenty-first century began. Export sales had plummeted from around 145 million bottles in 1990 to nearer 107 million by the end of the decade. Furthermore, a crisis atmosphere had spread across the region's 200,000 acres (81,000 ha) of low-lying vineyards, which roll westward from near Angoulême to the Atlantic coast. Overproduction was running at 25 percent, prices paid to grape growers had plunged, and government aid had been requested.

This was a sorry state of affairs for a drink that had long traded on its image of aristocratic sublimity. Then again, the image itself was part of the problem. Quite simply, cognac producers never got to grips with a modern era in which dark spirits are considered old hat. And their relentless attempts to promote cognac as evermore sophisticated, evermore ethereal (a key word in the cognac lexicon), simply put the drink even farther beyond most people's financial and aspirational reach.

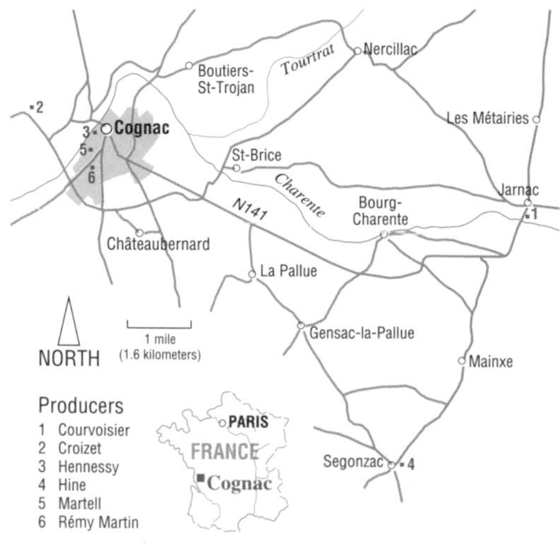

The promotional attempts were, however, understandable. They were dictated by a tradition that began when Dutch traders pioneered distillation in Charentes in the early seventeenth century. In the eighteenth century, the English and Irish came to the region to exploit cognac's potential, and Jean Martell (from Jersey), Thomas Hine (England) and James Hennessy (Ireland) all set up businesses that still exist today. In 1909, the production area was defined, and 25 years later the six constituent *crus* were recognized. This fuelled cognac's growing popularity which, in turn, in the late 1970s and 1980s, attracted the attention of the multinationals that now dominate the sector.

Production in the Cognac *crus*

The cognac production zone, which centers on the town of the same name, divides into six on the basis of climate and, especially, the concentration of chalk in the soil. The soils with the heaviest concentrations resemble those of Champagne, and are therefore known as Grande Champagne and Petite Champagne. The former has the most chalk and provides the finest, most delicate cognacs. Cognac from the Petite Champagne tends to have a more floral bouquet and a touch less finesse. (Fine Champagne is a mix of these *crus*, including a minimum of 50 percent Grande Champagne.)

The smallest *cru* in size, though not production, is the Borderies. Its cognac is rounder and more robust than those of the Champagnes, with a distinctive bouquet of violets, and ages more quickly. The Fins Bois is the largest producer, though quality varies; its cognac is marked by aromas of crushed grapes and is much used in blending. Encircling the other zones, the Bons Bois *cru* yields more rustic produce, while near the ocean the Bois Ordinaires/Communs supplies the most basic fare.

Once vinified, cognac wine is double-distilled in copper pot-stills. Afterward, it measures 70 percent alcohol, so it has to be diluted during aging, usually with distilled water. The length of aging varies, but can last for decades. As a result of evaporation during aging, each year about 2 percent of the cognac in the region's storehouses simply disappears into thin air—the equivalent of about 23 million bottles! The folk in Cognac call it "the angels' share."

Although single-vintage and single-*cru* cognacs are becoming fashionable, most cognacs are made from different *crus* and vintages. The traditional cognac classifications relate to the length of aging. VS (Very Special) or three stars means that the youngest brandy in the blend has been aged for at least two years; the youngest brandy in a VSOP (Very Superior Old Pale) blend has been aged for four years. A Napoléon has had a minimum aging of six years, though it is more usually seven to fifteen. This is the stepping stone from VSOP to XO (Extra Old), whose youngest component must have been aged for six years, though it's not unusual for the actual minimum to be nearer twenty-five years.

A man, fallen on hard times, sold his art collection but kept his cellar. When asked why he did not sell his wine, he said, "A man can live without art, but not without culture."

ANONYMOUS

Almost all cognac is sold by *négociants*, who usually buy in grapes or *eaux-de-vie*, though some also have their own vineyards. The market is dominated by the "Big Four" (Hennessy, Rémy Martin, Martell and Courvoisier), which are responsible for 70 percent of sales. These companies have led the way in dealing with the crisis, mainly by producing new styles of cognac aimed at a new market: women and the young. At the same time, the houses continue to make hugely expensive, antique fare, a reminder of cognac's superb, ethereal, dimension.

COURVOISIER

Established **1805** ***Owner*** **Allied Domecq** ***Production*** **1 million cases**

Napoleon visited Courvoisier's business in 1811, thus began the link between the emperor and cognac. The house continues to justify its imperial connections with a fine and aromatic range. From a VS with fruit and flower tones, it runs through the complexity of the flagship Napoleon to an XO Impérial of almost exotic character.

CROIZET

Established **1805** ***Owners*** **Eymard family** ***Production*** **45,000 cases**

Croizet offers exceptional cognacs in the Napoleon category and above. It also has pre-phylloxera stock and is one of few houses to sell single-vintage produce. If you're looking for a 1928 or 1944, this is a good place to start.

HENNESSY

Established **1765** ***Owner*** **LVMH** ***Production*** **3 million cases**

Since 1998, cognac's biggest producer has consolidated its hold in the US, created three single-distillery cognacs (Camp Romain, Izambard and Le Peu) and produced one of the most interesting of the "young-generation" cognacs, the Pure White. It has also enhanced its reputation for complex premium cognacs with the top-end Grande Champagne XO.

HINE

Established **1763** ***Owner*** **CL World Brands Ltd**
Production **60,000 cases**

This house retains its unbeatable reputation for cognacs of delicacy, elegance and great age. Rare & Delicate is as its name suggests, but rounded out with structured mellowness, while Antique balances light and shade, and displays floral notes as well as hints of leather.

MARTELL

Established **1715** ***Owner*** **Seagram** ***Production*** **1.25 million cases**

Martell is best known for its long-standing Cordon Bleu blend, but has recently sought to attract young drinkers with the excellent Odys and Artys brands, as well as new-wave connoisseurs with the Réserve de J&F Martell, a flowery, restrained, single-growth cognac. Création and the infinitely subtle L'Art de Martell maintain the company's presence at the very top of the market.

RÉMY MARTIN

Established **1724** ***Owner*** **Rémy Cointreau** ***Production*** **1.5 million cases**

The only house whose produce is all at least Fine Champagne, Rémy has nevertheless affixed its centaur emblem to new-era cognacs—notably, the floral and spicily fruity Trek. Meanwhile, Rémy Silver (cognac "pre-mixed with vodka and a "secret ingredient") is a shot at entering the cocktail market. But Rémy's most notable achievement remains the Louis XIII: a Grande Champagne of astonishingly rich, concentrated aromas made from *eaux-de-vie* at least 50 and up to 100 years old.

Regional Dozen

QUALITY COGNACS

Camus XO
Courvoisier XO Impérial
Delamain Pale & Dry XO
Fournier 1946 Grande Champagne
Hennessy Grande Champagne XO
Rémy Martin Louis XIII

BEST VALUE COGNACS

Camus VS
Denis Charpentier VS
Courvoisier VS
Hennessy Pure White
Hine Rare & Delicate
Martell Cordon Bleu

BELOW: *Barrels of century-old* eaux-de-vie, *which is added to blends of XO cognacs.*

Bordeaux

JAMES LAWTHER MW

Bordeaux has been synonymous with wine for centuries. The Romans sowed the seeds of an embryonic industry more than 2,000 years ago and since then Bordeaux has evolved into the largest fine-wine region in the world. Wine is Bordeaux's *raison d'être*.

To the outside world, however, Bordeaux's reputation rests squarely on a group of illustrious châteaux and their highly sought-after and increasingly expensive wines. The likes of Margaux, Lafite and Pétrus certainly turn out benchmark products—firm, long-lived, finely balanced and for the most part red. But they are merely the tip of the iceberg, representing just 5 percent of Bordeaux's total production. Below the waterline lies a vast range of wines, including excellent value offerings from the *petites appellations* as well as a large quantity of far-from-consistent generic bordeaux blends. About 85 percent of the region's output is red; the rest is mainly dry and sweet white, with a little rosé, *clairet* and sparkling *crémant*.

History

The Romans may have been the first to cultivate the vine in Bordeaux, but it was under English rule that trade in wine initially developed. In 1152, Eléanor, Duchess of Aquitaine, married Henry Plantagenet, the future King of England, thereby ceding her territories to England. In return, various concessions were offered by the English Crown, resulting in a flourishing trade between Bordeaux and England.

This golden period came to an end when the French army defeated the English at the Battle of Castillon in 1453. In the seventeenth century, the Dutch, in particular, became a major force, initiating a number of changes in wine styles and channels of distribution. They also introduced sulfur wicks for sterilizing barrels and, most notably, helped drain the marshland of the Médoc, enabling the region to develop as a major winegrowing district.

The eighteenth century provided Bordeaux's second golden era. A new, powerful moneyed class, the *noblesse de robe*, were keen to invest in vineyards. Also, wines from individual estates were increasingly recognized and sought out by wealthy Europeans. Trade in "new French clarets," as they were known, lured a different kind of merchant to Bordeaux. Originating mainly from Britain, Ireland, Holland and Germany, these entrepreneurs set up businesses in and around the Quai des Chartrons. Some of these merchant houses, such as Johnson and Barton, exist to this day. Growing prosperity led to a spate of building in Bordeaux, and much of the city's imposing architecture dates from this period.

In 1855, a classification system was introduced, which ranked wines from the top châteaux in the Médoc and Sauternes according to their market price. (The most expensive were classed as Premiers Crus, then came Deuxièmes Crus, and so on.) Then disaster: phylloxera in the 1870s and downy mildew toward the end

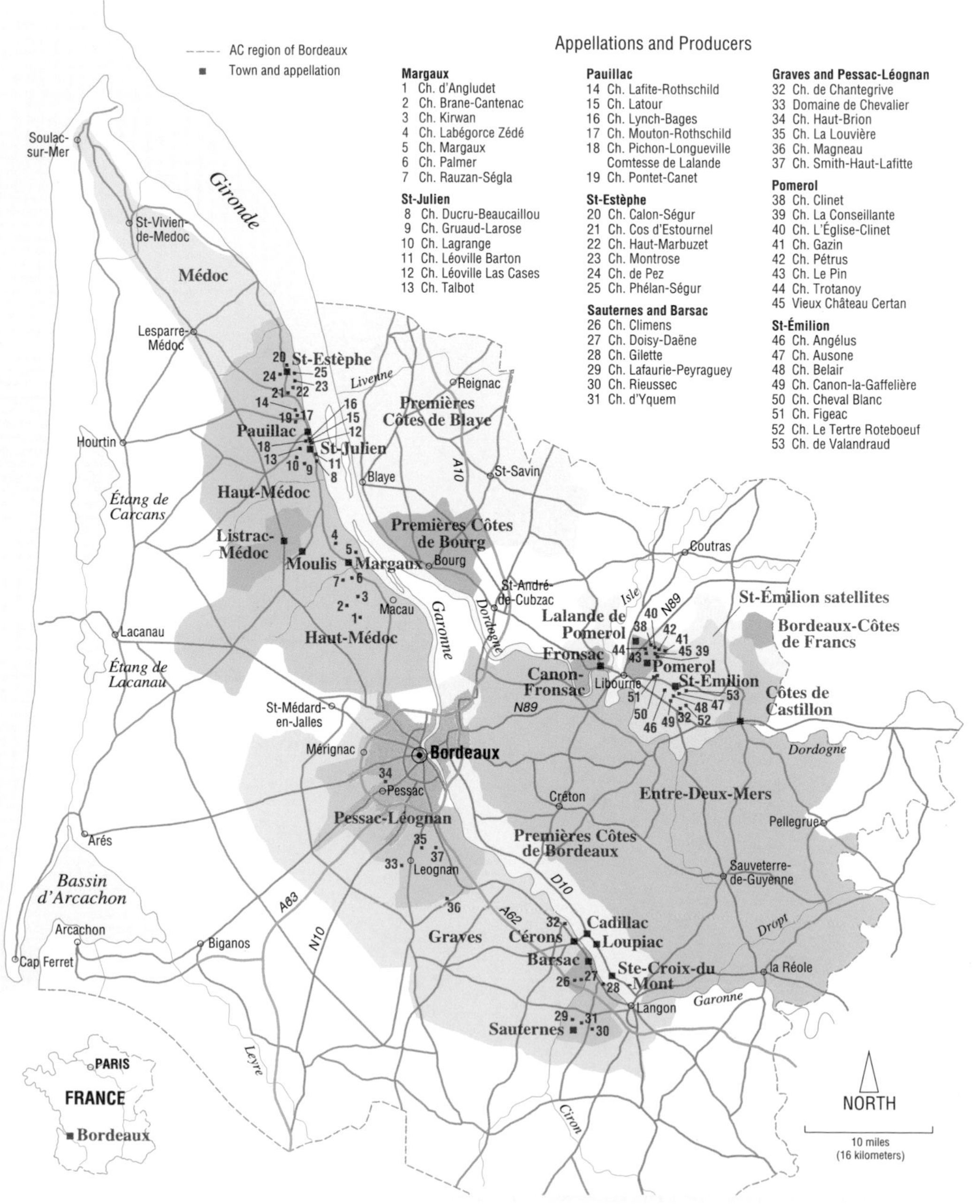

of the century devastated the region's vineyards. Viticulturalists used American rootstock to reconstruct, and it was probably around this time that cabernet sauvignon, cabernet franc, merlot, sémillon, sauvignon blanc and muscadelle became the principal Bordeaux grape varieties.

The twentieth century saw many setbacks—falling prices, overcropping, war, depression, the oil crisis—but there were also positives. In 1936, the system of *appellation contrôlée* was established, which delimited boundaries, defined work practices and, to a degree, set standards of quality. The 1960s saw châteaux owners and *négociants* financing development by selling wines as futures (*en primeur*), and in the 1970s the practice of bottling wines at the châteaux became compulsory.

The qualitative and commercial success of a series of vintages during the 1980s led to important new markets opening up in countries such as Japan. Also, land prices increased and there was a frenzy of investment in the region's vineyards and wineries, with institutional investors becoming significant new owners. Furthermore, a younger, more skilled generation arrived to fill technical and management positions.

Landscape and climate

The Bordeaux region is in the Gironde department of southwestern France, extending from the Pointe de Grave in the northwest to Langon in the southeast, and is crossed by the Dordogne and Garonne rivers. The vineyards are situated along these waterways in an area known as the Entre-Deux-Mers. Most of Bordeaux is flat or undulating, there are no steep slopes, and generally soil types determine which variety of grape is planted. On the "left bank" (the Médoc and Graves), the soils are mainly pebbles, gravel and sand and are generally poor, but they retain heat and have good filtration properties, ideal for late-ripening cabernet sauvignon. On the "right bank" (St-Émilion, Pomerol and Fronsac), the soils are mainly of clay, limestone, sand and pockets of gravel, and are cooler, making them more suited to early-ripening merlot.

Bordeaux has a temperate maritime climate made milder by the warming influence of the Gulf Stream. Rainfall is abundant, summers are warm, and winter rarely drops below freezing. The absence of extremes means that the grapes ripen only to a certain level of intensity, resulting in wines that are subtle and reserved. Cold winter snaps and spring frosts are a danger, but July to early September is the critical period for ripening. Often it coincides with a rainy spell, creating an anxious finish to the growing season. In fall, morning mists provoke the onset of noble rot (*Botrytis cinerea*) needed for sweet white wines.

ABOVE: Some of the top estates have their own cooperages where the barriques are made.

BELOW: At most of Bordeaux's leading vineyards, grapes are normally harvested by hand.

Vines and wines

The production of red wines has increased dramatically over the last 30 years, with merlot being the most widely planted grape. Its supple fruit and higher alcohol content add weight and substance to a blend, while its softness can make a wine more approachable. It adapts well to the cooler clay-limestone soils of the right bank and Entre-Deux-Mers, where it is dominant.

RIGHT: The practice of ploughing between rows of vines has been reintroduced to many areas.

Cabernet sauvignon is probably Bordeaux's most famous red variety, being most firmly associated with the great wines of the Médoc and Graves: it is less sensitive to spring frosts than merlot, and it ripens later, but it needs the assistance of warmer soils to come to full maturity. Its small, thick-skinned grapes provide color, tannin, and a firm but finely edged texture and bouquet.

Cabernet franc also plays a particularly significant role on the right bank, where it partners merlot in St-Émilion and Pomerol blends. When fully ripe, it adds elegance and a fruity complexity. Other red varieties include petit verdot and malbec.

Unlike wines made here in the past, the great red wines of Bordeaux today are quite capable of aging for several decades, and become gradually more harmonious and complex with time.

White grape varieties now make up only around 15 percent of Bordeaux's vineyards. Sémillon is still the principal variety, particularly in the sweet-wine appellations. A productive grape, it makes wines with a citrus flavor and aroma when vinified dry; however, because it is particularly susceptible to noble rot, it is more widely used to make sweet wines that are rich, unctuous, and redolent of honey, raisins and tropical fruits. Sauvignon blanc is the only white variety that is planted more widely now than in the past. Small amounts are blended with sémillon in sweet wines to supply added zest and aroma. However, in areas such as the Entre-Deux-Mers, sauvignon blanc is used to create a crisp, dry, aromatic, single-variety wine.

The other white varieties are now less significant. Muscadelle is used to create a more complex aroma in sweet wines such as Cadillac and Ste-Croix-du-Mont. Colombard and ugni blanc are used in generic bordeaux blends. There are also some experimental plantings of sauvignon gris (thought to be a muscat clone), which producers use for its fruit and heady aroma.

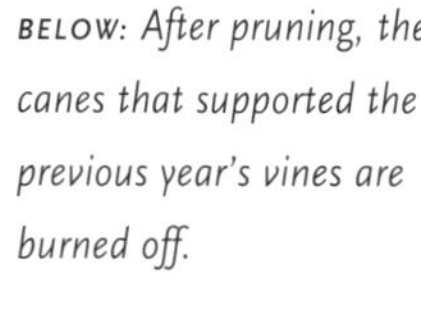

BELOW: After pruning, the canes that supported the previous year's vines are burned off.

Appellations and viticulture

Bordeaux's system of *appellation contrôlée* was established in 1936. As in other parts of France, each appellation is the subject of a ministerial decree that stipulates the geographical delimitation of the appellation, authorized grape varieties, methods of cultivation and vinification, base yield, minimum natural level of alcohol, minimum and maximum degrees of alcohol after fermentation, and labeling procedure, which is now controlled by European Union legislation.

While complying with these directives, the producer must apply for appellation status every year by declaring the harvest and requesting a certificate of approval. This is granted following the analysis and tasting of wines. If the certificate is refused—a sensitive issue, as the tasting panels are usually made up of fellow winegrowers—the producer can submit the wine for approval in a lower-graded appellation. If this too fails, the wine must be sold as a simple table wine (*vin de table*).

Virtually all of the 284,050 acres (115,000 ha) under vine in Bordeaux are delimited as *appellation contrôlée,* with less than 2 percent delimited as *vin de table*. There are 57 different appellations, ranging from regional (for example, Bordeaux and Bordeaux Supérieur) to subregional (Haut-Médoc, for instance) and communal or village (such as Pauillac and Fronsac). Each has its own set of directives and each has a winegrowers' association, or *syndicat viticole*, that defends and promotes the appellation.

Considerable progress has been made in viticulture over the last decade, with the more assiduous producers realizing that good wine is made in the vineyard. There has been much greater investment in planting, equipment and labor; fungal diseases have been better contained; and management has improved. Overcropping is still a problem, but grapes are now allowed more time to ripen: traditionally, wine-growers waited 100 days after flowering before harvesting, but most now allow 110 days.

Vine density varies according to the soil type and the economic imperatives of the producer. In the Médoc, the density may be as high as 4,000 vines per acre (10,000 vines per ha), whereas in St-Émilion, between 2,000 and 2,400 vines per acre (5,000 and 6,000 vines per ha) is normal. In the Entre-Deux-Mers, where economic difficulties resulted in the pulling up of vines in the 1960s and 1970s, there are still some vineyards with as little as 800 vines per acre (2,000 per ha). However, the general tendency is to increase density to provide competition for the vine.

The majority of Bordeaux's vineyards are Guyot-trained, either to one or two canes. Cordon-training is used in some of the more mechanized vineyards, while the lyre system also has its advocates. Pruning is usually carried out by hand, although occasionally some mechanical prepruning occurs. Herbicides are still widely used for weed control, but chemical fertilizers are used less frequently and organic manuring has been reintroduced. Growers are once again working the soils and ploughing between rows of vines. At the same time, the use of grass cover between rows to regulate water supply to the vines is favored in some regions, this is especially the case where erosion is a problem.

Bordeaux's damp climate means that fungal diseases are a perennial threat. Grey rot, oidium and mildew are the most common, but excoriose and eutypa dieback also attack susceptible varieties such as cabernet sauvignon. Other dangers include the animal parasites, grape moth and red spider-mite, and the viral disease known as court-noué, or fanleaf degeneration. Such environmental problems make a completely organic approach to viticulture difficult, but an increasing number of producers are embracing the idea of the "*lutte raisonnée*." This strategy involves limiting chemical spraying to periods when climatic conditions render it most effective, with the timing being based on local weather forecasts. Other innovations include the use of pheromone capsules that disorient the male grape moth, thus preventing the fertilization of eggs, and the introduction of a white spider-mite, the typhlodrome, to try and combat the red spider-mite.

Increased expenditure on labor has occurred mainly in the realm of canopy management. Although vine-trimming is normally mechanized, there has been an increase in shoot-thinning, the removal of excess buds and leaf-stripping, all of which are done by hand. Green harvesting to reduce the number of bunches per vine has also become a more common practice.

ABOVE: *Regular early morning mists in Sauternes contribute to the formation of botrytis.*

BELOW: *During winter, vineyard workers prune the vines and gather cuttings for grafting.*

ABOVE: *In many wineries, an Archimedes' screw is used to deliver the grapes to the crusher.*

BELOW: *Oak barrels line the cavernous cellars of Château Mouton-Rothschild in Pauillac.*

Winemaking

Scientific methods now enable growers to time the harvest of various parcels of vines more precisely, and the wider use of sorting tables, which can be applied to both machine- and hand-picked grapes, has allowed winemakers to be more selective. Each grape variety is vinified separately, as are grapes from different parcels of land if sufficient tank space is available. The fruit is destemmed and crushed, and then pumped or gravity-fed into fermentation tanks or *cuves*. The tanks may be made of cement, stainless steel, or wood. Each material has its own attributes and champions: for example, Pétrus is vinified in cement, Haut-Brion in stainless steel, and Margaux in wood. Sulfur dioxide (SO_2) is widely used as an additive to protect against oxidation and bacteria.

Alcoholic fermentation lasts an average of eight to ten days. Natural yeasts are used and, if necessary, a yeast starter, or *pied de cuve*, may be taken from one tank and added to the others. Following fermentation and maceration, the free-run wine is drained off and the remaining marc is pressed. The press wine is retained for blending purposes, with between 5 and 10 percent being used in the final blend. The wine then undergoes malolactic fermentation either in tank or, increasingly, in new oak barrels. The wine is then aged for anything up to 24 months in French oak barrels or *barriques*. A choice of oak is available (Limousin, Nièvre, or Allier) and producers often buy from a number of cooperages, both to ensure supply and to increase complexity. American oak is used at some châteaux, but rarely by the top producers. During the aging process, the wine is racked off its lees into a fresh barrel every three or four months. It is also clarified or fined using egg whites or a similar albumin preparation. Prior to bottling, the wine normally undergoes a light filtration.

An important task during the early stages of barrel maturation is the selection and blending for the principal wine. The selection process has become steadily more rigorous, with the *grand vin* now representing as little as 30 to 40 percent of total production at top estates.

The procedure for making dry white wines generally follows principles employed around the world, although EU regulations dictate that residual sugar in dry wine must not exceed 0.04 ounces per gallon [4 g per liter]. Variations practiced in Bordeaux include hand harvesting, and machine harvesting and barrel fermentation.

The sweet, rich wines of the best estates in Sauternes and Barsac—and occasionally across the river in Cadillac, Loupiac, and Ste-Croix-du-Mont—are made from grapes affected by noble rot. After selective harvesting, the grapes are pressed and then fermented, either in

French regional cuisine

Much wine is at its best when drunk with food. The rich, robust, rustic cuisine of southwestern France is a good match for its sturdy wines: foods like confit of duck, foie gras from the Gers, ham and chocolate from Bayonne, and prunes from Agen. Gascony is known for garbure, *a rich vegetable soup, and for sheep's cheese. The east is home to the hearty and filling dish known as cassoulet, a stew of beans, confit of duck and sausage.*

Bordeaux's regional fare is rich, warm, and hearty, and red bordeaux, with its fresh, tannic edge, is a natural foil. Red meat, duck, and game often feature. Typical dishes include foie gras, entrecôte *steak grilled over vine cuttings, and milk-fed Pauillac lamb. In fall, cèpe mushrooms are sought-after; spring is asparagus season. A crisp white wine from the Graves or Entre-Deux-Mers is the perfect accompaniment to fish or seafood dishes, such as oysters and lampreys.*

The Mediterranean climate strongly influences Languedoc-Roussillon's local cuisine. Here, fish soups are a specialty as is creamed salt cod, brandade de morue. *Game is eaten when in season, and vegetables, in particular, aubergines, peppers, and tomatoes, are important year round. Meat and fish are usually grilled. Roussillon displays a strong Catalan influence, with grilled pepper salad and crème catalan, a form of crème brulée, among the local specialties.*

Jura has a strong gastronomic tradition that has been integral to the success of its wines, which demand food. Poulsard, a very pale red wine, can be surprisingly good when combined with the right dish, such as smoked Morteau sausage. Comté is a cheese with a strong, nutty flavor perfect for vin jaune. *Bresse's chicken in a cream and* vin jaune *sauce is a local specialty.*

Alsace's French and German cultural mix is seen in its gastronomy. The emphasis is a blend of German heartiness and French refinement: spicy sausages, foie gras, rich stews, and choucroute *(like sauerkraut). Alsatian gewürztraminers are excellent with many rich local dishes or Munster cheese. Tokay (pinot gris) is often drunk with foie gras, which it complements perfectly.*

LEFT: *A simple lunch of paté, fresh bread and tomatoes just off the vine is enhanced by a glass of wine.*

stainless steel, or, increasingly at the top estates, in new or relatively new oak barrels. The fermentation process is necessarily long and slow. When the wine has reached the desired alcohol-sugar balance, the fermentation process is halted by reducing the temperature, racking, and adding sulfur dioxide. Aging in barrel then continues for another two or three years.

The Place de Bordeaux

The Bordeaux wine trade is unique in that it has its own marketplace, the Place de Bordeaux, where wines are sold in bulk and bottle, and as futures. Producers sell to *négociants*, who then sell to distributors in France or importers overseas. The transaction between producer and *négociant* is brokered by a middleman, the *courtier*, who receives a 2 percent commission on the price paid by the purchaser. About 400 *négociants* (including 150 of consequence) now handle 75 percent of the region's production, providing both châteaux wines and wines for commercial brands. The latter are purchased from producers and co-operatives, then blended and bottled in the merchants' cellars.

In the past, châteaux wines were also bought by the *négociants* and aged and bottled in their cellars. However, the growth of château bottling and the cost of holding inventory put an end to this tradition; wines from the top estates and less prestigious châteaux with a market rating are now sold mainly as futures, and dispatched to the purchaser 18 to 24 months after the transaction. The buoyancy of the futures market depends on the quality of the vintage, demand and the economic climate at the time. *Négociants* selling futures usually work on a minimum 12–15 percent margin but occasionally take a loss, as occurred following the overpriced 1997 vintage.

The classifications

Several classification systems are in use in Bordeaux. The most famous is the 1855 classification for red wines of the Médoc and sweet white wines of Sauternes, but others operate in St-Émilion and the Graves. Even the Crus Bourgeois of the Médoc have a grading, although it is limited by a European Union directive to the use of that term. Pomerol is the only major appellation without a classification. Each ranking has its own history and set of controls; the most important are explained in the box features on the following pages.

BELOW: *Fermentation tanks in the cellars of Château Mouton-Rothschild. The Rothschilds pioneered the practice of châteaux bottling.*

The 1855 classification

This classification was based on commercial considerations rather than any qualitative assessment. It was compiled in 1855, when wines from Bordeaux were presented at the Universal Exhibition in Paris and Emperor Napoleon III requested a classification. The listing was drawn up by the Union of Bordeaux Brokers and based on over 100 years of trading statistics (brokers may have been ranking wines unofficially since at least 1730). Sixty châteaux from the Médoc and one (Haut-Brion) from the Graves were classified in five different grades, while twenty-six from Sauternes and Barsac were presented in two grades. The châteaux were ranked according to the trading price they commanded at the time; this original order has been retained here. Only one change has been made to the list since it was compiled: in 1973, Mouton-Rothschild was upgraded from Deuxième Cru to Premier Cru.

THE MÉDOC

Premiers Crus (First Growths)

Château Lafite-Rothschild	Pauillac
Château Margaux	Margaux
Château Latour	Pauillac
Château Haut-Brion	Pessac-Léognan
Château Mouton-Rothschild (upgraded in 1973)	Pauillac

Deuxièmes Crus (Second Growths)

Château Rauzan-Ségla	Margaux
Château Rauzan-Gassies	Margaux
Château Léoville Las Cases	St-Julien
Château Léoville Poyferré	St-Julien
Château Léoville Barton	St-Julien
Château Durfort-Vivens	Margaux
Château Gruaud-Larose	St-Julien
Château Lascombes	Margaux
Château Brane-Cantenac	Margaux
Château Pichon-Longueville Baron	Pauillac
Château Pichon-Longueville Comtesse de Lalande	Pauillac
Château Ducru-Beaucaillou	St-Julien
Château Cos d'Estournel	St-Estèphe
Château Montrose	St-Estèphe

Troisièmes Crus (Third Growths)

Château Kirwan	Margaux
Château d'Issan	Margaux
Château Lagrange	St-Julien
Château Langoa Barton	St-Julien
Château Giscours	Margaux
Château Malescot-St-Exupéry	Margaux
Château Boyd-Cantenac	Margaux
Château Cantenac-Brown	Margaux
Château Palmer	Margaux
Château La Lagune	Haut-Médoc
Château Desmirail	Margaux
Château Calon-Ségur	St-Estèphe
Château Ferrière	Margaux
Château Marquis d'Alesme-Becker	Margaux

Quatrièmes Crus (Fourth Growths)

Château St-Pierre	St-Julien
Château Talbot	St-Julien
Château Branaire	St-Julien
Château Duhart-Milon	Pauillac
Château Pouget	Margaux
Château La Tour Carnet	Haut-Médoc
Château Lafon-Rochet	St-Estèphe
Château Beychevelle	St-Julien
Château Prieuré-Lichine	Margaux
Château Marquis de Terme	Margaux

Cinquièmes Crus (Fifth Growths)

Château Pontet-Canet	Pauillac
Château Batailley	Pauillac
Château Haut-Batailley	Pauillac
Château Grand-Puy-Lacoste	Pauillac
Château Grand-Puy-Ducasse	Pauillac
Château Lynch-Bages	Pauillac
Château Lynch-Moussas	Pauillac
Château Dauzac	Margaux
Château d'Armailhac	Pauillac
Château du Tertre	Margaux
Château Haut-Bages-Libéral	Pauillac
Château Pédesclaux	Pauillac
Château Belgrave	Haut-Médoc
Château Camensac	Haut-Médoc
Château Cos Labory	St-Estèphe
Château Clerc Milon	Pauillac
Château Croizet-Bages	Pauillac
Château Cantemerle	Haut-Médoc

SAUTERNES AND BARSAC

Premier Cru Supérieur (Superior First Growth)

Château d'Yquem	Sauternes

Premiers Crus (First Growths)

Château La Tour Blanche	Sauternes
Château Lafaurie-Peyraguey	Sauternes
Château Clos Haut-Peyraguey	Sauternes
Château Rayne Vigneau	Sauternes
Château Suduiraut	Sauternes
Château Coutet	Barsac
Château Climens	Barsac
Château Guiraud	Sauternes
Château Rieussec	Sauternes
Château Rabaud-Promis	Sauternes
Château Sigalas-Rabaud	Sauternes

Deuxièmes Crus (Second Growths)

Château de Myrat*	Sauternes
Château Doisy-Daëne*	Sauternes
Château Doisy-Dubroca*	Sauternes
Château Doisy-Védrines*	Sauternes
Château d'Arche	Sauternes
Château Filhot	Sauternes
Château Broustet	Barsac
Château Nairac	Barsac
Château Caillou	Barsac
Château Suau	Barsac
Château de Malle	Sauternes
Château Romer du Hayot	Sauternes
Château Lamothe	Sauternes
Château Lamothe Guignard	Sauternes

* Châteaux located in Barsac which use the Sauternes label

BELOW: Château Pichon-Longueville (Baron), with its elegant spires and ornamental lake.

ABOVE: *The imposing façade of Château Margaux, the appellation's most productive winery.*

MAJOR APPELLATIONS

Margaux

Margaux is the most southerly and extensive of the communal appellations in the Médoc, with approximately 3,340 acres (1,352 ha) under production. The vineyards are spread through five communes: Arsac, Labarde, Cantenac, Soussans and Margaux itself. Margaux's gravel and sand soils are poorer than those farther north, which accounts for the area's generally lighter-bodied and more fragrant style of red wine. The soils and warmer local climate suit late-ripening cabernet sauvignon and petit verdot.

Twenty-one Margaux châteaux were included in the 1855 classification, including Château Margaux, a Premier Cru which today supplies around 70 percent of production. Margaux has often been accused of underachieving, but since the 1990s a younger generation has come to the helm and there has been greater level of investment and commitment. As a result, this is once again an appellation to watch.

A meal without wine is like a day without sunshine.

ANTHELME BRILLAT SAVARIN (1755–1826)

CHÂTEAU MARGAUX

Owners **the Mentzelopoulos family and associates** ***Production*** **33,000 cases** ***Vineyard area*** **193 acres (78 ha); 75 percent cabernet sauvignon, 20 percent merlot, 5 percent petit verdot and cabernet franc**

This magnificent estate was commissioned by Marquis de la Colonel in 1810, and was often referred to as the Versailles of the Médoc. During the 1960s and 1970s highly variable wines were produced; however, since the Château was purchased by André Mentzelopoulos in 1977, it has probably been the most consistent of the Premiers Crus. The property is managed by André's daughter, Corinne, with the assistance of technical director Paul Pontallier. In recent years, the selection process has become more rigorous, with only 50 percent of the production going into the *grand vin* and the rest into the second wine, Pavillon Rouge. Both of these wonderful wines combine power and elegance with a purity of fruit and finely honed structure. The château also produces 3,300 cases of a white wine, Pavillon Blanc, made from 30 acres (12 ha) of barrel-fermented sauvignon blanc.

CHÂTEAU PALMER

Owner **SCI Château Palmer** ***Production*** **18,000 cases** ***Vineyard area*** **112 acres (45 ha); 55 percent cabernet sauvignon, 40 percent merlot, 5 percent petit verdot**

Established in the early nineteenth century by Englishman General Charles Palmer, this estate has regularly surpassed its Troisième Cru classification. The wines have been remarkably consistent, and for a period in the 1960s and 1970s were probably the best in the Margaux appellation. The large quantity of merlot grown on the estate accounts for Château Palmer's famous velvety texture, and with only one-third new oak barrels used for aging, the oak always remains discreet.

Since 1938, the château has been owned by a consortium of French, English and Dutch families. A new vatroom with 33 conically shaped stainless-steel tanks was completed in 1995.

ABOVE: *Tending to the vines on the estate of Château Léoville Las Cases, St-Julien.*

CHÂTEAU RAUZAN-SÉGLA

Owner **the Wertheimer family** ***Production*** **15,000 cases** ***Vineyard area*** **121 acres (49 ha); 61 percent cabernet sauvignon, 35 percent merlot, 4 percent petit verdot and cabernet franc**

In 1855, Château Rauzan-Ségla was considered the appellation's leading producer after Château Margaux, and classified as a second growth. Although it regained form sporadically in the 1980s, it has only begun to realize its full potential since it was acquired by the Wertheimer family, owners of Chanel, in 1994. A massive program of investment has left no stone unturned: vineyards have been drained and replanted, cellars renovated, new equipment installed and the proportion of new oak barrels increased to around 70 percent. Production from the estate's younger vines now goes into a second wine called Ségla. The high percentage of merlot in the main blend (up to 40 percent) endows Rauzan-Ségla with the body and texture to complement its elegant bouquet.

BELOW: *The head winemaker outside the historic winery at Château Branaire, St-Julien.*

Other Margaux producers of note include Bel Air Marquis d'Aligre, D'Anglutet, Brane-Cantenac, Dauzac, Durfort-Vivens, Ferrière, Giscours, La Gurgue, d'Issan, Kirwan, Labégorce, Lascombes, Malescot-St-Exupéry, Marquis de Terme, Monbrison, Prieuré-Lichine, Siran and du Tertre.

St-Julien

St-Julien can rightfully lay claim to having been the most consistent appellation in Bordeaux during the past 15 years. No fewer than 11 Classed Growths are found here, representing 80 percent of the appellation's production. But that is not the whole story: success requires a superior location and highly committed producers, and fortunately St-Julien has both.

The appellation's 2,223 acres (900 ha) are situated on two plateaux located between Pauillac to the north and the Haut-Médoc to the south, and close to the warming influence of the waters of the Gironde Estuary. A southeasterly exposure and free-draining, gravelly soils enhance the ripening cycle, contributing to a mellow fruit character in the red wines that is backed by a firm, structure with great potential for aging. Since the 1980s, the appellation's châteaux owners have made the most of these conditions by investing heavily in new equipmement for their vineyards and cellars.

CHÂTEAU DUCRU-BEAUCAILLOU

Owner **the Borie family** ***Production*** **18,000 cases** ***Vineyard area*** **123 acres (50 ha); 65 percent cabernet sauvignon, 25 percent merlot, 5 percent cabernet franc, 5 percent petit verdot**

Owned by the Borie family since 1942, this Deuxième Cru occupies a prime location, close to the Gironde Estuary at the southern end of the appellation. It is named for the *"beaux cailloux"*—the coarse chunks of quartz, flint and other rocks that are clearly visible in the vineyard's soil.

The estate's fortunes were revived during the 1950s by Jean-Eugène Borie, with the assistance of enologist Émile Peynaud, and their work is now being continued by Borie's son, François-Xavier. Wood contamination in the cellars caused some irregularity in late-1980s vintages, but new cellars and improvements in the selection process have seen Ducru-Beaucaillou return to top form. The wines are rich, ripe and elegant but need at least ten years to develop.

CHÂTEAU GRUAUD-LAROSE

Owners **the Merlaut family** ***Production*** **38,000 cases** ***Vineyard area*** **203 acres (82 ha); 55 percent cabernet sauvignon, 31 percent merlot, 10 percent cabernet franc, 2 percent petit verdot, 2 percent malbec**

Gruaud-Larose is probably the most full-bodied, fruity and muscular wine in St-Julien. This can be partly attributed to its location in the southern half of the appellation, where the soils are slightly heavier. Over the last 18 years the ownership has changed hands four times; the present owners, the Merlaut family, purchased the property from the industrial conglomerate Alcatel-Alstom in 1997. The latter was responsible for a massive program of investment in 1993, which included improved drainage, new machinery, the installation of a weather station and 14 new wooden vats. During vinification the wines undergo a long period of maceration. The estate uses only 30 percent new oak barrels for aging.

CHÂTEAU LÉOVILLE BARTON

Owner **Anthony Barton** ***Production*** **21,000 cases**
Vineyard area **116 acres (47 ha); 72 percent cabernet sauvignon, 20 percent merlot, 8 percent cabernet franc**

This Deuxième Cru has been owned by the Barton family since 1826 and run by Anthony Barton since 1982. The vineyard, which at one time formed part of the vast Léoville estate, has a high percentage of old vines. The estate has no château or cellars, so the wine is made at Troisième Cru Château Langoa Barton, also owned by the Barton family. Wooden vats are used for vinification, and the wine is then aged in 50 percent new oak barrels.

Anthony Barton and manager Michel Raoult have made the winemaking process steadily more rigorous, with the result that wines are now richer, fuller and more firmly structured.

Other St-Julien producers of note include Beychevelle, Branaire, La Bridane, Glana, Gloria, Lalande-Borie, Langoa Barton, Léoville Poyferré and St-Pierre.

Pauillac

Pauillac, for many, provides the quintessential wine of the Médoc: firm and powerful, slightly austere in youth, made for aging, and with a distinct scent of blackcurrant and cigar box. Significantly, this appellation is home to three Premiers Crus—Lafite, Mouton-Rothschild and Latour—as well as 15 other classified estates.

Bounded by St-Estèphe to the north and St-Julien to the south, Pauillac's 2,890 acres (1,170 ha) of vineyard are divided into two zones. North of the town of Pauillac, where both Lafite and Mouton are located, the land is higher (80 feet [24 m]), the vineyards farther from the estuary, and the gravel soils rest on a bed of sandy marl and limestone. To the south, home of Latour among others, the land is significantly lower but closer to the estuary, and the gravel soils are somewhat heavier and deeper and contain some very large pebbles. While the characteristics of each area add different nuances to the wines, both are ideal for cultivating the appellation's principal grape variety, cabernet sauvignon.

ABOVE: *Château Lafite's course gravel soils are typical of those of northern Pauillac.*

BELOW: *Bottles from vintages of the 1790s are still held in the cellars of Château Lafite-Rothschild.*

ABOVE: *Exquisite Château Latour, with its extensive vineyards and seventeenth-century tower.*

CHÂTEAU LAFITE-ROTHSCHILD

Owners **Barons de Rothschild** ***Production*** **20,000 cases** ***Vineyard area*** **247 acres (100 ha); 72 percent cabernet sauvignon, 23 percent merlot, 3 percent cabernet franc, 2 percent petit verdot**

The most northerly of Pauillac's three Premiers Crus, Lafite has been owned by the Rothschilds since 1868 and is presently run by Eric de Rothschild. Most of the vineyard is planted on an undulating gravel knoll which faces the Gironde Estuary to the east and extends toward the Breuil River in the north. Whether it is a result of the topography or the higher percentage of limestone in the subsoil, Lafite has always been lighter in style than either Mouton or Latour, and possessed a greater elegance; it also has a huge capacity for aging. Since 1995, manager Charles Chevallier and his team have refined their viticulture, resulting in a wine of greater weight and structure. The estate's second wine is known as Carruades.

CHÂTEAU LATOUR

Owner **François Pinault** ***Production*** **33,000 cases** ***Vineyard area*** **160 acres (65 ha); 75 percent cabernet sauvignon, 20 percent merlot, 5 percent cabernet franc and petit verdot**

Château Latour is the epitome of a classic Pauillac wine: deep color; blackcurrant, cedar and mineral bouquet; subdued power; and firm structure for long aging. The vineyard, too, has a classic profile with a high proportion of cabernet sauvignon, a southeasterly exposure, deep gravel soils, and close proximity to the warming influence of the Gironde Estuary. Its heart is the 116-acre (47-ha) Enclos, which surrounds the château. Wines for the Grand Vin de Château Latour are produced from this area, while the excellent second wine, Les Forts de Latour, and a third wine, simply labeled Pauillac, are produced from other parcels.

Château Latour is named for a square-shaped, fourteenth-century fortification, but the present tower dates from the seventeenth century. After 30 years of British ownership, Latour was acquired by French businessman François Pinault in 1993.

CHÂTEAU MOUTON-ROTHSCHILD

Owner **Baronne Philippine de Rothschild** ***Production*** **25,000 cases** ***Vineyard area*** **185 acres (75 ha); 80 percent cabernet sauvignon, 10 percent cabernet franc, 8 percent merlot, 2 percent petit verdot**

In 1853, Baron Nathaniel de Rothschild purchased this vineyard and changed the name from Brane-Mouton to Mouton-Rothschild. Classified as a Deuxième Cru in 1855, it was eventually upgraded to Premier Cru in 1973. This was mainly due to the work and persistence of Baron Philippe de Rothschild, who took over the estate in 1922, introduced château bottling in 1924, initiated the idea of artist-designed labels in 1945, and generally improved the quality and dimensions of the wines. He was succeeded by his daughter, Philippine de Rothschild, in 1988.

Mouton has the power and concentration of Pauillac but an opulence and panache that sets it apart from Lafite, whose vineyard has the same geological profile. A second label, Le Petit Mouton, was introduced in the 1990s and a small quantity of white wine, L'Aile d'Argent, is also produced.

Other Pauillac producers of note include d'Armailhac, Batailley, Clerc Milon, Duhart-Milon, Fonbadet, Grand-Puy-Ducasse, Grand-Puy-Lacoste, Haut-Bages-Libéral, Haut-Batailley, La Fleur Milon, Pibran, Pichon-Longueville Baron and Pichon-Longueville Comtesse de Lalande.

St-Estèphe

St-Estèphe is the most northerly of the Médoc's four principal communal appellations. Its varied soil structure includes gravel hillocks near the estuary; a bedrock of limestone, the *calcaire de St-Estèphe*, which outcrops in certain areas; and deposits of sand and clay, particularly in the west and north of the appellation. These variations influence the choice of grape varieties and add certain nuances to the wines. Cabernet sauvignon is still the most common variety but, given the preponderance of cooler soils, merlot has gained favor and now represents 35 percent of the 3,038 acres (1,230 ha) under production.

There are only five Classed Growths, which together produce 20 percent of the total output. The lion's share of 54 percent is generated by the Crus Bourgeois, with a further 17 percent coming from the local co-operative. St-Estèphe wines are generally fruity and full-bodied but with a firm tannic edge. This edge can be a little aggressive, though modern winemaking methods and grape selection have alleviated this problem.

CHÂTEAU CALON-SÉGUR

Owner Madame Capbern-Gasqueton Production 25,000 cases Vineyard area 136 acres (55 ha); 60 percent cabernet sauvignon, 30 percent merlot, 10 percent cabernet franc

The most northerly of the Classed Growths, Calon is also one of the appellation's oldest estates, its origins dating back to Gallo-Roman times. In the eighteenth century, it was owned by the powerful Ségur family, proprietors of Lafite and Latour. Georges Capbern-Gasqueton acquired the property in 1894 and it remains in the same family today.

The wines are firm, powerful and rich in the better vintages, but have tended toward leanness at other times. Fortunately, recent changes, including work in the vineyard, the inauguration of a new vatroom in 1999, the introduction of partial malolactic fermentation in barrel, and an increase in the percentage of new oak for aging have gone some way to remedying this problem.

ABOVE: *Carvings on the wall of the Château Cos d'Estournel in St-Estéphe.*

BELOW: *Cos d'Estournel's unusual winery was inspired by Asian architecture.*

CHÂTEAU COS D'ESTOURNEL

***Owners* Taillan Group *Production* 25,000 cases *Vineyard area* 161 acres (65 ha); 60 percent cabernet sauvignon, 40 percent merlot**

Cos, which in the old Gascon tongue means "hill of pebbles," was founded in 1811 by Louis Gaspard d'Estournel, whose fascination with eastern Asia led to the construction of the distinctive pagoda-like winery. The recent success of Cos is mainly due to co-owner Bruno Prats, who managed the estate from 1970 until it was sold to the Merlaut family (in association with an Argentinian group, Cavas de Santa Maria) in 1998. Prats' son, Jean-Guillaume, remains as general manager.

The wines are dark, rich and opulent, the high percentage of merlot adding an uncharacteristic (for the appellation) suavity and the well-judged oak an exotic, spicy nuance. The second wine, Les Pagodes de Cos, was baptized in 1994. Previously, the young vines were vinified with those of a separate estate, Château de Marbuzet, and sold as the second label under this name.

CHÂTEAU MONTROSE

***Owner* Jean-Louis Charmolüe *Production* 27,000 cases *Vineyard area* 168 acres (68 ha); 65 percent cabernet sauvignon, 25 percent merlot, 10 percent cabernet franc**

The vineyard of this Deuxième Cru has exactly the same profile as that of Château Latour or the Grand Clos of Château Léoville Las Cases: deep gravel soils, south-easterly exposure and close proximity to the Gironde Estuary. Like those of Latour, Château Montrose's wines are firm and powerful, dominated by cabernet sauvignon, and have great potential for aging. In recent years, later picking of riper grapes has mellowed what used to be a tough exterior. The estate's second wine, La Dame de Montrose, is also worth seeking out. The property has been owned by the Charmolüe family since 1896.

CHÂTEAU PHÉLAN-SÉGUR

Owners Gardinier family Production 33,000 cases Vineyard area 163 acres (66 ha); 60 percent cabernet sauvignon, 30 percent merlot, 10 percent cabernet franc

Much of the recent success here can be attributed to the Gardinier family, who purchased the estate in 1985. Having survived a disasterous contamination of wines by chemical spray, they have completely renovated the property and lifted the quality of their produce. The wines are now concentrated and possess poise and finesse. A second wine, Frank Phélan, was introduced in 1986.

Other St-Estèphes producers of note include Le Boscq, Cos Labory, Haut-Beauséjour, Lafon-Rochet, Le Crock, Lilian-Ladouys, Marbuzet, Meyney, Les Ormes de Pez and Tour de Pez.

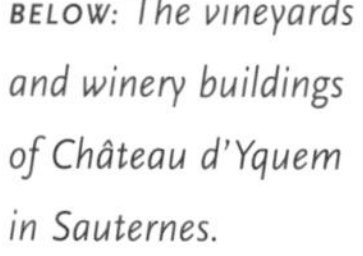

BELOW: The vineyards and winery buildings of Château d'Yquem in Sauternes.

Sauternes and Barsac

Situated 25 miles (40 km) southeast of the city of Bordeaux and encircled by vineyards of the Graves, the five communes of Bommes, Fargues, Sauternes, Preignac and Barsac are authorized to make the rich, opulent wines known as Sauternes and Barsac. (Producers in the commune of Barsac can label wines either Barsac or Sauternes.) If ever there was a product of nature, it is these wines, for they are the direct result of a unique combination of climatic influences. In fall, as the cool waters of the Ciron run into the warmer Garonne, mists form that provoke the onset of noble rot, or *Botrytis cinerea*. This fungal spore reduces the water content of the grape, increasing its sugar levels, acidity and flavor. The haphazard occurrence of this natural process means that the grapes have to be hand-picked selectively which in turn means that the wines are costly to make and in certain years the top châteaux are unable to declare a vintage. The success of several vintages in the 1980s and 1990s, however, has supplied funds for investment that were lacking in the past.

There are currently approximately 5,558 acres (2,250 ha) under production, with maximum yields restricted to 1.4 tons per acre (25 hl per ha). Sémillon is the principal grape variety; a little sauvignon blanc is normally added to increase aroma and acidity, and occasionally muscadelle is added too. The lower-lying land and higher limestone content in the soils generally make barsac a lighter wine than sauternes.

CHÂTEAU CLIMENS, BARSAC

Owner **Bérénice Lurton** ***Production*** **4,500 cases** ***Vineyard area*** **72 acres (29 ha); 100 percent sémillon**

Climens is the quintessential barsac: rich and concentrated, and displaying unparalleled finesse and delicacy as well as increasing complexity as it ages. The vineyard is located at the highest point of the Barsac plateau, on a soil composed of fissured limestone that provides good natural drainage. Lucien Lurton purchased this first growth in 1971 and provided the financial security that allowed the estate to return to a stricter system of grape selection; the property is now run by his daughter Bérénice. The wines, produced uniquely from sémillon, are fermented and aged in oak barrels, 50 percent of which are renewed yearly. In some years, a second wine, Les Cyprès de Climens, is produced.

CHÂTEAU LAFAURIE-PEYRAGUEY, SAUTERNES

Owner **Domaines Cordier** ***Production*** **6,000 cases** ***Vineyard area*** **99 acres (40 ha); 90 percent sémillon, 5 percent sauvignon blanc, 5 percent muscadelle**

The property is situated on an exposed hillock in Haut-Bommes, and includes a château that dates from the thirteenth century. In 1978, the estate began using oak casks again for fermentation; it has since increased the proportion of new oak to around 50 percent. In addition, the picking has become increasingly selective. Since the notable 1983 vintage, Lafaurie-Peyraguey has consistently turned out wines that are rich, full and balanced and have wonderful fruit expression.

ABOVE: Grapes affected by noble rot produce the great sweet wines of Sauternes and Barsac.

CHÂTEAU D'YQUEM, SAUTERNES

Owners **Group LVMH and Lur-Saluces family** ***Production*** **7,500 cases** ***Vineyard area*** **262 acres (106 ha); 80 percent sémillon, 20 percent sauvignon blanc**

Singled out as a Premier Cru Supérieur in the 1855 classification, Yquem owes its celebrated status to the continuity provided by the Lur-Saluces family (owners since 1785), the precision with which the *domaine* is run, and its geographical situation—the vineyard is located in one block on a prominent knoll that provides excellent ripening conditions. Yields here rarely exceed 0.5 tons per acre (9 hl per ha), the equivalent of just one glass of wine per vine, and in certain difficult years (1910, 1915, 1930, 1951, 1952, 1964, 1972, 1974 and 1992) no Yquem was produced. The wines are fermented and aged for three-and-a-half years in 100 percent new oak barrels, and are the richest and most powerful in the appellation. Their capacity to age is legendary. The majority shareholding in Yquem was sold in 1996 to the luxury group LVMH, but Comte Alexandre de Lur-Saluces retains an interest.

Other Sauternes and Barsac producers of note include Bastor-Lamontagne, Clos Haut-Peyraguey, Coutet, Cru Barréjats, Doisy-Védrines, Fargues, Guiraud, Haut-Bergeron, les Justices, de Malle, de Myrat, Nairac, Rabaud-Promis, Raymond-Lafon, Rayne Vigneau, Sigalas-Rabaud, Suduiraut and La Tour Blanche.

BELOW: In recent years, most producers have increased the proportion of new oak barrels in use in their cellars.

ABOVE: *Château Olivier, a Cru Classé, is classified for both its red and white wines.*

The 1959 classification of the Graves

This classification was undertaken by the INAO (Institut National des Appellations d'Origine). It was first ratified in 1953 for red wines only; dry white wines were included in 1959. The system is simple and grants all 16 châteaux Cru Classé (Classed Growth) status. Some estates are classified for both red and white wines, others for only one kind. All the châteaux are located in the Pessac-Léognan appellation of the northern Graves, which only came into existence in 1987. Because the system has not been updated since 1959, it cannot be regarded as a fair reflection of the current market standing of these wines.

THE CRUS CLASSÉS (CLASSED GROWTHS) OF THE GRAVES

Château Bouscaut	(red and white)
Château Carbonnieux	(red and white)
Château Couhins	(white)
Château Couhins-Lurton	(white)
Château de Fieuzal	(red)
Château Haut-Bailly	(red)
Château Haut-Brion	(red)
Château Laville Haut-Brion	(white)
Château Malartic-Lagravière	(red and white)
Château La Mission Haut-Brion	(red)
Château Olivier	(red and white)
Château Pape Clément	(red)
Château Smith-Haut-Lafitte	(red)
Château La Tour Haut-Brion	(red)
Château La Tour-Martillac	(red and white)
Domaine de Chevalier	(red and white)

The Graves and Pessac-Léognan

The Graves is Bordeaux's oldest viticultural zone, its vineyards dating back to at least the Middle Ages. It extends for 30 miles (50 km) southeast of the city of Bordeaux and is bounded to the east by the Garonne River and to the west by the Landes forest. The region takes its name from its gravel soils, which are particularly common around the fringes of the city.

In 1987, the northern sector of the Graves became a separate appellation, Pessac-Léognan. It now has about 3,260 acres (1,320 ha) under vine and has seen considerable investment in the last ten years. Red wine represents around 80 percent of production, and there is a limited output of top-quality white. The 1959 Graves Crus Classés are all located here.

BELOW: *At first light, mist from the Garonne drifts across the vineyards of Pessac-Léognan.*

The Graves appellation is more varied, both in terms of soil types and wine quality. It is also more extensive, with 5,410 acres (2,190 ha) under red and 2,320 acres (940 ha) for dry white vines; a further 1,150 acres (465 ha) are allotted to sweet Graves Supérieur.

The red wines of the Graves and Pessac-Léognan are similar to those of the Médoc and just as impressive at the top level. Cabernet sauvignon is the dominant red variety, although plantings of merlot are on the increase in the Graves.

The dry whites, made from sauvignon blanc and sémillon, have a citrus and mineral nuance but they gain extra weight and finesse when barrel-fermented and aged on lees.

Because the whites are more signifcant in this region than elsewhere in Bordeaux, separate figures have been provided in the following producer entries for red and white wine production.

CHÂTEAU DE CHANTEGRIVE, GRAVES

Owners Françoise and Henri Lévèque _Production_ 34,000 cases (17,000 red, 17,000 white) _Vineyard area_ 106 acres (44 ha) of red (55 percent cabernet sauvignon, 35 percent merlot, 10 percent cabernet franc), 114 acres (46 ha) of white (50 percent sémillon, 40 percent sauvignon blanc, 10 percent muscadelle)

Françoise and Henri Lévèque built this estate from scratch in 1967 and have steadily expanded it to the point where it is now the largest in the Graves.

The regular white wine is crisp and fruity, but of most interest is the Cuvée Caroline, a special bottling of barrel-fermented sémillon and sauvignon blanc. In certain years it can stand alongside the best from Pessac-Léognan. The red has been of less interest, but in 1998 the yields were reduced and the wines now appear richer and riper.

CHÂTEAU HAUT-BRION, PESSAC-LÉOGNAN

Owner **Domaine Clarence Dillon** ***Production*** **12,800 cases (12,000 red, 800 white)** ***Vineyard area*** **106 acres (43 ha) of red (45 percent cabernet sauvignon, 37 percent merlot, 18 percent cabernet franc), 7.4 acres (3 ha) of white (63 percent sémillon, 37 percent sauvignon blanc)**

Established in the sixteenth century and classified as a first growth in 1855, Haut-Brion is *the* great estate of the Graves region. It was bought by the American Clarence Dillon in 1935 and is now administered by his granddaughter Joan, the Duchesse de Mouchy. The vineyard is situated on two southeast-facing gravel hills and surrounded by Bordeaux's suburban sprawl. Average temperatures are slightly higher here than in the Médoc, allowing the grapes to attain greater levels of maturity. They are then vinified in a modern *cuverie* that was purpose-built by manager Jean-Bernard Delmas and opened in 1991. The red wine is always finely textured with smooth tannins, ripe fruit and a slightly burnt, roasted note. The white is full and complex. The Dillon family also own Châteaux La Mission Haut-Brion, Laville Haut-Brion and La Tour Haut-Brion.

CHÂTEAU SMITH-HAUT-LAFITTE, PESSAC-LÉOGNAN

Owners **Daniel and Florence Cathiard** ***Production*** **11,000 cases (8,500 red, 2,500 white)** ***Vineyard area*** **111 acres (45 ha) of red (55 percent cabernet sauvignon, 35 percent merlot, 10 percent cabernet franc), 25 acres (10 ha) of white (100 percent sauvignon blanc)**

Following its purchase by Daniel and Florence Cathiard in 1990, this estate became one of the revelations of the 1990s. No expense has been spared to improve the wines: the vineyard has been reorganized, yields reduced and organic methods introduced; winemaking facilities have been modernized; and the percentage of new oak barrels has been increased—50 percent are now provided by the estate's own cooperage, which opened in 1995. The barrel-fermented white is rich and aromatic and contains a tiny percentage of sauvignon gris. Since 1994, the red has gained in both density and finesse.

Other Graves producers of note include Archambeau, d'Ardennes, Bichon-Cassignols, Brondelle, Clos Floridène, Le Bonnat, Léhoul, Rahoul, Respide Médeville, St-Robert, du Seuil, Vieux Château Gaubert and Villa Bel Air.

Other Pessac-Léognan producers of note include Carbonnieux, Les Carmes Haut-Brion, de Fieuzal, de France, La Garde, Haut-Bailly, Haut-Bergey, Larrivet Haut-Brion, Latour-Martillac, Laville Haut-Brion, Malartic-Lagravière, La Mission Haut-Brion, Olivier, Pape Clément, Le Thil Comte Clary and La Tour Haut-Brion.

ABOVE: *Bringing in the harvest by hand at the Château Certan-de-May in Pomerol.*

Pomerol

The tiny appellation of Pomerol produces some of the finest and most sought-after wines in the world. Dominated by merlot, the best of which are rich, sweet and unctuous, the layered fruit extract adding gloss to a firm, tannic structure. Only 1,927 acres (780 ha) of Pomerol, located on a gently sloping plateau northeast Libourne, are under production. The clay and gravel soils of the center and east, the highest area, produce the richest wines, while the sandy soils to the west and south yield wines that are lighter in style. A ferruginous sand known as *crasse de fer*, which is found throughout the region, also provides added vigor. There is no official classification in Pomerol, but Pétrus heads the list of an unofficial hierarchy. The producers' properties are generally small and unassuming, the average holding no more than 12 acres (5 ha).

ABOVE: *Eighty percent of plantings in the Pessac-Léognan apellation are red grape varieties.*

CHÂTEAU CLINET

Owners **the Arcaute family** ***Production*** **3,500 cases** ***Vineyard area*** **22 acres (9 ha); 75 percent merlot, 15 percent cabernet sauvignon, 10 percent cabernet franc**

Rich, powerful and intense, Clinet has been one of the outstanding producers in Pomerol during the last 15 years. Its style changed in the 1980s when Jean-Michel Arcaute, with the assistance of enologist Michel Rolland, imposed new work methods. The grapes are now picked extremely ripe and given a long period of maceration for maximum extract, and the wine is aged in new oak barrels for at least 24 months.

CHÂTEAU PÉTRUS

Owners **Ets Jean-Pierre Moueix and Madame Lily Lacoste** ***Production*** **4,000 cases** ***Vineyard area*** **27 acres (11 ha); 95 percent merlot, 5 percent cabernet franc**

Pétrus was virtually unknown on the international market prior to the Second World War, but is now the outstanding estate in the Pomerol and Bordeaux's most expensive wine. Produced almost entirely from merlot, it is big, powerful and brooding, with layers of rich extract and firm but fine tannins, and it ages extremely well. Two factors contribute to the continuation of the Pétrus myth: the vineyard and *négociant* Jean-Pierre Moueix. The vineyard is located on the highest part of the Pomerol plateau on a unique deposit of ferruginous clay—the "Pétrus buttonhole" as it is known locally—on which merlot thrives. Moueix provides the marketing strategy and invaluable technical expertise: the merchant house's team of pickers is able to harvest the grapes at optimum ripeness in just half a day. The wines are then vinified in cement tanks and aged in 100 percent new oak barrels.

CHÂTEAU LE PIN

Owner **Jacques Thienpont** ***Production*** **700 cases** ***Vineyard area*** **5 acres (2 ha); 92 percent merlot, 8 percent cabernet franc**

Its limited volume, velvety texture and almost burgundian intensity of raspberry and cherry fruit have made Le Pin one of the region's biggest sensations of the past 15 years. Occasionally, prices for Le Pin even surpass those for Pétrus—and this for a *domaine* created in 1979!

The vineyard is located on sand and gravel soils not far from Vieux Château Certan. The yields are kept low (2 tons per acre [35 hl per ha]), the grapes vinified in temperature-controlled stainless steel vats, and the wine run off into 100 percent new oak barrels, where it undergoes malolactic fermentation and matures for a period of up to 18 months.

VIEUX CHÂTEAU CERTAN

Owners **Thienpont family** ***Production*** **4,500 cases** ***Vineyard area*** **33 acres (13.5 ha); 60 percent merlot, 30 percent cabernet franc, 10 percent cabernet sauvignon**

The high percentage of cabernet in this wine provides a distinctive style that is more characteristic of the Médoc than Pomerol. The property, which dates back to the sixteenth century, was acquired by Belgian wine merchant Georges Thienpont in 1924. It is ideally located on the high plateau, next to Pétrus, and has a complexity of soils that includes pure clay, gravel, clay-gravel and ancient sands. Each parcel of the vineyard is worked according to soil type, grape variety and age of vine.

Other Pomerol producers of note include Beauregard, Le Bon Pasteur, Bourgneuf-Vayron, Certan de May, Clos l'Église, La Croix de Gay, La Croix du Casse, L'Évangile, La Fleur-Pétrus, Gombaude-Guillot, Lafleur, Latour à Pomerol, Mazeyres, Montviel, Petit Village, La Pointe and de Sales.

BELOW: *Château Figeac's vineyards include a high proportion of cabernets sauvignon and franc.*

ABOVE: *The cool, humid St-Émilion region is best suited to early-ripening grapes.*

St-Émilion

St-Émilion is Bordeaux's most historic wine region, and vine cultivation has occurred here since Gallo-Roman times. The zone is located around nine villages or communes, including the town of St-Émilion, which was granted administrative control over the region by Edward I of England in 1289. The whole area was declared a World Heritage site by UNESCO in 1999.

There are 13,585 acres (5,500 ha) under production and four AOCs: Premier Grand Cru Classe A and B, Grand Cru Classe and St-Émilion. The latter requires a higher minimum-alcohol content (11 percent), lower yields (3 tons per acre [53 hl per ha]) and the approval of two tasting panels. It accounts for 40 percent of production and is obligatory for classified wines. The St-Émilion classification is reviewed every ten years and has two levels: the Premier Grand Cru Classé (13 wines) and the Grand Cru Classé (55 wines).

Merlot is the dominant grape variety followed by cabernet franc, but there is a wide variety of wine styles, defined mainly by site and winemaking philosophy. For example, in the northwest, adjacent to Pomerol, a pocket of gravelly soils provides elegant, cabernet-dominated wines, as exemplified by Châteaux Cheval Blanc and Figeac, while on the limestone plateau and côtes, the merlot-dominated wines are full-bodied, fresh and made for long aging. The properties are generally small family run affairs, and, consequently, the local co-operative is also a major producer.

CHÂTEAU ANGÉLUS

Owner Boüard family _Production_ 9,500 cases _Vineyard area_ 58 acres (23 ha); 50 percent merlot, 47 percent cabernet franc, 3 percent cabernet sauvignon

Promoted to Premier Grand Cru Classé in 1996, Angélus is St-Émilion's modern success story. In the 1980s, Hubert de Boüard and his cousin Jean-Bernard Grenié took over the family property and introduced new practices in the vineyard, including lower yields and a riper harvest. Changes in the cellars saw the period of maceration increased; a second wine was launched to improve selection (Carillon de l'Angélus); and the proportion of new oak barrels was increased to 100 percent. This transformed the château from a middling Grand Cru Classé into a top estate, and set the standard for a more contemporary style of St-Émilion: deeper in color, richer and more concentrated.

CHÂTEAU AUSONE

Owner Vauthier family _Production_ 2,000 cases _Vineyard area_ 17 acres (7 ha); 50 percent merlot, 50 percent cabernet franc

Ausone and Cheval Blanc are the only two estates in the St-Émilion classification to have been designated Premier Grand Cru Classé A. The château takes its name from the fourth-century Roman poet Ausonius (Decimus Magnus), and is located on the steep southern slopes of St-Émilion. The southeasterly exposure of the vineyard and the limestone, clay and sand soils shape the character of the wine—powerful but fine, and slow to

ABOVE: *The unusual mix of gravel, sand and clay in the vineyard at Château Cheval Blanc contributes to a distinctive style of wine.*

mature. Since Alain Vauthier took charge of production in 1996, the wines have gained in color, weight and fruit expression.

CHÂTEAU CHEVAL BLANC

Owners Albert Frère and Bernard Arnault **Production** 12,000 cases **Vineyard area** 89 acres (36 ha); 60 percent cabernet franc, 40 percent merlot

Known for its silky, elegant style and long aging potential, Cheval Blanc has been St-Émilion's top wine for the last 50 years. It owes its originality to the estate's soil types, mainly ancient gravel, sand and clay, and the high percentage of cabernet franc in the blend. The vineyard was first cultivated in the eighteenth century and an extensive drainage system was installed in the late nineteenth century, around the time when the first cabernet franc grapes were planted. The estate was then owned by the Fourcaud-Laussac family, whose association with the property continued until 1998, when it was sold to businessmen Albert Frère and Bernard Arnault. Manager Pierre Lurton has ensured a high degree of continuity during the last decade. Yields are kept very low, and a second wine, Le Petit Cheval, permits further selection.

CHÂTEAU FIGEAC

Owner Thierry Manoncourt **Production** 10,000 cases **Vineyard area** 99 acres (40 ha); 35 percent cabernet franc, 35 percent cabernet sauvignon, 30 percent merlot

In the eighteenth century, the estate comprised some 494 acres (200 ha), including what is now Château Cheval Blanc. When the present owner started replanting in 1947, the nature of the *terroir* led him to select an unusually high proportion of cabernet franc and cabernet sauvignon. These produce a wine that is more *Médocain* in style, displaying elegance, balance and depth of fruit in good years, a slight herbaceousness in mediocre vintages and a deceptive ability to age.

The classification of St-Émilion

The first classification in St-Émilion took place in 1955, 100 years after the introduction of the Médoc system. Unlike that of the Médoc, this system is revised every ten years or so, most recently in 1996. Modifications have been also made between reviews, as occurred in 1969 and 1985.

The classification consists of only two grades: Premier Grand Cru Classé (with an indicator of A or B status) and Grand Cru Classé. There are currently 13 of the former (Châteaux Angélus and Beau-Séjour-Bécot having been promoted in 1996) and 55 of the latter. To be considered for classification, a winery must already hold the St-Émilion Grand Cru appellation certificate. It must then make a presentation, including samples from the last ten vintages, for review by a commission nominated by the INAO.

THE 1996 CLASSIFICATION

Premiers Grands Crus Classés (First Great Classed Growths) A

Château Ausone
Château Cheval Blanc

Premiers Grands Crus Classés (First Great Classed Growths) B

Château Angélus
Château Beau-Séjour-Bécot
Château Beauséjour (Duffau-Lagarrose)
Château Belair
Château Canon
Château Figeac
Château La Gaffelière
Château Magdelaine
Château Pavie
Château Trottevieille
Clos Fourtet

Grands Crus Classés (Great Classed Growths)

Château L'Arrosée
Château Balestard-La-Tonnelle
Château Bellevue
Château Bergat
Château Berliquet
Château Cadet-Bon
Château Cadet-Piola
Château Canon-La-Gaffelière
Château Cap de Mourlin
Château Chauvin
Château La Clotte
Château La Clusière
Château Corbin
Château Corbin-Michotte
Château La Couspaude
Couvent des Jacobins
Château Curé-Bon
Château Dassault
Château La Dominique
Château Faurie-de-Souchard
Château Fonplégade
Château Fonroque
Château Franc-Mayne
Château Grand Mayne
Château Grandes-Murailles
Château Grand Pontet
Château Guadet St-Julien
Château Haut-Corbin
Château Haut-Sarpe
Château Lamarzelle
Château Laniote
Château Larcis-Ducasse
Château Larmande
Château Laroque
Château Laroze
Château Matras
Château Moulin-du-Cadet
Château Pavie-Decesse
Château Pavie-Macquin
Château Petit-Faurie-de-Soutard
Château Le Prieuré
Château Ripeau
Château St-Georges-Côte-Pavie
Château La Serre
Château Soutard
Château Tertre-Daugay
Château La Tour-Figeac
Château La Tour du Pin-Figeac (Giraud-Belivier)
Château La Tour du Pin-Figeac (Moueix)
Château Troplong-Mondot
Château Villemaurine
Château Yon-Figeac
Clos des Jacobins
Clos de l'Oratoire
Clos Saint-Martin

Other St-Émilion producers of note include L'Arrosée, Balestard-la-Tonnelle, Beau-Séjour-Bécot, Canon, Clos Fourtet, La Dominique, Faugères, Fleur Cardinale, La Gaffelière, Grand Mayne, Grand Pontet, Larcis-Ducasse, Larmande, Laroze, Magdelaine, Monbousquet, La Mondotte, Moulin St-Georges, Pavie, Pavie-Macquin, Pipeau, Soutard, La Tour Figeac and Troplong-Mondot.

MINOR APPELLATIONS

The Médoc (formerly Bas-Médoc) appellation has 635 vine growers, two-thirds of whom belong to the co-operative system. The wines, uniquely red, are usually fruity and forward. The Haut-Médoc appellation's gravelly soils have the potential to produce red wines of Classed Growth standard, as demonstrated by Château Sociando-Mallet. The wines of the Listrac-Médoc are firm and slightly austere, but the tendency of late has been to plant and use a higher proportion of merlot in order to soften them. Moulis produces cabernet sauvignon-dominated wines that are of a high quality, as well as a light and fruity merlot.

Sweet white wine appellations include Cérons, with rare wines that can be elegant and concentrated, Cadillac, with wines that vary from fresh, fruity and semisweet to richly botrytized; Loupiac, with consistent, fresh, fruity, and sweet wines; and Ste-Croix-du-Mont, which can produce rich, concentrated wines, but the quality can vary—their best is superb.

Premières Côtes de Bordeaux produces some sweet white wine, but the merlot-dominated reds have a bright, aromatic fruit character, and are either firm or lightly structured. A beautiful part of bordeaux, it is also one of the best value-for-money appellations.

The Entre-Deux-Mers region produces quite a large volume of generic red Bordeaux and also a dry white wine produced from sauvignon blanc, sémillon, and muscadelle. The Côtes de Castillon's merlot-based wines are solid and fruity. Neighboring Bordeaux-Côtes de Francs has some good red and dry white wines. Wines can be a little rustic in the St-Émilion "satellites," and Fronsac and Canon-Fronsac.

The Côtes de Bourg has full-bodied reds with good color and structure; the best are aged in oak. A little dry white Côtes de Bourg is produced. Premières Côtes de Blaye's wines are less substantial than those of Bourg.

The Bordeaux and Bordeaux Supérieur appellations produce 50 percent of the region's wine. Quality varies, and styles range from light and fruity wines to richer, oak-aged offerings. Red wine is the main product.

ABOVE: *The vineyards at Château Loudenne, one of the top producers in the Médoc appellation.*

BELOW: *Merlot has overtaken cabernet sauvignon as the Médoc's leading variety.*

The Southwest

JIM BUDD

The vineyards of southwestern France are dispersed over a wide area, stretching from the edge of Sauternes in Bordeaux to Toulouse in the southeast and to the

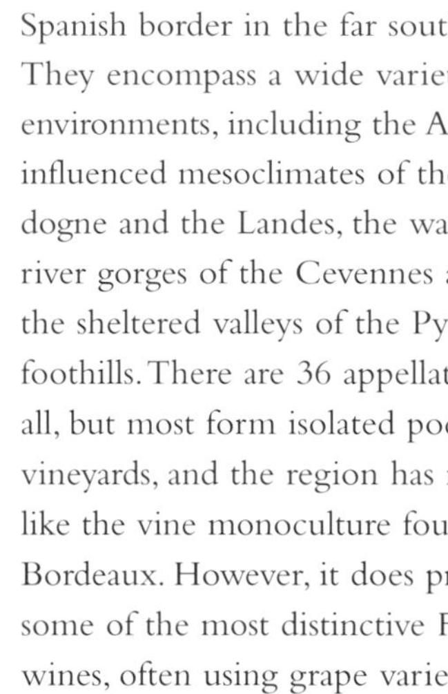

Spanish border in the far southwest. They encompass a wide variety of environments, including the Atlantic-influenced mesoclimates of the Dordogne and the Landes, the warmer river gorges of the Cevennes and the sheltered valleys of the Pyrenean foothills. There are 36 appellations in all, but most form isolated pockets of vineyards, and the region has nothing like the vine monoculture found in Bordeaux. However, it does produce some of the most distinctive French wines, often using grape varieties found nowhere else.

***ABOVE:** The mountainous Irouléguy appellation has potential for rapid growth in the near future.*

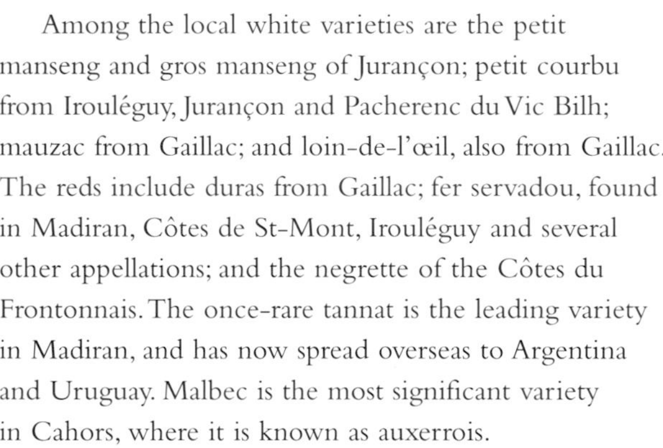

Among the local white varieties are the petit manseng and gros manseng of Jurançon; petit courbu from Irouléguy, Jurançon and Pacherenc du Vic Bilh; mauzac from Gaillac; and loin-de-l'œil, also from Gaillac. The reds include duras from Gaillac; fer servadou, found in Madiran, Côtes de St-Mont, Irouléguy and several other appellations; and the negrette of the Côtes du Frontonnais. The once-rare tannat is the leading variety in Madiran, and has now spread overseas to Argentina and Uruguay. Malbec is the most significant variety in Cahors, where it is known as auxerrois.

The Southwest region can be divided into three main areas: the so-called "satellite" vineyards of Bordeaux; the vineyards of the upper Garonne and its tributaries; and the southern appellations of the Landes, Gascogne and the Pays Basque.

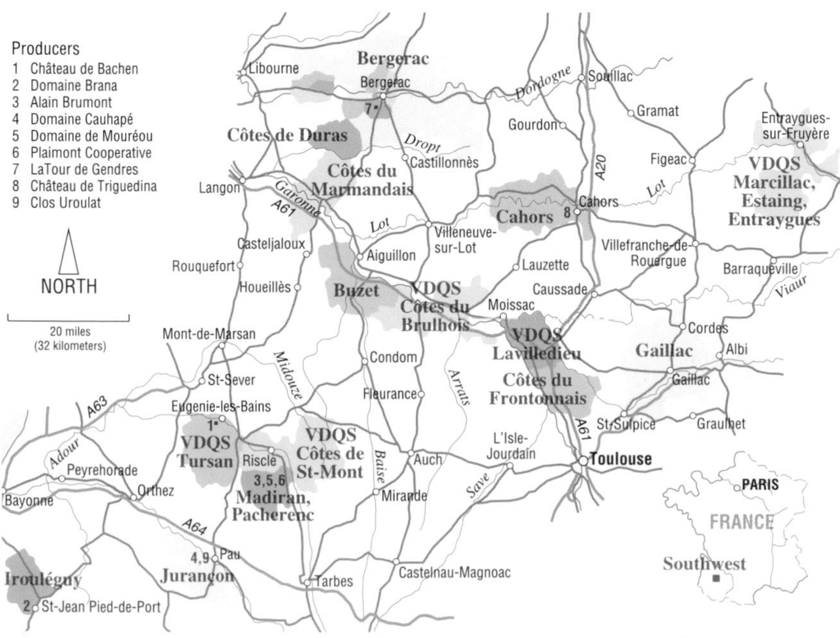

The Bordeaux "satellites"

These areas lie close to the Bordeaux vineyards, grow a similar mix of grape varieties and make comparable wines that often represent better value than their Bordeaux equivalents. They include the various appellations around the town of Bergerac, in the Dordogne Valley; the Côtes de Duras, around the town of Duras, between the Dordogne and the Garonne; the Côtes de Marmandais, centered on the town of Marmande on the Garonne; and Buzet, between the towns of Damazan and Agen.

White wines are made principally from sauvignon blanc, sémillon and a little muscadelle; the reds are normally a blend of merlot, cabernet sauvignon and cabernet franc, with the early-ripening merlot usually the most important component in the blend.

Pécharmant, to the northeast of Bergerac, is for reds only; these are some of the best in the region and age well, while Bergerac's standard has improved considerably. Côtes de Montravel, Haut-Montravel, Saussignac, and Monbazillac are sweet-wine appellations; the best Monbazillac is a rich, honeyed mouthful.

Montravel is mainly for dry whites as is the Côte de Duras, both places are best suited to dry whites, in particular sauvignon blanc. Most of the Côtes du Marmandais's production is red. Buzet's production is dominated by red wines; the remainder is white and rosé.

The Garonne and its tributaries

Winemaking on the northernmost tributary of the Garonne, the Lot, centers on Cahors. The area was once known for its "black wine," which owed its name to the dark auxerrois (malbec) grape and also to the practice of boiling the wine, which improved its keeping capacity and deepened its color. In 1956, a severe frost almost brought production to a halt, but Cahors has now recovered and has 10,467 acres (4,236 ha). The appellation is for reds only; it permits up to 30 percent of merlot to be added to soften the auxerrois. Although Cahors produces some light, easy-drinking wines, the best producers favor concentrated, powerful fare that needs time in oak and then bottle.

Farther up the Lot Valley the Aveyron department produces powerful, rustic reds, mainly from fer servadou.

North of Toulouse between the Garonne and the Tarn, the Côtes du Frontonnais appellation uses négrette, a red grape variety, which is blended with cabernet franc and cabernet sauvignon, gamay, malbec, mauzac and syrah. The wines range from soft and light to those that need two or three years' aging. The leading producers are Châteaux Baudare, Bellevue la Forêt, Ferran, Le Roc, Montauriol and the Cave de Fronton.

Northwest of Frontonnais, Lavilledieu and Côtes du Brulhois produce mainly red wines. To the east lies Gaillac which produces an enormous array of styles from a wide range of grapes. The area's most interesting producer is the Plageoles estate, which concentrates on mauzac, ondenc and duras.

The Landes, Gascogne and the Pays Basque

This area is home to some of the most dynamic producers in the Southwest. The best of the wines, particularly those from Madiran, are powerful and robust. The vineyards went into decline after the First World War—Madiran all but disappeared—but they are now enjoying a renaissance.

One of the region's recent success stories is the Côtes de Gascogne *vin de pays*, which is now sold throughout northern Europe. Most of the production is white. Colombard is the principal variety but ugni blanc, chardonnay and gros manseng are also used. Generally, the *vin de pays* is light and citric, and made to be drunk young.

Production in nearby Tursan VDQS appellation is about 65 percent red or rosé; the white is made from baroque, which is found only in Tursan. The principal producer is the Tursan Co-operative in Geaune.

To the southeast lie Madiran, a red-wine appellation, and the much smaller dry- and sweet-wine appellation of Pacherenc. The chief red grape here is the appropriately named tannat, a decidedly robust and tannic variety capable of producing complex, powerful wines; these need around a decade of aging to show their best and respond well to long-aging in oak. Permitted varieties for Pacherenc include arrufiac, petit and gros manseng, bordelais, sauvignon and sémillon. Greater emphasis is now being placed on the local varieties, and some remarkable sweet wines are being made by growers who delay picking until December.

Côtes de St-Mont is often described as a junior Madiran because the red is made mainly from tannat and the appellation lies immediately to the north. However, these reds are considerably softer and need much less time to age. There is also a white made from local varieties, and a small amount of rosé. The Plaimont Co-operative is the chief producer.

The best Jurançon is one of the country's most elegant and complex whites. It is made from three varieties: petit and gros manseng, and petit courbu. Traditionally, it was a sweet wine made from late-harvested grapes, mainly petit manseng, picked in November and December with the sweetness coming from *passerillage*. A dry wine, Jurançon sec, was created during the difficult years in the middle of the nineteenth century. Gros manseng is the chief variety used and it now accounts for 75 percent of the production. Partly as a result of its high level of acidity, both styles of Jurançon can age well.

The small Pyrenean appellation of Irouléguy has around 500 acres (200 ha) in production, although the appellation has a potential area of 3,030 acres (1,226 ha). The reds and rosés are made from cabernet franc, cabernet sauvignon and tannat. They tend to be less muscular versions of Madiran and show their best after several years aging. The whites are made from petit courbu and gros and petit manseng, and are usually crisp and lemony.

ABOVE: Viewed from Massat, parallel ranges rise toward the heights of the Pyrenees.

BELOW: Fresh truffles are an expensive delicacy in many parts of the Southwest.

ABOVE: *The Southwest's vineyards are planted with distinctive local grape varieties.*

CHÂTEAU DE BACHEN, VDQS TURSAN

Established **1988** ***Owner*** **Michel Guérard** ***Production*** **NA** ***Vineyard area*** **42 acres (17 ha)**

Michel Guérard, one of France's best-known chefs, is the owner of a restaurant and hotel at Eugenie-les-Bains and an Armagnac vineyard and distillery near Cazaubon in the Bas Armagnac. He bought Château de Bachen in 1983, built an impressive winery in Palladian style and produced his first vintage in 1988. The wines include an unoaked Château de Bachen and the Baron de Bachen, which is fermented and aged in new oak. The latter is more concentrated, and complex; it benefits from two to three years in bottle. The former should be drunk young and goes well with shellfish.

Regional Dozen

QUALITY WINES

- Château du Cèdre Le Cèdre Cahors red
- Château Montus Cuvée Prestige Madiran red
- Robert Plageoles Vin d'Autan de Robert Plageoles et Fils Doux Gaillac white
- Château Tirecul la Gravière Cuvée Madame Monbazillac white
- Clos Triguedina Prince Probus red
- Clos Uroulat Jourançon white

BEST VALUE WINES

- Château de Gueyze Les Vignerons de Buzet Buzet red
- Jean-Luc Matha Le Vieux Porche Marcillac red
- Château de Sabazan Producteurs Plaimont Côtes de St-Mont red
- Château St-Didier Parnac Cahors red
- Domaine de Tariquet Gros Manseng VDP des Côtes de Gascogne white
- Château Tour des Gendres Bergerac Sec white

DOMAINE BRANA, IROULÉGUY

Established **1985** ***Owners*** **the Brana family** ***Production*** **NA** ***Vineyard area*** **54 acres (22 ha)**

The Brana family set up a *negoçiant* business at Ustaritz in 1897, moving to St-Jean Pied de Port in 1920. In 1974, Étienne Brana started to distill high-quality fruit *eaux de vies* and began to plan a vineyard. The first wines were made in 1989. When Étienne died in 1992, his son Jean took over the winemaking, and his daughter Martine became the distiller. Both red and white irouléguy are made. The red is a blend of cabernet franc, cabernet sauvignon and tannat and is aged in oak for 12 months. The white is made from petit courbu and gros manseng.

DOMAINE ALAIN BRUNONT, MADIRAN

Established **1980** ***Owner*** **Alain Brumont** ***Production*** **NA** ***Vineyard area*** **195 acres (79 ha)**

Alain Brumont has played a leading role in the revival of the fortunes of the Southwest. He made his name with his Montus Prestige and Bouscassé Vieille Vignes. Both are 100 percent tannat and aged in new oak for at least a year. He also has other excellent wines, including a range of *vin de pays* from the Côtes de Gascogne.

DOMAINE CAUHAPÉ, JURANÇON

Established **1980** ***Owner*** **Henri Ramonteau** ***Production*** **NA** ***Vineyard area*** **62 acres (25 ha)**

Henri Ramonteau has done much to raise the international profile of Jurançon with his excellent range of wines. There are four dry whites: three from 100 percent gros manseng (one of which is made from old vines) and one from 100 percent petit manseng fermented in new oak. The sweet-wine range is headed by Noblesse de Petit Manseng and Quintessence, which are made exclusively from petit manseng, and the Vieilles Vignes, which is half petit manseng and half gros manseng.

DOMAINE DE MOURÉOU, MADIRAN

Established **1968** ***Owner*** **Patrick Ducorneau** ***Production*** **NA** ***Vineyard area*** **35 acres (14 ha)**

Patrick Ducourneau makes elegant, powerful and well-balanced wines, especially Chapelle Lenclos, which is made from pure tannat and ages well—at least ten to fifteen years after good vintages. But he is likely to be best remembered as the inventor of the micro-oxygenation system. This feeds a minute but continuous dose of oxygen to a wine as it matures in vat. It is of particular use in stainless steel vats, as it keeps the level of oxygen constant and reduces the need for racking. Initially developed to help soften the powerful tannins in tannat, this system is being used increasingly in France and in other parts of the world to soften and round out wines without using costly barrels.

PLAIMONT CO-OPERATIVE, MADIRAN

Established **1970** ***Owner*** **Plaimont Producteurs** ***Production*** **NA** ***Vineyard area*** **NA**

The Plaimont Co-operative in the Adour Valley has done much, under the leadership of André Dubosc, to develop both VDQS Côtes de St-Mont and VDP des Côtes de Gascogne. It was Dubosc who foresaw the decline of Armagnac and realized that Gascogne could yield easy-drinking, everyday white wines. More recently, as well as investing in vinification centers, the co-operative has helped growers to improve their viticultural practices and hence the quality of their grapes. The Plaimont range includes some madiran, but it's the red Côtes de St-Mont wines that offer the greatest interest and value. Particularly of interest is the wine at the top of the range, Château de Sabrezan.

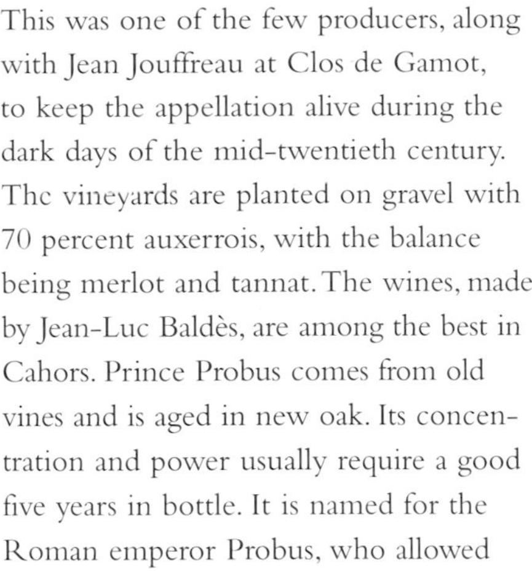

LA TOUR DE GENDRES, BERGERAC

Established **NA** ***Owner*** **SCEA de Conti** ***Production*** **NA** ***Vineyard area*** **100 acres (40 ha)**

Luc de Conti is one of a number of producers who have shown that Bergerac can at times outshine Bordeaux. His vineyards, which lie to the south of Monbazillac, are run mainly on organic principles wherever possible. The grape varieties planted are sauvignon blanc, sémillon, merlot and cabernet sauvignon. The white wines from this producer range from La Tour de Gendres, which is a good-value, pure sémillon, to Moulin des Dames, which is a blend of sémillon and sauvignon, and the rich, barrel-fermented Anthologia, which is mainly sauvignon blanc and always expensive. The red wines include La Gloire de Mon Père, which is chiefly merlot, and Moulin des Dames, which is a blend of cabernet sauvignon, cabernet franc and merlot.

CHÂTEAU DE TRIGUEDINA, CAHORS

Established **1830** ***Owners*** **the Baldès family** ***Production*** **NA** ***Vineyard area*** **99 acres (40 ha)**

This was one of the few producers, along with Jean Jouffreau at Clos de Gamot, to keep the appellation alive during the dark days of the mid-twentieth century. The vineyards are planted on gravel with 70 percent auxerrois, with the balance being merlot and tannat. The wines, made by Jean-Luc Baldès, are among the best in Cahors. Prince Probus comes from old vines and is aged in new oak. Its concentration and power usually require a good five years in bottle. It is named for the Roman emperor Probus, who allowed vines to be planted in Quercy in AD 280.

CLOS UROULAT, JURANÇON

Established **1983** ***Owner*** **Charles Hours** ***Production*** **NA** ***Vineyard area*** **18.5 acres (7.5 ha)**

Charles Hours contents himself with making just two wines: Cuvée Marie, a Jurançon sec, and the sweet Clos Uroulat; both are fermented in barrel. The vineyard is planted with petit courbu and the two mansengs, and yields are kept low, which explains the concentration and complexity that supports a thrilling purity of flavor in all Hours' wines.

BELOW: *Winegrowing areas near the southwest coast tend to have mild, wet climates.*

Languedoc-Roussillon

JIM BUDD

Although some 370,000 acres (150,000 ha) of vines have been pulled up in the past decade, Languedoc-Roussillon remains the world's largest wine region. About 620,000 acres (250,000 ha) of vines lie between the Rhône delta and the Spanish border at Banyuls—nearly two and half times the area of vines currently planted in Australia and just a little less than the entire US vineyard. After 150 years devoted to producing mainly cheap red table wines, the last 15 years has seen a shift toward Mediterranean specialties and major international varietals. In the process, Languedoc-Roussillon has become France's most dynamic and exciting wine region.

Drink wine, drink poetry, drink virtue.

Attributed to CHARLES BAUDELAIRE *(1821–1867)*

Landscape and climate

Although lumped together administratively, Languedoc and Roussillon are two distinct areas, historically and geographically. Roussillon was part of Spain from the thirteenth century until the Treaty of the Pyrenees in 1659 when it was ceded to France, and it has strong links with Catalonia on the other side of the border. Its geography is dominated by the Pyrenees, in particular by the Canigou mountain massif, and its vineyards are located mainly in narrow valleys. In contrast, Languedoc's vines are planted mainly on the broad coastal plains, although some of the higher-quality wines come from the inland hills, or *coteaux*.

Languedoc-Roussillon has a Mediterranean climate, with most of its rain falling in winter and very little occurring between the beginning of May and mid-August. The plains are the hottest and most arid areas of France, with an average annual temperature of 57°F (14°C), and the dry climate is often accentuated by the *tramontane*, an inland wind that blows from the northwest. Indeed, parts of Languedoc are so arid that vines and olives are the only viable crops.

Throughout the region, drought can be a problem in summer, particularly as French and EU regulations do not allow appellation vines to be irrigated. Rains in late August and early September can make the harvest difficult, and winter storms sometimes damage vines: in mid-November, 1999, the equivalent of an average year's rain fell in 36 hours, causing widespread destruction in the vineyards of Corbières and Minervois. Violent hailstorms also occur: parts of Roussillon were badly hit in May 1999.

Generally, Languedoc-Roussillon remains best suited to the production of red wines, as well as rosés for summer drinking. Despite modern methods, whites still tend to lack acidity and freshness.

History

Along with those of Provence, the vineyards of Languedoc-Roussillon are the oldest in France. Vines were first planted here by the Greeks near Narbonne during the fifth century BC and have been an important part of the regional economy ever since. During the

BELOW: *The Castle of Puilaurens in the high Corbières was once a refuge for Cathar "heretics."*

eighteenth and early nineteenth centuries, the area had a reputation for quality wine, most of which came from the hillsides, where the soils are poorer and the temperatures more moderate than elsewhere in the region.

In the mid-nineteenth century, several factors combined to transform the Languedoc-Roussillon wine industry and the regional economy as a whole. The development of heavy industry in the northeast created a substantial thirst among workers—by mid-century, annual French wine consumption per capita was around 32 gallons (120 l)—and the opening of a railroad link to Paris in 1850 allowed southern produce to more readily reach the capital and the industrial north. Soon, Languedoc began to supply northern France with cheap red wine—known as *le gros rouge*—made principally from aramon and alicante bouchet. As the yields were high, the wine was usually thin and had to be bolstered by more full-bodied reds from Algeria.

The destruction of the region's vineyards by phylloxera during the latter half of the nineteenth century merely accelerated the decline of the *coteaux* and the move to producing high-volume, low-quality *vin de table* on the plains. The American rootstock used to reconstruct the vines did not grow well in the limestone soils on the hillsides, and this coupled with the markedly higher costs of growing vines on the *coteaux* gave the plains a significant economic advantage.

Wine production continued to focus on *le gros rouge* until the late twentieth century. Then, in 1962, Algeria gained independence, and the supply of powerful red wines was cut off. More significantly, various changes in French lifestyle during the 1970s caused the demand for cheap red wine to collapse. These included the decline of heavy industry; the development of a more sophisticated taste among the broad population—drinkers were now consuming smaller quantities of better wines; and a growing fashion for drinking whisky rather than wine as an aperitif. These trends have continued: by 1998, per capita consumption of wine in France had declined to around 16 gallons (60 l) from around 30 gallons (112 l) in 1970.

Vines and wines

With the cheap table wine market in terminal decline, Languedoc-Roussillon has been forced to change course, and in the past 15 years there has been a dramatic move toward higher-quality produce. This change has been driven both by far-sighted local producers and by newcomers and investors from other parts of France, Europe and even Australia and California.

The change has taken two main forms: the plains that used to produce the oceans of *gros rouge* are now planted with international varieties, and the vineyards on the *coteaux* have been revived. The shift to international varieties, which include cabernet sauvignon, chardonnay,

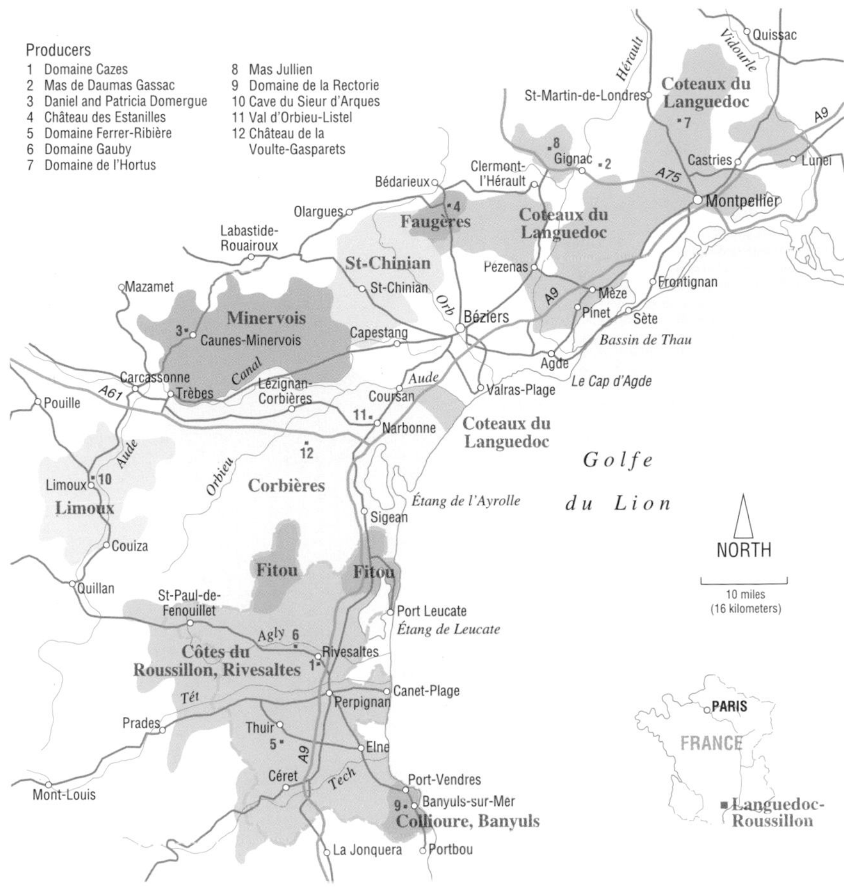

merlot and syrah, is partly the result of the introduction of the *vins de pays* classification (see p. 248) which, unlike local appellation laws, permits usage of these grapes. Varietal *vins de pays* from the plains of Languedoc-Roussillon have been very successful on export markets, especially in northern Europe.

On the *coteaux*, where wines were traditionally made mainly from carignan, new grape varieties, mainly from the Rhône, such as syrah, grenache, mourvèdre, vermentino and viognier, have been planted for use as flavor boosters (*cépages améliorateurs*) in blends. These varieties once grew in Languedoc-Roussillon, but were wiped out by phylloxera and largely replaced with aramon, alicante bouchet and carignan. There is now also a growing acceptance that carignan is worth cultivating; but unfortunately a lot of old carignan vines were pulled out in the late 1980s and early 1990s, and replaced with new varieties such as syrah. Because growers have to wait at least 40 years for carignan to produce satisfactory juice, no one is replanting it.

The enormous potential of the *coteaux* has, however, been realized over the past decade. Producers are now turning out wines of concentration and character, often interwoven with

BELOW: *Few crops other than vines flourish in the region's generally arid, gravelly soils.*

ABOVE: The village of Minerve in the Minervoise appellation is perched above the Cesse River.

the scents—especially rosemary and thyme—of the region's characteristic vegetation, the scrubby *garrigue*. Notable wine-producing regions on the hillsides include the Pic St-Loup, some 15 miles (25 km) north of Montpellier; the schistose hills of Faugères; and nearby St-Chinian. To the west, significant areas include the terraces of the Minervois, which overlook the Valley of the Aude, and the vineyards of the dramatically varied Corbières region, which extends from the shores of the Mediterranean to the gentle slopes of the Aude Valley and upward into the mountains. Another important area is the coastal bluff of La Clape, close to Narbonne.

Appellations

Most of the appellation wines are red and they tend to be blends chosen from grenache, carignan, mourvèdre, syrah, and occasionally cinsault. Although appellation restrictions have limited the excessive planting of cabernet sauvignon, chardonnay and merlot, they have, at the same time, prevented growers from experimenting with different varieties of grapes.

Roussillon is also noted for its fortified wines, known locally as *vins doux naturels*; however, the sweetness is not natural but is due to the addition of pure alcohol. Among the most important appellations for fortified wines are Rivesaltes and Muscat de Rivesaltes; however, Banyuls is the best known. At one time, the production of various proprietary brands of aperitif, such as Dubonnet, was a significant activity.

BELOW: The less fertile soils of the coteaux are better suited to viticulture than those of the plains.

Regional cuisine

The major influences on the cuisine of Languedoc-Roussillon are olive oil (of which the region is a major producer), Mediterranean fish and seafood, and the intense summer heat.

Generally, the climate is not suited to heartier dishes. Fishing is a major industry in the region, and fish that feature prominently on local menus include lotte (monkfish), racasse, red mullet, sea bass, sea bream, squid and sardines—fish soups are a specialty. Game is eaten when in season, and vegetables, particularly aubergines, peppers and tomatoes, are important year-round.

DOMAINE CAZES, RIVESALTES, ROUSSILLON

Established **NA** ***Owners*** **André and Bernard Cazes** ***Production*** **66,700 cases** ***Vineyard area*** **395 acres (160 ha)**

This estate has recently begun converting its entire vineyard to the biodynamic system. Once this is completed, Domaine Cazes may be the largest biodynamic winemaker in the world. It currently produces some 20 different wines, ranging from *vins de pays* through Côtes du Roussillon and Côtes du Roussillon Villages to some very fine *vins doux naturels*. Aimé Cazes, their top fortified wine, is made from grenache blanc and is aged for more than 20 years before it is released. Although it is a *vin de pays*, Le Credo is the estate's top red; it is made from cabernet sauvignon, merlot and syrah.

MAS DE DAUMAS GASSAC, VDP DE L'HÉRAULT, LANGUEDOC

Established **1974** ***Owners*** **Aimé and Véronique Guibert** ***Production*** **15,000 cases** ***Vineyard area*** **87 acres (35 ha)**

Whether Mas de Daumas Gassac is really the best wine produced in Languedoc-Roussillon is open to debate; however, there is no doubt that it was the wines made here during the 1980s that alerted enthusiasts to the remarkable developments taking place in the Midi.

When Aimé and Véronique Guibert bought this property in 1970, they had no intention of making wine; it was only when the special qualities of the soil were pointed out to them that they decided to plant vines. These produced their first vintage in 1978. The red is mainly cabernet sauvignon, malbec, merlot and syrah; the white, introduced later, is mainly viognier, chardonnay and muscat. Collaborating with local co-operatives, the Guibert's produce affordable wines for everyday consumption under names including Figaro and Terrasses de Guilheim.

DOMAINE GAUBY, CÔTES DU ROUSSILLON VILLAGES, ROUSSILLON

Established **NA** ***Owner*** **Gérard Gauby** ***Production*** **6,700 cases** ***Vineyard area*** **87 acres (35 ha)**

In the early 1990s, Domaine Gauby wines were rather severe, with hard tannins overwhelming the fruit. More recently, however, they have softened, allowing the fruit to come to the fore. The transformation is mainly the result of improvements in the vineyards, which are run on organic principles. The pick of the range are a powerful Côtes de Roussillon Villages; the white Cuvée Centenaire, a rich wine made from grenache blanc which displays fruit and honey flavors; and La Muntada, made from syrah. Most Gauby whites are now designated *vin de pays* as they invariably exceed the low 12.5 percent limit set for Côtes du Roussillon.

DOMAINE DE L'HORTUS, COTEAUX DU LANGUEDOC (PIC ST-LOUP), LANGUEDOC

Established **1981** ***Owner*** **Jean Orliac** ***Production*** **NA** ***Vineyard area*** **74 acres (30 ha)**

Jean Orliac is among the top producers in the Pic St-Loup. The vineyards here are mainly planted with syrah, mourvèdre and grenache. The Cuvée Classique, a blend of these three red varieties, is matured in stainless steel vats, whereas the Grande Cuvée is made from mourvèdre and syrah, and spends 15 months or so in new oak. Orliac also makes a promising barrel-fermented white (Grande Cuvée), blend of chardonnay and viognier. Pic St-Loup's high-altitude location means that acidity levels remain high, making it well suited to white-wine production.

DOMAINE DE LA RECTORIE, COLLIOURE AND BANYULS, ROUSSILLON

Established **NA** ***Owners*** **Marc and Thierry Parcé** ***Production*** **NA** ***Vineyard area*** **54 acres (22 ha)**

At one time, the fame of the wines of Collioure and Banyuls rested almost entirely upon the efforts of the late Dr André Parcé. His relatives, Marc and Thierry Parcé at Domaine de la Rectorie, have taken over the mantle. They are now established as the area's top winemakers. Their Banyuls Cuvée Parcé Frères can be enjoyed young, but the impressive Collioure will repay long aging. The Cuvée Leon Parcé, aged in oak for 18 months, has a robust structure and also ages well. An outstanding *vin de pays*, Cuvée l'Argile, is made from grenache gris.

CAVE DU SIEUR D'ARQUES, LIMOUX, LANGUEDOC

Established **1946** ***Owner*** **Co-operative of 500 members** ***Production*** **1.6 million cases** ***Vineyard area*** **12,350 acres (5,000 ha)**

One of the most efficient co-operatives in France. It offers a wide range of varietal *vin de pays* from chardonnay, chenin, mauzac, cabernet sauvignon and merlot. It also produces a barrel-fermented Toques et Clochers Chardonnay, as well as individual-vineyard, barrel-fermented AC Limoux chardonnays. In addition, it makes 90 percent of all sparkling Blanquette de Limoux and Crémant de Limoux, plus some small quantities of *méthode ancestrale* sparkling wine.

Other producers in this region are Val d'Orbieu-Listel (Languedoc- Roussillon); Mas Jullien (Coteaux du Languedoc, Languedoc); Daniel and Patricia Domergue (Minervois, Languedoc); Château des Estanilles (Faugeres, Languedoc); Domaine Ferrer-Ribière (Côtes du Roussillon, Roussillon); and de la Voulte-Gasparets.

Regional Dozen

- Corbieres de Boncaillou, Les Vignerons de Villesque de Corbieres red
- Domaine Borie de Maurel Cuvée Sylla Minervois red
- Mas de Daumas Gassac red
- Aimé Cazes Domaine Cazes Rivesaltes fortified
- Château des Estanilles Faugères red
- Domaine de la Coste Cuvée Selectionnée Coteaux du Languedoc St-Christol red
- Domaine Gauby La Muntada Côtes du Roussillon Villages red
- Domaine de l'Hortus Grande Cuvée Coteaux du Languedoc Pic St-Loup red
- Mas Jullien Les Vignes Oubliées Coteaux du Languedoc white
- Cellier des Templiers Cuvée Président Henry Vidal Banyuls fortified
- Château de la Voulte-Gasparets Cuvée Romain Pauc Corbières red
- Toques et Clochers Limoux Chardonnay

BELOW: Vines and typical Mediterranean scrubland surround a ruined castle at Tuchan in Fitou.

ABOVE: *The local fishing industry provides a variety of seafood to accompany Provence's much-improved rosés and whites.*

Provence

ANTHONY PEREGRINE

Provence is one of France's prettiest playgrounds and for years its mainly rosé wines had a merely playful reputation. No one, least of all the producers, took them very seriously; they were light fare for sundrenched vacationers. There is, though, another, deeper side to Provence and some wines are now reflecting this. Without sacrificing any of their characteristic freshness, the rosés (which make up 75 percent of production) have gained a gastronomic legitimacy—most notably within the context of high-tone Provençal cuisine, but also as accompaniments to East Asian dishes. Meanwhile, the improvement in red wines has spread outward from the Bandol appellation over much of the region, and a few terrific whites have even emerged. Provençal wines remain fun, but now display far greater depth, substance and consistency.

Winegrowing in Provence is, and has always been, geographically and politically fractured. The region boasts eight appellations (Côtes de Provence, Coteaux d'Aix-en-Provence, Coteaux Varois, Bandol, Les Baux-de-Provence, Cassis, Bellet and Palette), few of which get along with each other, and none of which shares any common ground with local *vins de pays* administrators. In total, the appellations make approximately 29 million gallons (110 million l) each year. *Vin de pays* accounts for 11.6 million gallons (44 million l), and the regional *vins de table* 10.6 million gallons (40 million l).

Landscape and climate

Warm summers and relatively mild winters provide 3,000 hours of sun a year—good conditions for grape-growing overall. But there are many nuances, for Provence is a disparate region. In the alpine foothills, for instance, winters can be tough; and the mistral wind whistling down the Rhône Valley can bend strong men in two. Yet it can also be a godsend: after short, violent Mediterranean storms, the blasting wind quickly dries vines, keeping them disease-free. Summers can be very hot, particularly in the inland, though nearer the coast, the torrid conditions are softened by moist sea breezes.

If the Provençal climate is varied, its *terroirs* are more so. Though mainly limestone and arid, they range from the beautiful terraced slopes overlooking the sea at Bandol and Cassis to the Var uplands, where vines dispute space with lavender and *garrigue*, and the pebbly soil is colored red by iron oxide. The Côtes de Provence appellation alone has four distinct zones: the coast, the inland valley, the Var hills and, off to the west, the Ste-Victoire district, dominated by the mountain of the same name that so enchanted local lad Paul Cézanne.

Wines and vines

Although most of Provence's production is fresh, fruity rosé—the Var department is the world's number-one

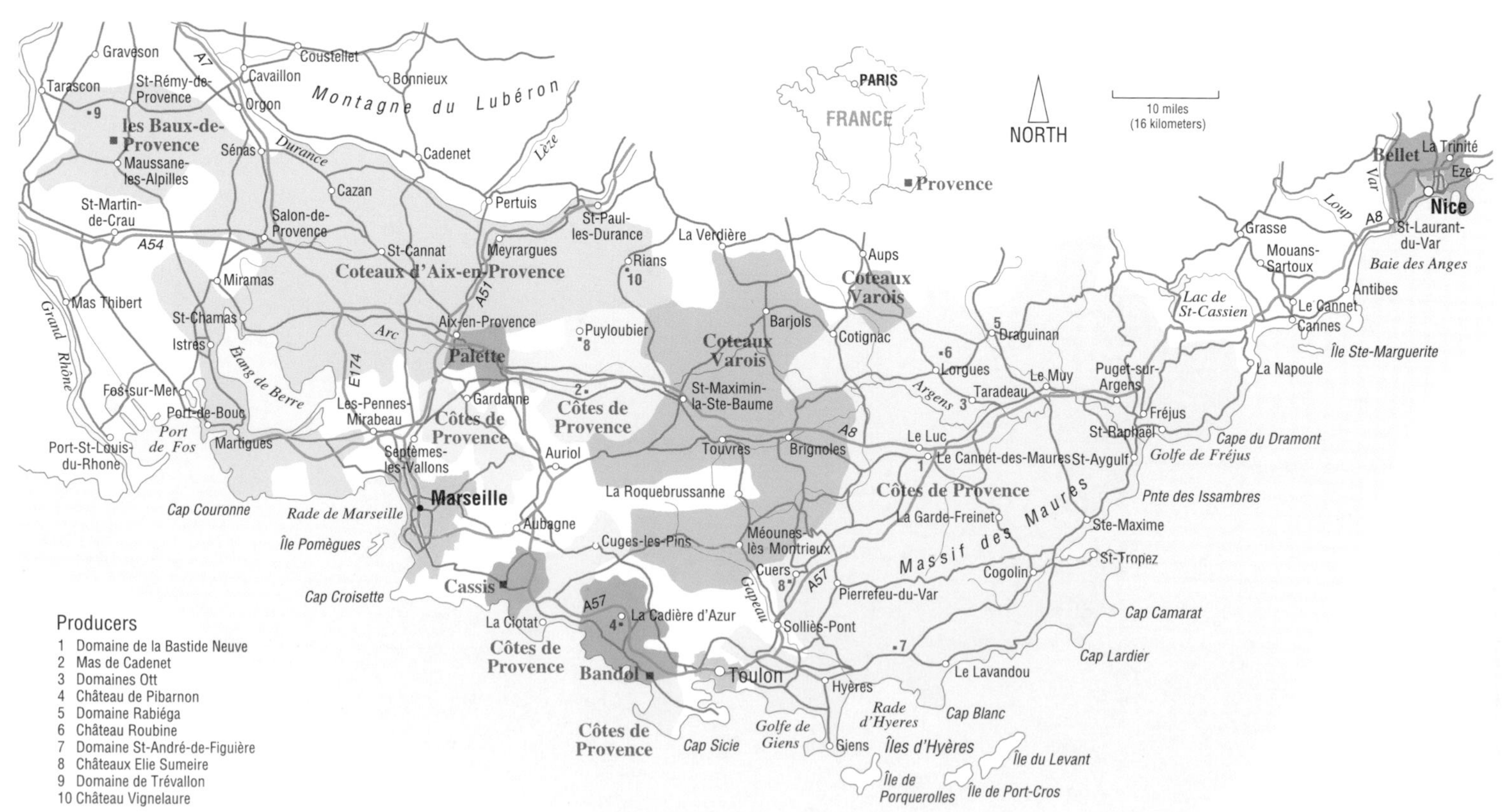

pink-wine region—it also includes dry, aromatic whites from areas such as Cassis, and elegant, powerful reds, capable of long aging, from Bandol and, increasingly, other zones. Even the rosé producers are now looking for greater structure, finesse, freshness and fruit in their wines.

The range of quality produce is now huge, as is the permitted range of grape varieties. The Côtes de Provence appellation, for instance, allows 13 varieties. Across the region, the main rosé and red varieties are grenache, mourvèdre, cinsault, carignan, the local tibouren and syrah. Of late, cabernet sauvignon has also crept in, though it remains a suspect outsider to more puritanical producers. White wine, which makes up 5 percent of the total, comes mainly from clairette, ugni blanc, the wonderfully aromatic rolle, bourboulenc, sémillon and sauvignon.

Eighteen Provençal estates have the right to call their wines Crus Classés. They gained this privilege in 1955, after petitioning the authorities. Much to the annoyance of other producers who have been denied access to the classification, none of these *domaines* is subject to any form of quality control. Certain of the better Crus Classés recently agreed to monitor each other's standards and thereby prove that they merit their status. The truth is that many do, some don't: here, at least, Cru Classé is still not the guarantee it should be.

DOMAINES OTT

Established **1912** ***Owners*** **the Ott family** ***Production*** **52,000 cases** ***Vineyard area*** **420 acres (170 ha)**

In 1912 Marcel Ott founded one of the region's finest family-run winemaking empires. Later the Otts added the white-producing Clos Mireille (also Côtes de Provence) and Château Romassan in Bandol to the stable, while building an unbeatable reputation for quality and consistency. The rosé, Cœur de Grain, has been their worldwide calling card, and the Blanc de Blancs and Bandol reds justify prices that are somewhat above the Provençal average.

CHÂTEAU DE PIBARNON

Established **1978** ***Owners*** **de St-Victor family** ***Production*** **20,000 cases** ***Vineyard area*** **111 acres (45 ha)**

If Bandol is the most prestigious of Provençal appellations, it's because it is known for red wines, with thanks due to a small group of quality-minded trailblazers keen to restore mourvèdre t0o primacy. The limestone soils of this estate now harness the power of mourvèdre to produce wines with finesse and structure; they represent an exemplary combination of *terroir*, grape variety and exceptional winemaking. The rosé is powerful, spicy and fresh, and quite the equal of the outstanding reds.

ABOVE: In Bandol, vineyards climb rugged ranges just a short distance from the ocean.

DOMAINE DE TRÉVALLON

Established **1973** ***Owners*** **the Durrbach family** ***Production*** **4,200 cases** ***Vineyard area*** **49 acres (20 ha)**

Eloi Durrbach fashioned his vineyard from the limestone of the northern Alpilles hills. His idiosyncratic, organic-influenced ideas create rich, tannic, but wonderfully elegant wines that age for years. Made with low-yielding cabernet sauvignon and syrah, fermented for an extended period and aged for 18–22 months, these are world-class reds. Falling foul of appellation rules, they are sold as *vin de pays*, yet the wines are the undoubted stars of Provence, and expensive.

Regional Best

QUALITY WINES

Chateau Simone Palette white
Domaine Tempier Bandol red
Domaine Rabiéga Clos d'Ière Cuvée I red
Domaine de Trévallon red

BEST VALUE WINES

Château Coussin rosé
Domaine St-André de Figuière Cuvée des Princes rosé
Château Vignelaure red

CHÂTEAU VIGNELAURE

Established **1995** ***Owners*** **the O'Brien family** ***Production*** **30,000 cases** ***Vineyard area*** **148 acres (60 ha)**

This estate has a reputation for bordeaux-tinged reds. These incorporate beautifully balanced cabernet sauvignon, syrah and grenache, and are barrel-aged for 18 months, creating a concentrated wine that will age splendidly beyond ten years. The headline wine is AC, but, due to their high cabernet content, the other *cuvées* are classified VDP Coteaux du Verdon. Château Vignelaure also produces a fine rosé.

Other noteworthy producers in Provence are Domaine de la Bastide Neuve, Mas de Cadenet, Domaine Rabiéga, Domaine St-André-de-Figuière and Châteaux Elie Sumeire.

BELOW: A wide range of mesoclimates and soils allows local farmers to grow diverse crops.

The Rhône

SIMON WOODS

The Rhône Valley is an area of contrasts, of ancient and modern, of classical French rural scenery and industrial sprawl, of steep, stark slopes in the north and generous rolling hills in the south, of the splendor of outstanding estate-grown Châteauneuf-du-Pape and the shame of mass-produced, inferior examples.

Until comparatively recently, wine lovers have been somewhat reticent in embracing this fascinating area. If their experience of the region is based on that staple of French café life, Côtes du Rhône, it's not hard to see why. But taste the finest wines from Châteauneuf and from other appellations such as Côte Rôtie and Hermitage, and it is not possible to deny that the Rhône deserves the same recognition as France's other great red-wine regions, Bordeaux and Burgundy. Indeed, at its best, the Rhône offers the authority and longevity of the former with the sensual pleasures of the latter, and usually undercuts both in price.

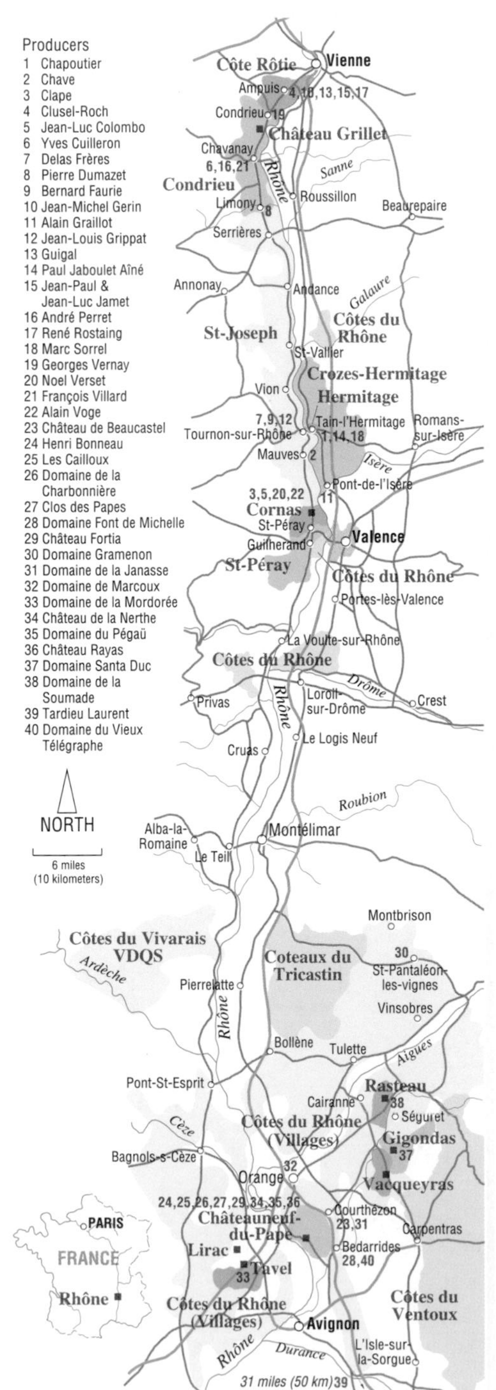

The Rhône winemaking region begins in eastern central France near Vienne to the south of Lyon and then spreads southward toward the Mediterranean, finishing in a rather sprawling fashion around Avignon. The region splits conveniently, both geographically and in terms of the wines produced, into two distinct subregions: the northern and southern Rhône.

The northern Rhône runs from Vienne, home of Côte Rôtie, southward to St-Péray, which lies just across the river from the town of Valence. The steep slopes overlooking the river are home to red wines of power and elegance made from the syrah grape. Whites are very much in the minority here, but the best, made from viognier, marsanne and rousanne, can be every bit as compelling as the reds. From just south of Montélimar, the start of the southern Rhône, the air gradually fills with the aromas of herbs, the valley flattens out, and the vines stretch away from the river, mainly to the east. Here, as in the north, red wines vastly outnumber whites, although grenache is the principal variety. Whites, with a few notable exceptions, seldom approach the reds in quality, this is the home of France's best and most famous *vin doux naturel*, Muscat de Beaumes de Venise. Most wines labeled simply Côtes du Rhône also hail from this southern sector.

What makes the Rhône one of the most exciting wine regions in the world is the progress that was made during the last part of the twentieth century, and the potential for further improvement in the twenty-first. Both the Californians and Australians may have played a large part in making grenache, syrah and viognier fashionable, but it is the Rhône producers who still create the benchmarks for these varieties and who are making better examples with each vintage. And, most refreshingly, in a wine world where too many vignerons think nothing of slapping exorbitant price-tags on their wines, the Rhône Valley remains a happy hunting ground for those who are guided by value for money rather than the whims of fashion.

History

This area has a very long history of winemaking—its wines were praised by Pliny the Elder in AD 71. It was after Louis XIII (1601–43) visited Tain that hermitage of both colors rose in popularity throughout Europe. The red wine was then also much in demand in Bordeaux for "improving" the local produce, and wines that had been *hermitagé* (hermitaged) sold for higher prices than unblended clarets. In 1787 Thomas Jefferson, then US Ambassador to France, eulogized both red and white hermitage. He praised the red for "its full body" and "exquisite flavor," while he declared the white to be the world's finest. By the end of the nineteenth century, phylloxera caused havoc, then wars and depression meant the Rhône entered the last half of the twentieth century in a pitiful state. However, things did change. In 1978, the first release of Marc Guigal's Côte Rôtie La Landonne, arguably the finest of the company's stunning trio of single-vineyard wines, set new standards for the Rhône and established it as a fully fledged fine wine region.

Since then there have been other new winemakers of excellence, such as the Chapoutiers, who have produced excellent prestige *cuvées*. Improved techniques and the additional number of winemakers in the area are likely to see the southern Rhône continue to rise in prominence.

ABOVE: *The town of Tain, on the Rhône River, from among the adjoining vineyards.*

Landscape and climate

The vine-growing regions in the northern sector are generally cooler, wetter and steeper than those of the southern sector, the *Méridionale*. Indeed, the only common factors in the two regions are the river and the often vicious winds which rip branches from vines, so trees are often planted as windbreaks; however, the winds also dry the vines and protect them from spring frosts. The climate in the north is continental and the best sites, such as those in Côte Rôtie and Hermitage, are steep slopes angled south or southeast and often overlooking the river so that the vines benefit from reflected as well as direct heat. In the warmer southern region, some of the vineyards face partly north to avoid too much heat.

Viticulture

Producers fall roughly into three different camps. Traditionalists do things as they have always been done, modernists use the latest gizmos and techniques, and pragmatists weigh up the pros and cons of each approach and use what they think will work best for them. But they all agree that the lower the yields in the vineyards, the better the quality.

Stainless steel, old wooden vats, and concrete are all used for fermenting syrah in the north, the choice being a personal preference on the part of the producer. Fermentation temperatures are generally high, while total maceration times vary from a few days to up to three weeks after fermentation has stopped. Traditional southern producers follow a similar method, but others prefer to put some or all of the fruit through carbonic maceration, which produces lighter and fruitier wines.

Traditionalists age their wines in large, old barrels; modernists often prefer new oak, although relatively few do so. Commercial pressures often mean that wines are bottled earlier than a producer would prefer. Also, while quantities produced in most northern Rhône cellars allow wines to be bottled in just one batch, this is not the case at many southern *domaines*, where some wines are still bottled to order over a period of many months. This practice, which sees huge variation between bottles, is becoming less prevalent. Advances in vinification technology have had a particularly beneficial effect on Rhône white wines. Dull, heavy, oversulfured, and downright faulty whites are disappearing. Some producers now choose to make different batches of wine and blend them. So a fresh, aromatic, fruity portion that has been fermented at a low temperature in stainless steel might be blended with a barrel-fermented and aged *cuvée* that has less fruitiness but greater weight and more complex, nutty flavors.

LEFT: *A stainless steel spittoon, designed to avoid splashes.*

RIGHT: *Lush vineyards with stone building, near Tain, Rhône Valley.*

Northern appellations and producers

In the main, red wine from the northern Rhône means syrah. However the Chave family has plantings of zinfandel on the hill of Hermitage, and Californian Jim Clendenen of Au Bon Climat feels that the *terroir* of Crozes-Hermitage is ideally suited for the Italian grape teroldego.

A number of the red-wine appellations do permit white grapes to be included in the blend. Marsanne and roussanne can be used in Hermitage and Crozes-Hermitage (both up to 15 percent) and St-Joseph (up to 10 percent), although few producers make use of such an allowance. Côte Rôtie can contain up to 20 percent viognier although its use is not widespread.

Côte Rôtie is the most northerly of the appellations. The aspect and incline of the slopes (in the best vineyard sites at least) ensure that the grapes ripen satisfactorily more often than not. Yet, while no one would describe the wines as lightweights, they seldom achieve the muscle of those 25 miles (40 km) or so downstream at Hermitage. They do, however, tend to be more elegant, and are marked by a heady perfume, sometimes of violets, sometimes of blossom. Where viognier has been used in the blend, its aromas are always secondary to those of syrah, although it does bring a softness to the wines that helps them to mature faster.

ABOVE: *Wine bottle with its wax capping intact.*

Soils in the vineyards north of the town of Ampuis, in what is known as the Côte Brune, have more clay and iron, whereas those of the Côte Blonde, to the south, tend to be sandier. As a consequence, Côte Brune wines tend to be sturdier than the more refined offerings from the Côte Blonde. Most of the growers here (and indeed throughout the Rhône) come from a long winemaking tradition, and wood is, for the most part, used with a sensitivity born from generations of experience. A three-year-old wine may have the toasty, vanilla flavors of new oak, but it will seldom be dominated by them. The style of a wine also depends on factors such as the calibre of the vintage and the influence of the winemaker, but good young Côte Rôtie should be reasonably full-bodied, packed with the smoky plum, berry, blackcurrant and orange-peel characters of syrah.

Côte Rôtie can be quite seductive at a tender age, but drinking it on release is a mistake. Even poorer vintages need five years before they begin to show their mettle, while with great vintages, a decade of patience pays off and, thanks to the tannin and acidity, the wines can happily be kept for much longer.

Côte Rôtie's rival for top spot in the northern Rhône is the majestic Hermitage. Côte Rôtie is the queen to Hermitage's king and, at their best, both are superlative wines. As in Côte Rôtie, there is considerable difference between the various parts of the appellation. The two best vineyards are the granite-based Les Bessards, which yield sturdy, spicy reds, and the limestone soil of Le Méal, the source of more perfumed supple wines. You can now find single-vineyard *cuvées* bearing these names, as well as those of other plots, such as Les Greffieux and L'Hermite. However, many producers still consider that the best hermitage is a blend of grapes from various sites. The vogue for new oak found in Côte Rôtie is less apparent in Hermitage.

Overall, it's warmer on the hill of Hermitage than on the slopes above Ampuis, and this is reflected in richer, fuller, more tannic wines. There are some of the same smoky fruit flavors, but there are also more spicy, cedary notes, which with bottle age can make the wines seem similar to the cabernet-sauvignon-based wines of Bordeaux. Although red hermitage may lack the perfume of Côte Rôtie, it is certainly not an uncouth brute of a wine; however, it does require plenty of time in bottle to unravel before you'll get a glimpse of its finesse. Wines from a great vintage, such as 1978, can still taste as if they are some way from their peak, and the top 1990s seem to be evolving in a similar fashion. Given the price her-

granite-rich vineyards around the village of Gervans or the stony plateau around Les Chassis and Les Sept Chemins, have very little in common with those from the flat, alluvial plains south of the town of Tain l'Hermitage, where the machine-harvesters roam. Unfortunately, vineyard designation has still to take off here, so pick your producer with care. A bottle labeled Crozes-Hermitage could contain a wine with much the same flavors and finesse as hermitage itself, albeit one that is ready to drink somewhat sooner; it could also contain something not far removed from basic Beaujolais.

Diversity of *terroir* is also an issue in St-Joseph. The appellation used to consist of about 222 acres (90 ha) of vineyards mostly on terraced, granite-rich slopes between the towns of Mauves and Vion. However, in 1969 it was extended to a whopping 17,300 acres (7,000 ha) running along the west bank of the Rhône from just south of the village of Condrieu all the way to the boundary with Cornas. Much of the new land was unsuitable for quality wine and remained unplanted, but the appearance of vines in such places prompted the local growers' syndicate to apply for another boundary change in 1994, which reduced the area by more than half. Many of the best wines still come from the original pre-1969 core of vineyards, although some of the new sites in the northern reaches that overlap part of the Condrieu appellation are showing promise.

St-Joseph wines vary enormously. Some are light, fresh and full of raspberry flavors, intended for early drinking and almost capable of taking a light chill. Others are more powerful and tannic, with the raspberry joined by black-

mitage now commands, it makes sense to give it the time it needs, a minimum of eight years from vintage and, for the good years, considerably longer.

Hermitage may not be a brute, but Cornas can be. The granite soils in this appellation on the west bank of the Rhône are the same as those found in Hermitage but Cornas is considerably warmer and drier. The best vineyards are on terraced south- to southeast-facing slopes, and are home to vines whose considerable age and, hence, deep roots are a boon in a district where drought can cause problems during hot vintages.

This combination of heat, old vines and rustic winemaking has traditionally resulted in massive, black wines with undoubted concentration of black-fruit flavor, but often with palate-numbing levels of tannin. Even an average vintage takes ten years to mature. Traditional Cornas can be a very worthwhile and sensibly priced wine.

In recent years, however, a more user-friendly style of Cornas has emerged, thanks largely to the effort of enologist Jean-Luc Colombo. A combination of techniques, including picking riper fruit, destemming all grapes prior to fermentation, lengthy maceration and aging in new oak has resulted in wines that seem to have the intensity of flavor of the traditional style without the rough edges. Debate rages as to whether such wines are quintessential Cornas. Both types at their best—Clape in the old style, Colombo's Les Ruchets in the new—are excellent.

Crozes-Hermitage is the largest of the northern appellations by a considerable margin. The diversity of *terroir* within its boundaries means that there's no such thing as a typical Crozes. The finest wines, from the

BELOW: *Gathering the harvest on the terraces near Cornas, Rhône Valley.*

ABOVE: Hermitage, both red and white, produced by the Chapoutier winery.

currant, cherry and plum, and need five years to show their best, although it is a rare St-Joseph that will last beyond ten years.

White wines are in a minority in the northern Rhône and fall into two distinct camps. Condrieu and Château Grillet are made entirely from the viognier grape, while Hermitage, Crozes-Hermitage, St-Joseph and St-Péray use marsanne and roussanne. "Exotic" is the tired cliché most often used for Condrieu, but exotic it undoubtedly is—or should be. Making great viognier is a tricky business, and not all succeed. The grapes need to be ripe enough for the development of the tell-tale musky perfume, yet not so ripe that sugar levels—and therefore alcohol levels—soar while acidity all but disappears.

Picked too early, Condrieu is just another white wine. Picked too late, it can become an ungainly, overweight caricature. Picked just right, it is a heady delight, rich and redolent of dried apricots, peaches and pears with perhaps a dollop of honey. Condrieu is at its best in its youth, so aim to drink it before its fourth birthday.

The famous estate of Château Grillet lies close to the village of Condrieu and, unusually, has its own appellation. Given the superbly sited vineyards and the prices the wine manages to command, it really should be better. There were signs of improvement in the mid-1990s, but the wine is still not as ripe and concentrated as it should be, and Château Grillet still has some way to go to catch up with the star performers of Condrieu.

White hermitage stands as one of the world's least well-known great wines. Marsanne is the preferred grape, although the use of roussanne is increasing, perhaps because of the success that Château de Beaucastel in Châteauneuf-du-Pape has enjoyed with this variety. A young white hermitage is full-bodied and creamy, packed with honeyed peach and apricot flavors. An adolescent white hermitage can be something of a disappointment: an eight-year-old wine, for example, can often seem to have lost its fruit without gaining any extra complexity. Patience is all that is required, as white hermitage can last as long as the red. From 15 years onward, aromas and flavors of nuts, flowers, toast and more appear, and the wine can then survive happily for at least another decade.

BELOW: In front of the Chapoutier winery.

A few estates produce a hermitage *vin de paille* ("straw wine"), made by drying whole bunches of grapes on straw mats before crushing and fermenting. These wines have intense flavors of butter, orange marmalade, nuts, apricots, peaches and more, and will outlast even the regular *cuvées* of white hermitage.

The other whites of the northern Rhône—Crozes-Hermitage, St-Joseph and St-Péray—only seldom approach the quality of Hermitage. Crozes is the most promising of the trio, offering wines with weight and flavor that can age well for five or six years. Chapoutier's St-Joseph Les Granits serves as a stunning reminder of what is possible. Clape's St-Péray is the best still wine in this lackluster appellation. Of its *méthode champenoise* wines, also made from marsanne and roussanne, sparkling-wine authority Tom Stevenson says they are "... made from the wrong grapes grown on the wrong soil."

CHAPOUTIER

Established **1808** ***Owners*** **the Chapoutier family** ***Production*** **30,000 cases** ***Vineyard area*** **173 acres (70 ha)**

The extensive Chapoutier family *domaines* are biodynamically farmed, and the *cuvées* made here—Ermitage Le Pavillon (red), Hermitage Cuvée de l'Orée (white), St-Joseph Les Granits (red and white), Crozes-Hermitage Les Varonniers (red), Côte Rôtie La Mordorée, and Châteauneuf-du-Pape Barbe Rac—are each among the top half-dozen wines made in each appellation. The regular releases from Côtes du Rhône and Côtes du Ventoux levels upward are also reliably good.

CHAVE

Established **1481** ***Owners*** **Gérard and Jean-Louis Chave** ***Production*** **4,000 cases** ***Vineyard area*** **37 acres (15 ha)**

Chave makes exemplary hermitage, both red and white, with each being capable of lasting for 20 years or longer. Since 1990, good vintages have seen a small parcel of the wine being given a sojourn in new oak and the result is the superb but rare Cuvée Cathelin. There are also small quantities of a ripe, supple St-Joseph and, from the 1997 vintage onward, rather larger amounts of a distinctly affordable Côtes du Rhône called Mon Cœur.

ABOVE: *Built of local stone, the village of Côtes du Rhône seems to grow out of the landscape.*

DELAS FRÈRES

Established **1835** ***Owner*** **Louis Roederer** ***Production*** **121,000 cases** ***Vineyard area*** **35 acres (14 ha)**

With Jacques Grange (ex-Chapoutier and Colombo) in charge of the cellars, there has been a much-needed surge in quality. Hermitage Les Bessards remains the finest wine. Once you needed to choose carefully among the others, but everything is now of a high standard.

GUIGAL

Established **1946** ***Owner*** **Marcel Guigal** ***Production*** **340,000 cases** ***Vineyard area*** **35 acres (14 ha)**

The Côte Rôties are fine wines with high prices. La Mouline has the most viognier and is the lightest and most perfumed, La Turque has more muscle, and La Landonne is the massive tannic monster built for the very long haul. The less pricey Côte Brune et Blonde *cuvée* is a lovely wine. Château d'Ampuis *cuvée* sits in between. From holdings in Condrieu comes delicious wine, with the partly barrel-fermented and aged La Doriane *cuvée* ranking as one of the stars.

RENÉ ROSTAING

Established 1971 Owner René Rostaing Production 3,250 cases Vineyard area 20 acres (8 ha)

René Rostaing's Côte Rôties are now beginning to get the attention they deserve. From a selection of vineyards, which includes vines more than 80 years old, he makes four *cuvées*: regular, Côte Blonde, La Viallière, and La Landonne—all richly fruited and supple. Rostaing also produces small amounts of fine condrieu.

MARC SORREL

Established **1928** ***Owner*** **Marc Sorrel** ***Production*** **1,600 cases** ***Vineyard area*** **10 acres (4 ha)**

Not to be confused with his brother Jean-Michel, who also has holdings in a number of the same vineyards, Marc Sorrel makes fine hermitage, as well as some delicious crozes-hermitage. The top red is the dense, sweet hermitage Le Gréal, made from a mixture of fruit (including some marsanne) from the Le Méal and Les Greffieux vineyards. The top white is the long-lived and powerful 100 percent marsanne Hermitage Les Rocoules.

GEORGES VERNAY

Established **1953** ***Owner*** **Christine Vernay** ***Production*** **8,000 cases** ***Vineyard area*** **40 acres (16 ha)**

This is the reference point for condrieu. Harvest takes place as late as possible to accentuate viognier's peach and apricot characters. A regular *cuvée* is bottled when young, but the two top wines, Les Chaillées de l'Enfer (The Terraces of Hell) and Coteau de Vernon, spend extra time in cask on their lees. Both emerge in aromatic splendor, and drink well for up to five years.

Other northern producers are Clape, Pierre Dumazet, Clusel-Roch, Jean-Luc Colombo, Yves Cuilleron, Delas Frères, Bernard Faurie, Jean-Michel Gerin, Alain Graillot, Jean-Louis Grippat, Jean-Paul and Jean-Luc Jamet, Andre Perret, Noel Verset, François Villard and Alain Voge.

Regional Dozen

NORTHERN RHÔNE

Chapoutier Hermitage Vin de Paille
Chapoutier St-Joseph Rouge Les Granits
Chave Hermitage Blanc
Chave Hermitage Rouge
Clape Cornas
Jean-Luc Colombo Cornas Les Ruchets
Yves Cuilleron Condrieu Les Chaillets Vieilles Vignes
Jean-Michel Gerin Côte Rôtie Les Grandes Places
Guigal Côte Rôtie La Turque
Paul Jaboulet Aîné Hermitage La Chapelle
René Rostaing Côte Rôtie La Landonne
Marc Sorrel Hermitage Le Gréal

ABOVE: *The ruins of an old stone fort in the southern Rhône Valley. The Romans were the first to grow wine grapes in the area.*

Up the Drôme

On the Drôme, Brézème-Côtes du Rhône is a one-man-band appellation near Livron-sur-Drôme. Here Jean-Marie Lombard makes syrah reds and marsanne and roussanne whites that are as good as many in more famous northern Rhône appellations. Farther upstream are some appellations that have little in common with other Rhône wines. Châtillon-en-Diois is another appellation dominated by one producer, in this instance the Cave Co-operative de Die. Its Aligoté and Chardonnay are better than the gamay-based red and rosé, but none of the wines can be recommended. The sparkling wine formerly called Clairette de Die and now known as Crémant de Die is slightly better, but being made from the lackluster clairette, it lacks style. Clairette de Die Tradition, or Clairette de Die Méthode Dioise Ancestrale as it is now sold, must include at least 75 percent muscat blanc à petits grains and is far more interesting. The *méthode dioise ancestrale* involves halting fermentation partway through and bottling the wine with residual sugar. The fermentation continues in bottle, producing the bubbles; subsequently, the wine is filtered to remove the yeast before being transferred to a fresh bottle, still with some residual sweetness. The result is France's answer to Italy's Asti Spumante, a delicious, frothy wine with a peachy, grapey flavor.

Southern appellations and producers

Wines such as Côte Rôtie, Hermitage and Condrieu ensure that the northern Rhône enjoys great prestige. However, its production is dwarfed by that of the southern sector of the valley, which makes more than 95 percent of all Rhône wines, the vast majority of them red. If syrah dominates the north, then the south is emphatically grenache country. One explanation for its ubiquity is that the beefy, high-alcohol wines it produces were much in demand until as recently as the 1960s for bolstering the wines of chilly Burgundy.

Ripening grenache in the southern warmth is seldom a problem, but making high-quality wine from this variety presents more of a challenge. When over-cropped, it produces wines that have a reasonable level of alcohol, but not much color or flavor. Color and slightly jammy, berry flavors start to appear as the yield decreases, but since grenache doesn't have especially high levels of tannin in its skins, by that time the wine often lacks the structure to support them. There are two ways of providing grenache with backbone. One is to slash yields even further to levels where the sheer strength of flavor carries the wines along. The other is to blend it with other grapes such as syrah and mourvèdre. This method has an additional advantage: grenache by itself is prone to oxidation, and both syrah and mourvèdre act as antioxidants to counter this.

Both methods have their adherents in this most famous appellation of the southern Rhône, Châteauneuf-du-Pape. As well as as grenache, 12 other grape varieties are allowed for Châteauneuf, namely syrah, mourvèdre, cinsault, counoise, vaccarèse, terret noir and muscardin (all red grape varieties); and clairette, bourboulenc, roussanne, picpoul and picardan (all white). This extensive list simply reflects what was in the vineyards when the appellation laws were drawn up, rather than being an indication of what the quintessential Châteauneuf-du-Pape should contain.

In the early twentieth century, Commander Joseph Ducos, whose property included Château la Nerte—today known as Château de la Nerthe—devised a formula for the ideal Châteauneuf. This contained 20 percent cinsault and grenache for "warmth, liqueur-like sweetness and mellowness;" 40 percent syrah, mourvèdre, muscardin and vaccarèse for "solidity, durability and color, accompanied by a straightforward, almost thirst-quenching flavor;" 30 percent counoise and picpoul for "vinosity, charm, freshness and accentuation of bouquet;" and 10 percent clairette and bourboulenc for "finesse, fire and sparkle."

Today, few producers make use of all 13 varieties, Château de Beaucastel being a notable exception. A normal Châteauneuf would be 70 percent grenache, with syrah and mourvèdre making up most of the remainder and the other varieties being used only in minute amounts. Some producers exclude other grapes entirely, while others include less than one-third grenache.

Lusty fruit infused with the character of thyme, bay and other southern herbs is found in most Châteauneuf but, thanks to the many permutations of grape varieties and variations in winemaking styles, there is no such thing as a textbook wine. And for every quality-minded producer of Châteauneuf, there are are several more for

No flying saucers

In 1954, the wine producers issued an extraordinary decree, which was translated by John Livingstone-Learmonth in his book, The Wines of the Rhône *(Faber & Faber, 1992) as follows:*

"Article 1. The flying overhead, landing and taking off of aeronautical machines called 'flying saucers' or 'flying cigars,' of whatever nationality they may be, is strictly forbidden on the territory of the commune of Châteauneuf-du-Pape."

"Article 2. Any aeronautical machine—'flying saucer' or 'flying cigar'—that lands on the territory of the commune will be immediately taken off to the pound."

whom quantity is more important. Disappointing as this can be, it does highlight the vast and still largely untapped potential of the appellation.

Châteauneufs made using a proportion of carbonic maceration are ready to drink sooner than traditionally fermented versions and tend to be less intensely flavored. In contrast, old-fashioned versions, aged in large, old wooden casks and often made with a high proportion of fruit from old vines and not destemmed are massive beasts packed with herby, spicy red- and black-fruit flavors. These need ten years or so in bottle before they show their warm, welcoming side.

Châteauneuf's increasing popularity has prompted many producers to release prestige *cuvées*. Here again, the range of styles is enormous. There's a world of difference between Chapoutier's 100 percent Grenache Barbe Rac and Beaucastel's Hommage à Jacques Perrin, which can be as much as 70 percent mourvèdre with only 15 percent grenache. Pleasingly, few suffer from excessive levels of new oak; indeed, over-oaking hardly ever occurs in Châteauneuf. Prices for such wines may seem high, but not when compared with those for top burgundy and bordeaux, and the quality is usually excellent.

ABOVE: *Old-fashioned hand plows are still used among the vines on difficult terrain.*

Châteauneuf is, without doubt, the finest appellation in the southern Rhône, but it no longer has a monopoly on quality. Gigondas is the most successful of the pretenders to Châteauneuf's throne. The range of grapes permitted here is even wider than in Châteauneuf. In practice, the blends tend to be similar, with a large proportion of grenache (but, according to the appellation rules, no more than 80 percent) bolstered by at least 15 percent syrah and mourvèdre. Gigondas is generally cooler than in Châteauneuf, so syrah can make up a higher proportion of the blend without dominating. But these cooler conditions make it more difficult to ripen mourvèdre.

Although the finest Gigondas can be mistaken for good Châteauneuf, the wines tend to be less full-bodied, with sweeter fruit, and take a shorter time to reach their peak. They are still broad-shouldered though, and most can safely be kept for ten years at least. Cash-strapped wine lovers looking for gutsy reds to replenish their stocks couldn't do much better than a few cases of 1998 Gigondas from a top *domaine*. However, here, as in Châteauneuf (and indeed throughout the southern Rhône), the diversity of styles and blends is huge, and it is important to pick your producer with care. The number of those who have the inclination (not to mention the francs) to raise quality levels is rising, but too

BELOW: *Vines trained on wires, Gigondas AC.*

RIGHT: An early corkscrew designed to fit easily and surreptitiously into a lady's handbag.

much potentially good wine still deteriorates in the large, musty old barrels of the town's many cellars.

Neighboring Vacqueyras formerly came under the Côtes du Rhône-Villages appellation but it was elevated to full AC status in 1990. Vacqueyras is to Gigondas as Gigondas is to Châteauneuf—based on roughly similar blends, but more rustic, ready to drink sooner, and cheaper. Top wines will last into their second decade, but most are at their best at around five to seven years old.

Lirac lies across the Rhône from Châteauneuf and is the least well-known of the main southern-Rhône appellations. A few wines, especially those of Domaine de la Mordorée, show that this appellation could be able to take on Vacqueyras and even Gigondas, but few producers are as yet fully exploiting its true potential.

Most wines labeled as Côtes du Rhône hail from the southern Rhône. Ninety-six percent of them are red, and these range from insipid to inspiring, from bland table wine to declassified Côte Rôtie or Châteauneuf-du-Pape. A simple and effective rule of thumb is that the producers who make good wines in a loftier appellation generally make the best Côtes du Rhône. Domaines Gramenon and Réméjeanne, which don't have vineyards elsewhere and make only Côtes du Rhône, are excellent exceptions to this rule. They and a number of other estates now produce *cuvées* that are 100 percent syrah, and the quality being achieved is increasingly impressive. We're still not talking Hermitage or Côte Rôtie, but the best can stand comparison with wines from St-Joseph and Crozes-Hermitage.

The 16 southern villages that are considered to be superior to the general standard and are entitled to append their name to the Côtes du Rhône-Villages appellation are Beaumes de Venise, Cairanne, Chusclan, Laudun, Rasteau, Roaix, Rochegude, Rousset-les-Vignes, Sablet, St-Gervais, St-Maurice-sur-Eygues, St-Pantaléon-les-Vignes, Séguret, Valréas, Vinsobres and Visan. The wines follow the general grenache-based trend of southern Rhône wines and, once again, quality and style vary enormously.

The other red-wine appellations of the greater Rhône Valley, namely Coteaux du Pierrevert, Coteaux du Tricastin, Côtes du Luberon, Côtes du Ventoux and Côtes du Vivarais, produce wines very much in the style—or styles—of Côtes du Rhône. Few of these are remarkable, but the wines from such well-known Rhône producers as Chapoutier and the Perrins of Château de Beaucastel (under the La Vieille Ferme label) can be excellent value. With the exception of Châteauneuf-du-Pape, all the southern Rhône red-wine appellations are allowed to make rosé wine using the same grape varieties. In addition, Tavel, Lirac's neighbor, is a rosé-only district. Rhône rosés have plenty of guts and can be wonderfully juicy and fresh, packed with thirst-quenching raspberry and strawberry flavors. Unfortunately, most are spoiled by clumsy vinification and lose the joy of youth that is the essence of rosé. Quite why Tavel has a reputation as a wine that can be aged escapes most sane wine drinkers.

The majority of white wines from the southern Rhône are also best in the flush of youth. The most

BELOW: Fall sunset in Rasteau, one of the 16 villages in the Côtes du Rhône appellation.

widely planted varieties are grenache blanc, which produces rich, full-bodied wines with a floral hint; the softer, lighter clairette; and bourboulenc, which provides body and acidity. The early harvesting and modern winemaking that many estates now employ result in fairly full-bodied but not especially intensely flavored wines that are best drunk within a year of release.

Finer white Rhônes with greater potential for aging do exist, and the vast majority are to be found in the appellation of Châteauneuf-du-Pape. Many include large proportions of roussanne, a variety that is prone to oxidation but is slowly gaining popularity among vignerons for its full-fleshed wines with aromas and flavors of flowers, nuts, peaches and cream. Some producers ferment and age some of their wine in new oak barrels, and then blend with unoaked *cuvées* to excellent effect. Such wines buck the southern white trend in that they keep happily for eight years or even more.

Quality whites are quite hard to find outside Châteauneuf. The Côtes du Rhône and Côtes du Rhône-Villages can provide happy hunting grounds, not least because viognier, outlawed in Châteauneuf, is permitted here. But once again, the best advice is try before you buy. Perhaps the best-known white wine of the southern Rhône, and arguably the most consistent, is Muscat de Beaumes de Venise, made from the muscat blanc à petits grains. This is a *vin doux naturel*, made by adding grape spirit to a partly fermented wine, resulting in a heady concoction with a minimum of 15 percent alcohol and 14.6 ounces per gallon (110 g per l) of unfermented sugar. It's wonderfully rich and floral, with flavors of apricot, marmalade and barley sugar, and although certainly sweet, it is seldom cloying.

The region's other *vin doux naturel* is Rasteau, made from at least 90 percent grenache. Grenache comes in both red and white forms, so Rasteau appears in various colors, and there is also a separate appellation, Rasteau Rancio, for wines that have been aged for longer periods. Port-like these are not: they are raw, sweet, fiery wines to warm you up on a cold day. Age mellows them slightly, but none approaches the quality of Muscat de Beaumes de Venise.

ABOVE: *Intricate terracing exposes the vines to the maximum possible warmth and sunlight.*

DOMAINE DE LA CHARBONNIÈRE

Established 1912 Owner Michel Maret Production 5,000 cases Vineyard area 54 acres (22 ha)

Michel Maret sprang to prominence in the 1990s for his ripe, herby Châteauneufs. Mourvèdre plays a prominent part—as much as 25 percent—in most of his wines, although the finest *cuvée*, the Vieilles Vignes, is mostly grenache. The *domaine* also makes fine Vacqueyras.

LEFT: *Wines from southern producer, Domaine de la Janasse.*

ABOVE: *Vines in the southern Rhône Valley.*

DOMAINE FONT DE MICHELLE

Established **1950** ***Owners*** **Jean and Michel Gonnet** ***Production*** **10,000 cases** ***Vineyard area*** **74 acres (30 ha)**

Jean and Michel Gonnet make a crisp, fruity white and a modern-style, smoky, spicy red with cherry and berry flavors. In homage to their father, they make Cuvée Étienne Gonnet, the red a deliciously aromatic and full-bodied wine, the white fleshy and perhaps slightly overoaked.

CHÂTEAU FORTIA

Established **Eighteenth century** ***Owner*** **Baron Le Roy de Boiseaumarie** ***Production*** **6,000 cases** ***Vineyard area*** **67 acres (27 ha)**

It was Baron Pierre Le Roy de Boiseaumarie of Château Fortia who, in 1923, drew up the rules that eventually developed into France's system of *appellation contrôlée*. Since 1994, his grandson Bruno, with Jean-Luc Colombo, has been making ripe, concentrated, but supple wines that have enhanced the reputation.

DOMAINE GRAMENON

Established **1979** ***Owners*** **Philippe and Michèle Laurent** ***Production*** **8,000 cases** ***Vineyard area*** **54 acres (22 ha)**

Philippe Laurent is one of the finest producers of Côtes du Rhône. Several red *cuvées* are made, all of them rich, concentrated, and far superior to the average Châteauneuf-du-Pape. The finest are Les Ceps Centennaires (from a 100-year-old grenache vineyard) and Cuvée des Laurentides (grenache plus 30 percent syrah). Gramenon recently introduced a late-harvest Cuvée Pascal and a full-bodied white, heavy with viognier.

DOMAINE DE MARCOUX

Established **Thirteenth century** ***Owner*** **SCEA Armenier** ***Production*** **3,300 cases** ***Vineyard area*** **45 acres (18 ha)**

Philippe Armenier runs one of the finest estates in Châteauneuf-du-Pape. He began experimenting with biodynamic viticulture in 1990, and now the whole estate is run on these principles. Maybe this, combined with the old vines and low yields, is what gives his wines such intensity of spicy, plummy, blackcurrant-and-cherry flavors, even in less than favorable vintages. The Vieilles Vignes *cuvée* is spectacularly good, while the white, in which the fleshy roussanne makes its presence felt, is also excellent.

DOMAINE DU PÉGAÜ

Established **Late seventeenth century** ***Owners*** **Paul and Laurence Feraud** ***Production*** **5,500 cases** ***Vineyard area*** **45 acres (18 ha)**

Paul and Laurence Feraud make traditional Châteauneuf from scattered vineyards that include some plots dating back to 1902. The reds are fermented and aged in large old oak *foudres* (barrels), for two years in the case of the Cuvée Réservée and for up to six years for Cuvée Laurence. These are thick, spicy, fruity wines that need eight years to show their best and will drink well for at least a decade after that. New wood is used with a portion of the rich, waxy grenache-blanc-based white.

CHÂTEAU RAYAS

Established **1890** ***Owner*** **Emmanuel Reynaud** ***Production*** **1,000 cases** ***Vineyard area*** **30 acres (12 ha)**

A policy of miserly yields and almost 100 percent grenache established the sweet and stylish Rayas in the top league of Châteauneufs. Pignan, from a separate vineyard, is a fine wine, and cheaper; the two côtes du rhônes from Domaine Fon Salette, one a blend of 50 percent grenache with mourvèdre and syrah, the other a thick, smoky, long-lived 100 percent syrah, are also relative bargains.

DOMAINE SANTA DUC

Established **NA** ***Owner*** **Yves Gras** ***Production*** **7,000 cases** ***Vineyard area*** **47 acres (19 ha)**

Gigondas is an appellation with a growing reputation, in no small part thanks to the work done by Yves Gras at this excellent estate. Old vines, low yields and ultra-ripe fruit are the secrets here, and the result is wines with powerful structures and fruit flavors, which need several years in bottle to soften. In good vintages, Santa Duc produces a Cuvée Prestige des Hautes Garrigues, which spends time in more new oak and contains a high

Regional Dozen

BEST VALUE WINES

- Château de Beaucastel Côtes du Rhône Blanc Coudoulet de Beaucastel
- Château de Beaucastel Côtes du Rhône Rouge Coudoulet de Beaucastel
- Clape Côtes du Rhône Blanc
- Domaine de Durban Muscat de Beaumes de Venise
- Jean-Michel Gerin Côtes du Rhône Rouge
- Alain Graillot Crozes-Hermitage Rouge
- Domaine Gramenon Côtes du Rhône Rouge Laurentides
- Guigal Côtes du Rhône Rouge
- Paul Jaboulet Aîné Crozes-Hermitage Rouge Domaine de Thalabert
- Domaine de la Janasse Vin de Pays de l'Orange
- Domaine de la Mordorée Lirac Rouge
- Domaine Santa Duc Côtes du Rhône Rouge

proportion of mourvèdre. Bargain hunters should look for their stylish Côtes du Rhône.

DOMAINE DE LA SOUMADE

Established **1979** ***Owner*** **André Romero** ***Production*** **10,000 cases** ***Vineyard area*** **64 acres (26 ha)**

André Romero makes two *cuvées* of *vin doux naturel*, but it is his three Côtes du Rhône-Villages reds that really merit attention. The basic wine is soft and friendly and is best drunk in the first five years of its life, whereas the Cuvée Prestige is more serious, full-bodied, and slightly leathery. The top wine is Cuvée Confiance, a wonderfully juicy blend of ancient grenache with about 20 percent syrah.

TARDIEU LAURENT

Established **1996** ***Owner*** **Michel Tardieu** ***Production*** **5,000 cases** ***Vineyard area*** **None**

A recent arrival on the Rhône landscape, this estate is the brainchild of pastry chef turned Burgundy *négociant* Dominique Laurent and Michel Tardieu, who is largely responsible for looking after the wines. Although based in Lourmarin in the southern Rhône, the company sources wine throughout the Rhône Valley. Quantities are small but the quality is high, with prices to match. The Côtes du Rhône Cuvée Guy Louis is an admirable introduction to a fine range.

ABOVE: *Wine aging in the cellars of Château de la Nerthe, Châteauneuf-du-Pape.*

DOMAINE DU VIEUX TÉLÉGRAPHE

Established **1900** ***Owners*** **Daniel and Frédéric Brunier** ***Production*** **22,000 cases** ***Vineyard area*** **178 acres (72 ha)**

This estate produces one of the more restrained Châteauneufs, a wine with lovely cherry and raspberry fruit infused with the aromas of Provençal herbs. The 1993 vintage saw a new second label, Vieux Mas des Papes; a prestige *cuvée,* Hippolyte, appeared in 1994. Vieux Télégraphe, a white, is a fresh, floral wine best drunk young.

Other southern Rhône producers are Les Cailloux, Clos des Papes, Domaines de la Janasse and de la Mordorée, and Châteaux de Beaucastel and de la Nerthe.

BELOW: *The substantial Château des Fines Roches, in the Châteauneuf-du-Pape appellation.*

ABOVE: *Beaujolais is named for the town of Beaujeu, which was founded in the tenth century.*

Beaujolais

CATHERINE FALLIS MS

From the gluggable, tooth-staining *nouveau* wines dispatched to the far reaches of the globe each November, to the serious, cellarworthy selections from the region's best *crus*, Beaujolais wines are, almost without exception, red, soft, fruit-driven and light—truly, wines with enormously wide appeal.

Although classified as a part of Burgundy, the wines and residents of Beaujolais are vastly different from their northern neighbours. On a cusp between the serious, cold north and the precocious sunny Mediterranean, their personalities, the lifestyle, climate, soils, principal grape varieties, viticulture, production and marketing are all unique.

BELOW: *The church of the village of Fleurie occupies a prominent position amid local vineyards.*

History

Vineyards were first planted in Beaujolais during the Roman occupation, and Benedictine Monks tended vineyards here in the seventh century. Winegrowing continued under the Dukes of Beaujeu, who ruled from the town of the same name from the tenth century.

In 1395, Philip the Bold, Duke of Burgundy issued an edict forbidding the use of the gamay grape in the Côte d'Or. This enabled Beaujolais to distinguish itself from Burgundy by specializing in wine made mainly from gamay. This affordable quaff soon found favor with thrifty Lyonnais and by the mid-twentieth century had seduced even the haughtiest of Parisians. By the 1970s, the British had been charmed, and in the 1980s, Americans, Japanese and Europeans were won over. Beaujolais gained a following in Asia in the 1990s, where consumers were drawn to red wine by reports of its health benefits.

Today, Germany is the leading importer (taking 26 percent of production), Switzerland is the second-largest customer and Japan the third-largest. Exports to the UK have declined, but sales to North America, the Netherlands and Italy are stable.

Landscape and climate

French wine authorities divide Burgundy into four departments: the Yonne (Chablis), the Côte d'Or (Côte de Nuits and Côte de Beaune), the Saone-et-Loire (Côte Chalonnaise and Maconnais regions), and the Rhône department (Beaujolais)—not to be confused with the Rhône Valley. Considered part of Burgundy, Beaujolais is the region's largest producer, yielding 40 percent of its output from 54,000 acres (22,000 ha) in the flatter southernmost district of Beaujolais, which is known as Beaujolais Bas. Here, boatloads of simple AC Beaujolais, the basic appellation, and Beaujolais Supérieur, which has an extra 0.5 percent of alcohol, are sold most often as Beaujolais Nouveau, the simple, grapey wine that is rushed to market 60 days after the just-fermented juice hits the bottle. This area's rich soils don't favor the production of high-quality gamay, but the warm climate helps the grapes ripen to maturity.

Haut Beaujolais, to the north, is hillier, with granite-based subsoils and easy-draining sandy topsoils, on which gamay thrives. Its climate is generally temperate and sunny, though summer hailstorms occasionally wreak havoc. Thirty-nine communes, or villages, in the area qualify for the superior Beaujolais-Villages appellation, and an additional ten communes are singled out as *crus*. Like the Premier and Grand Crus of Burgundy, these are considered the jewels of the region.

Winemaking and wine styles

Ninety-eight percent of Beaujolais is planted with gamay noir à jus blanc, a gamay not grown elsewhere. Two percent is planted with chardonnay, used mainly for Beaujolais Blanc. Aligoté is also allowed, but rarely planted. After ten years, vines are left to develop independently without training or trellising. Grapes are usually harvested by hand.

Small growers are the dominant source of fruit, which they sell to *negoçiants*. Few contracts exist, and each year the growers have an anxious wait to see if their crop is up to snuff. Major buyers can make or break an entire year's worth of work.

The grapes are normally fermented by carbonic maceration. The maceration time is absolutely minimal—four days for Beaujolais Nouveau and up to ten days for a *cru* wine. The juice is run off immediately, then blended with the press wine. Chaptalization is widely employed, especially in low-quality wines.

Beaujolais is a good introduction to red wines. Fans of whites and rosés enjoy this fruity, smooth, silky, perfumed wine, especially chilled. Beaujolais Nouveau is best known (but least impressive)—it has to be drunk young. Beaujolais-Villages can be good, and keeps for up to two years. The most characterful wines are from the *crus*. Differing *terroirs* alter the character of similar wines: Chiroubles is delicate, Brouilly is full-flavored, Côte-de-Brouilly is earthy, Julienas has wild aromatics, Fleurie is elegant and full-bodied, St-Amour is less fruity, Chenas is ageworthy, and Morgon and Moulin-à-Vent are powerful, solid and ageworthy. Regnie is still establishing its identity. After 3–5 years, the top *crus* take on the characteristics of well-aged Rhine or Côte de Beaune wines.

Recently, demand for *cru* wines has increased as interest in Beaujolais Nouveau has dwindled. This is understandable as the *cru* wines are usually a bargain and almost guaranteed to give pleasure, while the quality of the *nouveau* wines is highly variable.

GEORGES DUBŒUF

Established **1964** ***Owners*** **Georges Dubœuf and family** ***Production*** **2.6 million cases** ***Vineyard area*** **NA**

Georges Dubœuf works with over 600 growers to produce a dizzying array of wines—always around, affordable, and reliable. His *cru* bottlings are at the top of their class; the Morgon, for example, is lean and juicy with cranberry and licorice flavors, becoming softer and subtler after three to four years in bottle.

LOUIS JADOT

Established **1859** ***Owner*** **Kobrand** ***Production*** **NA** ***Vineyard area*** **NA**

For many, the wines of Jacques Lardière are the first taste of Burgundy on their lips. Jadot's wines are good value and reliable. Lardière's passion comes through in the Château des Jacques' Moulin-à-Vent—it has great intensity of fruit when young and ages superbly. His trusty Beaujolais-Villages should be on the required drinking list of every blossoming youth.

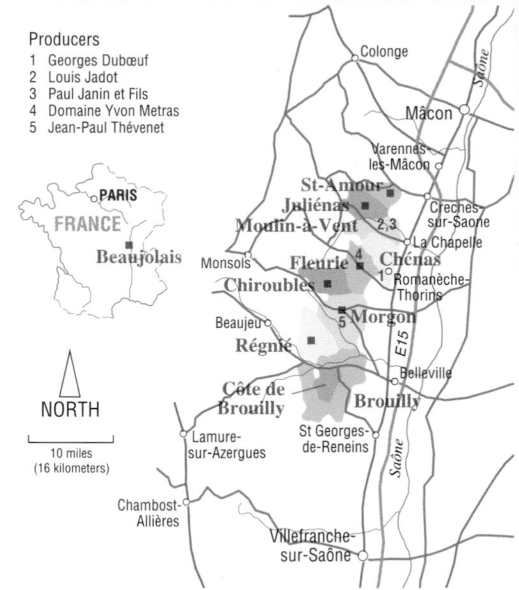

PAUL JANIN ET FILS

Established **1925** ***Owners*** **Paul Janin and family** ***Production*** **1,200 cases** ***Vineyard area*** **25 acres acres (10 ha)**

Janin's vineyard, Domaine des Vignes du Tremblay, is located on granite-based hillsides in Moulin-à-Vent and was planted by his grandparents; it is now farmed biodynamically. The wine is bold and characterful: after four to five years it displays aromas and flavors of incense, cigar box, cranberries and orange rind; a lithe, soft texture; and a long finish.

DOMAINE YVON METRAS

Established **NA** ***Owner*** **Yvon Metras** ***Production*** **600 cases** ***Vineyard area*** **3.75 acres (1.5 ha)**

Metras' vineyard is known locally as Grille Midi, or "roasting at midday," a reference to its sunny location. It produces inky, concentrated Fleurie, which is rarely chaptalized. Metras belongs to a group of growers known as the Gang of Four. It follows organic principles and avoids using sulfur or yeast during fermentation. His Fleurie shows floral, raspberry and cherry flavors and a lush texture, with enough acid and tannins for aging.

JEAN-PAUL THÉVENET

Established **1870** ***Owner*** **Jean-Paul Thévenet** ***Production*** **2,000 cases** ***Vineyard area*** **13 acres (5 ha)**

Another member of the Gang of Four, Jean-Paul Thévenet produces two Morgon *cuvées:* Tradition and Vieilles Vignes. The latter is made from 70-year-old vines and aged in oak for six to eight months. Intense, cedary and grapey when young, it softens and becomes even more elegant over two to three years.

Regional Dozen

QUALITY WINES

Guy Breton Morgan Vielles Vignes
Georges Dubœuf Morgon
Georges Dubœuf Moulin-à-Vent
Jean Foillard Morgon
Louis Jadot Chateau des Jacques Moulin-à-Vent
Marcel La Pierre Morgon

BEST VALUE WINES

Chateau de La Chaize Brouilly
Georges Dubœuf Jean Descombes Morgon
Sylvan Fessy Beaujolais-Villages
Louis Jadot Beaujolais-Villages Jadot
Paul Janin Clos du Tremblay Moulin-à-Vent
Louis Latour Morgon Les Charmes

Burgundy

JASPER MORRIS MW

Burgundy produces some of the greatest red and white wines of the world, mostly from two grape varieties: pinot noir and chardonnay. It is a region full of paradox: steeped in tradition yet equipped with modern research stations; simple to comprehend in some respects (there are only two main grapes), yet complex in others (many hundreds of individually named vineyards are divided up between many thousands of producers). The word itself is tremendously evocative, suggesting a deep red color (though many of the wines are a light, bright cherry red), a sense of winter warmth, an almost imperial majesty. It conjures up images of cobwebbed stone cellars with high, vaulted ceilings; tiled roofs on imposing bourgeois mansions; small villages dominated by churches; and gnarled peasants working among the vines all hours of the day. One such worker, the late, widely respected André Mussy, whose working life as a vigneron in Pommard lasted more than 70 years, started at the age of thirteen with a 72-hour working week and never grew out of the habit.

BELOW: The picturesque village of Nuits-St-Georges in the appellation of the same name.

When all is well, the wines of Burgundy can be the most majestic of all—Le Chambertin delights in the cliché of "The King of Wines; The Wine of Kings"—yet disappointments have been all too frequent. In 1869, the *Blue Guide* to the wines of the department of the Côte d'Or reproached the local winemakers for apathy, resistance to new ideas and healthy methods of cultivation, and a preference for quantity over quality. A century later, Anthony Hanson, in the first edition of his book on Burgundy, wrote in much the same language. Fortunately, Burgundy is currently enjoying a golden age, and the region has never been in better hands than today. More producers, whether growers or merchants, are making finer wine than ever before. This resurgence of quality is particularly noticeable in the region's red wines.

Burgundy was once a great independent duchy, nearly a separate kingdom, that stretched from the foothills of the Alps to Flanders. Today, it is a province of France, where it is known as Bourgogne (*la Bourgogne* refers to the region of Burgundy; *le Bourgogne* to the wine, burgundy). The four departments that make up administrative Burgundy are the Yonne, Nièvre, Côte d'Or and Saône et Loire. Although there are vineyards in the Nièvre, notably at Pouilly-Fumé, from a winemaking point of view they are considered part of the Loire.

The vineyards of Burgundy are usually divided into five groups. Those of the Yonne department are the farthest north; they include the appellations of Chablis, Sauvignon-de-St-Bris and generic Bourgogne, and some recently restored outlying vineyards near the towns of Joigny and Vézelay. Most of the wines produced here are white. To the south, in the department of the Côte d'Or are the Côte de Nuits and the Côte de Beaune. The former runs from the southern outskirts of Dijon to just beyond the town of Nuits-St-Georges; the latter takes over north of Beaune and continues southward through Chassagne-Montrachet, Santenay and Maranges. In both cases, the vineyards lie in a narrow strip that runs along the east-facing hillsides.

South of the market town of Chagny is a handful of villages that forms a loose grouping named the Côte Chalonnaise. The fifth and final region is the Mâconnais, where the hillsides are planted with vines and the valleys are used for growing corn or grazing Charollais cattle and sheep. Here, more than 40 widely scattered villages produce the largest volume of white wine in the whole of Burgundy.

The cities of Burgundy—Dijon, Auxerre, Chalon-sur-Saône and Mâcon—show little evidence of being winemaking centers. It is rather the smaller towns, such as Beaune and Nuits-St-Georges, and certain large villages that the wine seeker must head for.

Landscape and climate

Located in eastern central France, Burgundy has a generally continental climate, with cold winters and warm summers. Overall, the temperature is cooler than in maritime Bordeaux, so Burgundy is very much at the northern limit of red-wine-producing regions.

Most of Burgundy is underpinned by limestone and some of the best soils for winemaking are the Kimmeridgian limestones found in Chablis and the oolitic limestones of the Côte d'Or. The best vineyards of the Mâconnais are found where Bajocian and Bathonian limestone crop up.

Burgundy is the region that best exemplifies the French concept of *terroir*, and it is fascinating to sample the difference between one vineyard and another only 50 yards (46 m) away. Besides soil, the wine's flavor is determined by such factors as the vineyard's exposure to the sun, its slope, aspect, lay of the land and drainage—all these variables play a part in creating a wine even before human intervention, in the form of varying viticultural practices, further shapes the style.

Vines and wines

The two great grapes of Burgundy are chardonnay for white wines and pinot noir for reds. Chardonnay is certainly the most sought-after grape in the world, and it is native to Burgundy. It has many advantages: it is relatively easy to grow, can set a reasonable crop without obvious detriment to quality, ripens more often than not, produces a full-bodied wine that appeals to both experts and beginners alike, and it can be made in a wide variety of different styles.

The Yonne accounts for just under one-third of Burgundy's whites, most of which is chablis. The Saône et Loire, which incorporates the Côte Chalonnaise and the Mâconnais, produces over half the whites. The most famous part of Burgundy, the Côte d'Or, represents about15 percent of white wine production, but it supplies the best quality—Puligny-Montrachet, Chassagne-Montrachet, Corton-Charlemagne and Meursault make Burgundy's great white wines.

Another white grape used in Burgundy is aligoté, traditionally used to make a light, tart wine that is served by the *pichet* (jug) in cafés. After chardonnay, the most significant white-wine grapes are members of the pinot family, particularly pinot gris and pinot blanc. These are mutations of the original red grape (pinot noir).

Pinot noir is much more difficult to grow than chardonnay and, although Burgundy is generally thought to be ideal for this grape, even here success is not guaranteed. Because the pinot skins are relatively thin, tannin generally plays a lesser part in burgundy's ability to age than acidity. Certain years do have high tannin levels but in some instances the fruit never comes into balance with the dryness of the tannin. Only some vintages offer the perfect combination of rich, fully ripe fruit and a decent structure for long-term aging.

Since a wine's color is in part derived from the grape's skin, red burgundy tends to be pale. Winemakers who macerate for maximum color often also extract coarser tannins.

The hallmark of great pinot noir is its beguiling fragrance, which, when the wines are young, covers a whole register of red fruits, from cherries of different sorts through red currants to raspberries, strawberries, and plums. As the wines age, the details of the fragrance emerge. At Premier Cru level or above, it should be multilayered: a wonderful bouquet should slowly unfold,

ABOVE: *Made mainly from chardonnay, white burgundy typically has a golden hue.*

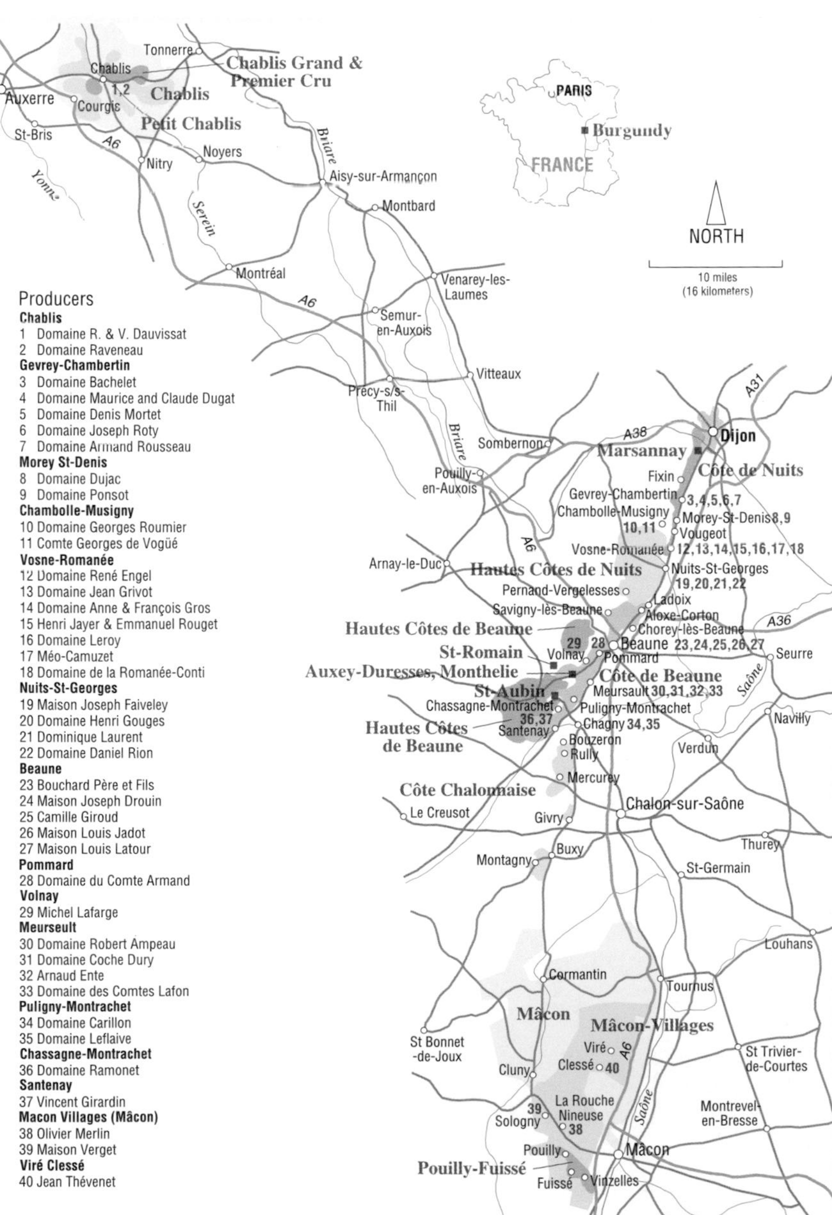

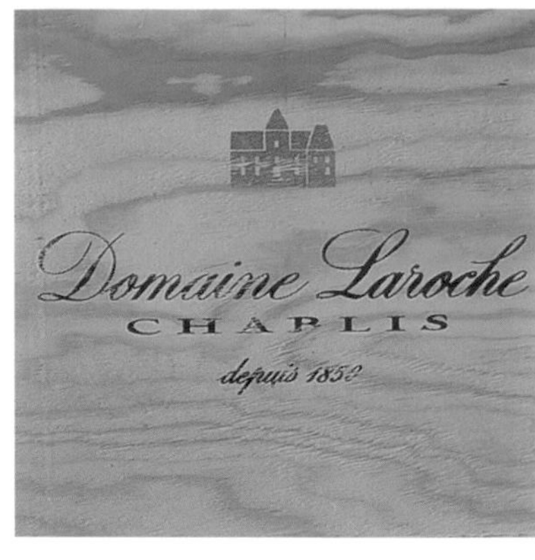

ABOVE: *Domaine Laroche is one of the leading producers in Chablis.*

its core of fruit edged by a decadent leafy, gamey or truffley aroma of decay. Above all, there should be a long, graceful, and lingering finish.

Viticulture and winemaking

Many growers here have switched to organic methods, and a handful of estates, including some of the region's flagship names (Lafon, Leflaive and Leroy), have espoused the use of biodynamic principles. The harvest takes place between mid-September and early October, varying with the area. After harvest, the white grapes are pressed, left overnight to settle (a process known in French as *débourbage*), then run off into tanks or barrels for fermentation. Throughout the region, white wines are still allowed to ferment using natural yeasts. Most cellars are warmed slightly to encourage fermentation. In the last few years, most producers have returned to the formerly standard practice of lees stirring (*bâtonnage*), which nourishes the wine, fleshes it out a bit, and ensures that the natural antioxidant function of the yeast cells acts on all the wine. White wines almost always undergo malolactic fermentation, then the wines are racked and left on fine lees until bottling.

Red grapes may be lightly sulfured when they leave the vineyard, and in warm years they may need to be cooled on arrival at the cellar so that the juice can macerate on the skins for a few days before fermentation begins. Fermentation usually takes place in open-topped vats and is accompanied by regular punching down (*pigeage*). The wine remains in vat for fermentation and maceration for between one and four weeks; it is then run off into barrel, where malolactic fermentation takes place, for further maturation. One racking is performed after the malolactic fermentation; another if the wine needs subsequent aeration.

BELOW: *Vineyards stretch to the horizon in Chablis.*

Growers, co-ops and merchants

The label on a bottle of burgundy gives the name of the producer but you may have to dig a little deeper to find out if the wine has come from an individual grower, a co-operative, or a merchant (*négociant*). Growers' wines are normally identified by words such as *propriétaire-récoltant* (owner-grower) or *mise en bouteilles au domaine* (bottled at the estate), whereas a merchant's wines usually bear the words *négociant-éleveur*. Wines from co-operatives are sometimes disguised as if they were from individual producers, but normally the label will refer to a *cave co-operative, producteurs réunis* or *groupement de producteurs*.

Far more burgundy is marketed by co-operatives and *négociants* than by individual growers. The leading *négociants* sell burgundian wines made with fruit from their own vineyards, and with grapes and wine bought from other suppliers.

Appellations

Almost all the vineyards of Burgundy fall within *appellation contrôlée* regulations. At the bottom level are the generic appellations—Bourgogne Blanc and Rouge, Bourgogne Aligoté and Passetoutgrains, Hautes Côtes de Nuits and Côtes de Beaune, and Mâcon. At the next level are the communal or village appellations, which include such famous names as Gevrey-Chambertin and Puligny-Montrachet. Excepting the Mâconnais district, the best vineyards of each village are classified as Premiers Crus. The very best vineyards are classified as Grand Cru. However, the status of any given wine depends on the potential quality of the patch of vineyard from which it came. Appellation laws also specify where vines can be planted, which grape varieties are allowed, how they must be pruned, what yields are permitted, and minimum sugar levels.

THE YONNE

The most northerly of Burgundy's departments, the Yonne rarely experiences enough warmth to ripen red grapes, but it is home to one of the most famous of all white wines, chablis. Its location also makes it the most logical place in Burgundy for a major production center of sparkling wine.

DOMAINE RAVENEAU

Owner **Jean-Marie Raveneau** ***Production*** **4,000 cases** ***Vineyard area*** **20 acres (8 ha)**

François Raveneau, now retired, established this *domaine* as the greatest name in Chablis, and his son Jean-Marie is continuing the good work. Old barrels are still used to make fascinating, rich, complex chablis from the Grands Crus of Valmur, Les Clos and Blanchots, and Premiers Crus such as Chapelots and Fôrets. Twenty- or thirty-year-old wines from Raveneau *père* are still fabulous.

Other reliable chablis producers include Domaines Adhémar Boudin, Defaix, Droin, Grossot, Laroche, Michel, Picq and Vocoret, as well as the co-operative La Chablisienne.

ABOVE: *The historic town of Chablis, which has given its name to a type of white wine.*

Bourgogne

The best areas are currently enjoying something of a renaissance. They are, for reds only, Irancy, and, for reds and whites, Côtes d'Auxerre, Epineuil, Coulanges-La-Vineuse, Chitry, and a bit farther afield, Vézelay and Côte St-Jacques. The village of Chitry is also locally well known for its Bourgogne Aligoté.

Sauvignon-de-St-Bris

Sauvignon-de-St-Bris is the only wine in Burgundy that has VDQS status; it is also the only wine in the region that is made from sauvignon blanc. The best grower is J.-H. Goisot.

CÔTE DE NUITS

The department of the Côte d'Or (the Slope of Gold) is somewhat romantically named for the vine-covered escarpment that rises from the valley of the Saône below. By custom, this is divided into two halves (the boundary is in fact the ancient dividing line between the bishoprics of Langres and Autun): the Côte de Nuits and the Côte de Beaune. As well as the major appellations described below, numerous vineyards in the Côte d'Or are located wherever favorable sites can be found in the hills and valleys of the plateau behind the famous slope.

The Côte de Nuits makes Burgundy's greatest red wines from villages such as Gevrey-Chambertin, Vosne-Romanée and Nuits-St-Georges, and the Grands Crus of Chambertin, Musigny and La Romanée-Conti—all located in a narrow band of vineyards rarely more than half a mile (1 km) wide.

Côte de Nuits Villages

Although many villages in the Côte de Beaune can market their wines either under their own village name or as Côte de Beaune Villages, the less-favored communes of the Côte de Nuits are permitted to use only the general appellation of Côte de Nuits Villages.

These communes are Fixin (in part) and Brochon (in part) at the northern end of the Côte de Nuits, along with Prémeaux-Prissey (in part), Corgoloin and Comblanchien to the south. There is a tiny amount of white Côte de Nuits Villages made, but the vast majority of the wine produced is a light, refreshing red wine made for early drinking.

Chablis

The key to chablis is the soil the grapes grow on: Kimmeridgian soil, a limestone-clay mix, full of tiny marine fossils, which gives the wine its energetic, flinty character. Another fossil-free, local soil produces wines without the authentic chablis character. There was almost civil war in Chablis in the early 1970s when a group of vignerons set about expanding the appellation to include slopes on this soil. The purists were horrified, but eventually the expansionists won out.

Most straight chablis wines can be drunk fairly young, though some producers make them to keep. Premier Cru wines usually benefit from two or three years in bottle. Chablis Grand Cru wines, the highest classification, are powerful and concentrated, and need to be kept for five or more years—not something you usually think of doing with chablis.

ABOVE: *The view across the vineyards to the town of Nuits-St-Georges in the Côte de Nuits.*

Marsannay

The vineyards here are in danger of being overwhelmed by the urban sprawl of Dijon. The appellation covers all three colors, though the whites are modest and the reds usually on the light side; there are no Premier or Grand Cru vineyards. Originally, Marsannay's reputation was built on its rosé wines. The best grower in the village is Bruno Clair, who has vineyards up and down the Côte. Other good sources for Marsannay are Domaines Charlopin, Coillot, Collotte, Guyard and Naddef.

Fixin

The wines of Fixin are much more substantial than those of Marsannay—deeper in color, with greater depth of fruit and noticeably more tannin, which means they need three to five years in bottle before drinking. They resemble Gevrey-Chambertin, but cost much less. The best vineyards are the Premiers Crus of Les Arvelets, Les Hervelets, Clos de la Perrière, Clos du Chapitre and Clos Napoleon; and interesting growers are Berthaut and Gelin.

Gevrey-Chambertin

The wines of Gevrey-Chambertin, when properly made, are among the longest-lived burgundies. Deeper in color than most, they are not immediately appealing and do not display the soft red fruit one might expect; instead, they are more full-bodied and the fruit is sometimes masked by a fair dose of tannin. After several years in bottle, however, the classical, autumnal, gently decaying flavors of great burgundy usually develop. Good vintages should be kept for at least five years.

Gevrey-Chambertin is blessed with eight Grands Crus: Chambertin and Chambertin Clos de Bèze lead the pack, making majestic, powerful, profound wines that require between 15 and 30 years maturation in the best vintages. Ruchottes-Chambert in and Griotte-Chambertin have very thin soils, so the wines are lighter in color but wonderfully perfumed. Latricières-Chambertin and Mazis- (or Mazy-) Chambertin are a touch fuller and richer. The most seductive is Charmes-Chambertin, although it can disappoint—as Chapelle-Chambertin usually does.

The best Premier Cru, which some think better than all but the top two Grands Crus, is Clos St-Jacques, which lies on a separate slope. Other good Premier Cru vineyards are Cazetiers, Lavaux St-Jacques, Estournelles St-Jacques and Combottes.

DOMAINE DENIS MORTET

Owner **Denis Mortet** ***Production*** **4,000 cases** ***Vineyard area*** **25 acres (10 ha)**

Despite having inherited a *domaine* with a modest reputation, Denis Mortet has risen to fame with his deeply colored, quite heavily extracted wines made from a range of village Gevrey-Chambertin vineyards and a tiny bit of Le Chambertin. The most recent vintages indicate that he is searching for a touch more refinement along with the power.

DOMAINE JOSEPH ROTY

Owner **Joseph Roty** ***Production*** **3,200 cases** ***Vineyard area*** **20 acres (8 ha)**

Joseph Roty's forceful personality shows through in the character of his wines, which were dark, concentrated and oaky even in the early 1980s when such a style was rare in Burgundy. Roty's range of single-vineyard Gevrey-Chambertin wines is supplemented by tiny amounts of Griottes-Chambertin, Mazy-Chambertin and a wonderful Charmes-Chambertin made from very old vines and labelled *très vieilles vignes*.

Other recommended producers include Bernard Dugat-Py, Alain Burguet, Philippe Charlopin, Michel Esmonin et Fille, Dominique Gallois, Géantet-Pansiot, Domaine Hereszytn and Christian Serafin.

Morey St-Denis

The wines here are usually described as having the elegance of Chambolle with the structure of Gevrey-Chambertin, but do have not quite as much of either.

Good Premier Cru vineyards include Clos de la Bussière (Roumier), Clos des Ormes (Lignier) and Les Millandes (Amiot), but the pride of the village is its range of Grands Crus. Two of these are monopolies: Clos de Tart belongs exclusively to the Mommessin family and makes worthy wine in great vintages, slightly dull wine in other years; the Saier family's Clos des Lambrays, on the other hand, seems to be returning to consistent form. The others are Clos St-Denis and Clos de la Roche, plus a part of Bonnes Mares that is mostly in Chambolle-Musigny. It was from Clos St-Denis that Morey derived part of its name.

DOMAINE DUJAC

***Owner* Jacques Seysses *Production* 4,500 cases**
***Vineyard area* 28 acres (11.5 ha)**

A *domaine* put together by Jacques Seysses since 1968, it consists of Clos de la Roche, Clos St-Denis, Bonnes Mares, Charmes-Chambertin, Echézeaux, Chambolle-Musigny Les Gruenchers, Vosne-Romanée Les Beaux-monts, Gevrey-Chambertin Les Combottes and Morey St-Denis. Dujac's controversial wines are frequently light in color when young and carry the aroma of the stalks, which are not removed—a rarity nowadays. After a few years in bottle, however, a magnificent perfume transcends any youthful awkwardness.

Other notable producers in Mory St-Denis include Domaines Perrot-Minot, Hubert Lignier, Georges Lignier and Jean Raphet.

Chambolle-Musigny

A typical Chambolle-Musigny is the most elegant wine in Burgundy. The soil in this appellation incudes a high proportion of active chalk and not much clay, so the wines tend not to be deep-colored nor especially full-bodied; however, they make up for this with an exquisite, lacy delicacy and a sublime fragrance.

There are two Grands Crus—Musigny and Bonnes Mares—and some outstanding Premier Cru vineyards. Le Musigny harnesses all of the fragrance that typifies Chambolle to sumptuous weight and body. This is one of Burgundy's most majestic wines, conjuring up the image of an iron fist in a velvet glove. Such wines need to age for a minimum of 15 years. De Vogüé, Mugnier, Drouhin and Jadot are the finest producers. Bonnes Mares, on the Morey St-Denis side of the village, is relatively full-bodied and structured and will develop some of the untamed characteristics of Morey. De Vogüé, Roumier, Groffier and Jadot are the leading producers of the wine, which again should be kept for a decade or more.

ABOVE: *One of the boundaries of the Grand Cru vineyards of Chambertin.*

The Premier Cru Les Amoureuses is the sensual understudy to Le Musigny. Every bit as seductive, it matures more quickly and can thrill the palate even in its first five years. Once again, the best sources are de Vogüé, Roumier, Mugnier, Groffier, Drouhin and Jadot. Les Charmes comes close behind Les Amoureuses, followed by Les Cras, Les Sentiers, Les Feussellotes and Les Fuées. The best producers of village Chambolle-Musigny are Roumier, Mugnier, Groffier, Ghislaine Barthod, Pierre Bertheau and Patrice Rion.

COMTE GEORGES DE VOGÜÉ

***Owner* Baronne de Ladoucette *Production* 3,600 cases**
***Vineyard area* 30 acres (12 ha)**

This impressive *domaine* is to Chambolle-Musigny what Domaine de la Romanée-Conti is to Vosne-Romanée. It makes grand Le Musigny, Bonnes Mares, Chambolle-Musigny Les Amoureuses, Chambolle-Musigny and a little white Musigny. Nowadays the reds have immense concentration of fruit, which seems to come from the vineyard—there is no sense of overextraction or of coarse use of oak here. Naturally massive, they should be kept for many years. Avoid most vintages of the 1970s and 1980s, but even the lesser vintages of the 1990s have been most impressive.

BELOW: *Vineyard managers carry out winter maintenance work at Domaine Dujac.*

ABOVE: *The entrance to one of the many holdings in the historic Clos de Vougeot Grand Cru.*

Vougeot

Cistercian monks identified this as prime vineyard land as early as the twelfth century, and in the fourteenth century they enclosed the land with a stone wall, or *clos*. Today, there are at least 80 different proprietors and quality varies widely from producer to producer, depending on their winemaking skills and the location of their holdings.

Clos de Vougeot is not a seductive wine when young. It is deep in color, powerful and concentrated, with a fairly tannic structure. Rather than red fruits, it displays black fruits, chocolate and even coffee. Good examples will age for up to 50 years, but this is more of a blockbuster than a subtly suggestive wine.

The best producers are Anne Gros, René Engel, Méo-Camuzet, Jadot, Leroy and Faiveley. Look out also for the wines of Domaine de la Vougeraie, owned by Jean-Claude Boisset and made from the 1999 vintage onward by Pascal Marchand.

Regional Dozen

CÔTE DE NUITS

Domaine Anne & François Gros Richebourg
Domaine Bertagna Clos de Vougeot
Domaine Denis Mortet Gevrey-Chambertin
Domaine Dujac Chambolle Musigny
Henri Jayer Echezeaux
Domaine Ponsot Clos de la Roche Vieilles Vignes
Domaine de la Romanée Conti Romanée Conti
Emmanuel Rouget Echezeaux
Domaine Georges Roumier Bonnes Mares
Domaine Armand Rousseau Chambertin
Frederic Esmonin Ruchottes Chambertin
Comte Georges de Vogüé Musigny

Vosne-Romanée

If Chambolle-Musigny epitomises finesse and Gevrey-Chambertin *gravitas*, only Vosne-Romanée can combine the two qualities. The wines have a striking elegance on top of a brilliantly concentrated structure, without ever seeming heavy. Village-level Vosne-Romanée is fine, balanced and attractive quite early; the Grands Crus are exceptionally long-lived. Four are owned entirely by single *domaines*: La Romanée-Conti and La Tâche by Domaine de la Romanée-Conti; La Grande Rue (promoted from Premier Cru in 1992) by Domaine Lamarche; and La Romanée by the Liger-Belair family, though the house of Bouchard Père et Fils is responsible for bottling and marketing.

The Grand Cru vineyards of Richebourg make a wonderfully rich, profound wine, and Romanée-St-Vivant, whose 23 acres (9.3 ha) yield a wine that is a touch lighter and very stylish, both have a variety of owners. Domaine de la Romanée-Conti, Leroy and Hudelot-Noellat produce both wines. Anne Gros, Grivot and Méo-Camuzet produce excellent examples of Richebourg; very fine Romanée-St-Vivant can be found *chez* Drouhin and Arnoux.

By convention, the only two vineyards in the commune of Flagey-Echézeaux are considered part of Vosne-Romanée. They are both Grands Crus, Echézeaux and Grands Echézeaux. Though the former with 93 acres (38 ha) is a little too large to be worthy of this status. Reliable, often exciting wines from these vineyards are made by Domaine de la Romanée-Conti, René Engel (both), Drouhin (Grands Echézeaux), Rouget, Dujac, Grivot and Confuron-Cotétidot (all Echézeaux).

The outstanding Premier Cru vineyards here, with the leading exponents given in brackets, are: Malconsorts (Hudelot-Noellat, Thomas-Moillard), Clos de Réas (Michel Gros), Cros Parentoux (Méo-Camuzet, Henri Jayer, Emmanuel Rouget), Les Brulées (Engel, Grivot, Leroy, Méo-Camuzet), Beauxmonts (Leroy, Rouget, Rion, Jadot), and Suchots (Arnoux, Grivot, Jadot).

All of the above producers, plus Domaines Cathiard, Clavelier, Confuron-Cotétidot, Forey and various Mugnerets, also make outstanding village Vosne-Romanée.

HENRI JAYER & EMMANUEL ROUGET

Owner **Emmanuel Rouget** ***Production*** **2,500 cases** ***Vineyard area*** **17 acres (7 ha)**

Now in retirement, Henri Jayer became the most famous of all growers for his wonderfully rich, perfumed and marvellously harmonious red wines. His nephew, Emmanuel Rouget, is his heir both to the vineyards and the style. The wines include Echézeaux, Vosne-Romanée Les Beaumonts, Vosne-Romanée Cros Parentoux, Vosne-Romanée and Nuits-St-Georges.

DOMAINE LEROY

Owner **Lalou Bize-Leroy** ***Production*** **5,000 cases** ***Vineyard area*** **56 acres (22.5 ha)**

In 1998, Domaine Leroy purchased Domaine Charles Noellat, which included Richebourg, Romanée-St-Vivant, Clos de Vougeot, Vosne-Romanée Beauxmonts, Vosne-Romanée Les Brulées and Nuits-St-Georges Boudots. More recent acquisitions have added Le Musigny, Le Chambertin, Latricières Chambertin, Clos de la Roche and Volnay-Santenots. The Leroy estate is run biodynamically with tiny yields; the wines have extraordinary concentration and longevity—and astronomical prices.

DOMAINE DE LA ROMANÉE-CONTI

***Owners* de Villaine and Leroy families *Production* 6,500 cases**
***Vineyard area* 63 acres (25.5 ha)**

This is the grandest *domaine* of them all, making nothing but Grand Cru wines, including the wines from the two vineyards that it owns outright, La Romanée-Conti and La Tâche. The other wines include Richebourg, Romanée-St-Vivant, Grands Echézeaux, Echézeaux and Le Montrachet. Yields are kept low and stems are left on during vinification. This is a practice that is now rare; it can give the wines a slightly austere edge when young, but it seems to provide structure for the long term. Even the most modest of the wines is wonderfully perfumed, silky and gracious. The top wines have the same delicacy, to which they add a massive, powerful framework that requires years of bottle age for them to reach perfection.

Nuits-St-Georges

The capital of the Côte-de-Nuits, Nuits-St-Georges is home to a number of the region's *négociants*, notably Faiveley and Boisset, as well as all the houses that have been taken over by the latter.

The village has no Grands Crus, although Les St-Georges would be promoted by some authorities and Les Vaucrains and Les Cailles are of comparable quality. The Nuits-St-Georges appellation extends south to include much of the commune of Prémeaux. The soil in Nuits-St-Georges is richer than in neighboring Vosne-Romanée, with a higher clay content. As a result, the wines are deeper-colored, full-bodied, sturdy, a little more tannic and a little less fine. All are worth aging for the medium term, and in the case of traditionalist producers such as Gouges, for several decades.

Half a dozen *domaines* produce white Nuits-St-Georges, which was first made by Henri Gouges from pinot noir that had degenerated into pinot blanc. Domaine de l'Arlot and Domaine Daniel Rion also make interesting examples.

MAISON JOSEPH FAIVELEY

***Owner* François Faiveley *Production* NA**
***Vineyard area* 285 acres (115 ha)**

Though technically a *négociant*, Maison Joseph Faiveley has sufficient vineyards of its own to supply most of its needs. The red wines are deep in color and sometimes quite tannic, making them a trifle ungainly in their youth but capable of long aging. The range includes a fine selection of Grands Crus, a number of Nuits-St-Georges including the whole production of Clos de la Maréchale, and a major holding of Mercurey in the Côte Chalonnaise. Only a handful of white wines are produced, including Mercurey Blanc and a little exquisite Corton-Charlemagne.

BELOW: The historic Clos de Vougeot Grand Cru vineyard has at least 80 registered owners.

DOMAINE HENRI GOUGES

Owners **Christian and Pierre Gouges** ***Production*** **5,500 cases**
Vineyard area **36 acres (14.5 ha)**

Gouge wines are not always appreciated because they are made for the long term and sometimes lack youthful appeal. But the superb range of Nuits-St-Georges Premiers Crus, notably Les St-Georges, Vaucrains, Clos des Porrets St-Georges and Pruliers, will reward long aging. The *domaine* also makes a small quantity of interesting white Nuits-St-Georges from pinot blanc.

DOMINIQUE LAURENT

Owner **Dominique Laurent** ***Production*** **NA** ***Vineyard area*** **None**

This former pastry chef turned *mini-négociant* specializes in small batches of red wines sourced from low-yielding, old vines. Laurent is a devotee of new oak, and has been celebrated by some for using what has been described as "200 percent new wood"—meaning that he racks his wine from one new barrel into another brand new one. The wines are certainly concentrated and can be fabulous, but sometimes the taste of the vineyard is lost behind the style of vinification and maturation.

Other top producers include Robert Chevillon (fruity wines from eight Premier Cru vineyards including Les St-Georges, Les Cailles and Vaucrains); Robert Arnoux (full, oaky Les Corvées-Pagets and Les Procès); Domaine de l'Arlot (fine, perfumed Clos de l'Arlot and Clos des Forêts St-Georges); Domaine Daniel Rion (modern structured wines from Haut Pruliers, Clos de Argillières and Vignes Rondes); and from neighboring Vosne-Romanée, Grivot (Les Boudots, Les Pruliers and Les Roncières).

CÔTE DE BEAUNE

The Côte de Beaune begins northwest of the town of Beaune and stretches southwest into the northern Sâone et Loire near the town of Chagny. This is again an excellent source of red wines, although none can match the greatest reds of the Côte de Nuits. However, the outstanding wines here are the whites from Montrachet vineyards, Meursault and Corton-Charlemagne.

Côte de Beaune Villages

This is a catch-all appellation for red wines coming from 14 villages within the Côte de Beaune. These are either major white-wine producers (Meursault, Puligny-Montrachet, Chassagne-Montrachet) that also make some red wine, or else villages of lesser fame (north of Beaune: Ladoix, Pernand-Vergelesses, Savigny-lès-Beaune and Chorey-lès-Beaune; to the south: Monthelie, Auxey-Duresses, Blagny, St-Aubin, St-Romain, Santenay and Maranges) whose own names, which they can opt to use, are not strong brands. Confusingly, there is also a small appellation (for both colors) called Côte de Beaune, which covers a handful of vineyards rather too high up on the hillside above Beaune to yield top wine.

Ladoix

The Ladoix vineyards are located on the eastern slope of the hill of Corton and indeed almost all the vineyards of merit are classified as Corton, including Rognets and Vergennes, or as Corton-Charlemagne. Some village and Premier Cru vineyards are classified as Ladoix, but these are rarely seen. The best-known growers are Prince de Mérode, Domaines Capitain-Gagnerot, Edmond Cornu, Maldant, Mallard and Nudant.

BELOW: *The village of Pernand-Vergelesses is tucked into a side valley off the main slope.*

Pernand-Vergelesses

This village has two vineyards of note. The first is the "En Charlemagne" part of the Grand Cru Corton-Charlemagne, which produces one of Burgundy's most thrilling white wines. The outstanding producer in the village is Bonneau du Martray; Dubreuil Fontaine, Marey, Rollin and Rapet also make good wine. The second significant vineyard, the Premier Cru Les Vergelesses, which lies across the valley and faces due east, is the source of the best red wines. Chandon de Briailles makes the best example. Otherwise, the red and white wines of Pernand-Vergelesses can be rather angular.

Aloxe-Corton

The village and Premier Cru wines of Aloxe-Corton are a little expensive for their quality. Aloxe is the headquarters for the *négociants* Louis Latour and La Reine Pedauque as well as for Domaines Senard, Voarick and Follin-Arvelet. However, the local jewels are the Grands Crus Corton-Charlemagne (white) and Corton (mostly red), though both are shared with neighboring Pernand-Vergelesses and Ladoix.

Domaine Bonneau du Martray, Maison Louis Latour and Maison Louis Jadot produce the most impressive Corton-Charlemagne in reasonable quantity; smaller quantities from Michel Juillot, Coche-Dury, Tollot-Beaut, Faiveley and Roumier can also be excellent. A great Corton-Charlemagne, best drunk after a decade or more in bottle, will combine a scintillating mineral quality with depth of flavor and Grand Cru richness.

The red Grand Cru, Corton, covers a number of subdivisions and it could be argued that these should either become Grands Crus in their own right or else be demoted. The best of them are Le Corton (Bonneau du Martray and Méo-Camuzet), Corton-Bressandes (Prince de Mérode and Comte Senard) and Corton Clos du Roi (Prince de Mérode and Comte Senard), along with the Corton-Pougets of Maison Louis Jadot, Corton Clos des Cortons of Maison Joseph Faiveley and the Corton Clos de la Vigne au Saint of Maison Louis Latour. A bottle which is labelled simply Corton, without the "Le," could be from one or more of the subdivisions.

Savigny-lès-Beaune

Savigny is a sound bet for good-quality red burgundy at an affordable price. The wines are attractive when they are young (especially those from Premier Cru vineyards such as Lavières), yet they are sturdy enough to age well (particularly Peuillets and Dominodes). The best producers in the village are Domaine Chandon de Briailles, Simon Bize et Fils, Jean-Marc Pavelot, Jean-Jacques and Philippe Girard, and Luc Camus-Brochon. The Savigny Narbantons of Leroy and the Savigny Dominodes of Bruno Clair are also excellent. The small quantity of white Savigny is of less interest.

Chorey-lès-Beaune

Single-vineyard wines are rarely if ever encountered here. Most of the production is red, and consists of a fruity, Côte-de-Beaune-style burgundy best drunk quite young. The leading growers in the village are Tollot-Beaut, Jacques Germain at the Château de Chorey-lès-Beaune and Arnoux Père et Fils.

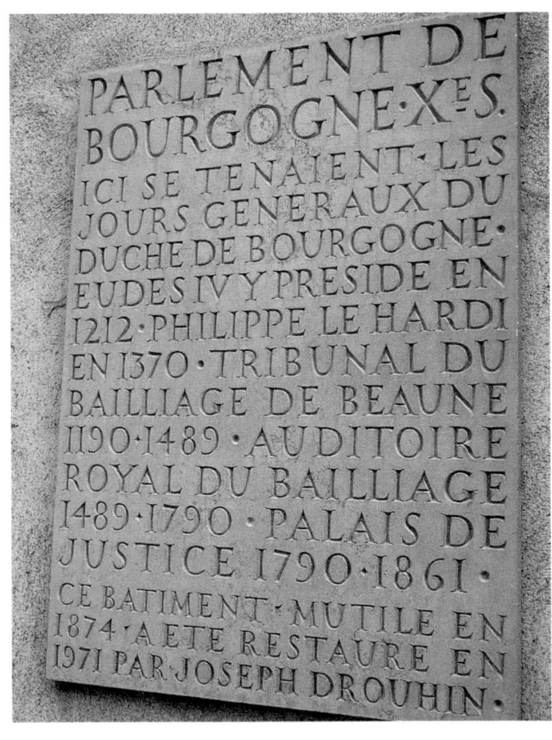

ABOVE: *This plaque outside the cellars of Joseph Drouhin in Beaune commemorates the long and distinguished history of the building.*

Les Trois Glorieuses

Burgundy is also famous for its festivals, most notably Les Trois Glorieuses, the "Three Glorious Feasts," which take place during the weekend of the Hospices de Beaune charity auction, held on the third Sunday in November.

The first feast is the Saturday-night celebration organized by the Chevaliers de Tastevin in their headquarters, the Clos de Vougeot. Guests enjoy abundant food, plenty of wine, rather too many speeches, and some cheerful singing from a local group called "Les Joyeux Bourguignons."

On the Sunday, the auction itself takes place in Les Halles, the covered market opposite the Hôtel Dieu. This is a long, drawn-out affair in which barrels of new wine from the vineyards belonging to the Hospices de Beaune are sold off at relatively elevated prices (reflecting the charitable purpose of the auction) which, however, provide some indication of the price levels that can be expected in the new season. Another formal dinner follows, and is again washed down with much wine and song.

The third and most entertaining feast is the Paulée de Meursault, held in the Château de Meursault at lunchtime on the Monday. A substantial meal is served to the 600-odd guests, who each bring bottles (or cases) of their own wines, including both recent vintages and older ones. As the bottles are passed up and down the tables, "Les Joyeux Bourguignons" once more provide the musical accompaniment. Afterward, many of the cellars in the village are opened so that revellers can continue to explore the merits of Meursault wines.

ABOVE: *Southern Burgundy, where temperatures are generally higher than in the north.*

Beaune

The capital of winegrowing Burgundy, Beaune is home to most of the major *négociants*. The vineyards themselves are not among the most distinguished of the Côte: there is a fair amount of sand in the soil, especially in the northern part of the appellation, so the grapes tend to mature fairly quickly. The wines are sound, middle-of-the-road examples of red burgundy. There are no Grands Crus but a plethora of Premiers Crus among which Grèves, Fèves, Clos du Roi, Bressandes and Teurons stand out. The four great *négociant* houses of Beaune are Bouchard Père et Fils, Joseph Drouhin, Louis Jadot and Louis Latour.

MAISON LOUIS JADOT

Owner **the Kopf family** ***Production*** **NA** ***Vineyard area*** **148 acres (60 ha)**

Maison Louis Jadot makes powerful wines including very good Beaune Clos des Ursules, Beaune Grèves and Beaune Boucherottes and Corton-Pougets, plus such Grands Crus from the Côte de Nuits as Chambertin Clos de Bèze and Le Musigny. The estate's white wines are unusual in that the malolactic fermentation is often deliberately blocked. Particularly impressive are their Chevalier-Montrachet Les Demoiselles, Corton-Charlemagne, Chassagne-Montrachet and, at an inexpensive level, Rully.

Pommard

Pommard wines fetch the highest prices in the Côte de Beaune after Corton, despite the fact that their relatively high tannin content, which requires substantial aging, makes them unfashionable. They are firm, deep wines that are slow to mature and have little immediate charm.

The best vineyards are Les Rugiens, south of the village, whose stony red soil produces a Pommard with great depth of flavor, and the various Epenots vineyards to the north: Grands Epenots, Petits Epenots and the Clos des Epeneaux. Here the slope is gentler and the wines finer, if less rich.

DOMAINE DU COMTE ARMAND

Owner **Comte Armand** ***Production*** **NA** ***Vineyard Area*** **NA**

Comte Armand is noted for its immensely rich, black, tannic Pommard Clos des Epeneaux, to which it has sole rights and which for a long period was its only wine. Now, it has additional red wines from Auxey-Duresses and Volnay, along with a little white wine. Between 1985 and 1998, the wines were made by the talented Pascal Marchand; his successor, Benjamin Leroux, looks set to maintain or even improve his high standards.

Other leading sources are Domaine de Courcel (Pommard Rugiens and Pommard Grands Epenots), Domaine Coste-Caumartin (Clos des Boucherottes),

Domaine Parent (Epenots, Pézerolles) and Jean-Marc Boillot (fine Pommard from Rugiens, Saussilles and Jarolières), who is possibly better known for his range of white wines. Outside the village Michel Lafarge, Marquis d'Angerville and Hubert de Montille in Volnay are also all excellent sources of Premier Cru Pommard.

Volnay

The Côte de Beaune's most elegant wines are produced in Volnay, which is totally different from neighboring Pommard. Comparisons can more easily be drawn with Chambolle-Musigny in the Côte de Nuits: in both cases, the wines lack deep color but are wonderfully perfumed, subtle and complex, and, despite their appeal when young, can age very well. In the best examples, a fine structure is overlaid with the gorgeous, velvety texture of ripe fruit. There are no Grands Crus in Volnay, but half a dozen Premiers Crus stand out: Les Caillerets (including the Clos des 60 Ouvrées belonging to Domaine de la Pousse d'Or); Clos des Chênes (outstanding examples come from Michel Lafarge as well as Comtes Lafon); Taillepieds (the best come from Marquis d'Angerville, Hubert de Montille and Carré Courbin); and Champans (especially de Montille and Lafon).

The other leading vineyard, Santenots, is in fact over the border in Meursault but is allowed to use the name of Volnay.

MICHEL LAFARGE

Owner **Michel Lafarge** ***Production*** **4,000 cases** ***Vineyard Area*** **25 acres (10 ha)**

The wines here are the finest in Volnay—perhaps in the Côte de Beaune. They are not overextracted or overoaked, yet are dark in color and intense in flavor. Lafarge produces Beaune Grèves and Pommard Les Pézérolles, plus a fine range of Volnays, topped by a superb Clos des Chênes, a benchmark for Volnay.

Monthelie

This village sits on the hill above Meursault. The local reds have a slightly harder edge and not quite the same depth of fruit as Volnays. The best examples come from Darviot-Perrin, de Suremain and Garaudet, and from Lafon in Meursault. Les Duresses is the best vineyard.

Auxey-Duresses

"Duresses" (which is derived from Les Duresses in Monthelie) refers to a certain hardness found in both red and white wines of the village. The wines are good value only in warm years. Jean-Pierre Diconne, the Prunier family, various Lafouges and Maison Leroy are all worth investigating.

St-Romain

The vineyards of St-Romain are significantly higher than the rest of the Côte, so ripeness is harder to achieve and the style tends to be lean. There are no Premier or Grand Cru vineyards here; production is divided fairly equally between reds and whites. St-Romain's leading winegrower is Alain Gras.

Meursault

The largest great white-wine village of the Côte d'Or, Meursault produces full-bodied, round, satisfying wine each year. There may be no Grands Crus, but there are many excellent vineyards and more competent growers than either Puligny- or Chassagne-Montrachet can boast. Mature meursault (five to ten years old) is buttery and nutty; when younger, it is rounded and weighty—the full bouquet needs time to develop.

Three of Meursault's Premier Cru vineyards stand out. Genevrières has light, stony soil that yields wines with a thrilling, racy, mineral quality, abundant finesse and not too much weight. Try those made by Lafon, François Jobard and Rémi Jobard. Charmes has a soft, rich texture. Look for the same producers plus Ampeau, Roulot and Darviot-Perrin. Perrières combines the best of both the others, but outdoes both. The top producers are Lafon, Coche-Dury, Grivault (for their Clos des Perrières), Morey and Roulot. Other good Premier Cru vineyards are Poruzot and Goutte d'Or.

One of Meursault's great strengths is its village wine: Tesson (from Bouzereau, Fichet, Roulot and Pierre Morey), Chevalières (Coche-Dury and Fichet), Narvaux (Coche Dury, Javillier and Leroy) and Clos de la Barre (Lafon).

Most producers in Meursault have underground cellars where they keep their wine in barrel for two winters. These wines often settle during the second winter, and require little stabilization before bottling; they also seem to gain in richness and longevity. Some red is produced, mostly for local consumption. Santenots is the red vineyard of real quality—it uses the name Volnay-Santenots.

BELOW: A cellar-hand records fluctuations in temperature on the outside of a barrel.

ABOVE: Burning off the dead wood in fall at Domaine Robert Ampeau, Côte de Beaune.

At the southern end of Meursault lies Blagny. The white wines produced here are designated as Meursault Blagny Premier Cru, a status they generally do not deserve, and the red wines, which are mostly light and austere and sometimes have a delicious cherry perfume, are called Blagny.

DOMAINE COCHE DURY

Owner **Jean-François Coche Dury** ***Production*** **3,500 cases**
Vineyard area **22 acres (9 ha)**

Dury makes hyper-elegant, fine and exciting Meursault from Les Perrières (Premier Cru), Les Narvaux, Les Rougeots and other vineyards, in addition to a tiny amount of Grand Cru Corton-Charlemagne. These wines have a near-perfect delineation of detail and much more power than the attractive floral bouquet would suggest. Increasingly good reds, mostly from lesser appellations are also made.

Puligny-Montrachet

The most famous of the white wine villages is Puligny, which, since the late nineteenth century, has been allowed to append the noble name of Montrachet. The Grand Montrachet vineyard, only 20 acres (8 ha) in size, has been considered the most sublime of Burgundy's white-wine vineyards since the early eighteenth century. To recommend producers is really just to tease, since only the extraordinarily rich can afford a bottle, but the wines of Lafon, Ramonet, Domaine de la Romanée-Conti, Leflaive, Marquis de Laguiche, Baron Thénard and Bouchard Père et Fils, should live up to the vineyard's reputation. Do not be in a hurry to drink a fine vintage—any time in its first 50 years will do.

Just uphill from Le Montrachet is the Grand Cru of Chevalier-Montrachet, where the soil is thinner and the wines not quite so opulent; however, they can still be enormously impressive, particularly those from Domaine Leflaive, Michel Niellon, Louis Jadot and Louis Latour. The last two producers share a special and much sought-after patch known as Les Demoiselles. Just below Le Montrachet are the Grands Crus of Bâtard-Montrachet, Bienvenues-Bâtard-Montrachet and Criots-Bâtard-Montrachet. The last-named is in fact entirely in the commune of Chassagne-Montrachet; Le Montrachet and Bâtard-Montrachet are shared between the two villages. The wines of the various Bâtards are a little more approachable than Chevalier-Montrachet, but also slightly less fine. Give them a decade of bottle age before opening.

Most consumers look to Puligny-Montrachet for more affordable Premier Cru and village wines. Puligny has a fine range of the former: Les Caillerets (particularly from Hubert de Montille and Michel Bouzereau); Les Pucelles (especially from Domaine Leflaive); Les Combettes (Leflaive and Sauzet); Les Folatières (Leflaive, Chavy and Pernot); and Les Demoiselles. In these vineyards, the wines combine a marvellous floral perfume and elegance with a steely backbone that promises both concentration and longevity.

The village wines have some flowery elegance but less concentration. Carillon and Jean-Marc Boillot are among the most reliable sources of fine Puligny-Montrachet village wines. Good *négociant* selections are available from Jadot, Drouhin and Leflaive.

DOMAINE CARILLON

Owner **Louis Carillon** ***Production*** **5,000 cases**
Vineyard Area **30 acres (12 ha)**

The Carillons have been a reliable source of Puligny-Montrachet for several generations (since at least 1632, they claim), but over the last 15 years they have risen to close to the top of the pile thanks to their fine, pure, white wines, which typify the respective vineyard sites—from village Puligny through the Premier Crus Les Combettes, Champs-Canet, Champ-Gain, Perrières and Referts, to the Grand Cru Bienvenues-Bâtard-Montrachet. The wines are delicious to drink quite young, yet hold together well for a decade.

Regional Dozen

CÔTE DE BEAUNE (RED)

Domaine du Comte Armand Pommard Clos des Epeneaux
Tollot-Beaut Chorey-lès-Beaune
Chandon de Briailles Pernand Vergelesses Île de Vergelesses
Maison Joseph Faiveley Corton Clos des Cortons
Vincent Girardin Santenay Gravières
Michel Lafarge Volnay Clos des Chênes
Domaine des Comtes Lafon Volnay-Santenots-du-Milieu
Méo-Camuzet Corton
Hubert de Montille Volnay-Champans
Domaine Muzard Santenay Clos de Tavannes
J.-M. Pavelot Savigny-lès-Beaune La Dominode
Nicolas Potel Bourgogne Rouge

St-Aubin

This village is best known for its white wines, which are similar to a lesser Puligny-Montrachet. However the fruity, if sometimes lean, red wines account for more than half the total production. Look out for the Premiers Crus En Remilly, Murgers Dents de Chien, La Chatenière and (for reds) Les Frionnes. Notable growers include Marc Colin, Hubert Lamy, Gérard Thomas and Dominique Derain.

Chassagne-Montrachet

The international fame of Chassagne-Montrachet rests on its white wines, which undoubtedly stems from the Grands Crus Le Montrachet, Bâtard-Montrachet and Criots-Bâtard-Montrachet, which lie partly or (in the case of the last) wholly within Chassagne-Montrachet. There is also a handful of top Premiers Crus such as Les Caillerets, Les Chaumées, Remilly, Blanchot, Vergers and Chenevottes—which make excellent white wine. Fine white Chassagne-Montrachet has the steely backbone of Puligny-Montrachet and slightly more weight, but lacks the floral character and, often, the elegance. In recent years the production of white Chassagne-Montrachet has overtaken that of the red.

The problem is that the reds here, even when good, do not come close to the best whites. Red Chassagne-Montrachet can be beautifully colored and fruity in cask, but in bottle tannins seem to remove the charm. The best vineyards for reds are Clos St-Jean and Morgeots.

DOMAINE RAMONET

Owner **the Ramonet family** ***Production*** **7,000 cases**
Vineyard area **42 acres (17 ha)**

Wines here develop superb concentration and complexity with bottle age: whites from Le Montrachet, Bâtard-Montrachet, Bienvenues- Bâtard-Montrachet; Premier Cru Chassagne-Montrachet from Les Ruchottes, Les Caillerets, Les Chaumées and Morgeot; and the red Premiers Crus Morgeot, Clos de la Boudriotte and Clos St-Jean.

Other good Chassagne-Montrachet producers include families with multiple *domaines* (Gagnards, Colins, Moreys, Pillots, Jouards and Coffinets) and some smaller producers, such as Michel Niellon and Guy Amiot-Bonfils.

Santenay

Geologists have identified rock strata in Santenay that are similar to those of the Côte de Nuits, but the reds, while generally full-bodied, tend toward the rustic. The best vineyards are Les Gravières, La Comme, Clos des Tavannes and Clos Rousseau. White Santenay can be interesting.

VINCENT GIRARDIN

Owner **Vincent Girardin** ***Production*** **NA** ***Vineyard area*** **NA**

Having established a reputation for the quality of his red and white wines, Vincent Girardin satisfied growing demand by setting up as a *négociant*. The wines are generally oaky but still full of fruit, include an impressive Chassagne-Montrachet.

Other Santenay producers include Lucien Muzard et Fils and Claude Maréchal.

Maranges

Three communes—Cheilly, Dezize and Sampigny—share the Premier Cru Maranges, and their former appellations have been grouped together under this name. Most of the wine here is red; it can be deep in color and full of fruit but is usually tannic and somewhat rustic. A little white is also made.

BELOW: Some of the finest reds in the Côte de Beaune come from the Meursault area.

ABOVE: *Mist shrouds the vineyards surrounding the village of Fuissé in the Mâconnais.*

CÔTE CHALONNAISE

Five villages make up the area called the Côte Chalonnaise, named for the nearest large town, Chalon-sur-Saône. Both red and white wines are produced here, mostly for early consumption. As yet, there are not enough good growers to put this region squarely on the map, and the best wines often come from the *négociants*. Wines produced outside the five villages are sold under the name of Bourgogne Côte Chalonnaise.

Bouzeron

This small village is noted for its aligoté, the lesser and thinner of the burgundian white grapes, which is, however, attractive in its youth for its firm, tangy character. Having first been allowed to add its name to a label alongside Bourgogne Aligoté, Bouzeron now has its own appellation, but only for this grape. Aubert de Vilaine is the best producer.

BELOW: *Chardonnay grapes ripening on the vine.*

Rully

The first major village south of Chagny is Rully, where red and white wines are produced in equal quantities along with some sparkling wine. The white wines are light and fruity but generally do not age well beyond two or three years. The red wines are also no more than medium-bodied and rely on fruit rather than structure; yet they can be extremely pleasing. Good addresses for Rully include the Château de Rully, Jacqueson, and *négociants* such as Olivier Leflaive and Louis Jadot.

Mercurey

The best and most ageworthy red wines of the Côte Chalonnaise are to be found in Mercurey, though they need a soft hand during vinification to produce sufficient fruit without too much tannin. Two *négociants* have major holdings in Mercurey: Faiveley, which produces several high-quality *cuvées* such as La Croix Jacquelet and La Framboisière; and Rodet, which makes and distributes the Mercurey wines of the Château de Chamirey. Among the growers, various members of the Juillot family have impressed, but they could do with a little more competition. White Mercurey accounts for just 10 percent of production but should not be ignored. The white wines can be quite full-bodied, with an attractive hint of licorice.

Givry

This was the favorite wine of King Henri IV of France, doubtless because his mistress came from Givry. The reds usually have good fruit backed by a reasonably tannic structure and can age for three to five years. The best vineyards are Clos Jus, Clos de la Servoisine and Clos Salomon. The best producers are Joblot, François Lumpp, Vincent Lumpp, Ragot, Mouton, Sarrazin and Chofflet-Valdenaire. A small amount of attractive white wine is made.

Montagny

Only white wines are produced in Montagny. They can be brisk and steely rather than soft and round, and should usually be drunk young. Louis Latour's Montagny is extremely reliable, and Stephane Aladame is clearly a rising star. In addition, the de Buxy co-operative has long been a fine source, along with Domaines Michel, Roy and Vachet.

MÂCONNAIS

The limestone hills west of the city of Mâcon are given over to arable and livestock farming, but the most suitable slopes are reserved for vineyards. Most of the production is white and inexpensive, save for fashionable Pouilly-Fuissé, and made from chardonnay. Red Mâcon and Mâcon Supérieur, both of which may be followed on labels by the name of the village of production, are made from the gamay grape, while wines made from pinot noir are labeled Bourgogne Rouge.

Mâcon Villages

The vast majority of white Mâcon wines are labeled Mâcon Villages. Producers also have the option of using the name of whichever of the 41 specified villages their wine comes from. Those most commonly seen labels are Mâcon Lugny (from the co-operative and Louis Latour), La Roche Vineuse (Merlin), Chaintré (Valette), Chardonnay and Prissé.

Most Mâcon Villages is made from high yields, vinified in stainless steel and bottled early, providing inexpensive but unremarkable chardonnay. However, a group of growers led by Jean Thévenet and Olivier Merlin has shown that the soils of the best villages can produce fine white burgundy if yields are restricted and skillful barrel fermentation and maturation are applied. Such wines can age for up to 10 years.

OLIVIER MERLIN

***Established* 1987 *Owner* Olivier Merlin *Production* NA**
***Vineyard area* NA**

Olivier Merlin, based in La Roche Vineuse, has established a reputation as one of the most serious producers of high-quality, barrel-aged Mâcon. In order to make some Pouilly-Fuissé, the top appellation in this area, he took out a *négociant* licence in 1997 which allows him to buy in grapes. The wines are gently oaky after up to 18 months in barrel, yet always showing refinement and balanced acidity. His principal wine is an excellent Mâcon La Roche Vineuse Vielles Vignes.

Viré-Clessé

The adjacent villages of Viré and Clessé used to be part of Mâcon Villages, but as of the 1998 vintage were promoted to appellation status. Both have long been known for making some of the richest and most appealing of Mâcon wines, especially those from the excellent co-operative and such growers as Bonhomme and Thévenet.

JEAN THÉVENET

***Owner* Jean Thévenet *Production* NA**
***Vineyard area* NA**

Clessé-based Thévenet's specialty is late-picked wines, sometimes botrytis affected, as in the Cuvée Levroutée. The residual sugar in his wines is deliberate rather than accidental, and should not be seen as an underhand way of ensuring mass appreciation of his very limited stock of wines. Not everybody approves locally and the rules for the new appellation of Viré-Clessé forbid residual sugar.

St-Véran

This appellation was only created in 1973, taking in vineyards on both sides of Pouilly-Fuissé. Those to the north are mostly on classical burgundian limestone soils. Those to the south are on red, sandy, granitic soils more typical of Beaujolais and much less suited to chardonnay—so choose carefully. Domaine des Deux Roches and Domaine Corsin are excellent sources. St-Veran is usually less expensive and often better than Pouilly-Fuisse.

Pouilly-Fuissé

This is the most famous appellation in the Mâconnais. It covers the communes of Chaintré, Vergisson and Solutré as well as the two villages that make up its name. The wines are generally rich, full-bodied, heady and powerful, especially those from the south-facing vineyards of Chaintré or the sun-trap of Fuissé. Those from Vergisson ripen less easily, as the vineyards are less well exposed, but this provides balance in hot years.

Wines (and prices) vary enormously from some fairly ordinary co-operative *cuvées* to the best selections of leading growers such as Château de Fuissé, Michel Forest, Robert Denogent, Gérard Valette and Madame Ferret. The two satellite appellations of Pouilly-Loché and Pouilly-Vinzelles are of lesser quality and importance.

Regional Dozen

CÔTE CHALONNAISE & MÂCONNAIS

- Stéphane Aladame Montagny Les Coères
- Cave de Buxy Montagny
- Château de Chamirey Mercurey (red and white)
- Michel Forest Pouilly-Fuissé Les Crays
- Château de Fuissé Pouilly-Fuissé Vieilles Vignes
- Domaine Guffens-Heynen Pouilly-Fuissé Les Petits Croux
- Maison Louis Jadot Rully Blanc
- Domaine Joblot Givry Clos de la Servoisine (red)
- Michel Juillot Mercurey Clos des Barraults (red)
- Mâcon la Roche Vineuse vieilles vignes
- Gérard Valette Pouilly-Fuissé le Clos de Mr Noly Vieilles Vignes
- Maison Verget Mâcon Villages Tête de Cuvée

BELOW: The Mâconnais produces mainly white wines.

ABOVE: *Vin de paille, a Jura specialty, is made from grapes that have been dried on straw mats.*

Jura, Savoie & Bugey

WINK LORCH

Located on the eastern fringes of France, in the foothills of the Alps, the wine regions of Jura, Savoie and Bugey are out on a limb. Yet their isolation is at least in part responsible for the distinctive and intriguing nature of their wines.

JURA

The vineyards of Jura, for example, produce one of France's most curious, sought-after wines, the sherry-like *vin jaune* (yellow wine), as well as luscious, sweet *vin de paille* (straw-wine), and dry whites, reds and sparkling wines from both burgundian and rare, indigenous grape varieties. Today, the industry centers on the town of Arbois, once home to Louis Pasteur, widely acknowledged as the father of the modern wine industry for his work on fermentation.

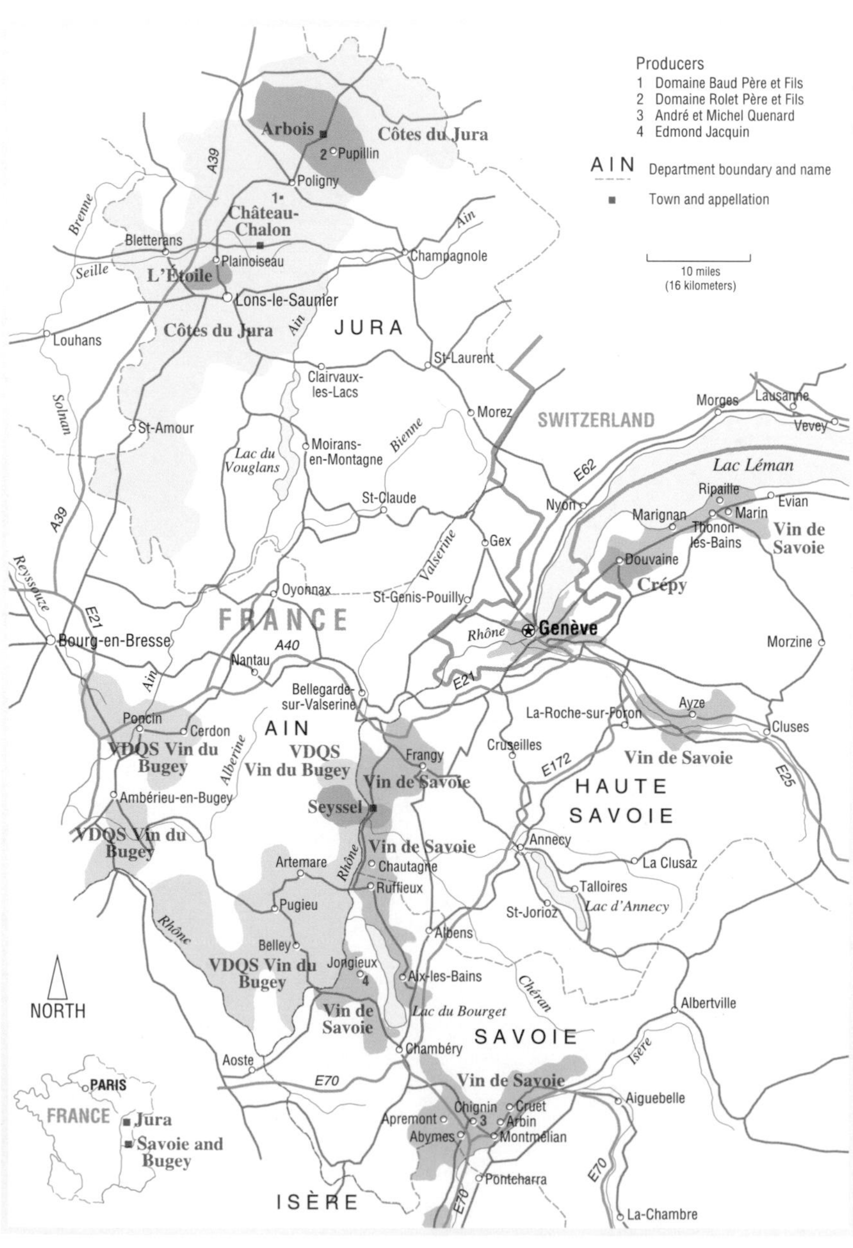

Jura is both the name of the department and of the mountain range that straddles France and Switzerland. It is also the derivation of the term "Jurassic", and both Jurassic and Triassic limestone form the basis of the local geology. The landscape is both dramatic and gentle, with vineyards sited, sometimes quite steeply, on the southern and southwestern slopes, at altitudes similar to those in Burgundy. With a continental climate bringing warm summers and cold winters, there is some risk of frost to older and more sensitive vines, both in winter and spring.

Traditionally, Jura red wines were blends, but today many are single varietals. Poulsard is the most widely planted red grape, followed by pinot noir and trousseau. Producers recommend aging all reds for several years. Trousseau provides the most interesting, displaying structure, almost animal flavors and dark red fruit.

Most Jura white winemakers prefer to make wines that have the slightly oxidized or nutty flavors associated with aging in old wood. Wines are usually varietal chardonnays or savagnins, or a blend. Like the reds, whites are sold with at least two years' cellar aging. Crémant du Jura is usually made with chardonnay and is similar to a delicate Crémant de Bourgogne, the best being creamy and fruity with well-integrated bubbles. Good examples of *vin de paille* rate among the finest sweet wines. *Vin jaune* is the apogee of Jura winemaking; distinctly yellow, dry, and concentrated, with flavors of spice and nuts, and it ages well.

Producers

The largest of the Jura *négociants* is Henri Maire, who owns about 740 acres (300 ha) of vines and markets nearly one-third of Jura's production. There are five wine co-operatives, and the rest of the production is in the hands of small, private *domaines*. About 60 percent of Jura's wines are sold in the wider administrative region of Franche-Comté, much of it through cellar-door sales. Less than 5 percent is exported. The producers below make the full range of Jura wines.

DOMAINE BAUD PÈRE ET FILS, VOITEUR

Established **1978** ***Owners*** **Alain and Jean-Michel Baud** ***Production*** **8,000 cases** ***Vineyard area*** **40 acres (16 ha)**

Still operating vineyards that his family has owned since the eighteenth century, Alain-Michel Baud produces 80 percent white wines. He is a traditionalist—even his chardonnay spends 18 months in old wood before it goes on sale. His Cuvée Tradition blend of savagnin and chardonnay is a nutty white wine style, and he also makes two great examples of *vins jaunes*: a Côtes du Jura and a Château-Chalon.

ABOVE: Outside of the growing season, Jura producers must protect vines against frost.

DOMAINE ROLET PÈRE ET FILS, ARBOIS

Established **1940s** ***Owners*** **the Rolet family** ***Production*** **30,000 cases** ***Vineyard area*** **153 acres (62 ha)**

The region's second-largest producer, Rolet has vineyards in Arbois and farther south in the Côtes du Jura and L'Étoile. The trousseau variety now provides its most successful red, the Arbois Trousseau, notable for its powerful structure. The whites are of a traditional style, and the *vin jaune* is exemplary.

SAVOIE AND BUGEY

The region's vineyards are located on south-facing slopes, and some enjoy an almost Mediterranean climate—peach and almond trees thrive in the area. The lower alpine pastures also abound with herbs, which are used in the wine-based dry French vermouth made in and named Chambéry.

The vineyards of Bugey lie west of the River Rhône in the Ain department, and are less influenced by alpine weather. With no large cities or tourist industry, it has been harder to establish markets for Bugey wines.

Savoie is planted with 80 percent white grapes, the most important of which is jacquère. Other white varieties grown are altesse (also called roussette, believed to originate from Cyprus); chasselas, chardonnay (also widespread in Bugey); roussanne (here called bergeron); gringet (related to Jura's savagnin) and molette. The reds are gamay, pinot noir andalso the exciting local variety, mondeuse.

The best Savoie white is altesse, sold as Roussette de Savoie. With a similar structure to chardonnay, altesse is made in various styles: with residual sugar, old-oak aging, or dry and fresh with a nutty, fruity character. In Bugey, chardonnay is the most successful white; some is light and fresh, some is vinified in oak.

Most Savoie reds are simple and fruity, particularly those from gamay and pinot noir; the best come from Chautagne and Jongieux. Mondeuse provides more interesting reds, and some producers are now recognizing the value of older vines and lower yields, as well as longer skin maceration and oak maturation. Mondeuse has an earthy flavor, allied with blackberry and blueberry, and a spicy touch not unlike syrah, even when unoaked. Bugey reds—generally made from gamay, pinot noir, or mondeuse—are light, early-drinking fare.

Sparkling wines are also made in Savoie, especially in Seyssel. In the *cru* of Ayze, gringet provides a more aromatic sparkling wine. Bugey sparklers include *méthode traditionnelle* wines.

Regional Best

Domaine Baud Père et Fils Côtes du Jura Tradition Blanc
Domaine Berthet-Bondet Château-Chalon
Château de l'Étoile L'Étoile Crémant du Jura
Domaine de Montbourgeau L'Étoile
Desiré Petit et Fils Arbois-Pupillin Vin de Paille
Domaine Rolet Père et Fils Arbois Trusseau

Producers

Savoie and Bugey have several *négociants*, some good co-operatives and a number of *domaines* that produce and bottle their own wine. The following have good ranges from different grapes.

EDMOND JACQUIN ET FILS, JONGIEUX

Established **NA** ***Owners*** **the Jacquin family** ***Production*** **NA** ***Vineyard area*** **47 acres (19 ha)**

Both Jacquin sons have studied enology and are committed to the family estate. Roussette is a specialty, and their Marestel is a concentrated, fruity style balanced by lively acidity.

ANDRÉ & MICHEL QUENARD, CHIGNIN

Established **1960s** ***Owners*** **André and Michel Quenard** ***Production*** **12,000 cases** ***Vineyard area*** **49 acres (20 ha)**

André and son Michel are consistently good producers of Chignin Bergero. They also make reds from mondeuse, which generally require a couple of years in bottle to soften the tannins.

BELOW: Savoie's growers plant mainly white varieties, with jacquère being the most significant.

ABOVE: *The Trois Châteaux d'Eguisheim crown the hill above Husseren-les-Châteaux.*

Alsace

ROGER VOSS

When you sample Alsatian wines, you feel as though you are getting a snapshot of central European history in a glass. There is the Germanic bottle, tall and fluted. There are the Germanic grape varieties: riesling, gewürztraminer and sylvaner. And there are the German surnames: Hugel, Dopff, Humbrecht. Yet, the addresses on the labels are French. The language is French. And so is the style of the wine.

This is a reflection of Alsace's status as a long-disputed territory, caught in a perpetual tug-of-war between Germany and France. Four times in the past 140 years the region has changed hands, and although it has been resolutely French since the Second World War, from a winemaking point of view the stylistic conundrum remains. This is the only part of France that is permitted to plant riesling, for example, even though it is obvious that this is a great grape variety that could prosper in many other French wine regions.

BELOW: *The Alsace Wine Route extends 112 miles (180 km) from Marlenheim to Thann.*

Alsace is the most important white-wine region in France, with an astonishing 37,050 acres (15,000 ha) of vines producing over 160 million bottles of AOC wine annually. That should place it at least as high in the white-wine stakes as Burgundy or Sancerre (and many wine connoisseurs would argue that Alsatian wines are better and more interesting than either of these popular styles). Yet, Alsace is curiously neglected, even by the French, and, probably as result of the stylistic confusion, nobody is quite sure how to rank the wines.

The wines of Alsace are predominantly dry, and fall into either Alsace or Alsace Grand Cru categories. Wines designated as Grand Cru may be dry or slightly off dry (as is the case quite often with Zind-Humbrecht); all dry wines here are generally high in alcohol. There are also two distinct types of late harvest wine: vendanges tardive and selection de grains noble. Alsatian wines are labeled varietally as mandated by their unique AOC regulations.

Vines and wines

Alsace grape varieties are divided into two categories: the noble varieties—gewürztraminer, riesling, pinot gris and muscat—and the lesser varieties. Apart from pinot noir, all are white. Gewürztraminer has brought more fame to the region than any other grape variety. In Alsace, the wine has high alcohol and a distinctive, spicy, full, oily taste. Sometimes it also has a bitter finish, and there is a dryness in even the sweetest examples.

Riesling provides the finest wine in Alsace: bone dry, with a flinty, steely taste, it is usually very fresh and frequently acidic when young, but softens with age, developing into an absolutely superb wine.

The Alsatians' favorite wine, pinot gris, is full, rich, soft, and well-balanced, with high acidity, a touch of pepper, moderately high alcohol, and an ability to age over a long period.

Alsace muscat is dry, yet with a honeyed tone; a perfect combination of sweetness and lightness, it is delicious as an aperitif wine but it is rare.

Pinot blanc grapes produce some of the region's most drinkable wines. These are relatively low in alcohol, fresh-tasting and soft, and have a pleasing touch of acidity and not too pronounced a character. Sylvaner is widely planted in Alsace and produces a neutral, reliable wine that is good for quaffing. It has a smoky, herby taste and a soft, low-acid, fruit flavor.

In Alsace, red and rosé wines are all made from pinot noir and some respectable reds are finally being made. Sparkling whites and some sweeter white styles are also produced.

Appellations and classifications

Alsace's appellation system is relatively simple, but was once even simpler: formerly, all wine came under the single Alsace appellation. Today, the general *appellation contrôlée* covers all vineyards save those that are designated Alsace Grand Cru or Crémant. Any of the permitted grape varieties grown in any village in any vineyard can qualify for the Alsace appellation, making it the largest white-wine appellation in France.

Alsace Grand Cru covers specified vineyards for particular grape varieties. In other words, if Grand Cru vineyard X is designated as Grand Cru only for riesling, any gewürztraminer produced by that vineyard will be simple AC Alsace. Grand Cru wines can be 100 percent from one vineyard (in which case the vineyard will be named on the label) or from a number of Grand Cru vineyards (in which case it will simply be called Alsace Grand Cru). All Alsace Grand Cru wines must be 100 percent from one grape variety, and only the noble varieties can be used. Permitted yields are lower than for AC Alsace, at 3.7 tons per acre (65 hl per ha).

Crémant d'Alsace is an appellation for sparkling wine. It must be made by the classic method of secondary fermentation in the bottle, using grapes grown only in the Alsace appellation area. The permitted varieties are pinot blanc, pinot auxerrois, pinot noir, pinot gris, riesling and chardonnay, although Crémant d'Alsace is normally made from pinot blanc and pinot auxerrois.

Sweeter wines made from bunches or selected berries that have particularly high levels of sugar and potential alcohol are classified as Vendange Tardive or Sélection des Grains Nobles, the former being whole bunch, the latter single berry. These categories more or less correspond to the German categories of Beerenauslese and Trockenbeerenauslese, with the vital difference that they are richer and never as sweet as their German equivalents. Both wines, but particularly Sélection des Grains Nobles, may contain botrytis-affected grapes.

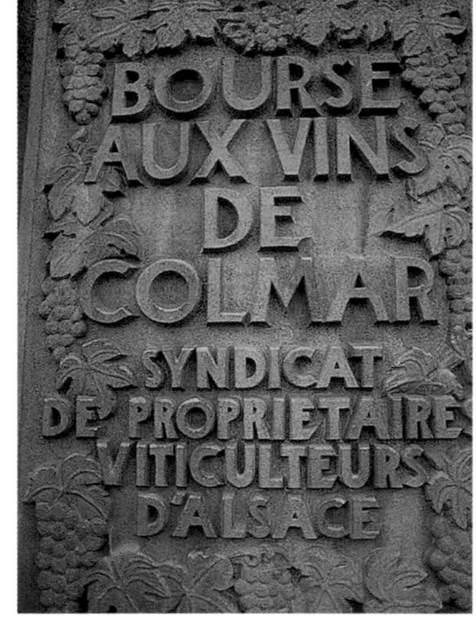

ABOVE: *The Bourse aux Vins (Wine Exchange), a trading center in Colmar, was built in 1609.*

LÉON BEYER

Established **1867** ***Owners*** **the Beyer family** ***Production*** **60,000 cases** ***Vineyard area*** **173 acres (70 ha)**

This *négociant* firm continues the wine activities of the Beyer family, who first arrived in Eguisheim in 1580. Directed today by Léon Beyer and his son Marc, it is best known for its dry, elegant style of wine, expressed both in the top Cuvée des Comtes d'Eguisheim and in the well-made Léon Beyer and Réserve ranges. The firm is particularly noted for its Gewürztraminer as well as its Vendange Tardive wines. After a brief spell during the early 1990s when some of the wines were inconsistent, Beyer returned to top form with the 1997 vintage.

DOMAINE MARCEL DEISS

Established **1949** ***Owner*** **Marcel Deiss** ***Production*** **10,000 cases** ***Vineyard area*** **49 acres (20 ha)**

Marcel Deiss makes extravagant wines from fine vineyards around Bergheim. His greatest success is his riesling, but he also created the Grand Vin d'Altenberg de Bergheim, a blended wine that encapsulates the vineyard much more than the grape variety.

RIGHT: Nielluccio, Corsica's most planted grape variety, is a type of sangiovese.

Corsica

ANTHONY PEREGRINE

Just over 20 years ago, wines from Corsican were predominantly rustic items, the products of a mountainous Mediterranean island with a reputation for beautiful, rugged scenery, political instability and endless vendettas. However in recent years, the wines have improved significantly, becoming more worthy of a viticultural tradition that stretches back approximately 2,500 years.

Regional Best

QUALITY WINES

Domaine Gentile Sélection Noble red
De Peretti della Rocca Cuvée Alexandra red
Domaine de Torraccia Oriu red

BEST VALUE WINES

Domaine Fiumicicoli rosé
Domaine de Pratavone white
Terra Vecchia red

Corsicans both ancient and modern have benefited from the Mediterranean's climate—warm sunshine and maritime humidity. And although the wild, tortuous terrain, which was perfect for the bandits of Corsican folklore, is mainly granitic (especially in the south and west) there is also some schistose land to the northeast and some limestone in between.

Two-thirds of Corsica's vineyards have been restructured under a replanting program. Although this has included international varieties such as cabernet sauvignon and chardonnay, the emphasis has generally been on traditional grapes. The dense, tannic nielluccio (known as sangiovese in Tuscany) and the more supple, sophisticated (and indigenous) sciacarello have reassumed their primacy in Corsican reds and rosés, while vermentino once again characterizes the ample dry whites. Simultaneously, winemaking techniques have developed immeasurably, so that even the more modest wines—which once either descaled the throat or passed down it unnoticed—generally, these days, boast freshness and balance.

Producers
1 Clos Capitoro
2 Domaine Fiumicicoli
3 Domaine de Tanella
4 Domaine de Torraccia

The overall effects of these developments have been twofold. Firstly, the island now produces an improving range of *vins de pays,* which is classified as VDP de l'Île de Beauté. These wines now account for 54 percent of Corsica's annual production of 9.24 million gallons (35 million l), and are usually at least honest, consistent and refreshing. They include a good selection of varietal wines, notably those made from the traditional grapes mentioned above, and an interesting range of double-variety wines. Cabernet sauvi-

gnon and nielluccio may seem unlikely partners but they can work well together.

Secondly, and more importantly, the island's appellation wines (26 percent of total production) now proudly embody the often craggy hillside terroirs, the grape varieties grown there, and the local cultures. Some of the reds are darkly robust (generally those with nielluccio to the fore), others are lighter and spicier (usually those made with sciacarello), and the best rosés marry fruitiness and structure. Whites are in the minority but can range from the fruity and nervous to the more aromatically complex.

Corsica's appellation structure is complex, reflecting the diversity of its vineyards and terrain. Vin de Corse is the generic, catch-all category, though, in practice, its supple reds and racy rosés come mainly from the cooperatives on the east coast. It accounts for 56 percent of Corsican AOCs.

Within the Vin de Corse are five subregional classifications: Calvi, with supple, sunny wines; Sartène, which offers characterful reds and rosés; Figari, whose dry, windy granite plateau produces well-structured fare; Porto-Vecchio, with elegant reds and aromatic rosés; and tiny Coteaux du Cap Corse, whose whites have very floral aromas.

In addition, the island boasts two independent *crus*. Ajaccio is the home territory of the sciacarello grape and makes silky wines which can age well. Patrimonio is perhaps the best-known of Corsican appellations; the nielluccio grape here produces rich, powerful red wines and the district's rosés are among the classiest on the island.

CLOS CAPITORO

Established **1856** ***Owners*** **the Bianchetti family** ***Production*** **22,000 cases** ***Vineyard area*** **120 acres (50 ha)**

Jacques Bianchetti currently directs the family estate near Ajaccio, where the sciacarello grape (literally, crunchy to eat) is king and red wines are consequently lighter in color than other Corsican fare. Despite this, they lack nothing in structure or staying power.

Bianchetti's rosés combine sophistication and festive fruitiness of the best of their breed.

DOMAINE FUIMICICOLI

Established **1962** ***Owners*** **the Andréani family** ***Production*** **20,000 cases** ***Vineyard area*** **108 acres (45 ha)**

Félix Andréani assumed control of what is now the dominant property in the Sartène appellation in 1962, and has since gained a top-line reputation. In collaboration with his son Simon, he produces reds from sciacarello, nielluccio and grenache which support spicy elegance with strength and length, as well as rosés that clearly demonstrate how intense sciacarello can be.

DOMAINE DE TANELLA

Established **1850** ***Owners*** **De Perretti della Rocca family** ***Production*** **22,000 cases** ***Vineyard area*** **144 acres (60 ha)**

Originally established in 1850 and with a solid reputation since that time, the leading producer in the Figari appellation has recently experienced wholesale restructuring. Fortunately the quality of its Cuvée Alexandra range has not suffered a jot. Named after the daughter of the house, the *cuvée* comes in all three colors, all of which are regularly cited among the island's top wines. The outstanding red, in which syrah has been added to the two traditional Corsican varieties, is a wine of real breeding; it displays structured elegance and is at once deeply aromatic and built to last.

DOMAINE DE TORRACCIA

Established **1964** ***Owner*** **Christian Imbert** ***Production*** **22,200 cases** ***Vineyard area*** **103 acres (43 ha)**

After a varied early career, Christian Imbert landed on the coast near Porto-Vecchio 36 years ago. Since then, he's been a leader in the island's viticulture. His own wines all speak forcefully of their *terroir*—and of Imbert's dedication. The red, a mixture of (mainly) nielluccio and some sciacarello, develops richness and power without losing finesse or balance—with potential to age for year.

ABOVE: Corsica's most interesting white wines are made from vermentino, an Italian variety.

BELOW: Fall leaves create a colorful contrast with empty wine bottles.

Regional Dozen

QUALITY WINES

Domaine de l'Aigle Pinot Noir Haute Vallée de l'Aude
Cuvée l'Argile Frères Parcé VDP des Côtes Catalanes
Domaine Cazes Le Credo VDP des Côtes Catalanes
Mas de Daumas Gassac Haute Vallée du Gassac VDP de l'Hérault
Domaine de Moulines Viognier, VDP de l'Hérault
Domaine de Trévallon VDP des Bouches du Rhône

BEST VALUE WINES

Les Vignerons Ardechois Syrah Cuvée Prestige VDP des Coteaux de l'Ardeche
Domaine de Bachellery Cabernet Sauvignon VDP d'Oc
Les Vignerons de Branceilles Mille et une Pierres VDP de Corrèze
Domaine Couillaud, Chardonnay, VDP du Jardin de la France
Domaine des Hauts de Seyr Le Montaillant Chardonnay VDP des Coteaux Charitois
James Herrick Syrah Mille Passum VDP d'Oc

Vins de Pays

JIM BUDD

In use since the 1930 but not formally recognized until 1979, the *vin de pays* (VDP) classification added another layer to the pyramid of categories used to define wine quality in France. *Vin de pays*—literally "country wine"—occupies a position above basic *vin de table* but below VDQS and *appellation contrôlée.*

Found throughout France—with the notable exceptions of Bordeaux, the Côte d'Or, Champagne and Alsace—*vins de pays* are classified as departmental, regional, or zonal. Thirty-nine denominations cover departments. In four areas, neighboring departments have agreed to group together to form a regional denomination. There are four regional *vin de pays*, Jardin de la France, Comte Tolosan, d'Oc, and Comtes Rhodaniens, and, to make matters confusing, 141 sub-appellations. From time to time, *vins de pays* are upgraded to VDQS, and from there to full AOC status.

The classification regulations include an overall yield limit of 5.1 tons per acre (90 hl per ha), although individual regions can specify lower yields; a natural minimum alcohol level of 9 percent (10 percent for the Mediterranean region); and a maximum alcohol content of 15 percent, although individual regions may set lower limits. Each department has its own list of permitted grapes, normally including local varieties plus some international ones. Generally, this allows producers much greater freedom than the appellation rules.

There are some constraints, however. Certain seemingly appropriate varieties are banned—viognier cannot be used in the Loire, for example. The words "château" or "*clos*" cannot be used on the label, nor can an individual vineyard be mentioned. Furthermore, in some regions, such as the Loire, the maximum alcohol permitted is 12.5 percent. This can be difficult to achieve in ripe years, particularly for producers who want to keep their yields low or pick their fruit at the optimum time. In 1996, the naming of a second grape variety on the label was permitted; yet it is still illegal to name a third or a fourth and the French wine establishment remains dismissive of varietal wines (*vins de cépage*).

For the most part, however, producers have taken to the *vin de pays* classification with relish, and it has grown rapidly. Today, almost 30 percent of French wine is *vin de pays*; about 65 percent of this is red, 17 percent rosé and 18 percent white.

Few *vins de pays* have attained the status of Italy's so-called "super *vini da tavola*", which have been awarded the IGT (Indicazione Geographica Tipica) denomination and are now among the country's most expensive wines. But this situation could change, especially in southern France where strict appellation laws have encouraged a number of leading producers to adopt the new classification. For example, since 1994 wine from Eloi Dürrbach's Domaine de Trévallon in Provence has been sold as a VDP des Bouches-du-Rhône instead of AC Les Baux-de-Provence, because its high proportion of cabernet sauvignon disqualifies it from the appellation. Dürrbach is probably the most high-profile producer to opt for the *vin de pays* status, but others in the Midi, such as Gérard Gauby and Domaine Cazes in the Roussillon are following suit.

ANIVIT, the French association of *vin de pays* producers, divides the country into a number of areas, which are shown on the map.

ACKERMAN-LAURANCE, VDP DU JARDIN DE LA FRANCE, LOIRE

Established **1811** ***Owner*** **Rémy Pannier Group**
Production **NA** ***Vineyard area*** **NA**

Founded in 1811, this is the oldest sparkling-wine house in Saumur and one of the biggest of the Loire *négociants*. VDP du Jardin de la France accounts for 25 percent of production; the principal varieties are chardonnay, chenin and cabernet franc.

DOMAINE DE LA BAUME, VDP D'OC, LANGUEDOC

Established **1989** ***Owner*** **Hardy Wine Company** ***Production*** **NA** ***Vineyard area*** **45 acres (18 ha)**

This estate produces two ranges of varietal wines: La Baume and Domaine de la Baume. The La Baume range is made from fruit purchased from outside growers, and includes five wines: chardonnay, sauvignon blanc, cabernet sauvignon, merlot and syrah. Wines produced from the estate's own vineyards are sold as Domaine de la Baume and include a merlot and a chardonnay viognier.

DOMAINE DE LA CHEVALIÈRE, VDP D'OC, LANGUEDOC

Established **1995** ***Owner*** **Michel Laroche**
Production **NA** ***Vineyard area*** **15 acres (6 ha)**

Michel Laroche is one of Alsace's leading chablis producers. The majority of the grapes are sourced from 740 acres (300 ha) owned by a number of growers in various parts of Languedoc. Laroche is convinced that blending is the key to success here. The 1996 Merlot, for instance, came from eight different areas. The small vineyard at the property is planted with chardonnay, roussanne, vermentino, viognier, cabernet sauvignon, merlot and syrah, which will eventually be used for prestige *cuvées*.

Other notable producers in the category include Fortant de France, James Herrick (both VDP D'OC, Languedoc); and Domaine de Tariquet (VDP Côte de Gascogne, Southwest).

ABOVE: *Languedoc-Roussillon;* vin de pays *allows producers more freedom.*

OPPOSITE PAGE: *The most successful* vin de pays *have been international varietals from the south.*

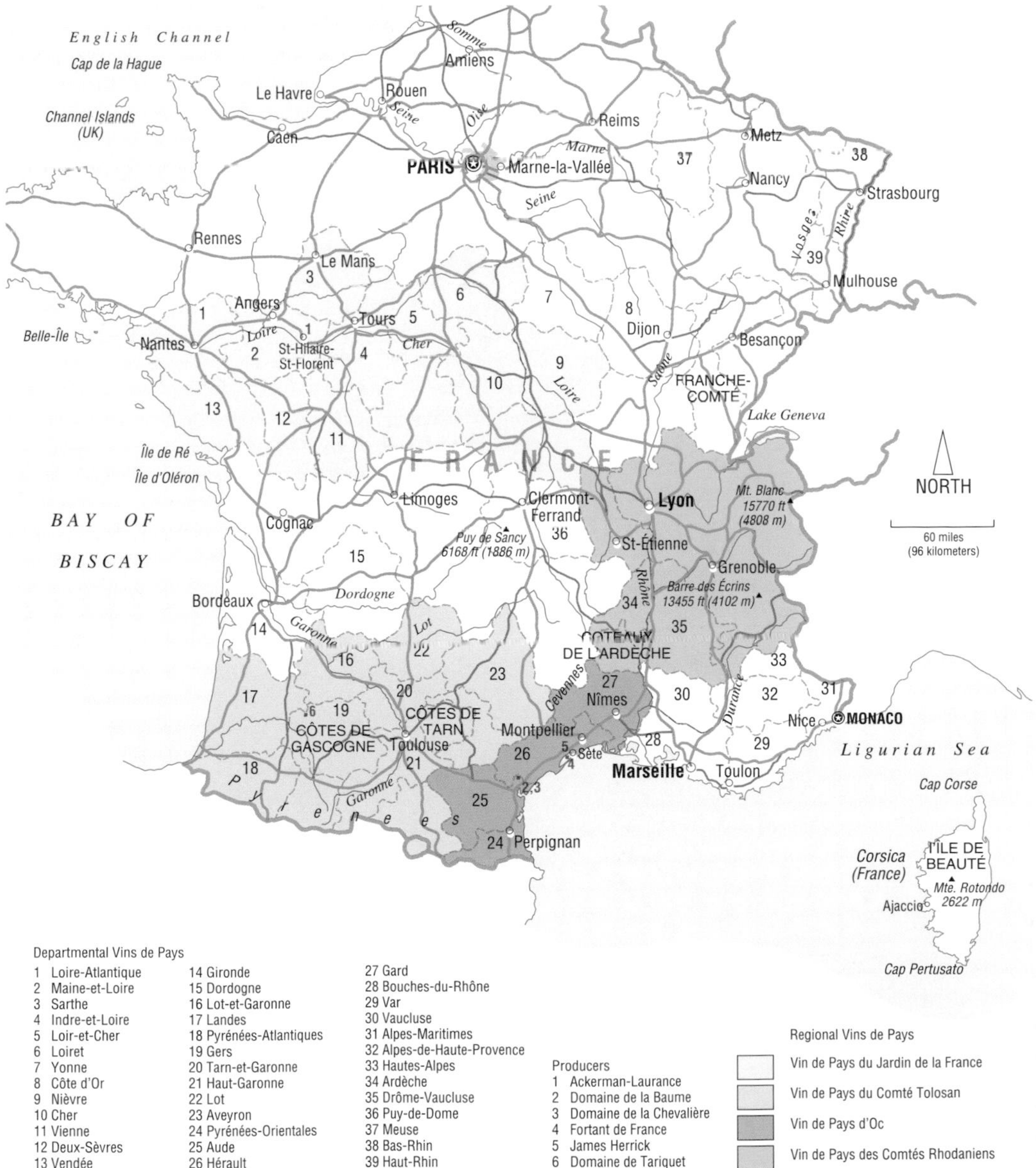

Picking grapes above Zeltingen-Rachtig in the Mosel Valley.

Germany

ABOVE: *An old oak barrel decorated with carved motifs in a winemaking theme.*

are vestiges of Roman wineries and other artifacts, and in other parts of Germany there is archeological confirmation that vineyards have been present for 2,000 years or more.

German wine has always been expensive, and demand for it during periods of prosperity pre-1914 kept prices buoyant. It also encouraged counterfeiters, just as in France, where the amount of Châteauneuf-du-Pape available before strict regulations were introduced always exceeded the quantity of wine the region could conceivably have produced. Wine laws had to be introduced in 1901 to combat such fraud.

Post World War II, new crossed grape varieties ripened early and were genetically selected to produce high sugar levels. This was a grape-grower's dream: vast crops of very sweet wines. But being heavy and sickly, a proliferation of wines from these new varieties—such as ortega, optima, bacchus and siegerrebe—did nothing for the reputation of German sweet wine. Subsequently, advances in viticulture combined with innovations in winery equipment meant that the taste of quality German sweet wine, traditionally due to incomplete fermentations that left residual sugar in the wine, could now be replicated by technology.

In the 1980s and 1990s there was a trend toward greater diversity in the wines of Germany. Dry white wines, even from regions better suited to off-dry or sweet wines, became quite fashionable. Much German red wine, even the highly praised spätburgunders from the Rheingau and Ahr, struck outsiders as thin and weedy, although there were exceptions in ripe vintages. But from the 1980s some good, if rarely world-class, red wines not only from spätburgunder, but also from new varieties like the dornfelder, began to be grown in some of the warmer regions.

The choice of styles today is greater than it would have been a century ago, and the experimentation of the 1980s and 1990s has settled down to a steady exploitation of appropriate grapes in appropriate sites.

Landscape and climate

Good German wine is very site-sensitive, and the nuances of site and microclimate count for much. So certain sites have always been acclaimed as especially fine. For instance, except in the Pfalz and in Baden, the German climate is cool, so every nuance of exposition and climate must be exploited to the maximum. This explains why only certain slopes along the Mosel River's banks are planted with vines; along the opposite side the sunshine is too patchy to allow the grapes to ripen. The best vineyards in the Rheingau face south and are planted on the steepest slopes.

BELOW: *The magnificent twelfth-century cellars of Kloster Eberbach, Rheingau.*

With such variations come nuances in taste and structure. In the Middle Mosel, the wines of Graach are usually identifiable as a touch broader and more ample than those from neighboring Wehlen. Within the large Brauneberger Juffer vineyard is a central patch that, it has long been acknowledged, usually provides better wines than the rest of the site: this is the parcel honored with its own name of Brauneberger Juffer-Sonnenuhr.

Germany's marginal or extreme climate means grapes do not always ripen easily. Many red wines could thus be mistaken for rosés; without some balancing residual sugar, while the rieslings of the Saar and Ruwer can be uncompromisingly harsh and tart. The acidity that can be so refreshing and zesty in a well-balanced riesling can be tooth-achingly unpleasant in a riesling made from unripe grapes. The greatest German wines have always been made on its climatic edges, though, and a great vintage gives wines that balance fruitiness and acidity.

Vines and wines

Although riesling is the most popular wine in Germany, there are other wines of note as well. Eiswein (ice wine) is a relatively new phenomenon and was just a freak of nature until the 1970s, when some estates began leaving parcels of vines untouched in corners of the vineyard that were most prone to frost. Strict regulations dictated the depth and longevity of the frost required before the resulting wine could be classified as eiswein. This style of wine still remains fashionable, despite the exceptionally high production costs.

The more traditional, and indeed more complex, beerenauslese and trockenbeerenauslese are often produced in tiny quantities. They might be poured for honored guests or perhaps conserved for a future generation. Sometimes they are offered at auction where high prices win recognition for the estate. Sylvaner has quite a distinguished pedigree in Germany and is best known as an earthy, vigorous, dry wine that is well suited to accompany food. In southern Germany however the pinot varieties do well: spätburgunder (pinot noir), weissburgunder (pinot blanc) and grauer burgunder (pinot gris).

Grauer burgunder is rarely improved by aging in *barriques*, but the German consumer is quite keen on the style. When vinified as a sweet wine, it can give extremely fat, unctuous, figgy wines at beerenauslese and trockenbeerenauslese levels.

In Württemberg, lemberger can make a lively cherryish wine of considerable character. The other common red variety here is trollinger, which produces pallid wines that appeal mostly to local consumers. Pinot meunier, known in Germany as schwarzriesling, is also found in Württemberg and Baden, but as a dry red wine it can be somewhat neutral. There are swathes of portugieser in many southern vineyards; its wine is light, fruity and innocuous.

ABOVE: The church steeple dominates the township of Zeltingen, in the Mosel Valley.

With white wines, rieslaner has high acidity and makes brilliant sweet wines that are very close in character to riesling, in regions such as Franken and the Pfalz. Scheurebe is known to yield a somewhat grapefruity dry wine, especially in the Pfalz region, and can also make exceedingly good sweet wines.

Chardonnay is a relative newcomer to Germany, but it can give quite good wines in the Pfalz and Baden as long as it is not smothered in new oak.

Some German sparkling wines—such as those from Breuer in the Rheingau, Lindenhof in the Nahe and Koehler-Ruprecht in the Pfalz, among a number of others—are of very acceptable quality.

Wine laws

The 1971 wine law placed German wine production into three categories: Tafelwein (the most basic), Qualitätswein (QbA) and the superior Qualitätswein mit Prädikat (QmP). The "Prädikat" consisted of further quality categories, rising from kabinett to trockenbeeren-

ABOVE: *Grapes do well beside the Mosel River where the banks plunge steeply down to the water's edge.*

auslese. The sole criterion for inclusion in any category was grape sugar at harvest and therein lay the fatal flaw. Unfortunately, the laws meant that vast amounts of undistinguished wine could proudly carry the label Qualitätswein. This dross, often dolled up in fancy bottles with fancy names, including the now infamous Liebfraumilch, ended up on supermarket shelves and the consumer began to associate German "quality wine" with the sugar-water on offer. And since it was usually the cheapest wine on the shelves, the consumer couldn't see the point in paying two or three times as much for some other "quality wine" from Germany.

As in other parts of the grape-growing world, the name of the estate has become the best guarantee of quality. It is scarcely conceivable that properties such as Robert Weil or Maximin Grünhaus will market a mediocre wine and the shrewd consumer should opt for a modest category from a top estate in preference to a grander appellation from an unknown grower, whose yields may be three times as high.

BELOW: *Grape pickers in the Mosel Valley.*

There is great debate within Germany as to the best way forward. Vineyard classification benefits the well-established estates with holdings in the best sites, whereas a conscientious producer with no exceptional vineyards but a good track record for quality may feel himself penalized by such a classification. No doubt these debates will continue. Meanwhile, the gradual process of undoing the worst damage inflicted by the 1971 wine laws and those who abused them is getting underway.

These long-term abuses as well as the climatic variations between regions make further generalizations about wine style very tricky.

Viticultural practices

These are often a function of terrain. The steep sites, from which most of the best wine emanates, have to be cultivated and harvested manually. On flatter land, especially in the Rheinhessen and the Pfalz, mechanization is usual. Green-harvesting and other post-pruning measures intended to reduce yields are relatively new in Germany and there is much debate as to the appropriate yields for, say, a good-quality riesling. Whereas yields of 1,600 gallons per acre (150 hl per ha) are perfectly feasible, most growers would see yields of 650 to 750 gallons (6,000 to 7,000 l) as being more compatible with producing decent quality. In some vineyards green cover has been planted, either to combat erosion or to provide competition for the hungry vine roots and so reduce yield.

Given the marginal climate of many of Germany's wine regions, it is not surprising that organic or biodynamic viticulture has made little headway. The strong possibility of cool rainy spells also increases the likelihood of rot and disease and few growers are prepared to eliminate spraying or other treatments from their vineyards. However, there are estates, such as Heyl zu Herrnsheim and Graf von Kanitz, that are wholly or partly committed to organic viticulture.

Winemaking procedures are relatively uncontroversial. There is near-universal agreement that for such varieties as riesling, müller-thurgau and sylvaner, *barriques* are anathema. Many traditional estates retain their large oval casks, often up to 100 years old, in which all their wines are fermented and aged. They argue that these large casks allow the wine to breathe and mature gracefully without imparting any trace of oakiness. Other producers favor a more reductive approach and have banished wood in favor of stainless steel. There are some outstanding producers in both camps and many employ both tanks and casks.

The pinot varieties and red wines, most growers acknowledge, benefit from some wood-aging, but the kind of aging varies greatly. The presence of residual sugar in many wines means that technical options such as chilling, sterile filtration or centrifuging are still employed. But dependence on technology is less unquestioning than it would have been even 20 years ago and German wine from top estates is a product of considerable purity.

ABOVE: *Bins of spätburgunder, ready for collection.*

Riesling

As far as Germany is concerned, riesling is the king. Although its late-ripening character can cause problems when inclement weather dogs the fall months, the long growing season it craves can yield wines of superlative structure. The grapes can be physiologically ripe without attaining exceptional sugar levels. A great Mosel riesling may have only 7° (or 7 percent) of alcohol; a Rheingau or Nahe wine has perhaps 10°. Yet this does not entail any loss of intensity.

As long as yields are kept to a sensible level so that there is no trace of dilution or unripeness, that intensity is provided by the racy acidity allied to the mouth-watering fruitiness of the riesling grape. There is no white variety quite as versatile as riesling. In warmer regions it can produce rich, dry wines of considerable power. The mighty dry rieslings of Alsace and the Wachau in Austria show this to be so, though in some vintages dry rieslings from the Pfalz can come close to matching their power. But the German dry rieslings are more graceful and elegant than those from elsewhere in the world, with the emphasis on finesse, not power.

In the more northerly regions, the wines need some balancing residual sugar. In the Rheingau the estates that formed the Charta Association in the 1970s promoted an off-dry style (known as halbtrocken in German). This wine was intended to be better adapted to consumption with food than the sweeter styles of riesling. Good white wine is all about balance. For example, some rieslings from the Mosel–Saar–Ruwer have surprisingly high levels of residual sugar and yet the wine does not taste especially sweet; this is because of the equally high levels of acidity and extract. The precise balance of any wine is partly the result of the attributes of the grapes when harvested but it is also subject to the choices then made by the producer.

Where riesling astonishes most is in its capacity to produce very long-lived and unashamedly sweet wines. It's a risky business, but the top estates will leave grapes on the vine until perilously late in the fall. If they are lucky, the grapes will have shriveled or become botrytized, provoking a concentration of sugar, as well as the production of other chemical compounds such as glycerol. These very late-harvested wines—beerenauslese or trockenbeerenauslese—are so high in sugar that they ferment with difficulty and are often even lower in alcohol than traditional riesling styles. Their acidity is very high too, allowing them to age for decades, becoming gradually more honeyed and unctuous. A great beerenauslesen or trockenbeerenauslesen from a classic vintage, even at 50 or 100 years old, can be a mind-blowing experience, with an infinitely complex range of aromas and flavors. Even a more modest riesling of kabinett quality, if well made, can easily age over 20 years.

ABOVE: *The highly verstile riesling grapes.*

LEFT: *The last bottle of riesling from the great 1917 vintage at Kloster Eberbach.*

Mosel–Saar–Ruwer

The Mosel River twists and turns on its leisurely way from Koblenz toward Luxembourg. Vineyards are planted on the best-exposed nearby slatey slopes—and, regrettably, on some flat land stretching away from the river. More thrive along the slopes beside its two tributaries, the Saar and Ruwer, which have been tossed into the administrative region of the Mosel–Saar–Ruwer.

ABOVE: This elaborate old fountain in Bernkastel celebrates the bounty of the vine.

Despite the impressive size of the region, there is surprising homogeneity in the character of its riesling wines. Although half the vineyards are planted with other varieties, mostly müller-thurgau, the Mosel–Saar–Ruwer is, or should be, pre-eminently riesling territory. Nowhere else in the world does riesling display such razor-sharp intensity of flavor. Although the noble wines from the Rheingau may dispute the claim, many would argue that Mosel rieslings are the finest.

The Mosel River itself is divided into the Lower, Middle and Upper Mosel—and the greatest of these is the Middle or Mittelmosel (M-M). Most of the estates, especially in the Lower Mosel, are small, and the largest properties were formerly ecclesiastical or educational foundations, which used their vineyard profits to fund charitable activities. Instead of aristocratic estates that once dominated the Rheingau region, many of the Mosel's best vineyards have been in the hands of clans such as the Prüms or Pauly-Bergweilers for generations.

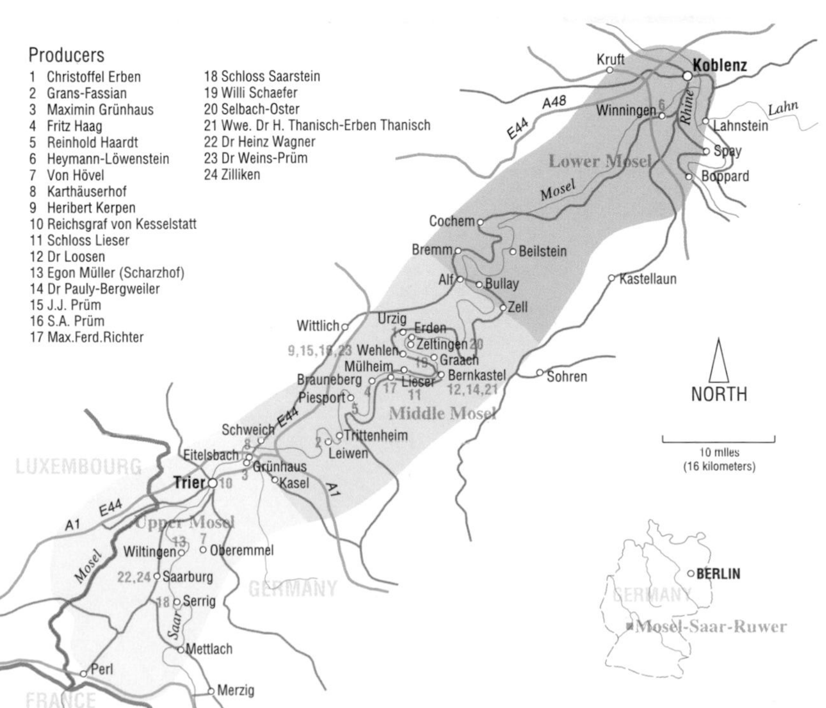

The Lower Mosel encompasses the stretch of the river between Koblenz and Zell and has less of the slate that characterizes the Middle Mosel. Its wines rarely ascend the heights scaled by those from the Middle Mosel, but some villages produce high-quality riesling, notably Zell, Cochem and Bullay. The wines tend to be light and delicate, without the steeliness of the finest rieslings.

The wine heartland lies in the Middle Mosel, a succession of river bends from Zell to just north of Trier, with a succession of celebrated villages, of which the best known are Wehlen, Bernkastel and Piesport. Here the slatey soils perform their dual function of imbuing the wines with a characteristic mineral tang and of reflecting the warmth of the day back onto the vines as daylight fades.

The Upper Mosel is a more amorphous region, following the river south from Trier. Riesling is less dominant here than in other sections of the Mosel, and müller-thurgau and elbling are commonly encountered. Although some good wines emanate from Trier itself and Konz, both along the Mosel, the best rieslings from the region come from the two tributaries: the Ruwer, flowing into the Mosel just north of Trier, and the Saar, entering at Konz southwest of Trier.

These are chilly valleys, especially the Saar, so the nuances of exposition and incline become even more important than in the Middle Mosel. In some years the grapes struggle to reach ripeness, but when they finally do, they are known to give the most elegant and racy wines of the entire region.

Despite the northerly climate, sublime sweet rieslings can be produced in certain vintages. These great rarities fetch very high prices at auction.

Villages of Middle Mosel

Bernkastel's busy streets don't encroach on the slatey vineyards towering above it. Doctor is the best-known site and its wines are the most expensive, but others, such as Lay, come close in quality with steely, fruity, quintessential Mosel riesling.

Brauneberg was made famous by winemaker Fritz Haag, but its celebrity is ancient. Powerful, long-lived wines. Best site: Juffer-Sonnenuhr.

Erden faces Urzig and is best known for its rich and long-lived rieslings from Prälat vineyard.

Graach has a broad band of superb vineyards between Bernkastel and Wehlen, producing wines a tad richer but less elegant than its neighbors. Best sites: Himmelreich and Josephshöfer.

Piesport comprises a succession of vineyards facing south across the river. Goldtröpfchen is best known but its neighbors produce a similar standard. Many wines have a mineral, aniseed quality.

Trittenheim's mostly steep vineyards give its wines delicacy and finesse. The best site is Apotheke.

Urzig's slatey soil is mixed with red clay, giving wines of unusual spiciness and exotic flavor.

Wehlen is perfectly exposed, and Wehlener Sonnenuhr is one of the classic sites of the region, producing the most exquisite rieslings.

Zeltingen, a neighbor of Wehlen, produces wines of comparable finesse, especially from its best vineyard, the Sonnenuhr.

Kasel, Ruwer, is the home of the Nies'chen vineyard, which regularly delivers rieslings with enticing delicacy and elegance.

Saarburg, Saar, is the source of good steely wines, especially from its top vineyard, Rausch.

Serrig, Saar, south of Saarburg, produces lean, tight rieslings that need years to evolve.

Wiltingen, Saar, has many good sites, but the most celebrated, justly, is the great hill of the Scharzhofberg, source of the Saar's most ethereal rieslings and most intense eisweins.

MAXIMIN GRÜNHAUS, GRÜNHAUS

Owner **Dr Carl Von Schubert**
Production **9,000 cases**
Vineyard area **84 acres (34 ha)**

This estate is admired within Germany for its dry rieslings, but it is the marvelous auslesen and eisweins that generate the most excitement for everyone outside Germany. Von Schubert bottles auslese from individual casks under a rather confusing cask number. The price indicates quality.

ABOVE: *A vineyard worker tastes a bunch of freshly picked grapes.*

FRITZ HAAG, BRAUNEBERG

Owner **Wilhelm Haag** ***Production*** **5,000 cases**
Vineyard area **17 acres (7 ha)**

Wilhelm Haag produces some powerful wines of intense flavor and long complex aftertastes. All his best wines come from the Juffer-Sonnenuhr vineyard. The Fritz Haag label has become a guarantee of classic, long-lived riesling. And the sweet wines are sensational.

BELOW: *Looking across the Mosel River toward Trittenheim, in the southern Middle Mosel.*

RIGHT: The church at Piesport. The town sits in a great amphitheater of vineyards.

REICHSGRAF VON KESSELSTATT, TRIER

Owner **Annegret Reh-Gartner** ***Production*** **33,000 cases**
Vineyard area **141 acres (57 ha)**

Annegret Reh-Gartner has imposed high standards in the vineyard and winery. Kesselstatt owns vineyards throughout the Mosel–Saar–Ruwer, and wines from Kaseler Nies'chen, Scharzhofberg, Josephshöfer, Piesporter Goldtröpfchen, and Bernkasteler Doctor can be recommended without hesitation.

DR LOOSEN, BERNKASTEL

Owner **Ernst Loosen** ***Production*** **6,000 cases** ***Vineyard area*** **25 acres (10 ha)**

The dynamic Ernst Loosen is focused on quality above all else, ruthlessly cutting yields and harvesting as late as possible. Other estates occasionally surpass Loosen in finesse but few can match the sheer brilliance and concentration of his wines, from the humblest kabinett to his majestic sweet wines.

Regional Dozen

QUALITY WINES

- Brauneberger Juffer-Sonnenuhr Riesling Beerenauslese (Fritz Haag)
- Eitelsbacher Karthäuserhof Riesling Auslese (Karthäuserhof)
- Erdener Prälat Riesling Auslese (Dr Loosen)
- Maximin Grünhauser Abtsberg Riesling Eiswein (Maximin Grünhaus)
- Scharzhofberger Riesling Beerenauslese (Egon Müller)
- Wehlener Sonnenuhr Riesling Auslese (J. J. Prüm)

BEST VALUE WINES

- Erdener Treppchen Riesling Kabinett (Dr Loosen)
- Scharzhofberger Riesling Kabinett (Kesselstatt)
- Serriger Schloss Saarsteiner Riesling Auslese (Schloss Saarstein)
- Wehlener Sonnenuhr Riesling Kabinett (Kerpen)
- Wintricher Ohligsberg Riesling Spätlese (Haart)
- Zeltinger Sonnenuhr Riesling Spätlese (Selbach-Oster)

EGON MÜLLER (SCHARZHOF), WILTINGEN

Owners **Egon Müller family** **Production** **4,000 cases**
Vineyard area **20 acres (8 ha)**

A legendary estate, distinguished by the astonishing quality of its wines—and astonishing prices. In a beautiful old manor house, the Egon Müllers coax the utmost complexity and refined structure from their incomparable and indestructible sweet wines, although the QbA and kabinett are usually of lesser interest.

J. J. PRÜM, WEHLEN

Owner **Manfred Prüm** ***Production*** **10,000 cases**
Vineyard area **35 acres (14 ha)**

Thanks to the gentle prickle of natural carbon dioxide in these wines, they can be deceptively youthful and can actually age for decades. In great vintages these can be the finest expressions of the Middle Mosel, supremely elegant distillations of the steep slatey soils of the Wehlener Sonnenuhr.

SELBACH-OSTER, ZELTINGEN

Owner **Johannes Selbach** ***Production*** **6,500 cases**
Vineyard area **25 acres (10 ha)**

Johannes Selbach is a shrewd *negociant* as well as an estate owner. All of his wines are of good quality, but those from his vineyards in Wehlen, Zeltingen, and Graach are often outstanding. Selbach-Oster demonstrates the high quality of the Zeltingen sites, which can rival those of neighboring Wehlen. The wines are accessible when young, but they age well.

WWE. DR H. THANISCH–ERBEN THANISCH, BERNKASTEL

Owner **Sofia Thanisch Spier** ***Production*** **4,000 cases**
Vineyard area **15 acres (6 ha)**

There are two estates with almost identical names and labels, and this is the better of the two (it sports the VDP logo on its label). It is best known for rich, firm wines of great distinction from the Bernkasteler Doctor vineyard. Buyers pay a premium for the illustrious name.

There are many other excellent wine producers in the Mosel–Saar–Ruwer region including Dr Pauly-Bergweiler (Bernkastel); Christoffel Erben (Urzig); Grans-Fassian (Leiwen); Reinhold Haart (Piesport); Von Hövel (Oberemmel); Karthäuserhof (Eitelsbach); Heymann Löwenstein (Winningen); Heribert Kerpen, S. A. Prüm, Dr Weins-Prüm (all Wehlen); Max. Ferd. Richter (Mülheim); Willi Schaefer (Graach); Schloss Lieser (Lieser); Schloss Saarstein (Serrig); Dr Heinz Wagner and Zilliken (both Saarburg).

Nahe

The Nahe is one of Germany's more amorphous regions. With its vast geological variation, there is little uniformity of style. Some of the best wines, with fine extract and raciness, come from the volcanic and slatey soils found around Niederhausen and Schlossböckelheim. The best wines, inevitably, are rieslings, but this variety accounts for less than one-third of the area planted. Many other varieties are grown, including müller-thurgau, sylvaner, grauer burgunder and more recent varieties such as kerner. Some red grapes are grown but standards are not high.

Nahe has a growing reputation for stunning eiswein and other very sweet styles. Compared with wines from the Rheingau or Mosel, prices remain very reasonable, but the growing reputation of the Nahe for stunning eiswein and other sweet styles may prompt an upward movement in prices. However, at many estates the full potential for high-quality wines has not yet been realized.

CRUSIUS, TRAISEN

***Owner* Dr Peter Crusius *Production* 6,500 cases**
***Vineyard area* 30 acres (12 ha)**

This highly regarded estate's top wine is invariably the riesling from Traiser Bastei, which has a distinctive earthy mineral tone allied to great vivacity and finesse. Almost as fine are the wines from Traiser Rotenfels and from Schlossböckelheimer Felsenberg.

SCHLOSSGUT DIEL, BURG LAYEN

***Owner* Armin Diel *Production* 7,500 cases**
***Vineyard area* 37 acres (15 ha)**

While not abandoning his great fondness for the dry wines, Armin Diel has also been making wines in a more classic style from his Dorsheim sites. However, devotees of the *barrique*-aged Burgundian varieties will find these here, too. The range is topped by some exceptional but very pricey sweet wines.

DÖNNHOFF, OBERHAUSEN

***Owner* Helmut Dönnhoff**
***Production* 7,000 cases**
***Vineyard area* 32 acres (13 ha)**

This is the Nahe's most outstanding producer. Some dry wines are produced—pinot blanc and pinot gris as well as riesling—but the glory of this estate is the riesling. These wines show an exceptional balance of fruit and acidity, and develop considerable complexity as they mature. In suitable vintages, Dönnhoff also produces some dazzling sweet wines.

Other producers of quality wine in the Nahe region include Emrich-Schönleber, Götelmann, Kruger-Rumpf, Gutsverwaltung Niederhausen-Schlossböckelheim.

Regional Dozen

QUALITY WINES

Monzinger Frühlingsplätzchen Riesling Auslese (Emrich-Schönleber)
Münsterer Dautenpflänzer Riesling Auslese (Kruger-Rumpf)
Niederhäuser Hermannsberg Riesling Eiswein (Gutsverwaltung Niederhausen-Schlossböckelheim)
Oberhäuser Brücke Riesling Eiswein (Dönnhoff)
Riesling Auslese (Sibyl)
Traiser Bastei Riesling Spätlese (Crusius)

BEST VALUE WINES

Monzinger Frühlingsplätzchen Riesling Kabinett (Emrich-Schönleber)
Münsterer Pittersberg Riesling Spätlese Trocken (Kruger-Rumpf)
Münsterer Rheinberg Riesling Spätlese (Göttelmann)
Niederhäuser Hermannshöhle Riesling Spätlese (Dönnhoff)
Norheimer Dellchen Riesling Auslese (Lötzbeyer)
Schlossböckelheimer Kupfergrube Riesling Spätlese (Gutsverwaltung Niederhausen-Schlossböckelheim)

BELOW: Protecting reisling grapes from birds, Nahe.

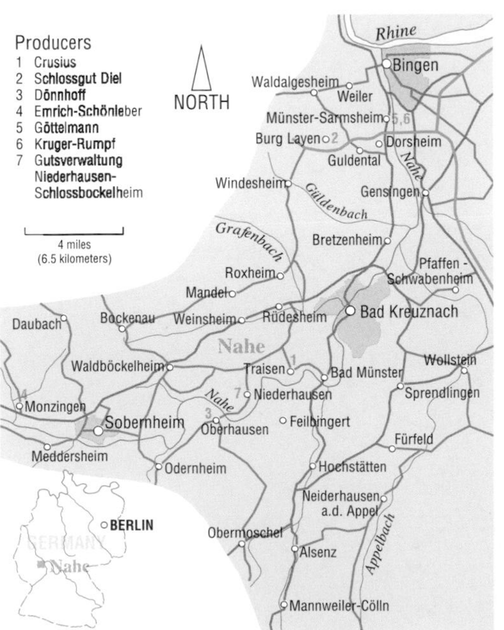

ABOVE: *Village of Rüdesheim, near Bad Kreuznach, is overlooked by steep vineyards.*

Rheingau

West of the twin cities of Mainz and Wiesbaden, the northern banks of the Rhine are swathed in an almost uninterrupted band of vineyards for about 22 miles (35 km) as far as the picturesque village of Rüdesheim, with its exceptionally steep vineyards. The vineyards of Hochheim, just east of Mainz, are also part of the Rheingau. Beyond Rüdesheim the river turns north and the vineyards peter out a short way on in the village of Lorch. The vineyards closest to the river are gently sloping, but there are many steeper patches rising into the Taunus mountains and, after about 2.5 miles (4 km), the height and exposure become unsuitable for viticulture. The lower sites benefit from richer soils, but the higher vineyards enjoy more sunshine than the sometimes mist-shrouded riverbanks.

The Rheingau is, by German standards, quite a small region, about 7,900 acres (3,200 ha). But it has become synonymous with riesling, which is by far the dominant variety, although around the village of Assmannshausen spätburgunder (pinot noir) is a highly regarded local specialty. Historically, the Rheingau is a more important flagship for fine riesling than any other German wine region, but in recent decades it has been eclipsed by the best Mosel and Saar estates; the warmer Pfalz has also provided strong competition.

The Rheingau's flagship is the magnificent Kloster Eberbach, buried deep in the forests just behind the most northerly band of vineyards. It has also long been used as a cultural and educational center. The accessibility of the region from some of Germany's largest and most prosperous cities has made it a focus for gastronomic festivals, held in some of the Rheingau's most magnificent cellars and monasteries.

VILLAGES OF THE RHEINGAU

Assmannshausen is a special case in the Rheingau, as the most widely planted grape here is red, spätburgunder (pinot noir). In fact spätburgunder constitutes half the half the vineyards on this estate. For all its celebrity the wine can be light, even weedy, and can often be disappointing, but quality has improved over time. In ripe years it can be surprisingly structured and subtle and capable of benefiting from *barrique*-aging.

Erbach is deservedly renowned for its excellent Marcobrunn vineyard, low-lying but located where it enjoys maximum sunshine. The wines are sumptuous and very long-lived.

Hattenheim is home to one of the celebrated Steinberg, solely owned by the Staatsweingut. Nussbrunnen and Wisselbrunnen often come close in quality. The wines tend to be rich and powerful.

Hochheim's best-known site is the Königin Victoria Berg. The wines are sturdy, built to last, but can lack the elegance of the best Rheingaus.

Johannisberg is dominated by the lordly Schloss Johannisberg, but wines from the Schloss are often found to be eclipsed by those from smaller estates in the village.

Kiedrich's vineyards have long had a fine reputation, but it is the success of Robert Weil in the 1990s that has really put them on the map—the Gräfenberg can deliver great sweet wines.

Lorch, just around the corner from the Rheingau, produces spicy rieslings that can be bargains compared with their illustrious cousins to the east.

Oestrich has more vineyard area than most other Rheingau villages. Its wines can be patchy, but the sweet wines from the Lenchen site are exquisite.

Rauenthal's best vineyard is Baiken. The Staatsweingut, in an old monastery at Kloster Eberbach, is the principal producer.

Rüdesheim's vineyards are among the finest in the Rheingau—powerful, extracted wines that can be the epitome of Rheingau riesling.

Winkel, gateway to Schloss Vollrads, produces some lovely wines from sites such as Hasensprung.

GEORG BREUER, RÜDESHEIM

Owner **Bernhard Breuer** ***Production*** **7,000 cases** ***Vineyard area*** **57 acres (23 ha)**

Bernhard Breuer, a wine historian and author as well as producer, was the man behind the Charta Association and the attempt to restore the reputation of the Rheingau as a great white-wine region. A fervent advocate of vineyard classification, he uses only the names of the top Rüdesheim vineyards on his labels. Anything from less than first-rate sites is bottled under the estate name. His dry wines are exemplary, never showing harshness or lack of ripeness. And his nobly sweet wines can be extraordinary—and understandably expensive.

To enjoy wine... what is needed is a sense of smell, a sense of taste, and an eye for color. All else is experience and personal preference

CYRIL RAY (1908–1991), *Ray on Wine*

GRAF VON KANITZ, LORCH

Owner **Carl Albrecht Graf von Kanitz** ***Production*** **6,500 cases** ***Vineyard area*** **35 acres (14 ha)**

This organic estate has long focused on riesling wines. Lorch is as close in microclimate to the Mittelrhein as the Rheingau, and there is a strong slate component in the soils. All this shows in the wines, which combine vivid fruit with lively acidity. The Renaissance Hilchenhaus on the property has been turned into the estate's restaurant, and a good place in which to enjoy the wines with food in a stylish setting.

SCHLOSS JOHANNISBERG, JOHANNISBERG

Owner **Fürst von Metternich** ***Production*** **20,000 cases** ***Vineyard area*** **86 acres (35 ha)**

One of the largest and most historic estates in the Rheingau, the *domaine* is dominated by its large Schloss, visible from miles around; the cellars beneath the castle are equally magnificent. The grapes, all riesling, are grown on the bank of vineyards spreading down from the castle terraces to the river. However, the wines are not as splendid as the setting. The quality is sound and at the top level of eiswein or beerenauslese can be outstanding, but given the high prices charged across the board for the Schloss wines, they hardly represent good value.

ABOVE: *Kloster Eberbach's twelfth-century cellar is part of a former Cistercian monastery.*

AUGUST KESSELER, ASSMANNSHAUSEN

Owner **August Kesseler** ***Production*** **7,500 cases** ***Vineyard area*** **40 acres (16 ha)**

Based in Assmannshausen, it is not surprising that August Kesseler has focused on red wines. Indeed, spätburgunder constitutes half the vineyards on this estate. These are not the watery pallid reds that were common here 20 years ago, but well-structured *barrique*-aged wines that command high prices. Kesseler also makes luscious rieslings from excellent sites in Rüdesheim.

KNYPHAUSEN, ERBACH

Owner **Gerko Freiherr zu Knyphausen** ***Production*** **10,000 cases** ***Vineyard area*** **54 acres (22 ha)**

Gerko zu Knyphausen is such a charming man and his ancient home so beautiful that it is impossible to visit the estate without conceiving a great affection for the wines. Produced from a range of good sites in Erbach,

BELOW: *From historic Schloss Johannisberg the vines run down to the river in orderly rows.*

Kiedrich and Hattenheim, the wines are not in the very first rank, but are invariably elegant and shapely. These are classic examples of firm Rheingau Riesling.

PETER JAKOB KUHN, OESTRICH

Owner **Peter Jakob Kuhn** ***Production*** **7,000 cases**
Vineyard area **30 acres (12 ha)**

Kuhn has quickly made a reputation for himself with his skilfully made dry rieslings, which have proved immensely popular in Germany. He also produces sweet wines that manage to be both rich and bracing. Unlike the dry wines, which all originate in Oestricher Doosberg or Lenchen, the sweet styles are bottled without a vineyard designation, which gives Kuhn more flexibility as well as simplifying life for the consumer.

JOSEF LEITZ, RÜDESHEIM

Owner **Johannes Leitz** ***Production*** **3,000 cases**
Vineyard area **15 acres (6 ha)**

Johannes Leitz is a well-traveled and widely experienced winemaker, so it is not surprising that he is up with the latest winemaking trends. The use of indigenous yeasts is rare among German wine estates, which prefer technological certainties to the vagaries of nature, but their use is routine practice here. Nor should one discount the splendid potential of his vineyards, which lie in some of the steepest sections of Rüdesheim.

BALTHASAR RESS, HATTENHEIM

Owner **Stefan Ress** ***Production*** **18,000 cases**
Vineyard area **82 acres (33 ha)**

The engaging Stefan Ress has never faltered in his enthusiasm for spreading the good word about Rheingau wines wherever he travels. With several outstanding sites in Oestrich, Rüdesheim and Hattenheim, he can easily produce a large range of wines, which, if rarely in the very top rank, are consistent, well-made and capable of giving great drinking pleasure. His sweeter wines often show wonderful delicacy as well as richness of fruit.

ROBERT WEIL, KIEDRICH

Manager **Wilhelm Weil** ***Production*** **30,000 cases**
Vineyard area **131 acres (53 ha)**

The rise to stardom of this estate has been spectacular. Its vineyards, most notably the Kiedricher Gräfenberg, are outstanding. Wilhelm Weil has also insisted on ripeness levels far above the minimum prescribed by the wine laws, so his auslesen are more likely to be declassified beerenauslesen. All the wines are good, even the modest kabinett, but it's at the top of the range that Weil excels, with a simply breathtaking range of nobly sweet wines. Prices are as staggering as quality.

Other significant producers in the Rheingau region include J. B. Becker (Walluf); Domdechant Werner'sches Weingut, Franz Küntsler (both Hoccheim); Johannishof (Johannisberg); and Schloss Vollrads (Oestrich-Winkel).

Regional Dozen

Erbacher Marcobrunn Riesling Spätlese (Schloss Reinhartshausen)
Hochheimer Kirchenstück Riesling Spätlese (Künstler)
Johannisberger Goldatzel Riesling Kabinett (Johannishof)
Johannisberger Klaus Riesling Spätlese (Prinz von Hessen)
Kiedricher Gräfenberg Riesling Trockenbeerenauslese (Weil)
Kiedricher Sandgrub Riesling Spätlese (Knyphausen)
Lorcher Krone Riesling Spätlese (von Kanitz)
Oestricher Doosberg Riesling Beerenauslese (Ress)
Riesling Eiswein (P. J. Kuhn)
Rüdesheimer Berg Rottland Riesling Auslese Trocken (Leitz)
Rüdesheimer Berg Rottland Riesling Spätlese (Kesseler)
Rüdesheimer Berg Schlossberg Riesling Erstes Gewächs (Breuer)

Wine auction

Kloster Eberbach, the magnificent twelfth-century Cistercian monastery, has a rich viticultural history as one of the most highly regarded wine estates of the Middle Ages. Now home to the German Wine Academy and Rheingau Wine Society, it hosts the world-renowned Die Glorige Tage, a three-day wine auction. Die Glorige Tage attracts legions of gourmands and wine industry luminaries such as Michael Broadbent, Jancis Robinson, and Hugh Johnson, who descend upon the abbey to taste, and bid on, Charta rieslings and wines with self-imposed restrictions on residual sugar (no more than 3 grams/liter total acidity). There are also blind-tasting elimination rounds for overall quality.

RIGHT: At wine auctions held at Kloster Eberbach's cellars, the finest wines from Rheingau estates are sold.

Rheinhessen

The famous vineyards of Rheinhessen cover more than 64,000 acres (26,000 ha), making it nine times larger than the Rheingau and the source of one-quarter of all German wine production. There are excellent producers and vineyards on the eastern fringes of Rheinhessen as well, but the vast swathes of vineyards in the central and western parts of the zone are mostly dedicated to cheap mass-produced wine.

Riesling is a minor player here, accounting for less than 10 percent of plantings. About a quarter of the vineyards are stocked with the often neutral müller-thurgau; sylvaner, which can deliver very good wines if grown in the right site, is also widely planted. Elsewhere, Rheinhessen is home to the crossings developed some years ago (bacchus, kerner, huxelrebe and many others) to generate high yields of early-ripening grapes; some of these varieties are also frost-resistant, enabling them to be planted in very fertile soils that are better suited to growing potatoes. A little red wine, usually undistinguished, is also produced here.

Nonetheless, excellent wine can be found in the Rheinhessen region, much of which is sensibly priced, perhaps reflecting the low esteem in which the region as a whole is regarded. In the north, near Bingen, one can find some good riesling sites. The most distinctive wines come from the so-called Rheinfront, the string of riverside villages south of Mainz: Nackenheim, Nierstein and Oppenheim. Some of the vineyards here have reddish loam soil, which gives the wines a bracing earthiness that can be very appealing. Sylvaner can be delicious here. The notorious Niersteiner Grosses Domtal Grosslage has done great damage to the district's reputation.

Rheinhessen is also the birthplace of Liebfraumilch, although legally a wine bearing that label can be produced from other northern regions, too. Made entirely for export markets, Liebfraumilch must be produced from müller-thurgau, sylvaner and kerner, but riesling can also be used in the blend (although not many growers would want to use this noble variety in such a low-priced wine). The historic Liebfrau vineyards situated in the center of Worms once had a good reputation. The firm of Valckenberg, present owner of the vineyards, is making a gallant attempt to rescue its good name.

For years growers of the Rheinhessen interior made a good living from their overcropped vineyards, but bulk wine prices tumbled in the 1990s and some growers are now losing money, however high their yields. Some of the over-production disappears into "Euro-blends," but it is increasingly clear that the market for insipid, sugary wine is dwindling. This will mean short-term pain for many growers, but perhaps the overall consequences for the German industry will be beneficial.

VILLAGES OF THE RHEINHESSEN

Bingen's rieslings bear some resemblance to those from the Rheingau, just across the river from Rüdesheim, but they rarely attain the same finesse.

Nackenheim's best site is Rothenberg, blessed with the zone's famous red soils. Gunderloch is the best-known producer in this Rheinfront village.

Nierstein is famous, but be warned, most of the bottles labeled Nierstein don't contain a single drop from this celebrated village. Authentic Nierstein riesling or sylvaner can be excellent, so always look for the top vineyard names of Oelberg, Hipping, Brudersberg and Pettental.

Oppenheim's chalky soils are well adapted to the riesling, which is well represented in this Rheinfront village. However, only a few of the steepest vineyards are of outstanding quality.

ABOVE: *The ornate cathedral at Worms. The town marks the southern limit of the Rheinhessen wine region.*

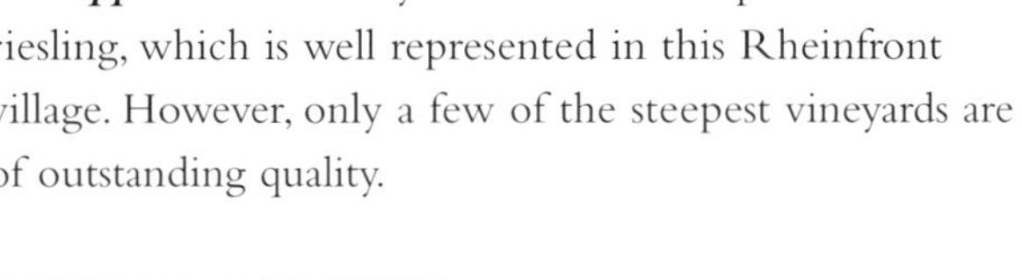

BALBACH, NIERSTEIN

Manager/lessor **Fritz Hasselbach** ***Production*** **8,000 cases**
Vineyard area **32 acres (13 ha)**

Balbach went into a gradual decline in the early 1990s, but in 1996 the estate was leased by Fritz Hasselbach of the Gunderloch *domaine* (see below). He has taken advantage of the excellent vineyards owned by Balbach to revive the reputation of the property. Hasselbach will probably purchase the vineyards eventually. Riesling is the dominant variety and Hasselbach has rightly focused on it, producing a fine range of fairly broad, succulent wines in the late 1990s.

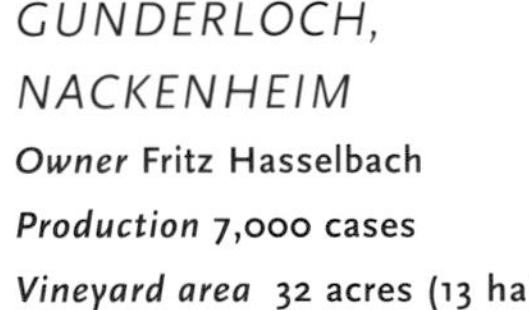

GUNDERLOCH, NACKENHEIM

Owner **Fritz Hasselbach**
Production **7,000 cases**
Vineyard area **32 acres (13 ha)**

The Hasselbachs have done wonders at this property. Although the estate owns vineyards in Nierstein, its top wines come from the reddish soil of the Nackenheimer Rothenberg site. Their standard, off-dry riesling is labeled "Jean-Baptiste" and does offer good value, but the top wines are the sweeter styles from Rothenberg. The wines are well-structured and require a few years to open up.

RIGHT: *Science lends winemakers a hand at the Department of Viticulture's State Research Institute in Ghisenheim.*

HEYL ZU HERRNSHEIM, NIERSTEIN

Owner **Markus Ahr** ***Production*** **17,000 cases** ***Vineyard area*** **92 acres (37 ha)**

Once the most celebrated estate in the Rheinhessen, it was brought to its best by Peter von Weymarn. An enthusiast for dry, often austere wines, mostly from riesling and sylvaner, he also released sweeter styles. In the mid-1990s the property was bought by the Ahr family, who have been vigorously building on von Weymarn's firm foundations. The top site is usually Brudersberg, but there are also outstanding wines from Pettental and Oelberg.

Regional Dozen

- Binger Scharlachberg Riesling Spätlese (Villa Sachsen)
- Dalsheimer Hubacker Riesling Eiswein (Keller)
- Nackenheimer Rothenberg Riesling Auslese (Gunderloch)
- Niersteiner Auglangen Riesling Spätlese (Sankt Antony)
- Niersteiner Hipping Riesling Auslese (Balbach)
- Niersteiner Hipping Riesling Spätlese (Schneider)
- Niersteiner Pettental Riesling Auslese (Franz Karl Schmitt)
- Niersteiner Pettental Riesling Auslese (Heyl zu Herrnsheim)
- Oppenheimer Herrenberg Riesling Spätlese (Kühling-Gillot)
- Rheinriver Selection QBA (Fritz Hasselbach)
- Riesling Kabinett Halbtrocken Jean Baptiste (Gunderloch)
- Rieslaner Auslese (Schales)

KELLER, FLÖRSHEIM–DALSHEIM

Owner **Klaus Keller** ***Production*** **8,000 cases** ***Vineyard area*** **30 acres (12 ha)**

This long-established estate is based on Dalsheim. Although not one of the most renowned Rheinhessen villages, lying just west of Worms, the Kellers have won an enviable reputation for producing intense and succulent sweet rieslings.

KÜHLING-GILLOT, BODENHEIM

Owners **the Gillot family** ***Production*** **6,500 cases** ***Vineyard area*** **22 acres (9 ha)**

The Gillot family's vineyards lie mostly in Oppenheim, just south of Nierstein. The top site is often the well-known Sackträger. A wide range of wines is produced, but the best tend to be the rieslings, which are made in a full range of styles. The sweeter wines are quite opulent and lush, with a slight suggestion of tropical fruits.

SANKT ANTONY, NIERSTEIN

Owner **MAN Corporation** ***Production*** **12,000 cases** ***Vineyard area*** **57 acres (23 ha)**

A large estate owned by a Munich corporation, Sankt Antony has recently made some excellent rieslings from its best vineyards, notably Pettental and Oelberg. Many of the wines are aged in large casks in the traditional manner. It has enjoyed considerable success with its drier styles.

SCHALES, FLÖRSHEIM-DALSHEIM

Owners **the Schales family** ***Production*** **25,000 cases** ***Vineyard area*** **119 acres (48 ha)**

Although not in the very first rank, the estate is typical of the best of the domaines inland from the Rhein. The Schales cultivate a huge range of grape varieties and vinify them in many different styles. Although sometimes a bit hit-and-miss, there is good rieslaner and a quite bizarre sparkling eiswein. The estate has a small but interesting wine museum.

BELOW: *Louis Guntrum winery on the banks of the Rhine, Nierstein, in the Rheinhessen region.*

Pfalz

The Pfalz is the largest German wine region after Rheinhessen. Not surprisingly, a good deal of mediocre wine is produced in the less-favored localities and for much the same reasons as in Rheinhessen: large vineyards on essentially flat land are planted with high-yielding and early-ripening varieties best suited to bulk wines. Even before the planting of those varieties, much of the Pfalz region was regarded primarily as a source of cheap blending wine and the reputation of the region was far from distinguished. Even so, there is a far higher proportion of fine wine made in the Pfalz than in its northern neighbor and observers presently find it to be the country's most exciting wine region.

The quality heart of the region lies in the stretch of vineyards just south of Bad Dürkheim, through the villages of Wachenheim, Forst, Deidesheim and Ruppertsberg. Here are the great estates of the Pfalz and the source of most of the area's greatest wines. Other excellent vineyards can be found just north of Bad Dürkheim in the villages of Kallstadt and Ungstein.

But whereas 20 years ago few would have paid much attention to the other sectors of the Pfalz, today there is wide recognition that these other parts, notably in the Südliche Weinstrasse in the south around Landau, are capable of producing wines of high quality, although not all are in the classic riesling mold. In the past the southern part of the Pfalz was dominated by co-operatives; they still exist, but many growers have broken away and set up, with increasing success, on their own. Nonetheless, average yields in the south remain high and there is ample room for improvement.

Riesling is more significant here than in Rheinhessen, although with only 20 percent of plantings it is still not a major player. On the other hand, there is no doubt that the southern sector in particular is well suited to the classic burgundian varieties, for which the potential has yet to be fully expressed. Since 1992 chardonnay has been permitted as a commercial variety and quite a few estates have planted it, to the dismay of some traditionalists. The best reds are spätburgunder, although the grape is still not as widely planted as portugieser or dornfelder. Portugieser rarely yields wine of much interest or structure and is often vinified as a rosé, but dornfelder can be as enjoyable as a ripe Beaujolais-type as long as yields are kept under control. There is also a smattering of cabernet sauvignon, but growing it remains an exercise in perversity, since there is no evidence that the Pfalz is well suited to this variety.

The climatic conditions that make the Pfalz so appropriate for burgundian varieties also means that rieslings here have a different structure from those found farther north. The grapes mature at higher must weights, making it feasible to produce fully dry rieslings with no hint of tartness. Levels of acidity are not as fierce as in the Mosel or the Mittelrhein, so the wines tend to taste broader and fleshier. Throughout the region riesling combines fruitiness, opulence and stylishness, especially in its sweeter manifestations. Top producers avoid flabbiness by maintaining lower yields and an impressive concentration of fruit. In some years, sweet wines of the most astounding syrupy richness can be made.

Fifteen years ago the Pfalz, for all its potential, produced far too many disappointing wines. That has all changed and many observers now find it the country's most exciting wine region. Formerly somnolent great estates such as von Buhl and Bassermann-Jordan have bounced back, once again producing a wide range of stimulating wines.

ABOVE: Riesling grapes, prized for their versatility.

LEFT Riedel reisling glass. Riedel, founded in 1756, is one of the world's finest glassware companies.

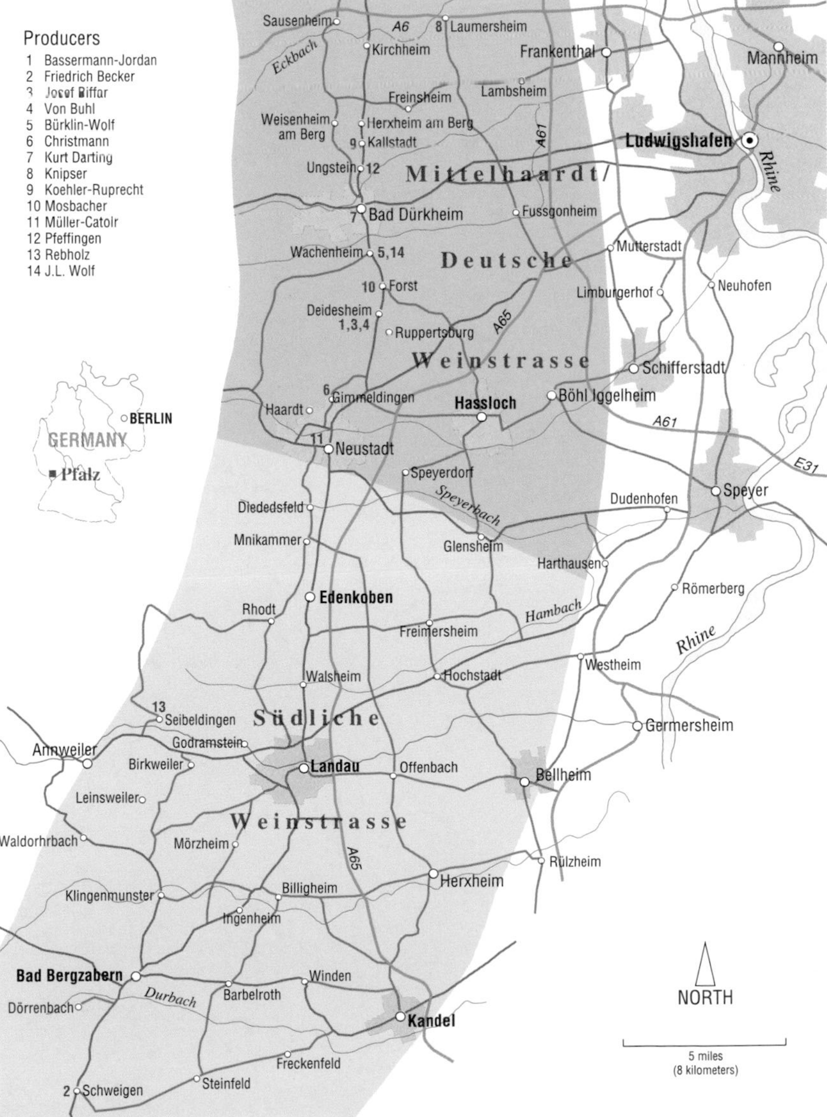

ABOVE: The village of Ranschbach with some of its sloping vineyards in the background.

ABOVE: J. L. Wolf 1996 and 1997 Rieslings; the first vintages under the management of Ernst Loosen.

Other estates that were not very well known in previous decades—Knipser, Christmann, Mosbacher, Biffar and Rebholz—are now well established and reliable sources of excellent wines. One innovative estate, Müller-Catoir, has for some years been demonstrating what a truly remarkable winemaker can do even with vineyards that are rated in the top rank.

Villages of the Pfalz

Deidesheim, just south of Forst, is a handsome town with a clutch of fine vineyards that are marginally warmer than those of its neighbor to the north, including Herrgottsacker, Mäushöhle and Leinhöhle.

Forst has a complex palette of soils—basalt as well as loam—which gives distinctive wines of remarkable elegance and richness. The best sites include Jesuitengarten, Ungeheuer, Pechstein and Kirchenstück. Von Buhl is a major proprietor here.

Kallstadt, north of Bad Dürkheim, is best known for the range of wines made from its best site, the chalky Saumagen, by Koehler-Ruprecht.

Ruppertsberg is essentially a satellite of Deidesheim. It is a good source of riesling, especially from top sites Reiterpfad and Gaisböhl. Some detect an earthiness in the wines from this village.

Ungstein, south of Kallstadt, has some steep sites such as the excellent Herrenberg. Both riesling and scheurebe deliver exceptional results here.

Wachenheim, just south of Bad Dürkheim, has some vineyards that deliver exceptionally ripe and full-bodied rieslings with considerable elegance. Top sites include Goldbächel and Gerümpel.

BASSERMANN-JORDAN, DEIDESHEIM

Owner **Margrit von Bassermann-Jordan** ***Production*** **30,000 cases**
Vineyard area **104 acres (42 ha)**

Still owned by the founding family after almost three hundred years, this grand estate has no truck with grape varieties other than riesling. Although based in Deidesheim, its best vineyards are situated in Forst and Ruppertsberg. The wines were decidedly dull in the 1980s, but have certainly improved since the arrival of a new winemaker at the estate.

VON BUHL, DEIDESHEIM

Owner **Reichsfreiherr Georg Enoch von und zu Gutenberg**
Production **30,000 cases** ***Vineyard area*** **141 acres (57 ha)**

This estate, with vineyards in Forst, Ruppertsberg and Deidesheim, was in the doldrums for much of the 1970s and 80s, but von Buhl is once again in the forefront of estates in the Pfalz region. A new winemaker, Frank John, was taken on in the mid-1990s. He has produced some dazzling wines, from dry rieslings to sumptuous trockenbeerenauslesen. John's main change is to harvest fruit later—this ensures high levels of ripeness, but can also mean smaller crops.

BÜRKLIN-WOLF, WACHENHEIM

Owner **Bettina Bürklin-Wolf Guradze** ***Production*** **60,000 cases** ***Vineyard area*** **235 acres (95 ha)**

Bürklin-Wolf has never let its standards slip. Its top wines are made by whole-cluster pressing, a technique which delivers a cleaner, more aromatic and more elegant fruit. A very large property, it can produce wines in a variety of styles. Its dry wines have quite a following, but its sweeter styles are more popular outside Germany. In some exceptional vintages, its nobly sweet wines and eisweins are sensational. Riesling dominates, but there are also decent reds made from spätburgunder and dornfelder.

KOEHLER-RUPRECHT, KALLSTADT

Owner **Bernd Philippi** ***Production*** **6,000 cases** ***Vineyard area*** **25 acres (10 ha)**

Bernd Philippi, an international wine consultant as well as a winemaker, is an individualist. The core of his production remains rieslings from the splendid Saumagen vineyard, made in every conceivable style according to the vintage. They are powerfully structured wines capable of great longevity. But Philippi also makes a range of *barrique* wines, including chardonnay, spätburgunder, and weisser and grauer burgunder, and his sweet wines—such as the occasional spätburgunder eiswein—can be extraordinary. To avoid confusion, *barrique* wines are sold under the Philippi rather than the estate label. Sample the wines in the Weincastell, the family's fine restaurant adjoining the winery.

MÜLLER-CATOIR, NEUSTADT

Owner **Jakob Heinrich Catoir** ***Production*** **11,000 cases** ***Vineyard area*** **50 acres (20 ha)**

The estate's vineyards in Mussbach and Gimmeldingen are not in the top tier of Pfalz growths, yet winemaker Hans-Gunter Schwartz routinely produces exceptional wines. Riesling is the dominant grape, but Schwartz also works his magic with grauer burgunder, muskateller and scheurebe. His rieslaner is considered to be the finest in Germany. The yields are low, which accounts for their concentration, but another part of the formula is Schwartz's willingness to trust the wine to make itself and his unwillingness to use the usual technical battery.

PFEFFINGEN, UNGSTEIN

Owner **Doris Eymael** ***Production*** **7,500 cases** ***Vineyard area*** **27 acres (11 ha)**

Doris Fuhrmann-Eymael runs this well-regarded estate. After a bad patch while its vineyards, replanted in the late 1980s, were attaining maturity, Pfeffingen is back on form. As well as rich spicy riesling from Ungsteiner Herrenberg, the estate produces robust sylvaner and plump, sappy scheurebe. A little spätburgunder and dornfelder have been planted and they will be *barrique*-aged.

J. L. WOLF, WACHENHEIM

Owners **the Sturm family (Ernst Loosen, manager)** ***Production*** **4,000 cases** ***Vineyard area*** **25 acres (10 ha)**

This was one of the more lackluster estates in the core of the Pfalz until Ernst Loosen of Bernkastel and a partner took it over in 1996. Its sites include such prime vineyards as Forster Ungeheuer and Jesuitengarten and Wachenheimer Gerümpel. Riesling is by far the most important variety. Initial vintages have been sound rather than brilliant, but Loosen is unlikely to rest until he has restored the estate to its proper rank.

Other recommended producers in the Pfalz region include Friedrich Becker (Schweigen); Josef Biffar (Deidesheim); Christmann (Gimmeldingen); Kurt Darting (Bad Dürkheim); Knipser (Laumersheim); Mosbacher (Forst); and Rebholz (Siebeldingen).

Regional Dozen

QUALITY WINES

- Forster Ungeheuer Riesling Trockenbeerenauslese (von Buhl)
- Mussbacher Eselshaut Rieslanre Auslese (Müller-Catoir)
- Riesling Estate (Burklin Wolf)
- Ruppertsberger Reiterpfad Riesling Spätlese Trocken (von Buhl)
- Ruppertsberger Reiterpfad Riesling Trockenbeeren-auslese (Bassermann-Jordan)
- Wachenheimer Gerümpel Riesling Eiswein (Bürklin-Wolf)

BEST VALUE WINES

- Forster Pechstein Riesling Auslese (Mosbacher)
- Kallstadter Saumagen Riesling Spätlese (Koehler-Ruprecht)
- Ruppertsberger Reiterpfad Riesling Spätlese Trocken (Christmann)
- Ungsteiner Herrenberg Riesling Auslese (Darting)
- Wachenheimer Gerümpel Riesling Eiswein (Bürklin-Wolf)
- Wachenheimer Goldbächel Riesling Spätlese (Biffar)

LEFT: Vines trained on wires, a labor-intensive but often necessary task.

Franken

ABOVE: Many of the great vineyards in Franken grow on very steep sites.

Franken (or Franconia) is a Bavarian region surrounding the splendid baroque city of Würzburg. The River Main loops through the region, with most vineyards on steep sites overlooking the river and benefiting from the warmth reflected by it. The soils are varied, but fall into three main types: sandstone, limestone and marl. These soils influence the grape varieties planted, as well as the flavor and structure of the wines.

Franken enjoys an essentially continental climate: winters are cold and prolonged, bringing a risk of spring frosts, while summers can be blisteringly hot. Harvesting rarely begins before October and often continues until the end of November.

Müller-thurgau is the most widely planted variety, delivering fresh, straightforward wines that can have a light mineral tone and a refreshing acidity. But Franken's specialty is sylvaner, originally brought here from Austria in the seventeenth century. Overcropped sylvaner can be neutral in character, but in Franken it can have a fine mineral edge. Inevitably it is at its best and definitely most enjoyable when yields are kept low. Riesling can also be delicious here, but it can be planted only in the best sites because it ripens so late.

Over the past decades there has been considerable vineyard expansion and, sadly, it is the lesser varieties, such as kerner and bacchus, that have been planted. More resistant to frost than riesling and sylvaner, they have been employed in flatter sites previously rejected as unsuitable for viticulture. Surprisingly, bacchus can deliver quite good results here and the off-dry aromatic wine it produces is popular locally.

For centuries Franken wine has been consigned to a dumpy bottle called the bocksbeutel, which has hindered the wine's international reputation. This is a shame, since the quality of the best wines is extremely high. Most are dry, but have the body and structure to keep any harshness at bay. They have an almost earthy mineral quality that is directly derived from the splendid vineyards.

There are also some magnificent sweet wines, which are intense, structured and long-lived.

Parts of Franken, especially in the western zones, are also well-suited to red wines. Spätburgunder is the principal grape, but a new variety, domina, is also popular. The best red wines are aged in *barriques* and command high prices. White burgundian varieties are also grown and these, too, are often fermented and aged in *barriques*, with considerable success.

BÜRGERSPITAL, WÜRZBURG

***Manager* Rudolf Friess *Production* 85,000 cases**
***Vineyard area* 356 acres (144 ha)**

Established in 1319 as a charitable institution, its activities are funded by selling wines from its vast estate. One third of the vineyards are planted with riesling, which is not typical of Franken. This was also the first large estate to specialize in weissburgunder. The wines, as always in Franken, are predominantly dry. There are some outstanding sweet wines from sylvaner, grauer burgunder and other varieties. Reds are undistinguished and quality has been far from exceptional, but the appointment of a new cellarmaster may help to improve performance.

JULIUSSPITAL, WÜRZBURG

***Manager* Horst Kolesch *Production* 80,000 cases**
***Vineyard area* 250 acres (100 ha)**

Run with great aplomb by Horst Kolesch, the ancient Juliusspital is currently the best of the large Würzburg estates. Like Bürgerspital, this is primarily a charitable foundation, supported by its wine production. It has extensive holdings in almost all the best sites in Franken and glories in its 64 acres (26 ha) in Würzburger Stein. It is a conservative estate, having no truck with blends or brands, but there is no question that the quality of the wines is brilliant. Riesling and sylvaner are the star turns, but there are also exceptional wines from weissburgunder and rieslaner. Nobly sweet wines are rarities here, but when they are made they are magnificent.

FÜRST LÖWENSTEIN, KREUZWERTHEIM

***Owner* Alois Konstantin Fürst zu Löwenstein *Production* 18,000 cases *Vineyard area* 67 acres (27 ha)**

Since the mid-1990s a determined attempt has been made to improve the performance of a once lackluster estate. Richly earthy sylvaner comes from the great Homburger Kallmuth site, but this princely estate has good vineyards in many other parts of Franken, as well as in Baden. Other than the rare sweet wines, all varieties are vinified in a totally dry style and the top

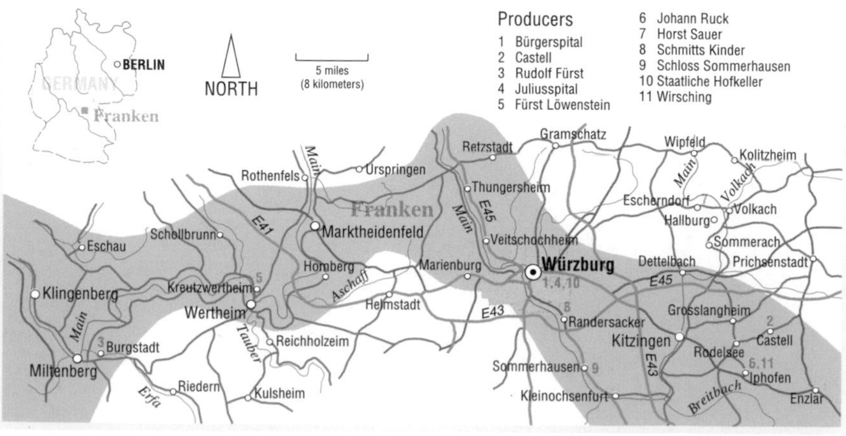

range is bottled under the Asphodel label, referring to the rare flower that grows in the sheltered Kallmuth. There is also some good spätburgunder that is aged in mostly new *barriques*.

JOHANN RUCK, IPHOFEN

Owners **Ruck family** ***Production*** **7,000 cases** ***Vineyard area*** **35 acres (14 ha)**

Johann Ruck traces his family way back to the year 945, but they think of themselves as relative newcomers to Iphofen, having arrived in 1839. Ruck produces classic Franken wines, taut, elegant and mostly dry. Yields are kept low, so the wines are finely concentrated. No wood is used, except for Ruck's pride and joy, a parcel of weissburgunder vines that are 40 years old. He handles this wine with special care and vinifies it in small oak.

HORST SAUER, ESCHERNDORF

Owner **Horst Sauer** ***Production*** **6,000 cases** ***Vineyard area*** **22 acres (9 ha)**

Sauer is a rising star, producing impeccable riesling and sylvaner from his vineyards in the outstanding Escherndorfer Lump site near Würzburg. His harvesters check through the vineyards repeatedly to ensure that only the ripest fruit is picked. The wines are all aged on the fine lees in steel tanks to retain their freshness and purity of fruit. Sauer also makes nobly sweet wines of sensational quality, but they are hard to come by as, sadly, he makes only very tiny quantities.

SCHMITTS KINDER, RANDERSACKER

Owner **Karl Martin Schmitt** ***Production*** **10,000 cases** ***Vineyard area*** **35 acres (14 ha)**

Sylvaner is the main variety here, but Schmitt also does well with riesling, rieslaner and even bacchus. For his top wines and for the sweet wines, he likes to use *barriques*, although oaked müller-thurgau is not a great success. Nor are the red wines, since the soils here are not suited to red varieties, but the dry white wines are of the highest quality.

SCHLOSS SOMMERHAUSEN, SOMMERHAUSEN

Owners **Steinmann family** ***Production*** **13,000 cases** ***Vineyard area*** **50 acres (20 ha)**

Owned since 1968 by the same family, the Schloss estates produce very good sylvaner and riesling and a wide range of burgundian varieties, as well as a well-known range of sparkling wines. The best of these wines are produced from riesling and auxerrois. In the top years there are some excellent and noble sweet wines from chardonnay, rieslaner and scheurebe.

WIRSCHING, IPHOFEN

Owner **Dr Heinrich Wirsching** ***Production*** **36,000 cases** ***Vineyard area*** **173 acres (70 ha)**

After some initial disappointing years, this large private estate is gradually returning to form under the direction of enologist Uwe Mateus. The winemaking here is less interventionist than at most other large estates and this allows a certain spicy complex fruitiness to shine forth. Sylvaner and riesling are very good dry wines and there is attractive traminer and rieslaner in a sweeter style. Wirsching is rightly proud of its low-yielding grauer burgunder, aged for 15 months in *barriques*. The reds are also of above-average quality.

Other notable producers in Franken include Castell (Castell); Rudolf Fürst (Burgstadt); and Staatliche Hofkeller (Würzburg).

Regional Dozen

Bürgstadter Centgrafenberg Spätburgunder Trocken (Fürst)
Bürgstadter Centgrafenberg Weisser Burgunder Spätlese Trocken (Fürst)
Casteller Kugelspiel Sylvaner Eiswein (Castell)
Escherndorfer Lump Riesling Beerenauslese (Sauer)
Homburger Kallmuth Sylvaner Spätlese Trocken (Löwenstein)
Iphofer Julius-Echter-Berg Sylvaner Kabinett Trocken (Ruck)
Iphofer Julius-Echter-Berg Sylvaner Spätlese Trocken (Wirsching)
Randersackerer Pfülben Rieslaner Beerenauslese (Bürgerspital)
Randersackerer Pfülben Riesling Kabinett Trocken (Schmitts Kinder)
Sommerhäuser Steinbach Riesling Spätlese Trocken (Schloss Sommerhausen)
Würzburger Stein Riesling Beerenauslese (Juliusspital)
Würzburger Stein Sylvaner Spätlese Trocken (Staatlicher Hofkeller)

LEFT: In the western parts of Franken the main grape variety grown is spätburgunder.

ABOVE: Vineyards rise steeply behind the town of Besigheim, near Stuttgart.

Other German Regions

WÜRTTEMBERG

Of all the major German wine regions, Württemberg is the least known. Its vineyards are scattered, with the best near Stuttgart and Heilbronn. Although some good, and even exceptional, riesling is produced, especially around Stuttgart, this is essentially red-wine country. An unimpressive red grape, trollinger, gives a pale red easily mistaken for rosé. Other varieties cultivated are spätburgunder (pinot noir), schwarzriesling (pinot meunier), lemberger, and the mutation of schwarzriesling known as samtrot. Many of the best examples are aged in small oak barrels and can have surprising richness and extraction.

GRAF ADELMANN, KLEINBOTTWAR

Owner Michael Graf Adelmann Production 10,000 cases
Vineyard area 44 acres (18 ha)

Based in the exquisite Schaubeck castle, this has been one of the region's leading estates for several decades. Adelmann harvests as late as possible, so these are wines of richness and great concentration. The dry rieslings are excellent and there is some lovely traminer and muskateller, but the best wines are oak-aged red cuvées. "Herbst im Park" is intended to be drunk with game and is supple and lush. A bit more structured is the "Vignette", an exceptionally elegant blend of lemberger and samtrot.

RIGHT: Trollinger grapes, Württemberg's most commonly planted red variety.

NEIPPERG, SCHWAIGERN

Owner Karl Eugen Erbgraf zu Neipperg Production 20,000 cases
Vineyard area 77 acres (31 ha)

The vineyards are clustered around the ancient Schloss Neipperg. Although riesling is made here, this is not Neipperg's strength. Instead, Graf von Neipperg prefers to produce varietal red wines and has little interest in the fashionable blended reds. An enthusiast for local traditions, he also ages his best reds in barrels crafted from oak trees grown in the family's own forests. The top wines are usually lemberger and samtrot.

HESSISCHE BERGSTRASSE

This very small region clustered around Bensheim is planted mostly with riesling, but burgundian varieties also do well here. Staatsweingut is an exceptionally consistent producer, and the best wines emerge from Heppenheimer Centgericht. The winery specializes in eiswein. Another reliable estate is Simon-Bürkle, which offers a wide range of red and white wines at reasonable prices. The town of Bensheim also has its own winery, making good riesling and burgundian wines from its chalky Kalkgasse site.

AHR

The River Ahr flows into the Rhine at Linz, to the northwest of Koblenz, its terraced rocky slopes planted with vines. The warming reflections off its craggy cliffs help bring the grapes to maturity. This most northerly region is best known for red wines. The area is very popular within Germany, largely because the area is exceedingly pretty and studded with inns, making it a pleasant outing for the day-trippers.

Spätburgunder (pinot noir) is the focus, with some riesling and portugieser. A handful of estates make pinot noirs that are increasingly rich and burgundian in style. The best wines in Ahr are quite expensive.

NELLES, HEIMERSHEIM

***Owner* Thomas Nelles *Production* 3,000 cases**
***Vineyard area* 12 acres (5 ha)**

Although spätburgunder is planted in only half the Nelles vineyards, they are the base of the best wines. Bottled without vineyard designation but with an arcane numbering system, these are pinot noirs of substance and elegance. The "B-52" is often the best wine in the range. The prices are less extravagant than those of Deutzerhof and the "Rubis" bottling offers a lively, simple pinot noir at an affordable price.

MITTELRHEIN

Mittelrhein has some dazzling scenery. Riverside villages crouch beneath steep vineyards and castle-capped cliffs; vineyards are strung out along the Rhine around

Koblenz. Wines from vines grown on slatey soils around Bacharach, in the far south, are often among the best. The village of Boppard is capable of occasionally producing notable sweet wines. The Mittelrhein offers racy, pleasurable rieslings. Their marked acidity gives them a freshness that is appealing when young and helps the wines to age quite well. Prices are reasonable.

TONI JOST, BACHARACH

***Owner* Peter Jost *Production* 4,500 cases**
***Vineyard area* 22 acres (9 ha)**

Long the leader of the pack, Peter Jost remains the leading grower, although his pre-eminence is increasingly being challenged by other quality-conscious estates. Jost makes a full range of wines, from dry to very sweet, and all are of reliable quality. He is best known for his amazingly sumptuous dessert wines, especially the Riesling Trockenbeerenauslese from Bacharacher Hahn.

> *Mixing one's wines may be a mistake, but old and new wisdom mix admirably.*
> BERTHOLT BRECHT (1898–1956)

SAALE-UNSTRUT

To the west of Leipzig, this is the most northerly wine region in continental Europe. The climate can be harsh, so early-ripening varieties dominate. Devastating spring frosts mean yields in some years are greatly reduced. Sixteenth-century commentators complained of the wine's sourness and little has changed since. Müller-thurgau is the dominant variety. Astonishingly, the leading estate, Lützkendorf, occasionally succeeds in producing a beerenauslese from sylvaner grapes.

SACHSEN

Here, too, spring frosts can slash yields to uneconomic levels, and Sachsen has yet to establish any reputation for quality. Müller-thurgau is the dominant variety in this region. Riesling is a significant variety, and the white burgundian varieties, as well as traminer, are also quite widely encountered.

The Zimmerling estate bottles all its production as dry table wine. In Meissen there is a weingalerie near the cathedral, where many of the wines can be sampled.

Other significant producers include Dautel (Bönnigheim); Karl Haidle (Kernen-Stetten); Wöhrwag (Untertürkheim); Deutzerhof (Mayschoss); and Weingart (Spay).

Regional Dozen

- Cuvée C [cabernet blend] (Aldinger)
- Cuvée Vignette [red] (Adelmann)
- Granat [red] (Schwegler)
- Kleinbottwarer Süssmund Riesling Spätlese Trocken (Adelmann)
- Kreation [red] (Dautel)
- Lemberger Auslese Trocken (Hohenlohe-Ohringen)
- Neipperger Schlossberg Lemberger Trocken (Neipperg)
- Philipp [red] (Wöhrwag)
- Riesling Eiswein (Feindert)
- Schnaiter Burghalde Spätburgunder Auslese Trocken (Haidle)
- Schwaigerner Ruthe Riesling Spätlese Trocken (Neipperg)
- Untertürkheimer Herzogenberg Riesling Spätlese Trocken (Wöhrwag)

BELOW: A bend in the River Neckar, with the town of Neckarsulm in the background.

Vineyards surround this picturesque small village in the Austrian countryside.

Austria

ABOVE: *Pure, clear Austrian schnapps is a profitable sideline for Austrian wineries. It is made from distilling grape skins, then fermenting the liquid.*

Austria

GILES MACDONOGH

Austria produces some of the most enticing sweet and dry white wines in Europe, as well as increasingly interesting reds, which make up around 20 percent of the output. A small, significant producer, Austria makes about the same quantity of wine as Bordeaux. Grapes were planted in the area we now call Austria as early as Celtic times and wine received another boost from the Romans.

It was the wine-loving Emperor Probus who first encouraged vine-growing in the area when idle soldiers were set to work planting vines on the warm Pannonian plain in the east. The Barbarian invasions naturally set back developments somewhat, but by the end of the first millennium Charlemagne's armies had established Christianity on both sides of the Danube. In the wake of the armies came the great monasteries and with the monks came the vineyards.

At one time Austrian wines enjoyed a huge reputation, until the popularity of Heurigen (the local wine bars run by individual growers) led many growers to concentrate more on bulk than quality. Between the two world wars, Austria established a reputation for hospitality and good cheer that appealed chiefly to the Germans. Sweet, or off-dry wines were the rule, but later Wachau and South Styria developed completely dry white wines, while Burgenland proved its ability to make convincing reds. Production of sweet wines is now chiefly limited to the area around the shallow Neusiedlersee.

Landscape and climate

With a continental climate, Austria has a long growing season. Top growers in the Wachau, for example, may still be picking at the end of November. The Wachau and parts of the Kremstal are composed of steep primary rock soils where grapes grown on horizontal terraces produce racy wines. Most vineyards in Lower Austria are found close to the River Danube, on ridges of loess and volcanic rock that provide relief to a largely flat region.

In Burgenland, black grapes, such as cabernet sauvignon, merlot, syrah, and nebbiolo, have little problem achieving good levels of ripeness when grown close to the warm lake of Neusiedlersee.

The Leitha Hills

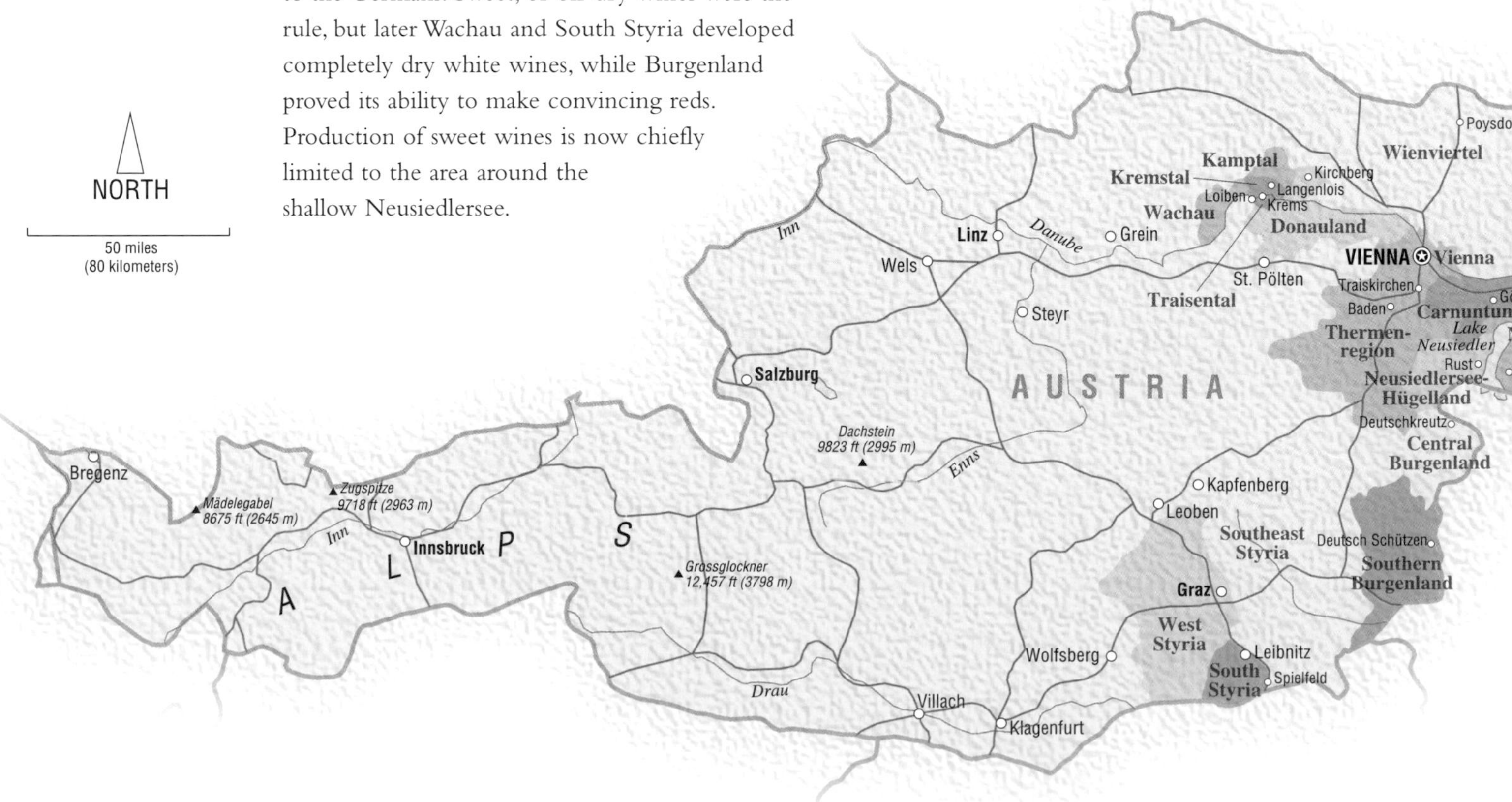

to the north and west are chalky and here both chardonnay and pinot noir have been successful. Central and Southern Burgenland are predominantly red-wine areas. The chief grape grown here is the blaufränkisch.

Vines and wines

Austria has many indigenous varieties providing a nice distraction from the globalization of tastes. On heavy soils such as those of the Weinviertel, grüner veltliner produces sappy, refreshing wines with a distinctly peppery bouquet. On the primary rock soils of the Wachau, however, it is so different in character that tasters often believe they are drinking top white burgundies. Riesling is an important white grape, while chardonnay, known as morillon, has a long tradition in Styria. Weiss- and grauburgunder, or pinots blanc and gris, have a longer tradition and often produce better results.

Neuburger is sometimes claimed as a pinot. Vinified dry or affected by botrytis, it can be superb. In Burgenland and Styria the workhorse grape is welschriesling, which can be excellent both when well-vinified and in sweeter styles.

The most widely planted red grape is zweigelt, a crossing of St Laurent and blaufränkisch. Low yields can produce stunning results. Blaufränkisch is seen as the number-one quality cultivar, but it tends to dry out in barriques. In West Styria there is blauer wildbacher, which is generally vinified as an acid rosé called schilcher.

Winemaking

Austrians like wines with a refreshing acidity. Flavors are more angular than those from, say, Australia. Oaking became very common in the late eighties and barriques were often used to age quite light, unsuitable wines. Many of Austria's best growers never use barriques; riesling and grüner veltliner are generally thought not to need it. In Styria the classical style with sauvignon blanc or morillon (chardonnay) has been to age in oak, concrete or stainless steel. Many reds are also "oak aged."

With very few firms able to supply a large amount of wine of consistent quality, Austria's strength now lies in high-quality niche products. With the average holding being less than 5 acres (2 ha), most Austrians cannot hope to lay hands on some of the more highly rated wines. Yet even with just 15 acres (6 ha), a grower will make up to half a dozen wines, ranging from dry whites to reds and botrytis-affected whites or eiswein. This means that production is limited, and demand (and prices) for the top quality wines is very high.

At the other end of the scale, in the Heurige, wine is drunk very young and it is very cheap. These places are often so profitable that there is little incentive to labor over making good wine. On the other hand, some makers reinvest their profits in properly made wines.

ABOVE: *Many producers shun mechanical harvesting, preferring to use grapes picked by hand.*

LEFT: *A Bohemian coloured tumbler with gilt decoration.*

Austrian wines are graded by levels of natural residual sweetness. In some areas there are as yet unofficial classifications of vineyards on the basis of the French cru system.

There are 16 wine-producing regions in Austria: these are Vienna, Thermenregion, Carnuntum, Donauland, Weinviertel, Kamptal, Kremstal, Wachau, Traisental, Neusiedlersee, Neusiedlersee–Hügelland, Central and Southern Burgenland, and also Southeast, West and South Styria.

KARL ALPHART, TRAISKIRCHEN, THERMENREGION

Owner **Karl Alphart** ***Production*** **4,445 cases** ***Vineyard area*** **25 acres (10 ha)**

The Thermenregion derives its name from its warm springs and spas. It is a little suntrap protected by the last outriders of the Alps and grapes ripen a little too well here, meaning either too much sugar, or too much alcohol. Despite the difficulties, Alphart makes it seem easy to make great wine. His first loves are the curious duo of zierfandler and rotgipfler, two local grapes found pretty well nowhere else. He vinifies them

BELOW: *The alpine village of Karten.*

together and apart, always imbuing them with an exciting spiciness. But that is not the end of the story, and there is exciting riesling from the steep slopes, good chardonnay and, once in a while, marvelous beerenauslesen and trockenbeerenauslesen.

WILLI BRÜNDLMAYER, LANGENLOIS, KAMPTAL

Owners **Bründlmayer family** ***Production*** **21,000 cases**
Vineyard area **123 acres (50 ha)**

ABOVE: Grüner veltliner grapes, are Austria's most widely planted cultivar. This remarkably versatile grape accounts for a little more than a third of the area under vine.

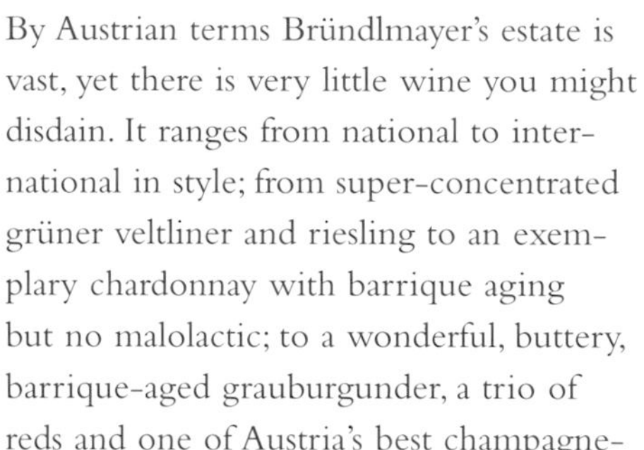

By Austrian terms Bründlmayer's estate is vast, yet there is very little wine you might disdain. It ranges from national to international in style; from super-concentrated grüner veltliner and riesling to an exemplary chardonnay with barrique aging but no malolactic; to a wonderful, buttery, barrique-aged grauburgunder, a trio of reds and one of Austria's best champagne-style sparklers. When the year is up to it, he also makes glorious dessert wines.

KARL FRITSCH, KIRCHBERG AM WAGRAM, DONAULAND, DONAULAND

Owners **Fritsch family** ***Production*** **2,500 cases**
Vineyard area **17 acres (7 ha)**

The Wagram, a long, south-facing, loess ridge overlooking the Danube, produces some exemplary grüner veltliner. The Fritsches, father and son, have built up a huge reputation over the past few years for their whites. They also make a few red wines, but the best is still a wine like the Schlossberg with its redolence of pineapples and grapefruit; or Perfektion (a name that might be asking for trouble), which is a silent Auslese, with up to 14 percent alcohol, and with a huge bouquet of pepper and angelica.

> *Wine comes in at the mouth.*
> *And love comes in at the eye;*
> *That's all we shall know for truth*
> *Before we grow old and die.*
>
> WILLIAM BUTLER YEATS *(1865–1939),*
> *The Green Helmet and Other Poems*
> *A Drinking Song*

RIGHT: Hand-picking riesling grapes in Lower Austria.

RIGHT: Sidestreet in the village of Heiligenstadt.

LUIS KRACHER, ILLMITZ, NEUSIEDLERSEE

Owner **Luis Kracher** ***Production*** **NA**
Vineyard area **18 acres (7.5 ha), plus purchased grapes in good years**

Now that he has turned his hand to production in California, Luis Kracher is the Austrian winemaker best-known abroad. He is the pope of Austrian sweet wine and in some years he makes more trockenbeerenauslesen than the rest of Germany. He has not only his skill to thank, but also the special conditions around his home village, where the mists settle on the stagnant ponds and botrytis sets in most years. The wines divide into new-oak fermented Nouvelle Vague, and the Zwischen den Seen range, made in traditional acacia wood casks.

F. X. PICHLER, LOIBEN, WACHAU

Owner **F. X. Pichler** ***Production*** **5,500 cases**
Vineyard area **18 acres (7.5 ha)**

Austrian winelovers would almost certainly cite F. X. as their greatest winemaker, yet he produces little wine. F. X. makes great riesling and grüner veltliner on steep sites in the beautiful Wachau. He is an austere, unrelenting man, but his determination shows in the great concentration of the wines. The best of a great year is marked "M" for "monumental." These wines are rarest of all.

ERNST TRIEBAUMER, RUST, NEUSIEDLERSEE–HÜGELLAND

Owners **Triebaumer family** ***Production*** **4,600 cases** ***Vineyard area*** **27 acres (11 ha)**

Rust is the home of Ausbruch, but there is more to it than great sweet wines. On its warm soils black grapes ripen superbly, producing good dry whites. Triebaumer's make superb Ausbruch, often with high alcohol levels, but in the Marienthal they also make Austria's best blaufränkisch, a barrel-fermented chardonnay and a lovely traminer. Ernst Triebaumer shares his cellars with his son Herbert, who is now also making fine Ausbruch.

FRITZ WIENINGER, WIEN STAMMERSDORF, VIENNA

Owner Fritz Wieninger Production 7,220 cases Vineyard area 32 acres (13 ha)

Vienna's best winemaker, Fritz Wieninger, harvests his grapes on steep, perfect south-facing slopes. Although his family runs a profitable Heurige, he makes few concessions to the traditional offering, "Mischsatz"—a sort of vinous stew. After training in California, Wieninger is keen to show he can make new-wave chardonnay, pinot noir and cabernet within Vienna's walls.

Regional Best

- Grüner Veltliner, Willi Bründlmayer
- Loibner Berg Grüner Veltliner, F. X. Pichler
- Marienthal Blaufränkisch, Ernst Triebaumer
- Perfektion Grüner Veltliner, Karl Fritsch
- Riesling, Alzinger
- Riesling, Martin Nigl
- Riesling Smaragd Loibenberg, Knoll
- Riesling Steinriegl Smaragd, Prager
- St Laurent Reserve, Josef Umathum
- Weissburgunder, Ludwig Neumayer
- Weisser Berg Weissburgunder, Helmut Taubenschuss
- Welschriesling/Chardonnay Days of Wine and Roses, Alois Kracher
- Welschriesling/Chardonnay Grand Cuvée #6 TBA, Alois Kracher
- Zweigelt Schilfwein Opitz One, Willi Opitz

MARTIN NIGL, SENFTENBERG, KREMSTAL

Owner **Martin Nigl** ***Production*** **3,900–5,000 cases** ***Vineyard area*** **23 acres (9.5 ha)**

Nigl is typical of modern Austria: a decade ago he was unknown. He is still very young and yet he has already established a reputation as one of the country's best winemakers. His grapes grow on the best land in the Krems Valley, on primary rock soils that produce the raciest grüner veltliners and rieslings imaginable. Most of it is bone-dry, but every now and then out comes a trockenbeerenauslese or an eiswein. He makes two wines with less appeal: a semi-sweet chardonnay, and a trendy, but misguided, sauvignon blanc.

HELMUT TAUBENSCHUSS, POYSDORF, WEINVIERTEL

Owner **Helmut Taubenschuss** ***Production*** **5,550–6,650 cases** ***Vineyard area*** **25 acres (10 ha)**

Poysdorf on the Brünn Road provides the base wine for much of Austria's sparkling sekt. While some local is very sour, Helmut seems to have no trouble at all making well-rounded balanced wines here on the Czech border. He makes lovely grüner veltliners bursting with flavor, but his best wines are weissburgunders. They can be massive, but they are massively good, too.

Other significant producers for the remaining regions include Hans Pitnauer (Donauland-Carnuntum); Ludwig Neumayer (Traisental); Engelbert Gesellmann (Central Bugenland); Krutzler (Southern Burgenland); Georg Winkler-Hermaden (Southeast Styria); Erich and Walter Polz (South Styria); and Domaine Müller (West Styria).

BELOW: *Picking riesling grapes by hand at Wolkersdorf in Austria.*

Many vineyards, like these near Lake Geneva, benefit from particular microclimates, provided by proximity to water, which reflects warmth.

Switzerland

ABOVE: *Wine tastings attract both locals and tourists to visit the wineries. Many are set in picturesque locations.*

Switzerland

WINK LORCH

Vineyards still thrive in the canton of Valais and on the shores of lakes Geneva, Neuchâtel, Zürich and Constance where Romans once cultivated them. Today, the most mountainous country in Europe finds space for more than 37,000 acres (15,000 ha) of vineyards in its valleys and foothills. Most vineyards are planted at altitudes common in Alsace and Burgundy.

A variety of wine styles are produced in Switzerland, reflecting its central geographic location, having borders with France (Alsace, Haute Savoie and Jura); Germany (Baden); western Austria; and Northern Italy.

Switzerland's vineyards lie between the 45° and 47°N latitudes, potentially ideal for quality viticulture. Generally the climate is temperate or continental, with plenty of sunshine and rainfall at the right time of year, cold winters and warm summers, though with considerable vintage variation. The appearance in some valleys of the *Föhn*, a warm alpine wind, can hasten ripening dramatically. Many soils are of glacial origin and broken-up slate, schist and large stones are very common. The variety of soil types accounts for the marked differences in character in the chasselas wines.

Wine regions

Wine regions in Switzerland are divided, first into the three main language divisions, French, German, and Italian, and then further into cantons. French-speaking Switzerland accounts for about 77 percent of the total, from which about 83 percent of Switzerland's wine is produced.

Valais is the most prolific wine canton and it also has some of the most picturesque vineyards. Some of Europe's highest vineyards are in the Haut-Valais, below the ski resorts of Zermatt and Saas-Fee. The region's greatest density of vineyards is on the south-facing slopes of the upper Rhône Valley, which runs east–west between Leuk (Loèche) and Martigny. The wine center and also the capital of the canton is Sion.

ABOVE: *Packers carefully prepare pinot noir grapes for transport; this is a grape the vigneron must treat well.*

Vaud has four main vineyard regions, the three largest close to Lake Geneva (from the west, La Côte, Lavaux and Chablais) and with the smallest close to Lake Neuchâtel. Lakes have a most important climatic influence, as they regulate temperature and increase the effects of the sun by reflection. The Chablais area also may be affected by the *Föhn*.

Geneva is close to three growing areas. Satigny, Switzerland's largest grape-growing community, is located at Mandement. Geneva's other two areas are Entre Arve et Rhône (between the Arve and Rhône rivers) and Entre Arve et Lac. Viticulture in this canton, with a landscape of rolling hills, is easier and more mechanized than elsewhere. There is plenty of sunshine and the nearby mountains deflect clouds, giving relatively low rainfall. Lake Geneva protects the vineyards from spring frosts and the best vineyards are on hillsides that warm rapidly in the morning sunshine.

Neuchâtel lies on the northern shores of the lakes of Neuchâtel and Bienne and south of the Jura mountains. The area has a fairly dry climate, but lacks the intensity of sunshine enjoyed by more southerly cantons.

German-speaking Switzerland has vineyards scattered across 18 cantons, with significant plantings in Zürich, Schaffhausen, Aargau, Graubünden (Grisons), Thurgau, and St Gallen (by Lake Constance). Here the climate is marginal for viticulture, though proximity to the Rhine River in the north, to various lakes, and the influence of the *Föhn* in the east, help certain vineyards.

Almost all of the vineyards in Italian-speaking Switzerland are in Ticino, the country's fourth-largest wine-producing canton. Sopraceneri and Sottoceneri, north and south of Monte Ceneri, have scattered plots, mostly on terraces, many of which are currently being reconstructed to aid mechanization. With the climate influenced by the Mediterranean, there are more sunshine hours than anywhere in Switzerland, but the rainfall is higher, too.

LEFT: *Colored cut crystal glass dating from 1900–1930.*

Vines and wines (white)

Chasselas is grown widely in the French-speaking cantons, notably in Vaud, where it dominates the

LEFT: *Vaud's Lavaux region on the slopes above Lake Geneva, where the vines are said to receive three suns—from the sky, and reflected off the lake and stone walls.*

ABOVE: *The village of Féchy, Vaud, beside Lake Geneva.*

vineyards. The wine's character derives much more from the soil type than from the grape. Malolactic fermentation is used to lower acidity and create a softer, creamier mouth-feel. Almost all chasselas is dry and fendant from the Valais can vary from soft and fruity (sometimes lacking in acidity) to a much more intense, mineral or stony flavor.

The Grand Crus of Dézaley and Calamin provide intensity in the first and elegance in the second, but nearby villages of Epesses and Saint-Saphorin can produce equally good, structured and honeyed wines. Yvorne and Aigle with steep vineyards in Chablais also produce excellent chasselas. Young chasselas often has a slight spritz and good examples benefit from two or more years aging.

Riesling-sylvaner, known elsewhere as müller-thurgau, is the first recorded vine crossing. It was made by Dr Müller of Thurgau, to suit marginal climates. It is most prevalent in German-speaking parts where it produces a dry or medium-dry, flowery wine to drink young. When yields are well controlled, the wines have good aromatic flavor.

Sylvaner thrives on steep, stony sites and produces grapes with considerably higher natural sugar levels than chasselas. In Valais, where it has always been revered, sylvaner wines are labeled, Johannisberg. Sylvaner can be made into dry, medium or perfumed late-harvest wines.

Chardonnay, although widely planted in Valais during the 1970s, does better in Geneva and Neuchâtel where both dry light and elegant styles are made and, less successfully, oak-matured wines.

Pinot gris has long been grown in Valais, where sweeter styles are called malvoisie. It does well in the warmer parts of German Switzerland.

Marsanne has thrived for years in the Upper Rhône Valley yielding wines labeled Ermitage (or Hermitage). Highly alcoholic, these dry or sweet wines develop vivid dried apricot or peach tones.

Regional Best

- Aigle Les Murailles, Henri Badoux & Fils, Vaud
- Chamoson Pinot Noir Rénommée de Saint-Pierre, René Favre et Fils, Valais
- Chamoson Petite Arvine, René Favre et Fils, Valais
- Château Lichten, Rouvinez, Valais
- Dardagny Le Bertholier Rouge Domaine Les Hutins, Geneva
- Dardagny Pinot Noir Reserve, Domaine Les Hutins, Geneva
- Dézaley L'Arbalette, Jean et Pierre Testuz, Vaud
- Dézaley-Marsens De La Tour, Les Frères Dubois, Vaud
- Epesses Clos du Boux, Luc Massy, Vaud
- Heida Gletscherwein, Oskar Chanton, Valais
- Johannisberg Moelleux, Domaine du Mont d'Or, Valais
- Merlot del Ticino Riflessi d'Epoca, I Vini di Guido Brivio, Ticino
- Petite Arvine Sous l'Escalier, Domaine du Mont d'Or, Valais
- Syrah Cayas, Bon Père Germanier, Valais
- Vétroz Amigne Mitis, Bon Père Germanier, Valais

Vines and wines (red)

Pinot noir is especially favored in German Switzerland, where it accounts for 70 percent of plantings. Thermovinification is widely practiced to give color but no tannin and this means most wines are rather lacking in flavor. Where producers with good sites treat pinot better, results are good. Also important in French Switzerland, it is Neuchâtel's only permitted red grape giving, notably, an excellent dry rosé, Oeil de Perdrix. It is gaining ground in Vaud, especially in La Côte and is the most-planted red in Valais, where much goes into the dôle and goron blends.

Gamay is grown widely in French Switzerland and used almost exclusively for blends in Valais, but Geneva successfully produces a characteristic fruity varietal with good acid balance.

Merlot is now the principal variety in Ticino. Good Ticino merlots show lively acidity, soft tannins and succulent fruit flavors, but many are light, fruity and rather thin. Several producers are making structured merlot, some with oak aging.

Syrah is causing excitement in Valais. Small quantities have been grown there for many years, but not given much attention. There are now about 125 acres (50 ha), mostly in Valais, on prime, slopes for maximum sunshine.

Gamaret and ***garanoir*** are two red wine crossings with white reichensteiner (itself a crossing) and red gamay in their parentage. They have proved remarkably successful, particularly in Geneva and Vaud. Used sometimes in blends and sometimes pure, they can produce deep-colored reds with good black fruit character and structure to cope with oak aging. In the Valais the crossing diolinoir is also gaining ground.

Specialty grapes

More than 50 varieties grow in the varied topography and soils of Valais; several are ancient and found nowhere else. Exciting white obscurities include petite arvine (also grown in Aosta, Italy), amigne (only 50 acres/20 ha in the world, all in Valais) and païen or heida (probably the savagnin from Jura). Both petite arvine and amigne can be made dry or medium-sweet to sweet, described as "mi-flétri" or "flétri" meaning "shriveled on the vine." Petite arvine, grown across Valais, has crisp acidity, good fruit concentration and an almost salty flavor. Amigne, almost all grown in Grand Cru vineyards of Vétroz, can show an attractive mandarin flavor and has proved particularly good when vinified sweet. Heida is grown in the high vineyards of Visperterminen and on these steep vineyard slopes it produces a dry wine of astonishing power with strong aromatic flavors. Now, plantings of païen (as it is called in the French part) are being developed elsewhere in Valais. For reds, the most interesting obscurities making a comeback are cornalin and humagne.

And Noah he often said to his wife when he sat down to dine, "I don't care where the water goes if it doesn't get into the wine."

G. K. CHESTERTON *(1874–1936), Wine and Water*

Producers

Switzerland has several thousand vineyard owners, many with tiny plots. Most are either part of a wine co-operative, or pass their crop over to a local *négociant*. In Valais alone about 700 producers make and sell their own wine. The following producers make a range that can be recommended, as can Bon Père Germanier and René Favre & Fils, both in Valais.

DOMAINE LES HUTINS, GENEVA

Established 1976 _Owners_ Jean and Pierre Hutin _Production_ 12,000 cases _Vineyard area_ 44 acres (18 ha)

Based in Dardagny, close to the French border, Jean and Pierre Hutin were among the first Swiss to plant sauvignon blanc. They produce both non-oaked and barrique versions of sauvignon blanc, chardonnay and pinot noir, the latter most successfully. Their best chasselas, Le Bertholier, is fresh and creamy. Le Bertholier Rouge, 80 percent gamaret with cabernet sauvignon, is aged partly in new barriques giving fabulous depth and complexity. Viognier and merlot are the latest challenge.

DOMAINE DU MONT D'OR, VALAIS

Established 1848 _Owners_ Domaine du Mont d'Or S. A. (majority Schenk S. A.) _Production_ 16,000 cases _Vineyard area_ 50 acres (20 ha)

The vineyards of this famous old domaine are located in prime south-facing, steep sites. It has always made reliable fendant and dôle, but its specialty is late-harvest wine, from several varieties, wherever possible from botrytized grapes. Its signature wine is Johannisberg from sylvaner, which shows a tropical fruit character. The fine Petite Arvine Sous L'Escalier ("below the steps") ages superbly.

ABOVE: Pickers taking a break.

JEAN & PIERRE TESTUZ, VAUD

Established 1845 _Owners_ J. & P. Testuz S. A. (100% owned by Testuz family) _Production_ 200,000 cases _Vineyard area_ 147 acres (60 ha) (some leased)

A large firm of growers and *négociants* based in the Grand Cru vineyards of Dézaley in Lavaux, Testuz specializes in chasselas, but also produces a range of other varietals. Run by Jean-Philippe, a thirteenth-generation Testuz, the firm takes its chasselas seriously. A wine with a subtly different character, reflecting various soil types and aspects, is produced from each major Lavaux appellation.

BELOW: Terraced vineyards at Sion, the center of the Valais wine region.

Vineyards near the town of Montebelluna in the heart of the Veneto in North Central Italy.

Italy

A L P S
DOLOMITES
Bolzano
Trentino-Alto Adige
Trento
Matterhorn 14,684 ft (4477 m)
Mt Rosa 15,199 ft (4634 m)
Mt Bianco 15,770 ft (4808 m)
Lake Maggiore
Lake Como
Valle d'Aosta
Franciacorta
Lake Garda
Adige
Udine
Friuli-Venezia Giulia
Trieste
Bergamo
Monza
Milan
Brescia
Valpolicella
Vicenza
Mestre
Venice
Piedmont
Novara
Lugana
Verona
Soave
Padua
Gulf of Venice
Turin
Po
Piacenza
Emilia-Romagna
Parma
Ferrara
Asti
Piedmont
Reggio nell'Emilia
Modena
Bologna
Emilia-Romagna
Genoa
APENNINES
Savona
Emilia-Romagna
Liguria
Liguria
La Spézia
Rimini
SAN MARINO
ADRIATIC SEA
Prato
Florence
Pisa
Livorno
Tuscany
Arezzo
Ancona
Tevere
Siena
Marche
Lake Trasimeno
Perugia
Umbria
Elba
Tuscany
Orvieto
Teramo
Terni
Pescara
Corsica (France)
L'Aquila
Abruzzo
Lazio
ROME
Monti dei Frentani
Lazio
Molise
Campobasso
Foggia
Campania
Sardinia
TYRRHENIAN SEA
Mt Vesuvius 4201 ft (1281 m)
Basilicata
Puglia
Naples
Torre del Greco
Sassari
Ischia
Campania
Salerno
Potenza
Sardinia
Appennino Lucano
Campania
Mt del Papa 6576 ft (2005 m)
Punta La Marmora 6015 ft (1834 m)
Calabria
Sardinia
Cagliari
Cosenza
Calabria
Catanzaro
Lipari Islands
Messina
Palermo
Trapani
Calabria
Reggio di Calabria
Bianco
Sicily
Sicily
Mt Etna 10,899 ft (3323 m)
Sicily
Catania
NORTH
Siracuse
Sicily
60 miles (96 kilometers)
Pantelleria

Italy

MAUREEN ASHLEY MW

ABOVE: *Michelangelo's David (1504), Florence*

There are mixed feelings and opinions about Italian wines: whereas some people regard them as confusing and complex, others happily embrace the astounding number of grape varieties and profusion of wines produced. In addition, the country's wine zones are hugely varied.

Italy is geographically complex. To the north, the well-drained lower slopes of the bordering Alps provide prime grape-growing territory before they give way to the plains of the Po Valley, about the only part of Italy where grapes are not consistently grown. This entire northern part has a somewhat gentle continental climate with marked inconsistencies from year to year giving pronounced vintage variations.

The long, narrow peninsular part of the country is defined by the Apennine mountain chain that forms its spine. There are numerous hill ranges and comparatively little flat ground. In some places the mountains fall right to the sea, creating the most dramatic of scenery and growing conditions.

While Italy's climate is naturally categorized as Mediterranean, the great variety of altitudes and exposures gives a far greater spread of climatic conditions than might be expected.

Much of the glorious lack of consistency in Italy's wine production derives from its history. Wine has been produced on its lands for several thousand years, at least since the time of the Phoenicians and Greeks. Yet Italy has been united politically only since the 1860s, and socially since the arrival of television over half a century ago. Even now a journey of 50 miles (80 km) can seem like 500 (800 km), so frequent are the changes in dialects and eating habits.

Italy's wine scene today is principally the result of two major, relatively recent movements. The first followed the devastation of the Second World War; in the economic boom that accompanied reconstruction, partly from necessity the wine producers' motto appeared to become "more is better," and the industry was aimed firmly at ever greater quantities, with hardly a thought given to quality. The second was the realization that this path was dreadfully flawed and that survival lay in high quality. This change, often called the Italian wine renaissance, started in the mid 1970s and hit its peak in the late 1980s. However, it must be said that a few corners of the country are learning the lesson only now; the old philosophy left its mark mainly in the vineyards, where mediocre but high-producing varieties sometimes squeezed out the more characterful grape varieties.

Italy has a vast heritage of grape varieties, possessing a wealth of indigenous vines as well as the varieties more often seen worldwide. Which varieties ended up where hundreds of years ago, depended not only on the suitability of growing conditions but also on how well the wines made from a particular grape variety suited the local diet.

LEFT: *A Greco–Roman amphora from around 450 BC, used to store and carry wine.*

BELOW: *Snowcapped mountains form a stunning backdrop to this estate in Piedmont.*

ABOVE: The River Arno, Florence, Tuscany. Chianti, especially Chianti Classico, is the region's linchpin.

The rediscovery and repropagation of the less well-known varieties, many of them rendered almost extinct during the quantity-driven days, is now in full swing. Often these are "troublesome" varieties, in the sense that they are naturally low-yielding, ripen with difficulty or are prone to disease. In compensation they may well give wines of incomparable flavor or, used in a blend, turn a good wine into an exciting one.

Dozens of varieties can be considered emblematic of one or more regions—examples are Piedmont's nebbiolo, sangiovese of Tuscany and nero d'avola in Sicily. International varieties such as cabernet sauvignon, merlot and syrah were planted here long before they were planted even in France, but are most often encountered in Tuscan blends. Pinot noir and chardonnay are planted for sparkling wine production in Lombardy; chardonnay on its own is not typical of Italian wine.

ABOVE: Mounted police in Florence, Tuscany.

In the early stages of the quantity-to-quality shift the emphasis was on winemaking, a vast amount of investment going into cellar equipment and the acquisition of technical know-how. Out went the old concrete vats and in came stainless steel vats, automatic temperature control and all the other baggage of the standard modern winemaking plant. On most estates the changeover took no more than a year or two, and while it was achieved with little interruption to production, there were huge effects on the wines produced. Some altered so much they became almost unrecognizable.

The next stage reached to the core of the matter: the vineyards. Revamping a vineyard is a much longer and more complicated procedure. Most estates have had to start from scratch to find the best combinations of rootstock and variety for their heterogeneous terrains, the most suitable clones and optimal planting density. Such research can take years and the vineyard must be replanted in stages to avoid massive interruptions to production. The improvements this stage brings will no doubt continue to emerge over the next decade. One thing is clear, however, the direction in vineyard plantings is toward high density. A few wine producers took the "more is better" theory to the extreme, planting up to 25,000 vines or more per acre (62,000 vines per ha), regardless of the cost or effect on cultivation efficiency.

Regions and Styles

Italy's wine laws follow the standard EU breakdown into "quality wine" and "table wine." Quality wine Italy has two categories, DOC *(denominazione di origine controllata)* and the higher-level DOCG *(denominazione di origine garantita)*. At the beginning of 2000 there were over 300 DOCs, wines with basic controls on origin, grape varieties and style, and several cultivation and winemaking parameters. Increasingly, larger DOCs are becoming nested with, for example, a DOC zone containing one or more subzonal DOCs which have tighter production constraints. In theory the nesting can continue right down to single-vineyard DOCs, but it will be some time before this level is reached.

DOCG was conceived as a class apart to represent the top wines. Currently either an entire zone may gain the additional qualification or at some stage along the nesting process a subzone can move from DOC to DOCG. Originally, though, zones had to be promoted whole or not at all and this caused some undeserving wines to gain their *garantita* along with other, more worthy ones. Perhaps the best—or worst—example is that of Chianti. Good wines from the Classico heartland and the higher quality subzones, lesser wines from the lower quality subzones and poor stuff from the periphery, became DOCG together. This means that the "G" does not guarantee much, although producers still cherish the qualification and keenly seek promotion to it.

At the table-wine end of the spectrum, simple VdT *(vino da tavola)* is about as basic as you can get. A large and increasing number of wines fall into the higher subcategory, IGT *(indicazione geografica tipica)*. Conceived to offer broadly regional wine styles, which to some extent it does (although there are regional DOCs too), just as often it is used as a sort of catch-all category, especially for wines that don't fit into their DOC for some reason (usually the grape varieties used). Hence the quality can be anything from mundane to marvellous. The only sensible advice is to ignore the category and go by the name of the producer.

Wine trends come and go in Italy but there are always talking points which, given the impassioned nature of most Italian discussion, often become the subject of intense debate. Recently, the use of the classic varieties provoked argument. On one side were those who saw use of the innovative varieties as a way of making Italian wines more readily acceptable on the international market; on the other were those who saw them as compromising Italy's unique wine styles. It is now generally accepted that international varieties have their place but that the future of Italian wine lies in the individuality provided by the indigenous grapes.

The use of the *barrique* is a current talking point. Traditionally, Italian wines, if aged at all, were put in large wooden barrels (*botti*), which were used for decades. *Botti* were commonly made of oak. Today, there is scarcely an estate that hasn't replaced or supplemented its *botti* stock with *barriques*—here used to mean small casks of new oak, usually but not always French. While most winemakers seem convinced that they are needed to produce high-quality wines, a growing voice holds that many Italian grape varieties are not well-suited to the *barrique* treatment. Even with those that are, say dissenters, the *barrique* tends to homogenize styles, squashing individuality with its oaky overlay.

BELOW: Winemaker Clerico Francesco tastes some of his own very good product.

There is also discussion about roving enologists. Producers of all sizes are increasingly placing their trust in well-known, highly skilled contract winemakers to guide production. While this does ensure that a wine is competently made, producers risk their wines reflecting their enologist's ideas on style and character rather than their own, and resembling others made by him. Worse, the enologists most in demand are taking on dozens of estates and cannot

BELOW: The Italian climate, broadly categorized as Mediterranean, has great regional variation.

ABOVE: *Terraced vines trained over ancient stone pillars.*

possibly give detailed personal attention to each one of them. It must be admitted that scores of estates have seen their wines improve out of all recognition.

Even sweet wines have come under the microscope. The classic method for creating the additional grape sugar necessary to produce a sweet (or strong) wine is to pick the grapes when normally ripe (sometimes even slightly underripe) and leave them to dry out until sufficient concentration has been reached. In the north the bunches are either hung from hooks or laid out on shallow racks in airy indoor locations. The drying process, called *appassimento*, is slow, lasting up to four months. In the hotter south the grapes are laid out on racks out of doors, and the *appassimento* is much faster, sometimes lasting just two to three weeks. The resulting *passito* wines can be delicately or richly sweet but they retain freshness and rarely cloy. Increasing numbers of producers, however, lured by the siren song of "renowned international style," are turning to late harvesting to ensure high sugar content, and once more the local traditional methods are having to fight for their place.

One thing does not brook debate, however. In Italy wine is conceived and made as a food accompaniment. Drinking wine on its own is a habit for foreigners, not Latins. Consequently, many wines that taste tart, light, dry, austere, or crisp on their own suddenly spring into life when enjoyed with food.

Italy is split into 20 administrative regions. While these do not often tally with viticultural zones it has become customary to use the regional breakdown when discussing Italian wines and this convention is followed here, even if somewhat loosely.

Barolo traditions

Dining at the home of a top producer in a small but world-recognized wine region is a fascinating experience. The characters behind the famous brands can often leave a longer-lasting impression than the wine. The best hosts and hostesses understand the fine art of making every guest feel important, but one or two attendees may be elevated to the special rank of "guest of honor." In Barolo, these privileged few are treated with the leftover wine! The locals feel that overnight aeration greatly enhances their wine, smoothing out the tannins and allowing more flavor to come through, so they save open, unfinished bottles at the end of the night, reserving them for their special guests the next day.

Piedmont and Northwest Italy

At the center of northwestern Italy, the Piedmont region's heart is the zones of Barolo and Barbaresco, names that for many represent the peak of Italian winemaking. Parts of Piedmont are mountainous but the main wine zones cluster to the south and east of Turin, an area of sharply defined hilly outcrops intersected by flat river valleys.

Most wines are single varietals. Three varieties, all red, stand out: nebbiolo, barbera and dolcetto. Of these, nebbiolo is the most illustrious, classically making slow-developing wines of intensity, austerity, and great refinement. Barbera is often aged in oak to soften the wine, while dolcetto's fruitiness is usually enjoyed while the wine is young. Other indigenous red grapes of note include grignolino, freisa, brachetto and croatina.

Leading the white grapes is moscato bianco, the white muscat that here produces the lightest, freshest, grapiest wine imaginable. Cortese is best past its first year or two. Arneis and favorito are also grown, and erbaluce, more rarely.

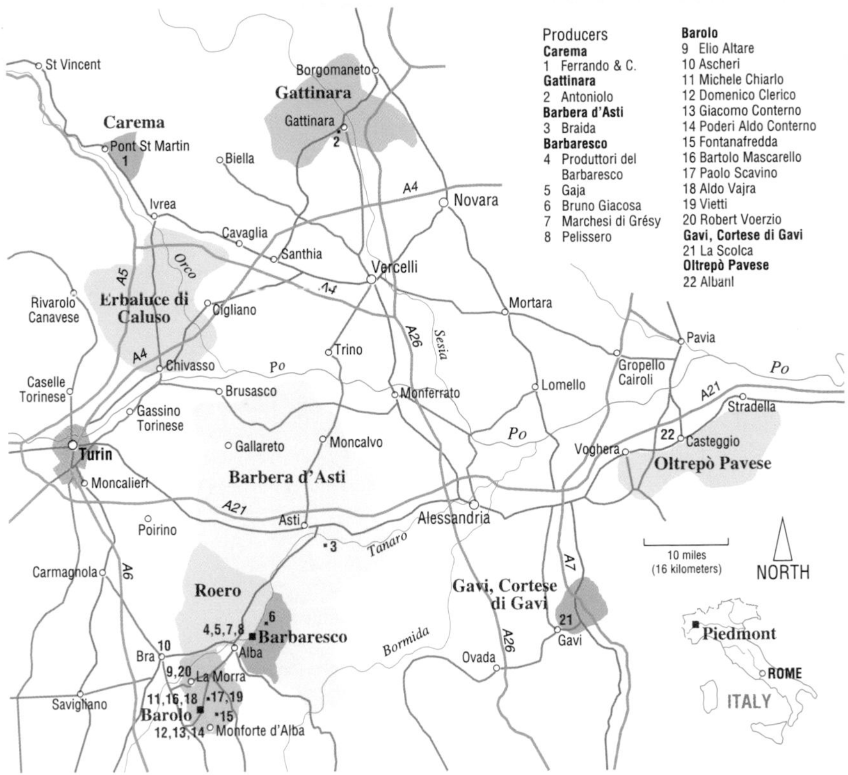

BAROLO AND BARBARESCO

Nowhere does nebbiolo show its class as much as in the two zones of Barolo and Barbaresco. And nowhere else in Italy is there such a tight mesh of small vineyards, each vineyard firmly stamping its personality onto its wines, although nebbiolo and its subvarieties (lampia, michet and rosé) are the only grapes used. Barolo's western wines are marked by greater aroma and finesse and develop quicker, while those from the east have greater structure, body, power, and longevity. Barbaresco too shows marked variation in terrain and grapes. Differences in maceration and oaking mean there is no typical style. However, overall barolo is considered a little chunkier and fuller, more powerful and slower-aging than the more refined barbaresco.

MOSCATO WINES

Moscato-based wines are grown in most of Italy, but the Piedmont area, Asti in particular, produces the best Asti spumante (spumante means "sparkling"). A fresh, light, sweet, frothy dessert wine, it is produced from moscato bianco grapes. Asti should be drunk as fresh as possible. An even lighter, more elegant, and more delicate version is the dessert wine moscato d'asti.

LEFT: The shuttered winery building on the estate of the Marchesi di Grésy, Piedmont.

ALBANI, OLTREPÒ PAVESE

Established **1992** ***Owner*** **Riccardo Albani** ***Production*** **4,500–5,300 cases** ***Vineyard area*** **37 acres (15 ha)**

Riccardo Albani's carefully nurtured estate, though a new arrival, has eclipsed the competition with its superbly refined wines of sheer class. There are just three: his slightly sparkling, off-dry Bonarda; the stylish, slow-developing, varietally pure rhine riesling; and Vigna della Casona, mainly from barbera, a wine that balances intensity and elegance with aplomb.

Regional Dozen

Barbaresco Sori San Lorenzo (Gaja)
Barbaresco Vigneti in Rio Sordo (Produttori del Barbaresco)
Barbera d' Alba Vittoria (Gianfranco Alessandria)
Barbera d' Asti Superiore Montruc (Franco M. Martinetti)
Barolo (Vietti)
Barolo Vigneto Arborina (Elio Altare)
Barolo Riserva Gran Bussia (Poderi Aldo Conterno)
Brachetto d' Acqui (Braida)
Dolcetto d' Alba Barturot (Ca' Viola)
Gavi dei Gavi Etichetta Nera (La Scolca)
Langhe Rosso Monpra (Conterno Fantino)
Roero Arneis Bricco delle Ciligie (Almondo)

ANTONIOLO, GATTINARA

Established **1949** ***Owners*** **the Antoniolo family** ***Production*** **5,000 cases** ***Vineyard area*** **37 acres (15 ha)**

Coming from this Gattinara producer is Coste della Sesia Nebbiolo Juvenia, a wine from nebbiolo that does not require long aging. The estate's leading wine, the Gattinara *cru* Osso San Grato, has plentiful, soft, red-berried fruitiness to offset its natural austerity.

ELIO ALTARE, BAROLO

Established **1948** ***Owner*** **Elio Altare** ***Production*** **3,000 cases** ***Vineyard area*** **11 acres (4.5 ha)**

Elio Altare is of the short-maceration school in Barolo. The wines are supple, complex, well-fruited, and refined. Top of the range is the *cru* Barolo Vigneto Arborina. Barbera d'Alba and Dolcetto d'Alba are also fruit-forward and most attractively balanced.

BRAIDA, BARBERA D'ASTI

Established **1961** ***Owners*** **the Bologna family** ***Production*** **25,000 cases** ***Vineyard area*** **50 acres + 20 leased (20 + 8 ha)**

This pioneer of barbera in *barrique* makes Barbera d'Asti Bricco dell'Uccellone (a fat, deep, spicy wine) and the tighter-knit Bricco della Bigotta and late-harvested Ai Suma. Young lively Barbera La Monella and finely balanced Moscato d'Asti show the breadth of the range.

BELOW: *The colorful chapel of Santissima Madonna delle Grazie, Barolo, Piedmont.*

PODERI ALDO CONTERNO, BAROLO

Established **1969** ***Owner*** **Aldo Conterno** ***Production*** **10,000–12,500 cases** ***Vineyard area*** **55 acres (23 ha)**

Aldo Conterno's wines are quite simply stunning, with a wealth of ripe fruit that balances the classic Barolo astringency and acts as counterpoint to the classic Barbera acidity. Wines from this Barolo concern are in very high demand

FERRANDO & C., CAREMA

Established **1900** ***Owners*** **the Ferrando family** ***Production*** **4,500 cases** ***Vineyard area*** **7.5 acres + 10 leased (3 + 4 ha)**

Luigi Ferrando, practically the only commercial producer of Carema, has three still versions of Erbaluce di Caluso: a brut sparkling wine from erbaluce; a late harvest, lightly sweet Erbaluce; and a Caluso Passito.

FONTANAFREDDA, BAROLO

Established **1878** ***Owners*** **Amministrazione Immobiliare SpA** ***Production*** **600,000 cases** ***Vineyard area*** **170 acres (68 ha)**

This winery is a landmark in Barolo. Wines are good value and an excellent introduction to the type (notably Barolo Serralunga d'Alba, a blend) especially for those wary of more austere versions. Barolo *crus* La Delizia, La Villa, Lazzarito, Gattinera and La Rosa top a long list.

GAJA, BARBARESCO

Established **1859** ***Owner*** **Angelo Gaja** ***Production*** **20,000 cases** ***Vineyard area*** **135 acres (55 ha)**

The charismatic Angelo Gaja holds a degree in enology from the Enological Institute of Alba and a Master's in economics from the University of Torino. His contribution to the wine scene, and not just in Barbaresco, is almost impossible to summarize in a few words. An acute brain, an enquiring mind, an uncompromising attitude to quality and a keenly directed sense of marketing have brought his wines head and shoulders above the competition and made him one of the most respected and sought-after characters in Italy. The wines are duly expensive but the combination of balance, complexity and class is unparalleled.

BRUNO GIACOSA, BARBARESCO

Established **1900** ***Owner*** **Bruno Giacosa** ***Production*** **37,000–42,000 cases** ***Vineyard area*** **37 acres (15 ha)**

Giacosa's philosophy was always to seek the best growers from the best sites and buy in grapes, but his ideas have now softened a little and he has bought 22 acres (9 ha) of vineyard in Serralunga (Barolo). The complex, floral, spicy, firm Barbaresco *cru* Santo Stefano di Neive is exemplary and stands out in a fairly large range.

MARCHESI DI GRÉSY, BARBARESCO

Established **1973** ***Owner*** **Alberto di Grésy** ***Production*** **13,500 cases**
Vineyard area **72 acres (29 ha)**

The di Grésy family settled in Piedmont the seventeenth century and have been grape growers ever since. It was only in 1973 that the estate started to vinify. Now, they make highly individual, light, graceful wines from well-sited vineyards. Crus Gaiun, Camp Gros, and Martinenga are highly acclaimed and a good Moscato d'Asti, La Serra, is made but di Grésy is now investing extra effort in chardonnay, sauvignon, and cabernet sauvignon.

PAOLO SCAVINO, BAROLO

Established **1921** ***Owner*** **Enrico Scavino** ***Production*** **5,000 cases**
Vineyard area **22 acres (9 ha)**

These are dense and elegantly perfumed wines with broad appeal. Scavino owns plots on some of Barolo's best sites: Cannubi, Bric del Fiasc and Rocche dell'Annunziata.

LA SCOLCA, GAVI, CORTESE DI GAVI

Established **1919** ***Owner*** **Giorgio Soldati** ***Production*** **16,500–21,000 cases** ***Vineyard area*** **86 acres (35 ha)**

Gavi's emergence as a wine of note derives from the efforts of this Cortese di Gavi estate. Scolca's best Gavi is the black label Etichetta Nera. Like most gavis, it matures into a firm, fleshy, spicily fruity wine of good structure: a red-wine drinker's white. Also outstanding is a finely tuned brut sparkling wine.

ALDO VAJRA, BAROLO

Established 1972 Owners Vajra family Production 7,500 cases
Vineyard area 50 acres (20 ha)

Aldo Vajra produces some of Barolo's most elegant, refined and stylish wines, lacking in neither intensity nor longevity. The beautifully constructed Barolo *cru* Bricco delle Viole leads a fine range of reds from nebbiolo, barbera and dolcetto, while Kié is undoubtedly one of the best examples of Freisa.

ABOVE: Signor Gianfranca Barile of Barolo seeks out truffles with his canine assistant Stella.

VIETTI, BAROLO

Established **1905** ***Owners*** **Corrado e Alfredo Vietti & C.**
Production **7,000 cases (+ 4,500 from bought-in grapes)**
Vineyard area **55 acres (22 ha)**

Wine gives courage and makes men more apt for passion.
OVID (43 BC–AD 17)

Vietti was the first in recent times to see the potential of arneis, and actively sought out plots of the variety. Burgundian in style, the beautifully balanced, perfumed, silky and elegant Vietti Barolos, especially from the *crus* Rocche, Brunate and Castiglione, are breathtaking.

Also noteworthy are Produttori del Barbaresco, Pelissero (both Barbaresco); Domenico Clerico, Giacomo Conterno, Cantine Oddero and Roberto Voerzio (all Barolo).

BELOW: Vineyards and winery buildings set in the landscape typical of Piedmont.

"VVV"

An easy way to remember the region of origin and the grape variety of Valpolicella is to think "V." Valpolicella wine is from the Veneto region. It is typically a light-bodied, unoaked, bitter cherry-imbued, refreshing dry red wine, ideal for lighter dishes with garlic. Innovative producers release a "souped up" valpolicella called ripasso, an impressive, richer, more deeply flavored and rounder wine made by refermenting valpolicella on dried grape skins, giving higher alcohol and extract. Completing the trio is amarone, made from the ripest grapes that are then dried on straw mats giving a potent, warm, mouthfilling wine with a slightly bitter finish.

ABOVE: *Snow dusts the vines near the winery at Monteforte Soave Classico, Veneto region.*

North Central Italy

In the central part of northern Italy, Lake Garda, Italy's largest lake, warms the local vineyards and separates the more rural region of Veneto, with its major vineyard areas of Valpolicella and Soave, from Lombardy to the west. South of the lake is the wine producing zone, Lugana. The wine, made from trebbiano di lugana, is usually unoaked and enjoyed young and crisp, but can repay aging for a few years. Nudging the lake to the northwest of Lugana is the Bianco di Custoza zone where an intriguing mix of grapes gives zip to a gently fruited white. Nearby, the southern part of Bardolino offers a similar style, a little lighter, more linear, and more herbaceous. Bardolino also lends itself to vinification as a pale rosé called Bardolino Chiaretto, a sheer delight, yet poorly known.

In the Valpolicella heartland, the wine is from a three-plus grape blend, and corvina is the most important. Versatile in style, valpolicella can be made for drinking as a young, fresh, vibrant red wine or as a fuller, rounder, longer-aged wine. Amarone della Valpolicella is a highly traditional wine; amarone retains the cherry-like characteristics of valpolicella but is stronger and port-like. Sweet recioto is another variation. Soave, a little further east, uses predominantly garganega grapes to produce its dry whites. The popularity of soave and valpolicella has caused the regions' vineyards to spread beyond the heartland Classico areas out on to the surrounding plains—these non-Classico wines have less to offer.

Beyond Soave and Valpolicella, single-varietal wines are the norm. The most prominent region is Breganze, which produces a huge array of red and white varietal wines.

Colli Trevigiani, north of Venice, is the tiny realm of the prosecco grape. Prosecco wines are most frequently sparkling, the style a deliberately light, youthful fruitiness. The natural aperitif throughout Italy, the wine can be anything from bone-dry to fairly sweet. Conegliano's wines are softer, Valdobbiadene's tighter and more elegant, but the differences are not marked. Franciacorta's sparkling wine openly sought to emulate champagne—with remarkable success.

The sweetness of prosecco wines is classically achieved by drying the grapes for longer than for amarone, creating such a concentration of sugars that the yeasts are unable to ferment to dryness, although it is not unheard of for producers to halt the fermentation. Recioto is a niche wine which is produced in small quantities. The name itself derives from *recie*, a dialect word for the "ears" of the grape bunch, the part that ripens most fully.

Regional Dozen

- Amarone della Valpolicella (Masi)
- Breganze Cabernet Sauvignon Ferrata (Maculan)
- Franciacorta Gran Cuvée Brut (Bellavista)
- La Poja (Allegrini)
- Lugana I Frati (Ca' dei Frati)
- Maurizio Zanella (Ca' del Bosco)
- Prosecco di Valdobbiadene Extra Dry Vigneti del Fol (Bisol)
- Recioto della Valpolicella Classico (Tommaso Bussola)
- Recioto di Soave I Capitelli (Anselmi)
- Soave Classico Superiore La Rocca (Pieropan)
- Soave Classico Superiore Vigneto Du Lot (Giuseppe Inama)
- Valpolicella Classico Superiore Sant' Urbano (F.lli Speri)

RIGHT: *Wine bottles and their protective straw.*

Soave also has its recioto, at its best giving a floral, gently honeyed sweetness of finesse but this too is a tiny proportion of the normal dry type. It is made predominantly from garganega grapes with, optionally, a small proportion of trebbiano di soave and some others. Soave's heartland lies on the steep slopes to the north and east of the castellated village of Soave itself.

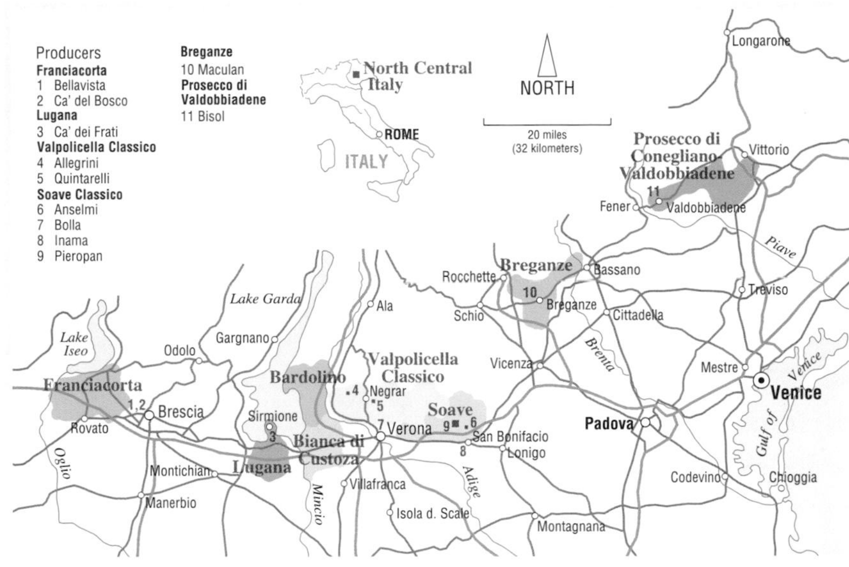

ALLEGRINI, VALPOLICELLA CLASSICO

Established **1920** ***Owners*** **the Allegrini family** ***Production*** **30,000 cases** ***Vineyard area*** **60 acres (24 ha)**

Allegrini makes a warm, spicy, full but supple wine from one of Valpolicella's top sites. La Poja is an excellent red of 100 percent corvina. Allegrini wines in general are marked by great vibrancy.

BELLAVISTA, FRANCIACORTA

Established **1977** ***Owner*** **Vittorio Moretti** ***Production*** **62,500 cases** ***Vineyard area*** **290 acres (117 ha)**

Using champagne for inspiration, the Bellavista sparkling wines are silky, graceful, supremely elegant and very long—equal in quality but different in style from Ca' del Bosco. They also produce a top-rate range of still wines using cabernet sauvignon, chardonnay and pinot nero.

BISOL, PROSECCO DI VALDOBBIADENE

Established **1875** ***Owners*** **the Bisol family** ***Production*** **40,000 cases** ***Vineyard area*** **114 acres (46 ha)**

Bisol offers a wide array of great wines. Both tank-method and classic-method sparklers are produced, plus Prosecco ranging from sweet to dry, from still to fully sparkling.

CA' DEI FRATI, LUGANA

Established **1956** ***Owners*** **Pietro Dal Cero and Sons** ***Production*** **21,000 cases** ***Vineyard area*** **90 acres (36 ha)**

Here are elegant full wines of youthful charm but evident staying power, especially the Lugana Brolettino from late-picked grapes given *barrique* aging. These are complemented by the oak-free, beautifully crafted Lugana I Frati. Also gaining plaudits is Pratto.

MACULAN, BREGANZE

Established **1933** ***Owner*** **Fausto Maculan** ***Production*** **30,000 cases** ***Vineyard area*** **173 acres (70 ha) part owned, part leased, part other arrangements with growers.**

A large range of characterful wines can be found at Breganze's Maculan, once famed for the sweet Torcolato, the even sweeter Acini Nobili, and the delicate Dindarello.

PIEROPAN, SOAVE CLASSICO

Established **1876** ***Owner*** **Leonildo Pieropan** ***Production*** **18,500 cases** ***Vineyard area*** **74 acres (30 ha)**

The wines here are beautifully crafted and well-knit, giving texture and depth to the Soave character. Pieropan has a firm belief in trebbiano di soave and was primarily responsible for saving it from extinction. He also believes strongly in the individual personalities that wines from single vineyards can achieve, as borne out by the two *cru* Soaves, Vigneto Calvarino and Vigneto La Rocca, slow-developing, concentrated, complex wines of great class. The Recioto di Soave is considered archetypal.

Other good producers in the region are Ca' del Bosco (Franciacorta); Masi (Valpolicello Classico); Anselmi, Bolla and Inama (all Soave Classico).

LEFT: Imposing colonnaded buildings lining a street in Traviso, northern Italy.

lightweight wine. Lagrein also finds its ideal growing conditions near Bolzano—lean and firm with plentiful fruit and good aging potential. On the Trentino side, marzemino makes a midweight red for simple quaffing but is better when grapes are grown in the Vallagarina, farther south. Teroldego thrives on the Rotaliano Plain and makes a deep, firm, and rather well-structured wine of good acidity, richly berried with a herbal tang.

However, the region's image comes from its whites: pure-toned, with varietal character that can be piercingly fresh and with more penetrating perfume than most Italian white wines. Chardonnay is now capturing the largest slice of vineyard area. Trentino is also important for sparkling wine production, mostly from pinot bianco, chardonnay, pinot nero, and pinot meunier.

ABOVE: *Verdant vineyards contrast dramatically with snow-covered mountains in the north.*

Trentino–Alto Adige

The region of Trentino–Alto Adige is Italy's northernmost. It links two provinces that once were part of Austria. The region is mountainous, and the vineyard lands follow the Adige river valley down from the gorges of the north, broadening as the altitude drops, where vines become much more prolific.

Nearly all wines from Trentino–Alto Adige are single-varietals of three main groups: French origin (chardonnay, sauvignon, cabernet franc, cabernet sauvignon, pinot nero), German origin (müller-thurgau, rhine riesling, sylvaner), and Italian or local origin (pinot bianco, malvasia, pinot grigio, moscato giallo, moscato rosa, rebo, schiava, lagrein, marzemino, nosiola, traminer aromatico, teroldego).

The local variety schiava is the most prolific and is particularly widely diffused in Alto Adige. It makes a lightish colored, fresh,

> *In vino veritas.*
> *(There is truth in wine.)*
> PLINY THE ELDER (AD 23–79)

Regional Best

Alto Adige Chardonnay St Valentin (Cantina Produttori San Michele Appiano)
Alto Adige Lagrein Scuro Riserva Untermoserhof (Georg Ramoser)
Gewürztraminer Kolbenhof (Hofstätter)
San Leonardo (Tenuta San Leonardo)
Teroldego Rotaliano Sgarzon (Foradori)
Trentino Pinot Grigio (Cesconi)
Trentino Pinot Nero (Maso Cantanghel)
Trento Riserva Giulio Ferrari (Ferrari)

ALTO ADIGE

LAGEDER

Established **1855** ***Owner*** **Alois Lageder** ***Production*** **80,000 cases**
Vineyard area **42 acres (17 ha) + bought-in grapes**

This large merchant house is moving steadily towards vineyard holdings and has several of note, the best known being Löwengang. There has also been investment in Casòn Hirschprunn, a separate estate. The estate wines have great individuality of character; the rest of the range, which is made up over 20 wines, is well-typed and of good quality.

ABBAZIA DI NOVACELLA

Established **1142** ***Owner*** **Canonici Regolari Agostiniani di Novacella**
Production **37,500 cases** ***Vineyard area*** **45 acres (18 ha)**

From its foundation in the middle of the twelfth century, the work of the Abbey of Novacella has included grape cultivation and winemaking. It is the prime exponent of the purity of aroma and freshness that Alto Adige wines can achieve. As well as being the focal point for research and development in Valle Isarco, this winery is the only commercial producer of any size north of the Isarco Valley.

TRENTINO

FERRARI

Established **1902** ***Owners*** **the Lunelli brothers** ***Production*** **250,000–290,000 cases** ***Vineyard area*** **190 acres (77 ha)**

This Trentino company, which passed from the Ferrari family to the Lunelli family in 1952, has always concentrated on sparkling wine at the top end of the market. The Ferrari sparklers now rival the best in Italy. A separate estate, Lunelli, has been set up recently, producing a range of still wines in line with the enterprise's reputation.

LEFT: A basket of tools used in grape husbandry.

FORADORI

Established **1880** ***Owner*** **Elisabetta Foradori** ***Production*** **11,000 cases** ***Vineyard area*** **37 acres (15 ha)**

If the fortunes of Teroldego Rotaliano have taken several strides forward in the past 15 years or so it is all down to Elisabetta Foradori who, convinced that the area could produce far better than the standard output suggested, has single-handedly pushed quality. The wines are stupendous, from the straight Teroldego Rotaliano through *crus* Sgarzon and Morei to Granato, the flagship. All have a superb suppleness of fruit combined with firm structure and robust body.

TENUTA SAN LEONARDO

Established **1870** ***Owners*** **the Marquises Guerrieri Gonzaga** ***Production*** **8,000 cases** ***Vineyard area*** **44 acres (18 ha)**

Vines have been grown around this property in southern Trentino since at least the tenth century. The current owner, the Marquis Carlo Guerrieri Gonzaga, cultivates only merlot and cabernets sauvignon and franc and makes oaky, hugely powerful, slow-maturing wines which are a long way from Trentino norms.

POJER & SANDRI

Established **1975** ***Owners*** **Sandri Fiorentino and Mario Pojer** ***Production*** **20,000 cases** ***Vineyard area*** **57 acres (23 ha)**

With high-sited vineyards at Faedo in northern Trentino, the steely, intensely perfumed delicacy of Pojer & Sandri's wines confound all those who claim there is a distinct difference between the styles of Alto Adige and Trentino.

DE TARCZAL

Established **1700** ***Owner*** **Ruggeri dell'Adamo de Tarczal** ***Production*** **10,000 cases** ***Vineyard area*** **44 acres (18 ha)**

Though initially famous for Pragiara, a cabernet/merlot blend, De Tarczal's forte is Marzemino, the most enjoyable and most dangerously drinkable of the area. He also produces a more serious Marzemino called Husar from selected grapes, and a small range of other varietals.

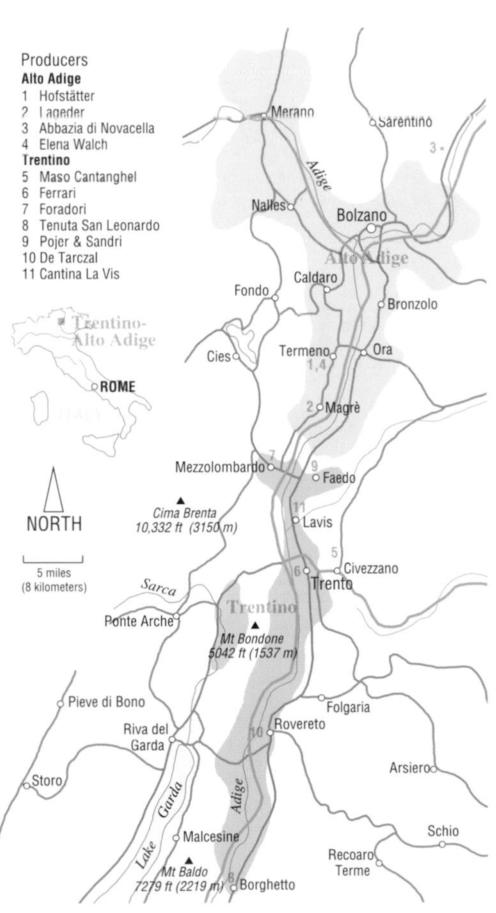

CANTINA LA VIS

Established **1948** ***Owners*** **Cooperative, 800 members** ***Production*** **250,000 cases** ***Vineyard area*** **1,975 acres (800 ha)**

This co-operative is responsible for about 10 percent of the entire production of Trentino yet the quality is unimpeachable, mainly because in 1985 a go-ahead management embarked on the "Quality Project" with the renowned viticultural/winemaking research institute of San Michele all' Adige. In 1990 the "Zoning Project" followed. It aimed at identifying which terrains best suited which varieties. Four ranges are produced, among which the La Vis line is reliably good and the Ritratti line remarkably good.

Other significant producers in the Trentino–Alto Adige region are Hofstätter, Elena Walch (both Alto Adige); and Maso Cantanghel (Trentino).

LEFT: Buying fresh grapes at the markets.

Friuli–Venezia Giulia

ABOVE: *There is a long-held belief that healthy soil has a beneficial effect on both the wine and its drinker. Winemaker at Ronco del Gelso checks local conditions.*

Friuli–Venezia Giulia (usually called simply Friuli) is to white wine what Piedmont and Tuscany are to red. The whites are classically restrained in tone, the epitome of refinement, and most are of them are single-varietals. Recent years have seen considerable developments with Friuli's reds, however, with their quality beginning to approach that of the whites. Perhaps this should not be surprising, for the emphasis on white is relatively modern.

Vines and wines

The almost 30 varieties grown in Friuli comprise the expected internationals, a small group of Italian origin (pinot bianco, pinot grigio, riesling italico, moscato giallo, moscato rosa) and a large group of local grape varieties. Among the red varieties, refosco dal peduncolo rosso (which differs from refosco d'istria) is the best-known. It makes chunky, brambly, herby wines. The most exciting is schioppettino (also called ribolla nera). Slow to come round, its wines are muscular, packed with ripe fruit, spicy and peppery. Tazzelenghe ("tonguecutter") is strongly tannic when young but mellows if allowed sufficient aging. Other native varieties include pignolo and franconia.

The most important of the local white varieties is tocai friulano. Its wines are often drunk young, when they have a lively florality, but after a few years they develop a nuttiness with hints of fennel and overall are far more interesting. By 2006 EU regulations will disallow the use of the term "tocai" here as its connections to Tokay and Tokaji in Hungary are misleading; also some wines under this label are blends. According to Galet, the grape is actually sauvignon vert.

In the past, ribolla gialla was almost always restricted to blends, being "too acidic." Increasing numbers of producers are realizing that, handled correctly, it can produce remarkable wines with an almost chardonnay-like butteriness but with a leaner, crisper edge and a fine lemony fruitiness. Verduzzo, also criticized for its acidity, comes into its own in Colli Orientali where it is fleshier, slightly nutty, with rich peach-like fruit. It can age for over a decade and matures to a deep, honeyed fruitiness, especially in the Cialla subzone. In the Ramandolo subzone it becomes a sweet wine from dried grapes, which enhances the honeyed softness.

For sweet wines picolot reigns supreme here. It is a troublesome variety, often flowering incompletely, prey to disease and yielding poorly. Handled properly, its wines can be superb—delicate, elegant, floral, dry-finishing, leaving the mouth perfectly clean, the antithesis of sauternes-type sweetness. Other local whites include malvasia istriana and vitovska.

While there is nothing exceptional today in the winemaking techniques of Friuli, Collio was the pioneer of cool, controlled white wine vinification in Italy; this approach was once known nationally as the metodo friulano, the Friuli method.

MARCO FELLUGA/RUSSIZ SUPERIORE/ CASTELLO DI BUTTRIO, COLLIO

Established **1905/1964/1994** ***Owners*** **the Felluga family** ***Production*** **58,000/20,850/2,100 cases** ***Vineyard area*** **334/158/52 acres (135/64/21 ha)**

Marco Felluga and Russiz Superiore (producing more intense wines) are both in Collio; Castello di Buttrio adds Colli Orientali to the portfolio. Early results here are distinctly promising.

KANTE, CARSO

Established **1980** ***Owner*** **Edi Kante** ***Production*** **2,500 cases** ***Vineyard area*** **18 acres (7 ha)**

Vines here grow at 820 feet (250 m) in a sheltered site. Kante works primarily with the classic malvasia istriana and terrano, and the rare indigenous grape, vitovska. The estate also grows chardonnay and sauvignon.

EDI KEBER, COLLIO

Established **1957** ***Owner*** **Edi Keber** ***Production*** **4,200 cases** ***Vineyard area*** **25 acres (10 ha)**

One of Collio's rising stars, Keber concentrates on the varieties best suited to his terrain. He now produces a fabulously refined tocai and a richly fruited merlot. There is also a white blend and a red blend of similar quality.

BELOW: *A cart loaded with old trellis poles, Colli Orientali del Friuli, Friuli–Venezia Giulia.*

ABOVE: *Terracotta and white-washed winery buildings; a part of the landscape in Colli Orientali del Friuli.*

Regional Dozen

Carso Malvasia (Kante)
Colli Orientali del Friuli Chardonnay Vigneto Ronc di Juri (Girolamo Dorigo)
Colli Orientali del Friuli Merlot Baolar (Pierpaolo Pecorari)
Colli Orientali del Friuli Rosazzo Bianco Terre Alte (Livio Felluga)
Colli Orientali del Friuli Rosso Sacrisassi (Le Due Terre)
Colli Orientali del Friuli Sauvignon (Miani)
Collio Pinot Bianco Amrita (Mario Schiopetto)
Collio Pinot Grigio (Puiatti)
Collio Pinot Grigio (Villa Russiz)
Friuli Isonzo Pinot Bianco (Mauro Drius)
Friuli Isonzo Sauvignon Vieris (Vie di Romans)
Vintage Tunina (Vinnaioli Jermann)

LIVON, GRAVE

Established **1960** ***Owners*** **the Livon family** ***Production*** **80,000 cases** ***Vineyard area*** **370 acres (150 ha)**

This large company has holdings in Collio, Colli Orientali, and Grave, and cellars each zone. The wines are of reliably good quality throughout the large range, particularly the *crus*, but keep a watch for the non-*barriqued* whites destined for long aging.

VIE DI ROMANS, ISONZO

Established **1976** ***Owners*** **the Gallo family** ***Production*** **5,850 cases** ***Vineyard area*** **40 acres (16 ha)**

Gianfranco Gallo has an exceptional, exquisitely crafted range, which is limited to varietal chardonnay, pinot grigio, sauvignon and tocai, along with a white blend, Flores di Uis, and a red blend, Voos dai Ciamps. This is an Isonzo estate capable of reaching Collio quality.

SCHIOPETTO, COLLIO

Established **1964** ***Owner*** **Mario Schiopetto** ***Production*** **18,000 cases** ***Vineyard area*** **57 acres (23 ha)**

Mario Schiopetto brought metodo friulano to the area: cool-temperature, controlled fermentation. Schiopetto wines are purely styled, long, and classy, and certainly live up to the almost awe-inspiring reputation of this estate.

LE VIGNE DI ZAMÒ, COLLI ORIENTALI

Established **1985/NA/1981** ***Owners*** **the Pontoni family** ***Production*** **4,200/NA/8,500 cases** ***Vineyard area*** **25/NA/37 acres (10/NA/15 ha)**

The name Le Vigne di Zamò refers to a grouping of three estates. Each of the three estates has a fairly limited range of varieties chosen to maximize the potential of its site, although schioppettino shines at all three. This aside, at Vigne dal Leon the pinot bianco stands out; merlot marks out Zamò & Zamò (and the white blends here are most notable too). At Ronco del Gnemiz there is the glorious müller-thurgau.

Other good producers in Friuli are Jermann; Borgo Magredo, Pighin (both Graves); Drius, Ronco del Gelso (both Isonzo); Villa Russiz, Gravner, Puiatti (all Collio); Ronchi di Cialla, Livio Felluga, Colli Orientali del Friuli, Giovanni Dri, and Miani (all Colli Orientali).

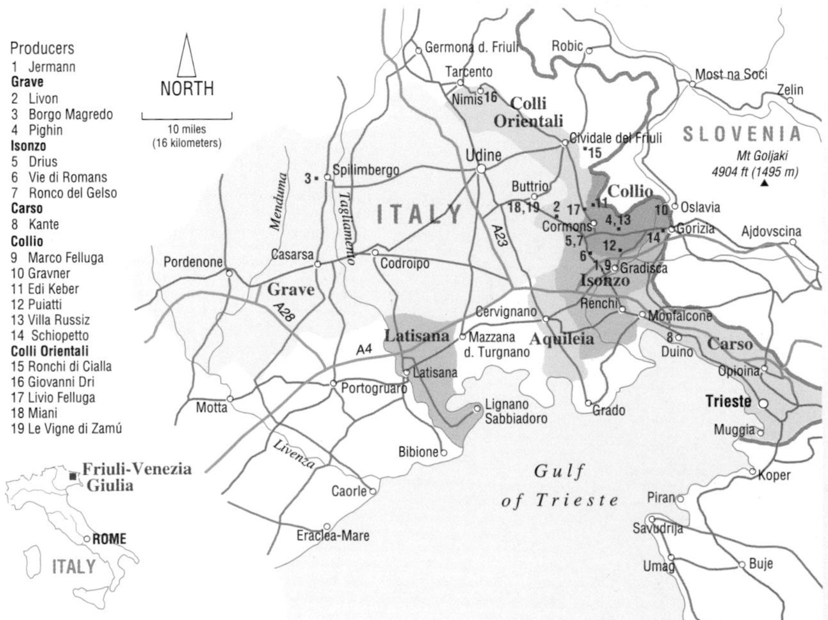

Emilia–Romagna

ABOVE: *Italy's great classic cheese, Parmigiano reggiano, is prized worldwide.*

Whatever system one might use to classify Italy, the region of Emilia–Romagna doesn't fit. It is a long, straggly region, almost bisecting the country and stretching for more than 150 miles (250 km) from Piedmont in the northwest to the Adriatic Sea and the Marche in the east. It is largely bordered to the north by the broad, rambling Po River and its flat, fertile valley, while the more southerly parts cover some of the more impenetrable reaches of the Apennines.

In the far west lies the zone of Colli Piacentini, with similar grape varieties and wine styles to neighboring Oltrepò Pavese, except for guturnio, its own unique barbera/bonarda blend. In the center is the Colli Bolognesi—its core is the quality subzone of Zola Predosa. The wines, mainly single-varietals, come principally from the indigenous variety, pignoletto. A fair amount of barbera is grown, while the international varieties (cabernet sauvignon, merlot, chardonnay, sauvignon and riesling) produce excellent, well-fruited wines.

Growing across Romagna in the east are trebbiano di romagna, albana di romagna, sangiovese di Romagna, cagnina di romagna and pagadebit di romagna. The trebbiano grown here rarely produces much more than easy-drinking wine. Albana is a middle-ranking white variety that requires considerable dedication and tenacity to produce wines of more than passing interest. Most of Romagna's sangiovese is a different strain from Tuscany's and these wines can have a lively rusticity to them.

BELOW: *A rustic villa in a vineyard, Emilia–Romagna.*

Landscape and climate

Emilia–Romagna's topography and climate vary enormously. Even splitting it into its natural divisions—Emilia to the west of Bologna, its hub, and Romagna, east of Bologna—does not help a great deal.

The image of Emilia–Romagna, however, is of highly fertile, perfectly flat, hazy countryside, extending through the Po Valley, with pin-straight roads and dotted with occasional plane trees. This terrain, fine for fruit tree cultivation and livestock rearing, is famous for Parma ham (prosciutto di Parma) and Parmesan cheese (Parmigiano reggiano) but not, in general, for vines. The vineyard areas are sparsely clustered on the poorer soils of hilly outcrops, but not on the cold Apennine slopes.

Lambrusco

Several strains of lambrusco are grown over a fair swathe of central–eastern and northeastern Italy but the area is largely concentrated near Modena. Its wine has become famous as something akin to sweetish, fizzy pop, a style that developed from cold weather halting natural fermentation. Not all lambrusco is like this; there are some dry versions around and some where the sweetness doesn't mask the wine's intrinsic fresh acidity and cherry-like character. There are three main strains: sorbara is often made dryer than most and has good perfume and character; grasaparossa di Castelvetro is more fully flavored and often used for the sweeter wines; salamino di Santa Croce has both richness and acidity. White and pink are, in theory, made from the red lambrusco grape, but cheating does go on.

FUGAZZA, COLLI PIACENTINI

Established **1920** ***Owners*** **the Fugazza sisters** ***Production*** **12,500 bottles** ***Vineyard area*** **210 acres (85 ha)**

Maria Giulia and Giovannella Fugazza's land straddles the border between Emilia's Colli Piacentini and Lombardy's Oltrepò Pavese so they have formed two estates, Romito in the former and Castello di Luzzano in Oltrepò. Maria Giulia looks after the vineyards and Giovannella the cellars. Best wines are from bonarda and barbera, leading naturally to good gutturnio. They also work well with malvasia and moscato.

MANICARDI, LAMBRUSCO

Established **1980** ***Owners*** **the Manicardi family** ***Production*** **6,500 cases** ***Vineyard area*** **42 acres (17 ha)**

This small estate is well known for its good quality aceto balsamico (balsamic vinegar). A move in management from Enzo Manicardi to his daughters Livia and Raffaella has provoked a change of emphasis and an upturn in the quality of the wines. All are from the Castelvetro sub-area and Lambrusco di Castelvetro strain. There is a dry version as well as the more common *amabile*.

TRE MONTI, ROMAGNA

Established **1972** ***Owners*** **Davide & Vittorio Navicella** ***Production*** **25,000 cases** ***Vineyard area*** **114 acres (46 ha)**

The estate is split into two plots, one on the first rises behind Imola, the other on the hills behind Forlì, about 18 miles (29 km) away, with good, southern exposures and altitudes around 650 feet (200 m). The largish range combines well-made wines from indigenous varieties such as albana and sangiovese; intense, *barriqued* international varietals such as chardonnay and cabernet sauvignon; and, blends of the two, notably salcerella (albana/chardonnay) and boldo (sangiovese/cabernet).

FATTORIA PARADISO, ROMAGNA

Established **1940** ***Owner*** **Mario Pezzi** ***Production*** **29,000 cases** ***Vineyard area*** **100 acres (40 ha)**

The Pezzi family overturned cynicism about the quality of wines from Romagna. The *cru* Sangiovese di Romagna, Vigna delle Lepri, was well above all competition because it was made from the Tuscan strain of sangiovese. Mario Pezzi wisely repropagated the disparaged pagadebit. He also discovered a deep, richly fruited variety he dubbed barbarossa, from what appeared to be a natural mutation of a single plant in his vineyards.

MORO RINALDO RINALDINI, LAMBRUSCO

Established **1972** ***Owner*** **Rinaldo Rinaldini** ***Production*** **12,500 cases** ***Vineyard area*** **37 acres (15 ha)**

This is one of the few estates still making "serious" sparkling lambrusco (dry), with its second fermentation being in bottle rather than in tank. Rinaldini also produces sparkling chardonnay, dry sparkling malvasia and a lightly sparkling pinot, all with bottle fermentation.

VIGNETO DELLE TERRE ROSSE, COLLI BOLOGNESI

Established **1961** ***Owners*** **the Vallania family** ***Production*** **5,800 cases** ***Vineyard area*** **49 acres (20 ha)**

Brother and sister Giovanni and Elisabetta Vallania practice vine cultivation as near to organic as is possible, use only varieties that suit their terrain (in the prime sub-zone of Zola Predosa) and give those varieties full expression by avoiding any oak in their aging. This approach gives rise to beautifully fruited, cleanly structured and long-lived cabernet sauvignon, notably in the Cuvée Enrico Vallania (named after their father), refined chardonnay, a surprisingly complex malvasia, intriguing pinot grigio and wonderful, multilayered, minerally, balanced late-harvest riesling. Nevertheless, it is his Viognier, from one of Italy's first plantings, that Giovanni Vallania is most proud of.

Other excellent producers found in the Emilia–Romagna region include La Stoppa (Colli Piacentini); Cavicchioli (Lambrusco); and Fattoria Zerbina (Romagna).

ABOVE: *Vines staked individually, Emilia–Romagna.*

Regional Best

Albana di Romagna Passito Scacco Matto (Fattoria Zerbina)
Colli Bolognesi Merlot (Tenuta Bonzara)
Colli d'Imola Cabernet Turico Tre Monti)
Il Tornese Chardonnay Drei Dona (Tenuta La Palazza)
Lambrusco di Sorbara Vigna del Cristo (Cavicchioli)
Marzieno Ravenna Rosso (Fattoria Zerbina)

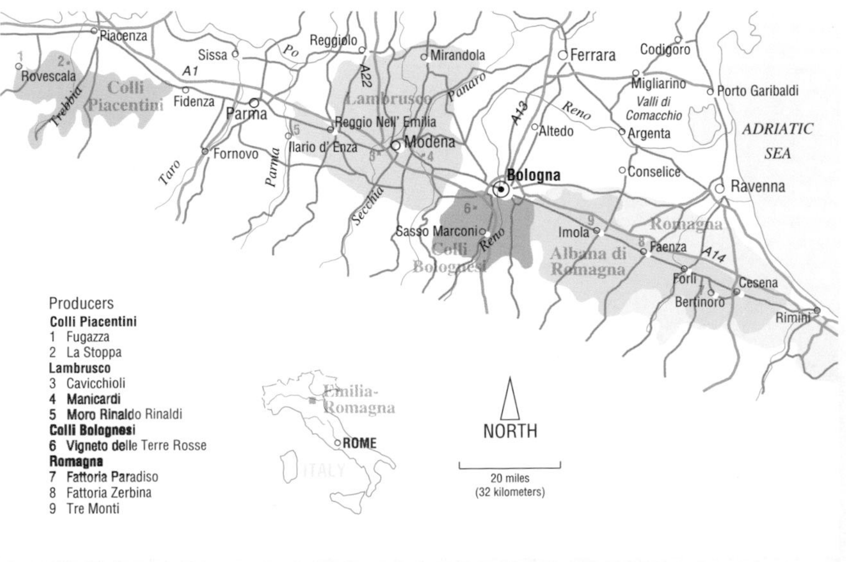

RIGHT: Florence and the River Arno viewed from the Piazzale Michelangelo.

Tuscany

The heart of Tuscany is its central hills: Chianti's southerly massifs of Montalcino and Montepulciano. The soul is the sangiovese grape. Some liken its aromas to fresh tea with an overlay of prunes, sometimes plums or cherries. It is often notably spicy, with a good swathe of acidity that should be balanced by ripe tannins. The Sangiovese grape makes lively wines but every extra ounce of quality requires greater care and skill, so a stunning sangiovese remains a challenge. Other red grapes traditionally grown in the area include canaiolo, mammolo, ciliegiolo and colorino.

The primary white variety is trebbiano toscano, fine as a neutral base in blends. Traditionally it was partnered with malvasia del chianti, which makes soft, round, gently perfumed wines. Malvasia and trebbiano are used to good effect in Vin Santo, a wine made from passito grapes; some are dry, traditional styles are sweet.

Brunello di montalcino is one of Italy's most distinguished wines. It is rich, ripe, mouth-filling, powerful, and intense. The "younger brother" rosso di montalcino is zippier, fruitier and cheaper. Bolgheri is unusual because it is the only Tuscan area not dominated by sangiovese. Bolgheri's cabernet-based Sassicaia, born in 1968, showed the way forward for this region. Carmignano, once notable for its finesse, is now moving toward greater attack and presence. In the Maremma, in Tuscany's south, morellino is grown, and Morellino di Scansano is comparatively soft, round, open, and cherry-like. The Parrina zone produces sangiovese-based reds of midweight and some good whites.

The most important area for white wine production is the zone of San Gimignano. The Vernaccia di San Gimignano can be pale-hued, light, clean, and fresh or deep, ripe, round, and fat.

Because many Tuscan wines do not comply with the DOC(G) labeling constraints, producers create wines that fall under either "Super-Tuscan" or one of the hundreds of new "IGT" categories.

Producers

Carmignano
1 Fattoria Selvapiana
2 Marchesi di Frescobaldi
3 Ruffino
4 Tenuta di Capezzana

Chianti Classico
5 Agricola Querciabella
6 Castello di Ama
7 Antinori
8 Castello di Brolio
9 Fattoria di Felsina
10 Fontodi
11 Isole e Olena
12 Montevertine
13 Castello di Volpaia

San Gimignano
14 Ponte a Rondolino

Bolgheri
15 Tenuta dell'Ornellaia
16 Tenuta San Guido

Montalcino
17 Castello Banfi
18 Biondi Santi
19 Casato Prime Donne
20 Costanti
21 Il Poggione

Montepulciano
22 Avignonesi
23 Poderi Boscarelli
24 Poliziano

Morellino di Scansano
25 Le Pupille

Colline di Lucchese
26 Tenuta di Valgiano

Chianti and Chianti Classico

Any discussion of the wines of Tuscany has to begin with Chianti and especially Chianti Classico, the region's linchpin. The Chianti Classico district covers the land between Florence and Siena. Non-Classico Chianti covers a far wider and more variable area, about 75 miles (120 km) west to east from the coast to Arezzo, and a similar distance north to south, from Pistoia to south of Montalcino. Most of it falls into one of eight subzones including Chianti Colli Senesi, Chianti Montabano, Chianti Colli Aretini and Chianti Rufina. "Chianti" is a misnomer for much of the territory and its use irritates the true Chianti folk, the "Chiantigiani." As the name became devalued in the 1970s and 1980s, many producers preferred not to use the denomination. Rufina apart, the wines are usually somewhat lighter than the Classico Chiantis and tend to be easy drinking, without great structure or weight. When Chianti was upgraded to DOCG in 1984, the whole area, Classico and non-Classico, was promoted. This caused innumerable protests at the time and is now recognized as a serious mistake, although amendments since have seen the criteria for Chianti Classico tightened. Chianti is made from sangiovese but not exclusively; the inclusion of small quantities of canailo, trebbiano and malvasia is typical. Adding white grapes is a throwback to the nineteenth century, when the wine was preferred light, fresh and youthful. Only in the Classico zone is 100 percent sangiovese permitted. The DOCG also allows for a small percentage of "other" varieties, usually cabernet sauvignon.

Within the geological structure of Chianti Classico two soil types mark out the best sites: *galestro*, a clay-schist, and the limestone *alberese*. The communes of Radda, Gaiole and Castellina form "the golden triangle," the heart of the heart of Chianti. They are surrounded by Castelnuovo Berardenga, Barberino Val d'Elsa, Greve and Panzano, with San Casciano farther north.

While not all wines display the black cockerel symbol (known in Italy as *gallo nero*), those that do belong to the Classico's marketing consortium, an influential and remarkably competent body. The symbol derives from historical Florence–Siena animosities: one day horsemen were to depart from both cities at dawn (announced by cock-crow) and the place where they met defined the border between the two territories. The Florentines trained their black cockerel to crow early and so gained the lion's share of the land.

CASTELLO DI AMA, CARMIGNANO

Established **1970s** ***Owners*** **Castello di Ama SpA**
Production **33,000 cases** ***Vineyard area*** **235 acres (96 ha)**

Ama wines differ from most chianti; stalkier, leaner, and with a more restrained fruitiness that can give them noticeable refinement. The estate has three distinctive chianti classico *crus*, plus merlot, pinot nero, sauvignon and chardonnay.

ANTINORI, CARMIGNANO

Established **1300s** ***Owners*** **Marchesi Antinori** ***Production*** **1.1–1.15 million cases** ***Vineyard area*** **c.850 acres (350 ha) plus grapes bought-in (c.60%)**

Antinori produces immensely drinkable wines with broad appeal. Santa Cristina and Chianti Classico Peppoli are popular; Solaia (cabernet/sangiovese) and Tignanello (sangiovese/cabernet) have proved the estate's worth at the higher end of the market.

CASTELLO BANFI, MONTALCINO

Established **1978** ***Owners*** **Banfi Vintners USA (Mariani brothers)**
Production **650,000 cases** ***Vineyard area*** **2,000 acres (800 ha)**

The arrival of Banfi stirred up Montalcino. Where vineyards were generally small and scattered, Banfi bought up about 7,000 acres (2,800 ha) of land and planted extensively. About 370 acres (150 ha) of this land are dedicated exclusively to brunello di montalcino. The cellar, one of Italy's largest, houses over 3,000 *barriques* and hundreds of larger barrels. Banfi spearheaded the revival of the moscadello di montalcino. The range of wines produced here is large and all are well-made and unimpeachable in type.

ABOVE: The centuries-old winery Castello di Volpaia reflected in a chianti bottle which also displays the black cockerel symbol.

BELOW: A hilltop town in Chianti, surrounded by vineyards and the cypresses that are emblematic of Tuscany.

ABOVE: Cypresses line the road to the vineyard Castello di Volpaia in Chianti.

TENUTA DELL'ORNELLAIA, BOLGHERI

Established **late 1970s** ***Owner*** **Marchese Ludovico Antinori** ***Production*** **32,500 cases** ***Vineyard area*** **170 acres (70 ha)**

The Marchese Ludovico Antinori's "California style" Ornellaia (85 percent cabernet sauvignon/merlot/ cabernet franc) is fatter, riper, and punchier than Sassicaia but less complex. The Bolgheri estate also stands out for Le Volte (cabernet sauvignon/ merlot), the intense Masseto (merlot), and the racy Poggio alle Gazze (sauvignon).

LE PUPILLE, MORELLINO DI SCANSANO

Established **1972** ***Owners*** **the Gentili family** ***Production*** **6,000–6,500 cases** ***Vineyard area*** **40 acres (16 ha)**

Le Pupille sets the tone in Scansano. Always refining the approach, the wines here are big and punchy yet they have style and character. Morellino is made in three versions. There is also the highly regarded Saffredi (cabernet/merlot/alicante) and Solalto, a sweet wine from the blend sauvignon/traminer/sémillon.

BIONDI SANTI, MONTALCINO

Established **1700s** ***Owners*** **Biondi Santi SpA** ***Production*** **28,500 cases** ***Vineyard area*** **110 acres (45 ha)**

As the "father" of brunello di montalcino, Biondi Santi is held almost in awe by many in the industry. The firm is legendary for the longevity of the wines. The range (previously just consisting of Brunello and Rosso) has been enhanced by a number of other wines, especially Sassoalloro (sangiovese).

TENUTA DI CAPEZZANA, CARMIGNANO

Established **At least 12 centuries ago; under current ownership since 1926** ***Owners*** **Conti Contini Bonacossi** ***Production*** **42,000 cases** ***Vineyard area*** **c.220 acres (90 ha)**

Conte Ugo Contini Bonacossi is the principal producer in Carmignano and he has advanced the area's style: the wines are supremely elegant, but with good grip and fine aging potential. The lively Barco Reale di Carmignano and the drinkable deep rosé, Vin Ruspo, stand out.

Regional Dozen

- Brunello di Montalcino (Costanti)
- Chianti Classico Riserva Castello di Fonterutoli (Mazzei)
- Chianti Classico Riserva Rancia (Fattoria di Felsina)
- Giallo dei Muri (Tenuta di Valgiano)
- Monsanto Chianti Classico Riserva
- Morellino di Scansano (Le Pupille)
- Poggio alla Gazze (Ornellaia)
- Sassicaia (Tenuta San Guido)
- Tignanello (Antinori)
- Vernaccia di San Gimignano (Teruzzi e Puthod)
- Vin Santo (Isole e Olena)
- Vino Nobile di Montepulciano Vigna del Nocio (Boscarelli)

ISOLE E OLENA, CARMIGNANO

Established **1971** ***Owner*** **Paolo de Marchi** ***Production*** **16,500 cases** ***Vineyard area*** **110 acres (45 ha)**

Paolo de Marchi has developed a particularly lively, fruit-forward style, allied with great depth and complexity. Super-Tuscan Cepparello (100 percent sangiovese) is extremely concentrated and slow-developing; the rich Vin Santo is one of the region's best. His syrah is one of the most intriguing expressions of the grape in Italy.

PONTE A RONDOLINO (ALSO KNOWN AS TERUZZI E PUTHOD), SAN GIMIGNANO

Established **1974** ***Owners*** **Enrico Teruzzi and Carmen Puthod** ***Production*** **25,000 cases** ***Vineyard area*** **85 + 8.5 acres leased (35 + 3.5 ha)**

The round, rich style of Teruzzi's Vernaccia brought the estate to prominence, but now it is the overtly oaked Terre di Tufi version that has attained the greater critical acclaim—an amazing achievement for Enrico Teruzzi, who started making wine almost for fun.

TENUTA DI VALGIANO, COLLINE LUCCHESI

Established **NA** ***Owners*** **NA** ***Production*** **3,500 cases** ***Vineyard area*** **25 acres (10 ha)**

Produced in Colline Lucchesi, the three Valgiano wines reach high levels of refinement and individuality. There is a racy, savory white, Giallo dei Muri; a vibrant and spicy red, Rosso di Palistorti; and the firmer, Scasso dei Casari.

Other significant producers include Fattoria Selvapiana, Ruffino (both Carmignano); Poliziano, Poderi Boscarelli (both Montepulciano); Casato Prime Donna, Costanti, Il Poggione (all Montalcino); Fontodi, Castello di Brolio, Fattoria di Felsina, Monsanto, Montevertin, Castello de Volpaia (all Chianti Classico); and Tenuta San Guido (Bolgheri).

Central Italy

The central part of the Italian peninsula includes the regions of Marche, Umbria and Lazio (sometimes called Latium). Widespread plantings of sangiovese and trebbiano form the base for much of the wine, but each region has at least one variety indigenous to one or more zones, which put their stamp on the wines.

MARCHE

Marche is dominated by verdicchio, crisply acidic, softly fruited with flavors of various green and yellow fruits, and gently creamy but with good power behind. The main growing area, Verdicchio dei Castelli di Jesi, is fairly extensive, the vineyards mostly lying west of the village of Jesi along two roughly parallel ranges 820–1,600 feet (250–500 m) high. The area of Verdicchio di Matelica is smaller; it lies further inland near the border with Umbria and produces less than 10 percent of the quantity of the Castelli di Jesi. Its wines are generally agreed to be superior: more muscular, more intense and deeper.

Reds take second place here, yet there are two of note. Rosso conero is made almost exclusively from montepulciano, a grape producing a deeply colored, deeply flavored, richly fruited but well-structured, brambly red. Rosso piceno's best wines come from a small area called Rosso Piceno Superior.

BONCI, VERDICCHIO DEI CASTELLI DI JESI

***Established* 1962 *Owners* the Bonci family *Production* 25,000 cases *Vineyard area* 86 acres (35 ha)**

This is one of Jesi's rising stars. The vineyards are at 1,500 feet (450 m) in some of the zone's best sites, with two of the sites given over to research under the guidance of Milan University. The standard verdicchio is clean and well-styled but the estate's flair is shown by their verdicchio *crus*, Le Case and the perfumed, full, structured, warm, softly balanced San Michele. An attractive, sweet, passito verdicchio and a finely tuned brut sparkling verdicchio complete the range.

COCCI GRIFONI, ROSSO PICENO SUPERIORE

***Established* 1969 *Owner* Guido Cocci Grifoni *Production* 25,000 cases *Vineyard area* 100 acres (40 ha)**

Cocci Grifoni is one of the longest standing estates in the Piceno Superiore area. The wines have improved steadily over the years and now set the standards in the zone with their perfumed, full-bodied, ripely fruited style. The estate also works to good effect with the white wines of the area.

LEFT: Early version of the open-frame bottle opener.

MARCHETTI, ROSSO CONERO

***Established* c.1900 *Owners* the Marchetti family *Production* 4,000 cases *Vineyard area* 30 acres (12 ha)**

Since the first bottlings in the 1960s, the Marchetti wines have set the standard for Rosso Conero. Once they were full, soft and deep, but as son Maurizio progressively took over from father Mario the style became

BELOW LEFT: An avenue of trees lines the entrance to the vineyards at Torgiano, Umbria, Central Italy.

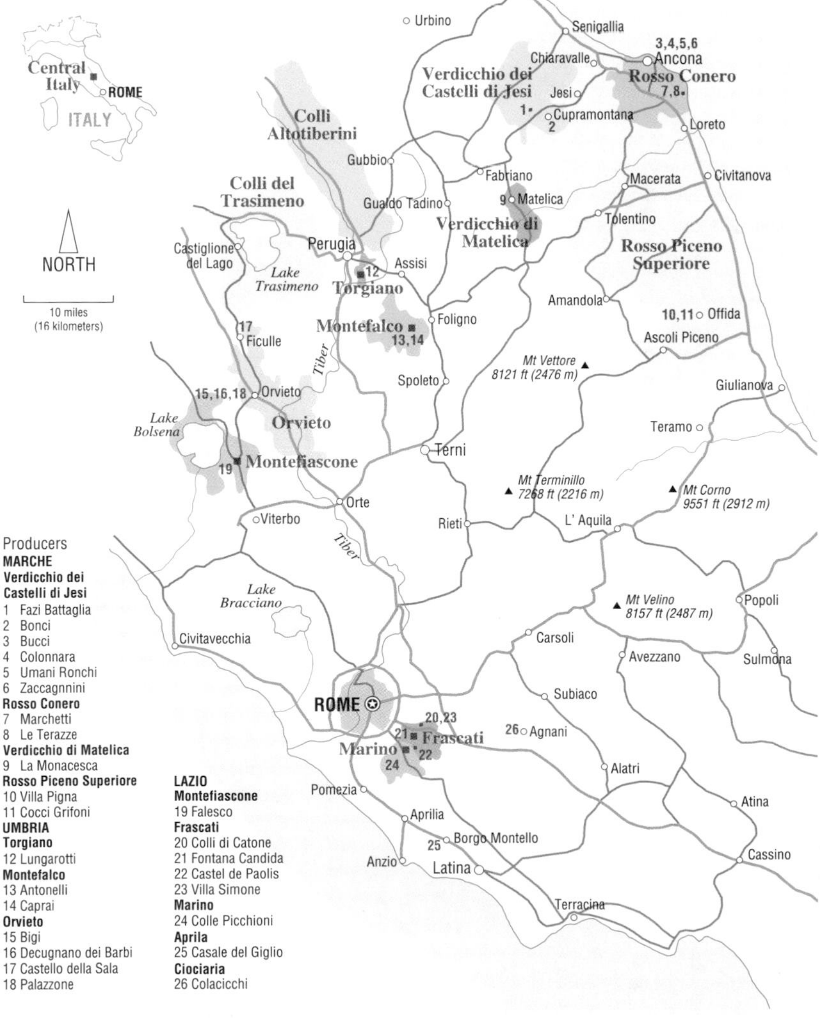

ABOVE: *The small town of Poggio Lavarino straddles a terraced hill in Umbria.*

somewhat fresher and punchier while the intrinsic quality and longevity remained. Maurizio introduced the Rosso Conero selection, Villa Bonomi, now the estate's leading wine. A small amount of Verdicchio dei Castelli di Jesi is made from bought-in grapes.

LA MONACESCA, VERDICCHIO DI MATELICA

Established **1966** ***Owner*** **Casimiro Cifola** ***Production*** **9,000 cases** ***Vineyard area*** **55 acres (22 ha)**

This estate began as a hobby for Casimiro Cifola but soon became his main occupation. It is now competently managed by his son Aldo. La Monacesca has long been the example par excellence of Verdicchio di Matelica in the zone. Until recently the estate has concentrated almost exclusively on the verdicchio grape, but is now beginning to work with red grapes.

Regional Dozen

- Cervara della Sala (Castello della Sala)
- Frascati Superiore (Colli di Catone)
- Frascati Superiore Vigna Adriana (Castel de Paolis)
- Orvieto Classico Campo del Guardiano (Palazzone)
- Orvieto Classico Pourriture Noble (Decugnano dei Barbi)
- Quattro Mori (Castel de Paolis)
- Rubino (La Palazzola)
- Sagrantino di Montefalc (Arnaldo Caprai)
- Torgiano Rosso Riserva Vigna Monticchio (Lungarotti)
- Verdicchio dei Castelli di Jesi Classico (Bucci)
- Verdicchio dei Castelli di Jesi Classico Superiore Casal di Serra (Umani Ronchi)
- Verdicchio di Matelica (La Monacesca)

UMANI RONCHI, VERDICCHIO DEI CASTELLI DI JESI

Established **1955** ***Owners*** **the Bernetti family** ***Production*** **350,000 cases** ***Vineyard area*** **370 + 100 acres leased (150 + 40 ha) + grapes bought in**

This colossus of the Marche scene has an equally high reputation for its Verdicchio and its Rosso Conero. It is the latter that is currently attracting greater attention in its three variants: the well-typed base version, the richer *cru* San Lorenzo and the oaked Cumaro. Under the guidance of consultant enologist Giacomo Tachis their new wine, Pèlago (cabernet sauvignon/montepulciano/merlot), is achieving acclaim. Among the verdicchios, *cru* Casal di Serra stands out, but the entire range is excellent value for money.

ZACCAGNINI, VERDICCHIO DEI CASTELLI DI JESI

Established **1974** ***Owners*** **the Zaccagnini brothers** ***Production*** **18,000 cases** ***Vineyard area*** **70 acres (28 ha)**

Silvio and Mario Zaccagnini were among the first in the area to work with single-vineyard, high-quality verdicchio wines. Their oak-free *cru* Salmagina, intense, characterful, finely balanced and of depth, is still one of the best. In addition there are two finely honed sparkling verdicchios, Brut and Metodo Tradizionale.

UMBRIA

Much of Umbria is formed of tightly packed, rounded hills, cut through by the upper reaches of the River Tiber. Lake Trasimeno and the northern part of the river have adjacent vineyards, Colli del Trasimeno and Colli Altotiberini respectively. The wines include varietals from chardonnay, pinot grigio, riesling italico, cabernet sauvignon and pinot nero, plus red torgiano made from a sangiovese-based blend, and white torgiano from trebbiano (mostly) and grechetto. Grechetto, a native white variety, makes punchy but rounded and rather nutty wines of good character. Its red counterpart is sagrantino, a magnificent variety that makes big, ripe, black-fruited wines of tremendous depth, length and vigor. It is the powerhouse behind the red wines of the Montefalco zone.

In the south, Colli Amerini is good value, but most significant here is Orvieto, which turns out well-made trebbiano-based wines. Occasionally the vineyards are affected by noble rot, prompting fully sweet, botrytized styles of Orvieto, so impressive, richly but not cloyingly sweet and beautifully floral, that a few estates now produce botrytized styles in most years, whether noble rot appears naturally or not.

CAPRAI, MONTEFALCO

Established **1971** ***Owners*** **the Caprai family** ***Production*** **62,500 cases** ***Vineyard area*** **200 acres (80 ha)**

Arnaldo Caprai, a fabrics industrialist, bought this estate in 1971, and gradually added adjacent land. He concentrated on sagrantino to become one of Montefalco's leading producers, especially with Sagrantino di Montefalco Passito. When his son Marco took over the styles of the wines changed, bringing even greater success. The Sagrantino di Montefalco is now *barriqued*, huge in power and intensity and made for the long haul, especially the Sagrantino di Montefalco 25 Anni.

LUNGAROTTI, TORGIANO

Established **1950** ***Owners*** **the Lungarotti family** ***Production*** **200,000 cases** ***Vineyard area*** **750 acres (300 ha)**

Lungarotti is quite simply synonymous with Torgiano, the village and the wine. Within the village the family owns a famed hotel and restaurant, Le Tre Vaselle, and one of Italy's best equipped wine museums. The wine names, Torre di Giano (white) and Rubesco (red), may even be better known than the denomination itself; the *riserva*-level wines, most notably *cru* Vigna Monticchio, have starry reputations, and the entire range is held in high consideration, although recent vintages have not quite hit the mark.

CASTELLO DELLA SALA, ORVIETO

Established **1977** ***Owner*** **Marchese Piero Antinori** ***Production*** **50,000 cases** ***Vineyard area*** **350 acres (140 ha)**

ABOVE: *Upright oak barrels in the famous Torgiano winery, Lungarotti.*

Castello della Sala is indeed a castle, medieval, fortressed and built around 1350. It was bought by Tuscany's famous Antinori family in 1940 and turned over to wine production in 1977. Although part of Piero Antinori's aim was to add Orvieto Classico to his range of Tuscan wines, most of the grapes planted on the clayey soils were chardonnay and sauvignon. The resultant wines, perfectly constructed, have won endless awards, especially Cervaro della Sala, from chardonnay (with a little grechetto). Muffato della Sala is from sauvignon, grechetto and others, botrytized. A pinot nero has also gained renown.

LAZIO

The important wines of Lazio, the region of Rome, are produced near the capital on the cool slopes of the hills rising close to its southeastern suburbs. In prime position is Frascati, whose fame did not arise solely from intrinsic superiority—its proximity to Rome was just as significant. Much frascati remains a commodity wine but an increasing proportion is of considerably finer quality.

LEFT: *Striking geometry in the vineyards of Torgiano, Umbria, Central Italy.*

There is more variety in the reds with considerable use being made of sangiovese and montepulciano, increasing plantings of merlot, and canaiolo and ciliegiolo taking supporting roles, especially in the north of the region. Lazio's indigenous red is cesanese, a wild, rustic variety of assured potential, if only someone could tame it. The curious red aleatico, grown only on the northwest shores of Lake Bolsena, produces a deep, richly fruity, lively but soft dessert wine which is sometimes liquoroso (fortified).

FONTANA CANDIDA, FRASCATI

Established **1958** ***Owner*** **Gruppo Italiano Vini** ***Production*** **625,000 cases** ***Vineyard area*** **225 acres (91 ha) + grapes bought in**

Fontana Candida is responsible for almost half of all frascati produced, and exports about two-thirds of its production. The company's wine-maker, Francesco Bardi, ensures good quality, well-styled wines throughout. The *cru* Santa Teresa, with 30 percent malvasia del lazio, is regularly one of the best frascatis on the market. The Frascati Terre dei Grifi, lighter and fresher, has a higher proportion of trebbiano; also from the Terre dei Grifi range is a broad but nuanced wine made from 100 percent malvasia del lazio.

RIGHT: The wine museum owned and run by Cantine Lungarotti in Torgiano.

COLACICCHI, CIOCIARIA

Established **1950** ***Owners*** **the Trimani family** ***Production*** **1,600 cases** ***Vineyard area*** **12 acres (5 ha)**

The Trimani family run one of Rome's best stocked wine shops, plus an adjacent wine bar. The tiny but highly prestigious Colacicchi estate is a quite recent acquisition and the aim is to ensure that its wines, especially the flagship Torre Ercolana (cabernet sauvignon/merlot/cesanese), always match their lofty reputations. The wines are not released until they are ready for drinking; for Torre Ercolana, this means after about eight years. A younger red, Romagnano Rosso, is made from the same varieties, and a white, Romagnano Bianco, from a blend of local grapes.

FALESCO, MONTEFIASCONE

Established **1979** ***Owner*** **Riccardo Cotarella** ***Production*** **20,000 cases** ***Vineyard area*** **All grapes bought in**

Riccardo Cotarella is one of Italy's most esteemed consultant enologists and he imposes strict controls on his grape growers. His Est! Est!! Est!!! first brought the wine out of disrepute and there is now a *cru* version, Poggio dei Gelsi, nuanced and ripely fruity. He also produces a varietal Grechetto and Vitiano (merlot/cabernet sauvignon/sangiovese), but the flagship wine is Montiano (100 percent merlot), a punchy giant.

CASALE DEL GIGLIO, APRILIA

Established **1968** ***Owners*** **the Santarelli family** ***Production*** **37,500–50,000 cases** ***Vineyard area*** **300 acres (120 ha)**

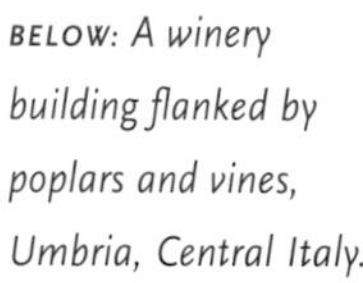

BELOW: A winery building flanked by poplars and vines, Umbria, Central Italy.

The year 1984 marked the beginning of this estate in its current form when it embarked on a major research project to establish the varieties best suited to its lands, near the coast in Aprilia, about 30 miles (50 km) southeast of Rome. Now working with a range of international varieties, its best known wine is Satrico (chardonnay/trebbiano).

COLLE PICCHIONI, MARINO

Established **1976** ***Owners*** **Paola & Armando di Mauro** ***Production*** **7,500 cases** ***Vineyard area*** **22 acres (9 ha)**

Paola di Mauro's wines, intense, complex, long-lived and fascinating, are the result not just of attentive vineyard management, intelligent vinification and careful aging but of reliance on the "minor" grapes of the zone. Marino Etichetta Verde, the estate's base wine, is far superior to the competition. Marino Etichetta Oro is several notches richer and deeper; Le Vignole is slow-developing and quite exceptional. Its red partner, Vigna del Vassallo, is made from merlot, cabernet sauvignon and cabernet franc. The same grapes form the base of the fine Colle Picchioni Rosso.

VILLA SIMONE, FRASCATI

Established **1980** ***Owners*** **the Costantini family** ***Production*** **10,000 cases** ***Vineyard area*** **50 acres (20 ha)**

Piero Costantini bought the Villa Simone with the express intent of making a frascati superior to all others. He replanted the vineyards with a proportion of malvasia del lazio and modernized the cellar. The resultant wines are elegant, individually styled and cleanly aromatic, especially the *crus* Vigneto Filonardi and Vigna dei Preti.

Other good producers in Central Italy include Fazi Battaglia, Bucci, Colonnara, Le Terazze, Villa Pigna (all Marche); Antonelli, Bigi, Colli di Catone, Palazzone (all Umbria); and Castel de Paolis (Lazio).

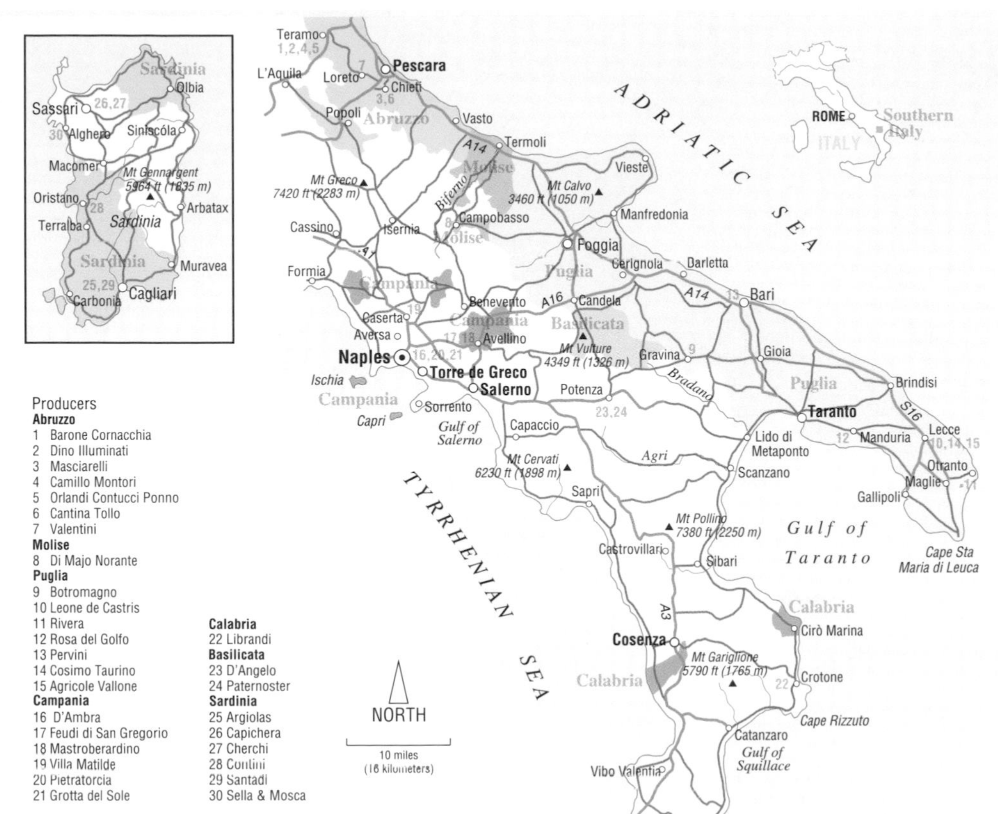

ABOVE: *Green bottles with red wax caps in the laboratory at Cantine Di Marco, Martina Franca, Puglia.*

Southern Italy

The south has long been regarded as the sleeping giant of Italy. Despite an abundance of grape varieties of indisputable quality, it has taken an unconscionably long time for a critical mass of good wine to be produced. The southern Italian regions comprise Abruzzo, Molise and Puglia, heading south from the Marche along the Adriatic coast; Campania and Calabria, south from Lazio along the western coast; Basilicata, the instep, joining the heel of Puglia to the toe of Calabria; and the island of Sardinia. Sicily, the other main island, is treated separately.

ABRUZZO, PUGLIA AND MOLISE

Abruzzo is one of Italy's most beautiful regions, with sandy beaches and high peaks. Here montepulciano finds its greatest expression. The wines are most structured and probably at their most typical around Pescara, while in L'Aquila they are lighter and more elegant. With white wine in Abruzzo, practically the only denomination is trebbiano d'abruzzo. Controguerra is produced only in Abruzzo's northeast corner: the red is from montepulciano blended with some cabernet sauvignon and/or merlot; the white is from trebbiano toscano with some of the indigenous variety, passerina.

Puglia is the south's go-ahead wine region, with a string of native grape varieties. Here, the center of attention is the narrow Salento Peninsula in the far south. The indigenous red variety, negroamaro, the "bitter-black," was renowned for deeply colored, impenetrably intense, bitter-finishing, and long-lived wines that needed a touch of the aromatic red malvasia to make them approachable. Negroamaro is now being shaped into a riper and fruitier wine.

The Salento's traditional wines made from primitivo are robust, mouth-filling, richly fruity, and strongly spicy red wines that are either dry (or off-dry) and strongly alcoholic, or sweet and fairly strongly alcoholic. Further north, uva di troia is the prime red grape, making a firm, stylish, minerally wine. Its white partner is pampanuto. They are at their best in Castel del Monte wines. Puglia also produces some of Italy's best rosés.

Molise is Italy's ugly-duckling region; there is one producer of note, Di Majo Norante.

CAMILLO MONTORI

Established **1879** ***Owner*** **Camillo Montori** ***Production*** **40,000 cases** ***Vineyard area*** **100 acres (40 ha) + grapes bought in**

Montori was the powerhouse behind the recognition of Colline Teramane as a Montepulciano subzone and also the setting up of a separate DOC for Controguerra. His attention to detail has ensured that his wines have long been in Abruzzo's top rank, especially his leading Fonte Cupa line, but a recent changeover to a more overtly oaky style has tended to knock them off-key. Montori is one of the few producers making Trebbiano d'Abruzzo worthy of note.

Regional Dozen

- Aglianico del Vulture (D'Angelo)
- Carignano del Sulcis Tre Torri (Cantina Sociale di Santadi)
- Greco del Tufo (Mastroberadino)
- Montepulciano d'Abruzzo Riparossa (Dino Illuminati)
- Primitivo di Manduria Archidamo (Pervini)
- Salice Salentino Rosso Riserva Donna Lisa (Leone de Castris)
- Taurasi (Feudi di San Gregorio)
- Terra Riserva Leverano (Conti Zecca)
- Torbato di Alghero Terre Bianche (Sella & Mosca)
- Turriga IGT (Antonio Argiolas)
- Vermentino di Gallura (Capichera)
- Vigna del Feudo (Felline)

RIGHT: *Many of the old buildings in Puglia feature exquisitely decorated facades as shown in this intricate example from the town of Martina Franca.*

LEONE DE CASTRIS

Established **1665** ***Owner*** **Salvatore Leone de Castris** ***Production*** **250,000 cases** ***Vineyard area*** **1,100 acres (450 ha)**

The estate took on its current form in 1925 and gained fame half a century ago when it created Five Roses, a soft but fully flavored rosé that established Puglia's reputation for pink wines. Leone de Castris is also credited with shaping Salice Salentino. The estate is now renowned for the *barrique*-aged red Donna Lisa Salice Salentino Riserva, intense, structured, spicy and deep.

COSIMO TAURINO

Established **late 1800s** ***Owners*** **the Taurino family** ***Production*** **75,000 cases** ***Vineyard area*** **270 acres (110 ha)**

The estate took on its present form in the 1970s when the cellars were constructed. Cosimo Taurino was the architect of the wines. Against all received wisdom in the area at the time he invested heavily in equipment and vineyards, turning his wines into some of Puglia's best. The estate's emblem is Patriglione, a big, overtly rich, chocolatey, spicy wine, while the leaner, firmer Notarpanaro is more typical of modern handling of negroamaro. A handful of other wines, all well-made, complete Taurino's range.

ROSA DEL GOLFO

Established **1939** ***Owners*** **Lina and Damiano Calò** ***Production*** **8,500 cases** ***Vineyard area*** **Grapes bought-in**

Rosa del Golfo is the name of both the company and its leading wine, showing a conviction in the potential and marketability of pink wine that is hard to match. Rosa del Golfo (the wine) is one of Italy's top rosés. From negroamaro and malvasia nera, it is comparatively deeply colored, ripely perfumed, mid-weight and pure-toned with strawberry-like fruit. Considerable work is being done on negroamaro-based reds and a verdeca-based white.

DI MAJO NORANTE

Established **1960s** ***Owner*** **Alessio di Majo** ***Production*** **50,000 cases** ***Vineyard area*** **150 acres (60 ha)**

Molise's sole producer of any standing cultivates organically and, apart from a couple of wines that fit into the Biferno DOC, has concentrated on varietals from the south's most prized grape varieties: falanghina, fiano, greco, aglianico and moscato. The wines have always been individual and characterful but quality has often been variable. The arrival of Riccardo Cotarella as consultant enologist has given the wines a nudge toward greater fruit and depth.

MASCIARELLI

Established **1981** ***Owner*** **Gianni Masciarelli** ***Production*** **50,000 cases** ***Vineyard area*** **85 + 37 acres leased (35 + 15 ha)**

Gianni Masciarelli's grandfather planted vines in the 1930s but the estate took shape in 1981 when wines were first bottled. Masciarelli pays meticulous attention to vine cultivation, with the result that the wines have great structure and complexity. He is often cited for a celebrated chardonnay, Marina Cvetic, named after his wife who works with him. The leading wine is Montepulciano d'Abruzzo Villa Gemma, which has remarkable elegance and power. Several others are produced; all are consistently well-made.

VALENTINI

Established **1650** ***Owner*** **Edoardo Valentini** ***Production*** **0–4,000 cases** ***Vineyard area*** **155 acres (63 ha)**

Valentini handcrafts his wines into some of the most exquisite bottles to be found anywhere. With his main income from other sources, he can afford to be as fussy as he likes and handles only the peak of his grapes, sending the rest to a local co-operative. He releases his wines only when he considers them ready for drinking. The Montepulciano d'Abruzzo is legendary: slow-developing, with great longevity and outstanding complexity; while the Trebbiano d'Abruzzo is an astonishingly rich, structured, deeply perfumed and multi-layered wine.

BELOW: *Distinctive trulli storehouses outside the town of Locorotondo, Puglia.*

ABOVE: *In Puglia, wine bottles grace the walls of these stone trulli buildings which house some local shops.*

CAMPANIA AND CALABRIA

Northern Campania was the home of Italy's most famous wine in Roman days—the revived falerno matches its ancient Roman forebear as closely as possible. White Falerno del Massico is floral, with elegant but pervasive fruit, notable depth, and good longevity. The red is refined and well structured. Three of Campania's most important wines, Taurasi (from aglianico), Greco di tufo (greco), and Fiano di Avellino (fiano), come from the hill territory inland near Avellino. All three improve with age. Other important wine areas in Campania include the island of Ischia, home of two white varieties, biancolella and forastera, and Aversa, home of a lemony fresh asprinio.

Practically the only wine in Calabria with an international reputation is Cirò, both red and white Cirò being prime examples of Calabria's indigenous varieties, the red gaglioppo and white greco.

Eyes of the wolf

Campania, with Naples as its capital, is a wine region that was once known as the producer of some of the finest wines of the Mediterranean basin. Today the region is not quite as well known for quality wines, but still has plenty of legend and lore. Campania Felix, as the Romans called it, is the home of a dry white wine called "Lachryma Christi." The wine was said to be so good it would bring tears to the eyes of Christ. Interestingly, the grape variety used to make Lachryma Christi is "coda di volpe," or "eyes of the wolf."

FEUDI DI SAN GREGORIO

Established **1986** ***Owners*** **Capaldo and Ercolino families** ***Production*** **85,000 cases** ***Vineyard area*** **200 acres (80 ha)**

Within a few years this company has moved into the limelight to become one of the best known Campanian names. The wines from this estate are reliable, carefully made, well typed and well priced. They are led by Campanaro and Pietracalda, both Fiano di Avellino, Serpico (aglianico/piedirosso/sangiovese) and Taurasi.

GROTTA DEL SOLE

Established **1989** ***Owners*** **the Martusciello family** ***Production*** **50,000 cases** ***Vineyard area*** **17 acres (7 ha)**

Grotta del Sole produces a large range of wines from throughout Campania but its interest lies in reinforcing the image of the area's traditional wines and restoring those fallen from favor—thus it has been the force behind the revival of traditional, tree-trained Asprinio (sparkling as well as still) and has also put much effort into the much maligned Lacryma Christi del Vesuvio. Unusually, a Piedirosso Passito is also produced.

LIBRANDI

Established **1950** ***Owners*** **the Librandi family** ***Production*** **125,000 cases** ***Vineyard area*** **160 acres (65 ha)**

In this introspective region the outward-looking attitude of the Librandi family has brought them to prominence. Opinion is divided on whether their top wine is the half-modernist Gravello, from a blend of gaglioppo with 40 percent cabernet sauvignon, or the strictly traditional Duca Sanfelice, exclusively from gaglioppo. Similarly,

ABOVE: *Fellini Alberello 1998; Puglia's traditional style wines are returning to prominence.*

ABOVE: Puglia stretches 220 miles (360 km) to Italy's heel tip.

there are as many fans of their Critone (chardonnay/sauvignon) and the softly attractive rosé Terre Lontane (gaglioppo/cabernet franc) as there are of the classic white, rosé and red Cirò. Le Pasulle is a finely honeyed, rich but not cloying sweet wine made from mantonico.

MASTROBERARDINO

Established **1878** ***Owners*** **Antonio, Carlo and Pietro Mastroberardino** ***Production*** **150,000 cases** ***Vineyard area*** **150 acres (60 ha) + grapes bought in**

Mastroberardino, historically one of the major names on the Italian wine scene, for years was practically the only representative of the south to have a reputation beyond local boundaries. It was also Mastroberardino that introduced Avellino's three leading wines: Taurasi, Fiano di Avellino and Greco di Tufo. The company now has considerable competition, with several of its former grape suppliers now making their own wine. The wines are reliably good if not exceptional quality, although older vintages of Taurasi show great longevity.

BASILICATA

Basilicata is almost a one-grape (aglianico), one-wine (aglianico del vulture) region. The wines are initially tannic with firm balancing acidity, full and powerful, minerally and darkly fruity. However, it almost certainly has the potential for wines of considerably greater distinction once the necessary research into the best clones and so on has been done.

RIGHT: A basket of olives; local produce in Southern Italy.

PATERNOSTER

Established **1925** ***Owners*** **the Paternoster family** ***Production*** **10,000–12,500 cases** ***Vineyard area*** **16 acres (6.5 ha)**

The Paternoster wines, when on form (which these days happens ever more regularly), excel for attack, structure, density and deep, ripe fruitiness. The selection Aglianico del Vulture Don Anselmo is produced only when the vintage warrants it but the standard Aglianico, made each year, is more classically styled. There is a white wine, Bianco di Corte, from fiano, and a sparkling moscato.

SARDINIA

For a long time Sardinia's wine fell into two categories: light, fresh, innocuous whites and heavy reds, usually from the cannonau variety, much appreciated by the locals. Cannonau is Sardinia's best known red grape, producing warm, broad, often alcoholic reds. Monica also makes lively drinkable red wines.

Among the white grapes, vermentino at its best expresses a lively, peach-like, almost buttery character. Torbato gives firm, creamy, lightly spicy wines. There is much demand for sweet and fortified wines, some of the most interesting being made from malvasia and moscato. Vernaccia di oristano is often compared with sherry.

ARGIOLAS

Established **1938** ***Owners*** **Argiolas & C. SaS** ***Production*** **75,000 cases** ***Vineyard area*** **540 acres (220 ha)**

Originally providing bulk wine to other estates, Argiolas started bottling in 1990 and took on the services of Giacomo Tachis, one of the top Italian consultant enologists. The wines are made predominantly from vermentino, nuragus, monica and cannonau and are of fine quality throughout, the top of the range being the *barrique*-aged red Turriga, from cannonau, carignano and others, and the partially *barrique*-aged white Angialis, from nasco and malvasia.

CONTINI

Established **1898** ***Owners*** **the Contini family** ***Production*** **c.30,000 cases** ***Vineyard area*** **NA**

Despite the unfashionability of the style and the poor offerings from much of the competition, Contini has managed to keep the sherry-like Vernaccia di Oristano a live force. The wines, especially the Riservas, have an intense nuttiness, great individuality and complexity. The company has about half-a-dozen other wines, mainly from vermentino, cannonau and nièddera.

SELLA & MOSCA

Established **1899** ***Owners*** **Sella & Mosca SpA** ***Production*** **500,000 cases** ***Vineyard area*** **1,235 acres (500 ha)**

Sella & Mosca has been the leading estate of Sardinia, both in size and image, for generations, and has an extensive range of wines. This is about the only producer to work consistently with torbato, notably in the wine Terre Bianche. Anghelu Ruju, strong and port-like, from partially dried cannonau, practically symbolizes the estate but Marchese di Villamarina (cabernet sauvignon) is gaining respect.

Sicily

The island of Sicily, at the heart of the Mediterranean, furnished the ancients with the vital triumvirate of life: grain, grape and olive. It has been invaded by practically every power from the Phoenicians onwards, leaving its inhabitants with very mixed feelings toward authority. Even Garibaldi, in his successful campaign to unify Italy, made his first landing in Sicily to fight the Bourbons.

ABOVE: *Tending the vines on a chilly morning.*

Vines and wines

Sicily's master grape is nero d'avola. Only now are people coming to truly appreciate it. It yields deep color and intensely ripe, blackberry-like fruit with an undernote of brown sugar, and can give high alcohol. Other red grapes are frappato, the light-hued nerello mascalese and perricone (or pignatello).

Sicily produces far more white wine than red, however, and the grape seen most widely is catarratto. While it can make wines lacking grace, it can also turn out well-structured, well rounded wines with a good fruit core. More generally appreciated, particularly for its elegant, floral perfumes, is inzolia.

Grillo is easily the best grape for marsala production, yet restrictions mean most marsala houses primarily use catarratto. The sweet wines of the Aeolian archipelago to the northeast are made from malvasia and those of the island of Pantelleria from zibibbo, the local name for muscat of alexandria.

Good wines are produced in a number of different locations on the island. The hills behind Palermo give wines full of character; Pachino (in the southeast) has rich, full nero d'avola; Cerasuola di Vittoria's blend of nero d'avola and frappato is developing; the zone of Contea di Scafani has many different wine types; and Etna's wines are improving all the time.

Marsala has been both Sicily's fortune and its downfall. It brought prosperity and renown in the nineteenth century after the British formulated the basic model of the wine and created a market for it; it became a mark of shame in the later twentieth century when it was relegated to the kitchen, its quality far too poor for actual drinking.

MARCO DE BARTOLI–MARSALA/PANTELLERIA, MOSCATO DI PANTELLERIA

Established **1978** ***Owner*** **Marco de Bartoli** ***Production*** **5,000 cases** ***Vineyard area*** **60 acres (25 ha)**

Marsala has been restored to a wine of quality, thanks to Marco de Bartoli. With Vecchio Samperi, a marsala-type wine based on the grillo grape, de Bartoli put marsala back on the world map. He did the same for Pantelleria. Vecchio Samperi 20 Anni (20 years old, from solera) is fine, as is the Moscato Passito di Pantelleria Bukkuram. There are other wines in the range.

CARAVAGLIO, MALVASIA DELLE LIPARI

Established **NA** ***Owner*** **Antonino Caravaglio** ***Production*** **NA** ***Vineyard area*** **NA**

A local hero on the island of Salina and an emerging winemaker of note in Sicily, Caravaglio is hardly known beyond. Yet he makes archetypal Malvasia delle Lipari, both Naturale and Passito, and a respectable dry white, Salina Bianco.

COS, CERASUOLO DI VITTORIA

Established **1980** ***Owner*** **Giusto Occhipinti** ***Production*** **20,000 cases** ***Vineyard area*** **50 acres (20 ha)**

In the 1980s Giusto Occhipinti aspired to make Cerasuolo di Vittoria the way he remembered it at his

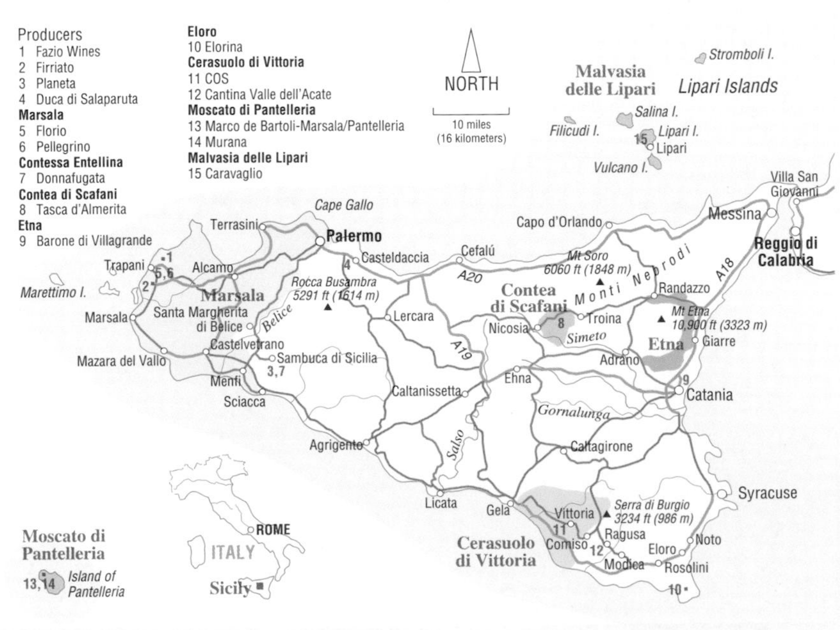

ABOVE: *Cleanliness in the cellar is paramount.*

BELOW: *A streetside stall in northern Sicily.*

grandparents' table, rather than the dull, often oxidized wine he saw all around him. He gradually built Cos into by far the best Vittoria estate, the model others now try to emulate. Demand now regularly outstrips supply and the range has broadened to include varietal inzolia, chardonnay and cabernet and some stunning nero d'avola.

CANTINA VALLE DELL'ACATE, CERASUOLO DI VITTORIA

Established 1981 **Owners** the Jacono family **Production** 16,500 cases in 1999 (increasing to 50,000 in the next few years) **Vineyard area** 300 acres (120 ha)

In the past few years Valle dell'Acate has turned into one of the most go-ahead estates in Italy, primarily due to the frenetically active Gaetana, daughter of the owner. The Cerasuolo di Vittoria aims more at fruit than weight compared with its counterparts but is always well balanced, well-integrated and attractive. There is also a very successful light and lively varietal, Frappato. The estate makes a good inzolia and a couple of other wines.

DONNAFUGATA, CONTESSA ENTELLINA

Established 1851 **Owners** the Rallo family **Production** 62,500 cases **Vineyard area** 260 acres (105 ha)

The Rallo family's roots have long been in the production of marsala but with this fourth generation the emphasis has changed to non-fortified wines. The range is broad, led by Tancredi (made from nero d'avola/cabernet sauvignon) and Chiaranda del Merlo (inzolia/chardonnay) with Contessa Entelina Chardonnay La Fuga and Contessa Entelina Vigna di Gabri (inzolia) top of the support team. There is also attractive Moscato di Pantelleria and a powerful barriqued nero d'avola called Mille e Una Notte.

ELORINA, ELORO

Established 1978 **Owners** Cooperative **Production** 16,500 cases **Vineyard area** 620 acres (250 ha)

Originally producing strong and powerful wines for blending, an enlightened directorship has moved the emphasis within the past decade toward quality and bottled output. The wines are improving steadily, with a fresh and clean inzolia-based white and a well-structured red Eloro. The leading wine is Pachino, a massive wine that amply demonstrates the positive attributes of nero d'avola grown so far south (and some of its problems).

FIRRIATO

Established 1982 **Owners** Di Gaetano brothers **Production** 350,000 cases **Vineyard area** 175 acres (70 ha); grapes bought-in from a further 980 acres (400 ha)

Firriato's wines are receiving rapturous reviews yet are still excellent value for money. A primarily Antipodean winemaking team led by Kym Milne gives the wines an international sheen that enables the estate to export almost 75 percent of its production, a range covering 30 labels. The emphasis at the quality end is on indigenous/international blends. The Santagostino red is from nero d'avola and syrah, the white from catarratto and chardonnay; Altavilla della Corte red also uses nero d'avola, this time with cabernet sauvignon, while the white blends grillo with chardonnay.

ABOVE: Grapes thrive on Sicily's cool slopes.

MURANA, MOSCATO DI PANTELLERIA

Established **1984** ***Owner*** **Salvatore Murana** ***Production*** **3,750 cases** ***Vineyard area*** **18.5 acres (7.5 ha)**

Prior to 1984, Salvatore Murana sent all of his grapes, grown on some of Pantelleria's best sites, to the co-operative. When he started to produce his own wines they immediately provoked interest and now his range, made exclusively from zibibbo, gains the highest plaudits. The range is led by the *cru* Moscato Passito di Pantelleria, Martingana, lusciously rich and amazingly intense; followed closely by the *cru* Khamma and the lighter, more aromatic Mueggen. The delicate Turbè is non-passito, as is the dryish Gadì.

PELLEGRINO, MARSALA

Established **1880** ***Owners*** **the Pellegrino family** ***Production*** **NA** ***Vineyard area*** **990 acres (400 ha)**

Family-run and modern in its thinking, this well-known marsala house is now concentrating as much on non-fortified wines as on its backbone fortifieds, leading to an extensive range. The most startling wine in the range of this winery is Ruby, a sweet rubino (red) marsala fine that provokes very mixed reactions.

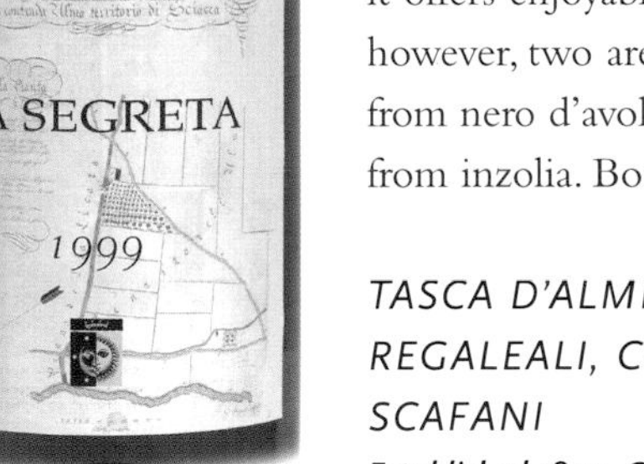

PLANETA

Established **1990s (first vintage 1995)** ***Owners*** **the Planeta family** ***Production*** **62,500 cases** ***Vineyard area*** **500 acres (200 ha) plus 150 acres (60 ha) currently not in use**

Founded by three youngsters, Planeta is an Italian phenomenon. In just a few years it has become one of the country's most esteemed estates, with impeccable wines throughout. There are excellent, purely toned, international varietals (cabernet sauvignon, merlot and, especially, chardonnay) but Planeta's skills show more in the blends of (mainly) native with non-native grapes: La Segreta Bianco (grecanico/cataratto/chardonnay), La Segreta Rosso (nero d'avola/merlot), Santa Cecilia (nero d'avola/syrah) and Alastro (grecanico/cataratto).

DUCA DI SALAPARUTA

Established **1824** ***Owners*** **The Region of Sicily** ***Production*** **700,000 cases** ***Vineyard area*** **All grapes bought-in**

This company's brand, Corvo, was at one time synonymous with Sicilian wine. Mostly it offers enjoyable but unexceptional wines, however, two are superior: Duca d'Enrico, from nero d'avola, and Bianca di Valguarnera, from inzolia. Both are heavily oaked.

TASCA D'ALMERITA/ REGALEALI, CONTEA DI SCAFANI

Established **1830** ***Owners*** **the Tasca family** ***Production*** **210,000 cases** ***Vineyard area*** **545 acres (220 ha)**

Tasca d'Almerita is best-known for its Regaleali. The wines produced here are excellent; the flagship Rosso del Conte (nero d'avola/perricone) is full, punchy, and spicy, while Nozze d'Oro from Tasca (probably sauvignonasse) and inzolia, is rich, buttery and herbal. The varietals cabernet sauvignon and chardonnay are both big, concentrated and of impeccable varietal character.

Other noteworthy producers in Sicily include Fazio Wines, Florio, Marsala and Barone de Villagrande.

Regional Dozen

- Cerasuolo di Vittoria (COS)
- Cerasuolo di Vittoria (Valle del Acate)
- Frappato (Cantina Valle dell'Acate)
- Litra (Abbazia di Sant'Anastasia)
- Marsala Superiore Riserva Vecchioflora (Vinicola Italiana Florio)
- Mille e Una Notte (Tenuta di Donnafugata)
- Moscato Passito di Pantelleria Bukkuram (Marco de Bartoli)
- Nero d'Avola (Settesoli)
- Nozze d'Oro (Tasca d'Almerita)
- Passito de Pantelleria Solidea (D'Ancona)
- Santagostino Rosso (Firriato)
- Torre dei Venti Rosso (Fazio Wines)

A wide selection of fine food and wine is carried by this shop in Queviures, Barcelona, in Catalonia.

Spain

ABOVE: *Trees from the countryside around Catalonia are an important source of cork.*

RIGHT: *An attractively decorated wine glass from the nineteenth century.*

(Anatolia) across the Mediterranean in clay amphorae, bartering it along the north coast of Africa and the south coast of Europe for commodities such as wheat, olives, sandalwood, perfumes, carpets and whatever else could profitably be traded. The Pillars of Hercules (the ancient name for the promontories flanking the Strait of Gibraltar) were at the very edge of the world of they then knew. But all that was soon to change when these early traders began to travel farther, venturing south to do business with the scattered tribes of the west African coast.

Before long it became expedient for them to have a permanent base at the western end of the Mediterranean, and they established the city of Gadier (modern-day Cádiz) around the year 1100 BC. The city grew in importance and wealth at what was then the crossroads of world trade, and migrants from Greece began to arrive. It is not known whether the founders of Gadier or the new inhabitants planted vines in the area around the city (now the area where sherry is produced) but by about 500 BC wine was being made there, based on the wines of the Middle East and the eastern Mediterranean—sweet and naturally strong, as it needed to be to survive rolling sea journeys, a hot climate and inadequately sealed clay jars.

As trade and early civilization spread inland, other areas of what was to become Spain developed their own agriculture, including vineyards and ways of making wine. The basic method of making wine was very simple and still survives today in some country areas: a stone trough was excavated from a hillside as a receptacle for the harvested grapes, which were then trodden on and squashed. The cloud of carbon dioxide gas released by the fermentation process blanketed the juice and prevented oxidation and, once the process was complete, a plug was removed from the side of the trough to allow the wine to run off into suitable vessels which would typically have been clay or earthenware jars. These were then left so that fermentation could complete in its own good time and, when the cloud of gas had dissipated, the jars would be topped up to brim-full to provide an airtight seal. This, and the

small surface area of the mouth, reduced oxidation and was a reasonably efficient way of keeping the wine drinkable. Moving it about was a different matter, but as most wine was made, sold and drunk locally, this was not a problem. So it was to continue until the arrival of the Romans.

Rome annexed Spain after a long and bloody war with Carthage but was in full control by the end of the third century BC, and it was the Romans who turned winemaking from a cottage industry into a major business. This was because it was becoming prohibitively expensive to transport wine for the occupying legions from Rome. The obvious solution was to make it locally, and this is what the Romans did, even doing some early work in researching which vine varieties were best suited to which soil. In this way the primitive local winemaking methods were "industrialized" on a relatively large scale.

The next major influence on Spain's viticulture was by the invasion of Moors from North Africa in AD 711. Their occupation peaked in the AD 929 and then receded southeastwards until they were finally expelled from their last stronghold in Granada in 1492. The intervening years had seen variously prohibition, vineyards turned over to the production of table grapes, and even occasional business ventures in which Moorish governors permitted the making of wine for export to Christian-ruled areas of Spain. However, the Moors' major contribution to Spanish viticulture was the introduction of distilling, which happened some time after AD 900.

The Moors used the process to obtain the dry extract residue for use in art, design and cosmetics, and the spirit for antiseptic and medicinal purposes, but the winemakers found quite a different use for it. They discovered that the problem of oxidation of wine could be solved by the simple expedient of fortifying it with grape spirit. This preserved the wine's traditional sweetness, increased its alcoholic strength and made it more easily transportable, which was an important consideration with the gradual opening up of export markets.

By the time the Moors left, the fortified wines of southwestern Spain were reckoned the world's finest and were finding their way far across the seas as the age of exploration got under way.

Landscape and climate

Spain is the third most mountainous country in Europe, after Albania and Switzerland, and this highland characteristic brings with it a wealth of microclimates and individual parcels of *terreño* (what the French call *terroir*) which make for wines of particular individuality.

In the north, the climate is dictated by the Cordillera Cantábrica, a series of mountain ranges which divide the vast upland plateau of central Spain from the north and northwest. This region is subject to the winds and rain coming from the Bay of Biscay and is known as "green Spain" because of its verdant pastures and dense woodlands. By Spanish standards, this is a cool, wet area which is ideal for the cultivation of grapes for white wines. The two great rivers which drain this area are the Ebro, which flows into the sea just south of Tarragona in Catalonia, and the Duero, which flows westwards into Portugal and out into the Atlantic at Oporto. These two rivers water around half of Spain's finest vineyards.

ABOVE: *Earthenware containers are still used for fermenting grapes in some parts of Spain.*

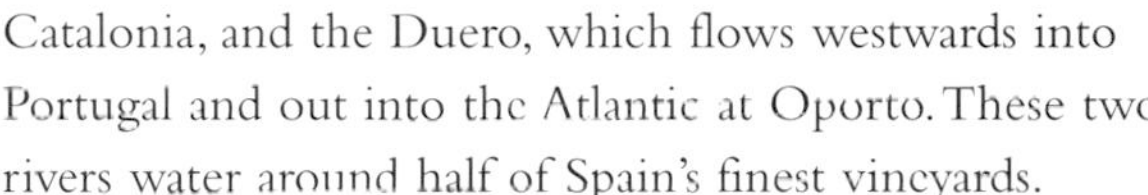

Immediately south of the Cordillera Cantábrica are the areas which have achieved most in the export market for Spain over the last century or so. Rioja and Navarra straddle the Ebro on the south side of the mountains, where the clay soil is rich in chalk and iron in the highlands and the climate is continental, with long, hot summers and short, very cold winters with most rainfall concentrated in the spring and autumn. Lowland areas here tend to be alluvial with sandy soil. On the west side, the vineyards of Ribera del Duero are farther south but higher in altitude, mitigating the effects of the sun on the vines with cooler night-time temperatures.

BELOW: *Rio Vero in Aragón. The cooler climate on the steep slopes here can produce outstanding wines from many different grape varieties.*

South to Madrid and beyond lies the mostly flat plateau of central Spain, averaging 2,000 feet (600 m) above sea level, surrounded by a ring of mountain ranges and with a climate which is extreme continental—over 100°F (38°C) in the summer and as low as –4°F (–20°C) in the winter. The wind slices across the great plain of La Mancha with a vengeance in season, hence the famous windmills of the region, so ineffectually attacked by the legendary Don Quixote.

I love everything that's old: old friends, old times, old manners, old books, old wine.
OLIVER GOLDSMITH (1782–1874), *She Stoops to Conquer*

The eastern seaboard climate is warm and humid, with frequent rains along the coast and the lowland vineyards in Catalonia, and hotter and drier in the Levant. Higher altitudes inland from the coast provide benefits for growing finer grapes, even this far south—as the land rises, temperature falls, and although highland vineyards get all the ripening heat of of the sun, they have a wider temperature range between day and night. This "rests" the vines so that the nutrients are still in the soil the next morning, when they can feed the grapes rather than the vine. Soils here are limestone-based, providing the basic carbonate which underpins the world's greatest vineyards. The highlands of Catalonia provide one of the best hot-climate bedrocks for vines—schistose comes to the surface in Priorato, Alella and parts of the high Penedès—and its fragmented structure holds water and provides a refuge and a drink for the vine roots in the arid heat of summer.

Andalusia is the most consistently hot of all the regions, with a semi-arid climate and rivers which habit-ually dry up in the summer. It includes Jeréz (sherry country) and thus some of the oldest vineyards in Europe. Its saving grace (in wine-making terms) is the astonishingly chalk-rich soil of the province of Cádiz. This has provided the unique conditions for the production of a wine which has, at a conservative estimate, been made continuously for some 2,500 years. The grape is the palomino, grown in the "golden triangle" between Jeréz de La Frontera and the coastal towns of Puerto de St María and Sanlúcar de Barrameda. Other grapes grown in the Jeréz region include the pedro ximénez (PX) and the moscatel, which are used in sweetening wines but also may be found on their own. Typically, moscatel will have been fortified during fermentation to provide a naturally rich, sweet wine, and PX will have been dried in the sun before fermentation, providing a wine of intense color, richness and sweetness. Elsewhere, clay, chalk and lime-

BELOW: *Sheep graze between rows of dormant vines, Costa Brava.*

stone dominate the soils while traditional super-ripe grapes and high-strength wines denote the viticultural style.

The Canaries, 60 miles (100 km) off the coast of northwest Africa, have been under the control of Spain since the fifteenth century. There are seven islands in the archipelago. Of these, Lanzarote has the most dramatic landscape of any vineyard area in the world. The soil is made up of black volcanic ash and the vines are planted in hollows scooped out of it and surrounded with low walls to protect them from the wind. Red and white wines are made here, including sweet malvasía and moscatel from sun-dried grapes in the old Canary-sack style.

ABOVE: *Stainless steel fermentation tanks such as these are widely used although some producers still prefer traditional oak barrels.*

Wines: sherry, rioja and cava

SHERRY

Sherry owes its early prominence as an export wine to the *solera* system, in which wines from the new vintage are introduced into a *criadera*, or "nursery," which is already partly filled with wine from the previous vintage. The new wine takes on the characteristics of the old and this mixture is, in turn, passed to another, older *criadera* in the same way. Eventually, the wine passes into the *solera*—the final row of barrels—from which the *saca* will be withdrawn. The end result is a wine of impressive consistency, with a maturity that is out of all proportion to its actual age—the result of this careful fractional blending process. The ancient winemakers of the eastern Mediterranean used a similar system which they called *nama*—the process of leaving some of the previous year's wine in the jar when adding the new vintage. The *solera* system replaced it when good-quality wooden barrels started to become readily available.

Jeréz/Xérès/Sherry y Manzanilla de Sanlúcar de Barrameda is the long-winded official name for the sherry denomination of origin, "copyrighting" the wine's name in Spanish, French and English as well as encompassing the *manzanilla* wines. Sherry has been through a very difficult time in the closing years of the twentieth century, partly due to changing fashions and partly, it has to be said, as a result of complacency in the industry, but its innate quality and the *solera* system now make it one of the world's best-value fine wines. There are several different styles of sherry:

Fino is one of the palest and driest of wines; it is lightly fortified (after complete natural fermentation) to 16–17 percent abv (alcohol by volume). The grapes will have grown a thin film of yeast called *flor* during their time in the bodega which gives the wine a fresh, yeasty edge, most prominent in the *manzanillas* from Sanlúcar, where it is drunk as a table wine with seafood.

Amontillados are wines which started out as *finos* but which have been allowed to age for 10 to 15 years or longer. These may achieve anything up to 18 percent abv or even more, and have a long, dry, powerful style which never ventures into richness. Sadly, it's also a term used by mass-market blenders to denote a style of "medium" sherry—a term which is unlikely to appeal to many.

Olorosos are wines which have not been allowed to grow a yeasty *flor* coating and will have been fortified to 18 percent abv. They have a rich (though not sweet), nutty character and can age for many decades.

Palo cortado is an unusual type of wine which starts out growing *flor*, like a *fino*, but then loses it and develops in the *oloroso* style. These are some of the finest wines of Jeréz—rich, complex and long-lived.

Cream and ***pale cream*** are blended wines catering to the mass market, usually with an *oloroso* base (pale creams are likely to have a *fino* base), mixed with sweetening wines and tailored to the needs of the export customer. The best of them may be very good. The rest tend to be very dull indeed.

LEFT: *Old casks are sometimes used to age traditional wines after fermentation.*

RIOJA

For rioja, the best grapes—mainly tempranillo and graciano—tend to come from the Alta and Alavesa areas; mazuelo and garnacha come from the warmer, drier Rioja Baja. Famous-name wines consist of a

ABOVE: *Riddling—inverting the bottle and gently shaking it—is a process which dislodges the deposit of sediment in cava, Spain's most famous sparkling wine.*

mixture of most or all of these varieties. The old *reservas*, at their best, have a wonderful mellow softness and age with grace. In the Alavesa region, however, they often make delicious red wines from pure tempranillo and drink them young. White and pink rioja are also made, of which the white, made usually from viura (macabeo) and malvasiá riojana, is most prominent. Traditional whites are rich, spicy, oaky, and aromatic. Modern styles may have just a touch of oak or none at all to maintain the natural freshness of the grape.

CAVA

Cava's birthplace was Catalonia, in the late 1800s; it mostly still comes from this area. Traditional cava continues to be made from any or all of the major three Catalan grape varieties: parellada, xarel-lo, and macabeo (viura). Chardonnay is also used by some producers. Cava must be made by the *método tradicional* and spend nine months on its lees before it can be released. Producers do particularly well making modestly priced wines that drink splendidly while young. There is a trend toward older, richer, more complex wines.

BELOW: *Roses planted at the end of a row of vines act as a biological control against mildew.*

Wine law

Spain's wine laws fall into the standard European pattern, although a great deal of work is done outside the system and new, regional wines and maverick winemakers are threatening the whole edifice of wine regulation. This is happening not just in Spain but throughout Europe.

QUALITY WINES

The letters VCPRD stand for Vinos de Calidad Producido en Regiones Determinades as defined by the European Commission. (QWPSR, the English equivalent, stands for "Quality Wine Produced in Specific Regions.") Each region has a Consejo Regulador (Regulating Council) which includes members from the producing bodegas, local government and technicians. This council decides on what type of grapes can be planted, where they can be planted and aging methods. At the beginning of the year 2000 Spain had 57 accredited VCPRD wines. Within this group, there are two more categories:

Denominación de Origen (DO) This term means "Denomination of Origin" and identifies the wine as a genuine product of its area under the control of the Consejo Regulador. This is equivalent to the AOC *(Appellation d'Origine Contrôlée)* in France and the DOC *(Denominazione de Origine Controllata)* in Italy. There are 56 *Denominación de Origens* in Spain.

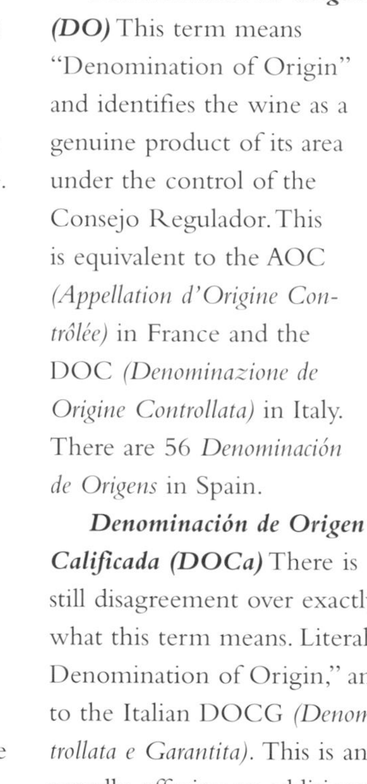

Denominación de Origen Calificada (DOCa) There is still disagreement over exactly what this term means. Literally, it translates as "Qualified Denomination of Origin," and is theoretically equivalent to the Italian DOCG *(Denominazione de Origine Controllata e Garantita)*. This is an upper-level grade, supposedly offering an additional guarantee of quality to the customer. Rioja was elevated to this grade in 1991 but, so far, no other wine has followed suit, probably because no one could agree on what the DOCa actually meant. Even as the arguments rage on, there has been a palpable improvement in the quality of the wines.

TABLE WINES

This category divides into four:

Vino de la Tierra (VdlT), or "country wines," are equivalent to the French *Vins de Pays de Zone* and in

Aging regulations

Joven *means the wine has had less than six months in oak casks, or none at all.* Crianza *has at least six months in oak; white and pink must spend a year in the bodega, and red* crianza *two years. White and pink* reserva *must spend six months in oak and two years in the bodega; red* reserva *three years in the bodega (at least one in both oak and in bottle).* Gran reserva *wines spend an extra year in the bodega; red* gran reserva *at least two years in oak and three in bottle.*

Spain the term applies to wines with sufficient local style and character to make them stand out individually. Controls for these are not only much less stringent than for DO wines, they are also administered by the local office of the Ministry of Agriculture. There are about two dozen such areas and many are actively seeking elevation to DO status.

Vino Comarcal (VC), or "local wines," are made in areas larger than a VdlT zone (equivalent to the French *Vins de Pays de Région* and *Vins de Pays de Département)* and these are subject to a more relaxed administration. There are about two dozen of these, the most prominent of which are understandably seeking promotion to DO status.

Vino de Mesa de ... (VdM de), or "table wine from ..." is a legal nicety to allow the mavericks to put a vintage date on their wines. For example, the Yllera family call their wine (a red wine made in a white-wine area) VdM de Castilla-León.

Vino de Mesa (VdM) simply means "table wine." It may only specify what color it is and that it is produced in Spain. No regional grape variety or vintage qualifications are permitted.

Table-wine areas tipped for promotion in the early years of this century include:

VdlT Manchuela, a large area in eastern Castilla-La Mancha, contiguous with the DO Utiel Requena; it has had a provisional DO for many years. The main wines are reds made from bobal with some cencibel (the local word for tempranillo) and monastrell.

VdlT Valdejalón, in the west of Zaragoza (Aragón) has always been bulk-wine country but, as ever, there are those maverick bodegas trying to do something better, mainly around the northwestern town of Moncayo.

VC Ribera de Arlanza is a region in Burgos (Castilla-León) which formerly shipped large quantities of wine to neighboring DO zones in the days when it was legal to do so. In the search for a new rôle, ambitious bodegas are planting tinto del país and lobbying for promotion.

VdM Medina del Campo is the name currently being used by red wine producers in the Rueda area, where the DO is for white wines only. It is expected to be admitted to DO status in due course. The production area is the same as that for Rueda, and the wines are mainly made from tinto fino (tempranillo).

ABOVE: Grand architecture and an expanding wine industry were two of the legacies of the Roman occupation in Spain.

LEFT: Some processes are still done by hand: a decorative tassel is added to a cava bottle.

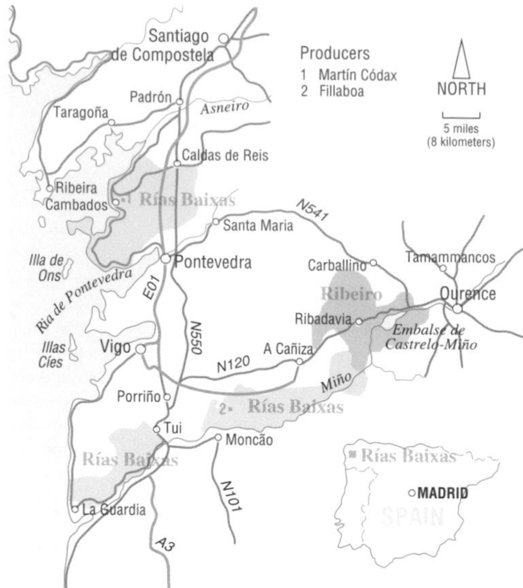

ABOVE: *Specialized hand tools are still needed for a variety of tasks in the wine trade.*

Galicia and the Basque Country

RÍAS BAIXAS

Galicia is close to Portugal and separated from its nearest Spanish neighbor, Castilla-León, by mountains. Although in the past its wines have shared an affinity with vinho verde, nowadays new winemaking techniques and an enthusiasm for older native grape varieties have resulted in its own distinctive wine styles.

There are five DO zones—Rías Baixas, Ribeiro, Ribiera Sacra, Valdeorras and Val do Monterrei (the most recent)—and the best wines in all of them are the whites, made from the albariño and the godello. At the eastern end of the region, the northern Basque provinces of Vizcaya (Bizkaia in Basque) and Guetaria (Getaria) on the coast produce a very small amount of a unique wine called chacolí (txakoli). There are two DOs—Chacolí de Vizcaya and Chacolí de Guetaria.

The peachy, fresh, crisp albariño grape put Rías Baixas on the vinous map, after growers and winemakers bit the bullet of accepting lower production in return for better wines. There are suggestions that this is indeed the riesling of Germany, brought by monks establishing monasteries along the pilgrim route of the Camino de Santiago, this has never been verified, although there are strong similarities. The wines here vie with those of Rueda for the title of the best whites of Spain.

MARTÍN CÓDAX

Established **1986** ***Owners*** **Local shareholders** ***Production*** **11,000 cases** ***Vineyard area*** **395 acres (160 ha)**

Named after the man who first wrote music on paper, this winery produces the most popular wine on its home patch, as well being one of the best of its kind. Made only from the albariño grape, the wines are of excellent quality. The range includes Martín Códax—a single-vineyard wine called Burgáns, Gallaecia, a late-harvest version, and Organistrum, a barrel-fermented wine with three months on the lees. Best wines: the entire range.

FILLABOA

Established **1988** ***Owners*** **Private shareholders** ***Production*** **28,000 cases** ***Vineyard area*** **69 acres (28 ha)**

This is an attractive vineyard on a small private granja (estate) with the vines trained on the *silvo* system—a semi-pergola style with wires strung between small monoliths of the lovely pink, quartz-flecked granite which underpins most of the best vineyards in the Condado del Tea district. Kiwi-fruit was planted to provide an income while waiting for the vines to mature. Best wine: albariño.

RIGHT: *The cultivation of olive groves and the growing of grapes are two of the oldest forms of agriculture in Europe.*

OTHER GALICIAN REGIONS

Ribeiro's best wines are whites made from godello—second only to the albariño in quality—and treixadura. New investment has made Ribeiro a region to watch. Stunningly beautiful Ribeira Sacra sits on the gorge of the rivers Sil and Miño. It features incredibly steep, slate-based vineyard slopes and historic monastic ruins. The best wines here are very good but few, with great albariño whites and promising mencía reds. In Veldeorras, a few bodegas are working hard to establish the region as a center for quality white wines made from godello and reds from mencía. Tiny Val do Monterrei makes mainly bland wines, however, there are a few quality white wines, made from doña blanca and verdello.

GARGALO, MONTERREI

Established **1998** ***Owners*** **Private shareholders** ***Production*** **17,500 cases** ***Vineyard area*** **49 acres (20 ha)**

This is a new enterprise in this slowly emerging region. Winemaker Mónica Carballo Coede makes a white wine from treixadura, godello and doña blanca and a red from tempranillo, mencía and a little bastardo. It's too soon to say what is achievable, but early results are promising. Best wine: Terra de Gargalo white.

ADEGAS MOURE, RIBEIRA SACRA

Established **1980** ***Owners*** **Private shareholders** ***Production*** **22,000 cases** ***Vineyard area*** **15 acres (6 ha)**

Adegas Moure, with its immaculately terraced vineyards, is situated in a lovely spot, high up on the banks of the River Miño. In the summer José-Manuel Moure takes his guests to the top of the hill and serves a light lunch with his own albariño overlooking the bend in the river. He makes three wines under the Abadia da Cova label: the white albariño and two reds from the mencía, one joven and one crianza. Best wines: all are excellent.

A. PORTELA, RIBEIRO

Established **1987** ***Owners*** **Antonio González Pousa and Agustín Formigó Raña** ***Production*** **25,000 cases** ***Vineyard area*** **20 acres (8 ha)**

The bulk of this bodega's production is Señorío de Beade, made from 40 percent jeréz (palomino), a grape which harks back to the Franco régime when growers were encouraged to plant the highest yielding varieties regardless of the quality. However, the other 60 percent is made up of equal parts treixadura, torrontés and godello, all of which (especially the last) have considerable claims to quality. There's also a red under the same label made from caiño, ferrón and sousón. Best wines: Primacia de Beade (treixadura).

A. TAPADA, VALDEORRAS

Established **1989** ***Owners*** **Local shareholders** ***Production*** **7,500 cases** ***Vineyard area*** **25 acres (10 ha)**

This is a very sharp, state-of-the-art winery which is surrounded by its own small estate of vineyards. There are two wines, both called Guitian, one joven and one barrel-fermented with six months on the lees. This is probably the most expensive wine from Valdeorras, and possibly the best. Best wines: both Guitians.

Regional Dozen

Abadia da Cova Albariño, Moure
Albariño, Martín Códax
Fillaboa Albariño, Fillaboa
Guitian, A. Tapada
Lagar de Cervera Albariño, Lagar de Fornelos
Señorío de Otxaran, Virgen de l'Orea
Terra do Gargalo, Gargalo
Txomin Etxaniz
Valdamor Albariño, Valdamor
Vilerma
Viña Godeval, Godeval
Viña Mein

LEFT: The tempranillo grape, grown widely, is used in many of Spain's most famous wines.

Basque wining and dining

At ten in the morning a crowd is starting to form as locals tuck into a few tapas and rinse them down with thimbles full of tart, spritzy white wine. This is the scene in San Sebastian, Spain, as well as in numerous other Basque taverns in the northwest parts of Spain. The wine is called chacoli (Txacolina de Guetaria in Basque), an obscure white fiercely protected from oblivion by stubborn farmers along the Bay of Biscay. How surprised they might be to learn that their humble wine is highly sought after at its release each year by sommeliers in Paris and San Francisco, who scramble to lock up their allocations and brag among their colleagues about how many cases they got, and who go on to serve that simple wine in fine hand-blown Austrian crystal, no less.

ABOVE: *Vineyards have been part of the agricultural landscape of Spain for centuries.*

Other Castilla-León Regions

RUEDA

This is the land of the verdejo, a grape which was simply waiting for technology to catch up with it. In the old days it oxidized so fast that the winemakers gave up, and made a sherry-type wine, supplementing it with the high-cropping palomino grape and making rueda pálido (light and dry) and rueda dorada (softer and darker), semi-fortified wines which still have a niche market. However, Riscal revolutionized the area with inert gas and cold fermentation technology, as well as introducing the sauvignon. The best rueda today is likely to have been made from grapes picked in the early hours of the morning, before sunrise, blanketed with nitrogen or some other inert gas in the trailer in the vineyard, and chilled to about 60°F (15°C) before going for a very gentle pressing in a pneumatic press. Some wines are given a six-month dressing in oak, others are delivered fresh and crisp to the market in the spring after the vintage. This is arguably the best white wine of modern Spain (but see also Rías Baixas). Only white wines are made with the DO, although (often very good) red wines are made under the new (1999) VdlT Medina del Campo. This classification is shortly tipped to become a DO in its own right for red and pink wines, made from tempranillo, garnacha, cabernet sauvignon and merlot.

BELONDRADE Y LURTON

Established **1984** ***Owners*** **Didier Belondrade and Brigitte Lurton-Belondrade** ***Production*** **2,500 cases** ***Vineyard area*** **30 acres (12 ha)**

Why should a young French couple want to make wine in Rueda? They say it's because it was something different, more of a challenge than setting up in their native Bordeaux, and they both love the area. Brigitte Lurton-Belondrade is the winemaker, along with her brother, Jacques, who is consultant winemaker at a number of bodegas in Ribera del Duero and Rueda. The wine is 100 percent verdejo in the modern style, and simply called Belondrade y Lurton. It's barrel-fermented and then left for a year on the lees, and is very good indeed. Best wine: Belondrade y Lurton.

CASTILLA LA VIEJA

Established **1976** ***Owners*** **the Sanz family** ***Production*** **225,000 cases** ***Vineyard area*** **247 acres (100 ha)**

Sanz family wines have had considerable success internationally thanks to some careful innovation and some inspired winemaking. Today, the company turns out some of the region's very best wines under the Bornos label. Best wines: Bornos Sauvignon Blanc; Palacio de Bornos Rueda Superior.

MARQUÉS DE RISCAL–VINOS BLANCOS DE CASTILLA

Established **1972** ***Owners*** **Vinos de los Herederos del Marqués de Riscal** ***Production*** **180,000 cases** ***Vineyard area*** **420 acres (170 ha)**

Francisco "Paco" Hurtado de Amezaga, current head of the Riscal family, wanted to make a white wine worthy of his family name but he didn't like the traditional oaked or modern squeaky-clean whites being made in Rioja, so he looked all over northern Spain, and finally settled on Rueda, attracted by the verdejo grape, which he thought showed tremendous potential. Today, Riscal wines are among the best in the region, and feature a sauvignon, a verdejo (with some viura, or macabeo) and an oak-aged Reserva Limousin Verdejo with 11 months in the cask. All are sold under the Marqués de Riscal label. Best wines: Reserva Limousin, Sauvignon.

TORO

Big and beefy, as you'd expect from a region named "Bull," there are white and pink wines here but the major interest is in the reds, made from the tinta de toro. This is the tempranillo but grown here in hotter, lower-altitude vineyards which give a thicker skin to the grape and more extract to the wine. The cabernet sauvignon and garnacha (mainly for pink wines) are also grown in this region, and cabernet/tempranillo blends (although denied the DO) can be excellent.

FARIÑA

Established **1942** ***Owners*** **the Fariña family** ***Production*** **30,000+ cases** ***Vineyard area*** **988 acres (400 ha)**

Manuel Fariña, the best-known winemaker in the region, was one of the first in Toro to espouse new technology. Colegiata is the name for *jovenes* in white, pink and red; Gran Colegiata is for *reservas* and *gran reservas* and a "semi-*crianza*" (a red wine which has had oak age but less than the regulation six months). There's also a premium *joven*, Primero, which is made from the best selected grapes. Best wines: Primero, Gran Colegiata.

CIGALES

Famous for its (excellent) pink wines, Cigales' best wines are, nevertheless, its reds which are made from the ubiquitous tinto del país (tempranillo) with, here and there, an admixture of garnacha and cabernet sauvignon, which is classified as "experimental."

BIERZO

In the far northwest of the region, Bierzo owes more to the style of Valdeorras in neighboring Galicia than to the hefty wines of lower Castilla-León. Fresh whites from godello and doña blanca and (mainly) light reds made from mencía do most of the business here.

PEREZ CARAMES

Established **1986** ***Owner*** **Antonia Barredo Lence** ***Production*** **13,500 cases** ***Vineyard area*** **79 acres (32 ha)**

The "maverick" tendency is on show here: most of this bodega's wines don't carry the DO Bierzo because they're made from "forbidden" grapes such as cabernet sauvignon, merlot and pinot noir, although there's also the local mencía and a maceración carbonica wine called Consules de Roma. However, the best tend to be the non-DO wines, under the label Casar de Santa Inés. Best wines: Casar de Santa Inés Pinot Noir, Merlot. The following wines are currently only allowed to be classified as Vino de Mesa de Castilla-León.

MAURO

Established **1980** ***Owners*** **the García Fernández family** ***Production*** **13,000 cases** ***Vineyard area*** **86 acres (35 ha)**

This is another bodega which has built a reputation for excellence since its foundation, not least because the winemaker is the ubiquitous Mariano García, late of Vega Sicilia. Unlike its "neighbor" in Sardón, however, Mauro grows only tempranillo and garnacha, and the wines are made more in the traditional way of Ribera del Duero, even though the bodega is well outside the region. The winemaking is immaculate and the vines are now at their peak of maturity for producing good grapes. There are three wines: Mauro is a *crianza* with 13 months in the cask; Mauro Vendimia Seleccionada, although it's still labeled *crianza*, is made from best-selected grapes, with 24 months in the cask. The latest departure, San Roman, has 12 months in oak and is made from 90 percent tinta de toro

ABADIA RETUERTA

Established **1996** ***Owner*** **Sandoz** ***Production*** **70,000 cases** ***Vineyard area*** **504 acres (204 ha)**

This is the old vineyard estate of the twelfth-century Abbey (Abadia) of St María. It was taken over in the late 1980s by Sandoz who decided to re-establish the vineyard and build a new winery with the latest high-quality installations. In a short time they have succeeded brilliantly. The vineyard has tempranillo, cabernet sauvignon and a little merlot and, unfettered by the regulations appertaining to the DO Ribera del Duero (the western boundary of which is a mere 6 miles (10 km) away, winemaker Angel Anocibar Beloqui does as he pleases, and what he does certainly pleases a lot of people. The wines are all called Abadia Retuerta. Best wines: the entire range, but especially El Campanario, El Palomar, Pago Negralada and Pago Valdebellón.

Regional Dozen

Abadia Retuerto Pago Negralada
Alejandro Fernandez Pesquera
Alejandro Fernandez Condado de Haza
Alion
Atauta Ungrafted
Dominio de Pingus, Pingus
Ismael Arroyo Val Sotillo
Mauro Terreus, Pago de Cueva Bajo
Perez Pascuas Vina Pedroso
Protos
Vega Sicilia Reserva Especial
Vega Sicilia Unico

LEFT: *Cristal Bota, a distinctively Spanish fashion in wine vessels, are used for drinking from, as well as for storing the wine.*

BELOW: *Collecting wine from the local co-operative is still part of the Sunday routine.*

North-Central Spain

RIOJA

Immediately south of the Cordillera Cantábrica on the Ebro is an area which has achieved most in the export market for Spain over the last century and more. The climate here is continental and the clay soil is rich in chalk. Rioja was classified under the new system in 1926 and is going through radical changes. Good producers are listed below; more are shown on the map.

ABOVE: *Corks are used to hold sulphur pellets, burned in the barrel to preserve the wine and to prevent bacteria.*

BELOW: *A wine press crushes the grapes to release the sugar, the first stage in winemaking.*

MARQUÉS DE CÁCERES–UNION VITIVINÍCOLA

Established **1970** ***Owners*** **the Forner family** ***Production*** **65,000 cases** ***Vineyard area*** **NA**

This bodega changed the face of Rioja when Enrique Forner moved back to Spain from Bordeaux and decided to make a "village wine," buying in grapes from growers in the locality and using minimal oak in the aging process. The bodega was the first to feature full-scale stainless steel technology. Enrique's original ambitions have mellowed a little with maturity and Cáceres now turns out some exemplary lightly oaked white wines, including the barrel-fermented Antea, as well as an impressive *gran reserva*. However, the wines from this bodega still tend not to spend much more time than the statutory minimum in the cask. Best wines: Gran Reserva, Gaudium Reserva.

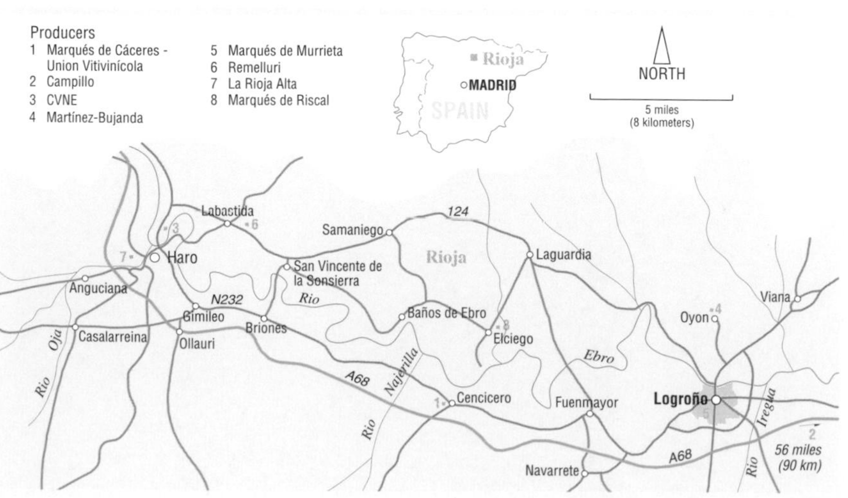

Rioja in threes

Understanding Rioja is as easy as one, two, three. There are three wine-growing regions—Rioja Alta, Alavesa, and Rioja Baja; three types of wine—white or "blanco," rosé or "rosado," and red or "tinto." And there are three main grape varieties for the red Rioja—tempranillo, garnacha and mazuelo. There are three quality levels for red rioja as well, based on minimum aging required by the Consejo Regulador. Crianza, which translates loosely to "cradle," refers to the youngest style and must be aged a minimum of one year in barrel and one in bottle. Reserva indicates a minimum of one year in barrel and two in bottle; while gran reserva indicates a minimum of two years in barrel plus three in bottle. Aging requirements are stricter in Rioja than any other region in Spain.

CVNE (COMPAÑÍA VINÍCOLA DEL NORTE DE ESPAÑA)

Established **1879** ***Owners*** **the Real de Asúa family** ***Production*** **667,000 cases** ***Vineyard area*** **1,364 acres (552 ha)**

This is one of Rioja's most respected companies. The wines are classic *rioja*, using the full mix of grapes, with the Viña Real range sourcing most of its tempranillo from the Rioja Alavesa and Imperial from the Rioja Alta. Everything is first-class from this exceptional bodega, but some are more first-class than others. Best wines: *reservas* and *gran reservas* in the Imperial and Viña Real ranges; Real de Asúa Reserva; Contino.

MARTÍNEZ-BUJANDA

Established **1889** ***Owners*** **the Martínez Bujanda family** ***Production*** **250,000 cases** ***Vineyard area*** **988 acres (400 ha)**

An old firm with the latest equipment, their wines range from a solid everyday range to some excellent new-wave stuff, including a barrel-fermented viura (macabeo), a varietal garnacha *reserva* with 20 months in oak, and a new *gran reserva* which is openly 50/50 tempranillo/ cabernet sauvignon. Best wines: Vendimia Seleccionada Gran Reserva; Finca de Valpiedra; Valdemar.

MARQUÉS DE MURRIETA

Established **1872** ***Owner*** **Dominios Creixell** ***Production*** **400,000 cases** ***Vineyard area*** **445 acres (180 ha)**

This elegant bodega has been extended, new vineyards planted and the wines revamped to appeal to the modern market without sacrificing quality. The company also owns Pazo de Barrantes in the

DO Rías Baixas, in Galicia. Best wines: Reservas; Castillo Ygay Gran Reservas.

REMELLURI

Established **1968** ***Owner*** **J. Rodríguez Salis** ***Production*** **33,000 cases** ***Vineyard area*** **260 acres (105 ha)**

Remelluri's bodega makes only *reservas*. It supplies about 80 percent of its own grapes, mostly tempranillo. The winemaking is a mix of traditional and modern, using refurbished oak vats and stainless steel; the wine typically spends around two years in *barricas*. The style and character of the wines are classics for Basque Country rioja.

LA RIOJA ALTA

Established **1890** ***Owners*** **the Aranzábal family** ***Production*** **250,000 cases** ***Vineyard area*** **740 acres (300 ha)**

A member of the Rioja "aristocracy," whose wines serves as a benchmark for many others. The very best wines are still fined with egg-whites and racked by hand; in the cellar next door automatic systems perform the same tasks. The wines are a mix of tempranillo, mazuelo, graciano and garnacha in varying proportions, and aging is done in a mixture of new and old oak (with an average age of six years). *Crianzas* normally have two years, *reservas* three and *gran reservas* four in oak. Best wines: everything, but especially Viña Ardanza; Grandes Reservas 890 and 904.

MARQUÉS DE RISCAL

Established **1860** ***Owners*** **the Hurtado de Amezaga family** ***Production*** **300,000 cases** ***Vineyard area*** **519 acres (210 ha)**

This was the first bodega built to make rioja wine by the "bordeaux method." The earliest plantations were cabernet sauvignon and tempranillo. The wines went through a difficult patch in the late 1970s—some of the old oak had become tainted with a fungal growth—but were back on form by the mid-1980s. Best wines: Barón de Chirel Reserva (60 percent tempranillo, 40 percent "other" grapes); Marqués de Riscal Reserva.

Another significant producer in Rioja is Campillo, their best wines are Campillo, Reserva, Reserva Especial and Gran Reserva.

ABOVE: Rows of vines follow the curves of the landscape in northern Spain.

Regional Dozen

Conde de Valdemar Reserva
Cune Contino Reserva
Cune Monopole Rioja Blanco
Finca Allende Aurus
Marques de Caceres Guadium Gran Vino Red
Marques de Murrieta Castillo Ygay Gran Reserva
Martinez-Bujanda Garnacha
Muga Prado Enea Gran Reserva
Muga Torre Muga
Remondo Palacios Rioja Blanco Placet
Roda I
Telmos Rodriguez Altos de Lanzaga

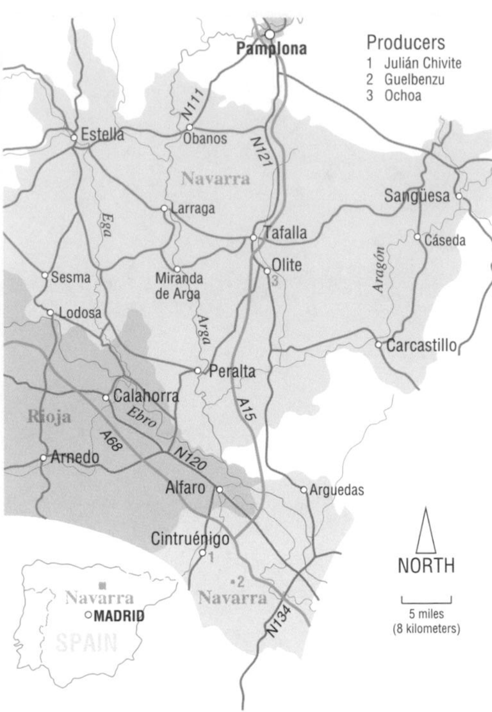

ABOVE: *The soft greens of a vineyard near Maneru contrast with the drier landscape around it.*

NAVARRA

Once under the shadow of neighboring Rioja, Navarra has reinvented itself with a vengeance as a source of some of Spain's most interesting new wines. Thanks to support for the regional government through the enological research station in Olite, the range of wines has never been more exciting.

JULIÁN CHIVITE

Established **1647** ***Owners*** **the Chivite family** ***Production*** **175,000 cases** ***Vineyard area*** **865 acres (350 ha)**

As recently as the early 1980s this company was the only serious exporter from Navarra and even today, given the massive explosion in new ideas and experimentation from this DO zone, the company holds a commanding lead in international recognition as well as size. The present company actually dates from 1860 and released a special edition—Colección 125—to mark the firm's 125th birthday in 1985. A barrel-fermented chardonnay with 11 months on the lees, and a tempranillo/merlot/cabernet *reserva* with, typically, 14 months have been made in every good year since then. Indeed, there is also a special *gran reserva* made from pure tempranillo aged for two years in oak, and a splendid rich *vendímia tardía* (late vintage) moscatel with ten months in the barrel. The basic range is called Gran Feudo and features a particularly good pink wine made only from 100 percent garnacha. Best wines: Colección 125 (the whole range—red, white, moscatel); Gran Feudo Rosado and Moscatel.

GUELBENZU

Established **1851** ***Owners*** **the Guelbenzu family** ***Production*** **25,000 cases** ***Vineyard area*** **104 acres (40 ha)**

This boutique winery can be found beside a lovely old house opposite the bullring in the small town of Cascante in the south of the region. The house wine is a *crianza*, mainly tempranillo; Guelbenzu EVO is a *crianza* dominated by cabernet sauvignon; Guelbenzu Jardín is a garnacha wine made from vines over 30 years old; and newcomer Guelbenzu Lautus, a tempranillo/merlot/cabernet/garnacha *reserva*. Best wines: Lautus; EVO.

OCHOA

Established **1845** ***Owners*** **Javier and Mariví Ochoa** ***Production*** **89,000 cases** ***Vineyard area*** **299 acres (121 ha)**

The Ochoa family has been in the wine business for several centuries but the modern-day company dates from 1986. Javier Ochoa has been one of the most tireless campaigners for quality both in Navarra and abroad. Ochoa was instrumental in setting up the research establishment EVENA (Estación de Viticultura y enologia de Navarra) which has done so much to improve quality and bring in new ideas to the district, and he's applied these in his own family vineyards too. He grows viura (the name Riojanos have for macabeo) and chardonnay for whites; tempranillo, garnacha, cabernet sauvignon and merlot for reds. He also pioneered the sweet moscatel wines which have been winning prizes all over the world. Best wines: Reserva; Gran Reserva; Moscatel.

Catalonia

PENEDÈS

Penedès (and rising star Priorato) has the lead in volume, reliability, innovation and quality-control throughout Catalonia. Every Catalan grape, almost every Spanish grape and many north European grapes are grown here in the myriad microclimates of the Baix-Penedès, Mitja-Penedès and Alt-Penedès, up to heights of 2,600 feet (800 m). The range of soils and altitudes provides perfect growing conditions for everything from the lightweight white wines for the beachfront market to impressive cabernet and chardonnay wines which can hold their vinous heads up anywhere in the world.

ABOVE: *Barrels line the cellar at the Torres Winery in Catalonia.*

JANÉ VENTURA

Established **1914** ***Owners*** **the Jané Ventura family** ***Production*** **24,000 cases** ***Vineyard area*** **27 acres (11 ha)**

This family firm turns out some excellent wines, especially cabernet sauvignon made in the new-wave style of Penedès, a barrel-fermented white made mainly from macabeo and an exemplary young white in the classic Catalan style. The company is small enough to have hands-on control of production under Benjamín Jané Ventura. Best wines: all the range, especially Cabernet Sauvignon and Finca els Camps barrel-fermented white.

CAVAS NAVERAN (SADEVE)

Established **1986** ***Owner*** **Mitchell Guillerán, shareholders** ***Production*** **5,000 cases** ***Vineyard area*** **210 acres (85 ha)**

As with many companies based in this area, Naveran is mainly a cava company, but makes some still wines under the DO Penedès: these may be small in number but they are big in quality. The winemaking here in this estate strictly new-wave and focused on "international" grape varieties including viognier as well as chardonnay, cabernet and merlot. Best wines: Don Pablo Reserva; Naveran Crianza.

MIGUEL TORRES

Established **1870** ***Owners*** **the Torres family** ***Production*** **2,5000,000 cases** ***Vineyard area*** **3,212 acres (1,300 ha)**

This is the company which did more than most to bring Spanish wine to the world after the Spanish Civil War, and its wines are now sold in more than 85 countries as a result. The present head of the family, Miguel A. Torres, has built on the solid foundation left by his father and extended the company's operations to Chile and the United States, where his sister, Marimar Torres, runs a brilliantly successful operation in California. Miguel was among the first to plant cabernet sauvignon and chardonnay in Catalonia but he also has a plantation of over 100 native Catalan varieties with which he

BELOW: *The gentle grace of fall colors on the vines near Poboleda, in Catalonia.*

ABOVE: *Tiny underground wine cellars, northwest Spain.*

experiments on a regular basis. The winery at Pacs del Penedès is an object-lesson in the marriage of new technology with traditional style and quality, and Torres wines are regular prizewinners in international competitions. Best wines: Fransola (sauvignon); Gran Viña Sol (chardonnay); Viña Esmeralda (moscatel/ gewürztraminer); Waltraud (riesling); Atrium (merlot); Gran Coronas, Mas la Plana (both cabernet sauvignon); Milmanda (chardonnay from Conca de Barberà).

Regional Best

Alvaro Palacios Finca Dofi Priorato
Alvaro Palacios Las Terrasses Priorato
Alvaro Palacios L'Ermita Priorato
Clos Martinet Priorato
Clos Mogador Priorato
Cordoniu Non Plus Ultra Cava Penedes
Costers del Siurana Clos de L'Obac Priorato
Jaume Serra Reserva Penedes
Mas Igneus Priorato
Scala Dei Priorato
Segura Viudas Heredad Reserva Brut Cava Penedes
Torres Mas La Plan Gran Coronas Cabernet Sauvignon Penedes

Other Catalonian Regions

CAVA

The Cava DO is defined by grape type and production method rather than the area, although since 1991, over 90 percent of all cava vineyards have been found in Catalonia itself. Most cava comes from the area around St Sadurní d'Anoia located in the province of Barcelona.

CODORNÍU

Established **1551** ***Owners*** **the Raventós family** ***Production*** **3,750,000 cases** ***Vineyard area*** **2,965 acres (1,200 ha)**

This is now the biggest of the cava companies, challenged only by Freixenet. The company's estate in St Sadurní is in idyllic landscape, housed in art nouveau buildings, and possesses the biggest cellars in the world, totaling 15 miles (25 km) on five underground levels. But this old-world charm hides a cutting-edge approach to the wine, with constant experiment and innovation. Codorníu is said to have introduced the first chardonnay to cava and is experimenting with pinot noir as well as selecting its own clones of the classic "big three" grapes (parellada, xarel-lo and macabeo). Best wines: Cuvée Raventós; Non Plus Ultra; Raïmat Gran Brut.

FREIXENET

Established **1889** ***Owners*** **the Ferrer family** ***Production*** **11,000,000 cases** ***Vineyard area*** **642 acres (260 ha)**

This is the other "big name" cava house (along with Codorníu) and the biggest sparkling wine producer in the world, with companies in the US, Mexico, France and Australia. Its most famous wine is Cordon Negro. The Freixenet group includes Segura Viudas and Castellblanch which are run as separate operations. In general, Freixenet is against the use of chardonnay in cava, although its top-of-the-range *reserva real* contains about 20 percent of the grape. The latest development is a red-grape/white-grape monastrell/xarel-lo which promises well. Best wines: Reserva Real; Cuvée DS; Segura Viudas Reserva Heredad.

RIGHT: *The best wines in the Empordà-Costa Brava region are the reds.*

GRAMONA

Established **1921** ***Owners*** **the Gramona family** ***Production*** **28,000 cases** ***Vineyard area*** **72 acres (29 ha)**

This is a small family-owned concern turning out relatively small quantities of impeccable wine in the best artesanal style. The grapes are the classic three and even the basic wine is aged for 18 months—double the legal minimum for cava. The top-of-the-range Celler Batlle, unusually, is made without any parellada—

just 70 percent xarel-lo and 30 percent macabeo. Best wines: Tres Lustros; Celler Batlle.

JOSEP MARÍA RAVENTÓS I BLANC,

Established **1986** ***Owner*** **Manuel Raventós i Negra** ***Production*** **24,000 cases** ***Vineyard area*** **217 acres (88 ha)**

Scion of the Raventós family of Codorníu fame, Josep-María decided to make his own way in the world and set up business hardly a stone's throw from the family estate. His taste in architecture is more modern but no less inspiring than that of his forbears, and his wines, similarly, show great style and panache. He grows chardonnay as well as the native grapes and has established a name for the company very early on. Best wines: Reserva; Gran Reserva; Reserva Personal Manuel Raventós.

JUVÉ Y CAMPS

Established **1921** ***Owners*** **the Juvé y Camps family** ***Production*** **200,000 cases** ***Vineyard area*** **1,235 acres (500 ha)**

This vineyard supports both cava and still wines made under the DO Penedès, but it is best known for its cava. The style is classic in the most formal sense of the word: a proper regard for tradition but with modern wine-making skills and long, slow, careful maturation for any-thing up to five years. A Juvé y Camps wine is likely to be the top cava on many a restaurant wine list. Best wines: Reserva de la Familia; Gran Juvé y Camps.

AGUSTÍ TORELLÓ

Established **1955** ***Owners*** **the Torelló Llopart family** ***Production*** **60,000 cases** ***Vineyard area*** **272 acres (110 ha)**

This is a company which makes an "estate" cava from its own vineyards at Can Marti de Baix just outside St Sadurní. Don Agustí himself is still in charge and the family provides most of the impetus for some of the Anoia valley's best wines. Only the native "big three" Catalan varieties are grown. The company's international fame was enhanced by the fabulously expensive Kripta (which was presented in a bottle in the shape of an amphora), proving that a relatively small producer can compete in quality terms with the big names of the cava industry. Some say that Kripta and Torelló's other masterpiece, Mata, are the finest cavas currently in production. Best wines: Kripta, Mata.

ABOVE: *Modern stainless steel vats hold the wine in Freixenet's extensive cellars at St Sadurni.*

ALELLA

This area had a promising early start, although it is much reduced in size these days owing to urban sprawl from the city of Barcelona—its biggest market—immediately to the south. Alella wines are mainly white and made from pansá blanca (xarel-lo) and garnacha blanca grapes. There is also a substantial amount of chardonnay. The wines are fresh and light: new-wave examples may be barrel-fermented. There is some small amount of red, mainly made from ull de llebre (tempranillo).

EMPORDÀ-COSTA BRAVA

Empordà-Costa Brava is on the border between Catalonia and France, an area which has reinvented itself as a dynamic and experimental zone. The best wines here tend to be the reds, made from tempranillo, cabernet sauvignon and merlot. The local classic is a sweet red made from sun-dried garnacha grapes called garnatxa del empordà, very much in the style of the *vins doux naturelles* made across the border in France.

BELOW: *Freixenet is one of the largest sparkling wine producers in the world.*

ABOVE: Bullfighting, as well as wine drinking, is an integral part of Spanish culture.

CAVAS DEL CASTILLO DE PERELADA

Established **1923** ***Owners*** **the Suqué-Matue family** ***Production*** **110,000 cases** ***Vineyard area*** **247 acres (100 ha)**

A magnificent castle in Perelada is the head office of the Perelada wine company, which has built a remarkable reputation for quality in all its wines. Cava is made in the cellars but most of the vinous work is carried out in a more prosaic winery with modern equipment. The vineyards grow tempranillo, garnacha, cariñena and macabeo as well as cabernet sauvignon, merlot, chardonnay and sauvignon blanc. Best wines: Castillo Perelada Reserva; cabernet sauvignon.

CONCA DE BARBERÀ

This highland area found in the province of Girona produces mainly *joven* wines in all three colors although there is the odd exception: Miguel Torres' barrel-fermented Milmanda Chardonnay comes from here, and there are continuing experiments with oak-aged reds made from tempranillo and garnacha, often with an admixture of cabernet sauvignon and merlot.

RIGHT: A leaf from the syrah vine, a grape that is widely grown in the Catalonia region.

CONCAVINS

Established **1988** ***Owner*** **Luis Carbonell Figueras** ***Production*** **280,000 cases** ***Vineyard area*** **NA**

Two separate ranges of wine are made here. First come the early-harvest supermarket blends of macabeo, parellada and chardonnay, which are put through the system quickly. Then comes the main harvest, most likely cabernet sauvignon, merlot and tempranillo. These are given the full malolactic treatment followed by extended caskage, typically 12–18 months for *crianzas* and up to two years for *reservas*. The wines are very good and quality control is excellent. Best wines: Castillo de Montblanc Cabernet Merlot; Via Aurelia Masia les Comes.

COSTERS DEL SEGRE

Cynics have suggested that the only reason this area was awarded the DO (in 1988) was because it was the home of Raïmat, the giant estate with Californian-inspired techniques and some admittedly excellent wines. Costers del Segre is fragmented into four subzones around the city of Lleida (Lérida): Raïmat, Artesa (both in the province of Lleida), Valls de Riu Corb and Les Garrigues (in Tarragona province). Some smaller firms are, however, beginning to appear. The wines come in all three colors; the best reds are generally made from tempranillo, cabernet sauvignon and merlot and the best whites from chardonnay and the "big three" Catalan grapes.

RAÏMAT

Established **1918** ***Owners*** **the Codorníu family** ***Production*** **300,000 cases** ***Vineyard area*** **3,706 acres (1,500 ha)**

This winery looks as if it might have come from another planet: mirrored walls, vines on the roof, neoclassical portals, and indoor water features. The wines here are Californian-style and aren't bad; arguably the best (Abadia) is a tempranillo/cabernet mix; also good is Mas Castell Reserva (cabernet sauvignon). They also make cava here.

PLA DE BAGES

This is a relatively small zone in the province of Barcelona with a reputation for making sound if unexceptional wines in the past. However, excellent work has been done with the picapoll (Spanish for the French picpoul or piquepoul) grape for white wines and the cabernet sauvignon for reds—perhaps we shall hear more.

MASIES DE AVINYÓ

Established **1983** ***Owners*** **the Roqueta family** ***Production*** **8,000 cases** ***Vineyard area*** **99 acres (40 ha)**

This is a small but very promising company which was making export wines under the Ramon Roqueta label for many years before re-forming under the present name. The family has made wine for centuries at the Masia Roqueta (the family farmhouse) and opened a retail shop in Manresa in 1898 to sell it. They also installed the first automatic bottling plant, in 1964, and became a company formally in 1983. Wines today are sold under the company name and made from macabeo, picapoll and chardonnay for whites; garnacha, tempranillo, merlot and cabernet sauvignon for reds. Best wines: Picapoll; Cabernet Sauvignon/ Tempranillo Crianza.

LEFT: A much patched stone wall protects vines from the wind, as it has done for centuries.

PRIORATO

This is an ancient and beautiful region with eight centuries of wine-making tradition, high in the hills of the province of Tarragona and home to one of the toughest, blackest and longest-lived wines of Spain. In the same region, in the hilltop town of Gratallops, century-old garnacha vines and high-technology plantations of cabernet, merlot and syrah are producing some of the best new-wave wines of Spain.

BODEGAS ALVARO PALACIOS

Established **1989** ***Owner*** **Alvaro Palacios** ***Production*** **12,000 cases** ***Vineyard area*** **99 acres (40 ha)**

Alvaro's wines are all magnificent. L'Ermita is now possibly the most expensive red wine in Spain, beating even the fabled Vega Sicilia. It is made from 100-year-old garnacha vines in a steep natural amphitheater located on ancient schistose bedrock. The finished wine has 15 percent cabernet sauvignon for aroma and 5 percent cariñena (the Rioja name for mazuelo) for color, and spends 15 months in oak. Finca Dofi, the "estate" wine, is made with syrah and merlot as well as cabernet and cariñena. Las Terrasses is the mainstream wine, made from garnacha, cariñena, and cabernet sauvignon.

TARRAGONA

This region's fame rested on a single wine, now known as Tarragona Clásico. This is a fortified red wine made from garnacha grapes and stored in oak vats for a minimum of 12 years.

Elsewhere, the DO produces all types of wine in all three colors, though 70 percent of Tarragona's wine production is white. Grapes grown include tempranillo, garnacha, cariñena and also cabernet and merlot. White wines tend to be made from the "big three" Catalan grapes (parellada, xarel-lo and macabeo) and/or chardonnay. Sweet whites are made from moscatel.

CELLER CO-OPERATIU DEL MASROIG

Established **1917** ***Owners*** **Co-op members** ***Production*** **225,000 cases** ***Vineyard area*** **1,235 acres (500 ha)**

There's been a good deal of change in the co-ops in Tarragona and this is an example of how new thinking in the winery and the vineyards is allowing these formerly bureaucratic and hidebound organizations to compete on the world stage. The grapes are the local specialties—garnacha blanca for whites and tempranillo (here called ull de llebre) and cariñena for reds—but the wines here speak for themselves. Best wine: Masroig Les Sorts.

TERRA ALTA

This is a remote area of sleepy local co-ops (although the main co-op in Gandesa is doing impressive work and is housed in a splendid Gaudíesque building). However, there are stirrings in the undergrowth and one or two "boutique" wineries are starting to make their names. The wines are generally reds made from hefty local grapes—cariñena and garnacha—along with tempranillo and, in the more forward-looking wineries, cabernet and merlot. Most white wine is made from garnacha blanca and parellada, although there is some very good macabeo and some experimental chardonnay.

PIÑOL

Established **1940** ***Owner*** **Josefina Piñol** ***Production*** **22,000 cases** ***Vineyard area*** **62 acres (25 ha)**

Among many innovations here are an interesting light, sweet wine called Josefina Piñol, made from over-ripe garnacha blanca, and Viñ Orosina, a dry-fermented moscatel. The top red wines are named L'Avi Arrufi (Grandfather Arrufi). Best wines: L'Avi Arrufi Crianza; Nuestra Señora del Portal.

Other recommended Catalonian producers include Rovellats (Cava), Castell del Remei (Costers del Segre) and Mas Martinet Viticultores (Priorata).

BELOW: Vineyards in Terra Alta, one of the eight DOs in Catalonia.

ABOVE: *Parasol pines (Pinus pinea) grace the very flat open fields in the southern part of La Mancha, which is due south of Madrid.*

Castilla-La Mancha

LA MANCHA & VALDEPEÑAS

In the 1980s, La Mancha was still regarded as little more than a bulk-wine producer for the cafés and bars of Madrid, but it reinvented itself in the 1990s and, although there's still a lot of fairly basic wine being turned out, some of the best-value everyday wines in Spain are now being made here.

Famous for its fabulously warm, ripe and modestly priced *reservas* and *gran reservas*, Valdepeñas has resisted the temptation to diversify, though there are signs, especially among the smaller companies, that new ideas are on the way. In the meantime, the traditional wines of this area must be among the best value-for-money in the world.

Regional Dozen

- Allozo Gran Reserva, Bodegas Centro-Españolas
- Castillo de Alhambra Cencibel, Vinícola de Castilla
- Castillo de Almansa Reserva, Piqueras
- Corcovo Cencibel Joven, J. A. Megía e Hijos
- Eméritus, Marqués de Griñón
- Estola Gran Reserva, Bodegas Ayuso
- Señorío de Mariscal Crianza, Bodegas Mariscal
- Vega Moragona Crianza, Co-op La Magdalena
- Vegaval Plata Reserva, Miguel Calatayud
- Viña Albali Reserva, Bodegas Felix Solis
- Viña Lastra, Co-op La Invencible
- Yuntero Reserva, Co-op N. P. Jesús del Perdón

VINÍCOLA DE CASTILLA, LA MANCHA

Established **1976** ***Owners*** **Private shareholders**
Production **900,000 cases** ***Vineyard area*** **494 acres (200 ha)**

Living proof that big can be beautiful, this bodega was founded by the old RuMaSA group which was taken over by the government in 1983 to avoid its imminent collapse, and its holdings sold off. Vinícola de Castilla was bought by financiers, who could see which way the wind was blowing. Even though some of the technology is now old-fashioned, it was so ahead of its time in those days that it still looks like a space-age installation. Today's spotless modern atrium and offices sit beside gleaming stainless steel equipment and complex computer controls. The wines have achieved a good deal in international competition. The company buys in most of its grapes and makes wine from viura, airén, chardonnay and sauvignon blanc (whites); and garnacha, cencibel (the local word for tempranillo), cabernet and merlot (reds). Best wines: Señorío de Guadianeja Reserve, Gran Reserva; Castilla de Alhambra Rosado, Tinto.

FELIX SOLIS, VALDEPEÑAS

Established **1952** ***Owners*** **the Solis family**
Production **11,000,000 cases** ***Vineyard area*** **1,730 acres (700 ha)**

As you drive along the N-IV between Madrid and Córdoba a mighty steel city rears up against the open sky on the outskirts of Valdepeñas. This is Bodegas Felix Solis, undergoing yet another expansion as a further 200 acres (80 ha) of land disappear under new buildings and storage warehouses, including the first fully automated, robot-staffed dispatch warehouse in Spain which will be able to handle 20,000 pallets of wine. Solis is the second-biggest wine company in Spain, after Bodegas y Bebidas but B & B owns half a dozen wineries, whereas Solis has just the one … for now. There are a number of ranges of wines, including Peñasol (everyday-quality table wines), Diego de Almagro, Los Molinos and the most famous brand—and some of the best-value red wine to come out of Spain—Viña Albali. Best wines: Viña Albali Crianza, Cabernet Sauvignon, Tempranillo (*joven*), Diego de Almagro Crianza.

Other Castilla-La Mancha Regions

ALMANSA

There are other bodegas in Almansa but only one has any profile outside the area. Making use of only local

RIGHT: *Widely spaced vineyards cut down the amount of maintenance time needed.*

grapes and making wine in the traditional way, Piqueras has shown that it can be done.

PIQUERAS

Established **1915** ***Owners*** **the Piqueras family** ***Production*** **167,000 cases** ***Vineyard area*** **248 acres (100 ha)**

Almansa is often seen as a bit of "one-horse" DO as, year after year, the only bodega which makes itself felt in a wider market is this one. Winemaker Juan Pablo Bonete Piqueras has made it his business to succeed even if his peers are lagging behind. He grows (and buys) airén and macabeo for white wine and cencibel (the local word for tempranillo) and monastrell for red. The quality is excellent and there seems to be no good reason why other bodegas have not emerged to challenge for the leadership but, in the meantime, Piqueras reigns in this part of Spain. Best wines: Castillo de Almansa Crianza, Reserva.

VDLT SIERRA DE ALCARAZ

MANUEL MANZANEQUE

Established **1992** ***Owner*** **Manuel Manzaneque** ***Production*** **12,000 cases** ***Vineyard area*** **84 acres (34 ha)**

At El Bonillo, these vineyards flourish at altitudes of 3,000–3,280 feet (900–1,000 m). The results have been widely admired: Manzaneque grows chardonnay as well as cabernet sauvignon, merlot, tempranillo and syrah and his wines are exemplary. Best wines: Chardonnay; Finca Elez Crianza (mainly cabernet); Gran Reserva.

VDLT DE CASTILLA

After much lobbying by several prominent producers, the new Vino de la Tierra zone of Castilla was approved by the provisional government in 1999. The idea is that, rather in the manner of the Vin de Pays d'Oc in France, individual producers will now be able to experiment more, with less supervision, than they would be able to under DO regulation.

DEHESA DEL CARRIZAL

Established **1987** ***Owner*** **Marcial Gómez Sequeira** ***Production*** **4,200 cases** ***Vineyard area*** **32 acres (13 ha)**

Ignacio de Miguel Poch, who makes the wine here, does only one thing but does it very well—that is, to make a world-class cabernet sauvignon in these unclassified lands, some 30 miles (50 km) north-west of the city of Ciudad Real. Dehesa del Carrizal's reputation has steadily advanced, to the point where its wines consistently challenge the finest wines of Spain in international tastings. The wine is made from 100 percent cabernet and spends, typically, 18 months in oak. Best wines: all of them.

VDM DE TOLEDO

MARQUÉS DE GRIÑÓN

Established **1972** ***Owners*** **the Falcó family** ***Production*** **12,500 cases** ***Vineyard area*** **104 acres (42 ha)**

Carlos Falcó de Fernández y Córdova, Marqués de Griñón and a grandee of Spain, has confounded the critics ever since his first commercial vintage in 1982. Feeling that the DO laws were a little too constricting, he decided to make wine the way he wanted it. The results have been outstanding, and his example set the tone for a whole generation of "maverick" winemakers who were to change the face of Spanish wine before the end of the century. Today, the Marqués grows cabernet, merlot, syrah and petit verdot and makes varietals as well as a new wine made from cabernet, syrah and petit verdot. Indeed, this last venture was so successful that in the year 2000 he began regrafting his chardonnay vines to petit verdot.

Another project begun in 2000 was the planting of a new clone of graciano, so the future for the wines of the Dominio de Valdepusa is entirely red. Carlos Falcó is also involved with the Arco Bodegas group, making similarly unclassified wines in Castilla-León as well as mainstream DOCa wines in Rueda and Rioja. Anything which carries the Griñón name may be relied upon without question. Best wines: everything, but especially Dominio de Valdepusa Cabernet Sauvignon, Syrah; Emeritus.

ABOVE: *Despite the difficult and often windy conditions, Castilla-La Mancha is one of Spain's largest producers of wine.*

Andalusia

JERÉZ

Jeréz/Xérès/Sherry y Manzanilla de Sanlúcar de Barrameda

About 20 companies now control the sherry business, under about 75 brand names. The wines themselves are as good as, or better than, they have ever been, even if nowadays the choice is not so wide as it once was.

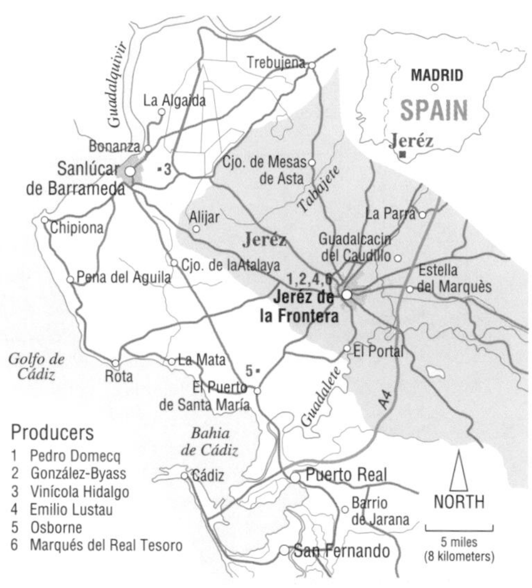

PEDRO DOMECQ

Established **1730** ***Owner*** **Allied-Domecq** ***Production*** **600,000 cases** ***Vineyard area*** **988 acres (400 ha)**

In spite of its membership of the multinational Allied-Domecq group, this bodega has managed to maintain its individuality, albeit with a reduced range of wines to accommodate the other members of the group (which includes the British company John Harvey, of Bristol Cream fame). In common with many another major company the recent upturn in interest for "premium" sherry has encouraged Domecq to expand its quality range beyond the best-selling Fino La Ina. Best wines: Fino La Ina; Amontillado 51-1°; Sibarita Oloroso; Palo Cortado Capuchino; Venerable PX.

BELOW: Vina el Caballo, a Jeréz winery. The 1980s and 1990s were a period of change for many sherry producers.

GONZÁLEZ-BYASS

Established **1835** ***Owners*** **the González family** ***Production*** **890,000 cases** ***Vineyard area*** **2,523 acres (1,021 ha)**

This company, with its large-scale and beautiful bodega in the middle of Jeréz, went through a difficult financial patch in the 1980s at a time when outside investors were involved. However, the stock is now all back in the hands of the family and sound leadership has restored the company to its former pre-eminence. González-Byass claims to have produced the first *fino* in the modern style (Tio Pepe) in the 1850s, and has an impressive collection of ancient *soleras*. Their latest development is the "Añadas" collection of vintage sherries. Best wines: Tio Pepe; Amontillado del Duque; Apóstoles Dry Oloroso; Matúsalem Rich Old Oloroso.

VINÍCOLA HIDALGO

Established **1792** ***Owners*** **the Hidalgo family** ***Production*** **150,000 cases** ***Vineyard area*** **494 acres (200 ha)**

This company has been a leading producer of *manzanilla* for many years. The current head of the family, Javier Hidalgo, has an independent streak which has kept the company in the forefront of traditional winemaking while others have gone for the mass-market. His young wines have a freshness and lightness which make them very drinkable with food, especially with fish in one of the seafront restaurants in Sanlúcar. He also produces the very rare *manzanilla*, *amontillado* and *oloroso* styles. The family vineyards are in the district of Torrebreva and some of the vines are 80 years old. Best wines: La Gitana Manzanilla; Amontillado Viejo; Napoleon Oloroso; Palo Cortado Viejo.

EMILIO LUSTAU

Established **1896** ***Owners*** **Luís Caballero group** ***Production*** **200,000 cases** ***Vineyard area*** **420 acres (170 ha)**

This house has an excellent reputation for quality wines. Under the late Rafael Balao it established the "Almacenista" range of wines, bought from small producers and brokers and bottled in short runs for the "premium" sherry market, which has been a brilliant success. When the Caballero group bought Lustau in 1990, there were worries that it might be subsumed into the core business (which is "own label") but in the event this has not happened. The bodega remains a law unto itself and, with Caballero's backing, has gone from strength to strength. Best wines: all wines are among the best in the Jeréz region, but particularly Manzanilla Pasada Manuel Cuevas Jurado; Papirusa Manzanilla; Amontillado Escuadrilla; Moscatel Superior Emilín; Pedro Ximénez San Emilio.

ABOVE: *The cellars of Pedro Domecq, a company famous for its sherry for over two centuries.*

OSBORNE

Established **1772** ***Owners*** **the Osborne family** ***Production*** **750,000 cases** ***Vineyard area*** **494 acres (200 ha)**

An old firm in a magnificently restored bodega building, Osborne still possesses some splendid old *soleras* and makes some excellent wine, besides being famous for its brandies. Its brand identity is well known for its silhouette bulls (which used to carry a slogan until roadside advertising was banned) which dot the countryside all over Spain. The company owns the brand-name Duff-Gordon, which is better known in some export markets than the main company name. Osborne took over Bobadilla in the mid-1990s. Best wines: Fino Quinta; AOS Solera Amontillado; Alonso El Sabio Oloroso; P Triangulo, P Oloroso.

MARQUÉS DEL REAL TESORO

Established **1897** ***Owner*** **José Estévez de los Reyes** ***Production*** **700,000 cases** ***Vineyard area*** **1,003 acres (406 ha)**

José Estévez bought the residuals of this dormant company in the 1980s and went on to buy the *soleras* of Tio Mateo (an excellent *fino* from the ancient house of Palomino & Vergara) from John Harvey, which was undergoing yet another metamorphosis within what was to become Allied-Domecq. These were rehoused in a smart new bodega on the Cádiz road. His latest acquisition is the house of Valdespino in its entirety, including the classic Inocente Fino, and it seems likely that Valdespino will continue to be a separate entity. Best wines: Tio Mateo Fino; Amontillado del Principe; Inocente Fino (Valdespino); Solera 1842 Oloroso (Valdespino).

Other Andalusian Regions

MONTILLA-MORILES

Montilla is the mainstay wine of the Andalusian region—the wines are modestly priced and are sold in dry, medium, and sweet styles. Unfortified, montilla achieves up to 15 percent alcohol by volume (abv) by natural fermentation. The grape here is the PX (pedro ximénez) and the Montilla area produces the ancient thick, black PX wines with exemplary grace. The best wines of Montilla are made in the fortified styles—*amontillado*, *oloroso*, *fino*, and cream.

ALVEAR

Established **1729** ***Owners*** **the Alvear family** ***Production*** **333,000 cases** ***Vineyard area*** **618 acres (250 ha)**

The approach at Alvear is meticulous, with the result that it releases some of the region's finest wines. Producing montilla, Alvear is

Regional Dozen

Amontillado del Duque, González-Byass
Amontillado Selección Imperial, José Gallego-Góngora
Capataz Fino, Alvear
Don PX Gran Reserva, Toro Albalá
Gran Barquero Amontillado, Perez Barquero
Inocente Fino, Valdespino, Marqués del Real Tesoro
La Gitana Manzanilla, Vinícola Hidalgo
Málaga Virgen, López Hermanos
Manilva Moscatel, Bodegas Castillo de la Duquesa
Principe Alfonso, Bodega las Monjas
Royal Ambrosante Dulce, Sandeman
Sibarita Oloroso, Pedro Domecq

ABOVE: Seville, at the heart of Andalusia has a heritage of flamenco and bullfighting.

wines. However, the main business hereabouts seems to be seasoning oak casks for the Scotch whisky industry: two years of *oloroso* wine in a new cask provides what a good malt needs.

VC ALJARAFE

There are a few independent bodegas working outside the mainstream wine-producing areas of Andalusia. Most of them have a long way to go before they achieve international recognition.

JOSÉ GALLEGO-GÓNGORA

Established **1682** ***Owners*** **the Gallego-Góngora family** ***Production*** **200,000 cases** ***Vineyard area*** **296 acres (120 ha)**

Although the grape used here is the garrido fino, the wines are made very much in the Andaluz *generoso* style, and the wines are named "*fino*" and "*amontillado*," in the manner of sherry and montilla.

In spite of its obscurity, the wines are astonishingly good: there are *jovenes afrutados* in the new fresh and crisp style, but the fortified wines are still the best: these are Amontillado Muy Viejo Selección Imperial and PX Dulce Añejo Selección Imperial.

Another important bodega in Montilla-Moriles is Perez Barquera, noted for its *fino*, *amontillado*, *oloroso* and PX (all under the Gran Barquero label).

also a pioneer of the *joven afrutado* style. The best wines here are Capataz Fino; Solera Fundación Amontillado; Pelayo Oloroso.

MÁLAGA

Peaking in the nineteenth century, the wines of this region have since been in decline. The grape is the pedro ximénez—but sunned and then fortified during fermentation, it produces a wine of almost toffee-like richness. The best wines are aged in a *solera* but are becoming harder to find.

> *Alonso of Aragon was wont to say in commendation of age, that age appears to be best in four things—old wood best to burn, old wine to drink, old friends to trust, and old authors to read.*
>
> FRANCIS BACON (1561–1626), *Apothegms*

LÓPEZ HERMANOS

Established **1885** ***Owners*** **the Burgos López family** ***Production*** **110,000 cases** ***Vineyard area*** **618 acres (250 ha)**

Rekindling interest in the wonderful classic wines of Málaga, López Hermanos also produces a "pale cream" oloroso and a "dry" (more medium-dry) style as well. A new moscatel wine is being developed under the brand Pico Plata. Best wines: Trajinero Oloroso; Cartojal Pale Cream; Málaga Virgen.

CONDADO DE HUELVA

As in Montilla, producers here have turned to light, fruity *jovenes afrutados* and unfortified wines for the supermarket trade, although there is still a modest export bulk market in South America for the fortified

RIGHT: Only old oak barrels are considered good enough to mature vintage sherries.

Other Spanish Regions

VALENCIA

Valencia is an autonomous Mediterranean region, the wineries here are among the most technologically advanced in Europe. Alicante was once known for high-strength, sweet white wines, made from moscatel, and a legendary but expensive dessert red called fondillón, made from sun-dried monastrell grapes and aged for at least eight years. Modern Alicante also turns out fresh, crisp whites made from merseguera, airén and macabeo. The best wines are probably reds made from monastrell, garnacha, bobal and sometimes cabernet sauvignon. Utiel-Requena is famed for beefy reds made from the bobal. The Valencia DO is the supermarket wine capital of Spain, and tailor-made wines include a light, fresh, crisp, dry white made from the merseguera, a rich, sweet, fortified moscatel, a *crianza* red from tempranillo and cabernet or anything in between.

VICENTE GANDIA PLA, UTIEL-REQUENA

Established **1885** ***Owners*** **the Gandía family** ***Production*** **20,000 cases** ***Vineyard area*** **247 acres (100 ha)**

This big company was once based in the city of Valencia and makes wines under both DO names; the best-known from Valencia is probably Castillo de Liria. The main business is large-scale exports, and the company has a new bodega with all the latest equipment. However, the bodega does also produce a range of its own wines, including a white macabeo and reds from tempranillo, cabernet sauvignon and monastrell. Best wine: Ceremonia Crianza.

SCHENK, VALENCIA

Established **1927** ***Owner*** **Schenk group** ***Production*** **2,000,000 cases** ***Vineyard area*** **NA**

This is a Swiss-owned company and part of a group which has wine interests all over the world. In common with most big Valenciano wine houses it produces large quantities of bulk wines for export as well as for selling all over Spain, but it also has its own range of wines, under the Cavas de Murviedro label. There are whites made from moscatel and merseguera and reds from monastrell, tempranillo and bobal. Best wines: Estrella (moscatel dulce); Los Monteros Crianza.

GUTIÉRREZ DE LA VEGA, ALICANTE

Established **1978** ***Owner*** **Pilar Sapena Sanchez** ***Production*** **8,000 cases** ***Vineyard area*** **25 acres (10 ha)**

This is a very small-scale bodega but it has an excellent reputation for elevating the sometimes mundane moscatel de Valencia into a high art, under the Casta Diva label. Viña Ulises Crianza made from cabernet sauvignon, giró, merlot tempranillo and monastrell is a very good red. Best wine: Casta Diva Cosecha Miel Dulce.

MURCIA

ABOVE: An exuberant chalk drawing on a barrel, a reminder that in some places winemaking is still small-scale and individual.

Jumilla now makes good—even great—wine from the humble monastrell grape, showing reserves of spiciness and sheer rich fruit. Wines from garnacha and tempranillo are of exemplary quality and at silly prices. Yecla owes its current modest prominence to just one leading bodega. The monastrell here has been teased out to give softness, fruit, and a ripe, spicy fragrance as well as aging well in oak. There is some pleasant white, the best of which tends to be made from macabeo. The monastrell grape has done the trick in Bullas too, although there's also tempranillo and garnacha varieties, as well as some experimentation with cabernet, merlot and syrah. White wines in this region are predominantly made from macabeo.

CASTAÑO, YECLA

Established **1985** ***Owners*** **the Castaño family** ***Production*** **333,000 cases** ***Vineyard area*** **791 acres (320 ha)**

Ramón Castano has been doing his bit to put Yecla on the map and has been exporting his wines for the better part of 20 years. Although the company as presently constituted was only set up in 1985, the Castaños have been in the wine business since at least 1950. Innovation,

BELOW: The ruins of ancient fortresses, built to repel Moslem invaders from the south, are a familiar sight in many parts of Spain.

ABOVE: *A cellar built into the side of a hillside creates a cool storage room for wine.*

as always, has been the key to success: the company grows monastrell, cabernet sauvignon, tempranillo and merlot and makes a white *joven* from macabeo as well as an unusual semi-sweet pink from monastrell. Its great strength, however, is the reds with *crianzas* and *reservas* under the Pozuelo label. Best wines: Castaño Monastrell (joven); Hecula (monastrell/tempranillo/merlot).

HUERTAS, JUMILLA

Established **1996** ***Owner*** **Antolin Huertas Manzaneque** ***Production*** **1,000,000 cases** ***Vineyard area*** **1,920 acres (777 ha)**

Although this is a large-scale bodega selling its wine all over Spain, its own vineyards provide only 4 percent of its needs in terms of grapes. Big though it is, it can still turn out some startlingly good wines. The best are the reds, all made entirely from monastrell. This is another bodega which has shown that with the correct handling, monastrell can be made into a truly excellent *joven* wine for (almost) immediate drinking. Best wines: Aranzo Crianza; Rodrejo (red joven).

AGAPITO RICO, JUMILLA

Established **1989** ***Owners*** **Juan Sierva, Agapito Rico Martínez** ***Production*** **Production 45,000 cases** ***Vineyard area*** **247 acres (100 ha)**

Under careful husbandry and vinification the monastrell grape has shown itself to be capable of great things, and this is one of the bodegas which made that change happen. The vineyards are at an altitude of 2,300 feet (700 m), which helps to provide a good temperature range during the ripening season, and the winery is very much state of the art. The wines are called Carchelo and there is a *joven* made from monastrell and tempranillo, a *crianza* with some added cabernet sauvignon and varietal merlots with and without *crianza*, as well as a varietal syrah without oak. Best wines: the whole range, but especially merlot and syrah.

RIGHT: *Tempranillo grapes, used in many blends, make richly colored, long-lived wines.*

MADRID AND EXTREMADURA

Bodegas in Vinos de Madrid now produce some stylish wines at moderate prices ideally suited to house-wine in the tapas bars of the city of Madrid. The better wines tend to be *joven* or occasionally *crianza* reds, made from tempranillo/tinto fino. However, the best wines come from Tierra de Barros in the Ribera del Guadiana DO.

INVIOSA, RIBERA DEL GUADIANA

Established **1931** ***Owners*** **the Díaz family** ***Production*** **85,000 cases** ***Vineyard area*** **1,112 acres (450 ha)**

This was the first bodega to recognize that the old VdlT Tierra de Barros wasn't going to get anywhere turning out the same old bulk wines it had made for generations. Marcelino Díaz, the current head of the family, took the decision in the early 1980s to branch out and explore the opportunities offered by "international" grape varieties and new technology. He planted chardonnay and sauvignon blanc alongside the native cayetana and pardina, cabernet sauvignon, merlot and tempranillo and even graciano alongside the garnacha, and invested in stainless steel kit and new oak barrels. The results astonished everyone: the export market took the wines to its heart and today Bodegas InViOSA (Industrias Vinícolas del Oeste, SA) is the leading producer in the region. Best wines: Lar de Barros (white); Lar de Oro (range).

BALEARIC ISLANDS

Binissalem DO on Majorca—Spain's first offshore DO—got its ticket in 1991, but it wasn't until much later that the major bodegas of the region finished renewing their equipment and looking to markets beyond the peninsula. Most of the land is planted in mantonegro, a grape not found elsewhere in Spain but ubiquitous here and in the Pla i Llevant de Mallorca DO. The wines it produces—with a little help from tempranillo and monastrell—are good to very good in quality and, with judicious use of oak, age well. There is some white wine made from moll (prensal), parellada and macabeo but this is, essentially, red-wine country.

alejandría and frontignan) for their white wine and callet, fogoneu, tempranillo, mantonegro and cabernet sauvignon for the reds. Best wines: Mont Ferrutx Crianza; Ses Ferritges Reserva.

ARAGÓN

The unique microclimates and rich soils of Somontano, which is located on the south side of the Pyrenees, make it possible to produce outstanding wine from almost any grape here. Smart, modern wineries are making this an exciting new Spanish region. In the lowlands, Cariñena has achieved modest success for its red wines, made mainly from garnacha. There's also tempranillo, a bit of cabernet sauvignon and a promising local called juan ibáñez. Campo de Borja has some decent reds, made mainly from garnacha. One or two bodegas in Calatayud are turning out good-quality wines at modest prices. The best wines in the region tend to be the reds made from tempranillo and/or garnacha, and monastrell.

Regional Dozen

Borsao Tinto, Borsao Borja
Chardonnay, Manuel Manzaneque
El Grifo Moscatel de Ana, El Grifo
Enate Reserva Especial, Viñedos y Crianzas del Alto Aragón
Finca Luzón
Jose L. Ferrer Tinto de Crianza, Franja Roja
Monte Ducay, San Valero Co-op
Señorío de Requena
Valdegracia, Co-op San Marcos de Almendralejo
Viña Alone Rosado, Co-op de Alicante
Viña Maín Tempranillo, Orusco
Viña Norte, Insulares Tenerife

LEFT: The village of Maluenda in Aragón is in the heart of wine country.

MACIA BATLE, BINISSALEM

Established **1998** ***Owners*** **the Batle family** ***Production*** **27,000 cases** ***Vineyard area*** **124 acres (50 ha)**

This small new family bodega is making great strides, especially when you consider that winemaker Agnau Calmés is working with the native Mallorquí grapes: moll (or prensal) for white wines; mantonegro and callet for pinks and reds. All the wines are under the Macia Batle name, and the company is already doing some export business in northern Europe. Best wines: Macia Batle red (two months in oak), white (*joven*).

VINYES I BODEGUES MIQUEL OLIVER, PLA I LLEVANT DE MALLORCA

Established **1912** ***Owners*** **the Oliver family** ***Production*** **8,500 cases** ***Vineyard area*** **25 acres (10 ha)**

This is another small family concern: Miquel and Pilar Oliver share the winemaking duties and turn out some refreshingly different wines from this newly promoted area where much else of the production is singularly underwhelming. The Olivers grow moscatel (both

VENTA D'AUBERT, VDLT BAJO ARAGÓN

Established **1987** ***Owner*** **the Mühlemann family** ***Production*** **6,000 cases** ***Vineyard area*** **69 acres (28 ha)**

This is a small bodega working away in a location which hasn't shown much promise for a while; the only other producer is a co-op, itself on the small side. But winemaker Stefan Dorst has worked hard with his small plantation of chardonnay, viognier, garnacha blanca, cabernet sauvignon, merlot, garnacha tinta and syrah and produced wines of a quality that would shame many a more famously situated bodega. Venta d'Aubert El Serrats is a white *crianza*, mainly chardonnay and viognier; Venta d'Aubert red is a cabernet/garnacha/syrah mix. Best wine: Domus Reserva (cabernet/merlot/garnacha/syrah).

BELOW: Sediment forms in the bottle during the secondary fermentation of sparkling wine. It is later disgorged after riddling.

ABOVE: *Vineyards near the village of Alarban in Arugón form a patchwork of color.*

CRIANZAS Y VIÑEDOS ST CRISTO SOCIEDAD CO-OP, CAMPO DE BORJA

Established 1956 _Owners_ Co-op members _Production_ 280,000 cases _Vineyard area_ 2,928 acres (1,185 ha)

Co-ops are traditionally slow to change their ways, but this one has moved with the times and installed new equipment and adopted a modern approach to wine producing. Its members grow macabeo, moscatel, garnacha and tempranillo and turn out some good wines under the hands of winemaker Modesto Francés Bernabeu. Best wine: Moscatel Ainzón Dulce.

BODEGA PIRINEOS, SOMONTANO

Established 1993 _Owners_ Co-op Somontano de Sobrabre, Instituto Aragonés de Fomento, Vinedos y Crianza de Alto Aragón (main shareholders) _Production_ 450,000 cases _Vineyard area_ 124 acres (50 ha)

This was once the local Co-operativa Sobrarbe-Somontano, privatized in 1993 and subsequently revolutionized in its winemaking (old concrete vats have been replaced with stainless steel). Today, the former members of the co-op are shareholders, but they deliver their grapes at vintage time just the same: macabeo and chardonnay for whites, moristel, tempranillo, garnacha, merlot and cabernet sauvignon for reds. Best wines: Bodega Pirineos Merlot/Cabernet; Montesierra Crianza.

SOLAR DE URBEZO, CARIÑENA

Established 1995 _Owners_ Private shareholders _Production_ 89,000 cases _Vineyard area_ 247 acres (100 ha)

This is a mainly family affair, with Santiago Gracia in charge of the business and María-Asunción Gracia in charge of the winemaking. The company has taken a different approach to the traditional one favored by producers in this DO zone in the past, and planted chardonnay, merlot, cabernet sauvignon and tempranillo as well as the ubiquitous garnacha. Going with the trend for younger, fresher wines there's an excellent *joven* made, rather surprisingly, from cabernet, tempranillo and garnacha, as well as a chardonnay with just one month in oak and a merlot/cabernet/tempranillo *crianza*. Best wines: Solar de Urbezo Crianza; Viña Urbezo (*joven*).

VIÑAS DEL VERO, SOMONTANO

Established 1986 _Owners_ Private and institutional shareholders _Production_ 125,000 cases _Vineyard area_ 1,359 acres (550 ha)

This was a new start-up company funded by institutional finance to take advantage of the liberal regulations governing what could and could not be done in the then new DO of Somontano. An initial experimental plantation and bodega produced excellent results, giving way to the massive installation of today. The company grows chardonnay, gewürztraminer and local varieties for white wines, cabernet sauvignon, tempranillo, moristel, merlot and pinot noir for reds, and the winemaking, by Pedro Aibar, is innovative and pin-sharp. The wines are sold under the Viñas del Vero label. Best wines: the whole range, but especially the chardonnay, gewürztraminer, Clarión (*joven* white), Gran Vos Reserva.

CANARY ISLANDS

All but one of the seven islands in the archipelago (Fuerteventura) now make wine under the DO Regulations and Tacoronte-Acentejo, Tenerife, the largest, has five DOs. Local wines are subsidized by the regional government, and many of them are excellent.

However, they are little known in export markets due to the prohibitive cost of transporting them to mainland Europe. Wineries in the Ycoden-Daute-Isora DO produce mainly fruity dry whites. Lanzarote, despite its inhospitable landscape, has an island-wide DO.

LEFT: Filling bladders for the restaurant trade, a significant customer for many wineries.

EL GRIFO, LANZAROTE

Established **1775** ***Owners*** **the Rodríguez-Bethencourt family** ***Production*** **50,000 cases** ***Vineyard area*** **99 acres (40 ha)**

This is Lanzarote's leading bodega and carries on a tradition started by the same family some five generations ago. The bodega has a small museum, is full of new technology and the winemaking style is innovative. El Grifo is at the forefront in new-wave red and white wines, but its finest work is reserved for good old-fashioned Canary-sack made from malvasía grapes. Best wines: El Grifo Dulce; El Grifo Moscatel de Ana.

INSULARES TENERIFE, TACORONTE-ACENTEJO, TENERIFE

Established **1992** ***Owners*** **500 local shareholder/growers** ***Production*** **56,000 cases** ***Vineyard area*** **1,235 acres (500 ha)**

This is the modern face of the co-operative: Insulares Tenerife is not a bureaucratic dinosaur burdened with endless committees but a limited company running its own affairs, and very well too. The bodega is smart, new and fitted with the latest equipment with plenty of room for extra capacity when the need arises. The wines are among the best on the island and the bodega has serious ambitions to export, but the distance (and therefore cost) from the Canaries to the peninsula is the most daunting aspect. Best wines: Viña Norte (red and pink).

CUEVA DEL REY, YCODEN-DAUTE-ISORA

Established **1990** ***Owner*** **Antonio Fernándo González** ***Production*** **2,500 cases** ***Vineyard area*** **35 acres (14 ha)**

This is the size of operation which makes "boutique" wineries look as if they're on an industrial scale. Antonio González has built his own installation using small fiberglass tanks, and temperature control is effected by a compressor made from an old freezer. His wines, however, are an excellent example of modern-style hands-on winemaking—light, fresh and fruity and ideally suited to the subtropical climate of the island. He makes just two wines: Cueva del Rey white (listán blanco) and red (listán negro).

TAJINASTE SAT, YCODEN-DAUTE-ISORA

Established **1993** ***Owners*** **Local shareholders** ***Production*** **13,000 cases** ***Vineyard area*** **198 acres (80 ha)**

This is a small company, though it is building a reputation for well-made fresh whites from the listán blanco grape and fruity reds from listán negro. Although the bodega has some new oak casks these tend to be used for fermentation, the rest of the winemaking is completely modern, with stainless steel installations. The best wine is made by the process of *maceración carbónica*. Best wine: Viña Donia Tinto.

VALLEORO, VALLE DE LA OROTAVA

Established **1988** ***Owners*** **52 co-operative shareholders** ***Production*** **67,000 cases** ***Vineyard area*** **297 acres (120 ha)**

This is a Sociedad Agraria de Transformación (SAT)—a kind of halfway house between an old-fashioned co-op and a limited company. It is known for its fresh light whites. The wines tend to be *jovenes* made in all three colors for the ever-thirsty tourist market. They are made from the listán blanco and listán negro, but there is some experimentation here, including barrel-fermentation for some of the white wines and *maceración carbonica* for some of the reds. The brand-name is Gran Tehyda, called after the towering crater of the volcano, Mount Teide. Best wines: Gran Tehyda Rosado (red).

BELOW: Lush valleys and ancient villages are typical features of south-west Spain.

The Tua Valley offers spectacular views of ancient vineyards in the upper Douro Valley.

Portugal

RIGHT: *Portugal's centuries' old tradition of winemaking is celebrated in many of its blue and white tilescapes.*

interests in more than one region. They are Sogrape, currently the biggest wine company in Portugal; and the Symington group, which could be easily described as the "royal family" of fortified wines in Portugal.

Landscape and climate

The country divides roughly in half, to the north and south of the Tagus River. The north is mountainous while the south is lower but climbs toward a central plain. The climate divides on similar lines: north of the Tagus there is more temperate influence, while in the south, the climate is more Mediterranean, with milder winters. In wine terms, Portugal can be split roughly into five mainland regions—the north, the area from the Douro to the Tagus Rivers; the center, Lisbon and the Tagus Valley; Setúbal and the south; the Algarve; and the islands of Madeira and the Azores.

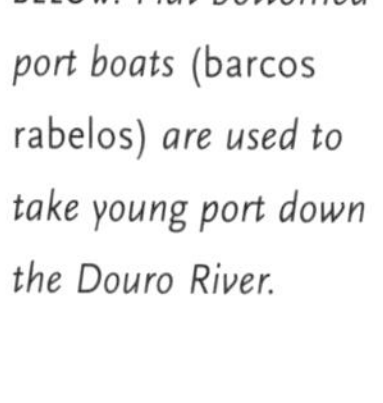

In the north, the land climbs from the west coast toward the Spanish border into granite mountains with outcrops of schist in the highlands of the port country. The great contrast here in winemaking is between the light, fresh, usually fizzy wines of Vinho Verde, where vinho verde ("green wine") is grown, and the heavyweights of the Douro, including port. Port country is some of the most beautiful and spectacular in the world. The River Corgo flows into the Douro near where the town of Régua splits the main production area of DOC Porto into two: Baixo Corgo, the area around the town and the confluence, is the westernmost area for port production and also the coolest and wettest. Cima Corgo, upstream from Régua, is the heartland of top-quality port production, centered around the town of Pinhão.

One of the oldest-established fine-wine areas lies between the points at which the rivers Douro and Tagus cross the Spanish border. Dão and Bairrada are prominent wine areas in this mountainous landscape.

In the country's center, the region of Estremadura stretches along the coast north of Lisbon. It is home to a vast array of grapes and has a reputation for decent, if unexciting, everyday wines.

Setúbal and the south covers almost a third of Portugal. This region is mainly undulating plain, fertile and heavily farmed. Setúbal has seen some of the most

BELOW: *Flat-bottomed port boats* (barcos rabelos) *are used to take young port down the Douro River.*

innovative and forward-thinking new ideas in recent years, creating some splendid wines and maintaining its reputation for the classic moscatel.

The Algarve is a very hot region of craggy inlets. Its winemaking tradition dates back to the days when fortified wines were shipped over to Spain. The biggest threat here to quality winemaking is the tourist market, to cater to which a large amount of unexciting and ordinary wine is produced.

Madeira is a spectacularly beautiful volcanic island closer to Morocco than Portugal. Wine grapes are grown on terraced slopes, often in high and apparently inaccessible places. It's about the last place on earth you'd expect to find one of the world's greatest wines. The climate here is temperate, though often humid.

The Azores is an archipelago in the Atlantic, about 870 miles (1,400 km) west of Portugal, and consists of nine main islands, volcanic in origin. The climate is subtropical with high humidity.

Wines

PORT

There are many theories surrounding the invention of port, whatever the truth of the matter, methods of making port today remain largely traditional, though there is fierce argument over whether the grapes are better pressed and fermented in steel tanks or pressed by foot in lagares (stone troughs) as they have been for centuries. One method tries to satisfy both sides of the argument by combining technology and tradition in the form of stainless steel tanks with machinery the same size and shape as a human footprint complete with toes to press the grapes. Another high-tech version has robot "feet" on hydraulic legs which are put to work in the *lagares* without needing to pause for rest.

Whichever method is used to press the grapes, the must is fermented to about 6–8 percent abv (alcohol by volume) and run off into holding tanks which are already a quarter full of a neutral grape spirit, *aguardiente*. This stalls fermentation without adding flavors or aromas to the wine. Then, after a suitable period of rest, the wine is passed to casks or tanks for maturation.

A bewildering variety of grapes may be used to make port, but only half a dozen are generally accepted to be in the front rank: touriga franca, tinta roriz, mourisco, bastardo and tinta cão and everyone's favorite, touriga nacional. Other top-class varieties are tinta francisca, tinta barroca, tinta amarela, periquita (also known as castelão frances) and sousão. There are nearly 30 varieties permitted for red wines and 20 for white. Most white port is made from a mixture which is likely to include gouveio, malvasia and rabigato (also known as rabo de ovelha).

All vineyards in port country are classified and

ABOVE: Bragança Castle, in the medieval town of Bragança in the northeast of Portugal.

graded according to the quality they normally produce. Points are awarded (or taken away) for altitude, yields, soil types, age and nature of vines and other factors which are deemed to affect the final quality of the grapes. The final scores are then banded into Grades A to F, and growers paid on a sliding scale according to the quality of what they produce.

Port is aged and classified according to its quality:

Vintage port is a single-vintage wine from the very best years. It spends two years in cask and the rest in bottle. Vintage ports are undoubtedly the region's greatest wines.

BELOW: Harvest time in the steep vineyards at Quinta Do Noval, in the Douro Valley.

Single-quinta is made from the grapes of an individual *quinta* ("farm"). It has become popular in recent years to make a single-*quinta* in the years which are not quite great enough to make a full vintage. (An exception would be Quinta do Noval which is the name of the estate as well as that of its finest wines.)

Colheita means "harvest"—that is, wine produced from the harvest of a single vintage. (It cannot be called "vintage" simply because that would confuse it with vintage port.) *Colheita* ports are single-vintage wines aged in wood until just before bottling. These may be very old, tawny-colored and delicately nutty in flavor.

ABOVE: The winter task of pruning over-long shoots encourages vines to grow in straight rows.

Tawny, as its name implies, is a lighter style of port, blended from different vintages and aged in wood for six to seven years before bottling and sale. There are some very fine old tawnies of 20, 30 and 40 years old.

ABOVE: Tinta negra mole grapes, the most widely grown variety in Madeira, arrive for vinification.

Late-bottled vintage is a vintage port, typically from a second-string year and aged in wood for four to six years or so before release.

Vintage character describes a port made "in the vintage style" but blended from a number of years.

Ruby is a basic everyday port wine which may be any age at all, and it can be variable in quality. The best rubies will have been aged for around four years.

MADEIRA

The four noble varieties used to make madeira are malvasia (known by the English as malmsey), boal, verdelho and sercial. As well, there have always been plantations of terrantez, bastardo and moscatel on Madeira, as well as listrão on the neighboring island of Porto Santo. However, the area planted to all these grape varieties added together is insignificant when compared to the area planted with the most common grape in Madeira—the tinta negra mole.

As with many fortified wines, the heating and cooling effects of travel in the tropics during the age of exploration seemed to improve the quality of the wine. This discovery led to the unique methods of maturation used on the island ever since. Grapes are bought from small farmers and the price paid reflects the quality of the grape. The noble varieties are fermented separately, often in oak casks or vats. Tinta negra mole is now typically fermented in concrete vats or stainless steel. The wines are fortified to 17–18% abv (alcohol by volume) during fermentation, as with port, although the moment chosen for fortification varies according to the dryness required in the finished wine.

BELOW: A very old vintage boal, one of the four "noble" grape varieties grown in Madeira.

Estufa (meaning "stove") is the name of the unique method which Madeira producers use to reproduce the gentle heating and cooling effects of a sea voyage in the tropics. Carried out incorrectly, it can seriously damage the wine, and there are those violently opposed to it in any form. Done gently, using the very latest equipment, however, it can certainly speed up the wine's development. A good modern installation will hold the wine in stainless steel tanks with a water-jacket containing hot water. The tank is heated gently to about 113°F (45°C) and then returned to the ambient temperature over a period of, maybe, six months. This allows the wine to develop without bringing out unwanted flavors. Noble wines are usually aged by the *canteiro* system, in which casks of the wine are racked into heated warehouses and allowed to adjust to the changing ambient temperature. In either case the wines must be aged for three years before sale.

Have some madeira

Producers of madeira must be proud to know their product is found in almost every restaurant, hotel, and cruise ship on the planet. Unfortunately, this globally known wine is most likely a rather low-end, commercial grade product destined for the kitchen, not the dining room. Young Turks on the Ilha da Madeira, or Island of the Woods, are hacking through the jungle of government red tape to introduce the world at large to their world-class wines, the single varietal sercials, verdelhos, boals and malmseys, from the finest vineyards, heated gently by the tropical climate instead of furnaces or hot tanks. The finest madeiras are one of the wine world's remaining bargains. A well-aged sercial or verdelho, for example, is less than the price of an ordinary chardonnay, and will stay fresh for years after opening.

Colheitas (see Port, the previous page, for a definition) are single-vintage wines made from the noble varieties. Those from the very best years have been known to survive for up to 200 years. By law, they must be stored in cask for a minimum of 20 years and in bottle for a further two years before release. Madeira made from terrantez and moscatel grapes is governed by the same regulations; it is rare and usually found only as *colheita* wine.

Some ***solera*** wines are the result of a system of winemaking which comes from Jeréz country. Wines from a series of "scales," or rows, of increasingly old barrels are blended with younger wines of the same type. In effect, new wine goes in at one end and old wine comes out of the other after a period of many years. In this way the new wine takes on the characteristics of the old and matures much more quickly and with better quality control. Some *solera* wines may carry the date of foundation of the *solera*. These are now rare but some of the older wines are still available.

Malmsey, ***boal***, ***verdelho*** and ***sercial*** must be made from 85 percent of the named grape. They are usually sold as 5-year-old, 10-year-old, 15-year-old and *colheita*.

Sweet, ***medium-sweet***, ***medium-dry*** and ***dry*** madeiras are wines made from tinta negra mole—the financial foundation of the wine industry—and the four levels of sweetness are supposed to represent the styles of the four noble grapes.

ABOVE: *The old flat-bottomed port boats (barcos rabelos) at Porto, across the river from Vila Nova de Gaia.*

Wine law

Several administrations over the past century have tried to organize the wine industry, with only limited success. However, in 1999 all the anomalies were sorted out and the new administrative body is the Instituto da Vinha e do Vinho (IVV) and the current terminology is as follows.

QUALITY WINE

The letters VQPRD stand for Vinho de Qualidade Produzidos em Regiões Determinadas (QWPSR in English—"Quality Wines Produced in Specific Regions"). This embraces two categories:

Denominação de Origem Controlada (DOC) means "denomination of controlled origin" and is the equivalent of Spain's DO. The 22 regions so classified include the traditional areas of winegrowing as well as some new ones. They are each policed by a Regional Commission which makes decisions about planting, yield and wine styles. The two largest DOC regions (Ribatejo and Alentejo) are further subdivided (into six and eight subregions respectively), making a total of 36 DOC areas.

LEFT: *Treading grapes at Quinta do Noval, Douro Valley.*

Indicação de Provenencia Regulamentada (IPR) is a category created for emergent wine areas which may eventually seek promotion. Some are administered by their own Regional Commission, others directly by the IVV. There are currently nine regions in this classification. Regulations are slightly more relaxed than those for the DOC although IPRs still have quality wine status.

TABLE WINE

This category divides into two categories:

Vinho Regional (VR) are country wines from fairly large areas. The regulations in this category are particularly important in that they allow growers and winemakers much more flexibility in the wines that they make as well as allowing a vintage date, some kind of regional name and the mention of grape variety/ies to appear on the label. Some of Portugal's most exciting new wines come under this apparently humble classification. Nine of them cover virtually the whole country, and they are administered directly by the IVV.

Vinho de Mesa (VdM) is a simple table wine. It may be made in and blended from grapes from any part of Portugal. There are few controls on the way it is made (except restrictions on gross yield) although, under European law, these wines may not carry any regional name (except the name of the country) or vintage date or grape variety. Vinho de Mesa Espumante (VdME) is classified simply as "sparkling table wine," with the same regulations as VdM, because there is no quality wine classification for sparkling wine in Portugal.

The North

VR MINHO

This is a country-wine area in the northwest. Its borders roughly coincide with those of the DOC Vinho Verde but regulation here is much less stringent and winemakers are experimenting with a whole range of grape varieties which go beyond those permitted in DOC wines.

Vinho Verde

This area is best known for its slightly under-ripe ("green") wines with a bit of slightly sparkling *spritzig* character. The wines are mainly white and the best of them are made from the loureiro, trajaduro and alvarinho grape. Other grapes include azal and rabigato.

ABOVE: *Sandeman's famous cloaked figure gives the brand an instantly recognisable identity.*

QUINTA DE ALDERIZ

Established **NA** ***Owner*** **S.A. de Casa Pinheiro** ***Production*** **6,000 cases** ***Vineyard area*** **25 acres (10 ha)**

From Monçao, along the Minho to the west of Melgaço, this is where much of the best alvarinho grows. The Sociedade Agrícola da Casa Pinheiro, which is based at the quinta, makes this excellent example. Best wine: Quinta de Alderiz Alvarinho.

SOGRAPE

Established **1947** ***Owners*** **Sogrape** ***Production*** **3,719,812 cases** ***Vineyard area*** **988 acres (400 ha)**

After a family split in 1979, Sogrape went on to develop its own vinho verde—Morgadio da Torre, made from 100 percent alvarinho—at its winery in Barcelos. Aveleda is still made at the quinta in Penafiel and the company now sells both brands. Best wine: Morgadio da Torre.

BELOW: *The Douro River has been an aquatic highway for the wine trade for centuries.*

VR TRÁS-OS-MONTES

In the northeast of Portugal, country wines are light whites in the vinho verde style as well as heavyweight whites and reds largely unseen outside their home region. The southern part includes the Douro Valley. Wine from here may be labeled "Vinho Regional Trás-os-Montes/Terras Durienses". The area includes Chaves, Valpaços and Planalto-Mirandes IPRs.

Douro

Such has been the interest and investment here—often by outsiders—that the best wines of the region are now being made and sold by single-*quinta* producers, and Douro wines are beginning to be accepted as some of Portugal's finest. Douro seems destined to become one of Europe's great red-wine areas.

QUINTA DO CRASTO

Established **1615** ***Owners*** **Jorge and Leonor Roquette** ***Production*** **19,000 cases** ***Vineyard area*** **123 acres (50 ha)**

This lovely Douro estate with beautifully restored house and chapel is set on the site of an ancient Roman fortress overlooking the river. With the help of Australian winemaker Dominic Morris, recent releases of Vinho da Pont, Touriga Nacional and Maria Teresa, from 70-year old vines on original terracing, have garnered international acclaim and are the new benchmarks in dry Douro red. Their LBV port is one of the best in the region.

A. A. FERREIRA S. A.

Established **1751** ***Owners*** **Sogrape** ***Production*** **60,000 cases** ***Vineyard area*** **370 acres (150 ha)**

This Douro offshoot of the port house Ferreira makes what was for many years Portugal's finest dry red wine—Barca Velha. It uses the finest grapes in only the finest years. The wine spends 18 months in French oak and a further seven or eight years in bottle. Other wines are Reserva Ferreirinha, Callabriga and Vinha Grande.

NIEPOORT

Established **1842** ***Owners*** **the Niepoort family** ***Production*** **5,000 cases** ***Vineyard area*** **62 acres (25 ha)**

Winemaker Dirk Niepoort makes a hefty red called Redoma at the Quinta do Carril. Unusually, he makes a white counterpart from gouveio and rabigato (rabo de ovelha) at the Quinta de Napolés. There's also a red made in the traditional manner (in lagares) from tinta roriz and touriga franca grapes.

RAMOS PINTO

Established **1880** ***Owner*** **Champagne Louis Roederer** ***Production*** **108,330 cases** ***Vineyard area*** **494 acres (200 ha)**

Here, wines are made here from a mixture of grapes drawn from Quinta da Ervamoira in the Côa Valley

LEFT: Pinhao Valley, Alto Douro. The number of single-estate wineries has increased with the relaxation of government bureaucracy and entry to the European Union.

(douro superior) and Quinta de Bom Retiro in the Torto Valley (cima corgo). The former provides grapes with freshness and acidity, the latter with weight, ripeness, and structure, and the result is known as Duas Quintas. The best wine here is Duas Quintas Reserva.

Porto

DOC Porto shares the same boundaries as DOC Douro in the subregion of VR Trás-os-Montes and these two areas dominate wine production, as very little wine is made under the VR regulations.

FERREIRA

Established **1751** ***Owner*** **Sogrape** ***Production*** **NA** ***Vineyard area*** **NA**

Antónia Adelaide Ferreira, the great-granddaughter of the founder, José Ferreira, consolidated the foundations of this company in the early nineteenth century. It is now under the guidance of Antónia's great-great-grandson, Vito Olazebal, and his son, Francisco. Grapes for Ferreira port come from four quintas—do Porto (bought in 1863); do Seixo (1979); de Leida and do Caedo (1990). Best wines: LBV; Duque de Bragança 20-year-old tawny; vintages.

FONSECA GUIMARAENS

Established **1822** ***Owner*** **Taylor, Fladgate & Yeatman**
Production **NA** ***Vineyard area*** **NA**

Fonseca has its own house style and its own sources of grapes—most notably the Quinta do Cruzeiro and the Quinta do Santo Antônio in the Pinhão Valley. Premium Ruby Bin 27 is its most famous name, but its aged tawnies are legendary, as is the late-bottled vintage, Fonseca-Guimaraens.

TAYLOR, FLADGATE & YEATMAN

Established **1692** ***Owner*** **Alistair Robertson**
Production **NA** ***Vineyard area*** **NA**

In the Douro, near Régua, Taylor's is generally recognized as the top port company. Major brands are LBV and some splendid old tawnies, but the jewels are wines produced by the two quintas, Quinta da Terra Faita and Quinta de Vargellas. The latter turns out some of the finest wines in the region.

Other significant producers in the North include António Esteves Ferreira (Vinho Verde); Vinha do Fojo, Montez Champalimaud, Quinta do Valado (all Douro); Graham's and Quinta do Noval (both Porto).

Regional Dozen

Broadbent Vintage Port
Ferreira "Barca Velha" Douro Red Table Wine
Ferreira "Dona Antonia" Reserva Tawny Port
Prats & Symington "Chryseia" Douro Red Table Wine
Quinta das Arcas Vinho Verde White Table Wine
Quinta do Noval "Nacional" Vintage Port
Quinta do Crasto LBV Port
Quinta do Crasto "Vinho da Pont" Red Table Wine
Quinta do Crasto "Touriga Nacional" Douro Red Table Wine
Ramos Pinto "Duas Quintas" Douro Red Table Wine
Sandeman Quinta do Vau Vintage Port
Vallardo Vinho Branco Douro White Table Wine

Historic Barca Velha

Portugal's Douro is most famous for the sweet, fortified port wine, but one firm, A. A. Ferreira, had staked its claim on a dry red, Barca Velha. This is one of Portugal's most expensive table wines and is made by Ferreira at Quinta do Vale de Meao. Just across the border are the vineyards for Spain's most expensive wine, Vega Sicilia. Barca Velha (the old barge) is made with the same grapes used in port, primarily touriga nacional and tinta roriz (which is also known as tempranillo or tinto fino across the border). The wine is ripe, spicy and has notes of mint, chocolate and earth. Production is limited, so the wine is hard to find. Nonetheless, it has served as inspiration to the fledgling table wine industry of the Douro.

The Douro to the Tagus

VR BEIRAS

This region covers the whole of the north-central part of Portugal, and wines made under the Vinho Regional epithet come in a huge array of styles, from sleepy local co-ops to some new-wave, experimental wineries. There are also some exciting new wines being made in the DOC regions within Beiras which are classified as VR because they don't fit in with current DOC regulations.

The VR Beiras area includes within it (from north to south): Távora/Varosa, Beira Interior, Dão and Bairrada DOCs and Lafões IPR.

RIGHT: Wines from Dão are enjoying a renaissance with the change of wine laws.

SOCIEDADE AGRICOLA DE SANTAR

Established **1790** ***Owner*** **Soc. Agricola de Santar** ***Production*** **77,780 cases** ***Vineyard area*** **247 acres (100 ha)**

This is a single-estate winery, completely redesigned in the 1990s and concentrating on varietal wines under the hands of winemaker Pedro de Vasconcellos e Souza. Best wines: Castas de Santar Alfrocheiro Preto, Touriga Nacional.

Regional Dozen

Arinto, Quinta de Dom Carlos
Buçaco Reserva, Hotel Palace do Buçaco
Cartuxa, Fundação Eugénio de Almeida
Encruzado, Quinta dos Roques
Garrafeira, Casa de Saima
Marquês de Borba, João Portugal Ramos
Quinta de Cabriz
Quinta da Pellada Touriga Nacional, Quinta de Saes
Quinta de Murta
Quinta dos Carvalhais Encruzado White Table Wine (Dão)
Tinto Bruto, Caves Aliança
Vinha Barossa, Luís Pato

Távora/Varosa

This area, which incorporates the former IPR areas of Varosa and Encostas da Nave, is mainly known for Douro-style reds and whites made from similar selections of grapes. However, the region is emerging, astonishingly enough, as a producer of some of Portugal's best sparkling wines, made from malvasia, chardonnay, sercial, pinot noir, and others, by the traditional method. This may be a future area of development.

CAVES DE MURGANHEIRA, VDME

Established **1974** ***Owners*** **Partinvest, O. da Costa Lourenco** ***Production*** **83,000 cases** ***Vineyard area*** **59 acres (24 ha)**

This company, in the district of Varosa, has made its name in new-wave "classic method" sparkling wines (what used to be called, in more enlightened times, *méthode champenoise*), none of which are entitled to any kind of official quality classification but must be labeled VdME. The company produces one of Portugal's best wines, made from malvasia, chardonnay, sercial and pinto, with several months in oak after the first fermentation and a year on the lees after the second. Best wine: Murganheira Varosa.

Beira Interior

Incorporating the former IPR zones of Pinhel, Castelo Rodrigo and Cova da Beira, this is a very large and varied area, covering much of the eastern part of the region from the Coa in the north to the Tagus in the south. Wines here range from some decent, full reds in the north (Castelo Rodrigo) through from co-op whites and reds and some rather uninspiring sparklers (Pinhel) to a wide selection in the large Cova da Beira zone.

Dão

One of Portugal's longest-serving wine areas fell into disrepute over years of official bureaucracy when only the co-ops could buy grapes from independent growers. This meant that independent winemakers had to rely on their own resources to support their needs. This changed in the mid-1990s and some interesting new wines began to appear, although the co-ops still make most of the wine. Some new single-*quinta* wines are showing particularly well and Dão may be on its way back. The best wines are solid reds made from touriga nacional and any one of a number of other grapes, including bastardo, jaen and tinta roriz. The best whites are made from cold-fermented encruzado.

QUINTA DOS ROQUES

Established **1989** ***Owners*** **Oliveira and Lorenço families** ***Production*** **4,500 cases** ***Vineyard area*** **99 acres (40 ha)**

The wines here show tremendous promise. Winemaking concentrates on quality reds made from touriga nacional, tinta roriz, tinta cão and others, although there are good whites made from bical, malvasia and sercial. Best wines: Touriga Nacional; Tinta Roriz.

RIGHT: Dão vineyards benefit from long hot summers and wet winters.

LEFT: *The famous wines of the Hotel Palace Do Buçaco are only available to guests.*

Bairrada

This ancient wine-producing region in northern Portugal suffered from delimitation in the eighteenth century, but reinvented itself early in the twentieth century and is now one of the country's most important and innovative areas. Most of its production is red wine, and most of these are made mainly from the local baga grape which, at its best, provides a wine of good color with a ripe fruit and considerable aging potential. Some of Portugal's most forward-thinking winemakers work in this area. White bairrada, which can also be very good, is produced here, and is generally made from the fernão pires (also known as the Maria Gomes) grape.

CAVES ALIANÇA

Established **1927** ***Owners*** **the Neves family** ***Production*** **833 cases** ***Vineyard area*** **25 acres (10 ha)**

This is a family-run company making wine here in Bairrada and also in Dão and the Alentejo. The winemaker is Francisco Antunes and he makes crisp dry whites from bical and chardonnay, as well as reds from baga and (under the VR Beiras) cabernet sauvignon. Best wines: Aliança Garrafeira (Bairrada); Galeria Cabernet Sauvignon (Beiras).

HOTEL PALACE DO BUÇACO (VDM)

Established **1917** ***Owners*** **Almeida group** ***Production*** **6,000 cases** ***Vineyard area*** **37 acres (15 ha)**

This is a mind-boggling, post-baroque, forest-fantasy palace built deep in the woodlands of the Serra de Buçaco as a country retreat for Carlos I. It was leased to Alexandre d'Almeida in 1917 and he turned it into a hotel and vineyard. The wines remain more or less as Almeida first created them. The red is made from baga, tinta pinheira and bastardo, pressed and fermented in stone *lagares* and aged for three years in enormous vats made from oak harvested from the surrounding forest. The hotel lists vintages from 1945 onwards, and there are those who claim that to eat the suckling pig and to drink the red wines of the Palace do Buçaco is to experience the best gastronomy in all of Portugal. Best wines: all of them.

Other significant producers in the region include Quinta de Foz de De Arouce (Beiras); Quinta das Maias, Caves Messias, Quinta de Saes (all Dão); Casa Agíicola de Saima, Luís Pato, Caves Primavera and Caves São João (all Bairrada).

BELOW LEFT: *Wine tourism in Portugal is increasing along with the popularity of its wines.*

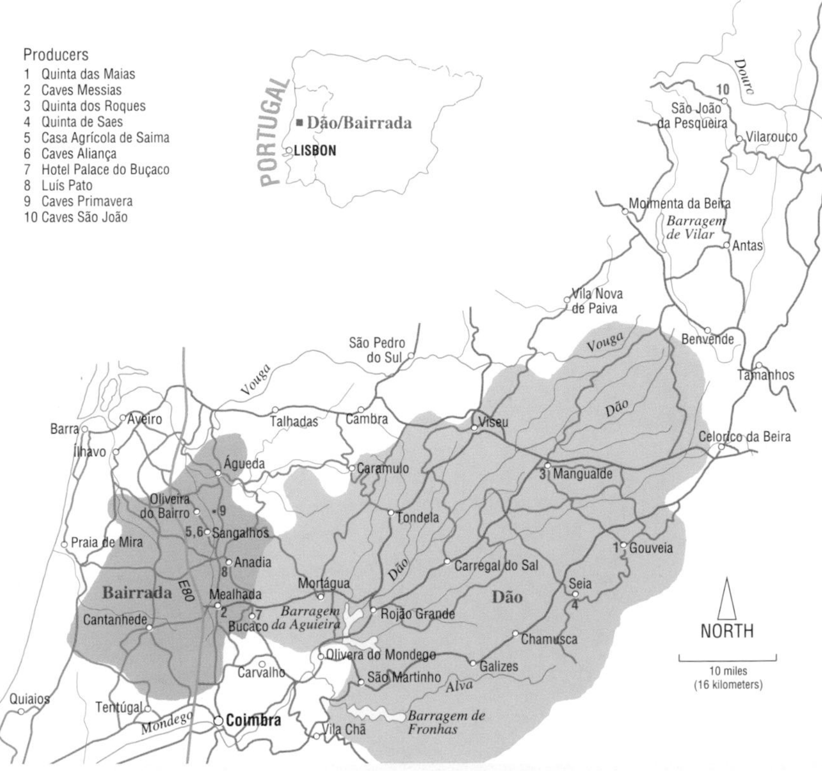

ABOVE: *The fertile soils of the Tagus Valley provide the ideal growing conditions for vines.*

RIGHT: *Secateurs for pruning vines and hand-picking grapes.*

Lisbon & Tagus Valley

VR ESTREMADURA

Estremadura is home to a huge range of grapes and decent, everyday wines. It has two IPR zones—Encostas d'Aire and Alcobaça—and eight DOC areas. Obidos has some decent reds; Lourinhã is considered Portugal's best brandy area; and Torres Vedras is a high-production area that is quite undistingushed. Alenquer has some promising wines made mainly from arinto, fernão pires, vital (white) and joão de santarém (red). Arruda, close to Lisbon, makes red wines of youthful charm, while Bucelas produces dry white wines made mainly from the arinto grape. Colares' best is red—dark, hard and tannic when young, maturing after a decade or more. Carcavelos, on the edge of Lisbon, has all but disappeared and the wine is not easy to find.

QUINTA DA BARÃO

Established 1973 Owners Guimarães family Production NA Vineyard area NA

If you're quick, you may find one or two of the semi-fortified wines of this fabled quinta still on sale as the encroaching concrete of Lisbon moves ever outward. As recently as 1989 there was a vintage, under the hands of Manuel Vieira, but since then little has been heard. If you find it, drink it. Best wines: anything you can find.

QUINTA DE PANCAS

Established 1973 Owners Soc. Agrícola Porto da Luz Production 20,000 cases Vineyard area 111 acres (45 ha)

This lovely old estate produces outstanding wines in two styles: classic, made from arinto and jampal (white) and tinta roriz and touriga nacional (red), and "new-wave," made from chardonnay and cabernet sauvignon. Best wines: Quinta de Pancas Cabernet Sauvignon, Touriga Nacional, Tinta Roriz.

QUINTA DA MURTA

Established 1995 Owner Cockburn Smithes Production 7,000 cases Vineyard area 37 acres (15 ha)

Winemaker Francisco Castelo Branco makes serious white wines here from arinto and a bit of esgana cão (sercial) and rabo de ovelha (rabigato). The wine is sold under the quinta name. Best wines: everything is reliable.

VR RIBATEJANO

The VR Ribatejano area includes within it Ribatejo/Tomar, site of a great convent–castle, an area once famous for its fairly hefty red wines but sadly no longer. Ribatejo/Almeirim has value-for-money everyday wines while Ribatejo/Chamusca is dominated by co-op wines. Almost half the DOC Ribatejo's wine comes from Ribatejo/Cartaxo, a source of good, everyday white and red wines. Ribatejo/Coruche has producers experimenting with a botrytized white made from fernão pires.

CASA CADAVAL

Established NA Owners Local shareholders Production 30,000 cases Vineyard area 173 acres (70 ha)

This is the Ribatejano area double-act of João Portugal Ramos and Rui Reguinga, making wines of international quality from pinot noir, cabernet sauvignon and trincadeira. Best wines: the entire range.

QUINTA GRANDE

Established NA Owners Local shareholders Production 1,400 cases Vineyard area NA

This is a small producer specializing in one major wine, also called Quinta Grande. It's made in the traditional way in stone lagares from trincadeira, periquita (joão de santarém/castelão frances) and grand noir, before spending some time in small casks of Portuguese oak. It ages with consummate grace. Best wine: Quinta Grande.

Setúbal & the South

VR TERRAS DO SADO

This region includes Palmela, in the north, which makes excellent reds from periquita and fresh, crisp whites from fernão pires. In the south, Setúbal still makes great classic sweet wine in the traditional way, fortified during fermentation (like port) and then allowed to macerate on its skins to give the classic muscat flavor.

JP VINHOS

Established **1922** ***Owners*** **M. and A. Avillez** ***Production*** **1,111,000 cases** ***Vineyard area*** **1,235 acres (500 ha)**

As well as "mainstream" styles of wine, this company makes Cova de Ursa, a barrel-fermented chardonnay, Quinta de Bacalhoa, a cabernet/merlot, and Má Partilha, a pure merlot. It also makes fortified moscatel de setúbal but, as most of the wines break many of the rules governing the DOC Setúbal, they tend to be labeled with the regional name of Terras do Sado. Best wines: JP Moscatel de Setúbal; JP Tinta Miúda; Má Partilha.

PEGOS CLAROS

Established **NA** ***Owners*** **Local shareholders** ***Production*** **36,000 cases** ***Vineyard area*** **198 acres (80 ha)**

The company's best wine is 100 percent periquita, aged for a year in oak and sold under the Pegos Claros label. Best wine: Pegos Claros Periquita.

VR ALENTEJANO

The wines made in this vast area of east central Portugal may be humble country wines or declassified (or unclassifiable) wines from the eight DOC regions within it. Alentejo/Portalegre has some white wine made mainly from fernão pires grapes. Alentejo/Borba offers red wines with fruit, freshness and a balanced acidity and decent whites. Alentejo/Redondo's reds have a pleasantly ripe, fruity freshness. Alentejo/Evora has good periquita and trincadeira reds and reasonable whites; watch this region for quality wines in the near future. Other DOCs in the area include Alentejo/Reguengos, Alentejo/Granja-Amareleja, Alentejo/Vidigueira and Alentejo/Moura.

ABOVE: These Portuguese wine bottles have woven "gloves" and handles making them considerably easier to pour from.

QUINTA DO CARMO

Established **1986** ***Owners*** **the Bastos family 50 percent, Domaines Baron de Rothschild 50 percent** ***Production*** **35,000 cases** ***Vineyard area*** **232 acres (94 ha)**

The Rothschilds bought a half share in this family estate in 1992 and installed new technology and French winemakers. The company grows alicante bouschet, aragonês (tempranillo), trincadeira and periquita (joão de santarém/ castelão frances) and ages the wine in oak. Best wine: Quinta do Carmo.

VR MADEIRA

Why Madeira needs a VR when it has an island-wide DOC is not clear—perhaps it makes it easier for maverick winemakers to do their own thing outside the DOC. Such winemakers are, for the moment, conspicuous by their absence.

ARTUR BARROS & SOUSA

Established **1881** ***Owners*** **the Sousa family** ***Production*** **500 cases** ***Vineyard area*** **11 acres (4.5 ha)**

This very small producer is turning out excellent wines, made in the *lagar* and aged by the *canteiro* method. The company has *reservas* aged for ten years or more and some wonderful *colheitas* dating back to the 1930s. Best wines: *colheitas*.

Regional Dozen

Blandy's (any 10-year-old), Madeira Wine Company
Carcavelos, Quinta do Barão
Catarina, JP Vinhos
Colheitas, Oliveira
Lancers, JP Vinhos
Madeira, Artur Barros & Sousa
Malmsey (10 or 15-year-old), Henriques & Henriques
Moscatel de Setúbal, José Maria de Fonseca
Moscatel de Setúbal, JP Vinhos
Pêra Manca, Fundação Eugénio Almeida
Silva Vinhos Old Vintage wines, Barbeito
Vale de Judia, Co-op Agrícola de Santa Isidro de Pegões

LEFT: The traditional craft of a cooper is essential in building and maintaining the oak barrels still preferred by many winemakers.

BARBEITO

Established **1946** ***Owners*** **Shareholders, the Barbeito family** ***Production*** **NA** ***Vineyard area*** **NA**

Now Japanese-owned and mostly serving the Japanese market, Barbeito nevertheless has several venerable wines in its cellars, including one allegedly from the 1795 vintage. More approachable and affordable is the splendid 1957, but all are good. Best wines: *colheitas*, 100-year-old malmsey.

Other producers include Co-op Agrícola de Santo Isidro de Pegões (Palmela), Cortes de Cima, Esperão, Soc. Agricola da Herdade dos Coelheiros (all VR Alentejano); Henriques & Henriques and Madeira Wine Company.

A sheltered site is one of the keys to successful grape-growing in England and Wales.

Other European

Winemaking Countries

Other European Winemaking Countries

ABOVE: *A striking blue cellar door—with lock and warning—in the Tokaj region.*

There is a great diversity in the climate, quality and types of wine produced in the countries included in this chapter. Although Britain imports a wide range of wines at all price levels from around the world, it does have its own modest wine industry which is supported by Her Majesty the Queen, who often serves English wine to visiting foreign dignitaries.

Central European winemakers are picking up the pieces after decades of communism had left them with collectivized vineyards and a dearth of the up-to-date equipment, hard currency and expertise that are required for successful wine production in today's world. But in the last decade or so, old identities and traditions of quality are being resurrected. Only Hungary has a great reputation, which is based upon the dessert wine tojaki (tokay), one of the world's greatest dessert wines. Slovenia deserves a better reputation than it has. And while Slovakia has declined as a wine producer, its entry into the European Union should see a big improvement in quality. The Czech Republic's vineyard area has also decreased in recent years, but the country may have a bright future.

In Eastern Europe, in the past attaining the necessities of life has understandably taken precedence over the production of fine wines. Financial support through joint ventures and the investment of foreign capital will be needed to bring the wine industry into the twenty-first century. Bulgaria has the longest history of export-friendly wines, and Moldova has at least as much potential. Romania's problem in the past has been lack of consistency. To date, the Ukraine and Russia have focused on local markets but they might yet prove to be sleeping giants.

Greece has had a long and distinguished winemaking history and has unique grape varieties found nowhere else in the world. Recent developments have shown that when modern winemaking and improvements in the vineyard are added to the Greek equation, the wines begin to look very attractive to consumers around the globe.

In Turkey, only 3 percent of its grape production is turned into wine—and not very good wine at that. Wine counts for little in Turkey; the locals seem to prefer their alcohol in the form of brandy. Cyprus appears to be one big missed opportunity as far as wine goes: it has a captive tourist market, but the wine isn't quite up to standard. Malta's wine production is small scale, but there are signs that more interesting wines are being made.

On the whole, the countries in this chapter have the potential to produce world-class wine, and they are, for the most part, well on their way. Only time will tell which ones will become the real successes.

OPPOSITE PAGE: *Winemaking and vineyards in parts of today's Greece look much as they would have a hundred years ago.*

BELOW: *Vineyards in the foothills near Tocal-Tokaj, Hungary's most well-known wine region.*

ENGLAND & WALES

ABOVE: *Pomp and ceremony in London. Although Her Majesty the Queen often serves English wines to visiting dignitaries, neither her government nor her subjects are as supportive.*

British Wine is the legal term for "made wine," that is, made in Britain from imported grape concentrate. Still sold in the UK, it is a source of much confusion on labels. A wine labeled English Wine must be made from fresh grapes grown in English vineyards.

The vineyard area in England and Wales was almost non-existent 50 years ago. Today it covers about 2,170 acres (878 ha) and there are now around 400 vineyards of which only 14 are more than 25 acres (10 ha).

Over the past 20 years or so, several wineries have proved that good-quality wine can be made from grapes grown in well-sited vineyards, despite the climate. Initially, all the efforts were with light, fresh, dry and medium-dry fruity white wines, which has become a definitive style. However, specialties such as late-harvest or lightly oaked white wines, unusual reds and traditional-method sparkling wines have enjoyed many accolades.

Fill ev'ry glass,
for wine inspires us,
And fires us
With courage, love and joy.

JOHN GAY (1685–1732),
The Beggar's Opera

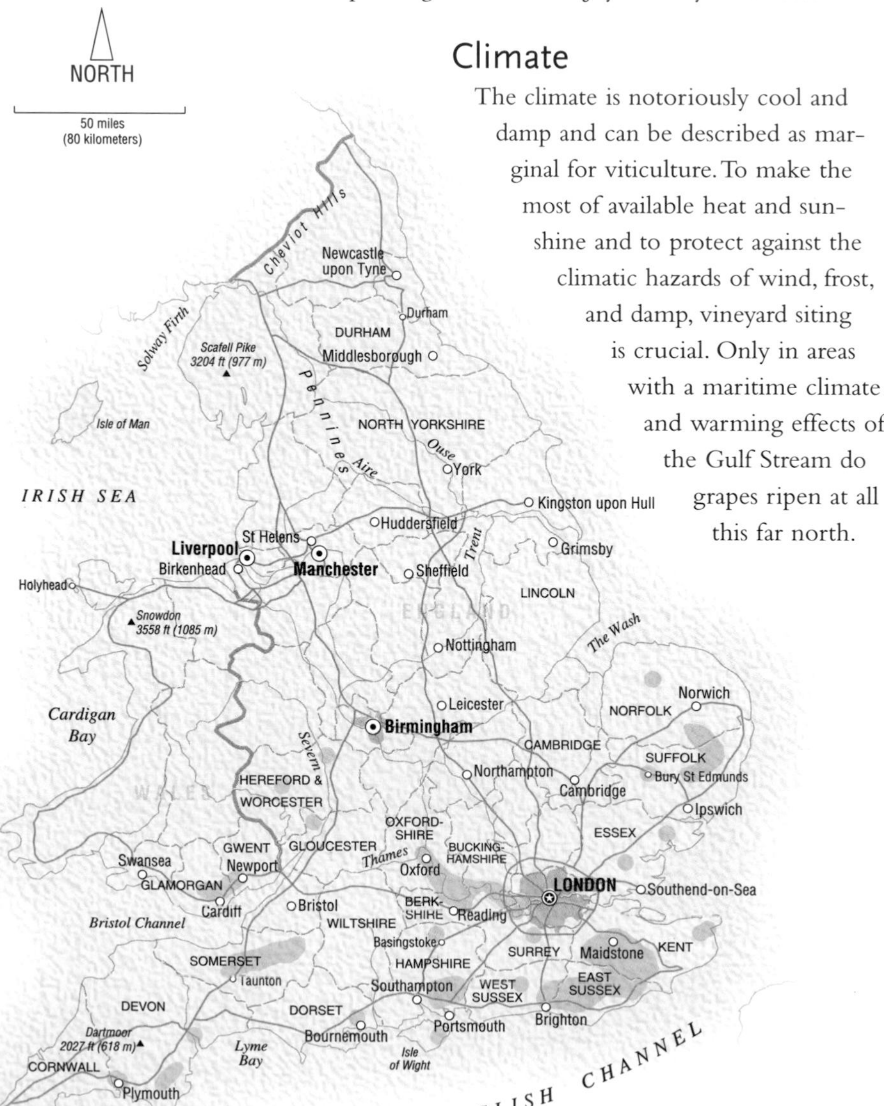

Climate

The climate is notoriously cool and damp and can be described as marginal for viticulture. To make the most of available heat and sunshine and to protect against the climatic hazards of wind, frost, and damp, vineyard siting is crucial. Only in areas with a maritime climate and warming effects of the Gulf Stream do grapes ripen at all this far north. However, the long growing season is ideal for flavor development in certain varieties. Production is erratic due to the variability of the weather.

Vines and wine laws

Most of the white varieties grown are of German origin, including müller-thurgau with 13 percent of total plantings, reichensteiner (12 percent), bacchus (10 percent), and schönburger (8 percent), with huxelrebe, ortega, ehrenfelser, faberrebe and siegerrebe among the others planted. The main non-Germanic white grape is the hybrid seyval, the third-most important variety with 11 percent of plantings. Madeleine angevine, a table grape, has 7 percent of plantings, while the only classic variety with plantings of any size is chardonnay with 4 percent, mainly for use in sparkling wines.

Most of the German crossings give floral or fruit flavors; some are quite leafy in character. White wines are light both in alcohol and flavor. Today, the dry and off-dry whites do better than medium styles. High acidity enables these wines to age well, and they often develop a better balance with one to four years of bottle age.

A few wineries have achieved success with good dessert wines from botrytis-affected grapes. These dessert wines tend to be low in alcohol with vibrant honey and fruit flavors and high acidity balancing the sweetness.

Pinot noir is the most planted red grape, with tiny amounts of merlot and cabernet sauvignon being the other classics. Red wines have been a struggle but there have been some successes. There are many dry and medium-dry rosés made, and the best are light and fresh with delicate strawberry fruit.

Good-quality traditional-method sparkling wines are made from base wine blends of German crossings, some also with seyval. Some producers have persevered with chardonnay and pinot noir and the resulting sparkling wines show tremendous quality. Other varieties are also proving good, such as auxerrois, pinot blanc, pinot meunier and gamay.

Regions

Vineyards are dispersed mainly south of a line from East Anglia, south of Birmingham, to south Wales. Many are sited not because they are in a particularly good place for growing vines, but because they are close to a tourist attraction, or simply on land owned by someone passionate about growing vines. The world's most northerly "commercial" vineyard is in Durham in northeast England, close to latitude 55°N.

About 60 percent of England's vineyards and most of the larger wineries are in the populous southeast. The counties of Kent, East Sussex and Surrey have been

LEFT: *Peter Hall among the vines at Breaky Bottom, Northtease, Sussex.*

the most successful—each has more than 250 acres (100 ha). The Thames Valley is the warmest vineyard region in the country. The counties of West Sussex and Hampshire are also important.

East Anglia has more than 250 acres (100 ha). The land is flat and fertile giving good yields but the region experiences strong winds. The counties in the Wessex region and the far southwestern counties of Devon and Cornwall have more than 250 acres (100 ha) among them. There are wide variations in climate with fierce westerly winds, so sites must be carefully chosen.

Moving north, the only significant counties are Gloucestershire, home to Three Choirs Vineyards, one of England's largest wineries, and Worcestershire. Wales has 57 acres (23 ha) split among 16 owners and four wineries.

Producers

Most producers sell only locally, from the farm gate and through local shops, pubs and restaurants. There is a steadily growing trend to extend facilities offered at vineyards to include other tourist-oriented attractions. This not only assists wine sales, but also provides much-needed extra revenue. A few producers have developed trade nationally and some export their product, but most UK retailers still do not stock English wines.

While some producers restrict themselves to estate wines, others include purchased grapes in their blends. As elsewhere, this is not always clear on the labels. Those producers mentioned below have had an important impact on the industry in England and Wales, and their wines are available beyond the cellar door. Equally important is Chapel Down Wines, the country's largest producer of English wines, using grapes from their own and others' vineyards.

DENBIES WINE ESTATE, SURREY

Established **1986** ***Owner*** **Denbies Wine Estate** ***Production*** **29,200 cases** ***Vineyard area*** **265 acres (108 ha)**

Denbies Wine Estate's biggest successes have been with the large-production and good-value Surrey Gold (a medium-dry blend) and a Special Late-Harvested white from a blend of Germanic varieties, including the late ripening optima and ortega. Pinot noir also does well, on its own and as a blend with dornfelder. Wines are from estate-grown grapes.

NYETIMBER VINEYARD, SUSSEX

Established **1990** ***Owners*** **Stuart and Sandy Moss** ***Production*** **4,200 cases** ***Vineyard area*** **40 acres (16 ha)**

Nyetimber is England's largest dedicated sparkling wine producer. The wines have at least three years on yeast in bottle and more aging before release. The complex Première Cuvée Blanc de Blancs is creamy, spicy, and beautifully balanced. The Classic Cuvée is equally stylish, but richer.

VALLEY VINEYARDS, BERKSHIRE

Established **1979** ***Owners*** **Jon Leighton and partners** ***Production*** **4,200 cases** ***Vineyard area*** **25 acres (10 ha) plus 5 acres (2 ha) leased in Surrey**

Valley's range includes Regatta, a fresh, aromatic dry white wine. The Heritage range (made from purchased grapes) includes one of England's consistently best oaked whites, Heritage Fumé, and a good-quality sparkling wine. The limited edition Clocktower wines include a fine sparkling white gamay, one of the country's top pinot noirs and a luscious dessert wine, labeled Botrytis.

Regional Best

Bearsted Vineyard Brut NV, Kent
Beenleigh Red (Sharpham Partnership), Devon
Breaky Bottom Seyval Brut, Sussex
Camel Valley Vineyard Seyval Dry, Cornwall
Davenport Vineyard Horsmonden Dry, Sussex
Hidden Springs Dark Fields Red, Sussex

BELOW: *A worker in the vineyard at Wootton, in Somerset.*

ABOVE: *Vertically trained vines, Znovín Znojmo, Moravia (Czech Republic).*

CENTRAL EUROPE

CZECH REPUBLIC

During 40 years of communist control, wine was produced here at the lowest common denominator level. Despite a Wine Act, which came into force in 1995, and the privatization of most wineries, the rate of change has been somewhat sluggish.

Notwithstanding a preponderance of poor product, some things are improving in the Czech Republic. The development and cloning of several new varieties that are more resistant to frost, fungi and diseases is one example. Another positive sign is the increase in foreign capital that has recently found its way into the country.

Wines and producers

The main growing regions are in Southern Moravia and the much smaller Bohemian region.

The traditional white grape varieties grown here are riesling, pinot gris, pinot blanc, gewürztraminer, sauvignon blanc, welsch-riesling, grüner veltliner, müller-thurgau, neuburger, sylvaner and Moravian muscat, along with a number of local grape crossings, such as aurelius (riesling crossed with neuburger) or palava (gewürztraminer with müller-thurgau). Chardonnay is becoming more predominant, making inroads into the Czech wine industry.

Reds include regional favorites such as modrý portugal, frankovka, svatovavřinecké, and the crosses of the latter two cultivars (andré and zweigeltrebe), not to mention cabernet sauvignon, which is not at its best here. Pinot noir, however, expresses itself surprisingly well, especially in the Bohemian region, its ideal *terroir.*

RIGHT: *Ruby red flashing has been used in the design of this Bohemian wine decanter from the late nineteenth century.*

SLOVAKIA

Slovakia "divorced" Czechoslovakia in 1993, having been an integral part of it for most of the twentieth century. It has much in common with its former other half: the same recent history, plantings of similar grape varieties, similar languages, and by and large the same economic conditions still prevail in the two countries. Prior to the "velvet revolution" in 1989, Slovakia had 74,000 acres (30,000 ha) under vine, while today it has 24,380 acres (9,687 ha) of registered vineyard planting—the country has ceased to be self-sufficient in the production of wine.

Wines and producers

The six growing regions of Slovakia are Lesser Carpathia, Southern Slovakia, Central Slovakia, Nitra, Eastern Slovakia and Tokaj. Tokaj straddles Slovakia and Hungary, however most of it is located in Hungary. Wine laws, which came into force in 1996, classify wines into the following: table wines, quality varietal wines, quality brand wines, quality blends, wines with special attributes, sparkling wines, aromatized wines and Tokaj wines.

Grape varieties planted are similar to those in the Czech Republic, with the addition of irsai oliver, leányka, lipovina (hárslevelű), furmint, bouviertraube, and local crossings, such as devín, dunaj and alibernet.

HUNGARY

Located close to the very center of Europe, Hungary has been subjected to a diversity of influences that have long shaped its wine production. Despite its checkered political history, viticulture thrived throughout the centuries, even under the communists—though quality suffered. However, between the mid-1980s and 1991 Hungary lost close to 75 percent of its wine exports, largely due to the collapse of the Soviet system. Widespread bankruptcy followed; some estimates put total vineyard losses at up to 25 percent. But privatization laws and the sale of vineyards and wineries enabled a much slimmed-down industry to survive. The search for quality is now the driving force behind production.

The wine areas are evenly distributed throughout the country, except to the east of the Tisza River, and show considerable geological diversity.

Climate

Hungary has a broadly temperate climate that varies from wet temperate in the west to continental in the east and Mediterranean in the south. Spring comes early, and the summers tend to be long and the winters short. In Tokaj-Hegyalja, autumnal sunshine and mists favor the formation of botrytis.

Vines and wines

The vineyard area is about 333,450 acres (135,000 ha), yielding a total annual production of 99 million gallons (375 million l), of which about 21 million gallons (80 million l) are exported. Hungary used to be mainly a producer of white wines, then red wine production began to increase in the 1960s, with new cabernet sauvignon and cabernet franc plantings, and in the late 1980s it increased rapidly. It is now over 30 percent of the total production, and is soon expected to overtake white wine production.

Rosé wine production has declined to a very small percentage of the total. Apart from tokaji and bikavér, which are traditional blends, Hungarian wines are generally sold under their varietal names or, occasionally, as blends bearing a proprietary name.

Of the grape varieties recognized in Hungary, 35 of them are white and 15 are red. They include the following, with Hungarian names appearing in brackets.

White: Rhine riesling (rajnairizling), Italian riesling (olaszrizling), sylvaner (zöld szilváni), müller-thurgau (rizlingszilváni), gewürztraminer (tramini), pinot gris (szürkebarát), pinot blanc (weissburgunder), chardonnay, sauvignon blanc, sémillon, chasselas, muscat ottonel (ottonel muskotály), yellow muscat (sárga muskotály) and grüner muscateller (zöld veltelini).

Red: Cabernet sauvignon, cabernet franc, merlot (médoc noir), pinot noir (nágyburgundi or blauburgunder), lemberger (kékfrankos), blauportugieser (kékoportó) and zweigelt.

The following are either native Hungarian grape varieties, or found almost exclusively in the region.

White: Furmint, ezerjó, hárslevelű, juhfark, kéknyelű, oremus, irsai olivér, leányka, király-leányka, csaba gyöngye, cserszegi fűszeres, cirfadli, kövidinka, kunleány and zefír.

Red: Kadarka.

Appellations and producers

There are currently 23 appellations in Hungary, the newest being Bortermohelyk, granted in mid-2000. State laws prescribe types and quality categories, compositional standards, production methods, yields, labeling conventions and levels of quality control. There is also a register of vineyards and wineries. Hungary's 23 appellations fall rather conveniently into six groups.

The Northeast includes Mátraalja, Bükkalja and Eger; the Northwest: Sopron, Pannonhalma Sokoróalja, Aszá-Neszmély, Mór, Eytek-Buda,and Somló; Lake Balaton: Badacsony, Balatonfüred-Csopak, Balatonfeld-videk, Dél-Balaton and Balatonmelléke; the Southwest: Szekszárd, Tolna, Mecsekalja, and Villány-Siklós; Central South: Hajós-Baja, Csongrád and Kiskunság; and Tokaj-Hegyalja.

Tokaj-Hegyalja

This region, declared a World Heritage site, produces Hungary's most famous wine, tokaji (or tokay, as it is known elsewhere). Today, Tokaj-Hegyalja has 12,350 acres (5,000 planted ha) under vine, of which 83 percent is owned by independent grape-growers. Out of more than a score of producers, ten foreign-owned joint-venture companies share about 10 percent of the appellation area. Hungarian producers hold the remaining area.

BELOW: *Selecting and making the best wines—just one of the vineyard worker's many tasks.*

ABOVE: *Rows of vines leading towards the winery buildings, Balascony region.*

BELOW: *Harvesting grapes below trellised vines, which provide some welcome shade.*

Tokaji is made from hárslevelű, furmint, sarga muskotály, and, occasionally, oremus. The first two are the base for the sweet aszú, on which the reputation of tokaji rests. Traditionally, this was made by picking botrytized grapes which, under the pressure of their own weight, slowly provided small quantities of a barely alcoholic syrup called Eszencia. The grapes were then mashed to a paste and added in hodfuls (*puttonyos*) of approximately 55 pounds (25 kg) to 36-gallon (136-l) casks of the one-year-old base wine to macerate. After racking, the resulting wine was matured in cask for three years or longer, then stored, then as now, in rock-hewn galleried cellars up to 600 years old. The sweetness of the resulting aszú wines was measured by the number of *puttonyos* added, aszú eszencia being the highest quality, followed by tokaji aszú. Some of the new producers have modified the traditional method, with excellent results.

Regional Dozen

- Balatonboglári Borgazdasági Rt, Chapel Hill Barrique Fermented Chardonnay
- Bock Pince, Villányi Cabernet Sauvignon
- Chateau Disnoko, Tokaji Aszu Ezsencia
- Gere Attila, Villányi Cabernet Sauvignon Barrique
- GIA Kft, Egri Barrique Chardonnay
- GIA Kft, Egri Cabernet Sauvignon
- Hilltop Neszmély Rt, Bin AK28 Sauvignon Blanc
- Hilltop Neszmély Rt, Riverview Kékfrankos
- Royal Tokaji Wine Company Kft, Nyulászó Vineyard, 5 puttonyos Aszú
- Szent Donatus Pincészet Kft, Balatonlellei Cabernet Sauvignon Reserve
- Szent Donatus Pincészet Kft, Lellei Oak Aged Chardonnay
- Tiffan's Bt, Cabernet Sauvignon/Cabernet Franc Grand Selection

SLOVENIA

With a vineyard area of around 58,000 acres (23,000 ha), the Slovenian wine industry is well managed and quality is assured: under Slovenian wine law only the best wines may be bottled in 75 cl (about 26 fl oz) bottles. These generally bear the seal of the PSVVS (Business Association for Viticulture and Wine Production), an organization that polices itself quite effectively.

Vines and wines

There are three wine areas in Slovenia, all of which press against the country's borders—the center of Slovenia produces no wine. The Littoral, or Primorska, region makes predominantly red wines; its climate is Mediterranean, though tempered by the nearness of the Alps. It has four subregions: the Brda hills in the north, which are a continuation of Friuli in Italy; Karst, tucked in behind Trieste; Vipava, further inland from Karst; and Koper, which occupies Slovenia's only stretch of coast. Barbera, refosco, cabernet sauvignon and merlot are responsible for most of the reds in this region, reds for which high acidity and high tannin are favored, in the Italian style. Pinot blanc and rebula (a local name for ribolla), picolit, malvaziji (malvasia), yellow muscat, chardonnay, pinot gris, furlaner tokaj (tocai friuliano) and others make the often very stylish whites.

The Drava Valley, or Podravje, is the other major region, and has a more continental climate, between them, these two regions produce some 85 percent of Slovenia's wine. Subregions here are Maribor, Sredjne (Central) Slovenske, Radgona-Kapela, Prekmurske, Ljutomer and Haloze. Wine styles vary according to whether regions border Styria in Austria, or Hungary where the hills are an extension of Styria. Here, light, clean, acidic wines are the norm; elsewhere, the wines are fatter and more flowery, and often sweeter. Ljutomer's best known wine is its Laski Rizling, which gave the region a bad name for decades. When made properly, however, it can be fresh, weighty and tasty. Other grapes grown in this region include gewürztraminer, pinot blanc, sauvignon blanc, riesling and šipon (probably an alias for Hungary's furmint), which makes a fiery, lively wine that deserves a wider audience.

The smallest region, the Sava Valley or Posavje, is divided into the subregions of Dolenjsko, Bela Krajina, Smarje and Bizeljsko. Summers are hot and autumns warm and sunny here; grapes include laski rizling, pinot blanc, sauvignon blanc and chardonnay for whites, and blaufränkisch, pinot noir, portugieser, gamay, kerner and

ABOVE: Hvar Island, pictured on the labels of the local winery Plenkovic Wines by Sv. Nadjela in Croatia.

zweigelt, as well as less familiar varieties such as rumeni plavec, seatlovrenka and zametovka for reds.

With an amenable climate and landscape, plus the enthusiasm of its winemakers, the future for wine in this small country looks very healthy.

CROATIA

War interrupted this once significant producer of wine with a thriving export market to Germany and Britain. However, since the cessation of hostilities there has again been a rapid rise in the country's wine production.

Of the two distinct growing regions in Croatia, the main one is Kontinentalna Hrvatska (Inland Croatia), which covers much of the eastern half of the country and incorporates seven districts. The other, Primorska Hrvatska (Coastal Croatia), has four districts, extends along the seaboard and includes all the country's islands.

The cooler and more fertile inland area produces mainly white wine (95 percent), especially from the dull laski rizling, or welschriesling, whereas 70 percent of coastal production is red wine. The inland region also produces fruity, straw-colored kutjevacka graševina from Kutjevo, some respectable gewürztraminer, pinot blanc, sauvignon blanc, johannisberg or Rhine riesling, and even muscat ottonel.

Interesting reds from the coast include wines from the plavac mali vine. Both dingač and postup from the Peljesac Peninsula are well regarded—the full international potential of these two wines, as well as wine from the Dalmatian sémillon grape, is yet to be fully explored.

BOSNIA AND HERZEGOVINA

Prior to the misery and upheaval of war, the vineyards in the south of the country covered 12,350 acres (5,000 ha) around coastal Mostar and Dubrovnik and farther inland. By 1997, declared production figures had halved to 1.4 million gallons (5.4 million l). Red wines have always been always less than persuasive, mainly due to the popularity of the unimpressive blatina grape, but white wines made from zilavka—one of no less than nine internationally recognized wine grapes starting with "z"—display its typical and welcome acidity. Both varieties are mainly used for popular Samotok rosé wines. Today, the future looks bright.

SERBIA AND MONTENEGRO

In line with the area's cultural leanings, most of Serbia's wine was in the past flavor-designed to suit Russian tastes. Only the three northern regions of Serbia, influenced by neighboring Hungary and Romania, enjoyed acceptance in the wider world.

The majority of vineyards follow the northerly course of the river Morava, from its source near Pristina in Kosovo to its confluence with the Danube, east of Belgrade. The southern regions concentrate on red wines, while the more northerly regions are planted primarily with white grapes. Viticultural practices are not modern, and are still mainly carried out through huge underfunded co-operatives.

Of Serbia's indigenous grapes, probably the finest is red prokupac, found everywhere south of the Danube valley. It is often used to lend a fruity taste to a blend with pinot noir or gamay. When used as a single variety, it is usually only lightly fermented to produce zupska ruzica rosé. A highly regarded white grape, smederevka, produces medium-sweet fruity wines and is grown in over 90 percent of the vineyards in the area around the town of Smederevo.

The Vojvodina region grows quite a number of mainly white grapes, and achieves some success with

ABOVE: *Southern Central Europe, where land is flatter, and the weather is drier and warmer.*

both traminers and merlots. Most of the remaining Serbian vineyards are planted with "European" varieties; some display very unusual taste and bouquet signatures.

In Montenegro, wine production is small, though three regions are defined. The traditional crmnicko crno wine from Lake Skadar is of the greatest significance. It is now called crnogorski vranac, and is made using the vranac grape.

MACEDONIA

"Close to ideal" would accurately describe Macedonia's grape-growing potential, in terms of landscape and climate, especially for red wines (which make up 80 percent of Macedonia's output). Whites also have potential. Unfortunately, the country's potential is likely to remain unrealized until there is sufficient political stability to make outside investment attractive.

The 75,000 acres (30,000 ha) of vineyards here are said to produce more than 27 million gallons (100 million l) of wine—few outside the country have ever tasted these. The vast majority (about 90 percent) of red wine is produced from indigenous vranac and kratosija varieties—the two, blended, produce kratosija, the country's most popular wine. Some cabernet sauvignon, merlot and grenache are also available.

The most common white varieties are laski riesling and local smederevka, often blended; small quantities of chardonnay and sauvignon blanc are also planted. Belan, from white grenache, is also popular—the zilavka variety, however, probably has greater potential.

RIGHT: *A fifth century* BC *black glaze kylix—drinking cup—from Attica.*

EASTERN EUROPE

ROMANIA

"The next Chile" or "the new Burgundy"? During the 1990s, these and other epithets were attached to the Romanian wine industry. However, storage and aging are low grade, and consistency is a problem—pinot noir can be full and savory and merlot can be grassy and herbaceous. Of the six main wine regions, only three export regularly and are of a quality that can be monitored.

Wine regions

In Muntenia, Dealul Mare is by far the major area, which is also large in terms of red wine production. At Tohani (linked to the excellent Ceptura winery), grapes are macerated below 82°F (28°C) to ensure clean fruit flavors. The Urlati winery specializes in well-extracted merlot and cabernet sauvignon. Petroade, a subdistrict, produces a golden, honeyed sweet wine from the tamîosa grape.

In the Dobrudja region, vineyards of the Murfatlar area produce rich, luscious white and late harvest wines. The Murfatlar winery majors in a range of floral versions of pinot gris and riesling italico.

Transylvania is a white wine area, with the best from the Tarnave Valley. Styles tend toward the Germanic, with a flinty acidity in the better examples. In the south, Apold de Sus produces a lively *méthode traditionelle* sparkling wine.

Northern Moldavia is predominantly white wine country, with the area producing the famous Cotnari wine. The Odobesti area makes a good grapefruity, spicy feteăscă albă variety. Cotesti produces an attractive minty-flavored merlot.

The Drăgăsăni vineyards, in the Oltenia region, produce sauvignon blanc and some late harvest wines. Also in Oltenia, the Drincea area produces adequate examples of merlot and pinot noir.

Banat is a region that includes flat areas where table wines—Teremia and Recăs—are produced and hillier sites where white wines are made from the flourishing local creătă grape.

BULGARIA

Bulgarian wine tastes different these days. Where once the country produced dark, rich oaked cabernets, now they are fresher, younger and more fruity. Which you prefer depends on your personal inclination, but the reasons for the change matter.

The de-monopolization of the Bulgarian wine industry in the 1990s led to increased production, but not necessarily to better quality and variety. Investment in local wineries has been immense, particularly by the biggest export company, Domaine Boyar. It received US $30.5 million from the European Bank for Reconstruction and Development in 1999. Wine companies throughout Bulgaria now intend to invest in the vineyards, although issues of land ownership are still being resolved.

My Friends should drink a dozen of claret on my Tomb.

John Keats (1795–1821), letter to Benjamin Bailey, August 14, 1819

Wine regions

NORTHERN REGION

Seven of the 28 Controliran regions are here. The area produces well-balanced, structured reds, particularly at the Russe winery. It produces elegant cabernet-based reds and clean chardonnays. Nearby Svishtov produces red wines only, from the excellent Gorchivka vineyard. Farther south is Suhindol, which specializes in cabernet sauvignon and produces one of the best wines in Bulgaria—Czar Simeon.

EASTERN REGION

This is a major white wine area. The pick of the local wineries is Pomorie, making floral, viscous chardonnays. Schumen has plain varietals that are much better than the branded Premium Oak wines, and Targovischte makes a promising sauvignon blanc.

SOUTHERN REGION

Perushtitza is excellent for local grape varieties such as the rich mulberry-like mavrud and the lively, appley misket. At Iambol high-tech equipment is used to produce fruity, clean cabernet sauvignons. Oriachovitza vineyards produce some of the best cabernet sauvignon and merlot in Bulgaria, for the Stara Zagora winery

SUB-BALKAN REGION

Sliven is one of the biggest wineries in Bulgaria. It mostly turns out clean, well-made red wine (cabernet sauvignon and merlot). Slaviantzi produces some of the country's best chardonnays.

SOUTHWESTERN REGION

The tasty, spicy melnik grape is a local variety that has potential, particularly at Damianitza. This winery is deep in the south of the country. The quality sometimes varies due to the heat, but some vineyards in the region are planted at an altitude of up to 3,300 feet (1,000 m), which gives them the potential for greater longevity and improved concentration.

MOLDOVA

Many ex-USSR countries around southeastern Europe and the Black Sea warrant the description "have potential," but none more so than Moldova. Its flat lands and temperatures coupled with annual rainfall provide almost ideal (by European standards) growing conditions.

Of all ex-USSR countries, Moldova is most similar to Hungary, Romania and Bulgaria, in that it has quantities of "European" varieties already established—cabernet sauvignon, merlot and pinot noir for reds, and chardonnay, aligoté, sauvignon blanc, pinot gris, muscat ottonel, riesling and gewürztraminer for whites.

Additionally, Moldova has probably the best selection of quality grapes indigenous to countries around the Black Sea—saperavi, black sereskia, and the teinturier variety gamay fréaux, plus the ubiquitous rkatsiteli and feteăscă. Six winemaking districts are delineated: Pucar, Balti, Ialoveni, Stauceni, Cricova, Romanesti and Hincesti.

UKRAINE

Like most countries around the Black Sea, wine production in this area actually stretches back into pre-history. After early tribes created settlements and developed viticulture, continued warfare and tribal movement conspired against systematic growth, and it

Regional Dozen

Damianitza Melnik
Iambol Cabernet Sauvignon Royal Reserve
Perushtitza Pulden Cabernet Sauvignon Mavrud
Pomorie Barrel Fermented Chardonnay
Russe Cabernet Sauvignon, Yantra Valley
Russe Reserve Chardonnay
Schumen Chardonnay & Aliogoté
Slaviantzi Barrel Fermented Chardonnay
Sliven Young Vatted Cabernet Sauvignon
Stara Zagora Boyar Cabernet Sauvignon Special Reserve, Oriochovitza
Suhindol Cabernet Sauvignon
Svishtov Cabernet Sauvignon Special Reserve, Gorchivka

BELOW: These merlot vines have been extensively hand pruned and thinned.

Regional Dozen

Ceptura Merlot
Ceptura Unoaked Feteasca Neagra
Judvei Gewürttraminer
Jidvei Muscat Ottonel
Jidvei Sauvignon BlancUrlati Cabernet Sauvignon
Murfatlar Barrel Fermented Chardonnay
Murfatlar Pinot Gris
Murfatlar Sauvignon Blanc
Tohani Pinot Noir
Tohani Sangiovese
Urlati Cabernet Sauvignon
Urlati Merlot

ABOVE RIGHT: The harvest awaiting processing.

was not until modern times that wine and the vine became significant in the agricultural life of the region.

Vines and wines

The major growing areas of Crimea, Odessa, Kherson, Nikolayev, Transcarpathia and Zaporozh'ye account for 90 percent of the vineyard area. Around 60 viticultural regions have been specified, and over 50 wine varieties have now been approved.

Traditional varieties such as rkatsiteli and saperavi, and European varieties such as cabernet sauvignon, gewürztraminer, and aligoté are grown, as well as bastardo and sercial for fortified production, and a raft of indigenous and Magaratch-developed varieties. Products are often varietally named—cabernet kolchuginskoie, aligoté zolotaia blaka, rkatsiteli inkermanskoie, for example. One of the best blends is alushta, which uses cabernet sauvignon, morrastel and saperavi. Sparkling wine production is still important. The most commonly used varieties are pinot noir, riesling, fetiaska and aligoté. Around 50 million bottles a year of sparkling wine are produced, originating from Kiev, Odessa, Kharkov, Sevastopol, Artemovska and Sudak.

BELOW: A sizeable Eastern European vineyard with new spring growth.

RUSSIA

"Russia" is a surprisingly unspecific name, sometimes being used to refer to the USSR or the Soviet Union, the previous association of communist states, and even now inaccurately applied to its successor, the CIS or Confederation of Independent States (12 states out of the previous 16). All states and regions within the CIS produce wine, and have varying degrees of self-determination, but Moscow's influence can still be quickly felt if political aspirations become too pronounced. Russia includes Belorussia (also called Belarus or White Russia), which is sometimes quoted separately in wine statistics—the OIV, for example, lists Belorussia with 5 million gallons (19 million l) in 1997—but in fact Belorussia is merely a processor of transported grapes, having no vineyards of its own.

The five significant vineyard areas in Russia (in descending order of importance) are: Dagestan, along the Caspian Sea coast from Derbent to Makhachkala; the Krasnodar region, which embraces the Kuban valley from inland Maykop and Krasnodar itself to Novorossiysk on the Black Sea; Stavropol, an inland area northwest of Pyatigorsk, from the valley of the Kuban to the valley of the Terek; the Don valley, around Rostov to the Ukraine border; and Chechnya-Ingushetia, where there are likely to be few remaining vineyards, due to constant recent warfare. These regions represent 95 percent of Russian production, the balance split between Kabardino-Balkaria and Ossetia, further north.

Vines and wines

In the Krasnodar region, the Abrau district is known for dry riesling, cabernet and Soviet sparkling wine (*champanskoje*). Up the coast at At Anapa (Krasnodar), riesling is the specialty, while down the coast at Gelendzhik, aligoté features. The Stavropol region offers both dry riesling and sylvaner alongside muscatel sweet wines. The Rostov (Don valley) region also offers sweet wines, the best known being Ruby of the Don, while the Caspian coast around Makhachkala (Dagestan) is almost entirely sweet wine country.

ABOVE: *The private cellar storing the estate owners' selection.*

SOUTHERN EUROPE

GREECE

Wine has been an integral part of Greek culture for over 3,000 years, partly because of Greece's geographic location has made it a natural crossroads for many different cultures. Throughout the ages, the fortunes of Greek wine have followed the country's often tumultuous history, closely mirroring its rises and falls, its successes and failures.

Greece is mountainous; most of its quality vineyards are found between sea level and up to an altitude of 2,800 feet (850 m). With a tremendous diversity of soil types and a generally maritime climate, much of the country is still blessed with an almost ideal climate for grape farming, as hail, fog and snow are rare.

Vines and wines

An annual wine production of 103 million gallons (389.3 million l) makes Greece the sixth-largest wine producer in Europe. A wide spectrum—encompassing all known classes and styles—is produced: it breaks down to roughly 70 percent white, 5 percent rosé, 3 percent sweet, and 22 percent red. Sparkling wines are the most underdeveloped category.

Greece's native grapes provide the raw material for some fascinating wines. Approximately 300 indigenous varieties have been identified, but currently only about 30 of these are used commercially.

Important white grapes here are assyrtiko, athiri, roditis, savatiano, vilana, robola, debina and muscat. Saved from the brink of extinction are the elegant lagorthi and the semiaromatic malagousia, while the blanc de gris moscofilero, with its grapey fruit and natural high acidity, is exclusive to Mantinia. Recently, varieties such as chardonnay, sauvignon blanc, viognier and sémillon have been introduced—these grapes are used as blends or for producing varietal wines.

The finest red grapes are aghiorghitiko and xynomavro, which are principally found in the two top red wine appellations, Neméa and Náoussa. Others include kotsifali and mandelaria. The first cabernet sauvignon plantings, at Averoff and Domaine Carras, date from 1963. More recently, cabernet franc and merlot were added; the most sighted new plantings now are syrah.

Greece used the French model for its appellation system. Thus it has 28 Appellations of Origin, two Appellations by Tradition, and more than 70 *vin de pays* (topikos oenos).

LEFT: *An English glass encased in colored cut crystal dates from the period 1900-1930.*

ABOVE: *A typical white-washed home in Greece.*

MAINLAND GREECE

Drama

Drama was resurrected as a wine region in the 1980s, largely due to two leading estates: those of Nikos Lazaridis and brother, Kosta Lazaridis.

Nikos Lazaridis has a postmodernist winery that would not look out of place in Napa: it has a spacious cellar, a large art gallery, plus several tasting rooms and halls for lectures and seminars. Ktima Kosta Lazaridis produces wines that are soft, with a fruit-driven style. The hugely successful fruity Amethystos white is the mainstay. The best red is Cava Amethystos.

Epanomi-Thessaloniki

Domaine Geravassiliou produces an impressive range of fruit-driven white wines. The cult-status wine named for the estate is a blend of steely assyrtiko and the white peach and mint taste of malagousia.

Goumenissa

J. Boutari Wineries S. A. has planted xynomavro and negoska varieties. They make a crisp, light- to medium-weight red wine; the best is Ktima Filiria.

Náoussa

The wines of Náoussa have a long history, although vintages vary enormously in quality. This was the first region to be granted appellation status in 1971. This is the home of the finest long-lasting xynomavro wines. Notable producers include Ktima Kir-Yanni, J. Boutari & Son, Ktima Karydas, Dalamaras and Melitzanis.

Amyndeo

This is a very cool region, which consistently produces wine high in malic acid. Aromatic whites are made from roditis, chardonnay, sauvignon blanc, gewürztraminer and blanc de noir; excellent rosés and reds are produced from xynomavro. White wines are more consistent; rosés and reds are good only in the top vintages. Sparkling wines, both *cuve close* and *méthode classique*, are improving. Producers of note in this region include the refurbished Amyndeo Co-Op and Grippa Wines.

Velvendos

This is xynomavro country for reds and rosés. Obscure local red varieties, such as moscomavro, are also grown. A significant producer here is Ktima Voyatzis.

Krania

Ktima Katsaros features organically farmed vineyards. A blend of cabernet sauvignon and merlot—a velvety smooth, cask-aged, smoky red—was their only wine until a 1999 *barrique* chardonnay appeared.

Zitsa

This cool plateau is almost all given over to debina, producing still and fizzy light-bodied crisp wines, noted for their white pepper on the nose and green apple freshness on the palate. Zitsa Co-Op is a significant producer in the area.

Attica

Attica is home to large *négociants* as well as a growing number of quality wine estates including Evharis, Kokotos and Strofilia. With the growth of Athens, vine-planted land has shrunk to half its original 30,000 acres (12,000 ha). D. Kourtakis is a large merchant here.

How simple and frugal a thing is happiness: a glass of wine, a roast chestnut, a wretched little brazier, the sound of the sea . . . All that is required to feel that here and now is happiness is a simple, frugal heart.

NIKOS KAZANTZAKIS (1885–1957), *Zorba the Greek*

THE PELOPONNESE

This region produces almost 29 percent of all Greek wine, and is the home of three quality appellations: Neméa, Pátras and Mantinia.

Neméa

Neméa is the region of the largest quality red wine appellation. It is planted exclusively with the richly colored, smooth tannin aghiorghitiko. Neméa has a varied terrain, with two distinct vineyards: Neméa valley floor and high Neméa. Gaia Wines, in Koutsi, is notable for its affable Notios range, dark and smoky Gaia Estate and hand-crafted Ritinitis Nobilis.

Pátras

This major port is home to light, crisp, dry wines and to Mavrodaphne dessert wines. In Vassilikos, Antonopoulos is a quality producer making a range of delicate whites, including Adoli Ghis.

Mantinia

This 2,130 feet (650 m) plateau in the center of the Peloponnese is home to the grapey blanc de gris variety

Regional Dozen

Antonopoulos Adoli Ghis
Domaine Gerovassiliou Malagousia
Domaine Tselepos Nemea
Gaia Wines Gaia Estate
Ktima-Kir Yianni Estate Akakies Xinomavro
Kostas Lazaridis Amethystos Cava
Mercouri Mercouri Estate
Oenoforos Asprolithi
Nikos Lazaridis Magico Vouno
Roxanne Matsa Estate Laoutari
Samos Co-Op Samos Nectar
Sigalas Mezzo

moscofilero, whose aroma has the spice of a light gewürztraminer and a (dry) muscat. Natural acidity is high. The rose petal muscat aroma is more apparent in ripe vintages. Tselepos Vineyards & Winery is a fine estate, producing a more concentrated Mantinia than any other on the market, with a fruit-derived "smokiness" on the nose.

THE AEGEAN ISLANDS

Limnos

Limnos is a volcanic island producing sweet, sundried and fortified muscat of alexandria wines. It features two growers: the Co-Op, which specializes in the sweeter versions, and Honas-Kyathos, which concentrates on bone-dry wines. Samos is home to the finest muscat from the muscat blanc, a petit grain. Top label Nectar, made with sundried grapes, is not fortified, and has peachy muscat flavors, followed by a very long finish.

Santorini

Santorini is a freakish volcanic island that has top quality vineyards planted with assyrtiko, the finest Greek white grape. There are two appellations here: the dry Santorini and the luscious, sweet, cask-aged Vinsanto. Gaia Wines' Santorini winery is located in a magnificent stone building, a former tomato paste canning factory, and produces the trendsetting, bone-dry Thalassitis. Sigalas is the recently constructed winery, in Kampos, near Oia, of mathematics teacher Paris Sigalas. His cask-fermented Vareli Oia is one the finest wooded Greek white wines. He is also producing very good Mezzo, a less sweet wine than Vinsanto.

Crete

There is a new momentum in this wine-producing island these days. Ktima Lyrarakis, inland from Heraklio at Alagni, focuses on near-extinct white varieties such as daphni and plyto, and produces the wonderful Syrah-Kotsifali. Creta Olympias produces quality Vilana-sourced dry whites. At Ziros, in Sitia, organic producer Ekonomou makes perhaps the finest Vilana in Crete, plus the quirky, pale-colored Liatiko "red."

THE IONIAN SEA ISLANDS

Cephalonia

Cephalonia is a verdant island whose best vineyards are to be found on limestone soils. Ungrafted high robola, with its trademark lemon and flint *terroir*, is unique in the Greek vineyard. Gentilini, in Minies, is a pioneer boutique winery. Vineyards and winemaking duties are overseen by Gabrielle Beamish, from Britain, who is producing a fruity and delicate Gentilini Classico and a new Syrah. Metaxa, in Mavrata, is another forward-thinking producer, and offers the rare white Zakynthino.

The best wine here is Robola, with a modernist peachy aroma and a flinty aftertaste.

ABOVE: *Bush vineyards on the white soils of Cyprus.*

MALTA

With entry into the European Union, winemaking practices on Malta have improved, and local winemakers are gaining international recognition. The Maltese islands consist of Malta, which is the largest island at 150 square miles (390 sq km), plus the much smaller islands of Gozo and Comino. This trio of tiny islands—62 miles (100 km) south of Sicily and 180 miles (290 km) north of Tripoli, in Libya—was host to one of the oldest civilizations in the Mediterranean, dating back to around 5,000 BC. Now Malta is an island haven for winter-weary travelers and home to some world-class, high quality, unique wines.

Vines and wines

Locally grown white table grapes ghirghentina and gennarua and red gellewza were in the past blended with grapes imported from Italy, with no indication of this on the label. Local authorities are now cracking down on this, and there is an increased focus on new

BELOW: *Vineyards in the Peloponnese, where almost a third of Greece's wines are produced.*

ABOVE: *Fields near Zeebug in the center of the island of Malta.*

plantings of grapes including chardonnay, cabernet sauvignon, pinot bianco, trebbiano and syrah.

Winemaking practices are improving, and local winemakers are gaining recognition on the international wine scene. For the local market, among the best-known wines are Emmanuel Delicata's Paradise Bay Red Wine and Gellewza Frizzante. Delicata and Marsovin together control about 90 percent of the local wine market.

RIGHT: *Rams head ryton dipping cup, late fourth century BC.*

Meridiana, an enterprise created by visionary Maltese wine expert Mark Miceli-Farrugia, is producing international-style wines, including barrel-fermented chardonnays, cabernet sauvignons and merlots. Successful smaller producers include the Dacoutros Group, Farmers Wine Co-Op, Hal-Caprat, Master Wine and Three Barrels.

TURKEY

If Noah did indeed plant a vineyard on the slopes of Mount Ararat, then Turkey could reasonably claim to be the cradle of viticulture. Today, Turkey has the fifth-largest area of vines in the world, but its predominantly Muslim lifestyle dictates that the majority of grapes are used for nonalcoholic products. Of the 3 percent fermented into wine, at least a quarter is distilled into local brandy or the aniseed-flavored spirit, raki. White wines consumed domestically tend to be heavily oxidized and over-aged, while reds are relatively alcoholic and oversulfured. Export-quality wines are produced only fitfully and are seldom widely available.

Appellations and producers

Turkey's seven official wine districts are Thrace-Marmara, the Aegean Coast, the Mediterranean Coast, the Black Sea Coast, Ankara, Central Anatolia and Eastern Anatolia. Thrace-Marmara produces 40 percent of Turkey's wines and, unusually, it focuses on clairette, sémillon, riesling, gamay and pinot noir. The searingly hot Aegean Coast yields European varieties such as sémillon, grenache and carignan. On the Mediterranean Coast, tourism is more important than winemaking. Both the Black Sea Coast and the Ankara region have considerable potential for grape growing. Vineyards in Central Anatolia are located at up to

4,000 feet (1,250 m), and suffer huge temperature extremes. Eastern Anatolia, bordering Georgia and Armenia, yields only 374 gallons per acre (3500 l per ha). The nationalized wine industry is administered by Tekel. Private producers are few, with the best known and most reputable being Kavaklidere, Doluca and Diren in Anatolia. The charmingly named hosbag (Thrace gamay) and buzbag (local varieties from Eastern Anatolia) are valued domestically; the most consistent wines come from Doluca. A quality wine scheme has been introduced, but it seems to be limited to state-owned products.

CYPRUS

Cypriot winemakers have produced few outstanding wines, despite the fact that they have been making wine for around 4,000 years. The earliest archaeological evidence of viticulture here dates to the second millennium BC. The wine trade flourished, undeterred by repeated invasions, until the Turks invaded the island in 1571 and imposed restrictions on alcohol. When the British took control in 1878, the situation began to improve. However, by the interwar years, as Europe was resuming full-scale production, Cypriot winemaking had entered a decline. Recent EU membership bodes well for a complete turnaround.

Vines and wines

The principal grape-growing areas in Cyprus lie on the southeastern plain and the lower slopes of the Troodos Mountains, up to 4,265 feet (1,300 m). The irrigated plains are superfertile and capable of awe-inspiring tonnages, although these are normally sold as table grapes. There is potential for quality wine production at higher altitudes.

Nearly three-quarters of Cypriot vineyards contain mavro (the Greek word for "black"), one of the world's least impressive grape varieties. White xinisteri is the next most widely planted variety—it is undistinguished and sensitive to overripeness, but can produce a lightly fragrant wine. Both palomino and the ancient malvasia are frequently used to improve xinisteri's performance.

Appellations and producers

Six viticultural regions have been created in Cyprus: Pitsilia (the highest), with its subregion Madhari; Troodos North; Marathasa; Commandaria; Troodos South, with subregions Afames and Laona; and Troodos West, with its subregions Ambelitis, Vounitis Panayias and Laona Kathhikas. Most of the island's produce is vinified by one of the four large companies based in Limassol (KEO, ETKO, SODA, and LOEL) all co-operatives or quasi-co-operatives. There are also a few boutique-style wineries.

Production methods are improving, though transportation methods in particular leave a lot to be desired. Trade restrictions are yet another problem, as Cypriot agricultural authorities retain a legislative stranglehold on wine production, not least through extraordinary vine importation controls.

LEFT: The front doors of a winery in Crete, an island whose wine is improving.

Island treasure

Commandaria, one of the world's oldest sundried or raisinated wines, is a Cypriot specialty. The Greek poet Hesiod (circa 800 BC) recommended this procedure for drying the grapes: "Show them to the sun ten days and nights, then cover them over for five, and on the sixth day draw off into vessels the gifts of joyful Dionysus." The word Commandaria derives from the Castle of Kolossi, built as the Grande Commanderie of the Knights of St John of Jerusalem in the twelfth century. The lands surrounding the castle were the primary source of Nama, which gradually became known as Vin de la Commanderie, or Commandaria. Today, despite legislation defining the permitted growing area and production method, the quality and quantity of Commandaria has declined.

By law, Commandaria must spend a minimum of two years in wood; in practice it may undergo a three-tier *solera* aging procedure. Before bottling, it is examined and approved, whereupon it will be sold in wine shops for a very small sum. Watch for quality and prices to rise with the modernization of the industry.

BELOW: These young vines in Cyprus are staked, and will soon be wired as well.

Harvesting grapes at the Bouchard Finalyson vineyards in Overberg.

South Africa

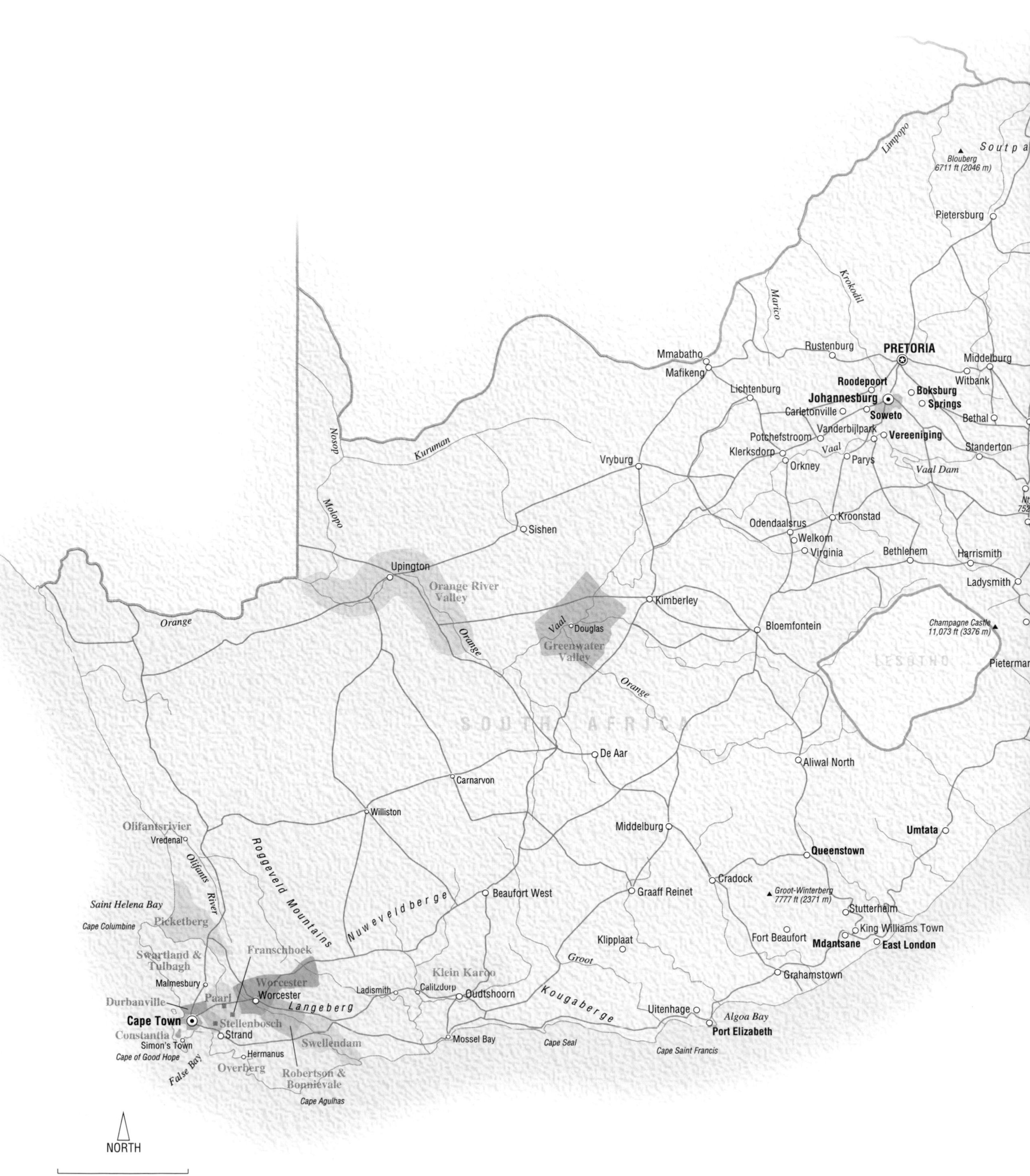

PRETORIA
Johannesburg
Soweto
Roodepoort
Boksburg
Springs
Vereeniging
Carletonville
Vanderbijlpark
Potchefstroom
Klerksdorp
Orkney
Parys
Vaal
Vaal Dam
Rustenburg
Mmabatho
Mafikeng
Lichtenburg
Middelburg
Witbank
Bethal
Standerton
Pietersburg
Blouberg
6711 ft (2046 m)
Limpopo
Krokodil
Marico
Vryburg
Kuruman
Nosop
Molopo
Sishen
Upington
Orange River Valley
Orange
Kimberley
Douglas
Greenwater Valley
Bloemfontein
Odendaalsrus
Welkom
Virginia
Kroonstad
Bethlehem
Harrismith
Ladysmith
Champagne Castle
11,073 ft (3376 m)
LESOTHO
SOUTH AFRICA
De Aar
Aliwal North
Carnarvon
Williston
Olifantsrivier
Vredenal
Olifants River
Roggeveld Mountains
Nuweveldberge
Beaufort West
Graaff Reinet
Middelburg
Cradock
Queenstown
Umtata
Groot-Winterberg
7777 ft (2371 m)
Stutterheim
King Williams Town
Mdantsane
East London
Fort Beaufort
Klipplaat
Groot
Grahamstown
Saint Helena Bay
Cape Columbine
Piketberg
Swartland & Tulbagh
Franschhoek
Malmesbury
Durbanville
Paarl
Worcester
Klein Karoo
Ladismith
Calitzdorp
Oudtshoorn
Langeberg
Kougaberge
Uitenhage
Algoa Bay
Port Elizabeth
Cape Town
Stellenbosch
Constantia
Strand
Simon's Town
Cape of Good Hope
Hermanus
False Bay
Overberg
Swellendam
Robertson & Bonnievale
Cape Agulhas
Mossel Bay
Cape Seal
Cape Saint Francis
NORTH
50 miles
(80 kilometers)

South Africa

MICHAEL FRIDJHON

The birth of the wine industry and the formal white settlement of the Cape went hand-in-hand in the mid-seventeenth century. Table Bay had been chosen by the Dutch East India Company as a convenient location to re-supply its trading ships on the long sea route between Europe and the East.

The Cape's first commander was Johan Van Riebeeck, a former ship's doctor. He and his expedition anchored at the foot of Table Mountain in April 1652. It is possible that Van Riebeeck brought grape seeds or even cuttings with him. Certainly, from the moment of his arrival he wrote with some enthusiasm about the agricultural potential of the Cape and urged the Company's Directors, the Lords Seventeen, to procure young trees and vine cuttings for him. The motivation for this request was pragmatic, fitting in with the original purpose of the settlement. Wine was a common enough beverage in the maritime world: it improved the ship's drinking water, stale after being transported in casks for several months; it had known antiseptic properties, useful in cases of gastro-intestinal illness; and it was held to be valuable in the treatment of scurvy.

Wines were customarily loaded in Amsterdam. The minimum amount, as stipulated by Company regulations, was sufficient to provide each crew member with a weekly ration. Much of what was available in the Dutch market at the time, at least that within the Company's procurement budget, turned to vinegar before it reached the equator. Van Riebeeck's halfway station was always destined to have a viticultural dimension, even though no one in his original party had any direct experience of growing grapes or winemaking.

The first successful consignment of vine cuttings reached the Cape in July 1655. Source material is believed to have been supplied from France, Germany, Bohemia and Spain. Muscat and muscadel types were probably included in the parcel. It was from these vines that Cape wine was first produced. On February 2, 1659, Van Riebeeck's logbook records both the quantity—4 gallons (15 l)—and the varietal (muscadel). Despite a resounding silence as to its quality, the Commander seems to have been sufficiently inspired to seek out additional land for vineyards. Thus began the wine industry in South Africa.

In the following centuries the industry's fortunes, especially in terms of quality, waxed and waned.

ABOVE: *Harvesting sauvignon grapes in the Klein Karoo region of South Africa.*

BELOW: *Agricultural land in West Cape Province.*

The KWV

Founded in 1918, the "Co-operative Wine Growers' Association of South Africa" came to be known by its Afrikaans initials, KWV. From the outset, this ultimately powerful organization set about establishing a growers' cartel. Its stated purpose was to regulate the sale of wine and brandy so as to ensure an adequate return for its members, who, in turn, pledged that they would not sell their produce below the price determined by their directors. Within a year the organization was converted to a company. Its success, from a grower's perspective, was immediate and gratifying—the floor price for wine almost doubled.

In its first few years the KWV gained considerable ground. However, when the post-war boom ended and demand and wine prices both dropped, some of the members opposed the regulations and others operated where possible beyond their ambit. By 1922 the company was converted back to a co-operative but found itself without the power to discipline its members.

Clearly, statutory powers were needed, so in 1924 Parliament passed a Bill "to provide for the control and management of the wine and spirit industry." This was the first of the laws and amendments (others followed in 1928, 1940, 1946, 1957 and 1970) that entrenched the KWV and eventually enabled it to control every element of South Africa's wine and spirit industry.

Over time the KWV came to determine the minimum prices for all grape products—first distilling wine, then so-called "good wine" and, finally, even grapes destined for juice concentrate. Since it was a buyer of last resort it obtained the right to fix the total tonnage of a particular property. (This regulation was never applied to enhance quality, since these production quotas permitted yields that were sometimes as high as 20 tons per acre/50 tonnes per ha.) The quota system also allowed the KWV to determine where, and by whom, vines could be planted. The result was that vineyards could be established only in traditional wine-producing areas, with the occasional exception, such as the Orange River irrigation scheme.

The KWV may have protected the country's growers from the full impact of market forces, but it did so at a vast cost to the country's fine-wine business. Minimum-price guarantees and a system that focused on yield, in potential alcohol, permitted the survival of the least efficient and undermined the initiative of the more adventurous. The imposition of trade sanctions against South Africa, mainly in the 1980s, postponed full recognition of how costly the KWV's regime had been. As the rest of the wine world came to understand—and meet—the quality expectations of the international market, South Africa languished in a vacuum. In the meantime, the KWV's wealth grew as it used price-fixing mechanisms to provide cash flow for its expansion. In 1996, when KWV announced its intention of converting from a co-operative to a company (with a view to distributing wealth acquired over nearly eight decades to its members), the Minister of Agriculture opposed the scheme of arrangement in the Cape High Court. He argued that KWV's assets were public in character and in part had been acquired as a result of its statutory authority. The KWV denied this, but a year later reached a settlement from which was born the South African Wine Industry Trust (largely funded by contributions from KWV). By agreement, KWV was then relieved of its statutory role.

ABOVE: Chardonnay in a lab beaker, awaiting analysis.

RIGHT: White grape vines growing on solid supports, South Africa. Today previously disadvantaged workers are emerging as a new group of grape farmers and wine-makers.

LEFT: A harvest of sauvignon grapes at the Bouchard Finlayson wineyards in the Overberg region.

Great estates gained international recognition, then succumbed to neglect, to be revived at a later stage. In the twentieth century, political and economic isolation was a major factor in wine quality, as was the stranglehold of the Co-operative Wine Growers' Association of South Africa.

Finally free from political strangleholds, the 1990s brought an incredible transformation to the Cape wine industry. Unfortunately, many producers so eager to reach the international marketplace sent inferior quality, mass-produced wines. Realizing their mistakes, producers are working diligently to showcase only top quality products. Winemakers are traveling more, local wine consumption is growing, and exports to the US alone were reported to be up 75 percent in 2002.

> *He makes grass grow for the cattle, and plants for man to cultivate—bringing forth food from the earth: wine that gladdens the heart of man.*
>
> OLD TESTAMENT, THE BOOK OF PSALMS

Pinotage has cleaned up its act, but really does not have the physical capability of producing world class wine. Shiraz, on the other hand, is poised to become the signature cultivar of South Africa, either on its own, or as a "Cape Blend" with cabernet sauvignon. Paul Pontallier and Michel Rolland, "Flying Winemakers" from Bordeaux, are working to upgrade Bordeaux blends, and the quality of sauvignon blanc is rapidly improving. Also notable is a spectacular rise in quality and availability of *méthode champenoise (méthode cap classique)* sparkling wines, as well as a lively renaissance of classic dessert wines.

Things are cleaning up in the vineyards as well. Over 95 percent of the Cape's wine grape farmers are members of the new Integrated Production of Wine (IPW), a group of research bodies, wine growers, wine producers, government and suppliers of chemicals and fertilizers. The IPW is looking to produce grapes profitably but in an environmentally sensitive way. Black empowerment is taking place with the support of the South African Wine Industry Trust (SAWIT). Previously disadvantaged workers are emerging in the new rainbow nation as wine farmers and winemakers. Cape wine farmers are establishing joint ventures and training them in viticulture and vinification. Communities living in winemaking regions are also benefiting from new ventures including New Beginnings, Freedom Road, Fair Valley, Helderkruin, Thandi, Tukulu, Uitzicht and Winds of Change; proceeds from the sales of these labels are used to improve local quality of life. KWV and Distell, formed in 2001 by the merging of Stellenbosch Farmers' Winery (SFW) and Distillers Corporation, are significantly invested in the success of these ventures. Distell is also a founding member of WIETA (South African Wine Industry Ethical Trade Association), and oversees living conditions on wine farms.

BELOW: On the road to Delheim Wines, Stellenbosch. Delheim were one of the three founder members of the Stellenbosch Wine Route, which has done so much to develop the wine industry in South Africa.

ABOVE: Outbuildings at Steenberg Winery, one of the Cape's oldest farms. A rigorous replanting program is showing gratifying results.

Constantia

The Constantia region, indisputably the cradle of wine culture in South Africa, was until recently on the brink of extinction. By the 1970s there was just one surviving winery, Groot Constantia, and it depended on generous government handouts to survive. With a substantially cooler climate than Stellenbosch and Paarl, and a virus endemic to the Cape vineyards, grapes ripened unevenly and irregularly. Evidence of Groot Constantia's financial troubles discouraged the neighboring landowners from seeking redemption through grape growing. The turnaround in fortunes for the region, when it came, was swift, and the results have been so gratifying that even in this relatively short time it seems impossible to visualize the depressed conditions from which the Constantia phoenix arose.

Regional Dozen

QUALITY WINES

Agusta Wines Chardonnay
Boekenhoutskloof Syrah
Boschendal Shiraz
Eikenhof Cabernet Sauvignon
La Motte Millennium
L'Ormarins Cabernet Sauvignon

BEST VALUE WINES

Dieu Donne Chardonnay
Eikenhof Bush Vine Sémillon
Franschhoek Vineyards Pinotage
Mont Rochelle Blanc de Blanc
L'Ormarins Blanc Fumé
Von Ortloff Chardonnay

BUITENVERWACHTING

Established **1796** ***Owners*** **C. and R. Müller, Trustees, Buitenverwachting Farm Trust** ***Production*** **60,000 cases** ***Vineyard area*** **250 acres (100 ha)**

Buitenverwachting has played a key role in the restoration of the Constantia region and the renewed reputation of Cape wines as a whole. Where possible the vineyard at Buitenverwachting focuses on organic farming methods. Some of its white wines are consistent front rankers, notably the rhine riesling, sauvignon blanc and chardonnay. Several vintages of the proprietary red, a blend of cabernet franc and cabernet sauvignon sold under the brand name Christine, have come to enjoy almost cult status; an earlier merlot vintage won the Diners Club Winemaker of the Year Award for the previous cellarmaster, Jean Daneel.

KLEIN CONSTANTIA ESTATE

Established **1823** ***Owners*** **Duggie and Lowell Jooste** ***Production*** **45,000 cases** ***Vineyard area*** **184 acres (74.5 ha)**

Duggie Jooste purchased a run-down and derelict Klein Constantia and immediately began planting vineyards and planning a winery. The first vintage, the 1986, reminded the Cape of the extraordinary potential of Constantia: the sauvignon blanc won the trophy for the best white wine at the national young wine show; a year later the 1986 cabernet sauvignon carried off the trophy for the best wine on show. Klein Constantia has subsequently acquired a fine reputation for its Vin de Constance, a muscat de frontignan dessert wine—it is sweet, but not cloying, a beautifully structured botrytis-free late-harvested beverage. It has done more than any other wine to bring prominence to the Constantia area.

Other significant producers in the Constantia region include Constantia Uitsig and Steenberg Vineyards.

Paarl

There has been long-standing rivalry between Paarl and Stellenbosch for supremacy in the South African wine industry, although Paarl is characterized by medium-sized cellars producing good, rather than extraordinary, wine. Still, the appearance of Glen Carlou and Veenwouden, and the revolution wrought by Charles Back at Fairview—the most innovative of Paarl wineries—all suggest that an era of boutique wines of the highest quality is imminent.

Situated farther inland than Stellenbosch, Paarl is warmer and its wines are more robust. Bounded by Wellington (north), Franschhoek (east), and Stellenbosch (south), Paarl is too spread out to offer the same homogeneity of style that characterizes Constantia. The Agter-Paarl vineyards near Wellington, for example, are much warmer than the sites adjacent to Stellenbosch.

BACKSBERG ESTATE

Established **1916** ***Owner*** **Michael Back** ***Production*** **95,000 cases** ***Vineyard area*** **408 acres (165 ha)**

The late Sydney Back worked to establish the integrity of site-specific viticulture in South Africa. He led the replanting revolution that followed the importation of quality chardonnay, sauvignon blanc and merlot in the 1980s. He also set up social responsibility programs—long before they were fashionable—and Back's son Michael has maintained this policy. Backsberg's vineyard workers produce and manage their own separate brand, sold under the Freedom Road label.

CENTER: The entrance sign for Nederburg Winery, famed for its annual auction, the most important event on the yearly wine calendar.

NEDERBURG WINES

Established **1791** ***Owner*** **Distell** ***Production*** **800,000 cases** ***Vineyard area*** **1,730 acres (700 ha)**

Nederburg is South Africa's largest premium winery. The first of the modern high-volume deluxe brands, this leviathan came to dominate the fine-wine industry in the 1960s and 1970s. For three decades, the cellarmaster of that era, Gunther Brözel, produced everything from German-style whites to cabernet and cabernet blends that rival even the best wines of modern, virus-free vineyards. Among his many innovations was a wine called Edelkeur, a botrytized chenin blanc still traded only at the annual Nederburg Auction. Even the auction is a reflection of Brözel's drive. Launched in 1975, it showcases the most complete array of South Africa's best wines.

Nederburg Auction

Open to retail and restaurant wine buyers from all over the world, the Nederburg Auction has for close to 30 years provided international attention for the Cape's best wines while raising money for charity. In 1975, winemaker Louis Martini of Napa Valley, California, observed the auction and left with the idea of setting up something similar back home. Always eager to assist his colleagues, organizer and industry spokesman Bennie Howard sent his auction manager to Napa to help oversee the first Napa Valley Wine Auction.

ABOVE: Rows of vines in a valley sheltered by a rugged mountain range.

PLAISIR DE MERLE, SIMONSBERG

Established **1964** ***Owners*** **Distell** ***Production*** **35,000 cases** ***Vineyard area*** **988 acres (400 ha)**

Close to Backsberg on the Franschhoek side of Paarl, Plaisir functions mainly as a supply farm to Nederburg. Replanting programs revealed specific vineyard blocks capable of producing super-premium wines. Accordingly, a small winery was established near the homestead to process this fruit. Paul Pontallier, Director of Château Margaux and consultant to the group, took a more hands-on role for the first few vintages and these reds show great concentration, with a richness and texture typical of the best Paarl wines.

VILLIERA WINE

Established **1928** ***Owners*** **Grier family** ***Production*** **100,000 cases** ***Vineyard area*** **741 acres (300 ha)**

Villiera is one of the country's most popular good-value, high-quality operations. Cellar-master Jeff Grier won the Diners Club Winemaker of the Year award and the Chenin Challenge in successive years. Notwithstanding show successes, pricing is surprisingly modest. The *méthode champenoise* bubbly, frequently the country's top-rated *cap classique,* sells for little more than the big-brand charmat wines produced in industrial cellars.

Other notable producers in the Paarl wine region include Glen Carlou Vineyards, Fairview, Veenwouden and Welgemeend Estate.

Regional Dozen

QUALITY WINES

Backsberg Klein Babylonstoren Cabernet Sauvignon-Merlot
Fairview Solitude Shiraz
Glen Carlou Chardonnay
Nederburg Edelkeur Noble Harvest
Plaisir de Merle Cabernet Sauvignon
Villiera Blanc Fume

BEST VALUE WINES

Backsberg Freedom Road Sauvignon Blanc
Landskroon Port
Nederburg Cabernet Sauvignon
Seidelberg Sauvignon Blanc
Villiera Chenin Blanc

ABOVE: *The potential of cooler-climate vineyards, such as these in Franschhoek, was largely unappreciated until fairly recent times.*

Franschhoek

Settled by French Huguenots before the end of the seventeenth century, this region has only recently become a meaningful player on the Cape wine scene. The most obvious reason for this is that its cooler climate placed it at a disadvantage for most of the twentieth century when the industry was driven by the KWV's minimum wine price arrangements. Since payments were made at that time on the basis of liters of wine at 10 percent alcohol, the areas that flourished were those with enough water and sunshine to stretch the crop and pump up the sugars. As viticulture became less lucrative, farmers turned to orchards for an income. Tucked away in a valley, the town itself was also relatively inaccessible.

The 1980s saw vast changes, many brought about by exactly those elements that had retarded its development. The discovery that quality wine production was not dependent on the KWV's purchase criteria focused attention on cooler regions. Franschhoek's unspoilt charm attracted wealthy investors for whom the extra distance from Cape Town was a positive advantage. The growers banded together under the banner of the Vignerons of Franschhoek. The village soon developed a more overt Huguenot/Cape Dutch/French feel as the old farm names were revived; translated Franschhoek means "French corner."

The success of the marketing efforts of small growers in this area led to an enormous increase in land prices and a proliferation of regional wines. Some of the producers who initially delivered their grapes to the co-operative for vinification have now built their own cellars; other long-established properties have replaced orchards with vineyards and today Franschhoek boasts some of the country's best-known wines.

Franschhoek is also the gourmet capital of wine country. It has an annual cheese festival. The town has become a popular choice for family day trips from Constantia, especially on weekends.

Regional Dozen

QUALITY WINES

Agusta Wines Chardonnay
Boekenhoutskloof Syrah
Boschendal Shiraz
Eikenhof Cabernet Sauvignon
La Motte Millennium
L'Ormarins Cabernet Sauvignon

BEST VALUE WINES

Dieu Donne Chardonnay
Eikenhof Bush Vine Sémillon
Franschhoek Vineyards Pinotage
Mont Rochelle Blanc de Blanc
L'Ormarins Blanc Fumé
Von Ortloff Chardonnay

BOSCHENDAL, GROOT DRAKENSTEIN

Established **1976** ***Owner*** **Anglo American Corporation (Amfarms)**
Production **205,000 cases** ***Vineyard area*** **1,235 acres (500 ha)**

Located near the boundaries of Paarl and Stellenbosch, Boschendal came to prominence in the early 1980s through the sale of South Africa's first blanc de noir, which had immediate appeal for a wide segment of the market. The cellar is now better known for its white wines, most of which are respectable, rather than exceptional examples of a standard range of varietal and blended wines. Initially classified as an estate, its commercial success made the purchase of non-estate grapes almost inevitable. While most of its vineyards are situated within the area, it now buys fruit from growers throughout the Coastal Region.

LA MOTTE ESTATE

Established **1695** ***Owner*** **Hanneli Koegelenberg (née Rupert)**
Production **15,000 cases** **Vineyard area 257 acres (104 ha)**

The estate makes some very good reds, of which the shiraz and the médoc blend (sold as Millennium) are consistently the best examples. Both of the old Rupert family properties have been beautifully restored, and both vinify and bottle their wines on the estate. The other property is L'Ormarins Estate.

Other significant producers in the Franschhoek region include Bellingham, Boekenhoutskloof and La Bri.

RIGHT: *The grand Manor House, Boschendal Estate, near Franschhoek's boundaries with Paarl and Stellenbosch.*

Stellenbosch

Some 30 miles (50 km) northeast of Cape Town, Stellenbosch boasts several properties identified in land grants made in the last two decades of the seventeenth century. While few boast three centuries of viticulture, several have been associated with quality winemaking for much of this time.

Known as the "Bordeaux" of South Africa, the area is divided into four sub-wards, of which Simonsberg has emerged as the frontrunner (appellation status is pending). Each of the subregions experiences a distinctly different climate due to maritime influences or to the location of ridges, cliffs, or valleys. Stellenbosch soils also vary considerably, and within a very small area there can be several different soil types. Almost all are acidic and it is now standard vineyard practice to add a great deal of lime at the time of replanting. Uneven ripening of the grapes has its origins as much in geology as in canopy management and viticultural practices.

There are now some 80 wineries in the Stellenbosch region. Ten years ago the number was roughly half. Given the flux and excitement, it is easy to understand why the area is regarded as the showcase of Cape wine. Some of the big brands of yesteryear, although falling behind, still produce creditable wine; the newcomers must work twice as hard simply to get noticed. Long-established contract growers suddenly decide to build their own cellars and make new wines from old plantings. Investors from other industries acquire run-down properties and breathe new life into them. In this sense Stellenbosch lies at the real heart of new-era South African wine.

DELHEIM WINES, SIMONSBERG

Established **1930** ***Owners*** **H. O. Hoheisen and M. H. Sperling** ***Production*** **66,000 cases** ***Vineyard area*** **371 acres (150 ha)**

Spatz Sperling was as happy to win an award for the worst-taste wine label in the industry as he was to take home a gold medal at the national wine show. Recent improvements, mainly in red-wine production, have encouraged Sperling to draw a more marked distinction between the popular and prestige sides of his business. Using separate vineyards across the valley at Klapmutskop, he aims to establish the Vera Cruz estate for his premium wines, retaining the Delheim name for the tourist trade.

DISTELL

Established **2001** ***Owners*** **Merger of Distillers Corporation and Stellenbosch Farmers' Winery** ***Vineyard area*** **3,706 acres (1500 ha) company owned farms**

This is the leading producer of fine wines and spirits in South Africa; it has a 40 percent share of South Africa's premium and super-premium wine markets. Distell is supported by an international team of winemakers; a sophisticated nursery; involvement in IPW (Integrated Production of Wine), a system for improving vineyard conditions; and is founding member of WIETA (South

Regional Dozen

QUALITY WINES

Engelbrecht-Els Ernie Els
Grangehurst Pinotage
Kanonkop Pinotage
Kevin Arnold Nadine Shiraz
Stellenzicht Syrah
Rustenberg Peter Barlow

BEST VALUE WINES

Fleur du Cap Noble Late Harvest
J. C. Le Roux Pongracz Method Cap Classique Brut nv
Ken Forrester Sauvignon Blanc
Neetlingshoff Lord Neethling Cabernet Sauvignon
Simonsig Method Cap Classique Brut nv
Simunye Sauvignon Blanc

CENTER: *The always enticing process of withdrawing the cork from the bottle.*

BELOW: *Newly planted vineyard, Stellenbosch region. The area is regarded as the "Bordeaux" of South Africa and the showcase of Cape wine.*

ABOVE: *Rows of vines in a valley sheltered by a rugged mountain range.*

African Wine Industry Ethical Trade Association). Distell brands include Fleur du Cap, Nederburg, Plaisir de Merle and Tukulu, a new empowerment project giving black taverners, wine farm workers and their community ownership of the premier Papkuilsfontein farm in Darling.

NEIL ELLIS WINES, JONKERSHOEK VALLEY

Established **1990** ***Owners*** **Neil Ellis Trust, Oude Nektar, London Stone (Pty) Ltd** ***Production*** **35,000 cases** ***Vineyard area*** **237 acres (96 ha), plus 74 acres (30 ha) elsewhere**

A relative newcomer, Neil Ellis is a site-specific négociant-winemaker operation. Ellis ran an itinerant winemaking set-up until he met up with Hans Peter Schröder. The latter had recently acquired the Oude Nektar Estate, with its somewhat run-down vineyards and cellar. A partnership has been established that has changed the rankings of Cape producers.

Ellis' wines now dominate the awards. His Reserve reds (mostly from the Oude Nektar vineyards) represent pretty much the acme of current Stellenbosch achievement, while his regular range is almost as impressive. Most of the reds are made from Stellenbosch fruit, but

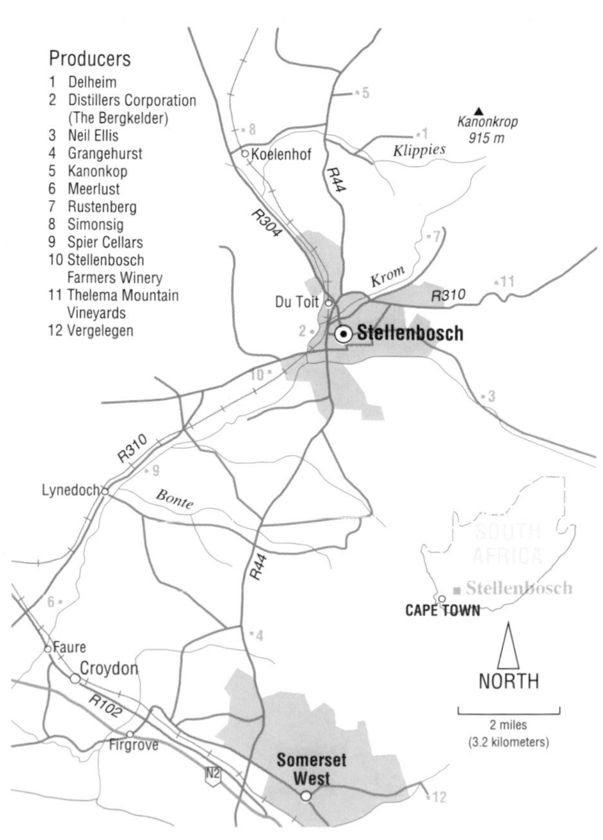

there are white wines from Elgin and a sauvignon blanc from Groenekloof on the West Coast, near Darling.

KANONKOP ESTATE

Established 1910 **Owners** J. and P. Krige **Production** 30,000 cases **Vineyard area** 346 acres (140 ha)

Almost alone, Kanonkop Estate established pinotage as a varietal worthy of international repute; it is also very much one of the country's putative "first growths." In the mid-twentieth century bush-vine vineyards were established with planting material from the original pinot noir–cinsault crossing. From its first commercial bottlings, the 1973 vintage, Kanonkop was clearly a leading red-wine site with a particular potential for dense, almost Rhône-like pinotage. However, it was only in the late 1980s that winemaker Beyers Truter invested the varietal with the kind of vinification and wood aging needed to bring out the fruit, concentration and complexity of which the grape is clearly capable. Successive vintages of show-stopping quality—especially among the cuvées reserved for the Cape Winemakers Guild annual auction—have produced an international market for this wine and for the varietal.

Kanonkop's reputation does not rest solely on the quality of its Guild Pinotage. The regular cuvée is often as impressive and its other reds, notably the cabernet and the Paul Sauer Fleur (a cabernet blend), sell well in the super-premium segment of the market.

SIMONSIG ESTATE

Established 1953 **Owners** Malan family **Production** 160,000 cases **Vineyard area** 667 acres (270 ha)

Simonsig Estate was the first South African cellar to make a bottle-fermented sparkling wine, and it has been in the avant-garde of most of the country's vineyard and cellar developments. When times were tough they offered house brands and second labels. They elected to operate as a wine estate, using the certification system—with its promise of site-specific viticulture. They participated in every high-profile selling opportunity, from the annual Nederburg Auction to the Cape Winemakers Guild sale. The breadth of their current range has enabled them to fill every niche in the spectrum.

ABOVE: Stellenbosch cabernet sauvignon: Jordan 1993 and the boutique Grangehurst.

THELEMA MOUNTAIN VINEYARDS

Established 1983 **Owners** McLean Family Trust and G. Webb **Production** 25,000 cases **Vineyard area** 124 acres (50 ha)

A comparative newcomer on the wine scene, Thelema has swiftly eclipsed most of its competitors. Modern vineyard preparation, proper and consistent viticultural practices, and inspired winemaking have all combined to produce this cutting-edge brand. A decade after the release of its first vintage, Thelema had won every award of significance in the country.

Some other producers of note in the region include Grangehurst, Helderberg-Stellenbosch; Meerlust Estate, Faure-Stellenbosch; Rustenberg Wines; Simunye; Spier Cellars; Vergelegen, Helderberg; and Warwick.

BELOW: Neil Ellis produces an impressive range of quality red wines from these vineyards in the Jonkershoek Valley, Stellenbosch.

ABOVE: *Many of the older wineries have artifacts, such as these beautifully carved barrels, dating from earlier times.*

Robertson–Bonnievale

The Robertson–Bonnievale region, less than two hours' drive from Cape Town, is an area in transition. Some of South Africa's best chardonnays are produced here; their quality is attributed to limestone in the ridge similar to that found in Burgundian soils. The success of chardonnay producers and other newly successful producers has encouraged bulk-grape farmers to look at producing and selling their own wines. Given the extensive replanting programs undertaken by the leading producers in recent years, it is fair to assume that both product profile and brand leaders will change dramatically.

The region was traditionally a brandy and fortified wine zone, a result both of its climate and the economics of the wine industry. The semi-desert inland areas lie beyond a cordon of mountains that shields them from much of the rainfall of the coastal region. Irrigation water from the Breede and Hex rivers has turned the region into a market garden: much of the country's best fruit is produced in these fertile valleys.

Regional Dozen

QUALITY WINES

- De Wetshof Chardonnay
- Graham Beck Method Cap Classique Brut nv
- Graham Beck The Ridge Shiraz
- Springfield Chardonnay Methode Ancien
- Weltevrede Oude Weltevreden Chardonnay
- Zandvliet Kalkveld Shiraz

BEST VALUE WINES

- Astonvale Chardonnay (Zandvliet Estate)
- De Wetshof Estate Mine d'Or Riesling
- Long Mountain Gecko Ridge Chardonnay
- Nuy Muscadel
- Weltevrede Chardonnay
- Weltevrede Sauvignon Blanc

GRAHAM BECK WINES, ROBERTSON

Established **1983** ***Owner*** **Graham Beck** ***Production*** **150,000 cases** ***Vineyard area*** **432 acres (175 ha)**

Graham Beck's Robertson operation showcases the best of the new-generation wines in the region. Initially dedicated to *cap classique (méthode champenoise)* production, it slowly widened its range to offer red and white wines in several categories. A shiraz—marketed as The Ridge Shiraz has already collected several awards.

But for all its recent successes with reds, the operation is still strongly identified with bubblies. There are several cuvées, including an experimental sparkling pinotage inspired by the sparkling shiraz of Australian producers. The more standard fizz is still oak-fermented, with even the bottom-of-the-range assured of two years on lees. The winery at Robertson also produces one of the Cape's best and most popular muscadels.

WELTEVREDE ESTATE, ROBERTSON–BONNIEVALE

Established **1926** ***Owner*** **Lourens Jonker** ***Production*** **33,000 cases** ***Vineyard area*** **250 acres (100 ha)**

Like most other properties in the region, this estate once focused solely on white and fortified wines. Recent plantings of cabernet sauvignon and merlot indicate a change in direction. Good chardonnay, concentrated rieslings, and an array of fortified muscats comprise the better wines in Weltevrede Estate's range.

DE WETSHOF ESTATE, ROBERTSON

Established **1947** ***Owner*** **Danie De Wet** ***Production*** **35,000 cases** ***Vineyard area*** **371 acres (150 ha)**

In the early 1970s, most of the cellar's wines were sold in bulk. Today the cellar is the undisputed success story of the region. De Wetshof Estate's best wines are generally held to be chardonnays, which are offered in a range of styles from unoaked to wood-fermented and barrel-aged. Surprisingly, the estate also produces a couple of very fine rieslings. One is marketed as Mine d'Or, with mosel-like acidity masking the sugar, while the other is a botrytized noble late-harvest.

Some other producers of note in the region include Springfield Estate and Zandvliet Estate.

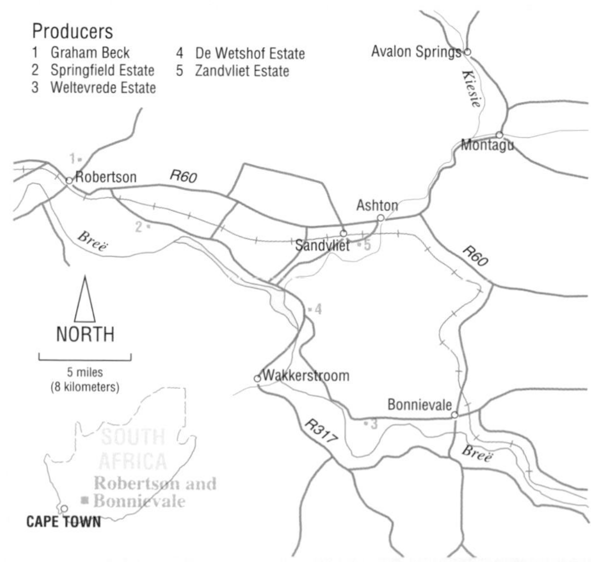

Other South African Regions

DURBANVILLE

Among the scattered appellations outside the established premium wine areas are several of the Cape's best producers. Durbanville used to be home to many growers before being overtaken by urban sprawl. There is a resurgence of interest in production, on a boutique scale.

Meerendal has long been associated with one of the country's best-known shiraz wines, and as early as the 1970s produced good pinotage. Altydgedacht, a long-established estate, was for years the only cellar in the Cape to offer a barbera. Cabernet sauvignon and chardonnay have done well more recently.

DURBANVILLE HILLS

Established **1998** ***Owners*** **Distillers Corp (7 farms)** ***Production*** **Not yet available** ***Vineyard area*** **Grapes from the 7 owner farms**

Probably the most important development in the area has been the Durbanville Hills cellar, which crushes grapes from several growers as well as many of the established producers. The winery will breathe life into the region and will help to ensure that Durbanville fruit retains its appellation, instead of vanishing into a "Coastal Region" blend. Early releases show fine chardonnay and sauvignon blanc, with impressive reds waiting in the wings.

SWARTLAND AND TULBAGH

This traditional West Coast region is also seeing something of a boom: five years ago a few co-operatives and one estate represented all the productive capacity. Now, winemakers from elsewhere are discovering the virtues of this area's relatively cool-climate fruit. New wineries have sprung up, and replanting programs are replacing non-premium varietals with merlot and sauvignon blanc.

TWEE JONGE GEZELLEN ESTATE, TULBAGH

Established **1710** ***Owners*** **Krone family** ***Production*** **40,000 cases** ***Vineyard area*** **677 acres (274 ha)**

Tulbagh is one of the country's most beautiful and least spoilt Cape Dutch villages. In the 1960s and 1970s the appellation was considered one of the best sources of white grapes in the country. This estate's premium brand, a 50/50 blend of pinot noir and chardonnay, which is made without preservatives, sells under the Krone Borealis label.

LEFT: Rocky ground makes cultivation difficult at Twee Jonge Gezellen Estate, Tulbagh.

BELOW: The Red Hills area, near Calitzdorp, in Klein Karoo, is home to several of the Cape's best port cellars.

KLEIN

The town of Calitzdorp has come to be known as the port capital of South Africa. The scene of the country's annual port festival, Calitzdorp is home to several of the Cape's best port cellars, including Axe Hill, Boplaas and Die Krans.

HAMILTON RUSSELL VINEYARDS, HERMANUS

Established **1976** ***Owner*** **Anthony Hamilton Russell** ***Production*** **15,000 cases** ***Vineyard area*** **158 acres (64 ha)**

Hamilton Russell recognized the importance of a slow and prolonged ripening season on fruit quality. He was one of the first chardonnay and pinot producers in the Cape. Now, over two decades later, while other cellars are often seen outperforming the Hamilton Russell wines, those who seek more restrained qualities still regard them as classics.

Other producers include Allesverloren Estate, Spice Route Wine Company, Beaumont Wines, Paul Cluver Estate and Goedvertrouw Estate.

Regional Dozen

QUALITY WINES

Bouchard Finlayson Pinot Noir
Deetlefs Method Cap Classique Brut nv
De Toren Fusion V
Hamilton Russell Pinot Noir
Rupert & Rothschild Baron Edmund
Slanghoek Hanepoot Jerepiko

BEST VALUE WINES

Beaumont Chenin Blanc
Brampton Chardonnay
Drakensig Cabernet Sauvignon
Graham Beck Sauvignon Blanc
Spice Route Syrah
Twee Jonge Gezllen Krone Borealis Method Cap Classique Brut nv

Tending the vines at Petersons Wines in the Hunter Valley, New South Wales.

Australia

ABOVE: An outside tasting area at Leasingham in the Clare Valley, South Australia.

Australia

Although wine has been made in Australia since shortly after the first European settlers arrived with the First Fleet in 1788, the culture of table-wine drinking is a relatively recent phenomenon. Large-scale wine production did not begin in earnest until the late 1960s. Perhaps because of its short history, Australian winemakers have readily embraced technological innovations, and have steered away from European traditions to produce interregional blends.

The last 20 years have seen the emergence of very large companies, through mergers, takeovers and expansion—some more successful than others. Southcorp is the largest and one of the major wine producers in the world, after the merger with Rosemount. Hardy's Wine Company is now part of Constellation Brands, one of the world's largest, while Orlando Wyndham (itself owned by French giant Pernod Ricard), Beringer Blass and McGuigan Simeon Wines, whose production is largely sold in bulk, all combine to produce more than three-quarters of the Australian production.

McWilliams and Yalumba are among the number of renowned middle-ranking producers which are still family owned. However, while there are now almost 1,800 wineries in Australia, 98 percent of them produce less than 5 percent of all wine. This concentration of production is also mirrored geographically.

BELOW: The Charles Melton Wines vineyard located in the world-renowned Barossa Valley, South Australia.

At one extreme, the state of South Australia makes more than half of all Australian wine and is home to the largest producers. At the other, Tasmania, with 4.6 percent of the wineries, has only 0.5 percent of production.

What is often forgotten in the pursuit of top wines like Penfold's Grange and Henschke's Hill of Grace is that half of all wine consumed in Australia is bulk wine, usually purchased in 1 gallon (4 l) casks. The basis of this wine—and many of the cheaper bottles of Australian wine sold in supermarkets around the world—is the multi-regional blend. "Wine of southeastern Australia" on a label means that the wine could come from anywhere except Western Australia, that is, from any of 98 percent of the nation's vineyard area. However, this does not mean the wines are of poorer quality—these fruity, accessible wines have revolutionized the international wine market in the last two decades—and even Australia's greatest wine, Grange, is traditionally a blend from a number of regions. These mass-produced wines could not exist without the viticultural development of Australia's vast irrigated areas.

Darwin
Palmerston
Arnhem Land
Joseph Bonaparte Gulf
Daly
Katherine
Roper
Gulf of Carpentaria
KIMBERLEY
Lake Argyle
King Leopold Ranges
Ord
Victoria
Fitzroy
Mt Broome
Northern Territory
Barkly Tableland
Mitchell
Cairns
Karumba
Mt Bartle Frere
5299 ft (1615 m)
Leichhardt
Flinders
Townsville
Tanami Desert
Tennant Creek
Mount Isa
GREAT DIVIDING RANGE
Lake Dalrymple
Mt Dalrymple
4190 ft (1277 m)
Mackay
Georgina
Queensland
Lake Mackay
DESERT
Diamantina
Longreach
Rockhampton
Gladstone
MacDonnell Ranges
Alice Springs
Gibson Desert
Lake Amadeus
Finke
Simpson Desert
Cooper
Bundaberg
Katatjuta (Mt Olga)
3497 ft (1066 m)
Uluru (Ayers Rock)
2831 ft (863 m)
Mt Woodroffe
4708 ft (1435 m)
Musgrave Ranges
Alberga
Warburton
Charleville
Maryborough
South Burnett
Kingaroy
Gympie
GREAT VICTORIA DESERT
Marla
Strzelcki Desert
Bulloo
Paroo
Warrego
Balonne
Nambour
Caboolture
Toowoomba
Brisbane
Warwick
Nerang
Lake Eyre
Coober Pedy
South Australia
Flinders Ranges
Granite Belt
Ballina
Lake Rebecca
Lake Torrens
Lake Frome
Darling
Namoi
Round Mtn
5203 ft (1586 m)
Grafton
Sawtell
Armidale
Nullarbor Plain
Eucla
Ceduna
St Mary Peak
3832 ft (1168 m)
New South Wales
Macquarie
Tamworth
Northern Rivers
Port Macquarie
Great Australian Bight
Port Augusta
Broken Hill
Whyalla
Port Pirie
The Barossa
Clare Valley
Riverland
Dubbo
Mudgee
Muswellbrook
Hunter Valley
Maitland
Central Ranges
Lachlan
Orange
Cessnock
Newcastle
Bathurst
Katoomba
Spencer Gulf
Gawler
Mildura
Northwest Victoria
Big Rivers
Griffith
Cowra
SYDNEY
Port Lincoln
Adelaide
Adelaide Hills
Murray Bridge
Cootamundra
Wagga Wagga
Goulburn
Wollongong
McLaren Vale
Langhorne Creek
Victoria
Murray
Rutherglen & NE Victoria
CANBERRA
Australian Capital Territory
Central Victoria
Echuca
Albury
Horsham
Wangaratta
Wodonga
Southern NSW
Coonawarra & the Limestone Coast
Bendigo
Mt Hotham
6125 ft (1867 m)
Mt Kosciuszko
7312 ft (2229 m)
South Coast
Penola
Grampians & Pyrenees
Ballarat
Yarra Valley
Bairnsdale
Mount Gambier
Portland
Geelong
Melbourne
Warrnambool
Port Phillip
Moe
Sale
Gippsland
Mornington Peninsula
Bass Strait
Burnie
Devonport
Launceston
Mt Ossa
5305 ft (1617 m)
Tasmania
Hobart
NORTH
200 miles
(320 kilometers)

Australian wine regions

Australia is a large country, so despite the distinctive national approach to wine, Australian wines are not all the same. Margaret River and Hunter Valley wines differ as much as Bordeaux and Mosel do. The three most important wine-producing states are South Australia, Victoria and New South Wales. As well as bulk production, they each have specific premium wine regions, while Tasmania and Western Australia are almost solely devoted to premium production.

In South Australia, the Clare Valley is renowned for its riesling, and the warmer Barossa Valley and McLaren Vale make big wines, chiefly from shiraz. In the cool Adelaide Hills, chardonnay and pinot noir show high quality. The cooler Coonawarra and surrounding Limestone Coast have an affinity with cabernet and cabernet blends. Riverland is the state's workhorse.

In Victoria, the Western Victoria zone includes the Grampians—well-known for its sparkling wines—and the Pyrenees. Fortified wines are the specialty in the hot region of Rutherglen. The state is best known for its fairly disparate cooler wine regions, like the Yarra Valley and Mornington Peninsula. Also cooler are the Gippsland, Macedon, and Geelong regions, which concentrate on pinot noir and chardonnay, while the warm Central Victoria region produces powerful and fruity reds.

Historically, the Hunter Valley was the only noted area in New South Wales—for its classic sémillons and shiraz. More recently, geographically diverse zones have been developed ranging from the subtropical Northern Rivers to the South Coast.

In Western Australia, the cooler southern regions are making high-quality table wine. The Margaret River region has gained much international recognition for its cabernet-based wines and chardonnay. The more recently developed Great Southern region is becoming known for its shiraz and riesling.

Queensland's most prominent wine-producing region, the Granite Belt, makes a range of wines. Other regions rely on grape varieties that can thrive in hot, humid conditions.

Tiny Tasmania, home of the small-scale enthusiast, is proving to be a stellar region for sparkling wines, while chardonnay and pinot noir are also important for table wines. Aromatic varieties like riesling also thrive, while pinot gris offers much promise.

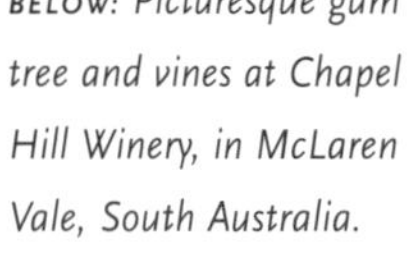

BELOW: Picturesque gum tree and vines at Chapel Hill Winery, in McLaren Vale, South Australia.

Major companies

SOUTHCORP WINES

For forty years, the massive wine producer we know as Southcorp, Australia's largest wine company, has engaged in a seemingly never-ending corporate two-step with mergers, acquisitions and sales. The result is a portfolio of exceptional brands such as Penfolds, Lindemans, Wynns, Devil's Lair, Coldstream Hills, Seppelts, Leo Buring, Seaview, Rosemount, Queen Adelaide and many more.

Unlike most of Australia's large producers, which had their genesis in a small winery established in the early days of the local wine industry, Southcorp is more an amalgamation of many different producers. It means that not only are almost all regions and styles represented but the company has some of Australia's great iconic wines, such as the famous Grange.

The $1.5 billion acquisition of Rosemount in 2001 was seen by some as a form of reverse takeover and has proved harder to swallow than first anticipated.

ORLANDO WYNDHAM

Until recently, Orlando Wyndham was the only major Australian wine producer in foreign hands, namely the French giant, Pernod Ricard. Pernod Ricard purchased Orlando in 1989 and the following year added Wyndham Estate. In the portfolio are producers such as Morris from Rutherglen, Montrose and Richmond Grove but the wine that has had the greatest impact from this company is the ubiquitous Jacob's Creek. This wine has led the Australian export push and is instantly recognizable as one of the world's best value and most successful brands.

THE HARDY WINE COMPANY

In 2003, the giant American producer Constellation Brands acquired BRL Hardy, changing the name to the Hardy Wine Company, and thereby formed what many believe to be the largest wine company in the world. It was a long way to that from the first wines made by English immigrant, Thomas Hardy in the mid-1850s.

The portfolio includes wines such as the environmentally friendly Banrock Station and value orientated Nottage Hill as well as an extraordinary array of quality labels such as Leasingham, Houghton's, Eileen Hardy, Crofters, Moondah Brook and Yarra Burn. Sparkling winemaker, Ed Carr, has established himself as the best in the land with Arras, the company's flagship.

BERINGER BLASS

Beringer Blass, the wine division of Fosters, has been on the path of expansion for decades. When Mildara merged with Wolf Blass in 1991, it brought together many leading brands and winemakers. There was much more to come before Fosters bought the company in 1996 and then in 2000, picked up the massive American producer, Beringer Wines, for $2.7 billion. Among the labels are Wolf Blass, Saltram, T'Gallant, Ingoldby, Maglieri, Krondorf, Yarra Ridge, Balgownie and the New Zealand based Matua Valley. Another controversial purchase was mail-order company, Cellarmasters, in 1997.

LEFT: Giant steel vats house Orlando Wines' huge production.

MCWILLIAMS

The sixth generation producer, McWilliams, is not quite in the same league as our other major companies in terms of size but they are, since the 2001 takeover of Rosemount by Southcorp, the country's largest family-owned wine producer. Their origins at Hanwood are celebrated by the naming of Australia's best value ranges after it. McWilliams struggled for many years to throw off their staid image as a fortified wine producer. In this they have been successful and have expanded to include quality wineries in a number of top regions, such as Brands in Coonawarra and Lillydale Vineyards in the Yarra Valley while establishing Barwang at Hilltops. Their Hunter range from Mt Pleasant, especially the Lovedale and Elizabeth sémillons are stars.

BELOW: Hardy's Chateau Reynella in South Australia is the headquarters for Hardy Wine Company.

ABOVE: *Margaret River's Amberley Estate vineyard bordered by a dam.*

WESTERN AUSTRALIA

Margaret River

PETER FORRESTAL

In a little over 30 years, Margaret River, which previously depended on dairying and forestry, has become a flourishing center for the wine industry, as well as a significant tourist destination. A key factor in this development has been the ability of the region's wineries to produce top-quality wines. Although the area is responsible for only about one percent of Australia's production, its wines account for 20 percent of the premium market. The cost of production is high, because yields are low and most wineries are small, and there is a consequent impact on economies of scale. Margaret River cabernet sauvignon and chardonnay are particularly highly regarded, with the region producing many of the country's best examples of these varietals. Its delicious sémillon/sauvignon blanc blends are popular on restaurant wine lists throughout Australia and overseas.

Margaret River's climate is the most maritime-influenced of any Australian wine region. It has a low mean annual temperature range and a long, dry period from October to April. Soils are mainly gravelly, or gritty sandy loam. Its major problems come with the strong salty winds in spring, which affect budburst and keep yields low. Chardonnay is especially affected by this.

A major development of the last decade has been the entry into the region of the major Australian wine companies. In 1996, Southcorp purchased the high-profile Devil's Lair while the Hardy Wine Company has 50 percent of Brookland Valley; McWilliams has also been involved in making quality wine from the region. All of these companies have vowed to maintain quality.

Regional Dozen

QUALITY WINES

Cape Mentelle Cabernet Sauvignon
Cullen Cabernet Merlot
Devil's Lair Chardonnay
Leeuwin Estate Chardonnay
Moss Wood Cabernet Sauvignon
Pierro Chardonnay

BEST VALUE WINES

Amberley Sémillon Sauvignon Blanc
Evans & Tate Classic Dry White
Sandalford Verdelho
Vasse Felix Sémillon
Voyager Sémillon
Chateau Xanadu Sémillon Sauvignon Blanc

CAPE MENTELLE

Established **1970** ***Owners*** **Veuve Clicquot** ***Production*** **65,000 cases** ***Vineyard area*** **297 acres (120 ha)**

The Cape Mentelle's vineyard was one of the region's first. Its winery hit the national spotlight by winning Australia's prestigious Jimmy Watson Trophy in consecutive years, with its 1982 and 1983 Cabernet Sauvignon. Founder David Hohnen has moved on and the reins have fallen to another high-profile member of the Australian wine industry, Dr Tony Jordan. The cabernet sauvignon is one of the region's finest and they produce some impressive whites, especially its powerful and complex chardonnay and a classy sémillon sauvignon blanc.

CULLEN

Established **1971** ***Owners*** **the Cullen family** ***Production*** **16,000 cases** ***Vineyard area*** **70 acres (28 ha)**

Cullen has become one of the country's best wineries. First Dr Kevin Cullen and then his wife, Diana, guided the fortunes of the winery, but their youngest daughter, Vanya, has been winemaker since 1989. Highly regarded as a show judge, Vanya has transformed Cullen into one of Australia's finest boutique wineries. Their complex, classically structured, velvety cabernet merlot is among the country's best, the underrated chardonnay is one of Australia's most impressive, while the wood-aged sauvignon blanc sémillon has an enthusiastic following for its beautifully integrated oak and ripe, juicy flavors.

HOWARD PARK WINES

Established **1986** ***Owners*** **Jeff and Amy Burch** ***Vineyard area*** **185 acres (75 ha)**

Howard Park Wines is one of the West's most significant producers. The riesling, one of Australia's best half dozen, has a tight, dry style, full of flavor; the cabernet merlot, also highly regarded, is a full-bodied, opulent and powerful red that demands cellaring. The Madfish label is popular, with an unwooded and wooded chardonnay, pinot noir and shiraz. White and red blends are well made, fruity, medium-priced wines.

LEEUWIN ESTATE

Established **1969** ***Owners*** **the Horgan family** ***Production*** **35,000 cases** ***Vineyard area*** **370 acres (150 ha)**

This showcase winery, venue for an annual concert featuring international artists, acts as a magnet for tourists. While the entrepreneurial energy of Denis and Tricia Horgan has done much to promote Leeuwin Estate, its reputation rests on the quality of its Art Series Chardonnay, regarded by many commentators as the best produced in Australia. Since the first release in 1980, these opulent, full-flavored and complex whites age more gracefully than any other Australian chardonnay. Leeuwin's Prelude Chardonnay and the Art Series Cabernet Sauvignon are also highly regarded.

MOSS WOOD

Established **1969** ***Owners*** **Keith and Clare Mugford** ***Production*** **5,500 cases** ***Vineyard area*** **72 acres (29 ha)**

Moss Wood is among Australia's leading boutique wineries, and its vineyard is one of the country's most distinguished viticultural sites. While the chardonnay and sémillon are both highly sought after, the cabernet is recognized as one of the best produced in Australia. Nearby Ribbon Vale has been purchased and will be marketed as a separate vineyard.

ABOVE: The entrance to Hay Shed Hill Vineyard, Margaret River.

XANADU

Established **1977** ***Owners*** **Chateau Xanadu Wines Ltd** ***Production*** **47,000 cases** ***Vineyard area*** **343 acres (139 ha)**

Expansion is the key word at Xanadu since the public company takeover. In the 1980s, Xanadu had a reputation for its whites, but improved vineyard management under Conor Lagan and winemaker, Jürg Muggli, improved the quality of the reds. The cabernets (especially the Reserve) are among the region's best, while the oak-matured sémillon, the sémillon sauvignon blanc and chardonnay are highly recommended.

Other significant producers in the Margaret River region include Amberley Estate, Brookland Valley Vineyard, Devil's Lair Wines, Evans & Tate, Hay Shed Hill Vineyard, Pierro and Voyager Estate.

BELOW LEFT: Vineyard at Cullen, Margaret River. Cullen is regarded as one of Australia's best wineries.

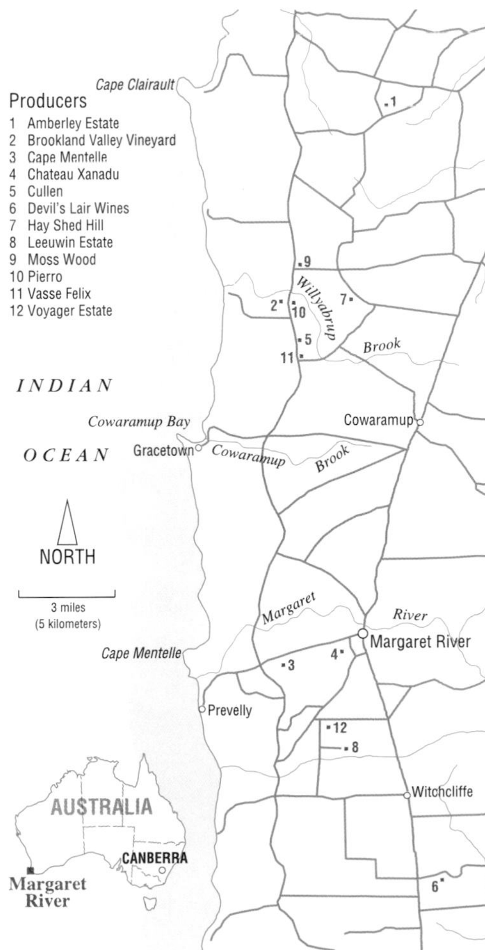

RIGHT: *The winery at Goundrey Wines provides a backdrop for the vineyards.*

Great Southern

PETER FORRESTAL

Great Southern is Western Australia's coolest and Australia's largest viticultural region. It consists of five subregions centered around Mount Barker, with Denmark, Frankland, Albany and the Porongurups all at least a half-hour drive away. While the climate of both Denmark and Albany are moderated by the sea, Frankland and Mount Barker experience more continental conditions. Soils are usually loams derived from granite and gneissic rocks, or lateritic gravelly sandy loams.

Given the size of the region, different subregions appear more suitable to some varieties than others. Mount Barker has been particularly successful as a producer of riesling, cabernet sauvignon, pinot noir, and shiraz; Denmark with chardonnay and pinot noir; Frankland with riesling, cabernets and shiraz; Albany with chardonnay and pinot noir; and the Porongurups with riesling.

The last decade or so has seen significant change. Many of the growers have become more involved in the wine industry and are seeking greater control over wine production by having their own wineries. From mature vineyards such as Forest Hill at Mount Barker, Westfield (leased to Houghton) and Alkoomi at Frankland, Bouverie and Wyjup (Plantagenet), and Windy Hill (Goundrey), the quality of fruit is so impressive that there has been widespread development in recent years. The region is becoming an important producer of premium wines, and its best are stunningly good.

Regional Best

QUALITY WINES

Frankland Estate Olmo's Reward
Goundrey Reserve Shiraz
Harewood Chardonnay
Howard Park Riesling
Plantagenet Shiraz
Plantagenet Riesling
Wignalls Reserve Pinot Noir

BEST VALUE WINES

Alkoomi Sauvignon Blanc
Castle Rock Riesling
Gilberts Shiraz
Karriview Pinot Noir
Pattersons Pinot Noir
Springviews Riesling

Producers
1 Alkoomi
2 Frankland Estate
3 Goundrey Wines
4 Howard Park Wines
5 Plantagenet Wines
6 Wignalls Wines

GOUNDREY WINES

Established **1978** ***Owner*** **Vincorp** ***Production*** **200,000 cases** ***Vineyard area*** **482 acres (195 ha)**

Nowhere in Great Southern has there been expansion such as that seen at Goundrey since its acquisition by American, Jack Bendat. The winery's capacity has been increased threefold and vineyard plantings have proceeded apace. In three years, production has risen from 33,000 to more than 200,000 cases. While it has not been possible to expand this rapidly using only Western Australian fruit, it is the intention at Goundrey to satisfy demand from local grapes as soon as this is possible. Wines are available at all prices, with Goundrey's Reserve Shiraz being the standout red, while the Unwooded Chardonnay completely dominates that niche.

PLANTAGENET WINES

Established **1974** ***Owners*** **Lionel Samson Pty Ltd** ***Production*** **40,000 cases** ***Vineyard area*** **291 acres (118 ha)**

Although he has just sold his share in the business, Plantagenet owes a major debt to its founder, Tony Smith. More than 25 years of pioneering endeavor have established Plantagenet as one of the state's preeminent wineries. As a contract winemaker for up to as many as 20 vineyards, Plantagenet has been a major force for quality winemaking in the region. The winery produces several very good to outstanding wines, notably its cabernet sauvignon, shiraz and riesling. All the Plantagenet wines offer consistent high quality and good value, as does their Omrah range.

Other significant producers in the Great Southern Region include Alkoomi, Frankland Estate and Wignalls Wines.

Other Western Australian Regions

PETER FORRESTAL

SWAN VALLEY

The Swan Valley is a flat alluvial plain, with deep, loamy, moisture-retentive soils. Its hot Mediterranean climate is best suited to verdelho, chenin blanc and fortifieds, although chardonnay and shiraz can also be impressive.

For historical reasons and because of its proximity to Perth, two of the state's largest companies, Houghton (owned by the Hardy Wine Company) and the independent Sandalford, have their headquarters in Swan Valley. Otherwise, the wineries of the area are quite small, family-owned businesses that offer modestly priced wines of very good to reasonable quality at the cellar door.

HOUGHTON WINE COMPANY

Established **1836** ***Owners*** **BRL Hardy** ***Production*** **500,000 cases**
Vineyard area **1,186 acres (480 ha)**

Houghton is by far the largest and most influential wine company in the west, as it owns, leases or buys fruit from vineyards in virtually all regions in the state. Significant investment in winemaking equipment and vineyard development over the past 20 years and exemplary winemaking and viticulture have meant that Houghton makes outstanding wines at every price. The super-premium Jack Mann red blend is as good as it gets, while the Crofters and Moondah Brook range includes many excellent wines, and those from Pemberton offer great promise.

SANDALFORD WINES

Established **1840** ***Owners*** **Peter and Debra Prendiville** ***Production*** **70,000 cases**
Vineyard area **282 acres (114 ha)**

Sandalford, one of the Western Australia's oldest wineries, is currently undergoing a revival of fortunes. Since the Prendivilles have taken over, there has been substantial investment in the vineyards (especially in Margaret River), a major upgrading of the winery and development of tourist facilities. The quality of the wines, which are sourced from most of the state's viticultural regions, has risen dramatically. They are sound, well-made wines representing good value.

ABOVE: An old flat-topped wagon with barrels at Peel Estate, near the Geographe region.

GEOGRAPHE

Geographe covers a wide and diverse region from Capel to the Ferguson Valley in the Bunbury hinterland, the farmlands of Donnybrook, and the dairy country around Harvey. Vineyards are being planted here at an astonishing rate.

The coastal strip from Capel to Harvey, with its fertile soils and warm temperatures moderated by sea breezes, is best suited to merlot, chardonnay and verdelho.

In the Ferguson Valley and the hills behind Harvey, vineyards have been planted between 820 and 985 feet (250 and 300 m) above sea level. The most suited grape varieties appear to be chardonnay, shiraz, sémillon and sauvignon blanc. Willow Bridge is the largest winery in Ferguson Valley.

BELOW: Vines growing in the Swan Valley, Houghton Wine Company.

ABOVE: Vines at Lamont Winery which also boasts a stylish cellar door, art gallery and restaurant.

the Whispering Hill Riesling, which is one of the best sourced from Great Southern. The Capel Vale wines represent good value, especially the tropical-fruited sauvignon blanc sémillon, the smooth rich merlot and the earthy, spicy shiraz.

PEMBERTON

The Pemberton region includes the Manjimup area, which is ideal for grape growing, having a comparable climate to Bordeaux. The Pemberton area, though, is cooler and wetter, with less sunshine. There is still debate about which grape varieties are most suitable for the region. Recommendations include cabernet varieties, shiraz, and chardonnay for Manjimup, and pinot noir and cabernet varieties (especially franc and merlot) for Pemberton. Chardonnay and pinot noir have proved successful as a sparkling wine base.

The stars of the region to date have been winemakers who established their reputations elsewhere. Moss Wood founder Bill Pannell and his son Dan have established Picardy, which has produced some stunning merlot cabernet, shiraz and pinot noir, further complicating the debate. Their best wine so far is a stunning, velvety merlot cabernet. Both John Kosovich (Westfield) and John Brocksopp (Leeuwin Estate) have planted vineyards here. Kosovich's Bronzewing Chardonnay has been superb, while Brocksopp has made tiny quantities of a fruity roussane and a fine, medium-bodied shiraz with clear varietal definition. Keith Mugford produces a fine, taut chardonnay and a spicy, savory pinot from the Lefroy Brook vineyard, sold under the Moss Wood label.

Donnybrook is a warm area for growing grapes. Orchards occupy the valley flats and vineyards the undulating slopes. David Hohnen, formerly of Cape Mentelle, believes the area is suited to the production of medium-price dry reds and he likes its shiraz, cabernet, zinfandel and grenache.

CAPEL VALE

Established **1974** ***Owners*** **Dr Peter and Elizabeth Pratten** ***Production*** **85,000 cases** ***Vineyard area*** **407 acres (165 ha)**

Capel Vale, one of the west's largest producers, now sources 85 percent of its production from its own vineyards in Geographe, Pemberton, Mount Barker and Margaret River. The pick of the reserve range is the Whispering Hill Riesling (continued above).

WESTFIELD

Established **1922** ***Owners*** **the Kosovich family** ***Production*** **4,500 cases** ***Vineyard area*** **30 acres (12 ha)**

John Kosovich at Westfield has continued to defy expectation by regularly producing outstanding wines in the unfashionable Swan Valley. Few would pick the Westfield Chardonnay as a warm-climate wine; fewer would expect it to age as gracefully as it does. The Liqueur Muscat is one of Australia's best, a rarity for a wine that does not come from Rutherglen. Kosovich has recently been joined by his son, Anthony, and together they operate the Swan Valley property and the new Bronzewing vineyard at Manjimup.

Other producers of note include Lamont Winery, Westfield (both Swan Valley) and Peel Estate (Geographe).

BELOW RIGHT: Westfield Winery produces a liqueur muscat that rivals those of Rutherglen in Victoria.

Regional Dozen

- Paul Conti Late Harvest Muscat
- Lamont Vintage Port
- Maiden Wood Pinot Chardonnay
- Mann Méthode Champenoise
- Moss Wood 'Lefroy Brook' Pinot Noir
- Picardy Merlot Cabernet
- Salitage Pinot Noir
- Sandalford Elements Shiraz Cabernet
- Smithbrook Merlot
- Talijancich Julian James Red Liqueur
- Westfield Bronzewing Chardonnay
- Westfield Chardonnay

SOUTH AUSTRALIA

Clare Valley

SALLY MARDEN

The Clare Valley is a pretty, winding, wooded region two hours' drive north of Adelaide, with a history of winemaking that dates back to the time of first European settlement. It is a curious region climatically and stylistically. Set in the middle of the dry mid-north wheat belt of South Australia, with hot summers and little ground water, Clare somehow manages to produce wines—such as its best-performing and best-known wine, riesling—that appear to come from a considerably cooler, wetter climate like that found in the famous Mosel region in Germany. This odd characteristic is attributed to cool afternoon breezes that blow through the Clare Valley in the warmer months, slowing and prolonging grape ripening.

Clare's main Australian competitor in the riesling stakes lies an hour away in the Eden Valley. Examples from both regions are regarded as Australian classics, but they differ somewhat in style: Eden Valley's are all restrained lime juice and steely in character, whereas Clare's add floral, perfumed, and spicy characters to the citrus aspects. Riesling is not the only star in Clare; it also produces big, firm, peppery shiraz and elegant, minty cabernets, both with plenty of backbone.

The Clare Valley is a mix of the large and small, as well as the old and new, but the most renowned producers have maintained their independence and remain small operations.

JIM BARRY WINES

Established **1959** ***Owners*** **the Barry family** ***Production*** **85,000 cases** ***Vineyard area*** **521 acres (211 ha)**

Originally gaining a reputation for its Watervale Riesling, Jim Barry Wines is now best known for its big, high-quality, full-bodied reds, the most highly sought after of which is The Armagh. A further 27 acres (11 ha) have recently been purchased in the Coonawarra.

Shiraz

From workhorse to doghouse to superstar, Australia's shiraz (syrah in France's Rhône Valley) has seen it all. The backbone of Australian wine for decades, even the classic cabernet region, Coonawarra, built its reputation on shiraz. When the trend turned to cool-climate wines in the 1980s, many old vines were pulled out. Then in the 1990s, regions like Barossa and McLaren Vale came into their own as the world woke up to the joy of rich, opulent, full-flavored shiraz.

GROSSET WINES

Established **1981** ***Owners*** **Jeffrey Grosset** ***Production*** **8,000 cases** ***Vineyard area*** **49 acres (20 ha)**

When it comes to Australian riesling, Jeffrey Grosset is the undisputed king. His superb wines have brought him numerous awards, including Riesling Winemaker of the Year at the 1998 Riesling Summit in the grape's German heartland. He makes two styles, one from Watervale and one from Polish Hill; both have the elegance and complexity of great riesling. Grosset's other wines include his highly acclaimed cabernet blend, Gaia, and the fragrant Adelaide Hills Pinot Noir.

PIKES WINES

Established **1984** ***Owners*** **the Pike family** ***Production*** **29,000 cases** ***Vineyard area*** **104 acres (42 ha)**

Pikes Wines is located in one of the cooler parts of Clare, resulting in a longer ripening

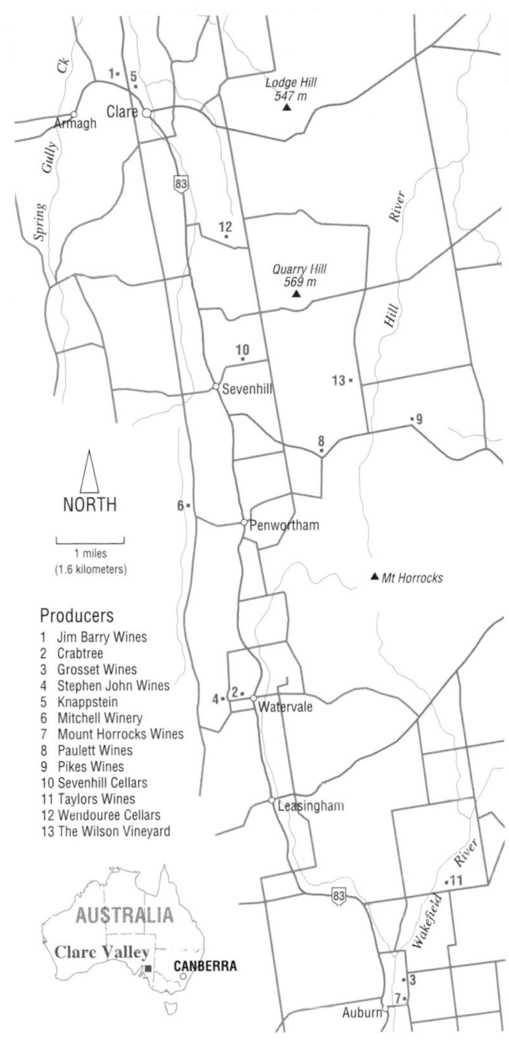

LEFT: *The tasting room at Jim Barry Wines features their high-quality gutsy red wines.*

ABOVE: *Rows of vines at Pikes Polish Hill vineyard stretch away towards the surrounding hills.*

season for grapes and a later harvest than most. This produces intense flavors, complexity, and fine acidity, resulting in elegant, long-lived wines. Highlights are riesling and a complex funky shiraz. Ten acres (4 ha) have been planted in the Adelaide Hills.

TAYLORS WINES

Established **1969** ***Owners*** **the Taylor family** ***Production*** **230,000 cases** ***Vineyard area*** **1,360 acres (550 ha)**

Taylors Wines dominates both the local industry and the southern end of the Clare Valley. The first wine released under the Taylors label, the 1973 Cabernet, won gold medals at every national Australian wine show. Since then, the company's reputation for producing high-quality red wines has grown, though today the emphasis is as much on white wines. A premium range under the St Andrews label was launched in 1999.

WENDOUREE CELLARS

Established **1895** ***Owners*** **Tony and Lita Brady** ***Production*** **2,500 cases** ***Vineyard area*** **30 acres (12 ha)**

Tony Brady makes small quantities of huge, powerful red wines, which are regarded as among Australia's best and sell out on release. The range includes cabernet, malbec, mataro (mourvèdre), and shiraz, plus varying blends of the four. There is also a redoubtable vintage port style made with muscat of alexandria. All wines age beautifully.

Other significant producers in the Clare Valley include Crabtree, Stephen John Wines, Knappstein, Mitchell Winery, Mount Horrocks Wines, O'Leary Walker, Paulett Wines, Sevenhill Cellars and the Wilson Vineyard.

Regional Dozen

QUALITY WINES

Jim Barry The Armagh
Crabtree Watervale Riesling
Grosset Polish Hill/Watervale Riesling
Mitchell Peppertree Vineyard Shiraz
Pike's Reserve Riesling
Wendouree Cellars Shiraz

BEST VALUE WINES

Annie's Lane Riesling
Galah Wines Shiraz
Knappstein Riesling
Leasingham Riesling
Pauletts Cabernet Merlot
Skillogalee Riesling

RIGHT: *Grosset Wines' cellar door is open for only about six weeks in the year.*

The Barossa

SALLY MARDEN

The Barossa—consisting of the Barossa and Eden Valleys—can justifiably claim to be Australia's best-known wine region, and is arguably its most important. Here, among the neat vineyards and rolling hills an hour northeast of Adelaide, are more than 50 wineries, including the home bases and headquarters of most of the country's leading wine companies. Australia's finest and most famous wines also come from here, especially the gloriously opulent shiraz wines that have brought such acclaim to Australia.

Fortified wines were the Barossa's mainstay for a long time, but from the 1950s, revolutionary winemakers started to produce the table wines that were to become the region's benchmarks—robust, full-bodied shiraz and steely, dry riesling. These two wine styles remain Barossa classics, and are known throughout the world.

During the late 1970s and the early 1980s, demand for the Barossa's big sturdy reds declined as people discovered chardonnay and sought dry whites. This resulted in substantial amounts of Barossa old shiraz, grenache and mourvèdre vines—the backbone of the old fortified industry—being ripped out, along with other less suitable varieties. Thankfully, not everyone followed suit. A number of winemakers and growers either set up their own small independent wineries or started producing wines that highlighted their Barossa heritage. In doing so, they brought the region back to its roots and played a significant part in turning its fortunes around again.

The wines those producers made then, and continue to make now, exemplify the Barossa: big blockbuster reds packed full of spice, tannin, rich fruit, and depth—wines with tar and leather and chocolate. These opulent full-bodied beauties have made the Barossa into a thriving premium winemaking region of global importance.

Peter Lehmann

Peter Lehmann, dubbed the Baron of the Barossa, is one of Australia's wine legends. These days it is hard to fathom that the Barossa ever needed saving, but many believe that without Lehmann's faith and efforts the Barossa was doomed. After years with both Yalumba and Saltram, whom he controversially left when its then multinational owners refused to honor grape contracts, he formed his own company. The team includes wife Margaret and son Doug as well as long-term winemaker Andrew Wigan. Peter Lehmann Wines is now a major producer in the region. His Stonewell Shiraz is one of the Barossa's great reds, while the Peter Lehmann Reserve Riesling has been awarded accolades around the globe. The entire Australian wine industry owes this man a debt of gratitude.

But a "riesling revival" is leading to wider distribution and acceptance, with the Australian charge being led by the Eden Valley region and its northern neighbor, the Clare Valley wine region.

The Barossa Valley, with its Mediterranean climate, has brown fertile soils that will grow just about anything that is planted. Apart from shiraz, the grapes that do best are other rhône varieties. Cabernet sauvignon can be

BELOW: *Tidy vines in widely spaced rows show off the Barossa Valley's fertile brown soil.*

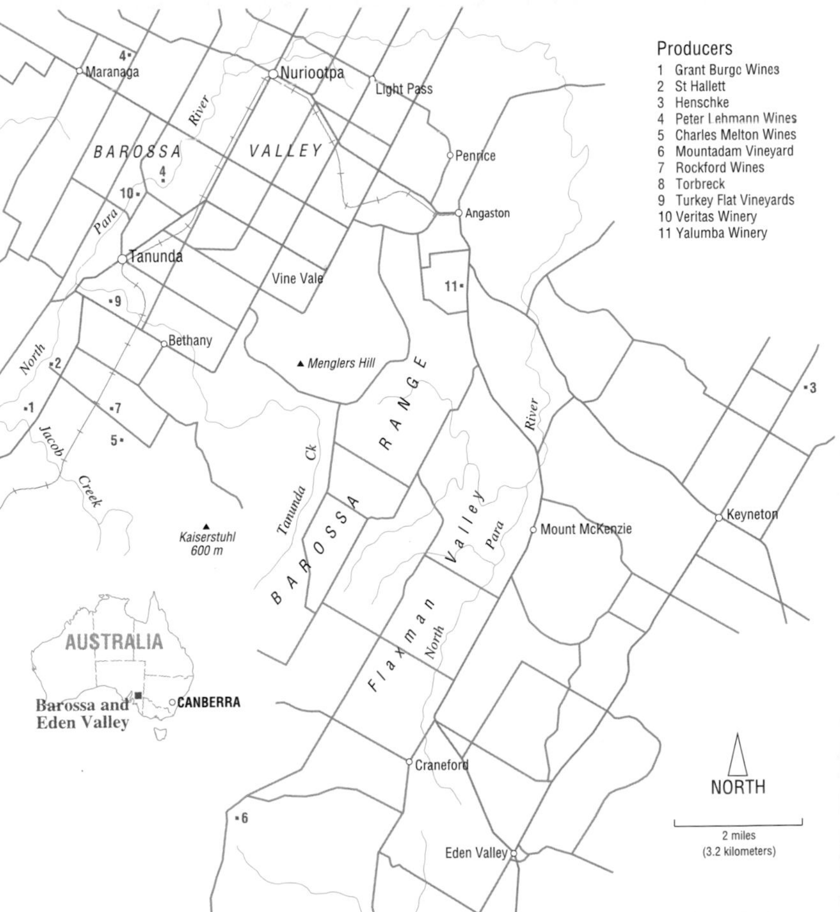

Settlement of the Barossa

At first glance, the Barossa seems dichotomous. There are two regions within it, each producing distinctive styles of wine. The Eden Valley is high-altitude hill country, producing elegant, structured wines, in particular rieslings. The Barossa Valley is on the valley floor, where classic, full-bodied old-vine shiraz and grenache are the order of the day. Each area was settled in the late 1830s by two very different groups of migrants, with their own particular cultures, lifestyles, and religions. Up in the hills it was English farmers and gentry, while down in the valley it was mainly German-speaking peasant farmers from Silesia (now part of Poland and eastern Germany) who established delightful European-style villages and settlements.

But cultural differences didn't seem to stand in the way too much here. Mixed hamlets, villages, and townships sprang up, farms were established, and the settlers developed a strong sense of community. Equally importantly, they quickly realized that grape vines were one of the most suitable and flourishing crops, whether in the hills or the valley. For the English, bottles and casks from Bordeaux and Burgundy suffered badly on their passage through the tropics. And for the Silesians, viticulture and winemaking were as much a part of their tradition as sausage-making or pickling vegetables. So, via this unexpectedly successful intertwining and establishment of lifestyle and cultures, the first Barossa wines were made in the 1840s, and many of the same vineyards planted then are still being worked today. Some of the oldest vines in the world can be found here, and many of the 500-plus growers producing grapes in the Barossa today are fifth- and sixth-generation descendants of the original settlers. However, there was a time when the harmony of the Barossa faced its own unique pressures.

The sense of community spirit that had been built up since settlement was severely tested by tensions between English descendants and those with German heritage during World War II. But the desire to maintain the community was strong, and organizations and events were started to rekindle a sense of unity, including the biennial Barossa Vintage Festival that still thrives today. The Silesian influence has given the area a unique food culture, and Australia's most distinctive regional cuisine. It has shaped the landscape with its mix of vineyards, historic cottages and churches, and provided the force behind some of Australia's most successful wine companies.

ripe and full-bodied. The most prevalent white grape is sémillon, which traditionally has received a large dose of oak. These days, both oaked and unoaked are produced, and the best provide a luscious, lemony mouthfeel.

In the Eden Valley, cooler temperatures give a longer growing season, and, together with rocky, acidic soil and significant winter rainfall, create ideal conditions for top riesling. But it also suits shiraz, cabernet and chardonnay, resulting in wines that are tighter and more elegant than their Barossa Valley brethren. Once almost extinct in its native Rhône Valley, viognier is also thriving in the Eden Valley, especially at the hands of Yalumba.

BELOW: *Steel vats and oak barrels fill Charles Melton Wines' outdoor processing center.*

In the latter part of the 1990s, the division between the Barossa and Eden Valleys was made. The Geographic Indications provide security against misuse of the names by other regions or wineries, and the delineation of vineyard land guards against rampant growth.

HENSCHKE, EDEN VALLEY

Established **1868** ***Owners*** **C. A. Henschke & Co.** ***Production*** **40,000 cases** ***Vineyard area*** **285 acres (115 ha)**

Cyril Henschke was one of the Australian wine industry's true pioneers in the 1950s, developing and marketing, among others, quality single-vineyard table wines from two of his best sites—Mount Edelstone and Hill of Grace. A generation on, Stephen and Prue Henschke have built on those foundations in stellar fashion, and their wines are among the best anywhere.

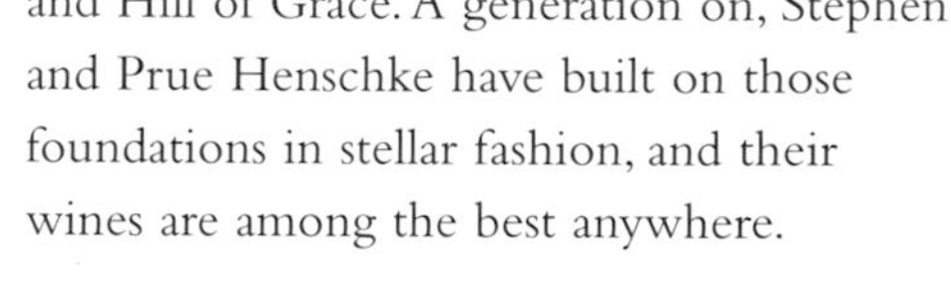

MOUNTADAM VINEYARD, EDEN VALLEY

Established **1972** ***Owners*** **David & Adam Wynn Pty Ltd**
Production **50,000 cases**
Vineyard area **125 acres (50 ha)**

David Wynn developed Mountadam on the beautiful High Eden Ridge after an exhaustive search throughout Australia for the best vineyard site to grow chardonnay. His son Adam became winemaker in 1984 after successfully completing his winemaking studies in Bordeaux. After nearly three decades, Mountadam is firmly established as one of Australia's super-premium wine companies, producing a range of elegant and refined wines. Mountadam Chardonnay sits

happily with the greats (and with considerably less fuss and price hype than some newer super-premiums).

CHARLES MELTON WINES, BAROSSA VALLEY

Established **1984** ***Owners*** **Charles Melton Wines** ***Production*** **7,000—8,000 cases** ***Vineyard area*** **72 acres (29 ha)**

In 1984, after a ten-year apprenticeship under Peter Lehmann, Charlie Melton wanted to take a new approach with grapes and wine styles that were being neglected elsewhere in the Australian industry. Using and cherishing old dry-grown grenache and shiraz grapes, he's become the Barossa's very own Rhône Ranger, and his grenache/shiraz/mourvèdre blend Nine Popes has reached cult status.

GRANT BURGE WINES, BAROSSA VALLEY

Established **1985** ***Owners*** **Grant Burge Wines Pty Ltd** ***Production*** **100,000 cases** ***Vineyard area*** **815 acres (330 ha)**

A fifth-generation Barossa Valley winemaker, Grant Burge is Barossan to his bootstraps. His family heritage of winemaking started with his great-great grandfather, John Burge, who settled in the Barossa in 1854 on one of the first vineyards established in the area. Today, Grant and his wife Helen operate the largest privately owned vineyard network in the Barossa. His winemaking history has recently come full circle. In 1972, he teamed up with Ian Wilson and purchased the fledgling Krondorf winery. After 14 years, they had built it into a national brand and sold it to the Mildara Group. In 1988, Burge started his own premium wine business, Grant Burge Wines, which has been such a success that, in late 1999, he was able to buy back Krondorf.

ROCKFORD WINES, BAROSSA VALLEY

Established **1984** ***Owners*** **Tanunda Vintners Pty Ltd** ***Production*** **20,000 cases** ***Vineyard area*** **59 acres (24 ha)**

Robert O'Callaghan has played a critical role in preserving the old plantings of Barossa shiraz that are vital to his full-bodied, richly flavored wines. The winery itself is a superb collection of stone and galvanized iron buildings containing restored nineteenth-century equipment—from old stationary engine-driven crushers to slate open fermenters and century-old wooden basket presses—used to make Basket Press Shiraz, Australia's best red sparkler, the Black Shiraz and the rhône blend, Moppa Springs.

Other significant producers in the Barossa and Eden Valleys include Peter Lehmann Wines, St Hallett, Torbreck, Turkey Flat Vineyards, Veritas Winery and Yalumba.

ABOVE: *Mountadam Vineyard offers spectacular views of the Eden Valley from the High Eden Ridge.*

LEFT: *A rusted old stencil, used for identifying the contents of barrels.*

Regional Dozen

QUALITY WINES

Henschke Hill of Grace
Irvine Grand Merlot
Charles Melton Nine Popes
Mountadam Chardonnay
Rockford Basket Press Shiraz
St Hallett Old Block Shiraz

BEST VALUE WINES

Elderton Golden Sémillon
Peter Lehmann Clancys
Charles Melton Rosé of Virginia
Richmond Grove Barossa Riesling
Seppelt DP117 Show Fino
Wolf Blass Gold Label Riesling

Adelaide Hills

SALLY MARDEN

The Adelaide Hills wine region lies less than a half-hour drive from the city of Adelaide up in the steep, wooded ranges that border the South Australian capital's eastern edge. It stretches from Mount Pleasant in the neighboring northerly wine region of Eden Valley, down to Mount Compass and the hills behind McLaren Vale in the south. Its restrained, lifted whites and elegant reds are attracting increasing international acclaim. Some of Australia's most respected winemakers have major interests in the area.

This is one of Australia's most picturesque wine regions. Oaks, green pastures, and a fair bit of mist and rain give a European feel to the area, and there are numerous microclimates and subregions. Any generalization about conditions and suitable varieties is hazardous, but the region's cool, moist climate provides excellent results from the most widely planted white grape, chardonnay, including two of Australia's most prestigious and expensive wines—Petaluma Tiers and Penfolds Yattarna. Riesling is successful here also, showing lime-blossom characters when young and aging well, and nowhere else in Australia can match the Adelaide Hills for sauvignon blanc. It also produces fruit and base wine for the country's better sparkling wines. Pinot noir from the Adelaide Hills is regarded as some of best in the land.

Regional Dozen

QUALITY WINES

Ashton Hills Reserve Pinot Noir
Chain of Ponds Ledge Shiraz
Lenswood Vineyards Chardonnay
Petaluma Tiers Chardonnay
Nepenthe Lenswood Sémillon
Geoff Weaver Chardonnay

BEST VALUE WINES

Bridgewater Mill Chardonnay
Chain of Ponds Riesling
Henschke Greens Hill Riesling
Pibbin Rosé
Shaw and Smith Sauvignon Blanc
Talunga Shiraz

KNAPPSTEIN LENSWOOD VINEYARDS

Established **1981** ***Owners*** **Tim and Annie Knappstein** ***Production*** **8,000 cases** ***Vineyard area*** **66 acres (26.7 ha)**

Tim Knappstein has been quietly making his presence felt in the Australian wine industry for nearly 40 years. Single-handedly revolutionizing the wines of his family's company, Stanley Wines of Clare, he took the Australian wine show circuit by storm during the late 1960s and early 1970s with his Leasingham bin label wines. In 1976, he set up on his own in Clare and established his

BELOW: A vintage truck signs the way to the tasting room at Hillstowe Wines.

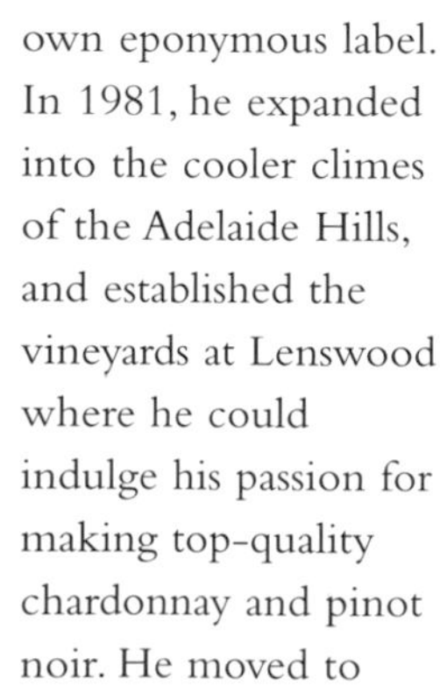

own eponymous label. In 1981, he expanded into the cooler climes of the Adelaide Hills, and established the vineyards at Lenswood where he could indulge his passion for making top-quality chardonnay and pinot noir. He moved to Lenswood after the sale of his Clare Valley winery. The resulting wines are consistently good and classic in style, particularly the chardonnay, riesling, cabernet sauvignon and pinot noir.

NEPENTHE VINEYARDS

Established **1994** ***Owner*** **James Tweddell** ***Production*** **6,500 cases** ***Vineyard area*** **62 acres (25 ha)**

One of the brightest new stars in the South Australian firmament, Nepenthe, named after an ancient Egyptian herbal drink with legendary powers, has swiftly gained cult status, and their wines sometimes sell out within hours of release. Peter Leske is the man behind them,

Australian practice of blending wines/regions

Unburdened by any appellation system, Australia has developed its wine industry as desired. This freedom has allowed winemakers to blend wines in ways that their European counterparts would find unthinkable—and illegal. Not only can different grapes be blended in any manner the winemaker chooses, so too can grapes from different regions end up in the same wine. All that is required is that label integrity be respected. Hence, a wine may include cabernet from Western Australia, merlot from Tasmania, and shiraz from New South Wales. Freedom of choice has also led to such traditional Australian styles as cabernet/shiraz and sémillon/chardonnay blends.

working at Nepenthe's state-of-the-art, environmentally friendly Lenswood winery to produce wines with great structure and class. Chardonnay, pinot noir and sémillon all attract attention, but so do the lesser known varietals, including pinot gris and zinfandel. The Fugue, a cabernet merlot/blend, is also good, but needs aging and decanting.

PETALUMA LTD

Established **1976** ***Owners*** **Lion Nathan** ***Production*** **30,000 cases** ***Vineyard area*** **309 acres (125 ha)**

One of Australia's best known and respected wine producers, Brian Croser established Petaluma in Adelaide Hills' Piccadilly Valley subregion in 1976. Prior to its recent purchase by Lion Nathan, Petaluma acquired a number of well known labels. Brian Croser has been the driving force throughout. Fruit is sourced from several regions, with the Adelaide Hills vineyards yielding premium grapes for stellar chardonnay (including the rare Tiers), the Croser Pinot Noir/Chardonnay sparkler, Clare the Riesling and Coonawarra the Cabernet Merlot. Petaluma's second label is Bridgewater Mill.

SHAW & SMITH

Established **1989** ***Owners*** **Martin Shaw and Michael Hill-Smith** ***Production*** **24,000 cases** ***Vineyard area*** **95 acres (38.5 ha)**

These two Australian wine legends specialize in white wine production. Shaw, formerly a winemaker at Petaluma, and Hill-Smith, a writer, judge, producer, consultant and master of wine, started the business determined to concentrate on sauvignon blanc and chardonnay. They quickly gained a reputation for producing modern, clean classics of both. Their chardonnay is balanced; creamy and smooth, with multiple layers of subtle flavors, while their sauvignon blanc is a match for New Zealand's finest. Merlot is the pick of the reds.

GEOFF WEAVER

Established **1982** ***Owners*** **Geoff and Judith Weaver** ***Production*** **5,000 cases** ***Vineyard area*** **34 acres (14 ha)**

Geoff Weaver is a firm adherent to the old maxim that good wine is made in the vineyard. He aims to make sure that each grape variety is allowed to express its classic characteristics through fresh, complex wines. The theory works well, resulting in chardonnay that shows rich, buttery characters and white peach fruit, sauvignon blanc that's tight, green, peppery and pungent, and riesling with balanced fruit and citrus flavors.

Other notable producers in the Hills include Ashton Hills Vineyard, Chain of Ponds Wines, Hillstowe Wines and Paracombe Wines.

ABOVE: A timber mill once stood on the site of Hillstowe Wines' Adelaide Hills vineyards.

Sparkling red—a very Australian wine

Known for decades as sparkling burgundy, these rich, velvety wines are very Australian. Once highly popular, they became an endangered species in the 1970s as the market was repelled by a flood of poor quality, oversweet lookalikes. Seppelt, who had always led the way and whose wines from the 1940s and 1960s now bring huge prices at auction, maintained the faith. A few other believers joined them, and gradually other wineries dipped a toe in the water. Now, producers from all over the country offer "spurgles." Although shiraz is the most popular grape, many other red varieties are used to make sparkling reds.

ABOVE: *A traditional-style wooden veranda adorns the winery building at d'Arenberg Wines.*

McLaren Vale

SALLY MARDEN

Most Australian wine regions take their influence from the migrants who settled there. In McLaren Vale it was a group of Englishmen who started the ball rolling. Two in particular laid the foundations for the region—John Reynell, who first planted vines in the area in 1838, and Thomas Hardy, whose influence has been integral to the region since he bought and developed the Tintara vineyards and winery in 1876.

Bordered to the east by the southern ranges of the Adelaide Hills and to the west by the Gulf of St Vincent, the landscape of McLaren Vale varies from steep ranges and gorges to wide open plains, with beaches and cliffs, rivers, hills, olive groves, orchards and ocean views in between. The terrain is undulating and the soil types vary widely. There is also significant climatic variation in this region, due to differing degrees of exposure to or protection from the nearby sea and its cooling influence. Summer rainfall is low, so irrigation of the vineyards is generally necessary.

Because of this geographical and climatic diversity, nearly all grape varieties flourish here, and especially those suited to premium styles. The resulting wines tend to be intense, full-flavored reds and powerful, fruit-driven whites. Shiraz is a mainstay, producing deep-colored, richly flavored wines, with distinctive velvety characters. Cabernet sauvignon tends to be smooth, with a ripe richness and hints of chocolate, and merlot also does well. Among the whites, chardonnay excels, producing classic examples at many levels, from big, rich, buttery, toasty wines to elegant, peach-flavored, fruit-driven examples. The region also produces some good fortifieds, and is home to a wide range of sparkling wines. As in so many regions worldwide, pinot noir struggles to graduate from being a sparkling wine component to a fully-fledged varietal red wine.

McLaren Vale's wineries are a mixed bunch, with everything from one-man cellar door operations to corporate behemoths. But the biggest of all of them is Hardy Wine Company, the current incarnation of the company started by Thomas Hardy in the mid-1800s. In addition, Southcorp has a significant stake in the region as has Beringer. But most of the wineries are considerably smaller, resulting in a range and variety of wines that reflects the diversity of the region and its producers.

Regional Dozen

QUALITY WINES

- Chapel Hill The Vicar Cabernet Sauvignon Shiraz
- Clarendon Hills Piggott Range Vineyard Shiraz
- Fox Creek JSM Shiraz Cabernets
- Rosemount GSM Grenache Shiraz Mourvèdre
- Tatachilla Clarendon Vineyard Merlot
- Wirra Wirra RSW Shiraz

BEST VALUE WINES

- Chapel Hill Verdelho
- d'Arenberg d'Arry's Original Shiraz Grenache
- Maglieri Chardonnay
- Scarpantoni Block 3 Shiraz
- Shottesbrooke Chardonnay
- Tatachilla Growers Chenin Sémillon Sauvignon Blanc

D'ARENBERG WINES

Established **1912** ***Owners*** **d'Arenberg Wines Pty Ltd** ***Production*** **120,000 cases** ***Vineyard area*** **291 acres (118 ha)**

A McLaren Vale stalwart since 1912, d'Arenberg has managed to move gracefully and intelligently with the

times. It was d'Arry Osborn who built up the business from the 1950s onwards, making big earthy reds and fortifieds, but his son Chester has held sway since the mid-1980s. Chester rejuvenated the old cellars and vineyards, brought in small stainless steel tanks and gave the winemaking a bit of a revamp. Both the whites and reds have since attracted increasing acclaim, both in Australia and overseas.

ABOVE LEFT: *Wine being tested at Chapel Hill Winery.*

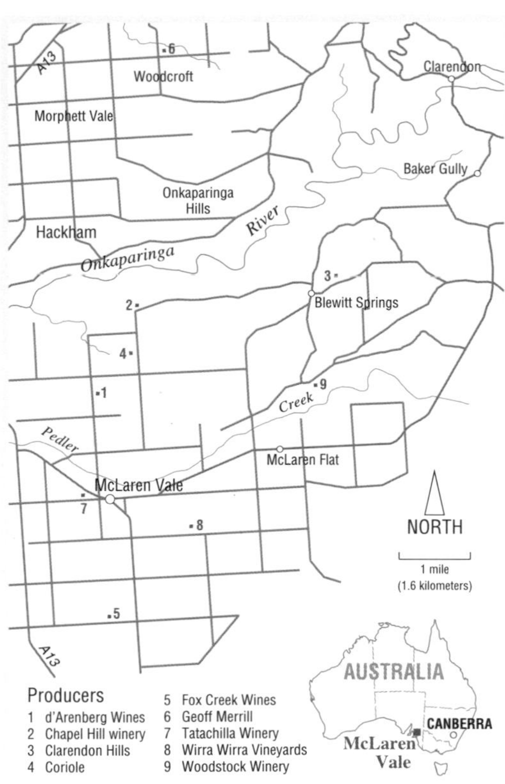

CHAPEL HILL WINERY

Established **1977** ***Owners*** **Gerard Industries Pty Ltd** ***Production*** **60,000 cases** ***Vineyard area*** **108 acres (44 ha)**

The redoubtably down-to-earth Pam Dunsford is probably heartily sick of reading this, but she will always be the first woman in Australia to have graduated as an enologist. In 1987, she moved to Chapel Hill, where she designed one of the most sensible (all machinery either glides or slides), yet graceful, wineries in the area, and tucked it unobtrusively into the side of the hill. Her wines are always robust, balanced and fine, whether the traditionally styled shiraz, cabernet sauvignon and blends, or chardonnay (with and without wood). She also makes a very good verdelho.

CLARENDON HILLS

Established **1970** ***Owners*** **Clarendon Hills Nominees Pty Ltd** ***Production*** **18,000 cases** ***Vineyard area*** **NA**

Always in the sought after category, the red wines from Clarendon Hills have become even more scarce in recent years, thanks largely to a string of recommendations from influential commentators, especially in the US. Situated on the northern fringes of McLaren Vale, the Clarendon Hills winery takes fruit from small plots of old vines in the hilly slopes bordering the Adelaide Hills region. The resulting wines are huge, intense, complex, multi-layered beasts which often owe more in style to French winemaking than Australian. Clarendon Hills' wines are not for the faint-hearted or the financially challenged.

LEFT: *The tasting room at Tatachilla Winery, which was named Australian Winery of the Year for 1996–97.*

TATACHILLA WINERY

Established **1901** ***Owners*** **Lion Nathan** ***Production*** **100,000 cases** ***Vineyard area*** **79 acres (32 ha)**

In recent years Tatachilla has really found its level. Owned for many years by a local growers co-operative, it was bought in 1993 by a consortium, then re-vamped and re-opened in 1995. Since then the wines have steadily improved and regularly do extremely well on the Australian wine show circuit. It was named Australian Winery of the Year for 1996–97 by *Vogue Entertaining* magazine. Cabernet sauvignon and merlot are particularly good.

WIRRA WIRRA VINEYARDS

Established **1894** ***Owners*** **Greg and Roger Trott** ***Production*** **60,000 cases** ***Vineyard area*** **123 acres (50 ha)**

Wirra Wirra, established by noted cricketer Robert Strangeways Wigley, was revived and restored by Greg and Roger Trott in 1969. They, with former winemaker Ben Riggs, current winemaker Samantha Connew and MD Tim James, have been responsible for increasingly good wines, both white and red, including the popular Church Block cabernet blend and the rich and creamy Cousins sparkling pinot noir/chardonnay.

Some significant producers in the region include Coriole, Fox Creek Wines, Geoff Merrill and Woodstock Winery.

RIGHT: *The carefully tended vineyard at Bowen Estate is hand pruned.*

Coonawarra and the Limestone Coast

ALEX MITCHELL

Coonawarra is known throughout Australia and the world for its elegant yet richly flavored cabernet sauvignon. Its fame rests on a narrow strip of paprika-colored soil: terra rossa. Loam overlays well-draining limestone and a high water table, and produces exceptional grape development and characters. It is only about 12.5 miles (20 km) long and 1 mile (1.5 km) wide, narrowing at each end, with the soil varying in depth from a few inches to 3 feet (a few centimeters to a meter).

John Riddoch discovered the region's viticultural potential, planting grape vines, largely shiraz and cabernet sauvignon, in 1890. He built the limestone winery that remains at Wynns Coonawarra Estate today.

Although Coonawarra is more well known, the Padthaway region, 53 miles (85 km) north, now produces more grapes. Seppelt was the first to plant vines there, in 1963. The suitability of the soil and climate for grape growing was soon evident, though not for reds, but for white varieties, notably chardonnay. Hardys and Lindemans have invested in the Padthaway region.

RIGHT: *An autumn leaf from a shiraz vine.*

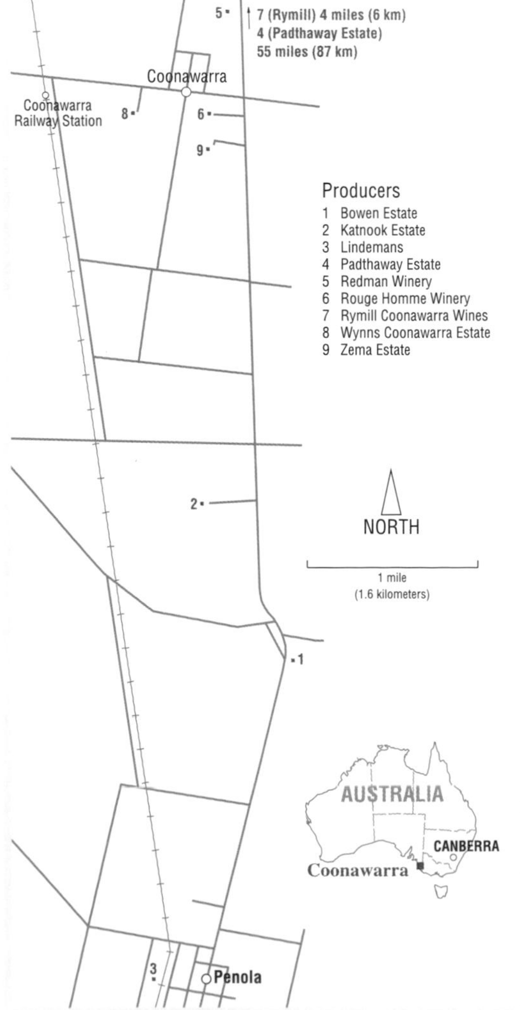

Less than 18.5 miles (30 km) from the coast, Mount Gambier is South Australia's southernmost viticultural region and awaits assessment of its full potential. There are five small producers, with chardonnay and cabernet sauvignon dominating plantings. The Mount Benson area, on the coast, is one of Australia's newest. Lindemans planted experimental vines in 1978, and Southcorp remains a significant investor, along with Cellarmaster Wines and, more recently, M. Chapoutier & Co., one of France's most notable Rhône Valley producers.

The region's early reputation was built on shiraz but by the 1960s, cabernet sauvignon had eclipsed it and this is one district that has never looked back. The cool climate and terra rossa combine to give distinctive perfume and complexity to the wines. Coonawarra cabernet displays the blackcurrants, plums, cassis, and chocolatey richness of the variety, but is frequently tinged with hints of mint and eucalyptus.

Though somewhat of a bridesmaid to cabernet, shiraz from the Limestone Coast has a fine history and remains a powerfully spicy form of the variety. Riesling from this area is surprisingly good, in a fruity and fragrant style made by only a few producers, most notably Wynns and Hollick. Rymill and Katnook Estate persist with sauvignon blanc. Chardonnay has seen mixed fortunes in the Coonawarra region but it has become the forte of Padthaway, where it makes elegant but fruity still wines and complex sparkling wines. Mount Benson and Robe are still experimenting, but some recently released shiraz has been surprisingly lush, especially when treated with French oak.

BOWEN ESTATE, COONAWARRA

Established **1972** ***Owners*** **Doug and Joy Bowen** ***Production*** **15,000 cases** ***Vineyard area*** **90 acres (33 ha)**

The family-owned and managed Bowen Estate has a well earned reputation for wines that reflect the premium nature of Coonawarra fruit when it is carefully tended, hand pruned and sensitively handled. Doug Bowen was a young Roseworthy graduate when he purchased and planted his plot of terra rossa in 1972. Bowen's wines have layers of intense flavor, a lush mouthfeel and remarkable length, and will further reward those who have the patience to cellar them carefully.

KATNOOK ESTATE, COONAWARRA

Established **1890s** ***Owner*** **Wingara Wine Group** ***Production*** **60,000 cases** ***Vineyard area*** **988 acres (400 ha)**

The Katnook Estate name is derived from the original property established by John Riddoch in Coonawarra in the 1860s, although the Katnook brand was not established until 1979. The second vintage of Riddoch's wines was made in the woolshed at Katnook, a building that still constitutes part of the winery complex, as does John Riddoch's homestead. The estate produces some of Coonawarra's most intensely flavored and painstakingly crafted wines. A Jimmy Watson trophy for the 1997 Shiraz highlights the caliber of the wines. Odyssey and Prodigy, wines of huge flavor and structure yet with fine balance and complexity, are made from the top one percent of hand-selected cabernet fruit.

LEFT: Grapes are shoveled into a crusher at Padthaway Estate.

LINDEMANS, COONAWARRA

Established **1908** ***Owner*** **Southcorp Wines** ***Production*** **9,000 cases** ***Vineyard area*** **250 acres (100 ha)**

British immigrant and Australian viticultural pioneer, Dr Henry John Lindeman planted his Cawarra vineyards in the Hunter Valley of NSW in 1843. His name is now one of Southcorp's most successful brands. The Lindemans Coonawarra trio of Pyrus, Limestone Ridge and St George, the brand's flagship wines, are crafted from premium Coonawarra fruit. St George is one of Australia's classic single vineyard cabernets and shows rich plums, chocolate and smoky wood on the palate.

PADTHAWAY ESTATE, PADTHAWAY

Established **1979** ***Owners*** **Dale Baker and Ian Gray** ***Production*** **6,000 cases** ***Vineyard area*** **125 acres (50 ha)**

The site of settler Robert Lawson's sheep property, this vineyard was the area's sole attraction until recently. The gracious Padthaway Estate Homestead built in 1882 remained the Lawson family residence until 1980, when it was sold for use as luxury accommodation. Padthaway Estate's sparkling wine demonstrates the potential of the area for success with cool-climate white grapes.

WYNNS COONAWARRA ESTATE, COONAWARRA

Established **1891** ***Owners*** **Southcorp Wines** ***Production*** **380,000 cases** ***Vineyard area*** **2,223 acres (900 ha)**

No visit to Coonawarra is complete without a pilgrimage to the historic limestone building, the first winery in the area, completed by John Riddoch in 1896. It was a facility much admired in its day. After the death of its founder in 1901, the property declined until Samuel Wynn and his son David purchased it in 1951. Their success in the following years was the impetus for investment in Coonawarra by many other companies. The classic shiraz beloved by many as Wynns Hermitage remains a benchmark, and the black label Cabernet Sauvignon is collected by aficionados, as are the premium John Riddoch Cabernet Sauvignon and Michael Shiraz.

Some significant producers in Coonawarra and the Limestone Coast include Redman Winery, Rymill Coonawarra Wines and Zema Estate.

Regional Best

QUALITY WINES

Bowen Estate Cabernet Sauvignon
Hollick Ravenswood Cabernet Sauvignon
Katnook Estate Odyssey Cabernet Sauvignon
Majella Cabernet Sauvignon
Parker First Growth Cabernet Sauvignon
Wynns John Riddoch Cabernet Sauvignon

BEST VALUE WINES

Lindemans St George Cabernet Sauvignon
Penley Estate Hyland Shiraz
Redman Cabernet Sauvignon
Rymill Merlot Cabernet
Wynns Coonawarra Estate Shiraz
Zema Estate Cluny Cabernets

BELOW: Triple gables appear on the Wynns Coonawarra Estate label.

ABOVE: *This tasting room offers a geometric display of resting bottles.*

Other South Australian Regions

RIVERLAND

SALLY MARDEN

Regional Dozen

- Angove's Classic Reserve Chardonnay
- Banrock Station Sparkling Chardonnay
- Banrock Station Shiraz
- Bonneyview Cabernet Petit Verdot
- Kingston Estate Cabernet Sauvignon
- Kingston Estate Merlot
- Normans Lone Gum Vineyard Unwooded Chardonnay
- Normans Lone Gum Vineyard Cabernet Merlot
- Renmano Chairman's Selection Reserve Chardonnay
- Yalumba Oxford Landing Limited Release Merlot
- Yalumba Oxford Landing Limited Release Sémillon
- Yalumba Oxford Landing Sauvignon Blanc

With so much emphasis placed on the fashionable regions producing premium wine, it would be easy to forget that the driving force in Australia's wine industry is the far less glamorous, vast open space of the Riverland. These endless acres of vines, watered by the Murray River, pump out more than half of South Australia's grapes and a third of the country's total crush. These vineyards provide the fruit for the Australian wines that most people, at home and abroad, drink most of: the wines are the big name brands, the bags-in-boxes, the everyday quaffers. They are honest, enjoyable, good-value wines that are full of flavor.

It's hot and dry here, but the brown sandy loam soils are reasonably fertile. Rainfall is low and evaporation high, so there is little risk of disease. The main concern for the future of the Riverland is the health of the Murray River, where water levels are dropping and salinity levels are rising. It is hoped that new, more sensitive irrigation systems will help to alleviate the pressures on this invaluable resource.

RIGHT: *Plump grapes destined for the crusher.*

ANGOVE'S

Established **1886** ***Owners*** **the Angove family** ***Production*** **750,000 cases** ***Vineyard area*** **1,260 acres (510 ha)**

This is one of Australia's largest privately owned wine companies, with a very successful range of good-value varietals, fortified wines and spirits, including Australia's best-known brandy, St Agnes. Labels include the Classic Reserve, Stonegate, Sarnia Farm, Butterfly Ridge and Misty Vineyards ranges.

BANROCK STATION

Established **1994** ***Owners*** **Hardy Wine Company** ***Production*** **1.5 million cases** ***Vineyard area*** **615 acres (250 ha)**

Banrock Station is a groundbreaking vineyard property, wetland reserve and visitor center. Everything has been done with the environment and conservation in mind. The wines themselves show what the region can achieve with the right handling; there is a delightful sparkling chardonnay, and fresh, modern examples of unwooded chardonnay, shiraz, cabernet/merlot and sémillon/chardonnay. These are good wines made with environmental common sense and marketing genius.

BERRI ESTATES

Established **1922** ***Owners*** **the Hardy Wine Company** ***Production*** **7,920,000 cases** ***Vineyard area*** **NA**

This was originally a growers' co-operative formed by soldiers returning from the First World War. The company merged with Riverland giant Renmano in 1982. Berri is Australia's largest single winery and distillery and can process 77,000 tons (70,000 t) of grapes every year, with storage room for 18.5 million gallons (70 million l).

BONNEYVIEW WINES

Established **1976** ***Owners*** **Robert Minns** ***Production*** **5,000 cases** ***Vineyard area*** **6 acres (2.5 ha)**

Not your average Riverland winery, this. The boutique Bonneyview was established by English cricketer Robert Minns on the shores of Lake Bonney. Not only is its size and style rather incongruous, so is its range of wines, which rely on the comparatively rare petit verdot. As well as straight varietals, Bonneyview Wines also produces blends with merlot and cabernet sauvignon. With a popular cellar door and restaurant, Bonneyview makes an interesting contrast to the industrial-scale enterprises of its nearest neighbors.

Other significant producers in the region include Kingston Estate Wines, Normans Lone Gum Winery and Renmano Winery.

VICTORIA

Grampians and Pyrenees

ALEX MITCHELL

The landscape in this area varies from flat golden pasture to rugged granite escarpment. The winters are cold and wet, the summers are cool and dry, and spring frosts are not uncommon. The average annual rainfall is low, and vines struggle without supplementary irrigation.

Flavors of the highly praised premium shiraz vary from region to region, but are always of juicy berry fruits. Cabernet sauvignon is often minty, tinged with eucalyptus and generally riddled with purple fruit flavors.

Sauvignon blanc from the Pyrenees is distinctive. A flinty dryness enriched by soft tropical fruit flavors suggests that this area may become a source of great varietal interest.

Ballarat's cooler temperatures result in pinot noirs of superb complexity. More recent plantings of sangiovese, pinot grigio and viognier are adding interest. The remote far southwest has a maritime climate and is sparsely planted so far. The Seppelt vineyards at Drumborg are most significant.

DALWHINNIE WINERY, PYRENEES

Established **1976** ***Owners*** **David and Jenny Jones** ***Production*** **4,500 cases** ***Vineyard area*** **62 acres (25 ha)**

Winemaker David Jones produces outstanding shiraz, cabernet sauvignon and chardonnay that show regional definition and intensity of fruit flavor, reflecting low-yield viticultural practices. Dalwhinnie's Eagle Series Shiraz is only released in exceptional years.

MOUNT LANGI GHIRAN WINERY, GRAMPIANS

Established **1970** ***Owners*** **the Rathbone family** ***Production*** **25,000 cases** ***Vineyard area*** **198 acres (80 ha)**

Winemaker Trevor Mast's premium shiraz is one of Australia's finest cool-climate reds, and it can be difficult to obtain, while the Cliff Edge Shiraz is fast building a fine reputation. The cabernet merlot and riesling are regional benchmarks. Recent releases of pinot grigio and sangiovese show the area's potential for these varieties.

SEPPELT GREAT WESTERN, GRAMPIANS

Established **1865** ***Owners*** **Southcorp Wines Pty Ltd** ***Production*** **2 million cases** ***Vineyard area*** **790 acres (320 ha)**

Here, 2 miles (3 km) of heritage-listed "drives" (granite tunnels) hold more than 8,000 gallons (30,000 l) of maturing sparkling wines. The large Seppelt production plant processes fruit from many regions, but estate-grown fruit stars in both the still and sparkling shiraz.

Some significant producers in the Grampians and Pyrenees regions include Bests Wines, Blue Pyrenees Estate and Redbank Winery.

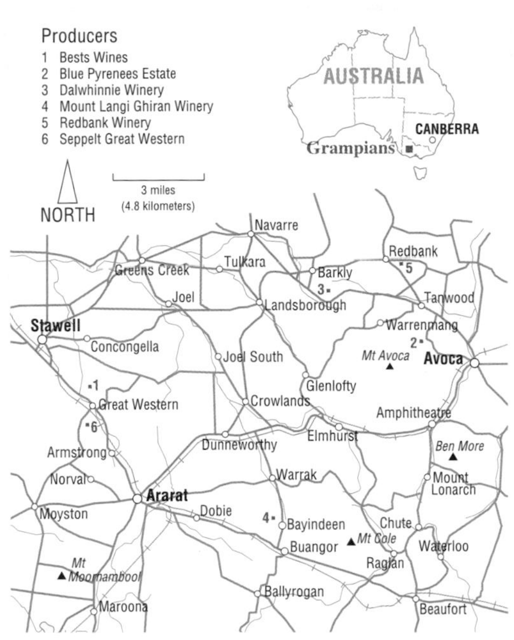

BELOW LEFT: The Dalwhinnie vineyard in the Pyrenees.

Regional Dozen

Bests Bin o Shiraz
Blue Pyrenees Estate Red Blend
Cathcart Ridge Merlot
Dalwhinnie Eagle Series Shiraz
Garden Gully Sparkling Red
Mount Avoca Sauvignon Blanc
Mount Langi Ghiran Shiraz
Redbank Sally's Paddock Red Blend
Seppelt Great Western Shiraz
Seppelt Show Reserve Sparkling Shiraz
Summerfield Shiraz
Taltarni Merlot

Producers
1 All Saints Estate
2 Baileys of Glenrowan
3 Brown Brothers Milawa Vineyard
4 R.L. Buller & Son
5 Campbells Wines
6 Chambers Rosewood Winery
7 Giaconda Vineyard
8 Morris Wines
9 Pfieffer Wines

ABOVE: *The tasting room at Brown Brothers Milawa Vineyard.*

Rutherglen & North East Victoria

ALEX MITCHELL

The history of North East Victorian viticulture is littered with names that to this day evoke the region—Brown, Morris, Sutherland Smith and Campbell. The first records of vines in the area are from 1851, and by 1870 Rutherglen was the largest vineyard area in the colony.

Rutherglen and Glenrowan are the epitome of a hot, continental climate; spring frosts can be a problem and rainfall is low. The Ovens Valley, overlooked by Mount Buffalo, has the high rainfall and cooler temperatures of an elevated region. The King Valley reflects its mountainous landscape, varying from sparse to abundant rainfall and from sterile to exceptionally fertile soils. Viticultural techniques vary throughout the North East region in response to these microclimates.

Brown Brothers plantings at Milawa serve as a mini-nursery for Italian grape varieties in Victoria. They include nebbiolo, dolcetto, barbera, aleatico and moscato, plus the Spanish variety graciano.

Rutherglen has also specialized in durif and shiraz to make its superb vintage ports, and transforms the brown muscat grape into rich, dark, barrel-aged liqueur muscats that are unique to North East Victoria. The local version of tokay, also a liqueur, is a product of the muscadelle grape; nowhere else in the world is it put to this use.

RIGHT: *An unusual wine bottle containing original liqueur from 1914.*

Regional Dozen

- All Saints Show Reserve Muscat and Tokay
- Baileys of Glenrowan Founders Muscat and Tokay
- Brown Brothers Very Old Liqueur Muscat and Vintage Port
- Bullers Museum Release Muscat
- Campbells Isabella Tokay and Merchant Prince Muscat
- Campbells The Barkly Durif
- Chambers Rosewood Rare Muscat and Tokay
- Giaconda Chardonnay and Pinot Noir
- Morris Old Premium Muscat and Tokay
- Pfieffer Christopher's Vintage Port
- Stanton & Killeen Special Old Liqueur Muscat
- Stanton & Killeen Vintage Port

BROWN BROTHERS MILAWA VINEYARD, KING VALLEY

Established **1889** ***Owners*** **the Brown family** ***Production*** **900,000 cases** ***Vineyard area*** **1,255 acres (508 ha)**

One of Australia's most successful and innovative family operations, Brown Brothers sources fruit from many of the surrounding regions, always acknowledging special vineyards on the labels. Consistency of quality and a kaleidoscope of varietals and styles have made them firm favorites with wine lovers.

GIACONDA VINEYARD, OVENS VALLEY

Established **1985** ***Owner*** **Rick Kinzbrunner** ***Production*** **1,000 cases** ***Vineyard area*** **19 acres (7 ha)**

For many, Giaconda makes Australia's best wines. They are eagerly sought after by those on the mailing list and also by restaurants. One of the country's most opulently flavored, although elegantly structured, chardonnays is complemented by a surprisingly Burgundian pinot noir. Early shiraz releases have been stunning.

MORRIS WINES, RUTHERGLEN

Established **1859** ***Owners*** **Orlando Wyndham Group** ***Production*** **60,000 cases** ***Vineyard area*** **250 acres (100 ha)**

Veteran winemaker David Morris is an ebullient character who produces fortifieds that are benchmarks of Australia. His table wines, especially the rich, full-bodied durif, boast a loyal following.

Other significant producers in Rutherglen and North East Victoria include Baileys of Glenrowan; All Saints Estate, R. L. Buller and Son, Campbells Wines, Chambers Rosewood Winery and Pfieffer Wines (all Rutherglen).

Yarra Valley

KATE MCINTYRE

In 1838 William Ryrie established Victoria's first commercial vineyard at the Yering cattle station in the Yarra Valley. Others followed—St Huberts, Yeringberg—and the Yarra Valley went on to enjoy international success in the late 1800s, winning gold medals at European wine shows. However, a combination of economic depression, the threat of phylloxera, and the temperance movement brought an end to the valley's wine history.

In the 1970s, the Yarra Valley returned to wine, and today it is one of Australia's most successful and diverse wine-producing regions. Its undulating hills contain small boutique wineries and larger, more commercial enterprises. Close to Melbourne, it has become an attractive tourist destination, with the Yarra Valley Vignerons Association ensuring the success of festivals such as Grape Grazing (in early March).

The combination of good soil and a cool temperate climate makes the Yarra Valley ideal for growing grapes and making premium wine. The warmest vineyards can ripen cabernet sauvignon and shiraz admirably, while cooler sites produce leaner wines and are better for pinot noir and chardonnay. Along with merlot, these are the predominant grape varieties grown in the valley. Sauvignon blanc, pinot gris, marsanne, and roussanne have been planted recently, but have not generally taken off yet.

The Yarra Valley is one of Australia's premium sites for sparkling wines and was selected by Champagne houses Devaux and Moët & Chandon as the site for their Australian sparkling wine ventures—Yarrabank and Domaine Chandon.

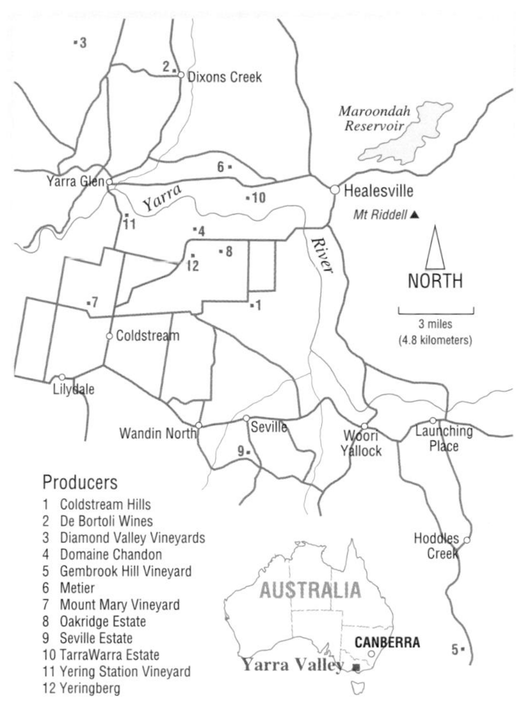

DE BORTOLI WINES

Established **1987** ***Owners*** **the De Bortoli family** ***Production*** **150,000 cases** ***Vineyard area*** **more than 840 acres (340 ha)**

De Bortoli, one of the biggest players in the Valley, does not sacrifice quality for quantity and produces excellent wines across its range. There is the occasional premium release followed by the excellent and always good-value Yarra Valley wines; then Gulf Station and the cheaper, fruit-driven Windy Peak wines. The top of the range shows a lot of new oak, which falls into balance with age. Their Reserve Shiraz won the 1997 Jimmy Watson award.

LEFT: *Grapes for the best wines are picked by hand.*

COLDSTREAM HILLS

Established **1985** ***Owners*** **Southcorp Wines Pty Ltd** ***Production*** **50,000 cases** ***Vineyard area*** **114 acres (46 ha)**

Founded by James Halliday, one of Australia's wine industry greats, Coldstream Hills is one of the Yarra's best-known wineries. Halliday established the winery and vineyard to specialize in limited-production, premium-quality pinot noir, chardonnay and cabernet sauvignon/merlot. In 1996, Southcorp acquired the vineyard and the brand, while retaining Halliday as head winemaker. Coldstream Hills has recently included a merlot, a sauvignon blanc and a pinot gris in its portfolio, but it is the old stalwarts—chardonnay and pinot noir—that continue to excel. Current winemaker Paul Lapsley is ensuring the quality of the wines remains high.

DOMAINE CHANDON

Established **1987** ***Owners*** **Moet et Chandon** ***Production*** **120,000 cases** ***Vineyard area*** **198 acres (80 ha)**

Moët & Chandon purchased the Green Point vineyard in 1987 and planted the traditional champagne varieties—pinot noir, chardonnay and pinot meunier. In 1994 they established another vineyard in the Strathbogie Ranges. Chandon has always asserted they are not attempting to make a clone of champagne, but

Regional Dozen

QUALITY WINES

- Diamond Valley Close Planted Pinot Noir
- Mount Mary Cabernets Quintet
- Oakridge Reserve Cabernet
- Seville Estate Shiraz
- TarraWarra Pinot Noir
- TarraWarra Chardonnay
- Yering Station Reserve Pinot Noir
- Yering Station Reserve Shir Viognier

BEST VALUE WINES

- Coldstream Hills Chardonnay
- Domaine Chandon (sparkling)
- Gembrook Hill Pinot Noir
- Gulf Station Shiraz
- St Hubert's Cabernet Merlot
- Yarra Burn Pinot Noir Chardonnay

to produce the best Australian sparkling wines using traditional methods. Reserves of older wines are being built up, and the wines are becoming world class.

MOUNT MARY VINEYARD

Established **1971** ***Owners*** **John and Marli Middleton** ***Production*** **3,500 cases** ***Vineyard area*** **30 acres (12 ha)**

Dr John Middleton's wines are some of the greatest in Australia. His intense Cabernets Quintet (cabernet sauvignon/cabernet franc/merlot/malbec/petit verdot) always lives up to its reputation, as does his long-living pinot noir. The wines are available only by mail order, at exclusive restaurants or sometimes at auctions.

SEVILLE ESTATE

Established **1972** ***Owners*** **Brokenwood Wines Pty Ltd and Peter McMahon** ***Production*** **2,500 cases** ***Vineyard area*** **20 acres (8 ha)**

Dr Peter McMahon shared a medical practice with Dr John Middleton (Mount Mary) in the 1950s and also shared Middleton's aspirations to create great wine. The vineyard was planted in 1972 and McMahon retired in 1982 to be a full-time winemaker. In 1997 the McMahons sold a controlling share of the estate to Brokenwood Wines, but continue to be involved in a consulting role. The Seville Estate Shiraz is everything you could want from a shiraz—rich, with spicy black pepper and ripe savory fruit, wonderful depth, length and complexity.

The soft extractive note of an aged cork being withdrawn has the true sound of a man opening his heart.

William Samuel Benwell, JOURNEY TO WINE IN VICTORIA

TARRAWARRA ESTATE

Established **1983** ***Owner*** **Marc Besen** ***Production*** **6,000 cases** ***Vineyard area*** **72 acres (29 ha)**

Tarrawarra, under the expert supervision of winemaker Clare Halloran, is regarded as one of the top producers of pinot noir in the Yarra Valley and indeed in Australia. The Tarrawarra Pinot Noir is powerful yet complex, with excellent structure supporting intense red and black berry fruit and brambly characters. Their chardonnay is definitely one of Australia's most underrated. Tarrawarra Estate's wines are made to last and are at their best with a little age.

BELOW: *The cellar door facilities at Domaine Chandon Winery have spectacular views of manicured vineyards and gardens with the rest of Yarra Valley in the distance.*

YERING STATION VINEYARD

Established **1838, re-established 1987** ***Owners*** **the Rathbone family** ***Production*** **15,000 cases** ***Vineyard area*** **284 acres (115 ha)**

The historic site of Victoria's first winery, Yering Station is not resting on its laurels. Winemaker Tom Carson produces a range of wines, some of which—the Yering Station Reserve Pinot Noir in particular—are superb. The pinot and chardonnay in the Reserve range are complex and lovely. Yering Station's winery and restaurant facility rivals the grandeur of Domaine Chandon, a rivalry also manifested in Yering Station's joint venture with Devaux Champagne to produce the elegantly delicious Yarrabank Cuvée. The Reserve Shiraz Viognier has quickly proved itself to be one of the very finest in the country.

Other significant producers in the Yarra Valley include Diamond Valley Vineyards, Gembrook Hill Vineyard, Metier, Oakridge Estate and Yeringberg.

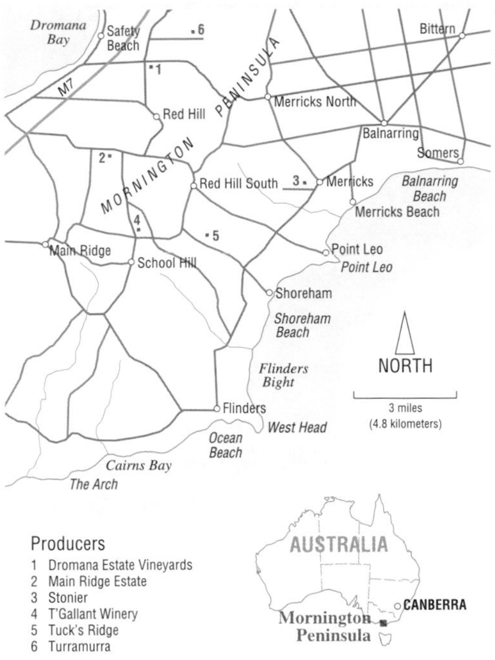

Mornington Peninsula

KATE MCINTYRE

This is a young and a boutique winery region that boasts more than 100 vineyards, all less than two hours from Melbourne. Many producers here are crafting elegant and complex wines. Quality improves with every vintage as vines become established, promising greatness.

The Peninsula is hilly, and the often marginal climate is cool to cold, with a maritime influence. A small region, it can be broken into at least five not as yet classified subregions: Moorooduc Downs, Red Hill, Dromana, Merricks and Main Ridge. The subregions show diverse soil types and microclimates, and the wines reflect these differences.

The region specializes in medium-bodied, dry table wines and is beginning to have success with sparkling wines. The predominant and most successful grape varieties are chardonnay and pinot noir. The latter already shows good complexity and structure, ranging in style from elegant and ethereal to huge, rich, and impressive. Chardonnay ranges from crisp, fruit-driven, unoaked wines, with a fruit spectrum from citrus and melon through to tropical pineapple aromas and flavors. Shiraz and sauvignon blanc are enjoying success in the warmer sites. Pinot gris, which does very well in the climate here, is touted as the "next big thing".

ABOVE LEFT: *Main Ridge Winery produces elegant complex wines from a marginal site.*

DROMANA ESTATE VINEYARDS

Established **1982** ***Owners*** **Crittenden Family** ***Production*** **10,300 cases** ***Vineyard area*** **12 acres (4.9 ha)**

Dromana Estate boasts the largest range of wines on sale on the Mornington Peninsula, from the lower-priced Schinus range through the Dromana Estate range to the Reserve wines. Made from estate-grown fruit and fermented by natural yeasts, the Reserve Chardonnay is particularly complex and rich. A range of outstanding wines made from Italian grape varieties is also produced.

T'GALLANT WINERY

Established **1990** ***Owners*** **Beringer Blass** ***Production*** **10,000 cases** ***Vineyard area*** **55 acres (20 ha)**

T'Gallant produces fresh, fruit-driven, unoaked chardonnay and several versions of pinot gris, including the Tribute, a homage to the Alsace wines made from this variety. They also produce a pinot grigio in a crisper, more flinty Italian style. Their pinot noir gets better each year, with rich, soft, dark berry fruit and velvety tannins.

Other notable producers here include Main Ridge Estate, Stonier, Tuck's Ridge at Red Hill and Turramurra.

Regional Dozen

QUALITY WINES

Dromana Estate Reserve Chardonnay
Main Ridge Half Acre Pinot Noir
Merricks Estate Shiraz
Moorooduc Chardonnay
Stonier Reserve Pinot Noir
Tuck's Ridge Pinot Noir

BEST VALUE WINES

Hann's Creek Pinot Noir
Osborns Vineyard Chardonnay
Red Hill Estate Pinot Noir
Stonier Pinot Noir
T'Gallant Tribute Pinot Gris
Turramurra Sauvignon Blanc

LEFT: *The picturesque Merricks vineyard on Mornington Peninsula, with the winery garden in the foreground.*

Other Victorian Regions

ALEX MITCHELL

GIPPSLAND

Gippsland, spreading over a large area of the state's southeastern corner, is Victoria's most recent viticultural area of rebirth, with current plantings beginning in the 1970s. The region's isolation and scattered nature of the wineries has kept it from achieving wider recognition.

Cool-climate classics chardonnay and pinot noir dominate production here. Spiciness and complexity characterize the fruit flavors. However, rainfall, soils, temperature and terrain do vary considerably, reflecting the size of the zone and proximity to the coast. Likewise, styles vary with *terroir*, but production of sparkling wine in the region is negligible.

Regional Dozen

Bass Phillip Chardonnay
Bass Phillip Pinot Noir
Wild Dog Winery Barrel-fermented Chardonnay
Cleveland Winery Macedon Brut
Cleveland Winery Pinot Noir
Craiglee Shiraz
Cobaw Ridge Chardonnay
Cobaw Ridge Shiraz
Cope-Williams r.o.m.s.e.y Brut
Hanging Rock Winery Macedon Cuvée
Knight Granite Hills Riesling
Rochford Pinot Noir

BASS PHILLIP WINES

Established **1979** ***Owners*** **Phillip and Sairung Jones** ***Production*** **1,400 cases** ***Vineyard area*** **58 acres (23.5 ha)**

Some declare Bass Phillip Pinot Noir to be without equal in Australia. It is certainly a labor of love for winemaker Phillip Jones, whose closely planted vines require traditional hand-pruning and harvesting. His chardonnay is also made with distinction.

MACEDON

The elevation of the Macedon Ranges makes it one of Australia's coldest regions. Wind chill, autumn frosts and unforgiving granite soils add to the challenge and lack appeal for larger companies.

The region's forte is sparkling wine made from the traditional combination of chardonnay and pinot noir. Wines are crisp and intensely flavored. An acid backbone gives elegance to whites. Pinot noir can be earthy and complex, and Shiraz, which has a cult following, shows spice, surprising fruit weight and soft tannins.

BELOW: A tractor brings in a load of grapes at Tahbilk Wines.

HANGING ROCK WINERY, MACEDON

Established **1982** ***Owners*** **John and Anne Ellis** ***Production*** **15,000 cases** ***Vineyard area*** **39 acres (16 ha)**

The large production here reflects sourcing of fruit from other wine regions. Winemaker John Ellis' wines are of consistently good quality. The Macedon Cuvée is a standout and the shiraz from Heathcote is highly regarded.

GEELONG

As one of Australia's most southerly regions, Geelong enjoys a long ripening period, allowing grapes to develop complexity and depth of flavor. Strongly maritime influenced, the *terroir* offers scant summer rainfall, chill winds, and poor clay soils. When Geelong wine is good, it is very good. Predictably, pinot noir and chardonnay are grown with distinction in the southerly climate.

BANNOCKBURN VINEYARDS

Established **1974** ***Owners*** **the Hooper Family** ***Production*** **7,000 cases** ***Vineyard area*** **67 acres (27 ha)**

Winemaker Gary Farr frequently works the vintage in Burgundy when his work at Bannockburn is done. The exceptional quality and complexity of his Pinot Noir, Chardonnay and Shiraz demonstrate his skill in realizing the potential of grapes from Geelong. These are cult wines from a producer who tends to avoid the trappings of the marketplace.

CENTRAL VICTORIA

The warm climate of Central Victoria's lower regions makes it highly suitable for red wines with powerful fruit flavors, particularly shiraz and cabernet.

Since the 1960s, the Bendigo region, with its undulating hills and dense eucalyptus forest, has become home to many small wineries that produce limited quantities of high-quality wine.

Marsanne grown in commercial quantities is exclusive to the flat, fertile land of the Goulburn Valley. Tahbilk and Mitchelton produce some of Victoria's best value and most interesting whites from this variety, their aged marsanne is a rare treat for collectors.

The Central Victorian Mountain Country is influenced by altitude which ranges from 1,000 to 6,000 feet (300 to 1,800 m). Yields are lower, frosts are a concern, and most vineyards experience snow in winter. The Mountain Country specializes in cooler climate varieties—chardonnay is its forte for both still and sparkling wines. Riesling and gewürztraminer are sought after for their crisp and fresh fruit flavors and balanced acid.

ABOVE: Nicholson River Winery in Gippsland uses minimal preservatives in its opulent chardonnays.

The red wines of Central Victoria often show distinctive minty, herbaceous characters. The wines tend to be strongly colored and have powerful fruit flavors. Shiraz occupies the most acreage, closely followed by cabernet sauvignon. The warmer areas produce generous yields, but strong sunshine and low rainfall require canopy management.

JASPER HILL VINEYARD, BENDIGO

Established **1976** ***Owners*** **Ron and Elva Laughton** ***Production*** **3,000 cases** ***Vineyard area*** **57 acres (23 ha)**

Two separate shiraz vineyards named after the Laughtons' daughters produce the much lauded and deliciously different Emily's Paddock and Georgia's Paddock wines. The vines are not irrigated and so produce only small quantities of grapes, which are carefully pressed and softly oaked—they are benchmark reds of the region.

TAHBILK WINES, GOULBURN VALLEY

Established **1860** ***Owners*** **the Purbrick Family** ***Production*** **100,000 cases** ***Vineyard area*** **449 acres (182 ha)**

This is one of the country's most beautiful and historic wineries, which still occupies some of the original buildings. Some of the oldest vines in the country remain producing the intensely flavored, outstanding Tahbilk 1860 Vines Shiraz. The marsanne is a bargain and a collectors' favorite, aging to honeyed richness.

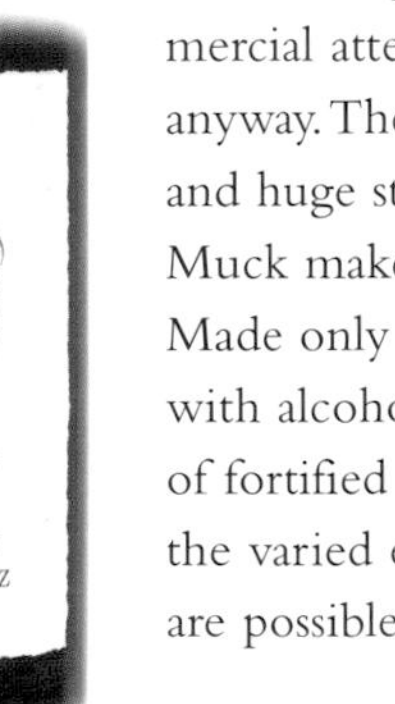

MITCHELTON WINERY, GOULBURN VALLEY

Established **1969** ***Owners*** **Petaluma Ltd** ***Production*** **200,000 cases** ***Vineyard area*** **350 acres (142 ha)**

Mitchelton is the largest producer of the area, with a reputation for quality and distinctive regional flavor profiles. Winemaker Don Lewis produces a huge range, including the Valley's specialty, white marsanne. The shiraz, cabernet and riesling are all outstanding.

WILD DUCK CREEK ESTATE, BENDIGO

Established **1980** ***Owners*** **Diana and David Anderson** ***Production*** **500 cases** ***Vineyard area*** **10 acres (4 ha)**

This small producer eschews commercial attention but receives it anyway. The intense concentration and huge structure of the Duck Muck make it a collectors' item. Made only in exceptional years and with alcohol levels approaching that of fortified wine, it demonstrates the varied expressions of shiraz that are possible in the Bendigo region.

Other producers in the region include Delatite (Central Victoria); Lyre Bird Hill Wines, Nicholson River Winery, Phillip Island Vineyard & Winery (all Gippsland); Cope-Williams, Knight Granite Hills Wines, Virgin Hills (all Macedon); and Craiglee (Sunbury).

Regional Dozen

Bannockburn Pinot Noir
Delatite Dead Man's Hill Gewürztraminer
Hanging Rock Heathcote Shiraz
Heathcote Winery Curagee
Idyll Vineyard Shiraz
Jasper Hill Emily's Paddock Shiraz
Mitchelton Print Label Shiraz
Mitchelton Blackwood Park Riesling
Prince Albert Vineyard Pinot Noir
Scotchmans Hill Chardonnay
Chateau Tahbilk Marsanne
Wild Duck Creek Estate Duck Muck

ABOVE: Vineyards and rose gardens at Tyrell's, Hunter Valley.

NEW SOUTH WALES

Hunter Valley

KEN GARGETT

The Hunter Valley is one of Australia's best-known wine areas, and its proximity to Sydney ensures its position as Australia's most visited wine region. Its unique sémillons have captured the hearts of wine lovers everywhere.

Until 1963, Hunter wineries were large commercial enterprises. In that year, however, Dr Max Lake launched Lake's Folly, Australia's first "boutique" winery, an event that would change the face of the country's winemaking.

Despite the Hunter Valley's extensive plantings, dozens of wineries, and a host of cellar door operations, many people think the Hunter is unsuitable for viticulture. The reasons are many, including a high probability of rain during harvest. There is no doubt that site selection is critical and, notwithstanding the current proliferation of new plantings, the area under vine today is smaller than it was 30 years ago.

If there is one white grape upon which the Lower Hunter has built its reputation, it is sémillon. Chardonnay is now more extensively planted, but aged Hunter sémillon is justifiably world famous. In time, these wines pick up toast, honey, butter, and lemon characters that are utterly entrancing. Over the years, Tyrrell's, McWilliams, Lindemans, Rothbury, Brokenwood and others have excelled at the style. The district's chardonnay is also popular, but its richness is not to the taste of every palate. Verdelho is likely to prove the pick of the other whites in years to come.

Regional Dozen

QUALITY WINES

Brokenwood Graveyard Shiraz
McWilliams Mount Pleasant Lovedale Sémillon
Rosemount Roxburgh Chardonnay
Scarborough Chardonnay
Tyrrell's Vat 1 Sémillon
Tyrrell's Vat 47 Chardonnay

BEST VALUE WINES

Brokenwood Sémillon
Drayton's Family Shiraz
Lindemans Hunter River Sémillon
McWilliams Mount Pleasant Elizabeth Sémillon
Margan Family Sémillon
Pepper Tree Shiraz

Hunter shiraz is as distinctive as the region's sémillon. Indeed, the Hunter's earthy, leathery flavors envelop all of its reds but work best with shiraz. It seems improbable that pinot noir could work in the Hunter, and most agree that it doesn't and that it loses varietal character. But many wineries—notably Tyrrell's—persist in planting the variety. Many of the great O'Shea wines and some of Lindemans finest "Hunter River Burgundies" contain a small percentage of pinot.

Grapes were successfully grown in the Upper Hunter in the second half of the nineteenth century, but production had ceased by 1910. The shift in tastes from table to fortified wine was also significant. Penfolds moved here from the Lower Hunter in 1960 but struggled. Their focus was on red wines but subsequent experience has shown that the region is best suited to whites. They also learned the hard way that irrigation is imperative. As with the Lower Hunter, there is a potential problem with rain during vintage in the Upper, but the overall rainfall is lower. The Upper Hunter has proved itself to be well suited to both chardonnay and sémillon.

Hunter sémillon

Sémillon is the grape blended with sauvignon blanc to produce the white wines of Bordeaux and Sauternes. In Australia, it makes the finest botrytized styles but is better known as a dry table wine, reaching its pinnacle with the Hunter Valley's unique and long-lived wines. When young, Hunter sémillons, usually unwooded, can be crisp, pleasing, and have gentle citrus flavors. However, there is little to suggest that they will blossom into wonderful, toasty, complex wines after five or ten years of bottle aging. Lindemans and Rothbury made many of the great wines of the 1960s and 1970s. Today's classics come from Tyrrell's, McWilliams and Brokenwood.

Hunter Valley development

Although grape growing in New South Wales began soon after the arrival of the First Fleet in 1788, with vines planted near what is now Circular Quay on Sydney Harbour, the New South Wales wine industry first grew to prominence in the Hunter Valley. The Hunter was settled soon after it was named in 1797, but the focus then was coal, not wine. It wasn't until the 1830s that James Busby, considered to be the father of Australian viticulture, and several others planted vines.

The Pokolbin and Rothbury subregions, now the center of the Lower Hunter vineyard area, weren't planted until the 1860s. The early vineyards proved encouraging, and the Hunter Valley Viticultural Association was formed in 1847. George Wyndham founded the Dalwood vineyards, which later belonged for a period to Penfolds, and Dan Tyrrell made his first vintage in 1883—at the age of 14—beginning an amazing run of 76 consecutive vintages. At that time, the Hunter Valley was seen as ideal for grapes—it was hot, disease-free, and the rainfall is believed to have been more appropriate than that of today. The Lower Hunter has endured its ups and downs, but it has never suffered total failure like so many early Australian wine regions in Victoria and South Australia.

In 1921, one of Australia's greatest winemakers made his appearance. After studying in France, Maurice O'Shea returned to the Hunter to run the Mount Pleasant vineyards and winery his family had purchased. The vineyards had been established in 1880 by another legendary Hunter figure, Charles King. O'Shea joined with McWilliams in 1932, which was a difficult time in the Hunter as the market had changed considerably and 85 percent of production was devoted to fortifieds. The area under vines decreased from almost 2,600 acres (1,050 ha) in the mid-1920s to just over half that a decade later. Although consumers in the 1940s and 1950s were not seeking the wines O'Shea and others were producing, the wines he made at that time are eagerly sought after at auctions today.

BROKENWOOD WINES, LOWER HUNTER

Established **1970** ***Owners*** **private syndicate** ***Production*** **60,000 cases** ***Vineyard area*** **49 acres (20 ha)**

A flagship winery for the Hunter Valley wine region, Brokenwood has also long sourced fruit from around the nation for its wines. The single-vineyard Graveyard Shiraz stands out. In extreme demand, this wine has established itself as the region's top shiraz. The sémillon is also well received.

LEFT: The McWilliams Mt Pleasant vineyards at Pokolbin in the Hunter Valley.

LAKE'S FOLLY, LOWER HUNTER

Established **1963** ***Owner*** **Peter Fogarty** ***Production*** **4,000 cases** ***Vineyard area*** **27 acres (11 ha)**

Australia's first boutique winery, and the forerunner of so many more, changed the face of the wine industry in Australia and quickly established a cult following. Two wines are made here, Cabernet, which is a blend of petit verdot, cabernet sauvignon, shiraz and merlot; and 100 percent Chardonnay. Both of these wines benefit from extended cellaring, and the quality has never been higher.

TYRRELL'S VINEYARDS, LOWER HUNTER

Established **1858** ***Owners*** **Bruce Tyrrell** ***Production*** **750,000 cases** ***Vineyard area*** **684 acres (277 ha)**

Edward Tyrrell planted the first vines on this estate in 1858. In 1883, at age 14, Dan Tyrrell took over the winemaking and worked 76 consecutive vintages before nephew Murray took over. When Murray died he was succeeded by his son Bruce. Shiraz and sémillon (especially their Vat 1 Sémillon) are stars, but the pioneering Vat 47 Chardonnay is one of Australia's finest.

Significant producers in the Hunter Valley include Allandale Winery, Bimbadgen Estate, Drayton's Family Wines, Glenguin Wine Company, Margan Family Winegrowers, Pendarves Estate and Petersons Wines.

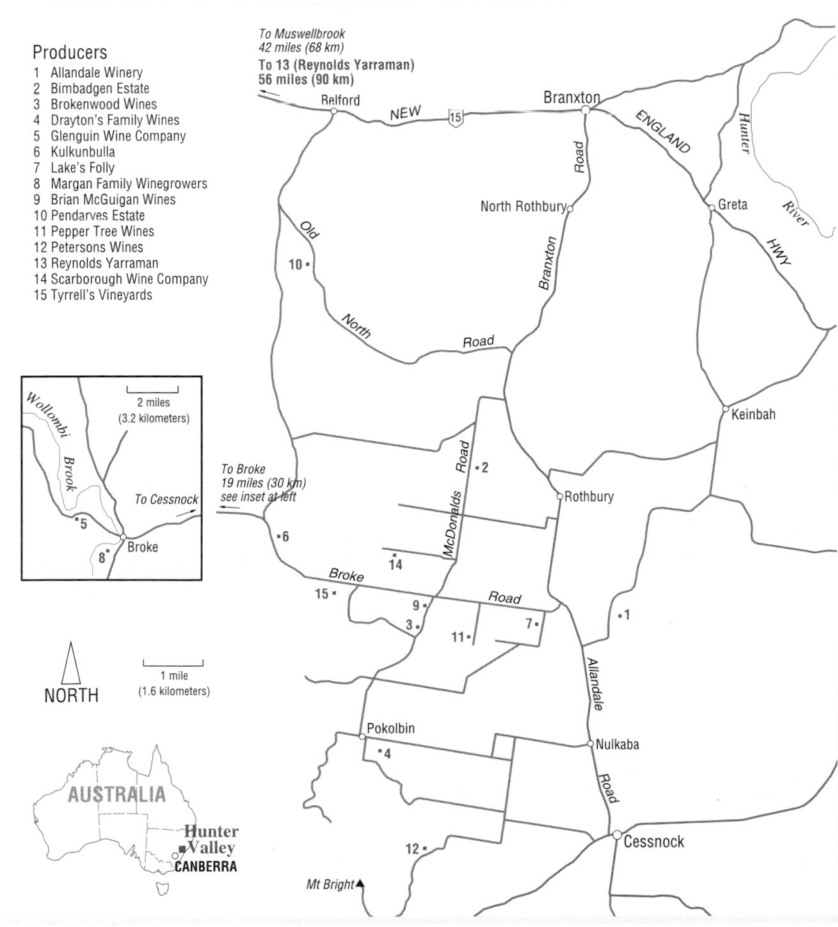

Regional Dozen

QUALITY WINES

Clonakilla Shiraz/Viognier
De Bortoli Noble One
Glenguin Merlot
Huntington Estate Reserve Shiraz
Rosemount Hill of Gold Chardonnay
Rosemount Mountain Blue Shiraz Cabernet

BEST VALUE WINES

Cranswick Estate Vignette Cabernet Merlot
Huntington Estate Cabernet Sauvignon
Miranda Mirrool Creek Shiraz Cabernet
Poet's Corner Shiraz Cabernet
Rothbury Estate Cowra Chardonnay
Westend Richland Chardonnay

Other New South Wales Regions

KEN GARGETT

NORTHERN RIVERS

Grape growing was revived at Hastings River by the Cassegrain family in the 1980s. Significant rainfall and high humidity can be a problem, which is one reason why the Cassegrains turned to chambourcin, a grape that is highly resistant to mildew and produces a wine of intense color and flavor. Both chardonnay and sémillon have been successful in some vintages.

CASSEGRAIN VINEYARDS, HASTINGS RIVER

Established **1980** ***Owners*** **Cassegrain family**
Vineyard area **30 acres (12 ha)**

Cassegrain led the winemaking revival in the region. Early vintages were variable but the wines have been more consistent in recent years. The range includes sparkling, rosé and chardonnay; however, it is the chambourcin that has gained prominence.

CENTRAL RANGES

The Central Ranges regions all lie about 185 miles (300 km) inland in an area west to northwest of Sydney. One of them, Mudgee, is among Australia's oldest viticultural regions. The other two, Cowra and Orange, are relative newcomers.

Mudgee is noted for cabernet sauvignon; shiraz has also done well, and there are significant plantings of chardonnay. The winery most likely to bring Mudgee to the attention of the world is Rosemount Estate, with its superb Mountain Blue Shiraz Cabernet and the Hill of Gold range.

In Cowra, chardonnay is by far the predominant grape and was responsible for the early Petaluma Chardonnays. The region quickly made a name for itself with some exciting releases by Rothbury Estate in the Hunter Valley. Other notable outside producers also make wines from Cowra fruit.

The region of Orange is centered around Mt Canobolas. Much of the production of the district goes to large outside producers, such as Rosemount and Rothbury. Chardonnay plantings far exceed all others and have produced some memorable wines. Cabernet sauvignon is also now established, and shiraz looks promising.

BELOW: The Cassegrain Vineyards in northern New South Wales.

LEFT: *A sign for cellar door sales at de Bortoli in the Riverina Big Rivers district*

HUNTINGTON ESTATE, MUDGEE
Established **1969** ***Owners*** **Bob and Wendy Roberts**
Vineyard area **104 acres (42 ha)**

Several decades ago Bob Roberts revived quality winemaking in Mudgee. His wines, particularly his underpriced reds, have been successful and age beautifully.

LOWE FAMILY WINE CO, MUDGEE
Established **1987** ***Owners*** **David Lowe and Jane Wilson**
Production **4,000 cases** ***Vineyard area*** **37 acres (15 ha)**

David Lowe began his career at Rothbury Estate in the Hunter Valley and rose to become chief winemaker before turning to consultant winemaking for numerous small producers, something he still does. He and his wife and co-winemaker, Jane Wilson, have been making wine from their Mudgee fruit, supplemented with fruit from the Hunter and Orange since 1987. They established a winery in late 1999.

BIG RIVERS

Big Rivers region in the Riverina is one of the heroes of the Australian wine industry. A lot of wine from the region ends up in ubiquitous casks, but it also produces much "sunshine in a bottle"—flavorful, great-value wines that sell well. The most widely planted grapes are shiraz, chardonnay and sémillon. Big Rivers has stunned critics and the public alike with its botrytis sémillons. Pioneered in 1982 by the de Bortoli family, these luscious and concentrated dessert-style wines are world class and have propelled the district into another dimension, drawing it to the attention of wine lovers around the world.

DE BORTOLI
Established **1928** ***Owners*** **de Bortoli family**
Vineyard area **675 acres (250 ha)**

If ever a wine company has made the leap from a producer of nondescript bulk wine to the top shelf, this is it. Much of de Bortoli's production is intended for the volume market, but its astonishing botrytis sémillon Noble One, changed public perception of both de Bortoli and the Big Rivers wine region forever.

SOUTHERN NEW SOUTH WALES

The three regions that comprise Southern New South Wales—Hilltops, Canberra District, and Tumbarumba—each show distinctive characteristics and are grouped together for geographical rather than viticultural reasons.

In 1975, grape growing was reintroduced to Hilltops, and to date chardonnay, cabernet sauvignon and especially shiraz have proved most successful. The McWilliams Barwang wines have established the potential of the region.

The Canberra District is the most established wine region in Southern New South Wales. Chardonnay, shiraz, cabernet sauvignon, and riesling have done well, and there is some support for pinot noir and sauvignon blanc. The development of Kamberra, the ACT winery of the Hardy Wine Company, will greatly assist the profile of the region.

High and remote, Tumbarumba is one of the cooler regions in Australia, and most of its grapes go into sparkling wines. Sauvignon blanc is the predominant table wine to date, but chardonnay could eventually become the most prominent white, and pinot noir has potential.

ABOVE: *The entrance to one of the highest wineries in Australia, Lark Hill, Canberra District.*

SOUTH COAST

A relative newcomer, the South Coast zone has climate problems—summer rainfall, humidity, rot and mildew. Consequently the area's winemakers have been attracted to chambourcin, but chardonnay, shiraz and cabernet sauvignon have all done well in good vintages. Some wineries, notably Coolangatta Estate and Cambewarra Estate, are producing quality wines. The South Coast also contains the outlying Sydney region, where Vicarys Winery has operated since 1923.

Other significant producers include Bloodwood, Cowra Estate, Andrew Harris Vineyards and Huntington Estate (all Central Ranges); Charles Sturt University, Cranswick Estate and Miranda Wines (both Big Rivers); Clonakilla and Lark Hill (both Southern New South Wales).

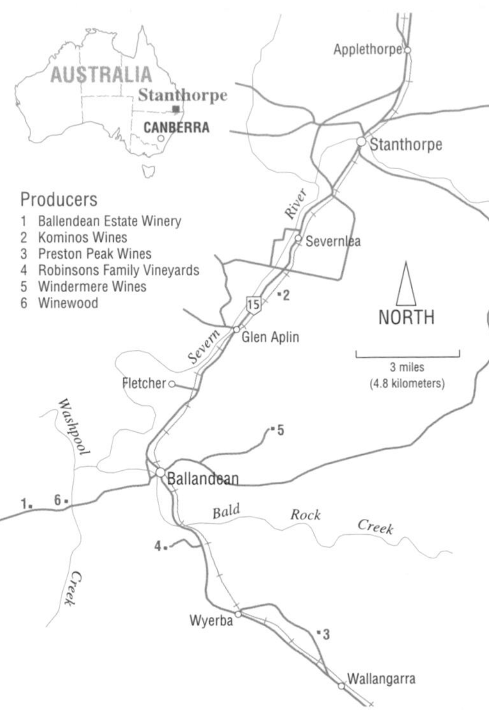

ABOVE: One of many panoramic vineyard views in Queensland's Granite Belt.

Queensland

KEN GARGETT

Grapes were first planted at Romavilla, Queensland's oldest continually operating winery, in 1863. More recently there has been an explosion of vineyards across the state, some in the most unlikely locations. Conditions in this huge state vary enormously. The Granite Belt is one of the highest wine regions in the country and cooler than coastal districts. In the Burnett, rain during harvest and the possibility of hail are potential problems. Western Queensland is hot and dry. Even in the established Granite Belt, it is too early to identify the most successful varieties. Cabernet sauvignon and shiraz dominate, and merlot is showing much potential, with all doing well at the tiny Boireann. Robert Channon Wines and Jimbour Estate are other producers to follow. There is some interest in red Italian varieties, and chambourcin's ability to withstand rain and humidity has given it a following outside the Granite Belt. Sémillon and chardonnay are by far the most successful whites.

Regional Dozen

- Ballandean Late Harvest Sylvaner
- Boireann Grenache Shiraz Mourvèdre
- Boireann Shiraz Viognier
- Robert Channon Verdelho
- Granite Ridge Cabernet Sauvignon
- Jimbour Shiraz
- Kominos Shiraz
- Preston Peak Chardonnay
- Romavilla Very Old Tawny Port
- Sirromet Merlot
- Sirromet Pinot Gris
- Windermere Sangiovese Cabernet

GRANITE BELT PRODUCERS

BALLANDEAN ESTATE WINERY

Established **1968** ***Owners*** **Angelo & Mary Puglisi** ***Production*** **9,000 cases** ***Vineyard area*** **84 acres (34 ha)**

Angelo Puglisi helped establish which grape varieties are best suited to the Granite Belt. The best wines are the Black Label Cabernet and Chardonnay, while the idiosyncratic Late Harvest Sylvaner has its supporters.

KOMINOS WINES

Established **1976** ***Owner*** **Tony Comino** ***Vineyard area*** **37 acres (15 ha)**

Red wines, particularly shiraz, impress more than white wines. Tony Comino has a serious interest in Greek varieties, and his Vin Doux is in the style of the dessert wine from the island of Samos.

OTHER QUEENSLAND PRODUCERS

SIRROMET WINES, BRISBANE

Established **2000** ***Owner*** **Sirromet Wines Pty Ltd** ***Production*** **21,600 cases** ***Vineyard area*** **351 acres (142 ha)**

Sirromet Wines, with its state-of-the-art winery, was developed as part of a tourist complex. Chambourcin has been planted in the hot, humid surrounding vineyards, and 20 different grape varieties have been planted at Ballandean. Sirromet has quickly established itself as the face of Queensland wine.

ROMAVILLA WINERY, SOUTHEAST QUEENSLAND

Established **1863** ***Owners*** **David and Joy Wall** ***Production*** **2,500 cases** ***Vineyard area*** **25 acres (10 ha)**

In this very old winery, ancient oak barrels stand alongside the latest stainless steel equipment. Romavilla's wide range encompasses some delicate whites, mid-weight reds that strive for elegance, and heavenly fortifieds.

Other significant producers in Queensland include Robinsons Family Vineyards, Windermere Wines, Winewood, Stone Ridge Vineyards (all Granite Belt); Barambah Ridge Winery and Vineyards (South Burnett), Clovelly Estate (Burnett) and Mount Tamborine Winery & Vineyard (Southeast Queensland).

Tasmania

MICHELE ROUND

Tasmania is a small island with a sublime landscape, situated off the southeast corner of mainland Australia. Its cool-temperate climate and long growing season aids in the production of some very elegant wines. Although geographic indications denote it as one region, it can be divided into six subregions: the Northwest, Tamar Valley, Pipers Brook/River, East Coast, Derwent/Coal River Valleys and the Huon Valley.

Experience and experimentation have pared down the grape selections in Tasmania's varied regions. Cabernet plantings are limited to the warmer slopes of the Tamar Valley, Coal River Valley and East Coast. Pinot noir growers have found that a combination of micro-climate and clonal selection is producing wines with layered bouquets and subtle, lingering flavors. Riesling is emerging as a star variety, with excellent examples from the Derwent/Coal River Valleys and Pipers Brook area.

A benchmark chardonnay style is yet to emerge; at present it is finding its expression alongside pinot noir in Tasmania's sparkling wine industry. The island has made its mark as Australia's finest region for sparkling wines.

LEFT: A rainbow crowns a typical Tasmanian winter vineyard scene.

FREYCINET VINEYARD

Established **1980** ***Owners*** **Geoff and Sue Bull** ***Production*** **8,000 cases** ***Vineyard area*** **22 acres (9 ha)**

Consistently making one of the best pinot noirs in the country, Freycinet Vineyard's national reputation is enhanced by its chardonnay, riesling and the full-flavored sparkling Radenti. Winemaker Claudio Radenti is married to the Bull family's winemaker daughter Lindy and he has continued to ensure the success of this small vineyard. The East Coast region is naturally warm and this, coupled with the vineyard's sun-embracing amphitheater, gives the team ample opportunity to work with ripe fruit—something of a luxury in Tasmania's mostly marginal climate.

PIPERS BROOK VINEYARD

Established **1974** ***Owner*** **Kreglinger** ***Production*** **60,000 cases** ***Vineyard area*** **452 acres (183 ha)**

Pipers Brook Vineyard boasts a range of wines from several labels, including Ninth Island. An ongoing search for great pinot noir is complemented by the refined package of pinot gris, gewürztraminer, and a well-pedigreed riesling, which are marketed as an Alsatian trio. Several tiers of quality are available from Pipers Brook, ranging right up to the single-vineyard Summit Chardonnay, the luxurious bubbly Pirie, and a super-premium pinot noir.

Other significant producers in Tasmania include Stefano Lubiana, Moorilla Estate and Stoney Vineyard.

Regional Dozen

Arras Riesling
Freycinet Vineyard Pinot Noir
Moorilla Pinot Noir
Panorama Pinot Noir
Pipers Brook Vineyard Gewürztraminer
Pirie
Springvale Pinot Noir
Stefano Lubiana Reserve Chardonnay
Stefano Lubiana Vintage Brut
Stoney Vineyard Domaine A Cabernet Sauvignon
Wellington Iced Riesling
Winstead Riesling

BELOW: Vineyards of the Derwent/Coal River Valleys.

Perelle Lake Hayes vineyard in Central Otago experiences cold but dry winters.

New Zealand

Another setback in the development of the wine industry was the emergence of the New Zealand Temperance Society. Formed in 1836, the society was particularly influential between 1881 and 1918, when restrictive liquor legislation was in place. However, soldiers returning from World War I bolstered opposition to the society, and it began to lose power before a ban on all alcohol took effect; its influence finally dwindled during the 1920s and 1930s.

The wine industry was also inhibited by the country's conservative licensing laws. Until 1881 winery sales were illegal and the only outlets for alcohol were hotels. It was only in 1955 that permission was granted for specialist shops to sell wine; and in 1960 restaurants were finally granted licenses to do the same. Since 1990 supermarkets have been permitted to sell wine.

New Zealand's modern wine industry really began with the planting of vines in Marlborough in 1973 by Montana Wines. This was followed in the 1980s by small plantings in other areas such as Wairarapa/Wellington, Canterbury/Waipara, Central Otago and Northland. Since then, the wine industry has grown spectacularly throughout the country.

By the turn of the century New Zealand's wine exports had grown significantly, reaching 4.4 million gallons (16.6 million l). Three-quarters of this went to the United Kingdom, but the United States is also becoming an important market.

Climatic variations

Generally, wine-producing regions in the North Island are warmer and wetter than those in the South Island. The exception to this is the Wairarapa/Wellington region, which is located at a similar latitude to Nelson and Marlborough at the top of the South Island.

Marlborough, Martinborough in the Wairarapa, and Gisborne have the country's most consistent conditions for grape growing, with high levels of sunshine, low rainfall and little risk of frost around vintage time. Canterbury and Central Otago in the southern half of the South Island have long been considered marginal for grape growing due to the relatively high risk of frost, low heat summation and the consequent lack of consistent annual grape quality and production. But as growers succeed in matching grape varieties with specific sites, some consistency is starting to show. Central Otago is New Zealand's only wine-producing region with a continental climate. This means that frost is a constant threat around vintage time, which can be as late as June. The vintage takes place between February and May throughout the rest of the country, depending on the grape variety and region.

BELOW: *Mills Reef Winery, Waikato/Bay of Plenty.*

Drip irrigation is not only permitted but is essential on many of the country's stonier vineyards. This is particularly so in the drier areas of Marlborough, Canterbury/Waipara, Wairarapa/Wellington, Hawkes Bay and Central Otago.

Vines and viticulture

In 2003, New Zealand had a total (producing) vineyard area of 38,233 acres (15,479 ha). Almost three-quarters of the vines are planted in the country's largest and fastest-growing wine regions—Marlborough, Hawkes Bay, Gisborne and Otago, which is the fastest growing of the newer regions.

White grape varieties account for a majority of plantings with sauvignon blanc topping the list by a significant margin, followed by chardonnay, reversing the position of a few years ago. The once prominent müller-thurgau diminishes every year. Others showing increases recently include pinot gris, riesling, gewürztraminer and sémillon, though all are far behind the major two.

Red-grape plantings are currently dominated by pinot noir, which may soon overtake chardonnay as the most prevalent variety in the country. Merlot has eclipsed cabernet sauvignon and syrah continues to expand albeit from a small base. Other grape varieties grown in relatively small quantities throughout New Zealand include breidecker (a hybrid of seibel and müller-thurgau), chasselas, chenin blanc, flora, palomino, pinot gris, reichensteiner, sylvaner, blauburger, cabernet franc, malbec, pinotage and syrah.

New Zealand soils are naturally highly fertile. As a result, many of the country's vines suffer from high vigor and overcropping, which tend to produce some overtly herbaceous wines. The country's newest vineyards are planted on less fertile sites, including stony soils that would previously have been considered inappropriate for grape growing.

Vine vigor can still be a problem, but many growers now use it to their advantage to produce high yields and make large quantities of wine. Others have developed techniques to combat associated problems, including judicious pruning, careful choice of trellising systems and the growth of various grass species such as chicory (whose long tap roots draw water away from the grape vines) between vine rows. Some of the country's top-quality chardonnays now come from high-vigor sites. Low-vigor soils needing fertilization can be ministered to with organic fertilizers.

The biggest problems faced by grape growers are botrytis, powdery mildew and downy mildew, all of which are exacerbated by the generally high humidity. Consequently, the principal challenge facing the New Zealand wine industry is to develop more environmentally friendly vineyard practices. In working toward this, the Winegrowers of New Zealand Society set up the Integrated Wine Production (IWP) scheme in 1995. The scheme provides grape growers with guidelines for managing their vineyards in much more a sustainable manner, including recommendations for minimizing the use of fungicides and pesticides.

ABOVE: Montana Wines in the Auckland wine region is New Zealand's largest winery.

BELOW: A winemaker surveys his domain.

ABOVE: Stainless-steel fermentation tanks tower over the vines at the House of Nobilo in Kumeu.

Auckland

Auckland is the name of New Zealand's largest city and also its most diverse wine-producing region. The latter incorporates the subregions of Northland and Matakana in the north; the far-flung Great Barrier Island; and Greater Auckland, Kumeu/Huapai, Henderson and Waiheke Island. Currently, Auckland has about 89 wineries and around 3 percent of the national vineyard area.

Northland's wineries are generally small, and most concentrate on the production of red wines, mainly the cabernet-sauvignon- and merlot-dominated blends, plus a little pinotage and shiraz. Müller-thurgau, sémillon, chardonnay, and gewürztraminer are among the whites made in small quantities.

The country's most northerly winery, Okahu Estate, produces high-quality reds, including shiraz- and cabernet-sauvignon-dominated blends, as well as a range of other reds made from pinotage, merlot and chambourcin. Farther south, there are several vineyards and wineries around Kerikeri and near Whangarei.

The Matakana subregion produces small amounts of top-quality red wine. Relatively new wineries here (mostly small) are concentrating on pinot gris, chardonnay, riesling and cabernet-based reds.

Great Barrier Island is home only to one operational vineyard, which yields small quantities of cabernet sauvignon. However, several small vineyards are currently under development at the island.

The subregions around the city of Auckland—Greater Auckland, Kumeu/Huapai and Henderson—are not renowned for good viticultural conditions. The Greater Auckland subregion includes the recently developed Clevedon area, which is planted mainly with red grape varieties such as cabernet sauvignon, malbec, merlot and a handful of Italian grape varieties, including sangiovese and nebbiolo.

Waiheke Island, situated in the Hauraki Gulf, concentrates on cabernet sauvignon, cabernet franc, malbec, merlot and chardonnay. Some winemakers are trialing pinot noir, plus sangiovese and other Italian varieties. The quantities of wine made are tiny but, although variable, can be among the country's best.

Regional Dozen

QUALITY WINES

Goldwater Esslin Merlot
Goldwater Estate Cabernet Sauvignon/Merlot
Fenton Cabernet
Kumeu River Maté's Chardonnay
Stonyridge Larose Cabernet
Villa Maria Reserve Barrique Fermented Chardonnay
Vina Alta Retico Amarone-style Cabernet Franc, Merlot UC

BEST VALUE WINES

Collards Chenin Blanc
Kumeu Brajkovich Cabernet Franc
Kumeu Brajkovich Signature Series Chardonnay
Kumeu Brajkovich Signature Series Merlot
Nobilo Huapai Valley Pinotage

KUMEU RIVER WINES

Established **1944** ***Owners*** **Melba Brajkovich and family**
Vineyard area **96 acres (39 ha)**

Kumeu River is one of New Zealand's finest small wineries. All Kumeu River Chardonnays, which have attracted international plaudits, are 100 percent whole bunch pressed; wild yeast, barrel, and malolactic fermented; then lees and oak aged. Stylistically, all these wines share seamless textures, fine balance and buttery flavors. The basic "lightly wooded" Brajkovich signature series is aged in four-year-old French oak, whereas the creamy Kumeu River (mendoza clone) shows a stronger new-oak influence than the purposely subdued, subtly nutty, long-lived Dijon Clone 95 Maté's Vineyard. Merlot and cabernet franc, along with malbec, make up the winery's top red, Melba. Recent pinot noir and pinot gris (that do not see oak) releases suggest a promising future with these varietals. Brajkovich has been one of the pioneers of screwcap closures in New Zealand.

MATUA VALLEY WINES

Established **1973** ***Owner*** **Beringer Blass Wine Estates**
Vineyard area **350 acres (864 ha)**

Matua is where New Zealand's renowned Sauvignon Blanc was born. Both the top-label Ararimu Chardonnay and Cabernet Merlot are produced only in exceptional years and are stylish, flavor-filled, concentrated, and smooth. The Judd Estate Chardonnay, a single vineyard wine along with the Matheson trio, is a classic, big-fruited wine. The new Innovator series provides an outlet for ongoing experiments with small-batch production. Matua's Unwooded Chardonnay pioneered this style in New Zealand and remains one of the best, vibrantly pure, mid-priced examples available. There are attractive and attractively priced regional and varietal wines such as the Eastern Bays Chardonnay and the Hawkes Bay Sauvignon Blanc. The Shingle Peak range is from Marlborough fruit.

MONTANA WINES

Established **1944** ***Owner*** **Allied Domecq** ***Vineyard area*** **7,410-plus acres (3,000-plus ha)**

Montana is New Zealand's largest winery and most sophisticated international brand. It produces over 50 percent of all of the country's wine and employs over 1,000 people. The company's international branding strength lies above its bulk wines, starting with the Montana range, which is regionally and varietally typical, and moving up through the stylish Saints, Montana Reserve and Church Road ranges, and the "letter-designated" single-vineyard Estate wines. All deliver focused fruit flavors, well-balanced and refined textures, and crisp acids, using each region's varietal strengths, for example, Marlborough's chardonnay, pinot noir and sauvignon blanc; and Gisborne's sémillon.

Sparkling wines are made primarily from traditional champagne grapes, with the bargain-priced Lindauer (which includes chenin blanc) and the rich, biscuity, Lindauer Reserve (pinot noir and chardonnay) among the country's best-value bubblies.

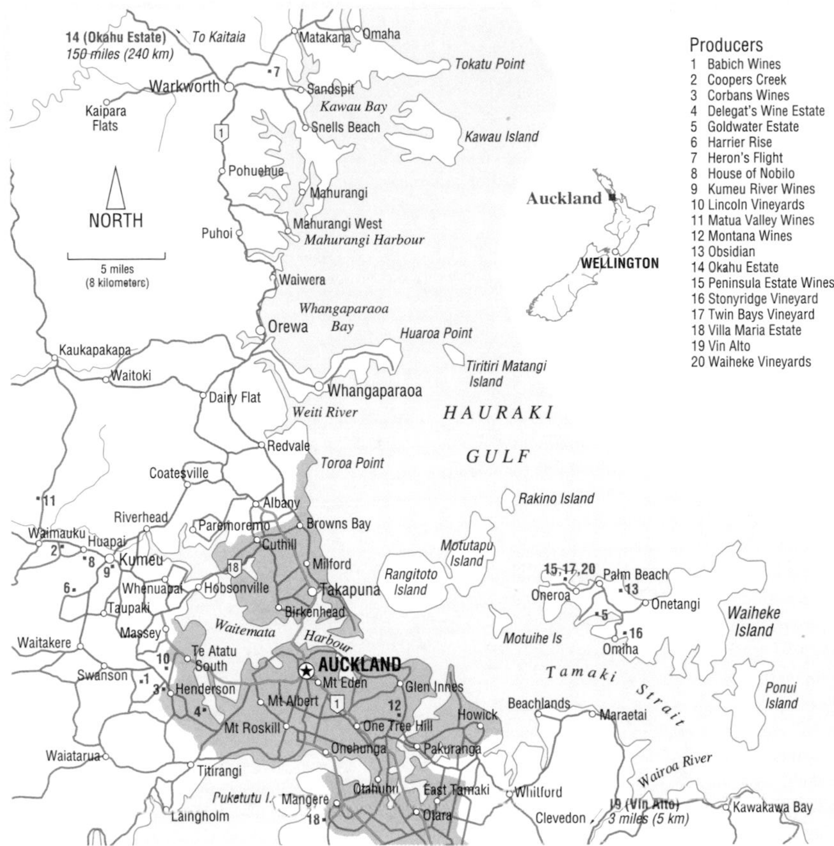

STONYRIDGE VINEYARD

Established **1982** ***Owner*** **Stephen White**
Vineyard area **34 acres (13.6 ha)**

Stephen White's Waiheke flagship, Larose Cabernet, is one of New Zealand's more expensive and certainly highest profile wines. Larose is defined by condensed textures and multileveled flavors and is stacked full of fine-grained tannins; it ages superbly. The Airfield label is a more forward style and is usually very good in its own right. A limited-quantity syrah is also produced.

VILLA MARIA ESTATE

Established **1961** ***Owner*** **George Fistonich**
Vineyard area **185 acres (75 ha)**

Villa Maria's solid Private Bin varietal ranges increasingly have an uncluttered, elegant, nervier style. The midrange Cellar Selection Sauvignon Blanc, Chardonnay and Riesling are generally excellent, with very pure varietal expressions. The top-flight reserve range, made only in good years, consistently produces two of New Zealand's best sauvignon blancs: the zesty, unwooded, leafy, passionfruit-laden Clifford Bay, and the deeper, darker, sweatier, more savory Wairau Valley. Both the riesling and the gewürztraminer in this range combine power with intensity and elegant restraint. Finally, the Noble Riesling shows a multilayered, well-structured palate.

Other producers of significance in the Auckland region include Arahura Vineyards, Ascension, Babich Wines, Brick Bay, Collards, Corbans Wines, Coopers Creek, Delegat's Wine Estate, Fenton, Goldwater Estate, Harrier Rise, Heron's Flight, House of Nobilo, Hyperion, Lincoln Vineyards, Obsidian, Odyssey, Okahu Estate, Peninsula Estate Wines, Providence, Twin Bays Vineyard, Vin Alto and Waiheke Vineyards.

ABOVE: *Stonyridge is the source of New Zealand's most expensive red wine, Larose Cabernet.*

LEFT: *The Goldwater Estate was the first vineyard to be planted on Waiheke Island, in 1970.*

ABOVE: *Plantings in the Firstland vineyards have shifted away from red varieties to whites.*

Waikato/Bay of Plenty

Situated a short distance south of the city of Auckland, the neighboring districts of Waikato and Bay of Plenty make up New Zealand's smallest wine region. It includes 13 widely scattered wineries and 345 acres (140 ha) of vineyards—less than one percent of the national total. Most of the wineries are very small, although there are some larger establishments which source their grapes from farther afield. The region is divided into four subregions: Te Kauwhata, Hamilton, the Bay of Plenty and the Mangatawhiri Valley.

> *... a new friend is as new wine; when it is old, thou shalt drink it with pleasure.*
>
> Old Testament

The Te Kauwhata area has relatively high levels of sunshine and few frosts, but is very humid and wet. Many of the wineries use canopy management and vineyard spraying programs to counter the damp conditions; others turn the climate to their advantage to produce some of New Zealand's finest botrytized dessert wines. Te Kauwhata is also renowned for its heavy clay loams, which favor chardonnay.

The city of Hamilton serves a farming community and a fast-growing urban population. There are only a few vineyards located nearby; all are small and sited on heavy clay-loam soils best suited to chardonnay. Although there is plenty of sunshine, rainfall levels are similar to those in Te Kauwhata and high humidity usually results in regular fogs.

The Bay of Plenty region has rich, fertile soils and experiences high levels of sunshine but also high levels of rainfall and humidity, particularly during the ripening cycle. As a result of these less-than-ideal conditions, wine production has not yet been pursued vigorously here.

The most northerly subregion in the Bay of Plenty is the Mangatawhiri Valley. This secluded, fertile valley is home to just one winery, Firstland. It obtains most of its grapes from Hawkes Bay and Marlborough, but is growing increasing quantities of good-quality pinot noir.

The most planted grape variety in the Waikato/Bay of Plenty region is chardonnay followed by cabernet sauvignon and sauvignon blanc.

FIRSTLAND

Established **1976 (formerly De Redcliffe Winery)** ***Owner*** **Ed Aster** ***Vineyard area*** **95 acres (38.5 ha)**

Strengths here lie in white wines, particularly sémillon, although the home vineyard also produces the stylish, fruity Mangatawhiri Chardonnay. Both the Marlborough Riesling and the Marlborough Sauvignon Blanc are fruit focused, crisply structured, and relatively underpriced. The 20-year-old Millennium Reserve Tawny Port is New Zealand's best.

MORTON ESTATE WINES

Established **1982** ***Owner*** **John Coney**
Vineyard area **850 acres (344 ha)**

Morton Estate is renowned for consistent quality across a broad range of varietals, and has a solid reputation for sparkling wines. At the bottom of the three-tier output, the Mill Road range offers generally good quality and value; the unwooded chardonnay is the star. The mainstay White Label has a Marlborough range, including a crisply herbaceous sauvignon blanc. The Hawkes Bay range includes a syrah and a rich, flowery, vanilla-and-oak-filled chardonnay. In the top-end Black Label range, a creamy, deeply viscous, meltaway chardonnay is consistently among the country's finest, and the merlot is the pick of the reds. Morton Estate's fine *méthode champenoise* range includes, among others, a good-value, finely balanced NV brut.

Other producers of significance in the region include Mills Reef Winery and Rongopai Wines.

Regional Best

Rongopai Winemakers Reserve Botrytised Chardonnay
Rongopai Winemakers Reserve Botrytised Riesling

Gisborne and Hawkes Bay

The east-coast wine regions of Gisborne and Hawkes Bay on New Zealand's North Island are close to each other geographically but distant relations when it comes to the wines they produce.

Gisborne is the country's third-largest grape-growing region, with 11.7 percent of the total New Zealand vineyard area. There are now 16 wineries in the region. Traditionally a bulk grape-growing area where müller-thurgau and muscat ruled the viticultural roost, it is now known as the country's chardonnay capital.

Soils here are generally volcanic, but vary widely. The success of white-grape varieties reflects Gisborne's status as a cool-climate grape-growing area. Chardonnay is the most planted variety, with 56 percent of the vineyard area, a significant increase in recent years. This is matched by increases in pinot noir, sémillon, gewürztraminer and merlot, though from considerably smaller bases. Concurrently, chenin blanc, müller-thurgau, muscat, and sauvignon are decreasing. The gewürztraminer produced here vies with that of Marlborough as New Zealand's best. Similarly, the chardonnay rivals the best offerings from Hawkes Bay and Marlborough, and, with its intense melon and tropical fruit flavors, is certainly the most distinctive of those made in New Zealand. Of the reds, merlot has so far shown the most promise. Plantings of pinot noir are predicted to increase faster than merlot, but mainly to provide a base for sparkling wines.

Hawkes Bay currently accounts for 24 percent of the total New Zealand vineyard area, a small percentage decrease in recent years but it remains an expanding region. It also produces the country's most diverse range of wines, from tropical sauvignon blanc and elegant chardonnay to gutsy merlot and cabernet-based reds and some surprisingly exciting syrah.

There are 56 wineries in the Hawkes Bay area, however, most of them are relatively small. Hawkes Bay has traditionally been seen as the most promising region in New Zealand for cabernet- and merlot-based red wines, but the quality depends on where the grapes are grown. The soils here are all alluvial and vary greatly. A smattering of well-drained limestone soils provides some of the country's most impressive chardonnay, merlot, cabernet and syrah. The stony soils of the Gimblett Gravels area are home to an increasing number of wineries whose focus is on the red varietals: cabernet franc, cabernet sauvignon, malbec and merlot.

Generally, Hawkes Bay has a cool maritime climate and the highest average hours of sunshine in New Zealand. Chardonnay is the most widely planted grape variety, with 27 percent of the area's current vineyard plantings, and is predicted to increase. Cabernet sauvignon (16 percent) has recently been overtaken by the more suitable merlot (21 percent) while sauvignon blanc (9%), which produces wines that are more tropical in flavor and softer in texture than the more intense Marlborough style, is likely to decrease in importance. The success of syrah will no doubt see plantings increase, while the other red varieties are likely to lose ground to merlot and to a lesser extent, cabernet sauvignon.

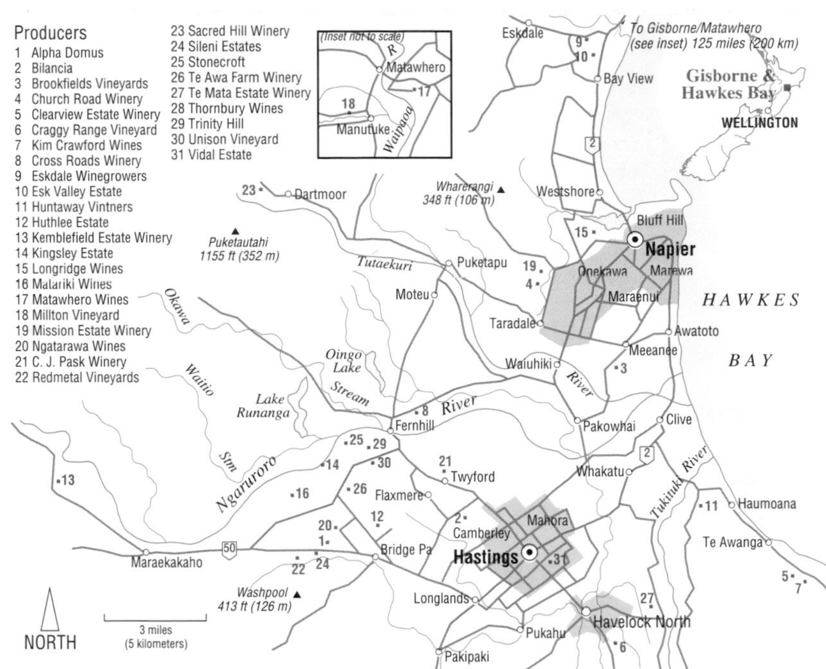

CRAGGY RANGE VINEYARDS

Established **1998** ***Owners*** **Terry Peabody and Steve Smith MW**
Production **4,000 cases** ***Vineyard area*** **494 acres (200 ha)**

This extraordinarily beautiful winery set forth with a vision to produce nothing but the highest quality, single vineyard wines. Marlborough-sourced first releases include the condensed, minerally Rapaura Road Riesling from 20-year-old fruit; a classic, pungent-with-sweat-and-passionfruit sauvignon; and a well-focused, beautifully balanced Strugglers Flat Pinot Noir. The Hawkes Bay Chardonnay is beautifully integrated with underplayed oak.

BELOW: Inside the winery at Craggy Bay Vineyards.

C. J. PASK WINERY

Established **1982** ***Owners*** **Chris Pask, Kate Radburn and John Benton** ***Production*** **35,000 cases**
Vineyard area **220 acres (90 ha)**

Chris Pask planted Gimblett Road's first grapes in 1982. In 1990 his appointment of winemaker Kate Radburn heralded considerable improvement in wine quality. Pask's strength lies in standard-range and reserve-quality merlot and cabernet sauvignon and in a 70 percent cabernet/merlot blend. Remarkably consistent, the base range can closely match the reserve's

Regional Best

QUALITY WINES

Corbans Cottage Block Gisborne Chardonnay
Craggy Range Sophia Merlot
Craggy Range Le Sol Syrah
Millton Barrel-Fermented Chenin Blanc
Montana Ormond Chardonnay
Morton Estate Black Label Chardonnay
Stonecroft Gewürztraminer
Te Mata Coleraine cabernet sauvignon, merlot

BEST VALUE WINES

Babich Mara Estate Syrah
Corbans Huntaway Pinot Gris
Esk Valley Chardonnay
Matua Unwooded Chardonnay
Ngatarawa The Stables Sauvignon Blanc
Phoenix Gewürztraminer

quality level in hot years. All show vibrant varietal characters with generous, but not overpowering, well-integrated sweet oak, with the reserve range more concentrated and structured to age.

Pask Chardonnay is a fruit-driven, very lightly oaked style, whereas the more powerful French-oak-fermented Reserve Chardonnay is buttery, and displays a deep, multilayered complexity. Pask also produces an inexpensive but good-quality, ageworthy chenin blanc. Gimblett Gravels fruit features in several of the very best wines.

SILENI ESTATES

Established **1997** ***Owners*** **Avery, Cowper and Edmonds families** ***Production*** **5,040 cases** ***Vineyard area*** **262 acres (106 ha)**

Sileni, one of Hawkes Bay's newer wineries, has achieved excellent early results with its team of winemaking specialists. The wines move from the basic Cellar Selection to the Estate Selection (chardonnays from both are worth following) to the expensive but superb 'EV' wines, led by the EV Merlot. Sileni Estates' production is expected to double over the next few years.

TE MATA ESTATE WINERY

Established **1896** ***Owners*** **Buck and Morris families** ***Production*** **28,000 cases** ***Vineyard area*** **296 acres (120 ha)**

Te Mata's Cabernet/Merlot blend is a benchmark for all other New Zealand bordeaux-style blends. A three-tiered red range begins with the bottom-end cabernet sauvignon/merlot, often excellent value as a result of catching spillage from the upper-tier Coleraine and Awatea. Both of these wines are blended cabernet sauvignon, merlot and cabernet franc, defined by seamless, smooth textures, complexity and concentration. Elston Chardonnay is a fully French-oak and malolactic fermented, long-lived wine with earthy and buttery characteristics. Te Mata Chardonnay is excellent value. The Bullnose Syrah is reaching the highest levels of style and quality.

Terroir

The concept of terroir is alive and well in New Zealand. A group of 34 wineries and growers banded together to promote themselves as a subregion of Hawkes Bay, known as Gimblett Gravels. Vineyards must be 95 percent within the defined region before their wines can display the GG logo. This 1,976 acre (800 ha) district differs from surrounding areas as it consists of gravelly soils which encourage thermal conductivity, resulting in temperatures three degrees warmer than the rest of the district. The subregion is now the site for some of New Zealand's best shiraz and bordeaux blend wines.

Other important producers in the Gisborne and Hawkes Bay region include Alpha Domus, Bilancia, Brookfields Vineyards, Church Road Winery, Clearview Estate Winery, Kim Crawford Wines, Cross Roads Winery, Eskdale Winegrowers, Esk Valley Estate, Huntaway Vintners, Huthlee Estate, Kemblefield Estate Winery, Kingsley Estate, Longridge Wines, Matariki Wines, Matawhero Wines, Millton Vineyard, Mission Estate Winery, Ngatarawa Wines, Redmetal Vineyards, Sacred Hill Winery, Stonecroft, Te Awa Farm Winery, Thornbury Wines, Trinity Hill, Unison Vineyard and Vidal Estate.

BELOW: *Sileni's stylish modernist winery houses restaurants and conference facilities.*

Wairarapa/Wellington

ABOVE: *The small town of Martinborough is the "capital" of the Wairarapa wine region.*

Like New Zealand's own presence in the wine world, Wairarapa/Wellington (formerly known as Martinborough), has forged a reputation that far outweighs its level of production. The 44 wine producers in the region constitute 10.5 percent of the country's winemakers, but only 3.6 percent of the country's vines. Moreover, the region's average vineyard size is less than half the national average. It is the North Island's coolest and driest winemaking region. Although some local winemakers believe in the potential of cabernet sauvignon and merlot, most have pinned their hopes on pinot noir (the most planted grape variety) and chardonnay. There are two particular pinot noir styles here: one tends to be more intensely fruit-driven and have higher alcohol, whereas the other is generally earthier and lighter.

The region's best chardonnays are stylistically complex, with flavors ranging beyond the realm of more fruit-driven styles. Sauvignon blanc also thrives, producing wines that are intense in flavor. Many growers are also committed to high-quality, low-cropped riesling, which performs extremely well. Wairarapa/Wellington's pinot gris is among the best in the country. Also outstanding is the tiny quantity of gewürztraminer.

ATA RANGI

Established **1980** ***Owners*** **Clive Paton, Phyll Pattie, Alison Paton and Oliver Masters** ***Production*** **5,000 cases** ***Vineyard area*** **82 acres (33 ha)**

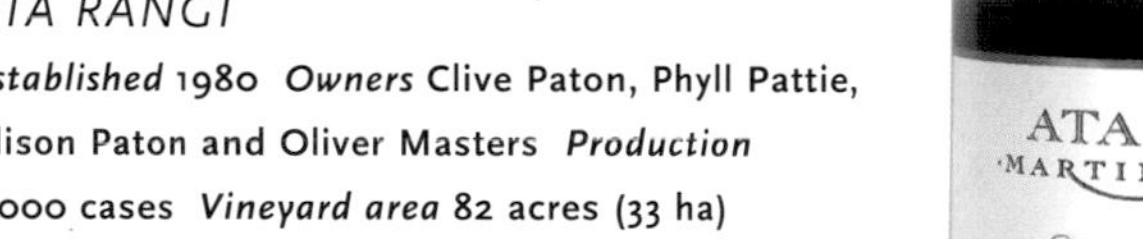

Ata Rangi's Pinot Noirs are among the best in the southern hemisphere. Their styles are consistently complex, multi-layered, and richly textured. Ata Rangi also produces two barrel-fermented chardonnays: Craighall is designed for bottle maturation and marked by a savory complexity, while Petrie is for early drinking and has fruit to the fore. The savory Célèbre is cabernet/merlot based, untypically spiced with syrah, sangiovese and nebbiolo, and contrasts with a charming rosé made from a similar blend. Recent additions to the range include a powerful pinot gris and a pure-fruit, young-vine pinot noir.

DRY RIVER WINES

Established **1979** ***Owners*** **Reg Oliver and Julian Robertson** ***Production*** **3,900 cases** ***Vineyard area*** **27 acres (11 ha)**

Chief winemaker, Neil McCallum, produces stiffly spined, dark and brooding pinot noir that has achieved cult status. Low cropping from bunch-thinning and leaf-plucking ensure Dry River wines are deep in extract, concentrated and complex. All are crafted for long bottle maturation (between five and ten years) and err on the side of austerity.

MARTINBOROUGH VINEYARD

Established **1980** ***Owners*** **180 Shareholders, Claire Campbell, and Russel and Sue Schultz** ***Production*** **6,336 cases** ***Vineyard area*** **247 acres (100 ha)**

Both the Martinborough Vineyard Pinot Noir and the Reserve Pinot Noir are never as ripe and powerful as they could be, but always the more interesting for it. Among other varietals, the chardonnay is consistently rich and well structured for mature drinking, while the pinot gris is one of New Zealand's finest. The Martinborough Vineyard Riesling and Late Harvest Riesling are also among the best in their categories. Larry McKenna, Martinborough's former winemaker, joined with other partners in setting up "The Escarpment," on Te Muna Road, southeast of Martinborough township. Their early pinot noir and pinot gris are promising wines. Early efforts with riesling indicate it will be a success here.

Other notable producers in the region include Alana Estate, Alexander Vineyard, Benfield & Delamare, Hau Ariki, Lintz Estate, Margrain Vineyard, Murdoch James Estate, Nga Waka, Palliser Estate, Stratford Wines, Te Kairanga Wines and Voss Estate.

Regional Dozen

QUALITY WINES

Ata Rangi Pinot Noir
Dry River Gewürztraminer
Dry River Pinot Gris
Dry River Pinot Noir
The Escarpment Pinot Noir
Martinborough Vineyards Reserve Pinot Noir
Palliser Estate Sauvignon Blanc

BEST VALUE WINES

Alexander Dusty Road Cabernet Franc UC
Margrain Riesling UC
Palliser Estate Riesling
Pencarrow Chardonnay
Pencarrow Sauvignon Blanc
Stratford Riesling UC

ABOVE: *A fine riesling and a sauvignon blanc are among the highlights of Allan Scott's range.*

Marlborough

Located on the northeastern tip of the South Island and centered on the Wairau Valley and the town of Blenheim, Marlborough is New Zealand's largest wine region and home to its most famous viticultural product, Marlborough Sauvignon Blanc, which has wowed the wine world. Marlborough is only the second-largest wine-producing area, but in terms of vineyard plantings it is by far the largest, with 16,492 acres (6,677 ha) and climbing. Its subregions are Renwick/Rapaura, Fairhall, Brancott Valley, Omaka, the newish Waihopai, Awatere Valley and the Kaikoura Ranges.

One of Marlborough's greatest viticultural strengths is its free-draining alluvial soil, and variations in its makeup account for a stylistically diverse range of wines. It has a relatively cool maritime climate with abundant sunshine.

Sauvignon blanc is Marlborough's most widely planted grape variety, accounting for 51 percent of total vineyard area. The second most planted variety is chardonnay, followed by pinot noir, riesling and much smaller quantities of other varieties; the once important cabernet sauvignon is in decline.

With few exceptions, the sauvignon blanc from the Marlborough region tends to be more intense in flavor and have higher acid levels than sauvignon blanc produced in other parts of New Zealand. A new style of sauvignon blanc is slowly emerging that has more oak and malolactic fermentation influences, and can be aged. Marlborough's chardonnay can be of a very high quality, as can the riesling, which many winemakers believe has great potential.

Regional Best

QUALITY WINES

Cloudy Bay Sauvignon Blanc
Corbans Cottage Block Noble Riesling
Dog Point Section 94 Sauvignon Blanc
Framingham Classic Riesling UC
Fromm La Strada Reserve Pinot Noir
Pelorus (sparkling)
Villa Maria Reserve Marlborough Chardonnay
Villa Maria Wairau Reserve Sauvignon Blanc

BEST VALUE WINES

Babich Marlborough Sauvignon Blanc
Grove Mill Sanctuary Riesling
Matua Shingle Peak Pinot Gris
Montana Lindauer Reserve Méthode Champenoise
Mount Riley Sauvignon Blanc
Selaks Drylands Chardonnay

When it comes to red wines, winemakers traditionally pinned their hopes on cabernet sauvignon but it has been eclipsed by pinot noir and even merlot. Plantings of pinot noir have now claimed a place among the country's best.

CELLIER LE BRUN

Established **1980** ***Owner*** **Recene Paint** ***Production*** **21,600 cases**
Vineyard area **99 acres (42 ha)**

Style and quality are hallmarks here. The reasonably priced, well-made Terrace Road range includes a sauvignon blanc, chardonnay, *méthode traditionnelle* and a pinot noir that is consistently among New Zealand's best buys. The sparkling range draws on chardonnay, pinot meunier, and/or pinot noir, includes a medium-bodied, yeasty brut NV; the Brut Tache, a pinot-dominated rosé; and the crisp, elegant Blanc de Blancs.

CLOUDY BAY

Established **1985** ***Owners*** **Cape Mentelle & Veuve Clicquot Ponsardin**
Production **100,800 cases** ***Vineyard area*** **247 acres (100 ha)**

All of Cloudy Bay's wines rank with the country's best. The sauvignon blanc is an explosion of mangoes, passionfruit, and pungent sweat, while the barrel-fermented Te Koko Sauvignon (pre-aged four years and on oak for 18 months) is quieter. The long-lived chardonnay is a flavor mix of low-yield fruit, French-oak fermentation, both wild and inoculated yeast, lees age, and partial malo. The Pelorus Méthode Traditionnelle, a barrel fermented pinot/chardonnay blend helped set a benchmark for top-end Kiwi bubblies. The pinot noir has steadily evolved a style that is multilayered, complex, and elegant. Made in small quantities, both the late harvest riesling and gewürztraminer are overlooked jewels.

FORREST ESTATE WINERY

***Established* 1989 *Owner* John Forrest *Production* 28,000 cases *Vineyard area* 222 acres (90 ha)**

John Forrest has a preference for transparently fruited, non-oaked wine, and his portfolio has consistently shown savory complexities, suppleness and structure. The winery's strengths include a densely textured, lees-aged sauvignon blanc that carries a touch of barrel-fermented sémillon; a lees-influenced, lightly oaked, partially malo-fermented chardonnay; and, in ripe years, a plummy, richly textured merlot. Forrest is also co-developing a vineyard and label in Hawkes Bay, producing a bordeaux-style blend branded Cornerstone.

FROMM WINERY

***Established* 1992 *Owners* Georg and Ruth Fromm *Production* 3,456 cases *Vineyard area* 15 acres (6 ha)**

Fromm's La Strada and, in good years, La Strada Reserve labels are marked by velvety textures, well-integrated fine tannins, rich flavors, and deep aromas. The consistency of La Strada Pinot Noir during the cool Marlborough 1995 and 1996 vintages had many local producers thinking they should pull out their cabernet and replace it with this grape. Fromm's radical approach quietly began a revolution that is only now yielding results.

HUIA VINEYARDS

***Established* 1996 *Owners* Claire and Mike Allan *Production* 7,600 cases *Vineyard area* 160 acres (65 ha)**

This winery is among the very best of Marlborough's producers. Winemaking here follows low-tech traditions, using natural yeast, minimal intervention, and no fining. Wines show great promise: the Dijon Clone 95/96 Chardonnay is subtle, minerally, long, and seamless with a fine viscosity; the gewürztraminer displays delicate

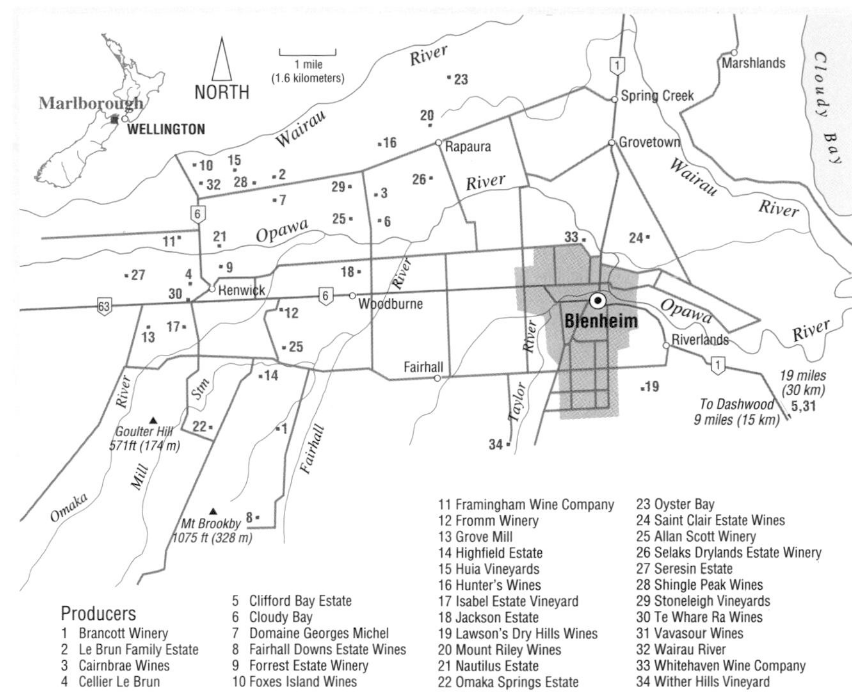

rose-like aromas but is explosive and nervy on the palate; the spicy pinot gris has similar palate weight; and the fine-grained pinot noir has mushroom characters.

ISABEL ESTATE VINEYARD

***Established* 1982 *Owners* Michael and Robyn Tiller *Production* 15,000 cases *Vineyard area* 198 acres (80 ha)**

Here, viticulture is paramount, intensive, and heading toward organic certification. Winemaking is *terroir*-oriented and non-interventionist, employing natural yeasts and soft handling. The three wines—chardonnay, sauvignon blanc and pinot noir—share a complex style, with transparent fruit underpinned by savory complexities, seamless textures, and great length.

SERESIN ESTATE

***Established* 1992 *Owner* Michael Seresin *Production* 15,840 cases *Vineyard area* 370 acres (150 ha)**

Intensive viticulture, clonal selection, and wild yeast ferments ensure complex and subtle, understated wines across Seresin's range. The varietally pure dry riesling is among Marlborough's top five, the sauvignon blanc (10 percent sémillon) is just as good, and the chardonnay, pinot gris, and pinot noir are distinguished by underplayed fruit, savoriness and balance.

There are many notable producers in this region, some of them are Le Brun Family Estate, Domaine Georges Michel, Grove Mill, Highfield Estate, Hunter's Wines, Lawson's Dry Hills Wines, Nautilus, Allan Scott Wines, Selaks Drylands Estate Winery, Shingle Peak Wines, Stoneleigh Vineyards, Te Whare Ra Wines, Vavsour Wines, Wairau River and Wither Hills.

LEFT: Trained vines at Hunter's Wines, which makes one of Marlborough's benchmark sauvignons.

RIGHT: Nelson's vineyards enjoy high levels of sunshine during the growing season.

Nelson

Since the early 1970s, Nelson has attracted a small but dedicated band of winemakers. There are now 26 wineries in the region; however, most of them are small, covering just 3 percent of New Zealand's total vineyard area. Although expansion has been slow compared to many regions, it is anticipated to make up lost ground in the next few years as plantings come on stream. Two long-established players, Seifried Estate and Neudorf Vineyards, dominate the region's production and profile.

Grapes are grown in two quite distinct areas around Nelson: the Waimea Plains and the Moutere Hills. Chardonnay is the most planted grape variety, followed by sauvignon blanc, pinot noir and riesling. Other grape varieties include cabernet franc, cabernet sauvignon, malbec, gewürztraminer, merlot, pinot gris and sémillon. White grapes have provided Nelson's most successful wines, with chardonnay and riesling being star performers, followed by sauvignon blanc.

Regional Dozen

QUALITY WINES

Greenhough Chardonnay UC
Greenhough Hope Pinot Noir UC
Neudorf Moutere Chardonnay
Neudorf Moutere Reserve Pinot Noir
Neudorf Sauvignon Blanc
Spencer Hill Tasman Bay Chardonnay

BEST VALUE WINES

Seifried Dry Riesling
Seifried Gewürztraminer
Seifried Gewürztraminer Ice Wine
Seifried Riesling
Waimea Estate Riesling UC
Waimea Estate Sauvignon Blanc UC

GREENHOUGH VINEYARD & WINERY

Established **1980** ***Owners*** **Andrew Greenhough and Jennifer Wheeler** ***Vineyard area*** **12.4 acres (5 ha)**

An existing vineyard was replanted with the clones and density determined to produce high-quality pinot noir, riesling, chardonnay and sauvignon blanc. The wines of the Reserve Hope Vineyard range are ripe, focused expressions of their respective varietals, with seamless textures, complexity, balance, and length—stars on the rise.

NEUDORF VINEYARDS

Established **1978** ***Owners*** **Tim and Judy Finn**
Vineyard area **62 acres (25 ha)**

Few would argue that Neudorf makes New Zealand's finest chardonnay. Both of its chardonnays share similar seamless textures and a meltaway finish, but the moutere is more savory and slower to develop than the brighter-fruited, more forward Nelson. The Brightwater Riesling and the sauvignon blanc are often among the country's top examples of these varietals. The floral Brightwater is particularly dense and very long, whereas the sauvignon has a finely etched structure and strong aromas.

Cork or screwcaps?

Winemakers around the globe are seeking closure to one of the most contentious issues facing the wine industry—to use natural corks, synthetic corks, or screw-caps. Groups of winemakers in New Zealand and Australia, tired of seeing their efforts spoilt by cork taint, are leading the push for screw-caps. In Australia, it was riesling producers in the Clare Valley; in New Zealand, sauvignon blanc makers from Marlborough. In both countries the use of these superior but controversial closures has quickly spread.

SEIFRIED ESTATE

Established **1973** ***Owners*** **Hermann and Agnes Seifried**
Production **80,000 cases** ***Vineyard area*** **247 acres (100 ha)**

The Seifried's have a gift for producing well priced, classy rieslings and gewürztraminers in a variety of dry, semidry, and late-harvested styles. The Old Coach Road range provides value for money, and the Winemaker's Collection has provided a successful forum for more serious varietal expression. Export success was followed by a UK-specific label called Redwood Valley, which has produced a trophy-winning sauvignon blanc and a highly regarded, barrel-fermented chardonnay.

WAIMEA ESTATES

Established **1997** ***Owner*** **Trevor Bolitho** ***Production*** **4,824 cases**
Vineyard area **190 acres (77 ha)**

Waimea Estates is being developed on land that was formerly a successful orchard on the Waimea Plains. The size of the operation and quality of the initial offerings suggest this is a winery to watch in future.

Other notable producers in the Nelson region include Denton Winery, Glover's Vineyard, McCashins, Spencer Hill Estate and Tohu Wines.

Canterbury/Waipara

The grape-growing areas of Canterbury and Waipara, on the east coast of New Zealand's South Island, are classified as a single entity, but in reality they are quite different. The soils, climates and styles of wine produced in each area have little in common; indeed, all they share is an ability to produce excellent chardonnay, pinot noir, riesling and, to a lesser extent, sauvignon blanc.

Together, Canterbury and Waipara form the country's (equal) fifth-largest wine-producing region, with just over 3.5 percent of the total vineyard area nationally. Currently, there are 42 wineries in Canterbury/Waipara. Canterbury has traditionally been the focus of grape growing and winemaking, but now Waipara is being recognized as a producer of top-quality wines.

There are two main winegrowing areas in Canterbury: Banks Peninsula and the Canterbury Plains. The soils are ably suited to chardonnay, pinot gris, pinot noir and riesling, but it's too early in the region's viticultural life to say which locations best suit individual varieties.

Canterbury's climate is cool maritime, with a low average annual rainfall. Frosts in both spring and autumn, and regular, hot, northwesterly winds and cool, easterly sea breezes can create problems. As a result, vintages tend to vary significantly from year to year. The most planted varieties are pinot noir, chardonnay and riesling, followed by pinot gris, sauvignon blanc and müller-thurgau. Waipara has lower rainfall and fewer frost problems than Canterbury, and is sheltered from the cool, easterly breezes. Southerly winds are a double-edged sword, as they can interfere with fruit-set but can virtually eliminate overcropping, resulting in more intensely flavored wines. The most planted grape variety in Waipara is sauvignon blanc, followed by riesling, chardonnay and pinot noir. Cabernet sauvignon is the next most-planted variety, despite the fact that the resulting wines tend to be relatively herbaceous in flavor.

GIESEN WINE ESTATE

Established **1981** ***Owners*** **Theo, Alex and Marcel Giesen**
Production **54,000 cases** ***Vineyard area*** **405 acres (164 ha)**

Giesen Wine Estate is Canterbury's largest operation. Its wines have always demonstrated a remarkable European sense of balance, finesse and restraint combined with clean, well-focused New Zealand fruit. The Marlborough Sauvignon Blanc is consistently one of New Zealand's best buys; so too is the low-yield, Pfalz-influenced, off-dry riesling. The vineyard consistently produces the dry botrytis that drives one of the country's best late-harvested rieslings. During the mid-1990s, Giesen found success with a complex pair of silky pinot noirs: one estate-grown, the second using fruit provided by Isabel Estate and other vineyards in Marlborough. Its restrained chardonnay is typical of the best Canterbury Reserves. Most Giesen wines need a few years bottle aging. The emphasis here has been on whites rather than reds.

ALAN MCCORKINDALE

Established **1996** ***Owner*** **Alan McCorkindale** ***Production*** **864 cases**
Vineyard area **10 acres (4 ha)**

Alan McCorkindale established a small vineyard in Waipara to make *méthode traditionnelle* sparklers from selected clones of chardonnay, pinot noir and pinot meunier. His first release, Millennium Brut, has an elegant style, savory flavors, and pronounced autolytic characters. McCorkindale also produces a riesling, chardonnay, pinot noir and sauvignon blanc. Besides that, he makes a number of the region's wines for other producers as well.

MOUNTFORD VINEYARD

Established **1990** ***Owners*** **Michael and Buffy Eaton**
Production **1,188 cases** ***Vineyard area*** **10 acres (4 ha)**

This is a tiny, tightly focused operation, incorporating tastefully designed accommodation. The winery specializes

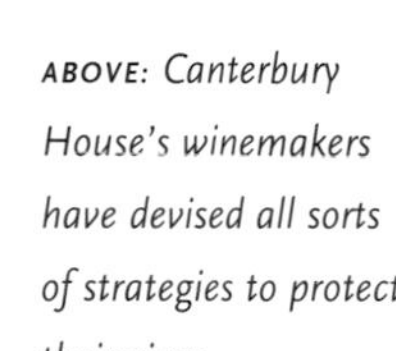

ABOVE: *Canterbury House's winemakers have devised all sorts of strategies to protect their vines.*

CENTER: *This unusual corkscrew, made in England in 1870, was patented as the Lund King.*

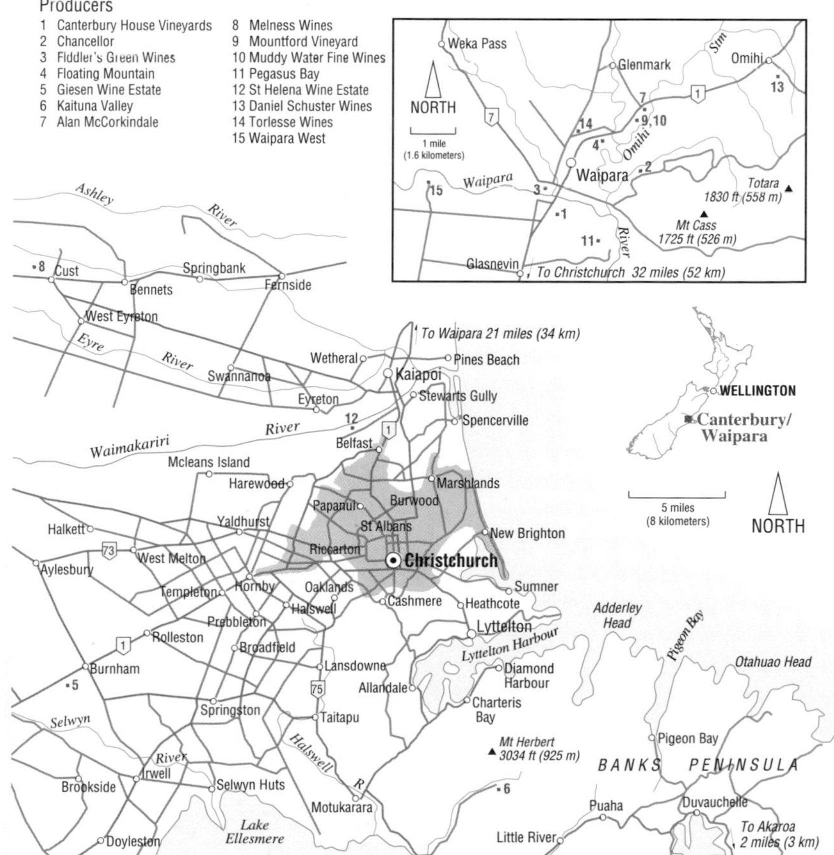

ABOVE: The Mountford Vineyard winery offers fine views of the rolling Canterbury countryside.

in only two varietals: chardonnay and pinot noir, both made by blind winemaker C. P. Lin, who is well known for his sharp sense of smell and taste. Although it is early days, the first pinot noirs have shown ripe cherry flavors, richness and concentration, and the chardonnay has tended toward a more obvious, full-on, buttery style.

PEGASUS BAY

Established **1992** ***Owners*** **Ivan and Chris Donaldson**
Production **19,440 cases** ***Vineyard area*** **86 acres (35 ha)**

Pegasus Bay has established itself in a very short period as one of New Zealand's top wineries and the star of the region. Generally, its wines are rich and ripe, but with added savory dimensions and multilayered complexities. Pegasus rieslings have been outstanding: both the Arias, the off-dry and the late-harvest, are marked by silky, seamless textures; complex, varietally focused aromas; and rich, minerally flavors. The savory chardonnay employs Burgundian oxidative techniques, whole-bunch pressing, and extended lees aging to construct complexity and drive length. In sharp contrast, the whopping great sauvignon blanc/sémillon reeks of mango, guava, and other tropical fruits. The unfiltered, voluptuous pinot noir is headed in the right direction, although it has tended toward excessive alcohol and overripe fruit flavors in hot vintages. In these same hot years, however, the cabernet sauvignon/merlot shines splendidly, possessing classic cigar-box and cedar aromas, and dense textures. A second label, Main Divide, drawn from declassified Pegasus Bay and Marlborough fruit, can represent good value.

Regional Best

QUALITY WINES

Giesen Botrytised Riesling
Giesen Reserve Pinot Noir
Mountford Pinot Noir
Pegasus Bay Aria Late Picked Riesling
Pegasus Bay Chardonnay
Pegasus Bay Pinot Noir
Pegasus Bay Riesling

BEST VALUE WINES

Corbans Private Bin Amberley Riesling
Giesen Canterbury Riesling
St Helena Pinot Blanc
St Helena Pinot Gris
St Helena Riesling
Torlese Gewürztraminer

DANIEL SCHUSTER WINES

Established **1984** ***Owners*** **Daniel and Mari Schuster** ***Production*** **4,536 cases** ***Vineyard area*** **35 acres (14 ha)**

Daniel Schuster is an internationally reknowned and respected "flying" viticulturist and coauthor of the classic work, *The Production of Grapes and Wine in Cool Climates*. As an early proponent of *terroir*-defined wine, and food-friendly styles, his views are often at odds with an industry known for its bold fruit. His Canterbury and pricey Selection range (chardonnay and pinot noir), made from the Omihi Hills fruit, show restraint and subtlety.

Other notable producers in the Canterbury/Waipara region include Canterbury House Vineyards, Chancellor, Fiddler's Green Wines, Floating Mountain, the Kaituna Valley, Melness Wines, Muddy Water Fine Wines, St Helena Wine Estate, Torlesse Wines, Waipara Springs Winery and Waipara West.

Central Otago

Central Otago is the most southerly grape-growing region in the world. It is also one of New Zealand's fastest growing regions, with 1,685 acres (682 ha), giving it 4.5 percent of total vineyards planted. This growth is fuelled by the extraordinary success of pinot noir, which occupies 63 percent of vineyards planted. Pinot noir is followed, in descending order, by chardonnay, pinot gris, riesling, and much smaller quantities of other varieties. Increases in vineyard area are expected to come mainly from plantings of pinot noir, pinot gris and riesling.

Central Otago has four main subregions: Gibbston, Wanaka, Alexandra and Cromwell, which is further divided into the three distinct areas of Bannockburn, Lowburn and Bendigo. A fifth subregion, Lake Hayes, has few plantings, most of which are devoted to sparkling wine production. The area's most planted subregion is Cromwell, with 60 percent of the total vineyard, followed by Gibbston with 27 percent, Alexandra with 8 percent, and Wanaka with 4 percent.

Viticulture is marginal in Otago, the country's only inland wine region. Most vineyards here lie between 650 and 1,000 feet (200 and 300 m) above sea level and are planted on hillsides to take advantage of the region's high levels of sunshine and to avoid frost.

Differences in the style of wines arising from slight variations in climate and soil in each of the subregions are slowly being noticed. Gibbston and Wanaka, which are home to the oldest vines and have the coolest climates, tend to produce more earthy, delicate styles of pinot noir compared to the more fruit-driven, lush styles emanating from other subregions. The warmest areas, Alexandra and Bannockburn, are already showing that they could also yield outstanding chardonnay and gewürztraminer.

Both the chardonnay and sauvignon blanc grown in Central Otago tend to be higher in acid than elsewhere in New Zealand, although both produce classic fruit-driven styles. Central Otago also has the potential to produce top-quality pinot gris, plantings of which are increasing. As tends to occur with pinot gris, styles vary widely, from fresh and bracingly acidic to opulent.

CHARD FARM

Established **1987** ***Owners*** **Rob and Greg Hay**
Vineyard area **74 acres (30 ha)**

Chard Farm's lees-stirred pinot gris, finely etched sauvignon blanc, and Judge and Jury Chardonnay are brilliant food wines, while the riesling and gewürztraminer often show great aromatic depth and a steely spine. The top pinot noirs (Finla Mor and Bragato) generally need time to marry textures and evolve savory characters. New secondary labels have also been introduced, covering single-vineyard wines from emerging hot spots such as Bannockburn, Lowburn and Lake Hayes.

FELTON ROAD WINES

Established **1991** ***Owners*** **Stewart and Kate Elms**
Vineyard area **74 acres (30 ha)**

Felton Road arrived on the scene with a flourish of concentrated pinot noirs and a pair of richly textured, highly aromatic, steely rieslings. Early success owes much to the winery's warm location, devotion to low-yield viticulture, and employment of traditional winemaking practices, including using wild yeasts to stamp *terroir* on the wines from inception. The wines from Felton Road have attracted huge critical success in the US.

GIBBSTON VALLEY WINES

Established **1981** ***Owner*** **Ross McKay**
Vineyard area **148 acres (60 ha)**

This is one of Central Otago's largest wineries. When the local vintage is strong, the wines are site specific; but in more difficult years, cross-blending helps fill in the gaps. Winemaker Grant Taylor's pinot noirs, which display the deep perfume, rich texture, and firm structure that typify cool-climate pinot, have won seven major international trophies. Other highlights from this winery include a finely balanced, complex riesling; a nervy, well-focused pinot gris; and the excellent-value, unwooded Greenstone Chardonnay.

Other significant producers include Amisfield Lake Hayes, Black Ridge Wines, Mount Edward, Olssen's of Bannockburn, Peregrine, Perrelle Lake Hayes, Quartz Reef, Rippon Vineyard and Two Paddocks.

Regional Dozen

Black Ridge Pinot Noir
Chard Farm Bragato Pinot Noir
Chard Farm Pinot Gris
Chard Farm Riesling
Felton Road Block Three Pinot Noir
Felton Road Chardonnay
Felton Road Dry Riesling
Gibbston Valley Reserve Pinot Noir
Quartz Reef Chauvet
Quartz Reef Pinot Noir
Rippon Pinot Noir
Two Paddocks Pinot Noir

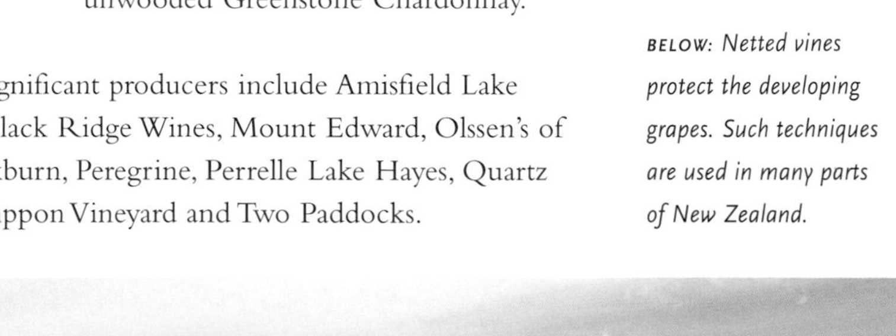

BELOW: *Netted vines protect the developing grapes. Such techniques are used in many parts of New Zealand.*

Enjoying Wine

STEVE CHARTERS MW

Above all, wine is designed to be enjoyed, preferably with entertaining companions and good food. However, although wine is often drunk in copious quantities in those circumstances, the issue of "tasting" arises for anyone who develops more than a passing interest in the subject.

Tasting is not drinking—the situation is different. It is not primarily a companionable activity (it can even be competitive) and ideally food should not be present, at least while tasting seriously. The purpose is also different. While drinking is for pleasure, tasting is primarily for assessment, allowing you to evaluate different wines.

HOW TO TASTE WINE

Tasting is more than just swilling the liquid into your mouth. There are in fact four senses used: sight, smell, taste and touch. Wine jargon has arisen around the whole process and these are dignified with the terms "appearance," "nose" and "palate" (which covers both taste and touch). Before you even take a sip, you may, using these criteria, be able to determine the wine's likely age, possible origin and the grape variety used, as well as the climate the grapes were produced in and how the wine was made and stored. Critically, you should also be able to establish if the wine is faulty or too old.

Anyone can taste. Many wine drinkers think that their palate may be defective, or that they will never have the ability to become good wine tasters. It is not true. Anyone can become a first-rate taster if they practice enough. Even though each palate is different and we all react to varying components in the wine with diverse responses, no palate is worse than another.

Sight

The first part of the process is to look carefully at the wine. Is its appearance cloudy or hazy? If it is, then it may be out of condition—although a slight haze on some red wines may merely mean that the wine-maker has chosen not to filter too harshly. A sediment in the bottom of the glass does not count as a haze, and is a perfectly normal part of the development of the wine in the bottle.

The depth of color gives clues about the wine. A deep red suggests a thick-skinned variety such as cabernet sauvignon or syrah. A paler color may simply be a variety like pinot noir or gamay. As red wines get older their color also fades, so this will give you more information about the wine. A pale, almost watery color in white wines hints at grapes grown in a cool area. A deep gold may be the result of a warmer climate, though it could also suggest some age on the wine and/or the use of oak as part of the aging process.

The hue of a wine is also important. A youthful red wine will probably have a purple-crimson character. With age, the wine progresses through shades of cherry or plum (still revealing some youth), through ruby to garnet and tawny. With white wines the reverse is true: the older the wine, the deeper its color becomes, and the lemon (and sometimes green) of youth becomes gold, then old-gold and amber. In any wine (other than fortified wines), a brown shade indicates the wine is too old.

ABOVE: Assessing sparkling wine—bubbles showing regular and persistent bead in a glass of champagne.

OPPOSITE: A winetasting at S. A. Prüm's winery in the Mosel region. The sense of smell is very important in assessing a wine.

Changing color with age

RIGHT: Penfold's Grange 1993 (right) and 1981 (far right). Penfold's Grange, first made by Max Schubert in the 1950s, is widely regarded as Australia's greatest red wine. The Grange from 1993 is a young red wine (although actually comparatively old) with a deep plum color and vibrant pink-crimson rim. The color of the older vintage Grange (1981) is no longer as deep: the hue has changed more to ruby, and there is a distinct brick tone about the rim, a clear sign of age.

RIGHT: Trimbach Riesling, cuvée "Frederic Emile" 1994 (right) and 1983 (far right), the great Alsace riesling made by Maison Trimbach. Cuvée "Frederic Emile" is named after a family member who brought the firm to prominence in the nineteenth century. The younger white wine (1994) has a very pale lemon hue, with a tinge of green (common in whites from a cooler climate). The older wine (1983) has a distinct gold-amber hue, betraying the impact of oxygen as it ages.

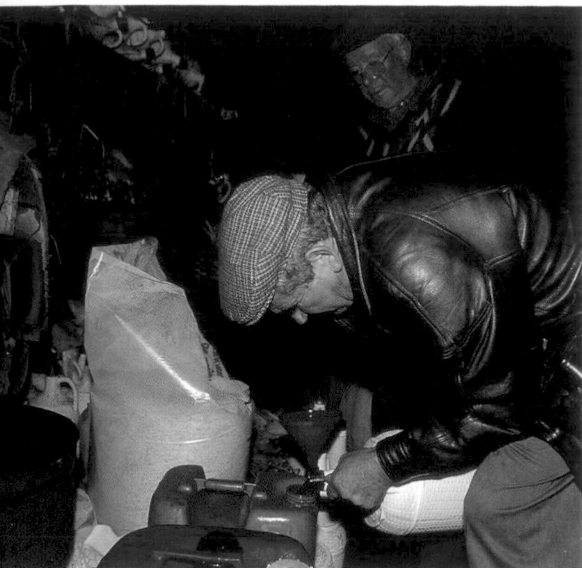

ABOVE: *Traditional distribution methods. "Bottling" in plastic containers for home consumption from a small winery in Portugal.*

Length Mediocre wines will fade fast, but a good wine has a flavor that will go on for about 15 seconds or longer.

Complexity Complexity refers to the layers of flavor in the wine. A simple syrah will only have one or two distinctive flavors—black fruit, for instance. A more complex one could also exhibit spice, coffee, cedar, black olive and tar. Complex wines also tend to have flavor patterns that then develop and change in the mouth, starting with fruit dominating, adding coffee and cedar, and ending on spice and tar, without the fruit flavor ever entirely being lost. Unfortunately, the more complex a wine is, the harder it can be to separate and analyze all the component flavors, even for the most experienced taster.

Not every high-quality wine will have all of these—and all but the most dreadful of wines should show some attributes of quality—but all good wines should at least have balance, intensity and generally length. The best will also show some complexity of flavor. Ideas of quality are complicated by differing cultural approaches to what is in the glass. A French drinker may place a lot of emphasis on the structure of the wine, and less on intense, ripe fruit. An Australian seeks great intensity, but may look less for structural harmony. An American is probably halfway between the two.

Conveying critical information about a wine can be done in many ways. Traditionally, wines were merely discussed in words, but these days points or stars are often used. In Australia, it is common to mark wines out of 20 (in practice, however, all wines get at least 10). In the United States, marks out of 100 are given (except, again, that the marking starts from halfway, so in practice one is only marking out of 50). Marks can be a useful aid to a quick personal assessment of a wine, but the danger is that they supplant the more informative process of describing the wine. Knowing that a wine has balanced acidity, firm tannins, quite a full body and intense and long black fruit and cedar characters conveys far more information than a wine score of 16/20 (or 80/100).

In many parts of the world wine shows are regularly used as a means of assessing wines. These can be an excellent way of helping the consumer make decisions about purchases, as well as helping successful producers sell their wines (note the number of bottles decorated with gold or silver medals in your local wine store). Some shows require judges to assess large classes—150 to 200 wines or more—very rapidly. This can also skew the show results because wines that are bold and forward are more easily appreciated than subtle and delicate ones, even if the latter actually have more complexity and balance.

THE RITUALS OF WINE

Choosing wine

The key factors in choosing a wine are the setting and context in which it will be drunk. Is it a casual drinks party in the garden, a barbecue or a more formal situation? Will there be food? Do the guests want to have wines to sip and think about, or merely to quench their thirst? Will you be serving wine on a warm summer's evening or will there be snow on the ground?

Riesling, for example, makes a light, crisp white wine, sometimes with a little residual sugar. It is great summer drinking, or with lighter foods at any time of the year. It provides some of the greatest value for money in terms of taste per dollar of any white wine in the world, but it is not invariably the best white to serve.

The subject of food and wine is much misunderstood. Historically, it has been hidebound with rules

RIGHT: *Buyers tasting wine before bidding at the most famous wine auction in the world, the Hospices de Beaune, in Burgundy.*

about what can and cannot be eaten and drunk together. There is a very strong reaction against this currently, with some experts even saying that any food can go with any wine as long as the food itself is in balance. It is therefore clearly an area fraught with difficulty.

A classic work on wine may suggest a good bordeaux or, possibly burgundy, for lamb, on the basis that the meat is roasted. But what if it is lamb tagine with quince? Or lamb daube, stewed in wine with herbs and olives? Or lamb curry? Each of those would probably clash with the traditional match; and if you had invested a lot of money in the wine you would probably be disappointed. The old adage that if you have a good wine you need a plain dish is probably the safest course. Consequently, your paramount rule of thumb should be to drink what you want with whatever you choose to eat, as long as the wine is a good one. As Australian wine producer and expert Len Evans said, "Life is too short to drink bad wine."

Another suggestion that may help match food and wine is to balance weight with weight. So a lighter-bodied wine will be preferable with seafood and very light cold meats, a medium-bodied wine will be better with fish and less fatty meats, and a full-bodied wine will complement heavier dishes such as casseroles and roasts. As for the color of the wine, some people will only drink red or white with their meal, and not both. Critically, however, it is often the sauce or key seasonings rather than the main component of the dish that should be considered when selecting the wine. Wine and food pairing has evolved naturally in Europe over many millennia. The reason rosé wines are popular in Provence, for example, is because, despite the fact that the region historically produces full-bodied reds, the locals need something to go with their bouillabaisse.

Food and wine generally go together well. Wine is an aid to digestion, and its acidity and tannin can complement the process of eating. Some foods clash with certain wines, but often there is a general symbiosis between food and wine. You may have an idea that a particular dish and a selected wine will work well together, and sometimes trial and error is the best way to find out. Sometimes by chance they just seem predestined to go with each other. The great matches—where the two just meld into each other—often seem to happen by accident. Enjoy it, and remember it, when it happens—it is serendipity.

LEFT: Champagne must be served chilled.

The rules for tasting

- ***Do not introduce intrusive smells***
  No perfume or aftershave: it really can distract your and other people's ability to smell and assess wine.
- ***Ensure there is good lighting***
  This is the only way for you to get a really good idea of the appearance of the wine.
- ***Be quiet***
  Talking may disturb others.
- ***Do not discuss the wines with others***
  This may prejudice them or you, and cause you to reach faulty conclusions. You can compare notes at the end.
- ***Write notes***
  To aid memory.
  To act as a reminder—especially if later decisions have to be made about it.
  To monitor the progress of the wine.
- ***Always spit if tasting more than a few wines***
  To avoid getting drunk.
- ***Think carefully about the wine***
  Start by analyzing the structure.
  Don't get sidetracked by the fruit aromas and flavors.
  Evaluate the quality and maturity of the wine.
  This is not primarily a case of whether or not you like it, but how good it is.
- ***Keep your glasses clean***
  Even detergent may affect the character of the wine.

Serving wine

CHILLING

Critical to enjoying wine is the temperature at which it should be served. In general today, we have a tendency to serve our white wines too cold on the basis that, like beer, they should refresh. Unfortunately, too cool a temperature deadens the flavor and aroma.

Conversely, we often serve our red wines too warm. The maxim that they should be at room temperature was established before the age of central heating or the move of the English-speaking world en masse into warm places like Australia. In the case of some of the red wines in particular, it means that 20 minutes in the refrigerator to take the warmth off may be a good idea. But chilling wine in the refrigerator for too long will dull its character. It is important to keep wine cool, but it should not be too cold. The bottle can go back in the refrigerator after opening, or place it in an ice bucket or vacuum cooler. As the wine warms up a little, the aromas are released. Too warm, however, and the aromas dissipate because the alcohol is evaporating too readily. Chilling makes sparkling wines appear less aggressive and maintains their fizz for longer, by reducing the apparent activity of acidity, as well as the activity of carbon dioxide.

RIGHT: Australian and New Zealand wines displaying their awards.

UNCORKING

The conventional corkscrew comes in all shapes and sizes. About the only rule is that it should be a complete spiral rather than a central column with a flanged screw around it because that will tend to push cork into the wine. "Waiters' friends" are simple, but not always the easiest to use. It is worth buying a corkscrew you feel happy with, because you may be using it regularly for many years. A foil cutter that removes the capsule easily is also an excellent investment. For those whose bank balance allows them to drink older wines regularly, a corkscrew that can deal with decaying corks is helpful. The style with two long thin metal blades that slip down between the cork and the neck of the bottle does this particularly well. Never shake a bottle of sparkling wine before opening it: at best, you will waste what is in the bottle; at worst, you are increasing the pressure on the cork. Never pry the cork open and let it pop into the air: eyes have been lost in this way. Instead, having removed the muzzle, hold the base of the bottle or grip the neck, with the bottle at a 45° angle. Grip the cork and gently twist it from the neck. The cork should escape with a faint hiss of gas and no loss of precious liquid.

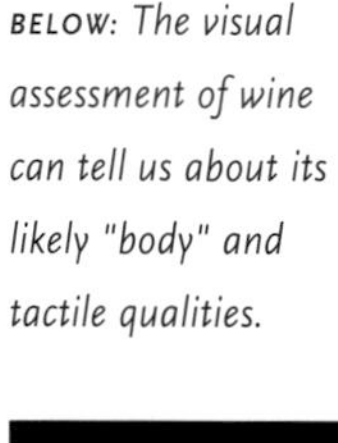

BELOW: The visual assessment of wine can tell us about its likely "body" and tactile qualities.

DECANTING

The next ritual of wine is decanting. Generally, one would only decant red wines, and mainly old red wines that have thrown a deposit or sediment. No one wants a glass tainted by gritty particles. The bottle should be left to stand for a while to allow the deposit to collect at its base, and then opened very gently to avoid disturbance. Pour off the wine carefully, leaving half an inch or so (a centimeter or two) in the bottle with the sediment. Decanting also has the benefit of blowing off the wine the temporary "bottle stink" that many wines develop with age, making them more immediately attractive before they get to the glass. With very old wines you should only decant immediately before service, otherwise what is left of the fruit aromas may dissipate very fast and the wine could lose its appeal. Wines of moderate age (say, six to 15 years old, depending on variety and vintage) will benefit from decanting about 30 minutes before service.

The second reason to decant wines attracts some controversy. A few wine lovers think that young red wines benefit from decanting an hour or so before drinking. This can speed the development of the wine by oxygen which normally takes some years in the bottle, integrating and softening the wine, making it more attractive. However, the weight of expert opinion is against it, saying it is better to allow the wine to develop in the glass. What is of no use is pulling the cork and standing the bottle, allowing the wine to "breathe." This has no impact on the wine, as the surface area of wine in the neck of the bottle is too small to change its character.

SAMPLING WINE

Commonly, before wine is shared, the person who is offering it will first pour a small sample and smell it. This is essential to ensure the wine is in good condition and not subject to cork taint.

Some wines (aromatic whites and fino sherries) may keep in the fridge for 24 hours, but no longer. Full-bodied whites and reds may keep for another day . More full-bodied fortified wines may keep for a few days, or maybe a week, but even a tawny port (made with long-term oxygen contact) will not remain fresh for long. If you like having a wine open to sip occasionally, then choose madeira. After the heating process, bacterial development and aging with air contact, no other "damage" can really occur. It is also a wonderful and much misunderstood drink.

Wine faults

Many faults can affect wine, though with good hygiene, modern methods of analysis, and a careful scientific approach to winemaking these should now be minimized.

Cork taint This fault is entirely outside the control of winemakers and is the bane of their lives. Essentially, a mold that occasionally exists in the cork combines with chlorine compounds (which may come from the cork processor, or the winery, or may just be in the air). The resulting chemical gives the wine a moldy smell, like wet hessian or damp cardboard, and can destroy its fruit flavors. Unfortunately, it does not always appear in a clear-cut form. It may occasionally just dull the wine, rather than ruin it.

Excess sulfur dioxide This used to plague many European wines, especially sweet ones. Sulfur dioxide is necessary to maintain freshness in the wine, but if added to excess it can give a burnt match character to the smell, and dull the fruit. Letting the wine breathe for a few minutes—especially by swirling it around in the glass—should help the fault blow off.

ABOVE: Wines from the middle of the last century: 1951 in Burgundy was actually a very poor year and not worth keeping!

Reading the label

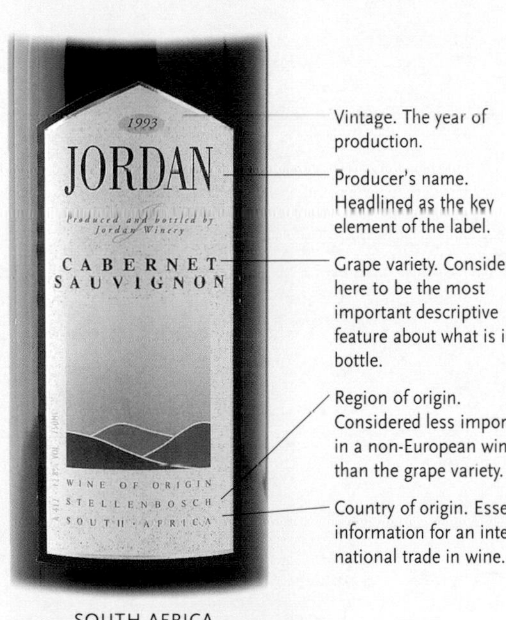

SOUTH AFRICA

UNITED STATES OF AMERICA

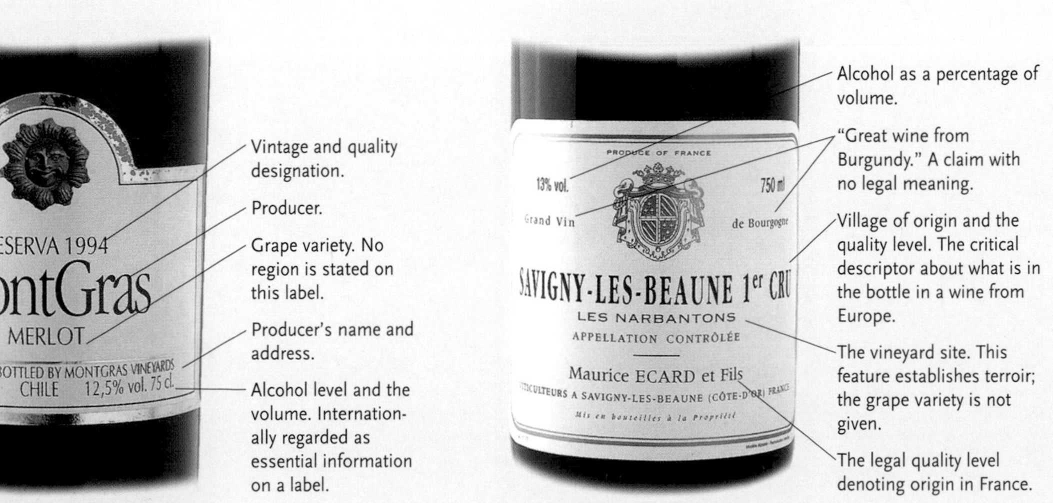

CHILE

FRANCE

Wine paraphernalia & glassware

The glassware in which the wine is served is critical. There was a fashion a few years ago to serve wine in small heavy water glasses. Nothing could be more designed to spoil the effect. These days, many glass producers make a living persuading aficionados that their glass, or series of glasses, is absolutely essential to the better enjoyment of wine. Often they are right, but even for those who cannot afford US$50 for a single glass, it is possible to improve one's enjoyment of wine if you stick to a few simple rules for glasses.

The ideal glass should have a tapering shape, being narrower at the top than at the base, to concentrate the aromas. The glass should be comparatively wide for red wines, to let air contact develop the wine, but less so for whites, where preserving the delicate aromatic

quality is essential to enjoying the wine. The glasses should not be made of cut glass, which distorts the appearance of the wine, but otherwise it helps the process of enjoyment if the glasses are esthetically appealing. The narrower the rim, the better the quality of glass and the delivery of wine to the mouth. For sparkling wines, the tall flute is ideal for preserving both their fizz and delicate aromas.

Never use a flat coupe as this shape allows the bubbles to disperse too quickly, reducing the drinker's enjoyment.

An efficient corkscrew and good glassware are essential items. A decanter and cooler are useful too, and a neck thermometer may be a help. Beyond that, ice jackets, wine preservers, aerators and the like are only for the most dedicated.

DECANTER
An attractive cut-glass container into which older red wines can be poured, to allow them to breathe, and to leave gritty deposit in the bottle, so it does not get poured into glasses.

SPARKLING WINE STOPPER
Designed to clip onto the flange at the top of a bottle of sparkling wine, so it is not blown off by the gas pressure. It inhibits fizz from escaping.

BEAUJOLAIS GLASS
Intended for fruity, less tannic reds; curved so that little development occurs in the glass from air contact, and the aromatic nature of the wine is preserved.

CHAMPAGNE FLUTE
Tall and thin, not to enhance the appearance of the bubbles, but to slow their dissipation into the air.

RED BURGUNDY GLASS
Half-way between the bordeaux glass (for big, tannic reds) and the beaujolais glass (fruity reds). This gives some air contact for older wines, but doesn't let the ethereal aromas be dissipated quickly.

RIESLING GLASS
Small and narrow, to protect the aromas of the most delicate aromatic white wines.

CHAMPAGNE CORK EXTRACTOR
Intended to give a grip on stubborn corks in sparkling wine bottles and ease their removal.

SMALL TASTING GLASSES
Designed for taking small samples of wine purely for tasting purpose; but it could also double as a glass for fortified wines.

SPARKLING WINE STOPPER

Sulfur compounds These can form either from residual sulfur in the vineyard or, more usually, as part of the process of fermentation, giving a "rotten egg" stink from hydrogen sulfide. At that stage, the problem can be easily cured. Unfortunately, if it is allowed to continue in the barrel, mercaptans may develop. These impart a foul garlic smell to the wine that cannot be removed.

Volatile acidity Few bacteria can survive in wine, but one that can (so long as oxygen is present) is acetobacter. This creates acetic acid (vinegar) which will not harm a wine in small doses (it may even add to its complexity), but in larger amounts gives the wine a sharp smell and a hard, bitter acid finish. It is easy to prevent in the winery but once it exists it cannot be eradicated.

Caskiness Sometimes a wine will smell or taste (on the finish) a bit woody or casky. A slightly unclean barrel or a faulty filter pad are among the main causes for this. However there is no excuse for poor winemaking, and the wine should be returned.

Storage

Sooner or later, anyone who develops a love for wine wants to keep a few bottles lying around. With time, those "few bottles" become a few cases. When those few cases expand into a few more, the issue arises about where and how to store it. There are a few basic rules.

Temperature Having a cool temperature to store wine is not as important as having a steady one, without much variation. Overt heat, and fluctuations, will accelerate the aging process and, at extremes, will damage the wine. A maximum temperature for mid-term storage is about 64°F (18°C); for the longer term, about 57°F (14°C) is best. Cellars are genuinely ideal, giving a constant cool, but not freezing, temperature.

Light Ultraviolet light can harm wine, giving it vegetal characters. For this reason, wine is often bottled in green or brown glass, but even then it should be kept away from light sources for long-term storage.

Vibration Movement is thought to damage wine. It is best to minimize movement of wine that is stored.

Position Bottles should be stored horizontally to keep the cork moist. This stops the cork from shrinking, thus keeping out air that could accelerate the oxidization process. (This does not apply to sparkling wine.)

Meeting these conditions can be difficult if you have limited space. Some commercial storage facilities actually often have wine stores. Whatever you do, never buy expensive wine to age and keep it in warm conditions for years on end in the hope that it will survive. It won't.

VINTAGES AND VINTAGE CHARTS

The term "vintage" does not describe a special wine—it merely means the year the grapes were picked. Almost all wines (except blended champagne and fortified wines) are therefore likely to be vintage wines.

Given the impact of the weather on grape quality (especially in more marginal climates), and therefore on the resulting wine, some years will make better wine than others. Part of the lore of connoisseurship involves learning by rote the good and the bad years.

Remember, quality wine is individual and subject to change. There will always be some producers who will make great wine in poor vintages, or fail in an otherwise great year.

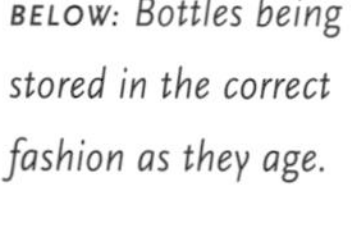

BELOW: Bottles being stored in the correct fashion as they age.

Wine Reference Table

While every effort has been made to provide an interesting selection of wines across many countries, tastes and price ranges, this list is by no means exhaustive. The table below is intended to be a guide only. The asterisks represent the approximate price of each wine in its country of origin. One asterisk represents easily affordable wines, two asterisks denote a moderate expense and three asterisks a more costly wine. Foods listed under compatible foods are intended only to be suggestions. Of course it is possible to drink any wine with any food; these are simply a guide.

UNITED STATES OF AMERICA

Wine name	Region	Style	Flavor/Bouquet	Compatible Foods	Price Range
Amity Pinot Blanc	Willamette Valley/Oregon	White	Apples, citrus, vanillin	Fish, chicken	**
Andrew Will Pepper Bridge Cabernet	Walla Walla Valley/ Washington State	Red	Plums, toasty, rich	Beef, lamb	***
Archery Arcus Estate Pinot Noir	Willamette Valley/Oregon	Red	Berry, jam, spicy	Chicken, veal, pork	***
Archery Premier Cuvée Pinot Noir	Willamette Valley/Oregon	Red	Berry, spicy, oaky	Chicken, veal, pork	***
Argyle Reserve Riesling	Willamette Valley/Oregon	White	Floral, fruity	Shellfish, fish	**
Barboursville Vineyards Pinot Grigio	Virginia	White	Citrus, floral	Shellfish, Asian	*
Bargetto Regan Vineyards Chardonnay	Santa Cruz Mountains, North Central Coast/California	White	Apples, spicy	Fish, chicken	**
Baron Herzog Lodi Zinfandel	Central Valley/California	Red	Berry, spicy	Pizza, beef, sausages	*
Basignani Winery Cabernet Sauvignon	Maryland	Red	Plums, spicy	Beef, pork, lamb	**
Baywood Cellars Lodi Vineyard Select Zinfandel	Central Valley/California	Red	Berry, spicy	Pizza, beef, sausages	*
Baywood Cellars Private Reserve California Port	Monterey/California	Fortified	Berry, jam	Dessert, nuts	*
Baywood Cellars Vineyard Select California Symphony	Monterey/California	White	Honey, floral	Salads, fruit	*
Beaux Frères Pinot Noir	Willamette Valley/Oregon	Red	Berry, fruity, oaky	Veal, pork, beef	***
Bedell Cellars Cabernet Franc	New York	Red	Plums, spicy	Pork, beef, veal	**
Bedell Cellars Eis (Riesling Dessert Wine) Clinton Vineyards Seyval	New York	Sweet	Sweet, honey, floral	Dessert	***
Bedell Cellars Merlot	New York	Red	Plums, vanillin	Pork, beef, lamb	**
Bella Vigna Lodi Vigna Antica Zinfandel	Central Valley/California	Red	Berry, spicy	Pizza, beef, sausages	**
Bernardus Carmel Valley Marinus Meritage	Monterey/California	Red	Rich, toasty	Lamb, beef, cheese	***
Bernardus Chardonnay	Monterey/California	White	Rich, buttery	Fish, chicken, veal	***
Bernardus Sauvignon Blanc	Monterey/California	White	Rich, citrus	Shellfish, fish, cheese	**
Biff and Scooter Abroad/Livermore Valley Cellars Yolo County Orange Muscat	Central Valley/California	Sweet	Honey, floral	Dessert	*
Big White House Arroyo Seco Vineyards Viognier	Monterey/California	White	Floral, tropical fruit	Fish, salads	**
Black Sheep Amador Clockspring Vineyard Zinfandel	Sierra Foothills/California	Red	Berry, spicy	Pizza, pork, veal	**
Black Sheep Sierra Foothills True Frogs Lily Pad White	Sierra Foothills/California	White	Floral, fruity	Shellfish, salads	*
Boeger Winery El Dorado Muscat Canelli	Sierra Foothills/California	Fortified	Floral, fruity	Dessert, nuts	*
Bogle Vineyards Colby Ranch Reserve Clarksburg Chardonnay	Central Valley/California	White	Butter, oaky	Chicken, fish, veal	*
Bonny Doon Vineyards Ca del Solo Big House Red	Monterey/California	Red	Plums, spicy	Pizza, pasta, beef, pork	**
Bonny Doon Vineyards Cardinal Zin Narly Old Vines Zinfandel	Contra Costa County San Francisco Bay/California	Red	Complex, spicy	Pizza, pork, veal	**
Bonny Doon Vineyards Clos de Gilroy Grenache	Santa Clara Valley, North Central Coast/California	Red	Berry, spicy	Asian, fish, pizza	*
Bonny Doon Vineyards Le Cigare Volant California	Santa Cruz Mountains, North Central Coast/California	Red	Jam, spicy	Pizza, beef, pork	**
Bonny Doon Vineyards Moscato Fior d'Arrancio Fortified Muscat	Monterey/California	Fortified	Fruity, floral	Dessert	**
Bonny Doon Vineyards Old Telegram Mourvedre	Contra Costa County San Francisco Bay/California	Red	Powerful, earthy	Beef, lamb, cheese	**
Bonny Doon Vineyards Sangiovese	Monterey/California	Red	Berry, spicy	Pizza, pasta, veal, pork	**
Bonny Doon Vineyards Vin de Glacière California Muscat	Santa Cruz Mountains, North Central Coast/California	White	Sweet, floral, complex	Cold meats, dessert	**
Boyer Pinot Noir	Monterey/California	Red	Berry, spicy	Fish, pork, chicken	**
Bridgeview Dry Gewürztraminer	Willamette Valley/Oregon	White	Spicy, floral	Asian, shellfish	*
Calera Central Coast Chardonnay	Monterey/California	White	Rich, tropical fruit	Fish, chicken	**
Calera Jensen Mount Harlan Pinot Noir	Monterey/California	Red	Complex, berry, spicy	Fish, pork, cheese	***
Calera Mount Harlan Chardonnay	Monterey/California	White	Elegant, floral	Fish, chicken, cheese	***
Calera Mount Harlan Viognier	Monterey/California	White	Rich, floral, stone fruit	Fruits, Asian, fish	***
Calera Selleck Mount Harlan Pinot Noir	Monterey/California	Red	Complex, berry, spicy	Fish, pork, cheese	***
Callaghan Buena Suerte (cabernet sauvignon/merlot/ cabernet franc)	Arizona	Red	Plums, vanillin	Veal, pork, beef	**
Camas Winery Tej Hopped Mead	Idaho	Sweet	Sweet, honey, wax	Dessert	**
Cameron Abbey Ridge Pinot Noir	Willamette Valley/Oregon	Red	Berry, spicy	Fish, chicken, pork	**
Campus Oaks Lodi Old Vine Zinfandel	Central Valley/California	Red	Berry, spicy	Pizza, beef, sausages	**

UNITED STATES OF AMERICA *(continued)*

Wine name	Region	Style	Flavor/Bouquet	Compatible Foods	Price Range
Canoe Ridge Reserve Merlot	Columbia Valley/ Washington State	Red	Smoky, intense, plums, cloves	Beef, lamb	**
Cayuse Cobblestone Vineyard Syrah	Walla Walla Valley/ Washington State	Red	Plums, smoky, spicy, oaky	Beef, lamb	**
Cedar Mountain Blanches Vineyard Cabernet Sauvignon	Livermore Valley, San Francisco Bay/California	Red	Complex, minerally	Beef, lamb, cheese	**
Cedar Mountain Cabernet Royal Dessert Wine	Livermore Valley, San Francisco Bay/California	Red	Sweet, fruity, rich	Dessert, nuts, cheese	**
Cedar Mountain Estate Chardonnay	Livermore Valley, San Francisco Bay/California	White	Crisp, rich, minerally	Fish, chicken	**
Cedar Mountain Library Reserve Cabernet Sauvignon	Livermore Valley, San Francisco Bay/California	Red	Elegant, earthy	Lamb, beef, cheese	***
Chaddsford Winery Pinot Grigio	Pennsylvania	White	Floral, nutty	Shellfish, Asian	**
Chaddsford Winery Merican (cabernet sauvignon/merlot)	Pennsylvania	Red	Plums, spicy	Beef, pork, veal	**
Chalet Débonné Pinot Gris	Ohio	White	Floral, nutty	Shellfish, fish	**
Chalone Vineyard Chalone Chardonnay	Monterey/California	White	Complex, rich	Fish, chicken	***
Chalone Vineyard Chalone Pinot Blanc	Monterey/California	White	Rich, nutty	Fish, chicken	***
Chalone Vineyard Chalone Pinot Noir	Monterey/California	Red	Complex, berry, spicy	Fish, pork, cheese	***
Chalone Vineyard The Pinnacles Chardonnay	Monterey/California	White	Rich, minerally	Fish, chicken	***
Charles B. Mitchell Vineyards El Dorado Semillon	Sierra Foothills/California	White	Wax, honey, citrus	Shellfish, fish	**
Charles Spinetta Winery Amador Barbera	Sierra Foothills/California	Red	Fruity, spicy	Pizza, pasta, pork	**
Charles Spinetta Winery Amador Zinfandel	Sierra Foothills/California	Red	Berry, spicy	Pizza, pork, veal	**
Chateau Grand Traverse Ice Wine	Michigan	Sweet	Sweet, rich, fruity	Dessert	**
Chateau Julien Sangiovese	Monterey/California	Red	Berry, fruity	Pizza, pasta, sausages	**
Chateau Ste Michelle Cold Creek Vineyard Riesling	Yakima Valley/ Washington State	White	Intense, floral, stone fruit	Asian, shellfish	**
Chateau Ste Michelle Reserve Merlot	Columbia Valley/ Washington State	Red	Rich, fruity, oaky	Beef, lamb	**
Chouinard Cabernet Sauvignon	Paso Robles, South Central Coast/California	Red	Jam, spicy	Beef, pork, lamb	**
Chouinard Lodi Mohr-Fry Ranch Zinfandel	Central Valley/California	Red	Berry, spicy	Chicken, veal, beef	**
Chouinard Orange Muscat	Paso Robles, South Central Coast/California	Fortified	Floral, rich	Dessert	**
Chouinard Vineyards Petite Sirah	Monterey/California	Red	Berry, peppery	Pizza, sausages, pork	**
Chouinard Vineyards San Francisco Bay Palomares Vineyards Chardonnay	Livermore Valley, San Francisco Bay/California	White	Citrus, apples, spicy	Fish, chicken	**
Clayton Lodi Petite Sirah	Central Valley/California	Red	Berry, peppery	Pizza, sausages	**
Cline Cellars Cotes d'Oakley Vin Rouge	Contra Costa County San Francisco Bay/California	Red	Fruity, peppery	Pizza, pasta, sausages	*
Cline Cellars Live Oak Vineyard Zinfandel	Contra Costa County San Francisco Bay/California	Red	Powerful, earthy	Lamb, beef, cheese	***
Cline Cellars Small Berry Mourvedre	Contra Costa County San Francisco Bay/California	Red	Powerful, spicy, mint	Lamb, beef, cheese	***
Cloninger Cellars Cabernet Sauvignon	Monterey/California	Red	Plums, toasty	Beef, pork, lamb	**
Clos du Val Napa-El Dorado-San Joaquin Zinfandel	Central Valley/California	Red	Berry, oaky	Beef, pork	**
Clos Tita Estate Pinot Noir	Santa Cruz Mountains, North Central Coast/California	Red	Earthy, minerally	Fish, pork, cheese	***
Clover Hill Vineyards & Winery Concord	Pennsylvania	Red	Fruity, spicy	Pizza, pasta, sausages	**
Colorado Cellars Merlot	Colorado	Red	Plums, herbaceous	Lamb, beef	**
Concannon Vineyard Reserve Assemblage Red Meritage	Livermore Valley, San Francisco Bay/California	Red	Plums, spicy	Veal, pork, beef	**
Concannon Vineyard Reserve Assemblage White Meritage	Livermore Valley, San Francisco Bay/California	White	Citrus, honey, spicy	Shellfish, fish, chicken	**
Concannon Vineyard Reserve Petite Sirah	Livermore Valley, San Francisco Bay/California	Red	Peppery, oaky	Pork, beef, lamb	**
Concannon Vineyard San Francisco Bay Selected Vineyards Sauvignon Blanc	Livermore Valley, San Francisco Bay/California	White	Stone fruit, minerally	Shellfish, salads	*
Cooper-Garrod Cabernet Franc	Santa Clara Valley, North Central Coast/California	Red	Plums, toasty	Beef, pork, veal	**
Cooper-Garrod Chardonnay	Santa Clara Valley, North Central Coast/California	White	Apples, toasty	Fish, chicken	**
Cronin Vineyards Pinot Noir	Santa Cruz Mountains, North Central Coast/California	Red	Berry, spicy	Pork, veal	***
David Bruce Central Coast Pinot Noir	Monterey/California	Red	Berry, oaky, spicy	Fish, pork, veal	**
Deaver Vineyards Golden Nectar 150-Year-Old Vine Zinfandel Port	Sierra Foothills/California	Fortified	Fruity, rich	Dessert	**
Delicato California Cabernet Sauvignon	Central Valley/California	Red	Plums, jam	Pizza, beef	*

UNITED STATES OF AMERICA *(continued)*

Wine name	Region	Style	Flavor/Bouquet	Compatible Foods	Price Range
Delille Chaleur Estate Meritage blend (cabernet sauvignon/merlot cabernet franc)	Yakima Valley/Washington State	Red	Berry, herbaceous, toasty, elegant	Beef, lamb	***
Delille Charleur Estate D2 (merlot/cabernet sauvignon/cabernet franc)	Yakima Valley/Washington State	Red	Plums, herbaceous, vanillin	Beef, lamb	**
Dobra Zemlja Amador Syrah	Sierra Foothills/California	Red	Plums, spicy	Pork, beef, lamb	**
Dobra Zemlja Amador Viognier	Sierra Foothills/California	White	Elegant, floral	Shellfish, fish, fruits	**
Domaine de la Terre Rouge Shenandoah Valley Sentinel Oak Vineyard Syrah	Sierra Foothills/California	Red	Earthy, gamey	Lamb, beef, cheese	***
Domaine Drouhin Cuvée Laurene Pinot Noir	Willamette Valley/Oregon	Red	Berry, jam, vanillin	Veal, pork, duck	***
Domaine Drouhin Pinot Noir	Willamette Valley/Oregon	Red	Berry, spicy, oaky	Chicken, veal, pork	***
Dr Frank's Vinifera Wine Cellars/Chateau Frank Riesling	New York	White	Crisp, floral, citrus	Shellfish, Asian	*
Dunham Cabernet Sauvignon III	Columbia Valley/Washington State	Red	Berry, herbaceous, intense, oaky	Beef, lamb	**
Edgefield Columbia Valley Syrah	Columbia Valley/Oregon	Red	Plums, smoky	Beef, lamb	**
Edmunds St John El Dorado Matagrano Vineyard Sangiovese	Sierra Foothills/California	Red	Complex, earthy	Beef, pork, veal	**
Edmunds St John El Dorado Wylie-Fenaughty Syrah	Sierra Foothills/California	Red	Powerful, minerally	Lamb, beef, cheese	***
Elk Cove Estate Reserve Pinot Noir	Willamette Valley/Oregon	Red	Berry, spicy	Veal, pork	**
Elliston Vineyards Sunol Valley Vineyard Pinot Gris	Livermore Valley, San Francisco Bay/California	White	Floral, nutty	Shellfish, Asian	**
Eola Hills Lodi Zinfandel	Central Valley/California	Red	Berry, spicy	Pizza, sausages, beef	*
Evesham Unfiltered Wood Cuvée J Pinot Noir	Willamette Valley/Oregon	Red	Berry, jam, complex	Chicken, veal, pork	***
Eyrie Pinot Gris	Willamette Valley/Oregon	White	Honey, nutty, crisp	Chicken, fish	*
Eyrie Pinot Meunier	Willamette Valley/Oregon	Red	Plums, berry, spicy	Fish, chicken, pork	**
Fall Creek Vineyards Meritus (merlot/cabernet malbec)	Texas	Red	Plums, herbaceous	Beef, pork, lamb	**
Fenestra Winery Semmonay (chardonnay/semillon)	Livermore Valley, San Francisco Bay/California	White	Complex, fruity	Fish, chicken	**
Fenestra Winery Zinfandel	Livermore Valley, San Francisco Bay/California	Red	Berry, spicy	Pizza, pork, veal	**
Ficklin Madera Vintage Port	Central Valley/California	Fortified	Berry, sweet	Dessert, cheese	**
Firelands Wine Co. Pinot Grigio	Ohio	White	Fruity, nutty	Shellfish, fish	**
Fitzpatrick Winery El Dorado Zinfandel	Sierra Foothills/California	Red	Berry, spicy	Pork, chicken, veal	**
Folie à Deux Shenandoah Valley Fiddletown Zinfandel	Sierra Foothills/California	Red	Berry, oaky	Pork, beef	**
Fox Run Vineyards Chardonnay	New York	White	Apples, vanillin	Fish, chicken	**
Fox Run Vineyards Reserve Pinot Noir	New York	Red	Berry, spicy	Fish, pork, veal	***
Foxen Sanford & Benedict Vineyard Pinot Noir	Santa Barbara County, South Central Coast/California	Red	Complex, earthy, spicy	Fish, pork, duck	***
Galante Carmel Valley Blackjack Cabernet Sauvignon	Monterey/California	Red	Powerful, complex	Lamb, beef, pork	***
Galante Carmel Valley Rancho Galante Cabernet Sauvignon	Monterey/California	Red	Rich, smoky	Lamb, beef, pork	**
Garre Vineyard and Winery Merlot	Livermore Valley, San Francisco Bay/California	Red	Plums, spicy	Pork, beef, lamb	**
Georis Winery Carmel Valley Merlot	Monterey/California	Red	Powerful, tannic	Lamb, cheese	***
Glen Fiona Columbia Valley Syrah (syrah/viognier)	Columbia Valley/Washington State	Red	Berry, spicy, floral, elegant	Chicken, veal, pork	**
Granite Springs Winery El Dorado Zinfandel	Sierra Foothills/California	Red	Berry, spicy	Pizza, pork, chicken	**
Hahn Estates Red Meritage	Monterey/California	Red	Rich, oaky	Pork, beef, lamb	***
Harpersfield Vineyard Gewurztraminer	Ohio	White	Floral, spicy	Shellfish, Asian	**
Hecker Pass Winery Petite Sirah Select	Santa Clara Valley, North Central Coast/California	Red	Berry, spicy	Pizza, pork, veal	**
Hedges Red Mountain Reserve (cabernet sauvignon/merlot/cabernet franc)	Yakima Valley/Washington State	Red	Fruity, oaky, rich	Beef, lamb	**
Heller Estate/Durney Carmel Valley Cachagua Cabernet Sauvignon	Monterey/California	Red	Complex, earthy	Lamb, beef, cheese	***
Heller Estate/Durney Carmel Valley Chardonnay	Monterey/California	White	Rich, minerally	Fish, chicken	***
Hermann J. Weimer Vineyard Chardonnay	New Mexico	White	Apples, buttery	Fish, chicken	**
Hermann J. Weimer Vineyard Late Harvest Riesling	New Mexico	White	Sweet, floral, honey	Dessert	**
Horton Vineyards Dionysius (Touriga Nacional Blend)	Virginia	Red	Berry, spicy	Veal, pork, beef	**
Horton Vineyards Viognier	Virginia	White	Stone fruit, floral, minerally	Shellfish, fruits	***
Ivan Tamas Trebbiano	Livermore Valley, San Francisco Bay/California	White	Floral, nutty	Shellfish, Asian	*
Ivan Tamas Zinfandel	Livermore Valley, San Francisco Bay/California	Red	Jam, spicy	Pizza, beef, chicken	*
J. Lohr Arroyo Seco Arroyo Vista Vineyard Chardonnay	Monterey/California	White	Buttery, oaky	Fish, chicken	**
J. Lohr Chardonnay	Monterey/California	White	Tropical fruit, buttery	Fish, chicken	*
J. Lohr Cypress California Chardonnay	Santa Clara Valley, North Central Coast/California	White	Apples, buttery	Fish, chicken	*
J. Lohr Lodi Cypress Zinfandel	Central Valley/California	Red	Berry, spicy	Pizza, sausages, beef	*

UNITED STATES OF AMERICA *(continued)*

Wine name	Region	Style	Flavor/Bouquet	Compatible Foods	Price Range
J. Lohr Wildflower Valdiguié	Monterey/California	Red	Fruity	Pizza, pasta	*
Jessie's Grove Lodi Fancy Quest Old Vine Zinfandel	Central Valley/California	Red	Berry, spicy	Sausages, beef	**
Jessie's Grove Lodi Reserve Westwind Old Vine Zinfandel	Central Valley/California	Red	Berry, complex	Beef, pork	**
Jessie's Grove Lodi Spenker Vineyard Royalty Old Vine Zinfandel	Central Valley/California	Red	Rich, toasty	Beef, pork, cheese	**
Jory Winery Syrah	Santa Clara Valley, North Central Coast/California	Red	Berry, spicy	Veal, pork, chicken	**
Joullian Carmel Valley Merlot	Monterey/California	Red	Plums, earthy	Lamb, beef, pork	***
Joullian Carmel Valley Sauvignon Blanc	Monterey/California	White	Citrus, honey, toasty	Fish, pasta	**
Joullian Carmel Valley Zinfandel	Monterey/California	Red	Berry, spicy	Pork, veal, pasta	**
Joullian Chardonnay	Monterey/California	White	Rich, minerally	Fish, chicken	**
Karly Amador Warrior Fires Zinfandel	Sierra Foothills/California	Red	Rich, fruity, smoky	Lamb, beef, cheese	***
Kathryn Kennedy California SHHH Chenin Blanc/Viognier	Santa Cruz Mountains, North Central Coast/California	White	Fruity, floral	Shellfish, Asian	**
Kathryn Kennedy Estate Cabernet Sauvignon	Santa Cruz Mountains, North Central Coast/California	Red	Elegant, powerful	Lamb, beef, cheese	***
Kathryn Kennedy Lateral Meritage	Santa Cruz Mountains, North Central Coast/California	Red	Elegant, earthy	Lamb, beef, cheese	***
Ken Wright Canary Hill Pinot Noir	Willamette Valley/Oregon	Red	Berry, earthy, oaky	Veal, pork, beef	***
Kestrel Signature Series Syrah	Yakima Valley/ Washington State	Red	Plums, smoky	Beef, lamb	**
Koenig Vineyards Zinfandel	Idaho	Red	Berry, spicy	Beef, pork	**
L'Ecole No 41 Barrel-fermented Semillon	Walla Walla Valley/ Washington State	White	Honey, wax, toasty	Chicken, fish	***
L. Mawby Vineyard Sparkling Wine	Michigan	Sparkling	Crisp, fruity	Fruit, Asian	**
Latcham Vineyards El Dorado Zinfandel Reserve	Sierra Foothills/California	Red	Berry, spicy	Pork, veal, beef	**
Lava Cap Winery El Dorado Muscat Canelli	Sierra Foothills/California	Fortified	Mandarin, honey, floral	Dessert, fruits	*
Leonetti Merlot	Walla Walla Valley/ Washington State	Red	Powerful, tannic	Beef, lamb	***
Livermore Valley Cellars/LVC One Oak Vineyard Merlot	Livermore Valley, San Francisco Bay/California	Red	Plums, spicy	Lamb, beef, pork	**
Livermore Valley Cellars/LVC Semillon/Chardonnay	Livermore Valley, San Francisco Bay/California	White	Apples, nutty, spicy	Shellfish, fish, chicken	**
Lockwood Cabernet Sauvignon	Monterey/California	Red	Plums, toasty	Pork, beef, lamb	**
Lockwood Chardonnay	Monterey/California	White	Fruity, oaky	Fish, chicken	**
Lockwood Pinot Blanc	Monterey/California	White	Apples, toasty	Fish, chicken	**
Lockwood Very Special Reserve Red Meritage	Monterey/California	Red	Rich, oaky	Lamb, beef, cheese	***
Logan Sleepy Hollow Vineyard Pinot Noir	Monterey/California	Red	Berry, toasty	Fish, pork	**
Longoria Cuvée Blues Cabernet Franc	Santa Barbara County, South Central Coast/California	Red	Powerful, oaky	Lamb, beef, cheese	**
Lucas Lodi Chardonnay	Central Valley/California	White	Apples, minerally	Fish, chicken, pasta	*
Lucas Lodi Old Vine Zinfandel	Central Valley/California	Red	Berry, spicy	Pizza, sausages, beef	*
Madrona Vineyards El Dorado Late Harvest Zinfandel	Sierra Foothills/California	Red	Sweet, fruity, rich	Dessert, nuts	**
Martin Ray Mariage California Chardonnay	Santa Cruz Mountains, North Central Coast/California	White	Apples, minerally	Fish, chicken	***
Mathews Cabernet Sauvignon Elerding Vineyard	Columbia Valley/ Washington State	Red	Berry, herbaceous, intense	Beef, lamb	**
McCrea Boushey Vineyard Syrah Viognier	Yakima Valley/ Washington State	Red	Berry, floral, spicy	Veal, pork, beef	**
McCrea Ciel du Cheval Vineyard Viognier	Yakima Valley/ Washington State	White	Floral, honey, stone fruit	Asian, fish	**
Mer et Soleil Central Coast Chardonnay	Monterey/California	White	Rich, buttery, toasty	Fish, chicken	***
Millbrook Vineyards & Winery Tokai	New York	White	Sweet, floral, nutty	Dessert	**
Mirassou Showcase Selection Harvest Reserve Pinot Noir	Monterey/California	Red	Berry, toasty	Fish, pork	**
Monterra San Bernabe Ranch Syrah	Monterey/California	Red	Jam, vanillin	Pizza, pork	*
Montevina Amador Brioso Zinfandel	Sierra Foothills/California	Red	Fruity, spicy	Pizza, pasta, beef, chicken, veal	*
Montevina Amador Sangiovese	Sierra Foothills/California	Red	Berry, spicy	Pork, chicken, veal, pizza	*
Montevina Amador Terra d'Oro Barbera	Sierra Foothills/California	Red	Earthy, spicy, oaky	Pork, veal, beef	**
Montevina Amador Terra d'Oro Deaver Ranch Vineyard Zinfandel	Sierra Foothills/California	Red	Complex, rich, earthy	Lamb, beef, cheese	**
Montevina Amador Terra d'Oro Sangiovese	Sierra Foothills/California	Red	Berry, oaky	Pork, veal, beef, pasta	**
Morgan Chardonnay	Monterey/California	White	Tropical fruit	Fish, chicken	**
Morgan Monterey/Sonoma Sauvignon Blanc	Monterey/California	White	Melon, citrus, toasty	Shellfish, fish, salads, cheese	**
Morgan Pinot Gris	Monterey/California	White	Floral, nutty	Shellfish, fish	**
Morgan Pinot Noir	Monterey/California	Red	Jam, spicy	Fish, pork, duck	**
Morgan Reserve Pinot Noir	Monterey/California	Red	Jam, oaky, rich	Fish, pork, duck	***

UNITED STATES OF AMERICA *(continued)*

Wine name	Region	Style	Flavor/Bouquet	Compatible Foods	Price Range
Mount Eden Edna Valley Macgregor Vineyard Chardonnay	Edna Valley, South Central Coast/California	White	Complex, oaky, tropical fruit	Fish, chicken, pasta	**
Mount Eden Santa Cruz Mountains Cabernet Sauvignon	Santa Cruz Mountains, North Central Coast/California	Red	Powerful, elegant	Lamb, beef, cheese	***
Mount Eden Santa Cruz Mountains Chardonnay	Santa Cruz Mountains, North Central Coast/California	White	Elegant, minerally	Fish, chicken	***
Mount Eden Santa Cruz Mountains Cuvée des Vielles Vignes Pinot Noir	Santa Cruz Mountains, North Central Coast/California	Red	Earthy, rich, spicy	Fish, pork, veal, cheese	***
Oakstone Winery El Dorado Meritage	Sierra Foothills/California	Red	Fruity, spicy	Beef, lamb, veal	**
Palmer Vineyards Pinot Blanc	New Mexico	White	Citrus, apples, vanillin	Fish, chicken	**
Paraiso Springs Santa Lucia Highlands Pinot Noir	Monterey/California	Red	Berry, spicy	Fish, pork, cheese	**
Paraiso Springs Santa Lucia Highlands Port Souzao	Monterey/California	Fortified	Caramelly	Nuts, cheese, dessert	*
Paraiso Springs Santa Lucia Highlands Reserve Pinot Blanc	Monterey/California	White	Nutty, oaky	Fish, chicken	**
Paraiso Springs Santa Lucia Highlands Syrah	Monterey/California	Red	Spicy, smoky	Veal, pork, cheese	**
Pend d'Oreille Bistro Rouge Red Table Wine	Idaho	Red	Fruity, jam	Pizza, pasta, pork	*
Pend d'Oreille Chardonnay	Idaho	White	Apples, buttery	Fish, chicken	**
Pend d'Oreille Pinot Noir	Idaho	Red	Berry, spicy	Fish, chicken, veal	**
Peninsula Cellars Chardonnay	Michigan	White	Apples, minerally	Fish, chicken	**
Perry Creek Vineyards El Dorado Nebbiolo	Sierra Foothills/California	Red	Licorice, jam	Pork, beef, lamb	**
Perry Creek Vineyards El Dorado Wenzell Vineyards Mourvedre	Sierra Foothills/California	Red	Rich, fruity, earthy	Lamb, beef, cheese	**
Perry Creek Vineyards El Dorado ZinMan Zinfandel	Sierra Foothills/California	Red	Berry, spicy	Pizza, pork, pasta	**
Phillips Vineyards California Symphony	Central Valley/California	White	Floral, fruity	Salads, fruits	*
Phillips Vineyards Lodi Cotes de Lodi Rhone Blush	Central Valley/California	Rosé	Fruity	Salads, shellfish	*
Phillips Vineyards Lodi Old Vine Carignan	Central Valley/California	Red	Earthy, spicy	Pizza, Mediterrerean	*
Pietra Santa California Sassolino Sangiovese/Cabernet Sauvignon	Monterey/California	Red	Rich, oaky	Pork, beef	***
Ponzi Pinot Gris	Willamette Valley/Oregon	White	Citrus, nutty, crisp	Shellfish, fish	**
Ponzi Reserve Pinot Noir	Willamette Valley/Oregon	Red	Berry, spicy, toasty	Veal, pork, beef	***
Quady Madera Electra Fortified Muscat	Central Valley/California	Fortified	Floral, zingy	Asian, cold meats, dessert	*
Quady Madera Elysium Fortified Muscat	Central Valley/California	Fortified	Spicy, floral	Dessert, cheese	*
Quady Madera Starboard Port	Central Valley/California	Fortified	Berry, rich	Nuts, cheese	*
Quilceda Creek Cabernet Sauvignon	Yakima Valley/ Washington State	Red	Berry, herbaceous, oaky	Pork, beef, lamb	**
R. H. Phillips California Dunnigan Hills Night Harvest Sauvignon Blanc	Central Valley/California	White	Sweet, floral, honey	Cold meats, cheese, dessert	*
Ravenswood Lodi Zinfandel	Central Valley/California	Red	Berry, spicy	Pizza, sausages, beef	**
Renaissance North Yuba Select Late Harvest Sauvignon Blanc	Sierra Foothills/California	White	Sweet, zingy, fruity	Cold meats, dessert	**
Renwood Winery Amador Clockspring Vineyard Sangiovese	Sierra Foothills/California	Red	Powerful, earthy	Pork, lamb	***
Retzlaff Vineyards Cabernet Sauvignon/Merlot	Livermore Valley, San Francisco Bay/California	Red	Elegant, earthy	Lamb, beef, cheese	***
Retzlaff Vineyards Chardonnay	Livermore Valley, San Francisco Bay/California	White	Apples, minerally	Fish, chicken	**
Retzlaff Vineyards Sauvignon Blanc	Livermore Valley, San Francisco Bay/California	White	Stone fruit, minerally	Shellfish, cheese	**
Rex Hill Reserve Pinot Noir	Willamette Valley/Oregon	Red	Berry, jam, vanillin	Veal, pork, beef	***
Ridge Bridgehead Mataro	Contra Costa County San Francisco Bay/California	Red	Elegant, rich, fruity	Lamb, beef, cheese	***
Ridge California Montebello Meritage	Santa Cruz Mountains, North Central Coast/California	Red	Complex, minerally	Lamb, beef, cheese	***
Ridge Santa Cruz Mountains Chardonnay	Santa Cruz Mountains, North Central Coast/California	White	Elegant, rich	Fish, chicken	***
Ridge Santa Cruz Mountains Merlot	Santa Cruz Mountains, North Central Coast/California	Red	Complex, spicy	Lamb, pork, veal	***
Ridge Zinfandel	Paso Robles, South Central Coast/California	Red	Powerful, oaky	Veal, pork, beef	***
Robert Mondavi Coastal Monterey Merlot	Monterey/California	Red	Plums, vanillin	Pork, beef, pizza	*
Robert Mondavi Coastal Monterey Syrah	Monterey/California	Red	Berry, vanillin	Pork, beef, pizza	*
Robert Talbott Cuvée Cynthia Chardonnay	Monterey/California	White	Apples, toasty	Fish, chicken	***
Robert Talbott Diamond T Estate Chardonnay	Monterey/California	White	Tropical fruit, toasty	Fish, chicken	***
Rosenblum Carla's Reserve Zinfandel	Contra Costa County San Francisco Bay/California	Red	Rich, fruity, spicy	Pizza, beef, veal, lamb	***
Rosenblum Chateau La Paws Cote du Bone Mourvedre	Contra Costa County San Francisco Bay/California	Red	Powerful, fruity	Lamb, beef, cheese	***
St Amant Lodi LBV Port	Central Valley/California	Fortified	Berry, rich	Nuts, cheese, dessert	*
St Amant Lodi Mohr-Fry Ranch Old Vines Zinfandel	Central Valley/California	Red	Berry, earthy	Lamb, beef, pork	**
St Julian Wine Co. Semi-Dry Riesling	Michigan	White	Honey, tropical fruit	Cheese, fruits, fish	*
Ste Chapelle Cabernet Sauvignon Winemaker's Series	Idaho	Red	Plums, toasty	Beef, pork, lamb	**

UNITED STATES OF AMERICA *(continued)*

Wine name	Region	Style	Flavor/Bouquet	Compatible Foods	Price Range
Ste Chapelle Chardonnay	Idaho	White	Apples, minerally	Fish, chicken	**
Ste Chapelle Merlot Winemaker's Series	Idaho	Red	Plums, oaky	Beef, pork, lamb	**
Sakonnet Vineyards Fumé Blanc (Vidal)	Rhode Island	White	Fruity, floral	Shellfish, fish	**
Sakonnet Vineyards Samson Brut (chardonnay/pinot noir)	Rhode Island	Sparkling	Crisp, rich	Shellfish, Asian	**
Sarah's Vineyard Estate Pinot Noir	Santa Clara Valley, North Central Coast/California	Red	Elegant, earthy	Fish, pork, cheese	***
Savannah-Chanel Laetitia Vineyards Chardonnay	Arroyo Grande, South Central Coast/California	White	Tropical fruit, oaky	Fish, chicken	**
Savannah-Chanel Late Harvest Cabernet Franc	Santa Cruz Mountains, North Central Coast/California	White	Sweet, fruity, spicy	Dessert, cheese	**
Savannah-Chanel Zinfandel	Paso Robles, South Central Coast/California	Red	Berry, spicy	Pizza, pork, veal	**
Sawtooth Riesling	Idaho	White	Floral, minerally	Shellfish, fruits	*
Sawtooth Semillon/Chardonnay	Idaho	White	Apples, honey	Fish, chicken	**
Scheid Vineyards Pinot Noir	Monterey/California	Red	Berry, spicy	Fish, pork, pizza	**
Scheid Vineyards San Lucas Chardonnay	Monterey/California	White	Apples, minerally	Fish, chicken	**
Seven Hills Merlot	Walla Walla Valley/ Washington State	Red	Plums, vanillin	Beef, lamb	**
Sharpe Hill Vineyard Select Late Harvest Stonington Vineyards Rosé	Connecticut	Rosé	Sweet, fruity, floral	Cheese, fruit, dessert	**
Shenandoah Vineyards Amador Cab-Shiraz	Sierra Foothills/California	Red	Complex, earthy	Lamb, beef, pork	**
Shenandoah Vineyards Amador Sangiovese	Sierra Foothills/California	Red	Berry, spicy, earthy	Pizza, pork, pasta, beef	**
Shenandoah Vineyards Amador Vintners Selection Zinfandel	Sierra Foothills/California	Red	Powerful, spicy	Lamb, beef, pork	**
Shenandoah Vineyards Amador Zingiovese	Sierra Foothills/California	Red	Fruity, spicy	Pizza, pork, pasta, veal	*
Sierra Vista Winery El Dorado Fleur de Montagne Rhone Red Blend	Sierra Foothills/California	Red	Berry, spicy	Pizza, pork, veal	**
Smith and Hook Viognier	Monterey/California	White	Floral, honey	Shellfish, fruits	**
Sobon Estate Shenandoah Valley Cougar Hill Zinfandel	Sierra Foothills/California	Red	Complex, spicy	Lamb, beef, pork	***
Sobon Estate Shenandoah Valley Fiddletown Zinfandel	Sierra Foothills/California	Red	Rich, fruity, spicy	Lamb, beef, pork	***
Sokol Blosser Redlands Pinot Noir	Willamette Valley/Oregon	Red	Berry, earthy, spicy	Veal, pork, beef	**
Solis Winery Estate Sangiovese	Santa Clara Valley, North Central Coast/California	Red	Berry, spicy	Pizza, pork, veal	**
Sonora Amador Story Vineyard Old Vine Zinfandel	Sierra Foothills/California	Red	Berry, earthy, spicy	Chicken, veal, pork	**
Sonora Amador Winery & Port Works Old Vine Zinfandel	Sierra Foothills/California	Red	Spicy, earthy	Chicken, veal, pork	**
South Hills/Hegy's Chenin Blanc	Idaho	White	Fruity, floral	Salads, shellfish	*
South Hills/Hegy's Pinot Noir	Idaho	Red	Berry, spicy	Fish, veal, pork	**
Spenker Family Winery Lodi Zinfandel	Central Valley/California	Red	Berry, spicy	Pizza, sausages, beef	**
Standing Stone Vineyards Gewurztraminer	New Mexico	White	Floral, spicy	Asian, fruits	**
Stephen Ross Bien Nacido Vineyard Pinot Noir	Santa Barbara County, South Central Coast/California	Red	Rich, earthy	Fish, pork, duck	**
Stone Hill Winery Norton	Missouri	Red	Fruity	Pizza, Asian	*
Stone Hill Winery Seyval	Missouri	White	Fruity, floral	Salads, fish	*
Stony Ridge Malvasia Bianca	Livermore Valley, San Francisco Bay/California	White	Apples, melon, minerally	Shellfish, salads	**
Stony Ridge Sangiovese Robusto Dessert Wine	Livermore Valley, San Francisco Bay/California	Fortified	Fruity, rich	Dessert, nuts, cheese	**
Storrs Ben Lomond Mountain Meyley Vineyard Chardonnay	Santa Cruz Mountains, North Central Coast/California	White	Elegant, tropical fruit	Fish, chicken	***
Story Winery Amador Picnic Hill Zinfandel	Sierra Foothills/California	Red	Berry, spicy	Pizza, pork, pasta, chicken	**
Story Winery Amador Alitia Zinfandel	Sierra Foothills/California	Red	Powerful, earthy	Chicken, veal, pork	**
Story Winery Amador Miss-Zin	Sierra Foothills/California	Red	Fruity, spicy	Pizza, pork, pasta, chicken	*
Story Winery Amador Sweet Mission	Sierra Foothills/California	Sweet	Sweet, fruity, tangy	Dessert, nuts, cheese	*
Talley Rincon Pinot Noir	Arroyo Grande, South Central Coast/California	Red	Berry, smoky	Fish, veal, pork	***
Taylor California Cellars Reserve Marsala	Monterey/California	Fortified	Tangy, nutty	Nuts, cheese, dessert	*
Testarossa Sleepy Hollow Vineyard Pinot Noir	Monterey/California	Red	Rich, berry, earthy	Fish, pork, cheese	***
Thackrey Pleiades VII Old Vines Red	Contra Costa County San Francisco Bay/California	Red	Fruity, rich, spicy	Chicken, veal, beef	**
Thomas Fogarty Gewurztraminer	Santa Cruz Mountains, North Central Coast/California	White	Floral, spicy	Shellfish, Asian	**
Thomas Kruse Brut Méthode Champenoise	Santa Clara Valley, North Central Coast/California	Sparkling	Crisp, citrus	Shellfish, Asian	**
Thunder Mountain Cabernet Sauvignon	Santa Cruz Mountains, North Central Coast/California	Red	Powerful, earthy	Lamb, beef, cheese	***
Treleaven Wines (King Ferry Winery) Barrel Fermented Chardonnay	New Mexico	White	Apples, toasty	Fish, chicken	**
Tria Vineyards Pinot Noir	Monterey/California	Red	Fruity, vanillin	Fish, chicken, pork, pizza	*

UNITED STATES OF AMERICA *(continued)*

Wine name	Region	Style	Flavor/Bouquet	Compatible Foods	Price Range
Turley Wine Cellars Lodi Spenker Vineyard Zinfandel	Central Valley/California	Red	Berry, rich	Cheese, lamb, dessert	***
Two Rivers Winery Cabernet Sauvignon	Colorado	Red	Berry, herbaceous	Beef, lamb	**
Unalii Lodi Hillside Estates Zinfandel	Central Valley/California	Red	Berry, spicy	Pizza, sausages, beef	**
Unionville Vineyards Seyval	New Jersey	White	Floral, grassy	Shellfish, salads	*
Venezio Vineyard El Dorado Zinfandel	Sierra Foothills/California	Red	Berry, spicy	Pizza, pork, pasta	**
Ventana Vineyards Syrah	Monterey/California	Red	Jam, spicy	Pork, chicken, pizza	*
Viano Vineyards Martinez Zinfandel	Contra Costa County San Francisco Bay/Californiaa	Red	Earthy, minerally	Lamb, beef, pork	*
Vigil Lodi Mohr-Fry Ranch Old Vines Zinfandel	Central Valley/California	Red	Berry, spicy	Pizza, sausages, beef	**
Vino Noceto Amador Riserva Sangiovese	Sierra Foothills/California	Red	Berry, earthy, spicy, oaky	Pork, veal, beef	**
Vino Noceto Amador Sangiovese	Sierra Foothills/California	Red	Berry, jam, spicy	Pizza, pork, veal, pasta	*
Vino Noceto Frivolo Sparkling Malvasia Bianca/Muscat	Sierra Foothills/California	Sparkling	Fruity, crisp	Shellfish, fruits, salads	*
Vino Noceto Rosato di Sangiovese	Sierra Foothills/California	Rosé	Fruity, floral	Shellfish, salads	*
Wallersheim Wine Co. Maréchal Foche	Wisconsin	Red	Fruity, tangy	Pizza, pasta, Asian	*
Waterbrook Meritage Red Mountain (cabernet franc/merlot)	Yakima Valley/ Washington State	Red	Plums, jam, oaky	Beef, lamb	**
Waterbrook Viognier	Walla Walla Valley/ Washington State	White	Floral, honey, stone fruit	Asian, fish	**
Wente Riva Ranch Reserve Arroyo Seco Chardonnay	Monterey/California	White	Tropical fruit, minerally	Fish, chicken	**
Wente Vineyards Cabernet Sauvignon	Livermore Valley, San Francisco Bay/California	Red	Spicy, toasty	Lamb, beef, pork	**
Wente Vineyards Charles Wetmore Reserve Cabernet Sauvignon	Livermore Valley, San Francisco Bay/California	Red	Rich, elegant	Lamb, beef, cheese	***
Wente Vineyards Herman Wente Reserve Chardonnay	Livermore Valley, San Francisco Bay/California	White	Complex, oaky`	Fish, chicken	***
Westover Vineyards San Francisco Bay Sunol Valley Vineyards Chardonnay	Livermore Valley, San Francisco Bay/California	White	Rich, fruity, minerally	Fish, chicken	**
Wolffer Estate/Sagpond Vineyards Merlot	New Mexico	Red	Plums, vanillin	Beef, pork, lamb	**
Wolffer Estate/Sagpond Vineyards Chardonnay	New Mexico	White	Apples, buttery	Fish, chicken	**
Woodbridge Robert Mondavi Lodi Barbera	Central Valley/California	Red	Plums, spicy	Pizza, sausages, Asian	*
Woodbridge Robert Mondavi Lodi Merlot	Central Valley/California	Red	Plums, licorice	Pizza, chicken, beef	*
Woodbridge Robert Mondavi Lodi Old Vine Zinfandel	Central Valley/California	Red	Berry, spicy	Pizza, sausages, beef	*
Woodbridge Robert Mondavi Lodi Sauvignon Blanc	Central Valley/California	White	Herbaceous, citrus	Shellfish, salads	*
Woodbridge Robert Mondavi Lodi Viognier	Central Valley/California	White	Floral, stone fruit	Fruit, salads	*
Woodward Canyon Celilo Vineyard Chardonnay	Columbia Valley/ Washington State	White	Apples, buttery, vanillin	Chicken, fish	**
Woodward Canyon Charbonneau (merlot/cabernet sauvignon)	Walla Walla Valley/ Washington State	Red	Berry, herbaceous, oaky	Beef, lamb	**
Woodward Canyon Merlot	Columbia Valley/ Washington State	Red	Berry, plum, oaky	Beef, lamb	**

CANADA

Wine name	Region	Style	Flavor/Bouquet	Compatible Foods	Price Range
Blue Mountain Vineyard and Cellars Reserve Pinot Blanc	British Columbia	White	Stone fruit, oaky	Cheese, fish	**
Blue Mountain Vineyard and Cellars Reserve Pinot Noir	British Columbia	Red	Jam, vanillin	Veal, pork, beef	**
Calona Vineyards Sandhill Pinot Blanc	Okanagan Valley/ British Columbia	White	Stone fruit, minerally	Shellfish, fish, chicken	**
Cave Spring Cellars Cabernet/Merlot	Niagara Peninsula/Ontario	Red	Earthy, berry	Beef, lamb	**
Cave Spring Cellars Chardonnay Reserve	Niagara Peninsula/Ontario	White	Fruity, oaky	Fish, chicken, veal	**
Cave Spring Cellars Estate Bottled Gewürztraminer	Niagara Peninsula/Ontario	White	Tropical fruit, floral	Cheese, fruit, Asian	**
Cave Spring Cellars Estate Bottled Reserve Riesling	Niagara Peninsula/Ontario	White	Fruity, minerally	Asian, shellfish	**
Cave Spring Cellars Gamay	Niagara Peninsula/Ontario	Red	Jam, berry	Pizza, Asian, chicken, veal, pork	*
Cave Spring Cellars Riesling Icewine	Niagara Peninsula/Ontario	White	Floral, tropical fruit	Dessert	***
Cedar Creek Estate Winery Cabernet Franc	Okanagan Valley/ British Columbia	Red	Berry, spicy	Veal, pork, chicken	**
Château des Charmes Late Harvest Riesling	Niagara Peninsula/Ontario	White	Floral, stone fruit	Cheese, dessert	** **
Colio Cabernet Franc	Lake Erie North Shore	Red	Berry, spicy	Pizza, beef, chicken	**
Colio Late Harvest Vidal	Ontario	White	Fruity, nutty	Dessert	**
D'Angelo Estate Cabernet Franc	Lake Erie North Shore	Red	Berry, spicy	Pizza, beef, chicken	**
Domaine Combret Cabernet Franc	British Columbia	Red	Berry, oaky	Beef, chicken, veal	**
Domaine Combret Chardonnay	British Columbia	White	Fruity, butter	Fish, chicken	**
Domaine Combret Riesling	British Columbia	White	Fruity	Cheese, pizza, fish	*
Domaine de Chaberton Estates Bacchus	Okanagan Valley/ British Columbia	White	Fruity	Pizza, pasta, Asian, cheese	**

CANADA *(continued)*

Wine name	Region	Style	Flavor/Bouquet	Compatible Foods	Price Range
Gehringer Bros. Estate Winery Auxerrois	Okanagan Valley/ British Columbia	White	Fruity, floral	Pizza, pasta, salads, chicken	*
Gray Monk Estate Winery Unwooded Chardonnay	Okanagan Valley/ British Columbia	White	Stone fruit, minerally	Shellfish, fish, chicken, veal	**
Hawthorne Mountain Vineyards Chardonnay	Okanagan Valley/ British Columbia	White	Butter, oaky	Fish, chicken, veal	**
Henry of Pelham Family Estate Reserve Baco Noir	Niagara Peninsula/Ontario	Red	Berry, earthy	Pasta, pork	**
Henry of Pelham Family Estate Reserve Baco Noir	Ontario	Red	Jam, spicy	Pizza, pasta, pork	**
Henry of Pelham Family Estate Reserve Riesling	Niagara Peninsula/Ontario	White	Floral, fruity	Asian, shellfish	**
Henry of Pelham Family Estate Riesling Icewine	Niagara Peninsula/Ontario	White	Floral, tropical fruit	Dessert	***
Henry of Pelham Family Estate Winery Barrel Fermented Chardonnay	Niagara Peninsula/Ontario	White	Fruity, oaky	Fish, chicken	**
Hernder Estate Wines Baco Noir	Ontario	Red	Fruity, spicy	Pizza, pasta, Asian	*
Hester Creek Estate Winery Reserve Pinot Blanc Icewine	Okanagan Valley/ British Columbia	White	Floral, nutty	Dessert	***
Hillebrand Estates Winery Glenlake Showcase Unfiltered Cabernet Sauvignon	Niagara Peninsula/Ontario	Red	Earthy, berry	Lamb, beef	**
Hillebrand Estates Winery Trius Chardonnay	Niagara Peninsula/Ontario	White	Fruity, oaky	Chicken, veal, pasta, fish	**
Hillside Estate Winery Late Harvest Vidal	Okanagan Valley/ British Columbia	White	Nutty, stone fruit	Dessert	**
IInniskillin Okanagan Vidal Icewine	Okanagan Valley/ British Columbia	White	Nutty, fruity, complex	Dessert	***
Inniskillin Wines Cabernet Franc	Niagara Peninsula/Ontario	Red	Berry, complex	Beef, veal, pork	**
Inniskillin Wines Culp Vyd. Chardonnay	Niagara Peninsula/Ontario	White	Stone fruit, vanillin	Fish, chicken, veal	**
Inniskillin Wines Founders' Reserve Pinot Noir	Niagara Peninsula/Ontario	Red	Berry, spicy	Pizza, veal, pork	**
Inniskillin Wines Vidal Icewine	Niagara Peninsula/Ontario	White	Nutty, tropical fruit, complex	Dessert	***
Jackson-Triggs Vintners Proprietors' Grand Reserve Chardonnay	Okanagan Valley/ British Columbia	White	Butter, oaky	Fish, chicken, veal	**
Jackson-Triggs Vintners Proprietors' Grand Reserve Merlot	Okanagan Valley/ British Columbia	Red	Berry, oaky, complex	Lamb, pork, beef	**
Jackson-Triggs Vintners Proprietors' Grand Reserve Riesling Icewine	Okanagan Valley/ British Columbia	White	Tropical fruit, floral	Dessert	***
Jackson-Triggs Vintners Proprietors' Reserve Chenin Blanc Icewine	Okanagan Valley/ British Columbia	White	Tropical fruit, floral	Dessert	**
Jackson-Triggs Vintners Proprietors' Reserve Merlot	Okanagan Valley/ British Columbia	Red	Berry, earthy	Lamb, beef	**
Jackson-Triggs Vintners Proprietors' Reserve Pinot Blanc	Okanagan Valley/ British Columbia	Red	Stone fruit, oaky	Fish, chicken, veal	**
Jackson-Triggs Vintners Proprietors' Reserve Riesling Icewine	Okanagan Valley/ British Columbia	White	Floral, tropical fruit	Dessert	***
Joseph's Estate Wines Vidal Icewine	Niagara Peninsula/Ontario	White	Nutty, tropical fruit, floral	Dessert	***
Kittling Ridge Estate Wines Marechal Foch	Ontario	Red	Berry, spicy	Pizza, pasta, Mediterranean	*
Konzelmann Estate Winery Late Harvest Riesling, Very Dry	Niagara Peninsula/Ontario	White	Floral, stone fruit	Asian, cheese	**
Lakeview Cellars Estate Winery Vinc Vyd. Reserve Chardonnay	Niagara Peninsula/Ontario	White	Butter, oaky	Fish, pasta, chicken	**
LeBlanc Estate Winery Vidal Icewine	Lake Erie North Shore	White	Citrus, tropical fruit, minerally	Dessert	***
Magnotta Barrel Fermented Chardonnay	Niagara Peninsula/Ontario	White	Fruity, oaky	Fish, chicken	**
Malivoire Winery Dry Late Harvest Gewürztraminer	Niagara Peninsula/Ontario	White	Tropical fruit, complex	Cheese, fruit, Asian	**
Malivoire Winery Gewürztraminer Icewine	Niagara Peninsula/Ontario	White	Tropical fruit, floral	Dessert	***
Marynissen Estate Winery Riesling	Niagara Peninsula/Ontario	White	Fruity, floral	Salads, Asian	*
Mission Hill Winery Grand Reserve Chardonnay	Okanagan Valley/ British Columbia	White	Butter, oaky	Fish, chicken, veal	**
Mission Hill Winery Grand Reserve Pinot Gris	Okanagan Valley/ British Columbia	White	Nutty, floral	Pasta, fish, veal	**
Mission Hill Winery Grand Reserve Pinot Noir	Okanagan Valley/ British Columbia	Red	Berry, oaky	Veal, chicken, pork	**
Mission Hill Winery Private Reserve Merlot	Okanagan Valley/ British Columbia	Red	Berry, oaky	Lamb, beef	**
Pelee Island Winery Cabernet Franc	Ontario	Red	Berry, spicy	Veal, pork	**
Peller Estates Founder's Series Chardonnay	Niagara Peninsula/Ontario	White	Fruity, butter	Fish, chicken	**
Peller Estates Wines Limited Edition Pinot Gris	Okanagan Valley/ British Columbia	White	Nutty, floral	Shellfish, fish, veal	**
Peller Estates Wines Trinity Icewine	Okanagan Valley/ British Columbia	White	Floral, fruity	Dessert	***
Pillitteri Estates Winery Baco Noir	Ontario	Red	Fruity, spicy	Pizza, pasta, Asian	*
Pillitteri Estates Winery Barrel Aged Chardonnay	Niagara Peninsula/Ontario	White	Fruity, oaky	Fish, chicken	**
Pillitteri Estates Winery Family Reserve Cabernet Franc	Niagara Peninsula/Ontario	Red	Berry, oaky	Veal, pork, pasta	**
Pillitteri Estates Winery Riesling Icewine	Niagara Peninsula/Ontario	White	Floral, tropical fruit	Dessert	***

CANADA (continued)

Wine name	Region	Style	Flavor/Bouquet	Compatible Foods	Price Range
Poplar Grove Cabernet Franc	British Columbia	Red	Berry, oaky	Beef, chicken, veal	**
Poplar Grove Chardonnay	British Columbia	White	Fruity, butter	Fish, chicken	**
Poplar Grove Merlot	British Columbia	Red	Berry, oaky	Veal, pork, lamb, beef	**
Quails' Gate Estate Winery Late Harvest Botrytis Affected Optima	Okanagan Valley/ British Columbia	White	Fruity, nutty	Dessert, cheese	***
Quails' Gate Estate Winery Limited Release Chenin Blanc	Okanagan Valley/ British Columbia	White	Fruity, floral	Pasta, salads, fish	**
Quails' Gate Estate Winery Limited Release Dry Riesling	Okanagan Valley/ British Columbia	White	Floral, tropical fruit	Shellfish, Asian	**
Quails' Gate Estate Winery Limited Release Meritage	Okanagan Valley/ British Columbia	Red	Oaky, berry, complex	Lamb, beef	**
Quails' Gate Estate Winery Limited Release Old Vines Foch	Okanagan Valley/ British Columbia	Red	Berry, spicy	Pizza, pasta, chicken	**
Reif Estate Winery Off Dry Riesling	Niagara Peninsula/Ontario	White	Floral, tropical fruit	Asian, cheese	*
Reif Estate Winery Riesling Icewine	Niagara Peninsula/Ontario	White	Floral, tropical fruit	Dessert	***
Reif Estate Winery Select Late Harvest Vidal	Ontario	White	Tropical fruit, nutty	Dessert	**
Reif Estate Winery Vidal Icewine	Niagara Peninsula/Ontario	White	Tropical fruit, floral	Dessert	***
St. Hubertus Estate Winery Gamay Rosé	Okanagan Valley/ British Columbia	Rosé	Fruity, floral	Antipasto, pizza, shellfish	*
St. Hubertus Estate Winery Oak Bay Chardonnay/Pinot Blanc	Okanagan Valley/ British Columbia	White	Fruity, minerally	Pasta, fish, chicken, veal	**
St. Hubertus Estate Winery Oak Bay Pinot Meunier	Okanagan Valley/ British Columbia	Red	Fruity, berry	Pizza, pasta, chicken	**
St. Hubertus Estate Winery Pinot Blanc/Riesling Icewine	Okanagan Valley/ British Columbia	White	Floral, complex	Dessert	***
Stonechurch Vineyards Pinot Noir	Niagara Peninsula/Ontario	Red	Berry, spicy	Chicken, veal	**
Stonechurch Vineyards Vidal Icewine	Niagara Peninsula/Ontario	White	Tropical fruit, nutty	Dessert	***
Stoney Ridge Cellars Barrel Fermented Gewurztraminer Icewine	Niagara Peninsula/Ontario	White	Tropical fruit, complex	Dessert	***
Stoney Ridge Cellars Butler's Grant Vyd. Reserve Pinot Noir	Niagara Peninsula/Ontario	Red	Berry, oaky	Veal, pork	**
Stoney Ridge Cellars Cuesta Old Vines Chardonnay	Niagara Peninsula/Ontario	White	Fruity, complex	Fish, chicken, veal	**
Stoney Ridge Cellars Reserve Pinot Noir	Niagara Peninsula/Ontario	Red	Berry, spicy, oaky	Pork, chicken	**
Stoney Ridge Cellars Select Late Harvest Vidal	Ontario	White	Tropical fruit, nutty	Dessert	**
Stoney Ridge Cellars Wismer Vyd. Cabernet Franc	Niagara Peninsula/Ontario	Red	Berry, oaky	Chicken, veal, pork	**
Strewn Pinot Blanc	Niagara Peninsula/Ontario	White	Stone fruit, minerally	Pasta, fish, chicken, veal	**
Sumac Ridge Estate Cabernet Sauvignon	Okanagan Valley/ British Columbia	Red	Berry, earthy, oaky	Lamb, beef	**
Sumac Ridge Estate Meritage White	Okanagan Valley/ British Columbia	White	Oaky, wax, stone fruit	Shellfish, fish, veal	**
Sumac Ridge Estate Okanagan Blush	Okanagan Valley/ British Columbia	Rosé	Berry, floral	Salads, pizza, pasta	*
Sumac Ridge Estate Pinot Blanc Icewine	Okanagan Valley/ British Columbia	White	Nutty, complex	Dessert	***
Summerhill Estate Winery Cipes Aurora Blanc de Blancs	Okanagan Valley/ British Columbia	White	Fruity, floral	Shellfish, veal	**
Summerhill Estate Winery Gewürztraminer Reserve	Okanagan Valley/ British Columbia	White	Tropical fruit, floral	Asian, fish, cheese	**
Summerhill Estate Winery Late Harvest Riesling Icewine	Okanagan Valley/ British Columbia	White	Floral, tropical fruit	Dessert	**
Summerhill Estate Winery Platinum Series Cabernet Sauvignon	Okanagan Valley/ British Columbia	Red	Berry, leather, oaky	Lamb, beef	**
Summerhill Estate Winery Platinum Series Pinot Noir	Okanagan Valley/ British Columbia	Red	Berry, spicy	Pork, veal	**
Summerhill Estate Winery Riesling Icewine	Okanagan Valley/ British Columbia	White	Floral, tropical fruit	Dessert	**
Thirty Bench Winery Reserve Cabernet Sauvignon	Niagara Peninsula/Ontario	Red	Berry, oaky	Lamb, beef	**
Tinhorn Creek Vineyards Cabernet Franc	Okanagan Valley/ British Columbia	Red	Berry, spicy	Veal, pork, chicken	**
Tinhorn Creek Vineyards Chardonnay	Okanagan Valley/ British Columbia	White	Butter, oaky	Fish, chicken, veal	**
Tinhorn Creek Vineyards Kerner Icewine	Okanagan Valley/ British Columbia	White	Spicy, fruity	Dessert	***
Tinhorn Creek Vineyards Merlot	Okanagan Valley/ British Columbia	Red	Berry, oaky	Pork, beef	**
Vineland Estates Gewürztraminer	Niagara Peninsula/Ontario	White	Tropical fruit, floral	Asian, cheese	*
Vineland Estates Semi-Dry Riesling	Niagara Peninsula/Ontario	White	Tropical fruit, floral	Asian, cheese	*
Vineland Estates Seyval Blanc	Ontario	White	Fruity, floral	Shellfish, fish, chicken	**
Wild Goose Vineyards and Winery Autumn Gold	Okanagan Valley/ British Columbia	White	Fruity, floral	Cheese, Asian	*

MEXICO AND SOUTH AMERICA

Wine name	Region	Style	Flavor/Bouquet	Compatible Foods	Price Range
MEXICO					
Bodegas de San Lorenzo Cabernet Sauvignon	Saltillo/Parras Valley	Red	Plums, earthy	Beef, lamb	**
Bodegas de Santo Tomás Cabernet Sauvignon	Ensenada/Baja California	Red	Plums, spicy	Pork, beef, lamb	**
Bodegas de Santo Tomás Chardonnay	Ensenada/Baja California	White	Apples, butter	Fish, chicken	**
Casa Pedro Domecq Chateau Domecq Cabernet Sauvignon	Mexico City	Red	Rich, elegant	Beef, lamb	***
Cavas de San Juan/Hidalgo Cabernet Sauvignon	San Juan del Río	Red	Plums, leathery	Beef, lamb	**
Cavas de San Juan/Hidalgo Carte Blanche	San Juan del Río	Sparkling	Crisp, stone fruit, yeasty	Shellfish, nuts	**
Cavas de Valmar Cabernet Sauvignon	Ensenada/Baja California	Red	Plums, leathery	Beef, lamb	**
L.A. Cetto Nebbiolo	Tijuana/Baja California	Red	Intense, licorice, minerally	Beef, lamb, cheese	**
L.A. Cetto Petite Sirah	Tijuana/Baja California	Red	Berry, spicy	Chicken, pork, beef	**
L.A. Cetto Zinfandel	Tijuana/Baja California	Red	Berry, spicy	Chicken, pork, beef	**
Monte Xanic Cabernet-Merlot	Enseneda/Baja California	Red	Berry, plums, earthy	Veal, pork, beef	**
Monte Xanic Chardonnay	Enseneda/Baja California	White	Apples, buttery	Fish, chicken	**
Salva Uiva Brut	San Juan del Río	Sparkling	Citrus, nutty, crisp	Shellfish, nuts	**
Vinedos San Marcos Brut	Saltillo/Parras Valley	Sparkling	Citrus, yeasty, crisp	Shellfish, nuts	**

CHILE

Wine name	Region	Style	Flavor/Bouquet	Compatible Foods	Price Range
Caliterra Cabernet Sauvignon	Central Valleys	Red	Minerally, spicy, elegant	Pork, beef	*
Caliterra Chardonnay	Central Valleys	White	Citrus, apples, crisp	Fish, chicken	*
Caliterra Merlot	Central Valleys	Red	Berry, tannic, herbaceous	Chicken, pork	*
Caliterra Merlot	Central Valleys	Red	Fruity, tannic	Chicken, pork	**
Caliterra Reserva Cabernet Sauvignon	Central Valleys	Red	Licorice, plums, minerally	Pork, beef	*
Casa Lapostolle Cuvée Alexandré Chardonnay	Casablanca Valley	White	Buttery, fruity, oaky	Fish, chicken	**
Casa Lapostolle Cabernet Sauvignon	Rapel Valley/Central Valleys	Red	Fruity, spicy, delicate	Beef, pork	**
Casa Lapostolle Chardonnay	Casablanca Valley	White	Buttery, yeasty, oaky	Fish, chicken	**
Casa Lapostolle Cuvée Alexandré Cabernet Sauvignon	Rapel Valley/Central Valleys	Red	Spicy, toasty, oaky	Veal, pork, beef	**
Casa Lapostolle Cuvée Alexandré Merlot	Rapel Valley/Central Valleys	Red	Fruity, oaky, rich	Pork, beef, lamb	**
Casa Lapostolle Merlot	Rapel Valley/Central Valleys	Red	Fruity, dill, intense	Pork, beef, lamb	**
Casa Lapostolle Sauvignon Blanc	Rapel Valley/Central Valleys	White	Melon, buttery, zingy	Shellfish, fish	*
Concho y Toro Amelia Chardonnay	Casablanca Valley	White	Buttery, toasty, tropical fruit	Fish, chicken	***
Concho y Toro Casillero del Diablo Cabernet Sauvignon	Maipo Valley/Central Valleys	Red	Fruity, minerally	Veal, pork, beef	*
Concho y Toro Casillero del Diablo Chardonnay	Casablanca Valley	White	Citrus, buttery	Shellfish, fish	**
Concho y Toro Casillero del Diablo Merlot	Maipo Valley/Central Valleys	Red	Berry, licorice, leathery	Beef, pork	*
Concho y Toro Don Melchar Puente Alto Vineyard Cabernet Sauvignon	Maipo Valley/Central Valleys	Red	Licorice, spicy, intense	Pork, beef	***
Concho y Toro Marques de Casa Concho Peumo Vineyard Merlot	Rapel Valley/Central Valleys	Red	Earthy, austere, minerally	Beef, pork	**
Concho y Toro Trio Cabernet Sauvignon	Maipo Valley/Central Valleys	Red	Berry, spicy, oaky	Pizza, veal	*
Cousino Macul Antiguas Reservas Cabernet Sauvignon	Maipo Valley/Central Valleys	Red	Fruity, oaky, minerally	Beef, lamb	**
Cousino Macul Finis Terrae	Maipo Valley/Central Valleys	Red	Minerally, licorice, toasty	Beef, lamb	***
Errazuriz Don Maximiano Cabernet Sauvignon	Anconcagua Valley	Red	Licorice, spicy, earthy, complex	Beef, lamb	***
Errazuriz Don Maximiano Merlot	Anconcagua Valley	Red	Fruity, earthy, oaky, rich	Beef, lamb	***
Errazuriz El Ciebo Estate Cabernet Sauvignon	Anconcagua Valley	Red	Fruity, spicy, complex	Beef, lamb	***
Errazuriz Reserva Chardonnay	Casablanca Valley	White	Tropical fruit, vanillin	Fish, chicken	**
Errazuriz Wild Ferment Chardonnay	Casablanca Valley	White	Apples, buttery, complex	Fish, chicken	**
La Palma Reserva Merlot	Rapel Valley/Central Valleys	Red	Fruity, rich	Veal, pork, beef	**
La Playa Cabernet Sauvignon	Maipo Valley/Central Valleys	Red	Fruity, spicy, minerally	Veal, pork, beef	*
Los Vascos Cabernet Sauvignon	Colchegua Valley	Red	Berry, oaky	Pizza, chicken	*
Los Vascos Cabernet Sauvignon	Colchegua Valley	Red	Fruity, minerally	Pizza, pasta	*
Luis Felipe Edwards Carmenere	Rapel Valley/Central Valleys	Red	Plums, berry, herbaceous	Beef, lamb	**
Luis Felipe Edwards Chardonnay	Rapel Valley/Central Valleys	White	Apples, minerally	Fish, Asian	**
Luis Felipe Edwards Pupilla Cabernet Sauvignon	Rapel Valley/Central Valleys	Red	Berry, plums, spicy	Pork, beef	**
Miguel Torres Manso de Velasco Cabernet Sauvignon	Carico Valley	Red	Fruity, minerally, herbaceous	Veal, pork, beef, lamb	**
Miguel Torres Maquetra Chardonnay	Maule Valley	White	Apples, toasty	Fish, chicken	**
Miguel Torres Santa Digna Brut	Maule Valley	Sparkling	Crisp, citrus	Shellfish, nuts	**
Miguel Torres Sauvignon Blanc	Curicó Valley	White	Herbaceous, zingy	Shellfish, cheese	*
Montes Alpha Cabernet Sauvignon	Curicó Valley	Red	Berry, oaky, rich	Beef, lamb	***
Montes Alpha Chardonnay	Curicó Valley	White	Stone fruit, buttery, vanillin	Fish, chicken	***
Montes Sauvignon Blanc	Curicó Valley	White	Grassy, melon, crisp	Shellfish, Asian	**
Montes Special Cuvée Merlot	Curicó Valley	Red	Berry, vanillin	Pizza, chicken	*
Pionero Cabernet Sauvignon	Central Valleys	Red	Fruity, spicy	Pizza, pasta	*
Santa Amelia Reserve Selection Chardonnay	Maule Valley	White	Grassy, citrus, crisp	Fish, pasta	*

CHILE (*Continued*)

Wine name	Region	Style	Flavor/Bouquet	Compatible Foods	Price Range
Santa Erna Reserve Cabernet Sauvignon	Maipo Valley/Central Valleys	Red	Berry, spicy, oaky	Veal, pork, beef	**
Santa Monica Tierra del Sol Reserva Chardonnay	Rancagua Valley	White	Apples, wax	Fish, chicken	**
Santa Rita Casa Real Old Vines Vineyard Cabernet Sauvignon	Maipo Valley/Central Valleys	Red	Intense, fruity, tannic	Beef, lamb	***
Santa Rita Late Harvest Semillon	Maipo Valley/Central Valleys	Sweet	Honey, wax, nutty, earthy	Fish, chicken	*
Santa Rita Medalla Real Chardonnay	Casablanca Valley	White	Citrus, melon, toasty, crisp	Fish, chicken	**
Santa Rita Medalla Real Special Reserve Cabernet Sauvignon	Maipo Valley/Central Valleys	Red	Berry, herbaceous, tannic	Pork, beef, lamb	**
Santa Rita Reserva Cabernet Sauvignon	Maipo Valley/Central Valleys	Red	Fruity, toasty, tannic	Pork, beef, lamb	**
Santa Rita Reserva Sauvignon Blanc	Maule Valley	White	Grassy, zingy	Shellfish, cheese	**
Valdevisio Barrel Select Malbec	Lontue	Red	Plums, spicy	Veal, pork, beef	**
Valdevisio Caballo Loco	Lontue	Red	Complex, intense, oaky	Beef, lamb	**
Valdevisio Reserve Cabernet Franc	Lontue	Red	Berry, toasty	Veal, pork, beef	**
Valdevisio Reserve Merlot	Lontue	Red	Plums, earthy, oaky	Pork, beef, lamb	**
Veramonte Merlot	Central Valleys	Red	Spicy, berry, herbaceous, elegant	Pizza, pasta	*
Viña Aquitania Cabernet Sauvignon	Maipo Valley/Central Valleys	Red	Plums, spicy	Pork, beef, lamb	**
Viña Calina Chardonnay	Rapel Valley/Central Valleys	White	Apples, crisp	Fish, Asian	*
Viña Calina Merlot	Maule Valley	Red	Fruity, herbaceous	Pizza, chicken	**
Viña Calina Selección de las Lomas Cabernet Franc	Maule Valley	Red	Fruity, toasty, elegant	Beef, lamb	***
Viña Calina Selección de las Lomas Cabernet Sauvignon	Rapel Valley/Central Valleys	Red	Spicy, fruity, intense	Pork, beef	**
Viña Calina Vicuña Vineyard Cabernet Sauvignon	Rapel Valley/Central Valleys	Red	Intense, fruity, toasty	Beef, lamb	***
Viña Gracia Barrique-Fermented Chardonnay	Bío-Bío Valley	White	Apples, buttery, oaky	Fish, chicken	**
Viña Gracia Chardonnay	Bío-Bío Valley	White	Apples, minerally	Fish, chicken	**
Viña Gracia Merlot	Bío-Bío Valley	Red	Plums, spicy	Chicken, veal	**
Viña La Rosa Cabernet Sauvignon	Rapel Valley/Central Valleys	Red	Plums, earthy, oaky	Pork, beef	**
Viña San Esteban President's Select Cabernet Sauvignon	Colchegua Valley	Red	Fruity, herbaceous, vanillin	Pork, beef	**
Viña San Pedro Castillo de Molina Reserva Chardonnay	Lontue	White	Fruity, buttery, toasty	Fish, chicken	*
Viña Santa Carolina Reserva Merlot	Maule Valley	Red	Berry, vanillin	Pork, veal, beef	*
Viña Tarapaca Chardonnay	Maipo Valley/Central Valleys	White	Apples, buttery, citrus	Fish, chicken	*
Viñedos J. Bouchon Chicureo Cabernet Sauvignon	Maule Valley	Red	Plums, berry, spicy	Pizza, chicken	*
Vista Sur Merlot	Central Valleys	Red	Plums, spicy	Chicken, pork, beef	**
Viu Manent Reserve Oak-Aged Malbec	Colchegua Valley	Red	Berry, toasty, zingy	Pork, beef	**
Walnut Crest Estate Selection Chardonnay	Casablanca Valley	White	Buttery, oaky	Fish, chicken	*

ARGENTINA

Wine name	Region	Style	Flavor/Bouquet	Compatible Foods	Price Range
Alamos Ridge Chardonnay	Mendoza	White	Apples, butter, spicy	Fish, chicken	*
Alamos Ridge Malbec	Mendoza	Red	Berry, plums, spicy	Chicken, veal, pork	*
Altos de les Hormigas Malbec	Mendoza	Red	Berry, spicy	Pizza, beef	*
Balbi Cabernet Sauvignon	Mendoza	Red	Berry, herbaceous, minerally	Pork, beef	**
Balbi Chardonnay	Mendoza	White	Citrus, minerally, zingy	Shellfish, fish	**
Balbi Malbec	Mendoza	Red	Berry, spicy	Pizza, chicken	**
Balbi Malbec-Syrah	Mendoza	Red	Floral, berry, fruity	Pizza, chicken, fish	*
Barral y Roca Malbec	Mendoza	Red	Berry, herbaceous, spicy	Pork, beef	**
Bodegas Curton Tempranillo-Malbec	Mendoza	Red	Berry, spicy	Pizza, beef	**
Bodegas Escorihuela Don Miguel Gascón Viognier	Mendoza	White	Tropical fruit, minerally, austere	Fish	**
Bodegas Etchart Arnaldo B Etchert Reserva	Cafayate	Red	Minerally, berry, herbaceous	Pork, beef, lamb	**
Bodegas Etchart Cafayate Chardonnay Barrel Fermented	Cafayate	White	Citrus, butter, toasty	Fish, chicken	**
Bodegas Etchart Rio de Plata Merlot	Mendoza	Red	Berry, spicy	Pizza, chicken	*
Bodegas Etchart Torrontes	Cafayate	White	Floral, tropical fruit	Asian, shellfish	*
Canale Malbec	Rio Negro	Red	Berry, earthy	Pork, beef, lamb	**
Catena Agrelo Vineyards Cabernet Sauvignon	Mendoza	Red	Berry, fruity, vanillin	Chicken, veal, pork	**
Catena Agrelo Vineyards Chardonnay	Mendoza	White	Fruity, oaky, butter	Fish, chicken	**
Catena Alta Malbec	Mendoza	Red	Complex, rich, earthy, oaky	Beef, lamb	***
Catena Lunlunta Vineyards Malbec	Mendoza	Red	Plums, fruity, rich, oaky	Beef, lamb	***
Finca Flinchman Dedicado	Maipu	Red	Berry, earthy, oaky	Beef, lamb	**
Finca Flinchman Reserva	Maipu	Red	Berry, herbaceous, oaky	Beef, lamb	**
Graffigna Cabernet Sauvignon-Merlot	San Juan	Red	Plums, spicy, oaky	Pork, beef, lamb	**
Graffigna Malbec	San Juan	Red	Berry, spicy	Veal, pork, beef	**
Hos de Medrano Viña Hormigas Reserva Malbec	Mendoza	Red	Fruity, intense, toasty	Pork, beef, lamb	***
Infinitus Malbec-Syrah	Patagonia	Red	Rich, berry, spicy	Veal, pork, beef	***
La Agricola Montepulciano	Mendoza	Red	Berry, earthy	Beef, lamb	*
Lavaque Cabernet Sauvignon-Merlot	Mendoza	Red	Berry, spicy, herbacous	Pork, beef, lamb	*
Mariposa Tapiz Reserve Malbec	Mendoza	Red	Berry, tannic	Beef, lamb	**

ARGENTINA (*Continued*)

Wine name	Region	Style	Flavor/Bouquet	Compatible Foods	Price Range
Michel Torino Don David Cabernet Sauvignon	Mendoza	Red	Berry, dill, oaky	Beef, lamb	**
Norton Barbera	Mendoza	Red	Berry, spicy	Pizza, chicken	*
Norton Privada	Mendoza	Red	Berry, herbaceous, oaky	Pork, beef	**
Proviar Chardonnay	Mendoza	White	Apples, minerally	Fish, chicken	**
Q Tempranillo	Mendoza	Red	Rich, berry, spicy, dill	Beef, pork	**
Rafael Malbec-Tempranillo	Mendoza	Red	Rich, plums, berry, leathery	Chicken, veal, pork	*
Santa Silva Barbera	Mendoza	Red	Berry, spicy	Pizza, chicken	**
Trapiche Fond de Cave Chardonnay	Mendoza	White	Apples, smoky, toasty	Fish, chicken	**
Trapiche Iscay Merlot-Malbec	Mendoza	Red	Rich, toasty, powerful	Veal, pork, beef	***
Trapiche Medalla Cabernet Sauvignon	Mendoza	Red	Berry, oaky, austere	Beef, lamb	**
Trapiche Medalla Chardonnay	Mendoza	White	Tropical fruit, toasty	Fish, chicken	**
Trapiche Medalla Merlot	Mendoza	Red	Berry, oaky, tannic	Veal, pork, beef	**
Trapiche Medalla Red	Mendoza	Red	Berry, minerally, oaky	Veal, pork, beef	**
Trapiche Oak Cask Cabernet Sauvignon	Mendoza	Red	Fruity, oaky	Pizza, beef	*
Trapiche Oak Cask Chardonnay	Mendoza	White	Apples, spicy	Fish, chicken	*
Trapiche Oak Cask Malbec	Mendoza	Red	Berry, oaky	Chicken, pork	*
Valentin Bianchi Cabernet Sauvignon	San Rafael	Red	Rich, spicy, oaky	Pork, beef	**
Valentin Bianchi Elsa Malbec	San Rafael	Red	Berry, fruity, vanillin	Pizza, beef	*
Valentin Bianchi Elsa Semillon Chardonnay	San Rafael	White	Citrus, minerally	Shellfish, fish	*
Valentin Bianchi Famiglia Bianchi Cabernet Sauvignon	San Rafael	Red	Intense, earthy, spicy, toasty	Beef, lamb	***
Valentin Bianchi Malbec	San Rafael	Red	Powerful, earthy	Beef, lamb	**
Valentin Bianchi Sauvignon Blanc	San Rafael	White	Citrus, minerally, crisp	Shellfish, fish	**
Valle del Condor Malbec	Mendoza	Red	Berry, spicy, rich	Pork, beef	**
Vinterra Merlot	San Juan	Red	Berry, vanillin	Pizza, beef	*
Weinert Cabernet Sauvignon	Mendoza	Red	Berry, earthy, toasty	Beef, lamb	**
Weinert Carrascal	Mendoza	Red	Earthy, minerally	Beef, lamb	**
Weinert Cevas de Weinert Gran Vino	Mendoza	Red	Mushroom, earthy, austere	Beef, lamb	**
Weinert Malbec	Mendoza	Red	Berry, gamey, leathery	Pork, beef, lamb	**

FRANCE

Wine name	Region	Style	Flavor/Bouquet	Compatible Foods	Price Range
Alfred Gratien Cuveé Paridis	Champagne	Sparkling	Berry, toasty, yeasty	Veal	**
Arbois Vin Jaune (André et Mireille Tissot)	Jura	White	Nutty, complex	Chicken	**
Auguste Clape St Peray	Rhône Valley	White	Floral, fruity	Shellfish, fish	**
Baud Père et Fils Côtes du Jura Chardonnay	Jura	White	Melon, spicy	Fish	**
Baud Père et Fils Côtes du Jura Tradition Blanc	Jura	White	Melon, fruity	Fish	**
Bergerac Château Tour des Gendres (Luc de Conti)	Bordeaux/Southwest France	Red	Berry, spicy	Cold meats	**
Bernède et Fils Cahors Clos la Coutale	Southwest France	Red	Herbaceous, spicy, earthy	Sausages	**
Billecart-Salmon Blanc de Blancs	Champagne	Sparkling	Citrus, elegant	Aperitif	**
Billecart-Salmon Cuvée N.F. Billecart	Champagne	Sparkling	Complex, citrus, berry, elegant	Fish	***
Billecart-Salmon Rosé	Champagne	Sparkling	Berry, floral	Lamb	**
Billecart-Salmon Rosé Cuvée Elizabeth	Champagne	Sparkling	Berry, complex, floral	Pork	**
Bisquit Cognac	Cognac	Brandy	Spirity, fiery, earthy	After dinner	***
Bollinger R.D.	Champagne	Sparkling	Complex, powerful, berry, yeasty	Chicken	***
Bollinger Special Cuvée	Champagne	Sparkling	Powerful, berry, apples, complex	Antipasto	**
Bollinger Vieilles Vignes Françaises	Champagne	Sparkling	Complex, berry, rich	Game	***
Bollinger Vintage	Champagne	Sparkling	Berry, complex, toasty, powerful	Fish	**
Bouvet-Ladubay Saumur Brut Trésor	Anjou-Saumur/Loire	Sparkling	Crisp, fruity, citrus	Aperitif	**
Bouvet-Ladubay Saumur-Champigny Les Non Pareils	Anjou-Saumur/Loire	Red	Berry, spicy	Cold meats, stew, offal	**
Campadieu Banyuls Grand Cru Cellier des Templiers Cuvée Amiral (Henry Vidal)	Roussillon	Fortified	Sweet, chocolatey	Chocolate	**
Camus Cognac	Cognac	Brandy	Spirity, complex, minerally	After dinner	***
Carillon Bienvenues Bâtard Montrachet	Puligny-Montrachet/Burgundy	White	Citrus, spicy	Fish	***
Carillon Puligny Montrachet Les Perrières	Puligny-Montrachet/Burgundy	White	Smoky, citrus	Chicken	**
Cattier Brut	Champagne	Sparkling	Yeasty, berry, floral	Shellfish	**
Cattier Clos du Moulin	Champagne	Sparkling	Berry, complex, powerful	Chicken	***
Cave Co-op de la Lavinière Minervois La Cave des Coteaux du Haut-Minervois	Languedoc	Red	Spicy, berry	Sausages	*
Cave Coopérative de Taradeau Oppidum	Côtes de Provence/Provence	Red	Berry, gamey	Stew	**
Cave de Cairanne Côtes du Rhône Villages Cuvée Temptation	Rhône Valley	Red	Berry, peppery, powerful	Beef, lamb	**
Cave de Chautagne Vin de Savoie Chautagne Gamay	Savoie	Red	Berry, spicy	Cold meats, stew, offal	**
Cave des Vignerons de Saumur Saumur Blanc les Pouches	Anjou-Saumur/Loire	White	Zingy, citrus, minerally	Fish	**
Cave Kientzheim-Kaysersberg Muscat Réserve	Alsace	White	Grapey, citrus	Chicken	**
Cave Vincole de Pfaffenheim et Gueberschwihr Gewurztraminer Grand Cru Goldert	Alsace	White	Spicy, chalky	Asian	**
Cave Vincole de Pfaffenheim et Gueberschwihr Gewuzrtraminer Grand Cru Zinnkoepfle Westhalten	Alsace	White	Spicy, floral	Asian	**

FRANCE (*Continued*)

Wine name	Region	Style	Flavor/Bouquet	Compatible Foods	Price Range
Chablis (A. Boudin)	Chablis/Burgundy	White	Minerally, spicy	Shellfish	**
Chablis (L. Michel)	Chablis/Burgundy	White	Citrus, minerally	Shellfish	**
Chandon de Briailles Pernand Vergelesses Ile de Vergelesses	Pernand-Vergelesses/Burgundy	Red	Minerally, floral	Veal	**
Chapoutier Châteauneuf-du-Pape La Bernadine	Rhône Valley	Red	Jam, peppery, rich	Beef, lamb	**
Chapoutier Côtes du Rhône Belleruche	Rhône Valley	Red	Berry, spicy, juicy	Pizza, chicken	*
Chapoutier Côtes du Rhône	Rhône Valley	White	Stone fruit, minerally	Fish, chicken	**
Château Angélus	St-Émilion/Bordeaux	Red	Minerally, plums	Lamb	**
Château Ausone	St-Émilion/Bordeaux	Red	Minerally, earthy, plums, herbaceous	Beef	***
Château Balestard-la-Tonnelle	St-Émilion/Bordeaux	Red	Herbaceous, minerally, spicy	Game	**
Château Bastor-Lamontagne	Sauternes, Barsac/Bordeaux	Sweet	Sweet, floral, mandarin	Dessert	***
Château Batailley	Pauillac/Bordeaux	Red	Berry, spicy, herbaceous	Stew	**
Château Beau-Séjour Bécot	St-Émilion/Bordeaux	Red	Minerally, tannic, herbaceous	Beef	**
Château Beaucastel Côtes du Rhône Coudoulet	Rhône Valley	Red	Berry, earthy, minerally, rich	Chicken, veal, pork	**
Château Beauregard	Pomerol/Bordeaux	Red	Spicy, minerally, plums	Lamb	**
Château Beauséjour	St-Émilion/Bordeaux	Red	Minerally, berry	Lamb	**
Château Bel Air	Entre-Deux-Mers/Bordeaux	Red	Herbaceous, berry	Stew	**
Château Bel-Air La Royère	Premières Côtes de Blaye/ Bordeaux	Red	Berry, fruity	Stew	**
Château Belgrave	Haut-Médoc/Bordeaux	Red	Berry, plums	Lamb	**
Château Beychevelle	St-Julien/Bordeaux	Red	Berry, herbaceous, tannic	Stew	**
Château Branaire	St-Julien/Bordeaux	Red	Berry, floral	Cheese	**
Château Brane-Cantenac	Margaux/Bordeaux	Red	Berry, herbaceous	Cold meats	**
Château Brondelle	Graves/Bordeaux	White	Citrus, herbaceous, vanillin	Fish, chicken	**
Château Calon (Montagne)	St-Émilion/Bordeaux	Red	Herbaceous, plums	Lamb	**
Château Calon-Ségur	St-Estèphe/Bordeaux	Red	Berry, tannic	Lamb	**
Château Camensac	Haut-Médoc/Bordeaux	Red	Minerally, berry	Cheese	**
Château Canon	St-Émilion/Bordeaux	Red	Smoky, berry	Cold meats	***
Château Canon-La Gaffelière	St-Émilion/Bordeaux	Red	Berry, herbaceous	Cold meats, stew, offal	**
Château Cantemerle	Haut-Médoc/Bordeaux	Red	Berry, spicy	Cold meats, stew, offal	**
Château Carbonnieux	Pessac-Léognan/Bordeaux	Red	Minerally, berry	Beef	**
Château Certan de May	Pomerol/Bordeaux	Red	Berry, floral, complex	Game	***
Château Cheval Blanc	St-Émilion/Bordeaux	Red	Minerally, berry, powerful, complex, herbaceous	Lamb	***
Château Clerc Milon	Pauillac/Bordeaux	Red	Berry, herbaceous	Lamb	**
Château Climens	Sauternes, Barsac/Bordeaux	Sweet	Sweet, complex, honey	Dessert	***
Château Clinet	Pomerol/Bordeaux	Red	Berry, tannic, minerally	Beef	***
Château Clos Haut-Peyraguey	Sauternes, Barsac/Bordeaux	Sweet	Sweet, honey, mandarin	Cheese	***
Château Cos d'Estournel	St-Estèphe/Bordeaux	Red	Minerally, tannic, herbaceous, berry	Beef	***
Château Cos Labory	St-Estèphe/Bordeaux	Red	Berry, tannic	Lamb	**
Château Couhins-Lurton	Pessac-Léognan/Bordeaux	Red	Berry, minerally	Pasta	**
Château Coutet	Sauternes, Barsac/Bordeaux	Sweet	Sweet, honey, mandarin	Dessert	***
Château d'Angludet	Margaux/Bordeaux	Red	Earthy, berry	Cheese	**
Château d'Archambeau	Graves/Bordeaux	White	Stone fruit, waxy, vanillin	Fish, chicken	**
Château d'Armailhac	Pauillac/Bordeaux	Red	Berry, tannic	Lamb	**
Château d'Epiré Savennières	Anjou-Saumur/Loire	White	Minerally, spicy	Shellfish	**
Château d'Issan	Margaux/Bordeaux	Red	Tannic, berry	Cold meats, stew, offal	**
Château d'Yquem	Sauternes, Barsac/Bordeaux	Sweet	Sweet, complex, honey, mandarin, citrus	Foie gras	***
Château Dauzac	Margaux/Bordeaux	Red	Plums, floral	Stew	**
Château de Bachen Tursan Baron de Bachen (Michel Guérard)	Landes, Gascogne and Pyrenees/Southwest France	White	Melon, oaky, spicy	Fish	**
Château de Chantegrive (also Cérons)	Graves/Bordeaux	White	Citrus, minerally	Fish	**
Château de Fesles Bonnezeaux Château de Fesles	Anjou-Saumur/Loire	Sweet	Sweet, apples, honey	Dessert	***
Château de Fieuzal	Pessac-Léognan/Bordeaux	Red	Minerally, tannic, herbaceous	Beef	***
Château de Francs	Bordeaux-Côtes de Francs/ Bordeaux	Red	Smoky, herbaceous	Sausages	**
Château de la Grille Chinon	Touraine/Loire	Red	Earthy, berry	Cold meats, stew, offal	*
Château de la Nerthe Châteauneuf-du-Pape Cuvée des Cadettes	Rhône Valley	Red	Berry, vanillin, powerful	Beef, lamb	**
Château de la Ragotière Muscadet de Sèvre et Maine	Pays Nantais/Loire	White	Citrus, minerally	Shellfish	**
Château de Malle	Sauternes, Barsac/Bordeaux	Sweet	Sweet, citrus	Dessert	***
Château de Myrat	Sauternes, Barsac/Bordeaux	Sweet	Sweet, fruity	Fruit	**
Château de Pibarnon (Eric de St Victor)	Bandol/Provence	Red	Earthy, berry	Stew	***
Château de Sales	Pomerol/Bordeaux	Red	Earthy, plums	Lamb	**
Château de Targé Saumur-Champigny	Anjou-Saumur/Loire	Red	Berry, plums	Stew	**
Château de Tracy Pouilly-Fumé	Center/Loire	White	Zingy, herbaceous	Pork	**
Château Doisy-Daëne	Sauternes, Barsac/Bordeaux	Sweet	Sweet, mandarin, minerally	Dessert	***
Château Doisy-Védrines	Sauternes, Barsac/Bordeaux	Sweet	Sweet, citrus, mandarin	Dessert	***
Château du Hureau Coteaux du Saumur	Anjou-Saumur/Loire	White	Medium-sweet, mandarin, minerally	Fruit	**

FRANCE (*Continued*)

Wine name	Region	Style	Flavor/Bouquet	Compatible Foods	Price Range
Château du Hureau Saumur-Champigny Cuvée Lisagathe	Anjou-Saumur/Loire	Red	Berry, fruity	Cold meats, stew, offal	**
Château du Tertre	Margaux/Bordeaux	Red	Berry, earthy	Cold meats	**
Château Ducru-Beaucaillou	St-Julien/Bordeaux	Red	Berry, minerally, herbaceous, tannic	Beef	***
Château Duhart-Milon	Pauillac/Bordeaux	Red	Berry, tannic	Beef	**
Château Durfort-Vivens	Margaux/Bordeaux	Red	Berry, herbaceous, tannic	Cold meats, stew, offal	**
Château Falfas	Côtes de Bourg/Bordeaux	Red	Herbaceous, plums	Pasta	*
Château Ferrière	Margaux/Bordeaux	Red	Berry, plums	Stew	**
Château Figeac	St-Émilion/Bordeaux	Red	Herbaceous, berry, minerally, tannic	Cheese	***
Château Fleur Cardinale	St-Émilion/Bordeaux	Red	Berry, spicy	Lamb	**
Château Garraud	Lalande de Pomerol/Bordeaux	Red	Berry, herbaceous	Lamb	**
Château Gaudrelle Vouvray Réserve Personelle Moelleux	Touraine/Loire	Sweet	Sweet, citrus, honey	Dessert	***
Château Giscours	Margaux/Bordeaux	Red	Plums, spicy	Lamb	**
Château Grand Mayne	St-Émilion/Bordeaux	Red	Berry, tannic	Stew	**
Château Grand-Puy-Ducasse	Pauillac/Bordeaux	Red	Berry, smoky	Beef	**
Château Grand-Puy-Lacoste	Pauillac/Bordeaux	Red	Plums, herbaceous, spicy	Lamb	**
Château Gruaud-Larose	St-Julien/Bordeaux	Red	Minerally, earthy, herbaceous, complex, tannic	Beef	***
Château Haut-Bages-Libéral	Pauillac/Bordeaux	Red	Herbaceous, berry	Cold meats, stew, offal	**
Château Haut-Bailly	Pessac-Léognan/Bordeaux	Red	Herbaceous, spicy, tannic	Cheese	**
Château Haut-Batailley	Pauillac/Bordeaux	Red	Berry, tannic	Cold meats, stew, offal	**
Château Haut-Beauséjour	St-Estèphe/Bordeaux	Red	Berry, spicy, herbaceous	Stew	**
Château Haut-Brion	Pessac-Léognan/Bordeaux	Red	Complex, tannic, minerally, berry	Lamb	***
Château Kirwan	Margaux/Bordeaux	Red	Tannic, herbaceous, berry	Lamb	**
Château l'Arrosée	St-Émilion/Bordeaux	Red	Berry, spicy, tannic	Cold meats, stew, offal	**
Château La Dominique	St-Émilion/Bordeaux	Red	Berry, spicy, complex	Lamb	***
Château La Fleur Milon	Pauillac/Bordeaux	Red	Berry, herbaceous	Stew	**
Château La Fleur Pétrus	Pomerol/Bordeaux	Red	Complex, berry, plums, herbaceous	Stew	***
Château La Gaffelière	St-Émilion/Bordeaux	Red	Minerally, berry, herbaceous	Lamb	**
Château La Lagune	Haut-Médoc/Bordeaux	Red	Berry, herbaceous, tannic	Game	**
Château La Mission Haut-Brion	Pessac-Léognan/Bordeaux	Red	Complex, tannic, herbaceous, minerally	Lamb	***
Château La Mondotte	St-Émilion/Bordeaux	Red	Herbaceous, berry, smoky,tannic	Beef	***
Château La Tour Blanche	Sauternes, Barsac/Bordeaux	Sweet	Sweet, honey, citrus	Dessert	***
Château La Tour Carnet	Haut-Médoc/Bordeaux	Red	Smoky, berry	Cold meats, stew, offal	**
Château La Tour Figeac	St-Émilion/Bordeaux	Red	Minerally, herbaceous, berry	Stew	***
Château La Tour Haut-Brion	Pessac-Léognan/Bordeaux	Red	Minerally, herbaceous, tannic	Lamb	**
Château Labégorce-Zédé	Margaux/Bordeaux	Red	Berry, smoky	Lamb	**
Château Lacombe-Noaillac	Médoc/Bordeaux	Red	Spicy, herbaceous, earthy	Pasta	**
Château Lafaurie-Peyraguey	Sauternes, Barsac/Bordeaux	Sweet	Sweet, mandarin, citrus	Cheese	***
Château Lafite-Rothschild	Pauillac/Bordeaux	Red	Complex, berry, smoky, tannic	Lamb	***
Château Lafleur	Pomerol/Bordeaux	Red	Minerally, plums, spicy	Lamb	***
Château Lafon-Rochet	St-Estèphe/Bordeaux	Red	Berry, spicy, herbaceous	Lamb	**
Château Lagrange	St-Julien/Bordeaux	Red	Berry, herbaceous, tannic	Lamb	**
Château Langoa Barton	St-Julien/Bordeaux	Red	Berry, smoky	Beef	**
Château Larcis Ducasse	St-Émilion/Bordeaux	Red	Berry, smoky	Cheese	**
Château Larmande	St-Émilion/Bordeaux	Red	Plums, herbaceous, spicy	Cheese	**
Château Lascombes	Margaux/Bordeaux	Red	Herbaceous, smoky, spicy	Beef	**
Château Latour à Pomerol	Pomerol/Bordeaux	Red	Complex, spicy, herbaceous, minerally	Beef	***
Château Latour	Pauillac/Bordeaux	Red	Complex, berry, powerful, tannic	Lamb	***
Château Latour-Martillac	Pessac-Léognan/Bordeaux	Red	Berry, tannic	Beef	**
Château Laville Haut-Brion	Pessac-Léognan/Bordeaux	Red	Minerally, berry, herbaceous	Game	***
Château Le Bon Pasteur	Pomerol/Bordeaux	Red	Tannic, spicy, berry	Beef	**
Château Le Bonnat	Graves/Bordeaux	White	Apples, melon, waxy, herbaceous	Fish, chicken	**
Château Le Pin	Pomerol/Bordeaux	Red	Complex, powerful, tannic, spicy, herbaceous	Cold meats, stew, offal	***
Château Léhoul	Graves/Bordeaux	Red	Spicy, plums	Pizza	**
Château Léoville Barton	St-Julien/Bordeaux	Red	Berry, complex, herbaceous, smoky	Lamb	**
Château Léoville Las Cases	St-Julien/Bordeaux	Red	Complex, minerally, herbaceous, berry	Lamb	***
Château Léoville Poyferré	St-Julien/Bordeaux	Red	Berry, herbaceous, minerally	Cold meats, stew, offal	**
Château Les Carmes Haut-Brion	Pessac-Léognan/Bordeaux	Red	Spicy, herbaceous, earthy	Cold meats, stew, offal	**
Château Les Justices	Sauternes, Barsac/Bordeaux	Sweet	Sweet, citrus	Fruit	**
Château Les Ormes-de-Pez	St-Estèphe/Bordeaux	Red	Minerally, tannic	Beef	**
Château Lilian-Ladouys	St-Estèphe/Bordeaux	Red	Tannic, floral, herbaceous	Game	**
Château Lynch-Bages	Pauillac/Bordeaux	Red	Berry, tannic, herbaceous	Lamb	***
Château Magdelaine	St-Émilion/Bordeaux	Red	Minerally, earthy, herbaceous	Lamb	***

FRANCE (*Continued*)

Wine name	Region	Style	Flavor/Bouquet	Compatible Foods	Price Range
Château Malartic-Lagravière	Pessac-Léognan/Bordeaux	Red	Minerally, herbaceous, tannic	Cold meats, stew, offal	**
Château Malescot-St-Exupéry	Margaux/Bordeaux	Red	Berry, spicy	Stew	**
Château Marbuzet	St-Estèphe/Bordeaux	Red	Berry, herbaceous, tannic	Cold meats, stew, offal	**
Château Margaux	Margaux/Bordeaux	Red	Complex, minerally, berry, tannic, spicy	Lamb	***
Château Marquis de Terme	Margaux/Bordeaux	Red	Berry, floral	Stew	**
Château Monbousquet	St-Émilion/Bordeaux	Red	Berry, herbaceous, tannic	Stew	**
Château Monbrison	Margaux/Bordeaux	Red	Berry, herbaceous	Cold meats, stew, offal	**
Château Montrose	St-Estèphe/Bordeaux	Red	Minerally, complex, powerful, berry	Beef	***
Château Moulin Haut-Laroque	Fronsac, Canon-Fronsac/ Bordeaux	Red	Herbaceous, berry	Beef	**
Château Moulin St-Georges	St-Émilion/Bordeaux	Red	Berry, plums	Beef	**
Château Mouton-Rothschild	Pauillac/Bordeaux	Red	Complex, berry, herbaceous, tannic, spicy	Lamb	***
Château Nairac	Sauternes, Barsac/Bordeaux	Sweet	Sweet, floral, citrus	Dessert	**
Château Palmer	Margaux/Bordeaux	Red	Complex, tannic, herbaceous, berry	Cheese	***
Château Pape Clément	Pessac-Léognan/Bordeaux	Red	Berry, minerally	Stew	**
Château Pavie	St-Émilion/Bordeaux	Red	Minerally, plums, herbaceous	Lamb	***
Château Pavie-Decesse	St-Émilion/Bordeaux	Red	Herbaceous, smoky	Stew	**
Château Pavie-Macquin	St-Émilion/Bordeaux	Red	Plums, berry	Pasta	**
Château Petit-Village	Pomerol/Bordeaux	Red	Berry, spicy	Sausages	**
Château Pétrus	Pomerol/Bordeaux	Red	Complex, spicy, herbaceous, berry, tannic	Game	***
Château Pibran	Pauillac/Bordeaux	Red	Berry, spicy	Stew	**
Château Pichon-Longueville (Comtesse de Lalande)	Pauillac/Bordeaux	Red	Berry, plums, complex, tannic	Lamb	***
Château Pichon-Longueville	Pauillac/Bordeaux	Red	Berry, smoky, tannic, herbaceous	Beef	***
Château Pierre Bise Quarts de Chaume	Anjou-Saumur/Loire	Sweet	Sweet, honey	Dessert	**
Château Pontet-Canet	Pauillac/Bordeaux	Red	Herbaceous, spicy	Cold meats	**
Château Prieuré-Lichine	Margaux/Bordeaux	Red	Berry, tannic	Lamb	**
Château Rabaud-Promis	Sauternes, Barsac/Bordeaux	Sweet	Sweet, citrus, mandarin	Dessert	**
Château Rahoul	Graves/Bordeaux	Red	Berry, herbaceous	Sausages	**
Château Rauzan Ségla	Margaux/Bordeaux	Red	Smoky, tannic	Cold meats	***
Château Rayas Châteauneuf-du-Pape	Rhône Valley	Red	Powerful, complex, berry, jam	Beef, lamb	***
Château Rayas Fonsolette Côtes du Rhône	Rhône Valley	Red	Berry, spicy, earthy, rich	Chicken, veal, pork	**
Château Rayas Pignan Châteauneuf-du-Pape	Rhône Valley	Red	Berry, jam, rich, intense	Beef, lamb	**
Château Raymond-Lafon	Sauternes, Barsac/Bordeaux	Sweet	Sweet, complex, honey	Foie gras	***
Château Rayne Vigneau	Sauternes, Barsac/Bordeaux	Sweet	Sweet, mandarin, honey	Dessert	***
Château Respide Médeville	Graves/Bordeaux	Red	Smoky, plums	Pasta	**
Château Rieussec	Sauternes, Barsac/Bordeaux	Sweet	Sweet, complex, honey, mandarin	Dessert	***
Château Roquefort	Bordeaux Supérieur/Bordeaux	Red	Spicy, earthy	Beef	**
Château Saint-Pierre	St-Julien/Bordeaux	Red	Plums, spicy, berry	Beef	**
Château Sigalas-Rabaud	Sauternes, Barsac/Bordeaux	Sweet	Sweet, citrus, floral	Dessert	**
Château Siran	Margaux/Bordeaux	Red	Berry, plums	Cold meats, stew, offal	**
Château Smith-Haut-Lafitte	Pessac-Léognan/Bordeaux	Red	Minerally, herbaceous, tannic	Beef	**
Château Soutard	St-Émilion/Bordeaux	Red	Plums, berry	Lamb	**
Château St-Robert	Graves/Bordeaux	White	Citrus, waxy, herbaceous, vanillin	Fish, chicken	**
Château Suau	Premières Côtes de Bordeaux/ Bordeaux	Red	Herbaceous, minerally	Pasta	**
Château Suduiraut	Sauternes, Barsac/Bordeaux	Sweet	Sweet, complex, citrus	Dessert	***
Château Talbot	St-Julien/Bordeaux	Red	Berry, herbaceous, minerally	Sausages	**
Château Troplong-Mondot	St-Émilion/Bordeaux	Red	Spicy, minerally, berry	Lamb	**
Château Vieux Robin	Médoc/Bordeaux	Red	Spicy, berry	Lamb	**
Château Vignelaure (David O'Brien/Hugh Ryman)	Coteaux d'Aix/Provence	Red	Berry, spicy, earthy	Pork	**
Clair Chambertin Clos de Bèze	Gevrey-Chambertin/Burgundy	Red	Spicy, minerally, berry	Duck	***
Clos Capitoro Rouge	Ajuccio/Corsica	Red	Spicy, earthy	Chicken, veal, pork	**
Clos de l'Oratoire	St-Émilion/Bordeaux	Red	Berry, spicy	Stew	**
Clos Floridène	Graves/Bordeaux	White	Spicy, minerally	Shellfish	**
Clos l'Eglise	Pomerol/Bordeaux	Red	Berry, minerally, herbaceous, tannic	Beef	***
Coche Dury Meursault	Meursault/Burgundy	White	Citrus, nutty	Fish	**
Coche Dury Meursault Perrières	Meursault/Burgundy	White	Complex, citrus, spicy	Fish	**
Coche Dury Volnay Premier cru	Volnay/Burgundy	Red	Spicy, gamey	Duck	**
Colin-Deleger Puligny Montrachet Les Demoiselles	Puligny-Montrachet/Burgundy	White	Spicy, citrus, nutty	Veal	**
Corbieres Château La Voulte-Gasparets Cuvée Romain Puic (Patrick Reverdy)	Languedoc	Red	Spicy, berry	Sausages	**
Corton Charlemagne (Louis Jadot)	Aloxe Corton/Burgundy	White	Citrus, floral, tropical fruit	Chicken	***
Corton Perrières (Michel Juillot)	Aloxe Corton/Burgundy	Red	Smoky, berry	Cold meats, stew, offal	***
Coteaux de l'Aubance Les Fontenelles (Christian et Agnès Papin)	Anjou-Saumur/Loire	Sweet	Minerally, sweet, apples	Cheese	**

FRANCE *(Continued)*

Wine name	Region	Style	Flavor/Bouquet	Compatible Foods	Price Range
Coteaux du Languedoc Château Saint-Martin de la Garrigue	Languedoc	Red	Berry, spicy	Pork	**
Coteaux du Languedoc Dom Clavel La Méjanelle (Pierre Clavel)	Languedoc	Red	Spicy, minerally	Stew	**
Coteaux du Languedoc La Clape Château Pech-Céleyran (Jacques de St Exupéry)	Languedoc	Red	Berry, earthy	Stew	*
Coteaux du Languedoc Mas Jullien Les Depierre (Olivier Jullien)	Languedoc	Red	Spicy, gamey	Lamb	**
Coteaux du Languedoc Mas Jullien Les Vignes Oubliées (Olivier Jullien)	Languedoc	Red	Smoky, spicy	Stew	*
Coteaux du Languedoc Pic St Loup Château Lascaux Noble Pierre	Languedoc	Red	Berry, spicy	Sausages	**
Coteaux du Languedoc Pic St Loup Domaine de l'Hortus (Jean Orliac)	Languedoc	Red	Gamey, earthy	Cold meats, stew, offal	**
Coteaux du Languedoc Pic St Loup Mas Bruguière	Languedoc	Red	Berry, herbaceous	Cold meats	*
Côtes de Bergerac Château Court-les-Muts	Bordeaux/Southwest France	Red	Berry, spicy	Veal	**
Côtes de Duras Dom du Grand Mayne Rouge (Andrew Gordon)	Bordeaux/Southwest France	Red	Spicy, berry	Pasta	**
Courvoisier Cognac	Cognac	Brandy	Spirity, complex, minerally	After dinner	***
Croizet Cognac	Cognac	Brandy	Spirity, minerally	After dinner	***
Cru Barréjats	Sauternes, Barsac/Bordeaux	Sweet	Sweet, citrus	Dessert	*
Delamotte Vintage	Champagne	Sparkling	Berry, citrus, crisp	Shellfish	**
Delas Frères Condrieu Clos Boucher	Rhône Valley	White	Stone fruit, floral, rich	Fish, fruits	**
Delas Frères Condrieu La Galopine	Rhône Valley	White	Stone fruit, minerally, elegant	Fish, fruits	**
Désiré Petit et Fils Arbois-Pupillin Vin de Paille	Jura	Sweet	Raisiny, complex, sweet	Nuts	***
Deutz Blanc de Blancs	Champagne	Sparkling	Citrus, elegant, crisp	Aperitif	**
Deutz Cuveé (William Deutz)	Champagne	Sparkling	Berry, complex, citrus	Veal	***
Deutz Vintage	Champagne	Sparkling	Berry, citrus	Fish	**
Domaine Alphonse Mellot Sancerre Génération XIX	Center/Loire	White	Grassy, citrus	Fish	***
Domaine André Ehrhart et Fils Tokay Pinot Gris Cuvée Elise	Alsace	White	Floral, citrus	Veal	**
Domaine Bernard Baudry Chinon les Grèzeaux	Touraine/Loire	Red	Berry, earthy, gamey	Stew	**
Domaine Cady Coteaux du Layon Saint-Aubin Cuvée Volupté	Anjou-Saumur/Loire	Sweet	Sweet, citrus, honey	Dessert	***
Domaine Charles Joguet Chinon les Varennes du Grand Clos	Touraine/Loire	Red	Herbaceous, berry, spicy, complex, earthy	Lamb	**
Domaine Couly-Dutheil Chinon Clos de l'Echo	Touraine/Loire	Red	Spicy, herbaceous, berry	Veal	**
Domaine de Chevalier	Pessac-Léognan/Bordeaux	Red	Berry, herbaceous, tannic, minerally	Beef	***
Domaine de l'Arlot Nuits St Georges Clos des Forêts St Georges	Nuits-St-Georges/Burgundy	Red	Spicy, gamey, berry	Duck	**
Domaine de l'Oratoire St Martin Côtes du Rhône Cairanne	Rhône Valley	Red	Berry, earthy, spicy	Pizza, chicken	**
Domaine de la Bastide Neuve (Jérome Paquette)	Côtes de Provence/Provence	Red	Berry, earthy	Stew	**
Domaine de la Bigotière Muscadet de Sèvre et Maine	Pays Nantais/Loire	White	Minerally, zingy, floral	Fish	*
Domaine de la Charbonnière Vacqueyras	Rhône Valley	Red	Berry, herbaceous, leathery, intense	Pork, beef, lamb	**
Domaine de la Janasse Châteauneuf-du-Pape	Rhône Valley	Red	Berry, peppery, earthy, spicy	Beef, lamb	**
Domaine de la Janasse Côtes-du-Rhône	Rhône Valley	Red	Berry, spicy	Pizza, chicken	*
Domaine de la Louvetrie Muscadet de Sèvre et Maine Clos du Château de la Carizière	Pays Nantais/Loire	White	Zingy, citrus	Fish	**
Domaine de la Mordorée Châteauneuf-du-Pape Cuvée de la Reine des Bois	Rhône Valley	Red	Berry, licorice, spicy, earthy	Pork, beef	**
Domaine de la Mordorée Lirac Cuvée de la Reine des Bois	Rhône Valley	Red	Berry, licorice, herbaceous	Veal, pork, beef	**
Domaine de la Mordorée Tavel	Rhône Valley	Rosé	Berry, rich, fruity	Asian, fish	**
Domaine de la Romanée Conti Echézeaux	Vosne-Romanée/Burgundy	Red	Complex, floral, spicy, earthy	Duck	***
Domaine de la Romanée Conti La Tâche	Vosne-Romanée/Burgundy	Red	Spicy, earthy, silky, complex	Duck	***
Domaine de la Romanée Conti Le Montrachet	Puligny-Montrachet/Burgundy	White	Minerally, complex, spicy, nutty	Fish	***
Domaine de la Romanée Conti Richebourg	Vosne-Romanée/Burgundy	Red	Gamey, spicy, complex	Gamey	***
Domaine de la Romanée Conti Romanée Conti	Vosne-Romanée/Burgundy	Red	Complex, spicy, earthy, minerally	Duck	***
Domaine de la Romanée Conti Romanée St Vivant	Vosne-Romanée/Burgundy	Red	Complex, minerally, smoky, earthy	Game	***
Domaine de la Romanée Conti Grands Echézeaux	Vosne-Romanée/Burgundy	Red	Spicy, complex, minerally, berry	Lamb	***
Domaine de Ladoucette Sancerre (Comte Lafond)	Center/Loire	White	Zingy, grassy	Cheese	**
Domaine de Tanella Cuvée Alexandra	Figari/Corsica	Red	Powerful, complex	Beef, lamb	***
Domaine de Torraccia Cuvée Oriu	Porto-Vecchio/Corsica	Red	Rich, smoky	Beef, lamb	***
Domaine de Trévallon (Eloi Durrbach)	Les Baux-de-Provence/Provence	Red	Berry, earthy	Pasta	**
Domaine des Aubuisières Vouvray sec Le Marigny	Touraine/Loire	White	Apples, citrus, minerally	Fish	**
Domaine des Baumard Anjou Blanc Clos de la Folie	Anjou-Saumur/Loire	White	Apples, citrus, minerally	Shellfish	**
Domaine des Baumard Coteaux du Layon Clos de Sainte Catherine	Anjou-Saumur/Loire	Sweet	Sweet, minerally, honey	Fruit	***
Domaine des Baumard Quarts de Chaume	Anjou-Saumur/Loire	Sweet	Sweet, honey, mandarin	Dessert	***
Domaine des Baumard Savennières Clos du Papillon	Anjou-Saumur/Loire	White	Minerally, citrus, complex	Veal	***
Domaine des Marroniers Riesling Kastelberg	Alsace	White	Citrus, spicy	Veal	**
Domaine Didier Dagueneau Pouilly-Fumé Astérôde	Center/Loire	White	Zingy, citrus, herbaceous	Mediterranean	***
Domaine Didier Dagueneau Pouilly-Fumé Pur Sang	Center/Loire	White	Minerally, citrus, spicy	Fish	***
Domaine Druet Bourgueil Grand Mont	Touraine/Loire	Red	Berry, gamey	Stew	**
Domaine du Caillou Châteauneuf-du-Pape	Rhône Valley	Red	Berry, floral, elegant	Beef, lamb	**
Domaine du Clos Naudin Vouvray Moelleux Réserve	Touraine/Loire	Sweet	Sweet, honey, minerally	Cheese	***

FRANCE (*Continued*)

Wine name	Region	Style	Flavor/Bouquet	Compatible Foods	Price Range
Domaine du Closel Savennières Clos du Papillon	Anjou-Saumur/Loire	White	Complex, minerally	Chicken	**
Domaine Fuimicicoli Rouge	Sartène/Corsica	Red	Spicy, elegant	Chicken, veal, pork	**
Domaine Henri Bourgeois Sanerre le M.D. de Bourgeois	Center/Loire	White	Minerally, floral	Veal	**
Domaine Jean Sipp Riesling Grand Cru Kirchberg	Alsace	White	Floral, citrus	Chicken	**
Domaine Jean-Max Roger Sancerre Le Grand Chemarin	Center/Loire	White	Citrus, cold tea	Fish	**
Domaine Jo Pithon Coteaux du Layon Saint-Lambert	Anjou-Saumur/Loire	Sweet	Sweet, honey, citrus	Cheese	***
Domaine Lucien Crochet Sancerre Rouge Prestige	Center/Loire	Red	Herbaceous, spicy, berry	Cold meats	**
Domaine Marcel Deiss Riesling Burg de Bergheim	Alsace	White	Floral, citrus, complex	Fish	**
Domaine Marcel Deiss Riesling Grand Cru Altenberg de Bergheim	Alsace	White	Complex, floral, minerally	Chicken	**
Domaine Masson-Blondelet Pouilly-Fumé Tradition Cullus	Center/Loire	White	Grassy, minerally	Salad	**
Domaine Ogereau Anjou Villages Prestige	Anjou-Saumur/Loire	Red	Berry, spicy, earthy	Stew	**
Domaine Ogereau Coteaux du Layon Saint-Lambert	Anjou-Saumur/Loire	Sweet	Sweet, citrus, minerally	Dessert	**
Domaine Ostertag Gewurztraminer Fronholz Vendanges Tardives	Alsace	White	Powerful, sweet, floral	Fruit	***
Domaine Ostertag Sylvaner Vieilles Vignes	Alsace	White	Floral, citrus	Cheese	**
Domaine Ostertag Tokay Pinot Gris Fronhoz	Alsace	White	Citrus, oily	Veal	**
Domaine Paul Antard Châteauneuf-du-Pape Cuvée Classique	Rhône Valley	Red	Powerful, jam, licorice	Beef, lamb	**
Domaine René Muré Gewurztraminer Schultzengass	Alsace	White	Minerally, chalky	Asian	**
Domaine René Muré Pinot Noir Clos Saint-Landelin	Alsace	Red	Berry, gamey	Cold meats	**
Domaine René Muré Riesling Grand Cru Vorbourg Clos Saint-Landelin	Alsace	White	Spicy, minerally	Asian	**
Domaine René Muré Sylvaner Clos Saint-Landelin Cuvée Oscar	Alsace	White	Floral, minerally	Fish	**
Domaine René Muré Tokay Pinot Gris Lutzeltal	Alsace	White	Floral, citrus	Fish	**
Domaine René-Noêl Legrand Saumur-Champigny Les Rogelins	Anjou-Saumur/Loire	Red	Berry, spicy	Stew	**
Domaine Richou Coteaux de l'Aubance Les Trois Demoiselles	Anjou-Saumur/Loire	Sweet	Sweet, citrus, apples	Dessert	**
Domaine Rolly Gassmann Muscat Moenchreben de Rorschwihr	Alsace	White	Floral, grapey	Fruit	**
Domaine Rolly Gassmann Pinot Noir de Rodern	Alsace	Red	Smoky, berry	Duck	**
Domaine Rolly Gassmann Riesling Kappelweg de Rorschwihr	Alsace	White	Floral, spicy	Pork	**
Domaine Schlumberger Gewurztraminer Cuvée Christine	Alsace	White	Smoky, spicy	Asian	***
Domaine Schlumberger Riesling Grand Cru Kessler	Alsace	White	Floral, minerally	Pasta	**
Domaine Schlumberger Tokay Pinot Gris Grand Cru Kitterle	Alsace	White	Spicy, oily	Fish	**
Domaine Schoffit Gewurztraminer Grand Cru Rangen Clos Saint-Théobald Vendanges Tardives	Alsace	White	Sweet, powerful, chalky	Fish	**
Domaine St André de Figuière (Alain Combard)	Côtes de Provence/Provence	Red	Berry, earthy	Pasta	**
Domaine Vacheron Sancerre Rouge	Center/Loire	Red	Berry, herbaceous	Cold meats, stew, offal	**
Domaine Vincent Pinard Sancerre Harmonie	Center/Loire	White	Zingy, herbaceous	Shellfish	**
Domaine Weinbach Riesling Grand Cru Schlossberg	Alsace	White	Complex, floral, minerally	Chicken	***
Domaine Weinbach Tokay Pinot Gris Quintessence de Grains Nobles	Alsace	Sweet	Sweet, complex, spicy	Dessert	***
Domaine Yannick Amirault Bourgueil Vieilles Vignes Petite Cave	Touraine/Loire	Red	Berry, earthy	Sausages	**
Domaine Yvon Metras Fleurie	Beaujolais	Red	Berry, floral, jam, earthy	Chicken, pork, veal, beef	**
Domaine Zind Humbrecht Gewurztraminer Hengst	Alsace	White	Complex, powerful, spicy	Veal	***
Domaine Zind-Humbrecht Gewurztraminer Grand Cru Goldert	Alsace	White	Powerful, complex, spicy	Cheese	***
Domaine Zind-Humbrecht Riesling Rangen de Thann Clos Saint-Urbain	Alsace	White	Powerful, minerally, floral	Fish	***
Domaine Zind-Humbrecht Tokay Pinot Gris Clos Jebsal Sélection de Grains Nobles	Alsace	Sweet	Sweet, complex, citrus, floral	Dessert	***
Domaine Zind-Humbrecht Tokay Pinot Gris Grand Cru Rangen de Thann Clos Saint-Urbain	Alsace	White	Spicy, oily, powerful	Chicken	***
Domaine Zind-Humbrecht Tokay Pinot Gris Windsbuhl	Alsace	White	Spicy, oily, complex	Chicken	***
Drouhin Beaune Clos des Mouches	Beaune/Burgundy	White	Minerally, citrus	Fish	**
Drouhin Puligny Montrachet	Puligny-Montrachet/Burgundy	White	Citrus, minerally	Pork	**
Dujac Clos de la Roche	Morey St-Denis/Burgundy	Red	Complex, gamey, earthy	Duck	***
Dujac Clos St Denis	Morey St-Denis/Burgundy	Red	Earthy, minerally, berry	Beef	***
Faiveley Corton Charlemagne	Aloxe Corton/Burgundy	White	Citrus, minerally, spicy	Veal	***
Gagnard-Delagrange Bâtard Montrachet	Chassagne Montrachet/ Burgundy	White	Complex, nutty, minerally	Fish	***
Gagnard-Delagrange Chassagne Morey	Chassagne Montrachet/ Burgundy	White	Nutty, spicy	Veal	**
Gaillac Domaine de Causse-Marines Delires D'Automme Doux (Patrice Lescarret)	Southwest France	Red	Spicy, berry	Sausages	**
Gardet Vintage	Champagne	Sparkling	Berry, citrus, crisp	Shellfish	**
Gautier Cognac	Cognac	Brandy	Spirity, complex	After dinner	***
Georges Du Boeuf Morgon	Beaujolais	Red	Jam, berry, intense	Chicken, veal, pork	**
Georges Du Boeuf Moulin-à-Vent	Beaujolais	Red	Berry, earthy, minerally	Chicken, veal, pork	**
Georges Vernay Condrieu Coteaux du Vernon	Rhône Valley	White	Stone fruit, minerally, powerful	Fish, fruits	**
Gevrey Chambertin (D. Mortet)	Gevrey-Chambertin/Burgundy	Red	Berry, licorice	Stew	**
Gouges Nuits St Georges Les St Georges	Nuits-St-Georges/Burgundy	Red	Earthy, berry	Game	**
Gouges Nuits St Georges Les St Porrets	Nuits-St-Georges/Burgundy	Red	Plums, berry	Cheese	**
Grossot Chablis	Chablis/Burgundy	White	Minerally, apples	Fish	**
Guigal Condrieu la Doriane	Rhône Valley	White	Stone fruit, minerally, oaky	Fish, chicken	***
Guigal Condrieu	Rhône Valley	White	Stone fruit, minerally, floral, complex	Fish, fruits	**

FRANCE (*Continued*)

Wine name	Region	Style	Flavor/Bouquet	Compatible Foods	Price Range
Guigal Côte-Rôtie Blonde et Brune	Rhône Valley	Red	Berry, smoky, rich, elegant	Beef, lamb	**
Guigal Côte-Rôtie La Landonne	Rhône Valley	Red	Berry, peppery, licorice, complex	Beef, lamb	***
Guigal Côte-Rôtie La Mouline	Rhône Valley	Red	Floral, berry, nutty, complex	Beef, lamb	***
Guigal Côte-Rôtie La Turque	Rhône Valley	Red	Berry, peppery, licorice, intense	Beef, lamb	***
Guigal Côtes du Rhône	Rhône Valley	Red	Fruity, berry, spicy	Pizza, chicken	*
Guigal Côtes du Rhône	Rhône Valley	White	Floral, stone fruit, crisp	Fish, chicken	*
Guigal Gigondas	Rhône Valley	Red	Berry, earthy, austere	Veal, pork, beef	**
Guigal Hermitage	Rhône Valley	Red	Berry, licorice, mushroom, rich	Beef, lamb	**
Heidsieck & Monopole Vintage	Champagne	Sparkling	Crisp, toasty, berry	Cheese	**
Hennessy Cognac	Cognac	Brandy	Spirity, fiery, minerally	After dinner	***
Hine Cognac	Cognac	Brandy	Spirity, minerally	After dinner	***
Hugel et Fils Gewurztraminer Sélection de Grains Nobles	Alsace	Sweet	Sweet, complex, citrus, spicy	Dessert	***
Hugel et Fils Riesling Sélection de Grains Nobles	Alsace	Sweet	Sweet, complex, powerful, floral	Dessert	***
Hugel et Fils Tokay Pinot Gris Hommage (Jean Hugel)	Alsace	White	Oily, floral	Cheese	***
Irouléguy Dom Brana (Jean et Adrienne Brana)	Landes, Gascogne and Pyrenees/Southwest France	Red	Berry, spicy	Cold meats, stew, offal	**
J. L. Chave Hermitage	Rhône Valley	Red	Complex, rich, earthy	Beef, lamb	***
Jacquesson Signature	Champagne	Sparkling	Complex, berry, powerful	Chicken	**
Jacquesson Signature Non Dosé	Champagne	Sparkling	Dry, austere, crisp, citrus	Shellfish	**
Jadot Beaune Boucherottes	Beaune/Burgundy	Red	Berry, earthy	Cheese	**
Jadot Beaune Clos des Ursules	Beaune/Burgundy	Red	Berry, earthy	Stew	**
Jadot Chevalier Montrachet Les Demoiselles	Puligny-Montrachet/Burgundy	White	Spicy, smoky	Chicken	***
Jadot Corton Pougets	Aloxe Corton/Burgundy	Red	Berry, leathery	Duck	***
Jadot Puligny Montrachet	Puligny-Montrachet/Burgundy	White	Minerally, spicy	Veal	**
Jamet Côte-Rôtie	Rhône Valley	Red	Jam, berry, earthy, complex	Beef, lamb	**
Jean-Luc Colombo Cornas Le Terre Brûlée	Rhône Valley	Red	Berry, spicy, minerally, complex	Beef, lamb	**
Jean-Luc Colombo Côtes du Rhône les Figuieres	Rhône Valley	White	Floral, stone fruit, rich	Fish, chicken	**
Jean-Luc Colombo Muscat de Rivesettes les Saintes	Rhône Valley	Sweet	Citrus, floral, intense, zingy	Dessert	*
Jean-Paul Thévenet Morgon Cuvée Cielles Vignes	Beaujolais	Red	Berry, spicy, intense	Chicken, fish, pork, pizza	**
Jurançon Bru-Baché L'Eminence (Claude Loustalot)	Landes, Gascogne and Pyrenees/Southwest France	Sweet	Sweet, citrus	Dessert	**
Jurançon Clos Uroulat (Charles Hours)	Landes, Gascogne and Pyrenees/Southwest France	Sweet	Sweet, honey	Fruit	**
Jurançon Dom Bellgarde Cuvée Thibault (Pascal Labasse)	Landes, Gascogne and Pyrenees/Southwest France	White	Citrus, minerally, zingy	Aperitif	**
Jurançon Dom Cauhapé Noblesse du Temps (Henri Ramonteau)	Landes, Gascogne and Pyrenees/Southwest France	Sweet	Sweet, honey	Fruit	**
Jurançon Dom Cauhapé Quintessence du Petit Manseng (Henri Ramonteau)	Landes, Gascogne and Pyrenees/Southwest France	Sweet	Sweet, citrus	Cheese	**
Jurançon Sec Clos Lapeyre (Jean-Bernard Larrieu)	Landes, Gascogne and Pyrenees/Southwest France	White	Zingy, citrus	Shellfish	**
Jurançon Sec Cuvée Marie (Charles Hours)	Landes, Gascogne and Pyrenees/Southwest France	White	Citrus, minerally, zingy	Aperitif	**
Jurançon Sec Dom Bellegarde (Pascal Labasse)	Landes, Gascogne and Pyrenees/Southwest France	White	Citrus, zingy	Aperitif	**
Jurançon Sec Dom Cauhapé Chant des Vignes (Henri Ramonteau)	Landes, Gascogne and Pyrenees/Southwest France	White	Minerally, spicy, citrus	Fish	**
Krug Clos du Mesnil	Champagne	Sparkling	Complex, citrus, yeasty, powerful	Shellfish	***
Krug Grande Cuvée	Champagne	Sparkling	Berry, complex, powerful	Fish	***
Krug Rosé	Champagne	Sparkling	Berry, complex, floral	Lamb	***
Krug Vintage	Champagne	Sparkling	Powerful, complex, berry	Game	***
Kuentz Bas Gewurztraminer Eichberg	Alsace	White	Spicy, minerally, floral	Veal	**
Kuentz Bas Riesling Grand Cru Pfersigberg	Alsace	White	Citrus, floral	Chicken	**
La Vieille Ferme Côtes du Lubéron	Rhône Valley	Red	Berry, spicy	Pizza, chicken	*
Lafarge Beaune Grèves	Beaune/Burgundy	Red	Plums, berry	Duck	**
Lafarge Volnay Clos des Chênes	Volnay/Burgundy	Red	Spicy, earthy	Stew	**
Lafarge Volnay Clos du Château des Ducs	Volnay/Burgundy	Red	Smoky, berry	Pasta	**
Langlois-Château Crémant de Loire Quadrille	Anjou-Saumur/Loire	Sparkling	Fruity, crisp, citrus	Aperitif	**
Latour Puligny Montrachet	Puligny-Montrachet/Burgundy	White	Citrus, smoky	Chicken	**
Laurent-Perrier Grand Siècle Vintage	Champagne	Sparkling	Berry, complex, yeasty	Fish	***
Limoux Dom de l'Aigle Classique (Jean-Louis Denois)	Languedoc	Sparkling	Crisp, citrus, minerally	Aperitif	**
Louis Jadot Château des Jacques Moulin-à-Vent	Beaujolais	Red	Berry, vanillin, complex	Pork, veal, beef	**
Louis Jadot Domaine du Monnet Brouilly	Beaujolais	Red	Berry, spicy, earthy	Pork, veal, beef	**
Louis Roederer Brut Premier NV	Champagne	Sparkling	Berry, citrus, minerally	Antipasto	**
Louis Roederer Cristal	Champagne	Sparkling	Complex, citrus, floral, crisp, elegant	Fish	***
Louis Roederer Cristal Rosé	Champagne	Sparkling	Berry, floral, complex	Lamb	***
Louis Roederer Rosé	Champagne	Sparkling	Floral, berry	Cheese	**
Louis Roederer Vintage	Champagne	Sparkling	Berry, citrus, complex	Fish	**
Maison Guy Saget Pouilly-Fumé Les Logères	Center/Loire	White	Zingy, citrus	Chicken	**
Maison Mollex Roussette de Savoie Seyssel La Taconnière	Savoie	White	Citrus, spicy	Shellfish	**

FRANCE (*Continued*)

Wine name	Region	Style	Flavor/Bouquet	Compatible Foods	Price Range
Maison Trimbach Riesling Clos Saint-Hune	Alsace	White	Citrus, floral, complex	Fish	***
Maison Trimbach Tokay Pinot Gris Réserve Personelle	Alsace	White	Smoky, citrus	Chicken	**
Marc Sorrel Hermitage	Rhône Valley	Red	Berry, rich, oaky	Beef, lamb	**
Martell Cognac	Cognac	Brandy	Spirity, berry, complex	After dinner	***
Mas de Cadenet (Guy Négrel)	Côtes de Provence/Provence	Red	Berry, spicy	Pizza	*
Merlin Macon La Roche Vineuse Vieilles Vignes	Maconnais/Burgundy	White	Minerally, tropical fruit	Mediterranean	**
Meursault Perrières (Comte Lafon)	Meursault/Burgundy	White	Citrus, spicy, minerally	Fish	***
Michel Chapoutier Condrieu	Rhône Valley	White	Floral, stone fruit, complex	Fish, fruits	**
Minervois Clos Centeilles (Patricia Boyer and Daniel Domergue)	Languedoc	Red	Gamey, earthy	Pizza	*
Moet & Chandon Brut NV	Champagne	Sparkling	Berry, earthy, yeasty	Fish	**
Moet & Chandon Dom Perignon	Champagne	Sparkling	Complex, citrus, berry, elegant, powerful	Fish	***
Moet & Chandon Dom Perignon Rosé	Champagne	Sparkling	Floral, berry, powerful, complex	Game	***
Moet & Chandon Rosé	Champagne	Sparkling	Floral, berry	Lamb	**
Moet & Chandon Vintage	Champagne	Sparkling	Berry, toasty, minerally	Chicken	**
Monbazillac Château Tirecul la Gravière (Claudie and Bruno Bilancini)	Bordeaux/Southwest France	Sweet	Sweet, honey	Dessert	**
Muscadet de Sèvre et Maine (Guy Bossard)	Pays Nantais/Loire	White	Minerally, floral, citrus	Shellfish	**
Paul Jaboulet Aîné Hermitage La Chapelle	Rhône Valley	Red	Berry, earthy, rich, complex	Beef, lamb	**
Paul Janin et Fils Moulin-a-Vent	Beaujolais	Red	Berry, powerful, citrus, minerally	Pork, veal, beef	**
Perrier-Jouet Belle-Epoque Rosé	Champagne	Sparkling	Floral, berry, complex	Game	***
Philipponnat Clos des Goisses	Champagne	Sparkling	Berry, complex, powerful, toasty	Duck	***
Philipponnat Vintage	Champagne	Sparkling	Berry, yeasty	Chicken	**
Piper-Heidsieck Vintage	Champagne	Sparkling	Berry, toasty	Chicken	**
Pol Roger Blanc de Chardonnay	Champagne	Sparkling	Citrus, elegant, complex	Aperitif	**
Pol Roger Brut NV (White Foil)	Champagne	Sparkling	Berry, floral, yeasty	Shellfish	**
Pol Roger Cuvée Sir Winston Churchill	Champagne	Sparkling	Powerful, complex, berry, rich	Duck	***
Pol Roger PR	Champagne	Sparkling	Complex, berry, yeasty	Cheese	**
Pol Roger Rosé	Champagne	Sparkling	Berry, floral	Game	**
Pol Roger Vintage	Champagne	Sparkling	Berry, complex, toasty	Fish	**
Pommery Cuvée Louise	Champagne	Sparkling	Complex, citrus, berry, elegant	Fish	***
Pommery Cuvée Louise Rosé	Champagne	Sparkling	Floral, berry, complex	Lamb	***
Pouilly Fuissé (Madame Ferret)	Maconnais/Burgundy	White	Minerally, citrus	Shellfish	**
Pouilly-Fumé Cuvée Majorum (Michel Redde et Fils)	Center/Loire	White	Herbaceous, grassy, citrus	Cheese	**
Pouilly-Fumé Domaine des Riaux (Jeannot Père et Fils)	Center/Loire	White	Citrus, grassy	Fish	**
Pouilly-Fumé Les Griottines (Michel Bailly)	Center/Loire	White	Zingy, grassy	Shellfish	**
Pousse d'Or Santenay Clos des Tavannes	Santenay/Burgundy	Red	Floral, minerally	Pasta	**
Ramonet Bâtard Montrachet	Chassagne Montrachet/ Burgundy	White	Complex, tropical fruit, smoky	Fish	***
Ramonet Chassagne Montrachet Cailleret	Chassagne Montrachet/ Burgundy	White	Spicy, citrus	Pork	**
Ramonet Le Montrachet	Puligny-Montrachet/Burgundy	White	Citrus, smoky, minerally	Chicken	***
Raveneau Chablis Les Clos	Chablis/Burgundy	White	Complex, nutty, minerally	Chicken	***
Rémy Martin Cognac	Cognac	Brandy	Spirity, fiery, earthy	After dinner	***
René Rostaing Condrieu	Rhône Valley	White	Stone fruit, minerally, floral, rich	Fish, fruits	**
René Rostaing Côte-Rôtie Côte Blonde	Rhône Valley	Red	Floral, berry, elegant, intense	Beef, lamb	***
Rolet Père et Fils Arbois Rouge Tradition	Jura	Red	Berry, spicy	Stew	**
Rolet Père et Fils Arbois Trousseau Memorial	Jura	Red	Berry, spicy	Veal	**
Rolet Père et Fils Arbois Vin Jaune	Jura	White	Complex, nutty	Veal	**
Roussette de Savoie Marestel (Noël Dupasquier)	Savoie	White	Zingy, citrus	Fish	**
Ruinart Brut	Champagne	Sparkling	Berry, yeasty	Veal	**
Ruinart Dom Ruinart	Champagne	Sparkling	Berry, citrus, elegant	Fish	***
Ruinart Dom Ruinart Rosé	Champagne	Sparkling	Floral, berry, complex	Lamb	***
Ruinart Vintage	Champagne	Sparkling	Berry, complex, toasty	Fish	**
St-Georges Château St-André Corbin	St-Émilion/Bordeaux	Red	Berry, plums	Cold meats	**
St-Georges Château St-Georges	St-Émilion/Bordeaux	Red	Spicy, herbaceous, plums	Cold meats	**
Southcorp VDP d'Oc James Herrick Chardonnay	Vin de Pays	White	Citrus, tropical fruit	Fish	**
Southcorp VDP d'Oc James Herrick Cuvée Simone	Vin de Pays	White	Tropical fruit, citrus	Veal	**
Taittinger Brut NV	Champagne	Sparkling	Citrus, floral, sweet	Aperitif	**
Taittinger Comtes de Champagne	Champagne	Sparkling	Citrus, floral, complex, powerful	Shellfish	***
Taittinger Comtes de Champagne Rosé	Champagne	Sparkling	Berry, complex, powerful	Duck	***
Taittinger Vintage	Champagne	Sparkling	Citrus, elegant, floral	Fish	**
Tardieu Laurent Comes Vieilles Vignes	Rhône Valley	Red	Floral, berry, mushroom, rich	Beef, lamb	**
Thevenet Macon Clessé Cuvée Levroutée	Maconnais/Burgundy	White	Minerally, mandarin	Pasta	**
VDP d'Oc Domaine de la Baume Syrah Tête de Cuvée (Hardy Wine Compant)	Vin de Pays	Red	Earthy, spicy	Pasta	**
VDP Herault Mas de Daumas Gassac (red) (Aimé Guibert)	Vin de Pays	Red	Berry, spicy, complex, tannic	Beef	***
VDP Herault Mas de Daumas Gassac (white)	Vin de Pays	White	Zingy, citrus, minerally	Fish	***
VDP Jardin de la France Dom de Bablut Chardonnay (Christophe Daviau)	Vin de Pays	White	Tropical fruit, melon	Fish	*
VDP Jardin de la France Michel Robineau Sauvignon	Vin de Pays	White	Berry, herbaceous	Shellfish	*

FRANCE (*Continued*)

Wine name	Region	Style	Flavor/Bouquet	Compatible Foods	Price Range
VDP Jardin de la France Rémy Pannier Chenin Blanc	Vin de Pays	White	Melon, apples	Aperitif	*
Veuve Clicquot Brut	Champagne	Sparkling	Berry, yeasty	Shellfish	**
Veuve Clicquot La Grande Dame	Champagne	Sparkling	Berry, complex, minerally	Game	***
Veuve Clicquot La Grande Dame Rosé	Champagne	Sparkling	Berry, powerful, floral, rich	Lamb	***
Veuve Clicquot Vintage	Champagne	Sparkling	Berry, toasty, complex	Fish	**
Vieux Château Certan	Pomerol/Bordeaux	Red	Herbaceous, berry, spicy, minerally, tannic	Beef	***
Vieux Château Champs de Mars	Côtes de Castillon/Bordeaux	Red	Spicy, plums	Pasta	**
Vieux Château Gaubert	Graves/Bordeaux	White	Citrus, minerally	Fish	**
Vieux Télégraphe Châteauneuf-du-Pape	Rhône Valley	Red	Berry, herbaceous, spicy, rich	Beef, lamb	**
Vignerons de Buzet Buzet Château de Gueyze	Bordeaux/Southwest France	Red	Earthy, berry	Sausages	*
Villa Bel Air	Graves/Bordeaux	White	Citrus, herbaceous, vanillin	Fish, chicken	**
Vouvray Cuvée Tries de Vendange (Didier Champalou)	Touraine/Loire	White	Citrus, crispy, minerally	Chicken	**
Vouvray La Cabane Noire (Thierry Cosme)	Touraine/Loire	White	Minerally, apples, citrus	Fish	**
Yves and Matilde Gangloff Côte-Rôtie Vieilles Vignes	Rhône Valley	Red	Berry, peppery, earthy, complex	Beef, lamb	**
Yves Cuilleron Condrieu les Ayguets	Rhône Valley	White	Stone fruit, minerally, rich	Fish, fruits	**
Yves Cuilleron Condrieu les Chaillets Vieilles Vignes	Rhône Valley	White	Stone fruit, rich, floral, complex	Fish, fruits	**
Yves Guilleron Côte-Rôtie "Bassenon"	Rhône Valley	Red	Intense, earthy, minerally	Beef, lamb	**

GERMANY

Wine name	Region	Style	Flavor/Bouquet	Compatible Foods	Price Range
Adelmann Cuvée Vignette Tafelwein	Württemberg	Red	Berry, spicy	Pizza	**
Allendorf Winkeler Jesuitengarten Riesling Kabinett	Rheingau	White	Spicy, minerally	Fish	**
Bacharacher Posten Riesling Auslese (Karl Heidrich)	Mittelrhein	White	Sweet, honey	Dessert	**
Balbach Niersteiner Hipping Riesling Auslese	Rheinhessen	Sweet	Sweet, citrus	Dessert	**
Balbach Niersteiner Pettental Riesling Kabinett	Rheinhessen	White	Apples, minerally	Veal	**
Bassermann-Jordan Forster Jesuitengarten Riesling Kabinett	Pfalz	White	Minerally, floral	Fish	**
Bassermann-Jordan Forster Jesuitengarten Riesling Spätlese	Pfalz	White	Sweet, floral	Asian	**
Bassermann-Jordan Forster Ungeheuer Riesling Eiswein	Pfalz	Sweet	Mandarin, honey, sweet	Dessert	***
Bassermann-Jordan Ruppertsberger Reiterpfad Riesling TBA	Pfalz	Sweet	Complex, sweet, mandarin	Dessert	***
Bercher Chardonnay Spätlese Trocken SE	Baden	White	Melon, smoky	Veal	**
Bercher-Schmidt Oberrotweiler Käsleberg Weisser Burgunder Spätlese Trocken	Baden	White	Floral, spicy	Pasta	**
Bernkasteler Doctor Riesling Auslese (J. Wegeler Erben)	Mosel-Saar-Ruwer	White	Sweet, minerally, floral	Dessert	**
Biffar Deidesheimer Kieselberg Riesling Auslese	Pfalz	White	Sweet, citrus, floral	Dessert	**
Biffar Deidesheimer Mäushöhle Riesling Eiswein	Pfalz	Sweet	Complex, sweet, mandarin	Dessert	***
Biffar Wachenheimer Goldbächel Riesling Spätlese	Pfalz	White	Sweet, floral	Fish	**
Boppарder Hamm Ohlenberg Riesling Kabinett (August Perll)	Mittelrhein	White	Zingy, citrus	Fish	**
Brauneberger Juffer-Sonnenuhr Riesling Kabinett (Fritz Haag)	Mosel-Saar-Ruwer	White	Floral, zingy	Fish	**
Breuer Rauenthaler Nonnenberg Riesling Erstes Gewächs	Rheingau	White	Citrus, floral	Fish	**
Breuer Riesling Brut	Rheingau	Sparkling	Crisp, fruity	Aperitif	**
Breuer Rüdesheimer Berg Schlossberg Riesling Erstes Gewächs	Rheingau	White	Citrus, floral	Fish	**
Breuer Rüdesheimer Bischofsberg Riesling TBA	Rheingau	Sweet	Sweet, honey	Dessert	***
Bürgerspital Randersackerer Pfülben Rieslaner Beerenauslese	Franken	Sweet	Floral, sweet, minerally	Dessert	***
Bürgerspital Würzburger Stein Riesling Spätlese	Franken	White	Sweet, citrus	Asian	**
Bürgerspital Würzburger Stein Riesling TBA	Franken	Sweet	Complex, honey, sweet	Dessert	***
Castell Casteller Kugelspiel Rieslaner Beerenauslese	Franken	Sweet	Sweet, honey	Dessert	***
Castell Casteller Kugelspiel Silvaner Eiswein	Franken	Sweet	Sweet, mandarin	Dessert	***
Castell Casteller Schlossberg Silvaner Spätlese Trocken	Franken	White	Citrus, minerally, floral	Veal	**
Christmann Deidesheimer Hohenmorgen Riesling Beerenauslese	Pfalz	Sweet	Mandarin, sweet, complex	Dessert	***
Christmann Ruppertsberger Reiterpfad Riesling Spätlese Trocken	Pfalz	White	Citrus, floral	Chicken	**
Christmann Ruppertsberger Reiterpfad Riesling TBA	Pfalz	Sweet	Mandarin, sweet, citrus	Dessert	***
Clüsserath-Weiler Trittenheimer Apotheke Riesling Spätlese	Mosel-Saar-Ruwer	White	Sweet, citrus, minerally	Cheese	**
Crusius Traiser Bastei Riesling Spätlese	Nahe	White	Sweet, floral	Cheese	**
Crusius Traiser Rotenfels Riesling Auslese	Nahe	White	Sweet, citrus, mandarin	Dessert	**
Crusius Traiser Rotenfels Riesling Spätlese Trocken	Nahe	White	Sweet, floral	Fish	**
Darting Dürkheimer Fronhof Scheurebe TBA	Pfalz	Sweet	Sweet, mandarin	Dessert	***
Darting Ungsteiner Herrenberg Riesling Auslese	Pfalz	White	Sweet, citrus	Dessert	**
Dautel Kreation Tafelwein	Württemberg	Red	Berry, smoky	Cold meats, stew, offal	**
Dautel Chardonnay Trocken	Württemberg	White	Melon, spicy	Pizza	**
Deinhard Ruppertsberger Reiterpfad Riesling Eiswein	Pfalz	Sweet	Sweet, mandarin	Dessert	***
Deutzerhof Spätburgunder Auslese Trocken Grand Duc Select	Ahr	Red	Berry, spicy	Pasta	**
Domdechant Werner Hochheimer Domdechaney Riesling Spätlese	Rheingau	White	Citrus, floral	Cheese	**
Dönnhoff Niederhäuser Hermannshöhle Riesling Spätlese	Nahe	White	Sweet, floral	Asian	**

GERMANY (*Continued*)

Wine name	Region	Style	Flavor/Bouquet	Compatible Foods	Price Range
Dönnhoff Niederhäuser Hermannshöhle Riesling Spätlese Trocken	Nahe	White	Floral, apples	Chicken	**
Dönnhoff Oberhäuser Brücke Riesling Eiswein	Nahe	Sweet	Honey, sweet, complex	Dessert	***
Dönnhoff Weisser Burgunder Spätlese Trocken	Nahe	White	Citrus, melon	Chicken	**
Dr Heger Achkarrer Schlossberg Grauer Burgunder Spätlese Trocken	Baden	White	Melon, apples	Veal	**
Dr Heger Achkarrer Schlossberg Silvaner Spätlese Trocken	Baden	White	Citrus, floral	Fish	**
Dr Heger Ihringer Winklerberg Muskateller TBA	Baden	Sweet	Mandarin, sweet, honey	Dessert	***
Dr Heger Ihringer Winklerberg Riesling Auslese	Baden	White	Sweet, honey	Dessert	**
Dr Heger Ihringer Winklerberg Riesling Beerenauslese	Baden	Sweet	Complex, sweet, mandarin	Dessert	***
Dr Loosen Erdener Prälat Riesling Auslese	Mosel-Saar-Ruwer	White	Sweet, minerally, citrus	Dessert	**
Dr Loosen Erdener Treppchen Riesling Spätlese	Mosel-Saar-Ruwer	White	Sweet, zingy, smoky	Fruit	**
Dr Loosen Urziger Würzgarten Riesling TBA	Mosel-Saar-Ruwer	Sweet	Minerally, complex, sweet	Dessert	***
Dr Loosen Wehlener Sonnenuhr Riesling Kabinett	Mosel-Saar-Ruwer	White	Apples, minerally, citrus	Chicken	**
Durbacher Winzergenossenschaft Durbacher Plauelrain Riesling Auslese	Baden	White	Honey, sweet, citrus	Dessert	**
Durbacher Winzergenossenschaft Durbacher Plauelrain Riesling Auslese Trocken	Baden	White	Floral, minerally	Dessert	**
Egon Müller Scharzhofberger Riesling Auslese	Mosel-Saar-Ruwer	White	Sweet, apples, minerally	Dessert	***
Egon Müller Scharzhofberger Riesling Eiswein	Mosel-Saar-Ruwer	Sweet	Complex, honey, sweet, minerally	Dessert	***
Egon Müller Scharzhofberger Riesling TBA	Mosel-Saar-Ruwer	Sweet	Complex, mandarin, sweet	Dessert	***
Emrich-Schönleber Monzinger Frühlingsplätzchen Riesling Auslese	Nahe	White	Sweet, floral	Dessert	**
F. Becker Schweigener Sonnenberg Riesling Spätlese	Pfalz	White	Sweet, citrus	Cheese	**
F. Becker Spätburgunder Tafelwein Trocken Reserve	Pfalz	Red	Berry, earthy	Cold meats, stew, offal	**
Forster Kirchenstück Riesling Auslese Trocken (Eugen Müller)	Pfalz	White	Citrus, spicy, floral	Fish	**
Forster Stift Riesling Eiswein (Eugen Müller)	Pfalz	Sweet	Sweet, mandarin	Dessert	***
Forster Ungeheuer Riesling Auslese Trocken (J.L. Wolf)	Pfalz	White	Citrus, spicy	Chicken	**
Fürst Bürgstadter Centgrafenberg Rieslaner Beerenauslese	Franken	Sweet	Mandarin, sweet, honey	Dessert	***
Fürst Burgstadter Centgrafenberg Riesling Spätlese Trocken	Franken	White	Citrus, floral	Fish	**
Fürst Bürgstadter Centgrafenberg Spätburgunder Trocken	Franken	Red	Spicy, berry, gamey	Cold meats, stew, offal	**
Fürst Bürgstadter Centgrafenberg Weisser Burgunder Spätlese Trocken	Franken	White	Melon, floral	Fish	**
Göttelmann Münsterer Rheinberg Riesling Spätlese	Nahe	White	Sweet, citrus	Fruit	**
Graacher Himmelreich Riesling Kabinett (Willi Schaeffer)	Mosel-Saar-Ruwer	White	Crisp, minerally, apples	Fish	**
Graacher Himmelreich Riesling Spätlese (J. J. Prüm)	Mosel-Saar-Ruwer	White	Floral, minerally, sweet	Cheese	**
Grans-Fassian Trittenheimer Apotheke Riesling Beerenauslese	Mosel-Saar-Ruwer	Sweet	Apples, honey, sweet	Dessert	***
Gutsverwaltung Niederhausen-Schlossböckelheim Niederhäuser Hermannsberg Riesling Eiswein	Nahe	Sweet	Sweet, mandarin	Dessert	***
Gutsverwaltung Niederhäuser Hermannshöhle Riesling Beerenauslese	Nahe	Sweet	Sweet, honey	Dessert	***
Gutsverwaltung Schlossböckelheimer Kupfergrube Riesling Spätlese	Nahe	White	Sweet, floral	Fish	**
Haidle Schnaiter Burghalde Spätburgunder Auslese Trocken	Württemberg	Red	Berry, game	Cold meats, stew, offal	**
Heyl zu Herrnsheim Niersteiner Pettental Riesling Auslese	Rheinhessen	Sweet	Minerally, sweet, citrus	Dessert	**
Heymann-Löwenstein Winninger Uhlen Riesling TBA	Mosel-Saar-Ruwer	Sweet	Complex, sweet, mandarin	Dessert	***
Hoensbroech Michelfelder Himmelberg Weisser Burgunder Spätlese Trocken	Baden	White	Citrus, minerally	Fish	**
Huber Chardonnay Trocken	Baden	White	Melon, citrus	Fish	**
Huber Malterer White	Baden	White	Melon, fruity	Pizza	**
Huber Spätburgunder Trocken Reserve	Baden	Red	Earthy, smoky	Game	**
J. Wegeler Erben Oestricher Lenchen Riesling TBA	Rheingau	Sweet	Complex, sweet, mandarin	Dessert	***
Johannishof Johannisberger Goldatzel Riesling Kabinett	Rheingau	White	Minerally, smoky, citrus	Veal	**
Johannishof Rüdesheimer Berg Rottland Riesling Auslese	Rheingau	White	Sweet, citrus, floral	Dessert	**
Johner Blauer Spätburgunder Trocken (S. J. Johner)	Baden	Red	Berry, spicy	Pasta	**
Johner Chardonnay Tafelwein	Baden	White	Fruity, citrus	Pasta	**
Johner Grauer Burgunder Tafelwein Trocken	Baden	White	Fruity, citrus	Pasta	**
Jost Bacharacher Hahn Riesling Auslese	Mittelrhein	White	Sweet, minerally	Dessert	**
Jost Bacharacher Hahn Riesling Kabinett	Mittelrhein	White	Zingy, minerally	Fish	**
Jost Bacharacher Hahn Riesling TBA	Mittelrhein	Sweet	Minerally, sweet, complex	Dessert	***
Juliusspital Randersackerer Pfülben Rieslaner Auslese	Franken	White	Sweet, minerally	Dessert	**
Juliusspital Würzburger Stein Riesling Beerenauslese	Franken	Sweet	Sweet, mandarin	Dessert	***
Juliusspital Würzburger Stein Riesling Spätlese Trocken	Franken	White	Minerally, floral	Chicken	**
Keller Dalsheimer Hubacker Riesling TBA	Rheinhessen	Sweet	Complex, sweet, mandarin	Dessert	***

GERMANY *(Continued)*

Wine name	Region	Style	Flavor/Bouquet	Compatible Foods	Price Range
Kesseler Assmannshäuser Höllenberg Spätburgunder Spätlese Trocken	Rheingau	Red	Spicy, gamey, berry	Cold meats, stew, offal	**
Kesseler Rüdesheimer Berg Rottland Riesling Spätlese	Rheingau	White	Sweet, citrus	Cheese	**
Kesseler Rüdesheimer Bischofsberg Riesling TBA	Rheingau	Sweet	Complex, sweet, honey	Dessert	***
Kesselstatt Josephshöfer Riesling Spätlese	Mosel-Saar-Ruwer	White	Sweet, floral	Chicken	**
Knipser Grauer Burgunder Tafelwein Trocken	Pfalz	White	Melon, citrus	Pizza	**
Knipser Grosskarlbacher Burgweg Spätburgunder Auslese Trocken	Pfalz	Red	Berry, spicy	Game	**
Knyphausen Erbacher Siegelsberg Riesling Eiswein	Rheingau	Sweet	Mandarin, citrus, sweet	Dessert	***
Knyphausen Kiedricher Sandgrub Riesling Spätlese	Rheingau	White	Sweet, citrus	Asian	**
Koehler-Ruprecht Grauer Burgunder Tafelwein Trocken	Pfalz	White	Fruity, melon	Chicken	**
Koehler-Ruprecht Kallstadter Saumagen Riesling Beerenauslese	Pfalz	Sweet	Honey, sweet, complex	Dessert	***
Koehler-Ruprecht Kallstadter Saumagen Riesling Spätlese	Pfalz	White	Sweet, apples, citrus	Fish	**
Koehler-Ruprecht Pinot Blanc Brut Philippi	Pfalz	Sparkling	Minerally, fruity, crisp	Aperitif	**
Königswingert Guldentaler Hipperich Riesling Spätlese Trocken	Nahe	White	Apples, minerally, floral	Veal	**
Kreuznacher Brückes Riesling Auslese (Paul Anheuser)	Nahe	White	Sweet, floral, minerally	Dessert	**
Krone Assmannshäuser Höllenberg Spätburgunder Spätlese	Rheingau	Red	Berry, spicy	Pork	**
Kruger-Rumpf Münsterer Dautenpflänzer Riesling Auslese	Nahe	White	Citrus, sweet	Dessert	**
Künstler Hochheimer Kirchenstück Riesling Spätlese	Rheingau	White	Sweet, citrus, floral	Asian	**
Laible Durbacher Plauelrain Riesling Eiswein	Baden	Sweet	Mandarin, honey, sweet	Dessert	***
Laible Durbacher Plauelrain Riesling Spätlese Trocken	Baden	White	Floral, citrus	Fish	**
Lämmlin-Schindler Chardonnay Spätlese Trocken	Baden	White	Citrus, melon	Fish	**
Le Gallais Wiltinger Braune Kupp Riesling Auslese	Mosel-Saar-Ruwer	White	Sweet, minerally, apples	Dessert	**
Leitz Rüdesheimer Berg Rottland Riesling Auslese	Rheingau	White	Floral, sweet	Dessert	**
Leitz Rüdesheimer Berg Rottland Riesling Auslese Trocken	Rheingau	White	Citrus, minerally, floral	Veal	**
Lindenhof Weisser Burgunder Brut	Nahe	Sparkling	Crisp, fruity	Aperitif	**
Löwenstein Homburger Kallmuth Silvaner Spätlese Trocken	Franken	White	Apples, citrus	Fish	**
Mathern Niederhäuser Rosenberg Riesling Auslese	Nahe	White	Sweet, floral	Dessert	**
Mathern Niederhäuser Rosenheck Riesling Spätlese Halbtrocken	Nahe	White	Floral, citrus	Fish	**
Maximin Grünhäuser Abtsberg Riesling Eiswein (Maximin Grünhaus)	Mosel-Saar-Ruwer	Sweet	Sweet, mandarin	Dessert	***
Maximin Grünhäuser Abtsberg Riesling Kabinett (Maximin Grünhaus)	Mosel-Saar-Ruwer	White	Minerally, apples, floral	Fish	**
Maximin Grünhäuser Herrenberg Riesling Spätlese (Maximin Grünhaus)	Mosel-Saar-Ruwer	White	Sweet, floral, citrus	Cheese	**
Messmer Burrweiler Schlossgarten Weisser Burgunder Spätlese Trocken Selection	Pfalz	White	Minerally, citrus	Chicken	**
Michel-Pfannebecker Flomborner Feuerberg Scheurebe Eiswein	Rheinhessen	Sweet	Mandarin, sweet	Dessert	***
Milz-Laurentiushof Neumagener Nusswingert Riesling Spätlese	Mosel-Saar-Ruwer	White	Sweet, minerally, smoky	Chicken	**
Mosbacher Forster Freundstück Riesling Eiswein	Pfalz	Sweet	Smoky, sweet, mandarin	Dessert	***
Mosbacher Forster Pechstein Riesling Auslese	Pfalz	White	Sweet, minerally	Dessert	**
Mosbacher Forster Ungeheuer Riesling Spätlese Trocken	Pfalz	White	Citrus, apples	Pork	**
Mülheimer Helenenkloster Riesling Eiswein (Max. Ferd. Richter)	Mosel-Saar-Ruwer	Sweet	Sweet, honey	Dessert	***
Müller-Catoir Haardter Bürgergarten Riesling Eiswein	Pfalz	Sweet	Minerally, sweet, floral	Dessert	***
Müller-Catoir Haardter Mandelring Scheurebe Eiswein	Pfalz	Sweet	Mandarin, sweet	Dessert	***
Müller-Catoir Mussbacher Eselshaut Rieslaner Auslese	Pfalz	White	Sweet, apples, honey	Dessert	**
Nägler Rüdesheimer Berg Roseneck Riesling Kabinett	Rheingau	White	Austere, minerally, citrus	Veal	**
Neipperg Neipperger Schlossberg Lemberger Trocken	Württemberg	Red	Berry, spicy	Game	**
Neipperg Schwaigerner Ruthe Riesling Spätlese Trocken	Württemberg	White	Citrus, floral	Chicken	**
Nelles Spätburgunder Trocken B52	Ahr	Red	Spicy, berry	Game	**
Nelles Spätburgunder Trocken Futura	Ahr	Red	Berry, earthy	Game	**
Niederhäuser Hermannshöhle Riesling Spätlese Trocken (Jakob Schneider)	Nahe	White	Citrus, apples	Chicken	**
Niersteiner Hipping Riesling Spätlese (Franz Karl Schmitt)	Rheinhessen	White	Sweet, floral	Dessert	**
Ockfener Bockstein Riesling Spätlese (Heinz Wagner)	Mosel-Saar-Ruwer	White	Sweet, floral	Fish	**
Oestricher Lenchen Riesling Auslese (J. Wegeler Erben)	Rheingau	White	Sweet, citrus, floral	Dessert	**
Oestricher Lenchen Riesling Eiswein (August Eser)	Rheingau	Sweet	Complex, mandarin, sweet	Dessert	***
P. J. Kuhn Riesling Eiswein	Rheingau	Sweet	Minerally, sweet, honey	Dessert	***
Pauly-Bergweiler Bernkasteler Alte Badstube am Doctorberg Riesling TBA	Mosel-Saar-Ruwer	Sweet	Honey, sweet, complex	Dessert	***
Pauly-Bergweiler Urziger Würzgarten Riesling TBA	Mosel-Saar-Ruwer	Sweet	Complex, honey, sweet	Dessert	***
Pfeffingen Ungsteiner Herrenberg Riesling Spätlese	Pfalz	White	Sweet, floral	Asian	**
Pfeffingen Ungsteiner Herrenberg Scheurebe Beerenauslese	Pfalz	Sweet	Mandarin, sweet	Dessert	***
Pfeffingen Ungsteiner Herrenberg Scheurebe Spätlese	Pfalz	White	Sweet, floral	Asian	**

GERMANY (*Continued*)

Wine name	Region	Style	Flavor/Bouquet	Compatible Foods	Price Range
Piesporter Goldtröpfchen Riesling Spätlese (Kurt Hain)	Mosel-Saar-Ruwer	White	Floral, minerally, citrus	Fish	**
Prinz zu Salm-Dalberg Wallhäuser Johannisberg Riesling Spätlese	Nahe	White	Sweet, floral	Fruit	**
R. Rebholz Spätburgunder Spätlese Trocken	Pfalz	Red	Berry, spicy	Pasta	**
Ratzenberger Steeger Sankt Jost Riesling Auslese	Mittelrhein	White	Sweet, mandarin, minerally	Dessert	**
Rebholz Chardonnay Spätlese Trocken R	Pfalz	White	Floral, spicy	Fish	**
Rebholz Siebeldinger im Sonnenschein Riesling Spätlese Trocken	Pfalz	White	Floral, minerally	Cold meats, stew, offal	**
Reinhold Haart Wintricher Ohligsberg Riesling Spätlese	Mosel-Saar-Ruwer	White	Sweet, floral	Asian	**
Ress Oestricher Doosberger TBA	Rheingau	Sweet	Complex, sweet, honey	Dessert	***
Ruck Iphofer Julius-Echter-Berg Scheurebe Spätlese Trocken	Franken	White	Floral, citrus	Veal	**
Ruck Iphofer Julius-Echter-Berg Silvaner Kabinett Trocken	Franken	White	Floral, minerally	Aperitif	**
Salwey Oberrotweiler Henkenberg Grauer Burgunder Spätlese Trocken Alte Reben	Baden	White	Citrus, floral, spicy	Fish	**
Salwey Oberrotweiler Kirchberg Riesling Spätlese Trocken	Baden	White	Floral, citrus	Cheese	**
Sankt Antony Niersteiner Auglangen Riesling Spätlese	Rheinhessen	White	Sweet, citrus	Fruit	**
Sauer Erschendorfer Lump Riesling Beerenauslese	Franken	Sweet	Sweet, honey	Dessert	***
Schaefer Wachenheimer Gerümpel Riesling Spätlese Trocken	Pfalz	White	Spicy, floral	Chicken	**
Schales Rieslaner Auslese	Rheinhessen	White	Sweet, citrus	Dessert	**
Schloss Johannisberger Riesling Auslese	Rheingau	White	Minerally, sweet, citrus, floral	Dessert	**
Schloss Johannisberger Riesling Beerenauslese	Rheingau	Sweet	Complex, honey, sweet	Dessert	***
Schloss Neuweier Neuweierer Mauerberg Riesling Spätlese Trocken Alte Reben	Baden	White	Floral, minerally	Cheese	**
Schloss Reinhartshausen Erbacher Siegelsberg Riesling Beerenauslese	Rheingau	Sweet	Mandarin, sweet, complex	Dessert	***
Schloss Saarstein Serriger Schloss Saarstein Riesling Spätlese	Mosel-Saar-Ruwer	White	Sweet, citrus, minerally	Fish	**
Schloss Sommerhausen Sommerhäuser Reifenstein Scheurebe Eiswein	Franken	Sweet	Sweet, mandarin	Dessert	***
Schloss Sommerhausen Sommerhäuser Steinbach Rieslaner TBA	Franken	Sweet	Complex, sweet, minerally	Dessert	***
Schloss Sommerhausen Sommerhäuser Steinbach Riesling Spätlese Trocken	Franken	White	Floral, citrus	Chicken	**
Schlumberger Weisser Burgunder Spätlese Trocken	Baden	White	Citrus, floral	Chicken	**
Schmidt Obermoscheler Schlossberg Riesling Kabinett	Nahe	White	Minerally, apples	Shellfish	**
Schmitt's Kinder Randersackerer Pfülben Riesling Auslese	Franken	Sweet	Honey, mandarin, sweet	Dessert	**
Schmitt's Kinder Randersackerer Pfülben Riesling Kabinett	Franken	White	Zingy, minerally	Fruit	**
Schmitt's Kinder Randersackerer Sonnenstuhl Rieslaner Beerenauslese	Franken	Sweet	Sweet, honey	Dessert	***
Selbach-Oster Zeltinger Sonnenuhr Riesling Spätlese	Mosel-Saar-Ruwer	White	Floral, sweet	Fruit	**
Selbach-Oster Zeltinger Sonnenuhr Riesling TBA	Mosel-Saar-Ruwer	Sweet	Complex, sweet, honey	Dessert	***
Staatlicher Hofkeller Würzburger Stein Riesling Auslese	Franken	White	Honey, sweet	Dessert	**
Staatlicher Hofkeller Würzburger Stein Silvaner Spätlese Trocken	Franken	White	Floral, minerally	Chicken	**
von Buhl Forster Jesuitengarten Riesling Eiswein	Pfalz	Sweet	Complex, sweet, minerally	Dessert	***
von Buhl Forster Ungeheuer Riesling Auslese	Pfalz	White	Sweet, minerally, floral	Dessert	**
von Buhl Forster Ungeheuer Riesling TBA	Pfalz	Sweet	Mandarin, sweet, honey	Dessert	***
von Buhl Ruppertsberger Reiterpfad Riesling Spätlese Trocken	Pfalz	White	Floral, minerally	Chicken	**
von Kanitz Lorcher Krone Riesling Spätlese	Rheingau	White	Floral, citrus	Cheese	**
Wachenheimer Gerümpel Riesling Spätlese (J. L. Wolf)	Pfalz	White	Sweet, minerally, apples	Fruit	**
Wallufer Walkenberg Riesling Spätlese Trocken (J. B. Becker)	Rheingau	White	Spicy, citrus	Chicken	**
Wallufer Walkenberg Riesling Spätlese Trocken (Toni Jost)	Rheingau	White	Floral, minerally	Chicken	**
Wehlener Sonnenuhr Riesling Auslese (J. J. Prüm)	Mosel-Saar-Ruwer	White	Sweet, minerally, apples	Dessert	***
Wehlener Sonnenuhr Riesling Auslese (S. A. Prüm)	Mosel-Saar-Ruwer	White	Sweet, citrus, minerally	Dessert	**
Wehlener Sonnenuhr Riesling Kabinett (S. A. Prüm)	Mosel-Saar-Ruwer	White	Minerally, apples	Veal	**
Weil Kiedricher Gräfenberg Riesling Auslese	Rheingau	White	Citrus, floral, sweet	Dessert	**
Weil Kiedricher Gräfenberg Riesling Eiswein	Rheingau	Sweet	Honey, sweet	Dessert	***
Weil Kiedricher Gräfenberg Riesling TBA	Rheingau	Sweet	Complex, sweet, mandarin	Dessert	***
Weins-Prüm Erdener Prälat Riesling Auslese	Mosel-Saar-Ruwer	White	Minerally, floral, sweet	Dessert	**
Weins-Prüm Wehlener Sonnenuhr Riesling Kabinett	Mosel-Saar-Ruwer	White	Citrus, minerally	Fish	**
Winzergenossenschaft Achkarren Achkarrer Schlossberg Grauer Burgunder Spätlese Trocken	Baden	White	Melon, smoky	Chicken	**
Winzergenossenschaft Alde Gott Sasbachwaldener Alde Gott Grauer Burgunder Spätlese Trocken	Baden	White	Minerally, melon	Fish	**
Winzergenossenschaft Alde Gott Sasbachwaldener Alde Gott Spätburgunder Burgunder Spätlese Trocken	Baden	White	Minerally, melon	Fish	**
Winzergenossenschaft Bischoffingen Bischoffinger Rosenkrantz Weisser Burgunder TBA	Baden	Sweet	Mandarin, sweet, honey	Dessert	***
Winzergenossenschaft Bischoffingen Bischoffinger Steinbuck Ruländer Auslese	Baden	White	Mandarin, sweet, citrus	Dessert	**

GERMANY *(Continued)*

Wine name	Region	Style	Flavor/Bouquet	Compatible Foods	Price Range
Winzergenossenschaft Britzingen Britzinger Sonnhole Grauer Burgunder Spätlese Trocken	Baden	White	Citrus, melon	Pork	**
Winzergenossenschaft Britzingen Britzinger Sonnhole Ruländer Beerenauslese	Baden	Sweet	Honey, sweet	Dessert	***
Winzergenossenschaft Königschaffhausen Königschaffhauser Hasenberg Ruländer TBA	Baden	Sweet	Sweet	Dessert	***
Winzergenossenschaft Königschaffhausen Königschaffhauser Steingrüble Spätburgunder Trocken Selection	Baden	Red	Gamey, spicy, berry	Fish	**
Winzergenossenschaft Pfaffenweiler Oberdürrenberg Grauer Burgunder Spätlese Trocken Primus	Baden	White	Citrus, minerally, spicy	Fish	**
Winzergenossenschaft Pfaffenweiler Oberdürrenberg Ruländer Eiswein	Baden	Sweet	Mandarin, sweet	Dessert	***
Wirsching Iphöfer Kronsberg Riesling Spätlese	Franken	White	Citrus, sweet	Fish	**
Wwe. H. Thanisch–Erben Thanisch Bernkasteler Badstube Riesling Kabinett	Mosel-Saar-Ruwer	White	Zingy, austere, minerally	Fish	**
Wwe. H. Thanisch–Erben Thanisch Bernkasteler Doctor Riesling Auslese	Mosel-Saar-Ruwer	Sweet	Honey, minerally, sweet, complex	Dessert	***
Zeltinger Sonnenuhr Riesling Auslese (J. J. Prüm)	Mosel-Saar-Ruwer	White	Sweet, minerally, citrus	Dessert	***
Zilliken Saarburger Rausch Riesling Eiswein	Mosel-Saar-Ruwer	Sweet	Mandarin, sweet, complex	Dessert	***
Zilliken Saarburger Rausch Riesling Spätlese	Mosel-Saar-Ruwer	White	Sweet, minerally	Asian	**

AUSTRIA

Wine name	Region	Style	Flavor/Bouquet	Compatible Foods	Price Range
Alzinger Steinertal Riesling	Wachau	White	Spicy, floral	Fish	**
Emmerich Knoll Schütt Riesling	Wachau	White	Floral, minerally	Fish	**
Ernst Triebaumer Marienthal Blaufränkisch	Neusiedlersee-Hügelland	Red	Earthy, tannic, oaky	Stew	**
F. X. Pichler Kellerberg Grüner Veltliner	Wachau	White	Floral, citrus	Fish	**
F. X. Pichler Kellerberg Riesling	Wachau	White	Minerally, citrus	Fish	**
F. X. Pichler Loibner Berg Grüner Veltliner	Wachau	White	Citrus, spicy, floral	Chicken	**
F. X. Pichler Steinertal Riesling	Wachau	White	Floral, citrus	Fish	**
Fritsch Perfektion Grüner Veltliner	Donauland	White	Crisp, citrus	Veal	**
Fritz Wieninger Grand Select Chardonnay	Vienna	White	Citrus, spicy, oaky	Chicken	**
Heidi Schröck Ausbruch	Neusiedlersee-Hügelland	Sweet	Sweet, rich	Dessert	***
Hiedler Spiegel Weissburgunder	Kamptal	White	Citrus, fruity	Pork	**
Karl Alphart Spätrot-Rotgipfler	Thermenregion	White	Floral, spicy	Fish	**
Kollwentz Tatschler Chardonnay	Neusiedlersee-Hügelland	White	Melon, oaky	Chicken	**
Lackner-Tinnacher Grauburgunder	South Styria	White	Spicy, citrus	Veal	**
Lagler Vordersieber Grüner Veltliner	Wachau	White	Spicy, complex, floral	Chicken	**
Lang Scheurebe Trockenbeerenauslese und Eiswein	Neusiedlersee	Sweet	Sweet, honey	Dessert	***
Mantlerhof Reisenthal Roter Veltliner	Kremstal	White	Citrus, minerally	Veal	**
Neumayer Weissburgunder	Traisental	White	Spicy, fruity	Veal	**
Nigl Riesling: Piri	Kremstal	White	Floral, citrus	Mediterranean	**
Polz Grassnitzberg Weissburgunder	South Styria	White	Minerally, spicy	Chicken	**
Polz Hochgrassnitzberg Morillon	South Styria	White	Floral, citrus	Fish	**
Polz Hochgrassnitzberg Sauvignon Blanc	South Styria	White	Grassy, crisp	Shellfish	**
Prieler Blaufränkisch	Neusiedlersee-Hügelland	White	Citrus, minerally	Fish	**
Reinisch Reserve Blauburgunder	Thermenregion	Red	Berry, earthy	Duck	**
Retzl Bergjuwel Riesling	Kamptal	White	Floral, minerally	Salads	**
Saahs Steiner Hund Riesling	Wachau	White	Citrus, minerally	Salads	**
Sepp Moser Gebling Chardonnay	Kremstal	White	Melon, citrus	Pork	**
Taubenschuss Weisser Berg Weissburgunder	Weinviertel	White	Spicy, citrus	Veal	**
Tement Grassnitzberg Weissburgunder	South Styria	White	Citrus, minerally	Fish	**
Willi Bründlmayer Chardonnay	Kamptal	White	Tropical fruit, melon	Chicken	**
Willi Bründlmayer Grüner Veltliner: Ried Lamm	Kamptal	White	Citrus, melon	Veal	**
Willi Bründlmayer Riesling: Zöbinger Heiligenstein	Kamptal	White	Floral, minerally	Shellfish	**
Wohlmuth Muskateller	South Styria	White	Grapey, minerally	Fish	**

SWITZERLAND

Wine name	Region	Style	Flavor/Bouquet	Compatible Foods	Price Range
Bon Père Germanier Syrah Cayas	Valais	Red	Earthy, spicy	Stew	**
Bon Père Germanier Vétroz Amigne Mitis	Valais	White	Sweet, toasty	Cheese	**
Domaine du Mont d'Or Petite Arvine Sous l'Escalier	Valais	White	Minerally, citrus	Fish	**
Domaine Les Hutins Dardagny Le Bertholier Rouge	Geneva	Red	Berry, spicy	Stew	**

SWITZERLAND (*Continued*)

Wine name	Region	Style	Flavor/Bouquet	Compatible Foods	Price Range
Domaine Les Hutins Pinot Noir	Geneva	Red	Gamey, smoky	Shellfish	**
Domaine Les Hutins Dardagny Sauvignon	Geneva	White	Crisp, citrus	Shellfish	**
Domaine Louis Bovard Dézaley Medinette	Vaud	White	Fruity, melon	Veal	**
Dupraz et Fils Coteau de Lully Gamaret	Geneva	Red	Berry, gamey	Cold meats, stew, offal	**
Fendant Les Murettes (Robert Gilliard)	Valais	White	Fruity, minerally	Chicken	**
Henri Badoux et Fils Aigle Pinot Noir	Vaud	Red	Gamey, berry	Duck	**
Les Perrières Peissy Chardonnay Futs de Chene	Geneva	White	Tropical, fruit, melon	Chicken	**
Les Perrières Peissy Gamay	Geneva	Red	Berry, fruity	Antipasto	**
Luc Massy L'Epesses Clos du Boux	Vaud	White	Floral, minerally	Chicken	**
Provins Brindamour Malvoisie de Sierre	Valais	White	Minerally, citrus	Fish	**
Provins Corbassieres Rouge	Valais	Red	Earthy, berry	Pasta	**
René Favre et Fils Chamoson Pinot Noir Rénommée Saint-Pierre	Valais	Red	Berry, gamey	Duck	**
St-Saphorin Roche Ronde (Jean et Pierre Testuz)	Vaud	White	Floral, citrus	Pork	**
Schaffhausen Hallauer Silberkelch Riesling-Sylvaner (Hans Schlatter)	Eastern Switzerland	White	Floral, citrus	Shellfish	**
Simon Maye et Fils Chamoson Syrah	Valais	Red	Earthy, spicy	Beef	**
Tamborini Merlot del Ticino Vigna Vecchia	Ticino	Red	Spicy, plums	Beef	**
Valsangiacomo Merlot del Ticino Vigneto Roncobello di Morbio	Ticino	Red	Plums, oaky	Pasta	**
Weinbau Nussbaumer Baselbieter Kluser Pinot Gris Barrique (Basel)	Eastern Switzerland	White	Melon, citrus, oaky	Fish	**
Yvorne Château Maison Blanche	Vaud	White	Citrus, spicy	Fish	**
Zürich Truttiker Pinot Noir Barrique (Zahner)	Eastern Switzerland	Red	Berry, oaky	Game	**

ITALY

Wine name	Region	Style	Flavor/Bouquet	Compatible Foods	Price Range
Allegrini La Poja IGT	Soave Classico, Valpolicella Classico/North Central Italy	Red	Berry, licorice, spicy	Pork, lamb	***
Almondo Roero Arneis DOC Bricco delle Ciligie	Piedmont/Northwest Italy	White	Citrus, nutty, floral	Fish, chicken	**
Alto Adige Lagrein Scuro Riserva DOC Untermoserhof (Georg Ramoser)	Trentino-Alto Adige	Red	Plums, spicy	Pizza, chicken	**
Amano Primitivo IGT (Mark Shannon)	Southern Italy	Red	Berry, earthy	Chicken, veal, pork	**
Anselmi Recioto di Soave DOC I Capitelli	Soave Classico, Valpolicella Classico/North Central Italy	Sweet	Sweet, honey, nutty, minerally, rich	Dessert	**
Antinori Tignanello IGT	Tuscany	Red	Elegant, spicy, toasty	Beef, lamb	***
Barbera d'Asti Superiore DOC Montruc (Franco M. Martinetti)	Piedmont/Northwest Italy	Red	Berry, spicy, crisp	Chicken, veal	**
Barolo DOCG Vigneto Arborina (Elio Altare)	Piedmont/Northwest Italy	Red	Berry, licorice, vanillin	Beef, lamb	***
Bartolo Mascarello Barolo DOCG	Piedmont/Northwest Italy	Red	Powerful, berry, spicy	Beef, lamb	***
Bellavista Franciacorta DOCG Gran Cuvée Brut	Soave Classico, Valpolicella Classico/North Central Italy	Sparkling	Stone fruit, yeasty, minerally	Shellfish, nuts	***
Bisol Prosecco di Valdobbiadene DOC Extra Dry Vigneti del Fol	Soave Classico, Valpolicella Classico/North Central Italy	Sparkling	Citrus, minerally, crisp	Shellfish	**
Boscarelli Vino Nobile di Montepulciano DOCG Vigna del Nocio	Tuscany	Red	Rich, earthy, leathery	Beef, lamb	***
Braida Brachetto d'Acqui DOC	Piedmont/Northwest Italy	Red	Berry, crisp, floral	Pizza, chicken	**
Ca' dei Frati Lugana DOC I Frati	Soave Classico, Valpolicella Classico/North Central Italy	White	Citrus, nutty, crisp	Fish, chicken	**
Ca' del Bosco Maurizio Zanella IGT	Soave Classico, Valpolicella Classico/North Central Italy	White	Stone fruit, rich, minerally	Fish, chicken	**
Ca'Viola Dolcetto d'Alba DOC Barturot	Piedmont/Northwest Italy	Red	Berry, peppery, crisp	Pasta, chicken, pork	**
Camillo Montori Montepulciano d'Abruzzo DOC Fonte Cupa	Southern Italy	Red	Fruity, spicy	Pizza, chicken	**
Cantina Produttori San Michele Appiano Alto Adige Chardonnay DOC St Valentin	Trentino-Alto Adige	White	Apples, citrus, minerally	Fish, chicken	**
Cantina Sociale di Santadi Carignano del Sulcis DOC Tre Torri	Southern Italy	Red	Rich, plums, earthy	Veal, pork, beef	**
Cantine Lungarotti Torgiano Rosso Riserva DOC Vigna Monticchio	Central Italy	Red	Berry, earthy, leathery	Beef, lamb	**
Castel de Paolis Frascati Superiore DOC Vigna Adriana	Central Italy	White	Citrus, crisp	Shellfish, fish	**
Castello della Sala Cervara della Sala IGT	Central Italy	White	Apples, minerally	Fish, chicken	**
Cavicchioli Lambrusco di Sorbara DOC Vigna del Cristo	Emilia-Romagna	Red	Berry, fruity, crisp	Veal, pork, beef	**
Cesconi Trentino Pinot Grigio DOC	Trentino-Alto Adige	White	Stone fruit, nutty	Shellfish, fish	**
Colli di Catone Frascati Superiore DOC	Central Italy	White	Citrus, crisp	Shellfish, fish	**
Conterno Fantino Langhe Rosso IGT Monpra	Piedmont/Northwest Italy	Red	Berry, licorice, elegant	Veal, pork, beef	**
COS Cerasuolo di Vittoria DOC	Sicily	Red	Berry, spicy, earthy	Veal, pork, beef	**
Costanti Brunello di Montalcino DOCG	Tuscany	Red	Intense, berry, leathery, earthy	Beef, lamb	***
D'Ancona Passito de Pantelleria DOC Solidea	Sicily	Sweet	Sweet, floral, wax, rich	Dessert, nuts	**
D'Angelo Aglianico del Vulture DOC	Southern Italy	Red	Berry, earthy, minerally	Veal, pork, beef	**
Fattoria di Felsina Chianti Classico Riserva DOCG Rancia	Tuscany	Red	Rich, berry, spicy, complex	Beef, lamb	***

ITALY *(Continued)*

Wine name	Region	Style	Flavor/Bouquet	Compatible Foods	Price Range
Fattoria Zerbina Albana di Romagna Passito DOCG Scacco Matto	Emilia-Romagna	Sweet	Sweet, honey, waxy, floral	Dessert	***
Fattoria Zerbina Marzieno Ravenna Rosso IGT	Emilia-Romagna	Red	Berry, spicy	Veal, pork, beef	**
Fazio Wines Torre dei Venti Rosso IGT	Sicily	Red	Berry, spicy	Veal, pork, beef	**
Feudi di San Gregorio Taurasi DOC	Southern Italy	Red	Rich, fruity, earthy	Beef, lamb	**
Firriato Santagostino Rosso IGT	Sicily	Red	Berry, spicy	Veal, pork, beef	**
Foradori Teroldego Rotaliano DOC Sgarzon	Trentino-Alto Adige	Red	Plums, jam	Chicken, veal, pork	**
Frescobaldi Nipozzano Chianti Rufina Riserva DOCG	Tuscany	Red	Berry, spicy, elegant	Beef, lamb	***
Friuli Isonzo Pinot Bianco DOC (Mauro Drius)	Friuli-Venezia Giulia	White	Apples, melon, crisp	Fish, chicken	**
Gaja Barbaresco DOCG Sori San Lorenzo	Piedmont/Northwest Italy	Red	Berry, licorice, earthy, rich	Beef, lamb	***
Gianfranco Alessandria Barbera d'Alba DOC Vittoria	Piedmont/Northwest Italy	Red	Jam, crisp, rich	Pizza, chicken	**
Girolamo Dorigo Colli Orientali del Friuli Chardonnay DOC Vigneto Ronc di Juri	Friuli-Venezia Giulia	White	Apples, butter, vanillin	Fish, chicken	**
Hofstatter Gewurztraminer DOC Kolbenhof	Trentino-Alto Adige	White	Floral, tropical fruit, spicy	Fish, pasta, Asian	**
Isole e Olena Vin Santo DOC	Tuscany	Sweet	Sweet, honey, wax, nutty	Dessert	**
Kante Carso Malvasia DOC	Friuli-Venezia Giulia	White	Floral, fruity	Asian, shellfish	**
La Monacesca Verdicchio di Matelica DOC	Central Italy	White	Stone fruit, melon	Shellfish, fish	**
La Scolca Gavi dei Gavi DOC Etichetta Nera	Piedmont/Northwest Italy	White	Stone fruit, nutty, rich	Fish, chicken	**
Le Due Terre Colli Orientali del Friuli Rosso Sacrisassi IGT	Friuli-Venezia Giulia	Red	Berry, spicy	Pizza, pasta	**
Le Pupille Morellino di Scansano DOC	Tuscany	Red	Plums, spicy	Pizza, chicken	**
Leone de Castris Salice Salentino Rosso Riserva DOC Donna Lisa	Southern Italy	Red	Powerful, earthy	Beef, lamb	**
Livio Felluga Colli Orientali del Friuli Rosazzo IGT Bianco Terre Alte	Friuli-Venezia Giulia	White	Citrus, crisp, stone fruit	Shellfish, fish	**
Maculan Breganze Cabernet Sauvignon DOC Ferrata	Soave Classico, Valpolicella Classico/North Central Italy	Red	Berry, herbaceous, toasty	Beef, lamb	**
Marco de Bartoli Moscato Passito di Pantelleria DOC Bukkuram	Sicily	White	Sweet, floral, fruity, elegant	Dessert	**
Maso Cantanghel Trentino Pinot Nero DOC	Trentino-Alto Adige	Red	Berry, spicy	Fish, chicken	**
Mastroberadino Greco del Tufo DOC	Southern Italy	White	Floral, nutty, minerally	Shellfish, fish	**
Mazzei Chianti Classico Riserva DOCG Castello di Fonterutoli	Tuscany	Red	Complex, licorice, earthy, spicy	Beef, lamb	***
Miani Colli Orientali del Friuli Sauvignon DOC	Friuli-Venezia Giulia	White	Grassy, zingy	Shellfish, cheese	**
Montepulciano d'Abruzzo DOC Riparossa (Dino Illuminati)	Southern Italy	Red	Fruity, spicy	Pizza, chicken	**
Ornellaia Poggio alla Gazze DOC	Tuscany	Red	Berry, spicy, earthy, toasty	Beef, lamb	***
Palazzone Orvieto Classico DOC Campo del Guardiano	Central Italy	White	Citrus, stone fruit, crisp	Shellfish, fish	**
Pervini Primitivo di Manduria DOC Archidamo	Southern Italy	Red	Berry, earthy	Chicken, veal, pork	**
Pieropan Soave Classico Superiore DOC La Rocca	Soave Classico, Valpolicella Classico/North Central Italy	White	Citrus, crisp, stone fruit	Shellfish, fish	**
Pierpaolo Pecorari Colli Orientali del Friuli Merlot IGT Baolar	Friuli-Venezia Giulia	Red	Plums, spicy	Veal, pork, beef	**
Planeta Chardonnay IGT	Sicily	White	Apples, minerally	Fish, chicken	**
Poderi Aldo Conterno Barolo Riserva DOCG Gran Bussia	Piedmont/Northwest Italy	Red	Complex, berry, spicy, earthy,	Beef, lamb	***
Produttori del Barbaresco Barbaresco DOCG Vigneti in Rio Sordo	Piedmont/Northwest Italy	Red	Berry, licorice, leathery, intense	Beef, lamb	***
Puiatti Collio Pinot Grigio DOC	Friuli-Venezia Giulia	White	Stone fruit, nutty, crisp	Fish, chicken	**
Quintarelli Amarone della Valpolicella DOCG	Soave Classico, Valpolicella Classico/North Central Italy	Red	Powerful, spicy, earthy	Pork, lamb, cheese	***
Sagrantino di Montefalco DOC (Arnaldo Caprai)	Central Italy	Red	Intense, berry, earthy, complex	Beef, lamb	**
Settesoli Nero d'Avola IGT	Sicily	Red	Plums, spicy, earthy	Beef, lamb	**
Tenuta Bonzara Colli Bolognesi Merlot DOC	Emilia-Romagna	Red	Plums, spicy	Chicken, veal, pork	**
Tenuta La Palazza Il Tornese Chardonnay IGT, Drei Dona	Emilia-Romagna	White	Apples, minerally	Fish, chicken	**
Tenuta San Guido Sassicaia DOC	Tuscany	Red	Berry, spicy, earthy, toasty	Beef, lamb	***
Tenute Capichera Vermentino di Gallura DOC	Southern Italy	White	Crisp, fruity	Shellfish, Asian	**
Teruzzi e Puthod Vernaccia di San Gimignano DOCG	Tuscany	White	Citrus, crisp	Shellfish, fish	**
Tommaso Bussola Recioto della Valpolicella Classico DOC	Soave Classico, Valpolicella Classico/North Central Italy	Red	Berry, licorice, leathery, intense	Beef, pork, lamb	**
Tre Monti Colli d'Imola Cabernet DOC Turico	Emilia-Romagna	Red	Berry, spicy	Pork, beef	**
Trebbiano d'Abruzzo DOC (Edoardo Valentini)	Southern Italy	White	Crisp, citrus, minerally	Shellfish, fish	**
Trebbiano d'Abruzzo DOC Marina Cvetic (Gianni Masciarelli)	Southern Italy	White	Crisp, fruity	Shellfish, fish	**
Turriga IGT (Antonio Argiolas)	Southern Italy	White	Fruity, nutty, elegant	Fish, chicken	**
Valpolicella Classico Superiore DOC Sant'Urbano (F. lli Speri)	Soave Classico, Valpolicella Classico/North Central Italy	Red	Berry, spicy	Pizza, chicken	**
Verdicchio dei Castelli di Jesi Classico DOC (F. lli Bucci)	Central Italy	White	Citrus, crisp	Shellfish, fish	**
Verdicchio dei Castelli di Jesi Classico Superiore DOC Casal di Serra, Umani Ronchi	Central Italy	White	Citrus, honey, crisp	Shellfish, fish	**
Vie di Romans Friuli Isonzo Sauvignon DOC Vieris	Friuli-Venezia Giulia	White	Grassy, zingy	Shellfish, cheese	**
Villa Russiz Collio Tocai Friulano DOC	Friuli-Venezia Giulia	White	Citrus, elegant	Shellfish, fish	**
Vinicola Italiana Florio Marsala Superiore Riserva DOC Vecchioflora	Sicily	Sweet	Sweet, intense, licorice, tangy	Cheese, dessert	**
Vinnaioli Jermann Vintage Tunina IGT	Friuli-Venezia Giulia	White	Rich, fruity, complex	Fish, chicken	***

SPAIN

Wine name	Region	Style	Flavor/Bouquet	Compatible Foods	Price Range
A Portella Viña Mein	Ribeiro/Galacia	White	Fruity, floral	Fish, chicken	**
A Tapada Guitian	Valdeorras/Galacia	White	Fruity, minerally	Chicken, fish	**
Abadia Retuerta Abado Retuerta Cuvée el Campanario	Castilla-León	Red	Berry, oaky	Pork, beef, cheese	***
Abadia Retuerta Abado Retuerta Cuvée el Palomar	Castilla-León	Red	Berry, oaky	Pork, beef, cheese	***
Abadia Retuerta Abado Retuerta Pago Negralada	Castilla-León	Red	Berry, oaky	Pork, beef, cheese	***
Abadia Retuerta	Castilla-León	Red	Berry, licorice	Pizza, pork, cheese	*
Abadia Retuerta Pago Valdebellon	Castilla-León	Red	Berry, oaky	Pork, beef, cheese	***
Agapito Rico Carchelo	Jumilla/Mercia	Red	Plums, jam	Pasta, pork	**
Agapito Rico Carchelo Merlot	Jumilla/Mercia	Red	Plums, vanillin	Pork, veal, beef	**
Agapito Rico Carchelo Syrah	Jumilla/Mercia	Red	Berry, spicy	Pork, lamb	**
Agustí Torelló Kripta	Cava/Catalonia	Sparkling	Crisp, minerally	Cold meats, shellfish	**
Agustí Torelló Mata	Cava/Catalonia	Sparkling	Crisp, minerally	Cold meats, shellfish	**
Alejandro Fernández Pesquera	Ribera del Duero/Castilla-León	Red	Plums, leathery, earthy	Lamb, beef, pork	**
Alvaro Palacios L'Ermita	Priorato/Catalonia	Red	Plums, oaky	Lamb, beef	***
Alvear Asunción	Montilla-Moriles/Andalucía	Fortified	Minerally, nutty	Cold meats, nuts	**
Alvear Carlos VII	Montilla-Moriles/Andalucía	Fortified	Minerally, nutty	Cold meats, nuts	**
Alvear CB	Montilla-Moriles/Andalucía	Fortified	Minerally, nutty	Cold meats, nuts	**
Alvear Pedro Ximénez 1830	Montilla-Moriles/Andalucía	Fortified	Sweet, caramelly	Dessert	**
Alvear Pedro Ximénez 1927	Montilla-Moriles/Andalucía	Fortified	Sweet, caramelly	Dessert	**
Alvear Pelayo	Montilla-Moriles/Andalucía	Fortified	Minerally, nutty	Cheese, nuts	**
Alvear Solera Fundación	Montilla-Moriles/Andalucía	Fortified	Complex, nutty	Cheese, nuts	**
Campillo Campillo	Rioja/Northeast Spain	Red	Berry, spicy	Veal, pork, beef	**
Campillo Reserva Especial	Rioja/Northeast Spain	Red	Earthy, spicy	Lamb, cheese	**
Casa de la Viña	Valdepeñas/Castilla-La Mancha	Red	Plums, earthy	Beef, lamb, pork	**
Castaño Hecula	Yecla/Murcia	Red	Plums, earthy	Beef, lamb, pork	**
Castell del Remei 1780	Costers del Serge/Catalonia	Red	Plums, spicy	Pork, veal, beef	**
Castelo de Medina Sauvignon	Rueda/Castilla-León	White	Herbaceous, spicy	Shellfish, fish	**
Castilla la Vieja Bornos Sauvignon	Rueda/Castilla-León	White	Herbaceous, zingy	Shellfish, salads	**
Cavas Naveran Don Pablo	Penedès/Catalonia	Red	Berry, spicy	Pizza, pork, beef	**
Cerrosol Doña Beatriz	Rueda/Castilla-León	White	Spicy, fruity	Shellfish, fish	**
Clos Mogador	Priorato/Catalonia	Red	Berry, vanillin	Pork, lamb, beef	**
Codorníu Cuvée Raventós	Cava/Catalonia	Sparkling	Crisp, nutty	Cold meats, fish	**
Codorníu Gran Codorníu	Cava/Catalonia	Sparkling	Yeasty, rich	Cold meats, shellfish, nuts	**
Codorníu Jaume de Codorníu	Cava/Catalonia	Sparkling	Crisp, nutty	Cold meats, cheese, fish, pasta	**
Codorníu Non Plus Ultra	Cava/Catalonia	Sparkling	Austere, minerally	Asian, shellfish	**
Compañía Vinícola del Norte de España Real de Asúa	Rioja/Northeast Spain	Red	Earthy, leathery	Lamb, beef, cheese	**
Compañía Vinícola del Norte de España Viña Real Oro	Rioja/Northeast Spain	Red	Plums, mushrooms	Lamb, cheese	**
Concavins Vía Aurelia Masía Les Combes	Conca de Barberà/Catalonia	Red	Berry, jam	Pork, beef	**
Dehesa de los Canónigos	Ribera del Duero/Castilla-León	Red	Plums, spicy	Lamb, beef, pork	**
Dehesa del Carrizal	Castilla-La Mancha	Red	Berry, earthy	Lamb, beef	**
Emilio Lustau Amontillado Escuadrilla	Jeréz/Andalucía	Fortified	Tangy, nutty	Cold meats, nuts	**
Emilio Lustau Moscatel Superior Emilín	Jeréz/Andalucía	Fortified	Sweet, rich	Fruits, dessert	**
Emilio Lustau Papirusa	Jeréz/Andalucía	Fortified	Tangy, yeasty	Nuts, cheese	**
Emilio Lustau Pedro Ximénez San Emilio	Jeréz/Andalucía	Fortified	Sweet, caramelly	Dessert	**
Emilio Lustau Península	Jeréz/Andalucía	Fortified	Minerally, nutty	Cold meats, nuts	**
Emilio Lustau Puerto Fino	Jeréz/Andalucía	Fortified	Tangy, nutty	Cold meats, nuts	**
Fariña Primero	Toro/Castilla-León	Red	Plums, spicy	Beef, lamb, pork	**
González Byass Apóstoles	Jeréz/Andalucía	Fortified	Minerally, nutty	Cold meats, nuts	**
González Byass Matusalem	Jeréz/Andalucía	Fortified	Minerally, nutty	Cold meats, nuts	**
González Byass Noë	Jeréz/Andalucía	Fortified	Minerally, nutty	cold meats, nuts	**
González Byass Solera 1847	Jeréz/Andalucía	Fortified	Complex, nutty	Cold meats, nuts	***
Gramona Celler Batlle	Cava/Catalonia	Sparkling	Crisp, minerally	Cold meats, shellfish	**
Gramona Tres Lustros	Cava/Catalonia	Sparkling	Crisp, minerally	Cold meats, shellfish	**
Guelbenzu Evo	Navarra	Red	Berry, spicy	Pizza, pasta, pork	**
Guelbenzu Lautus	Navarra	Red	Berry, vanillin	Pork, beef, lamb	**
Gutiérrez de la Vega Casta Diva Cosecha Miel	Alicante/Valencia	Fortified	Fruity, rich	Dessert	*
Hacienda Monasterio Dominio de Pingus	Ribera del Duero/Castilla-León	Red	Plums, oaky	Lamb, beef, pork	**
Hacienda Monasterio	Ribera del Duero/Castilla-León	Red	Plums, spicy	Lamb, beef, pork	**
Huertas Rodrejo	Jumilla/Mercia	Red	Plums, spicy	Pork, veal, beef	**
Insulares Tenerife Viña Norte	Tacoronte-Acentejo/ Canary Islands	Red	Jam, spicy	Beef, lamb, pork	**
Jané Ventura Brut Nature	Cava/Catalonia	Sparkling	Austere, stone fruit	Asian, shellfish	**
Jané Ventura Finca els Camps	Penedès/Catalonia	White	Crisp, fruity	Fish, chicken	**

SPAIN *(Continued)*

Wine name	Region	Style	Flavor/Bouquet	Compatible Foods	Price Range
Jané Ventura Gran Reserva	Cava/Catalonia	Sparkling	Yeasty, minerally	Nuts, sausages, cold meats	**
Jané Ventura	Penedès/Catalonia	Rosé	Fruity, floral	Salads, Asian	**
José Gallego Góngora Amontillado muy Viejo Selección Imperial	Aljarafe/Andalucía	Fortified	Fruity, rich	Dessert, nuts	*
José Gallego Góngora PX Dulce Añejo Selección Imperial	Aljarafe/Andalucía	Fortified	Sweet, rich	Dessert	*
Josep María Raventós Chardonnay Raventós i Blanc	Penedès/Catalonia	White	Apples, buttery	Fish, chicken	**
Josep María Raventós i Blanc	Cava/Catalonia	Sparkling	Crisp, minerally	Cold meats, shellfish	**
Julian Chivite Chivite Colección 125	Navarra	White	Stone fruit, minerally	Fish, chicken, pasta	**
Julian Chivite Gran Feudo	Navarra	Rosé	Fruity, floral	Salads, Asian, fish	**
Julian Chivite Gran Fuedo	Navarra	White	Tropical fruit, apples	Salads, fish, chicken	**
Juve y Camps Gran Juve Camps	Cava/Catalonia	Sparkling	Crisp, minerally	Cold meats, shellfish	**
La Rioja Alta Gran Reserva 904	Rioja/Northeast Spain	Red	Earthy, spicy	Beef, lamb, pork	***
La Rioja Alta Viña Ardanza	Rioja/Northeast Spain	Red	Plums, earthy	Beef, lamb, pork	**
López Cristobal	Ribera del Duero/Castilla-León	Red	Plums, spicy	Lamb, beef, pork	**
López Hermanos Málaga Virgen	Málaga/Andalucía	Fortified	Sweet, caramelly	Dessert, cheese	**
López Hermanos Trajinero	Málaga/Andalucía	Fortified	Sweet, caramelly	Dessert, cheese	**
Macia Batle	Binissalem/Balearic Islands	White	Fruity, floral	Fish, chicken, veal	**
Manuel Manzaneque Chardonnay	Sierra de Alcaraz/ Castilla-La Mancha	White	Fruity, vanillin	Chicken, fish	**
Manuel Manzaneque Finca Elez	Sierra de Alcaraz/ Castilla-La Mancha	Red	Berry, spicy	Veal, pork, beef	**
Marqués de Griñón Dominio de Valdepusa Cabernet Sauvignon	Toledo/Castilla-La Mancha	Red	Plums, leathery, earthy	Beef, lamb, pork	**
Marqués de Griñón Dominio de Valdepusa Syrah	Toledo/Castilla-La Mancha	Red	Berry, licorice, spicy	Veal, pork, beef	**
Marqués de Riscal Baron de Chirel	Rioja/Northeast Spain	Red	Plums, spicy	Beef, lamb, pork	**
Marqués de Riscal	Rioja/Northeast Spain	Red	Earthy, leathery	Beef, lamb, pork	**
Marqués del Real Tesoro Del Principe	Jeréz/Andalucía	Fortified	Minerally, nutty	Cheese, nuts	**
Martín Códax Burgans	Rías Baixas/Galacia	White	Minerally, tropical fruit	Shellfish, Asian	**
Martín Códax Organistrum	Rías Baixas/Galacia	White	Minerally, floral	Shellfish, fish	**
Martín Códax	Rías Baixas/Galacia	White	Minerally, floral	Shellfish, fish	**
Martínez-Bujanda Finca Valpiedra	Rioja/Northeast Spain	Red	Berry, licorice, oaky	Veal, pork, beef	***
Martínez-Bujanda Valdemar	Rioja/Northeast Spain	Red	Plums, earthy, spicy, oaky	Beef, lamb, pork	**
Martínez-Bujanda Vendímia Selecciónada	Rioja/Northeast Spain	Red	Complex, earthy	Beef, lamb, pork	***
Mas Martinet Vinicultors Clos Martinet	Priorato/Catalonia	Red	Berry, spicy	Pork, lamb, beef	**
Masroig Les Sorts	Tarragona/Catalonia	Red	Plums, spicy	Beef, lamb, pork	**
Mauro	Castilla-León	Red	Plums, spicy	Pork, beef, lamb	**
Mauro San Roman	Castilla-León	Red	Berry, spicy	Pizza, pork, beef	**
Mauro Vendímia Selecciónada	Castilla-León	Red	Plums, jam	Pork, veal, beef	**
Miguel Torres Atrium	Penedès/Catalonia	Red	Berry, spicy	Veal, chicken, pork	**
Miguel Torres Fransola	Penedès/Catalonia	White	Floral, spicy	Salads, shellfish	**
Miguel Torres Gran Coronas	Penedès/Catalonia	Red	Plums, earthy	Lamb, beef, pork	**
Miguel Torres Gran Viña Sol	Penedès/Catalonia	White	Rich, fruity	Pasta, chicken	**
Miguel Torres Grans Muralles	Conca de Barberà/Catalonia	Red	Plums, earthy	Pork, beef	**
Miguel Torres Mas la Plana Gran Coronas	Penedès/Catalonia	Red	Plums, toasty	Lamb, beef, pork	***
Miguel Torres Milmanda	Conca de Barberà/Catalonia	White	Buttery, toasty	Fish, pasta	***
Miguel Torres Viña Esmerelda	Penedès/Catalonia	White	Spicy, fruity	Shellfish, salads	**
Miguel Torres Waltraud	Penedès/Catalonia	White	Fruity, floral	Fish, chicken	**
Miquel Oliver Ses Ferritges	Pla i Llevant de Mallorca/ Balearic Islands	Red	Berry, spicy	Chicken, veal, beef	**
Ochoa Ochoa Moscatel	Navarra	Sweet	Fruity, rich	Dessert, cheese	**
Osborne y Cía Alonso el Sabio	Jeréz/Andalucía	Fortified	Minerally, nutty	Cold meats, nuts	**
Osborne y Cía Aos Solera	Jeréz/Andalucía	Fortified	Complex, rich	Cold meats, nuts	**
Osborne y Cía Bailen	Jeréz/Andalucía	Fortified	Minerally, nutty	Cold meats, nuts	**
Osborne y Cía Coquinero Dry	Jeréz/Andalucía	Fortified	Minerally, nutty	Cold meats, nuts	**
Osborne y Cía Fino Quinta	Jeréz/Andalucía	Fortified	Minerally, zingy	Cold meats, shellfish	**
Osborne y Cía Moscatel Fruta	Jeréz/Andalucía	Fortified	Sweet, rich	Fruits, dessert	**
Osborne y Cía P Triangulo P	Jeréz/Andalucía	Fortified	Minerally, nutty	Cold meats, nuts	**
Osborne y Cía Pedro Ximénez 1827	Jeréz/Andalucía	Fortified	Sweet, caramelly	Dessert	**
Osborne y Cía Solera India	Jeréz/Andalucía	Fortified	Rich, nutty	Cheese, nuts	**
Osborne y Cía Very Old Dry Oloroso	Jeréz/Andalucía	Fortified	Tangy, complex	Cheese, nuts	**
Pago de Carraovejas	Ribera del Duero/Castilla-León	Red	Plums, spicy	Lamb, beef, pork	**
Parxet Marqués de Alella Seco	Alella/Catalonia	White	Minerally, crisp	Salads, Asian, shellfish	**
Pazo de Señorans	Rías Baixas/Galacia	White	Minerally, floral	Shellfish, fish	**
Pedro Domecq Amontillado 51-1ª	Jeréz/Andalucía	Fortified	Tangy, nutty	Cold meats, nuts	**
Pedro Domecq Botaina	Jeréz/Andalucía	Fortified	Minerally, nutty	Cold meats, nuts	**
Pedro Domecq Capuchino	Jeréz/Andalucía	Fortified	Minerally, nutty	Cold meats, nuts	**

SPAIN (Continued)

Wine name	Region	Style	Flavor/Bouquet	Compatible Foods	Price Range
Pedro Domecq La Ina	Jeréz/Andalucía	Fortified	Minerally, zingy	Cold meats, nuts	**
Pedro Domecq Rio Viejo	Jeréz/Andalucía	Fortified	Minerally, nutty	Cold meats, nuts	**
Pedro Domecq Sibarita	Jeréz/Andalucía	Fortified	Nutty, rich	Cheese, nuts	**
Pedro Domecq Venerable	Jeréz/Andalucía	Fortified	Complex, rich	Cheese, nuts	**
Pere Guardiola Petit Floresta	Empordà-CB	Red	Berry, spicy	Pizza, pork, chicken	**
Perez Caramés Casar de Santa Inés	Bierzo/Castilla-León	Red	Berry, spicy	Pizza, pasta, pork	**
Pérez Barquero Gran Barquero Amontillado	Montilla-Moriles/Andalucía	Fortified	Tangy, nutty	Cold meats, nuts	**
Pérez Barquero Gran Barquero Cream	Montilla-Moriles/Andalucía	Fortified	Sweet, nutty	Dessert, cheese	**
Pérez Barquero Gran Barquero	Montilla-Moriles/Andalucía	Fortified	Minerally, nutty	Cold meats, nuts	**
Pérez Barquero Gran Barquero Pedro Ximénez	Montilla-Moriles/Andalucía	Fortified	Sweet, caramelly	Dessert	**
Pilar Aranda Amontillado 1730	Jeréz/Andalucía	Fortified	Tangy, nutty	Cold meats, nuts	**
Pilar Aranda Oloroso 1730	Jeréz/Andalucía	Fortified	Tangy, yeasty	Cheese, nuts	**
Piñol L'Avi Arrufi	Terra Alta/Catalonia	Red	Berry, spicy	Beef, lamb, pork	**
Piqueras Castillo de Almansa	Almansa/Castilla-La Mancha	Red	Plums, berry	Veal, pork, beef	**
Pirineos Señorío de Lazan	Somontano/Aragón	Red	Plums, spicy	Beef, lamb, pork	**
Primicia Viña Diezmo	Rioja/Northeast Spain	Red	Plums, spicy	Beef, lamb, pork	**
Raïmat Abadia	Costers del Serge/Catalonia	Red	Berry, earthy	Pork, veal, beef	**
Raïmat Cabernet Sauvignon	Costers del Serge/Catalonia	Red	Plums, leathery	Lamb, beef	**
Raïmat Casal	Costers del Serge/Catalonia	White	Floral, fruity	Fish, chicken	**
Raïmat Gran Brut	Cava/Catalonia	Sparkling	Crisp, minerally	Cold meats, shellfish	**
Raïmat Mas Castell	Costers del Serge/Catalonia	Red	Berry, earthy	Pork, beef	**
Rodero Carmelo Rodero	Ribera del Duero/Castilla-León	Red	Plums, spicy	Lamb, beef, pork	**
Rovellats Brut Nature	Cava/Catalonia	Sparkling	Austere, minerally	Asian, shellfish	**
Sandeman-Coprimar Royal Esmerelda	Jeréz/Andalucía	Fortified	Minerally, nutty	Cheese, nuts	**
Santa Eulalia Conde de Siruela	Ribera del Duero/Castilla-León	Red	Plums, earthy	Lamb, beef, pork	**
Segura Viudas Reserva Heredad (Freixenet)	Cava/Catalonia	Sparkling	Powerful, minerally	Fish, pasta, Asian	**
Sierra Cantabria	Rioja/Northeast Spain	Red	Plums, oaky	Beef, lamb, pork	**
Solar de Urbezo Viña Urbezo	Cariñena/Aragón	Red	Berry, plums	Pork, lamb	**
Torreblanca Masblanc	Cava/Catalonia	Sparkling	Crisp, rich	Cold meats, shellfish	**
Union de Cosecheros de Labastida Solagüen	Rioja/Northeast Spain	Red	Plums, spicy	Beef, lamb, pork	**
Union Viti-Vinícola Gaudium	Rioja/Northeast Spain	Red	Earthy, spicy	Beef, lamb, pork	**
Valpincia	Ribera del Duero/Castilla-León	Red	Plums, spicy	Lamb, beef, pork	**
Vega Sicilia Único	Ribera del Duero/Castilla-León	Red	Rich, complex, plums, earthy	Lamb, beef, cheese	***
Venta D'Aubert Domus	Bajo Aragón/Aragón	Red	Jam, spicy	Pork, beef, lamb	**
Venta d'Aubert el Serrats	Bajo Aragón/Aragón	White	Floral, fruity	Fish, pasta	**
Vicente Gandia Pla Ceremonia	Utiel-Requena/Valencia	Red	Plums, spicy	Beef, lamb, pork	**
Vilella de la Cartoixa Fra Fulco Selecció	Priorato/Catalonia	Red	Berry, spicy	Pork, lamb, beef	**
Viñas del Vero Cabernet Sauvignon	Somontano/Aragón	Red	Plums, spicy	Beef, lamb, pork	*
Viñas del Vero Chardonnay	Somontano/Aragón	White	Apples, buttery	Chicken, fish	*
Viñas del Vero Clarión	Somontano/Aragón	White	Fruity, floral	Chicken, fish	**
Viñas del Vero Gewürztraminer	Somontano/Aragón	White	Spicy, fruity	Asian, salads	*
Viñas del Vero Gran Vos	Somontano/Aragón	Red	Berry, spicy	Veal, chicken, pork	**
Vinícola de Castilla Castillo de Alhambra	La Mancha/Castilla-La Mancha	Red	Plums, jam	Pork, lamb, beef	**
Vinícola del Priorat L'Arc	Priorato/Catalonia	Red	Berry, spicy	Pork, lamb, beef	**
Vinícola Hidalgo y Cía Napoleon Pedro Ximénez	Jeréz/Andalucía	Fortified	Sweet, caramelly	Dessert	**
Vizcarra-Ramos Vizcarra	Ribera del Duero/Castilla-León	Red	Plums, spicy	Lamb, beef, cheese	**

PORTUGAL

Wine name	Region	Style	Flavor/Bouquet	Compatible Foods	Price Range
Adega Co-op. de Lagoa Afonso XIII	Algarve/Setúbal & the South	Fortified	Spirity, powerful, complex	Nuts	**
Adega Co-op. de Portalegre	Alentejano/Setúbal & the South	Red	Berry, spicy	Mediterranean	**
Alcântara Agrícola Morgado de Sta. Catherina	Bucelas/Lisbon & Tagus Valley	White	Floral, citrus	Fish	**
Alcântara Agrícola Prova Régia Arinto	Bucelas/Lisbon & Tagus Valley	White	Zingy, floral	Pasta	**
Alcântara Agrícola Quinta da Romeira Arinto	Estremadura/Lisbon & Tagus Valley	White	Crisp, citrus	Shellfish	*
Aleixo Brito Caldas Quinta da Baguinha Alvarinho	Vinho Verde/The North	White	Citrus, minerally	Fish	**
António Esteves Ferreirinha Soalheiro Alvarinho	Vinho Verde/The North	White	Crisp, minerally	Shellfish	**
António Gonçalves Faria Gonçalves Faria Reserva	Bairrada/The Douro to the Tagus	Red	Berry, gamey	Stew	**
Artur Barros & Sousa Madeira range, esp. Boal & Terrantez	Madeira/Setúbal & the South	Madeira	Nutty, complex	Cheese	**
Atíade da Costa Martins Semedo Quinta da Rigodeira	Bairrada/The Douro to the Tagus	Red	Spicy, tannic	Cold meats, stew, offal	**

PORTUGAL *(Continued)*

Wine name	Region	Style	Flavor/Bouquet	Compatible Foods	Price Range
Atíade da Costa Martins Semedo Quinta da Rigodeira	Bairrada/The Douro to the Tagus	White	Citrus, minerally	Fish	**
Barbeito Madeira range	Madeira/Setúbal & the South	Madeira	Nutty, spirity, complex	Aperitif	**
Barros Almeida Port range, esp. Colheitas	Porto/The North	Port	Sweet, nutty	Chese	**
Borges & Irmãa Port range	Porto/The North	Port	Sweet, spirity	Cheese	**
Borges Madeira range	Madeira/Setúbal & the South	Madeira	Complex, rich	Cheese	**
Burmester Port range, esp. Colheitas, Vintage	Porto/The North	Port	Spirity, sweet	Cheese	**
Cálem Port range, esp. Quinta de Foz	Porto/The North	Port	Spirity, sweet	Cheese	**
Casa Agrícola de Saima Casa de Saima Garrafeira	Bairrada/The Douro to the Tagus	Red	Smoky, tannic	Cold meats, stew, offal	**
Casa Agrícola de Saima Casa de Saima Garrafeira	Bairrada/The Douro to the Tagus	White	Crisp, citrus	Fish	*
Casa Burmester	Douro/The North	Red	Berry, plums	Veal	**
Casa Cadaval Cabernet Sauvignon	Ribatejano/Lisbon & Tagus Valley	Red	Berry, herbaceous	Cold meats	**
Casa Cadaval Trincadeira Preta	Ribatejano/Lisbon & Tagus Valley	Red	Spicy, smoky	Stew	**
Casa de Sezim Colheita Seleccionada	Vinho Verde/The North	White	Citrus, minerally	Shellfish	**
Casa Ferreirinha Barca Velha	Douro/The North	Red	Powerful, berry, spicy	Beef	***
Casa Ferreirinha Callabriga	Douro/The North	Red	Berry, earthy	Game	**
Casa Ferreirinha Quinta da Leda Touriga Nacional	Douro/The North	Red	Berry, tannic	Sausages	**
Casa Ferreirinha Reserva	Douro/The North	Red	Earthy, plums	Stew	**
Casa Ferreirinha Reserva Especial	Douro/The North	Red	Berry, tannic	Cold meats, stew, offal	**
Casa Ferreirinha Vinha Grande	Douro/The North	Red	Berry, spicy	Cold meats, stew, offal	**
Casal de Valle Pradinhos Valle Pradinhos	Trás-os-Montes/The North	Red	Berry, gamey	Game	*
Castas de Santar Alfrocheiro Preto	Beiras/The Douro to the Tagus	Red	Berry, spicy	Stew	**
Castas de Santar Touriga Nacional	Beiras/The Douro to the Tagus	Red	Gamey, berry	Cold meats	**
Caves Aliança Galeria Cabernet Sauvignon	Beiras/The Douro to the Tagus	Red	Berry, herbaceous	Beef	**
Caves Aliança Garrafeira	Bairrada/The Douro to the Tagus	Red	Berry, tannic	Stew	**
Caves de Murghaneira Murganheira Varosa	Távora-Varosa/The Douro to the Tagus	Sparkling	Fruity, citrus	Aperitif	**
Caves Messias Messias Reserva Touriga Nacional	Dão/The Douro to the Tagus	Red	Berry, tannic	Beef	**
Caves Messias Quinta do Cachão Tinta Roriz	Douro/The North	Red	Berry, tannic	Cheese	**
Caves Primavera Lda. Primavera Baga/Cabernet Sauvignon	Beiras/The Douro to the Tagus	Red	Berry, herbaceous	Game	**
Caves Primavera Lda. Primavera Beiras	Beiras/The Douro to the Tagus	White	Fruity, citrus, melon	Fish	**
Caves Primavera Lda. Primavera Garrafeira	Bairrada/The Douro to the Tagus	Red	Gamey, tannic	Cold meats	**
Caves Primavera Lda. Primavera Touriga Nacional	Bairrada/The Douro to the Tagus	Red	Berry, tannic	Beef	**
Caves São João Frei João Reserva	Bairrada/The Douro to the Tagus	Red	Spicy, herbaceous, tannic	Stew	**
Caves São João Poço do Lobo Cabernet Sauvignon	Beiras/The Douro to the Tagus	Red	Herbaceous, spicy, berry	Lamb	**
Caves São João Porta dos Cavaleiros Reserva Seleccionada	Dão/The Douro to the Tagus	Red	Berry, tannic	Stew	**
Caves São João Porta dos Cavaleiros Reserva Seleccionada	Dão/The Douro to the Tagus	White	Citrus, minerally	Fish	**
Caves São João Quinta do Poço do Lobo	Bairrada/The Douro to the Tagus	Red	Berry, smoky	Sausages	**
Caves São João Reserva	Bairrada/The Douro to the Tagus	Red	Earthy, spicy	Mediterranean	**
Churchill Port range, esp. Vintage	Porto/The North	Port	Spirity, sweet, complex	Cheese	**
Cockburn Smithes Port range, including Quinta dos Canais	Porto/The North	Port	Complex, sweet, spirity	Cheese	**
Coop. Agrícola de Santa Isidro de Pegões Vale de Judia	Terras do Sado/Setúbal & the South	White	Minerally, floral	Fish	**
Coop. de Cantanhede Marquês Marialva Baga Reserva	Bairrada/The Douro to the Tagus	Red	Berry, tannic	Cold meats, stew, offal	**
Coop. de Murça CRL Caves da Porca Garrafeira	Douro/The North	Red	Berry, spicy	Pizza	*
Coop. Regional de Monção Alvarinho Deu la Deu	Vinho Verde/The North	White	Crisp, citrus	Mediterranean	**
Croft Port range, including Delaforce	Porto/The North	Port	Spirity, sweet	Nuts	**
Da Silva Port range, esp. Colheitas	Porto/The North	Port	Sweet, spirity	Nuts	**
Domingos Alves de Sousa Quinta do Vale de Raposa Touriga Nacional	Douro/The North	Red	Berry, tannic	Veal	**
Dona Paterna	Vinho Verde/The North	White	Zingy, floral	Shellfish	**
Dow Port range, esp. Vintage	Porto/The North	Port	Rich, sweet, complex, spirity	Nuts	***
Dulcínea dos Santos Ferreirinha Sidónio de Sousa Reserva	Bairrada/The Douro to the Tagus	Red	Earthy, minerally	Sausages	**
Encostas de Paderne Alvarinho	Vinho Verde/The North	White	Fruity, crisp	Asian	**
Falua Tercius	Ribatejo	Red	Floral, zingy	Sausages	**

PORTUGAL *(Continued)*

Wine name	Region	Style	Flavor/Bouquet	Compatible Foods	Price Range
Ferreira Port range, esp. Vintage	Porto/The North	Port	Spirity, sweet	Cheese	**
Finagra Esporão Trincadeira	Alentejano/Setúbal & the South	Red	Spicy, earthy	Sausages	**
Fonseca Guimaraens Dom Prior	Douro/The North	White	Crisp, floral	Mediterranean	**
Fonseca Guimaraens Port range, esp. Vintage	Porto/The North	Port	Complex, powerful, rich, sweet	Cheese	***
Fundação Eugénio de Almeida Cartuxa	Évora /Setúbal & the South	White	Floral, citrus	Fish	**
Gassiot Port range, esp. Quinta da Eira Velha	Porto/The North	Port	Sweet, spirity	Cheese	**
Graham Port range, esp. Quinta dos Malvedos, Quinta del Vesúvio	Porto/The North	Port	Rich, complex, sweet, spirity	Cheese	***
Hans Kristian Jørgensen Cortes de Cima	Alentejano/Setúbal & the South	Red	Berry, gamey	Pasta	**
Henriques & Henriques Madeira range	Madeira/Setúbal & the South	Madeira	Rich, nutty, complex	Nuts	**
Herdade do Mouchão Dom Rafael	Alentejano/Setúbal & the South	Red	Spicy, floral	Pasta	**
Hotel Palace do Buçaco Buçaco Reserva	Bairrada/The Douro to the Tagus	Red	Earthy, minerally	Game	**
João Portugal Ramos Antão Vaz	Alentejano/Setúbal & the South	White	Crisp, citrus	Salads	**
João Portugal Ramos Aragonês	Alentejano/Setúbal & the South	Red	Earthy, smoky	Game	**
José Arnaldo Coutinho Quinta de Mosteirô	Douro/The North	Red	Spicy, berry	Sausages	**
José Bento dos Santos Monte d'Oiro Syrah	Estremadura/Lisbon & Tagus Valley	Red	Berry, spicy	Sausages	**
José Carlos de Morais Calheiros Cruz Quinta de Covelos Reserva	Douro/The North	Red	Earthy, tannic	Pasta	**
José Maria da Fonseca Colecção Privada Domingos Soares Franco	Terras do Sado/Setúbal & the South	Red	Berry, spicy	Cold meats, stew, offal	**
JP Vinhos Catarina	Terras do Sado/Setúbal & the South	White	Citrus, minerally	Chicken	**
JP Vinhos JP Arinto	Terras do Sado/Setúbal & the South	White	Floral, citrus	Salads	**
JP Vinhos JP Tinta Miúda	Palmela/Setúbal & the South	Red	Minerally, berry	Cold meats, stew, offal	**
JP Vinhos Má Partilha	Terras do Sado/Setúbal & the South	Red	Berry, gamey	Cold meats	**
JP Vinhos Moscatel de Setúbal Range, Vintage	Setúbal/Setúbal & the South	Fortified	Spirity, sweet	Nuts	**
JP Vinhos Tinto de Ânfora	Alentejano/Setúbal & the South	Red	Spicy, smoky	Pasta	**
Leacock, Rutherford & Miles Cossart Gordon Madeira range	Madeira/Setúbal & the South	Madeira	Nutty, complex	Nuts	**
Lemos & van Zeller Quinta do Vale D. Maria	Douro/The North	Red	Spicy, berry	Cold meats, stew, offal	**
Luis Pato Quinta do Ribeirinho Baga Pé Franco	Bairrada/The Douro to the Tagus	Red	Herbaceous, floral, spicy	Cold meats	**
Luis Pato Quinta do Ribeirinho Primeira Escolha	Bairrada/The Douro to the Tagus	Red	Berry, spicy	Lamb	**
Luis Pato Vinha Barrosa	Bairrada/The Douro to the Tagus	Red	Spicy, berry	Pasta	**
Luis Pato Vinha Pan	Bairrada/The Douro to the Tagus	Red	Tannic, berry	Veal	**
Luis Pato Vinha Velhas	Bairrada/The Douro to the Tagus	Red	Spicy, berry	Game	**
Mário Sérgio Alves Nuno Quinta das Bágeiras Especial Garrafeira	Bairrada/The Douro to the Tagus	Red	Berry, tannic	Cheese	**
Montez Champalimaud Lda. Quinta do Côtto	Douro/The North	Red	Spicy, minerally	Lamb	**
Murganheira Cerceal	Távora-Varosa/The Douro to the Tagus	White	Minerally, floral	Shellfish	**
Niepoort Passadouro	Douro/The North	Red	Spicy, earthy, tannic	Sausages	**
Niepoort Port range, esp. old tawnies, Quinta do Passadouro	Porto/The North	Port	Spirity, sweet	Cheese	**
Niepoort Port range, esp. Vintage	Porto/The North	Port	Sweet, spirity	Nuts	**
Niepoort Redoma	Douro/The North	Red	Spicy, earthy	Cheese	**
Niepoort Redoma Reserva	Douro/The North	White	Crisp, floral	Fish	**
Pedro Borges da Gama Quinta da Alameda Touriga Nacional	Dão/The Douro to the Tagus	Red	Smoky, tannic	Sausages	**
Poças Port range	Porto/The North	Port	Rich, spirity	Cheese	**
Provam Alvarinho Portal do Fidalgo	Vinho Verde/The North	White	Minerally, zingy	Salads	**
Provam Vinha Antiga Alvarinho Escolha	Vinho Verde/The North	White	Minerally, floral	Shellfish	**
Quarles Harris Port range, esp. old tawnies	Porto/The North	Port	Rich, nutty, spirity	Nuts	**
Quinta da Barão Carcavelos range, Old wines	Carcavelos/Lisbon & Tagus Valley	Fortified	Spirity, berry, nutty	Nuts	**
Quinta de Azevedo	Vinho Verde/The North	White	Zingy, minerally	Veal	**
Quinta de Foz de Arouce	Beiras/The Douro to the Tagus	Red	Spicy, berry	Stew	*
Quinta de Foz de Arouce	Beiras/The Douro to the Tagus	White	Citrus, crisp	Veal	**
Quinta de Murta	Bucelas/Lisbon & Tagus Valley	White	Crisp, floral	Salads	**
Quinta de Saes Quinta da Pellada 100% Jaen	Dão/The Douro to the Tagus	Red	Berry, spicy	Stew	**
Quinta de Saes Quinta da Pellada 100% Touriga Nacional	Dão/The Douro to the Tagus	Red	Berry, tannic	Cold meats, stew, offal	**
Quinta de Saes Quinta da Pellada Jaen/Touriga Nacional	Dão/The Douro to the Tagus	Red	Berry, smoky	Cold meats	**

PORTUGAL *(Continued)*

Wine name	Region	Style	Flavor/Bouquet	Compatible Foods	Price Range
Quinta de Saes Quinta da Pellada Tinta Roriz/Touriga Nacional	Dão/The Douro to the Tagus	Red	Berry, earthy	Stew	**
Quinta do Côtto	Porto/The North	Port	Spirity, sweet	Cheese	**
Quinta do Crasto	Porto/The North	Port	Sweet, spirity	Cheese	**
Quinta dos Roques Alfrocheiro Preto	Dão/The Douro to the Tagus	Red	Berry, gamey	Pasta	**
Quinta dos Roques Encruzado	Dão/The Douro to the Tagus	White	Spicy, smoky	Fish	**
Quinta dos Roques Tinto Cão	Dão/The Douro to the Tagus	Red	Spicy, gamey	Stew	**
Quinta dos Roques Touriga Nacional	Dão/The Douro to the Tagus	Red	Berry, tannic	Pasta	**
Quinta Grande	Ribatejano/Lisbon & Tagus Valley	Red	Berry, spicy	Cold meats, stew, offal	**
Ramos Pinto Duas Quintas	Douro/The North	Red	Berry, tannic	Sausages	**
Ramos Pinto Duas Quintas Reserva	Douro/The North	Red	Plums, tannic	Stew	**
Ramos-Pinto Port range, esp. Colheitas	Porto/The North	Port	Rich, nutty, spirity	Nuts	**
Sandeman Confradeiro	Douro/The North	Red	Berry, spicy	Cold meats, stew, offal	**
Silva Vinhos Madeira range	Madeira/Setúbal & the South	Madeira	Complex, nutty	Nuts	**
Smith-Woodhouse Port range, esp. Vintage	Porto/The North	Port	Rich, sweet, spirity	Nuts	**
Soc. Agrícola da Herdade dos Coelheiros Tapada de Coelheiros	Alentejano/Setúbal & the South	Red	Earthy, spicy	Mediterranean	**
Soc. Agrícola da Herdade dos Coelheiros Tapada de Coelheiros Garrafeira	Alentejano/Setúbal & the South	Red	Floral, earthy	Game	**
Soc. Agrícola da Quinta do Crasto Quinta do Crasto Red	Douro/The North	Red	Berry, tannic	Game	*
Soc. Agrícola Porto da Luz/Quinta de Pancas Quinta de Pancas Tinta Roriz	Estremadura/Lisbon & Tagus Valley	Red	Smoky, spicy	Cold meats, stew, offal	**
Sogrape Duque du Viseu	Dão/The Douro to the Tagus	Red	Berry, earthy	Cold meats, stew, offal	*
Sogrape Herdade do Peso Aragonês	Alentejo/Setúbal & the South	Red	Smoky, spicy	Pizza	*
Sogrape Morgadio da Torre Alvarinho	Vinho Verde/The North	White	Fruity, zingy	Shellfish	**
Sogrape Quinta de Pedralvites	Bairrada/The Douro to the Tagus	White	Crisp, floral	Salads	*
Sogrape Quinta dos Carvalhais Alfrocheiro Preto	Dão/The Douro to the Tagus	Red	Berry, plums	Sausages	**
Sogrape Quinta dos Carvalhais Encruzado	Dão/The Douro to the Tagus	White	Fruity, floral	Salads	*
Sogrape Quinta dos Carvalhais Reserva	Dão/The Douro to the Tagus	Red	Berry, plums	Lamb	**
Sogrape Quinta dos Carvalhais Tinta Roriz	Dão/The Douro to the Tagus	Red	Berry, spicy	Pasta	*
Sogrape Quinta dos Carvalhais Touriga Nacional	Dão/The Douro to the Tagus	Red	Berry, tannic	Stew	**
Sogrape Reserva	Douro/The North	White	Minerally, citrus	Salads	**
Sophia B. Vasconcellos/Casal Branco Capucho Cabernet Sauvignon	Almeirim/Lisbon & Tagus Valley	Red	Herbaceous, berry	Cold meats, stew, offal	**
Sophia B. Vasconcellos/Casal Branco Falcoaria Almeirim	Ribatejo/Almeirim	Red	Berry, spicy	Cold meats, stew, offal	**
Taylor's Port range, esp. Vintage, Quinta de Vargellas, Quinta da Terra Feita	Porto/The North	Port	Rich, complex, powerful, sweet	Cheese	***
Venâncio da Costa Lima Garrafeira	Palmela/Setúbal & the South	Red	Berry, spicy	Stew	**
Warre's Port range, esp. Quinta da Cavadinha	Porto/The North	Port	Sweet, rich, berry, complex	Cheese	***

ENGLAND AND WALES

Wine name	Region	Style	Flavor/Bouquet	Compatible Foods	Price Range
Breaky Bottom Seyval Brut	Sussex/Weald and Downland	Sparkling	Citrus, crisp	Shellfish, fish	**
Breaky Bottom Seyval Dry	Sussex/Weald and Downland	White	Grassy, tangy	Shellfish, Asian	**
Chapel Down Bacchus	Kent/Weald and Downland	White	Floral, fruity, herbaceous	Shellfish, fish, Asian	**
Chapel Down Epoch I	Kent/Weald and Downland	Red	Berry, plums, spicy	Veal, pork, beef	**
Chapel Down Epoch Vintage Brut	Kent/Weald and Downland	Sparkling	Citrus, minerally	Shellfish, nuts	**
Chapel Down Schönburger	Kent/Weald and Downland	White	Stone fruit, spicy	Asian, fish	**
Denbies Wine Estate Dornfelder/Pinot Noir	Surrey/Weald and Downland	Red	Fruity, spicy	Chicken, fish	**
Denbies Wine Estate Special Late Harvested	Surrey/Weald and Downland	Sweet	Fruity, honey, floral	Dessert	**
Denbies Wine Estate Surrey Gold	Surrey/Weald and Downland	White	Fruity, floral	Asian, fish	**
Denbines Wine Estate Pinot Blanc	Surrey/Weald and Downland	White	Stone fruit, nutty, minerally	Fish, chicken	**
Nyetimber Classic Cuvée Vintage Brut	Sussex/Weald and Downland	Sparkling	Citrus, minerally, yeasty	Shellfish, fish	***
Nyetimber Première Cuvée Blanc de Blancs Vintage Brut	Sussex/Weald and Downland	Sparkling	Apples, citrus, minerally, yeasty	Shellfish, nuts	***
Thames Valley Vineyards Clocktower Pinot Noir	Berkshire/Thames and Chiltern	Red	Berry, spicy	Fish, chicken, pork	**
Thames Valley Vineyards Heritage Brut	Berkshire/Thames and Chiltern	Sparkling	Citrus, crisp	Shellfish, fish	**
Thames Valley Vineyards Heritage Fumé	Berkshire/Thames and Chiltern	White	Fruity, oaky	Fish, chicken	**
Three Choirs Vineyards Phoenix/Seyval	Gloucestershire/Southwest and Wales	White	Grassy, tangy	Shellfish, Asian	**
Three Choirs Vineyards Siegerrebe	Gloucestershire/Southwest and Wales	White	Citrus, spicy, tangy	Shellfish, Asian	**

CENTRAL EUROPE

Wine name	Region	Style	Flavor/Bouquet	Compatible Foods	Price Range
CZECH REPUBLIC					
Chateau Roudnice Pinot Noir	Bohemia	Red	Berry, gamey	Cold meats, stew, offal	**
Chateau Valtice a.s. Sylvaner Spaetlese	Moravia	White	Floral, medium-sweet	Veal	**
Lobkowicz Winery Chateau Melnik Oak-fermented Pinot Blanc	Bohemia	White	Melon, oaky	Chicken	**
Mikros-vin Gruener Veltliner	Za cihelnou/Moravia	White	Spicy, crisp	Fish	**
Novy Saldorf Znojmo Spalkovy	Moravia	Red	Berry, earthy	Pasta	**
Obce Vinselekt Pinot Blanc Kabinet	Nemcicky/Moravia	White	Melon, medium-sweet	Fish	**
St Martin Straw-Wine Blauer Portugieser	Moravia	Red	Berry, rich	Cheese	**
Velke Bilovice Ing. Frantisek Madl Sauvignon	Moravia	White	Crisp, grassy	Shellfish	*
Velke Pavlovice Radomil Aloun Neuburger Spaetlese	Moravia	White	Citrus, medium-sweet	Veal	**
Velke Pavlovice S.S.V. Andre Spaetlese	Moravia	White	Medium-sweet, floral	Fish	**
Velke Pavlovice Vinium a. s. Pinot Blanc Kabinet	Moravia	White	Melon, minerally	Fish	**
Vendule Zernosecke Vinarstvi s.r.o Riesling Kabinet	Velke Zernoseky/Bohemia	White	Floral, minerally, spicy	Salads	**
Vinne Sklepy Rodiny Vino Schaler Blauer Portugieser (port-style wine)	Moravia	Red	Berry, rich	Cheese	**
Zlechov Tramin	Moravia	White	Floral, spicy	Pork	*
Znovin Znojmo Riesling Praedikat (spaetlese equivalent)	Sobes/Moravia	White	Sweet, floral		
SLOVAK REPUBLIC					
Ing. Vladimir Mrva Zelenec Riesling Kabinet	Slovak Republic	White	Floral, minerally	Fish	**
Pezinok Dornfelder	Slovak Republic	Red	Plums, smoky	Cold meats	**
Vino Nitra Barrique Cabernet Sauvignon	Slovak Republic	Red	Berry, herbaceous	Lamb	**
HUNGARY					
Aliscavin Borászati Rt Chardonnay Barrique	Szekszárd/The Southwest	White	Apples, vanillin	Fish, chicken	**
Bajor Pince Siklósi Rajnai Rizling	Villány-Siklós/The Southwest	White	Floral, fruity	Asian, shellfish	**
Balatonboglári Borgazdasági Rt Chapel Hill Cabernet Sauvignon Barrique Aged	Dél-Balaton/Lake Balaton	Red	Berry, oaky	Beef, lamb	**
Balatonboglári Borgazdasági Rt Chapel Hill Chardonnay Barrique Fermented	Dél-Balaton/Lake Balaton	White	Fruity, complex	Chicken, veal	**
Bock Pince Villányi Cabernet Sauvignon	Villány-Siklós/The Southwest	Red	Plums, spicy	Pork, beef, lamb	**
Ch Pajzos és Ch Megyer Rt Aszús under the Pajzos label Disznókő Rt Aszús	Tokaj-Hegyalja	Sweet	Honey, wax, floral, nutty	Dessert	***
Danubiana Bt Gyöngyös Estate Sauvignon Blanc	Mátraalja/The Northeast	White	Grassy, melon	Shellfish, fish	**
Dreyer Domaine Viticole Vaskapu Kastély Kadarka	Mecsekalja/The Southwest	Red	Berry, spicy	Chicken, veal, pork	**
Eberhardt György Pince Mohácsi Chardonnay	Mecsekalja/The Southwest	White	Apples, minerally	Fish, chicken	**
Európai Bortermelők Kft Bátaapati Estate Barrique Chardonnay	Tolna/The Southwest	White	Apples, vanillin	Fish, chicken	**
Fine Wine Borászati Vállalkozás Pécselyi Sémillon	Balatonfüred-Csopak/ Lake Balaton	White	Honey, nutty	Fish, chicken, veal	**
Franz Weninger Soproni Kékfrankos Barrique	Sopron/The Northwest	Red	Fruity, peppery, oaky	Pork, beef	**
Gere Attila Villányi Cabernet Sauvignon Barrique	Villány-Siklós/The Southwest	Red	Plums, toasty	Beef, lamb	**
Györgykovács Pince Hárslevelő	Somló/The Northwest	White	Floral, spicy	Fish, chicken	**
Heimann Ferenc Szekszárdi Bikavér	Szekszárd/The Southwest	Red	Berry, spicy	Chicken, veal, pork	**
Huba Szeremley Szürkebarát	Badacsony/Lake Balaton	White	Stone fruit, nutty	Fish, chicken	**
Hungarovin Rt François President Brut	Eytek-Buda/The Northwest	Sparkling	Citrus, minerally	Shellfish, nuts	**
Ódon Pince Olaszrizling	Balatonmelléke/Lake Balaton	White	Floral, rich	Asian, fish	**
Polgár Pince Kft Villányi Cabernet Sauvignon Barrique	Villány-Siklós/The Southwest	Red	Plums, oaky	Beef, lamb	**
Royal Tokaji Wine Company Kft Aszús	Tokaj-Hegyalja	Sweet	Honey, wax, floral, nutty	Dessert	***
Szent Donatus Pincészet Kft Balatonlellei Cabernet	Dél-Balaton/Lake Balaton	Red	Plums, earthy	Beef, lamb	**
Szent Orbán Pince Szürkebarát	Badacsony/Lake Balaton	White	Stone fruit, nutty	Fish, chicken	**
Szőlőskert Szövetkezet Borászati Üzem Nagyréde Pinot Gris Reserve	Mátraalja/The Northeast	White	Stone fruit, nutty	Fish, chicken	**
Takler Pince Szekszárdi Merlot	Szekszárd/The Southwest	Red	Plums, jam	Veal, pork, beef	**
Tamás Gere Villányi Merlot/Cabernet Franc	Villány-Siklós/The Southwest	Red	Plums, berry	Pork, beef, lamb	**
Thummerer Pince Egri Bikavér	Eger/The Northeast	Red	Berry, spicy	Chicken veal, pork	**
Tiffán's Bt Kékoportó Vylyan Rt Villányi Kékoportó Barrique	Villány-Siklós/The Southwest	Red	Powerful, oaky	Beef, lamb	**
Tokaj Kereskedőház Rt Aszús	Tokaj-Hegyalja	Sweet	Honey, wax, floral, nutty	Dessert	***
Tokaj Oremus Kft Aszús	Tokaj-Hegyalja	Sweet	Honey, wax, floral, nutty	Dessert	***
Vida Pince Szekszárdi Merlot	Szekszárd/The Southwest	Red	Plums, jam	Veal, pork, beef	**
Vinarium Rt Ch. Vincent Sparkling Brut	Dél-Balaton/Lake Balaton	Sparkling	Citrus, minerally	Shellfish, nuts	**
Vincze Béla Magánpincézete Egri Cabernet Sauvignon	Eger/The Northeast	Red	Plums, earthy	Beef, lamb	**
Vylyan Rt Villányi Cabernet Sauvignon	Villány-Siklós/The Southwest	Red	Plums, leathery	Pork, beef, lamb	**
Zwack Kft Egri Bikavér	Eger/The Northeast	Red	Berry, spicy	Chicken, veal, pork	**

CENTRAL EUROPE *(Continued)*

Wine name	Region	Style	Flavor/Bouquet	Compatible Foods	Price Range
SLOVENIA					
Barbara International No 1 Cuvée Speciale	Postavje	Sparkling	Crisp, citrus	Aperitif	**
Jeruzalem Ormoz VVS d.d. Renski Rizling	Podravje	White	Floral, minerally	Fish	**
Kapela d.d. Traminec	Podravje	White	Floral, spicy	Shellfish	**
Kemetijski Kombinat Ptuj Chardonnay	Podravje	White	Melon, citrus	Chicken	**
Kmecka Zadruga Krsko Cvicek	Postavje	Red	Berry, spicy	Game	*
Kmetijska Zadruga Chardonnay	Goriska Brda/Primorska	White	Tropical fruit, melon	Chicken	**
Kmetijski Kombinat Ptuj Rumeni Muscat	Podravje	White	Floral, citrus	Veal	**
Ljutomercan d.d. Ranina	Ljutomer/Podravje	White	Crisp, fruity	Fish	**
Radgonske Gorice d.d. Janzevec (blended wine)	Podravje	White	Citrus, floral	Pork	**
Slovenske Konjice Zlati Gric Renski Rizling–Jagodni Izbor	Podravje	Sweet	Sweet, citrus	Fruit	**
Stanko Curin Kog Traminec–Ledeno Vino	Podravje	Sweet	Floral, sweet	Cheese	*
Valter Zorin Poljcane Laski Rizling–Suhi Jagodni Izbor	Podravje	Sweet	Sweet, citrus	Cheese	**
Vinakoper Cabernet Sauvignon	Koper/Primorska	Red	Berry, herbaceous	Lamb	**
Vinakoper Chardonnay Prestige	Koper/Primorska	White	Tropical fruit, oaky	Chicken	**
Vino Brezice d.d. Chardonnay–Jagodni Izbor	Postavje	Sweet	Sweet, melon	Fruit	**
Vino Brezice d.d. Laski Rizling–Ledeno Vino	Postavje	Sweet	Sweet, citrus	Fruit	**
Vreel Sauvignon	Zgornje Hoce/Podravje	White	Zingy, citrus	Shellfish	*
MONTENEGRO					
Monte Cheval Pro Corde	Plantaze Agrokombinat Podg	Red	Earthy, spicy	Cold meats, stew, offal	**
Monte Cheval Vranac	Plantaze Agrokombinat Podg	Red	Berry, plums	Sausages	**

EASTERN EUROPE

Wine name	Region	Style	Flavor/Bouquet	Compatible Foods	Price Range
BULGARIA					
Assenovgrad Merlot Reserve	Southern Region	Red	Plums, earthy	Beef	**
Azbuka Sliven Cabernet Sauvignon	Sub-Balkan Region	Red	Berry, herbaceous	Pasta	**
Controliran Svischtov Cabernet Sauvignon	Northern Region	Red	Berry, herbaceous	Cold meats, stew	**
Controliran Yantra Valley Cabernet Sauvignon	Northern Region	Red	Berry, herbaceous	Cold meats	**
Damianiza Melnik	Southwestern Region	Red	Berry, earthy	Pasta	**
Domaine Boyar Iambol Premium Reserve Merlot Gamza	Southern Region	Red	Plums, spicy	Cheese	**
Domaine Boyar Iambol Premium Reserve Merlot	Southern Region	Red	Plums, oaky	Sausages	**
Domaine Boyar Schumen Premium Cuveé Cabernet Sauvignon	Eastern Region	Red	Berry, herbaceous	Lamb	**
Domaine Boyar Schumen Premium Oak Cabernet Sauvignon	Eastern Region	Red	Berry, herbaceous, oaky	Pasta	**
Domaine Boyar Schumen Premium Oak Chardonnay	Eastern Region	White	Tropical fruit, oaky	Veal	**
Domaine Boyar Schumen Premium Oak Merlot	Eastern Region	Red	Plums, oaky	Game	**
Perushtitza Cabernet Sauvignon Rubin	Southern Region	Red	Plums, herbaceous	Lamb	**
Preslav Khan Krum Chardonnay Reserve	Eastern Region	White	Tropical fruit, oaky	Chicken	**
Russe Azbuka Merlot	Northern Region	Red	Plums, spicy	Sausages	**
Russe Chardonnay	Northern Region	White	Tropical fruit, melon	Fish	*
Russe Chardonnay Reserve	Northern Region	White	Tropical fruit, oaky	Chicken	**
Sakar Azbuka Merlot	Southern Region	Red	Plums, spicy	Cheese	**
Sakar Controliran Merlot	Southern Region	Red	Plums, spicy	Pasta	*
Sliven Cabernet Sauvignon Reserve	Sub-Balkan Region	Red	Berry, tannic, herbaceous	Lamb	**
Sliven Young Vatted Cabernet Sauvignon	Sub-Balkan Region	Red	Berry, herbaceous	Sausages	**
Stambolovo Controliran Merlot	Southern Region	Red	Berry, plums	Cold meats, stew	*
Stambolovo Merlot Reserve	Southern Region	Red	Fruit cake, berry	Lamb	**
Suhindol Cabernet Sauvignon Estate Selection	Northern Region	Red	Berry, herbaceous, tannic	Beef	**
ROMANIA					
Carl Reh Winery River Route Pinot Grigio	Romania	White	Crisp, minerally	Fish	**
Dealul-Mare Premiat Merlot	Romania	Red	Berry, spicy	Chicken, veal, pork	*
Dealul-Mare Premiat Pinot Noir	Romania	Red	Berry, earthy, leathery	Fish, chicken	*
Dealul-Mare Valley of the Monks Merlot	Romania	Red	Berry, herbaceous	Chicken, veal, pork	*
Hanwood Group Idlerock Romanian Pinot Noir	Romania	Red	Berry, gamey	Duck	**
Murfatlar Pinot Gris	Romania	White	Floral, apples	Shellfish, fish	*
Rovit Special Reserve Pinot Noir	Romania	Red	Earthy, spicy	Game	**
St Ursula Lupu Negru Cabernet Sauvignon Merlot	Romania	Red	Berry, herbaceous	Lamb	**
Tirnave Blaj Muscat Attonel	Romania	White	Floral, honey, mint	Asian, fish	**

EASTERN EUROPE (Continued)

Wine name	Region	Style	Flavor/Bouquet	Compatible Foods	Price Range
GEORGIA					
Georgian Wines & Spirits Co Matrasa	Georgia	Red	Berry, earthy	Sausages	**
Georgian Wines & Spirits Co Pinot Noir	Georgia	Red	Berry, gamey	Cold meats, stew, offal	**

SOUTHERN EUROPE

Wine name	Region	Style	Flavor/Bouquet	Compatible Foods	Price Range
GREECE					
Ambelones Tselepos Mantinia	Mantinia/Peloponnese	White	Crisp, citrus, zingy	Shellfish, salads	**
Antonopoulos Adoli Ghis	Pàtras/Peloponnese	White	Apples, floral, complex, elegant	Fish, chicken	**
Babatzim Portogo Thessaloniki	Chalkidiki/Mainland Greece	Red	Earthy, peppery	Beef, lamb	**
Chateau Carras Cotes de Meliton	Macedonia	Red	Berry, earthy, herbaceous	Beef, lamb	**
Domaine Carras Cimnio Cotes de Meliton	Macedonia	Red	Berry, spicy	Pork, beef	**
Domaine Carras Melisanthi Cotes de Meliton	Macedonia	White	Honey, floral	Fish, chicken	**
Kostas Lazaridis Amethystos Cava	Drama/Mainland Greece	Red	Plums, berry, licorice, vanillin	Pork, beef, lamb	**
Ktima Gerovassiliou Viognier	Epanomi/Mainland Greece	White	Floral, fruity	Shellfish, Asian	**
Ktima Papaioannou Palea Klimata	Neméa/Peloponnese	Red	Berry, spicy	Veal, pork, beef	**
Nikos Lazaridis Magico Vouno	Drama/Macedonia	White	Fruity, floral, intense	Asian, fish	**
Oenoforos Asprolithi	Pàtras/Peloponnese	White	Melon, floral, honey	Shellfish, fish	**
Samos Co-op Samos Nectar	Samos/Aegean Islands	Sweet	Honey, floral, tropical fruit	Dessert	*
Semeli Chateau Semeli	Attica/Mainland Greece	Red	Rich, plums, earthy, oaky	Beef, lamb	**
Sigalas Mezzo	Santorini/Aegean Islands	White	Floral, honey, crisp	Shellfish, fish	**
MALTA					
Delicata Anchor Bay Rosé	Malta	Rosé	Fruity, berry	Antipasto	*
Delicata Chardonnay Superiore	Malta	White	Tropical fruit, citrus	Chicken	**
Delicata Fumé Blanc	Malta	White	Crisp, fruity	Shellfish	**
Delicata Golden Bay White	Malta	White	Fruity, melon	Shellfish	*
Delicata Grand Vin de Hauteville–Cabernet Sauvignon	Malta	Red	Berry, spicy	Sausages	**
Delicata Grand Vin de Hauteville–Oak Aged Chardonnay	Malta	White	Tropical fruit, oaky	Chicken	**
Delicata Green Label Dry	Malta	White	Zingy, citrus	Fish	*
Delicata Green Label Medium-Dry	Malta	White	Fruity, tropical fruit	Fish	**
Delicata Paradise Bay Red	Malta	Red	Earthy, berry	Pasta	**
Delicata Red Label Gellewza	Malta	Red	Berry, spicy	Pizza	**
Delicata Red Label Rosé	Malta	Rosé	Berry, fruity	Antipasto	*
Delicata Sauvignon Blanc	Malta	White	Zingy, grassy	Salads	**
Delicata St Paul's Bay White	Malta	White	Fruity, melon	Fish	*
Delicata Trebbiano Classico	Malta	White	Fruity, minerally	Pasta	*
Marsovin Antonin Blanc	Malta	White	Citrus, fruity	Salads	*
Marsovin Antonin Red	Malta	Red	Earthy, spicy	Pasta	*
Marsovin Cassar de Malte, Méthode Traditionelle	Malta	Sparkling	Crisp, fruity	Aperitif	**
Marsovin Cheval Franc	Malta	Red	Berry, herbaceous	Lamb	**
CYPRUS					
ETKO Despotika	Cyprus	Red	Berry, spicy	Cheese	**
ETKO Ino	Cyprus	Red	Spicy, earthy	Cold meats, stew, offal	**
ETKO Olympus	Cyprus	Red	Smoky, berry	Cold meats	**
ETKO Salera Red	Cyprus	Red	Berry, gamey	Pasta	*
ETKO Salera White	Cyprus	White	Floral, citrus	Fish	*
KEO Alkion	Cyprus	White	Crisp, citrus	Shellfish	*
KEO Cabernet Sauvignon	Cyprus	Red	Herbaceous, berry	Lamb	**
KEO Commanderie St John	Cyprus	Sweet	Sweet, honey, raisiny	Nuts	**
KEO Domaine d'Ahera	Cyprus	Red	Plums, berry	Cold meats, stew, offal	**
KEO Heritage	Cyprus	Red	Earthy, berry	Sausages	**
KEO Thisbe	Cyprus	White	Citrus, minerally	Chicken	**

SOUTH AFRICA

Wine name	Region	Style	Flavor/Bouquet	Compatible Foods	Price Range
Axe Hill Vintage Port	Klein Karoo	Fortified	Sweet, spirity	Nuts	**
Backsberg Cabernet Sauvignon	Paarl	Red	Berry, tannic, herbaceous	Lamb	**
Backsberg Merlot	Paarl	Red	Plums, fruity	Pasta	**

SOUTH AFRICA *(Continued)*

Wine name	Region	Style	Flavor/Bouquet	Compatible Foods	Price Range
Boplaas Port	Klein Karoo	Fortified	Sweet, raisiny	Cheese	**
Boplaas Vintage Reserve Port	Klein Karoo	Fortified	Sweet, spirity, fruity	Cheese	**
Boschendal Brut MCC	Franschhoek	Sparkling	Crisp, yeasty	Aperitif	**
Boschendal Chardonnay Reserve	Franschhoek	White	Tropical fruit, oaky, spicy	Veal	**
Boschendal Merlot	Franschhoek	Red	Berry, fruit cake	Lamb	**
Bouchard Finlayson Galpin Peak Pinot Noir	Walker Bay	Red	Smoky, berry	Duck	**
Brampton Sauvignon Blanc	Stellenbosch	White	Citrus, zingy	Shellfish	**
Buitenverwachting Chardonnay	Constantia	White	Melon, citrus	Chicken	**
Buitenverwachting Christine Red Blend	Constantia	Red	Berry, smoky	Cold meats, stew, offal	**
Clos Malverne Red Blend	Stellenbosch	Red	Berry, tannic	Pasta	**
Constantia Uitsig Reserve Chardonnay	Constantia	White	Melon, oaky	Chicken	**
Constantia Uitsig Reserve Semillon	Constantia	White	Citrus, grassy	Antipasto	**
Darling Cellars Groenkloof Pinotage	Swartland	Red	Spicy, earthy	Cold meats	**
De Trafford Shiraz	Stellenbosch	Red	Berry, earthy	Cold meats, stew, offal	**
De Wetshof d'Honneur Chardonnay	Robertson	White	Melon, citrus	Fish	**
De Wetshof Finesse Chardonnay	Robertson	White	Tropical fruit, melon	Fish	**
Delheim Cabernet Sauvignon	Stellenbosch	Red	Berry, herbaceous	Lamb	**
Delheim Gëwurztraminer	Stellenbosch	White	Spicy, floral	Asian	**
Delheim Merlot	Stellenbosch	Red	Plums, berry	Pizza	**
Delheim Shiraz	Stellenbosch	Red	Earthy, tannic, berry	Beef	**
Genesis Shiraz	Stellenbosch	Red	Earthy, minerally, berry	Beef	**
Glen Carlou (Reserve) Chardonnay	Paarl	White	Tropical fruit, oaky	Fish	**
Glen Carlou Grand Classique Red Blend	Paarl	Red	Berry, spicy	Veal	**
Glen Carlou Peter Devereux Chenin Blanc	Paarl	White	Apples, tropical fruit	Fish	**
Graham Beck Blanc de Blancs MCC	Robertson	Sparkling	Crisp, minerally, citrus	Aperitif	**
Graham Beck Pinotage	Coastal	Red	Earthy, berry	Sausages	**
Graham Beck Shiraz	Coastal	Red	Earthy, berry, spicy	Beef	**
Grangehurst CIWG Cabernet Sauvignon	Stellenbosch	Red	Berry, minerally, complex	Lamb	***
Grangehurst CIWG Pinotage	Stellenbosch	Red	Berry, earthy	Stew	**
Grangehurst Merlot	Stellenbosch	Red	Fruit cake, complex	Game	***
Groot Constantia Gewurztraminer	Constantia	White	Spicy, floral	Sausages	**
Groot Constantia Rhine Riesling	Constantia	White	Floral, citrus	Fish	**
Hamilton Russell Chardonnay	Walker Bay	White	Melon, tropical fruit	Fish	**
Hamilton Russell Pinot Noir	Walker Bay	Red	Berry, spicy	Duck	***
JC Le Roux Chardonnay MCC	Stellenbosch	Sparkling	Crisp, fruity	Aperitif	**
Kanonkop Cabernet Sauvignon	Stellenbosch	Red	Berry, complex, herbaceous	Lamb	**
Kanonkop CIWG Pinotage	Stellenbosch	Red	Earthy, berry	Stew	**
Kanonkop Pinotage	Stellenbosch	Red	Earthy, leathery	Stew	**
Karoo Die Krans Vintage Reserve Port	Klein Karoo	Fortified	Sweet, spirity, powerful	Nuts	**
Klein Constantia Rhine Riesling	Constantia	White	Floral, spicy	Fish	**
Klein Constantia Sauvignon Blanc	Constantia	White	Zingy, citrus	Shellfish	**
Klein Constantia Shiraz	Constantia	Red	Earthy, plums	Beef	**
Krone Borealis MCC	Tulbagh	Sparkling	Crisp, fruity	Aperitif	**
KWV Cathedral Cellars Cabernet Franc	Coastal	Red	Berry, herbaceous	Lamb	**
KWV Cathedral Cellars Merlot	Coastal	Red	Berry, plums	Beef	**
KWV Cathedral Cellars Pinotage	Coastal	Red	Berry, earthy	Cold meats, stew, offal	**
KWV Cathedral Cellars Port	Coastal	Fortified	Sweet, spirity	Nuts	**
KWV Cathedral Cellars Triptych Red Blend	Coastal	Red	Earthy, minerally, spicy	Lamb	**
L'Avenir Vin de Meurveur Dessert Wine	Stellenbosch	Sweet	Sweet, citrus	Dessert	**
Longridge Merlot	Stellenbosch	Red	Plum, berry	Lamb	**
Meerlust Rubicon Red Blend	Stellenbosch	Red	Spicy, earthy, oaky	Beef	**
Morgenhof Premier Selection Red Blend	Stellenbosch	Red	Earthy, berry	Cheese	**
Mulderbosch Steen op Hout Chenin Blanc	Stellenbosch	White	Tropical fruit, spicy	Cheese	**
Nederburg Auction Cabernet Sauvignon	Paarl	Red	Berry, herbaceous	Lamb	**
Nederburg Bin R115 Red Blend	Paarl	Red	Spicy, berry	Beef	**
Nederburg Bin R163 Cabernet Sauvignon	Paarl	Red	Berry, herbaceous, tannic	Lamb	**
Nederburg Bin S316 Noble Late Harvest	Paarl	Sweet	Sweet, citrus	Dessert	**
Nederburg Eminence Dessert Wine	Paarl	Sweet	Sweet, complex, mandarin	Dessert	***
Nederburg Gëwurztraminer	Paarl	White	Spicy, floral	Asian	**
Nederburg Noble Late Harvest Dessert Wine	Paarl	Sweet	Sweet, citrus	Dessert	**
Neil Ellis Cabernet Sauvignon	Stellenbosch	Red	Herbaceous, berry	Lamb	**
Neil Ellis Elgin Chardonnay	Elgin	White	Tropical fruit, melon	Fish	**
Neil Ellis Elgin Sauvignon Blanc	Elgin	White	Citrus, zingy	Shellfish	**

SOUTH AFRICA *(Continued)*

Wine name	Region	Style	Flavor/Bouquet	Compatible Foods	Price Range
Neil Ellis Groenekloof Sauvignon Blanc	Darling	White	Zingy, citrus	Shellfish	**
Neil Ellis Reserve Cabernet Sauvignon	Stellenbosch	Red	Herbaceous, oaky	Cold meats	**
Overgaauw Touirga Nacional Port	Stellenbosch	Fortified	Sweet, raisiny	Cheese	**
Paul Cluver Chardonnay	Elgin	White	Melon, citrus	Fish	**
Plaisir de Merle Cabernet Sauvignon	Franschhoek	Red	Herbaceous, tannic	Lamb	**
Pongrácz MCC	Stellenbosch	Sparkling	Crisp, fruity	Aperitif	**
Rustenberg Cabernet Sauvignon	Stellenbosch	Red	Herbaceous, berry	Lamb	**
Rustenberg Red Blend	Stellenbosch	Red	Earthy, berry	Sausages	**
Rusterberg Peter Barlow Red Blend	Stellenbosch	Red	Earthy, smoky	Cheese	**
Saxenburg Reserve Shiraz	Stellenbosch	Red	Berry, spicy	Cold meats	***
Simonsig Frans Malan Reserve Red Blend	Stellenbosch	Red	Earthy, berry, oaky	Lamb	**
Simonsig Pinotage	Stellenbosch	Red	Earthy, spicy	Cold meats, stew, offal	**
Simonsig Red Hill Pinotage	Stellenbosch	Red	Berry, earthy	Sausages	**
Simonsig Reserve Shiraz	Stellenbosch	Red	Earthy, spicy, oaky	Beef	**
Simonsig Shiraz	Stellenbosch	Red	Berry, earthy	Pasta	**
Simonsig Tiara Red Blend	Stellenbosch	Red	Fruity, berry	Cold meats	**
Simonsvlei Hercules Paragon Chardonnay	Paarl	White	Melon, tropical fruit	Fish	**
Southern Right Pinotage	Walker Bay	Red	Earthy, spicy	Cold meats, stew, offal	**
Spice Route Reserve Chenin Blanc	Swartland	White	Tropical fruit, melon	Fish	**
Spice Route Reserve Pinotage	Swartland	Red	Earthy, spicy	Pasta	**
Spier IV Spears Sauvignon Blanc	Stellenbosch	White	Zingy, citrus	Shellfish	**
Springfield Life From Stone Sauvignon Blanc	Robertson	White	Zingy, citrus	Shellfish	**
Steenberg Oaked Semillon	Constantia	White	Grassy, oaky	Veal	**
Steenberg Reserve Sauvignon Blanc	Constantia	White	Citrus, tropical fruit	Salads	**
Steenberg Sauvignon Blanc	Constantia	White	Zingy, citrus	Salads	**
Thelema Cabernet Sauvignon	Stellenbosch	Red	Herbaceous, berry	Cheese	***
Thelema Eds Reserve Chardonnay	Stellenbosch	White	Citrus, oaky	Veal	**
Thelema Reserve Chardonnay	Stellenbosch	White	Spicy, citrus, oaky	Chicken	***
Vergelegen Mill Race Red Red Blend	Stellenbosch	Red	Smoky, spicy	Sausages	**
Vergelegen Reserve Chardonnay	Stellenbosch	White	Melon, tropical fruit	Fish	**
Villiera Bush Vine Sauvignon Blanc	Paarl	White	Grassy, tropical fruit	Salads	**
Villiera Carte d'Or MCC	Paarl	Sparkling	Austere, crisp	Shellfish	**
Villiera Chenin Blanc	Paarl	White	Apples, citrus	Pasta	**
Villiera Sauvignon Blanc	Paarl	White	Zingy, citrus	Shellfish	**
Warwick Cabernet Franc	Stellenbosch	Red	Berry, herbaceous	Lamb	**
Warwick Chardonnay	Stellenbosch	White	Melon, tropical fruit	Fish	**
Warwick Trilogy Red Blend	Stellenbosch	Red	Earthy, smoky	Cold meats	**
Zandvliet Chardonnay	Robertson	White	Melon, minerally	Fish	**
Zandvliet Shiraz	Robertson	Red	Berry, tannic	Beef	**

AUSTRALIA

Wine name	Region	Style	Flavor/Bouquet	Compatible Foods	Price Range
Alkoomi Riesling	Western Australia	White	Floral	Shellfish	**
Alkoomi Sauvignon Blanc	Western Australia	White	Tropical fruit	Salads	**
All Saints Aleatico	North East Victoria/Victoria	Red	Fruity	Asian	**
All Saints Show Reserve Tokay	North East Victoria/Victoria	Fortified	Sweet, complex	Nuts	**
Allandale Chardonnay	New South Wales	White	Nutty, tropical fruit	Fish	**
Amberley Semillon Sauvignon Blanc	Western Australia	White	Tropical fruit	Shellfish	**
Amberley Shiraz	Western Australia	Red	Berry, earthy	Beef	**
Andrew Harris The Vision	New South Wales	Red	Oaky, complex, berry	Beef	***
Angove's Classic Reserve Cabernet Sauvignon	Riverland/South Australia	Red	Berry, plum	Stew	**
Angove's Classic Reserve Chardonnay	Riverland/South Australia	White	Tropical fruit	Pork	**
Angove's Classic Reserve Shiraz	Riverland/South Australia	Red	Berry, earthy	Pasta	**
Ashton Hills Chardonnay	Adelaide Hills/South Australia	White	Nutty, complex	Chicken	**
Ashton Hills Reserve Pinot Noir	Adelaide Hills/South Australia	Red	Spicy, berry	Duck	**
Baileys of Glenrowan 1920s Block Shiraz	North East Victoria/Victoria	Red	Powerful, berry, tannic	Stew	**
Baileys of Glenrowan Founders Muscat	North East Victoria/Victoria	Fortified	Sweet, complex, raisiny	Nuts	**
Balgownie Cabernet Sauvignon	Central Victoria	Red	Herbaceous, berry	Lamb	**
Balgownie Shiraz	Central Victoria	Red	Berry, spicy	Beef	**
Ballandean Black Label Cabernet Sauvignon	Queensland	Red	Berry, herbaceous	Lamb	**
Ballandean Black Label Chardonnay	Queensland	White	Melon, tropical fruit	Fish	**
Ballandean Late Harvest Sylvaner	Queensland	Sweet	Sweet, citrus	Fruit	**
Bannockburn Cabernet Sauvignon	Geelong/Victoria	Red	Minerally, berry, herbaceous	Lamb	**

AUSTRALIA *(Continued)*

Wine name	Region	Style	Flavor/Bouquet	Compatible Foods	Price Range
Bannockburn Chardonnay	Geelong/Victoria	White	Nutty, complex, melon	Fish	**
Bannockburn Pinot Noir	Geelong/Victoria	Red	Gamey, earthy, complex	Duck	**
Bannockburn Shiraz	Geelong/Victoria	Red	Complex, spicy, berry	Beef	**
Banrock Station Shiraz Cabernet	Riverland/South Australia	Red	Berry	Pizza	*
Banrock Station Shiraz	Riverland/South Australia	Red	Berry	Pizza	*
Banrock Station Sparkling Chardonnay	Riverland/South Australia	Sparkling	Citrus, melon	Salads	*
Barossa Valley Estate E Black Pepper Shiraz	Barossa/South Australia	Red	Berry, oaky, earthy	Beef	***
Barwang Shiraz	New South Wales	Red	Berry, spicy	Cold meats	**
Bass Phillip Chardonnay	Gippsland/Victoria	White	Melon, nutty	Fish	***
Bass Phillip Pinot Noir	Gippsland/Victoria	Red	Complex, berry, gamey	Duck	***
Bimbadgen Semillon	New South Wales	White	Citrus	Veal	**
Blass Adelaide Hills Cabernet Merlot	Adelaide Hills/South Australia	Red	Berry, spicy, oaky	Beef	**
Blass Barossa Valley Shiraz	Barossa/South Australia	Red	Berry, spicy, tannic	Beef	**
Blass Vineyard Selection Cabernet Sauvignon	Barossa/South Australia	Red	Berry, herbaceous, oaky	Sausages	**
Bloodwood Chardonnay	New South Wales	White	Tropical fruit, melon	Chicken	**
Bonneyview Chardonnay	Riverland/South Australia	White	Tropical fruit	Chicken	**
Bonneyview Petit Verdot Merlot	Riverland/South Australia	Red	Berry	Pasta	**
Botobolar Shiraz	New South Wales	Red	Berry, earthy	Cold meats, stew, offal	**
Bowen Estate Cabernet Sauvignon	Coonawarra/South Australia	Red	Berry, herbaceous, tannic, minerally	Lamb	**
Bowen Estate Chardonnay	Coonawarra/South Australia	White	Tropical fruit, nutty	Fish	**
Bowen Estate Shiraz	Coonawarra/South Australia	Red	Berry, spicy, tannic	Beef	**
Brokenwood Graveyard Shiraz	New South Wales	Red	Berry, complex, tannic	Beef	***
Brokenwood ILR Semillon	New South Wales	White	Complex, toasty, citrus	Pork	***
Brokenwood Semillon	New South Wales	White	Citrus	Fish	**
Brown Brothers Classic Release Cabernet Sauvignon	North East Victoria/Victoria	Red	Berry, herbaceous	Lamb	**
Brown Brothers Late Harvested Noble Riesling	North East Victoria/Victoria	Sweet	Sweet, complex, citrus	Dessert	**
Brown Brothers Late Harvested Orange Muscat and Flora	North East Victoria/Victoria	Sweet	Sweet, citrus	Fruit	**
Brown Brothers Shiraz	North East Victoria/Victoria	Red	Earthy, berry	Beef	**
Brown Brothers Very Old Liqueur Muscat	North East Victoria/Victoria	Fortified	Sweet, complex, raisiny	Nuts	**
Brown Brothers Vintage Port	North East Victoria/Victoria	Fortified	Sweet, licorice	Cheese	**
Cape Mentelle Semillon Sauvignon Blanc	Western Australia	White	Grassy, tropical fruit	Salads	**
Cape Mentelle Shiraz	Western Australia	Red	Earthy, berry	Stew	**
Cape Mentelle Zinfandel	Western Australia	Red	Earthy, berry	Beef	**
Capel Vale Riesling	Western Australia	White	Floral	Salads	**
Cassegrain Reserve Chambourcin	New South Wales	Red	Berry, plum	Cold meats	**
Cassegrain Reserve Chardonnay	New South Wales	White	Tropical fruit, melon	Fish	**
Chain of Ponds Amadeus Cabernet Sauvignon	Adelaide Hills/South Australia	Red	Herbaceous, berry	Lamb	**
Chain of Ponds Ledge Shiraz	Adelaide Hills/South Australia	Red	Spicy, berry	Beef	**
Chain of Ponds Riesling	Adelaide Hills/South Australia	White	Citrus, floral, zingy	Cheese	**
Chambers Rosewood Rare Muscat	North East Victoria/Victoria	Fortified	Raisiny, complex, sweet	Nuts	**
Chambers Rosewood Rare Tokay	North East Victoria/Victoria	Fortified	Complex, sweet, cold tea	Nuts	**
Chapel Hill Cabernet Sauvignon	McLaren Vale/South Australia	Red	Berry, herbaceous, complex	Lamb	**
Chapel Hill Shiraz	McLaren Vale/South Australia	Red	Berry, spicy	Beef	**
Chapel Hill The Vicar Cabernet Sauvignon Shiraz	McLaren Vale/South Australia	Red	Berry, spicy, tannic, oaky	Lamb	**
Charles Cimicky Shiraz	Barossa/South Australia	Red	Berry, plum	Stew	**
Charles Melton Nine Popes	Barossa/South Australia	Red	Berry, complex, earthy	Cold meats, stew, offal	**
Charles Melton Rose of Virginia	Barossa/South Australia	Rosé	Berry, floral	Cheese	**
Charles Melton Sparkling Red	Barossa/South Australia	Sparkling	Berry, smokey, powerful	Cold meats	**
Charles Sturt University Cabernet Sauvignon	New South Wales	Red	Berry, herbaceous	Sausages	**
Chateau Tahbilk Cabernet Sauvignon	Central Victoria	Red	Earthy, berry	Cold meats, stew, offal	**
Chateau Tahbilk Marsanne	Central Victoria	White	Citrus, tropical fruit	Antipasto	*
Chateau Xanadu Cabernet Reserve	Western Australia	Red	Berry, minerally, complex	Lamb	***
Chateau Xanadu Semillon	Western Australia	White	Grassy	Antipasto	**
Clarendon Hills Kangarilla Vineyard Old Vines Grenache	McLaren Vale/South Australia	Red	Berry, plum, powerful	Cold meats, stew, offal	***
Clarendon Hills Piggott Range Vineyard Shiraz	McLaren Vale/South Australia	Red	Spicy, berry, earthy, tannic, oaky	Sausages	***
Clonakilla Shiraz/Viognier	New South Wales	Red	Berry, minerally, complex	Veal	**
Clovelly Estate Left Field Chardonnay	Queensland	White	Fruity	Chicken	**
Cope-Williams R.O.M.S.E.Y. Brut	Macedon/Victoria	Sparkling	Crisp, complex, berry	Shellfish	**
Coriole Lalla Rookh Semillon	McLaren Vale/South Australia	White	Tropical fruit	Veal	**
Coriole Redstone Shiraz Cabernet Sauvignon Grenache Merlot	McLaren Vale/South Australia	Red	Berry, tannic	Stew	**
Cowra Estate Cabernet Franc Rosé	New South Wales	Rosé	Berry, fruity	Antipasto	**
Crabtree Watervale Shiraz Cabernet Sauvignon	Clare Valley/South Australia	Red	Berry, spicy	Stew	**
Cranswick Autumn Gold	New South Wales	Sweet	Citrus, mandarin, sweet	Fruit	**
Cullen Cabernet Merlot	Western Australia	Red	Complex, minerally, berry	Lamb	***

AUSTRALIA *(Continued)*

Wine name	Region	Style	Flavor/Bouquet	Compatible Foods	Price Range
Cullen Chardonnay	Western Australia	White	Nutty, complex, melon	Fish	**
D'Arenberg D'Arry's Original Shiraz Grenache	McLaren Vale/South Australia	Red	Berry, earthy	Sausages	*
D'Arenberg Peppermint Park Sparkling Chambourcin	McLaren Vale/South Australia	Sparkling	Fruit cake, berry	Cold meats	**
D'Arenberg Twenty Eight Road Mourvedre	McLaren Vale/South Australia	Red	Berry, spicy, oaky, tannic	Stew	**
Dalwhinnie Chardonnay	Grampians & Western Victoria/Victoria	White	Complex, melon, nutty	Fish	**
Dalwhinnie Eagle Series Shiraz	Grampians & Western Victoria/Victoria	Red	Complex, spicy, berry	Beef	***
Dalwhinnie Pinot Noir	Grampians & Western Victoria/Victoria	Red	Spicy, earthy, berry	Duck	**
De Bortoli Black Noble	New South Wales	Fortified	Sweet, raisiny, fruit cake	Nuts	**
De Bortoli Noble One	New South Wales	Sweet	Sweet, citrus, mandarin	Dessert	**
Devil's Lair Cabernet Sauvignon	Western Australia	Red	Minerally, herbaceous, earthy	Lamb	**
Devil's Lair Chardonnay	Western Australia	White	Melon, nutty	Fish	**
Evans & Tate Redbrook Semillon	Western Australia	White	Fruity, tropical fruit	Shellfish	**
Evans & Tate Shiraz	Western Australia	Red	Earthy, minerally	Beef	**
Evans Family Hunter Valley Chardonnay	New South Wales	White	Tropical fruit, melon	Fish	**
Fox Creek JSM Shiraz Cabernets	McLaren Vale/South Australia	Red	Berry, plum	Sausages	**
Fox Creek Vixen Sparkling Cabernet Sauvignon/Shiraz	McLaren Vale/South Australia	Sparkling	Plum, berry	Cold meats	**
Frankland Estate Olmo's Reward Bordeaux Blend	Western Australia	Red	Complex, herbaceous, berry	Lamb	**
Frankland Estate Riesling	Western Australia	White	Citrus, floral	Asian	**
Geoff Merrill Cabernet Merlot	McLaren Vale/South Australia	Red	Berry, herbaceous	Lamb	**
Geoff Weaver Chardonnay	Adelaide Hills/South Australia	White	Complex with tropical flavour	Fish	**
Geoff Weaver Sauvignon Blanc	Adelaide Hills/South Australia	White	Zingy, grassy	Shellfish	**
Giaconda Chardonnay	North East Victoria/Victoria	White	Complex, nutty, minerally, tropical fruit	Fish	***
Giaconda Pinot Noir	North East Victoria/Victoria	Red	Earthy, gamey, spicy, complex, berry	Duck	***
Glenara Cabernet Sauvignon Merlot	Adelaide Hills/South Australia	Red	Herbaceous, berry	Lamb	**
Glenguin Merlot	New South Wales	Red	Berry, fruit cake	Cold meats	**
Glenguin Semillon	New South Wales	White	Citrus, toasty	Shellfish	**
Goundrey Reserve Chardonnay	Western Australia	White	Melon, nutty	Chicken	**
Goundrey Reserve Shiraz	Western Australia	Red	Minerally, oaky, berry	Beef	**
Grant Burge The Holy Trinity Grenache Shiraz Mourvedre	Barossa/South Australia	Red	Earthy, berry, oaky	Cold meats, stew, offal	**
Grant Burge Zerk Semillon	Barossa/South Australia	White	Tropical fruit, oaky	Veal	**
Grosset Pinot Noir	Clare Valley/South Australia	Red	Berry, spicy, gamey	Duck	**
Grosset Polish Hill Riesling	Clare Valley/South Australia	White	Citrus, floral, complex, minerally	Shellfish	**
Hanging Rock Winery Macedon Cuvee	Macedon/Victoria	Fortified	Complex, yeasty, berry, powerful	Fish	***
Hanging Rock Winery Victoria Chardonnay	Macedon/Victoria	White	Melon, tropical fruit	Fish	**
Hardys Eileen Hardy Shiraz	McLaren Vale/South Australia	Red	Berry, tannic, complex, oaky	Beef	***
Hardys Tintara Shiraz	McLaren Vale/South Australia	Red	Powerful, tannic, earthy, berry	Beef	**
Hay Shed Hill Cabernet Sauvignon	Western Australia	Red	Berry	Pasta	**
Henschke Cyril Henschke Cabernet Sauvignon Merlot Cabernet Franc	Barossa/South Australia	Red	Berry, spicy	Lamb	**
Henschke Green's Hill Riesling	Adelaide Hills/South Australia	White	Citrus, floral	Asian	**
Henschke Hill of Grace	Barossa/South Australia	Red	Complex, berry, oaky, minerally	Beef	***
Henschke Julius Eden Valley Riesling	Barossa/South Australia	White	Citrus, floral	Shellfish	**
Henschke Mount Edelstone	Barossa/South Australia	Red	Complex, berry	Beef	***
Hillstowe Buxton Sauvignon Blanc	Adelaide Hills/South Australia	White	Grassy	Shellfish	**
Hillstowe Mary's Hundred Shiraz	McLaren Vale/South Australia	Red	Berry, tannic, powerful	Beef	**
Hillstowe Udys Mill Pinot Noir	Adelaide Hills/South Australia	Red	Berry, spicy	Game	**
Houghton Jack Mann Cabernet Sauvignon Malbec Shiraz	Western Australia	Red	Complex, berry, minerally, earthy	Lamb	***
Howard Park Cabernet Sauvignon Merlot	Western Australia	Red	Complex, herbaceous, minerally	Lamb	***
Howard Park Chardonnay	Western Australia	White	Nutty, complex, melon	Chicken	***
Huntington Estate Reserve Shiraz	New South Wales	Red	Berry, tannic, powerful, spicy	Beef	**
Huntington Estate Shiraz	New South Wales	Red	Berry, tannic, spicy	Stew	**
Jasper Hill Emily's Paddock Shiraz	Central Victoria	Red	Berry, complex, spicy	Beef	***
Jasper Hill Georgia's Paddock Riesling	Central Victoria	White	Citrus, floral	Shellfish	**
Jim Barry The Armagh	Clare Valley/South Australia	Red	Berry, spicy, complex, oaky, powerful, tannic	Beef	***
Jim Barry Watervale Riesling	Clare Valley/South Australia	White	Citrus, floral	Antipasto	**
Katnook Estate Cabernet Sauvignon	Coonawarra/South Australia	Red	Berry, oaky, herbaceous	Lamb	**
Katnook Estate Chardonnay Brut	Coonawarra/South Australia	Sparkling	Crisp, citrus, fruity	Shellfish	**
Katnook Estate Merlot	Coonawarra/South Australia	Red	Berry, fruit cake, tannic	Game	**

AUSTRALIA *(Continued)*

Wine name	Region	Style	Flavor/Bouquet	Compatible Foods	Price Range
Katnook Estate Riesling	Coonawarra/South Australia	White	Citrus, floral	Antipasto	**
Katnook Estate Sauvignon Blanc	Coonawarra/South Australia	White	Tropical fruit, zingy	Salads	**
Kay's Amery Cabernet Sauvignon	McLaren Vale/South Australia	Red	Berry, tannic	Lamb	**
Kingston Estate Merlot	Riverland/South Australia	Red	Berry, plum	Stew	*
Knappstein Enterprise Cabernet Sauvignon	Clare Valley/South Australia	Red	Berry, herbaceous	Lamb	**
Knappstein Enterprise Shiraz	Clare Valley/South Australia	Red	Berry, spicy	Beef	**
Knight Granite Hills Shiraz	Macedon/Victoria	Red	Spicy, peppery, berry	Beef	**
Knight Granite Hills Sparkling Pinot Noir Chardonnay	Macedon/Victoria	Sparkling	Crisp, yeasty	Aperitif	**
Kominos Shiraz	Queensland	Red	Berry, earthy	Sausages	**
Lake's Folly Cabernet	New South Wales	Red	Berry, leathery, herbaceous	Lamb	***
Lake's Folly Chardonnay	New South Wales	White	Tropical fruit, complex	Fish	***
Lamont Barrel-Fermented Chardonnay	Western Australia	White	Melon, oaky	Fish	**
Lark Hill Chardonnay	New South Wales	White	Melon, citrus	Chicken	**
Leeuwin Estate Art Series Cabernet Sauvignon	Western Australia	Red	Herbaceous, minerally	Lamb	***
Leeuwin Estate Art Series Chardonnay	Western Australia	White	Complex, nutty, tropical fruit, melon	Fish	***
Leo Buring Clare Valley Riesling	Clare Valley/South Australia	White	Floral	Asian	*
Leo Buring Clare Valley Shiraz	Clare Valley/South Australia	Red	Berry	Beef	**
Lindemans Hunter River Reserve Porphyry	New South Wales	Sweet	Sweet, floral, citrus	Fruit	**
Lindemans Hunter River Semillon	New South Wales	White	Citrus, toasty, complex	Fish	*
Lindemans Hunter River Shiraz	New South Wales	Red	Leathery, berry	Stew	**
Lindemans Limestone Ridge Shiraz Cabernet	Coonawarra/South Australia	Red	Spicy, berry, herbaceous	Beef	**
Lindemans St George Cabernet Sauvignon	Coonawarra/South Australia	Red	Herbaceous, berry, oaky	Lamb	**
Lowe Family Chardonnay	New South Wales	White	Melon, tropical fruit	Pork	**
Lyre Bird Hill Pinot Noir	Gippsland/Victoria	Red	Berry, spicy	Duck	**
Madew Riesling	New South Wales	White	Floral, citrus	Fruit	**
Maglieri Steve Maglieri Shiraz	McLaren Vale/South Australia	Red	Berry, tannic, complex	Beef	***
Margan Family Semillon	New South Wales	White	Citrus, zingy	Shellfish	**
Margan Family Shiraz	New South Wales	Red	Berry, earthy	Cold meats, stew, offal	**
Mildara Jamiesons Run Reserve Red Blend	Coonawarra/South Australia	Red	Berry, oaky, tannic	Beef	**
Mildara Robertson's Well Cabernet Sauvignon	Coonawarra/South Australia	Red	Tannic, berry, herbaceous	Lamb	**
Mildara Robertson's Well Shiraz	Coonawarra/South Australia	Red	Berry, spicy, plum	Cold meats	**
Miranda Golden Botrytis Semillon	New South Wales	Sweet	Mandarin, sweet	Dessert	**
Mitchell Peppertree Vineyard Shiraz	Clare Valley/South Australia	Red	Berry, spicy	Beef	**
Mitchell Watervale Riesling	Clare Valley/South Australia	White	Citrus, floral	Shellfish	**
Mitchelton Blackwood Park Botrytis Riesling	Central Victoria	Sweet	Sweet, citrus	Fruit	**
Mitchelton Blackwood Park Riesling	Central Victoria	White	Citrus, floral	Fish	*
Moondah Brook Cabernet Sauvignon	Western Australia	Red	Herbaceous, berry	Cold meats	**
Moondah Brook Shiraz	Western Australia	Red	Earthy, berry	Stew	**
Morris Old Premium Muscat	North East Victoria/Victoria	Fortified	Complex, sweet, raisiny	Nuts	**
Morris Sparkling Durif Shiraz	North East Victoria/Victoria	Sparkling	Earthy, berry, plum	Cold meats	**
Moss Wood Chardonnay	Western Australia	White	Nutty, tropical fruit	Fish	**
Moss Wood Semillon	Western Australia	White	Grassy, fruity	Asian	**
Mount Langi Ghiran Billi Billi Red Blend	Grampians & Western Victoria/Victoria	Red	Berry, earthy	Pasta	**
Mount Langi Ghiran Cabernet Merlot	Grampians & Western Victoria/Victoria	Red	Berry, minerally, herbaceous	Stew	**
Mount Langi Ghiran Pinot Grigio	Grampians & Western Victoria/Victoria	White	Tropical fruit, citrus	Antipasto	**
Mount Pleasant Lovedale Semillon	New South Wales	White	Complex, toasty, honey	Chicken	**
Mount Pleasant Maurice O'Shea Shiraz	New South Wales	Red	Berry, leathery	Beef	**
Mount Pleasant Rosehill Shiraz	New South Wales	Red	Berry, leathery	Stew	**
Mountadam Chardonnay	Barossa/South Australia	White	Nutty, complex, tropical fruit	Fish	**
Mountadam Pinot Noir	Barossa/South Australia	Red	Gamey, berry, spicy	Duck	**
Mt Tamborine Cedar Creek Chardonnay	Queensland	White	Fruity, tropical fruit	Fish	**
Mt Tamborine Tehembrin Merlot	Queensland	Red	Berry, fruit cake	Stew	**
Nepenthe Lenswood Pinot Noir	Adelaide Hills/South Australia	Red	Berry, spicy, gamey, complex	Duck	**
Nepenthe Lenswood Semillon	Adelaide Hills/South Australia	White	Tropical fruit, citrus	Antipasto	**
Nicholson River Chardonnay	Gippsland/Victoria	White	Complex, minerally	Chicken	***
Normans Lone Gum Vineyard Shiraz Cabernet	Riverland/South Australia	Red	Berry, earthy	Mediterranean	*
Orlando Steingarten Riesling	Barossa/South Australia	White	Citrus, minerally, floral	Fish	**
Paracombe Cabernet Franc	Adelaide Hills/South Australia	Red	Herbaceous	Sausages	**
Parker First Growth Cabernet Sauvignon	Coonawarra/South Australia	Red	Berry, herbaceous, complex, tannic, oaky	Lamb	***
Pauletts Cabernet Merlot	Clare Valley/South Australia	Red	Berry, herbaceous	Lamb	**
Pendarves Verdelho	New South Wales	White	Tropical fruit	Fish	**

AUSTRALIA *(Continued)*

Wine name	Region	Style	Flavor/Bouquet	Compatible Foods	Price Range
Penfolds Adelaide Hills Chardonnay	Adelaide Hills/South Australia	White	Nutty, tropical fruit	Chicken	**
Penfolds Bin 707	Barossa/South Australia	Red	Berry, minerally, tannic, oaky	Lamb	***
Penfolds Eden Valley Riesling	Barossa/South Australia	White	Citrus, floral	Chicken	**
Penfolds Grandfather Port	Barossa/South Australia	Fortified	Raisins, sweet, complex	Nuts	***
Penfolds Grange	Barossa/South Australia	Red	Complex, powerful, tannic, oaky, berry, earthy	Beef	***
Penfolds Old Vine Grenache Mourvedre Shiraz	Barossa/South Australia	Red	Berry, spicy, plum	Cold meats, stew, offal	**
Penfolds Yattarna Chardonnay	Adelaide Hills/South Australia	White	Complex, nutty, citrus, tropical fruit	Fish	***
Petaluma Chardonnay	Adelaide Hills/South Australia	White	Complex, nutty, melon	Fish	**
Petaluma Croser	Adelaide Hills/South Australia	Sparkling	Crisp, yeasty, citrus, austere	Aperitif	**
Peter Lehmann Semillon	Barossa/South Australia	White	Tropical fruit, oaky	Veal	*
Peter Lehmann Stonewell Shiraz	Barossa/South Australia	Red	Berry, oaky, complex, tannic	Beef	**
Peter Lehmann The Mentor	Barossa/South Australia	Red	Berry, oaky, plum	Stew	**
Petersons Chardonnay	New South Wales	White	Tropical fruit	Chicken	**
Pewsey Vale Riesling	Barossa/South Australia	White	Citrus, floral, minerally	Salads	**
Phillip Island Winery Chardonnay	Gippsland/Victoria	White	Melon, tropical fruit	Chicken	**
Pierro Chardonnay	Western Australia	White	Complex, nutty, melon	Chicken	***
Pierro Semillon Sauvignon Blanc	Western Australia	White	Zingy, grassy	Shellfish	**
Pike's Premio Sangiovese	Clare Valley/South Australia	Red	Berry, earthy, savoury	Mediterranean	**
Pike's Reserve Riesling	Clare Valley/South Australia	White	Citrus, floral, austere	Chicken	**
Plantagenet Cabernet Sauvignon	Western Australia	Red	Herbaceous, berry	Lamb	**
Plantagenet Omrah Chardonnay	Western Australia	White	Fruity, citrus	Salads	**
Renmano Chairman's Selection Reserve Chardonnay	Riverland/South Australia	White	Tropical fruit	Fish	*
Richmond Grove Cowra Chardonnay	New South Wales	White	Tropical fruit	Fish	**
Richmond Grove Watervale Riesling	Clare Valley/South Australia	White	Citrus, floral	Shellfish	*
Rimfire Shiraz	Queensland	Red	Berry, spicy	Beef	**
Robinsons Family Cabernet Sauvignon	Queensland	Red	Herbaceous, earthy, berry	Sausages	**
Rochford Chardonnay	Macedon/Victoria	White	Tropical fruit, complex	Fish	**
Rockford Black Shiraz	Barossa/South Australia	Sparkling	Powerful, plum, berry, earthy, complex	Cold meats	***
Rockford Dry Country Grenache	Barossa/South Australia	Red	Plum, berry, earthy	Cold meats, stew, offal	**
Romavilla Very Old Tawny Port	Queensland	Fortified	Sweet, raisiny, complex	Nuts	**
Rosemount Balmoral Syrah	McLaren Vale/South Australia	Red	Powerful, berry, spicy, oaky, complex	Beef	***
Rosemount Giant's Creek Chardonnay	New South Wales	White	Tropical fruit, citrus, melon	Chicken	**
Rosemount GSM Grenache Shiraz Mourvedre	McLaren Vale/South Australia	Red	Berry, tannic, spicy	Cold meats, stew, offal	**
Rosemount Hill of Gold Chardonnay	New South Wales	White	Tropical fruit, melon	Fish	**
Rosemount Hill of Gold Shiraz	New South Wales	Red	Berry, spicy, tannic	Beef	**
Rosemount Roxburgh Chardonnay	New South Wales	White	Melon, complex, nutty, toasty	Chicken	***
Rosemount Show Reserve Semillon	New South Wales	White	Tropical fruit, citrus	Fish	**
Rothbury Estate Brokenback Semillon	New South Wales	White	Citrus, minerally	Fish	**
Rothbury Estate Brokenback Shiraz	New South Wales	Red	Leathery, berry	Stew	**
Rymill Pinot Noir Chardonnay Sparkling	Coonawarra/South Australia	Sparkling	Crisp, yeasty, citrus	Aperitif	**
Saltram Mamre Brook Cabernet Sauvignon	Barossa/South Australia	Red	Berry	Stew	**
Saltram Mamre Brook Shiraz	Barossa/South Australia	Red	Berry, earthy	Stew	**
Sandalford Verdelho	Western Australia	White	Tropical fruit	Veal	**
Scotchmans Hill Pinot Noir	Geelong/Victoria	Red	Spicy, berry	Duck	**
Scotchmans Hill Sauvignon Blanc	Geelong/Victoria	White	Tropical fruit, citrus	Cheese	**
Seaview Edwards & Chaffey Shiraz	McLaren Vale/South Australia	Red	Berry, oaky, tannic	Beef	**
Seppelt DP90 Show Tawny	Barossa/South Australia	Fortified	Complex, nutty, sweet	Nuts	**
Seppelt Great Western Shiraz	Grampians & Western Victoria/Victoria	Red	Earthy, complex, spicy	Stew	**
Seppelt Original Sparkling Shiraz	Grampians & Western Victoria/Victoria	Sparkling	Fruity, berry	Nuts	**
Seppelt Para Liqueur Vintage Tawny Port	Barossa/South Australia	Fortified	Sweet, raisiny	Cheese	**
Seppelt Rhymney Sauvignon Blanc	Grampians & Western Victoria/Victoria	White	Zingy	Shellfish	**
Seppelt Sheoak Riesling	Grampians & Western Victoria/Victoria	White	Floral, citrus	Shellfish	**
Seppelt Sunday Creek Pinot Noir	Grampians & Western Victoria/Victoria	Red	Berry, spicy	Cold meats	**
Sevenhill Cellars Shiraz	Clare Valley/South Australia	Red	Berry, spicy, earthy	Stew	**
Shaw and Smith Sauvignon Blanc	Adelaide Hills/South Australia	White	Zingy, tropical fruit, herbaceous	Shellfish	**
Skillogalee Riesling	Clare Valley/South Australia	White	Citrus, floral	Fish	**
Stephen John Watervale Pedro Ximenez	Clare Valley/South Australia	White	Crisp, apple	Shellfish	**
Stone Ridge Chardonnay	Queensland	White	Tropical fruit, nutty	Fish	**

AUSTRALIA *(Continued)*

Wine name	Region	Style	Flavor/Bouquet	Compatible Foods	Price Range
Stone Ridge Shiraz	Queensland	Red	Berry, earthy, spicy, tannic	Beef	**
Taltarni Merlot	Grampians & Western Victoria/Victoria	Red	Berry, fruit cake	Lamb	**
Taltarni Reserve Cabernet Sauvignon Victoria/Victoria	Grampians & Western	Red	Berry, herbaceous, powerful, tannic	Lamb	**
Tatachilla Clarendon Vineyard Merlot	McLaren Vale/South Australia	Red	Berry, fruit cake, spicy	Stew	**
Taylors Cabernet Sauvignon	Clare Valley/South Australia	Red	Berry	Pasta	*
Tim Adams The Fergus Grenache	Clare Valley/South Australia	Red	Earthy, berry, plum	Cold meats, stew, offal	**
Torbreck Runrig	Barossa/South Australia	Red	Berry, earthy, tannic	Beef	**
Torbreck The Steading	Barossa/South Australia	Red	Berry, earthy, tannic, oaky, powerful	Beef	***
Turkey Flat Butcher's Block	Barossa/South Australia	Red	Berry, earthy	Beef	**
Turkey Flat Shiraz	Barossa/South Australia	Red	Berry, tannic, powerful	Beef	**
Tyrell's Rufus Stone McLaren Vale Shiraz	Clare Valley/South Australia	Red	Berry, spicy	Beef	**
Tyrell's Brokenback Shiraz	New South Wales	Red	Berry, leathery	Cold meats	**
Tyrell's Moon Mountain Chardonnay	New South Wales	White	Tropical fruit, nutty	Fish	**
Tyrell's Vat 9 Dry Red	New South Wales	Red	Berry, leathery, tannic	Stew	**
Tyrell's Vat 47 Chardonnay	New South Wales	White	Complex, tropical fruit, melon	Chicken	**
Vasse Felix Heytesbury Red	Western Australia	Red	Complex, herbaceous, minerally	Beef	***
Vasse Felix Noble Riesling	Western Australia	Sweet	Sweet, citrus	Dessert	**
Vasse Felix Semillon	Western Australia	White	Grassy	Salads	**
Vasse Felix Shiraz	Western Australia	Red	Earthy, berry	Beef	**
Veritas Bull's Blood Shiraz Mourvedre Pressings	Barossa/South Australia	Red	Tannic, powerful, berry	Stew	**
Virgin Hills Red Blend	Macedon/Victoria	Red	Herbaceous, minerally, berry	Lamb	**
Voyager Cabernet Sauvignon Merlot	Western Australia	Red	Herbaceous, minerally, berry	Lamb	**
Voyager Chardonnay	Western Australia	White	Tropical fruit	Chicken	**
Wendouree Cellars Shiraz	Clare Valley/South Australia	Red	Berry, complex, spicy, tannic, powerful	Beef	**
Westend Golden Mist Botrytis Semillon	New South Wales	Sweet	Citrus, sweet	Dessert	**
Westfield Chardonnay	Western Australia	White	Melon, fruity	Chicken	**
Westfield Liqueur Muscat	Western Australia	Fortified	Sweet	Nuts	**
Wild Duck Creek Estate Black Label Reserve Cabernet	Central Victoria	Red	Herbaceous, berry	Lamb	**
Wild Duck Creek Estate Duckmuck	Central Victoria	Red	Powerful, spicy, berry	Beef	***
Wild Duck Creek Estate The Blend Red	Central Victoria	Red	Berry, earthy	Stew	**
Windermere Sangiovese Cabernet	Queensland	Red	Berry, spicy, savoury	Pasta	**
Windermere Shiraz	Queensland	Red	Berry, spicy, tannic	Beef	**
Winewood Shiraz Marsanne	Queensland	Red	Berry, spicy	Stew	**
Wirra Wirra Chardonnay	McLaren Vale/South Australia	White	Nutty, tropical fruit, melon	Fish	**
Wirra Wirra RSW Shiraz	McLaren Vale/South Australia	Red	Berry, complex, spicy	Beef	**
Wolf Blass Black Label Cabernet Shiraz Merlot	Barossa/South Australia	Red	Berry, oaky	Lamb	***
Wolf Blass Gold Label Riesling	Barossa/South Australia	White	Crisp, citrus, floral	Fish	*
Woodstock The Stocks Shiraz	McLaren Vale/South Australia	Red	Berry, earthy, tannic	Sausages	**
Wynns John Riddoch Cabernet Sauvignon	Coonawarra/South Australia	Red	Complex, berry, herbaceous, l tannic, powerfu	Lamb	***
Wynns Michael Shiraz	Coonawarra/South Australia	Red	Oaky, berry, tannic	Stew	***
Wynns Riesling	Coonawarra/South Australia	White	Floral, citrus	Shellfish	**
Wynns Shiraz	Coonawarra/South Australia	Red	Berry, spicy, tannic	Cold meats, stew, offal	*
Yalumba Oxford Landing Limited Release Merlot	Riverland/South Australia	Red	Berry, earthy	Pasta	*
Yalumba Signature Cabernet Sauvignon Shiraz	Barossa/South Australia	Red	Berry, plum	Cold meats, stew, offal	**
Yalumba The Octavius	Barossa/South Australia	Red	Oaky, tannic, berry, powerful	Stew	***
Yellowglen Cuvée Victoria	Grampians & Western Victoria/Victoria	Sparkling	Crisp, yeasty	Antipasto	**

NEW ZEALAND

Wine name	Region	Style	Flavor/Bouquet	Compatible Foods	Price Range
Alan McCorkindale Pinot Noir	Canterbury/Waipara	Red	Spicy, berry	Game	**
Alana Estate Sauvignon Blanc	Martinborough	White	Zingy, grassy	Shellfish	**
Alexander Vineyard Pinot Noir	Martinborough	Red	Spicy, berry, earthy	Veal	**
Allan Scott Chardonnay	Marlborough	White	Melon, citrus	Shellfish	**
Alpha Domus The Navigator (merlot/malbec/cabernet franc)	Hawkes Bay	Red	Earthy, oaky, berry	Beef	**
Ata Rangi Celebre Cabernet Sauvignon Merlot Syrah	Martinborough	Red	Berry, oaky, spicy	Lamb	**
Ata Rangi Craighall Chardonnay	Martinborough	White	Citrus, melon, oaky	Chicken	***
Babich Irongate Cabernet Sauvignon Merlot	Gisborne/Hawkes Bay	Red	Herbaceous, berry	Lamb	**
Babich Patriarch Cabernet Sauvignon	Gisborne/Hawkes Bay	Red	Berry, earthy, herbaceous	Stew	**
Babich Patriarch Chardonnay	Gisborne/Hawkes Bay	White	Tropical fruit, citrus	Fish	**
Benfield & Delamare Cabernet Sauvignon Merlot	Martinborough	Red	Herbaceous, berry	Lamb	**

NEW ZEALAND *(Continued)*

Wine name	Region	Style	Flavor/Bouquet	Compatible Foods	Price Range
Black Ridge Gewurztraminer	Central Otago	White	Spicy, citrus	Sausages	**
Brick Bay Matakana Pinot Gris	Northland	White	Citrus, floral	Pork	**
Brookfields Gewurztraminer	Gisborne/Hawkes Bay	White	Floral, spicy	Sausages	**
Brookfields Marshall Bank Chardonnay	Gisborne/Hawkes Bay	White	Tropical fruit, citrus	Fish	**
C. J. Pask Reserve Chardonnay	Gisborne/Hawkes Bay	White	Toasty, ripe, citrus	Shellfish	***
C. J. Pask Reserve Merlot	Gisborne/Hawkes Bay	Red	Plums, tannic	Mushrooms	***
Cairnbrae Reserve Riesling	Marlborough	White	Citrus, minerally	Cheese	**
Cairnbrae The Stones Sauvignon Blanc	Marlborough	White	Grassy, citrus	Shellfish	**
Canterbury House Chardonnay	Canterbury/Waipara	White	Melon, tropical fruit	Fish	**
Chancellor Sauvignon Blanc	Canterbury/Waipara	White	Citrus, floral, zingy	Shellfish	**
Chard Farm Bragato Pinot Noir	Central Otago	Red	Berry, spicy	Game	**
Chard Farm Finla Mor Pinot Noir	Central Otago	Red	Berry, tannic	Game	**
Chard Farm Riesling	Central Otago	White	Citrus, floral	Fish	**
Church Road Chardonnay	Gisborne/Hawkes Bay	White	Citrus, oaky, spicy	Pork	**
Church Road Reserve Cabernet Sauvignon Merlot	Gisborne/Hawkes Bay	Red	Tannic, berry, smoky	Beef	***
Clearview Old Olive Block Cabernet Sauvignon Cabernet Franc	Gisborne/Hawkes Bay	Red	Ripe, berry, tannic	Cold meats, stew, offal	**
Clearview Reserve Cabernet Sauvignon	Gisborne/Hawkes Bay	Red	Berry, minerally	Lamb	**
Cloudy Bay Chardonnay	Marlborough	White	Melon, toasty	Fish	***
Cloudy Bay Pinot Noir	Marlborough	Red	Gamey, leathery	Duck	***
Coopers Creek Reserve Hawkes Bay Merlot Cabernet Franc	Gisborne/Hawkes Bay	Red	Plums, berry	Lamb	**
Corbans Cottage Block Marlborough Chardonnay	Marlborough	White	Melon, tropical fruit	Fish	**
Corbans Cottage Block Noble Riesling	Marlborough	Sweet	Mandarin, honey	Fruit	**
Corbans Private Bin Gisborne Chardonnay	Gisborne	White	Melon, citrus	Fish	**
Corbans Private Bin Marlborough Chardonnay	Marlborough	White	Melon, tropical fruit	Fish	**
Craggy Range Chardonnay	Gisborne/Hawkes Bay	White	Complex, minerally, spicy	Fish	***
Craggy Range Riesling	Marlborough	White	Citrus, floral, zingy, complex	Shellfish	***
Cross Roads Talisman (up to 6 varieties)	Hawkes Bay	Red	Oaky, berry, rich	Beef	***
Daniel Le Brun Vintage Brut Méthode Traditionnelle	Marlborough	Sparkling	Toasty, complex	Aperitif	***
Danniel Schuster Selection Chardonnay	Canterbury/Waipara	White	Tropical fruit, zingy	Chicken	**
Danniel Schuster Selection Pinot Noir	Canterbury/Waipara	Red	Cherry, plums, oaky	Duck	***
De Redcliffe Marlborough Riesling	Marlborough	White	Floral, citrus	Fish	**
Delegates Reserve Cabernet Sauvignon	Gisborne/Hawkes Bay	Red	Complex, berry, herbaceous	Lamb	**
Domaine Chandon Marlborough Brut Méthode Traditionnelle	Marlborough	Sparkling	Toasty, crisp, minerally	Aperitif	**
Domaine Georges Michel Chardonnay	Marlborough	White	Nutty, tropical fruit	Fish	**
Dry River Craighall Botrytis Riesling	Martinborough	Sweet	Sweet, honey	Dessert	**
Dry River Craighall Riesling	Martinborough	White	Floral, citrus	Fish	**
Dry River Syrah	Martinborough	Red	Plums, berry, earthy	Beef	***
Esk Valley The Terraces Malbec Merlot Cabernet franc	Gisborne/Hawkes Bay	Red	Berry, tannic, ripe	Beef	***
Fairhall Downs Sauvignon Blanc	Marlborough	White	Tropical fruit, zingy	Shellfish	**
Felton Road Block Three Pinot Noir	Central Otago	Red	Complex, berry, gamey	Duck	***
Felton Road Chardonnay	Central Otago	White	Oaky, tropical fruit	Veal	**
Fiddler's Green Riesling	Canterbury/Waipara	White	Floral	Asian	**
Forrest Estate Cornerstone Cabernet Sauvignon Merlot Cabernet Franc Malbec	Gisborne/Hawkes Bay	Red	Herbaceous, spicy	Pasta	**
Forrest Estate Sauvignon Blanc	Marlborough	White	Zingy, citrus, minerally	Shellfish	**
Forrest Merlot	Marlborough	Red	Berry, herbaceous	Lamb	**
Forrest Riesling	Marlborough	White	Floral, citrus	Aperitif	**
Forrest Semillon	Marlborough	White	Tropical fruit, grassy	Fish	**
Foxes Island Chardonnay	Marlborough	White	Citrus, spicy	Chicken	***
Framingham Classic Riesling	Marlborough	White	Floral, minerally	Fish	**
Fromm La Strada Chardonnay	Marlborough	White	Complex, nutty, tropical fruit	Veal	**
Fromm La Strada Merlot	Marlborough	Red	Berry, complex, spicy	Lamb	***
Fromm La Strada Riesling Auslese	Marlborough	Sweet	Sweet, citrus, floral	Dessert	**
Gibbston Valley Pinot Noir	Central Otago	Red	Spicy, berry	Game	**
Gibbston Valley Reserve Pinot Noir	Central Otago	Red	Complex, berry, earthy	Duck	***
Gibbston Valley Riesling	Central Otago	White	Citrus, zingy	Fish	**
Gibbston Valley Sauvignon Blanc	Central Otago	White	Zingy, grassy	Antipasto	**
Giesen Noble Late Harvest Riesling	Canterbury/Waipara	Sweet	Sweet, citrus	Dessert	**
Giesen Reserve Chardonnay	Canterbury/Waipara	White	Melon, tropical fruit	Chicken	**
Giesen Reserve Pinot Noir	Canterbury/Waipara	Red	Berry, earthy, gamey	Fish, veal, pork	***
Goldwater Zell Chardonnay	Waiheke Island	White	Nutty, melon	Fish	**
Greenhough Hope Pinot Noir	Nelson	Red	Berry, earthy	Game	**
Greenhough Sauvignon Blanc	Nelson	White	Zingy, grassy	Shellfish	**
Grove Mill Sauvignon Blanc	Marlborough	White	Citrus, zingy	Shellfish	**
Highfield Elstree Méthode Traditionnelle	Marlborough	Sparkling	Crisp, toasty	Aperitif	**

NEW ZEALAND *(Continued)*

Wine name	Region	Style	Flavor/Bouquet	Compatible Foods	Price Range
Huia Gewurztraminer	Marlborough	White	Floral, spicy, complex	Sausages	**
Huia Méthode Traditionnelle	Marlborough	Sparkling	Toasty, complex	Fish	***
Huia Sauvignon Blanc	Marlborough	White	Tropical fruit, spicy, zingy	Shellfish	**
Huntaway Gewurztraminer	Gisborne/Hawkes Bay	White	Spicy, floral	Asian	**
Hunters Brut Méthode Traditionnelle	Marlborough	Sparkling	Crisp, fruity	Aperitif	**
Hunters Sauvignon Blanc	Marlborough	White	Zingy, citrus	Shellfish	**
Huthlee Merlot	Gisborne/Hawkes Bay	Red	Fruit cake, berry	Cold meats, stew, offal	**
Isabel Estate Pinot Noir	Marlborough	Red	Spicy, oaky, berry	Cold meats	***
Isabel Estate Sauvignon Blanc	Marlborough	White	Zingy, spicy	Shellfish	**
Jackson Estate Sauvignon Blanc	Marlborough	White	Zingy, tropical fruit	Shellfish	**
Kaituna Valley Pinot Noir	Canterbury/Waipara	Red	Berry, plum	Sausages	**
Kawarau Estate Reserve Pinot Noir	Central Otago	Red	Oaky, spicy	Cold meats, stew, offal	**
Kemble Field Chardonnay	Gisborne/Hawkes Bay	White	Melon, citrus	Fish	**
Kim Crawford Unwooded Chardonnay	Marlborough	White	Melon, citrus	Fish	**
Kingsley Estate Cabernet Sauvignon	Gisborne/Hawkes Bay	Red	Berry, minerally	Beef	**
Kumeau Brajkovich Cabernet Franc	Auckland	Red	Herbaceous, berry	Cold meats	**
Kumeau Brajkovich Chardonnay	Auckland	White	Austere, citrus	Fish	**
Lawson's Dry Hills Riesling	Marlborough	White	Floral, citrus	Veal	**
Lawson's Dry Hills Sauvignon Blanc	Marlborough	White	Grassy, zingy	Shellfish	**
Le Brun Family No. 1 Méthode Traditionnelle	Marlborough	Sparkling	Toasty, berry, spicy	Shellfish	***
Lintz Vitesse Cabernet Sauvignon	Martinborough	Red	Berry, tannic, smoky	Venison	***
Margrain Merlot	Martinborough	Red	Plums, leathery	Cold meats, stew, offal	**
Martinborough Vineyard Chardonnay	Martinborough	White	Melon, nutty, complex	Chicken	**
Martinborough Vineyards Late Harvest Riesling	Martinborough	Sweet	Honey, mandarin, sweet	Dessert	**
Martinborough Vineyards Reserve Pinot Noir	Martinborough	Red	Oaky, berry, gamey	Duck	***
Matariki Anthology (syrah/merlot/cabernet sauvignon/ cabernet franc)	Gisborne/Hawkes Bay	Red	Smoky, berry	Cold meats	**
Matawhero Gewurztraminer	Gisborne/Hawkes Bay	White	Floral, citrus	Sausages	**
Matua Innovator Malbec	Gisborne/Hawkes Bay	Red	Earthy, berry	Cold meats, stew, offal	**
Matua Shingle Peak Pinot Blanc	Marlborough	White	Melon, fruity	Mediterranean	**
Matua Unwooded Chardonnay	Gisborne/Hawkes Bay	White	Stone fruit, melon	Fish	**
Matua Valley Matheson Reserve Sauvignon Blanc	Gisborne/Hawkes Bay	White	Zingy, citrus	Shellfish	**
Mills Reef Reserve Chardonnay	Gisborne/Hawkes Bay	White	Nutty, melon	Fish	**
Millton Barrel Fermented Chardonnay	Gisborne/Hawkes Bay	White	Nutty, spicy	Veal	**
Millton Barrel Fermented Chenin Blanc	Gisborne/Hawkes Bay	White	Melon, nutty, apples	Chicken	**
Mission Jewelstone Pinot Gris	Gisborne/Hawkes Bay	White	Citrus, spicy	Fish	**
Montana Patutahi Gewurztraminer	Gisborne/Hawkes Bay	White	Zingy, spicy	Asian	**
Montana Reserve Chardonnay	Marlborough	White	Nutty, minerally, citrus	Chicken	**
Montana Reserve Pinot Noir	Marlborough	Red	Berry, spicy, earthy	Game	**
Montana Tom Cabernet Sauvignon Merlot	Gisborne/Hawkes Bay	Red	Herbaceous, minerally	Lamb	**
Morton Estate Black Label Cabernet Sauvignon	Gisborne/Hawkes Bay	Red	Berry, complex	Beef	***
Morton Estate Black Label Chardonnay	Gisborne/Hawkes Bay	White	Citrus, nutty	Fish	**
Morton Estate Black Label Merlot Cabernet Sauvignon	Gisborne/Hawkes Bay	Red	Oaky, berry, plums	Beef	***
Morton Estate Black Label Méthode Traditionnelle	Gisborne/Hawkes Bay	Sparkling	Toasty, austere	Aperitif	**
Morton Estate RD Méthode Traditionnelle	Gisborne/Hawkes Bay	Sparkling	Crisp, toasty	Nuts	**
Morton Estate White Label Marlborough Sauvignon Blanc	Marlborough	White	Grassy, zingy	Shellfish	**
Morton White Label Hawkes Bay Chardonnay	Gisborne/Hawkes Bay	White	Melon, floral	Fish	**
Mountford Chardonnay	Canterbury/Waipara	White	Melon, tropical fruit	Pork	**
Mountford Pinot Noir	Canterbury/Waipara	Red	Berry, spicy	Duck	**
Muddy Water Pinot Noir	Canterbury/Waipara	Red	Earthy, berry	Pasta	**
Murdoch James Syrah	Martinborough	Red	Spicy, berry, earthy	Beef	**
Nautilus Chardonnay	Marlborough	White	Melon, tropical fruit	Fish	**
Neudorf Moutere Chardonnay	Nelson	White	Tropical fruit, toasty, nutty	Shellfish	***
Neudorf Moutere Late Harvest Riesling	Nelson	Sweet	Mandarin, sweet	Dessert	**
Neudorf Moutere Reserve Pinot Noir	Nelson	Red	Earthy, gamey, berry	Game	***
Neudorf Sauvignon Blanc	Nelson	White	Zingy, citrus, tropical fruit	Shellfish	**
Nevis Bluff Pinot Gris	Central Otago	White	Zingy, rich	Salads	**
Nga Waka Riesling	Martinborough	White	Floral, citrus	Mediterranean	**
Ngatarawa Alwyn Noble Harvest Riesling	Gisborne/Hawkes Bay	Sweet	Sweet, citrus	Dessert	**
Nobilos Grand Reserve Chardonnay	Gisborne/Hawkes Bay	White	Melon, oaky	Fish	**
Nobilos Icon Gewurztraminer	Marlborough	White	Spicy, floral, citrus	Asian	**
Okahu Pinotage	Northland/Auckland	Red	Berry, earthy	Pasta	**
Olssen's of Bannockburn Pinot Noir	Central Otago	Red	Fungal, berry	Pasta	**
Omaka Springs Chardonnay	Marlborough	White	Melon, fruity	Salads	*
Oyster Bay Chardonnay	Marlborough	White	Citrus, mandarin, oaky	Shellfish	**
Oyster Bay Sauvignon Blanc	Marlborough	White	Zingy, citrus, fruity	Shellfish	**

NEW ZEALAND *(Continued)*

Wine name	Region	Style	Flavor/Bouquet	Compatible Foods	Price Range
Palliser Estate Méthode Traditionnelle	Martinborough	Sparkling	Crisp, berry, citrus	Aperitif	**
Pegasus Bay Aria Late Picked Riesling	Canterbury/Waipara	Sweet	Sweet, mandarin	Dessert	**
Pegasus Bay Chardonnay	Canterbury/Waipara	White	Tropical fruit, melon	Fish	**
Pegasus Bay Finale Noble Chardonnay	Canterbury/Waipara	Sweet	Sweet, complex	Dessert	**
Pegasus Bay Prima Donna Pinot Noir	Canterbury/Waipara	Red	Berry, smoky, complex	Duck	***
Penisula Estate Cabernet Sauvignon Merlot	Waiheke Island	Red	Berry, tannic	Lamb	***
Peregrine Pinot Noir	Central Otago	Red	Spicy, berry	Sausages	**
Perrelle Lake Hayes Grand Cuvée Méthode Traditionnelle	Central Otago	Sparkling	Crisp, citrus	Aperitif	**
Quartz Reef Pinot Noir	Central Otago	Red	Berry, spicy	Duck	**
Redmetal Vineyards Basket Press Merlot Cabernet Franc	Gisborne/Hawkes Bay	Red	Berry, chocolate, tannic	Beef	***
Rippon Pinot Noir	Central Otago	Red	Berry, spicy	Duck	***
Rippon Sauvignon Blanc	Central Otago	White	Zingy, citrus	Cheese	**
Rongopai Winemakers Reserve Botrytised Chardonnay	Waikato/Bay of Plenty	Sweet	Sweet, mandarin	Dessert	***
Sacred Hill Barrel Fermented Sauvignon Blanc	Gisborne/Hawkes Bay	White	Tropical fruit, nutty	Chicken	**
Sacred Hill XS Noble Selection Riesling	Gisborne/Hawkes Bay	Sweet	Citrus, sweet	Dessert	**
Saint Clair Awatere Reserve Sauvignon Blanc	Marlborough	White	Grassy, zingy	Cheese	**
Seifried Barrel Fermented Chardonnay	Nelson	White	Melon, nutty	Veal	**
Seifried Winemaker's Collection Riesling	Nelson	White	Citrus, floral	Fruit	**
Seifried Winemaker's Collection Riesling Ice Wine	Nelson	Sweet	Sweet, citrus, floral	Dessert	**
Selaks Drylands Chardonnay	Marlborough	White	Melon, nutty	Fish	**
Selaks Drylands Sauvignon Blanc	Marlborough	White	Tropical fruit, zingy	Salads	**
Seresin Chardonnay	Marlborough	White	Nutty, melon, complex	Chicken	**
Seresin Noble Riesling	Marlborough	Sweet	Sweet, honey, citrus	Dessert	**
Seresin Pinot Noir	Marlborough	Red	Fungal, earthy, gamey	Duck	**
Seresin Riesling	Marlborough	White	Floral, citrus, spicy	Fish	**
Sileni Chardonnay	Gisborne/Hawkes Bay	White	Fruity, tropical fruit	Fish	**
Sileni Merlot Cabernet Sauvignon Cabernet Franc	Gisborne/Hawkes Bay	Red	Leathery, berry	Beef	***
St Helena Reserve Pinot Gris	Canterbury/Waipara	White	Tropical fruit, spicy	Salads	**
Stonecroft Gewurztraminer	Gisborne/Hawkes Bay	White	Floral, spicy	Asian	**
Stonecroft Syrah	Gisborne/Hawkes Bay	Red	Spicy, berry	Duck	***
Stoneleigh Sauvignon Blanc	Marlborough	White	Zingy, minerally	Shellfish	**
Stoneyridge Larose Cabernets (cabernet sauvignon/malbec/merlot/cabernet franc/petite verdot)	Waiheke Island	Red	Berry, complex, tannic, oaky	Lamb	***
Te Awa Farm Boundary (cabernet sauvignon/merlot/cabernet franc/malbec)	Hawkes Bay	Red	Herbaceous, berry	Beef	**
Te Awa Farm Merlot	Gisborne/Hawkes Bay	Red	Berry, spicy, herbaceous	Lamb	**
Te Awa Frontier Chardonnay	Gisborne/Hawkes Bay	White	Melon, nutty	Fish	**
Te Kairanga Reserve Pinot Noir	Martinborough	Red	Complex, berry, spicy	Duck	***
Te Mata Awatea Cabernet Sauvignon Merlot	Gisborne/Hawkes Bay	Red	Berry, herbaceous	Beef	***
Te Mata Cape Crest Sauvignon Blanc	Gisborne/Hawkes Bay	White	Zingy, grassy	Salads	**
Te Whare Ra Duke of Marlborough Chardonnay	Marlborough	White	Melon, oaky	Chicken	**
Thornbury Merlot	Gisborne/Hawkes Bay	Red	Herbaceous, plums	Venison	**
Thornbury Sauvignon Blanc	Marlborough	White	Grassy, tropical fruit	Cheese	**
Torlese Gewurztraminer	Canterbury/Waipara	White	Spicy, floral	Asian	**
Trinity Hill Cabernet Sauvignon	Gisborne/Hawkes Bay	Red	Berry, tannic	Pasta	***
Trinity Hill Gimbless Road Cabernet Sauvignon Merlot	Gisborne/Hawkes Bay	Red	Smoky, tannic	Venison	***
Two Paddocks Pinot Noir	Central Otago	Red	Spicy, gamey, earthy	Game	**
Unison Merlot Cabernet Sauvignon Syrah	Gisborne/Hawkes Bay	Red	Spicy, berry, oaky	Beef	**
Vavasour Dashwood Sauvignon Blanc	Marlborough	White	Zingy, tropical fruit	Fish	**
Vavasour Pinot Noir	Marlborough	Red	Gamey, berry	Duck	**
Vavasour Riesling	Marlborough	White	Citrus, floral	Veal	**
Vavasour Single Vineyard Sauvignon Blanc	Marlborough	White	Zingy, tropical fruit, citrus	Fish	**
Vidal Reseve Noble Semillon	Gisborne/Hawkes Bay	Sweet	Sweet, mandarin	Dessert	**
Vidal Sauvignon Blanc	Marlborough	White	Grassy, zingy	Cheese	**
Villa Maria Reserve Gewurztraminer	Gisborne/Hawkes Bay	White	Spicy, citrus	Asian	**
Villa Maria Reserve Hawkes Bay Cabernet Sauvignon Merlot	Gisborne/Hawkes Bay	Red	Berry, tannic	Beef	***
Villa Maria Reserve Marlborough Chardonnay	Marlborough	White	Melon, citrus	Pork	**
Villa Maria Reserve Noble Riesling	Marlborough	Sweet	Sweet, mandarin	Dessert	***
Villa Maria Wairau Valley Reserve Sauvignon Blanc	Marlborough	White	Zingy, minerally	Shellfish	**
Vina Alta Retico Amarone-style Cabernet Franc/Merlot	Auckland	Red	Berry, plums, rich	Cheese	**
Waiheke Vineyards Te Motu Cabernet Sauvignon Merlot	Waiheke Island/Auckland	Red	Berry, tannic	Lamb	***
Waipara West Chardonnay	Canterbury/Waipara	White	Tropical fruit, melon	Chicken	**
Whitehaven Single Vineyard Reserve Sauvignon Blanc	Marlborough	White	Zingy, grassy	Shellfish	**
William Hill Riesling	Central Otago	White	Floral, zingy	Fish	**
Winslow Turakrae Reserve Cabernet Sauvignon Cabernet Franc	Wairarapa/Wellington	Red	Earthy, berry, tannic	Lamb	***
Wither Hills Sauvignon Blanc	Marlborough	White	Zingy, minerally	Cheese	**

Glossary

STEVE CHARTERS MW

a.b.v. "Alcohol by volume," the standard form of measuring the alcohol level in a wine, given as a percentage.
AC Initials of *Appellation Controlée.*
Acid The component of substances which gives them a sharp, tangy taste. Lemons, for example, are very acidic. Acidity, mainly in the form of tartaric acid, is a key component of wine.
Acidification The process of adding acidity to juice or wine to make it taste fresher and prevent damage from bacteria and oxygen.
Adega (Portuguese) A cellar or winery.
Aguardiente (Spanish) A popular high-proof grape spirit produced by the continuous still method.
Air-bag press A cylindrical press which works by expanding a rubber bladder under air pressure. As the bladder expands it squeezes the grapes in the press, producing juice.
Alcohol by volume *see* a.b.v.
Amtliche prufungsnummer **(AP)** (German) The number which appears on every bottle of QbA or QmP wine. It signifies that the wine has passed the official taste tests.
Appellation A term used to describe a demarcated wine region, one where the boundaries of the region are mapped out. The term is originally French. *See also Appellation Controlée.*
Appellation Controlée (AC) (French) A demarcated wine region in France. For example, only wine made in the specifically defined area around Bordeaux can claim to be from the Bordeaux appellation. French appellation laws also prescribe various viticultural and winemaking practices for each AC.
Aromatic Literally a wine with a noticeable smell, but often used to describe wines with a very floral or spicy nose.
Artisanal Wine made by an artisan: the "crafted" result of small-scale, often traditional, production.
Assemblage (French) The term used for the blending of still wines prior to a secondary fermentation which will produce champagne or sparkling wine.
Aszú (Hungarian) Botrytized grapes. Most often encountered as tokay aszú (tokaji), Hungary's most famous sweet wine.
Ausbruch (Austrian) A notable wine made from botrytized grapes and considered to be more opulent than wines from the Beerenauslese category.
Auslese (German) One of the *Prädikats* of German wine law, literally meaning "selected harvest." In practice, a wine with greater must weight than is normal for German wines, and probably with noticeable sweetness and a hint of botrytis.
Autolysis The process resulting from the decomposition of dead yeast cells following fermentation. It gives a creamy texture and yeasty aromas to wine. It is especially important for sparkling wine which has undergone second fermentation by the traditional method.
Autolytic characters The aroma and flavor characters resulting from autolysis in sparkling wines.
Balance The relationship among the factors that make up the structure of a wine—the acid, residual sugar, tannin, alcohol, weight, texture and fruit intensity—when tasting it.
Barrel aging The process of aging wine in a barrel (usually of new or newish oak) rather than in a large tank and/or the bottle.
Barrel fermentation The process of fermenting wine in small oak barrels rather than tanks or vats. The process imparts a richness and creaminess to the texture of the wine, but if all new oak is used, this can be overdone.
Barrica (Spanish) *see Barrique.*
Barrique (French) A term originally used in Bordeaux but now commonly used worldwide for a barrel of 225 liters (60 gallons).
Base wine The wine, fermented dry, that will undergo a second fermentation to become sparkling wine.
Battonage (French) The stirring of yeast lees in barrel. It encourages the uptake of lees flavors in the wine, and prevents some faults developing in the wine.
Baumé (French) One of the methods of quantifying sugar levels in grape juice; the others are brix and *oeschle.* This method is used in France and Australia. One degree *baumé* is roughly equal to one percent of alcohol in the resulting wine.
Beerenauslese **(BA)** (German) One of the *Prädikats* of German wine law, literally "selected berries." This category implies the selection of botrytized grapes, to make intense and sweet wine.
Biodynamic A system of cultivation which is related to organic viticulture. It is based around viewing the soil as a living organism which should not be treated with inorganic substances. The system has a complex dogma, which is dismissed as superstition by some, but it has been adopted by some of the leading producers in France and elsewhere.
Bladder press *see* Air-bag press.
Blanc de Blancs (French) White wine from white grapes but attaches to champagnes made from 100 percent chardonnay grapes.
Blanc de Noirs (French) White wine from black (or red) grapes. In Champagne, it refers to wines made from pinot noir and/or pinot meunier, though there are not many. Bollinger's VVF is the classic example. It is possible to make white wine from these grapes as they, and almost all other "black" grapes, have "white" juice and pulp, the color of the wine eventually coming from skin content.
Bodega (Spanish) This word has many meanings: cellar, wine producer, merchant, store selling wine, tavern.
Bodeguero (Spanish) Proprietor of a *bodega.*
Botrytis Latin term for fungus, encompassing all the rots which can affect grapes and damage the resulting wine. In one form—noble rot—it does not harm the grapes, but produces a complex and sweet wine, commonly referred to as "botrytized."
Bottle shock The term for the impact of bottling on wine: the wine can become less aromatic or tasty in the few weeks after bottling.
Brix One of the methods of quantifying sugar levels in grape juice; the others are *baumé* and *oeschle.* This method is used by winemakers in the US and New Zealand as one component of assessing grape ripeness.
Brut (French) This term is used to denote dry or very dry champagne. Extra brut is even drier.
Cane The woody growth developing from vine shoots: it both produces the vine leaves and carries the bunches of grapes.
Canteiro (Portuguese) The eaves of the Madeira houses under which the island's great vintage wines must age for a minimum of 20 years in cask.
Cap The mixture of skins, stalks, and other matter which accumulates at the top of fermenting red must.
Carbonic maceration The process of starting to ferment juice in unbroken grapes, using enzymes rather than yeast; a full yeast fermentation follows once the alcohol level in the grapes reaches about 4 percent. It is traditionally used in Beaujolais, producing fruity wines with low tannin.
Cap The mixture of skins, stalks and other matter which accumulates at the top of fermenting red must.
Casa Vinacola (Italian) A producer who buys in grapes and even wine, rather than a producer that grows their own grapes.
Cava Spanish sparkling wine made in a number of regions by the traditional method.
Cepage (French) Grape varieties. *Encepagement* refers to the grape varieties that make up the blend of any wine. For example, the *encepagement* of a Bordeaux will include some or all of merlot, cabernet sauvignon, cabernet franc, petit verdot, and malbec.
Chaptalization The process of adding sugar to fermenting must to increase the resulting alcoholic strength of the wine.
Charmat A method of inducing the second fermentation, and thus creating sparkling wine, in large pressure tanks. This method reduces the production costs usually associated with the traditional method.
Clairet Deep rosé wine that is produced in Bordeaux.
Classic When used on German labels, at the discretion of the producer, it indicates the wine is dry, officially under 1.5 percent residual sugar. The term has been used since the year 2000.
Classico (Italian) The designation for the best part of any DOC region. The best known is Chianti Classico, which has attained a DOC rating of its own.
Climat (French) A term used particularly in Burgundy for a vineyard site, defined by its meso-climate as well as by its soil.
Clone Propagation of vines from an original mother vine. Some varieties, especially pinot noir, may have hundreds of clones. They will have different uses. For example, one clone of pinot noir may suit the production of sparkling wine while another may be more suited to table wine. Most serious producers of a grape such as pinot believe that it is of benefit to

the final wine for their vineyard to have a number of different clones.

Clos (French) A walled vineyard.

Cold stabilization The process whereby tartrate crystals are precipitated out of the wine (if not, they can leave small harmless crystals) by swift chilling.

Colheita (Portuguese) A tawny port which is not a blend of different years but which is "dated," that is, from a single vintage.

Commune (French) A term often associated with the small subregions of Bordeaux. They can be appellations in their own right.

Concentration The intensity and focus of flavor in a wine.

Condition The state of a wine being drunk; whether or not it has any faults.

Cordon A permanent branch of a vine, usually trained along a wire.

Cork taint A wine fault caused generally by the interaction of mold (originating from the cork) with chlorine compounds, causing a loss of fruit flavor and—to a greater or lesser extent—a damp, hessian-like smell on the wine.

Crémant (French) This term was banned in Champagne in the early 1990's. Prior to that, it had been used to describe wines with a lesser degree of pressure (resulting in less fizz). These wines are still made in Champagne but each producer will provide the wine with its own name. The term is still used for sparkling wines made outside the Champagne district. Examples are Crémant de Loire and Crémant d'Alsace.

Crianza (Spanish) The term for aging, and for the youngest official category of a wood-matured wine (used particularly in Rioja, and some other regions, such as Ribera del Duero).

Crossing A new variety produced by adding the pollen of one variety to the flowers of another and planting the resulting grape seeds. Müller-Thurgau is probably the most utilized crossing in the world. Note the difference between a crossing and a hybrid.

Cru (French) Literally "growth." Practically, this is difficult to translate, but usually it is used in a qualitative context, as in "premier cru"—"first growth"—which is a high-quality wine.

Cuvée (French) Derived from the term for a tank, this word now refers to a particular selection of wine. In Champagne it is the first selection of juice on pressing—the best for making sparkling wine.

Deacidification The process of reducing the acid level in wine, normally by malolactic fermentation or the addition of various compounds which cause acidity to deposit out.

Demarcation The process of defining the exact geographical limits of a wine region. *See also* Appellation.

Demi-sec (French) A term used for sweet sparkling wine or champagne.

Denominazione di Origine Controllata (Italian) DOC equates to France's Appellation d'Origine Contrôlée laws. Over three hundred have been proclaimed. As with the French system, the laws govern the viticulture and winemaking practices permitted in each DOC. The wines also undergo chemical analysis and tasting under controlled conditions before they can be called DOC.

Denominazione di Origine Controllata e Garantita (Italian) DOCG is the quality level above the DOC wines. The regulations for these wines (there are more than twenty such regions) are stricter than those for DOC wines.

Disgorgement The action of expelling frozen yeast lees from a bottle of wine which has undergone second fermentation, to ensure that the wine is not cloudy.

DOC Initials of Denominazione di Origine Controllata.

DOCG Initials of Denominazione di Origine Controllata e Garantita.

Domaine (French) Often used to denote a winery, commonly used in Burgundy. In Bordeaux, it is much more likely that they will be referred to as Châteaux. In southern France, the term, Mas, is often substituted.

Dosage (French) Just prior to corking, a small quantity of "*liqueur d'expedition*," of varying degrees of sweetness, is added to sparkling wines. This *dosage* will determine the final classification of sweetness of the wine.

Eau-de-Vie A spirit or brandy, usually clear and sometimes flavored, that is made from distilling wine or grape skins (known as pomace). Translated literally, it means "water of life." Where an eau-de-vie is particularly strongly flavored or powerful, it can be called a marc.

Einzellagen (German) Individual vineyard sites. The number of these sites in Germany is approaching 3,000. Germany's regions are divided first into *Berieche*, then *Grosslagen*, and finally *Einzellagen*.

Eiswein (German) An intensely sweet wine that is made from grapes which have been left to hang on the vine for an extended period of time. The production of *eiswein* is a risky business. The grapes are pressed while frozen and the tiny amount of juice that is extracted is extremely concentrated and high in acid. The wines, which will age for many years, are rare and very expensive because of this method of production. Canada also produces wines in this style, called ice wine.

En primeur (French) The first sale of wine in Bordeaux from each vintage, in which wine is sold to the customer while the wine is still in barrels in the châteaux' cellars.

Enology The science of wine production.

Enrichment The process of increasing the alcohol level of the wine, usually by chaptalization, to modify its structure.

Estufa (Portuguese) The method of heating madeira which accelerates its development; it gives madeira its characteristic style by caramelizing the sugars in the wine.

Ethyl alcohol Scientific classification of the predominant type of alcohol in wine. Often popularly referred to as ethanol.

Extract The dry matter which would remain were you to evaporate the liquid from a wine. The higher the sugar-free extract, the more flavor, body and phenolic components there are in the wine. However, over-extraction can cause a wine to be unbalanced, especially if it results in excessive phenolics.

Feinherb (German) A term denoting an off-dry wine.

Fermentation The chemical process involved in converting sugar to alcohol and carbon dioxide, brought about by the activity of yeast.

Filtration The process of removing unwanted matter (even matter as small as bacteria or yeast cells) from a wine by various methods of straining.

Finesse The term used to describe elegant delicacy in a wine.

Fining The process of removing undesirable particles (usually proteins or phenolics) dissolved in the wine.

Flor (Spanish) The layer of yeast which forms on the surface of Fino and Manzanilla sherries during aging. It helps inhibit oxidation and also plays a role in contributing to the final flavor of the wine.

Fortification The addition of spirit (normally grape spirit) to wine. This is normally done during fermentation, to a point where yeast cells die and fermentation stops. Wines produced in this way are referred to as "fortified."

Foxy A description often applied to wine from native American varieties where the wine has a wild, earthy, gamey, grapey character. The term is most often applied disparagingly.

Fractional blending The process whereby when some wine is extracted from a cask for bottling it is replaced by wine from a more recent blend, which in turn may be replaced by a yet more recent blend, and so on until wine from the current vintage is added to the youngest blend. The process is used particularly in the making of sherry.

Frizzante (Italian) Slightly sparkling wine, an example is prosecco.

Garrafeira (Portuguese) A wine which has been subject to additional aging—three years for red wine and one year for white—for that type of wine. Wines labeled "Garrafeira" are generally considered to be of better quality.

Generoso (Spanish and Portuguese) Fortified wine.

Glycerol A heavy liquid, which is related to alcohol, which may impart hints of sweetness to a wine.

Gran Reserva (Spanish) This term is used to denote a wine that has had extra aging. Specifically, this means two years in cask and three years in bottle for red wines; and rather less for whites.

Grand vin (French) Literally "big wine": this can be interpreted as a great, serious, or important wine. Also used in Bordeaux for the main wine (not the second wine) made by a château.

Granvas (Spanish) Sparkling wine made by either the tank method or the charmat method.

Green harvesting The process of removing some bunches on a vine to reduce the yield and enhance the ripening process in the bunches which remain.

Guyot-trained A method of training a vine which uses a new cane or canes each year to provide shoots and ultimately fruit; it is unlike cordon training, which uses a permanent branch.

Halbtrocken (German) Literally "half dry": in practice, a medium dry wine.

Harmony The sense of integration and equilibrium one gets when tasting a wine which is in balance.

Herbaceous A wine which tastes herbal, or of dried grass. Sometimes used in a derogatory way.

Hybrid A new vine produced from two parents, generally one *Vitis vinifera* (which provides almost all the grape varieties used for making wine) and the other a native American species. This was done to combine the best aspects of both varieties, and to increase the vines' resistance to phylloxera (in Europe in the late nineteenth century), but the hybrids produced poor wine; only a few, such as seyval blanc and chambourcin, make acceptable wine.

IGT (Italian) Initials for *Indicazione Geografica Tipica*.

Imbottigliato all'Origine (Italian) Estate bottled wine. The grapes must also have been grown on the property.

Indicazione Geografica Tipica **(IGT)** (Italian) A category of wines considered to equate to France's *vin de pays*. There are well over one hundred IGTs, and they are subject to regulations that are less strict than those for DOC and DOCG wines. Super Tuscans such as Sassicaia and Tignanello are high-profile IGT examples.

Jeropiga (Portuguese) Grape juice prevented from fermenting by fortification. Usually used to sweeten fortified wines.

Joven afrutado (Spanish) A young wine made to emphasize overt fruity characters.

Jug wine US wine of mediocre quality produced in bulk and sold cheaply.

Kabinett (German) The most basic of the *Prädikats* of German wine law, but still usually of higher quality than basic QbA wine. These are very light wines.

KWV Initials (from the name in Afrikaans) of the Cooperative Wine Growers' Association of South Africa.

Lagar (Portuguese) A shallow basin in which the grapes used for port can be trodden to release their juice and extract phenolics while fermentation takes place.

Late disgorgement A form of champagne which remains on its yeast lees in the bottle for many years. The champagne is then disgorged shortly before sale. The lees allow the champagne to age slowly, and may also impart further flavor complexity.

Lees The term literally means any debris that falls out of wine (including skins, pips etc), but it is often used to refer to the dead yeast cells deposited at the end of fermentation, (also known as yeast lees). *See also* Autolysis; *Battonage*.

Length The amount of time the taste of wine lingers in the mouth after it has been swallowed. A long wine is generally a wine of high quality.

Levada (Portuguese) An irrigation trench used in Madeira to take water to the vineyards.

Liqueur de Tirage (French) A blend of wine, sugar, and yeasts that is added to still wine, which the producer intends to be sparkling, to induce the second fermentation, hence providing the effervescence.

Liqueur d'Expedition (French) The wine which is used to top up a champagne bottle after disgorging and prior to final corking. It adds the *dosage*, which determines the final level of sweetness in the wine.

Low cropping Vines which are managed in order to produce lower yields (and therefore, theoretically, higher quality yields). Also called crop thinning.

Maceración carbonica (Spanish) *see* carbonic maceration.

Maceration The process of leaving must or wine with grape skins during or after fermentation in order to increase the taking up of phenolics.

Maderization A process by which wine is made to taste like madeira: oxidation is sped up by the addition of heat. The term is sometimes used pejoratively, to indicate excessive oxidation and consequent unpleasant taste.

Malolactic fermentation The conversion by bacteria of crisp malic acid into softer lactic acid, making the wine fuller. It is commonly used in making red wines, but only with discretion in whites wines

Mercaptans A wine fault stemming from a sulfur compound that causes an unpleasant garlic-like smell, and which is impossible to shift.

Meritage (US) A trademarked name for wine based on a blend of the traditional red varieties from Bordeaux—primarily cabernet sauvignon, cabernet franc and merlot. Most Meritage is made in California.

Méthode ancestrale (French) A traditional way of making sparkling wine which involves stopping the fermentation by chilling, leaving a wine that is fizzy, slightly sweet and cloudy (from the yeast lees). It is mainly used for Blanquette de Limoux.

Méthode champenoise (French) The traditional method of making sparkling wine as utilized in Champagne.

Méthode traditionelle (French) *see* Traditional method.

Methyl alcohol A form of alcohol found in wine, but is much less important than ethyl alcohol. PIt is more popularly known as methanol.

Método tradicional (Spanish) *see* Traditional method.

Millésime (French) A term used to denote a vintage wine in Champagne.

Minerally A tasting term used to describe wine flavors which are not fruity, oaky or floral, but which may be more reminiscent of sucking on a pebble.

Mistelle (French) Grape juice prevented from fermenting by fortification with spirit.

Moelleux (French) Sweet, but not luscious.

Mousse The bubbles on the surface of a sparkling wine. The term is also used to describe the feel of the bubbles in the mouth.

Must The liquid that is fermenting—neither pure juice nor finished wine.

Muzzle The wire restraint which contains the cork of a sparkling wine.

Négociant (French) A wine merchant.

Nematodes Microscopic insects which may damage a vine or, more dangerously, carry a disease which will infect the vine.

Noble A contraction of "noble rot," referring to wine which has undergone the beneficial effects of botrytis.

Nose A term used to describe the smell of a wine.

Oechsle One of the methods of quantifying sugar levels in grape juice; the others are *baumé* and brix. It is commonly used by winemakers in Germany and Central Europe as one component of assessing grape ripeness.

Organoleptic An adjective referring to the process of tasting.

Oxidation The dulling of the color, aroma and flavor of a wine which results from too much air contact.

Palate A term used to describe the taste of wine.

Pasada (Spanish) Describes sherry that has been well aged.

Passerillage (French) Concentrating the sugars in grapes by leaving them to hang on the bunches and partially dehydrate.

Passito (Italian) Wine made from half-dried grapes, which has the effect of concentrating them. The wine is almost always sweet.

pH The scientific measurement of acidity and alkalinity. Water (which is neutral) has a pH of 7. A pH of less than that means a substance is acidic (at a pH of 1 it would be very highly acidic), and a pH above 7 means the substance is alkaline. Wine generally has a pH between 2.9 and about 3.6 (sometimes a little higher).

Phenolics Substances extracted from the skins of grapes which provide the coloring (anthocyanins) and texture (tannins) for red wine.

Phylloxera An aphid, with nineteen lifecycles, which attacks and slowly kills the root system of a vine. There is no known cure and the only way to save the vineyards of Europe and many other countries in the nineteenth century was to graft the *Vitis vinifera* vines on to the rootstock of native American vines, from where the aphid originated. Otherwise, there would likely be no wine industry, as we know it today.

Power A tasting term referring to the combined weight and flavor intensity of the wine—and possibly the impact of its alcohol as well.

Prädikat (German) Literally a "distinction," given to QmP wines: essentially a marker of the sugar level and an indicator of the likely style of the wine. The term is used in Germany and Austria.

Pumping over A method of increasing phenolic extraction from black grapes by pumping must from the bottom of a tank and spraying it over the cap at the top.

Punching down A method of increasing phenolic extraction from black grapes by pressing the cap down into the must, thus increasing contact between the cap and the liquid.

***Qualitätswein bestimmter Anbaugebiete* (QbA)** (German) Literally "quality wine from a region:" the most basic level of quality wine in Germany and Austria.

***Qualitätswein mit Prädikat* (QmP)** (German) Higher in quality than QbA in both Germany and Austria, QmP wines are defined using an additional categorization, which is based essentially on the wine's must weight (sugar level). *See also Kabinett*; *Spätlese*; *Auslese*; *Beerenauslese*; *Trockenbeerenauslese*.

Quinta (Portuguese) Strictly speaking it means a farm, but can be used to indicate either a specific vineyard or a specific wine estate, the Port House of Quinta do Noval is a prime example.

Racking The process of moving wine from one container to another, generally leaving some deposit behind. Sometimes, though not invariably, some aeration is involved.

Recioto (Italian) A sweet wine made from dried grapes, most famously from the Soave and Valpolicella regions.

Reduction The process of maturing wine in an environment with no oxygen contact. As the oxygen dissolved in the wine is used up, further oxidation cannot occur. This environment helps preserve freshness in wine, but in certain environments off-odors can develop.

Remuage (French) French term for riddling. It can be achieved by hand or by machines (gyropalettes).

Reserva (Spanish) Red wine that has been aged for at least a year in cask and two years in bottle. White wines age for a shorter period. These wines are generally of higher quality than ordinary wines.

Residual sugar Sugar which remains in the finished wine after fermentation has been completed, giving some sweetness to it.

Riddling The process (in the traditional method) of slowly shaking the yeast lees to the neck of the bottle ready for disgorgement.

Saignée (French) The process of "bleeding off" some red must at the start of fermentation in order to achieve a greater concentration of phenolics.

Sec (French) Although it literally means dry, if it appears on a champagne label, it means a wine that is slightly sweet, certainly sweeter than brut.

Second fermentation The means of adding the fizz (in the traditional method), by adding more yeast and sugar to base wine in a bottle or tank, then capping it in order to trap the resulting carbon dioxide.

Selection (German) A term for dry wine, under 1.2 percent residual sweetness, which can only be used where the label details the vineyard in which the grapes were grown. The term can be used at the maker's discretion.

Sélection de Grains Nobles (French) The term used in Alsace for wines made from very late harvested fruit, which has been affected by botrytis. The wines are intense and can be very expensive.

Set The point, after the vine has flowered, when the fertilized flower heads begin to turn into minute berries.

Shy-bearing A vine which does not produce much fruit.

Solera system A system of fractional blending, used mainly with sherry, which allows younger wine to gradually be blended with, and refresh, older wine.

Sorting tables Tables set up at harvest on which grapes can be sorted before crushing, to remove any of unacceptable quality. *See also triage*.

Spätlese (German) One of the *Prädikats* of German wine law, literally "late picked."

Spritzig (German) Wine which has a prickle of carbon dioxide, without being fully sparkling.

Stabilization The process of ensuring that wine has no components which may give rise to haze, deposits or further microbial activity once bottled.

Structure In tasting, the relationship between the elements sensed in the mouth (sugar, acidity, tannin, alcohol, bitterness, weight and texture), as well as the flavor intensity of the wine.

Sur lie (French) Literally "on lees": a wine which has been matured for some time on its yeast lees.

Süssreserve (German) Literally "sweet reserve": unfermented grape juice or grape concentrate added to the wine before bottling to sweeten it.

Table wine In Europe, this is the legal classification of the most basic wine, which distinguishes it from "quality" wine. In some European Union countries, this can now refer to blended wines, called European table wines.

Tafelwein (German) *see* Table wine.

Tannin A phenolic compound which gives a textural character to (mainly red) wine—"furring" the teeth and gums in much the same way that stewed tea does. In balance within the wine, it is an essential part of the structure of red wine.

Texture A tasting term for the tactile sensation of wine in the mouth: relating particularly to tannin.

Traditional method The production of sparkling wine by the induction of a second fermentation in a bottle, which is then riddled and undergoes disgorgement.

Triage (French) The sorting of grapes during vintage to discard those of unacceptable quality. With botrytized wines, *triage* is used to delay the picking of grapes which have not yet adequately developed noble rot.

***Trockenbeerenauslese* (TBA)** (German) One of the *Prädikats* of German wine law, literally "selected dried berries": the name implies selection of botrytized grapes, to make very intense and sweet wine. This is the pinnacle of German and Austrian sweet wine, and commands extremely high prices.

Ullage The small gap between the cork and the wine (when the bottle is upright). The greater the ullage, the more chance of oxidation of the wine.

Vaslin press A cylindrical press which works by pulling together two plates from either end of the cylinder, thus squeezing the grapes contained between the plates.

Vendange (French) Harvest.

Vendange tardive (French) Late harvest. The term is used in Alsace, and equates to the German *spätlese*.

Veraison (French) A critical stage in the ripening process, when black grapes start to attain their color, and white grapes cease to be intense green and become translucent. From this point the grape size expands noticeably and the sugar content starts to increase dramatically.

***Verband Deutscher Prädikats und Qualitätsweingüter* (VDP)** A German growers' association that requires its members to meet far higher production and quality standards than those demanded by the wine laws.

Vigor Vines may have more or less vigor. A certain amount implies a healthy vine, but excessive vigor may result in too much foliage, which shades the bunches and may impede ripening. Some vines are naturally more vigorous than others.

Vin de pays (French) A category of table wine which is nevertheless allowed to state a region of origin. Its production—particularly its yield—is more controlled than that of table wine (although without the constraints imposed by the appellation system), in an attempt to produce better wine.

Vino joven afrutado (Spanish) Young, fruity wine.

Vin doux naturel (French) Literally, "a wine that is naturally sweet," but used to describe a kind of fortified wine where spirit is added to grape juice rather than to wine. In various forms this is made across much of the south of France, either from grenache or muscat.

Vintage The year in which the grapes used to produce wine were picked.

Vitis vinifera (Latin) Botanical classification for the wine vine. Almost all varieties used to make wine are members of this species.

Weight The apparent feeling of heaviness (or not) which a wine gives when in the mouth. It is related to the alcohol content of the wine.

Winkler–Amerine heat summation scale A system of viticultural climate classification for California, based on the average environmental temperature. Growing zones are graded into regions (I–V) using monthly averages of temperatures over 50° Fahrenheit (10°C) during the vine's growing season. Daily temperature surpluses are averaged then multiplied by the number of days per month. Accumulations of heat are measured in degree days. The fewer the degree days, the cooler the region.

I. Less than 2,500 degree days: Bordeaux, Reims, Carneros, Edna Valley.
II. 2,501–3,000 degree days: Asti in Piedmont, Auckland, St. Helena in Napa Valley.
III. 3,001–3,500 degree days: Calistoga in Napa Valley, Ukiah in Mendocino.
IV. 3,500–4,000 degree days: Capetown, Florence.
V. More than 4,000 degree days: Perth, San Joaquin Valley.

Yield The amount of grapes produced by a vineyard, normally indicated by tons per acre/tonnes per hectare/hectoliters per hectare. As a rule, high yields are considered to produce lesser wine than vineyards with low yields, but many other factors must be taken into account.

Index

Italic page numbers refer to maps. **Bold** page numbers refer to major geographic sections. Pictures have not been indexed. Vineyards are indexed under their full names, including the words Château and Domaine.

In general Italian names are entered in the index under *de*, *di* and *della*. Spanish names are entered under the main part of the name, with the *de* inverted. French names are entered under *Du*, *La* and *Le*, but *de* is inverted. Afrikaans names are entered under prefixes, but German names are usually entered under the name following the prefix. It is important to check all possible positions in the index, as common usage of specific names sometimes differs from the general rules.

D

Q

R

S

T